PENGUIN BOOKS

MARCEL PROU

George D. Painter was born in Birmingham in 1914 and educated at King Edward's School before gaining a First Class Honours degree in Classics at Trinity College, Cambridge. His professional career from 1938 to 1974 was spent as an Assistant Keeper in the British Library, where during the last twenty years he was in charge of the national collection of fifteenth-century printing. Although an international authority in this field, he is best known for his celebrated biographies of Marcel Proust, André Gide, William Caxton and Chateaubriand. He has also translated *Marcel Proust, Letters to His Mother* and *The Chelsea Way* by André Maurois.

One of the few writers to have received both the Duff Cooper Memorial Prize (for his biography of Proust) and the James Tait Black Memorial Prize (for *Chateaubriand: A Biography, Volume 1*), George D. Painter has been a Fellow of the Royal Society of Literature since 1965. He was awarded the OBE in 1974. He is now working on the second and third volumes of his life of Chateaubriand, the great French romantic writer and statesman.

George D. Painter

MARCEL PROUST

A BIOGRAPHY

PENGUIN BOOKS

PENGUIN BOOKS

Published by the Penguin Group
Penguin Books Ltd, 27 Wrights Lane, London w8 5TZ, England
Viking Penguin, a division of Penguin Books USA Inc.
375 Hudson Street, New York, New York 10014, USA
Penguin Books Australia Ltd, Ringwood, Victoria, Australia
Penguin Books Canada Ltd, 2801 John Street, Markham, Ontario, Canada L3R 1B4
Penguin Books (NZ) Ltd, 182–190 Wairau Road, Auckland 10, New Zealand

Penguin Books Ltd, Registered Offices: Harmondsworth, Middlesex, England

Volume 1 first published by Chatto & Windus 1959
Published in Peregrine Books 1977
Volume 2 first published by Chatto & Windus 1965
Published in Peregrine Books 1977
Published in one volume in Penguin Books 1983

This edition first published by Chatto & Windus 1989
Published in Penguin Books 1990
1 3 5 7 9 10 8 6 4 2

For my wife

JOAN PAINTER

CONTENTS

Preface to New Edition   *Page xv*

Preface to First Edition   *xix*

VOLUME I

1 The Garden of Auteuil   1

2 The Garden of Illiers   13

3 The Two Ways   29

4 The Garden of the Champs-Élysèes   40

5 Balbec and Condorcet   51

6 Bergotte and Doncières   65

7 The Student in Society   80

8 The Duchesse and Albertine   109

9 First Glimpses of the Cities of the Plain 120

10 The Guermantes Way   147

11 Descent into the Cities of the Plain 169

12 The Early Years of *Jean Santeuil*   192

13 The Dreyfus Case   221

14 Salvation through Ruskin   256

15 Saint-Loup   288

16 Time begins to be Lost   315

VOLUME II

1   Visits from Albertine (*December 1903-December 1904*)   1

2   Death of a Mother (*January-December 1905*)   29

3   The Watershed (*December 1905-January 1907*)   52

4   Balbec Revisited (*February-December 1907*)   72

5   Purification through Parody (*January-October 1908*)   98

6   By Way of Sainte-Beuve (*November 1908-August 1909*)   118

7   The Tea and the Madeleine (*January-December 1909*)   129

8   Mademoiselle de Saint-Loup (*January 1910-July 1912*)   154

9   Agony at Sunrise (*August 1912-August 1913*)   180

10 Agostinelli Vanishes (*September 1913-July 1914*)   199

11 The Death of Saint-Loup (*August 1914-January 1916*)   217

12 The Vinteuil Septet (*February 1916-March 1917*)   232

13 The Pit of Sodom (*March 1917-November 1918*)   251

14 The Prize (*November 1918-June 1920*)   283

15 The Dark Woman (*July 1920-October 1921*)   303

16 An Indian Summer (*October 1921-September 1922*)   327

17 The Two Ways Meet (*September-November 1922*)   353

Bibliography, Volumes I and II   365

References to Sources, Volume I   375

References to Sources, Volume II   388

Supplementary Select Annotated Bibliography   405

Indexes, Volume I
    Persons and Places   413
    Characters and Places   425

Indexes, Volume II
    Persons and Places   429
    Characters and Places   443

ACKNOWLEDGEMENTS

The author and publishers wish to thank the authors, copyright-owners and publishers of the works used or quoted. As stated in the original Preface, only published sources have been used, and these are fully listed and cited in the Bibliography and References to Sources.

PROUST'S

Place names used or adapted by Proust in A la Recherche du Temps Perdu for the stations of the Little Train, or for other features of the country near 'Balbec', are shown in italics.

Querqueville
Octeville-la-Venelle CHERBOURG *Brillevast*
Quettehou
Sottevast
VALOGNES
Bricquebec
Carquebuto *Englesqueville*
Luc-sur-mer
BAYEUX
Ouistreham
BALLEROY CAEN

Montsurvent
COUTANCES
Orne
Montmartin-sur-mer
Combray
Chanteloup
Hudimesnil
FALAISE

GRANVILLE

St. Jean-de-la-Haize

CANCALE

AVRANCHES

Mont
St. Michel PONTORSON

Miles
0   5   10   15   20   25   30

Railway
Sta.

The Coast of BALBEC

Luc-sur-mer

Lion-sur-mer

Riva-Bella

Le Homme
-sur-mer
Hermanville *Merville*
Ouistreham

Orne
Varaville

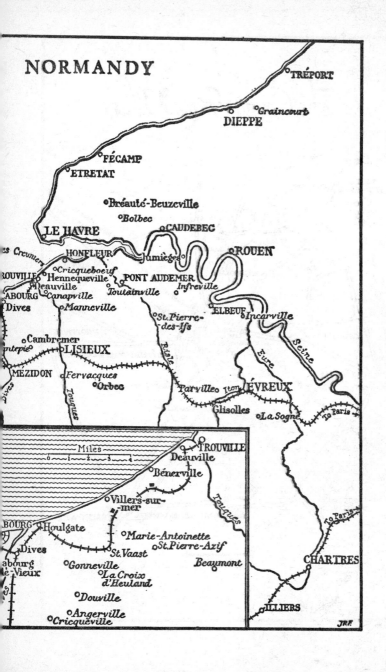

NORMANDY

TRÉPORT

Graincourt

DIEPPE

FÉCAMP

ETRETAT

Bréauté-Beuzeville

Bolbec

CAUDEBEC

LE HAVRE

HONFLEUR   Jumièges   ROUEN

es Creuses

Cricqueboeuf
TROUVILLE   Hennequeville   PONT AUDEMER
eauville   Infreville
ABOURG   Canapville   Toutainville
Dives   Manneville   ELBEUF   Incarville
                      St. Pierre-
                      des-Ifs   Seine

Cambremer   Eure
ntepie   LISIEUX
MEZIDON   Fervacques   Iton   ÉVREUX
          Orbec   Parville
                                        La Sogne   To Paris
                            Glisolles

          Miles
          0   1   2   3   4   TROUVILLE
                                        Deauville

                                        Bénerville

                                        Villers-sur-
                                        mer   Touques

BOURG   Houlgate
                      Marie-Antoinette   To Paris
Dives   St. Vaast   St. Pierre-Azif
abourg   Beaumont
e-Vieux   Gonneville
          La Croix   CHARTRES
          d'Heuland

          Douville

          Angerville   ILLIERS
          Cricqueville

JRF

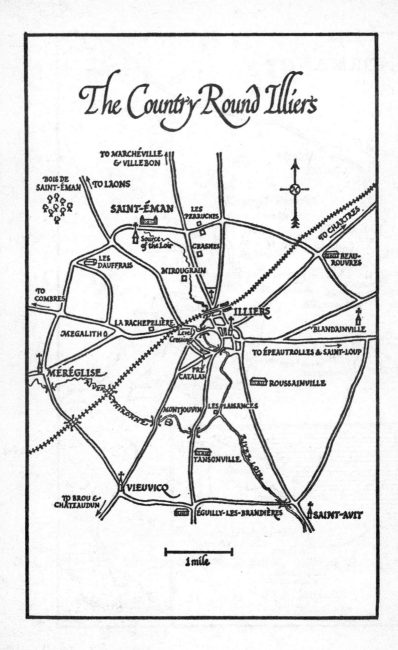

The Country Round Illiers

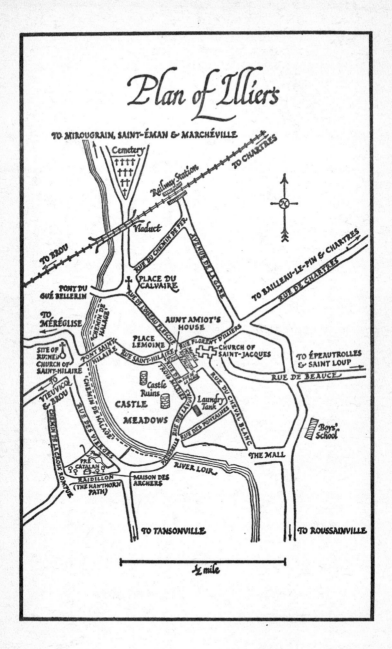

Plan of Illiers

PREFACE TO NEW EDITION

THIS biography of Marcel Proust was first published in English and American editions in two separate volumes, the first in 1959, the second in 1965. It has remained in print ever since, in Great Britain with Chatto and Windus or Penguin Books, in the United States successively with Atlantic Little Brown and Random House. French, German and Italian translations (published by Mercure de France, Suhrkamp, and Feltrinelli respectively) have likewise continued in print and reprint, together with versions in Spanish, Polish, and Japanese. The original text is here reprinted for the first time in one-volume hardback, giving the opportunity to add new updating material, including this preface, a supplementary select annotated bibliography, and a few minor typographical corrections.

I am surprised and grateful that my book has remained during three decades alive and well. I am conscious how much this survival is due to its publishers—in particular the angel Norah Smallwood, and now John Charlton—and above all to the fascination of its subject, Marcel Proust, who is incommensurably more interesting in himself than any book written about him. However, my work has not as yet been replaced or superseded as the only large-scale and detailed biography of Proust. It still retains, as I believe, much of the relative adequacy and validity of the already abundant but hitherto unexplored primary sources on which it was based. The ultimate biography of Proust must await completion of the current publications of Proust's correspondence and manuscripts, and the long labours of a wiser and younger biographer than myself. Even so, his materials, though vastly increased, will perhaps lead my successor to a narrative and to conclusions not fundamentally different from my own.

The chief advance in biographical source material during the last two decades is, of course, Philip Kolb's magisterial and magnificent edition of Proust's *Correspondance*, produced almost annually since 1970, and now (in 1988), having reached its sixteenth volume and the end of 1917, only a further six volumes and six years of Proust's life from completion. The letters here published (already 3418 by my count) nearly double the number previously available. Earlier editors of Proust's habitually dateless letters misdated, misread, mutilated and even falsified their texts, to an extent which could only be suspected or inferred, and is here first revealed and rectified by Kolb. Full and true texts are now presented in the real order of writing, with certain or probable dates supplied, and with annotations identifying persons and illuminating contexts. Chronology is regained, the lost sequence of events is restored, and Proust's life, so far as he committed it to letters, can be relived from day to day. His correspondence deserves to be read, with fascination and delight, as a major work, second only to *A la Recherche*; but it is also one of the most significant exhibitions in all literature of the raw material from which a great artist created his masterpiece—"the material of my experience," as the Narrator himself says, "which would also be the material of my book."

The eventual publication of Proust's manuscript drafts will bring another and last, enormous, daunting but vital text and task to Proust's most devoted readers and scholars, and to his ultimate biographer. These drafts, which record in vast complexity his first thoughts, afterthoughts, additions, enrichments and rejections, must not be allowed to replace his final and chosen version. Even so, their antecedent presence remains everywhere implicit beneath *A la Recherche*, revealing its evolution, its processes of creation, and even the last secrets of its meaning to its author. Their later stages give essential evidence for perfecting the text of volumes which Proust did not live to revise fully, and have been used for this purpose in the successive *Pléiade* editions and others. Their total publication, perhaps in facsimile as well as in print, is necessary, formidable, distant, but inevitable.

New evidence has so far tended to confirm my original findings. As I predicted, the typescript of Proust's penultimate volume, completed in June 1922 a few months before his death, since lost, and rediscovered only in 1986, was found to include the change of title, written in his own hand, from *La Fugitive* to *Albertine Disparue*.[1] In Albertine's letters to the Narrator after her flight, as I suggested, Proust was quoting Agostinelli's own words; and Kolb has since published the letter from Proust to Agostinelli (written unawares at the moment of the young man's fatal accident, 30 May 1914) which repeats these very words.[2] Authentic and well-satisfied ex-clients of Jupien-Le Cuziat's brothel wrote in the late 1960s to assure me that there was a real Man in Chains (whose feelings were hurt only when his tormentor stole from

---

[1] *MP* II 349, 358; *Assouline* 46; *Albertine Disparue*, ed. N. Mauriac (1988)
[2] *MP* II 212; *Lettres retrouvées*, ed. P. Kolb, pp. 97–104

him); the real Charlus (Montesquiou) came occasionally, but only for conversation; and the real Jupien proudly displayed a presentation copy of Proust's *Sésame et les Lys*, inscribed 'A mon petit Albert'.[1] Then again, as I later realised, the Vinteuil Septet must surely be modelled not only on the works by César Franck and Debussy with which I have compared it, but on Ravel's *Introduction and Allegro*, which alone resembles it in being for seven instruments including a harp. The harp in the Septet would have been singularly difficult to play, for Proust describes it as having horizontal strings.[2]

The manuscript archives apparently throw no light as yet on the most crucial and absorbing problems in the early evolution of *A la Recherche*. They seem not to include the primitive drafts on which Proust must have worked between the final abandonment of *Jean Santeuil* in 1902 and the beginnings of the mature *Combray* chapter in 1908. Even the published *Contre Sainte-Beuve* was compiled with skill and tact by Bernard de Fallois not from Proust's finished version or versions, which certainly existed but have since disappeared, but from the preliminary drafts on which these were based. Most intriguing and baffling of all, apparently no trace survives (except for various early versions of the final matinée in *Le Temps Retrouvé*) of the last third, intended to form the original third volume, of Proust's novel as it existed in 1912.[3] What was Albertine, and what her story, before the appearance, captivity, escape and death of Agostinelli in 1913–14? That she already existed, though with a different name, before real life uncannily repeated the already pre-existing events of Proust's novel, is absolutely certain. Proust's 1908 notebook predicts her imprisonment in the Narrator's home;[4] the fatal scene at Montjouvain was already in Proust's text, and intended to prepare the Narrator's agony at sunrise, long before Agostinelli's arrival; and she appears in the earliest sketches as chieftainess of the little band under the name Maria, which Proust in his own hand cancels in 1913 and alters to Albertine.[5] Perhaps the missing texts may yet come to light, as others have, in the possession of heirs or collectors.[6] Perhaps they are lost for ever, burned in the kitchen stove at 102 Boulevard Haussmann among the '32 black plush exercise-books'

[1] *MP* II 265, 270; cf. *Albaret* 235–40, *Léautaud* XII 125–6
[2] *MP* II 245–7; *Pléiade* III 251
[3] Winton, *Proust's Additions* I 12, n.4
[4] *Cahier de 1908*, ed. P. Kolb, pp. 49, 50, 135–6
[5] *Bonnet* I (1971) 198; *Bardèche* II 25–37
[6] *Assouline* 43, 46

destroyed at Proust's command by Céleste Albaret, or in the holocaust of 'manuscripts of which no other copy exists' at the time of his removal to rue Laurent-Pichat in May 1917.[1] However this may be, the evidence on which I based my own reconstructions of these missing materials still seems to me adequate, and is confirmed by these later amplifications.[2]

As I bid farewell to writing on Proust, I look back to a day in 1962 when I reached his death, and seemed not only to be bereaved but to die myself. A biographer's relationship with his subject is perhaps the deepest in his own experience outside the family, and he who writes more lives than one more deaths than one must die. Further still is the week in 1947 when I first encountered a volume of Proust's letters, found to my astonishment that it revealed a world that belonged to the raw material of his novel, and resolved to write his life with the intention or hope of experiencing it myself, and of discovering what *A la Recherche* meant to himself. Remotest, but still most vivid of all, is the moment sixty years ago in 1928, when I opened in our midland city public library a blue-and-gold-spined book mysteriously called *Swann's Way*, and found myself walking with the Narrator, an adolescent of my own age, among the cornfields and appletrees of the Méséglise Way. I have walked there ever since, as so many others have and many more will.

This new edition is again dedicated as before to my wife Joan Painter, now forty-seven years after our marriage. In the previous editions Volume One was inscribed also to Henry Reed (1914–86), Volume Two to Wynyard Browne (1911–64) and to Angus (later Sir Angus) Wilson, and I retain these additional dedications in remembrance of our youth and friendship in Proust.

Hove, 1988   GEORGE D. PAINTER

[1] *MP* II 288; *Lettres retrouvées* 10; *Cattaui* (B) 184; *Albaret* 324–5, 390
[2] *MP* II 237–41; see also *MP* II 44–5, 143–4, 208–9

BELIEVING that the published sources are now adequate in quantity and quality, but that the subject has never yet been treated with anything approaching scholarly method, I have endeavoured to write a definitive biography of Proust: a complete, exact and detailed narrative of his life, that is, based on every known or discoverable primary source, and on primary sources only. The mass of material is vast, complex and scattered. I have tried to winnow it, to extract all that is relevant, to place it in its organic and significant order, to preserve the main thread of the story through necessary digressions, and to serve the needs of both the general reader and the Proustian scholar. There seems to be no good reason why an interesting subject should be made boring in the name of scholarship, or why the most scrupulous accuracy should not be achievable without draining the life-blood from a living theme. Fortunately the quality of life was already abundant in the sources. I have invented nothing whatever; and even when I give the words of a conversation, or describe the state of the weather or a facial expression at a particular moment, I do so from evidence that seems reliable. I think I may claim that something like nine-tenths of the narrative here given is new to Proustian biography, or conversely that previous biographers have used only about one-tenth of the discoverable sources.

This is not intended as a controversial work: my purpose is to discover facts and elicit their meaning, and the larger part of this book is devoted to the plain narrative of Proust's life. But I must explain that my uncustomary approach to *A la Recherche du Temps Perdu*, my belief that Proust's novel cannot be fully understood without a knowledge of his life, is necessitated by the facts, and is not due to mere ignorance of the accepted clichés. It has become one of the dogmas of Proustian criticism that his novel can and must be treated as a closed system, containing in itself all the elements necessary for its understanding. To take two examples from many dozens, Monsieur X is praised for having 'emptied his mind'—did he have to empty it of so very much?— 'of all Proustian matter extraneous to the novel which he has set himself to examine'; "I do not propose," says Professor Y, "in this study, which is an attempt to interpret Proust's great novel, to discuss the external facts of his life." But they like to have it both ways. They use, and so does Professor Z, unproven biographical axioms for critical purposes: they argue (again to take one instance of many) from the supposed total homosexuality of the author, that the women loved by the Narrator are disguises of men loved by Proust, that they must therefore be psychologically unconvincing, and that Proust has falsified the whole drama of human love. I have not tried to deny Proust's homosexuality—on the contrary, I shall give the first full account of it based on evidence. But readers who have felt all along that Proust's picture of heterosexual love is valid and founded on personal experience will be glad to find their instinct justified. Here, then, is one among very many unrealised biographical facts about Proust the critical bearing of which is fundamental and indispensable. In general, however, there is no aspect of Proust or his work—his style, philosophy, character, morality, his attitude to music, painting, Ruskin, snobism and so on—which can be studied without an accurate and detailed knowledge of his life, or which has so far escaped distortion for lack of such knowledge.

This first volume is the place for analysis of the autobiographical material used by Proust in his novel: a discussion of his methods of synthesis will appear in the second volume, when the period at which he wrote it is reached. But it may be appropriate here to remark in advance on some of the further ways in which Proust's biography is significant for our understanding of *A la Recherche*. I hope those who judge this aspect of my work will consider whether the facts are true, rather than whether the critical approach demanded by the facts happens to be fashionable at the present moment.

I shall show that it is possible to identify and reconstruct from ample evidence the sources in Proust's real life for all major, and many minor characters, events and places in his novel. By discovering which aspects of his originals he chose or rejected, how he combined many models into each new figure, and most of all how he altered material reality to make it conform more closely to symbolic reality, we can observe the workings of his imagination at the very moment of creation." The 'closed system' Proustians have been egoistically contented to know of Proust's novel only what it means to themselves. It is surely relevant to learn what the novel meant to the author, to understand the special significance which, because they were part of his life and being, every character and episode had for Proust and still retains in its substance. What do they know of *A la Recherche* who only *A la Recherche* know?

A still more important consequence follows from the study of Proust's novel in the light of his biography. *A la Recherche* turns out to be not only based entirely on his own experiences: it is intended to be the symbolic story of his life, and occupies a place unique among great novels in that it is not, properly speaking, a fiction, but a creative autobiography. Proust believed, justifiably, that his life had the shape and meaning of a great work of art: it was his task to select, telescope and transmute the facts so that their universal significance should be revealed; and this revelation of the relationship between his own life and his unborn novel is one of the chief meanings of Time Regained. But though he invented nothing, he altered everything. His places and people are composite in space and time, constructed from various sources and from widely separate periods of his life. His purpose in so doing was not to falsify reality, but, on the contrary, to induce it to reveal the truths it so successfully hides in this world. Behind the diversity of the originals is an underlying unity, the quality which, he felt, they had in common, the Platonic ideal of which they were the obscure earthly symbols. He fused each group of particular cases into a complex, universal whole, and so disengaged the truth about the poetry of places, or love and jealousy, or the nature of duchesses, and, most of all, the meaning of the mystery of his own life. In my belief the facts demonstrated in the present biography compel us to take an entirely new view of Proust's novel. "A man's life of any worth is a continual allegory," said Keats: *A la Recherche* is the allegory of Proust's life, a work not of fiction but of imagination interpreting reality.

It would be absurd to suppose that Proust's greatness is in any degree lessened by his reliance on reality. His work is an illustration of Wordsworth's distinction between Fancy and Imagination —between the art which invents what has never existed and the art which discovers the inner meanings of what exists. We may or may not feel that Imagination is superior to Fancy; but we cannot possibly maintain that it is inferior. Proust was perhaps deficient in or indifferent to Fancy; but he was among the greatest masters of Imagination. It would be equally absurd to pretend that *A la Recherche* is a mere *roman à clef*—a novel, that is, which is a literal narrative of real events in which only the names are changed. As Proust himself explained to a friend, "there are no keys to the people in my novel; or rather, there are eight or ten keys to each character".

I do not apologise for the abundance of detail in this biography, not only because it is the function of a definitive biography to be complete, but because it was from the mass of such detail that Proust's novel was created. Dates of day, month and year (chronology, too, has to be regained) are given for every datable incident. I have tried to bring his friends and acquaintances to life as they were when he knew them, by describing their appearance, characters and subsequent careers, and by telling the social anecdotes which he revelled in and used in his novel. Sometimes it has been possible to discuss the synthesis of a Proustian character in one place, but usually the ingredients can only be mentioned as they occur in the chronological course of his life: collective references will be found, however, in the Index. Here, too, I have aimed at completeness: if Bergotte or Saint-Loup, for instance, have half a dozen or more originals, each contributing something of his own, I hope the reader would not wish me to conceal it. Often even the sources of the proper names are important, because they had some special significance in Proust's life, as indeed they have in his novel, of which two major sections are called Names of Places and Names of People. My enquiries into the sexual inversion, or Jewish, plebeian or noble birth of persons whom Proust knew, are necessitated by the nature of the case, and do not correspond to any prejudices or predilections on my own part.

It has been necessary to interrupt the main narrative with four long digressions: on the topography of Illiers, on Proust's hosts, hostesses and acquaintances in society, on the Dreyfus Affair, and on Proust's study of Ruskin; but these are subjects of fundamental importance in his life and novel, they could be treated in no other way, and I believe the digressions will be found not uninteresting in themselves. Sometimes the evidence on essential matters is unusually complex and intractable: my discussions of the order of composition and relationship to Proust's life of the stories in *Les Plaisirs et les Jours* and *Jean Santeuil*, and of a few points elsewhere, could not be made easy reading. But these passages are only a few pages of the whole, I have done my best to make them lucid and concise, and I can only ask the reader to take the occasional rough with the smooth.

To avoid needless repetition—and also, I confess, to avoid laying all my cards on the table before the game is finished—I have postponed giving a full bibliography of the sources used, together with detailed references for each statement, till the second and final volume, which will appear in six years' time. Occasionally, however, and usually in order to correct some predecessor's misstatement, I have given my sources in a footnote. I share the general reader's dislike of footnotes; but sometimes I have reluctantly relegated to the bottom of the page some discussion of a point of detail which would have interrupted the main narrative; and it seemed imperative to give references (to the standard *Plēïade* edition of the original text in three volumes) on each occasion when Proust introduced material from his life in particular passages of his novel. All translations from the French are my own.

I had already made my researches into the dating of Proust's letters and the originals of his characters before the appearance of those two monumental works, Professor Philip Kolb's *La Correspondance de Marcel Proust* (1949) and Antoine Adam's *Le Roman de Proust et le problème des clefs* (*Revue des Sciences humaines*, jan.-mars 1952, pp. 49-90). I have added to, re-examined and sometimes differed from their conclusions; but my debt to them, though limited, is great, and I acknowledge it with admiration and gratitude. In Chapters 2 and 3, along with other sources including my own visit to Illiers in September 1950, I have consulted P. L. Larcher's exquisite *Le Parfum de Combray* (1945). My chapter on Ruskin is independent of Jean Autret's *L'Influence de Ruskin sur la vie, les idées et l'œuvre de Marcel Proust* (1955), but I have made some use of his views on the extent of Proust's first-hand knowledge of Ruskin, Turner and Giotto. In Chapter 12 I have had the benefit of Professor Kolb's description of the original manuscript of *Jean Santeuil*, thanks to the kindness of Mr Miron Grindea, editor of *Adam*, who showed me the advance proofs of Professor Kolb's article in the special Proust number of his magazine.

I have dedicated this first volume to Henry Reed, my friend of more than thirty years, with whom I first read Proust in our schooldays. I have also remembered, after a gulf of twenty-two years, R. B. and her far-reaching question to me: "Who was Swann?"

GEORGE D. PAINTER

London,
May, 1959

VOLUME ONE

Le tombeau d'Albertine est près de mon berceau
MARCELINE DESBORDES-VALMORE

For

HENRY REED

Chapter 1

THE GARDEN OF AUTEUIL

THE doorway of the house where Louis Proust was born, in the Rue du Cheval Blanc at Illiers, is a single stone arch of exactly the same form as the double arch in the romanesque side-porch of the nearby church. It would be wrong to infer that there is something ecclesiastical about the houses of the people of Illiers; the truth is rather that there is something domestic about the church of Saint-Jacques. But the Prousts tended to have a vague connection with the church. When Louis Proust married Virginie Torcheux, about 1827, he moved to 11 Place du Marché, opposite Saint-Jacques, and sold spices, thread, sugar, wooden shoes and tallow-candles to his fellow-citizens; but in the room behind the shop he made wax-candles for all the worshippers in the parish, and dreamed of the day when his son would be a priest. His first child was a girl, Élisabeth, born 16 August 1828. His son Adrien was born on 18 March 1834, and in due course won a scholarship to the high school at Chartres, where he took his baccalaureate in letters and science. Towards the end of his life Adrien Proust made light of the honours with which his profession and his country had loaded him, and boasted of a distinction which somehow meant far more: "My name is in the roll of honour of the Collège de Chartres," he said. But, like his son Marcel after him, he could not fulfil his father's ambition; he decided that his vocation for the priesthood was insufficient and, without losing his Catholic faith, became a convert to science. In July 1853, two years before the death of Louis Proust, he passed the necessary certificate of aptitude for physical sciences and went to Paris to become a doctor. No Proust had ever left Illiers before him; it was a turning-point in a chain of events which led, deviously and inevitably, to *A la Recherche du Temps Perdu*.

The heroic age of French medicine was just beginning; the learned but hitherto Molièresque profession of healing was being transformed into an experimental, and therefore an exact, science, and the conquest of disease and the exploration of the mind already seemed possible. Among Adrien Proust's near contemporaries were men great in their day but now forgotten—Chauffard, Parrot, Vulpian—and others who are still remembered: Potain,[1] whom even Mme Verdurin thought second only to Dr Cottard as a diagnostician, and Charcot, the psychiatrist who taught Freud. One of his fellow-students sounds oddly familiar, and need only be spelt with a double 't' to become recognisable: his name was Cotard.

Adrien Proust took his doctorate of medicine on 29 December 1862 with a thesis on 'idiopathic pneumothorax'. He became *chef de clinique* at the Charité hospital in 1863, and on 14 March 1866 was admitted with special mention in the *concours d'agrégation*, the state examination for licence to teach in university schools of medicine. In the same year the third of the four great cholera epidemics of the nineteenth century reached France. Even in the largest and worst-hit towns only twenty in every thousand fell ill; but of every thousand sufferers, five hundred died. Dr Proust distinguished himself by his untiring devotion to duty and disregard of danger, and saw his patients die of a disease which could not be cured or prevented in the individual. In the career of every great specialist there is a moment of inspiration, inextricably compounded of desire to save the world and of personal ambition, in which his life-work is revealed to him. Dr Proust decided to prevent cholera in the mass by keeping it out of Europe; he took over from his masters Tardieu and Fauvel the principle of the *cordon sanitaire*, and invented the slogans which would make it intelligible and interesting to politicians. "The question of international hygiene passes and surpasses political frontiers," he announced, and "Egypt is Europe's barrier against cholera": M. de Norpois himself could not have put it more aptly. In 1869 the Minister of Agriculture and Commerce sent him to Persia, via St Petersburg and Astrakhan, to discover the routes by which previous epidemics had entered Russia. He travelled on horseback through appalling heat, and was received with special regard at Teheran by the Shah, who presented him with a magnificent Persian carpet, and by the Grand Vizier Ali Pasha at Constantinople. In August 1870, a few days before the disaster of Sedan, he received the red ribbon of the Légion d'Honneur from the

[1] *Pléiade*, I, 188

Empress Eugénie, and on 3 September, the day before the fall of the Second Empire, he married Jeanne Weil.

Mlle Weil was a beautiful and intelligent Jewess, aged twenty-one, fifteen years younger than Dr Proust. Her father, Nathé Weil, then aged fifty-four, was a wealthy stockbroker, whose family originally came from Metz in Lorraine; he became a surly old gentleman with a kind heart, on whom his grandson was to model M. Sandré in *Jean Santeuil*. Her mother, whose maiden name was Adèle Berncastel, then aged forty-five, was as gentle and self-sacrificing as Nathé Weil was independent and ungracious; next only to abnegation and her family Mme Nathé loved music and literature, especially the literature of the *grand siècle*, and above all the letters of Mme de Sévigné, in whom she recognised a motherly love like her own for her daughter. She handed on all her own qualities to Jeanne, including perhaps a preference for a husband who would be her own opposite, with whom her wifely devotion and her love of art would be safe, precisely because he had no special need for them. So Dr Proust was to advance towards fame in his profession, secured from the rear by his wife's loving admiration and her perfect management of his home: it was to be, for both, an extremely happy marriage.

Within a few weeks of her wedding Mme Proust was pregnant, and the times were hard for a young expectant mother. The victorious German army began the siege of Paris on 19 September, and for more than four months the city was cut off from the outside world. Meat, bread, fruit and milk became scarce, and though her parents were rich and her husband a doctor, it is unlikely that Mme Proust had the food she needed for herself and her unborn child. In the country round Illiers the Germans were campaigning against the Army of the Loire, and Dr Proust had no news of his widowed mother. In October they sacked Châteaudun, fifteen miles to the south, and occupied Chartres, fifteen miles to the north-east. Towards the end of December he sent a letter by balloon-post to a friend at Tours, a wholesale draper named Esnault: 'Has she left Illiers? Is she with you? Is she well? Such are the questions which I beg you to answer by pigeon-post and to add all the information you may have about any of my family.' From the address of this letter it seems that he and his wife were living at 8 Rue Roy, a little street running into the Boulevard Haussmann. They were never to move more than a few hundred yards from this point, and when nearly fifty years later their son Marcel was at last uprooted from the district sacred to his parents, it was the death of him.

After the hungry winter of the siege came the German entry into Paris and the troubled spring of the Commune. In May the Government forces of Citizen Thiers returned to the city, the 'Bloody Week' of street-fighting followed, and one morning as Dr Proust was walking to his work at the Charité he was narrowly missed by a stray bullet. His young wife was so over-come by the shock that it was thought advisable for them to move to the house of her uncle Louis Weil at 96 Rue La Fontaine, Auteuil, and here on 10 July 1871 Marcel Proust was born.

At first he was thought too weak to live, and long afterwards he liked to attribute his lifelong ill-health to his mother's priva-tions and anxiety during the siege and the Commune. Perhaps, from the beginning, she agreed with him, and felt responsible for history's injury to her unborn child; for she tried to redeem her guilt with exaggerated care. He grew to believe, resentfully, that she loved him best when he was ill and he tried to win her love by being ill. Meanwhile, however, he was soon well enough to enter the Catholic Church of his father. Mme Proust kept her Jewish faith out of devotion to her parents; but Marcel was duly christened at Saint-Louis d'Antin, the local church of their home in Paris. In after-life he would point with some pride to the certificate of his christening, and to the later certificate of confirm-ation, signed by the Archbishop of Paris himself. Yet he was always conscious of belonging, thanks to his mother, to two great proscribed nations, who once lived in neighbouring regions, till the wrath of God scattered them over the face of the earth; for her blood made him a tribesman of Abraham, her over-anxious love a native of the Cities of the Plain.

Their Paris home for nearly thirty years was a large apartment at 9 Boulevard Malesherbes. The boulevard is lined with chestnut-trees and commands a pleasant vista from the rear of the Madeleine to the domed church of Saint-Augustin, built the year before Proust's birth. 'One of the ugliest districts in Paris,' he called it in *Du Côté de chez Swann*; but even so, the 'violet belfry' of Saint-Augustin seen over the rooftops seemed to him 'to give this view of Paris the character of certain views of Rome by Piranesi'.[1] On

[1] *Pléiade*, I, 66

the ground floor was the tailor's shop of M. Eppler; next door was another, that of Sandt and Laborde (it was a family joke to call them 'Sandford and Merton'); and one of these no doubt suggested Jupien's shop in the lodger's wing of the Duchesse de Guermantes's mansion. The handsome double doors remain as they were in the 1870s, surmounted by a carved stone shield, framed in oak-leaves and bearing the number Nine. The house has seven storeys, each with its iron balustrade running the whole length of the façade. From the second-floor balcony Marcel was to watch the fitful appearances of the sunlight, augury of the afternoon's weather which would release him, if all went well, to play with the original of Gilberte Swann in the Champs-Élysées. On the opposite corner the Morriss column still stands, to which every morning he would run to study the theatre-bills, announcing 'the glittering white plume of *The Queen's Diamond Necklace* or the smooth, mysterious satin of *The Black Domino*'.[1] But these memories come from the 1880s; the important events of the '70s took place elsewhere, and only four incidents of this decade belong to 9 Boulevard Malesherbes.

The first was the birth on 24 May 1873, when Marcel was not yet two years old, of his brother Robert. Robert took after his father: he retained all through his life Dr Proust's narrow mouth, with the thick, pursed, kindly, Holbeinesque lips, which were to be seen only by rare glimpses beneath Marcel's moustache. The son who pleases and obeys is loved, no doubt, neither more nor less than the son who rouses anxiety and admiration; Robert was the son who obeyed. He became almost as eminent a surgeon as his father had been a physician and hygienist; he, too, was to be a Professor in the Faculty of Medicine and belong to the Légion d'Honneur. But perhaps one may see in Marcel as well as in Robert something of the surgeon who dissects in order to heal. Robert was to write a textbook on *The Surgery of the Female Genital Organs*; and it is a subject not entirely foreign to the Marcel who described the naked Albertine asleep. The relation-ship between the brothers was always affectionate, never intimate. There is an early photograph of Marcel, aged six, and Robert, aged four; Marcel, with bobbed hair in a fringe and a timid smile, wears a grey serge frock buttoning down the front, and lays his

[1] I, 73

arm protectively round his brother's neck; and Robert, in a frilly
white skirt, nestles against Marcel with a self-confident expression.
Witnesses have recorded that Marcel kept his protective attitude
towards Robert until the end of his life: 'it made one realise the
full force of the term "brotherly love",' wrote Lucien Daudet.
Marcel had no good reason for jealousy; his mother, though no
doubt she loved them both equally, knew that he needed her love
more than the easy-going Robert; Marcel was always her 'little
wolf', *mon petit loup*, and Robert was only *mon autre loup*. But
the shock of his brother's birth may have helped to make Marcel's
love for his mother so tyrannical and exorbitant; and he managed
to draw her into a kind of amiable conspiracy against his rival. In
the letters between Marcel and his mother Robert is a kind of
private joke: he has nicknames, such as Dick, or His Majesty, and
needs to be saved from the consequences of his rashness or sloth.
If anyone was jealous, Marcel decided, it must be Robert. In an
early draft of his novel he introduced Robert in his high chair,
complaining, with a piercing scream, that "Marcel has had more
chocolate blancmange than me!"[1] In *A la Recherche*, although no
doubt his reasons were mainly aesthetic, he preferred to abolish
Robert entirely.

The other three incidents may seem trivial, but are somehow
characteristic, and two were thought sufficiently important by
Proust to be introduced into *Jean Santeuil*. One New Year's Day
Marcel and Robert were enlisted to help in the distribution of New
Year gifts—a ceremony held particularly sacred in the Proust
family, and often alluded to in *A la Recherche*.[2] Mme Proust gave
Marcel a five-franc piece to take to her cousin's cook, but on the
way he saw a little bootblack, scarcely older than himself, looking
so cold and unhappy that he could not resist giving him the five-
franc piece. Mme Proust was furious, and punished him: he still
remembered the incident vividly forty years later, when he told
it to his housekeeper Céleste. All through his life he was to invite
the anger of his parents—even after they were dead—by the
extravagance of his generosity, and to purchase with pity and
money the love of the poor and unhappy. Then again, there was a
period in his early childhood when he was fascinated by the moon,
and begged to be given books on astronomy for his presents. One
winter afternoon, when Mme Proust was entertaining her friends

[1] *Contre Sainte-Beuve*, 296   [2] E.g. I, 52, 77, 486

in the drawing-room, she asked him to show them his 'books about the moon'. Marcel returned and proudly displayed not only the astronomy books, but also a little illustrated grammar, in which there was a picture of the moon with a nose and a funny face; for it seemed to him that this too, quite as much as the others, was 'a book about the moon'.[1] He was at the age—which he was so fortunate as never to outgrow—'when the world has not yet become something completely known and real, when it seems that an unfamiliar place in the real world might well give access to the world of the unreal'. One day his mother took him with her to the Deligny cold baths near the Pont de la Concorde; he was left in the waiting-room while she put on her bathing-costume, and then he was admitted to 'a vast liquid cavern', where the other bathing ladies and their cubicles receded to a seemingly endless distance. He felt he had come to the waters under the earth, 'the entrance to the polar seas'; and when his mother walked towards him, wearing a streaming rubber cap, and throwing kisses, he 'would not have been surprised to hear that he was the son of a water-goddess'.[2]

But the important events of the 1870s did not belong to the too familiar 'home' at 9 Boulevard Malesherbes. That island of bourgeois furniture in the desert of grey houses, however beloved, was too much the scene of a normal state of life to become a Paradise, which is a state of exception. Proust's Edens were the gardens of Auteuil and Illiers, which later became the gardens of Combray. He saw them only at holiday-times, and afterwards forfeited them eternally through the original sin of asthma; but if he had never lost them, they would never have become Paradise.

Auteuil, then as now, was a residential suburb between the western borders of Paris and the Bois de Boulogne; but then it still retained something of the country hamlet, now lost for ever, in which Molière and Boileau had their villas. In the months before Mme Proust moved there to have her baby, Auteuil had been twice bombarded, first by the Prussians, next, far more terribly, by the Government army from Versailles. On 24 May 1871 Edmond de Goncourt crossed Paris, still under shell-fire, with his faithful servant Pélagie, to find his house in the Boulevard Montmorency riddled with bullets, the doors on the second

[1] *Jean Santeuil*, vol. 1, 196   [2] *Jean Santeuil*, vol. 1, 193-4. The incident is also used in *Albertine Disparue* (*Pléiade*, III, 653).

floor blown to splinters by 'quite a little shell, one of the last to be fired', a crater in the middle of his lawn 'in which one could bury an elephant'. That night he watched, through the shattered branches of his garden trees, 'Paris in flames, looking like a Neapolitan gouache, on a sheet of black paper, of Vesuvius in eruption'. It was no doubt at this very time, when Paris was dangerous and Auteuil for the first time safe, that Mme Proust moved to the green suburban haven of 96 Rue La Fontaine.

It was a large house, 'about as tasteless as it possibly could be', in a big garden with formal gravel paths and flower-beds, and lawns, and trees which had grown too tall for the garden, and an ill-omened fountain, into whose shallow waters Marcel once fell when he was a child. One hot summer day in the early 1890s his second-cousin Valentine Thomson came to tea in the charge of her Aunt Laure.[1] Valentine was the daughter of Mme Proust's cousin Henriette Peigné-Crémieux, who married the politician Gaston Thomson, the Navy Minister of 1905-08; she was then a little girl and Marcel was in his early twenties. Marcel did the honours of the garden with a solemn and sacramental air: the flower-beds and the over-tall trees, both bad for his asthma, most of all the dreadful fountain, had become part of the mythology of his life. As he spoke of the fountain, Mme Proust joined in, and so did Aunt Laure; their faces, the amused child noticed, were serious, almost awed; for if the accident of the fountain had been important when it happened, it was surely still more important now, when the infant Marcel was submerged not only in its sinister waters, but in fifteen years of family history. Then he took the little girl indoors, and the ceremony proceeded. Each piece of 'grim, frumpy, solid furniture, smothered with frills of silk, dark and uninviting like a roomful of ancient, overdressed maiden aunts', had to be shown and explained, 'as if he were introducing me to dear friends'. So he was: he searched through life in vain for friends who would match the unending loyalty, the instant comprehension of his great-uncle's sideboards.

During the springs and summers of twenty-five years, whenever the family needed a holiday and Dr Proust was unable to leave Paris, they would move to Auteuil. Every morning the Doctor took the Auteuil-Madeleine omnibus, just opposite the

[1] Aunt Laure was Mme Proust's distant cousin Mme Charles Nathan, née Laure Rodrigues-Ely. See *Proust, Mme*, 36, note 2, 221.

house, and in less than an hour would be at his work in the Hôtel-
Dieu or the Charité hospital. He was ritually preceded by his
man-servant, running with dramatic gestures to stop the bus,
pleading with the driver to be patient, while behind him his master
waved a last au revoir to the children. These morning departures
became a family joke, a traditional story useful for the entertainment of visitors. As for arriving, 'I can't express the pleasure I
felt,' Proust wrote long afterwards, 'when after walking down the
Rue La Fontaine in the hot sun and the scent of the lime-trees, I
went upstairs to my room. There, in the twilight, coloured
mother-of-pearl by the glazed reflection of the Empire-blue satin
curtains (very inappropriate to their rural surroundings), the
unctuous air of the warm morning had just finished varnishing
and isolating the honest smells of the soap and the wardrobe with
its mirror-glass doors.' In the pantry there was cider, 'which we
drank from tumblers whose glass was so thick that one felt
tempted to bite them'. And in the dining-room 'the air was transparent and congealed, like an immaterial agate veined with the
scent of the cherries already piled high in the fruit dishes'. He was
fascinated by the little cut-glass prisms on which the knives and
forks were propped—'an exceedingly vulgar middle-class fashion,
but I liked it. Their iridescence did more than add mystery to the
odour of gruyère cheese and apricots. In the half light of the
dining-room these rainbow knife-rests threw peacock-feather
patterns on the walls, which seemed to me as miraculous as the
stained-glass windows in Rheims Cathedral.'[1]

In that room with the Empire-blue curtains, and the garden
with the over-tall chestnuts, when he was only seven years old,
the most important event in Proust's life happened. It told him
that love is doomed and happiness does not exist. He spent his
life, in his friendships, his love-affairs and relations with society,
in trying to disprove it, and only succeeded in perpetually reproducing it; till in his great novel he went back beyond it, to the
time outside Time where it had not yet happened, and therefore
could never happen. One summer evening at Auteuil Marcel's
mother was helping to entertain a medical colleague of Dr Proust,
and could not come up to his bedroom to give him his usual
good-night kiss. The anguished child watched the group in the
moonlit garden, as they talked and sipped their after-dinner

[1] *De David à Degas*, p. viii. Also mentioned in *A la Recherche*, III, 168.

liqueurs under the trees. He could not sleep; in vain he begged their man-servant to fetch his mother; till at last in desperation he opened the window and called to her: "*Ma petite maman*, I want you for a second." Rather than risk a worse scene, she came, urged by the good-natured Dr Proust, and tried to comfort him; but he broke into a fit of hysterical weeping, for the irrevocable harm was done. The servant looked in inquisitively, and his mother explained: "Master Marcel doesn't know himself what is the matter with him, or what he wants—it's his nerves." He felt a fierce joy that the act which he had felt to be a deliberate crime should be declared to be something beyond his control.

He wrote two accounts of this incident, which forms the opening scene both of *Jean Santeuil* and *A la Recherche du Temps Perdu*. The version in *Jean Santeuil* is more matter-of-fact and probably contains the literal truth; it has been followed above. In *Du Côté de chez Swann* the event is elaborated and joined to other scenes from other years, for there his purpose is to give its symbolic truth. The garden is at Combray, the bell in the garden-gate at Illiers is heard, the visitor is Swann, the servant Françoise; and the father, with a generosity which is all the more touching and noble because it is ungracious, unexpected, and 'regardless of the principles of international law', allows the mother to spend the night in her child's room, reading aloud his day after to-morrow's birthday present of George Sand's *François le Champi*. This final episode, though here it is aesthetically inseparable from the rest, does not occur in *Jean Santeuil*, where the narrative rings true—in the realm of literal truth, that is—without it. Yet the *François le Champi* incident is no less charged with the emotions of an actual memory. It happened on another night at Auteuil, when Marcel had a temperature, and the family doctor prescribed medicine to check his fever, and ordered: "Keep the boy on a light diet." Mme Proust said nothing and Marcel knew from her silence that she had already determined he should take no medicine and should eat nothing till the fever had gone. "My children," she would say on such occasions, "that doctor may be cleverer than I am, but I know what is right." So she gave Marcel nothing but milk, and read to him from *François le Champi* and *La Petite Fadette*. A few mornings later she decided he had a cool skin and a steady pulse; and he was allowed at last to eat a small boiled sole. An allusion in one of Proust's letters to his mother shows that the *François le Champi* incident occurred at Auteuil[1]; and the more important event of his mother's kiss also occurred there, and not at Illiers: not only because it is placed there in the unelaborated version of *Jean Santeuil*, but because even in *Du Côté de chez Swann* Proust has planted a characteristic clue which leads likewise to the house of Louis Weil. 'The wall of the staircase,' he tells us, 'on which I saw the light of my father's candle climbing, has long since been demolished.'[2] This is untrue of the house at Illiers, which survives to this day, but true of 96 Rue La Fontaine, which was pulled down late in the 1890s, when the new Avenue Mozart was driven through the middle of the garden.

To regard Marcel's loss and recovery of his mother's kiss as being, in itself, the decisive trauma of his early life, would be to over-simplify. Its importance is no doubt symbolic, as typifying, along with innumerable similar events which are unrecorded, a whole aspect of his childhood. Psycho-analysts might even regard it as a 'screen-memory', partly hiding and partly revealing some still earlier and deeper memory. Proust's own interpretation of it is not quite adequate: he regards it remorsefully as a first defeat in his mother's efforts to make him normal and self-reliant, as a first stage in the decline towards his legendary and non-existent 'lack of will-power'. We may suspect, however, that the child's anger went deeper than his remorse, that the true crux was not her final capitulation, but her initial refusal. Her concession was not an act of love, but a surrender to his blackmail. Henceforth, however often she might bring him his good-night kiss, he would always hate her for having denied it. In *Jean Santeuil* his resentment against his mother is open and unappeased; she was still alive when he wrote, and therefore he had not yet forgiven her, nor seen that not she but the very nature of human life was to blame for his anguish. But in *A la Recherche*, after she was dead and pardoned, he told the truth, when he said that somewhere inside him his sobbing had never ceased, that the 'metallic, shrill, interminable' sound of the visitors' bell in the garden gate had never stopped ringing.[3] In order to silence these sounds he sought everywhere for the infinite, unconditional love which he had lost; in order to hear them again he always increased his demands to the point at which they would be refused. Perhaps it was with the

---

[1] *Mme Proust*, p. 176   [2] I, 37
[3] III, 1046

unconscious purpose of regaining his mother's love, and of punishing her at the same time for withholding it, that he fell ill.

During another visit to Auteuil, when Marcel was nine years old, the family took a walk in the nearby Bois de Boulogne with some friends. On the way back he was seized by a fit of suffocation, and seemed on the point of dying before the eyes of his terrified father. His lifelong disease of asthma had begun. Medically speaking, his malady was involuntary and genuine; but asthma, we are told, is often closely linked to unconscious conflicts and desires, and for Proust it was to be, though a dread master, a faithful servant. In his attacks of asthma the same causes were at work as in his childhood fits of hysterical weeping; his unconscious mind was asking for his father's pity and his mother's love; and his breathlessness reproduced, perhaps, the moment of suffocation which comes equally from tears or from sexual pleasure. He sinned through his lungs, and in the end his lungs were to kill him. Other great writers, Flaubert and Dostoevsky, suffered from epilepsy, which stood in an inseparable and partly causal relation to their art. Asthma was Proust's epilepsy. In early years it was the mark of his difference from others, his appeal for love, his refuge from duties which were foreign to his still unconscious purpose; and in later life it helped him to withdraw from the world and to produce a work 'de si longue haleine'. Meanwhile, however, he was only a little boy choking and writhing in the scented air under the green leaves, in the deadly garden of spring.

Chapter 2

THE GARDEN OF ILLIERS

MARCEL'S grandfather at Illiers had died long ago, on 2 October 1855, when the future Dr Proust was still a young medical student in Paris: Louis Proust was never to know that his son would be successful and famous, any more than Dr Proust in his turn could know that his own beloved but disappointing child would be anything more than an idler in society and a dilettante in literature. Virginie Proust, the grandmother, kept the family grocer's shop at 11 Place du Marché, for eleven years more, until her son passed his *agrégation* in 1866 and became able to help in her support with his earnings. Then she retired to live in an apartment over a shop, only a few doors away, at No. 6; and there, in her front room with its esparto carpet and calico curtains, she sat by the window looking at the market-place below and the church opposite—against its walls at that time were the shops of the local hatter, the barber and the clockmaker—for twenty-three years. The church clock threw its hours and quarters down to the fortunate widow, as she watched the cobbled square which to the natives of Illiers is the hub of the universe. Her time was lost, so easily it passed, but never wasted. Even on ordinary days there was always someone passing, and on Friday market-day and Sunday mass-day everybody was passing; Friday and Sunday were never far away, and Easter or high summer, when her son brought his family from Paris, always came soon.

Her daughter Élisabeth had married in May 1847 a prosperous tradesman of Illiers, Jules Amiot. He kept a draper's shop at No. 14 in the market-place, and his dwelling-house was at No. 4 in the Rue du Saint-Esprit, which runs parallel with the market-place a few yards to the south-west, and is now called, after Proust's father, Rue du Docteur Proust. It was with Marcel's Aunt and Uncle Amiot that the family stayed when they visited Illiers.

They took the train from Paris via Chartres on the day before

Good Friday; and when they left the great cathedral on its grey plateau they travelled south-west for fifteen miles through the endless flat land of the Beauce. As they drew near to Illiers they watched through the carriage window for the first sight of the spire of Saint-Jacques; for 'Combray at a distance, seen from the train when we arrived there in the week before Easter, was nothing but a church that epitomised the town'.[1] It was the signal for Dr Proust to say: "Fold your rugs up, we shall be there in a minute"; and they hastily collected their luggage for leaving the train, which waited, as it still waits, only two minutes at Illiers, and then 'ran on over the viaduct, leaving behind it the frontiers of Christendom whose extreme limit, to me, was marked by Combray'.[2] After crossing the railway-line they walked down the Avenue de la Gare under the still leafless lime-trees, turned right into the Rue de Chartres, left across the market-place into the Rue de la Place; and there, on the opposite side of the Rue du Saint-Esprit, was the house of Aunt Amiot. The frozen travellers warmed themselves by the dining-room fire, while Uncle Jules tapped the barometer in hope that the fine weather would return, and Mme Proust ordered Marcel's hot-water bottle ("Not just hot, boiling") and his pillows ("So that he can't lie down even if he wants to, four if you have them, they can't be too high"). That night the child would wake with a beating heart, as the two booming notes with which Saint-Jacques chimes the quarters trembled on the dark air; to-morrow or the next day, to him as to the good people of Illiers who slept around him, habit would have made them inaudible.

His bed was screened by high white curtains, and covered in the daytime with flowered quilts, embroidered counterpanes and cambric pillowcases which he had to remove and drape over a chair, 'where they consented to spend the night', before he could go to bed. On a bedside table stood a blue glass tumbler and sugar-basin, with a water-jug to match, which his aunt always told Ernestine to empty on the day after his arrival, 'because the child might spill it'. On the mantelpiece was a clock muttering under a glass bell, so heavy that whenever the clock ran down they had to send for the clockmaker to wind it again; on the armchairs were little white antimacassars crocheted with roses, 'not without thorns', since they stuck to him whenever he sat down; and the window had three sets of impracticable curtains, which it was impossible to draw all at once. The whole room was full of objects 'which obviously hadn't been put there in the hope that they would be of use to anyone'; but their very uselessness gave them an individuality, a mysterious life of their own. On the wall hung an engraving of Prince Eugene, looking handsome and fierce in his military cloak. This picture Marcel innocently took to be unique, and was amazed one day to find its twin hanging in a railway refreshment-room, where it served to advertise a brand of biscuits; his uncle, he realised, must have received it, one among many, 'as a free gift from the munificent manufacturer'. A photograph of Botticelli's Primavera would have been much more in accordance with William Morris's precepts for interior decoration, as he afterwards confessed; 'but if I ever saw Prince Eugene again, I think he would have more to tell me than the Primavera'. The contents of his bedroom at Illiers had a quality more precious to him than beauty: they were raw material for his imagination. In the 1890s he was to go through a period of 'good taste'; afterwards, however, to the end of his life, he filled his rooms with hideous but sacred objects which spoke to him of his dead parents, his childhood, time lost. He had come into the world not to collect beauty ready-made, but to create it.

Marcel would spend the morning in his uncle's garden on the far side of the Loir or on walks with the family. When possible he would return before twelve-o'clock lunch to read in the dining-room by the fire, of which his uncle would soon be exclaiming: "That's what I like to see! I can do with a bit of a fire—it was pretty cold in the kitchen-garden at six o'clock this morning, I can tell you! And to think that it's nearly Easter!" Meanwhile the china plates on the wall refrained from interrupting the reading child; the sound of the pump in the garden only made him look up for a moment; but soon the servant came in to lay the table, the walkers returned from Méréglise, the letter-writers came downstairs. "Now then, put your book away, it's lunch-time," said Dr Proust, and they sat down to the delicious fowl which Ernestine, with cries of "Filthy beast", had yesterday murdered in the yard. Her cooking was exquisite, but Aunt Élisabeth's judgment was even more so. Sometimes she would only nibble at a dish, and then everyone knew that the verdict she refrained from giving must be unfavourable. The look of unshakeable and well-considered disapproval in her gentle eyes would send her husband into a rage; he would beg her ironically for her opinion, press her with questions, lose his temper; but she would rather have been burned at the stake than reveal her knowledge that there wasn't quite enough sugar in the pudding. After lunch the glass retort would be brought in, in which Jules Amiot insisted on making the coffee himself; it was 'like an instrument in a chemist's laboratory, except that it smelt good'; and later in the season Uncle Jules would mix the strawberries with cream cheese, of which Marcel was inordinately fond, stopping, 'with the experience of a colourist and the divination of a gourmand', when the mixture had reached exactly the right shade of pink.

It was only in the earlier years at Illiers that Aunt Élisabeth considered herself well enough to come down to meals, or indeed to take meals at all. She refused, step by step, to leave Illiers, her house, her room, and finally her bed; she existed, it seemed, solely on Vichy water, pepsin, lime-tea and the famous madeleines—a plump but diminutive sponge-cake in the form of a scallop-shell, which is still to be found in Illiers, partly, no doubt, because Proustian tourists have been found to welcome it with a mysterious enthusiasm.[1] Like her nephew after her, Aunt Élisabeth became an imaginary invalid, a voluntary prisoner in her bedroom, and died at last of a malady in which no one but the sufferer had ever quite believed. In the end, too late, she was operated upon by Dr Maunoury, the glory of the whole country-side and brother of the general who helped to save Paris in 1914; and everyone agreed at last that she had really been ill, for she died. It is an ironic fact that Marcel's hereditary neurasthenia, his tendency to an illness which was at once hypochondriac and genuine, was transmitted to him not by his sensitive over-loving mother, who nevertheless did so much to perpetuate his weakness, but from his euphoric, extravert father's side of the family.

Gradually Aunt Élisabeth had discouraged all her friends from calling, for they either annoyed her by believing that she was

[1] The scallop-shaped madeleine cake has been known in Illiers from time immemorial. Illiers was one of the halting-places on the mediaeval pilgrimage route from Paris to the shrine of St James the Apostle at Compostella in Spain. The church took its name from St James, and the madeleine-cake its shape from the shell worn by the pilgrims in their hats. Proust alludes to this in the madeleine incident (I, 45).

perfectly well, and only needed 'a brisk walk in the sunshine or a good red beefsteak', or distressed her by thinking she was really as ill as she said she was. Only two visitors were still welcome; one of them was the parish priest, Abbé, afterwards Canon Joseph Marquis, who took Marcel through his first steps in Latin and taught him the names of all the flowers in his garden. But even he exhausted the poor lady with his passion for the etymology of place-names, which so enthralled her nephew, or infuriated her by recommending the view from the tower of Saint-Jacques—as if she could ever climb those ninety-seven steps! In *Du Côté de chez Swann* he is said 'to be thinking of writing a book on the parish of Combray'[1]; and towards the end of his life, in 1907, he did indeed publish the result of his labours, in a large and learned volume called, simply, *Illiers*, which traces the history of the little town from prehistoric times to the building in the 1880s of the new boys' school.[2] But Aunt Élisabeth's most welcome visitor, who never tired her like the curé, who always pleased her by believing that she was ill and did not frighten her by thinking she might die, was the person who in *A la Recherche* is called Eulalie. She lived as servant-companion with the widowed Virginie Proust in the Place du Marché, and came every Sunday afternoon, in her nun-like black mantle and white coif, with news of the morning's mass and the week's gossip; and she left, to the intense disapproval of the jealous Ernestine, with a small gold coin discreetly palmed and pocketed.

Ernestine Gallou, Aunt Élisabeth's housekeeper, must have been still a young woman in Marcel's childhood, for in the early 1930s she was still alive, 'a little old lady, bowed and dwarfed with age, with a pale wrinkled face and fine grey eyes'. She could do nothing against the hated 'Eulalie', but in everything else she was the tyrant of the household. Her devotion to her mistress was profound, but years of familiarity had worn away her deference. The visitors from Paris, however, had never lost their prestige, and to them she was as obliging as she was severe to poor Aunt

---

[1] I, 103

[2] It is often supposed that the name of the curé at Combray (who in fact remains nameless) is Abbé Perdreau; but Abbé Perdreau, who is only mentioned once (I, 57), when Aunt Léonie sees his niece from her window, is a different person. A namesake of his was curé of Saint-Jacques at Illiers from 1777 to 1792.

Élisabeth, and never forgot that coffee and hot-water bottles should always be 'not just hot, but boiling'. "It's amazing how intelligent that girl is, and how well she understands things," Mme Proust would say. But she kept to herself the management of the other servants and all direct communication with her employers; if she was all smiles in the dining-room, in the kitchen she was merciless and treacherous to her unhappy inferiors. The other servants never stayed long; some left at the end of the first month, and only the bravest and most industrious could endure for as long as a year. Marcel observed her cruelty to the kitchen-maid with indignation and pity, which were tempered not only by his appreciation of her cooking, but by a secret complicity: it was the child's first sight of sadism, of the nerve of evil which runs, whether we are conscious of it or not, through all mankind, including ourselves, and which had been planted in him, once and for all, by his anger against his mother. Ernestine's talk was full of old words and turns of speech, which later he met again in Molière or Saint-Simon; her face had qualities of nobility and courage, credulity and cunning, which he recognised in the sculptures of Chartres or the porch of the imaginary Saint-André-des-Champs near Combray. She became for him a symbol of a bygone France, 'a mediaeval peasant who had survived to cook for us in the nineteenth century',[1] with a pedigree as ancient as that of any Guermantes. She was the first of a long line of family servants who together merged into Françoise; and her mistress, almost without modification, became Aunt Léonie.

The door of Ernestine's kitchen, 'a miniature temple of Venus overflowing with the offerings of the milkman and the green-grocer', opened on a little garden which was more like a court-yard, since most of it was paved, though space was found for a tiny lawn, a flower-bed of pansies and a chestnut-tree. There was no room here for Marcel's grandmother Weil to walk in the wind and rain, as she did in his novel, while her wicked relatives indoors tempted her husband to drink a glass of brandy; indeed, it is unlikely that she ever visited Illiers, and the scene of these events was certainly Uncle Louis Weil's more spacious garden at Auteuil. But here at Illiers, too, the family would sit with their liqueurs after dinner, on the cane garden-chairs at the iron garden-table; there was a family friend who would call, like

[1] I, 151

Swann, at this time in the evening; and for Marcel 'the drama of going to bed' and the anxious ceremony of his good-night kiss were enacted at Illiers as at Auteuil. Projecting from Ernestine's back-kitchen into the garden was a single-storeyed building, with windows of tinted glass, the cubby-hole of Uncle Jules and the studio of his son André, who painted. Jules Amiot had lived in Algeria as a young man, and his sanctum was adorned with native mats on the stone floor, with carved coconuts and photographs of palm-trees and mosques. After lunch, when the others took a siesta, and Dr Proust remarked, "It's strange, I don't feel well if I don't have a nap in the daytime," Uncle Jules would say, "I'd sooner walk ten miles than lie down now, it would give me a fever," and retire to his room, where he was supposed to be engaged in some important work. But when Marcel came to call him for the afternoon walk he would not reply at first, and then would answer in a startled voice, and come out rubbing his eyes; for the sleep he maligned had overtaken him on his wickerwork chaise-longue, by his hookah, as he arranged his photograph album or meditated on his fabulous youth.

The garden door opened into the Place Lemoine, where the Rue Saint-Hilaire, which continues the Rue de Chartres down to the river and the Pont Saint-Hilaire, meets the Rue des Trois Maries. It had a narrow grille through which one can still peep into the stone-flagged garden, and over it hung the famous jangling bell, which sounded automatically whenever one of the family came in 'without ringing'. Its interminable clanging could be heard in Mme Larcher's front room across the Place Lemoine, and she would always say to her visitors: "There goes Jules Amiot's doorbell"; it could never be mistaken for the 'double tinkle, timid, oval and gilded' of the visitors' bell. In his novel Proust brought the Auteuil garden and with it Swann to Combray, but he kept the garden gate of Illiers and the two bells, which took their place among the most potent symbols of Time Lost.

Past Aunt Amiot's front door ran the Rue du Saint-Esprit, 'monotonous and grey, with its three gritstone steps before nearly every door, like a furrow cut by a sculptor of gothic images in the very stone in which he has carved a crib or a calvary'. Next door to the right lived M. Pipereau, who gave his name to Dr Piperaud in Proust's novel; and next door to the left, on the street corner, was Legué's grocery, which Ernestine patronised when

she had no time to go as far as Mme Damoiseau's in the Rue de la
Place. In the hot summer afternoons, when Marcel was reading
in the darkness of his shuttered bedroom, his sense of the
brilliance of the sunlight outside would come from the din of M.
Legué's hammer, which 'seemed to scatter a distant shower of
scarlet stars', as he broke up old packing-cases in his yard. In the
novel Legué is called Camus; but there was indeed a grocer called
Camus elsewhere in Illiers, and nowadays one of his descendants
and namesakes keeps the grocery at Méréglise. Opposite, at No.3,
was the shop of M. Desvaux, the gunsmith, who embarrassed
Marcel whenever he went to his bedroom window by waving
amicably from his doorstep, where he would stand smoking his
pipe and chatting with the passers-by. At No. 1, on the corner
opposite Legué's, lived Mme Goupil, daughter of Dr Galopin,
after whom the former Rue de l'Oiseau Fléché, which continues
the Rue du Saint-Esprit in the direction of the railway, is now
called Rue du Docteur Galopin. She appears in the novel under
her own name, when Aunt Léonie sees her going to church,
wearing her new silk gown made in Châteaudun, and without an
umbrella, although a black cloud is looming behind the church
tower.[1] Her father is introduced as Dr Percepied, in whose
carriage Marcel has the revelation of the three spires of Martinville
le-Sec; but here Proust is playing one of his favourite tricks with
names, for at Illiers Percepied was really the name of the postman,
while at Combray Galopin is the pastrycook from whom Mme
Goupil buys a tart, and who owns the new dog, 'as clever as a
Christian', whose appearance so startles Aunt Léonie.[2] Mme
Goupil, who was on visiting terms with the Amiots, was a lady
of majestic demeanour and imperturbable dignity: "I don't think
she'd turn a hair if the church-spire fell on her head," a medical
friend of Dr Proust was heard to remark. She had married a
wealthy property-owner of Illiers, and in the novel it is at her
wedding, under the alias of Dr Percepied's daughter, that the
Narrator has his first sight of the Duchesse de Guermantes in the
chapel of Gilbert the Bad. Her waxen and hieratic face was said
to have inspired the figure of St Lucy, her patron saint, in the
stained-glass window by the pulpit in the church.

In the Rue de la Place, which leads from the Rue du Saint-
Esprit to the market-place, was a grocery kept by Mme

Damoiseau, the 'épicerie Borange' of Combray, which was also the telephone-exchange and the only bookshop in Illiers. On either side of the door, 'more mysterious and teeming with ideas than the porch of a cathedral', 'a mosaic of books and magazines'[1] still hangs. Friday, in our time, is still market-day; the cobblestones are strewn with straw, cauliflowers, hobnailed boots, ironmongery and carpets, and everyone in Illiers is there as stallholder or purchaser. When a visitor passes, however unobtrusive his appearance, all pause to stare in amazed hostility, with something of the emotion felt by Aunt Léonie when she saw from her window 'a dog she didn't know'. But later in the day, when he dares to show his face again, all is well and their glances are friendly; he has been identified as a *proustien anglais* who is staying at the Hôtel de l'Image, and he is no longer a strange dog.

The church of Saint-Jacques is half surrounded by the wide market-place, half built-in by ancient houses; and even the market-place side shows the traces, like shadows in time, of shops built by mediaeval squatters and pulled down since Proust's days. To the English visitor, accustomed to the little English parish-church, Saint-Jacques seems enormous; the roof of the nave, with the ugly modern clock whose Rhinegold chime is nevertheless so antique and beautiful, has an endless steep slope which recalls the churches of Holland. The spire rises on a square, buttressed tower with a turret at the side; it is in two tiers, resembling a large squat extinguisher on top of which has been placed a tall thin extinguisher; and above is a long mast with a weather-cock at the summit. No wonder that the spire comes into view at every side-street, at every road leading out of Illiers, and soars at an immense height, always with three or four jackdaws circling or alighting, over rooftops one would have thought steep enough to hide it. The asymmetry and oddity of the spire gives it the humble yet majestic air which made Aunt Amiot say: "If it played the piano, I'm sure it would play with real feeling"; and each new angle from which it is seen, 'like a solid surprised at an unknown moment of its revolution', seems intended by the unknown architect to be the best viewpoint of all.

The church of Saint-Jacques at Illiers is less ancient than Saint-Hilaire at Combray: it was built in the late eleventh century, restored in the fifteenth century by Florent d'Illiers, who left only

[1] I, 84

the romanesque doorway and a portion of wall from the older church, and has no Merovingian crypt, no golden cross presented by King Dagobert, no tomb of Sigebert's little daughter. Most of the interior, indeed, is of the nineteenth century, for it was 'restored' by Abbé Louis Carré and by his successor, the good Canon Marquis, who was determined, despite his passion for history and etymology, that his church should be absolutely modern.[1] Proust did not libel him when he made him say to Aunt Léonie: "I admit there are a few things in my church that are well worth a visit, but there are others that are getting very old."[2] The glass is modern, there is no stonework to be seen except the Canon's new altar, and the floor, once paved with the tombs of abbots and marquises of Illiers, is now covered with marble tiles. Nevertheless, this is not the vulgar, rootless nineteenth century of English church restoration, but one in which old traditions of magnificence and good taste were still alive. The panelling which conceals the walls is painted a faded purplish brown, adorned with golden lozenges, crosses and crowns; and though the purple is sombre, the vivid colour of the rest is dazzling and sumptuous to English Protestant eyes. In Proust's time some of the original stained glass still remained; but all is gone now, blown to pieces, along with the refugees from Belgium and the North herded in the market-place, by the exuberant Italian air-raids of June 1940; and the windows are still glassless, covered with the canvas and boarding so familiar in English churches since that year. Under the tower is a side-chapel sacred not to Gilbert the Bad, but to the Virgin. It is this chapel of the Virgin which was decorated with pink and white hawthorn in the 'month of Mary', and in which at Combray the Duchesse de Guermantes sat, 'in the intermittent, hot sunshine of a windy and rainy day', at the wedding of Dr Percepied's daughter.[3] The pews of the local nobility, the Goussencourts of Saint-Éman (which is Guermantes), and the squires of Tansonville, Éguilly-les-Brandières and Beaurouvre, were in fact in this chapel of the Virgin, and Marcel must often have seen the châtelaine of Saint-Éman sitting there at Sunday

---

[1] Abbé Carré (1850-72) provided the purple panelling and the Florent d'Illiers window in the choir. The further restoration was the work of Canon Marquis, who proudly declared: "in my opinion the correct principle of restoration is to harmonise the furnishings with the original style of the church".

[2] I, 103   [3] I, 174-8

mass, the first avatar of the Duchesse. Even the presence of
Gilbert the Bad is not far to seek. The arms of the marquises of
Illiers (or, six annulets azure, three, two and one) appear on the
seventeenth-century roofbeams; it was their first ancestor,
Geoffroy d'Illiers, builder of the castle of Illiers, who suggested
the desperate life and horrible end of Gilbert the Bad; and Basin,
the second Lord of Illiers, a contemporary of William the
Conqueror, gave his name to Gilbert's descendant, Basin, Duc de
Guermantes. The most celebrated member of the family was
Florent d'Illiers, who fought beside Joan of Arc (whose statue is
in the market-place outside the church-porch) as lieutenant of the
Bastard Dunois, and was buried in Saint-Jacques; he appears
along with Christ, Saint Jacques, Saint Hilaire and Miles d'Illiers,
Bishop of Chartres, in a window over the choir. From a female
cousin of Florent descended the poet Ronsard, and by the
Chantemesle branch the Marquises of Illiers were connected with
the Balzacs.[1] Throughout the seventeenth century they employed
the Prousts as their stewards and stood as godparents to their
children. The Lords of Illiers could not trace their descent as far
back as the Duchesse de Guermantes's ancestress Geneviève de
Brabant, wife of the eighth-century Count Palatine Siegfried,
whose wrongful accusation of adultery by the infamous Golo was
part of the repertoire of the magic lantern in Marcel's bedroom;
but they helped to create the Guermantes's, to ensure that Marcel,
in his childhood at Illiers, should see the French nobility as living
symbols of a mediaeval past, miraculous survivors of a glowing
window in a gothic church and the nursery-tales flashed in green
and scarlet on his bedroom wall.

Marcel's uncle made up for the minuteness of his back-garden
by possessing two other gardens. In the Rue des Lavoirs, which
continues the Rue des Trois Maries on the way to the River Loir,
and is so called from the stagnant oblong tank, surrounded by a
lean-to shelter, where the laundry of Illiers is washed, he had a
vegetable-garden; and at the far side of the river, on the edge of
open fields, was his pleasure-garden, the Pré Catelan, which he
proudly named after the famous enclosure in the Bois de Boulogne
at Paris.

As they walked down the Rue des Lavoirs to the Pré Catelan,

[1] Cf. II, 1053, for the probable emotions of M. de Charlus if he had learnt
that the Guermantes's were related to the Balzacs.

carrying their trowels and fishing-lines, Marcel and Robert passed on their right one of the two ruined towers of the castle of Illiers, built in 1019 by the wicked Geoffroy d'Illiers, Vicomte de Châteaudun, during his quarrel with Fulbert, Bishop of Chartres. The other tower, a hundred yards further along the meadows stretching between the town and the river, had an unhallowed significance for Marcel: it could be seen from the lavatory window at the top of the house, as he sat in the little room scented by a festoon of iris-roots from the banks of the garden-pond. Here, since it was the only place in the house where he was allowed to lock himself in, he would retire whenever he needed privacy to read, weep, or make his first experiments in the pleasures of sex—experiments which were not without their heroic side, since he was not sure at first that their rending delight would not be the death of him. In the morning he would vow not to give way to temptation; but after lunch, when he was replete with Ernestine's chicken, the idea would return, 'sending a mounting, delicious wave of blood to his heart', and he would climb again to his grotto of pleasure, where only the branches of flowering currant and the castle tower could see him. In his novel he transferred the under-ground chamber of the first tower to this second, and brought the ruined keep to the market-town of Roussainville-le-Pin, on the Méséglise Way, and surrounded it with woods; but the real Roussainville is a tiny hamlet a mile south of Illiers, without ruins, woods or market, a whole quarter of the compass away from Méréglise; and the suffix le-Pin comes from Bailleau-le-Pin, a village six miles north-east of Illiers on the road to Chartres. Perhaps the naughty boys and girls of the town, led by 'Théodore' (who was Victor, the errand-boy at Legué's grocery, choirboy at Saint-Jacques, and brother of Jules Amiot's gardener Ménard), played in these ruins at Illiers as at Combray, and Marcel with them; or perhaps it was only the thought of his forbidden pleasures in the lavatory that made Roussainville in the rain seem to be 'chastised like a village in the Old Testament by God the Father'.[1]

After the laundry-tank (on the left), the kitchen-garden, the castle ruins and a field of grazing cows (on the right), the Rue des Lavoirs ends in a wooden footbridge over the Loir, variously known as the Pont-Vieux, the Passerelle or the Grand' Planche,

[1] I, 152

and associated in the novel with Legrandin. There is a tradition at Illiers that in the days when this bridge was only a single plank and had no railings, the village drunkard would totter over it, crying "Lord, lord, let me across and I'll give up the drink"; but when he reached the other side he would begin to dance and sing, and shout "Now I can go on drinking!" On the far side of the bridge is a path leading upstream along the Loir, called at Combray the tow-path (*chemin de halage*); but it can never have been used for towing at Illiers, since a line of trees grows between it and the river, and the Loir here is too shallow for barges. A little further on the walled lane from the footbridge leads into the Rue des Vierges, which runs to the right towards the Pont Saint-Hilaire, while a turning left goes to Tansonville, two miles away to the south. But Tansonville gave no more than its name and its château to Swann's park, the original of which lies directly before us, on the opposite side of the Rue des Vierges: it is none other than Jules Amiot's pleasure-garden, the Pré Catelan.

Up the left-hand side of the Pré Catelan climbs a narrow lane, separated from the garden by a hedge of pink and white hawthorns. To Marcel the pink hawthorns seemed twice as beautiful as the white: similarly, he reflected, the pink iced biscuits at Mme Damoiseau's grocery were twice as expensive as the white. The hawthorns reminded him, too, of the colour of his favourite strawberries crushed with cream-cheese; and they seemed not only edible but holy; for just as they made the altar of Saint-Jacques look like a hedge in bloom in the month of Mary, so here in the *petit sentier* the hawthorn chapels took on something of the religious sanctity of the church. Their scent was not yet fatal to him, and once, when he was ill, his mother brought him branches of his beloved pink flower and laid them on his bed, a present from Ménard the gardener. Through the gaps in the hedge he could look down to the lawns and ornamental water; and perhaps once he saw there some little girl with reddish hair, freckles and a sly look, a first appearance of Gilberte. The Amiots and Prousts were often joined for picnics in the Pré Catelan by friends and their children; and all we know of Proust's method of fusing people from different periods of his life into single characters for his novel suggests that there was someone at Illiers who became the Gilberte of Combray.

Uncle Jules had laid out the flat lower part of his garden near the Rue des Vierges with lawns, gravel paths, dwarf palms, geranium-beds and an ornamental water, not a lake as in Swann's park, but a broadening, still hardly too wide for leaping, of a brook running into the Loir. This winding pond, now almost silted up, had a rustic bridge, water-lilies, swans and carp, so many that the children were allowed to fish for them—hence the fishing-line with its bobbing cork which the Narrator sees in the water by Gilberte[1]—and its banks were bordered with forget-me-nots and the blue and yellow irises whose roots scented the room at the top of the house. Along the paths were curious, turreted dove-cotes of variegated brick, modelled on the Arab pigeon-houses which Uncle Jules had seen in Algeria. Somewhere in this region Marcel and Robert planted a poplar sapling, for which Robert searched in vain more than fifty years later, among the other trees near the great catalpa, a fortnight before his death in 1935. The spire of Saint-Jacques, nearly half a mile away, shows through the trees, as it did at Tansonville.[2] There is a sound of gently falling water from a weir in the Loir near by.

Above the lawns was a steep hill covered with a dense copse of hazels, known as the Bois Pilou, where Marcel and Robert played at hide-and-seek, and sometimes frightened themselves into believing they were really lost. Near the left-hand side of the garden, separated by the hawthorn hedge from the *petit sentier*, a path with stone steps climbed the slope, a favourite haunt, nowadays at least, of long, fat, steel-grey slow-worms. Half-way up Uncle Jules had built an octagonal summer-house in red brick, the Maison des Archers. Its foundations were an artificial grotto, and the first floor was a furnished rest-room where Marcel could lie reading *Le Capitaine Fracasse* on a pink divan. Still further up the slope was a concrete tank which supplied water for the hose-pipes and fountains below. It was filled by a pump worked by horses, who every few days would plod round a circular track, one at each end of a rotating beam with the pump in the middle. When the horses were not working, only the shadow of the beam would turn with the sun: "You see, it's a kind of sundial," Uncle Jules told Marcel. At the bottom of the tank, when the water was low, Marcel could see a dim entanglement of pipes, green with water-weeds; a newt slept clinging to the sides, until he startled it and it leapt into the water. From the path by the tank, over the hawthorns of the *raidillon* to the left, meadows could be seen which were visible from nowhere else; and they seemed to Marcel a mysterious country set in the middle of the real world, like the underworld of water in which he had seen his mother bathing. A few yards further up the path, the park ended in a little plateau containing an immemorial asparagus-bed, beside which grew the strawberries of which his uncle was so proud. "They are *exquisite,*" Mme Proust would earnestly say; and "Yes, they *are* good," Uncle Jules would reply modestly, "they are real wood-strawberries." On the far side of the asparagus-bed the end of the garden was marked by a white gate, past which the landscape dramatically changed into mile upon mile of rolling plain: here was the Méréglise way.

There is no direct path to Méréglise here, however; the haw-thorn path turns sharply right at the white gate, and runs down-hill through land which then was green cornfields scattered with scarlet poppies, and now is allotment-gardens, into the main road from Illiers to Brou, here called Chemin de la Croix Rompue. This leads back to the outskirts of Illiers, and crosses the opposite end of the Rue des Vierges near the site of the church of Saint-Hilaire, demolished in the French Revolution, which gave its name to the church at Combray. Jules Amiot rescued carved stone from its ruins for the front gate of his Pré Catelan in the Rue des Vierges. Here a road to the left leads to Méréglise, and on the right is the Loir with its only road-bridge, the Pont Saint-Hilaire, over which it is delightful to lean and watch the trailing green water-weeds and the motionless trout. Here the Rue Saint-Hilaire leads from the bridge past the Place Lemoine and the Rue du Saint-Esprit to the market-place.

Sometimes, when the family walked back from picnic-tea in the Pré Catelan in the red twilight after sunset, Dr Proust would take them a longer way round. From the town-side of the Pont Saint-Hilaire another 'towing-path' leads up the Loir to a foot-bridge called the Pont du Gué Bellerin. Here is the triangular Place du Calvaire, with its cross and image of the Crucified, which in *Du Côté de chez Swann* becomes 'the Mall'. A road to Saint-Éman runs north under the railway viaduct and past the cemetery, where at Combray Dr Percepied once met the music-teacher Vinteuil; and the Rue de l'Oiseau-Fléché, named after an inn where the mediaeval archers of Illiers met to shoot at a bird tied to a pole, leads to the right towards the Rue du Saint-Esprit.[1] But the parents and the blissfully weary children would press forward along the Rue du Chemin de Fer into the Avenue de la Gare. As they looked back, the cross was silhouetted against the water of the Loir near the Gué Bellerin, lit crimson by the western sky, but in the Avenue de la Gare, which contains, as at Combray, 'the most attractive villas in the town', the moon was already shining. In every garden (for this is almost the only street at Illiers where the houses have front gardens) 'the moonlight, as in the paintings of Hubert Robert, scattered its broken staircases of white marble, its fountains, its iron gates left half-open'. Marcel was dragging his feet and dropping with sleep, and 'the scent of the lime-trees seemed like a reward which could only be won at the expense of great fatigue, and wasn't worth the effort'. At last Dr Proust would stop and say: "Where are we now?" No one knew; but the kind, bearded father would point with a laugh to their back-garden gate in the Place Lemoine, and Mme Proust, whose respect for her husband reached its peak when she considered his interest in meteorology or his sense of direction, would murmur: "My dear, you are amazing!"

[1] The Rue de l'Oiseau and its inn are among the Narrator's most persistent memories of Combray. Cf. I, 48, 55, 166; II, 531; III, 624, 856, 955

Chapter 3

THE TWO WAYS

TO the child Marcel the two favourite walks of the family seemed to be in diametrically opposite directions, so that no two points in the world could be so utterly separated as their never-reached destinations. Whether they left the house by the front door or by the garden-gate, they would turn one way for Méréglise and the other way for Saint-Éman. To Méréglise, since the Rue Saint-Hilaire, though a short-cut, was less interesting, they would go by the Rue des Lavoirs and the *passerelle*, up the hawthorn path beside the Pré Catelan, and along the Chemin de la Croix-Rompue to the Méréglise turning by the site of Saint-Hilaire. In his novel Proust called Méréglise 'Méséglise', for euphony; and as the way there went by the Pré Catelan, which he had transformed into Swann's park, he was able to say with truth that it was also Swann's Way.

A few yards from the Pont Saint-Hilaire the Méréglise way climbs a slope: behind, the spire of Saint-Jacques rises to its full height, and sends its last chime to the departing wanderer; but in front, past the level-crossing of the railway on its way to Brou, is the landscape of rolling plain already seen from the top of the hawthorn path, pierced by the spires of village churches and barred by dark woods on the far horizon. The air here has a limpid, milky quality which in England one breathes only in the West Country; and a warm wind, 'the tutelary genius of Combray', is always blowing. To the Narrator this wind seems to bring a message from Gilberte at Laon,[1] as well it might: for though Proust intended to lead his reader astray to the cathedral-town of Laon in Seine-et-Marne, 150 miles from Illiers, he was thinking privately of Laons at the northern end of Eure-et-Loire, near the birthplace of the husband of Mme Goupil; and the road to Laons may be seen from here. Can a daughter of Mme Goupil, or the niece with whom Aunt Léonie sees her walking, have been the first original of Gilberte?

[1] I, 145

Along the right-hand grass verge of the road, past a prehistoric standing-stone, is an endless line of apple-trees, surrounded in September by the red rings of fallen apples, and all
summer through by the circles of their shade: 'It was on the
Méséglise Way,' says the Narrator, 'that I first noticed the round
shadow which apple-trees cast on the sunlit ground.'[1] Later in
life Proust would drug himself for a week with veronal and
cafeine, in order to get up in the daytime and visit his favourite
trees in bloom on the outskirts of Paris; but he rode in a taxi
hermetically sealed to cut off their deadly scent, which in his
childhood he had loved with impunity.

Méréglise itself, however, far from being an important town
large enough to send the Duc de Guermantes to represent it in the
Chamber of Deputies, is a small hamlet of about forty houses, a
little church, and two or three shops, including nowadays the
grocery of M. Camus. Its gardens are coloured with russet
dahlias shedding their petals through wire netting, and with pink
laundry hanging up to dry. The Proustian magic somehow stops
short of this insignificant village; as in *Du Côté de chez Swann*, the
way to Méréglise is more important than Méréglise itself. 'Of
Méséglise,' says the Narrator, 'I never knew anything but the
Way.'[2] But the church of Méréglise, at least, has its part to play
in the most remarkable of all the manifestations of the Méséglise
Way.

The church of Saint-Jacques, which seemed lost for ever
behind the hill between the Pont Saint-Hilaire and the level-
crossing, has been in view again all along the road to Méréglise,
but never for long in the same place. The road winds imper-
ceptibly, and the spires and towers of Vieuvicq, Méréglise, Saint-
Éman and Marchéville, in a kind of ritual dance, change their
places incessantly in relation to Saint-Jacques and one another.
It is the phenomenon of the moving spires which the Narrator
sees in Dr Percepied's carriage, though there it takes place at the
centre, and here round the circumference of a circle. Along the
rough track of flint and sand which leads north-east to Saint-
Éman and Marchéville just before the standing-stone, the illusion
is even more bewildering; and this is the very route taken by Dr
Percepied on his way to his patient at 'Martinville-le-Sec'. It was
more than twenty years later that Proust saw the enchantment

[1] I, 146　　　　　　　　[2] I, 134

repeated, this time in the centripetal form which it takes in his novel, by the spires of Caen; but then, as we shall see, it was in the country near 'Balbec', after the deaths of his parents, and in a motor-car driven by the young chauffeur who was one of the originals of Albertine.

The Méréglise way, Dr Proust always said, was the finest view of a plain he had ever seen, while the Saint-Éman way was the very type of a river-landscape. The shortest route to Saint-Éman was by the Rue de l'Oiseau-Fléché to the Place du Calvaire and the cemetery, after which the path leads all the way by the banks of the Loir; but if they wished to see as much as possible of the river they could go first by the Rue des Lavoirs to the *passerelle*, and along the two 'towing-paths' to the Place du Calvaire again; and this, though the first half of it belongs to the Méréglise way, is the route Proust describes in his novel. But the Loir above Illiers soon becomes only a narrow though charming brook. For the river-scenery of the Guermantes Way he described the country downstream from the *passerelle*, with its motionless anglers, and water-lilies, and rowing-boats, and introduced the Pré Catelan a second time: this time it is the 'property thrown open to the public by its owner, who had made a hobby of aquatic gardening'.[1] A mile below Illiers, near Tansonville, the Thironne, which comes from beyond Méréglise and gave part of its name to the Vivonne of Combray, flows into the Loir. Where the two rivers meet is a garden called Les Plaisances, to which he obliquely refers in his description of the Guermantes Way: beside the water, he says, is 'une maison dite de plaisance', where a young woman, disappointed in love, has come 'in the popular phrase, to bury herself'; and he sees her standing pensively framed in her window, and looking up as the family passes.[2] Half a mile further up the Thironne is a water-mill, whose white front wreathed in climbing plants is reflected in a millpond covered with water-lilies, and whose name sends a shudder through Proust's readers: it is Montjouvin. The mysterious young woman really existed in the country round Illiers, though she lived neither at Montjouvin nor Les Plaisances, but at Mirougrain. In the novel her dwelling-place is a fusion of all three, while the girl herself has become two separate characters, one of whom is far more important than the forsaken maiden, who never reappears: she is none other than

[1] I, 169   [2] I, 170, 171

Mlle Vinteuil. This complex of topography and persons befits the complex of forbidden love which it embodies; for it is at 'Montjouvain', and through Vinteuil's daughter, that the innocent Combray is linked with the Cities of the Plain.

At Combray Mirougrain is a farm belonging to Aunt Léonie; it is one of her favourite daydreams that one day her house will be burned down with all the family in it, and that she will have time to escape at her leisure and go to spend the summer 'in her pretty farmhouse at Mirougrain, where there was a waterfall'.[1] At Illiers Mirougrain is a country-house called Le Rocher de Mirougrain, a mile up the Loir in the direction of Saint-Éman. The Loir broadens here into a still pool, crossed at one end by a wooden footbridge; on the far side is a steep slope, from which one can look down on the house; and, just as at Mlle Vinteuil's 'Montjouvain', there is a pond below the house, and a red-tiled gardener's hut by the pond. No one will ever know whether in real life Marcel hid in the bushes on the slope to spy on the lonely young lady of the house; but it is not unlikely that he did, and local gossip suggested that he might see something he ought not to see.

Her name was Juliette Joinville d'Artois, and in 1880, when Marcel was nine, she was in her early twenties. Her melancholy love of the past had taken a form which would horrify a modern archaeologist: she had collected prehistoric dolmens from the surrounding countryside, fortunately overlooking the one near Méréglise, and built with them a monstrous edifice in her garden, which she proudly called 'my temple'. 'In this fair-haired, frail, twenty-year-old child,' she remarks of herself in a volume called *A Journey through My Heart*, published in 1887, 'I see a soul longing to kill its body, a body doing all it can to bring rest to its weary soul. And in the colossal, awe-inspiring, defensive mass of my temple I see a savage desire to create a place of refuge, a shelter against further misfortunes.' Her only companion was a deaf-mute man-servant, whose presence gave rise to strange rumours in Illiers: she had chosen him, she said, from love of silence, and from desire to learn and teach the deaf-and-dumb language; but was it not rather, as scandal suggested, because he would be unable to tell what he saw at Mirougrain? Nothing more is known to-day of the morals, seventy years ago, of poor Mlle

[1] I, 116

Joinville d'Artois. She lived in a lonely house and was a subject for scandal: for the other qualities of Mlle Vinteuil, her homosexuality so closely united to her sadism, Proust had only to look in himself. We shall find him, many years later, inviting the partners of his pleasure to desecrate the images of his dead parents, as part of the ritual of his enjoyment; for the form of sadism which in Mlle Vinteuil seems hardly to deserve the name (since she cannot really hurt her dead father by encouraging her friend to spit on his photograph) was to him the most real, horrifying and irresistible.

In his novel Proust called Vinteuil's Mirougrain 'Montjouvain', and situated it on the Méséglise Way; whereas, since Mirougrain is in fact on the river in the direction of Saint-Éman, it would seem to belong of right to the Guermantes Way. But there are several links which made this change of place and name natural to his imagination. The road to Laons, which begins on the way to Méréglise, runs past Mirougrain; both Mirougrain and Montjouvin are on a river and by a pond; and in the eighteenth century the château of Montjouvin, of which nothing now remains but its water-mill, was owned by a certain Jean-Jacques Jouvet de Mirougrain. When Dr Percepied met Vinteuil by the cemetery, where he had gone to weep over his wife's grave, the unhappy music-teacher was a long way from Montjouvain, but little more than half a mile from Mirougrain.

Saint-Éman can be reached from Mirougrain either by following the road to Laons, or along the path by the bank of the Loir, or by the road which leads from the Place du Calvaire at Illiers past the cemetery. Half a mile beyond Mirougrain is the farm on the right of the road, 'at some distance from two other farms which were themselves close together', which seems to the Narrator one of the chief symbols of the Guermantes Way; for on their way back it is only half an hour from home, where dinner will be later than usual, as is the rule when they have walked towards Guermantes; he will be sent to bed immediately after the soup course, and his mother, 'kept at table just as though there had been company to dinner', will not come upstairs to give him his good-night kiss.[1] The isolated farm is called Crasne, and the two other farms are the hamlet of Les Perruches. At Les Perruches a turning left soon reaches Saint-Éman.

[1] I, 182-3

At Saint-Éman is the château of the Goussencourts, with its
towers in the shape which the French call pepper-pots. For the
vast woods which surround the country home of the Duchesse de
Guermantes, however, Proust was thinking of the forests which
half encircle Illiers on the edge of the highlands of the Perche a
few miles further west; and one of these is called the Bois de
Saint-Éman. At Saint-Éman, too, is one of the sources of the
Loir, which the Narrator first sees long after his childhood at
Combray, on his walk to Guermantes with Gilberte after her
marriage to Saint-Loup, near the verge of Time Regained. This
fabulous place, 'as extra-terrestrial as the gate of Hell', is in fact,
as he is so disappointed to find, 'nothing but a kind of laundry-
tank in which bubbles rise to the surface'.[1] But the most surprising
sight at Saint-Éman is a signpost which reads: 'Méréglise, 3 kilo-
metres.' Not content with their trick with the church spires, the
winding roads of the Méréglise way have succeeded in bringing
Méréglise nearer to Saint-Éman than either village is to Illiers.
Gilberte was quite serious when she said: "If you like we can go
to Guermantes by Méséglise, it is the nicest walk"; and when she
says: "If we took the road to the left and then turned to the right,
we should be at Guermantes in less than a quarter of an hour", she
is thinking of the track by the megalith, which is on the left
coming from Méréglise, and turns right, half-way to Saint-Éman,
at a hamlet called Les Dauffraies; though she is exaggerating the
shortness of the walk, which at any comfortable walking-speed
would take at least three-quarters of an hour. The 'perfect and
profound valley, carpeted with moonlight', in which they stop for
a moment, 'like two insects about to plunge into the blue calix of
a flower',[2] is the narrow ravine formed by the Loir a little below
Saint-Éman.

We have seen the streets and church of Illiers, the hawthorn
path and the garden pond, and have taken the two ways which,
after all, can so easily be made one. It is at first sight surprising
that the real landscape of Illiers should resemble so closely the
created, mythical and universal landscape of Combray; and
certainly in no other section of *A la Recherche du Temps Perdu* did
the literal truth need so little alteration in order to make it
coincide with the ideal truth. Partly this is because Proust saw
Illiers in childhood, when the visual object, which later serves

[1] III, 693   [2] III, 692-3

only to mask immaterial truth, is still able to reveal it: for to the
child's eye object and symbol are one and the same. Partly, too,
it is because he wrote of Combray after many years, when
memory had already performed its task of rejecting the in-
essential. Perhaps there is even some danger of exaggerating the
objectivity of the presence in the Illiers landscape of the symbols
Proust saw there: they are undoubtedly real outside this world,
but in this world may they not be illusions? Perhaps, as the Baron
de Charlus said of Combray, Illiers is only 'a little town like so
many others',[1] and if Proust had spent his childhood holidays in
one of those many other little towns, he would have extracted
the same truths from different symbols. And yet, at Illiers, the
church and grey streets and gardens of Combray are there for all
to see; the village spires perform their strange movement, the two
ways of rolling plain and narrow river lead for ever in opposite
directions, and nevertheless meet. In the real topography of
Illiers the mysterious significance of the symbolical landscape of
Combray was already latent. However, the differences between
Illiers and Combray are real and important; by observing them
we may detect Proust in the act of adjusting the truth of Illiers
to make it conform still more closely to the truth of Combray.

It was necessary first of all to set Combray free, to divert the
reader's attention and his own imagination from the real Illiers.
He planted clues which suggest that Combray is in Normandy or
Champagne; he invented new streets, the Rue Sainte-Hildegarde,
Rue de la Eretonnerie, Rue de Saintrailles, and changed the
position of old ones, so that the Rue du Saint-Esprit moves to
the back of Aunt Léonie's house, and the Mall, which at Illiers is
on the southern edge of the town, is to the north by the Place
du Calvaire. Saint-Jacques takes the name of the demolished
Saint-Hilaire. There is no equivalent near Illiers of the large town
of Thiberzy, whither Françoise had to go before dawn to fetch
the midwife for the kitchen-maid (although Combray, like Illiers,
is large enough to support a midwife of its own). There is no
village called Champieu on the Méréglise way, nor any church
of Saint-André-des-Champs, in the sculptured figures of whose
porch the Narrator could see Françoise and her philosophy,
Théodore the grocer's boy, and the peasant girl sheltering from
the rain, whom he longed in vain to meet alone. The original of

[1] III, 795

Saint-André has been variously identified as Notre-Dame-de-Champdé at Châteaudun, or Saint-Loup-de-Naud, or a little church in the Rue de la Maladrerie at Illiers; but Proust was no doubt thinking primarily of the porches of Chartres, and next of the concentrated essence of the gothic churches he visited in the early 1900s. 'In order to describe a single church, one needs to have seen a great many,'[1] he says in *Le Temps Retrouvé*; and even the church of Saint-Hilaire at Combray has paving from Lisieux and Dives, and stained glass from Évreux, Pont-Audemer and the Saint-Chapelle in Paris. He took the name of Combray from Combres, a village a few miles past Méréglise; but it suggests the Combourg of Chateaubriand's boyhood in Brittany, the Cambrai in Flanders of which his friend Bertrand de Fénelon's famous ancestor was bishop; and there is an actual Combray in Normandy near Lisieux. He generalised Illiers so that it should become universal, the paradise of innocent vision from which every human being is expelled at the end of his childhood. He shifted the known landscape of Illiers to give it the kaleidoscopic quality of a dream—the kind of dream in which, going a little past the furthest point reached in childhood walks on the outskirts of an inland industrial birthplace, we find ourselves in sight of Paris or the sea.

The most far-reaching adjustments occurred, however, not in the topography but in the people of Combray. Proust wished to make Combray a symbol of the family; and so that all the family should be there, he imported his maternal grandparents and Uncle Louis Weil (who, as Uncle Adolphe, takes possession of Jules Amiot's den in the garden), although it is probable that they never visited Illiers. Grandfather Weil, indeed, was notorious for never having spent a night away from Paris in all his eighty years, except during the siege of 1870, when he took his wife to Étampes for safety. Whether the great-aunt (who teases Swann for living near the Halle aux Vins) and Aunts Flora and Céline (who thank him so obscurely for the present of Asti) ever existed, remains unknown. Perhaps they too belonged to Paris and his mother's side of the family; though in *Journées de Lecture* the great-aunt seems identical with Aunt Élisabeth Amiot before she became bed-ridden. Jules Amiot disappears from the novel: since his garden had been made over to Swann, his function as 'the

[1] III, 907

gardening, early-rising uncle' had lapsed; and it is one of Aunt
Léonie's most terrible nightmares that 'her poor Octave', who is
long dead, should turn out to be still alive and insist on her taking
a walk every day.[1]

It was necessary also that Combray and its chapter should be
the whole novel in miniature, and contain the germs of all its
themes and events. For the rest of the novel the Narrator follows
up the ways on which he first set foot at Combray: however far
he seems to be leaving it behind, he is really circling back, and
Time Regained is also Combray regained. Characters who belong
chiefly, as did their originals in real life exclusively, to Paris,
appear also in Combray. Sometimes, as in the case of Swann, the
Duchesse de Guermantes or Gilberte, their connection with
Combray is aided by the existence at Illiers of persons in whom
Proust afterwards saw analogies with the corresponding person in
Paris: in each place there was a family friend, an unapproachable
noblewoman, a little girl he loved. Sometimes he was helped by
coincidences of history and geography: he named the Narrator's
friend, Robert de Saint-Loup-en-Bray, from Saint-Loup-de-Naud
in Seine-et-Marne, whose church he visited with a group of young
noblemen who collectively suggested his hero; but there is also a
village of Saint-Loup eight miles east of Illiers. He made Saint-
Loup marry Gilberte partly because one of the originals of Saint-
Loup in real life married one of the originals of Gilberte; but the
name was already linked with Tansonville, where the château
was occupied in 1710 by a certain Robert de Durcet after his
marriage with Claire de Saint-Loup. As for the suffix en-Bray, no
doubt it comes from Bourg-en-Bray near Saint-Loup-de-Naud;
but there is a River Braye which flows into the Loir some fifty
miles downstream from Illiers.

Sometimes characters seen at Combray, such as Charlus,
Odette or Legrandin, have originals with no possible association
with Illiers. Perhaps this is true of Vinteuil: Illiers was large
enough to possess a music-teacher, but there is no published
record of his existence. Legrandin can be identified with a person
who resembled him in every way, except that he had no link with
Illiers and was a doctor instead of an engineer. Dr Henri Cazalis
(1840-1909) was a professional friend of Dr Proust; but he was
also, under the pseudonym of Jean Lahor, a symbolist poet of

[1] I, 110

minor reputation and merit and an intimate friend of Mallarmé
and Francis Jammes; and he was noted for social climbing.

Illiers was more, even, than an earthly paradise lost, a symbol
of innocence, childhood, natural beauty and family affection for
loved ones since aged or dead. It gave Proust not only the first
chapter of his novel, but the philosophy of the whole: for it was
here that he had his first intimations of unconscious memory. At
first, as recorded in *Jean Santeuil*, the memory was preconscious
rather than unconscious, roused by the repetition of some sight
or feeling of the previous year, forgotten during the intervening
winter in Paris, but remembered instantly and without obstruc-
tion on his return to Illiers. He would see cordon apple-trees in
flower in the orchards of the Rue des Lavoirs, and recollect seeing
them a year ago; or at home in Paris he would hear buzzing flies
in his room, and they would call to mind his bedroom in the Rue
du Saint-Esprit, and the dazzling noise of M. Legué breaking up
his packing-cases next door. Memories of this kind only became
truly unconscious when they had been driven deeper by the
passage of years, by long periods in which they had no opportunity of recurring, and by changes in his personality. Then the
memory was mysterious, and not even recognisable at first as
memory; only prolonged effort could bring its source to consciousness, and the struggle was rewarded not only by the joy
and release of success, but by the intrinsic value of what was
discovered: a fragment of the past miraculously preserved in
eternity, a moment of time regained. Unconscious memory was
linked with other feelings of inexplicable delight in which
memory had no part, such as the ecstasies he owed to the moving
spires, or the 'little phrase' in what became the Vinteuil Sonata.
They revealed the existence, somewhere deep within him, of a
region in which beauty was real and eternal, uncontaminated by
disappointment, sin and death. Later in life these feelings became
more important than anything else in the world, more valuable
than the false enchantments of love or society: they were sign-
posts, marked with an unexpectedly short distance, to the only
true reality. If he could find his way back to their lost country,
his life would be justified and his sins forgiven.

But Illiers, like Time, had to be lost before it could be regained.
The break seems to have come when he was thirteen, after the
summer which was long known as 'the summer of Augustin

Thierry'. In the Pré Catelan, where in previous years he had lain in the hazel-copse by the asparagus-bed reading Dickens, George Eliot, or Gautier's *Le Capitaine Fracasse*, he was now captivated by *La Conquête de l'Angleterre par les Normands*, and *Récits des Temps Mérovingiens*. After the obligatory game of hide-and-seek, and the picnic tea, during which his book must be left unopened on the grass by the pool, Marcel would escape to read in a horn-beam-tree at the top of the garden; and the voices of the family calling him in vain had as little power to disturb him as the distant chimes of the church clock, 'which seemed to peal from some-where behind the blue sky'. But it was decided that Illiers was bad for his health. The Loir, Dr Proust declared, was a menace to the whole town; and his friends the hawthorns and the apple-trees in flower had turned against him, and punished his love with the agonies of asthma. Only sea or mountain air could cure him, and in future his holidays were spent with his grandmother on the coast of Normandy or with his mother at inland health-resorts. Perhaps his education also made the former impromptu visits to Illiers impossible; for he had now left his preparatory school for the Lycée Condorcet, and had outgrown the arithmetic lessons of the village optician, and Canon Marquis's tuition in Latin and the names of flowers. He saw Illiers again in rare visits, which continued till he was past thirty. But the spell was broken, and Illiers now resembled only the Combray of the sojourn at Tanson-ville with Gilberte de Saint-Loup: the Loir was 'a meagre, ugly stream', and the Méréglise and Saint-Éman ways had lost, or had not yet acquired, their meaning.

As he grew older, his memories of Illiers became ever more vivid and more vague, like the landscape of a dream. Geography changed, space was altered by time. In what street was the house of Aunt Élisabeth, at which end of Illiers was the Mall? The back-garden widened and stretched, and along its gravel paths his dead grandmother strode up and down in the rain; the family visitor had the melancholy, ironical face of Charles Haas. He built a country house in the Pré Catelan for Swann and Gilberte, and brought a Lesbian girl to Le Rocher de Mirougrain.

Chapter 4

THE GARDEN OF THE CHAMPS-ÉLYSÉES

MARCEL'S face was changing: it moved indeed in several directions and on several planes, as if uncertain of its destination. Would it take after his father, or his mother, or be a new individual—and if the last, should it be hysterical, cheerful, or gravely melancholy? There are four surviving photographs of the period between his tenth and twelfth years. In the first he is with Robert, who quietly hugs his brother's arm in an attitude which had hardly altered since the photograph in which Marcel was five and both were in frocks; but Marcel's face has a frozen frenzy which recalls the young Rimbaud, a timidity masked by arrogance and anger. It is about the time of his first attack of asthma in the Bois de Boulogne: is this the nervous face of the young asthmatic, jealous of his brother (for a child can be both fond and envious of his rival) and wooing his mother with fits of weeping rage—or, since the other photographs are so very different, is it only a normal boy trying to keep still for the photographer? Both brothers wear wide Eton collars over their shoulders, Lavallière cravats, and knee-breeches which leave an expanse of thin bare leg above their white socks and high buttoned boots. Their hair has been meticulously curled; perhaps this is the photograph of which he was thinking in *Du Côté de chez Swann*, when the Narrator tears out his curl-papers and spoils his velvet jacket and new hat embracing the hawthorns at Tansonville. Or perhaps it is the next, though now his hair is straight and worn in a fringe, for here are the new hat and the velvet jacket; and this, whether or not it is the Combray photograph, is certainly the one Céleste Albaret found when rummaging in the Narrator's drawer at Balbec: "He tried to make us think they always dressed him quite simply. And there, with his little cane, he's nothing but furs and laces, such as no prince ever wore!"[1] She might well think of a prince, for the morocco frame is covered with golden fleur-de-lis; he sits on the photographer's balustrade, the new hat beside him

[1] II, 848

and the toy riding-cane on his lap, with exquisite poetic intelligence in his face, as if he meditated on the spires of Martinville-le-Sec. It is one of the most moving of all portraits of genius in childhood, and the next two photographs are something of an anticlimax. Both were taken on the same day; he is with Robert, arm in arm again; they are in their black school-suits, and Marcel has a look of positively chirpy cheerfulness. He is eleven, and it is 1882, the year in which he entered the Lycée Condorcet.

For the past year or two he had attended a preparatory school, the Cours Pape-Carpentier, where one of his schoolfellows was Jacques Bizet, son of the composer of *Carmen*, who had died in 1875 soon after the disastrous failure of his opera. It was the custom for the little boys to be escorted to school by their mothers, so perhaps Marcel may have seen Jacques with his beautiful and intelligent mother, daughter of the Jewish composer Fromental Halévy, and future hostess of the Guermantes's. Six years later he would begin to frequent her salon, and she would become his friend for life; but now she was a lonely widow who shunned society.

His parents chose the Lycée Condorcet, no doubt, because it was so near home: the school entrance in the Rue de Caumartin, a few yards north from the Boulevard Haussmann, is hardly ten minutes' walk from 9 Boulevard Malesherbes. But, by a fortunate coincidence, no choice could have been happier for Marcel. Unlike the grim schools of the Left Bank, Louis-le-Grand, Henri-Quatre, Saint-Louis, or Stanislas, awful in their discipline and learning, Condorcet was considered a haven of liberty and culture. The beginning of lessons, the end of recreation were marked, it is true, by the traditional drum-roll; but even the drum, as Marcel's schoolfriend Robert Dreyfus remarks, 'seemed to invite us rather than order us into school'. The teachers were mostly minor literary figures, who seemed less determined to force knowledge into their pupils than eager to co-operate with them in the love and practice of literature; and towards the upper reaches of the school, in the classes of *rhétorique* and *philosophie*, the boys were allowed by their benevolent headmaster, Julien Giraud, to choose their own teacher.

There is a little documentary evidence on Marcel's early school-days, during the period of five years from his entry in October 1882 to the beginning of *rhétorique* in October 1887. He took two

years to reach Class Five, in which he made his first appearance
in the Condorcet roll of honour on 31 December 1884. Thanks
to this success, he seems to have gone up after only one term into
Class Three, in which he is again found on the roll of honour on
14 February 1885; but he stuck there for two years, reaching the
roll of honour once more on 28 February 1887. As he joined the
rhétorique class in the following October, he must have spent only
the summer term in Class Two; or perhaps, in the expression of
French schoolboy slang, he 'jumped' it altogether. No doubt this
irregular progress was caused by his ill-health: his school friend
Robert Dreyfus speaks of his prolonged absences, which often
prevented him from writing his end-of-term compositions. Moreover, 'he was a pupil full of fantasy, an elusive apprentice of
meditation and daydreams, inspired more by his delight in
reading, thinking and feeling than by any ambition to shine on
prize-days'. In *Jean Santeuil* the father's colleagues predict a
brilliant career at school for a boy who already knows Victor
Hugo and Alfred de Musset by heart; but Jean is punished for in-
attention, is bottom for French composition, and finishes his first
year without a single prize. Instead of writing the brief, correct
essays which are expected of him, he covers page after page,
intoxicated by his own facility and by 'the infinite and delicious
melancholy inspired by the burning of Joan of Arc or the speech
of the Constable de Bourbon'; and the composition he has written
with tears of enthusiasm is greeted by the laughter of the whole
class. He accuses himself of vanity and a desire to be admired,
which he considers he has inherited from his father's 'inoffensive
self-conceit'; and he cannot bear to think that the boy next to
him, who is rich, well-born and plays with real agate marbles,
might remain ignorant of his social successes. One morning, when
the class is deep in Hannibal's crossing of the Alps, he leans over
and whispers: "Do you know, I've had dinner with the headmaster!" "What's that you said?" the startled rich boy exclaims
aloud; the master calls them out, and asks what they were talking
about; and Jean feels ready to die of embarrassment and pride as
his companion mumbles: "Santeuil was saying he'd been to
dinner with the Head."[1] At last Jean's angry father sends him as
a boarder to the terrible Lycée Henri-Quatre; and though Dr
Proust never punished Marcel in this way, he may well have

[1] *Jean Santeuil*, vol. 1, 114-17

threatened it. Marcel's parents, like Jean's, decided at last that his failures were due not to ill-health, nor to idleness, but to 'lack of will-power'. They repeated the accusation so often that Marcel half believed it, and made it one of the characteristics of the heroes of both his novels; and his critics have believed it after him.

Perhaps Marcel's prolonged stay in Class Three was caused not by ill-health, still less by *manque de volonté*, but by the sorrows of love. His little playmate at Illiers was already lost in the past; but in the summer of 1886, when he was not quite fifteen,[1] he was seized by a passion for her counterpart in Paris which long afterwards, only a few years before his death, he still thought of as 'one of the two great loves of my life'. Her name was Marie de Benardaky, and he met her in the Champs-Élysées, where he used to play every afternoon after school (which ended at three o'clock), and on the Thursday half-holiday, with a group of schoolfellows from Condorcet and a little band of girls. The boys were later to have distinguished careers, if Robert Dreyfus, who was one of them, is to be believed: 'In our little group,' he says, 'which met so harmoniously near the roundabouts, there were future scholars, philosophers, industrialists, doctors, engineers, economists, politicians, barristers, generals, and an ambassador.' The ambassador was Maurice Herbette, the politician Paul Bénazet, and the philosopher was Léon Brunschwicg, editor of Pascal, who is said to have had much in common with Bloch in Proust's novel. There were also two who became minor poets, Louis de la Salle and Jean de Tinan. Among the girls were Antoinette and Lucie Faure, daughters of the deputy from Le Havre, who ten years later became President of the Republic, and Gabrielle Schwartz.

Lucie Faure was five years older than Marcel, while her sister Antoinette was his senior by only a year. His friendship with

---

[1] The earliest stage of his acquaintance with Mlle de Benardaky is dated by a letter to Antoinette Faure written on 15 July 1886. The date is fixed by his description of the famous review of the army at Longchamp by General Boulanger on 14 July 1886, which he saw, he says, 'yesterday'. 'I go to the Champs-Élysées nearly every day,' he writes; 'Blanche is still very sweet, with her angelic face so teasing and so resigned. Marie Benardaki [*sic*] is very pretty and more exuberant than ever. She *fought* Blanche with her fists the other day, and Blanche had to give in!'

Antoinette was at its height about eighteen months before the present period, and was a milder prefiguration of his love for Marie de Benardaky: in a photograph taken in the Parc Monceau, Mlle Faure, with a plumed hat and carrying an umbrella, is about fourteen, and Marcel, in a striped straw hat, is only thirteen. The Comtesse de Martel, otherwise the novelist Gyp, saw him playing with Antoinette in the Champs-Élysées, and was amused to meet the little boy a few days later buying the complete works of Molière and Lamartine in Calmann Lévy's bookshop in the Rue de Grammont[1]; where recognising her as a friend of Antoinette he greeted her with a pallid but charming smile. When Gyp next had tea with Mme Faure she asked who he was. "He's Dr Proust's son, I've known his mother for years," replied that lady, "he's amazingly intelligent, but unfortunately rather frail, and he's a great friend of Antoinette's." Marcel used to recite his favourite poems to Antoinette, and then ask timidly, "Did you like that?"; and in return she taught him how to make caramels. She could always make him obey her with a glance of her grey eyes, with their extraordinarily long lashes: "have you ever noticed Antoinette's eyelashes, madame?" he asked Gyp earnestly.

Marie de Benardaky and her younger sister Nelly were daughters of a Polish nobleman, Nicolas de Benardaky, who is said to have gained his wealth as a tea-merchant. He had once been master of ceremonies at the court of the Tsar, and was still entitled to be called 'Your Excellency'. M. de Benardaky lived at 65 Rue de Chaillot, which runs into the Avenue Marceau a quarter of a mile to the west of the Champs-Élysées; for these elysian lawns were the joint playground of the noble children of the west end of Paris and the bourgeois children of the centre. He had a reputation for arrogance, while his wife, whose maiden name was Lebrock, was said to care for nothing but champagne and love. She was statuesque and beautiful, and was remembered for her appearance at a fancy-dress ball as a Valkyrie, complete with spear. Her daughter Marie had long black hair and a rosy, laughing face; she can have had little outward resemblance to the red-haired, freckled and sullen Gilberte. As Proust remembered her long afterwards, she was fifteen when he fell in love with her, and

[1] The shop of Calmann Lévy, who later published *Les Plaisirs et les Jours*, was a favourite resort of Charles Haas, original of Swann, and of Anatole France, original of Bergotte.

perhaps he was right; for although according to Gotha she was born at Pavlovsk on 12 July 1874, and would therefore only have been twelve, Gotha is known to be less fallible on the ages of princes than on those of princesses, particularly when these belonged before their marriage only to the minor nobility.[1]

Except for the hooting torrent of automobiles which rushes past their gravel bank towards the Arc de Triomphe, the Champs-Élysées to-day are much the same as they were seventy years ago. The lawns by the Alcazar d'Été and the Théâtre des Ambassadeurs, on which Marcel played prisoner's base, are now railed off; but the laurel shrubberies of his games of hide-and-seek are still there, and the nymph of the fountain still arranges her long stony tresses. In the novel she is holding out a baby, and after the snowfall an icicle hangs from her hand, 'which seemed to explain her gesture'[2]; but in the real Champs-Élysées she is childless, and in order to make his joke, Proust had to present her with one of the three putti, carrying wheat, grapes and doves, who form the centre-piece of another fountain further up, by the Théâtre Marigny. The only surviving roundabout has been banished to this part of the park since Marcel's time. Near by is a cedar, bearing a notice which reads 'Probable age in 1950, 90 years': here, too, is something which saw Marcel at play with 'Gilberte', and could perhaps tell us whether their wrestling match in the shrubbery ever occurred, or whether, as he affirmed long afterwards, 'there was never anything in the least improper in my relations with her'. The wooden booths, lettered A to H, where ginger-bread, barley-sugar, toy drums and windmills were sold, still line the avenue under the chestnut-trees; and there is the public lavatory in which the Narrator's grandmother had her stroke, a dignified edifice of cast-iron painted green. Perhaps the Marquise, its guardian and hostess, was a real figure, and perhaps in real life Marcel was plunged into an ecstasy of unconscious memory when the musty odour of her 'salon' reminded him of Jules Amiot's den in the back-garden at Illiers. But the story of the Marquise's exclusiveness, her pride in 'choosing her society', is also told in *Jean Santeuil* of Mme Laudet, at whose farm, Les Aigneaux, the people of Étreuilles are served with refreshments on Sundays: "I only receive people I like," she says.[3]

[1] The *Almanach de Gotha* for 1900 even dates her birth as 1876.
[2] I, 398, 405   [3] *Jean Santeuil*, vol. 1, 23ᶜ

In the happy fields of the Champs-Élysées, the third of the gardens of his childhood, Marcel held court among his young friends. Leaving prisoner's base to those who preferred it, he would stroll along the gravel-walk by the Alcazar d'Été talking of Sarah Bernhardt and Mounet-Sully, and repeating the verses of his favourite poets. He already possessed his amazing verbal memory for poetry, and Musset, Hugo, Racine, Lamartine and Baudelaire were among his repertoire. The day of the symbolists had not yet arrived, though he knew the work of Verlaine; and his chief enthusiasm among living poets was Leconte de Lisle, greatest of the Parnassians, from whose prose translations of the Iliad and Odyssey the Homeric argot of Bloch is derived. 'He charmed his little companions,' says Robert Dreyfus, 'and he also rather baffled us. But most astonished of all were the grown-ups, who were unanimous in their rapture at the refinements of his courtesy, the complications of his good intentions. I see him now, very handsome and very sensitive to cold, smothered in jerseys and mufflers, rushing to meet our mothers or grandmothers, bowing at their approach and always finding the right words to touch their hearts, whether he broached subjects usually reserved for his elders, or merely enquired after their health.' The novelist Gyp saw him one day (though this was in the Parc Monceau) pinched and shivering with cold, clutching a hot roast potato in each of his frozen hands. In those days it was customary for Parisian ladies to stop on their way to the Opéra to buy roast potatoes, which they would keep in their muffs as a substitute for central heating during the performance; so this conduct was less eccentric than it might now seem. When he left he would present the potatoes to the chair-woman, by way of a tip: she grew to expect them, and would have been hurt if he had forgotten.

Soon, however, he would see Marie and Nelly de Benardaky hurrying through the trees ahead of the violet plume on the hat of their governess; he abandoned his recitation of Leconte de Lisle, or his talk of Sarah Bernhardt, and ran to join their game of prisoner's base. He would always try to be on Marie's side and to arrange for her to win; and once when he hesitated out of polite-ness and made as if to join her sister, the good-natured Nelly laughed and said "No, you're on Marie's side, it makes you so happy." Marie gave a mocking but indulgent smile, and he felt that his love, since it was thus publicly admitted, must surely be returned. On rainy days he would stand by the window at home, gazing in despair at the streaming balcony and the glistening Boulevard Malesherbes; till a pale ray of sunlight shone on the railings and cast a filigree shadow on the grey stone-work, which gradually brightened, like a crescendo in music, to 'the fixed and unalterable gold of a fine day'. He hurried to the Champs-‹ Élysées, and there was Marie already, greeting him with the familiar "Let's start playing at once, you're on my side."

In December came the snow, levelling the boulevard with the pavements and deadening the noise of the traffic. "There won't be anyone at the Champs-Élysées," said Mme Proust, "and if that's why you're looking at the sky, you can be sure Mlle de Benardaky won't come—they won't let her spoil her fine dresses just for that." Suppressing a desire to strike his unfeeling mother, Marcel replied: "No, I know she won't be there," and went, not so much in order to see Marie, as to view the white ruin of his hopes. The deserted lawns were deep in snow, and icicles hung from the naked protuberances of the cherubs on the fountain; but there, after all, was Marie advancing in front of her governess, with glowing cheeks and a fur toque over her long black hair. One by one their other friends arrived. Soon they were sliding on the glazed gravel paths, and throwing snowballs; and as he recalled with irony long afterwards, when Marie hurled down his neck the snowballs which he himself had given her, he felt it was a sign of predilection on her part, almost a declaration of their love, and that all their company knew it.

Every evening before he went to sleep he would say to himself "I shall see her to-morrow"; and if he woke in the small hours he would fall asleep again with the thought: "It's already to-day!" As he lay in bed he promised himself that to-morrow he would make a decisive step in his love, or at least memorise the elusive details of Marie's face; but when to-morrow came the afternoon would pass in the insignificant ritual of prisoner's base, and her face would have changed. 'He measured his pleasure in seeing her by the immensity of his desire to see her,' he wrote afterwards in *Jean Santeuil*, 'and by his grief at seeing her go; for he enjoyed her actual presence very little.'[1] Sometimes in the Champs-Élysées he felt that the little girl he saw was somehow a different person from the little girl he loved: such are the characteristic

[1] *Jean Santeuil*, vol. I, 89

symptoms of romantic love, which loves not a person but an ideal, a personified desire, a projection of one's self.

In February he was kept away from the Champs-Élysées by a bout of influenza; but his agony at the thought that Marie would be enjoying prisoner's base without him was happily relieved by the news that she was ill too. When he was convalescent a letter came from her asking him in her mother's name to tea, 'at five o'clock, on any day you wish'. He entered the house he had thought inaccessible for ever, outside which he had stood and stared on afternoons when Marie had stayed away from the Champs-Élysées, and whose number in the Rue de Chaillot, together with the name of that poetic street, had echoed in his thoughts with 'a painful and deleterious enchantment'. The staircase was dark, and in the profound obscurity of the vestibule it was impossible to tell whether the dim figure standing by a gothic sideboard was some footman waiting for his mistress to end her visit, or the master of the house himself. In the drawing-room the paintings on the ceiling, the coloured glass in the windows, the lap-dog and the tea-table seemed not only part of the beauty and mystery of his beloved and her mother, but also evidence of a social superiority of which Marie must never become aware. He tried in vain to persuade his parents to change their furniture and their habits; and then, reflecting that Marie would in all probability never visit them and learn the humiliating truth, he assured her next time that in his home as in hers there were loose-covers on the chairs, and chocolate was never served at tea-time. The awe-inspiring concierge bowed affably before him, her parents changed from 'implacable deities' into a lady and gentleman who urged him to come often, to 'teach Marie all about literature', and assured him that he had a good influence upon her. His parents, however, were not altogether content with this new acquaintance. Certainly, it was only proper that M. and Mme de Benardaky should admire the intelligence of Marcel; but they were out of his class, and perhaps not very favourable representatives of their own. "Mme de Benardaky has reached such a high position in society," said the witty Mlle de Malakoff, "that the only person you see in her house who isn't out of the top drawer is herself." Even Marcel himself, now or later, came to look critically on Marie's parents: there is a distinct resemblance between Odette Swann and her *louche* salon in *A l'Ombre*, and Mme de Benardaky

and the company she kept. There were to be at least two other
ladies who contributed to the character of Odette; but the one
who kept mixed company (Mme Hayman) was unmarried, and
the one who was married (Mme Straus) had a salon of extreme
distinction and was notoriously faithful to her husband.

In the spring of 1887 he ceased to see Marie. In *Jean Santeuil* it
is because his parents, alarmed at the unhappiness and emotional
instability caused by his passion, forbid their meetings, while in
A l'Ombre the Narrator, convinced at last that his friend does not
return his love, decides for himself never to see her again. Perhaps
both versions were true in real life; but for a time in his despair
Marcel wished to commit suicide, to throw himself from the
balcony of 9 Boulevard Malesherbes—the former barometer of
his hopes—on the pavement below; and when he recovered, his
life was irretrievably changed. His first attempt to love and be
loved by someone other than his mother—to escape, that is, from
incest—had failed. Ability to love a person of the opposite sex,
and of one's own age, is the only valid escape from the prison of
the family; and that way was now barred. If he were to risk loving
another young girl his suffering, his humiliation and his mother's
displeasure would only be repeated. No doubt he was doomed
even before he met Marie de Benardaky—if not by some ante-
natal predisposition, then by tensions whose work was done for
ever in his early childhood—to lifelong homosexuality. Perhaps,
too, as not infrequently happens in the puberty of a future homosexual, his unconscious mind had deliberately made a heterosexual choice which was certain to fail, in order to set itself free
for its true desire. In every homosexual, perhaps, there is a
heterosexual double, uppermost at first, who must be imprisoned
and made powerless before his stronger brother can come to life.
Marcel had tried to be 'normal': if he had failed, it was Marie's
fault for rejecting him; and his mother had wished it, and was
therefore partly to blame. He was absolved. But Marie had also
taught him to believe, perhaps rightly, that love, outside the
family, is the only feeling which can never be returned.

During most of his life he continued to be intermittently
fascinated by young girls. They inspired him with a mingled
attraction and repulsion, desire and fear, and a whole little band
of them invaded his novel; but there was safety in numbers. Once
and only once, after his mother's death, when he was at the

beginning of middle age, he thought for a time of marrying one, but decided to write his novel instead. Almost to the end of his life he continued, now and then, to fall in love with women; but somehow his choice always happened to be a respectable married lady, twenty years older than himself, or a high-class, equally safe and unattainable cocotte; or if he loved an unmarried woman of his own age or younger, then she was usually the fiancée or mistress of a friend. The married ladies or the cocotte, Freudians would say, were mother-images; and they would rightly add that a preference for women already bespoken to male friends is a typical symptom of homosexuality. These were substitutes for his mother, those were substitutes for his friends. But there was a rejected part of himself, forever prevented by stronger forces from coming to power, for which the young girls were also substitutes for Marie de Benardaky; and when he migrated to the Cities of the Plain he took with him a prisoner crushed beneath the weight of Time and Habit, a buried heterosexual boy who continued to cry unappeased for a little girl lost.

Chapter 5

BALBEC AND CONDORCET

AN inventory of the contents and condition of the fourteen-year-old Marcel's mind, in the period shortly before his meeting with Marie de Benardaky, has been preserved in a leaf of a confession-book belonging to Antoinette Faure, one of his playmates in the Champs-Élysées. The book was an import from Victorian England to anglomaniac Paris, and the twenty-five questions are printed in English—perhaps Marcel had already learned enough of the language from his mother to understand them, or perhaps Antoinette translated for him. He writes in a fluent, uninhibited hand, with precocious self-expression and wit; and words such as 'intelligence', 'naturalness', 'beauty', 'the land of the ideal' occur and recur, showing that he was accustomed to submit all questions to these touchstones. His 'favourite occupations' are 'reading, revery, poetry, the theatre'. His 'ideal of happiness' is 'to live near all the people I love, with the beauties of nature, plenty of books and music, and a French theatre near by'. His 'pet aversion' is 'people who have no feeling for goodness, and do not know the pleasures of affection'—perhaps he is thinking of Dr Proust. All this is nothing extraordinary, and no doubt others of Mlle Faure's young friends, those future politicians, generals and society hostesses, made no less idealistic entries. But Marcel's originality lay in the strength of will which would enable him to pursue his vision of goodness and beauty, deepened but unchanged, in later life, when others convince themselves that the quest is unimportant, or that life has given them what they sought. He would see that the Ideal is not to be found in the world of space and time, and press on to seek it elsewhere; and at this point the object of the search would become not happiness, but salvation.

His cultural tastes, however, remain immature. His 'favourite prose authors' are still George Sand and Augustin Thierry, for he is faithful to the memories of the night when his mother read *François le Champi* at his bedside, and the summer of Augustin

Thierry at Illiers. His favourite poet is Alfred de Musset, whom
Bloch tolerated only because he had written 'one absolutely
meaningless line'.[1] Among painters he mentions only the
execrable Meissonier, who became the idol of the French
bourgeoisie by painting pictures of fat red cardinals at supper,
and among musicians only Mozart (a great composer, but Proust
was by nature a Wagnerian) and Gounod, a Meissonier of music.
But the confession-album continues its inquisition, and two
entries reveal something of the cross-currents with which the boy
is striving. 'What is your idea of the depths of misery?' he is
asked, and replies 'to be separated from Mother'. 'For what fault
have you most indulgence?' it persists, and he answers: 'for the
private life of geniuses'. He was never to feel indulgence for his
own vices, never to separate sin from guilt; but here it is as if he
had some premonition that the time, thirty years ahead, when he
would descend to the lowest pits of Sodom, where love and
cruelty are imitated for hire, would coincide with—and perhaps
be indispensable to—the moment of revelation and victory.

Illiers, with its lilacs and hawthorns, was now a forbidden
country. Only the air of sea or mountains was safe for his asthma,
and he spent his holidays with his mother or grandmother on the
Normandy coast, at Dieppe, Tréport, Trouville or Cabourg, or
at Salies-de-Béarn in the Pyrenees. It is regrettable that so little
information concerning these seaside holidays of his 'teens has
survived, for he seems to have distilled from the summers of the
1880s many aspects of the first visit to Balbec in *A l'Ombre*. With
the sole exception of *Un Amour de Swann* (in which it is probable
that little came from his personal experience), there is no episode
in his novel where the materials for comparison with his real life
are so scanty. Evidence is not lacking, however, for the two salient
features of the Narrator's first holiday at Balbec, his relations with
his grandmother and the presence of the little band. In a letter to
his mother from Cabourg on 9 September 1891, two summers
after the death of Mme Nathé Weil, Proust wrote of 'those seaside holidays when grandmother and I, lost in one another,
walked battling with the wind and talking'. And in an early prose
piece he described 'some little girls I once watched at play by the
sea'. One was running with shuffling steps, pretending to be a
princess in a carriage, while another was chasing her to return a

muff which she had left behind, and shouting at the top of her voice: "Madame! Your Royal Highness has forgotten her muff! The Princess has forgotten her muff! Your muff, Princess!" And the first little girl thanked her with a smile, and took the muff with a dignified absence of surprise.[1] Perhaps these little girls may seem too childish to represent Albertine and her friends, who were, nevertheless, young enough to play at diabolo and ferret. But the idea of the little band is here, as well as in the Champs-Élysées; and we shall find Proust at play later with at least two more groups of young girls, one in Paris in 1891, the other at Cabourg in the late 1900s. In a conversation with André Gide, which we shall meet in its place many years later, he used expressions which have been taken to mean that the original little band was composed of boys; but in fact his words to Gide are only a general statement that in the heterosexual parts of his novel he used 'the feelings of tenderness and charm supplied by his homosexual memories'. We shall find that the female characters loved or desired by the Narrator invariably began, at least, as girls or women to whom Proust himself was attracted in real life: he never merely transposed them from boys or men, though he sometimes reinforced them with elements from his homosexual life.

In 1887, during the summer after his winter's love for Marie de Benardaky, Marcel visited the health-resort of Salies-de-Béarn with his mother. With them at the Hôtel de la Paix was Mme Proust's best friend, the beautiful wife of Anatole Catusse, later senator for the district of Tarn-et-Garonne. The two ladies shared a taste for music, a similar turn of wit, and that love of amiable gossip, of discussing the actions and motives of acquaintances and strangers, which is so valuable an example in the mother of a great novelist. In the conversation and singing of Mme Catusse Marcel found some consolation for 'the boredom which Salies inspires in one who hasn't enough "double muscles" (as Tartarin would say) to walk in the cool shade of the countryside near by, and find there the grain of poetry which is indispensable to one's existence, but is not to be found in the hotel terrace, with its silly chatter and tobacco smoke, where we spend all our time'. One day Mme Catusse promised to sing for him 'a little song if I begin her portrait in words, a big one if I finish it, and as many songs as I like if it is full-length'. His friends were calling him to join their

[1] *Chroniques*, 135

game of croquet in the hotel garden; but instead he sat down at the desk of Mlle Biraben, the proprietress, to write about Mme Catusse to his grandmother in Paris. The embarrassed boy describes the young woman's eyes, complexion, hair and figure for a reward ('the divine melodies of Massenet and Gounod') and in a manner ('it's frightfully difficult to rival Alfred de Musset') which recall the confession-album of the previous year. But the banalities of gallantry are mixed with the more interesting clichés of his new love for the Homeric translations of Leconte de Lisle; and as he swears 'by Artemis the white goddess and Pluto of the burning eyes', the voice of Bloch is heard. Perhaps his ardour is almost genuine, and he has already turned from the love of young girls to the pursuit of a mother-substitute; but soon he curses 'the genii hostile to the peace of mankind who have forced me to write such nonsense about someone I really like and who has been so kind to me'; and seeing the absurdity of the situation, he ends with a cheerful 'Good-morning, Grandmama, and how do you do?'

In the first half of 1887, cured of his first love, and of the no less detrimental habits of loitering on the way home from the Lycée Condorcet, spoiling his dinner by devouring rich cakes at a pâtisserie, and chatting for hours with the concierge, Marcel had begun to work hard at school. He was rewarded in July by a second prize for history and geography, a third for Latin and a fourth for 'general excellence'. His worst subject was mathematics; and when Robert, in his efforts to help his elder brother, entreated him: "Really, Marcel, you must at least *try* to understand," Marcel would reply: "Impossible!" A letter to his mother of 24 September, after his return from Salies-de-Béarn, shows him reading Loti, visiting the Louvre, and walking in the Bois de Boulogne, where his Great-Uncle Louis meets him in the Avenue des Acacias with his carriage. He is experimenting with his health: he has had 'transparent nights, with the conscious feeling that I am asleep, but am on the point of waking up', a sensation well known to the Narrator of *A la Recherche*; and then, one morning, he utters a cry of surprise on waking, because he has slept calmly and his mouth tastes fresh. The day before he had driven in the Bois in a closed carriage; and he draws the not very hygienic conclusion that he had better try to stop his open-air walks there. Perhaps it was in this summer that he accompanied Mme Catusse in the horse-omnibus from Auteuil to the Madeleine. He felt he ought to make polite conversation, and thought he was succeeding, until his mother's friend asked: "Are you going to talk like this all the way?"; 'after which cold shower', as he reminded her long afterwards, 'no further sound was heard but the rumbling of the bus on the cobbles of the Rue La Fontaine'.

In October he began his year of *rhétorique* at Condorcet, the first half of the two years' course leading to the baccalaureate—a year which Marcel airily described as 'a circular tour from Homer to André Chénier by way of Petronius'. The class was shared by rude M. Cucheval, polite M. Dauphiné—'It's really amusing to let oneself be guided by two such different minds,' he reported a year later to Robert Dreyfus—and the witty Maxime Gaucher. M. Cucheval was forthright, uncompromising, 'a real savage of a schoolmaster', and yet, 'however much you're Cuchevalised, it does you no harm. Don't think him a fool, just because he makes silly jokes, and is too much of a barbarian to enjoy exquisite combinations of syllables or verbal contours. He's a relief from those idiots who round off all their periods—a thing he can't and won't do. He's absolutely delightful, the ideal of a good teacher, and the very reverse of boring.'

Maxime Gaucher, who was literary critic on the *Revue Bleue*, and whom Marcel calls 'an infinitely free and charming intelligence', was the first to realise his pupil's exceptional talent. Week after week he made Marcel read his compositions aloud to the class, praising them, criticising them, and suddenly overcome by helpless laughter at some audacity of style. One of these pieces has survived, an essay on Corneille and Racine which shows remarkable maturity of thought and language. Proust is already writing his seamless, interwoven prose with sentences a hundred words long and virgin of paragraphs; and when he made Gisèle write her famous letter from Sophocles among the shades to Racine, beginning 'My dear friend', he may have been thinking of the subject of this essay, but hardly of its matter or style, in which there is nothing of which to be ashamed. Once he was even asked to read his latest composition to a visiting inspector from the Sorbonne, Eugène Manuel, a mediocre poet who put up for the Académie Française whenever there was a vacancy, but always in vain. The outraged inspector heard him to the end, and turning to M. Gaucher asked, "Haven't you anyone, even at the bottom

of your class, who can write French more clearly and correctly?";
only to receive the cutting and punning reply: "Sir, none of my
pupils is taught to write French like a Manual." M. Cucheval,
however, that 'ideal of a good teacher', did not at first return his
pupil's regard. Before the end of the October term 'a dozen silly
fools were writing decadent prose, M. Cucheval said I'd divided
the class into factions, and was a poisoner of young minds, and
some people even thought I was a poseur!' Marcel's essays were
greeted by storms of booing and applause—'if it hadn't been for
Gaucher they'd have massacred me'. After a few months M.
Cucheval began to come round; but just before the final examination he was heard to remark: "He'll get through, because he's only
a joker, but it'll be his fault if another fifteen of them are
ploughed."

In the summer of 1888, alas, Maxime Gaucher fell ill, and died
on 24 July. His place was taken till the end of term by M. Dupré,
who was 'affectionate, kind, and full of delicacy, but a bore'. He
knew the works of Leconte de Lisle, it was true, but 'what's the
use of hearing modern writers talked about by someone who likes
them with far too many reservations? It makes you tap your feet
and grind your teeth.' The other master in *rhétorique*, the cold,
thin and ceremonious M. Dauphiné, likewise admired Leconte de
Lisle, but thought him 'cuwious' and was puzzled by 'his taste for
the stwange and exotic'. M. Dauphiné lisped, and when his pupils
misbehaved would say "Monsieur Halévy and Monsieur Bizet,
I must ask you to withdwaw." These two, the son and nephew
of Bizet's widow, were particularly unruly, perhaps because
the innocent and blue-spectacled M. Martin, the school
superintendent, had told them: "With famous names like yours,
you know, you'll never be expelled."

There is a photograph of the class of M. Cucheval, a huge
pyramid of fifty boys, most of whom are older than Marcel. He is
an alert, asthenic child of sixteen, with narrow chest, sloping
shoulders, and collar turned up to keep out the draught. M.
Cucheval has the heavy dignity of a St Bernard dog with a beard.
Marcel is motionless, caught half-way between the little prince of
Illiers and the dandy of the 1890s; but soon the pyramid will col-
lapse, M. Cucheval will bark, the boy in the front row will put on
his bowler hat, and time will begin to pass. In the July examina-
tions of 1888 Marcel won first prize for French composition and

third prize for Latin and Greek. Was the other half of M. Cucheval's prophecy fulfilled, and did this success mean the failure of fifteen imitators?

Early in September his mother took Robert to Salies-de-Béarn, while Marcel stayed at Auteuil. He missed little, for the weather at Salies was unbearably hot; but during the first day of parting he wept, and was lectured by Great-Uncle Louis, who said his grief was 'sheer egotism'. 'This little psychological discovery caused him such pure joy of pride and self-satisfaction that he gave me a merciless sermon'. His grandfather was less severe and only called him a 'silly boy', while his grandmother shook her head with a smile and said: "It would take more than this to prove that you really love your mother!" But next morning he went to the Bois de Boulogne and laughed aloud with joy; the sun was out, the air was still cool, and he felt an unaccustomed pleasure in breathing and walking, just as in the long-lost summer of Augustin Thierry at Illiers. He sat on the grass by the smaller lake, reading *Le Mariage de Loti* and watching the violet shadow on the water, till the returning sunlight sparkled on lake and leaves. At lunch he behaved particularly well, and instead of the usual furious glares from his grandfather, there came only a mild rebuke ("You shouldn't *rub* so!") when he wiped away a few last tears with his handkerchief.

The servants, Victoire and Angélique, as he wrote to his mother, were convinced that he had a 'little friend' who would soon console him for her absence—and the servants were right. During this September he was interested in a pretty Viennese girl whom he had met at the Perrin dancing-school in the Rue de la Victoire, not far from Condorcet. The cynicism with which he wrote of her to Robert Dreyfus was no doubt assumed, but it does not suggest any profound feeling or enjoyment: 'I've had an extremely uncomplicated affair which ended very boringly in the inevitable way, and has given birth to an absorbing liaison that threatens to last at least a year, to the greater profit of café concerts and places of that kind to which one takes that kind of person.' Perhaps the 'platonic passion for a celebrated cocotte', which he mentions in the same letter, struck a little deeper. Her name was Léonie Closmesnil, and he watched her every afternoon driving along the Avenue des Acacias in the Bois, and alighting to walk in the Tir aux Pigeons, with her characteristic lingering step, and long skirts sweeping the gravel.[1] He tried to analyse her fascination, in which one may recognise the Freudian identification of the courtesan with the mother, in purely aesthetic terms: the rounded lines of her neck and shoulders were those of an Etruscan vase, the corner of her mouth was that of a Luini or Botticelli Virgin; the pink of her dress was more exquisite than the September sky above the Bois at six in the evening, and the blue of her hat-band reminded him of deep, still water. He wrote to her to inform her of his admiration, and she wrote back; then he sent a photograph, and she gave him several of herself, which he kept till the end of his life, in his album crammed with the images of women and men he had loved or liked, of picnics and house-parties, the records of his wasted time. For one moment of his novel she became Odette, whom Swann, too, was to compare to a Botticelli: Proust revealed to a friend that when Odette walks by the Tir aux Pigeons, 'letting the long train of her mauve skirt trail behind her', and the onlooking gentleman says to his friend: "I was in bed with her on the day MacMahon resigned",[2] she is Léonie Closmesnil.

He was already trying, tied to the cord which led so deeply and painfully to the bottom of his heart that it would always pull him back, to escape from the family. Perhaps he would never have wished or dared to devote his September to the pretty girl and the beautiful cocotte if his mother had been at home. But she had left him for a holiday with his young brother, for whom she was trying to find a riding-companion—perhaps young Eiffel ('his father built the Tower, you know!') would do? So Marcel good-humouredly sent on 'His Majesty's' new hunting-horn, which seemed much too big, more like a trumpet to be blown on Judgment Day: "It looks very funny and I can't think what it's for," said Victoire. Perhaps it was in this month that he ventured still further into the forbidden country of normal love, and retreated still more disenchanted. A schoolfellow persuaded him to visit a brothel, an incident which he recalled in his novel, when Bloch informs the Narrator to his amazement that 'women never ask for anything better than to make love', and by taking him to a house

---

[1] She wore a white lock of hair, intentionally bleached, on her forehead, and was known as 'the Butcheress', because her first lover had been a butcher. Odette, too, appears in the Bois 'with a single grey lock in her hair, now turned yellow' (I, 419).   [2] I, 420, 421

of ill fame performs a service which bears 'the same useful relation to love as that of handbooks on mediaeval towns to travel'.[1]But the experience was horrible; the proprietress had the face of a murderess, and when he left, he afterwards told his comrades (who thought the remark exquisitely absurd), "I felt as if I had left part of my moral being behind me."

In October 1888 he began his year of *philosophie* under Marie-Alphonse Darlu, 'the great philosopher', as he wrote in the preface to *Les Plaisirs et les Jours*, 'whose inspired words, more sure of survival than many a book, brought thought to birth in me and so many others'. Darlu was a bearded and spectacled little man with an energetic and highly coloured face; Anatole France said condescendingly of him that he 'had a pretty brain', little knowing that Darlu, with equal condescension, said the same of Anatole France. He had a strong southern accent, so that philosophy to him was 'phi-loh-soh-phy' and stupidity 'stoo-pi-di-ty'. On the desk in front of him he would place his top-hat, and take it as a concrete example for any abstruse doctrine he was expounding: as Fernand Gregh said, 'he brought the whole of philosophy, like a conjuror, out of that hat'. Marcel always remembered his explanation of the theories of Leibnitz: "Suppose my hat is a monad; well, I drop my handkerchief into the hat . . ."—but what the handkerchief represented we are not told. He would startle his pupils into thinking for themselves by a policy of severe sarcasm. Once, a year after Marcel's time, he announced that a certain composition came first, and then crushed the unhappy pupil with the words, perhaps a little too exalted for a schoolboy: "All the same, these are the fantasies of a sick brain, *aegri somnia*, a philosophy fit for Sganarelle!" Darlu's destructive and constructive criticism did more for Marcel than the delighted appreciation of Maxime Gaucher; and he surprised the boy by complaining not, like M. Cucheval, of the incoherence or eccentricity of his essays, but of their tendency to banality and loose metaphor—"all these bad habits you've picked up from magazines and reviews". "How can you write a phrase like 'the red conflagration of the sunset'? That sort of colouring is only fit for some little newspaper in the provinces, no, I won't say even that, in the colonies!" For when

---

[1] I, 575, 576. In *Jean Santeuil* (vol. 1, 130) he even gives the address of the brothel in the Rue Boudreau, which may well be correct, since that street was on his way home from Condorcet.

a writer tries to startle, he is likely only to utter a cliché. He will only be profoundly original when he seeks painfully for a universal truth; and this will be most universal when it is most personal. Darlu's influence on Marcel was crucial, and may be traced even into *A la Recherche du Temps Perdu*, not only in certain features of the character of Bergotte, but in the very core of the novel. This influence went beyond the mere adoption of his apparently contradictory doctrines, such as the importance of scientific discovery ("How agreeable it would be, to be a really intelligent scientist and get to the bottom of these things," Darlu would say) or the 'unreality of the sensible world'. Marcel learned that it is not sufficient for a great work of art to be poetic or moral: it must also be metaphysical; and the deepest theme of *A la Recherche* is the revelation of a purely metaphysical truth. He was no longer satisfied with vague sensations, but felt it his duty to discover and express their meaning; and if the Narrator refuses to rest content with his mysterious delight in the spires of Martinville or the taste of the madeleine, and persists in obstinate questioning till he conquers their secret, it is partly thanks to the teaching of Darlu. No doubt, however, Darlu only gave his pupil qualities which he possessed already, waiting for liberation; and the Socratic master would modestly conclude with: "But I'm not here to give you all this advice, my job is to teach you philosophy."

Meanwhile, not satisfied with writing 'decadent prose' for their homework, the pupils of Condorcet had been raising a crop of handwritten schoolboy magazines. In the words of a doggerel poem which appeared in one of them in 1890:

> '*Excuse me, sir, have we had showers?*
> *What are these fresh, poetic flowers? ...*
> *Let me explain, it's nothing new:*
> *The whole class writes, their master is Darlu.*'

The editors were Daniel Halévy and Jacques Bizet, though Marcel often appeared as contributor or member of the editorial board. The earliest was *Lundi*, 'an artistic and literary review', which began in 1887 and had a white cover with an elegant pen-and-ink drawing of two cupids allegorically supporting a folio volume open at Verlaine's line 'The eclectic triumph of the Beautiful'. In the spring of 1888 came the *Revue de Seconde* ('*Class Two Review*'), organ of the audacious new school of subtilitism, of which Halévy, aged fifteen, proclaimed himself the founder and leader. It died in March, at the thirteenth number; but from its ashes sprang the *Revue Verte*, written on the green paper, prescribed for the sake of his pupils' eyes and his own, by the master of Class Two, Eugène Lintilhac. Nothing of it survives but Mr Secretary Marcel's written, semi-humorous protest against Halévy's request, seconded by Bizet, for permission to copy certain articles for the good of posterity. The *Revue Verte*, he argues, 'unlike the so-called public press', is published not for financial gain nor in a large number of copies (this is no exaggeration, for there was never more than one copy, free of charge), but 'for the amusement of an extremely limited and select group'. These 'fleeting reflections of the mobility of imaginations at play' must be 'protected against the criticism of readers for whom they were never scribbled'; otherwise 'Mr Secretary will be under the regretful necessity of refusing his participation in a review so widely different from that in which he hitherto thought of collaborating.' But Daniel Halévy consoled himself in the 1920s for the early death of the *Revue Verte* by launching the famous *Cahiers Verts*, no. 68 of which was the *Souvenirs sur Marcel Proust* of their schoolfellow Robert Dreyfus.

The most important of these little magazines was the last, the *Revue Lilas*, named after the colour of the little twopenny exercise books, bought at the stationer's in the Passage du Havre near Condorcet, in which it was written. There is a persistent rumour that Marcel's essay on the spires of Martinville appeared in it; and though there is no actual evidence for this, it is just possible that the rumour may be based on reliable oral tradition, perhaps deriving from Daniel Halévy himself. But one of Marcel's contributions survives, dedicated 'to my dear friend Jacques Bizet', and headed 'for the *Revue Lilas*, to be destroyed after publication'. He imagines himself in his bedroom at the age of fifteen, oppressed by 'the horror of usual things', the banality of his lighted lamp, the noise of crockery in the next room, the dark violet sky with its gleaming stains of moonlight and stars. Then he is seventeen, it is the present, and everything is transformed: the Boulevard Malesherbes below his window, with 'the blue moonbeams dripping from the chestnut-trees', and the 'fresh, chill breathing of all these sleeping things', becomes a night-scene as exquisite as the moonlit garden of Combray, and 'usual things' are no longer horrible. 'I have made them sacred, and Nature too, because I could not conquer them. I have clothed them with my soul, with the inner splendour of images. I live in a sanctuary surrounded by a pageant. I am the centre of things, and each of them brings for my enjoyment sensations or sentiments that are magnificent or melancholy. I have glorious visions before my eyes.' This little sketch of the return of beauty and significance to things made sterile by habit touches one of the capital themes of Proust's art: it is already Time Regained in miniature.

His school friendships, however, gave him less satisfaction than his writing. 'There was something about him which we found unpleasant,' Daniel Halévy recalled many years after Proust's death; 'his kindnesses and tender attentions seemed mere mannerisms and poses, and we took occasion to tell him so to his face. Poor, unhappy boy, we were beastly to him.' In a minor episode of *Jean Santeuil* there are three boys whose intelligence the hero admires: they jostle him in the playground, and when he writes them 'such a beautiful, sincere and eloquent letter that tears came into his eyes as he wrote', only mock him the more. 'Jean did not understand that his craving for sympathy, his morbid and over-refined sensibility, which made him overflow with affection at the least show of kindness, were mistaken for hypocrisy, and only shocked and irritated these young people, in whom the indifference of their colder nature was accentuated by the heartlessness of youth.' So he takes his vengeance, in this novel of revenges, by making Jean meet one of them two years later, and find that he is silly after all.[1] But if Marcel suffered much in his schooldays from physical bullying, there would be other hints of it. At Condorcet, as in most French schools, violence was as unknown as other organised games; there was no worship of the strong and stupid, and intellectual prowess was respected and encouraged, even by the masters. His suffering came from his need to repeat with his fellow-creatures, in friendship as in love, the relationship he had known with his mother, the only one that could satisfy him, the only one that was impossible. A former schoolfellow told Jacques Émile Blanche, long afterwards, of his terror when he saw Marcel coming towards him, to take his hand and declare his need of 'a tyrannical and total affection'. And the bewildered little Halévy, two years his junior, saw him 'with his huge oriental eyes,

[1] *Jean Santeuil*, vol. 1, 325-7

his big white collar and flying cravat, as a sort of disturbed and disturbing archangel'. At first Halévy responded to Marcel's advances, then avoided him in alarm, only to bewilder him a month later with a shy 'good-morning'. And his cousin Bizet was just as bad: 'why did he say he was my friend, and then drop me completely? What do they want?—to get rid of me, annoy me, mystify me, or what? And I thought they were so nice!'

In the little, artificial world of childhood and school, love and friendship had disappointed him; but in the great real world outside, into which he would soon be released, perhaps love and friendship would be great and real also. Moreover, he had begun to see a third and last mirage of happiness from human relationships, in the realm of high society where those relationships might, it seemed, be considered and enjoyed as a work of art. In the autumn of 1888 he took his first tentative steps towards the Guermantes Way.

He might, if he wished, have found his admission through the ready-made connections of his father; for Dr Proust knew politicians such as Félix Faure, diplomats such as Camille Barrère and Gabriel Hanotaux, society physicians such as Dr Samuel Pozzi. Marcel met Dr Pozzi at dinner with his parents when he was only fifteen, and always remembered that his first 'dinner in town', no doubt a year or two later, had been with Pozzi in the Place Vendôme. But such an entry would have been too slow, humble and tainted, rather as if his Narrator had been reduced to meeting the Duchesse through the combined good offices of Mme Bontemps's husband, M. de Norpois and Dr Cottard. The high society of Paris was never as exclusive as it is symbolically represented in *A la Recherche*. Political, scientific or literary eminence, even mere intelligence or charm, were valid passports to the salons, and society was a career open to the talents. But Marcel wanted the *haut monde* to be more exclusive than it actually was, both to enhance its glamour and to increase his merit in arriving there; and for both these reasons, again, he wished to arrive suddenly and miraculously, and to be instantly accepted. This second wish was granted to him in real life, as to the Narrator in his novel; for Marcel was to discover that in this life all our desires are fulfilled, on the condition that they do not bring the happiness we expected from them.

The key to the Guermantes Way was absurdly simple: indeed,

its very obviousness may not only have answered his ambition, but have helped to create it. Two of his schoolfellows, Jacques Baignères and Jacques Bizet, happened to be sons of two of the chief mistresses of salons in the layer of society immediately below the nobility, where the upper bourgeoisie and the Faubourg Saint-Germain met on common ground. Jacques Baignères was the son of the prominent hostess Mme Laure Baignères, though not, if rumour was correct, of her husband. A visitor unaware of her intimate association with the Orleanist leader M. de Rémusat once asked: "Which does your son most resemble, yourself or M. Baignères?"; and she imperturbably replied "Jacques is just like his father." Jacques Bizet's widowed mother a few years earlier had married Émile Straus, a wealthy Jewish lawyer, after a long and ardent courtship: when asked why she had become his wife, she answered "Because it was the only way I could get him to leave me in peace." But Jacques Bizet remembered his mother saying: "Listen, my child, if I were to marry again, whom would you like best for a step-father?" "Émile," he replied without hesitation, and she kissed him, for she too preferred Émile Straus. Already, in the December of 1888, Marcel was inviting Mme Straus and Jacques Bizet to share his box with the other Jacques for the first night of Edmond de Goncourt's *Germinie Lacerteux* at the Odéon on the 15th; and to persuade her he added a characteristic piece of double-edged flattery: "I've found some lines in Vigny which even you ought to like, for they seem to have been written for your glorification—he must have foreseen you!"

When the news that Marcel was meeting academicians and showing 'an undue partiality for dukes' reached Condorcet, his schoolfellows felt he had betrayed the high ideals of the *Revue Lilas*. They mocked him to his face, but succeeded only in hurting his feelings, not in changing them, or in understanding that the power which drove him to the Guermantes Way was not snobism but genius. The legend that Proust was a society-writer and a snob had begun, and would be replaced by the truth of his greatness only in the last three years of his life, thirty years later. So his last year of school closes in umbrage and obscurity. In the baccalaureate exam he took a first prize for French composition; he began to choose beautiful cravats; and suddenly he was no longer a schoolboy, but a young man of eighteen with a moustache. He was abandoned by and tired of Bloch: it was time to find Saint-Loup.

Chapter 6

BERGOTTE AND DONCIÈRES

PROUST could never remember who had first taken him to the salon of Mme Arman de Caillavet. It was some time in the summer of 1889, and she greeted him with the remark she always served out for newcomers: "You'll find instruction as well as amusement here, it's just like a school prize-book." Then she introduced him to Anatole France, and he found to his disappointment that the writer whom he had imagined as 'a sweet singer with snowy locks' was a little man aged forty-five, of half-clerical, half-military appearance, with 'a red nose like a snail-shell and a pointed black beard'. From that moment of contrast between imagination and reality the character of Bergotte was to be born.

His hostess lived at 12 Avenue Hoche. Her maiden name was Léontine Lippmann, she had married the wealthy Albert Arman in 1868, and at this stage in her progress she was called simply Mme Arman. A few years later her husband added to the family surname the name of a vine-growing château on his country estate of Capian, and she was known as Mme Arman de Caillavet; and then the Arman was suppressed altogether and she became Mme de Caillavet, which sounded best of all. But she always professed that this self-ennobling of Albert's was absurd, and insisted to the end of her life on signing herself 'L. Arman Caillavet', accepting the 'Caillavet', it is true, but rejecting the 'de'.

In 1889 she was forty-two, still unaged and good-looking, loaded with pearls, with a small, intelligent head and short waved hair, and blue eyes which, although a little too prominent, had kept their air of mystery. Something of her imperious manner entered into Mme Verdurin. Mme Arman hurried to greet the proud and timid daughter of the dramatist Bjoernson with cries of "A Norwegian! What luck, what a recruit for my salon! You're just the number I need!" But whenever Mme Arman called on this desirable Viking, the servant always announced: "Madame regrets that she cannot receive Madame. She is in the middle of washing her hair." "Will this woman never finish washing her hair?" complained Mme Arman, but in vain.

Like Mme Verdurin, she felt herself persecuted by *les ennuyeux*. Strangely enough, however, these bores were not people whom she despaired of luring to her salon, but those she was anxious to expel from it; just as, at the age of three, she had tried to throw her baby brother out of the window, saying "He bores me." If the nobility were never to be seen at her receptions, it was chiefly because she didn't want them there, for her only ambition was to attract writers and politicians. In Proust's novel the Baron de Charlus visits Mme Verdurin partly as an act of enormous grace, partly for ends of his own; but in real life Comte Robert de Montesquiou, one of the chief originals of Charlus, was reduced to pleading for Mme Arman's favour, and cadged her invitations with little success. The letters in which he expresses his thwarted admiration and injured feelings, all in vain, are positively heart-rending. When he succeeded at last in enticing her and France to his mansion to meet his cousin, Comtesse Greffulhe, on whom Proust modelled several aspects of both the Duchesse and the Princesse de Guermantes, it was the culmination of seventeen years of hitherto fruitless intrigue. Mme Arman was perhaps an intellectual snob, but she was not a social one. Montesquiou was both: in wooing her it was France and her other pet lions he was after.

Her husband was noted for his sudden, alarming and often untimely appearances, and was therefore said to resemble a jack-in-a-box. M. Arman had a wart on his nose, the trailing ends of his cravat had been compared to the sails of a windmill, and his manner was humorously truculent; 'but he was a very good fellow,' writes Fernand Gregh, 'and there was more in him than people said'. Whenever he saw a new face among his wife's guests, he would pop up and say, "I am not Anatole France"; or he would introduce himself with, "I am the Master—I mean, of the house," and shout, "Monsieur France, here's another admirer for you!" He wrote the yachting column in *Le Figaro* under the preposterous pseudonym of Jip Topsail. He delighted in teasing France, who once helped him in his column with a few beauties of description which the editor carefully deleted. "Ha ha!" bellowed M. Arman, who had a strong southern accent, "you may be a great writer and an academician, but they couldn't find room for your blue skies and white clouds and sails like birds' wings!" "You know everything about the art of writing, M. Arman," France began with careful irony; but Mme Arman broke in with: "Hold your tongue, Albert, you're always saying something stupid." Clearly M. Arman shared several traits with that other great yachtsman, the bluff, teasing, hen-pecked M. Verdurin.

Mme Arman had captured France in 1886 from a rival hostess, Mme Aubernon de Nerville. For some years after their first meeting in 1876 the two ladies had been great friends, and Mme Aubernon, when complimented on her charming companion, would say complacently, "Yes, I invented her myself." But Mme Arman decided to set up her own salon, and their rupture was the late nineteenth-century equivalent of the quarrel between the ageing Mme du Deffand and the young Julie de Lespinasse. Along with France, she stole the younger Dumas, the dramatist, Professor Brochard of the Sorbonne, the critic Jules Lemaître and the playwright Pailleron. The others continued to frequent both salons, but France never returned to Mme Aubernon's. "Is it true," she taxed him, "that you tell everybody you'll never come to my house again because my dinners bore you?" "I may have said so, madam," replied the embarrassed France, "but I never meant it to be repeated."

For a few years Mme Arman was forced to tolerate the occasional visits of the great man's wife. At first Mme France was an exquisite blonde who was sometimes mistaken for France's daughter; but she put on weight, her teeth became repulsively irregular, and in her domineering presence France trembled and stammered more than ever. Then he ceased to speak to her or to notice her presence. One day in June 1892 she invaded his study, where he was writing his fortnightly article for the *Universel*, and called him by a word which he considered 'gross, unseemly and basely insulting'—some say the word was '*cocu*'. A little later she heard the street-door close, and ran to the window: France was already receding along the Rue Chalgrin, carrying his inkwell, pen and unfinished article on a tray; he still wore his slippers and skull-cap, and the cord of his dressing-gown trailed on the pavement behind him. On 2 August 1893 they were divorced. No doubt the fault was not entirely on France's side; but Proust might well write of Bergotte that he was said to have 'behaved cruelly to his wife'.[1] Henceforth France ate and spent his days at Mme

[1] I, 559

Arman's. They made love every morning at his bachelor home,
and then walked to Avenue Hoche for lunch. At tea-time he
would enter the drawing-room and say, "I happened to be passing
your house, and couldn't resist the pleasure of laying my delighted
homage at your feet"; but everybody knew he had been writing
in the library all afternoon. In Proust's novel this anecdote is told
of M. de Norpois and Mme de Villeparisis.[1]

Anatole France was timid, lazy and unambitious; but Mme
Arman, seized with the desire to create a great writer, made him
self-confident, industrious and famous. Did she make him great?
At least there is something in the faded prose of France, a joy, an
irony, a craftsmanship, which has enabled him, alone of the
secondary novelists of the French 1890s, to survive a little to-day.
In his novel Proust gave the guardianship of Bergotte, so like
Mme Arman's of France, not to Mme Verdurin but to Odette,
Swann's wife. Bergotte spends every day at Mme Swann's, 'on
exhibition', and her salon is built round him. She whispers to an
influential guest: "I'll speak to him, and he'll write an article for
you"; it is rumoured that she collaborates in his works; and the
Narrator tells us that 'between the elegance of Mme Swann's salon
and one whole aspect of the work of Bergotte there are relationships so close that each, for the old men of to-day, can become
alternately a commentary on the other.'[2] In all this Proust is
thinking of Mme Arman and France. He took the name of
Bergotte from M. Bergeret, the hero of France's tetralogy
L'Histoire Contemporaine; but it is also a near-anagram of
Bourget, a novelist whom he m..t, as we shall see, in association
with yet another original of Odette Swann. To people of Proust's
generation the name could not fail to suggest also the philosopher
Bergson, particularly to Proust himself, who was Bergson's
cousin by marriage; but although the influence of Bergson's
philosophy upon Proust's novel was considerable, there is little
more of Bergson in Bergotte. There is, however, something of
Renan, whom Proust visited on 17 January 1889, taking with him
the old Grecian's *Vie de Jésus*; and after a long conversation, of
which afterwards he had little to relate, he returned with the
volume signed by the author.[3] The snail-shell nose is Renan's,

[1] II, 221   [2] II, 743-5
[3] 'For Marcel Proust,' wrote Renan, who died in 1892, 'whom I ask to
keep an affectionate memory of me when I am no longer in this world.'

for the nose of Anatole France was quite different, being long, thin and a little to one side; and Bergotte's famous invocation to the Korai on the Acropolis was suggested by Renan's *Prière sur l'Acropole*. Bergotte's early essay on Racine, which Gilberte gives to the Narrator in a white packet tied with mauve ribbons, was a contribution by France, which was also printed separately, to an edition of Racine's works published in 1874.[1] Conversely, when M. de Norpois remarks that Bergotte has 'the subtlety of a deliquescent mandarin', Proust has in mind Lemaître's comparison of France to 'an extraordinarily learned and subtle mandarin'.

Was the influence of France upon Proust comparable to that of Bergotte on the Narrator? Many of France's themes—the unreality of the phenomenal world, the poetic nature of the past in which the only true reality is hidden, the impossibility of knowing another person, the continual process of change in the self, feelings and memory, his pessimism—are to be found in *A la Recherche*. The influence of his style is there long outgrown, but it is perceptible not only in Proust's early stories, written in the 1890s and collected in *Les Plaisirs et les Jours*, for which France wrote the preface, but even in *Jean Santeuil*. When the Narrator of *A la Recherche* speaks of 'a book I began to write', and of finding 'the equivalent in Bergotte of certain of my own phrases, whose quality was insufficient to determine me to continue it',[2] Proust is thinking of his unfinished *Jean Santeuil*; though no doubt the process was really in the reverse direction, and he had already found in France's novels the passages which he unconsciously reproduced in *Jean Santeuil*.

To the Narrator, however, the work of Bergotte was a discovery which was one of the foretastes of Time Regained, and gave him 'a joy that I felt I was experiencing in a deeper, vaster, more unified region of myself, from which all obstacles and separations seemed to have been removed'.[3] As we shall see, the only writer from whom Proust was to be granted a similar revelation—and that only a partial and temporary one, since the true revelation was to come from himself—was Ruskin, whom he

[1] But the reference in Bergotte's essay to the 'plastic nobility' and 'Delphic symbol' of Berma's acting in *Phèdre* comes from a critique by Jules Lemaître on Sarah Bernhardt's appearance in Racine's play at the Théâtre de la Renaissance in November 1893.

[2] I, 96   [3] I, 94

discovered ten years later. It is true that for a year or two France, along with Loti, was his favourite contemporary novelist. He never ceased to respect him, and he never replaced him with another, for when he outgrew France he turned to the masters of the past, to Balzac, Stendhal or Flaubert, or to the Russians, Tolstoy or Dostoevsky, or to English novelists, George Eliot and Hardy; and last of all to himself, for since Bergotte did not exist he was compelled, as a last resort, to become him. France was the only living novelist (except Barrès, who also contributed a little to Bergotte) whom he met and enthusiastically admired in early youth, and in gratitude he built the character of Bergotte, an apotheosis of France, around him. But he had to invent the greatness of Bergotte, in whose work, the magic of which is so subtly conveyed but so rarely demonstrated by quotation, there is something higher than France or any other French novelist of his time.

'On entering the drawing-room of Mme Arman,' wrote one of her guests, 'one had the impression of being in a railway-station, of which Anatole France was the stationmaster.' Mme Arman sat to the right of the fireplace, while France leaned against the mantelpiece, gesturing, stammering, hunting for the right word, but always holding forth. 'His conversation was that of a superior but crashing bore,' thought Henri de Regnier, who was however fond of talking himself; but to Fernand Gregh it seemed 'literally enchanting with its mixture of irony and kindness, wit and grace, naturalness and erudition, fantasy and good sense'. Towards Proust he adopted the paternal tone of Bergotte. "How do you manage to know so many things, Monsieur France?" asked Proust, and France replied: "It's quite simple, my dear Marcel. When I was your age I wasn't good-looking and popular like you. So instead of going into society I stayed at home and did nothing but read." No doubt he also uttered Bergotte's famous remark, that the pleasures of the mind would compensate for Marcel's ill-health. 'I would not exchange the painful pleasures of the intelligence for all the gay frivolities and empty experiences of the ordinary man,' he wrote in *Le Temps* of 9 November 1891. But when he said to Proust at Mme Arman's "You, Marcel, who love so much the things of the intelligence," his young friend interrupted: "I don't love the things of the intelligence at all; I only love life and movement."

Perhaps, however, the chief immediate influence upon his life which Proust encountered at this time in Mme Arman's salon was that of a person who was not there, her son Gaston. It can hardly be a coincidence that the military service of Gaston Arman, whom so far he had never met,[1] was immediately followed by that of Proust. Every Wednesday at Mme Arman's (for her day was the same as Mme Verdurin's) he would hear the latest news of Gaston in the army: his life in barracks at Versailles, the practical jokes for which he was so frequently confined to those barracks, the horrors and heroism of his route-marches and billeting in barns in the country of the Loire. He would see the photograph of Gaston on leave, standing in the sunlight on the balcony of 12 Avenue Hoche, fierce and resplendent in his artillery-man's uniform, the image of a rather portly Saint-Loup. Proust heard, admired and envied: why should he not do the same? He joined the army of his own free will, for with his father's influence he could easily have obtained exemption on the grounds of ill-health; and exemptions were also freely granted to those taking a university education. But it is true that unless he was either to spend three long years in military service or evade it altogether, the time was now or never.

The period of compulsory military service since 1872 had been five years, but for volunteers only one year. In practice, for more than half the total number of recruits, the full period of five years was not insisted upon, since it would have meant an intolerable strain upon finance and manpower.[2] Nevertheless, the only way in which one could be sure of serving only one year was to have parents rich enough to pay 1,500 francs (£60) for one's uniform and maintenance, to have been educated up to baccalaureate or equivalent standard, and to volunteer. Such volunteers served in

[1] So he said, more than thirty years later. But it seems certain that Gaston Arman was at Condorcet a year above Proust, for in her letters to her son, though she never names his school, Mme Arman mentions Élie Halévy, Léon Brunschwicg and Jacques Baignères as his schoolfellows. Proust must have known him there, but perhaps only by sight. Cf. also the entry for Gaston de Caillavet in *Qui êtes-vous?*, 1910-11.

[2] The class of each year was about 240,000 men: if each had served his full time the army, including 100,000 officers, N.C.O.s and long-service men, would have numbered 1,300,000 men. In fact, exemptions were numerous, many others were sent on indefinite leave after one year, and only about 500,000 were under arms at a time.

the ranks, but were treated as a kind of officer-cadet. If their training was satisfactory, they would pass out as sub-officers[1] in the reserve. They would then have to serve occasional periods of a month's training, and would gradually be promoted to lieutenant, captain or even higher rank. But on 15 July 1889 a law was passed limiting military service to three years and abolishing the *volontariat*. Proust seized the opportunity to volunteer before the new law became effective on 1 November, and on 15 November he was called to the colours in the 76th Infantry at Orleans. The following year of the discipline and love of comrades which to certain neurotics are so welcome was one of the happiest of his life.[2]

His way was smoothed by his status as a volunteer. Army officers regarded the young noblemen and sons of the upper bourgeoisie who made up the ranks of the *volontariat* as men of their own class and as future colleagues; and whether officially or not the volunteers were allowed to have batmen to take care of their uniform and equipment. His commanding officer, Colonel Arvers—'my excellent colonel'—was of a paternal and kindly disposition, and Trooper Proust had been recommended to his special care through the political contacts of Dr Proust. Colonel Arvers went so far as to grant him exemption, no doubt on medical grounds, from early morning parade and from jumping ditches when at riding-exercise. Another of his officers was Captain Walewski, a grandson of Napoleon by his amour with Marie Walewska. He was respected by his men not only for his glorious descent and personal resemblance to the great Emperor, but for his courtesy and kindness in command. He is an evident original of the Prince de Borodino at Doncières.[3] There was also

[1] The *sous-officier* was a senior N.C.O. of rank ranging from sergeant to sergeant-major.

[2] His army pay-book gives his height as five feet six inches (1·68 metres) on 11 November 1889. He may well have grown a little further by his twenty-first year. He was therefore of middle height, which explains why some of his friends have described him as tall, others as short. His hair and eyes, in the army's opinion, are 'chestnut' ('*châtains*'). A surviving lock of his hair, clipped from his dead body in November 1922, is very dark brown, almost black, with only a very few grey hairs.

[3] Count Walewski's mother had been a mistress of Napoleon III. Similarly, the Narrator remarks, 'the second Princesse de Borodino was thought to have bestowed her favours upon Napoleon III', and accounts by this for Borodino's facial resemblance to both Emperors (II, 129).

a Captain Saivrin, a friend of friends of Mme Proust, from whom she sometimes had indirect news of her 'little wolf'. In immediate command over Proust was Lieutenant de Cholet, a handsome young officer with black moustaches, who presented him at the end of his year with a signed photograph 'to Marcel Proust, volunteer cadet (*conditionnel*), from one of his torturers'. It was Cholet who once, like Saint-Loup,[1] hurt his feelings by saluting him coldly, pretending not to recognise him, in the street.

In theory the volunteers were strictly forbidden to take lodgings in town; but in practice they would hire a private room —Proust's was at Mme Renvoyzé's in the Rue des Bons Enfants near the cathedral—where they would dine and drink champagne or punch in the evening, while late-comers shaved and changed into their best uniforms in the adjoining dressing-rooms. When an officer met them on the stairs he would smile, seeming to cast a wistful eye on the champagne visible through the open door; and to make his good-will perfectly clear, he might even condescend to ask one of them for a light. "You ought to have asked him in, he'd have been quite welcome," someone would say afterwards, 'with the jesting air', as Proust wrote in *Jean Santeuil*, 'of a bourgeois saying to a friend who has just seen the Tsar of Russia drive past: "You should have brought him along to dinner, you could have told him I'd be delighted." '[2] A few yards from the Rue des Bons Enfants and the nearby much-restored cathedral, traditionally known as 'the ugliest in France', were the church and street of Saint-Euverte, after which Proust named in his novel the hostess who was the Baron de Charlus's pet aversion, and at whose reception Swann heard the Vinteuil Sonata. On the bank of the Loire two miles above the town is the Château de Saint-Loup.

In February an introduction from Dr Proust brought an invitation to dinner from the Prefect of the Loire, M. Boegner, to Proust and another gentleman-ranker named Mayrargues. Young Robert de Billy, a volunteer in the 30th Artillery stationed at Orleans, was also there, with his gaiters and buttons brilliantly polished, his white gloves newly washed, and the handle of his sabre resting in the regulation position in the crook of his arm.

[1] II, 138
[2] *Jean Santeuil*, vol. 2, 291

Mayrargues seemed smart enough, he thought, but the other guest had a greatcoat several times too large; 'his deportment and manner of speaking did not conform with the military ideal; he had enormous questioning eyes, and his flow of conversation was amiable and easy.' At first Proust's Condorcet ways did not please a youth who had recently left the formidable Lycée Saint Louis: the fellow talked of nothing but the delights of metaphysics, and the genius of a schoolmaster named Darlu. But soon they became fast friends, and compared this first encounter to the meeting of Bouvard and Pécuchet in Flaubert. Billy had had a strict French Protestant education: 'I owe it in great part to Marcel,' he says, 'if I knew the joy of thinking otherwise than in accordance with fixed principles.'

Incredible as it may seem, in view of his later ill-health and physical inactivity, Proust enjoyed his life in the army. 'It's curious,' he wrote to a friend fifteen years later, 'that you should have regarded the army as a prison, I as a paradise.' He swam, rode, fenced and marched, and rejoiced to be called '*mon vieux*' by the common soldiers his companions: he experienced, for one whole year, the delightful illusion of being normal and accepted. There was a new poetry in the grey autumnal landscape, in the daily scenes of life in the barrack-room, which he likened to the *genre* paintings of the Dutch School. 'The rural character of the places,' he wrote in *Les Plaisirs et les Jours*, 'the simplicity of some of my peasant-comrades, whose bodies were more beautiful and agile, their minds more original, their character more natural than those of the young men I had known before or knew later, the calm of a life in which occupations are more regulated and the imagination less trammelled than in any other, in which pleasure is the more constantly with us because we have no time to run about looking for it and so miss it altogether, all these things concur to make this period of my life a series of little pictures full of happy reality and a charm on which time has since shed its delicious sadness and its poetry.'[1] Orleans, with its cobbled streets, warm inns and misty views of the nearby countryside, became Doncières; and because he first came there in autumn, and overlaid Saint-Loup's garrison-town with later visits to Fontainebleau (1896), Versailles (1906 and 1908) and Lisieux (1907) which happened at the same

[1] *Les Plaisirs et les Jours*, 216

melancholy time of year, Doncières is a place where it is always autumn.[1]

Meanwhile his mother wrote to him, and he to her, every day. Her correspondence is full of gossip about home, as letters to a soldier in exile should be, but tantalisingly void of information about the addressee; and only one letter from Orleans of Trooper Proust, and that to his father, has survived. She describes Robert ('Proustovitch') unmercifully massaging his father's lumbago, and Dr Proust roaring, "You're hurting me like blazes! God in Heaven, how you're hurting me!" and then adding, "Why are you stopping? Get on with it, boy!" Or she asks the servant to prepare a fish dinner one Friday, when Catholic friends are coming, and remarks, 'Angélique will think I'm going to be converted!' She sends on a message from Anatole France, 'Tell Marcel I'm very fond of him'; and Lucie Faure, his playmate in the Champs-Élysées, says, 'Tell him the same from me.' Or she offers a little good advice; his father wishes him to cut down his intake of cream-cheese, so—'Think of a number, then halve it', or, most practical of all (had he been punished for neglecting to polish them?), 'Gaiters, gaiters, gaiters, gaiters!' She visited him regularly, and so occasionally did Robert Proust, Horace Finaly, with whom he had stayed at Ostend the previous August, and other friends.

His father's mother, Louis Proust's widow, had died at Illiers on 19 March 1889; but on 2 January 1890 came a more terrible loss, the death of his maternal grandmother, Mme Nathé Weil.

[1] Does Doncières also contain memories of a time when Proust was no longer a soldier himself, but the guest of a soldier? In 1893-94 his friends Louis de la Salle and Daniel Halévy served their year at Fontainebleau, while Pierre Lavallée was at Chartres; in 1894-95 Robert Proust was at Rheims with Fernand Gregh, Robert Dreyfus and other old friends; and in 1895 a pianist friend, Édouard Risler, who may perhaps have suggested the piano-playing Marquis de Poitiers in *Jean Santeuil*, served at Chartres. There is no direct evidence for such a visit, but there are plenty of months unaccounted for in the 1890s in which it might have occurred; and in *Jean Santeuil*, at least, the hero experiences army life both as a soldier and as a visiting onlooker. The name Doncières comes from a character in *Connaîs-toi*, a play by Paul Hervieu, whom Proust knew well, produced at the Comédie Française in 1909. Doncières is a junction on the line between Balbec and Paris, and its first syllable recalls the junction-town of Mézidon, sixteen miles south of Cabourg, where the branch-line from Cabourg joins the main line from Paris to Cherbourg.

At our last glimpse of the poor lady, a fortnight before, she is on a milk diet, and refusing even that, 'unless you can make it not taste of milk'. In memory of her beloved mother Mme Proust began to read and quote Mme de Sévigné, just as the Narrator's mother does in *Sodome et Gomorrhe*. ' "I know another mother who counts as nothing for herself, who has transmitted herself entirely to her children," ' she wrote—'Isn't that just like your grandmother? Only she wouldn't have *said* it!' Proust wept for his loss and his mother's grief, but was told: 'Think of her, by all means, and cherish her as I do: but don't let yourself go, and spend days in tears, because it's only bad for your nerves, and she wouldn't wish it. No, the more you think of her, the more it is your duty to be as she would like you to be, and act as she would like you to act.' But the last days of the grandmother in *Le Côté de Guermantes* are drawn chiefly, as will be seen, from the last illness of Mme Proust herself fifteen years later.

Almost every week-end Proust was able to come home on leave to Paris, which was less than two hours from Orleans by rail. On one of his first leaves he visited Mme Arman, and there at last met the famous Gaston, whose military service had just ended. 'Gaston was so charming to me that our friendship began immediately.' In the barrack-room Proust talked of nothing else and so impressed his batman and the corporal that they sent Gaston an address of homage for New Year's Day. Throughout that year Proust was to be seen at Sunday tea-time in Mme Arman's salon, buried in his uniform and the enormous cushions of one of her best armchairs. The weary head of the soldier lay back, drooping to one shoulder; his face was serious, his large brown eyes were melancholy; and then at the least pretext he would burst into his nervous but infectious laugh, and the pale face was lit up by his white teeth. At six o'clock Mme Arman would stuff him with cakes and sandwiches, and load him with more to take away—"You may need them in the train"; and then he would make the round of the drawing-room to say good-bye, embarrassed by the parcels and his képi, bustled from behind by Gaston. When at last Gaston tore him from the final benediction of Anatole France and pushed him downstairs, their cab had been waiting for more than half an hour. In the Rue du Faubourg Saint-Honoré there was a pastry-cook whose clock was always slow—they were reassured; but in the Rue Royale a restaurant clock was always fast, and they were plunged into despair. At the Gare d'Orléans Gaston hurried after his friend as far as the platform, chased by the angry cabman—they had promised him double, and now he was afraid of being bilked altogether. Then Gaston returned alone, having missed dinner in the cause of friendship.

One afternoon at Mme Arman's Proust was introduced to Gaston's fiancée, Mlle Jeanne Pouquet, and immediately began to compliment her effusively on her beauty. Blushing and frightened, the young girl walked away, only to be asked: "Are you turning your back on me because you're afraid I won't notice your lovely hair?" She complained to Gaston—"I think your friend Proust is horrid." "Not at all, he's delightful. Besides, even before he spoke to you, he told me you were simply charming!" Meanwhile Proust had been busy with Jeanne's mother, who now came up and said: "Young Monsieur Proust has quite made a conquest of me, and I've asked him to come and see us on his next leave." "Then I shall arrange to be out," replied the infuriated girl. But Proust, fascinated equally by her magnificent plaits of dark hair and by the fact that she already belonged to his friend, had fallen in love. 'Gilberte's plaits seemed to me a matchless work of art,' he wrote long afterwards; 'for a section of them, however infinitely small, what celestial herbal would I not have chosen as a reliquary!'[1]

Soon it was Gaston's turn to be angry. Proust had invited Jeanne and her mother ('or if she can't come, your governess or a maid will do just as well for a chaperone') to stay at Orleans, 'to visit the churches and museums and go hunting'. He would book rooms at the best hotel, and knew a tapestry-man and an antique-dealer who would make their apartment really comfortable: 'there's nothing extraordinary about that, is there?' He had discovered that she had cousins near Orleans, whose father, Louis Darblay, was an enthusiastic huntsman. Suddenly Proust developed a longing to ride to hounds, and intrigued for an introduction to M. Merle, their kennel-master. He found a château to let near Orleans, 'quite a small one': they must come and stay with him there, Gaston too, and all their friends. "But if the château is so small, how can we all come?"—and they never came. Next he tried to obtain her photograph, and Gaston was

[1] I, 503

furious again. Reduced to more indirect means, he proposed that all the girls of their set should exchange photographs with all the young men; and to set an example he arrived at Mme Pouquet's weekly dance with a packet of photographs of himself, which he proceeded to distribute. Their mothers hurried up with loud cries of horror, and all was to begin again. He began to scrape acquaintance with her most distant relatives; and a chorus of uncles, aunts and cousins, charmed by his assiduity, began to sing his praises. Perhaps they would invite him to their country-houses, perhaps there would be photograph-albums there, and then—"I shan't stick at theft," he said. He won the photograph only twenty years later, when Jeanne had ceased to resemble it, but even then he was still receiving New Year cards from the same obscure aunts in Périgord. 'To obtain Gilberte's photograph I committed acts of baseness which did not get me what I wanted, but involved me for the rest of my life with some extremely boring people.'[1]

In the summer of his army year he was given clerical work at divisional headquarters; 'but the Chief of Staff, not without reason, was exasperated by my handwriting, and threw me out'. On a sunny day, against the leafy trellis of a garden wall, he was photographed four times: no doubt these are the photographs he handed round at Mme Pouquet's dance. In one he is marking time in his greatcoat and képi, with an ingratiating smile, doing his best to look like a soldier in the chorus of some comic opera by Offenbach; in the second he wears a heavy sweater with collar and carries a riding-stock; in the third, inscribed 'to the one and only Gaston', he is pensively reading, and has slyly contrived to make the greatcoat look like a monk's habit, the book like a breviary.

That August Dr Proust was sent to investigate an outbreak of cholera in Spain, which recalls the Spanish tour of the Narrator's father with M. de Norpois in *A l'Ombre*.[2] He returned, still hot and dusty, announcing that 'travel is a delightful thing, because you're so glad to go, and so glad to come back'. It was a month of photographs: to compensate for one in which the photographer had made her grimace, Mme Proust sent her son another in which she had an air of inspiration. 'I look like Goethe,' she wittily wrote, 'gazing up at a fourth-floor window and saying "I am in love with one who is far above me.'" In September Proust spent a short leave with her at Cabourg, and immediately on his return to Orleans wrote to his father, who was staying at Aix-les-Bains at the country-house of Dr Cazalis. On his way to the station at Cabourg a group of housemaids, stirred by his soldier's uniform, had blown kisses, much to the horror of his mother's friends. 'So the maids of Orleans whom I had abandoned had their revenge, and I am punished—if M. Cazalis will allow me to quote one of his finest lines—"for scorning the rosebuds of their naked breasts".'[1]

For the last few months of his military service Proust was placed in the instruction-squad, with a view to promotion to the rank of *sous-officier*. 'I am having great difficulty in fixing my attention and learning by heart,' he told his father; and his final position was sixty-third in a squad of sixty-four. 'Because of my wretched health, I was such a mediocre soldier that I remained a mere private[2],' he wrote thirty years later. As a last incongruous episode of his life in the army, he begged Colonel Arvers to be allowed to stay on for a few months; alas, it could not be arranged. He was free to continue his climb into society and his wooing of Jeanne Pouquet; but his release seemed more like an expulsion from yet another paradise. Now he must try to satisfy not a fatherly colonel, but an actual father, who demanded that he should face the claims of adult life and adopt a bread-winning career.

[1] At Aix Dr Proust had met Maupassant: 'I hope you liked him,' writes his son; 'I've only met him twice, but he must know more or less who I am.' This is interesting, since the novelist C., who is the putative author of *Jean Santeuil*, so closely resembles Maupassant in appearance and habits. In *A la Recherche*, C.'s function is taken over by Elstir; and it will be seen later how an incident at Beg-Meil in 1895 caused the novelist to be changed into a painter. Proust's meetings with Maupassant were no doubt in the salon of Mme Straus, which Maupassant frequented in the late 1880s. For a time Maupassant was unsuccessfully in love with his hostess, and he made her one of the heroines in his last novel, *Fort comme la Mort*.

[2] As Proust was in an infantry regiment, he was not strictly speaking a 'trooper'; but the nickname was given him by his family, no doubt because his training included riding exercises.

Chapter 7

THE STUDENT IN SOCIETY

ON 20 November 1890, soon after his unwilling release from the army, Proust enrolled as a student in the Faculté de Droit at the Sorbonne. By way of having two strings to his bow he also joined the École des Sciences Politiques: at the end of his three years as a student, he thought, he would at least have the choice between two equally uninviting careers, the law and the diplomatic service. Among his fellow-students were Robert de Billy, Gabriel Trarieux, who became a symbolist poet, and Jean Boissonnas, a future ambassador. He listened with respect to the lectures of the distinguished historians, Anatole Leroy-Beaulieu and Albert Sorel, and of the philosophers Paul Desjardins and Henri Bergson. Bergson became his cousin-in-law when he married a niece of Mme Proust, Mlle Neuburger, in 1892. For the platitudes of Comte Albert Vandal, however, he felt only amused contempt: the object of his course, it seemed, was to teach the budding diplomat to think and speak like M. de Norpois. One morning Vandal was explaining the origin of the Russo-Turkish war of 1877. A Serb had been killed by a Turkish soldier when trying to draw water from a forbidden well: "Gentlemen," said Vandal, "from that well came a conflagration which set fire to the whole of Eastern Europe." Proust suddenly began to write in his hitherto virgin notebook, and Billy looking over read the following doggerel:

'For exquisite Vandal's Attic salt
Who cares a da⸱ ⸱n? Not Gabriel,
Robert, or Jean, or even Marcel,
Though he is serious to a fault.'

Vandal had a nervous trick of suddenly closing one eye, so that people thought he must be winking at them: a weakness shared by Dr Cottard, who made Swann fear they might have met on the stairs in a brothel, while Charlus suspected him of making immoral advances.[1] But as the four young men strolled back from

[1] I, 202; II, 919

the Left Bank they talked of more important subjects, of metaphysics and the symbolist movement and the Russian novel and
Ibsen. In these conversations, Billy remembered, Proust made
cunning use of the Socratic method of questioning, which he had
learned from Darlu, and so induced his friends to utter truths
which they were unaware of knowing.

Meanwhile he never missed the 'dancing-lesson' which Mme
Pouquet held every week, at ten in the evening, in her house at
62 Rue de Miromesnil. In fact there was neither dancing-master
nor lesson; but their hostess felt it was important not to call it
a soirée, as none of the girls there was old enough to 'come out'.
He arrived when everyone was leaving, for he only wanted to see
Jeanne, and persuade the willing Gaston to stay; and then they
talked with Jeanne and her mother, until M. Pouquet appeared,
in an affable rage, and asked "Are you going to bed to-day or
to-morrow?" "But, Papa, it's past midnight, so we're certain to
go to bed to-day," said Jeanne. M. Pouquet showed the wooers
the door with "Now then, young fellows, it's time you were
leaving," and old Louis, the alcoholic butler, would grumble:
"Monsieur ought to turn them out earlier; he doesn't realise that
these young people can stay in bed till nine, but we servants have
to be up with the sun." Proust was delighted with Louis's conversation, and gave him stupendous tips; but the old man would
say: "He's a nice lad enough, only he doesn't know his place. He's
always hanging round Mlle Jeanne, and Madame doesn't notice
anything—but M. Gaston can see what's going on." When
Proust was invited to tea he would arrive early for a talk with
Fifine, the chamber-maid, whom he admired because she refused
to steal one of the coveted photographs of Jeanne for him. When
the ladies arrived home they were told: "Monsieur Marcel's been
here for hours." "Why, where is he?" "In the linen-room with
Fifine!"

That winter Gaston, who was to become one of the most
popular writers of light comedy of his generation, devised a little
revue to be performed by their friends. Jeanne appeared as
Cleopatra and as a concierge; and a photograph survives of her
in the latter role, wearing a loud gown and a huge feathered
bonnet, round-faced, thick-lipped and eager in a pathetic moment
of time lost. Proust was given the important role of prompter,
but at the dress rehearsal he was overcome by enthusiasm at the

costumes which he now saw for the first time and the talent of
his friends. He interrupted every line with uncontrollable laughter
and cries of "Bravo!" At the end of the rehearsal the indignant
cast rounded upon him and took back the prompt-book. That
night he wrote an extremely bad poem, 'On a Young Lady who
this evening played Cleopatra, to the present trouble and future
damnation of a young man who happened to be present', containing the lines:

> '*You have dethroned the Queen of Nile, for you
> Are both the artist and the work of art.*'

Soon afterwards Gaston wrote for Jeanne a one-act play called
Colombine. They asked Proust to be Pierrot: "You're just right
for the part, you're so pale and your eyes are so big!"; but he
refused to act on the stage a character which he was already
playing in real life.

In the summer of 1891 he frequented with Gaston and Jeanne
a tennis-court in the Boulevard Bineau at Neuilly. Instead of
playing he sat under the trees with the girls in a group which the
others scornfully called 'gossips' corner' and 'the Court of Love'.
He was made responsible for the refreshments, and arrived
carrying a huge cardboard box of cakes; and when everyone was
hot with playing he was sent to a near-by café and returned
groaning and panting with a basket of beer and lemonade. Sometimes a tennis ball hurtled among the glasses and girls of the
Court of Love, and he would cry with justified indignation, "You
did that on purpose." He was photographed kneeling and
strumming on a tennis-racket for a guitar at the feet of Jeanne
standing on a chair, while Gabrielle Schwartz, Gabriel Trarieux
and the Daireaux and Dancognée girls struck attitudes around
them. His emotions among this little band later became associated
with Gilberte in the Champs-Élysées and the budding grove of
girls at Balbec. In 1912, when he was about to publish in *Le Figaro*
an early version of his love for Gilberte, he wrote to Jeanne:
'You will find amalgamated in it something of my feelings when
I wasn't sure whether you would be at the tennis-court. But
what's the use of recalling things which you took the absurd and
unkind course of pretending never to notice!"

After two years his relationship with Jeanne had become static
and thoroughly explored, and therefore uninteresting. Jeanne was

flattered and amused, but untouched by his love, and he ceased to love her. In May 1893, by which time he had pursued four more women and begun at last to love young men, she married Gaston. Proust was asked to be best man, but declined; he refused even to go to dinner in their new home, writing: "How could you invite me, Madame? If you didn't understand that I couldn't come, you will be equally unable to understand my reasons for declining!" It is rumoured that Gaston de Caillavet, like Robert de Saint-Loup, was not altogether a faithful husband, though his wife, unlike Gilberte, was thought too naïve to notice it. Once, it is said, when he went out for the first time after an illness, Jeanne asked him where he had spent the day. "I went to the Bois de Boulogne, my dear." "But it's been raining all day! What ever did you do there?" "Oh, I just sat on a seat." "Really, dear, do you think that was wise?" For Proust this marriage of the first friend and the first love of his early manhood was buried ever deeper beneath the weight of later events in which it had no part; until seventeen years later, when *A la Recherche* was already begun, he met the beautiful daughter of Gaston and Jeanne—as his Narrator met the daughter of Saint-Loup and Gilberte at the Princesse de Guermantes's final party—and realised its ideal significance. In real life the marriage was no miraculous reconciliation of two worlds: husband and wife were both from the same layer of the upper bourgeoisie, and it was Gaston who, through his mother, was half Jewish. But in his novel it became the symbol of the meeting of the two ways of Illiers and Combray, and the incarnation of that meeting in the person of Mlle de Saint-Loup.

In September 1891 Proust visited Cabourg, where he was overcome by memories of his boyhood holidays there with his dead grandmother, and wrote to his mother on the 9th the letter already quoted: 'How different it is from those seaside holidays when Grandmother and I, lost in one another, walked battling with the wind and talking.' These weeks correspond to the Narrator's delayed grief during the early part of his second visit to Balbec. Towards the end of the month he moved to Trouville for a stay at Mme Charlotte Baignères's villa Les Frémonts, high on a hill over the Channel, the original as we shall see later of La Raspelière with its 'three views'. On the promenade he was impressed by a rouged, middle-aged, great lady, whose sinuous figure seemed to coil about her parasol like a snake round a rod, and whose reticule was carried by a little negro page in red satin. She was the Princesse de Sagan, and he made her Mme de Villeparisis's friend the Princesse de Luxembourg. Soon, in a gown of a bygone, Second Empire elegance, the Princesse toiled up the hill to Les Frémonts from her Villa Persane with her great friend the Marquise de Galliffet, who was a first cousin of Mme Baignères. Both ladies were daughters of Second Empire financiers (the Princesse was a Seillière, the Marquise a Laffitte), separated from their husbands, and continuing in their middle fifties to lead lives of assiduous gallantry. We shall meet them again three chapters later, but may note meanwhile that another original of the Princesse de Luxembourg was Princesse Alice of Monaco, and that in *A la Recherche* the Luxembourgs as a family correspond to the royal house of Monaco.

Another visitor to Les Frémonts was the painter Jacques Émile Blanche, who came over from his parents' summer villa at Dieppe, where his friends among the English colony included Sickert, Beardsley, Whistler, Conder and Wilde. Blanche was ten years older than Proust, and had left Condorcet, where he had studied English under Mallarmé and philosophy under Victor Brochard (the chief original of Brichot), two years before Proust's arrival. They had likewise failed to meet at Auteuil, although the famous private lunatic asylum kept by Dr Antoine Blanche was only a few yards from Louis Weil's villa; and their paths had first crossed earlier in 1891 at the salons of Mme Straus, Princesse Mathilde and Mme Baignères. Blanche's parents were wealthy—"We have a hundred thousand francs a year, not counting our dear lunatics," his mother would say complacently. He was a burly, heavy-featured young man, sharp-tongued and vindictive, a talented and delightful painter, and destined later to be an almost equally brilliant writer; his work in both fields has lived. On 1 October at Les Frémonts, during the hour before dinner, he made a pencil sketch for the well-known portrait of Proust which he painted in his studio at Auteuil during the mornings of the following spring, and exhibited in the Salon des Artistes Français of 1893. After the sittings they would lunch with Dr Blanche, who from professional habit, and long familiarity with madmen of genius— Maupassant at this time was one of his inmates—would cry: "Now, Jacques, you must try not to upset him—pay no attention, my dear boy, keep absolutely calm, Jacques doesn't mean a word he's saying—just sip a glass of cold water and count up to a hundred!" Proust showed his naïve satisfaction with the painting in *Jean Santeuil*, in the description of his hero's portrait by 'Le Gandare': 'a radiant young man still posing before the whole of Paris . . . with eyes like fresh almonds . . . and features cool and luminous as a spring morning, a beauty not so much thoughtful as gently pensive'.[1] But the romantic and elegant young man-about-town of the oil portrait is Proust's ephemeral vision of himself on the Guermantes Way, at the Princesse de Wagram's ball; and Blanche showed keener divination in the pencil sketch of a hunched, unkempt youth, with a glare of terrifying intensity, in the hour before dinner at Les Frémonts. Proust saw a great deal of Blanche during 1892 at the salons of the hostesses named above and of Laure Hayman (Odette) and Mme Aubernon (Mme Verdurin); and he was presented with a photograph of his ugly companion inscribed: 'to his great friend Proust, '92'. Possibly Elstir as 'Monsieur Tiche' at Mme Verdurin's represents Blanche at Mme Baignères's. Their estrangement in 1893 was caused partly by Blanche's contempt for Proust's social ambitions, partly by Montesquiou, who had put Blanche on his black list; and it was prolonged some years later by their different views during the Dreyfus Affair, in which Blanche took the anti-Dreyfusist side.[2]

Towards the winter of 1891 Proust had already found a new subject of interest, and was not displeased to notice that Jeanne Pouquet was a little jealous, and that Gaston was jealous of her jealousy. His old great-uncle Louis Weil was the lover of a famous cocotte, to whom he had introduced his delighted great-nephew three years before, in the autumn of his last year at school. Proust now renewed the acquaintance, and turned from Gilberte to Odette.

Laure Hayman was a descendant of the English painter Francis Hayman (1708-76), who taught Gainsborough and was one of the founders of the Royal Academy. She was born in 1851 on a

---

[1] *Jean Santeuil*, vol. 3, 296-7. The rest of the passage corresponds accurately to the Blanche portrait, except that Jean wears a rose in his buttonhole, whereas Proust sported an orchid spray. In the name 'Le Gandare' Proust alludes to the society portraitist La Gandara.

[2] It is significant that all Blanche's published reminiscences of Proust relate either to the years 1891-92 or to the period after their reconciliation twenty years later, shortly before the war.

ranch in the Andes; her father, an engineer, died when she was still a child, and her mother, after trying in vain to live by giving piano-lessons, brought her up as a courtesan. Her lovers were quite as distinguished as the Grand Duke who supplied the cigarettes of Uncle Adolphe's lady in pink. They included the Duc d'Orléans, the King of Greece, Karageorgevitch, pretender to the Serbian throne, said to be the only man she really loved, Prince Karl Egon von Fürstenberg, the financier Raphael Bischoffsheim, and Michael Herbert, a secretary at the English embassy in Paris.[1] Albert Flament[2] called her 'the educator of dukes', and her lessons included not only the art of love but the correct use of language. Vicomte Charles de la Rochefoucauld wrote to her from Biarritz, with unconscious derangement of epithets: 'We're having torrential heat here,' to which she replied by return of post: 'The rain here has been positively torrid.' "He's got blue blood, all right," she would remark, "I can't even teach him to spell—and as for his French. . . !" Like Odette she lived in a little house in the Rue La Pérouse, with a back-entrance on the Rue Dumont d'Urville.

When Proust first met her, in the autumn of 1888, she was thirty-seven and he was seventeen: she was now just forty. She was plump but wasp-waisted,[3] and wore an extremely low décolletée with festoons of pearls dangling, three a side, from what little of her bosom was hidden from view. Her hair was ash-blonde, tied with a pink ribbon; her eyes were black, and when she was excited tended to open too wide—"I have almond eyes, but in the wrong direction," she would say with a laugh. She owned a large collection of china, and added Proust to it, calling him 'my little porcelain psychologist'. He replied by

[1] Michael Herbert, brother of Lord Pembroke and Lady Lonsdale, was astonished to find that he was not asked to contribute to her expenses, which were looked after by M. Bischoffsheim. "An English girl wouldn't have been satisfied with a banker," he declared admiringly.

[2] He saw her riding in the Bois, still beautiful, on the morning of 3 April 1899, and recorded the fact in his diary, adding: 'A handsome woman looks still more graceful on horseback.'

[3] As a photograph of this period shows. In a later photograph she is painfully haggard and thin, while the festoons of pearls have increased to five a side. But in earlier photographs she is exceedingly pretty and fluffy, though quite un-mysterious and not in the least like Botticelli's fresco of Jethro's daughter, to which Swann compared Odette.

comparing the what-not on which she kept her Saxe figurines to an altar: "we live in the century of Laure Hayman, and its reigning dynasty is Saxe," he said; and afterwards he made Odette collect Saxe, and say of any object whose appearance she liked: "How pretty that is, it's just like the flowers on a piece of Saxe." He was attracted not only by Mme Hayman's beauty but by her salon, which was full of dukes, club-men, writers and future academicians. One of these was Paul Bourget, who had described her in his short story *Gladys Harvey*: 'Gladys has something of the courtesan of the eighteenth century, and not too much of the ferociously calculating harlot of our brutal and positivist age.' In December 1888 she had given Proust, who now showed it to the horrified Jeanne Pouquet, a copy of *Gladys Harvey* bound in flower-embroidered silk from one of her petticoats, and inscribed 'You mustn't like everything in Gladys Harvey!'; and then she wrote of him to Bourget, enclosing the schoolboy's enthusiastic letter of thanks. 'Judging by his letter, your "little Marcel" must be simply delightful,' replied Bourget, and continued in the vein of Bergotte: 'but he must never allow his love of literature to die out. He will cease to like my books because he likes them too much; but may he never fall out of love with the beauty of art which he seeks in my unworthy self! And, though this advice coming via the lips of a Delilah may seem ironic, tell him to work and develop all that lies hidden in his already so admirable intelligence.' So Proust, while still a schoolboy, had been introduced by an original of Odette to an original of Bergotte.

Unlike Odette, Mme Hayman seems to have been an intelligent, sensible, witty and cultured woman. She was never supposed to have ruined anyone, and her lovers may have felt that she gave value for money. Her affection for Louis Weil was sincere, and whereas Odette as mistress of Uncle Adolphe was barred by the family, Laure Hayman was accepted by the Prousts. She was on visiting terms with Dr Proust, and would give him news of his son's activities; so that whenever Dr Adrien said with an air of impenetrable mystery, "You've been seen at . . .", or "They tell me you have . . .", Proust would know that Mme Hayman had called. Once, with the best intentions, she succeeded in thoroughly upsetting both father and son, by warning Dr Proust of Marcel's extravagance. The young man's allowance could be nothing like that of a Grand Duke; yet he insisted on loading her

with her favourite chrysanthemums and giving her lunch at the
most expensive restaurants. Jacques Émile Blanche hints that
Proust's affair with Mme Hayman was not merely platonic: it was
all a very long time ago, but Blanche, who was a friend of both
at this time, was perhaps in a position to know. It would not have
been the first nor the last time that Proust's relations with women
were physical; and it may be significant that in *Jean Santeuil* it is
the hero himself who undergoes with Mme Françoise S. the love-
affair which in *A la Recherche* was transferred to Swann and
Odette.

But admission to Mme Hayman's drawing-room was no pass-
port to society, for although dukes were there they were never
accompanied by their duchesses. Even Mme de Caillavet's salon
was a mere picture-frame for Anatole France. It is time to visit in
turn the four other salons in which at this period, in 1891 and
1892, Proust began to move towards the Guermantes Way.

Jeanne Pouquet was not the only beloved whom Proust tried
to make jealous by confiding the open secrets of his intimacy with
Mme Hayman. The flowers that deluged his great-uncle's mistress
had already fallen, in the winter and spring after he left the army,
on Mme Straus: once he succeeded in bringing them even to her
bedside, where she sat, 'beautiful as an angel with a slight indisposition,' and scolded him for his extravagance. But now, he
cuttingly explained, she mustn't think he loved her less because
the flowers had stopped. His daily walks with Mme Hayman and
the lunches that follow are so expensive that (except a franc's
worth of poppies for Mme Lemaire) he can't afford to buy any!
Mme Straus had rebuked him for his passion and dismissed him:
now, in November 1891, she announced that they were friends
as before. "You are unique, as in everything else, in the art of
making hearts vibrate till they break," he sighed, and explained
that his love for her was now only platonic: however, "one should
always show *great indulgence* for platonic love." Gradually she
began to appreciate the intelligence of her little Cherubino; and
Proust, in turn, freed from the unholy attraction of this beautiful
lady—for she resembled his mother in age, wit and Jewish birth,
and was the mother and aunt of his schoolfriends Bizet and
Halévy—became her friend for life. He began again to frequent
her salon, which was growing ever more brilliant: the way into
the Faubourg Saint-Germain was opening before him.

The social ascent of Fromental Halévy's daughter and Bizet's widow had been extraordinary, almost impossible; though she never forgot her middle-class musical origins, and once, when asked by a great lady whether she was fond of music, replied: "They played a great deal of it in my first family." Her portrait by Delaunay, white and appealing in widow's black, had created a sensation in the Salon of 1878: Degas found his way to the house in the Rue de Douai where she lived in retirement with her uncle Léon Halévy, and begged to be allowed to see her combing her hair. Then, as we have seen, Émile Straus, the favourite lawyer (and, it was said, the illegitimate half-brother) of the three Barons Rothschild, Alphonse, Edmond and Gustave, insisted on marrying her. He came up to town every morning with Joseph Reinach, who used to say: "I could always relax on the train with Émile—he did all the talking, it was Geneviève, Geneviève all the way." "You *must* see Geneviève," Straus told the Rothschilds, and soon all society was saying "We must see Geneviève." Long lines of carriages drew up in the Rue de Douai, and followed after their marriage in 1886 to their apartment in the Boulevard Haussmann, at the corner of the Avenue de Messine, opposite the statue of Shakespeare. Jacques Bizet, now a medical student, found it convenient to open a ground-floor window at dead of night and disappear along the boulevard on business best known to himself. In the morning, M. Straus would rise early to wait for him on the stairs, to the amusement of his indulgent mother: "Émile has such a sense of theatre," she said. Whether or not Jacques's escapades were connected with his friend, M. Straus decided first that Proust had a bad influence on his step-son, next that, on the whole, he had not. He made a call of reconciliation at 9 Boulevard Malesherbes, and amid the bronzes, potted palms, plush and mahogany of the drawing-room, looking for something to be polite about, noticed a little drawing by Henri Monnier. It was a present to Dr Proust from a grateful patient, Caran d'Ache, the caricaturist. "Charming, charming," murmured M. Straus.

Émile Straus was a slim little man with grey hair and a smile of extreme but amiable irony. His eyes, owing to a disability acquired in the Franco-Prussian war, were always half-closed. Like Swann he devoted his life and his enormous wealth to the clothing and social career of his wife: his friends recognised him immediately when they read the scene in *A l'Ombre* where Swann

peeps benevolently through the curtains at Odette's guests.[1]
There is, indeed, a distinct likeness between his photographs and
those of Charles Haas, the chief original of Swann. Both are
dressed with the same exquisite, imperceptible elegance; their
features are whimsical and Jewish; but M. Straus lacks the
melancholy, puzzled look of M. Haas. Sometimes, however, when
he asked his guests "Have you heard Geneviève's latest?" he
resembled for a moment the Duc de Guermantes saying the same
of his wife Oriane; and he would go on to explain, like the Duke,
that his wife's intelligence was admirable not so much for its wit
as for its sound common sense. He was an exceedingly but quite
unjustifiably jealous husband.

Mme Straus's wit is important, for Proust made it his chief
model for the celebrated 'Guermantes wit'. Some of her sayings
are repeated as chestnuts to this day, though their authorship is
forgotten. It was she who said: "I was just about to say the same
myself," when her former music-teacher Gounod remarked at a
performance of Massenet's *Hérodiade* that the passage they had
just heard was "perfectly octagonal"; or "I'd no idea you had
any," when the dramatist Pailleron, after reviling her friend Louis
Ganderax for a hostile article in the *Revue des Deux Mondes*, said:
"And now you can have your revenge on *my* friends." When it
was rumoured that the lady novelist Marcelle Tinayre was to be
given the cross of the Légion d'Honneur, she commented: "A
woman's breast was never meant to be honoured." Of a gentleman who pursued her with unwarranted optimism, she said:
"Poor Achille, it would be so much less trouble to make him
happy than it is to make him unhappy." Of her florist, who had
the same name as the general who shouted "*Merde*" when invited
to surrender at the Battle of Waterloo—so that the word was ever
afterwards known euphemistically as '*le mot de Cambronne*'—she
remarked, "She is so nicely spoken that she calls herself Cambronne." The Duchesse de Guermantes, then Princesse des
Laumes, makes a similar joke on the name of Mme de Cambremer
at Mme de Saint-Euverte's party.[2] When she uttered, or urged by
her husband repeated her 'latest', her face was that of the Duchesse
inviting and sharing the hearer's amusement. It was Mme Straus
who once put on black shoes instead of red when dressing for a
fancy-dress ball, and like the Duchesse was compelled by her

[1] I, 599   [2] I, 341

angry husband to change them; but it was in no such circumstances of cruelty and selfishness: Proust ran upstairs to fetch the red shoes, and all was well.

Mme Straus's beauty was wholly different from that of the Duchesse or Odette or any others of their originals. It resided in the sincerity of her expression, the fervour of her eyes ('like black stars', said Abel Hermant) and the elegance of her dress. The poetry of her little hats tied under the chin, her tubular skirts, her slim folded parasols, survives unfaded to this day in her photographs of the 1890s. Her features had lost the fresh youth of Delaunay's painting: they were gipsy-like, heavy, thick-lipped, but still fascinating. A nervous tic made her open her eyes wide and then suddenly screw them up, or protrude her lower lip, or bend her head abruptly to her left shoulder: Mme Albert Gillou compared her face to 'a sky disordered by summer lightning'.

In the huge rotunda drawing-room of the Boulevard Haussmann the walls were hung with eighteenth-century paintings by Nattier and Latour, side by side with Monets and the Delaunay portrait of the hostess—"Don't you agree that it's lovelier than the Mona Lisa?" Proust would ask his fellow-guests, as he leaned adoringly over her chair or sat on a cushion at her feet. Her salon consisted partly of writers and artists, partly of the Faubourg Saint-Germain. But it was neither literary, since she refused to talk literature, nor social, for the Faubourg was in the minority and came only as personal friends of the hostess. It was composed of persons whom she invited for the sake of their intelligence, and who came for the sake of hers. Henri Meilhac, who collaborated as Offenbach's librettist with her cousin Ludovic Halévy (Daniel's father), was almost one of the family: Proust refers several times to the 'Meilhac and Halévy style' of the Duchesse de Guermantes's wit.[1] Meilhac arrived with trailing laces, being too fat to tie his shoes, and exchanged epigrams with Forain, whom she had met through his master Degas. In his youth Forain had sheltered Rimbaud in his studio, until that atrocious young man left after defecating in his host's morning milk by way of farewell. He was now as famous for his savage wit as for his art. Among the men of letters were the dramatists Hervieu and Porto-Riche, the novelist Bourget, and the bearded, spectacled Louis Ganderax, the literary editor of the *Revue de Paris*. He was feared by his

[1] I, 334; II, 207, 495-6; III, 1009

contributors for the ruthlessness of his proof-corrections, "pursuing hiatuses," said Anatole France, "into the very interior of words"; and Jules Renard pretended that when frogs croaked in lily-ponds they were only repeating: "Ganderax! Ganderax!" One of her humbler friends was a gentle and melancholy musician named Ernest Guiraud, who once uttered a remark which in *A la Recherche* is made to the Narrator's grandmother.[1] Mme Straus had good-naturedly asked him to bring his illegitimate daughter to call on her. "Does she take after her mother?" she asked, and the naïve father replied: "I don't know, I never saw her dear mother without her hat on."

Among her nobler guests was Prince Auguste d'Arenberg, who appears in Odette's salon as the Prince d'Agrigente: Mme Straus had intrigued with her friends among the republican politicians to have him appointed president of the administrative council of the Suez Canal. Comte Othenin d'Haussonville would be there, absent-mindedly twirling his monocle and following a train of thought usually connected with his ancestress Madame de Staël, whose life he was exhuming from the archives at Coppet. Others included Princesse Mathilde, Louis de Turenne, and several English friends, Lord Lytton, the English ambassador, Lady de Grey, later Marchioness of Ripon, and Reggie Lister. But the three who most concern Proust and his novel were the Comtesse de Chevigné, Comtesse Greffulhe and Charles Haas. The first became the Duchesse de Guermantes, the second contributed to both the Duchesse and the Princesse de Guermantes, and the last was Charles Swann himself. At that time, however, Proust could only admire the two ladies from afar: to be invited with a great lady, he found, was not the same as being invited by her. But Haas, with whom he was never to become personally intimate, but who meant so much to his novel and his life, must be examined immediately.

Charles Haas was, as he himself used ironically to say, "the only Jew ever to be accepted by Parisian society without being immensely rich." He was, however, far from poor, for his father, a stockbroker, had left him a comfortable fortune. His gallantry in the Franco-Prussian war won him the entry to the exclusive Jockey Club, of which the only other members of his race were the Rothschilds. Earlier still he had moved in the court society

[1] I, 859

of the Second Empire: we have a glimpse of him in December 1863, playing in private theatricals at the Duc de Mouchy's country house, along with the Galliffets, the Pourtalès's, Gaston de Saint-Maurice, and other persons fashionable in their day. In 1868 Haas appears in Tissot's famous painting of the balcony of the Club in the Rue Royale,[1] with the Prince de Polignac and Saint-Maurice again ('the only two people in the picture, besides Haas, whom I knew personally,' Proust told Paul Brach in 1922), the Marquis's du Lau and de Ganay, General de Galliffet and others. He is tall and svelte, wise, sad and arrogant; he cocks his walking-cane on his right shoulder; he lolls astride in the french window of the balcony, ineffably elegant in grey top-hat and striped trousers. His hair was frizzled and reddish, and later as it receded turned pepper-and-salt colour. He had arched, amused but puzzled eyebrows, an upturned moustache into which he faintly smiled, and his nose, people would say, was hardly curved at all; but in his last days, when his skin stretched over it like parchment and his ancestry reappeared, it was found, like Swann's in his last illness, to be enormously hooked. He died in July 1902.

Haas frequented Mme Straus's salon during the late 1880s and early '90s, and Proust probably met him there. But he must also have seen him as the guest of several other hostesses: the Princesse Mathilde in the early '90s, and later, when Proust had succeeded in penetrating to the Faubourg Saint-Germain, the Princesse de Polignac, Comtesse Rosa de FitzJames, and Comtesse Greffulhe. Haas had met Mme Greffulhe's cousin Robert de Montesquiou as early as 1871, and was, we are told 'the darling of her coterie in the Rue d'Astorg'. Correspondingly in Proust's novel Swann is the intimate friend of the Duchesse de Guermantes, and one of the earliest friends of her cousin, the Baron de Charlus. Like Swann, Haas was also a favourite companion of Edward VII as Prince of Wales and of the Orleanist pretender to the throne of France, the Comte de Paris, who lived in exile at Twickenham. Apart from social life, his chief interests were woman-chasing and Italian painting, on both of which subjects he was regarded

---

[1] This club, although Saint-Loup (I, 772) thought Bloch senior might possibly belong to it ('his family considered it "lowering", and he knew several Israelites had been admitted'), was second only to the Jockey. The Cercle Agricole and Cercle de l'Union came next, and some of the best people liked to belong to all four, as did Swann (III, 199).

as a connoisseur. Once Saint-Maurice showed him a new acquisi-
tion, a horrible, blackened Italian daub, and proudly asked:
"What do you think it is?" "A joke in rather poor taste," replied
Haas, as did Swann to the Duc de Guermantes when shown his
new 'Velasquez'.[1]

In some respects Swann is to be differentiated from Haas. As
we have seen, Swann at Combray was suggested by a family
friend at Illiers. There is no evidence that Haas was acquainted
with the chief original of Odette, Laure Hayman, who was, however, so popular with his fellow-clubmen. It is doubtful whether
he knew, as Swann knew Uncle Adolphe, Proust's great-uncle
Louis Weil.[2] Haas's Odette was a Spanish lady of noble birth
from whom he had a daughter, who is said to be still living; but
he never married. In the Dreyfus Affair Swann had the loyalty
and courage to turn from those of his old friends who became
anti-Dreyfusards; but Haas, we are told by Jacques Émile Blanche,
joined his nationalist fellow-members of the Jockey Club in
cutting General de Galliffet when he became war minister in the
revisionist government of Waldeck-Rousseau.

In his novel Proust proclaimed Swann's origin in the famous
apostrophe to 'dear Charles Swann, whom I knew when I was
still so young and you were near the grave—it is because he
whom you must have thought a silly young man has made you
the hero of his volumes that people begin to talk of you again,
and that your name will perhaps live,' and in the allusion which
follows to Haas's presence in Tissot's painting.[3] He also characteristically gave the clue to their identity, as he did with so many of
the people in *A la Recherche*, by unobtrusively juxtaposing the
name of the character with that of the original: Swann, he tells us,
wears a grey top-hat of a shape which Delion makes only for him
and Charles Haas.[4] Those who had known Haas immediately
recognised him in Swann, whom Mme Straus insisted on calling
Swann-Haas. 'What, you recognised Haas?' Proust wrote to
Gabriel Astruc. Some, including Montesquiou, thought they

---

[1] II, 580
[2] The prevalent idea that he did seems to rest solely on a general remark
by Robert de Billy, that in his belief Proust learned from Louis Weil 'of the
structure of Jewish society and of the existence of Haas' (*Billy*, 64).
[3] III, 200
[4] II, 579

detected elements in Swann, particularly his erudition in art, which belonged to Charles Ephrussi; though Haas's own knowledge of art was quite sufficient to supply Swann's. Ephrussi edited the *Gazette des Beaux Arts*, an expensive art-magazine which every great lady kept open but unread on her table. He was a Polish Jew whose career was parallel to that of Haas, for he frequented much the same salons, but on a lower plane, for he was sought after less for his personal charm than as a fashionable art-expert. He was stout, bearded and ugly, his manner was ponderous and uncouth, and he was nicknamed 'Matame', not for any discreditable reason, but because he pronounced the word 'Madame' with a Polish accent.[1] It is difficult to think of any feature of Swann to be found in Ephrussi and not in Haas; except that Swann wrote an essay on Vermeer and Ephrussi one on Dürer, while Haas wrote nothing. Neither Haas nor Ephrussi were particularly interested in Vermeer: it was Proust himself who bestowed his own love of the Dutch master, as one of their saving graces, on both Swann and Bergotte.

Proust knew Ephrussi well, but was never intimate with Haas. He saw this mysterious and fascinating figure only from a distance and in his late middle age: in life as in his novel he learned from others of the days of his glory in the Second Empire—before his own birth and the Narrator's—of his great love and his illegitimate daughter, who supplied this feature to Gilberte. There is no trace of Swann-Haas in Proust's work until the beginnings of *A la Recherche* nearly twenty years later. But it may well be, as some have suggested, that he saw Haas even at this early period as a hero and an example, another self. Haas, like himself, was a Jew, a pariah by birth; yet by his own merits of intelligence and charm he had made society a career open to the talents. Whether or not he was aided by the inspiration of Haas, Proust set himself to do the same. Social acceptance was a symbol—though, as he was to discover, an illusory one—of salvation.

Another of Proust's early salons was that of Princesse Mathilde, Napoleon's niece, now in her seventies. Long ago she had been the hostess of Flaubert, Renan, Sainte-Beuve, Taine, Dumas Fils, Mérimée and Edmond de Goncourt, and her friends had called her 'Notre Dame des Arts'. All were now dead, except Goncourt

[1] The Prince von Faffenheim addresses Mme de Villeparisis as 'Matame la Marquise', (II 263).

and Taine, and with Taine she had quarrelled in 1887, after his series of hostile articles on her uncle, leaving on him the famous visiting-card marked P.P.C.[1] Her house was at 20 Rue de Berri, and her guests, with a nucleus of old Bonapartists such as Counts Benedetti and Primoli, now included the Straus's, Charles Haas, Ephrussi, Dr Pozzi, Ganderax, Bourget and Porto-Riche. Count Benedetti had been the French ambassador at Berlin in 1870, a post which he shared with M. de Norpois.[2] Count Joseph Primoli, a nephew of the Princess, was a bald-headed gentleman with a white beard, who looked rather like God the Father. He was despised for collecting postage-stamps, until people heard that he had sold his collection for a million francs; and he was addicted to the tiresome form of humour which consists in asking awkward questions with a straight face, and inviting deadly enemies to dinner on the same evening. His nickname was Gégé, which may be compared with the Babals, Grigris and Mamas of the Guermantes set. There was also a sprinkling of society from the Faubourg—the Gramonts, Rohans, Comte Louis de Turenne, a few others; but the majority of the Princess's titled guests were of the Napoleonic creation, with names mostly taken from battles— like the fictitious Iénas, whom Charlus called 'those people who are named after a bridge'[3]—on whom the Faubourg tended to look down: the Wagrams, Albuferas, Elchingens, Esslings, Murats.

The Princess was a portly little lady, with a startling resemblance to her uncle Napoleon. "If it weren't for him, I'd be selling oranges in the streets of Ajaccio," she would say in the gruff, plebeian, soldierly voice of the Bonapartes. She sat, wearing a string of black pearls, in a humble armchair to which her presence somehow gave the air of a throne. She liked to feel that she was no stickler for etiquette, and would allow the ladies only to begin the movement of a curtsey before pulling them up by main force for an embrace; while the gentlemen, once they had shown their intention of kissing her hand, would receive an informal hand-

[1] The newspapers got hold of the story, and various rude interpretations of the initials (which of course stand for '*Pour prendre congé*') were suggested: among the more innocent was '*Princesse pas contente*'. Taine tried to get sympathy from Renan, who only remarked: "My *Vie de Jésus* put me in bad odour with a *much* greater lady!"

[2] III, 637-9

[3] II, 564. Cf. I, 338

shake. If asked by some uninstructed, ultra-polite newcomer: "And how is your Imperial Highness's health?" she would growl: "Not so bad! How's yours?" Her last of several lovers, himself now dismissed for infidelity, had been Claudius Popelin, the artist in enamel to whom Heredia devoted a sonnet.[1] Proust became so affectionately appreciated by her that her disgruntled habitués referred to him, in allusion to the stage dynasty of Coquelin *aîné* and Coquelin *cadet*, as Popelin the Younger. She gave him a piece of silk from one of her dresses for a cravat, and another to Barrès.

In *A la Recherche* the Princess appears in her own person, when the Narrator is introduced to her by Swann and Odette in the Bois de Boulogne.[2] Her conversation on this occasion is a pot-pourri of her authentic sayings over a long period: the anecdote of Alfred de Musset coming to dinner dead-drunk and speechless; the quarrel with Taine in 1887; her remark when her favourite nephew Prince Louis Napoleon joined the Russian army—"just because there's already been a soldier in the family, that's no reason"; and the story of Tsar Nicolas II's visit to Napoleon's tomb at the Invalides, which occurred on 7 October 1896, when she refused an official invitation, saying, "I have my own keys." But she also supplied several traits for the Princesse de Parme, a name which was perhaps suggested to Proust by the connecting-link of imperial violets. The Princesse de Parme, unlike the Princesse Mathilde, traces her noble descent back to A.D. 63, and is a non-intellectual, who listens to the Duchesse de Guermantes's conversation with admiring amazement. But she too is a little dark lady, her mock-simple manner of salutation is Princesse Mathilde's, so is the inferior social level of her salon; and the Princesse de Parme has a comically stupid lady-in-waiting, Mme de Varambon, whose sayings were actually uttered by Princess Mathilde's attendant, the Baronne de Galbois. Mme de Galbois, who knitted and embroidered at the Princess's side for forty years, was the constant joy of her guests, though the Princess would crossly exclaim: "Really, Galbois, you're such a fool!" She claimed that Flaubert had read *Bouvard et Pécuchet* to her, and when everybody seemed incredulous corrected herself: "Well,

[1] The *Almanach de Gotha* even stated in 1879 that she had secretly married him, but the Princess immediately issued a denial.
[2] I, 541-4

perhaps he didn't read *Pécuchet*, but I'm quite sure he read
Bouvard." After a visit to the country she spoke of "a cow that
gave so much milk, everyone thought it must be a stallion!" In a
season of untimely rain she said: "You'd think the barometer had
stopped having any influence on the weather"; and on a cold
winter's day she assured the company that "it can't possibly snow,
they've spread salt on the pavements." The second and last of
these anecdotes are told of the Princesse de Parme's lady-in-
waiting Mme de Varambon.[1] Another of Mme de Galbois's
absurdities is given to the Comtesse de Monteriender, who says
to Swann of the musicians who perform the Vinteuil Sonata at
Mme de Sainte-Euverte's reception: "I've never seen anything so
amazing—except table-turning, of course."[2]

Of the literary and artistic bourgeois salons those of Mme
Aubernon de Nerville and Mme Lemaire, to both of which Proust
gained admission in 1892 or a little before, were supreme in their
prestige. A great artist is remembered, a great hostess is forgotten
when the last of her guests has died; yet each of these ladies
contributed to the immortal Mme Verdurin, and lives still in her.

Mme Lydie Aubernon had been blissfully parted from her
husband since 1867, and was in the habit of remarking that she
was looking forward to her 'golden separation'. M. Georges
Aubernon lived with their son Raoul, at Antibes, and his wife was
known as 'the Widow'. Until the end of the 1880s she was assisted
in the running of her salon by her mother, whose own drawing-
room had been famous in the 1840s under Louis Philippe. The
two ladies, in allusion to their republican sympathies and to
Molière's comedy, were called '*Les Précieuses Radicales*'. But
Mme Aubernon showed little positive interest in politics, and used
to say: "I'm a republican, but only in sheer desperation." After
old Mme de Nerville died she told Edmond de Goncourt: "I miss
her often, but only a little at a time"—a remark also uttered by
Swann's father after the death of his wife.[3] She received at her
house in the Avenue de Messine, later in the Rue d'Astorg, where
(incongruous conjunction) the Comtesse Greffulhe also lived, and
last at 11 Rue Montchanin. Along with her more brilliant guests
she entertained a hard core of mysterious elderly ladies, widows
of writers or friends of her dead mother, who sat in the back-

---

[1] II, 547; III, 1009   [2] I, 353
[3] I, 15

ground, like the pianist's aunt or Princesse Sherbatoff at Mme Verdurin's, and were known as 'my sacred monsters'. One of the monsters was once reproached for frivolity by her son, who felt that her name appeared far too frequently in the society columns of the newspapers. "You're quite right, my dear," she said, "to-morrow I'll give up going to funerals."

Mme Aubernon was a fat, lively little woman, with dimpled arms, and wore loud beribboned dresses and shoes with pompoms. "She looked like Queen Pomaré on the lavatory seat," Montesquiou used to say. She was sixty-seven in 1892, and was not unaware that her beauty had vanished: "I realised it," she said, "when men stopped raving about my face and only told me how intelligent I was." Her evening receptions on Wednesdays (Mme Verdurin's day) and Saturdays were preceded by a dinner for twelve persons, neither more nor less, for which the subject of conversation was announced in advance. The guests did not always take the custom as seriously as she wished. "What is your opini on of adultery?" she asked Mme Straus one week, when that happened to be the theme, and Mme Straus replied: "I'm so sorry, I prepared incest by mistake." Labiche, when asked what he thought of Shakespeare, enquired: "Why, is he marrying someone we know?" And d'Annunzio, when asked to talk about love, was even less forthcoming: "Read my books, madam," he said, "and let me get on with my food." Thinking a change of subject might thaw her guest, Mme Aubernon began to ask after his distinguished contemporaries. "Tell me about Fogazzaro," she implored. "Fogazzaro?" echoed the poet, "he's at Vicenza"; and the meal finished in frozen silence. When Mme Laure Baignères was asked the same question: "What do you think about love?" she could only reply, "I make it, often, but I never, never talk about it."[1] If conversation at the other end of the table became general, Mme Aubernon would ring her famous little bell[2] to secure attention for the speaker of the moment. Once, on his very first visit, Labiche was heard to murmur "I . . . I . . ." The Widow jingled with her bell and shouted: "Monsieur Labiche, you will have your turn in a minute." The speaker finished, and she said

[1] A remark attributed to Mme Leroi in *Le Côté de Guermantes* (II, 195).
[2] It was of silver, the handle was a figure of St Louis, and on the bell was engraved the maxim attributed to that king by Joinville: 'If you have anything worth saying, let everyone hear it; if not, be silent.'

graciously: "You may speak now, Monsieur Labiche." But the unhappy dramatist only mumbled: "I just wanted to ask for another helping of peas."

Mme Aubernon's salon was remarkable, like Mme Verdurin's, for the absence of beautiful women. "I provide conversation," she would say, "not love"; or, "Women are a subject men are too fond of getting on top of." But she was thought once to have been not averse to love in its time and place, and had been heard to announce: "I have a *glorious* body." To attend one's first dinner in the Rue d'Astorg was like sitting for an examination. Afterwards the result would be proclaimed: "Monsieur So-and-so dined very well," or "Monsieur So-and-so didn't dine at all well, he talked to the lady next to him." Proust, however, dined exceedingly well, and Mme Aubernon would say: "Marcel's epigrams are *definitive*." Now and then, like Mme Verdurin, she would hold a public execution of some offender, which would end in an outburst of tears, sometimes the victim's, sometimes the executioner's; for Mme Aubernon's rages were genuine, not cold-blooded like Mme Verdurin's. But she was not vindictive for long, and a few months later a whole series of criminals would be pardoned and reappear at what she called 'a dinner of forgiveness'. Silence, and being a bore, were the only unforgivable sins: after a series of boring visitors, she declared: "I've been outraged nine times this morning." But with her as with Mme Arman the word 'bore' had its ordinary meaning, and was not a euphemism for a person in high society who could not be lured to her salon. The Faubourg never appeared there, and there is no reason to believe that she ever missed it. Unlike Mme Verdurin, again, she did not pretend to be fond of music; but her amateur theatricals, which in *A la Recherche* are transferred to Mme de Villeparisis, were famous, and it is to her credit that the first performances of Ibsen's *A Doll's House* and *John Gabriel Borkman* took place in her drawing-room. It was at this time that a visitor found her engrossed in a volume of Ibsen: "Don't disturb me! I'm acquiring a Norwegian soul!"

In some points of detail, it is clear, Mme Aubernon differed from Mme Verdurin: she was unmusical, non-political, and in the social sense unsnobbish. She was capable, as Mme Verdurin was not, of a kind of wit; though her witticisms, it will be noticed, are remarkable chiefly for their unconscious absurdity, for she could never see that her jokes were always against herself. "The Aubernon hag had no sense of the ridiculous," declared Montesquiou, "because she was herself the very incarnation of every possible form of it." She was absurd through her very spontaneity, whereas Mme Verdurin was absurd through her pretence of spontaneity. But as a hostess of half-comic, half-terrifying vanity and despotism, Mme Aubernon was the chief original of Mme Verdurin. Moreover, it was among the band of her 'faithful', as she herself called them, that Proust knew a doctor like Cottard, a pedant like Brichot, and an invert like Charlus; and he met them not only at her receptions in Paris, but in a 'little train' on the way to her country-house.

The doctor was Dr Pozzi, whom we have already seen at Mme Straus's and Princesse Mathilde's, and giving the schoolboy Proust his first 'dinner in town'. He was, Léon Daudet says, 'talkative, hollow and reeking of hair-oil'. He resembled Cottard, who was 'constantly unfaithful to his wife', in that his flirtations with his lady patients were notorious: Mme Aubernon called him, after Molière's play, 'l'Amour Médecin'. He was vain of his good looks, and opinions varied as to his skill as a surgeon: 'I wouldn't have trusted him to cut my hair,' wrote Léon Daudet, 'especially if there'd been a mirror in the room.' His wife, who was a relative of Dr Cazalis (the original of Legrandin), resembled the kind, dutiful, silly Mme Cottard: Mme Aubernon called her 'Pozzi's mute'. He consoled her for his infidelities by saying: "I don't deceive you, my dear, I supplement you." His chief love was a lady in Belgium, and when he seemed overworked and despondent Mme Pozzi would timidly say, "I think a trip to Belgium would do you good." He was the most fashionable doctor of the upper bourgeoisie, as was Dr Le Reboulet (who as Dr Du Boulbon attended the Narrator's dying grandmother) of the Faubourg Saint-Germain; though Pozzi too had friends and patients in the Faubourg, who included Montesquiou himself.

The pedant was Victor Brochard, a professor at the Sorbonne and author of a standard work on the Greek sceptics. He had been the *philosophie* master at the Lycée Condorcet a few years before Proust's arrival there, and had thought the 'aces' of that time, such as Jacques Émile Blanche or Abel Hermant, unbeatable; but when he saw Proust, Fernand Gregh and their contemporaries at

Mme Aubernon's, he remarked to Blanche: "These young colts of 1889 are even more amazing than those of '79." He had been the star of Mme Arman's salon before the famous schism when she stole Anatole France from Mme Aubernon. He continued to frequent both ladies, for he had the courage to announce that he would abandon the first to forbid him to visit the other— "Women are bitches, but that's no reason why men should be puppets!" He was afflicted, like Brichot, by growing blindness and paralysis, which were attributed by malicious people, rightly or wrongly, to a discreditable cause. Brochard, peering through his thick spectacles and talking unendingly, was the image of Brichot.

"Brochard bores me, Doasan disgusts me," said Henri Becque. Baron Jacques Doasan was a cousin of Mme Aubernon's, who had been wealthy but had ruined himself for love of a Polish violinist: once, it was said, he had the walls of a box at the theatre covered with roses for this ungrateful young man. He was a tall, portly invert of virile appearance, looking "like a knight-at-arms in the Hundred Years War," said one of Mme Aubernon's habitués; but his face was bloated, blotched and heavily powdered, and newcomers were puzzled to find his hair and moustache changing from jet-black to white, and from white to jet-black again, though never simultaneously, for it did not occur to him to dye both at the same time. Nothing horrified him more than effeminacy in young men: "How I despise these little flunkeys of Des Esseintes," he would scream, perfidiously alluding to Montesquiou, who was reputed to be the original of the aesthete Des Esseintes in Huysmans's *A Rebours*. His perpetual, factitiously hostile talk about homosexuality was particularly embarrassing in public, on the little local train from the Gare Saint-Lazare in which Mme Aubernon's week-end guests made their way to her country-house, Cœur-Volant, at Louveciennes. "He can be witty —for ten minutes at a time, when you haven't seen him for a week," people said; but his wit, such as it was, was appallingly malicious, and sometimes his victims would hint that the Wednesdays might be more pleasant without him. "But don't you see," Mme Aubernon would say, "he's terribly unhappy, he'd starve if it weren't for me, and I find him so useful as a gentleman in waiting!" So he remained an immovable 'sacred monster' to the end, and was never relegated to what he called "the toy cupboard where Mme Aubernon puts away the dolls, male or female, that don't amuse her any more." Perhaps he could be induced to reform? Brochard was persuaded to give him a good talking to, "so that you can recover all the ground you've lost. People would soon forget your horrible language, and *everything else*, if you took as much trouble to be nice as you do to make enemies." Doasan listened without a word, till Brochard had quite finished, but only said, "It can't be helped, I prefer my vices to my friends." When Proust first attended a Wednesday he became aware that the dreadful Baron's eyes were staring at him, in a fixed, vacant gaze which pretended not to see him. He remembered the incident twenty years later when describing the meeting of Charlus and the Narrator at Balbec. But in 1892 at the Rue d'Astorg its significance must have been a little different: the eyes of Baron Doasan expressed not a questioning desire, but the recognition by one active invert of another. Proust was not a potential conquest, but a possible rival or even betrayer; and Doasan forbade his cousin to receive "that 'little Marcel'", but in vain. Montesquiou, the other original of Charlus, whom Proust was to meet a year later, was also an occasional guest of Mme Aubernon; but these two halves of Charlus were at daggers drawn, and it is said that Montesquiou's faithful secretary Gabriel d'Yturri was stolen by him from Doasan.

The train for Cœur-Volant, on which Doasan's conversation was so embarrassing for Proust and his fellow-guests, left Saint-Lazare at 5 p.m., stopped for several minutes at every local station, and took over an hour for the journey. At Louveciennes the guests disembarked, amid titters and elbow-nudging from bystanders convulsed by their incongruous appearance in full evening-dress, into three decrepit victorias sent by Mme Aubernon. As at La Raspelière, there was a long pull to the crest of the hill, where their hostess awaited them on the terrace. In her park was a lake with ducks, whose keep in bread was said by her cheating servants to cost a fortune—"It couldn't have been more expensive if I'd had illegitimate children," she declared— and a meadow with two pretty little cows. Just before dinner Doasan would say to the men: "Let's go and take a look at the cows"; and on the way each would step discreetly behind a tree, for indoor sanitation at Cœur-Volant was limited, and reserved for the ladies.

Mme Aubernon owned a seaside villa at Trouville, the Manoir de la Cour Brûlée, which helped to suggest Mme Verdurin's La Raspelière and to connect Mme Aubernon with the district of Balbec. It had a magnificent view of the Channel, but the 'three views' of La Raspelière belonged, as we shall see, to Les Frémonts near by. The Cour Brûlée was rented from Mme Aubernon by Mme Straus in 1892, and Proust perhaps saw it only as Mme Straus's guest. No doubt the week-ends at Cœur-Volant, preceded as they were by the journeys with Brochard and Doasan in the little train, contributed more than the summer parties at the Cour Brûlée to La Raspelière. We shall meet later, in their place, three other prototypes of the 'little train' of *Sodome et Gomorrhe*. The name of the villa hired by Mme Verdurin from the Cambremers came from La Rachepelière, a hamlet a mile west of Illiers on the Méréglise way.

To complete the foreshadowing of Mme Verdurin's salon in Mme Aubernon's it only remains to discover representatives of Swann and Odette among her guests. Paul Hervieu, the dramatist, was a little like Haas and Swann in appearance, with his rather frigid elegance, his upturned moustache ("Hervieu has tiny icicles in the corners of his moustache," said Fernand Gregh), his air of weary sadness and irony. The remark made by Swann to a girl in a brothel—"How sweet of you, you're wearing blue eyes to go with your sash"[1]—is modelled on a compliment of Hervieu at Mme Aubernon's to the Baronne de Jouvenel: "I see you're wearing black velvet eyes this evening." The lady on this occasion was not flattered, and replied: "Thanks very much—do you mean that I don't wear them every day?" At Mme Aubernon's Hervieu met and fell in love with the beautiful and talented Baronne Marguerite de Pierrebourg ("Mme de Pierrebourg is so eloquent," Mme Aubernon would say appreciatively). She was then thirty-five, and lived apart from her husband Aimery de Pierrebourg: Odette, it will be remembered, was herself the separated wife of Pierre de Verjus, Comte de Crécy, whom the Narrator met during his second visit to Balbec. The baroness deserted Mme Aubernon, taking Hervieu with her, and began, like Odette, a brilliant salon of her own, which Proust afterwards frequented. They never married, or lived together, and their love was life-long; but otherwise their story has clear analogies with that of

[1] I, 373

Swann and Odette.[1] Madeleine, her daughter by the Baron de Pierrebourg, married in 1910 Comte Georges de Lauris, a member of the group of young noblemen, the collective originals of Saint-Loup, whom Proust was to meet in the early 1900s. Perhaps this union helped to suggest the marriage of Odette's daughter and Saint-Loup.

The last of Proust's chief hostesses at this time was Mme Madeleine Lemaire. She conducted the most brilliant and crowded of the bourgeois salons, the only one where it was possible to meet in large numbers all but the most exclusive of the nobility. She began with a few fellow-artists, Puvis de Chavannes, Bonnat, Detaille, Georges Clairin, and the talented *genre* painter Jean Béraud, whose pictures of social life in clubs, soirées, the Opéra and the Bois are nowadays appreciated anew after fifty years of oblivion, and contributed to the paintings by Elstir on similar themes. But soon the Faubourg Saint-Germain arrived, because it was so delightful to meet artists, and then still more artists, because it was so delightful to meet the Faubourg. On Tuesdays from April to June her exiguous house at 31 Rue de Monceau was crowded to suffocation. The neighbouring streets were obstructed with waiting carriages, and ever more drew up, emitting duchesses and countesses with their consorts, the La Roche-foucaulds, Uzès's, Luynes's, Haussonvilles, Chevignés, Greffuhles. Thanks to some long-forgotten excuse for violating the building laws of Paris, Mme Lemaire's little house encroached upon the pavement far beyond its larger neighbours; but the passer-by, irritated here by being pushed into the gutter, would be consoled by the rural scent of the lilacs in her garden. Her receptions were held in a glass-roofed studio-annexe, which despite its huge size rapidly became overcrowded. A late-coming duchess might not only fail to find a seat, amid her hostess's cries of "A chair for Mme la Duchesse!" but even be forced out into the garden. There, pale in the light of lamps inside and street-lamps outside, hung the clusters of flowering lilac; and over the wall and across the street the dim masses of trees in Prince

---

[1] When Hervieu left, on days when Mme de Pierrebourg had company, she would see him to the door of her drawing-room and say, in the manner of Mme de Villeparisis with M. de Norpois: "You know the way, don't you?" Hervieu indeed knew the way, for she lived at 1 *bis* Avenue du Bois, and his own house was at No. 7.

Joachim Murat's garden made Mme Lemaire's yard seem like a glade in a forest.

She was a tall, energetic woman, with arched eyebrows, hair that was not all her own, a great deal of rouge, a spangled evening-gown that seemed to have been thrown on in a hurry, and the remains of pleasant good looks—though later she is said to have become hideous. All day she had indefatigably painted her flower-pieces, which were reputed to fetch 500 francs apiece, and enormous roses still stood in a corner of the studio posing in their glasses of water. "No one, except God, has created more roses," the younger Dumas had said (her daughter Suzette remarked long afterwards that Dumas was the only one of her mother's lovers she had felt quite certain about, "because she always called him 'Monsieur'"); and Montesquiou nicknamed her 'the Empress of roses'.

As a painter of flowers Madeleine Lemaire helped to suggest Mme de Villeparisis; but the chief original of Mme de Villeparisis, as will be seen later, only made artificial flowers. Mme Lemaire contributed more to Mme Verdurin. She was known as '*la Patronne*', 'the Mistress',[1] and she used to call the painter Clairin by the nickname given by Mme Verdurin to Brichot, 'Chochotte'. Like Mmes Arman and Aubernon, Mme Lemaire spoke incessantly of her dread of bores, '*les ennuyeux*'; but for her this word had the special sense given to it by Mme Verdurin, of people who felt too distinguished to come to her evenings. But like Mme Verdurin, though far more rapidly, she experienced a rise in social standing which made the numerous race of bores dwindle to the verge of extinction. She, too, was not averse to executions of un-satisfactory guests, which would be heralded in the Verdurin manner by ominous pronouncements of "The fact is, that man has lost his talent", or "that woman is a goose", or "I won't allow that sort of behaviour in my house". She frequently interfered in the private lives of her friends, though not as a rule to their detriment. She owned a magnificent country-house called Réveillon in Seine-et-Marne, where we shall see Proust a few years later, and her system of interior decoration there is said to have resembled Mme Verdurin's at La Raspelière. Alone of the hostesses we have so far met, she provided music as an essential

[1] She was also called, like Mme Aubernon and for the same reason, 'the Widow'.

part of her evenings, and saw to it that many a great artist was first launched in Paris by performing to the nobility in her house. She insisted on absolute silence during a recital, and would shout across the studio to suppress any offender; but as no memorialist has thought her own behaviour under the influence of music worthy of special attention, it is perhaps unlikely that she gave way to the pantomime of intense emotion attributed to Mme Verdurin. Indeed, if any incident in *A la Recherche* resembles a musical evening at Madeleine Lemaire's, it is rather the soirée at Mme de Saint-Euverte's in *Du Côté de chez Swann* than any Wednesday of Mme Verdurin's. One of her guests, Frédéric de Madrazo, known as 'Coco' to his friends, was an original of the sculptor Ski, the dabbler in all the arts, at Mme Verdurin's. Coco composed a little and sang a little, both very badly, and painted, rather better, a great deal: "This dear young man is so *artissstic*," Mme Lemaire would coo. He was a lifelong friend of Proust and of many friends of Proust: so the unsympathetic character of Ski seems to have had a more sympathetic original.

If a musical evening at Mme Lemaire's was very like the 'crush' at Mme de Saint-Euverte's, where Swann heard the Vinteuil Sonata for the second time, it is none the less certain that the chief original of that hapless lady was Marquise Diane de Saint-Paul. Like Mme de Saint-Euverte she was of excellent family, being born a Feydeau de Brou, and her company was as aristocratic as she pleased: it must be remembered that Mme de Saint-Euverte's salon was attended by the Duchesse, Bréauté, Swann and the rest of the Guermantes set, and it was only M. de Charlus who pretended, for his own sadistic pleasure, that her house was no better than a privy.[1] Mme de Saint-Paul gave concerts at which the greatest artists of the day performed, and dinners for academicians at which the food was not infrequently provided by the guests: "They bring me flowers, so why shouldn't they bring pheasants?" she said. Her biting tongue and her brilliance as a pianist were expressed in her nickname, the *Serpent à Sonates*, or sonata-snake —a pun which Proust gave to Swann's rival Forcheville, who had to explain it to the baffled Cottard.[2] Proust gave Mme de Saint-Euverte the forename, Diane, of her original, and took her surname from the Rue Saint-Euverte near his lodgings at Orleans

[1] II, 700

[2] I, 263. *Serpent à sonnettes*, of course, means 'rattlesnake'.

in his army year. At the Princesse de Guermantes's soirée M. de
Charlus taunts her with her 'mystic name'[1]; and Montesquiou had
once loudly exclaimed in Mme de Saint-Paul's hearing: "That she
should dare to call herself both Diana and Saint Paul is as
monstrous an insult to paganism as it is to Christianity!" In his
Figaro article of 11 May 1903 on Mme Lemaire's salon Proust was
to introduce the Marquise de Saint-Paul angling there for her next
week's guests (as Mme de Saint-Euverte did at the Princesse de
Guermantes's soirée), and promising the singer Gabrielle Krauss
'a fan painted by her own hands if she would promise to perform
at her next Thursday in the Rue Nitot'.

Mme Aubernon, nevertheless, remains the most important
model of Mme Verdurin; and the chief significance of Mme
Lemaire for Proust was that in her salon was the most accessible
entrance to the Guermantes Way. Already, in this spring of 1892,
he was beginning to meet the people whose recognition, he
obscurely hoped, might palliate the guilt of his Jewish blood, his
awakening perversion, and the memory of the moonlit night at
Auteuil.

[1] II, 700

Chapter 8

THE DUCHESSE AND ALBERTINE

EITHER at Mme Lemaire's or at Mme Straus's, for she was
to be seen, a celestial visitor from the Faubourg Saint-
Germain, at both these salons, Proust met Comtesse Laure de
Chevigné. He therefore had a perfect right to raise his hat when
he met her in the street, a better right than the Narrator's to salute
the Duchesse de Guermantes, whom he knew only by sight and
as the son of her bourgeois lodgers. On the first occasion their
morning meeting must have seemed to the hurrying countess a
negligible but natural occurrence, on the next a curious coincidence, on the third an ill-bred attempt, surprising in so elegant
a young man, to presume on a casual acquaintance with a social
superior. But when, day after day, she encountered the same lifted
straw-hat and dark, infatuated eyes, she realised the dreadful truth.
It was worse even than a snobbish persecution: the wretched
young man was in love with her.

He had discovered that Mme de Chevigné took her daily walk
along the Avenue de Marigny; and there he loitered every March
morning of 1892 under the budding chestnuts, until he saw her
erect shape gliding in the distance, carrying a case of visiting-
cards, with a hat trimmed with blue cornflowers over her radiant
blue eyes—'unpickable periwinkles sunlit by an azure smile'.
Sometimes, in the vain hope of disguising his subterfuge, he
would wait near her house at 34 Rue de Miromesnil—not un-
observed by Jeanne Pouquet, who lived at No. 62 in the same
street—or in the Avenue Gabriel beside the Champs-Élysées.
Once, on a morning when Mme de Chevigné unaccountably
failed to pass, he brought Robert de Billy to see her. He varied
his routine, walking sometimes on the opposite pavement, sometimes on the same side as the countess. One morning he would
stare greedily as soon as the blue hat appeared far away, while
next day he would notice her, with an ostentatious start of
surprise, only as they met and passed. Sometimes he lurked behind
the glass door of Émile Paul's bookshop, at the corner of the Rue

de Miromesnil and the Rue du Faubourg Saint-Honoré. Each day, when the countess drew near, his love combined with the pangs of guilt and danger which his conduct invited, to produce an agonising palpitation of the heart: as he confessed to her long afterwards, "I had a heart-attack every time I saw you." At last he unwisely ventured to stop and speak; but the embarrassed lady only uttered a furious: "FitzJames is expecting me," and sailed on to her morning call on Comte Robert de FitzJames, leaving him standing. Such was the end of this strange and pathetic love-affair. Next year, when the countess saw that his behaviour was normal, his infatuation ended, and his position in society more assured, she was perfectly charming, like the Duchesse at Mme de Villeparisis's matinée; and they remained on ostensibly friendly terms until twenty-eight years later, when with mixed feelings she found her former beauty and cruelty immortalised in the love of the Narrator for the Duchesse de Guermantes. Meanwhile, in a vain attempt to improve his status in her eyes, or at least to procure her photograph, he scraped acquaintance with Gustave and Jacques de Waru, the sons of her sister who was married to Comte Pierre de Waru—but with no more success than the Narrator when he sought similar help from the Duchesse's nephew Saint-Loup.[1]

In his half-incestuous pursuit of ladies old enough to be his mother Proust had now courted in turn a bourgeois hostess, a courtesan and a society beauty. He can hardly have hoped or wished for success with Mme Straus or Laure Hayman; but from the Comtesse de Chevigné a serious rebuff was even more inevitable, and he made it doubly humiliating by the absurd form he chose for his wooing.[2] He was bitterly and unforgettably hurt, and his rage and despised love remained unaltered in his unconscious mind until they should be called upon. The character of the Duchesse de Guermantes was created not only by aesthetic laws, but by a long memory for love and revenge. In 1920, as we shall see, he made sure that the elderly countess should see this and be duly offended; and to exacerbate and reconcile her he deployed his unfaded adoration and anger as if the incident in the

---

[1] II, 79, 103
[2] Nevertheless, he perhaps had daydreams of success with Mme de Chevigné: in an early version of *A la Recherche* the Comtesse de Guermantes, who later turned into the Duchesse, becomes the mistress of the hero.

Avenue Gabriel had happened only yesterday. But by employing an impossible means in pursuit of an unattainable object he had shown an unconscious desire for failure; and a possible latent motive is revealed by the effect that his failure soon produced. He was now deterred from falling in love with mother-images by the fear of reopening the wound he had goaded the countess into inflicting. He could still fall unsuccessfully in love with a young girl, and did so, for the last time for many years, in the following summer. But his concealed perversion had been using the self-sought failure of his early loves, however sincere they had been, to bar all ways that led from itself; and the process was now nearly complete.

Mme de Chevigné, now in her middle thirties, had married in 1879 Comte Adhéaume de Chevigné, a gentleman-in-waiting of the Comte de Chambord, the dispossessed heir to the throne of France, known to his adherents as Henri V. Count Adhéaume was a tall, bald gentleman with a pink, angular face, and a manner so breezy that when he came into the room people half expected the doors and windows to rattle. For eight months of the year, until his exiled master's death in 1883, he served at the gloomy castle of Frohsdorf in Austria, amid a parody of the frozen etiquette of Versailles. For a few weeks in every year his wife accompanied him, and so became well-acquainted with the ancient courtiers whom the Duchesse de Guermantes called 'the old Frohsdorfs'.[1] One day when driving out with her deaf mistress she remarked to their footman: "Oh, Joseph, how bored I'm going to be to-day," and was horrified when the royal lady, whose hearing happened to be better than usual that morning, replied: "My poor child, how sorry I am to hear it!" But for the rest of the year she was free in Paris. At first she preferred a some-what Bohemian society of artists and singers, but gradually she acquired the friendship of a group of elderly, intelligent clubmen who liked to hear her talk—'she is an eighteenth-century woman, whose emotions turn instantaneously into wit,' wrote Proust's friend Reynaldo Hahn. All were intimate friends of Charles Haas, though we are not told that he was among them. Punctually at two o'clock, immediately after lunch, her butler Gustave would admit the Marquis du Lau, Comte Joseph de Gontaut-Biron, Marquis Henri de Breteuil, Comte Costa de Beauregard and the rest; and all stayed until she turned them out at four, sitting each in his own chair in a circle round the countess. She sat bolt upright, smoking endless cigarettes of coarse 'caporal' tobacco through an amber holder, uttering the witticisms of which one would like to have more and better specimens, since they helped her to become the Duchesse de Guermantes. The clubmen were 'as jealous as tomcats', said her friend Barbara Lister, of any younger recruit to their number: "My old men growl when they smell fresh meat," declared the countess. Every New Year's Day they subscribed to add another string to her pearls, whose festoons grew ever more difficult to count as time went by: "I can number my friends and my years on them," she said. She, too, was jealous, and on first meeting the American heiress who had robbed her of a favourite clubman (the Marquis de Breteuil, who married a Miss Garner) she uttered the simple and deadly words: "Thank you for sparing me the sight of Henri's old age."

Comtesse Laure de Chevigné, although she differed from the Duchesse de Guermantes in being neither wealthy nor of particularly exalted rank, was regarded as one of the most distinguished ladies in Parisian society. She could hardly be said to have a salon, nor could it be denied that her company was 'mixed'; but she was felt to be so pre-eminently desirable either as guest or hostess, that wherever she chose to be was exclusive, and whatever company she chose to invite was fashionable. The Duchesse de Guermantes was descended from Geneviève de Brabant; but Mme de Chevigné, though her family belonged only to the provincial nobility, was of almost equally legendary birth. She was a Sade, and among her ancestors were her namesake Laura, to whom Petrarch wrote his sonnets, and the terrible Marquis de Sade of whom, rather creditably, she was equally proud. Her head displayed the fascinating ornithological qualities which Proust transferred to the Duchesse: her neck was long and birdlike, her nose was beaked, and her wide thin mouth, with its subtle pointed smile, was birdlike too. She had azure eyes and golden hair, worn high at the nape of the neck and with ringlets on the forehead. She wore the two kinds of clothing characteristic of the Duchesse: in her early years she favoured white, spangled, plumage-like satin and muslin, but later she discovered that dark grey tailored costumes, created by Creed, which she was the first to launch at Longchamp races, were more elegant still. Her voice was trenchant and hoarse, with a peasant-like roughness which, as Proust realised, came from her provincial ancestry, and was part of her supreme distinction; though Albert Flament prosaically explained it by her excessive cigarette smoking. Like the Duchesse she had two reputations, an early one for impregnable chastity, and another, which spread mysteriously when she was already ageing, for having had secret lovers. It was at this later period that one day, as she was crossing the street, a workman called out from his scaffolding: "Coo, what a lovely tart"; to which she replied: "Not so fast, young man, you haven't seen the front view!" Like the Duchesse, again, the countess was a friend of Queen Isabella of Spain, of Edward VII as Prince of Wales, and of the Grand-Duchess Wladimir, whom she appropriated each November on her arrival from St Petersburg, and advised on her clothes. "Where did your highness get that dress? It looks as if it came from Ménilmontant!"; and the Grand-Duchess was whisked back into her carriage and off to Worth's for refitting.

In May 1892, when the fatal words "FitzJames is expecting me" had already been spoken, Proust had the melancholy pleasure of reading in a little magazine called *Le Banquet* a sketch of Mme de Chevigné, which he had written a month or two earlier when his pursuit was just beginning. The genesis of the Duchesse is already visible: Mme de Chevigné has become Hippolyta, the beauty of Verona, who has a hooked, birdlike nose, piercing eyes and a sharp angle in her mouth when she laughs. He has seen her, as the Narrator was to see the Duchesse, in a box at the theatre, dressed in white gauze like folded wings, waving a white wing-like fan of feathers. She is a white peacock, a hawk with diamond eyes. Whenever he meets her nephew (Gustave de Waru), who has the same curved nose, thin lips, piercing eyes and too delicate skin, he is disturbed at recognising again this race issued from the union of a goddess and a bird. It is an epitome, using many identical words, of passages on the Duchesse and Saint-Loup which would not appear in *Le Côté de Guermantes* until twenty-eight years later.

Le Banquet was founded, in direct descent from the *Revue Lilas* and *Revue Verte*, the schoolboy magazines of three or four years before, by a group of Proust's former schoolfellows. As a compliment to the beloved M. Darlu, who had taught them all in their

respective years of *philosophie* at Condorcet, the title was
borrowed from the French name of Plato's *Symposium*. In theory
the magazine was to be directed by an editorial committee
consisting of Daniel Halévy, Robert Dreyfus and Proust; but
the management of the second number by Fernand Gregh, a
young poet who had reached Condorcet in the term after Proust
left in 1889, was found so successful that Gregh became sole
editor. Other contributors, several of whose names are still not
unknown to fame, included Jacques Bizet, Robert de Flers,
Gaston de Caillavet, Louis de la Salle, Gabriel Trarieux, Henri
Barbusse author of *Le Feu*, Henri Rabaud the composer, and
Léon Blum the socialist prime minister. Each gave ten francs
monthly, and four hundred copies of each number were hand-
somely printed for a mere hundred francs by Eugène Reiter, son
of Jacques Bizet's former wet-nurse, then director of the printing-
works of the newspaper *Le Temps*. Even so, Gregh took panic at
the sight of the bill for the first number, and ordered only two
hundred of the second, which is consequently even more un-
procurable to-day than the rest. Thereafter circulation rose to
safety-level, and Mme Straus's visitors, hearing of her son
Jacques's and nephew Daniel's new venture, would take out a
subscription with the same benevolent and fashionable air with
which they contributed to her charities. The company met above
Rouquette's bookshop at 71 Passage Choiseul, in a room magnificently surrounded by green and crimson rows of rare books in
glass-fronted bookcases. Jacques's friend Henri de Rothschild
procured them this privilege, and even offered to guarantee the
costs of printing if they would promise in return to accept his
articles; but they refused for the sake of independence.

Le Banquet ran from March 1892 till March 1893. It did not
always succeed in appearing monthly, and during this period of
thirteen months only eight numbers appeared. In each except the
fourth and eighth Proust contributed sketches and short stories,
all but two of which were collected in *Les Plaisirs et les Jours*,
and essays and reviews, mostly reprinted in *Chroniques*. Next to
the exuberant Gregh, who wrote under several pseudonyms as
well as his own name, he was the most assiduous contributor. Yet
his companions felt it was they who were writers by vocation,
while Proust, who appeared to give only a part of himself to his
art, could never be more than a talented amateur. 'He seemed to

us far more anxious to find a way into certain drawing-rooms of the nobility than to devote himself to literature,' wrote Robert Dreyfus. This unfortunate tendency could be detected even in his writing: his characters were duchesses and countesses with absurd names, with whom dazzling young heroes of independent means fell in love and were frequently loved in return. His prose style was as faded and artificial as it was graceful and highly finished; and he used it for subtle investigations into the psychology of snobism (was he for or against it?), and love and jealousy in high society. It was alarming to see in one so young so total a disenchantment, so final a disbelief in any values more real than those of the social marionette show he described. Perhaps most distressing of all, his work was already too nearly perfect: it left, as it seemed, almost no room for evolution into something more important; it could only become an ever more brilliant pastiche of Bourget and Anatole France. The judgment of his friends of *Le Banquet* would only be confirmed by his writings during the next ten years, by the remainder of *Les Plaisirs et les Jours* and, if they could have read it, *Jean Santeuil*. They may be pardoned for failing to foresee that he would attain greatness through revelation and metamorphosis.

And yet, *Le Banquet* contains the seeds of *A la Recherche*, however different they may seem, as is natural to seeds, from the future tree. Already Proust is trying to use his own experience of life as a metaphorical representation of universal truths: here is Mme Hayman as the courtesan Heldemone, Mme Straus as 'a lady whose intelligence was revealed only by a subtler grace', Mme de Chevigné as a bird-goddess; there is a glimpse of army-life, a child who jumps out of the window for love of a little girl, a band of girls at the seaside, a seascape in Normandy, with the shadows of the clouds and the 'pale pathways' left by the currents. Both these last reminiscences belong to a holiday in August 1892, when he went to Balbec, stayed at La Raspelière, and met Albertine.

She was the sister of one of his associates on *Le Banquet*, Horace Finaly, a former schoolfellow who was the son of a wealthy Jewish banker. Proust had spent part of September 1889 on a visit to the Finalys at Ostend, and on the following 13 December Horace had travelled down to Orleans to see his friend on military service. He was duly pumped on his return by Mme

Proust: 'but I'm afraid, such is his character,' she wrote, 'he stopped at the façade and never even tried to penetrate your inner condition'. He was a short, stout, melancholy young man, interested in metaphysics and fencing, and an ardent reader of Greek poets in the original. His father, Hugo Finaly, was a fat little man with short legs and side-whiskers. Fernand Gregh compared son and father to Hamlet and Polonius; but we may compare them to Bloch and Bloch senior. Horace Finaly became Director of the Bank of Paris and the Netherlands, and for a short period was even Minister of Finance. Proust rather lost sight of him in later years, and, as we shall see, used other models for the later aspects of Bloch; but he still found Horace useful when he needed advice on stocks and shares or a job for some young protégé. Prince André Poniatowski, who knew Finaly many years later, writes rather snobbishly of another character-istic which he shared with Bloch, 'his utter lack of manners, the uncontrollable ill-breeding characteristic of the millionaire who has never ceased to be a clerk'.

Mme Hugo Finaly's uncle, Baron Horace de Landau (1824-1903), had been the representative of the Rothschilds in the newly created Kingdom of Italy during the railway boom of the 1860s. He was an imposing, white-bearded old gentleman, who smoked an immense pipe that reached nearly to the floor; and Gregh, with his whim for finding Shakespearean equivalents for members of the Finaly family, compared him to King Lear. The Baron was devoted to his niece, to whom he willed his entire fortune, and had recently made her a present of Mme Baignères's villa at Trouville, Les Frémonts. He had bought the property for 200,000 francs from Arthur Baignères, and rewarded Proust for his services as intermediary in the deal with a superb walking-cane, a cross between a sceptre and a sugar-stick. It was said the Baron had given Les Frémonts to his niece to tease her ('*pour la taquiner*') as the outcome of a bet. "That's what I call *Taquin le Superbe*," exclaimed Arthur Baignères; and Proust treasured the epigram to give it to the Duchesse de Guermantes on the occasion of the Baron de Charlus's presenting the draughty château of Brézé to his sister Mme de Marsantes.[1] If Hugo and Horace

---

[1] II, 465. M. Nissim Bernard likewise paid for the Bloch's villa near Balbec, La Commanderie (I, 774; II, 842), and made Mme Bloch his sole heir (I, 773).

Finaly were Bloch father and son, it would follow (though nothing is known of his morals) that Baron Landau was Nissim Bernard. But Proust took the exquisitely Jewish name of Nissim from one of two banker brothers, Abraham and Nissim Camondo, who had come from Constantinople to live in a magnificent mansion in the Rue de Monceau, near Mme Lemaire, where they were to be seen strolling side by side in the garden, still wearing their fezzes.

Early in August 1892 Proust had passed the first part of his law exam with credit, but failed in the oral ('my family is awfully sick about it,' he wrote to Robert de Billy). On Sunday the 14th he left for Trouville with Louis de la Salle, armed, he told Billy, 'with Liberty ties of all possible shades', to spend a few weeks at Les Frémonts. The villa stood high above the sands of the Trouville bathing-beach, at the top of the hill at whose foot was the Hôtel des Roches Noires, where he had stayed with his grandmother in the summers of his childhood: it was one of the originals of the Grand Hotel at Balbec. But Les Frémonts itself possessed the celebrated three views of La Raspelière. Its wide bay-windows commanded three distinct prospects, the blue waters of the Channel, the coast past Cabourg as far as Lion-sur-Mer, and the inland orchards of Normandy. Other fellow-banqueters, Gregh and Trarieux, were staying near by with Jacques Bizet at the Manoir de la Cour Brûlée, which Mme Straus had hired for the season from Mme Aubernon. The walks and carriage-drives with Albertine and her friends, the flowerless, fruiting hawthorns and apple-trees of the hinterland of Balbec, belong to this summer. The young men visited the ivy-covered churches of Hennequeville and Criqueboeuf (the Carqueville to which Mme de Villeparisis takes the Narrator and his grandmother in her carriage),[1] on the way to Honfleur, and the mile-long avenues of pines and rhododendrons, above the estuary of the Seine, called Les Allées Marguerite; they went to the races at Deauville, where Proust bet and lost; and one of their companions was the first original of Albertine.

Horace Finaly's sister Marie was a pale, pretty girl with sea-green eyes, alternately gay and grave: Fernand Gregh gave her the role, in her Shakespearean family, of Ophelia. 'We were all more or less in love with Marie,' he writes; and for Proust it was

[1] I, 715

one of the very few occasions on which his love for a woman was returned, for Gregh says again: 'he and the charming Marie felt for one another a childish and reciprocated love'. It is characteristic of Proust that one of the first signs of their sympathy was a common regard for one of his friends, Robert de Billy: 'She talks about you and the nobility of your mind every day,' Proust wrote to Billy, 'in fact I'm quite amazed at the moral, indeed almost religious preoccupations of this girl.' For the first time his love was associated with music: the strange colour of Marie's eyes, the season of the year, the seascapes of their clifftop walks, seemed fully expressed by Fauré's setting of Baudelaire's *Chant d'Automne*. Fifty years later Gregh could still remember his friend ecstatically and discordantly humming, with half-closed eyes and head thrown back, '*J'aime de vos longs yeux la lumière verdâtre*.'[1] A few years afterwards Marie became the wife of a nobleman of Italian family, Thomas de Barbarin, and the mother of three children; in spite of her Jewish parentage she adopted, as Proust regretfully put it, 'anti-Dreyfusism in the name of good taste'; and she died of Spanish influenza at the end of the First World War.

A curious sketch called 'Moonlight Sonata' in *Les Plaisirs et les Jours*[2] relates to this summer, and was suggested by his brief love for Marie Finaly. After driving all day with the pale 'Assunta', the Narrator asks her to go home in the carriage and leave him to rest; he falls asleep near Honfleur in 'a double avenue of great trees, within sound of the sea'—the Allées Marguerite— dreams of an eery cold sunset, and wakes to find himself flooded in moonlight. Assunta returns, saying: "My brother had gone to bed, I was afraid you might be cold"; she wraps her cloak round him, puts her arm round his neck, and they walk weeping in the moonlight. Perhaps the game of ferret took place on the clifftop, as it does in *A l'Ombre*; but more probably it happened in Paris, as in *Jean Santeuil*,[3] for Proust's letters in the following winter show him playing party-games in a circle which apparently

---

[1] The Narrator (I, 674) associates another line of Baudelaire's poem with Balbec: 'I wondered whether Baudelaire's "ray of sunlight on the sea" was not the same that at this very moment was burning the sea like a topaz, fermenting it till it became as pale and milky as beer, as frothy as milk. . . .'

[2] Pp. 192-7

[3] *Pléiade*, I, 918-21; *Jean Santeuil*, vol. 3, 247-9

includes the Finalys. 'Mlle Finaly,' he told Billy at the year's end, 'looks like a painting by Rossetti, who is thus incongruously linked with Shakespeare, the indisputable creator of Horace!'

Proust's love for Marie Finaly can hardly have been of more than minor importance in his life, or its appearance in his letters and other biographical sources would have been less unobtrusive; but its influence on *A la Recherche* was considerable. In his life her position in time and place correspond to that of Albertine in his novel: his love for Marie came immediately after his successive wooings of originals of Gilberte, Odette and the Duchesse de Guermantes; and it happened during a summer on the Normandy coast and a winter in Paris. It was round the distant, half-obliterated figure of Marie Finaly that Albertine was to crystallise. And in its lasting effect this love was one of the turning-points of his life. After the fiasco of Mme de Chevigné he never again fell in love with an older woman; after Marie Finaly it was many years before he next fell in love with a girl. With relief and joy, in the spring of 1893, he took the only path that now lay open, the path he had been deviously and unconsciously seeking all the way from Marie de Benardaky to Marie Finaly. It led into the deep valley of the Cities of the Plain, still green and fertile, untouched as yet by the fire from heaven.

Chapter 9

FIRST GLIMPSES OF THE CITIES OF THE PLAIN

IN the latter half of 1892 Proust began again the series of ardent but still platonic friendships with young men which three years of apparently normal love for women had interrupted. It is probable that in his teens, like Gide, he had remained unaware of his destiny, perhaps ignorant even of the existence of homosexual love. At the Lycée Condorcet M. Darlu would mildly enquire, when he noticed the symptoms of yet another new attachment: "What number did you give him when he came through the door of your heart?" But his pupil, it seemed, was attracted only by intellectual and moral distinction, real or imagined; his utmost desire was for a declaration of exclusive mutual devotion, to be followed by long conversations about literature. If his advances were rejected, if the sacred fire disappointingly faded in Jacques Bizet or 'little Halévy', he turned with unquenchable optimism elsewhere. In his army year the sequence continued: Horace Finaly was closely followed by Gaston de Caillavet, as was Bloch by Saint-Loup. He appreciated at Orleans the simplicity and originality of his peasant comrades; though he did not follow the path thus suggested till fifteen years later, when his mother's death set him free to make friends among the working classes. Next comes the long interlude during which nothing is heard of male friends, when his heart was occupied in turn with Jeanne Pouquet, Mme Straus, Laure Hayman, the Comtesse de Chevigné and Marie Finaly. But from the autumn of 1892 the charming young men appear in uninterrupted succession for many years, handing on, like Grecian runners, the torch of friendship or love. Proust was nearing the period in his life which corresponds in his novel to the Narrator's detection of the true nature of M. de Charlus. It is probable that in this revelation, and the proliferation of Sodom throughout the novel which is its consequence, he symbolised his discovery of his own inversion. In 1893 he met the chief original of Charlus; in 1894 came his first undoubtedly homosexual love-affair.

His new friendships in 1892 were symptoms, though he could not know it, of the approaching change; and young Robert de Billy was the involuntary cause of their beginning. Billy, his fellow-soldier and fellow-student, was a Protestant from Alsace and a lover of mountaineering. In the summer vacation of 1891 he had visited Geneva, where his religion and noble birth enabled him to move in the aristocratic society of the Rue des Granges and to make friends with a young Swiss named Edgar Aubert. In the winter Aubert returned the visit, and was introduced by Billy and Proust to the salons of Mme Straus and the cousins Charlotte and Laure Baignères. His elegance, sincerity and cosmopolitan culture made him an instant success; but his qualities were appreciated by no one more than by Proust himself. Edgar knew English, the language of Dickens and George Eliot, whom Proust could read only in translation. He spoke it at the Finalys', and when he gave Proust a photograph of his austerely handsome features a few lines of an English poet were written on the back: 'the words seem rather sad to me,' Proust commented.[1] He learned from Aubert, moreover, of the intricate social structure of the Swiss Protestant upper classes: they were a fascinating replica in miniature of the Faubourg Saint-Germain, and yet, since their hierarchy was based not on a titled nobility but on the more abstract conception of 'good family', it resembled also the Jewish caste-system which included the Rothschilds, Charles Haas, the Finalys and Mme Proust's relatives. After cross-examining Aubert, Proust made researches of his own, and was particularly delighted when he could discover some scandalous secret in an otherwise respectable Huguenot family: "I'm telling you this for your own good, *mon petit Robert*," he would say to Billy with an air of innocence, "to save you from making some awful *gaffe*." But perhaps the most impressive characteristic of Edgar Aubert was his religious fervour: in his steady eyes Proust saw, together with irony, affection and disenchantment, the light of faith; he thought of his mother's and dead grandmother's grace and good works, and felt a vague remorse for sins he had not yet committed.

[1] The quotation was very probably from Rossetti's sonnet (*The House of Life*, XCVII):

> 'Look in my face; my name is Might-have-been;
> I am also called No-more, Too-late, Farewell.'

Cf. *Corr. Gén.*, III, 66

The three young men walked in the Tuileries gardens in the warm air of a new spring, or late at night endlessly saw one another home. Edgar, Proust always remembered, was 'so charming and witty and kind'; and though he would sometimes rebuke Marcel's sentimentality or curiosity with cutting sarcasm, he always made up for it with an affectionate glance or a shake of the hand. All too soon, however, it was time for Aubert's return to Geneva. He hoped for so much from life, and yet some presentiment made him uneasy, dejected, engagingly apprehensive. Of one thing, nevertheless, he was quite certain: "I shall come back next year *whatever happens*," he said. But he never did.

In August, when Proust was at Trouville with the Finalys, Billy joined Aubert at Saint-Moritz. The weather was delightful, they played tennis with a young Indian Rajah and climbed several mountains; and then, only a few days after their parting, on 18 September 1892, Aubert died of appendicitis. He met his end with extraordinary firmness; he sent Proust a keepsake through their friend Jean Boissonnas; but he never had a reply to the two letters he had written to Proust just before his illness began.

Instead, Proust could only write Billy a letter of condolence which showed regret rather than grief. He was, posthumously, a little jealous: Aubert, after all, had been Billy's friend, not his. Now he must find an Aubert of his own, and make sure that Billy knew about it: perhaps Billy could be made to feel jealous in return? Already at Les Frémonts, after receiving a ten-page letter from an unnamed correspondent, he had teasingly informed Billy, in a letter that Aubert would see: 'At last I've found the tender, letter-writing friend of my dreams. It's true he only puts one stamp on his envelopes, so I always have to pay 30 centimes— but what wouldn't one do when one really likes a person?' Early in 1893, when Billy had become a probationer in the French Embassy at Berlin, Proust had found another friend, 'who is everything to me that I should have been to X——, if he hadn't been so unfeeling. I refer to the young, charming, intelligent, kind, affectionate Robert de Flers.' In February he went with Flers to the Lenten sermons, on *'Living for Others'*, of Abbé Pierre Vignot, and greatly admired them, though not perhaps in the sense in which the preacher intended. Afterwards he frequently met the Abbé at the home of his Condorcet friend, Pierre

Lavallée. But in the spring, when 'the return of gentle sunlit days' gave him 'the exact illusion, to the point of hallucination, of the time when we used to see Edgar Aubert home', he met a young man who was very like Aubert indeed. He duly told Billy, who was about to visit Paris on leave; he also sent an oval seating-plan of an enormous dinner-party at 9 Boulevard Malesherbes for a select ten of his very best friends, and the names of seven more who came after dinner—'I'm afraid the list isn't quite complete,' he added apologetically. Willie Heath is in the place of honour on Mme Proust's left, while Proust is separated from them by Comte Charles de Grancey and Robert de Flers. Of the ten dinner-guests, four are counts (Grancey, Flers, Louis de la Salle and Gustave de Waru) and two viscounts; the after-dinner guests are all untitled. 'If only I'd known you were coming I'd have put off the dinner,' he said; but Billy was not allowed to meet Heath on this visit, and there was never to be another opportunity.

It was almost as if Aubert had fulfilled his promise of coming next year, *whatever happens*. Willie Heath was quite alarmingly like Aubert. He not only spoke English, he *was* English; he was deeply religious, like Edgar, though after a Protestant upbringing he had been converted to Catholicism at the tender age of twelve; and in his eyes there was the same look of melancholy premonition and resignation as in Aubert's. Of all their circle he was the most serious, and yet the most childlike, not only in the purity of his heart, but in his bursts of delightful, unselfconscious gaiety. Proust noted with some envy that the secret of making Willie laugh seemed denied to himself, whereas Charles de Grancey, with stories of his schooldays, could always send Willie into fits.

They met in the Bois de Boulogne. The morning sunlight slanted through the new leaves as Proust advanced to their meeting-place: there, under the trees, erect yet reposing in his pensive elegance, stood Willie, his eyes already fixed on his friend; and a strange thought came into Proust's mind. In 1891, the first year of their student life, Robert de Billy had shown him Van Dyck's portraits of young English cavaliers in the Louvre: "you see, Marcel," he had explained, "they're all going to be killed soon in the Civil War, and you can tell it in their faces." How like the doomed Duke of Richmond, standing under dark green foliage,

was Willie! 'Their elegance, like yours,' Proust wrote later, 'lies
not so much in their clothes as in their bodies, and their bodies
seem to have received it, and to continue unceasingly to receive
it, from their souls: for it is a moral elegance.' Then, as he watched
another characteristic attitude of Willie's, the raised finger pointing to some heavenly enigma, the impenetrably smiling eyes, he
thought of another favourite picture in the Louvre, in which
spirituality, mystery and sexual ambiguity are even more intensely
mingled: Willie was very like Leonardo's John the Baptist. When
they began to talk in the green glade, it was of a plan 'to live more
and more together, in a chosen group of highminded women and
men, somewhere too far away from stupidity, vice and malice for
their vulgar arrows ever to reach us'. But before this project
could be carried out, on 3 October 1893, still in Paris, Willie
Heath died of typhoid. His resemblance to Edgar Aubert was now
complete.

Meanwhile the spring of 1893 had brought—along with Abbé
Vignot's Lenten sermons, and hallucinatory memories of the dead
Aubert, and Willie's friendship, and the new leaves in the Bois—
the annual resumption of Mme Lemaire's Tuesdays. On Tuesday,
28 March, the event of the evening was a recital by Mlle Bartet
from the Comédie Française of poems from *Les Chauves-Souris*,
the first published volume of Comte Robert de Montesquiou-
Fezensac.[1] Moved by a mild interest in the verses and an intense
curiosity about their author, Proust joined the cooing ladies who
queued to congratulate the fluting count; and as Montesquiou's
appetite for flattery was only equalled by his predilection for
handsome young men, the new admirer was graciously received,
and his entreaty for permission to call was affably granted. Proust
was to meet many writers of more genuine talent, and a few of
genius; but in some ways this pseudo-poet and monster of vanity
was the most extraordinary person he ever met. For Count
Robert, as Proust perhaps obscurely realised as early as this very
Tuesday, had the makings of Palamède, Baron de Charlus.

Montesquiou, as he not infrequently explained, was a member
of one of the oldest families in the French nobility: it included a

---

[1] It was most incorrect, however, to call him by his full name. As the
Narrator remarks, 'a guest in a drawing-room proves that he is unfamiliar
with society if he refers to M. de Montesquiou as M. de Montesquiou-
Fezensac'. (II, 934).

comparatively recent ducal branch, whose title dated only from 1815, but now consisted mostly of innumerable counts and countesses with whom he was on terms of permanent enmity. He claimed descent from the Merovingian kings of France; but among his undoubted ancestors were the crusader Raimond-Aimeri de Montesquiou (*circa* 1190), Blaise de Montluc (1502-72), the marshal of France, massacrer of Protestants and author of the famous *Commentaires*, and Charles de Batz (1611-73), the original of D'Artagnan in *The Three Musketeers*. The château of Artagnan in the Hautes-Pyrénées was still in the possession of the family, and Montesquiou used it as his country-seat and occasional refuge from the fatigues of Paris. Various Montesquious of the *grand siècle* move through the memoirs of Saint-Simon; but the family reached its highest prominence in the church and army under Louis XVI. "There's one good thing about the French Revolution," Hervieu had been heard to remark one evening at Mme de Caillavet's, when Montesquiou was reciting his poems and leaning nobly against the mantelpiece: "if it hadn't happened, that man would have had us beating his ponds to keep the frogs quiet." But there were several scores of families of higher absolute position in the French society of Proust's time; and Count Robert's own social eminence was based partly on his snob-value as a titled intellectual, partly on his hypnotic power of imposing himself on the fashionable world, and partly on the gift his hated relatives possessed for intermarriage with the great. He was related by recent marriages to the ducal families of La Rochefoucauld, Bauffremont, Rohan-Chabot, Gramont, Feltre, Descars, Béthune, Maillé de la Tour Landry, Noailles and Rochechouart-Mortemart; to the princes of Caraman-Chimay, Faucigny-Lucinge, Bibesco and Brancovan; and through these to everyone else who mattered in the slightest. Charlus spoke of 'my cousin Clara de Chimay', 'my cousins the La Rochefoucaulds',[1] and so, incessantly, did Robert de Montesquiou. For the 1910 edition of *Qui êtes-vous* he wrote under his name: 'Allied to the greater part of the European aristocracy.' It was the simple truth.

Montesquiou was now thirty-eight, and the soirée at Mme Lemaire's was the first step in a campaign already long overdue, through which he hoped to exchange his notoriety as a beautiful aesthete for fame as a well-preserved poet. He was born in 1855,

[1] I, 764; III, 268

and became an ailing, frightened little boy, bullied by his father, schoolfellows and Jesuit teachers. In 1871, at the age of sixteen, he met Charles Haas, and was impressed by his wit and easy elegance: Proust, exaggerating a little, for Haas was more than twenty years Montesquiou's senior, made Charlus and Swann friends in their schooldays.[1] Desiring to surround himself with beauty, as a fitting mirror of the beauty he so admired in himself, he became a fanatic of interior decoration, a collector of bric-à-brac. He met Mallarmé late in the '70s, and in 1879 brightened the fatal illness of the poet's little son Anatole with the gift of a cockatoo named Semiramis. Mallarmé told Huysmans of this fantastic young aesthete, and the decadent novelist constructed *A Rebours* (1885) and the character of Des Esseintes about him. Mallarmé was perturbed lest the ultra-susceptible Montesquiou should be annoyed: but no, he was delighted. Yes, it was perfectly true that he had a room decorated as a snow-scene, with a polar-bear rug and a sleigh and mica hoar-frost ("when you went into that room you felt f-r-r-rozen!" his dear secretary Yturri would say). And yes, he did inlay the shell of a pet tortoise with turquoises, of which the poor creature died; and he *had* been known to wear a white velvet suit, with a bunch of violets in the neck of his shirt instead of a cravat. If anything aggrieved him, he revealed, it was that Mallarmé should have paid him only a single visit in search of material.

In the 1880s he met Edmond de Goncourt, and there are admiring glimpses of him in the Goncourt *Journal*, of a delicious absurdity only surpassed by the parody of the *Journal* read at Tansonville by the Narrator. There is an accidental meeting on 6 April 1887 with Montesquiou at Passy, 'in all the correctness of one of his supremely *chic* suitings': he was carrying what looked like a sumptuously bound prayer-book, but turned out to be a copy of one of Goncourt's own novels—'which is some slight compensation for all the setbacks I have had lately,' remarks the poor diarist. There is a visit on 7 July 1891 to Montesquiou's house in the Rue Franklin at Passy, where Proust was to visit him in April 1893. It was 'crammed with a hodge-podge of incongruous objects, old family portraits, Empire furniture, Japanese kakemonos and etchings by Whistler'. But the most amazing room of all was the bathroom, decorated with represen-

[1] III, 299

tations of the count's favourite flower, the hortensia, 'in every possible material and every conceivable art-form', and containing two objects which later must have filled Proust with a special *frisson* of amusement and envy: a glass cupboard with 'the tender pastel shades of a hundred cravats', and above it 'a photograph of La Rochefoucauld, the acrobat at the Cirque Mollier, in tights which do full justice to his elegant ephebic figure'.

Montesquiou was tall and thin—"I look like a greyhound in a greatcoat," he would say complacently. He had abandoned his former eccentricities of dress, and favoured dark grey suits whose harmonies and exquisite drapings made him more noticeable than ever. His hair was black, crisp and artificially waved; he had beetling black eyebrows like circumflex accents, and a moustache with upturned pointed ends, like the Kaiser's but larger. His face was white, long, hawk-like and finely drawn; his cheeks were rouged and delicately wrinkled, so that Proust, greatly to his annoyance, compared them to a moss-rose; and his mouth was small and red, with little black teeth which he hurriedly concealed with one hand whenever he laughed—a gesture unnecessarily copied by Proust, whose teeth were beautifully white in his youth. In these early days he used only a little powder and rouge. Everything in his appearance was studied, for the artist, he felt, should be himself a work of art. But as this strange, black and white nobleman chanted, swayed and gesticulated, he acted a whole series of puppet characters, as if manipulated on wires pulled by some other self in the ceiling: he was a Spanish hidalgo, a duellist, his ancestor D'Artagnan, a screeching black macaw, an angry spinster, the greatest living poet. The sobriety of his colour-scheme was mitigated by the coquetry of his lilac perfume and pastel-hued cravats: "I should like admiration for my person to reach the pitch of physical desire," he confessed.

Montesquiou had inherited from his family great wealth and a delight in spending it: it was one of the few traits he shared with his father, Comte Thierry de Montesquiou, who had once remarked when contemplating marriage with a young heiress: "She has 500,000 francs a year—with what I have that will make 50,000." The increasing splendour of his apartments and the receptions he gave in them sometimes involved him in temporary debt; but, as he said, "It's bad enough not to have any money, it would be too much if one had to deprive oneself of anything."

At such times he was capable of economy: he and Yturri might be seen devouring the cheapest lunch at the humble creamery opposite his apartment, or Yturri would go out and sell something. Sometimes the articles of his collection cost very little: Yturri found Mme de Montespan's pink marble bath in the garden of a Versailles convent, and paid for it with his own cast-off slipper which, he assured the nuns, had once belonged to the Pope. Sometimes they cost nothing at all. Worn out by Montesquiou's nagging, his exclamations of "Don't you see, it's *disgusting* to give away anything you can bear to part with," a noble lady would surrender an eighteenth-century drawing, a porcelain figurine, or a manuscript of Baudelaire; and he would carry off the precious object wrapped in tissue-paper.

The conversation of Montesquiou appealed both to the ear and the eye: it was like an aria by a great singer or a speech by a great actor, yet with something of a clown's antics or a madman's raving. He made beautiful gestures with his white-gloved hands; then he would remove the gloves, displaying a simple but curious ring; his gesticulation became ever more impassioned, till suddenly he would point heavenward: his voice rose like a trumpet in an orchestra, and passed into the soprano register of fortissimo violins; he stamped his foot, threw back his head, and emitted peal upon peal of shrill, maniacal laughter. He spoke of poetry and painting, of countesses' hats, of the splendour of his race, and of himself as its crowning glory. "I can't bear that man who's always telling me about his ancestors," Anatole France would complain; and Charles Haas, on request, would imitate Montesquiou saying, in the choicest accent of the *gratin*—it was a kind of incisive, yelping drawl—"My forebears used up all the family intelligence; my father had nothing left but the sense of his own grandeur; my brother hadn't even that, but had the decency to die young; while I—I have added to our ducal coron*et* the glorious coron*al* of a poet!" Very often he would recite his own verses; and when his hostess whispered: "How very beautiful!" he would reply: "Yes, it *is* a beautiful poem, and I will now recite it to you again." Sometimes he would stand on the staircase, like M. de Charlus at the Princesse de Guermantes's, and make distinctly audible comments on the arriving guests: "I see the Chanoinesse de Faudoas is wearing orange—no doubt she wishes to display the number of her quarters." Once he embarrassed an unfortunate maiden whose dress was garnished with imitation cherries: "I had no idea young girls were allowed to bear fruit." There was, indeed, even apart from his insolent delight in the pleasure of making enemies, his readiness to sacrifice his best friends for the sake of making an epigram, a streak of sadism in his nature. He used to visit his little nieces and say, "My dears, to-day we will play at pretending to cry." He would then mimic bitter sobs, his nieces would imitate him just for fun; and when their tears became real he would slip away, leaving them writhing in hysteria.

Montesquiou was by no means insensible to the beauty of women. He had adored Sarah Bernhardt in the days when she was still ravishingly pretty and young-looking: he had even gone to bed with her, an experience which was unhappily followed by a week of uncontrollable vomiting. He kept up a life-long, semi-mystical cult for the Comtesse de Castiglione, who had been the mistress of Napoleon III and many of his courtiers; she still lived on in the Place Vendôme, half-crazed, emerging only at night, lest people should see the ruin of her beauty. Among his most treasured possessions—along with La Gandara's drawing of Comtesse Greffulhe's chin and Boldini's painting of Yturri's legs in cycling breeches—was a plaster-cast of the Castiglione's knees. His *Les Chauves-Souris* was dedicated to the lovely Marquise Flavie de Casa-Fuerte, whose son Illan was to become one of his last young friends fifteen years later. In his middle age he was to be no less devoted to Eleanora Duse, Isadora Duncan and Ida Rubinstein. His sexual abnormality was so inconspicuous that after his death several of the people who had known him best denied its existence: "he was not an invert, but merely an introvert," says André Germain. In fact, Montesquiou's inversion may have been confined largely to his almost conjugal relations with his secretaries, and his attachments to other young men were perhaps often, if not invariably, platonic. Similarly, in *A la Recherche* the Narrator sometimes surprisingly conjectures that Charlus's liaison with Morel may have been entirely innocent. There is no hint in the life of Montesquiou of casual affairs with waiters, cabmen and other underlings: this feature of Charlus, like his burly physique, was derived from Baron Doasan.

The first of Count Robert's secretaries—followed after his death by the second and last—was Gabriel d'Yturri. The surname is a Basque word meaning a spring of fresh water, and the particle was added at Montesquiou's suggestion. Yturri was born on 12 March 1864 at Tucuman in the Argentine, brought up in Buenos Ayres, and emigrated at the age of fifteen to Paris. Baron Doasan found him serving behind a counter at the Magasins du Louvre, and persuaded him to become his secretary, only to have him stolen by Montesquiou—hence the undying enmity between the count and the baron. For twenty years, from 1885 till he died in harness in 1905, Yturri was the loyal friend and factotum (as was Jupien of the Baron de Charlus) of 'Mossou le Connte', as he called him in his indelible *rastaquouère* accent. At first his status and antecedents were difficult to explain. "From which house does M. d'Yturri derive?" asked the blue-blooded Comte Aimery de La Rochefoucauld, Montesquiou's cousin by marriage, only to be told by a malicious informant: "He derives from a 'house' in the Rue de Boccador!"[1] When Count Aimery pursued his enquiries by asking Yturri himself, the reply was even less satisfactory: "Why, I was ze secretary of ze Baron Doasan!" cried the young man with visible pride. But Yturri was so good-natured and faithful, and lasted so long, that in the end he was universally accepted and even liked. He was short, handsome and excitable; he had coffee-coloured eyes, a deathly pale olive face, a conspicuous mole tufted with hair, and a tendency to baldness against which he fought with desperate unsuccess. He exuded a strange odour of chloroform and rotten apples, which no one realised until too late to be a symptom of diabetes. His relationship with Montesquiou was clouded only by occasional tiffs and sulks, and by the fact that it was impossible to discover just where he went on his bicycle. Once there was a more prolonged absence, by train, and the poor count could only reply to an enquiring friend: "Gabriel has gone to Monte Carlo with a young person who seems to have an extremely bad influence on him."

In one respect Montesquiou's character stands in need of no defence. He invented and kept his own astonishing rules of life:

[1] Such was the rumour, all the more illuminating for being apocryphal. The truth of the story, as told by Montesquiou himself, is simply that, on the occasion of Montesquiou's duel with Henri de Regnier, Comte Aimery (anxious lest his cousin should be fighting a mere commoner) asked Yturri: "To what house does M. de Regnier belong?", and Yturri, deliberately misunderstanding, gave him Regnier's address: "No. 6 Rue du Boccador!"

he was, though of lesser calibre than the Baron de Charlus, an eccentric in his own right, and by far the most remarkable and original person in the empty milieu of the Faubourg Saint-Germain; he was witty, and brilliantly though not profoundly intelligent. But with some research it is possible to detect in him moral qualities which mitigate, though they do not redeem, his charlatanism. He was kind and loyal to his friends, during the short period before he quarrelled with them. He was brave and indomitable. But best of all was his selfless devotion to the artists and writers whom he considered his equals or even superiors. They included Mallarmé, Leconte de Lisle, Heredia, Coppée, Goncourt, Huysmans, Villiers de l'Isle Adam, Barbey d'Aurevilly, Verlaine, Regnier, d'Annunzio, Barrès, Gustave Moreau, Degas, Whistler and Forain: though the list shows no insight in advance of his time, it contains only one or two inferior names. He supported them with tireless propaganda; he supplied them with patrons and purchasers, and to the few who needed it he gave his own money. In return they respected his talent, perhaps more than it deserved, and defended him when taxed with their enjoyment of his company. "He says such marvellous things," said Barrès. "He's so foonny . . . and besides, he comes walking with me in the Bois, and there are so few people who can keep oop with me!" Whistler (one of the many originals of Elstir) painted two portraits of the count in 1891; and it is probable that Whistler was a decisive model for the definitive mask which Montesquiou adopted in the early '90s, and for the publicity campaign of readings, lectures and entertainments which had just opened at the time of his meeting with Proust. He borrowed Whistler's coiffure for his waving black hair, Whistler's moustache, his duellist's stance, his baying laugh with head thrown back, his ferocity and his epigrams, his gentle art of making enemies.

Montesquiou showed rather less abnegation and critical taste in his discoveries: they were mostly artists (he took good care never to 'discover' a writer) of little or secondary merit, whom he pushed with one eye on the credit they would do him. Among them were Helleu, an etcher and painter of real talent, La Gandara, who became a fashionable but execrable society-portraitist, Lobre, the painter of Versailles, and Gallé, the engraver of glass and the creator of Montesquiou's hortensia bathroom. The only one of his discoveries whose work still lives was Proust's friend, Jacques

Émile Blanche, a post-impressionist of enduring charm and originality, except for an unfortunate period during the Edwardian era when he imitated Sargent. The story of their final breach is instructive: it shows the pattern of a typical Montesquiou execution, and it has several features in common with the quarrel-scene of Charlus and the Narrator in *Le Côté de Guermantes*.

For a time Montesquiou called Blanche "the Lord's anointed". He commissioned a portrait of "a Beautiful Unknown—nobody must hear about her"—but when Blanche arrived for the sitting, shiver of little mossfronds, perfume of friendship, delicious fluting where. Similarly he had told her that her portraitist was "an unknown genius I've discovered". One morning, however, when Blanche at Montesquiou's earnest request had asked him to lunch to meet the composer Fauré, the unlucky painter encountered the Prince de Sagan, with his white gloves, white hair and white carnation, walking in the Bois, and invited him to come too. The prince and the count were deadly enemies: Montesquiou took one look, turned green with rage, and left, Fauré or no Fauré. They met once more, on the Ile des Cygnes at Passy, to return their correspondence and bid everlasting farewell: Montesquiou gave back Blanche's letters in a scented coffer of sandalwood, whereupon Blanche hurled Montesquiou's into the Seine. It was the opening day of the Universal Exhibition of 1889 and of its chief attraction, the Eiffel Tower. "If you had understood the tutelary importance of the man who hoped to reveal you to yourself," said Montesquiou mournfully, "it would have helped you to avoid the false steps in which you seem to take such pleasure. But as we shall never meet again, I will consecrate one last hour to you. Let us ascend to the first platform of the Eiffel Tower, and gaze upon the panorama of this tentacular Paris, in which I should have liked to show you the places to shun." And after the ascent Montesquiou saw Blanche home in a cab, as Charlus did the Narrator. Henceforth he exerted all his power to exclude the painter from society; he called him 'the Auteuil shaving-brush'; and when he saw one of his paintings in a noble lady's house he would say: "Isn't it high time you put this piece of linoleum under your bath-tub?"

All in all, Montesquiou was a hollow man. The terrifying, impenetrable façade of his vanity, his insolence, his perversity, covered nothing but the frightened small boy with whom he had irrevocably lost touch. If he had used his real sensibility and intelligence to remain true to himself—as did Proust, who in some ways was not unlike him—he might have possessed the genius in which he so firmly believed. Instead he only dressed, collected, scribbled, quarrelled, fascinated and terrorised. He possessed little of the Lear-like grandeur of Charlus: he was a pathetic, not a tragic figure. The character of the Baron de Charlus is rightly supposed to be, in some of its aspects, Proust's revenge upon Montesquiou; but it is also a generous and sincere tribute to the buried potentialities of Count Robert.

Early in April 1893, Proust received a copy of *Les Chauves-Souris* inscribed with a line from one of its most revealing poems: '*I am the sovereign of the transitory.*' In return he sent the first of a series of flattering letters which was to continue throughout the next twenty-eight years, until Montesquiou's death. 'You extend far beyond the frontiers of the type of the exquisite decadent in which you are usually depicted . . . this supreme refinement was never before linked with this creative energy, this almost seventeenth-century intellectuality . . . you are the sovereign not only of transitory, but of eternal things,' he wrote. Montesquiou believed it, Proust half-believed it, and it is not wholly untrue; for there are signs of all these qualities in *Les Chauves-Souris*, although they serve only to polish the mirror of Montesquiou's vanity. The poems are poetically worthless, but technically dazzling; they have no depth of feeling or significance, but their surface has a diamond-like hardness and brilliance. Their style is influenced by Montesquiou's favourite poets, Hugo ("your grandfather and I," he once shatteringly began to Georges Hugo), Mallarmé, Leconte de Lisle (who ironically called him 'the nobleman of letters'), Heredia; but he brought to it a shallow, arrogant preciosity which is all his own. Even the eternal things are there. The subject and method of Montesquiou's verses have some affinity with those of Proust's novel: he pursued, with a proliferation of metaphor and unexpected adjectives, the timeless reality which underlies the phenomenal world. The pursuit was always diverted by his self-adoration: whenever he reached the holy of holies it turned out to contain the graven image of a nobleman-poet; and the metaphors and adjectives were always showy and untrue. But he held, unable and unworthy as he was to turn it, one of the keys to Time Regained.

There were many reasons for Proust's flattery of the pathetic count. One was amiable: Proust longed to be liked and loved to give pleasure. Another was utilitarian: Montesquiou had the power, and if suitably handled might have the desire, to introduce him into the Faubourg Saint-Germain. Another was aesthetic, for Montesquiou was a model for Proust's own ambition at this time, to live simultaneously in the world of the imagination and in the world of society. There was a psychiatric motive, for Montesquiou resembled a madman who can only be appeased by repeated assurances that he is, in fact, Napoleon or Victor Hugo. But most of all Proust felt that his own destiny was linked to Montesquiou: as a person, Count Robert was a character in an undreamed-of novel; as a writer he unwittingly possessed a clue to the recovery of the Time which Proust had not yet lost.

It was not altogether easy to flatter him with success. Very soon —in a postcard sent on 28 April 1893—he forbade Proust to use the almost indispensable word 'nice' (*gentille*). He was inclined, from unhappy experience, to be suspicious, and was known to remark, as M. de Norpois did of the Narrator, that Proust was 'a hysterical flatterer'. He also became aware, shortly after his young friend's visit in mid-April to his exquisite house at Passy, that he was viewed with a misplaced sense of comedy. The pride of his garden in the Rue Franklin was a group of Japanese dwarf trees, tended by a real Japanese gardener named Hata: and it was a very mixed compliment to be told that his soul was 'a garden as rare and fastidious as the one in which you allowed me to walk the other day, except that it is *not* lacking in the tall trees of France'. He would have been still more annoyed if he could have foreseen that Proust's further remark, that his soul contained 'a morsel of blue sky', would be adapted for the use of Legrandin in *Du Côté de chez Swann*.[1]

The reasons for Proust's interest in Montesquiou were not only aesthetic and social. Even without the bathroom photograph of Larochefoucauld the acrobat, or the poems in *Les Chauves-Souris* devoted to eminent inverts such as Louis XIII, Wagner's Louis of Bavaria or Mr W. H., this keen diagnostician could detect that Montesquiou possessed the vice that he was himself about to acquire. A few allusions in Proust's letters suggest that in the early summer of 1893 Montesquiou administered the monu-

[1] I, 120

mental wigging on which the quarrel between Charlus and the
Narrator in *Le Côté de Guermantes* is based. It is very possible
that Proust detected beneath the count's anger the notes of
despised love; but the whole tenor of their subsequent relationship shows that his advances, if they were made, were veiled and
unsuccessful. Montesquiou must have realised, like Baron Doasan
before him, that his new friend was (or would soon be) like
himself an active, not a passive invert, a rival huntsman, not a
possible prey. The ostensible grounds of the dispute, both in real
life and in the novel, were a report that the disciple had been
talking scandal about the master. Montesquiou had good reason
to be touchy: in March 1895 the loyal Yturri felt compelled to
challenge Blanche to a duel on a charge of gossiping about his
relations with the count; though Blanche was soon able to convince Yturri's second, Henri de Regnier, that it was all a trick
of the malicious Comtesse Potocka and her friend Georges
Legrand. Charlus's speeches in the quarrel-scene, as elsewhere,
are a brilliant parody of Montesquiou; but several of the baron's
sayings in this episode are known to be favourite tags of the
terrible count's: Proust's letters show that they were uttered to
him at some time in the early 1890s, and it may well be that it
happened on this very occasion. One is: "Words repeated at
second-hand are seldom true"; another is "I have submitted you
to the supreme test of excessive amiability, the only one which
separates the wheat from the tares"; and another is Montesquiou's
infuriating quotation from Psalms ii, 10, with which he invariably
accompanied a warning or a complaint: "*Et nunc erudimini*"—
'Be ye now instructed.'

The quarrel with Montesquiou did not last long. In August
Proust made the best of two very different friendships by visiting
Saint-Moritz with Louis de la Salle, his companion at the
Finalys' the summer before, and Montesquiou. With the count
was one of his adored lady-friends, Mme Meredith Howland, an
intimate of Charles Haas and one of the very few Americans then
admitted to high society[1]; she and Montesquiou had been there
the previous year at the same time as Billy and Aubert, though the

[1] In *Le Temps Retrouvé*, when the Narrator reminds the Duchesse of a
hostess who had spoken ill of Mme Howland, Oriane bursts out laughing:
"Why, of course, Mme Howland had all the men in her salon, and your
friend was trying to lure them to her own!" (III, 1026).

two couples had not met. Proust and La Salle ascended the Righi by funicular and the Alp Grüm on foot, seeing from the summit a dim blue vista that led to Italy; and by the lake of Sils-Maria they watched a flight of pink butterflies cross the water and return. Then, after three weeks, the party moved for a last week to the Lake of Geneva, to find a miniature working-model of Parisian society: it was in expectation of this that Proust had defensively told Billy: 'I shall be meeting lots of women.' There was Laure Baignères in her Villa Quatorze at Clarens, after which (in allusion to the Belgian Comtesse Vilain-Quatorze whom Louis XIV ennobled after a delightful visit) she was nicknamed Comtesse Villa-Quatorze. At Amphion, in her Villa Bassaraba, was Princesse Rachel de Brancovan, who played Chopin so beautifully but so reluctantly, with a musical agony that recalls Mme Verdurin's. "Oh, not to-day, Monsieur, I couldn't!" she would cry: "Oh, what torture! No, it would kill me, feel my hands, they're frozen!" She was one of the leaders of musical society in Paris, a patroness of Paderewski, Fauré and Enesco. Perhaps Proust first met at this time her wild and pretty sixteen-year-old daughter Anna, the future poetess and Comtesse de Noailles, who was later to be his friend. But as he travelled from hostess to hostess round the lake he thought of Aubert's sad, ironic eyes, and reproached himself, as he wrote to Billy, for enjoying the beauty that poor Edgar would never see again.

In September he spent a fortnight with Mme Proust at the Hôtel des Roches Noires, Trouville, at the western end of the boarded promenade—an original of that on which the little band of girls walks at Balbec—which the society gossip columns called 'the summer boulevard of Paris'. Summer, however, was nearly over: evening mists rose in the valley behind the hotel, and the fireplaces, it seemed, were not intended to contain fires. There was only one lavatory to each storey, and the partitions between the bedrooms were too thin; but at least this meant that his mother would hear his tapping on the wall, as did his grandmother long ago, and visit him as soon as he woke. Perhaps he saw Marie Finaly again: at least, he nostalgically quoted to his father after his return Baudelaire's line, which he associated with her, about '*le soleil rayonnant sur la mer*'. But Dr Proust was in no mood for quotations. Marcel, if all went well, would soon pass his law diploma (in fact he took it on 10 October 1893, a week after Willy Heath's death); and the holiday at Trouville, after supplying a few hints for the second visit to Balbec, ended in an ultimatum, expressed with the well-meaning father's characteristic impatience and finality: Marcel must choose a career; he must show some will-power.

With an outbreak of genuine panic, and a mask of despairing obedience, Marcel showed so much will-power that in the end nothing happened. 'I had hoped, *mon cher petit papa*,' he wrote, 'to persuade you to allow me to continue the literary and philosophical studies for which I believe I am fitted.' But at this time he felt it no less essential that he should be allowed to pursue his social life. In *A la Recherche* the Narrator is determined not to go into the diplomatic service because he would have to live abroad and cease to see Gilberte; and here, no doubt, Proust remembers the year 1891, when it seemed likely that he would in due course enter the Ministry of Foreign Affairs, with his fellow-students Trarieux and Billy, and so be separated from Jeanne Pouquet. But in 1893 Jeanne was married and forgotten, and the danger had changed. 'I'm determined not to go abroad,' he told Billy; for it would mean renouncing not only the bourgeois hostesses he already possessed, but also the noble hostesses for whom he hoped. Nor could he endure a post that might make him socially unacceptable: 'isn't the magistrature too much looked down upon?' he pathetically asked Billy. 'As for going into a lawyer's office, I'd a thousand times rather it were a stockbroker's—you can be quite sure I wouldn't stay there three days,' he told Dr Proust. He did in fact begin training with a lawyer, a certain Maître Brunet, and endured it for a whole fortnight, but no longer; and for a time there was even some talk of buying him a lawyer's practice. He toyed with the grim idea of the Cour des Comptes, the Government accounting office which was traditionally regarded as being socially distinguished (Billy's father was a *conseiller référendaire* there); but 'the boredom would kill me', and mathematics had been his worst subject at Condorcet. At last, although Marcel promised to work seriously for 'the Foreign Affairs exam or the École des Chartes, the choice to be yours', poor Dr Proust realised it would be simpler to shelve the whole matter. It was agreed that Marcel should spend the next academic year studying for the *licence ès lettres*; and Proust was

not dissatisfied with this first step towards family acquiescence in
his literary career. As he told his father with unconscious foresight: 'anything but literature and philosophy for me would be
temps perdu'—Time Lost.

His progress as a writer had already reached a new stage. After
the demise of *Le Banquet*, in March 1893, several of the homeless
banqueters, including Gregh, Léon Blum, Jacques Baignères and
Proust himself, had been offered hospitality by the *Revue Blanche*.
This was a high-class, mildly *avant-garde* little review, founded
in 1891 by the wealthy Polish brothers Thadée and Alexandre
Natanson. Verlaine, Mallarmé, Heredia, Barrès, Jean Lorrain,
Pierre Louÿs and the young André Gide were among its contributors. Nine sketches by Proust, of the kind that had already
appeared in *Le Banquet*, were published in the *Revue Blanche* for
July-August 1893; a short story, *Mélancolique Villégiature de
Madame de Breyves*, was in the September number; and several
of another group of six sketches, which did not appear till
December 1893, were written before this September. The greater
part of what was to be *Les Plaisirs et les Jours* was therefore
already in existence by September 1893; and towards the end of
the month, encouraged by his year's reprieve from the horrors
of earning a living, Proust began to plan their publication in
volume form. He mentioned the idea to Mme Lemaire a few days
after Willie Heath's death on 3 October; and to his delight she
offered—or consented—to illustrate the book with the execrable
drawings and brushwork which would, he hoped, ensure its
success in fashionable circles. He immediately approached Heath's
family for permission to dedicate his volume to his dead friend:
'they seemed quite pleased with the suggestion,' he wrote to Billy
early in November, but a further application to Aubert's parents,
to ask that Edgar's name might be coupled with Willie's, came to
nothing.

Any attempt to distinguish autobiographical elements in the
Revue Blanche sketches must be made with caution. As a rule they
have the impersonal air of literary exercises, and there is little of
the special feeling which in Proust marks personal experience. The
love incidents—nearly all the sketches are about love—are
derivative from the contemporary high-society fiction of France
and Bourget, and contain almost nothing which can be linked
with Proust's emotional life at this time. Proust sometimes tells

his story from the heroine's point of view; but this well-worn device, used by so many heterosexual authors, need not necessarily be interpreted here as 'transposition'—the use, that is, of homosexual material in a heterosexual context. If the heroines were really Proust himself, they would be more alive; if their lovers were based on young men loved by Proust, they too would be less dull and conventional. Three pieces, however, share a similar and thoroughly Proustian theme, the crystallisation of love for an absent person. *Présence réelle* is set in the landscapes of the Engadine which Proust visited with Louis de la Salle, and is told in the first person; but not even the sex of the vague, faraway loved one is revealed. In *Rêve* the narrator dreams he is making love at Trouville with a Mme Dorothy B——, to whom he is indifferent in waking life, and on waking finds he is in love with her. In *Mélancolique Villégiature de Madame de Breyves*, which is dedicated to Mme Howland but was written before the visit to Saint-Moritz, the heroine is consumed with a passion for an insignificant nobleman whom she has met only once and then disliked. Perhaps this repetition of subject conceals some real experience; but perhaps Proust was merely experimenting in variations on a theme that interested him intellectually and instinctively.

Another sketch, the brief *Avant la nuit*, which Proust discreetly refrained from reprinting in *Les Plaisirs et les Jours*, concerns a situation that reappears in the Françoise episode of *Jean Santeuil*, in Swann's jealousy of Odette's past, and in the Narrator's life with Albertine. The heroine confesses to her secretly horrified lover, who tells the story, that she has had homosexual affairs with other women. Here, at least, is a possible instance of transposition; though whether the underlying circumstance is real or imagined, and whether Proust is confessing to a young man or a young man confessing to Proust, it would be hard to say. But *Avant la nuit* is also, with one exception, the first reference to the theme of Lesbianism which is of such importance in both *Jean Santeuil* and *A la Recherche*. It is often supposed that in *A la Recherche* the loves of Gomorrah are nothing but transpositions of the loves of Sodom. But if, as can be shown, the character of Albertine is based not only on transposition but also, and primarily, on Proust's affairs over a period of twenty years with a number of young women, it may well be that his painful interest in Lesbianism was likewise founded on real experience.[1]

It was perhaps in the winter of 1893-94 that Proust frequented the Saturdays of the great Parnassian Heredia at 11 *bis* Rue Balzac. Guests had the choice of two rooms: their host's study, full of poets and cigar-smoke, and the drawing-room, which Proust preferred, where Heredia's three lovely daughters, Hélène, Louise and Marie, were surrounded by a group of admiring young men. He met there Pierre Louÿs (who married Louise and ill-treated her), the symbolist Henri de Regnier, thirty years old, with a monocle and long drooping moustaches (who married Marie), and possibly André Gide, whom he might also have met with Paul Valéry and the painter Maurice Denis at the Finalys' in the winter of 1892. In parody of her father's campaign for election to the Académie Française Marie organised a secret society of her friends known as the Académie Canaque, which might be roughly translated as 'the Cannibal Academy'. She was Queen of the Academy, Proust was Perpetual Secretary, with the task of calling the meetings and keeping the minutes, and members included Pierre Louÿs, Regnier, Paul Valéry, Fernand Gregh, Léon Blum, the economist and banker Raphael Georges Lévy, the poet Ferdinand Hérold, and the young politicians Philippe and Daniel Berthelot. The formal speech of thanks for

[1] If this is so, then the experience of the confession must be looked for in the years before *Avant la nuit* was written; and indeed there seems to be little later evidence of Proust's acquaintance with Lesbians before an advanced stage in the composition of *A la Recherche*. There are a few slight and dubious indications that this early experience, if it occurred, may have been connected with Marie Finaly. There is a single short reference to female homosexuality in Proust's work before *Avant la nuit*, in the short story *Violante, ou la Mondanité*, in which the heroine is unsuccessfully assaulted by a Lesbian. *Violante* was published in *Le Banquet* in February 1893; and since it is perhaps the most mature of the *Le Banquet* pieces, it can hardly have been written before Proust's visit to the Finalys in August 1892. Violante is a young girl who is led astray from the life of the spirit and the imagination by a love of society; and although in this respect the character undoubtedly reflects Proust's own feelings of guilt, we have found him later accusing Marie Finaly of having taken the same wrong path. Perhaps, then, Violante resembles Marie Finaly in still other ways. Marie was the first original of Albertine; as her brother Horace was an original of Bloch, she may also have had some resemblance to Bloch's Lesbian sisters; and she may have activated the theme of the Proustian hero's jealousy of Lesbian infidelity which begins in *Avant la nuit* and ends in *Albertine Disparue*.

newly elected members which was a feature of the senior institution was replaced by a silent series of artistic and horrible grimaces; and it was unanimously agreed that the inaugural address of Paul Valéry was the finest ever seen in the Cannibal Academy. The members were bound by a pact of mutual assistance—'I trust I may never have reason to repent that I never joined,' remarked Robert de Billy many years later. The Academy soon dissolved; but Proust continued ever after to address Marie as 'My Queen'.

In November 1893 Proust devised a means of continuing his career in the *Revue Blanche*, of opening a new field in his writing, and of regaining the favour of the ever-ruffled Montesquiou. He would write a series of critical essays, and inaugurate it with an article entitled, with mingled paradox, irony and adulation, *La Simplicité de M. de Montesquiou*. Count Robert thought the plan excellent. No one had ever written a full-dress article on him before, and yes, Marcel was perfectly right: people considered his poetry obscure and excessively refined, but it was, in fact, divinely simple. Besides, if published in time, the article would serve as advance publicity for his new volume, *Le Chef des Odeurs Suaves*, due to appear in January 1894. Proust self-sacrificingly begged Natanson to substitute his essay for the six sketches in the December *Revue Blanche*; but the reluctant editor first refused, then consented, and then refused again. Now there would be no room even in the January number: Montesquiou and his simplicity would have to wait till February. As a last resort Proust approached Mme Straus's friend Louis Ganderax, who was about to revive the conservative *Revue de Paris* as a rival to the still more conservative *Revue des Deux Mondes*; but Ganderax would not bite, and now even the February *Revue Blanche* was full. *La Simplicité de M. de Montesquiou* did not appear till sixty years later, in *Contre Sainte-Beuve*.[1] Its theme, which perhaps explains the equal but opposite intransigences of Natanson and Ganderax, is that of Proust's first flattering letter to the count: Montesquiou, he maintains, is not an 1890s decadent but a seventeenth-century classic, and resembles Corneille (which is absurd) just as Baudelaire resembles Racine (which is very true).

With all his efforts Proust had succeeded only in barring against himself the doors of the *Revue Blanche*—in which he

[1] *Contre Sainte-Beuve*, 430-5.

appeared only once more, in 1896—and in aggrieving Montesquiou, who was never the man to take good intentions for good
deeds. "Your conceptions invariably result in abortions," the
count acidly remarked. Perhaps he was still nettled by a request
which Proust had made in the course of the *Revue Blanche*
negotiations. By December 1893 Proust was receiving invitations
from the Princesse de Wagram and her sister the Duchesse de
Gramont: this was a distinct upward step, though still far from
the top, for both these ladies had only been Rothschilds before
their marriages, and it was felt that their husbands had been a
little declassed by marrying outside the nobility into non-Aryan
money. Relying on these invitations and the credit of his still
unrejected article, he begged Montesquiou with would-be tact
'to be so kind, if you are there too, as to point out to me a few
of the ladies in whose circles your name is most frequently
mentioned—Comtesse Greffulhe, or the Princesse de Léon, for
instance'. In this he made two errors, one of greed and one of
social ignorance. Mme Greffulhe, Montesquiou's beloved cousin,
was perhaps the most distinguished lady in the whole of Parisian
society, and an introduction to her could only be the reward of
far higher merit than dear Marcel had yet shown. As for the
'Princesse de Léon', he should have known that since the death
of her father-in-law on the previous 6 August her correct title
was the Duchesse de Rohan. Proust was duly snubbed, and bided
his time; but he did not fail to note this curious feature in the
natural history of titled persons. Several of the French ducal
families had a repertoire of princely titles available for their heirs,
pending their succession to the dukedom; and when the future
Duchesse de Guermantes first appears in the early years of her
marriage, she is known as the Princesse des Laumes.

Meanwhile Montesquiou was arranging his own publicity. On
the afternoon of 17 January 1894, at the Théâtre de la Bodinière,
he gave a lecture on the poetry of Marceline Desbordes-Valmore,
whom he called 'the Christian Sappho'. He had read her poems
for the first time at twilight on a dusty road near Cannes, when
his adored Pauline de Montesquiou, his brother Gontran's wife,
was dying; and bursting into tears he had vowed to rescue the
poetess from undeserved neglect. 'I venture to assert,' he wrote
with some truth, 'that she owes her posthumous fame—the only
fame that really counts—to the incessant efforts that followed my

vow.' So Montesquiou began the movement which restored her to her rightful position as one of the most interesting lesser poets among the French romantics. Her lines

> *Je veux aller mourir aux lieux où je suis née;*
> *Le tombeau d'Albertine est près de mon berceau ...*

may well have helped in suggesting to Proust the name of his heroine and part of the subject of his novel. But the lecture was also a move in a campaign to save Montesquiou himself from neglect: 'the auditorium was a mosaic of celebrities,' he boasted. Everyone expected the count to appear in his famous green dress-coat, with one of his pink Liberty cravats. But to the astonishment of all he wore a customary suit of solemn black and looked, Proust thought, like a solicitor's clerk. He discreetly mentioned his surprise. "The feeling I had decided to arouse," Montesquiou magnificently explained, "was a disappointed expectation of the ridiculous."

In February, when his article was finally rejected, Proust invented another plan for recovering favour with Montesquiou. Whether or not the count last year had unsuccessfully tempted Proust, Proust now to his extreme annoyance tempted him. At the house of Comte Henri de Saussine, a dilettante composer and musical critic,[1] he had met a nineteen-year-old pianist named Léon Delafosse. The young virtuoso had given his first recital at the age of seven, had won a first prize at the Conservatoire when he was thirteen, and was now in search of a wealthy patron. Who could be more suitable than Montesquiou? By way of preparing the ground Delafosse set three of the *Chauves-Souris* poems to music[2]; on 10 February Proust notified Montesquiou of the fact; and at last, on 15 March, the two tempters were permitted to bring their homage to the Pavillon Montesquiou at Versailles. "Do let me turn the music while he sings," entreated Proust; but Montesquiou smelt a rat. It so happened, he announced, that only

[1] His salon at 14 Rue Saint-Guillaume is described in the sketch '*Éventail*' in *Les Plaisirs et les Jours*, 87-91

[2] Similarly Morel asks the Narrator if he knows of 'any poet with a big position among the nobs', takes a note of a suitable name, and writes that he is a fanatical admirer of his works, has set one of his sonnets to music, and would like him to arrange a performance at Comtesse——'s. But the outcome is different, for 'the poet took offence and did not answer his letter'. (Cf. II, 265-6).

one kind of music would suit his mood that afternoon, namely, the barrel-organ; and he carried them off to the nearby fair at Viroflay, where they wandered dejectedly among the booths, while the diabolical count listened in pretended ecstasy to the strains of the hurdy-gurdy. Soon the kind-hearted Yturri felt Mossou le Connte had gone far enough: "You're always the same, why don't you try to be nice to people!" he whispered crossly. So they returned, and Montesquiou, finding that the young man 'played with incomparable virtuosity, though he sang with the voice of a cat run over by a cab', decided the recital had been intended not as a practical joke but as a sincere tribute to his genius. He took Delafosse into his favour: "I venture to believe that your settings of my poems will last as long as the poems themselves," he prophesied sublimely and, alas, truly. A few days later he visited Delafosse and his doting mother in their huge, gloomy apartment near the Rue d'Antin, with its dining-room adorned only with a seating-plan of the Salle Érard and a grand-piano, 'like an ebony dolmen,' said Montesquiou, 'gleaming with the blackened blood of a paying public'. On 27 April, when Delafosse gave his opening recital at the Salle Érard, many of Montesquiou's friends were in the audience; and the critic from *Le Ménestrel* wrote: 'Simplicity, charm, elegance and distinction are the chief qualities of this brilliant young virtuoso.'

Léon Delafosse was a thin, vain, ambitious, blond young man, with icy blue eyes and diaphanously pale, supernaturally beautiful features. Proust had nicknamed him 'the Angel'. "How annoying it would be not to be famous," Delafosse would say—"an annoyance which he has frequently experienced since I threw him over," said Montesquiou after their subsequent breach. When he was playing, 'this little face, with its silly laugh, became trans-figured with superhuman beauty, and took on the pallor and remoteness of death'; but once the music stopped, Montesquiou almost disliked him. "Try to ensure," he would warn him, "that my love for your art may always prevail over my distaste for your person." The young pianist was clearly an important original of Charlie Morel. But the model for the suffering and moral ruin brought upon Charlus by Morel came from Baron Doasan and his Polish violinist, not from the relationship between Montes-quiou and Delafosse. Montesquiou loved in his protégés only himself as tyrant, impresario, Maecenas and Svengali; and we shall see him ending his attachment to Delafosse at a time of his own choosing, without regret, with delight in vengeance.

Meanwhile, however, Count Robert was in the first enthusiastic stage of a new friendship. 'For three years,' he afterwards confessed, 'Delafosse became part of my life.' Proust waited in vain for his reward: the cunning Montesquiou had swallowed the bait and rejected the hook. By way of a reminder he sent Delafosse to the count on 24 March with yet another angel, a rather battered plaster one from an eighteenth-century crêche. 'For those who have ears I am sure he can sing with the same witty voice as our little musician. His tailcoat reveals his wings by its complete absence. His little nose is damaged, but even if it were all there I'm afraid it wouldn't have the expressive dryness, the passionate thinness, the eloquent concision of the nose of our musician.' But Montesquiou was furious: '*our* little musician', indeed!—and at Mme Lemaire's Tuesday on 27 March he pointedly refrained from speaking to the giver of angels. On 17 April Proust tried again. He went straight from one of his lessons for the *licence ès lettres* to the private view of the Marie Antoinette exhibition at the Sedelmayer Gallery, hoping to see Montesquiou 'with one or two ladies who are themselves works of art'; but he arrived too late, when everyone had left except the proprietors, from whose angry glares he became aware that it was long past closing-time. When he first saw Comtesse Greffulhe, early in May, it was by his own efforts. She was at the Princesse de Wagram's, wearing a coiffure of mauve cattleyas, which gave her 'a somehow Polynesian grace'; but he did not dare ask to be presented to her. She was the most beautiful woman he had ever seen; he asked Montesquiou to tell her so; and the count realised that if he did not give this determined young man the introduction he craved for, someone or other soon would.

He was now preparing at the Pavillon Montesquiou the first of the magnificent fêtes which for the next two decades were to be considered among the most brilliant events of the social year. In theory it was in honour of Sarah Bernhardt and her temporary protégé, a Breton sailor named Yann Nibor who was to sing some original verses about storms and albatrosses. But the count saw his chance to support other, even more deserving causes. His own poems and those of Marceline Desbordes-Valmore, recited by Mlles Bartet and Reichenberg from the Comédie Française,

figured still more prominently in the programme; and when
Delafosse played everyone knew that the real guest of honour
was the Angel. As one of the many newspaper accounts put it,
whether innocently or not, 'M. Delafosse bore on his forehead the
kiss of M. de Montesquiou's Muse.' Round the temporary stage
in the garden, the Ephemeral Theatre as Montesquiou called it in
the printed programme, Proust now met many of the most
exclusive ladies of the Faubourg Saint-Germain: Comtesse Rosa
de FitzJames, for whom Mme de Chevigné had left him standing
in the Avenue Gabriel two years before, Comtesse Aimery de la
Rochefoucauld, Comtesse Potocka, Comtesse Mélanie de
Pourtalès, Marquise d' Hervey de Saint-Denis, and Comtesse
Greffulhe herself. Mme Greffulhe wore a mauve gown, the colour
of her favourite cattleyas (a preference which Proust later,
perhaps not without malice, transferred to Odette); and her
superb eyes shone, 'like black fireflies,' said Montesquiou, through
a veil to match. Proust was made to work for his introductions.
All afternoon he feverishly took notes on the ladies' dresses,
which he begged each of the lovely wearers to read and correct;
and after the party he hurried to the office of *Le Gaulois* with an
article ('*A Literary Fête at Versailles*') for next day's gossip
column. In the morning, alas, he found his article ruthlessly cut:
Mme Potocka was there, but stripped of her dress; Mme Howland
was gone altogether; and from the sentence which modestly began
'Among others present', the name of M. Marcel Proust had been
deleted.

The fête of 30 May 1894 was one of the crucial events of
Proust's youth. At last he had met several of the most brilliant
hostesses of the inner Faubourg Saint-Germain, including the
lady who was to supply important elements of both the Duchesse
and the Princesse de Guermantes. At breakfast next morning they
would read his appreciative account of their beauty and their
clothes; soon their invitation-cards would be stuck in the dining-
room mirror at 9 Boulevard Malesherbes. And he had seen them
gathered to do acquiescent homage to the latest homosexual
relationship of his powerful friend and sponsor. In the next few
months Proust would simultaneously reach the summit of the
Guermantes Way, and go down into the valley of the Cities of
the Plain.

Chapter 10

THE GUERMANTES WAY

FOR an unbroken period of four years, until he was turned away by growing ill-health, the stresses of the Dreyfus Case, and disillusion with the heartlessness of the Guermantes world, Proust moved with manifold delight in the high society of the Faubourg Saint-Germain. In his novel the social experiences of these years were distilled into three representative functions, the afternoon at Mme de Villeparisis's, the dinner at the Duchesse de Guermantes's, and the Princesse de Guermantes's soirée. The biographer, similarly, must abandon for the space of one chapter the chronological narrative of days and months; and conversely, in the description of the persons and groups Proust then encountered, he must analyse the chemical compounds of Proust's imagination into the human elements from which they were formed.

The agate-eyed Comtesse Élisabeth Greffulhe, when Proust met her at Montesquiou's Delafosse fête, was aged thirty-four. She was the eldest daughter of the Franco-Belgian Prince Joseph de Caraman-Chimay and his wife Marie de Montesquiou, Robert de Montesquiou's aunt: Count Robert was therefore her cousin, just as Charlus was the Duchesse de Guermantes's.[1] Her family was short of money, and had been forced to sell the ancestral Hôtel de Chimay on the Quai Malaquais and to marry into wealth. Her brother, now himself Prince Joseph after their father's death in 1892, had become the husband of an American heiress, Clara Ward, in 1890; but the princess was soon to raise a deplorable scandal by her affair with Jancsi Rigo, the swarthy, pockmarked violinist in Boldi's gipsy orchestra at Maxim's, with whom she eloped in 1896: "my dishonoured cousin Clara de Chimay, who has left her husband," says Charlus.[2] Élisabeth's marriage in 1878 to the fabulously wealthy Comte Henri Greffulhe was considered far more satisfactory.

[1] "I've got furniture that came to Basin from the Montesquious," says the Duchesse de Guermantes (I, 339). [2] I, 764

Her husband belonged to a Belgian banking family naturalised in France, whose nobility, like the Caraman-Chimays' princedom, dated only from the Restoration. His great-aunt Cordélia Greffulhe, wife of the Maréchal de Castellane, had been a mistress of Chateaubriand; and his father Charles Greffulhe, in collaboration with Charles Laffitte (a relative of Baron Doasan), was one of the original founders of the Jockey Club. Despite the comparative newness of his title, Comte Greffulhe had a leading position in society, and was the chief original of the Duc de Guermantes.

He was a tall, broad-shouldered man, with a yellow beard and an air of majesty and suppressed rage, which made Blanche compare him to a king in a pack of cards, while others likened him to Jove the Thunderer.[1] "He displaces more air than any ordinary mortal," said Barrès. His lordly affability was never more strikingly displayed than when he made the round of his electors, presenting them according to social position with a gold watch or a brace of pheasants from his château at Boisboudran. For many years he represented Melun in the Chamber of Deputies; similarly, the Duc de Guermantes was the member for Méséglise. Like the Duc, Comte Greffulhe was a tyrannical and unfaithful husband, overfond of the society of persons whom the countess disdainfully called 'the little ladies who make such good mattresses'. Once, many years later, an imprudent guest who felt sure that the still-dazzling Mme Greffulhe must be the mistress, and therefore mistook the ugly lady at the far end of the room for the wife, remarked feelingly to the countess: "Ah, Madame, now I've seen you, how I do sympathise with the count!" On another occasion Comte Greffulhe sent his valet to arrange a rendezvous with the beautiful actress Mlle Marsy. "Well, did you see her?" "Yes, Monsieur le Comte, she was sitting with the Prince de Sagan, while he had a footbath." "It's too bad," cried the outraged nobleman, in the words of the Duc de Guermantes complaining of Swann's Dreyfusism, "why, the man dines with us!" But his infidelities did not prevent him being jealous, though entirely without cause; and the brevity of his wife's appearances in society, which was often ascribed to hauteur, was in fact due to his insistence on her being home by eleven-thirty. He did not

[1] The Narrator frequently borrows this comparison for the Duc (e.g. II, 284, 683; III, 42, 1020).

care for Montesquiou and his friends, who descended on his Villa
La Case at Dieppe every September as soon as he left for the
shooting-season at Boisboudran. "They're a lot of Japs," he said,
meaning aesthetes.

Comtesse Greffulhe (the *gratin* pronounced the name
Greffeuille) was considered the supreme society beauty of her
time. As she sailed rapidly through a drawing-room the guests
could be heard murmuring: "Which way did she go? Did you
see her?" She had chestnut hair and dark mineral eyes, like agates
or topazes:

> '*Comtesse Greffulhe*
> *Is two dark glances wrapped in tulle,*'

wrote Montesquiou; but her features, though delicately chiselled,
were somewhat irregular, with a hint of wildness. She was fully
conscious of the uniqueness of her looks, but despaired of finding
an artist to do them justice: "However beautiful one is, there are
days when one looks hideous, and that's when they paint one!"
she exclaimed. She was sculpted by Falguière ("the head wasn't
very good, so I threw it away, but I've kept the shoulders"),
etched and pastelled by Helleu (an original of Elstir), and painted
by Laszlo, Hébert and other society portraitists. But only a poet
or a camera, she thought, could reproduce the loveliness she saw
reflected in her mirror or in the eyes of beholders. She was
particularly gratified, therefore, by a sonnet of Montesquiou
which ended: 'Fair lily, your black pistils are your eyes.' Turning
to her sister (the favourite lady-in-waiting of Queen Elisabeth of
Belgium), she remarked: "Quite a good likeness, Ghislaine, don't
you think?" and added to Montesquiou: "Only you and the sun
really understand me!" "I was glad she put me first," said
Montesquiou afterwards.

The countess and her cousin Count Robert were united by
mutual admiration and genuine affection: "She's the only person
with whom I have never succeeded in quarrelling," he would say.
Montesquiou had a great respect for her intelligence, though in
his belief she never read a book (Edmond de Goncourt thought
her extremely well-read, but that was because she talked to him
about his own novels), and picked up her knowledge through
conversation with learned guests. Like the Duchesse de Guermantes she invited scientists to dinner in her later years; and she

would be heard to remark afterwards: "Did you know that even iron suffers from fatigue?" She took a public interest in the arts, especially in music. She wrote a one-act play for a house-party at Boisboudran, and a book of confessions in which she showed such keen appreciation of her own beauty that Goncourt advised her not to publish.

As we have seen, many features of the Duchesse de Guermantes —her corn-coloured hair and cornflower eyes, her rasping voice. something of her wit, her style of dress, the Narrator's early love for her—derived from Mme de Chevigné. Most of the remainder —including her supreme position in society, her relations with her husband, her cousinship with Charlus-Montesquiou—came from Mme Greffulhe. She had the chiming silvery laugh of the Duchesse: "Mme Greffulhe's laugh sounds like the carillon at Bruges," said Proust, at a later time when he had heard both. Just as the Duc and Duchesse lived in the same house as Mme de Villeparisis—shared also by the Narrator's family and the tailor Jupien—so Comte Greffulhe dwelt in symbiosis at 8 Rue d'Astorg with his widowed mother (born a La Rochefoucauld) and his sisters, the Marquise de l'Aigle and the Princesse d'Arenberg (the wife of Mme Straus's friend, original of the Prince d'Agrigente). Duc Agénor de Gramont playfully called their house Vatican City. Like the Duchesse, Comtesse Greffulhe was famous for the exclusive coterie of her men-friends. Chief of them all was Charles Haas, the original of Swann, now, sixteen years after her marriage, a sick and ageing man. The others, some of whom were among the band of club-men who spent their afternoons with Mme de Chevigné, included the Marquis du Lau, Comte Costa de Beauregard, Comte Albert de Mun, Comte Louis de Turenne and Marquis Henri de Breteuil. The latter pair together made up Hannibal (Babal) de Bréauté. The good-natured but stupid Turenne had blue eyes and a yellow complexion, and wore Bréauté's monocle, 'which carried, glued to the other side, an infinitesimal gaze, swarming with affability, and never ceasing to beam at the height of the ceiling, the magnificence of the reception, the interestingness of the programme and the quality of the refreshments'.[1] Like Bréauté he was thought a connoisseur of objects of art, and loved to give advice with an air of expert knowledge on things he knew nothing whatever about:

[1] I, 327

the marriages he recommended always failed, the interior decorations looked hideous, and the investments immediately slumped. Breteuil, too, was a would-be connoisseur of art. Like Turenne and Haas he was an intimate friend of Edward VII as Prince of Wales; he had married an American heiress, Miss Garner, and was often to be seen at Sandringham shoots or Windsor Castle house-parties. He was witty and deformed, and once in *A la Recherche* Proust maliciously refers to him as Quasimodo de Breteuil, giving him the name of the Hunchback of Notre Dame.[1] The Marquis was present at the famous dinner-party given by Mme Greffulhe in 1910 to Edward VII and Queen Alexandra, at which the only other guest was the fashionable painter Detaille. In *Le Côté de Guermantes* this dinner is given by the Duchesse de Guermantes, and is quoted as a supreme example of her unconventionality[2]; but in real life the choice of guests was the King's, for he had been assured by experts in England that M. Detaille was the greatest living French painter.

Another member of the Greffulhe coterie, a particular friend of Charles Haas (with whom he appears in Tissot's painting) and of the Prince de Sagan, and a probable original of General de Froberville, was the boastful, loud-voiced and opportunist General Marquis de Galliffet. He wore a silver plate in his abdomen, the relic of a wound received at the Battle of Puebla in the Mexican war of 1863—no doubt Proust was thinking of this when he compared Froberville's monocle to 'a shell-splinter, a monstrous wound which it was splendid to have acquired, but indecent to exhibit'.[3] Curiosity as to the real dimensions of this silver plate, which some said was no larger than a twenty-franc piece, while others alleged it was a good six inches across, was thought to play some part in the General's enormous success with society ladies. He had married a Laffitte, a relative of Baron Doasan and Mme Aubernon; and when the priest in his nuptial address used the unfortunate words "When the inevitable hour of separation comes", the wedding-guests burst out laughing. Soon, when that inevitable hour came, Mme de Galliffet was living near her friend the Princesse de Sagan in the Manoir des Roches at Trouville, where Proust saw them in 1891, and receiving frequent visits from the Prince of Wales. Once the Prince de Sagan gave

[1] III, 587   [2] II, 430
[3] I, 326

a dinner to Mme de Chevigné's heroine, the Grand-Duchess Wladimir, and Galliffet. "Your Highness is sitting between the two biggest cuckolds in Europe," announced the Prince; but his remark was coldly received. The General had led the famous cavalry charge at Sedan, and taken part in the savage suppression of the Commune just before Proust's birth. Proust admired him for his wit, of which perhaps the best example is a silent one: when riding one afternoon in the Bois Galliffet met the unfrocked priest Monsignor Bauer, an acquaintance from Second Empire days, when he was the Empress Eugénie's chaplain. Mgr Bauer politely raised his hat; and the General with equal politeness made the sign of priestly benediction.

In several respects, however, Mme Greffulhe resembled not only the Duchesse, but the Duchesse's cousin, the Princesse de Guermantes. Her topaz eyes and statuesque beauty are given to the Princesse; so is her flamboyant style of dress, in which Mme Greffulhe contrasted with the sobriety of Mme de Chevigné as did the Princesse with the Duchesse. A characteristic anecdote of Comtesse Greffulhe is told of the Princesse de Guermantes in a rejected passage of *Sodome et Gomorrhe*.[1] "I shall know I've lost my beauty when people stop turning to stare at me in the street," the Comtesse told Mme Standish; and Mme Standish replied: "Never fear, my dear, so long as you dress as you do, people will always turn and stare!" The famous scene of the Princesse de Guermantes's box at the Opéra in *Le Côté de Guermantes* actually occurred, as we shall see, in May 1912: here the Princesse represents Mme Greffulhe, and the Duchesse Mme Standish. Elstir's portrait of the Princesse with the crescent moon of Diana in her hair[2] was a very bad painting of Mme Greffulhe by Hébert.[3] The Princesse's attitude in the Dreyfus Case was shared, as will be shown later, by Mme Greffulhe; and her chaste but pronounced affection for her cousin Montesquiou no doubt suggested the Princesse's unhappy passion for Charlus.

A later but equally important original of the Princesse was Comtesse Jean (Dolly) de Castellane, a half-sister of Boson de

---

[1] II, 1185   [2] II, 1183

[3] M. de Norpois at Mme de Villeparisis's, when he hears the Narrator declaring his admiration for Elstir's *Bunch of Radishes*, cries: "If you call that clever little sketch a masterpiece, what words will you have left for Hébert's *Virgin*?" (II, 223).

Talleyrand-Périgord, Prince de Sagan. Just as the Princesse de Guermantes was a Bavarian royalty, so Comtesse Dolly had married Karl Egon, Prince von Fürstenberg (the former lover of Laure Hayman), and had spent her youth in a German court. It was not till 1898, after her first husband's death, that she married Comte Jean de Castellane, her cousin and nephew, and became, in rivalry to Mme Greffulhe, one of the rulers of Parisian society. She was majestic, beautiful and Teutonic, and had retained the grand manner of a German princess. People called her 'Gräfin Jean', and she looked, says André Germain, 'as if she'd always just come back from a visit to Wotan'. The jealous Mme Greffulhe affected to confuse her with her less dazzling sister-in-law, and once, when Montesquiou was lamenting her absence from one of his fêtes ("She said she'd been asked to a shooting-party at Mme Porgès's, so I told her that there was some houses where it was absolutely inexcusable to go shooting, unless it was to shoot one's hostess!"), she enquired devastatingly "*Which* Mme de Castellane?"

For the feudal devotion of the Prince de Guermantes to questions of birth and etiquette, the 'almost fossil rigidity of his aristocratic prejudices' ("His ideas are out of this world," said the Duchesse),[1] Proust thought of Comte Aimery de La Rochefoucauld, whose extreme regard for precedence had caused him to be nicknamed 'Place-at-table'. Of a girl who had married beneath her for love he remarked: "A few nights of passion, and then a whole lifetime at the wrong end of the table." It was exceedingly important not to put Comte Aimery at the wrong end of the table: he was liable, if so insulted, to call for his carriage immediately after dinner; and once he was heard to enquire in a loud voice: "Does one get a helping of *everything* where I'm sitting?" Of the Luynes family, into which his aunt the Duchesse Yolande de Luynes had married, he observed: "They were mere nobodies in the year 1000."[2] When the Comtesse de Chabrillan asked whose was a portrait on his drawing-room wall, he replied: "That is Henry the Fourth, madam." "Really, I should never have recognised him." "I refer, Madam, to Henry, the Fourth

[1] II, 570, 523

[2] M. de Charles makes similar remarks about the Luynes family: "I ask you—a mere Alberti, who didn't manage to scrape the mud off his feet until Louis XIII!" (III, 233).

Duc de La Rochefoucauld." And the refusal of the Prince de Guermantes to greet Mme ('Tiny') de Hunolstein at the foot of his stairs[1] may be compared to Comte Aimery's advice to a friend on the correct manner to receive a certain bishop. "When His Grace came to our house my wife saw him out as far as the drawing-room door, and I took him to the front door. So I think *your* wife had better see him as far as the lobby, and *you'd* better take him right out into the street!" He, too, like the Prince de Guermantes, had a Bavarian princely title, though this was not granted till 1909. The incident of the Duc de Guermantes's insistence on attending the fancy-dress ball, in spite of repeated warnings from the Ladies with the Walking-sticks that poor 'Mama' d'Osmond is at death's door, was borrowed by Proust (with the addition of Mme Straus's red shoes) from an anecdote of Montesquiou's about his cousin Aimery. Montesquiou's brother Gontran was dying, but Comte Aimery felt unable to give up his plans for the evening. He was overtaken by a tactless informant, who cried "Gontran's dead!"; whereupon Comte Aimery merely pushed his wife (who was dressed as a queen-bee) up the steps, declared, in the Duc de Guermantes's very words, "People exaggerate!" and fled majestically into the ball.[2] Comte Aimery's son Gabriel, whom Proust met a few years later, was one of the many originals of Saint-Loup.

Other hints for various Guermantes's came from the Talley-rand-Périgord and Castellane families, who were closely related to one another, and more distantly to the Greffulhes. It is clear not only that Proust used individual Talleyrands and Castellanes in the creation of his characters, but that their interrelationships served decisively as a model for the general structure of the Guermantes family. Boson de Talleyrand-Périgord, Prince de Sagan, supplied elements both to the Duc de Guermantes and Charlus; he was half-brother to Comtesse Jean de Castellane, whose affinities with the Princesse de Guermantes have just been noted; he was a cousin of the Comtesse de Beaulaincourt, the chief original of Mme de Villeparisis; and Boni de Castellane, his nephew and heir, was an early original of the Duc de Guermantes's nephew and Mme de Villeparisis's great-nephew, Saint-Loup.

The Prince de Sagan, now in his sixties, was generally con-sidered the most consummate *grand seigneur* and arbiter of

[1] II, 530   [2] Cf. II, 725

elegance of his time. He was unintelligent and devoid of taste except in clothes; but as he had now been separated from his wealthy wife for fifteen years, he could no longer afford the best tailors, and the extraordinary distinction of his appearance came largely from his personal presence. The Prince frequented the foyer of the Comédie-Française, then a fashionable resort, adorned with antique furniture and old prints which made it look like Louis de Turenne's drawing-room. He stood astride in his velvet-collared greatcoat with white rose button-hole, twirling his monocle on a sensationally broad black ribbon, with his friends Robert de FitzJames, General de Galliffet, Charles Haas and Turenne; and after the performance they would depart severally with the actresses of the evening, with Mlle Reichenberg or Mlle Marsy. He lived in bachelor rooms over the Club in the Rue Royale, and with Charles Haas was a favourite of old Isabella, the flower-seller outside the Café Anglais. "You're a real gentleman," she told Boni de Castellane after Haas's death, "there's only you and the Prince de Sagan left of your sort, now Monsieur Haas has gone." His archaic Christian name, Boson, helped by its similar sound to give a contemporary ring to that of the Duc de Guermantes, which was borrowed from Basin, the eleventh-century Count of Illiers. But in his tragic last days the Prince came to resemble the fallen Baron de Charlus. In 1908 he had a paralytic stroke, and was willy-nilly taken back by the wife he had not seen since the 1880s. Looking like an aged, white-maned lion, he was pushed about in a wheel-chair, with bent head and dribbling mouth, as was Charlus by Jupien; he bowed, like Charlus, to all the wrong people, clutched the arms of his chair in a vain effort to rise, and mumbled "Delighted, I'm sure—delighted, I'm sure."

The Princesse de Sagan his wife, born Jeanne-Marguerite Seillière, came of a rich, *parvenu* family of Second Empire barons, related, like Mme de Galliffet, to Mme Aubernon and Baron Doasan. She spent the summer at her Villa Persane at Trouville and was to be seen walking on the front with her negro page, thus serving as a model for the Princesse de Luxembourg at Balbec. She gave a famous ball in 1885 at which all the guests—including Charles Haas, the Chevignés, Turenne, and the rest of the Guermantes set—were dressed as animals, and the whole of the Opéra ballet emerged from an enormous beehive. The Duchesse de Guermantes refers to her as 'my aunt Sagan', and Françoise, with her love of unsafe grammatical analogies, as 'the Sagante'.[1]

The Prince de Sagan's nephew, Boni de Castellane, was now and for the next twelve years the most brilliant young man in Parisian society. He had the golden hair, the dazzling pink complexion, the cold lapis-lazuli eyes, the flying monocle and darting movements, the tall, slim figure of Saint-Loup. His Rachel was Mlle Marsy, the actress, whom he had torn from the embraces of his admiring uncle Sagan and the furious Comte Greffulhe; like Saint-Loup he was blackballed at the Jockey Club, of which his mother's father, the Marquis de Juigné, had been vice-president for many years.

In 1895, when Boni's money was already growing short, he married an American millionaire heiress, Miss Anna Gould. She was short, thin and sallow, with a line of black hair down her spine—'like an Iroquois chieftainess,' people said; but Boni depilated, rouged and dressed her, and taught her to reply, when complimented on her appearance, "Nice of you to say so." Their monumental house in the Avenue du Bois was built to Boni's design, after the Petit Trianon at Versailles. "The staircase will be like the one at the Opéra, only bigger," she told enquirers. Boni went into politics as a royalist and anti-Semite; he gave receptions of a megalomaniac lavishness; but it seemed to some observers that he was riding for a fall. "You need to be used to it, if you're going to handle all that money," remarked Baron Alphonse de Rothschild. Later we shall have further glimpses of Proust's contact with Boni in the periods of his highest glory, his catastrophe and his pathetic, courageous sunset.

Boni de Castellane's great-aunt, Comtesse Sophie de Beaulaincourt, was the original of Mme de Villeparisis, the type of an old lady who has slowly and painfully regained a social position forfeited by the excesses of her youth. She was the daughter, born in 1818, of the Maréchal de Castellane and Comte Greffulhe's great-aunt Cordélia Greffulhe, who was the mistress of Comte Molé and of the great Chateaubriand: well might Mme de Villeparisis say "I remember M. Molé very well," and: "Chateaubriand often came to my father's house"![2] In 1836, under Louis

---

[1] II, 526, 207. Her ball is referred to ironically by Mme de Villeparisis in conversation with Bloch: "Is that what you'd call a great social solemnity?" she asks the Duchesse (II, 244).   [2] II, 192; I, 721

Philippe, she married the Marquis de Contades, whose descendant Vicomte Antoine de Contades was to become the husband of Marie de Benardaky's sister Nelly. Of one of her innumerable lovers Mme de Chevigné told Proust: "She ate him up, down to his last farm-rent." During the Second Empire she was the mistress of the Comte de Fleury, the French ambassador at St Petersburg—whose liaison with her suggested that of M. de Norpois with Mme de Villeparisis—and a friend of the Empress Eugénie and of Mérimée, a whole volume of whose letters are addressed to her. From the Comte de Coislin she had a son, whom she acknowledged and kept with her, despite the disapproval of the Faubourg. In 1859 she took her second but short-lived husband, the Comte de Beaulaincourt. Now, two generations after her wild youth, she was an ugly little old lady of seventy-six, with a purple face and big spectacles, like the aged Mme de Villeparisis seen at Venice by Mme Sazerat, whose father she had ruined; but she had succeeded, almost too late, in reconquering her position in society, and was visited by Princesse Mathilde, the ex-Empress Eugénie, and all the Faubourg. She lived in the Rue de Miromesnil, near Mme Straus, Mme de Chevigné and the Pouquets, and sat, wearing a black silk gown, a peasant-woman's bonnet and a white lace-edged apron, at a little desk piled high with paper petals and saucers of paint, making artificial flowers: "when you're no longer young, you have to find a hobby to keep you company," she told Edmond de Goncourt. The flowers were copies from nature, and bunches of roses and violets were sent for the purpose daily from her Château d'Acosta, near Princesse Mathilde's at Saint-Gratien. Proust made Mme de Villeparisis paint flowers, like Mme Lemaire: 'so that she wouldn't be *too* like Mme de Beaulaincourt,' he told Montesquiou in 1921. She watched her great-nephew Boni's career with a sardonic eye: "It's like dining in a red marble aquarium, with goldfish for footmen," she remarked after a visit to his Palais Rose at 45 Avenue du Bois; "and you should see Boni and his wife strutting up that staircase of theirs, with peacock-feathers stuck up their behinds!" She took a fancy to Proust and gave him valuable instruction, from her own unique knowledge, in the state of politics and society under Louis Philippe, Napoleon III and the young Third Republic.

In his account of a visit to Mme de Beaulaincourt (*Journal*, vol. 7, 155-7, 7 September 1887), Edmond de Goncourt wishes

'this witty old woman with her inexhaustible flow of talk' would
write her memoirs. She never did; and the Memoirs of Mme de
Villeparisis, and those of her equally fictitious sister Mme de
Beausergent, who was the Narrator's grandmother's favourite
author next to Mme de Sévigné, were both suggested by the
voluminous and rather boring *Mémoires* of the Comtesse de
Boigne, whose favourite nephew the Marquis d'Osmond[1] was a
friend of Proust's parents, whose great-nephew the Comte de
Maillé was his near neighbour in the Boulevard Malesherbes, and
whose niece the dowager Duchesse de Maillé, then in her
seventies, he often saw at the balls of the 1890s. "Mme de Beausergent, afterwards Mme d'Hazfeld, sister of Mme de Villeparisis,"
says Swann in the Goncourt *Journal* pastiche (III, 715); and the
sister of Mme de Beaulaincourt was, in fact, Comtesse Pauline de
Hatzfeldt.

Mme de Villeparisis's rival 'Alix', who attends her afternoon
receptions in the hope of stealing her guests, was Mme de
Chaponay: Proust characteristically mentions her by name,
together with Mme de Beaulaincourt, in juxtaposition with the
characters they suggested. Mme de Chaponay, like 'Alix', wore
her white hair piled high in Marie-Antoinette style, had the same
difficulty as Mme de Beaulaincourt, and for the same cause, in
recruiting her salon, and was famous for her social raids. But the
Christian name Alix came from Vicomtesse Alix de Janzé, who
was born (as the Narrator mentions of 'Alix') a Choiseul. Mme
de Janzé wrote a book on Alfred de Musset, and 'Alix' has written
one on Lamartine. She and Mme de Chaponay were the originals
of two of the 'Three Fates, with white, blue or red hair' who were
Mme de Villeparisis's friends and competitors: the third was Mme
de Blocqueville.[2]

---

[1] The Marquis d'Osmond appears in Mme de Cambremer's box at the
Opera as the charming young Marquis de Beausergent (II, 55), and again,
transformed by old age, at the Princesse de Guermantes's matinée (III, 938).
But Proust prefers to make the Narrator discover in *Le Temps Retrouvé* that
the favourite nephew for whom Mme de Beausergent wrote her memoirs
was none other than the Duc de Guermantes as a boy (III, 715, 717). In
Le Côté de Guermantes the Marquis d'Osmond (nicknamed 'Mama') is the
cousin of the Duc de Guermantes whose death, announced by the Ladies
with the Walking-sticks, does not prevent the Duc from taking the Duchesse
to the fancy-dress ball (II, 575).

[2] For the references in the foregoing paragraph cf. II, 202, 198, 197.

In real life Mme Blanche Leroi, who bows so coldly to poor Mme de Villeparisis and refuses to attend her salon,[1] was Mme Gaston (Clothilde) Legrand, *née* Fournes, known as 'Cloton' to the Faubourg. She was married to a wealthy owner of coal-mines —similarly Mme Leroi was the daughter of a timber-merchant.[2] Montesquiou owned her portrait, 'Mme Legrand returning from the races', by Mme Romaine Brooks. "Notice those romantic eyes glowing under her veil," he would say, "and how they are belied by the wryness of her mouth, embittered by chewing the cud of the vileness of humanity; in this painting one sees the fusion of defiant pride and compulsory diffidence!" As we have seen, the remark attributed to Mme Leroi—"My opinion of love? I make it, often, but never, never talk about it"[3]—was uttered by Laure Baignères to Mme Aubernon.

The *gratin* included persons who, without disgracing themselves openly like the poor Princesse Clara de Chimay, contrived to live a life as wild as Mme de Beaulaincourt's in a previous generation. One of the late arrivals at the Princesse de Guermantes's soirée is the Princesse d'Orvillers, in whom the Narrator recognises the lady with gentle blue eyes and opulent bosom who had made advances to him while pretending to look in a shop-window near his home. She appears many years later at the final matinée of the Princesse de Guermantes in *Le Temps Retrouvé*, still tender and magnificent, but 'hurrying to the grave', though here Proust forgetfully calls her the Princesse de Nassau. She was the Marquise d'Hervey de Saint-Denis, one of the guests at Montesquiou's fête in honour of Delafosse: she was invited at Proust's earnest request, so she may well have made eyes at him in real life. Her husband, the much-betrayed Marquis (1823-92), was an eminent Chinese scholar, and is mentioned under his own name as having given a Chinese vase to Charlus in his boyhood. Like the Princesse d'Orvillers, Mme d'Hervey was a natural daughter of the last reigning Duke of Parma.[4] She was rich, fair-haired and ever-youthful: people called her the Demi-Chevreul, in allusion to the long-lived chemist Michel Chevreul, whose hundredth birthday was celebrated in 1886. After her husband's death she became younger than ever, and married Mme de Chevigné's nephew Jacques de Waru, who was fifteen years her

[1] II, 186   [2] II, 273
[3] II, 195   [4] II, 373, 720, 721; III, 979-80; II, 718

junior, and one of the two brothers Proust had pursued because they had their aunt's blue eyes and beaked nose. Mme de Chevigné was not altogether pleased to acquire a niece several years older than herself, but was thought to console herself by the thought of the money it brought into the family.

Another salon in which Charles Haas, Breteuil, Turenne and the rest of Comtesse Greffulhe's set were to be met—together with Princesse Mathilde, the Grand-Duchess Wladimir and Comte Robert de FitzJames—was the Duchesse de la Trémoïlle's. "I don't say she's 'profound'," Swann tells Mme Verdurin, "but she's intelligent, and her husband is really cultured." The Duchesse looked like the White Queen in *Alice*, we are told by an English observer, and wouldn't have a mirror in the house. Mme de Chevigné stayed several months in every year at her Château de Serrant in Anjou. Her scholarly husband, who was the premier duke of France, senior even to the La Rochefoucaulds, was tall, bearded, refined and deaf. Charlus, greeting the arriving guests at the Princesse de Guermantes's, calls out: "Good evening, Mme de la Trémoïlle."[1]

When Charlus also says: "Good evening, my dear Herminie," he is addressing the Duchesse Herminie de Rohan-Chabot, the same who before her husband's succession was Princesse de Léon. It was she who gave, in the 1880s, the celebrated 'ball of the Princesse de Léon', which Swann mentions at Combray.[2] Boni de Castellane, still in his teens, had appeared there as the Maréchal de Saxe, in powdered wig, plumed hat and a purple cloak bordered with sables borrowed from Mlle Marsy. The company in her salon was mixed: her daughter, Princesse Marie Murat, was once forced to leave a message with the butler: "Tell Mother I couldn't get to her through all those poets." Even Verlaine might have appeared there, had not the absent-minded duchess invited him for the first time several years after his death. She was exceedingly kind-hearted, and when warned that one of her guests had been in prison, replied only: "Oh, poor dear, no wonder he looks so sad!" Once she helped a peasant-woman in the train to change her baby's napkins. "What is your name, kind lady?" asked the grateful mother. "The Duchesse de Rohan." "Well, I'm the Queen of Sheba." She worked for charities, presided on literary juries, and published several volumes of verses. "She's managed

[1] I, 260; II, 658   [2] I, 26, 98, 174

to persuade herself, in a well-meaning sort of way, that she's the muse Polyhymnia," said Montesquiou, who when presented with one of her books had simply returned his card, inscribed 'Yours in spite of everything.' Her husband, Duc Alain, would stop in front of any pretty face not previously known to him and say, "I bet you don't know who *I* am"; but the pretty face invariably replied, "You're the Duc de Rohan." He was particularly fond of foreign lady visitors. "After a month he gets tired of them," said his wife, "and then I have them on my hands for the rest of my life"—a remark which is also given to the Duchesse de Guermantes.[1]

Another Guermantes hostess was Comtesse Rosa de FitzJames, for whose sake (if not for her husband's, of whom she was supposed to be still fonder) Mme de Chevigné had left Proust standing in the Avenue Gabriel. Proust was presented to her by the old Marquise de Brantes; and the Comtesse de Pourtalès remembered him on this very occasion, 'extraordinarily pale, with a fringe of black hair over his huge black eyes'. Comtesse Rosa was a Jewess from Vienna, *née* Gutmann, and at first the Faubourg was inclined to find her unacceptable; but her husband was so unkind and unfaithful that they nicknamed her 'Rosa Malheur' (after the animal-painter Rosa Bonheur) and (except for the inflexible Comte Aimery de La Rochefoucauld, who said: "She wanted a salon, and all she's got is a dining-room") took her to their hearts. The German philosopher Count Keyserling, Bourget and the Abbé Mugnier were to be met in her house, together with the inevitable Charles Haas, Turenne and Marquis du Lau. Comtesse Rosa was plain, melancholy and not very intelligent: "Everyone says you're silly, my dear Rosa," said her best friend, "but I always tell them they exaggerate." She was said to keep a secret weapon in her desk: a list of all the Jewish marriages in the noble families of Europe. Her husband, Comte Robert de Fitz-James, when she began "In Vienna, where I was bred," would interrupt with "You mean, born." But he had no respect for anyone's feelings, and to a duchess who said, when her last daughter was engaged, "At last my girls are all placed," he retorted: "Yes, but not in the first three."

Comtesse Mélanie de Pourtalès was a surviving beauty of the Second Empire and had appeared in Winterhalter's famous

[1] III, 1006

painting of the Empress Eugénie's ladies-in-waiting. She was notorious for talking throughout the performance whenever she went to the opera; and Charles Haas, when invited to her box, had murmured: "Yes, I'd love to come, I've never heard you in *Faust*." She still wore imperial violets, and refused to allow her golden hair to turn white; and from force of habit she eyed young men, we are told, with 'matriarchal coquetry'. To an old priest who expressed his gratitude at meeting 'the beautiful Comtesse de Pourtalès of whom I've heard so much', she sighed: "Ah, M. le Curé, if you'd seen me forty years ago you would have said the Almighty created his masterpiece when He made me!" But she stood on her dignity, and when Reynaldo Hahn unfortunately used his friend Proust's favourite adjective of her she retorted: "My dear Reynaldo, you can say the Comtesse de Pourtalès is kind; you can say she is no ordinary woman; but you can't possibly call her *nice*!" Her guests comprised not only the Faubourg, but also Central European dignitaries—her friendship with Princesse Metternich was legendary—Protestants, such as Proust's *bête noire*, the Byzantine historian Gustave Schlumberger, and Bonapartist nobles—the Prince de Borodino at Doncières naturally dines with her whenever he visits Paris.[1] But she wisely refrained from mingling all these with the Faubourg; and the Duchesse de Guermantes says, complaining of the mixed company at her cousin the Princesse's soirée: "It's much better arranged at Mélanie Pourtalès's—she can invite the Holy Synod and the Oratoire chapel if she likes, but she doesn't ask us on the same day."[2]

One of the great ladies to whom Montesquiou was particularly devoted was Mme Greffulhe's friend and his own second cousin, Mme Standish (his cousin Bertrand had married her sister Émilie). Despite her foreign name (the Faubourg called her 'Missis'), she eminently belonged to the *gratin*, being a niece of the Duc des Cars, while her husband was the son of a Noailles. 'It would take a whole lecture,' says the Narrator, 'to explain to certain foolish young men why Mme Standish is at least as great a lady as the Duchesse de Doudeauville.'[3] She had been the mistress of General Galliffet and of Edward VII as Prince of Wales, and dressed (though people could never decide which imitated the other) exactly like the Princess of Wales, later Queen Alexandra, with

[1] II, 132   [2] II, 672   [3] II, 661

stringed bonnets, wasp-waist, curled fringe and high dog-collar. But when asked by admiring rivals where some amazingly elegant dress came from, she would say: "My maid ran it up for me." She was still beautiful, with a frigid, bolt-upright English manner.

Next to the La Trémoïlles and the La Rochefoucaulds the premier dukes of France were the Uzès's, the pronunciation of whose name by the *gratin* ('Uzaï', without the final 's') so astonishes and enraptures Legrandin's sister, the Marquise de Cambremer.[1] A former Duc d'Uzès, when the king expressed surprise that no Uzès had ever been Marshal of France, had replied: "Sire, we are always killed in battle too soon." The Dowager Duchesse Anne d'Uzès was a remote cousin of Adhéaume de Chevigné and granddaughter of the Veuve Clicquot of champagne fame; but first and foremost she was a Mortemart, of the family whose wit was so famous under Louis XIV. "I was so exasperated by Saint-Simon's incessant talk about the 'Mortemart wit', without once telling us in what it consisted," Proust says, "that I resolved to go one better and invent the Guermantes wit." The duchesse liked to be told, however untruthfully, that she had the Mortemart wit. She was a dumpy, formidable, horsy woman, a poetess, novelist, sculptress, yachtswoman, feminist, huntress and motorist: by the time of her death in 1933 at the age of 86 the grisly antlers of more than two thousand stags which she had slain in person had been nailed to the walls of her hunting-lodge in the Forest of Rambouillet; and in 1897 she became the first woman in France to hold a driving-licence for one of the new-fangled motor-carriages. She was thought to have been the mistress of General Boulanger (and of the old Prince Joseph de Caraman-Chimay and the Duc de La Trémoïlle), though she always denied it; but it was certain that she had contributed three million francs to the shifty general's lost cause. On another occasion she was more thrifty, to her lasting sorrow. Her son Jacques became infatuated with the cocotte Émilienne d'Alençon, who was exhibiting a troupe of performing white rabbits—though nobody had eyes for the rabbits—to enthusiastic crowds at the Cirque d'Été in the Champs-Élysées. Soon she was to be seen wearing the Uzès family jewels. With the best intentions the Duchesse packed her son off to the Congo; but the poor young man died of enteric

[1] II, 819

fever at Kabinda in the Sudan in 1893, in the fourteenth month of his journey across Africa. This suggested Saint-Loup's exile to Morocco as a punishment for his extravagant gifts to Rachel.

One of the companions of Charles Haas in Tissot's painting is Prince Edmond de Polignac; some say it was he who introduced Proust to Haas. He was the son of Charles X's reactionary minister, a kind, witty, rapidly ageing man, with the bearing of a great nobleman and the face of a scholar: "He looked like a castle-tower converted into a library," said Proust. The prince was devoted to music, and was himself a composer of some distinction, but lacked the money to have his works performed. Montesquiou and Comtesse Greffulhe arranged his wedding in December 1893 to Winnaretta Singer, the heiress to the Singer sewing-machine millions, whose sister Isabelle had married the Duc Decaze in 1888. Jacques Émile Blanche remembered the prince jumping over a chair at the Blanches' Dieppe villa, by way of proving he was still young enough to marry, and old Mme Blanche saying: "So the lute is going to marry the sewing-machine." However, their union was extremely happy, and the prince's compositions were now performed in their studio in the Rue Cortambert by full orchestras and choirs. Proust heard there Fauré's sonata, one of the models for the Vinteuil Sonata. He also recalled with delight the unexpected arrival of his Condorcet tyrant M. Cucheval, and the butler saying to the prince: "This gentleman says his name is Cucheval, ought I to announce him all the same?"; and indeed, when one thought of it, the school-master's name was hardly fit to be pronounced before ladies. In the studio hung the prince's favourite picture, a study by Monet of tulips in a field near Haarlem, snatched from him at a sale a few years before by Miss Singer and now providentially returned. A single point of difference marred their union: the princess loved fresh air, and the prince hated draughts. When his friends teased him for sitting in a corner of the studio, smothered with travelling-rugs as if in a railway-carriage, he would murmur with a smile: "Ah well, as Anaxagoras says, this life is a journey"; and Proust gave the remark to the dying Bergotte.[1]

Another salon which Proust entered about this time was that of Comtesse Pauline d'Haussonville, a daughter of the Duc d'Harcourt. She was tall, haughty and statuesque, was said to

[1] III, 184

have the smallest ears in Paris, and wore red to set off her dark hair and her celebrated blue eyes. We have already seen her husband, Comte Othenin, with his ironic smile, bright, inquisitive eyes and dangling monocle, at Mme Straus's. He was a member of the Académie Française, and their salon became the headquarters of the clique of nobly-born academicians, the so-called 'party of the dukes'. Although his was said to have been the voice that had voted the survival of the Third Republic in 1876 by a majority of one, M. d'Haussonville was a leader of the liberal Orleanists, with whom he united the legitimists after the death of the Comte de Chambord in 1883. He was the grandson of Mme de Staël's daughter Albertine, whose Proustian Christian name was shared by two other ladies known to Proust, Princesse Albertine de Broglie and Comtesse Albertine de Montebello. Both husband and wife were exceedingly courteous and kind-hearted, but none the less conscious of the importance of their position; and the new guest would be gratified by the depth of their bow, only to be snubbed by the 'gymnastic harmony' (as Proust called it) with which, after regaining the perpendicular, they leaned as far backwards as they had bowed forwards. Proust attributed the Haussonville bow to the Guermantes ladies, who had borrowed it, he tells us, from the Courvoisiers, and to the Duchesse de Réveillon in *Jean Santeuil*.[1] In the Haussonvilles' drawing-room in the Rue Saint-Dominique hung the portrait of M. d'Haussonville's ancestress, Béatrix de Lillebonne, abbess under Louis XIV of the exclusive convent of Remiremont. Proust gives this painting to Mme de Villeparisis, who stupefies Bloch by maintaining, a little exaggeratedly, that even the King's own daughter would not have been admitted to this nunnery, "because after its misalliance with the Medicis the House of France hadn't enough quarters".[2] It was an incident in the memoirs of the Count's father, which Proust read only in 1920—in his youth the elder M. d'Haussonville had stood in doubt outside Mme Delessert's house, wondering if he had really been invited to her reception— that suggested the Narrator's anxieties at the Princesse de Guermantes's soirée.[3] In 1907 we shall see Mme d'Haussonville

[1] II, 445; *Jean Santeuil*, vol. 1, 285. For Albertine de Staël, afterwards Duchesse de Broglie, and the Haussonvilles, cf. II, 275, and III, 968.
[2] II, 199
[3] II, 633, etc.

contributing for a moment to the character of Mme de Cambremer, and in 1920 her husband prefiguring the old age of the Duc de Guermantes.

One of the salons in which the *gratin* could meet the arts was that of the beautiful and cruel Comtesse Emmanuela Potocka, with whom Jacques Émile Blanche had had a heart-breaking love-affair in the early 1880s. Her riotous circle, which included Bourget, Dr Pozzi, Maupassant (one of her lovers), Béraud and Gervex (yet another original of Elstir), was known as the Maccabees (meaning Ghouls), and called her sometimes the Siren, sometimes, like Mme Verdurin, the Mistress. One of Proust's favourite anecdotes was Mme Potocka's belated reply to a theological argument of the philosopher Caro: as he was leaving she leaned over the banisters and spat downstairs on his bald head, shouting: "Take that for your Idea of God!" One evening at the Duchesse de La Trémoïlle's, when Mme Potocka graciously rose to greet the scholar Vaufreland, Mme de Chevigné uttered words adapted in one of the Duchesse de Guermantes's epigrams: "She's like the sun, she rises for one man just before going to bed for another."[1] On one of his visits to Mme Potocka Proust saw the Duchesse de Luynes's carriage and the Comtesse de Guerne's motor-car waiting outside, and had the extreme pleasure of hearing the hall-porter saying "Mme la Comtesse is out," to an unwanted caller and "Mme la Comtesse is expecting you," to himself. Towards the end of the 1890s the Siren moved to Auteuil in order to devote more time to the only creatures she ever really loved, her greyhounds. "Take care," said Reynaldo Hahn, "You're too malicious to live so far out." At first the *gratin* followed her, though with some grumbling: "It's charming out here," said Proust's friend Gabriel de La Rochefoucauld, "Is there anything one oughtn't to miss seeing in the vicinity?" She was to be seen in the morning mists of the Bois, her beauty fading, with a yelling pack of dogs around her and a huge collie straining on the leash. But in the end Reynaldo's warning was justified: during the Occupation, after forty years of isolation, the deserted countess and her last greyhound died of old age and hunger in the house at Auteuil. When their bodies were discovered at last, the rats had been at them.

The tale of the salons of the Faubourg Saint-Germain is com-

[1] II, 410

plete. We shall encounter most of them again, in their place and time, and see what further use Proust made of them in his novel. It remains to ask why he entered them, and why, indeed, this obscure, half-Jewish, bourgeois young man was ever allowed in.

We needs must love the highest when we see it. Unfortunately, it is not easy for the idealist young to discern which of the things they see—nature, art, love, friendship, the noble mind of the nobly born—is the highest. Proust pursued all these together, and thought for a long time to find some of them on the Guermantes Way. Perhaps, however they choose, the young are right; for the highest, whatever it be, is not of this earth, and it matters little in which of its earthly symbols they may seek it in vain. A drawing-room, it seemed to Proust, was itself a work of art, of which its habitués were both the performers and the creators, devising the formal movements of the mysterious ballet they danced, inventing the words of the frivolous but portentous drama they played. Then, too, there was the poetic glamour of meeting the modern equivalents of characters in Balzac, or the descendants and namesakes of noble personages of whom he had read in Saint-Simon's memoirs and Mme de Sévigné's letters. There was the intellectual fascination of unravelling the mechanisms of a world in which the interplay of human passions and conventions was so peculiarly intense and so exceptionally disguised. There was the need for enchantment and disenchantment, for the experiences which would go to make his unconceived novel. Perhaps deeper still (if an impulse from the Freudian unconscious can be said to be deeper than an impulse from the creative unconscious) was his need to prove that he was not a pariah, the anxious prompting of his inner guilt. He must be accepted where acceptance would be most difficult and failure most humiliating, in the company of the elect, in the Faubourg which was on earth the image, whether real or merely blasphemous, of the blessed saints in heaven. And he pursued the welcoming smile of a noble hostess as at Auteuil he had pursued his mother's kiss, and for the same reasons.

The influence of Montesquiou in introducing Proust to society has often been exaggerated. Count Robert acted, as we have seen, with the least possible energy and at the last possible moment, when Proust was on the point of attaining the highest levels of the Faubourg (having already reached the lower) by his own devices. Proust reproduced the situation accurately in his novel. The Narrator visits Mme de Villeparisis and dines at the Duchesse's unknown to Charlus, who still hopes, like Mephistopheles tempting Faust, to exact a mysterious and awful price for his services; and the baron has the supreme mortification of meeting him at the Princesse de Guermantes's, where, he had announced, "they never invite *anyone* unless I intervene".[1] Moreover, Montesquiou was not altogether a desirable sponsor. It would not be pleasant to be asked merely because a hostess was terrified of annoying the Count, and in the invidious capacity of his latest young man. Besides, if in a fit of enthusiasm Montesquiou compelled everyone to invite a protégé, he would soon in a fit of rage forbid anyone ever to invite him again. The evidence suggests that after the Delafosse fête, at which Proust met nearly all the ladies mentioned in this chapter, he went everywhere unaided, kept Montesquiou at a safe distance, and employed all his diplomacy in ensuring that the Count should *not* intervene. The uneasy knowledge that he had not, after all, been indispensable, was an important element in the mingled antipathy and admiration with which Montesquiou ever after regarded his 'dear Marcel'.

[1] II, 565

Chapter 11

DESCENT INTO THE CITIES OF THE PLAIN

DURING the summer of 1894, the period of his ascent to the heights of the Faubourg Saint-Germain, Proust continued simultaneously his descent towards Sodom. His uneasy friendship with Montesquiou, however, ceased to be a preponderant motive force, and the Count's honeymoon with Delafosse seemed a model to be avoided. Only politeness was maintained. In July he tried, unsuccessfully, to arrange a 'musical dinner' for the happy couple at the fashionable restaurant of Armenonville in the Bois de Boulogne. No doubt all three had been there before; for it was at Armenonville that the Verdurin's pianist used to play the Vinteuil Sonata to Odette and the 'faithful', so that ever afterwards, when Swann heard the 'little phrase', he could see 'the moonlight preventing the leaves from moving', and hear someone murmuring, "You can almost see to read the newspaper!"[1] Proust learned, too late, that Delafosse had left for London, where he gave a piano-recital on 12 July, while Montesquiou had been ill with laryngitis ('I should so have loved to bring you hot drinks and smoothe your pillow!'). He would be going to Saint-Moritz again in August—could Marcel come too? But Proust had more attractive plans.

Before these plans are revealed, a strange meeting in the previous spring must be mentioned. During the April of 1894, Oscar Wilde paid his last visit to Paris before his self-sought doom of the following year. It was the period of his most triumphant pride, when he felt himself to be, as he said, 'the King of Life', and only disaster could offer him a new experience. His bloated, gloriously insolent features were to be seen at Mme Straus's; and Proust dined with him one evening at Mme Arman de Caillavet's, where the two men eyed one another, as Fernand Gregh noticed, 'with a complex curiosity'. "You know," said Mme Arman afterwards, "Monsieur Wilde looks like a cross between the Apollo Belvedere and Albert Wolff." Everyone knew

[1] I, 533, 534

what she meant; for Albert Wolff, the art and theatre critic of
Le Figaro—'a creature of no religion, no country, and no sex', the
anti-Semite Drumont had written in *La France Juive*—was a fat,
fluting, corseted, rouged caricature of Wilde the pervert. Robert
de Billy, now back in Paris at the Foreign Ministry, remembered
Wilde confessing: "I find an ever-growing difficulty in expressing
my originality through my choice of waistcoats and cravats"; and
Billy was not sure that Oscar had not had some part, during a
previous visit, in the selection of a dove-grey cravat for the well-
known portrait which J. E. Blanche had painted of Proust two
years before. Wilde even visited 9 Boulevard Malesherbes, where,
like the Baron de Charlus,[1] he commented adversely on the
furniture, much to Proust's annoyance: "I don't think M. Wilde
has been well brought-up," he said afterwards. On the young
André Gide, Proust's elder by two years, the influence of Wilde's
conversation in preparing him for moral and spiritual liberation
had been crucial; for Wilde is Ménalque, the genius of heroic
hedonism, in *Les Nourritures Terrestres* and *L'Immoraliste*. He
failed to impress Proust: yet perhaps Wilde's glorying in his vice
may have taken some effect in that spring of 1894. Possibly there
is a little of Wilde in Charlus; and there is, more probably, something of the dangerous, beautiful Lord Alfred Douglas, who
accompanied Wilde, and was sometimes to be seen at the *Revue
Blanche* office in the Rue Laffitte, in Charlie Morel.

In August Montesquiou was at Saint-Moritz, which he
appreciated less than in the two previous years. "Switzerland is a
hideous country," he told the young Élisabeth de Gramont, Duc
Agénor's daughter and a future friend of Proust, who was staying
at the same hotel; "on the rare occasions when one does come
across a possible view, it's invariably blocked by an enormous
notice-board that says 'Hôtel Belle-Vue'!" But Proust was staying
at Mme Lemaire's château in the Marne, Réveillon, with Reynaldo
Hahn.

Hahn was a young man of nineteen, the favourite pupil of
Massenet at the Conservatoire, and already a singer, pianist and
composer of some distinction. He was a Jew, born at Caracas in
Venezuela, and now lived in Paris with his parents and several
sisters; he had brown eyes, pale brown skin, austerely handsome
features and a little dark moustache. Proust met him early this

[1] III, 387

summer at Mme Lemaire's Tuesdays in the Rue Monceau, where
Hahn's singing of his own song-cycle from poems of Verlaine,
Les Chansons Grises, immediately became the rage: he was to be
one of the chief performing stars of her musical evenings for the
next two decades. His voice was a light but rich tenor; he leaned
far back, playing his own accompaniment to his own songs, with
half-closed eyes and a convincing air of inspiration. A malicious
observer would notice that his singing head cocked from side to
side, like a bird's, as he darted keen glances through his long eyelashes at each member of his audience, to make sure that all were
properly mesmerised. But he possessed the serious charm, the
intelligence and moral distinction that Proust sought in the ideal
friend. Their friendship was passionate for the next two years,
and temperate but unclouded for the rest of Proust's life.

Réveillon was a rambling seventeenth-century country-house,
turreted and moated, with large formal flower-gardens surrounded
by dense forest. The interior decoration, in which real flowers
from the gardens alternated with painted flowers from Mme
Lemaire's brush, resembled that of La Raspelière under the reign
of Mme Verdurin.[1] On the first day Proust and Hahn took a walk
in the gardens, talking as they went, until they passed a crimson
border of Bengal roses, when Proust suddenly became silent.
"Would you be annoyed if I stayed behind a minute?" he asked,
in the sad, gentle, childish voice which was so characteristic of him.
"I want to have another look at those roses." When Reynaldo
returned, after walking all round the house, he found his friend
standing motionless, frowning and oblivious, biting one end of
his long moustache which he held between his teeth with his left
hand, still staring at the roses. Reynaldo passed by once more,
till he heard Marcel calling and running after him; with a feeling
of amused respect he divined that it would be better to ask no
questions about his friend's state of trance, and they resumed their
conversation as though nothing had happened.[2] Proust can hardly
have forgotten that there were Bengal roses in the Pré Catelan
at Illiers, so this curious episode cannot have been an onset of
unconscious memory, like the eating of the madeleine; it was,
rather, the kindred effort to wrest the secret of a natural object,

[1] II, 917, etc.
[2] Andrée shows similar tact when the Narrator wishes to contemplate the
hawthorns in the country near Balbec (I, 922); so does Saint-Loup (II, 157).

like the incident of the three trees near Balbec, or the spires on the horizon of the Méséglise Way.

Proust's stay at Réveillon lasted from 18 August to the middle of September, and was followed by ten days with his mother at the Hôtel des Roches Noires at Trouville, where he wrote a short story, *La Mort de Baldassare Silvande*, for *Les Plaisirs et les Jours*. He saw a great deal of Mme Straus at her villa, the Clos des Mûriers, but failed to persuade Reynaldo to visit him and continue his musical education. 'You will find me a much altered Marcel, musically speaking,' he wrote to Pierre Lavallée, 'in fact I'm Romeo-and-Julietising rather to excess, perhaps.' A tiresome event of this holiday was that his brother Robert, while staying at Rueil (a village on the Seine a few miles north of Paris), fell from his tandem-bicycle under a five-ton coal-wagon, which passed over his thigh without causing serious injury. Mme Proust hurried away to nurse him, and found his lower-class girl-friend already installed at his bedside, a situation which she accepted with supreme tact. Proust remembered the incident in *La Prisonnière*: the Narrator's mother, when the captive Albertine accompanied them on the train from Balbec to Paris, 'spoke kindly to my friend, like a mother whose son is gravely injured, and who is grateful to the young mistress who tends him with devoted care'.[1] Nevertheless, Mme Proust had Robert packed off to Uncle Louis's house at Auteuil as soon as he was fit to be moved. Proust returned to Paris on 25 September.

Proust's mention of *Romeo and Juliet* (in which the double meaning, if any, is certainly unconscious) no doubt refers to the opera by Gounod, to whose lineage Reynaldo belonged via his master Saint-Saëns. The musical preferences which Hahn hoped to inculcate in his friend were, by an odd coincidence, those which Proust had already held at the age of fifteen, under the influence of his mother and Mme Catusse, when he wrote in Antoinette Faure's confession-album: 'Favourite composers, Gounod and Mozart.' For Hahn was a Mozartian classicist, and in the delicate, traditional refinement of his own music he showed, by no means discreditably, his indifference to innovators such as Fauré and Debussy, and his antipathy to Wagner. Proust, on the other hand, was by now an ardent Wagnerian, devoted to Fauré and intrigued by Debussy, whose music, now just beginning to

[1] III, 13

be known, he was to admire intensely a decade later. 'Monsieur,
he wrote to Fauré about this time, 'I not only admire and venerate
your music, I am in love with it. Long before you met me you
used to thank me with a smile when, at a concert or an evening-
party, the clamour of my enthusiasm obliged your disdainful indifference to success to bow a fifth or sixth time to your audience!'
It was probably at Comte Henri de Saussine's, in 1893, that he
met Fauré, as he had also met Delafosse, for in real life Vinteuil
and Morel frequented one and the same salon. But the guest
Saussine admired even above Fauré was the Wagnerian pupil of
César Franck, Vincent d'Indy, whose name is echoed in the name
of Vinteuil. Under Saussine's influence Proust acquired the
enthusiasm for Wagner to which he was in any case born: it was
on 14 January 1894, at the Sunday Colonne concert, that he first
heard the Flower Maiden scene from *Parsifal*, which he recalled
in the episode in *Le Côté de Guermantes* where the lady guests of
the Duchesse ('their flesh appeared on either side of a sinuous
spray of mimosa or the petals of a full-blown rose') are compared
to the Flower Maidens.[1]

Hahn's attempt at re-education came, very fortunately, too late
to distract Proust from the musical aesthetic which suited his
nature and was to inform his novel. Reynaldo's traditionalism
was no doubt salutary for himself, but would only have been
disastrous for Proust: it could never have led to the invention of
Vinteuil. To please Reynaldo he did his best to like Saint-Saëns:
he wrote two articles in *Le Gaulois* of 14 January and 11
December 1895, in which, however, his attempts at praise only
succeeded in displaying his reservations. 'Saint-Saëns uses
archaism to legitimise modernity; he bestows upon a commonplace, step by step, through the ingenious, personal, sublime
appropriateness of his style, the value of an original creation ...
he is a musical humanist,' says Proust very truly. And yet, it was
from Reynaldo's tuition and from the charming, meritorious but
secondary music of Saint-Saëns, that the 'little phrase' of the
Vinteuil Sonata took its beginning.

It was perhaps at Mme Lemaire's, and played by Ysaye ('his
rendering is splendid, majestic and luminous, with admirable
form,' wrote Reynaldo in his diary), that Proust first heard the
Saint-Saëns Sonata in D Minor for violin and piano. His imagina-

[1] II, 423

tion was captured by the chief theme of the first movement, a
mediocre but haunting melody whose only musical merit is its
simplicity, and whose fascination comes from its very banality, like
that of a popular song or dance-tune, and its incessant repetition.

Afterwards, in Reynaldo's room at 6 Rue du Cirque, with its
enormous stone fireplace, or in the dining-room at 9 Boulevard
Malesherbes, Proust would say: "Play me that bit I like, Reynaldo
—you know, the 'little phrase'." So the little phrase of Saint-
Saëns became the 'national anthem' of his love for Reynaldo, as
Vinteuil's became that of Swann's love for Odette.[1]

---

[1] I, 218. In *Jean Santeuil* the hero's mistress, Françoise S., plays the Saint-
Saëns sonata under its own name, during an episode of jealous cross-
examination about her Lesbian loves which is retold in *A la Recherche* both
of Swann and Odette, and of the Narrator and Albertine. So it may be
conjectured that there is something of Proust's friendship for Reynaldo in
both Françoise and Albertine. Perhaps, too (though here the transposition
would be particularly devious and dubious), since Albertine and the Sonata
are associated through Mlle Vinteuil and her friend with homosexual
jealousy, it may be guessed that Proust quarrelled with Reynaldo over his
loyal attachment to his master Saint-Saëns, who, as was notorious, was
himself an invert. Another probable relic of Reynaldo in Françoise S. is the
episode of her musician friends, Vésale, Saint-Géron and Griffon, who
perform chamber-music in her apartment, with Françoise at the piano. But
at this point in their friendship no more than the possibility of some relation
between Françoise and Reynaldo can be inferred, and no definite conclusions
about events in real life between Hahn and Proust can be drawn from such
uncertain material. Indeed, the evidence against the connection is more
convincing. The scene of jealousy had already appeared in *Avant la nuit*,
written a year before Proust met Hahn. Françoise is much less closely allied
to Albertine than to Odette in *Un Amour de Swann*, who derives from a
very different region of Proust's life, from his flirtation with Mme Hayman,
his discoveries about the early life of Charles Haas, and most of all from his
imagination, for *Un Amour de Swann* is the only episode of *A la Recherche*
in which there is a large element of fiction. Proust's early association with
Hahn seems to have been free from quarrels, or any unhappiness except his
intermittent feelings of guilt towards his unsuspecting mother. Its passionate
stage ended two years later, when Proust found another young friend, and
a brief period of tension was followed by a loyal and lifelong comradeship.
Except for the few angry months in 1896 which ended their love, nothing
could be further from this most satisfactory and lasting of all Proust's
friendships than the torments inflicted by Françoise and Albertine.

Meanwhile the preparation of *Les Plaisirs et les Jours* was advancing rapidly. The long dedicatory foreword to Willie Heath was written in July 1894; Mme Lemaire was busy with her gracefully repellent brush-drawings; Anatole France used his personal influence to find a publisher; and Montesquiou generously consented to the quotation of his still unpublished verses to Mme Lemaire ('*the goddess and Vigée-Lebrun of flowers*'), 'which display,' wrote the grateful Proust, 'the sententious and subtle elegance, the vigorous sense of form, that so often in his work remind one of the seventeenth century'. But Count Robert refused to allow one of the stories to be dedicated to him, even with the inducement that France and Heredia would be among his fellow-dedicatees, and that his *bête noire* Blanche would be excluded; and in the end it was decided there should be no dedications of individual stories at all. The manuscript—although a few pieces were written and inserted later—was in the hands of the publisher Calmann Lévy by September. And when the year ended Proust found he no longer dreaded New Year's Day—that recurrent point in the spiral of time which in the long-past winter of Marie de Benardaky seemed the beginning of a new life, but afterwards became a mocking admonition that life could not be altered by the calendar alone. 'I used to feel,' he wrote to Montesquiou, 'that however the years change, our character remains the same; and that the future we dream and desire is merely the product of the very past from which we would like it to be so different, and only echoes all the bells of good and evil we have previously set ringing. But now it is with a keener consciousness of divine grace and human liberty, with faith in at least an inner Providence, that I begin the year.' For now the joy of Reynaldo's friendship reached out into an endless future, and the possibility of fame from writing seemed within his grasp.

His new love, however, happy and virtuous as it seemed, had its darker implications. Whether or not his previous friendships had been entirely platonic, they had been transitory, and had never touched his deepest emotions; he had often been in love with women; he could still regard himself as fundamentally normal. Now, once and for all, he must admit to himself that he was a homosexual, one of the exiled, scattered, outlawed inhabitants of Sodom, a race more tragic and despised even than the Jews. He was a criminal, and Reynaldo was his accomplice; they

belonged to the kin of Doasan and his Polish violinist, of
Montesquiou and Delafosse, Wilde and Lord Alfred. His previous
innocent friendships, from 'little Halévy' to Willie Heath, were
retrospectively debased into sublimations of a vicious desire.
Worst of all, he must now devote his life to an interminable effort
to conceal his real nature from his mother. If he succeeded,
would he not crucify her daily with his deceit? If he failed, would
he not, quite literally, kill her? He wrote a story in which he
killed first his mother, and then himself, almost as if this was the
only possible solution of his dilemma.

   La Confession d'une Jeune Fille is the only certain case of 'transposition' in Proust's early short stories: it is abundantly clear that
the heroine is Proust himself. She spends the summers of her
childhood in the garden of Les Oublis, which is one and the same
as the Pré Catelan at Illiers, the garden at Étreuilles in *Jean
Santeuil* (which is likewise called Les Oublis), and Swann's park
at Tansonville. There is the incident of the mother's good-night
kiss, 'an old habit which she had abandoned, because it gave me
too much pleasure and too much pain'. The girl is seduced at the
age of fifteen by a boy cousin—did this, too, happen to Proust,
and is such an incident alluded to when the Narrator presents the
proprietress of Bloch's brothel with Aunt Léonie's sofa, 'on which
I first tasted the pleasures of love with a little girl cousin'?[1] She
is tortured by indolence, procrastination and 'lack of will-power'.
'I gave myself time, and often felt wretched when I saw time
pass, but after all, there was so much of it still before me! . . .
Wishing to have will-power was not enough. What I ought to
have done was precisely what I could not do without will-power
—to will it.' She becomes addicted to 'the desiccating pleasures
of society'—'I went into society to calm myself after sinning, and
the moment I was calmed I sinned again.' She acquires a brutally
sensual fiancé, with her parents' consent, and is seduced once
more. Her mother, looking through the window, finds her in the
act and dies of a stroke; and the girl shoots herself, like the
Lesbian heroine of *Avant la nuit*.

   It is surely improbable, though several of Proust's biographers
have suggested it, that the melodramatic discovery occurred in
real life. The brutal fiancé is very far from the gentle Reynaldo;
and though Proust no doubt often ran the horrifying risk of

[1] I, 578

detection in his own home, the event could not have occurred without leaving a permanent scar—of which there is not the least trace—in the relations of mother and son. It is still more inconceivable, even granting his latent sadism towards his mother, that he could have recorded such an incident openly in the book in which he expected her to take pride and pleasure. His remorse, and his fear that the story might come true, were no doubt real enough, but the story itself shows that he succeeded in repressing them. Like the rest of *Les Plaisirs et les Jours* it has the sterile tone of a literary exercise: he had confessed to the world and to his mother as a sop to his conscience, and with no intention of being taken at his word. Nevertheless, *Confession d'une Jeune Fille* is the first clear sign of Proust's recognition of his own inversion. It is also, though he could scarcely have foreseen it, a first embryonic draft of *Jean Santeuil* and *A la Recherche*; the garden of Combray, the mother's kiss refused and extorted, the Guermantes Way and the Cities of the Plain, the obsession of Time Lost, his own life told as an allegory, all are there, though with suicide as the only solution. The final incident of the destroyer taken into the parents' house, the desecration of the mother, and the symbolic window, is a distant prefiguration both of Albertine as captive, and of Mlle Vinteuil's profanation of her dead father's portrait, seen by the Narrator through the window at Montjouvain.

By the New Year of 1895, as we have seen, Proust was already feeling 'a keener consciousness of divine grace and human liberty': he had come to terms with his remorse and accepted his destiny. He took Reynaldo to a careful selection of broadminded hostesses, including Mme Aubernon, Mme Straus and the rich, kind, malicious, white-haired old Marquise de Brantes— "She's worth a whole Council of Trent," her nephew Montesquiou would say with vague approbation. From January onwards they visited Count Robert himself, who was most affable, and was repaid with a shower of grateful letters for 'your kindness to my friend'. On 28 May, at Mme Lemaire's Tuesday, Proust's poem sequence *Portraits de Peintres* was recited, to a piano accompaniment composed by Hahn, in the august presence of Montesquiou and Anatole France. Proust's musician friend Édouard Risler was at the piano, having come up specially for the occasion from his military service at Chartres. Risler is presum-

ably the Marquis de Poitiers, the pianist soldier in *Jean Santeuil*[1];
and as a letter of this summer to Pierre Lavallée suggests that
Proust visited Chartres to dine with Risler, it is probable that
Chartres is one of the many garrison-towns which compose
Doncières in *Le Côté de Guermantes*. Proust's poems, on Paul
Potter, Cuyp, Watteau and Van Dyck (this last with a hint of
Willie Heath, 'erect yet reposing' in the green shade of the Bois
de Boulogne) are almost worthless imitations of Montesquiou, with
a few would-be suggestions of Mallarmé, and inferior to Hahn's
delicate accompaniment. But at least they show the sincerity of
Proust's admiration for Montesquiou's work—an admiration
which came not from bad taste, but from an instinctive knowledge
that Count Robert possessed a secret of supreme aesthetic importance, if only he could discover what it was. He also copied
Montesquiou in a way which was less gratifying to that very
susceptible model. His imitations of the Count's monologues,
with the harsh voice rising to an eldritch scream, the head flung
back and the final stamp of the foot, became a popular party-
piece; they were irresistibly comic, and at the same time hallucina-
torily accurate. Proust's pastiches of Montesquiou are still audible,
brought to the level of great art, in the speeches of the Baron de
Charlus. Of course the Count got wind of these performances:
Proust explained that he was merely quoting his marvellous
sayings to an admiring audience, and that quite involuntarily 'the
body was carried away by the soul, my voice and accent took on
the rhythm of the great thoughts I had for the moment borrowed
—if anyone has told you anything else, or mentioned the word
"caricature", I can only invoke your axiom, that words repeated at
second-hand are never true'.[2] Montesquiou pretended to take his
word for it, but: "I don't know why you should set yourself up as
the travelling-salesman of my wit," he persisted in complaining.

Proust spent one afternoon of this spring at the Jardin des
Plantes with his schoolfriend Pierre Lavallée and Reynaldo, and
contemplated the *colombes poignardées*, the doves with a red spot
as of blood on their breasts, in a recurrence of the trance in which

---

[1] *Jean Santeuil*, vol. 2, 293-7. Risler, as the pet pianist of Mme Lemaire's
salon, is also the pianist Dechambre at Mme Verdurin's. The Marquis de
Poitiers, forever cigarette-smoking as he plays, also resembles Reynaldo Hahn.

[2] An axiom uttered by the Baron de Charlus during his quarrel-scene
with the Narrator (II, 560).

he had gazed at the Bengal roses of Réveillon. "They look like nymphs who've stabbed themselves for love," said Reynaldo, "and some god has changed them into birds." At one time, in 1913, Proust thought of calling the second volume of *A la Recherche*, which was later divided into *A l'Ombre des Jeunes Filles en Fleurs* and *Le Côté de Guermantes*, *Les Colombes Poignardées*. He visited Lavallée at his parents' country-house at Segrez, Seine-et-Oise, when the trees were still in bud, and wrote the sketch '*Promenade*' in *Les Plaisirs et les Jours* in memory of the afternoon of his arrival. They walked among wood-anemones and cuckoo-flowers, watched eels and perch wandering in their green meadows of water-weed under the blue water of the streams, collected eggs in the farmyard and admired the jewelled, regal peacock. But during the night Proust had an attack of asthma, and in the morning, to everyone's amazement, he insisted on returning to Paris. His malady, after exiling him from Illiers and troubling his early schooldays, had spared him for nearly ten years, during which his health had been good, except for occasional stomach-pains and vague rheumatisms, both presumably of the same nervous origin. But now it was on its way back, summoned no doubt by the double guilt of society and Sodom. Already a year before, in the spring of 1894, as he complained in a letter to Montesquiou, he had suffered 'a horrible attack of choking, which lasted twenty-four hours'. Soon asthma would arrive in full force, and stay for ever.

In June 1895 began the pathetically comic episode of Proust's career as a librarian. He had taken his *licence ès lettres* in March, after a year of private lessons from M. Darlu, with the creditable placing of twenty-third in his year; his family, though with waning hope and vigour, still pressed him to choose a regular occupation, and it was probably Dr Proust's friend Gabriel Hanotaux, then Foreign Minister, and one of the originals of M. de Norpois, who suggested that a post at the Mazarine Library might suit this literary young man. The Mazarine was in the left wing of the Institut de France, the seat of the five Academies; and Sainte-Beuve himself had been a librarian there fifty years before.[1]

---

[1] No doubt he also had in mind the example of Anatole France, assistant at the Senate Library in the Luxembourg Palace from 1876 to 1890, when he resigned at the urgent request of the chief librarian, Charles Edmond, who complained: "Monsieur France hasn't catalogued a single book since 1882!"

Certainly the duties of an honorary unpaid assistant would be unlikely to interfere with his writing: the working day was of five hours, and attendance was required on a minimum of two and a maximum of five days in the week. Proust was interviewed in a competition for three vacancies on 28 May, and on 29 June was chosen third and last. Every now and then during the next four months, when he felt in the mood, and his health seemed equal to the strain, and (though this was seldom indeed) he was not away on holiday, he actually turned up for a chat with his busy but amiable colleagues and a browse among the Cardinal's books. The books, however, were dusty; and when he emerged on the Quai Conti to meet his new young friend Lucien Daudet, he would produce a throat-spray and counteract the ravages of the day with a cloud of vaporised eucalyptus. His colleagues, Paul Marais the incunabulist and Alfred Franklin the Chief Librarian, thought him nice but quite useless.

Early in July, however, Proust was already on holiday with his mother at Kreuznach, a German spa on the River Nahe, which flows into the Rhine at Bingen ten miles farther east. Robert de Billy came to stay a night with his young wife Jeanne, the daughter of Paul Mirabaud, governor of the Bank of France; they had married a month before, on 4 June, and were still on honeymoon. Mme Proust exerted all her charm, Billy talked about his experiences as a budding diplomat in Germany throughout lunch, and Proust said he must write them down immediately— "and your wife can go upstairs to rest". Billy wrote all afternoon: "It's very good, but you oughtn't to use so many adjectives," declared his friend, who was to make a practice, with such superb effect, of using three or four in a row. Then he produced his short story, *La Mort de Baldassare Silvande*, written at Trouville the previous September, to which Billy in turn made certain objections; they corrected it together in the lamplight, and ever afterwards Proust would say to Billy with a plaintive smile: "You never did like anything I write!" Billy remembered the visit to Kreuznach as the occasion of their first conversations on gothic architecture, which a little later was to become Proust's ruling passion for several years.

After Kreuznach Proust spent a fortnight with Reynaldo and his sister Maria in the forest of Saint-Germain-en-Laye at the Pavillon Louis XIV, a villa belonging to Reynaldo's married

sister Clarita, Mme Seminario, where he finished the revision of
La Mort de Baldassare Silvande. The figure of the dying
Baldassare, little Alexis's uncle with the riotous past, was no doubt
suggested (though Baldassare is a young man of thirty-six) by
the now aged and ailing Louis Weil; but he also contains elements
which recall the later years of Jean Santeuil and even Swann
himself; and in his musical career he is based on both Reynaldo
and Prince Edmond de Polignac. It was probably Baldassare's
gift of a pony to little Alexis (who is Proust as a child) which
made Reynaldo nickname his friend 'Pony': at first much to
Proust's distress ('Marcel the Pony sounds as bad as Jack the
Ripper'), though soon he grew to like it. The story was published
in the *Revue Hebdomadaire* of 29 October 1895, with the dedication 'To Reynaldo Hahn, poet, singer and musician', and earned
Proust 150 francs. This not inconsiderable sum was worth six
pounds then, but would to-day represent nearer fifty: it was an
argument to show his parents that even a writer's career might
be more remunerative than that of an honorary, unpaid librarian
on indefinitely prolonged leave.

Soon, from about 8 August to the end of the month, Proust
was staying with Reynaldo at Mme Lemaire's villa on the seafront at 32 Rue Aguado,[1] Dieppe. As a little bird, who was not
improbably Proust himself, informed the society columnist of *Le
Gaulois*: 'Everyone is talking about the well-known members of
Parisian society who happen to be at Dieppe just now. All Paris
is there, the Comte and Comtesse Louis de Talleyrand-Périgord,
Duc Josselin de Rohan, Madeleine Lemaire, and MM. Marcel
Proust and Reynaldo Hahn, who are the guests of that eminent
artist!' But Proust was collecting impressions for Balbec, and
composing a sketch called 'Underwood' for *Les Plaisirs et les
Jours*: 'Lying on our backs, with our heads pillowed in dead
leaves,' he wrote, 'we followed the joyous agility of our thoughts
as they climbed, without making a single leaf quiver, to the
highest branches, where they perched on the edge of the hazy sky,
beside a singing bird.' He wrote to Reynaldo's charming elder

---

[1] Through a misunderstanding of the words 'Petit-Abbeville (Dieppe)
August 1895' at the end of Proust's sketch *'Sous-Bois'* in *Les Plaisirs et les
Jours*, 232-4, it has been wrongly supposed that Mme Lemaire's villa
was called Petit-Abbeville. In fact the name is that of a village a mile or two
south-west of Dieppe.

sister Maria in a flirtatious cadenza of marine epithets—'O my sister Maria, confidant of my inmost thoughts'—she was reading his *Baldassare Silvande*—'lighthouse of wandering woes, star of kindness, halcyon of exiles, sea-breeze, song of mighty oarsmen, shiver of little mossfronds, perfume of friendship, delicious fluting of winds that bring lost ships to life . . .' and so on. 'Marcel is rather tight-chested, his father may advise against Brittany,' wrote Reynaldo to Maria on the 12th; and Mme Lemaire, with an inexorable hospitality worthy of Mme Verdurin at La Raspelière, reported on the 17th, 'Marcel is much better—if only they would give up the Brittany idea—at least I make them eat regular meals, which they wouldn't do at some dreadful little hotel.' But they refused to give up this 'Brittany idea'; they returned to Paris on 30 August and left almost immediately for Belle-Isle. The railway journey, like that of the first visit to Balbec, took all night; they stayed in the Hôtel de Bretagne at Palais, the chief port of the island.

No doubt the visit to Brittany was, for Proust, like the arrival at Balbec for the Narrator, the fulfilment of a childhood longing[1]: he would see Renan's 'land of the virtuous Armoricans, who dwell by a dark sea jagged with rocks, beaten by everlasting storms', and perhaps, too, its 'girls with eyes like green wells, in whose depths of undulating water-plants the blue sky is mirrored'. But at first they were more conscious of making a 'pilgrimage to the habitations made glorious by Sarah Bernhardt', as Proust wrote to Yturri; for Belle-Isle, an island ten miles from the coast opposite Quiberon, was the summer residence of the divine Sarah, and the home of the poetry-writing sailor whom she had brought to the Delafosse fête. But when they had made the customary excursions in a bumpy governess-cart, through the purple heather and golden gorse of the slate uplands, and the palm-trees of the warm valleys, and gazed on the Atlantic from the hair-raising cliffs, there was nothing left to do: the season was nearly over, and there was a dreadful smell of sardines. They fled to the mainland on 6 September and settled at Beg-Meil, a fashionable little *plage* across the bay from Concarneau. Proust had heard of the place from a friend of his parents, a banker and music-lover named André Bénac, who owned a château near by:

[1] In point of fact, Proust had already visited Brittany as a child, and seen Mont Saint-Michel when he was too little to appreciate it. (Cf. *Billy*, 115.)

similarly, in *Jean Santeuil*, Jean is recommended to visit Beg-Meil by his mother's friends the Sauvalgues.

Their hotel was a converted farmhouse, and M. Fermont the proprietor had the kindly bluffness of a farmer: soon Proust was treated as one of the family, just as he had been in Mme Renvoyzé's lodgings at Orleans. They stayed in the annexe a hundred yards from the main building, and *pension* was a mere two francs a day. Apple orchards descended to the edge of the sea, and the cider-like smell of rotting wind-falls mingled with the scent of seaweed. Proust made friends with a fisher-boy, who took him out into the bay at evening to hear the bells of Concarneau, and carefully avoided the shoals of jelly-fish which Proust hated, and kept a bottle of ink in his boat in case the young gentleman should wish to write. A shout of "Good-night, good fishing," came from a passing smack, and "Good-night, good fishing," Proust would blissfully call back. In the afternoons after their enormous lunch he lay hidden in the sand-dunes with Reynaldo, reading Balzac, and Carlyle's *Heroes and Hero-worship* in Izoulet-Loubatière's translation. They found that the absence of indoor sanitation was made still more serious by the prevalence of nettles.

Among the other guests at the hotel was a minor Franco-American marine painter, Alexander Harrison, whose *Blue Lake* they had already noticed in the Luxembourg Museum. 'He's stayed here for nine months every year for the last seventeen years,' wrote Reynaldo to his sister Maria. Half-serious, half-joking, they sent him a joint letter announcing their intense admiration for his work and begging to be allowed to meet him; and after dinner the amused but flattered painter joined them at their table. From this incident comes the meeting with the novelist C. at 'Kerengrimen' in *Jean Santeuil*, though C. himself is a memory of Maupassant in Normandy; and in *A l'Ombre* Harrison for a moment becomes Elstir, to whom the Narrator and Saint-Loup introduce themselves in the same way in the restaurant at Rivebelle. He recommended a trip to Penmarch—"a sort of mixture of Holland, the East Indies and Florida,"[1] he

[1] Similarly, when Elstir urges the Narrator to visit Carquethuit near Balbec in preference to the Pointe du Raz, he says of Carquethuit: "I don't know anything quite analogous to it in the rest of France, it reminds one more of certain aspects of Florida" (I, 854). Elstir at Rivebelle in the time when the restaurant is still a humble farm (I, 826) resembles Harrison at Beg-Meil.

said, referring to its sand-dunes and sub-tropical climate, "and a storm there is the sublimest thing you could see anywhere". When a storm came they duly went, by pony-trap, to the nearest station at Pont l'Abbé, and then on the little local railway to the Pointe de Penmarch. They crawled on hands and knees through the gale to the edge of the cliff; and below him Proust saw, instead of the expected violence and turmoil, a white procession of calm Alpine heights slowly surging and falling into the abyss, and thundering as they fell.

It was Beg-Meil that gave to Balbec—besides one syllable of its name—the Celtic mystery of its position. The mystery resides in the idea, and dissolves in the reality of Balbec, which is found when the Narrator visits it to be a charming but ordinary Normandy resort like Cabourg, Trouville or Dieppe. But when Legrandin speaks of "Balbec, the most ancient bone in the geological skeleton of our soil, the end of the world, the real country of the Cimmerians, that funereal shore famed for its numberless shipwrecks, the eternal realm of the sea-mists," and the Narrator as a child longs to take 'the beautiful, generous one-twenty-two train' which will land him at Balbec after an all-night journey, 'when the grey dawn rises on a raging sea', and then proceed to the Breton towns of Lannion, Pont-Aven and Quimperlé,[1] the yet unvisited Balbec is united with Beg-Meil. Brittany, also, was a land of many 'little trains', of which Proust travelled on at least two, that from Auray to Quiberon, whence he sailed to Belle-Isle, and that from Pont l'Abbé to Penmarch, when he went to meet the gale.

His return to Paris in mid-October was soon followed by a catastrophe. He had been absent from the Mazarine almost continuously since July, and had made delightful plans for still more leave; but now he heard that the third of the new attachés was to be transferred to the Ministry of Public Instruction for routine service in the registration of books deposited under the law of copyright. He informed his superior at the Ministry of his delicate state of health, and M. Franklin was invited to throw one of the two senior attachés to the wolves in his place. 'Monsieur Proust seemed to me to enjoy excellent health,' replied the inexorable Franklin, 'and if he has been concealing infirmities which render him unfit for his very light duties, he has only to resign.' Instead, Proust asked for further leave, invoking the all-powerful

[1] I, 130, 385-6

name of M. Hanotaux, then Foreign Minister; and just in time for his second visit to Réveillon, leave came.

Whether because she believed *Les Plaisirs et les Jours* would float her drawings to still wider fame, or because she liked people who liked Réveillon, Mme Lemaire had taken a temporary fancy to Proust. The invitation in October came because in August, at Dieppe, she could hardly bear to let him leave for Brittany. But on principle she preferred not to give invitations in the 'bad season', when the garden was past its best. Her daughter Suzette was detailed to speed the coming guests. 'It's fine, though cold, now,' she wrote to Maria Hahn on 19 October, 'but if they dawdle much longer winter will be here, this huge house will be full of draughts and gloom, and I'm afraid Mama won't want them to come—do tell Reynaldo to bring lots of warm clothes, just as if he were spending the winter at the North Pole.' The great chestnuts had turned colour, but still kept their leaves; and the branches, as Proust wrote in one of the last sketches for his coming book,[1] 'seemed like a magnificent comb clasping the flowing golden locks of the leaves'. The autumn visit to Réveillon was almost the last of the events in Proust's life which form the fundamental plot of *Jean Santeuil*. It may be assumed that most of the incidents in the 'Second Visit to Réveillon' of *Jean Santeuil* —the moonlight walks in the hills, the bedroom fires, the delicious food provided by the Duchesse ("I've got them to make you a *soufflé*, my dears, the least I can do is to see you eat well"), the storm that makes Jean long to set off immediately for Penmarch—really occurred. But it will no doubt never be known whether a fellow guest, a 'tall young woman of twenty-two, so kind, cheerful and healthy' really shared Proust's bed, or whether she, too, was a case of 'transposition'. On his return he applied to the Ministry for a whole year's leave, which was granted on 24 December 1895, for nothing could be refused to a protégé of M. Hanotaux.

Another event of the closing year was a dinner on 12 December at Alphonse Daudet's, with Edmond de Goncourt, who hardly spoke, the right-wing journalist Henri Rochefort, Montesquiou, who made the most peculiar serpentine gestures with his hands and chattered infuriatingly about ladies' fashions in the Second Empire, and Albert Flament, who tells the story. When they rose

[1] *'Les Marroniers'*, *P. et J.*, 234-5

from table Montesquiou made a beeline for Flament and asked: "Do you like poetry, and have you read mine?" At one a.m. in the cloakroom Proust gave an imitation of Count Robert's piercing screams to the Daudets' cousins, Adeline and Marthe Allard, muffling the noise against the hanging masses of overcoats. 'Before that evening I'd heard nothing but blame of Proust's idleness, his slavish devotion to Mme Lemaire, his uncontrollable passion for high society, his total lack of personality,' wrote Flament in his diary; but as Proust continued his imitations in the cab going home, Flament was impressed by 'the surprising profundity of his adjectives'.

After eighteen months of complete absorption in Reynaldo Hahn, Proust's interest was now turning to another young man. It was a year before, in the winter of 1894, at a dinner given by Charlotte Baignères, that Proust had first met the great Alphonse Daudet, in whose house Reynaldo was already a regular visitor. "Monsieur de Montesquiou was there," Mme Daudet told her sixteen-year-old son Lucien, "and a charming young man called Marcel Proust, extraordinarily well-read and with beautiful manners—and now go to sleep, dear boy, it's terribly late." Soon Proust was asked to one of the Daudets' Thursday at-homes, and Lucien, who was allowed to serve the coffee before being packed off to bed, remembered his moonlike paleness and jet-black hair, his over-large head drooping on his narrow shoulders, and his enormous eyes, which seemed to take in everything at once without actually looking at anything. "Never in all my days," declared Lucien's grandmother next morning, "have I met a young man so well brought up as that little Monsieur Proust." Lucien was a slim, frail youth, with a classic nose of which he was inordinately proud, and a tiny Chaplinesque moustache: 'a handsome boy,' Jules Renard had written in his journal for 2 March 1895, 'curled and pomaded, painted and powdered, with a little squeaky voice which he takes out of his waistcoat pocket'. He was intelligent, capricious and highly-strung, given to hysterical laughter and weeping, and, a little later, to unhappy relationships with young men of the working classes. His talent for painting and writing came to nothing, crushed by the superiority of his celebrated father and his kind but truculent elder brother, the anti-Semitic, proto-fascist Léon Daudet. Such was the brilliance of Lucien's conversation—'that astonishing windmill of words which was his only feat of creation'—that André Germain, who married his sister Edmée, thought he had a preponderant influence on the prose-style of Proust; but it is much more probable that the influence was in the opposite direction.

In the autumn of 1895 Lucien, now seventeen, and attending art-school with Albert Flament at the famous studio of M. Jullian, became sufficiently grown up to be interesting. He was invited to tea in Proust's bedroom, where Félicie Fitau, an old servant in a white bonnet, one of the originals of Françoise, brought a dish of cakes, and Proust offered for his entertainment an album of photographs of actresses, writers and society ladies, and the treasured copy of *Gladys Harvey* bound in Mme Hayman's petticoat. "Photographs bore me, I'd rather we talked," declared Lucien disconcertingly; they discussed Jullian's studio, their favourite authors, and Proust's health ("I hardly ever manage to get to the Mazarine Library"); and their friendship began. Soon they met every day. They went to the Louvre, where Proust revelled in Fra Angelico ("His yellows and pinks are creamy and comestible") or, as was Swann's habit, found like-nesses to people they knew in portraits by old masters. "Do you see this Ghirlandaio of the little boy and the old man with a polyp on his nose—it's the very image of the Marquis du Lau"[1]; and with a characteristic dilation of the nostrils Proust would add, "Ah, dear boy, it's *so* amusing to look at pictures!" For a New Year's present, on 31 December 1895, he sent Lucien an eighteenth-century ivory casket, carved with a young lady leaning on an urn and the words '*A l'amitié*'.

Lucien became aware of his brilliant friend's extraordinary simplicity of heart. Sometimes his kindness was absurd but touching: he invited the Daudets' aged maid-servant to an evening at the theatre; and when Lucien prevented him from carrying a heavy parcel for Alphonse Daudet's Italian valet Pietro (Proust always shook hands with the old man, and talked about Dante), he was hurt and angry—"You're violent and heartless," he cried. But sometimes his moral nobility took a dreadfully moving form. Lucien told, as a callous joke, an anecdote of a schoolfriend who was ashamed of a dowdy mother and

[1] Swann is struck by the resemblance between this picture and M. de Palancy (I, 223).

pretended, when she visited him in the school parlour, that she was a family servant. Proust hid his face in his hands, and Lucien thought he was laughing; but then he saw his friend's cheeks were streaming with tears. 'Marcel Proust was nearer to God than certain hard-hearted and haughty persons I know who are Christians,' he wrote long afterwards. But they shared a keen sense of the ridiculous, and collected clichés of the kind dear to M. de Norpois ('the Emerald Isle', 'our brave little soldiers', 'Albion' instead of England)—which they called *louchonneries*, 'because they make you blink, you know'—and also those of two slightly different varieties which are respectively characteristic of Professor Cottard ('raining cats and dogs', 'deaf as a post') and his wife ('my Abigail' for a maid, 'making an expedition' for a visit to Versailles). Their joint appreciation of people's absurdity brought on a distressing affliction: sooner or later, whenever they went out together, they lapsed into a paroxysm of hysterical laughter. Montesquiou invited them for an evening with Delafosse, and they saw fit to warn him, on the pretext that 'we might offend Delafosse', of their propensity to 'blind, agonising, irresistible *fou rire*'. They went, *fou rire* seized them, and Montesquiou never forgot or forgave 'this gross breach of decency'. He remembered the occasion when Lucien as a child (for Count Robert was an old friend of the family) had emptied a plate of bonbons into his top-hat—"He did it on purpose!" he had bitterly cried; and now he told everyone: "Lucien Daudet has a pernicious influence on Marcel Proust." And yet, for a time, just as he had wooed Proust himself, and then Reynaldo Hahn who by now was in disgrace, Montesquiou saw in Lucien a possibility of the longed-for disciple. But the mirage receded, and he sent Mme Daudet an exquisite rose with the message: 'You are a rose, your children are the thorns.' Long afterwards he likened Reynaldo and Lucien to the two thieves, the bad and the good, who were crucified on Calvary: Reynaldo was the bad thief, but Lucien, he hoped, would be with him in Paradise. Montesquiou's involvement with Lucien, however, had one permanent result. He introduced him to his admired Marquise de Casa-Fuerte, who in turn made him known to her aunt the Empress Eugénie; and poor Lucien discovered that his vocation was neither painting nor writing, but to attend the exiled Empress at Farnborough and Cap Martin to the end of her very long life.

Meanwhile, however, perhaps at first only by way of retaliation, Reynaldo himself was straying from their friendship. For a few months, in the spring and early summer of 1896, Proust suffered from excruciating jealousy, in which his anguished curiosity characteristically turned from the present to the past. 'I deserve your reproaches, oftener than you imagine,' he wrote, 'but if ever I do not deserve them, it is in those moments of torturing effort, when by watching a face, or linking one name with another, or reconstituting a past event, I endeavour to fill in the gaps in a life which is dearer to me than all else, but which will continue to cause me the most anxious sorrow until, even in its most innocent details, I know it all.' One evening in society Hahn insisted on staying to supper when Proust begged him to come home. "You'll regret this one day," declared the furious Reynaldo, only to be punished next morning by an appalling letter. 'I owe it to our former friendship not to let you commit such acts of stupidity, spite and cowardice without trying to arouse your conscience, and to persuade you—not to admit, for your pride forbids it—but at least to realise what you have done. . . . You don't see that when, after we say good-bye in the evening, I carry away with me the image of a Reynaldo who has ceased to care how he hurts me, I shall no longer have any obstacle to put in the way of my desires, and then nothing will stop me. . . . Overwhelmed with remorse for so many evil thoughts, so many weak and wicked intentions, I can't claim to be any better than you are'—and so on. This is the pattern of the many scenes of jealousy in *Les Plaisirs et les Jours*, some written before he met Hahn, all before this most serious of their quarrels: they had occurred, therefore, in Proust's earlier friendships, and we shall find them recurring in later attachments. But the situation revealed in these terrible letters leaves no doubt that in the Françoise episode of *Jean Santeuil*, in Swann's jealousy over Odette and the Narrator's over Albertine, Proust was remembering not only his total experience of love, but the rupture of his love for Reynaldo. His agonies, however, lasted only a few months: it was some consolation for his wounded pride to know that he, in the first place, had jilted Reynaldo, not Reynaldo him; and he still had Lucien. In July, as we shall see shortly, the worst was already over.

Only one obstacle now delayed the publication of *Les Plaisirs*

et les Jours: the whole book was now in the hands of Calmann
Lévy, with the exception of Anatole France's interminably
procrastinated preface. At last, with the help of Mme Arman de
Caillavet, Monsieur France was bullied into writing it. A
distressing rumour, indeed, which has persisted to this day,
declared that Mme Arman had perpetrated the whole preface herself—just as Odette was supposed 'by certain gentlemen of the
highest society to have collaborated, more or less, in Bergotte's
works'.[1] Only the last phrase, so the rumour went, was by France
himself. But the rumour-mongers were mistaken with regard to
this last phrase, about Mme Lemaire scattering 'roses and the
roses' dew;—'*les roses avec leur rosée*'—which is in fact a quotation from Villiers de l'Isle Adam's well-known poem *Les
Présents*; and they were probably equally wrong about the whole
preface, which has the inimitable rhythm and preciosity of the
master, doing his best to praise a book he does not altogether like
or understand. His efforts did Proust little good: for nearly a
quarter of a century he was thought of as the writer of whom
Anatole France had said: 'he lures us into a hot-house atmosphere,
among intelligent orchids whose strange and unhealthy beauty
has no roots in the soil ... there is something in him of a depraved
Bernardin de Saint-Pierre and an innocent Petronius'.

Les Plaisirs et les Jours was published on 13 June 1896, at what
was then the enormous price of 13 francs 50 centimes. Proust
gave away copies to most of the friends and acquaintances who
might otherwise have bought his book, and little of the remainder
of the edition was sold. There were very few reviews of this
luxury quarto. It was automatically praised in *Le Figaro*, *Le
Gaulois* and *Le Temps*, because the author was a diner-out, and
the illustrations were by Mme Lemaire. His former colleagues of
Le Banquet, regarding him as a talented traitor to literature,
mingled sarcasm with reluctant admiration: Léon Blum in the
Revue Blanche rebuked him for 'affectation and prettiness—his
gifts ought not to be wasted'; and Fernand Gregh in the *Revue de
Paris* made fun of his reliance on sponsors—'he has invited all
the fairies, without forgetting one, to the cradle of his newborn
book'. Charles Maurras, the future anti-Semitic nationalist, wrote
benevolently in the *Revue Encyclopédique* of his 'diversity of

[1] II, 745. It is true, however, that Mme Arman sometimes helped France
in his weekly articles for *L'Univers*.

talents', 'harmonious tonality', and 'pure, transparent language'—
'the new generation will have to acquire the habit of regarding
this young writer as one of its leaders'.[1] But Maurras at this time
was using Mme Arman's salon for the benefit of his career, and
could do no less for her protégé and France's preface. *Les Plaisirs
et les Jours* dropped stone-dead. Proust would not be famous till
a quarter of a century had passed.

To us, with our unfair advantage of after-knowledge, it is
possible to recognise an aspect of *Les Plaisirs et les Jours* which
was invisible to the Banqueters. We can observe, as his contemporaries did, that the author is immature, sentimental,
mannered, acquainted with malice and snobism from the inside,
and aged twenty-five. But we can also see, as they could not, that
these stories are reservoirs of Time Lost, a vat from which, after
their long steeping, Mme Frémer, Baldassare Silvande, Hippolyta,
Honoré will emerge utterly transfigured as Mme Verdurin, Uncle
Adolphe, Oriane de Guermantes, the Narrator. Illiers, Trouville
and Orleans tremble on the verge of becoming Combray, Balbec,
Doncières; and the young Proust is already speaking with
authority of Time, Jealousy, Habit, Oblivion, 'the ephemeral
efficacy of sorrow'. Yet his frivolous though melancholy title,
with its ironic allusion to Hesiod's *Works and Days*, expresses
only one of the double meanings of *Temps Perdu:* he is not yet
consciously aware of Time Lost, but he is remorsefully conscious
of Time Wasted.

[1] As Professor Kolb has pointed out, Maurras also accidentally hit upon
one of Proust's future titles: 'M. Marcel Proust,' he wrote, 'will be a new
witness to truth regained' (*'la vérité retrouvée'*).

Chapter 12

THE EARLY YEARS OF *JEAN SANTEUIL*

THE appearance of *Les Plaisirs et les Jours* was overshadowed in the Proust family by the sudden death, on 10 May 1896, of Great-Uncle Louis Weil. The poor old gentleman hardly knew he was ill. A cold turned to pneumonia overnight; he became unconscious, showed no signs of suffering, and at five in the afternoon departed this life of ladies in pink in Paris and leisured summers in the green garden of Auteuil. So the original of Uncle Adolphe lay, watched by his niece Mme Proust and his great-nephew Marcel, in his town house at 102 Boulevard Haussmann which was to be Proust's home ten years later; they guarded his lifeless body in the very bedroom, then with flesh-pink walls and gilded woodwork, where Proust would sleep by day and write *A la Recherche* all night. Meanwhile, by the terms of his will, the house went to his nephew, Mme Proust's brother, Georges Weil the lawyer.

In accordance with Louis Weil's Jewish faith there was no service for the dead, and he had even asked that his funeral should be 'no flowers by request'. It was an embarrassing moment when, just as the procession of hearse and cabs left 102 Boulevard Haussmann, a cyclist rode up to deliver a magnificent wreath from the lady in pink herself, Mme Hayman. She had shown great tact in not coming in person—'*of course* you wouldn't shock anyone, everybody who knows you admires and likes you, and my great-uncle was so fond of you,' Proust had written, 'but I'm afraid it might tire you, and there'll be so few other ladies there'. For a moment, when he saw the cyclist and the flowers, and thought of old times and the old gentleman, Proust burst into tears; then he took the wreath into his cab and followed his mother, who had left before the incident, to Père La Chaise, half hoping to fall into Mme Hayman's arms there after all. Mme Proust, not to be outdone in tact, had the wreath buried with the coffin; and at the year's end Proust sent Mme Hayman a valuable tie-pin ('I thought it might do for your hat') which had belonged

to Great-Uncle Louis. Among the old man's relics he also discovered a collection of photographs of pretty little, forgotten
actresses, each with a fond inscription, and kept them as a
souvenir. One was of a certain Marie van Zandt, a sweetly
innocent-looking young person in male travesty, with frilled,
knee-length pantaloons: an original of Elstir's sketch of Odette
as Miss Sacripant.[1]

Next month, on 30 June, death returned to take Mme Proust's
father, Nathé Weil. He was a square-faced, hook-nosed old man,
with clean-shaven, rat-trap lips, bristles of white beard from ear to
ear, and an expression of hard incorruptibility. It is said—and one
can almost hear the Narrator's great-aunt at Combray calling:
"Bathilde, come and stop your husband drinking cognac!"—that
he showed his good taste in wines by providing inferior stuff for
his family, while he kept a bottle of the best Bordeaux on the
floor at his feet for his own use. His reluctance to spend a night
away from home—which was inherited by his grandson—was
notorious: the only exception was during the siege of Paris in
1870-71, when he took his wife to Étampes for safety. Grandfather Weil liked to be strict towards Marcel in his earlier youth,
but when he saw the boy in any real distress would show an unexpected, rather touching sympathy. We need not doubt that
Nathé Weil, like M. Sandré in *Jean Santeuil* at the end of the
Marie Kossichef episode, shed tears when he saw Marcel in
despair over his parting with Marie de Benardaky. Proust reproached himself bitterly for his feeling of heartless indifference
at his grandfather's death, and was relieved to find himself, when
he entered the old man's empty room after the funeral, bursting
into uncontrollable weeping. But for Proust, despite his genuine
regret, the passing of Nathé Weil had its compensations: he was
able to tell Montesquiou, who was nagging him to attend the
inauguration of a monument to Marceline Desbordes-Valmore
at Douai on 13 July, that his mother would not hear of his 'going
to a celebration' in this time of mourning. He shamelessly begged

[1] Similarly in *A la Recherche* Morel, the son of Uncle Adolphe's valet,
brings the Narrator a bundle of photographs of actresses as a souvenir of the
dead man. They are inscribed 'To my best friend', and among them is a
reproduction of Elstir's portrait of Miss Sacripant (II, 264-5). Mlle van
Zandt was no doubt either a relative of the Amélie van Zandt who sang
Mignon and created the part of Lakmé at the Opéra Comique in 1883, or
the same person using a different Christian name.

her to corroborate his story if Montesquiou and Yturri, as they
threatened, should call to ask her to relent; but neither mourning
nor a new attack of asthma prevented him from a round of visits
to Mme Arman, Mme Lemaire, Reynaldo at Saint-Cloud, and his
publisher Calmann-Lévy. His mother, he told Reynaldo, seemed
to be taking her bereavements remarkably well: in fact, as he was
to realise a few months later, her heart was broken.

In August he spent a few weeks with her at Mont-Dore, a
health-resort in the mountains of the Puy-de-Dôme. Both as a
complete mental rest, and as an indirect communication with
Reynaldo, he read Reynaldo's favourite author, Dumas; he
challenged a fellow-guest at the hotel to a duel, without result;
and he received from Dr Cazalis, the original of Legrandin, an
over-gushing and under-paid telegram of thanks for a copy of
Les Plaisirs et les Jours, which cost Mme Proust three francs,
'thus offending,' as he wrote to Reynaldo, 'her twin instincts for
economy and concision'. But even in that mountain-air asthma
awaited him. Hay-making, several months late in the high hills,
was in full progress, and a violent attack of hay-fever drove him
back to Paris.

On the eve of his departure he wrote to Reynaldo—who was
now, after five weeks spent in Hamburg with Proust's blessing,
at Villers-sur-Mer near Cabourg—a letter which sounded the knell
of their love and marked the beginning of their friendship. They
had released one another from all vows of fidelity and chastity:
'it would be noble, perhaps, but it would not be natural at our
age to live as Tolstoy demands of us'. Proust had made the
condition that Reynaldo should confess any new lapses, while
poor Reynaldo, on the contrary, asked only that Proust should
keep quiet about his. 'In future you needn't tell me anything,'
Proust wrote, 'seeing it upsets you so. But you'll never find a
confessor more gentle, more understanding (alas!) and more un-
humiliating—since, if it hadn't been you who asked for silence,
and I for avowal, the situation would be reversed: your heart
would be the confessional, and I the sinner begging for absolution, for I am as weak as you, or weaker.'

In September Mme Proust continued her interrupted holiday
at Dieppe, bathing under medical orders, bruising her feet on the
pebbles, and walking like her dead mother in the wind and rain.
Proust stayed alone with the servants at home, smoking Espic

anti-asthma cigarettes, fumigating with Legras powders, and drugging himself to sleep with amyl, valerian and trional. He dreamed he was at a charity fête at Mme Hochon's (another original of Mme Verdurin), with Mme Lemaire on his arm and the actress Mme Pierson somewhere in the room, and awoke tortured with guilt for having gone into society when still in mourning. Old Félicie came to say the gas-man had called and she was alone in the house; but "I think I'll go down," she concluded, Françoise-like, "the man has such an honest face."

Early in October, when the family was united again, came a state occasion which in *A la Recherche*, where it is relegated to a period ten years earlier in the Narrator's life, became the visit of King Theodosius II. The Emperor Nicolas II of Russia came to Paris as the guest of Félix Faure, the father of Antoinette and Lucie, Proust's playmates in the time of Marie de Benardaky, and now President of the Republic. The trees in the Champs-Élysées were hung with coloured globes of celluloid, paper flowers, and garlands of the new electric lights—most of which, it was discovered when dusk fell, refused to work; and the pale, frigid, twenty-eight-year-old Tzar rode in the presidential landau through frenzied crowds, visibly alarmed at the violence of their cheering. The royalist Duc Honoré de Luynes said hopefully: "The Government has dropped a brick, you can see how the French people love monarchy"; but what the people loved was to have their republic treated as an equal by an emperor. The visit was engineered by the French ambassador at St Petersburg, Marquis Gustave de Montebello, the original of M. de Vaugoubert who arranged the visit of King Theodosius; and the noun 'affinities' which so enraptured M. de Norpois was suggested by the Tzar's equally vague reference (for the word 'alliance' was still taboo) to the 'precious links that unite our two nations'. Two originals of M. de Norpois, Armand Nisard, Marie de Benardaky's uncle by marriage, then director of political affairs at the Quai d'Orsay, and the Foreign Minister Gabriel Hanotaux, both friends of Dr Proust, were present at the state banquet at the Élysée Palace on 6 October when these momentous words were spoken; and it is more than likely that one or the other visited 9 Boulevard Malesherbes soon after, like M. de Norpois when he 'came to dinner for the first time', to dine on Félicie's spiced beef jelly and recount his emotions on hearing the Tzar say 'precious links'.

Another episode in the career of the Vaugouberts is taken from the Montebellos. Mme de Vaugoubert ruins her husband's career by insulting the French ministers' wives during a second visit of King Theodosius, when she monopolises the attention of her friend Queen Eudoxie.[1] Similarly, on the occasion of the reception held at Compiègne during Nicolas II's second state visit to France in September 1901, Mme de Montebello neglected to inform the ministers' wives that hats were *de rigueur*. The ladies disgraced themselves by appearing bareheaded; the only hats to be seen were those of the Empress Alexandra and Mme de Montebello; and it was rumoured that her husband's dismissal by the Combes government in 1902 was in retaliation for this unfortunate incident.[2]

On 19 October Proust went to Fontainebleau, with visions of sunlight on brown leaves, for a writing holiday at the Hôtel de France et d'Angleterre with Lucien's elder brother Léon. Léon Daudet remembered that week as a halcyon period of afternoon walks in the forest, evening drives by moonlight ('Proust, that most enchanting, fantastic and unreal of companions, was like a will-o'-the-wisp at my side in the victoria') and conversations by the fire in the deserted hotel lounge; and for Proust, too, it mellowed sufficiently to play its part in the creation of Doncières. But at the time it seemed a damp inferno of real and imaginary woes. The trees were annoyingly green, it never stopped raining, and they grimly took their daily walk, hearing the horns and baying of a distant hunt, under a steady downpour. His bed was a hateful four-poster, with suffocating curtains and a canopy that seemed always about to fall and crush him; it faced the wrong way; he had asthma and could not sleep. Lucien's longed-for visit on the 22nd ended in a tiff. There was nothing to read but a biography of the Du Barry, which seemed still to preserve the odour of railway-carriages and the excruciating melancholy of departure, for he had started it in the train. He sent urgent and intensely complicated orders to Mme Proust for the despatch of his umbrella, a tie-pin, watch, hat, four Balzacs, *Wilhelm Meister*, Shakespeare's *Julius Caesar* and George Eliot's *Middlemarch*, more money. Thirty francs vanished through a hole in his trouser-

[1] III, 246
[2] The true reason was the change of emphasis in relations with Russia necessitated by the new Entente Cordiale with England.

pocket—an accident which happened with such distressing regularity whenever he went on holiday without his parents, that one suspects him of prevarication to conceal extravagance which he dared not confess. 'The thought pursues me like a crime, a crime against you almost. I can quite understand people who commit suicide for nothing at all.' Mme Proust sent reassuring letters with '100 francs and 100,000 kisses', and offered to take a house for him at Versailles, or to send him to Illiers, 'where you were as miraculously well in the cold weather as you were ill in the hot'. And the weather that year, she pointed out, was quite as dreadful everywhere else as at Fontainebleau: indeed, Dr Proust (who shared the Narrator's father's passion for meteorology) had just made her read him a long article in the *Journal des Débats*, 'which sets out to prove that whenever the weather's bad there's always a reason for it!' But a few days later he returned home, defeated. There had been a real cause behind the misery for which he made so many absurd excuses; he had come suddenly, in another person, upon the abyss of irrevocability, of suffering greater than any of his own. He had experienced a first terrible glimpse of Time Lost.

On 20 October, the day after his departure, Mme Proust had crossed the Boulevard Malesherbes to Cerisier's bakery at No. 8 to telephone her son. 'But Cerisier's subscription didn't include calls outside Paris, and despite all my offers to the Ladies of the Telephone to pay extra, they banished me to the public cabin.' When the call at last reached Proust in the hotel at Fontainebleau he was already anxious and hypersensitised by a long wait. In the disembodied voice of his mother he detected for the first time the note of incurable grief for her dead parents, which at home in Paris the familiar sight of her cheerful, self-sacrificing face had made inaudible. 'When her poor voice reached me,' he wrote to Antoine Bibesco six years later, 'it was broken and bruised, for ever changed from the voice I had known, full of cracks and crevices; and it was only when I reconstituted in the telephone-receiver those shattered and bleeding fragments of words, that I had for the first time the horrible feeling of all that was broken inside her.' He had the thrift and presence of mind, however, to write down his experience immediately and send the manuscript, to his mother: 'please *keep* it, and remember where you put it because it will come in my novel'; and Mme Proust kept it, good-humouredly commenting: 'the story of a convict on his way to Devil's Island could hardly be more despairing'. The incident appears in *Jean Santeuil*, when the hero telephones to his mother from Beg-Meil: Proust even forgot to make the transposition from Fontainebleau to Beg-Meil complete, since Jean thinks of returning immediately to Paris and being with his mother in three hours' time, which would only be possible from Fontainebleau. But in *Jean Santeuil*, as is characteristic of that novel, the keynote is not Jean's awareness of his mother's grief, but his pity for himself. When the Narrator telephones his grandmother from Doncières, yet another theme has taken first place. The Ladies of the Telephone (the phrase is not Proust's own, but the usual Parisian expression, which we have just seen his mother using on this very occasion, for the girl operators at the exchange) have become supernatural deities of the underworld, 'the Danaids of the Invisible'. Perhaps Proust felt a hint of this at the time, for the experience of speaking to an absent person, as if to a talking wraith, through a little black trumpet, was still unusual enough to be uncanny. But in *Le Côté de Guermantes* the episode is a preparation for the death of the grandmother, and it was written after his mother's death.

Proust had now been writing *Jean Santeuil* for a year. As Professor Kolb's study of the original manuscript has shown, the whole of Part I[1] (from the mother's kiss to Jean's early schooldays) was written at Beg-Meil in September-October 1895[2]: it was for this, then, that Proust's friend the fisher-boy kept a bottle of ink in his boat. Some, at least, of Part VI (Jean and Henri's holiday at Beg-Meil) dates from the same time,[3] as also does Part

[1] It is convenient here to refer to *Jean Santeuil* by its 'parts', rather than by the volumes as published, except that page-references must of course be made by the volume.

[2] All six chapters are written mostly on the same cheap local paper ('I'm in a place called Beg-Meil, where you can't get paper,' Proust had written to Robert de Billy). Several pages are written on the backs of draft letters to M. Franklin of the Mazarine Library, asking for an extension of leave from 15 October to 15 December 1895—the leave Proust needed for his November visit to Réveillon.

[3] One page is written on the verso of a letter dated 10 October 1895, extending Proust's and Hahn's return-tickets for a further ten days— a concession for which Proust had characteristically applied direct to André Bénac, who was a member of the government railway commission.

VII, Chapter V ('*Une Petite Ville de Province*').[1] The introductory chapter (in which the novelist C. is met in Brittany, and after his death a few years later leaves the manuscript of the novel to his young friends) was not composed until March 1896, at the home of Léon Yeatman, to whom Proust immediately read it: 'Léon said it was typically "pony",' he told Reynaldo. This was written in a manuscript-book, no doubt the same of which he told his mother in August, 'I have paginated the first 90 pages.' In September he wrote the incident of the children's book with the picture of the moon with a funny face, which occurs in the Étreuilles section (Part II, Chapter IV); and a little later he had filled the 110 leaves of this book, 'besides the loose leaves I worked on before'. The loose leaves are no doubt Part I, written at Beg-Meil; so we may deduce that the exercise-book contained, besides the introductory chapter, all or most of Part II (Étreuilles). At this time—mid-September 1896—he was negotiating with Calmann-Lévy for the eventual publication of his novel, and thought that by working four hours a day he might finish it by 1 February 1897. At Fontainebleau in October 1896 he wrote, besides the telephone scene at Beg-Meil (Part VI, Chapter II), a part of the Charlotte Clissette episode in Part X. Part III, Chapter VIII ('*Une Séance à la Chambre*'), in which the Armenian massacres of August 1896 are mentioned, dates from shortly after his return to Paris. Since the next chapters which can be dated by

---

[1] It is written on the official notepaper of the yacht-club at Étel, a little port on the mainland opposite Belle-Isle. The place described in this chapter is evidently Fontainebleau, and was in fact called Fontainebleau in the original manuscript, though Proust later substituted the reading of the published version, 'Provins'. Ought we to assume that the chapter dates from after Proust's visit to Fontainebleau in October 1896, and that he had saved the paper from the year before? Probably not; for Jean's cheerful bedroom in the hotel, which comforts his homesickness and is clearly the original of the Narrator's room at Doncières, is very different from the hated room of October 1896; and the group of young officers whom he meets in the following pages, and who resemble so closely the Narrator's friends at Doncières, is equally foreign to the stay at Fontainebleau with Léon Daudet. But these features may well belong to an earlier visit to Fontainebleau, perhaps in the autumn of 1893, when his friends Louis de la Salle and Daniel Halévy were conscripts there. If so, there is no longer any need to doubt that this chapter was written at Beg-Meil; and, what is more, the mystery of the primary origin of Doncières is solved.

evidence now available belong mostly to Part VIII and begin in August 1897, we may reasonably assume that the interval between October 1896 and August 1897 was occupied with the composition of Parts IV, VI and VII, which describe the summer at Réveillon, the visit to Beg-Meil, and the second, winter stay at Réveillon.

With the exception of the Dreyfus Case episodes in Part V, Chapters V-IX and a few episodes in Parts VIII-X, the plot of *Jean Santeuil* is the story of Proust's own life up to the end of 1895. It is probable, therefore, that he foresaw and planned the greater part of his novel during the first few months of its composition. The material is the same as that used in the first half of *A la Recherche*, up to the end, say, of the Princesse de Guermantes's soirée in *Sodome et Gomorrhe*. But Proust's selection of it is often different: Charlus and Sodom appear only briefly in *Jean Santeuil*, for they were not fit reading for his mother in her lifetime; the Narrator's schooldays are rarely mentioned in *A la Recherche*; and the story of Swann and Odette is told of Jean and Françoise S. Proust had not yet discovered the master-theme of Time, which would enable him to bring creative imagination to bear upon reality. Because the novel is supposed to be the middle-aged novelist C.'s story of his own youth, there is a basic inconsistency in the time-scheme, far more serious than those in *A la Recherche*,[1] which the reader accepts as mysterious but credible loops in the dimension of Time. Jean is born in 1859, Henri meets the Dutch nun in 1866 (at least ten years too early); yet otherwise the time-scale is that of Proust's own life, and when Jean is in his early twenties he takes part in the events of the Dreyfus Case which belong to 1898. But it is more important to note that Proust is already wrestling with Time, than to complain that he does so without success.

The narrative opens, like *Confession d'une jeune fille* and *Du Côté de chez Swann*, with the crucial incident of the moonlit garden at Auteuil[2] and the mother's kiss refused and exacted. Then Grandfather Weil as M. Sandré deplores, one evening at

---

[1] E.g. the Narrator's encounter with the Lady in Pink, who is Odette before she met Swann, although Odette's affair with Swann happened before the Narrator's birth; the immense age of Odette and Mme Verdurin in *Le Temps Retrouvé*, etc.

[2] Here called Saint-Germain, but later (vol. 3, 307) Auteuil.

Dieppe,[1] the possibility that Jean may become a poet—"you might as well give him a rope and tell him to hang himself!" The year is 1866, and Jean is seven years old; but in Proust's own life this discussion belongs rather to 1893, when he was ordered to choose a career; and M. Santeuil's remark that 'the new Minister of Foreign Affairs has quite a good opinion of writers' is an allusion to Gabriel Hanotaux, who became Foreign Minister in May 1894 and gave the judiciously qualified support to Proust's literary career that is attributed in *A l'Ombre* to M. de Norpois. After a gap of seven years Jean falls in love with Marie Kossichef in the Champs-Élysées, and is parted from her not by his own decision (as was the Narrator from Gilberte) but by the cruelty of his parents. He is sent to the Lycée Henri-Quatre, where his schoolmaster Rustinlor speaks the Homeric language of Bloch; and he pays his unsuccessful visit to the brothel in the Rue Boudreau.

The Easter and May-month interlude at Étreuilles,[2] a half-way stage between Illiers and Combray, belongs both in Proust's own life and in *Du Côté de chez Swann* to the period before the Champs-Élysées, but is displaced in *Jean Santeuil* to the middle of the hero's schooldays. The house in which the family stays, which in real life was the property of Uncle Jules Amiot and in *Swann* was to be that of Aunt Léonie, belongs at one moment (for Proust was undecided) to Jean's paternal grandfather, and then to his father's brother-in-law and sister, the Sureaus. M. Sureau, like Jules Amiot, keeps a draper's shop in the market-place. The garden beyond the river, which later became Swann's Tansonville, and was never entered by the Narrator or his family, is here still owned, like the Pré Catelan at Illiers, by the 'early-rising, gardening uncle'. The servant, who like Françoise kills a chicken and ill-treats the kitchen-maid, is given the real Christian-name of her original, Ernestine Gallou. In many ways Étreuilles already resembles Combray: we meet, in turn, the buzzing flies and hammering in the street by which the hero in his darkened bed-room deduces the heat of the summer's day, the corn-poppy nodding in the plain, the strawberries and cream-cheese, the pink

[1] Nathé Weil paid at least one visit to Dieppe, but in accordance with his well-known habit left the same day, rather than spend a night away from Paris. (Cf. *Corr. Mme Proust*, 125.)

[2] The name Étreuilles is taken from Épeautrolles, a village five miles east of Illiers.

and white hawthorn-chapels, the orris-roots in the lavatory, the
magic-lantern with Golo and Geneviève de Brabant. But Swann,
Gilberte and the Duchesse de Guermantes are absent; there is no
Eulalie, and the invalid aunt, Mme Sureau, though she is allowed
in a brief episode to question Ernestine on the passers-by in the
street, is not given the importance of Aunt Léonie. Sunday mass
in the church is described, but not the church itself, nor the parish
priest. The Two Ways, along which the whole of *A la Recherche*
was to be constructed, remain un-thought of; the dancing spires
of Martinville-le-Sec remain invisible until Proust repeats the
experience at Caen in 1907; and Montjouvain receives only a
passing mention as a place where the family sometimes picnics.
The river is still named the Loir; and Proust sometimes forgets
himself, and calls the village Illiers, and himself not 'Jean' but 'I'.

When the story re-opens in Part III Jean is seventeen, and
beginning his year of *philosophie*. He meets his new schoolmaster,
M. Beulier,[1] who is modelled closely on Alphonse Darlu, and a
new schoolfellow, Henri, son of the Duc and Duchesse de
Réveillon. His parents forbid him to dine out with Henri, unjustly suspecting that the two boys mean to spend the evening
with prostitutes, and Jean quarrels with them violently. This
parental interference may well have occurred in Proust's late
teens, and is less likely to belong to the mid-1890s, when his
mother and father usually forbore to meddle with his private life;
but the other circumstances of the scene are taken, as we shall
see, from a quarrel which occurred in or about May 1897. In
Chapter VI Henri's name is suddenly changed to Bertrand de
Réveillon, and the character described, in particular his walking,
like Saint-Loup, along the partition in a restaurant to fetch Jean's
greatcoat, is recognisable as Bertrand de Fénelon. Proust perhaps
did not meet Fénelon until November 1901, and this chapter is
thus the only one in *Jean Santeuil* which seems likely to have
been written after he virtually abandoned his novel in the autumn
of 1899.

Part IV describes a summer visit to Réveillon, the château of
Henri's parents. Réveillon is modelled on Mme Lemaire's country-
house of the same name; and the visit corresponds to Proust's

[1] The episode in the classroom cannot have been written before 1897, for
it is clearly a counterblast to the opening chapter of Barrès's *Les Déracinés*,
which appeared in that year.

stay at Mme Lemaire's Réveillon with Reynaldo Hahn in August-September 1894. The story of the rosebush is told; Henri is an accomplished musician for the moment, to suit his identification here with Reynaldo; and a sister of Henri, Mlle de Réveillon, appears in place of Mme Lemaire's daughter Suzette. The visit to the farmyard and the peacock with the Duchesse is taken from Proust's stay with Pierre Lavallée at Segrez in April 1895. Anatole France, who had no business at Mme Lemaire's Réveillon, appears as the novelist Monsieur de Traves, and is severely criticised as 'an adept of materialist and sceptic philosophy' by the idealist Jean. But M. de Traves already prefigures Bergotte in 'the mysterious resemblance of all his books to one another', in the fact that 'neither his appearance, nor his conversation, nor anything that Jean heard of his life were in any way a continuation of the strange enchantment, the unique world into which he transported one from the very first pages of any of his books'. One of his absurdest shortcomings, as it seems to Jean, apparently with Proust's approval, is his habit of explaining the beauty of a great work by some minute, material detail ("Yes, it's beautiful, because Rome is such a very beautiful word, don't you think?" or "A lance, that's pretty fine, isn't it?"). Yet in *A la Recherche* this foible, which also belonged to Anatole France, is one of the symptoms of Bergotte's genius, and culminates in his obsession with the patch of yellow on the wall in Vermeer's View of Delft, which brought to the dying novelist both death and salvation. Another visitor at Réveillon is Jean's former schoolmaster Rustinlor, now more like Bloch than ever: when Jean admires Barrès, Rustinlor says, "A pretty bad egg, and the same goes for his books"; and despite his fierce hatred of the aristocracy he calls the Réveillons, after dining with them, "exquisite creatures, with a faraway mediaeval quality which I for one find intensely poetic".

Part V, a political interlude, consists of the downfall of the imaginary politician Charles Marie, followed by scenes from the Dreyfus Case belonging to 1898. The episode of the Marie scandal is no doubt based on the Panama affair of 1892, in which several prominent statesmen, including Floquet, Clemenceau, Freycinet and Maurice Rouvier (who, like Charles Marie, was Minister of Finance at the time and a bitter opponent of the proposed income tax), were accused of receiving bribes from the Panama Canal Company. The politicians implicated in the scandal were, unfortunately, the same who in 1889 had opposed and destroyed the nationalist and proto-fascist movement of General Boulanger. Panama was the second round in the struggle between right and left, army and anti-militarists, anti-Semites and Jews, Catholics and anti-clericals, royalists and republicans, nobility and bourgeois, of which the Dreyfus Case was to be the third. France was already, several years before the Dreyfus Case, in process of division into two hostile halves, of which Proust was committed, against the majority of his hostesses in the Faubourg Saint-Germain, to that of the Jews and the progressive intellectuals. But the division was not yet clear-cut at the time of Panama, when the nationalists to the right and socialists to the left were banded in unnatural union against the receivers of bribes. In so far as the extreme right and left oppositions were enemies of corruption, any decent bourgeois, including Proust himself, could not but support them. But in so far as their motives were impure, aiming at political revenge rather than justice, it was possible to sympathise with the politicians exposed in 1892, as Jean sympathises with Charles Marie, and to regard them as victims of a hypocritical intrigue. Although the chapters on the Dreyfus Case form a logical pendant to those on the Marie Scandal, it is doubtful whether they would have remained juxta-posed if Proust had completed his novel, since they are separated historically by an interval of nearly six years. The episode of the Affair will be noticed in its chronological place, at the beginning of 1898.

All but three chapters of Part VI are based with little alteration on Proust's holiday at Beg-Meil with Hahn in September-October 1895. But the telephone conversation with his mother in Chapter II is imported from the week with Léon Daudet at Fontainebleau in October 1896; Chapter VII, in which Jean finds himself with his mother a year later 'at a health-resort in a valley surrounded by high mountains', is a reminiscence of August 1896 at Mont-Dore; and Chapter VIII, 'Beg-Meil in Holland', recalls a visit to Holland in October 1898.

Most of the material for Part VII, the winter visit to Réveillon, comes from Proust's stay with Reynaldo Hahn at Mme Lemaire's château in November 1895. But the scenes of garrison life in Chapters IV-VI and IX, which form a preliminary sketch for Doncières, come from other periods in Proust's life, from his own military service at Orleans, and from visits to conscript friends, Risler at Chartres in 1895 and perhaps Louis de la Salle at Fontainebleau in 1893. The garrison-town is called Provins, 'two hours distant from Réveillon'—and in fact Provins was only some forty miles by rail from Mme Lemaire's Réveillon. But in the manuscript Proust first wrote 'Fontainebleau', and at first the town described is indeed Fontainebleau, with its Hôtel d'Angleterre 'in the Place d'Armes opposite the Château', and the cheerful vista of three rooms which reappears at Doncières. Proust has not yet decided precisely how the scenes of army-life are to be introduced into his novel: at one moment Jean is visiting officer friends with Henri de Réveillon, at another Henri himself is an officer, and then again Jean is a volunteer private not at Provins but at Orleans, walking from barracks, like Proust himself, through the Faubourg Bannier to his lodgings at Mme Renvoyzé's. Jean meets the Bonapartist Prince de Borodino, who is based on Captain Walewski at Orleans, and reappears at Doncières. One of the Réveillon episodes is among the last to be written in the whole novel: the young poetess of Chapter VIII, the Vicomtesse Gaspard de Réveillon, is Comtesse Mathieu (Anna) de Noailles, and the verses she has just published in the *Revue des Deux Mondes* are those by Mme de Noailles in the *Revue de Paris* for 1 February 1899.

'I mean you to be ever-present in my novel,' Proust wrote to Reynaldo Hahn in March 1896, 'like a god in disguise whom no mortal can recognise.' The metamorphosis of the Jewish, middle-class Reynaldo Hahn into the blue-blooded Henri de Réveillon, a prefiguration of Saint-Loup, is even more astonishing than that of Mme Lemaire—who produced in the opposite direction merges with Mme Verdurin—into the Duchesse de Réveillon his mother. Proust intended it, no doubt, as an apotheosis for his friend, and a wish-fulfilment for his own longing to love a Reynaldo of noble birth. The same desire, compounded from his twin vices of homosexuality and snobbism, which had caused him at first to invent Henri de Réveillon, led him afterwards to seek him out in real life. But it was not until several years later, in the early 1900s, that he made friends with the group of young aristocrats who were the collective models for Saint-Loup; and it remains paradoxically true of Saint-Loup that Proust created the character before he met the original.

Henri's parents present a similar paradox. From the benevolent but rapacious Mme-Verdurin-like hospitality of Mme Lemaire Proust created the Duchesse de Réveillon, with her "I've asked them to make a *soufflé*, my dears, the least I can do is to see you eat well"; and since the Widow had no husband, he presented her with a consort whose Olympian bonhomie and snobism are drawn from Comte Greffulhe. The Duc and Duchesse de Réveillon are a homely, dowdy couple; yet with their dukedom dating from the year 887, incredibly senior, by many centuries, even to that of the La Trémoïlles, their social prestige, their inexplicable, almost parental regard for the hero, they foreshadow the Duc and Duchesse de Guermantes. But here fate was less kind to Proust, or rather, his desire to provide himself with noble parent-substitutes was less practical than his desire for a noble Reynaldo-substitute. He was never to take the trouble to become the darling of a ducal château.

And so, through the second half of the 1890s, he worked upon a novel which he hoped would reveal the inner, universal meaning of his childhood and early manhood, a novel, that is, that tells the same story and has the same intention as *A la Recherche* itself. He hoped; but the meaning eluded him, buried deep and inaccessible beneath the vague excitement with which he wrote. He was still living in the illusory world of Time, floating on the dead sea of the phenomenal world and trying in vain to drown: he could not regain Time because he had not yet lost it. Between all the lines of *Jean Santeuil* is his effort to believe he is writing a great novel, his unwilling admission that his work is doomed from the beginning to sterility. There is something heroic in his premature endeavour, his four years' persistence, his ultimate abandonment of this marvellous failure. But as early as September 1896 he wrote to his mother: 'I can't see anything in it, and I feel sure the result will be detestable'; and *Jean Santeuil*, providentially, was not to be Proust's masterpiece, any more than it was to be delivered complete to Calmann-Lévy on 1 February 1897.

In December 1896 he met, without recognising her, the Ariadne whose thread was to lead him near to the heart of the labyrinth. The beautiful Marie Nordlinger, a young English cousin of Reynaldo Hahn, had arrived from darkest Manchester to study painting and sculpture in Paris; and one evening, when Proust called for his friend on the way to some soirée, he found her added to the group of Reynaldo and his sisters which he used to call 'Apollo surrounded by the Muses'. The visitor from the land of George Eliot and Willie Heath was short and slender, with delicate Pre-Raphaelite hands, dark eyes, full lips, and a look of warm sincerity and intelligence. For the eighteen months of her stay, although at this time they never ceased to call one another 'Monsieur' and 'Mademoiselle', she belonged to Proust's circle; and often, when he called on Mme Hahn, he came not to take Reynaldo away but to stay the evening. They talked endlessly about *vers libre*, metaphor, symbolism and gothic cathedrals (which Reynaldo, a classicist in everything, could not abide); they chose for one another the artists most fitted to paint their portraits, Titian for Marie, El Greco for Coco de Madrazo, Pisanello or Whistler for Proust; or they played paper-games. One evening each was asked to confess his worst faults. Coco freely admitted that his was laziness, and "Quite right, Coco!" everyone approved. Reynaldo's was jealousy, "jealousy and pride"; and Proust, following his friend on to this dangerous ground, declared with much insight: "I'm inordinately jealous, but if anything I'm too humble." They visited the Italian primitives and the Chardins at the Louvre, and the Monets at Durand-Ruel's gallery. One afternoon in July 1897 they went to tea, like the Narrator and Albertine with Elstir,[1] at Alexander Harrison's studio in the Rue Campagne-Première in Montparnasse, and inspected innumerable seascapes of Beg-Meil at dawn, noon and night. 'I little thought I was having tea with Elstir,' Marie Nordlinger wrote long afterwards. But at this early period in their friendship the true function of Miss Nordlinger as the Muse of England and harbinger of Ruskin remained unrecognised: indeed, Proust started on the wrong foot by asking whether she had seen Verlaine on his last visit to London. She had not, and received a reproachful gaze and a murmur of "Oh dear, what a pity!"

It was an unkind stroke of fate that, when he had already begun to forget the failure of his short stories, and thought only of the future glory of *Jean Santeuil*, he should be subjected to two distressing attacks on *Les Plaisirs et les Jours*. The first was an article in *Le Journal* on 3 February 1897, signed Raitif de la Bretonne, which everyone knew to be a pseudonym of the decadent novelist and infamous columnist Jean Lorrain. The real

[1] I, 870-6

object of Lorrain's malice, however, which only made it the more galling, was not Proust himself but Montesquiou.

Lorrain was a large, flaccid invert, rather in the manner of Baron Doasan, who was a great friend of his. He drugged, painted and powdered, and wore loads of jewelled rings on his fat, white, fish-like fingers. His lips were moist and red, his eyes were as blue as the circles that surrounded them; and over them hung extraordinary, paralytic eyelids, 'like the hoods on the front of an omnibus,' as Jules Renard said. Lorrain belonged to that dangerous type of invert which tries to avert scandal by pretending to be virile and accusing everyone else of perversion. In 1902, the year of *Pelléas and Mélisande*, he attacked the admirers of Debussy in an article shamelessly entitled '*Les Pelléastres*'; and in his volume of poems *Le Sang des Dieux* (1882) an ostentatiously heterosexual sonnet-sequence beginning '*Filles adorables du reve!*' was dedicated to Doasan, while another called 'Les Ephèbes', on the beautiful youths of classical antiquity—Ganymede, Alexis, Hylas, Antinous and others—was addressed with equal inappropriateness to Flaubert. Lorrain had many respectable friends, who forgave everything for his prose-style or pitied his unhappy life, and was received by some easy-going hostesses, though barred by most: "It's terrible," said Mme Germain, the banker's wife, "I hear he gives little dances for young persons in the artillery!" But he was a perilous acquaintance. On one occasion he asked Heredia to come to Mme de Poilly's soirée: "I'd rather not," replied Heredia lightly, "because, like Diana of the Ephesians, she has several rows of breasts, one above the other." Before long the poet was horrified to find his little joke quoted word for word in an article of Lorrain's, but used of poor Mme Aubernon, with whom Lorrain happened to have quarrelled, and of whom it was equally true; and as Lorrain had a genuine admiration for Heredia, he had added: 'as the great poet Heredia has so beautifully put it'.

It was the sonnet on Antinous that established contact between Lorrain and Montesquiou. Count Robert was so favourably impressed by the lines

> '*He has the narrow forehead and broad eyes*
> *Of passive striplings loved by perverse gods*'

that he asked to be allowed to call. The causes of their subsequent quarrel are obscure, for we are not compelled to believe the Count's explanation that Lorrain was hurt by his polite refusal to accept the dedication of a new book. Montesquiou soon found he was attacked by Lorrain on every opportunity both in print and in private. One such occasion was the publication in June 1896 of *Les Hortensias bleus*, which earned for Montesquiou from Léon Daudet the nickname of 'Hortensiou' (this was almost more damaging than Forain's 'Grotesquiou'). Proust, unfortunately, was mentioned with approbation in the preface, and Lorrain, leaping to conclusions as to the intimacy of their relationship, had referred to him in his review of 1 July as 'one of those pretty little society boys who've managed to get themselves pregnant with literature'. In *Le Journal* for 3 February 1897 appeared a still more serious libel. Lorrain wrote of the 'elegiac mawkishness' of *Les Plaisirs et les Jours*, 'those elegant, subtle little nothings, thwarted affections, vicarious flirtations, all in a precious and pretentious prose, with Mme Lemaire's flowers strewn by way of symbols all over the margins. All the same, M. Marcel Proust has had his preface from M. Anatole France, who wouldn't have done as much for Marcel Schwob, or Pierre Louÿs, or Maurice Barrès; but'—and here came the sting in the tail—'such is the way the world wags, and you may be sure that for his next volume M. Proust will extract a preface from the intransigent Alphonse Daudet himself, who won't be able to refuse this service either to Mme Lemaire or to his son Lucien.' Only the most inattentive of *Le Journal's* hundreds of thousands of readers could fail to understand that this was a public accusation of homosexuality, involving both Proust and Lucien Daudet. There was only one way to answer it, and to stop further attacks; and Proust sprang with alacrity to the defence of his friend's honour and his own. Only three days later, on the 6th, he fought a duel with his enemy.

It was a cold, rainy afternoon at the Tour de Villebon in the Bois de Meudon, a traditional duelling-ground for quarrelling Parisians. Lorrain's seconds were Paul Adam, the novelist, who was later on Proust's side in the Dreyfus Affair, and Octave Uzanne, the art-critic, who arrived half an hour late with a grey, drawn face, still under the influence of morphine. Proust's own seconds were a positive social triumph: he had succeeded in persuading Jean Béraud, the painter at Mme Lemaire's, not only

to act on his behalf but to bring his great friend, Gustave de
Borda, familiarly known as Sword-Thrust Borda. Thus, when the
Narrator tells Albertine of a duel he has fought, she remarks:
"What very high-class seconds!"[1] Borda had been for many
years an unbeatable challenger, and later a much sought-after
second in society duels: his assistance was a guarantee of social
distinction and, indeed, of virility. This time, however, the
weapon was pistols. The combatants exchanged two ineffective
shots at a distance of twenty-five yards, probably, as decency
demanded except in a life-and-death quarrel, firing into the air.
As *Le Figaro* reported on the 7th, 'no one was hurt, and the
seconds pronounced that this meeting put an end to the dispute'.
"Proust behaved very pluckily, though he wasn't physically
strong," Béraud told Robert Dreyfus many years later; Reynaldo,
who had come to see his friend through, wrote in his diary:
'Marcel's coolness and firmness during these three days seemed
incompatible with his nervous disposition, but did not surprise
me in the least'; and Robert de Flers, who was also present, wrote
to Gaston de Caillavet: 'Marcel was brave, frail and charming.'
Next morning letters of congratulation flowed in, including one
from Willy, otherwise Henri Gauthier-Villars, the witty, shifty
first husband of the young Colette; but this had to be kept from
Mme Arman, who had quarrelled with Willy and had already
given Proust a severe wigging for not dropping his acquaintance.

After the duel Lorrain let Proust lie, but assailed Montesquiou
with redoubled venom. In the April of 1897 Count Robert was
much in view. His verses on Delafosse's piano-playing, entitled
Flower-Quintet, appeared in *Le Figaro* on the 10th; and on the
23rd his portrait by Boldini—an almost spherical society-painter
of whom Mme Straus said "He looks like a toad in a strawberry-
bed"—was one of the sensations of the Spring Salon at the
Champ de Mars. Boldini had done his utmost to represent the
Count, fiercely contemplating a blue-porcelain-handled walking-
cane which he clutched like a rapier, as the image of his ancestor
d'Artagnan. But the fluidity of the subject's attitude was quite
embarrassing, and it was noticeable that his cuff-links, too, were
of blue porcelain to match. 'This year,' wrote Lorrain, 'M. Robert
de Montesquiou has confided the task of reproducing his elegant
silhouette to M. Boldini, that habitual distorter of little women

[1] II, 355

with nervous grimaces, sometimes known as the Paganini of the Peignoir.' On 4 May came the disaster of the Charity Bazaar. A fire started in a cinema booth ('The most amazing invention of the century, admission 50 centimes'); and in ten minutes the temporary building in the Cours la Reine, with its wooden walls, roof of tarred canvas and insufficient exits, was a charred ruin. One hundred and forty-three prominent figures in society, mostly ladies, were burned alive. Montesquiou—who would certainly have behaved with his undoubted courage and nobility if he had been there, but as it happened was not—was maliciously rumoured to have used his famous cane in forcing a way out. Lorrain, in an article on the 14th, gleefully resumed his criticism of the Boldini portrait. 'He seems hypnotised in adoration of his cane, that battle-axe for live ladies and tongs for removal of the corpses of dead ones, henceforth so dismally celebrated in the annals of masculine elegance.' So Montesquiou in turn had to fight a duel, not, strangely enough, with Lorrain but with Henri de Regnier. The Count had arranged on 5 June an afternoon visit to Baroness Adolphe de Rothschild's art-collection, during the course of which Delafosse obliged with a recital. While the guests were collecting their hats and sticks before leaving, Regnier's wife (*née* Marie de Heredia, a friend of Proust in her girlhood) took the opportunity to remark: "That's a splendid cane for a bazaar, you could hit dozens of women without breaking it"; and Regnier, instead of making peace, joined in with: "You'd look still better with a fan!" "I'd feel far more at home with a sword," replied Montesquiou with dignity; and swords it was, a more dangerous weapon in the etiquette of duelling than the pistols chosen by Lorrain.[1] They fought at the Pré aux Clercs in the Bois on 9 June, with Barrès as Montesquiou's second, Béraud, this time on the other side, as Regnier's, and Dr Pozzi in attendance as Montesquiou's doctor. Count Robert's idea of duelling was to whirl his sword like the sails of a windmill. A few moments after joining combat for the third time he received a wound in the thumb, bled profusely, and retired to Touraine to recuperate. The numerous spectators had included more than one priest sent by noble ladies to give 'Quiou-Quiou', in case of need, the last

[1] With pistols it was bad form not to miss your opponent, unless you had an exceptionally serious grievance; but with swords the combatants were in honour bound to go on fighting until one was hurt.

consolations of the Church. "It was one of the best fêtes I've ever given," he exulted. Curiously enough, he found it impossible to dislike Lorrain. Yturri, always glad to act as a dove of peace, was sent to negotiate, and they made it up. Despite a rather unfortunate dinner with Lorrain, during which he was several times called downstairs by blackmailers ("People keep bringing me proofs to correct," he mumbled to Montesquiou), they remained on affable terms until the deplorable Lorrain's death, from multiple anal fistulas, in 1906.

The recital at Mme de Rothschild's was the last given by Delafosse as Montesquiou's protégé. The young pianist had committed the unforgivable treachery of flirting with another patron: 'He threw himself,' said Montesquiou, 'not into the arms, for she can hardly be said to have had any, but at the feet, which were enormous, of an aged spinster of Swiss origin.' Their estrangement was very different from that between Charlus and Morel. Far from being heartbroken, Montesquiou dismissed the unhappy young man with vengeful delight, and when, one day, Delafosse found himself cut in public, the Count's explanation was unanswerable: "One bows when the Cross passes, but one does not expect the Cross to bow back." Visiting friends noted that the Angel's portrait had been transferred from the drawing-room to the lavatory, and that a sure means of giving pleasure to the Count was to speak ill of Delafosse. Mme Howland could call him 'that little "Defosse" girl' with impunity; Montesquiou referred to him no longer as 'the Angel' but as 'the Scrambled Egg'[1]; and during the Dreyfus Affair Proust curried favour by pretending that the famous reference in the 'Alexandrine' letter to 'that swine D——' alluded not to Dreyfus but to Delafosse.[2] The pianist's career, much to Montesquiou's disappointment, was not broken. He played for Countess Metternich at Vienna, in Paris at Princesse Rachel de Brancovan's musical evenings, where Proust continued to see him, and during the 1900s to Edwardian society in London, where he was a friend of Percy Grainger and

[1] *L'œuf brouillé*, '*brouillé*' meaning also 'someone with whom one has quarrelled'.

[2] The true identity of 'D——' in the letter signed Alexandrine from Schwartzkoppen to the Italian military attaché Panizzardi, written at an unknown date in 1891 or 1893, has never been established; but as he was engaged in selling maps of fortifications at a mere 10 fr. apiece, D—— must have been a very small-time spy.

Sargent. After the First World War, however, he declined with the fall of the Guermantes world on which he had lived; and the poverty and obscurity of his death in old age in 1955 were a belated consequence of his first fatal choice sixty-one years before, when instead of relying solely on his art he had sought the patronage of Montesquiou and high society.

Meanwhile the delayed results of *Les Plaisirs et les Jours* had caused Proust further distress, this time from his former comrades of *Le Banquet*. Jacques Bizet, now in his last year as a medical student and living in a bachelor-garret on the Quai Bourbon in the Ile Saint-Louis, had collaborated with Robert Dreyfus in a little revue for shadow-figures, after the manner popularised by the famous Chat-Noir cabaret in Montmartre. The paper figures were cut by distinguished artists, among them Forain and Jacques Émile Blanche; the lighting was provided by a fearsome cylinder of acetylene gas ("if that tube blows up, we'll all be buried in the ruins," Bizet warned); and the revue, which satirised the literary successes of their friends in the previous year, was wittily entitled '*The Laurels all are Cut*'. Fernand Gregh, who nobly accompanied at the piano, was one of the chief victims, for his first volume of poems, *La Maison de l'Enfance*, had just been hailed as a masterpiece. Proust, whose voice was imitated perfectly by Léon Yeatman behind the screen, was seen in grimacing silhouette talking to Ernest La Jeunesse: perhaps this partly accounted for his subsequent annoyance, for La Jeunesse was a malicious, falsetto-voiced, Jewish homosexual, unwashed, deformed, and notorious for his physical resemblance to a body-louse. "I have nothing but contempt for you," he had once declared to the critic Henri Bauer, who replied: "And I have nothing but mercury-ointment for you." So on three evenings, from 18 to 20 March 1897, an appreciative cross-section of literary and social Paris listened to the following:

PROUST. Have you read my book, Monsieur La Jeunesse?
LA JEUNESSE. No, it was too expensive.
PROUST. Oh dear, that's what everybody says. . . . And yet, a preface by M. France, 4 francs—pictures by Mme Lemaire, 4 francs—music by Reynaldo Hahn, 4 francs—prose by me, 1 franc—verses by me, 50 centimes—surely that's value for money?

LA JEUNESSE. Yes, but you get a lot more in the *Almanac Hachette*, and it only costs 2 francs 50.

PROUST (*laughing heartily*). Oh, very good! Oh, how it hurts me to laugh like that! How witty you are, Monsieur La Jeunesse! How delightful it must be, to be as witty as that!

Proust, when it was duly reported to him, was inconsolable. "They have hurt me enormously," he said, weeping, to Gaston de Caillavet at Mme Arman's next Wednesday; "I thought they were so nice—and they're utterly heartless!" But his distress, though disproportionate, was not unreasonable; for the apparently harmless mockery of his former schoolfriends was the anger of Bloch aware of the Narrator's preference for Saint-Loup.

A few weeks later, on 11 April, he paid a visit to two retired servants of the family in an old folks' home at Issy, accompanied by Albert Flament. Again Flament noticed his astonishing gift for mimicry and pastiche, 'like the touch of colour on a pencil-sketch by Forain', as he impersonated the ladies of the Faubourg Saint-Germain, or Mme Arman with her stricken "If only Marcel would work!" They waited in the garden by a bed of pansies— "The only flower I can smell without getting asthma," remarked Proust, and added as he inhaled one cupped in his hand: "It smells like skin." The old couple hurried up, overjoyed to see 'Monsieur Marcel'; he enquired after their wants, insisted on their wanting something, pressed a handful of crumpled banknotes into the old woman's hand, and promised, dancing from one foot to the other, to come again soon and stay longer. On the way back they stopped at a fair on the outskirts of Paris and devoured, under naphtha flares in the cold spring dusk, fried chipped potatoes from paper bags.

On 24 May Proust gave one of the spectacular dinners at 9 Boulevard Malesherbes to which he delighted to invite his best friends, anyone who happened to have done him a good turn recently, stars of the bourgeois salons, and a sprinkling of persons from the Faubourg Saint-Germain whose presence would flatter everyone. The friends were Reynaldo and Gaston; the benefactors were his seconds, Béraud and Borda; Anatole France and the Jewish dramatist Porto-Riche were the *salonnards*; and the flattering company comprised Montesquiou, Marquis Antoine de

Castellane (Boni's father) and Comte Louis de Turenne, original of Babal de Bréauté. The willingness of these distinguished noblemen to dine in Proust's bourgeois home proves two mutually contradictory facts: that the Guermantes set were more human, less exclusive in real life than in *A la Recherche*; and that Proust did not exaggerate his own social position when he portrayed the Narrator's. But the account in next morning's *Le Gaulois* suggests a vague cloud behind the scenes: the Marquis de Castellane left as early as possible for an engagement with his cousin, Boson Prince de Sagan; Mme Proust, still in mourning for her parents, was not to be seen; and 'the famous Dr Proust effaced himself, leaving his son to do the honours of this brilliant dinner-party, during which the most Parisian wit never ceased to sparkle'. Proust thriftily passed on the floral decorations to Mme Straus next morning.

It was about this time, and perhaps in consequence of the trouble and expense of this dinner, that Proust had the quarrel with his parents which in Part III, Chapter VII of *Jean Santeuil* is transposed to his schooldays. Mme Proust, in the humiliating presence of his father's valet Jean Blanc, reproached him for extravagance and ingratitude; Dr Proust, so easy-going by nature, but so violent when roused, joined in; and their son marched furiously out of the dining-room, slamming the door and smashing its panes of coloured glass to smithereens. In his bedroom he was carried away by a further paroxysm of rage and (as he wrote in *Jean Santeuil* and told his housekeeper Céleste many years later) seized from the mantelpiece a vase of Venetian glass given him by his mother and hurled it to the floor. 'We needn't think or speak of it again,' wrote Mme Proust in a letter of forgiveness, 'and we'll let the broken glass be what it is in the synagogue, a symbol of indestructible union.' She alluded to the Jewish ceremony of marriage, which includes the ritual breaking of a glass from which the bridal couple have drunk; and if her words were given their full, terrible meaning they would imply a mystic union with her son more valid than her marriage, in an alien faith, to his father. But their consequences need not be taken too seriously. Psycho-analysis had not yet been invented; and moreover, the malady in Proust's heart fed not on his present relationship with his mother but on the buried, unalterable fixation of his childhood.

Proust was among the three thousand guests at Boni de Castellane's famous ball in the Bois de Boulogne on 2 July. The ball was to celebrate the twenty-first birthday of Boni's reluctant wife ("I'm just as good as these princesses of yours!"), though the host and his uncle gave a different reason when they called on the President of the Municipal Council to extract permission for the use of the Bois. "What is the purpose of this ball?" asked the astonished functionary; and the Prince de Sagan replied, adjusting his monocle with Olympian impertinence: "This ball, Monsieur, will be given for pleasure . . . simply and solely for *pleasure*!" So 300,000 francs of Mme de Castellane's fortune were spent; the trees of the Bois were hung with 80,000 green Venetian lanterns, shining like unripe fruit; and the entire corps de ballet of the Opéra danced before the guests. The climax of the evening was when twenty-five swans, brought by Boni's neighbour Camille Groult, were released to beat their white wings among the lanterns, revellers and fountains of fire. But the loveliest swan of all was Mme Greffulhe, swathed in clouds of white tulle.

M. Groult was a millionaire art-collector, of jolly, piratical appearance, whose wealth came from flour and meat-paste. His collection was particularly remarkable for its eighteenth-century drawings and pastels, beneath which were displayed glass cases of transfixed butterflies. "These are signed Watteau, Nattier, Fragonard," M. Groult would say, "and these"—pointing to the butterflies—"are signed: God." Montesquiou, who frequently called with sight-seeing parties of his friends, was enamoured of a portrait of a young nobleman by Perroneau. "You can see the tooth-marks where that exquisite young mouth has been kissed," he announced, and the pretty Marquise de Jaucourt, leaning eagerly forward, cried "Where? Where? Show me!" M. Groult's most celebrated jest was on the occasion of Edward VII's visit to Paris in 1907. Henri de Breteuil (the other original of Hannibal de Bréauté) was asked to arrange lunch for the King at M. Groult's, to be followed by a tour of his pictures; and to make sure that no one unsuitable should be invited, he demanded a complete list of the guests. 'Don't worry,' M. Groult wrote back, alluding both to the source of his riches and to La Fontaine's fable of the miller and his son, in which the third party is their ass; 'There'll only be the miller, the miller's son, and you!' The story is told in *Le Côté de Guermantes* of the Prince de Luxembourg and his wife's grandfather, 'who had made that enormous fortune out of cereals and meat-pastes'.[1]

Later that month Proust was ill with asthma, his most serious attack as yet. It was at the time of this illness, on 15 July, that Reynaldo lost his father, Carlos Hahn. On one blazing afternoon Marie Nordlinger rode on her bicycle to the Hahns' villa at Saint-Cloud to enquire, and met Marcel just getting out of his closed cab on the same errand. He was grotesquely muffled in overcoat and scarves and writhing in the throes of an appalling attack of hay-fever. She begged him to come inside out of the sun; but "No, I'll wait here," he panted; "you go in and find out how he is, only for heaven's sake don't tell them I've come." As soon as possible she emerged with her report and Proust, gasping, choking and unannounced, drove straight back to Paris. As early as the winter before he had already begun his habit, from which he was never to succeed in curing himself, of working all night and sleeping by day. Henceforth he slept as a rule from eight in the morning till three in the afternoon; and at the time of his duel, as he told Montesquiou in 1905, his only anxiety had been lest he should have to fight in the morning, when he ought to be asleep. 'When they told me it was arranged for the afternoon, all my fears vanished.'

During the same summer, introduced by Reynaldo and accompanied by Marie Nordlinger, Proust frequented the salon of a cocotte who contributed a little to Odette. Méry Laurent, *née* Louviot, was born in 1849, married at the age of fifteen to Claude Laurent, an insolvent grocer, and separated from him seven months later. During the next twelve years or so she first posed in tights and spangles at the Théâtre du Châtelet, then put on more clothes to become an actress, and lastly took everything off to be an artist's model. Towards the end of the 1870s she became the mistress of the famous Dr Thomas Evans, Napoleon III's American dentist. Evans was wealthy, generous and free from jealousy; he installed Méry in an apartment near his own consulting-room in the Rue de Rome, but had no objection to her indulging her passion for painters and poets, so long as they were out of the way when he called, as he did every day, for lunch. She became a model and mistress of Manet, who introduced her to his friend Mallarmé. Manet painted several of his models in

[1] II, 537

male travesty; although Méry does not seem to have been among these, his association with her is doubtless another link with Elstir and his portrait of Odette as Miss Sacripant. A year after Manet's death in 1883, Mallarmé became her lover; she was the delight of his disappointed life until his own death in 1898.

It was to her charming villa, Les Talus, at 9 Boulevard Lannes near the Bois de Boulogne, that Reynaldo took Proust and Marie Nordlinger. Other guests have described Les Talus as a countrified little house with low ceilings and rustic furniture upholstered in flowered cretonne. But by 1897 Mme Laurent had become converted, like Odette, to Japanese art; and it was at Les Talus that Proust saw Odette's staircase with dark painted walls hung with oriental tapestries and Turkish beads, and the huge Japanese lantern suspended from a silken cord and lit, 'to provide her guests with the latest comforts of Western civilisation', Mlle Nordlinger remembered, 'with a gas-jet!' The large and small drawing-rooms, as at Odette's house in the Rue Lapérouse, were entered through a narrow lobby, the wall of which was covered by a gilded trellis, and lined with a long rectangular box from which grew a lofty row of pink, orange and white chrysanthemums.[1] In Mme Laurent's drawing-room was the same portrait of the hostess on a plush-draped easel as in Odette's[2]; though at Les Talus it was 'Manet's enchanting pastel of his beloved, wearing a little toque with a veil, through which emerged her dreamy eyes, her slightly tilted nose and greedy little mouth'.

Mme Laurent was a tall, pink and gold blonde, with regular features and arched eyebrows which made her look always surprised. So ardent and varied was her love of poets that George Moore called her 'Toute la Lyre'; though it was said that when she led Moore himself to her blue-satin bedroom he failed to take the hint, and stood looking like a gasping carp until she declared: "I don't think there's any point in our staying any longer in my bedroom," and led him out. Mallarmé, who had borne with equanimity her association with Gervex, Coppée, Dr Robin (Proust's father's friend, who owned her portrait as 'Autumn' by Manet) and so many more, was a little distressed by the new circle of Dreyfusist young men who were gathering round her; and in a letter of that summer in which he sent Méry an item of botanical information he added ironically: "This will give you a chance of showing off your knowledge in front of Proust." One evening Reynaldo took Proust, whose interest in Ruskin was already awakening, to Méry's to meet Whistler, Ruskin's arch-opponent since the famous libel-suit in 1878. "Ruskin knew nothing whatever about painting," Whistler asserted; but Proust cajoled him into 'saying a few nice things about Ruskin,' and when the painter left his grey kid gloves behind he appropriated them as a souvenir. Dr Evans died in November 1897, and Mallarmé on 9 September 1898; and this late flowering of Méry Laurent's salon had an early withering.

In August Proust stayed with his mother, as in 1895, at the Kurhaus Hôtel, Kreuznach. At first the weather was fine and dry, but he had asthma—it was because their rooms were on the ground floor, he decided. Then it was rainy and cold, yet the perverse malady receded. At Kreuznach he wrote Part VIII, Chapter V, of *Jean Santeuil*, '*Le Salon de la Duchesse de Réveillon*', and no doubt other episodes of his novel, for he told Léon Yeatman: "I haven't been able to write any letters, because I've been working so hard." All through this holiday, and even as late as October, when he went away with Hahn, Mme Lemaire was hoping to see Marcel and Reynaldo at Réveillon again. In vain she sent full instructions and times of trains, or deputed Suzette to beg Maria Hahn 'to *press* them and *hustle* them a bit'. But Réveillon had already yielded all its sweetness two years before, and they never came.

On 16 December 1897 Alphonse Daudet died, struck down after thirty years of respectable married life by the unforgiving *Spirochaeta pallida* caught in his Bohemian youth. For Proust Daudet's place as a writer was with Théophile Gautier and George Sand, whose works, though he had ceased to overvalue them, retained the irrecoverable but indestructible glamour of the dining-room fireside and the shady recesses of the Pré Catelan at Illiers. He continued all his life to quote Tartarin's 'double muscles', or 'hellish dark and smells of cheese' from *Jack*—he did not know that the Master had stolen the latter from *Handley Cross*. But when he came to know the dying writer personally he felt a new gratitude for his kindness, a respect for his heroic endurance of pain and paralysis. Alphonse Daudet, in turn, was charmed and impressed by Lucien's brilliant friend. From the first he kept Proust's letters with the cherished correspondence of great men,

which his family called 'the autographs'. "Marcel Proust's the
Devil Himself," he would remark with amused awe, when faced
with some new example of his psychological insight; and Proust
would be welcomed with a smile when he burst into the study
at 31 Rue de Bellechasse to enquire: "Do you know when Lucien
will be back from Jullian's?" "The great stumbling-block
('*écueil*') in your life, my dear boy, will be your health," he once
told Proust; and the saying supplied a theme for *Jean Santeuil* and
a hint for Bergotte's prophecy to the Narrator.

For three days Proust and Reynaldo rallied round the distraught and weeping Lucien. They saw Alphonse Daudet lying
in state, like Bergotte, on his flower-strewn bed: La Gandara was
sketching his friend for the last time, while Barrès stood in
mournful contemplation, and Hervieu in tears kissed the death-
cold forehead. In the funeral procession from Sainte-Clotilde to
Père la Chaise on the 21st they walked behind Zola, Drumont
and Anatole France, enemies united for a moment in their love
for the dead writer. From time to time Proust hurried forward
to take Lucien's arm; and that evening he called again to beg his
friend to try to sleep. An epoch was over; and as the deaths of
Calmette and Agostinelli seventeen years later seemed, for Proust,
to herald the World War, so the passing of Alphonse Daudet
marked the real beginning of the Dreyfus Affair, the end of the
cul-de-sac of the Guermantes Way.

Chapter 13

THE DREYFUS CASE

ON 26 September 1894 Mme Bastian, an elderly charwoman at the German Embassy in Paris, had delivered as usual the contents of the German military attaché's waste-paper basket to Major Henry, the second-in-command of the counter-espionage bureau of the French War Office euphemistically known as the Statistical Section. Usually her carrier-bag contained nothing more exciting than Colonel Schwartzkoppen's love-letters from Mme de Weede[1]; but this time Henry found a note, thereafter known as the *bordereau*, giving a list of five secret documents which the anonymous writer was willing to sell to the Germans. Some were about guns, some were about mobilisation: the Statistical Section decided, reasonably enough, that only a staff-officer who had recently served in the artillery could have had access to all the documents in question. Among four or five possible suspects was Captain Alfred Dreyfus, whose handwriting happened to resemble that of the *bordereau*; and besides, the man was a Jew. Dreyfus was arrested on 15 October, tried by court-martial on 19 December, sentenced to public degradation and life-imprisonment on the 22nd, and shipped to Devil's Island on 21 February 1895. He remained there in solitary confinement, hoping and despairing, for more than four years.

The case roused only temporary interest, and with the exception of Dreyfus's wife and brother none of his later supporters was inclined to quarrel with the verdict. The Jews, shocked and ashamed that one of their number should be a traitor, kept scrupulously quiet. The socialists, led by Jaurès, were at that time inclined to anti-Semitism on the assumption that all Jews were capitalists. They therefore attacked the Government, with the support of the opposition radical Clemenceau, for favouritism in

[1] She was the wife of the counsellor at the Dutch Embassy in Paris, and occasionally wrote letters to Schwartzkoppen's dictation when he did not wish the handwriting to be recognisable. The most important of these was the *petit bleu*.

not imposing the death-sentence. Even Major Picquart, the future champion of Dreyfus, disliked Jews; he was present at the court-martial and had been unfavourably impressed by the toneless voice in which Dreyfus had protested his innocence. The various army officers involved in the condemnation, including Major Henry, were perfectly sincere in their belief in his guilt. Rather than let a traitor escape, they felt justified in exaggerating the evidence against him; for its thinness, they thought, only showed the cleverness of the criminal. Their chief error had been failure to realise that the secret documents could have been procured by a person not entitled to possess them. In fact, they had been sold, and the *bordereau* written, by Major Esterhazy, an aggrieved and insolvent infantry officer who had never belonged either to the artillery or to the general staff. It was an unfortunate co-incidence that his handwriting had a superficial resemblance to Dreyfus's.

In July 1895 Major Georges Picquart was placed in charge of the so-called Statistical Section and ordered to re-examine the case against Dreyfus with a view to discovering a motive for the crime. Nothing turned up until March 1896, when the invaluable Mme Bastian brought from Schwartzkoppen's waste-paper basket the torn fragments of a *petit bleu*, or special delivery letter. It was addressed to Esterhazy. At first Picquart only suspected a new traitor; but in August he obtained specimens of Esterhazy's hand-writing and immediately recognised its identity with that of the *bordereau*. His superiors were willing to admit that Esterhazy might be guilty, but not that Dreyfus was innocent. In December Picquart was transferred to Tunisia, and knew his career was broken: "I shan't carry this secret with me to my grave," were his parting words. Meanwhile, from September 1896 onwards, Henry began forging new evidence against Dreyfus, some of which was designed to implicate Picquart as an accomplice. He believed he was acting for the best, that Picquart was a blundering meddler or worse, that Dreyfus was guilty; and he knew that his own reputation, not to mention that of his superiors and the whole army, was at stake. Picquart remained silent from a sense of military duty, though he left a confidential account of his discoveries with his lawyer, Leblois, 'in case anything should happen to me'. For yet another year the Dreyfus Case seemed stifled, as if for ever.

Suddenly, in November 1897, the Affair exploded. On the 9th Dreyfus's brother Mathieu published facsimiles of the *bordereau* for sale in the streets; on the 15th he denounced Esterhazy; on the 29th *Le Figaro* published damning photographs of the *bordereau* and of an old letter of Esterhazy to his mistress, in which he declared his ambition to die 'as a captain of Uhlans, sabring the French'. Clemenceau began a long series of articles in *L'Aurore*, demanding revision of the Dreyfus trial; Picquart was recalled from Tunisia under suspicion of conspiracy with the Dreyfusists; and the gallant Esterhazy, confident of War Office support, requested court-martial in order to clear his name. He was tried on 10-11 January 1898 and duly acquitted. On the 13th Picquart was arrested and confined in the Mont-Valérien fortress; and Zola's famous manifesto *I Accuse* appeared in *L'Aurore*. Next morning's issue contained the first instalment of the 'petition of the intellectuals', demanding the revision of the Dreyfus Case.

'I was the first Dreyfusard,' Proust later claimed, with pardonable exaggeration and pride, 'for it was I who went to ask Anatole France for his signature.' Proust and Gregh tackled France at Mme Arman's, in his little study on the third floor, where Mme Arman knitted in an armchair at his side. "Are you trying to get us all put in prison, young man?" he remarked to the ardent Gregh as he signed, while Mme Arman cried: "Don't do it, the Félix Faures will never forgive us!" The two Halévy brothers, Jacques Bizet, Robert de Flers, Léon Yeatman and Louis de la Salle also collected signatures and signed. They had met, along with Marcel and Robert Proust, every evening since the first day of Esterhazy's court-martial, in the upstairs room of the Café des Variétés to plan their campaign. For a whole week Dr Proust refused to speak to his sons: he was a confirmed anti-Dreyfusist, being a personal friend of almost every minister in the Government, and when asked for his own signature by a medical colleague had shown the canvasser to the door. But the 'manifesto of the hundred and four' organised by Proust and his friends was soon followed by half the professors in the Sorbonne, including Proust's schoolmaster Darlu, and Paul Desjardins whose philosophy lectures he had attended when studying for his *licence en droit*. Several artists, such as Montesquiou's friend Gallé, the glass-maker, Mme Lemaire's guest Jules Clairin, and the great

Monet (Elstir himself!) joined in.[1] By the end of the month the petition numbered three thousand names, and was attacked by Barrès in *Le Journal* for 1 February: 'the petition of the intellectuals is signed mostly by half-wits,' he wrote, and went on to call them 'the semi-intellectuals'.

From 7 to 23 February 1898 Zola was tried for defamation of the officers who had acquitted Esterhazy. 'The Dreyfus court-martial may have been unintelligent, but the Esterhazy court-martial was criminal,' he had written in *I Accuse*. His protest was not only a moral act of supreme courage and danger: it was also a tactical move of great skill. By forcing the Government to prosecute him on the Esterhazy question he hoped to enable his lawyers to bring out, in cross-examination of the army witnesses, the new evidence on the Dreyfus Case which was the essential need of the revisionists. Despite the judges' efforts, on instructions from above, to exclude all mention of Dreyfus, a few important facts came out: notably, the admission that Dreyfus had been illegally condemned, since part of the evidence had not been shown to the defence.[2]

A few weeks before Picquart's arrest Proust had been taken to the house of Zola's publisher, Gustave Charpentier, to meet Picquart in person. His admiration for the heroic officer was redoubled when he found he was a friend of Monsieur Darlu, interested in philosophy and music, and well-read. With great

---

[1] Among other signatories were Albert Bloch, '*licencié ès lois*, teacher in the Polytechnic school at Buenos Ayres', whose name Proust used for the character in *A la Recherche*, though there is no evidence that he knew him personally; Pierre Quillard, a poet whom Proust had met at Mallarmé's, and who spoke Bloch's Homeric jargon ("warrior of the shining greaves", of Pierre Louys in well-varnished shoes, or "thou of the swift chariot" to a friend alighting from an omnibus, and so on); also Jules Renard and André Gide.

[2] A no less vital consequence (and no doubt purpose) of Zola's action was that in the witness-box Picquart would be free at last to make his own discoveries public. He revealed the existence of the *petit bleu* (Schwartz-koppen's letter to Esterhazy), and told the court of his horrified amazement, on examining the Secret File against Dreyfus, at finding it contained not a shadow of proof. He also expressed his opinion that the letter from the Italian military attaché Panizzardi to Schwartzkoppen, asking him to 'say we've had nothing to do with this Jew . . . no one must ever know what happened with him', was spurious. It was in fact forged by Henry and is generally known as the '*faux-Henry*'.

difficulty he managed to smuggle a copy of *Les Plaisirs et les Jours* to Picquart's cell at Mont-Valérien; though whether or not the martyr's confinement was soothed by this gift remains unknown. All through the Zola trial he climbed with Louis de Robert each morning to the public gallery in the Palais de Justice, feeling the same pleasurable apprehension and mental tension as at the time of his examination for the *licence en droit*, and armed, as then, with a flask of coffee and a packet of sandwiches.[1]

Zola showed to less advantage in his trial than in the magnificent protest which had provoked it: alternately sulky and vain, he made unfortunate remarks such as: "I don't know the law, and I don't want to know it," or "I have won with my writings more victories than these generals who insult me." Proust had eyes only for the officers, the mistaken, unjust kindred of the spiritual fathers and elder brothers he had known at Orleans. The honour of the Army, he knew, could be saved only by admission of error, not by perpetuating injustice; yet it was with admiration mingled with his horror that he studied General de Boisdeffre, tall, elderly and handsome, with violet cheeks and a courteous manner, when on the morning of 18 February he swore to the genuineness of the *faux Henry* and threatened his resignation as Chief of General Staff if disbelieved. But the centre of the interminable trial was Picquart himself, the Angel of the Revision, as Dreyfusist hostesses had already begun to call him. In *Jean Santeuil*,[2] advancing in his sky-blue uniform towards the president of the court, 'with the light, rapid movement of a Spahi, as if he had just dismounted from his horse, his head on one side and glancing right and left with vague astonishment', Picquart has the air of Saint-Loup. In his scrupulous way of pausing to think before he answered, in order to discover not the most telling

---

[1] Robert de Billy was told a few years later by an informant in the inner circle of Reinach's assistants that Proust had been 'singled out to take an active part in the movement; but his ill-health prevented him from accepting'. Jean Santeuil attended the Zola trial with a watching-brief for Zola's lawyer: "Call for me in the morning," he says to his friend Durrieux as they leave the Palais de Justice, "I'll have finished the notes I'm taking for Labori by then" (vol. 2, p. 121). Perhaps Proust, too, had an official task to perform at the trial. In *A la Recherche* the Narrator's attitude to the Affair is more neutral, and Proust transferred his own attendance at the Zola trial, including the coffee and sandwiches, to Bloch (II, 234).

[2] Vol. 2, 134

reply but the very truth, he reminded Proust of Darlu; in his habits of reading and meditation he recalled Proust's own immersion in books at the firesides of Illiers and Orleans; and the ethical beauty of his conduct for which he was now in prison was that of the morality of Saint-André-des-Champs.

The intervention of Boisdeffre was decisive: Zola was found guilty and received the maximum penalty of a year's imprisonment and a 3,000 francs fine. He appealed on technical grounds, was retried with the same result on 18 July, and unwillingly, under pressure from his friends, fled to England, where he remained till the general amnesty eighteen months later. Picquart was released from prison and dismissed the service on 16 February. For several months the Affair was once again suppressed; but meanwhile revisionists and anti-revisionists gathered forces to prepare for the next inevitable explosion.

Already the heroic age of the Affair was ending. Revisionism became less and less a matter of justice, more and more a matter of politics. Since the Government had set its face against revision, revision could only be achieved through the fall of the Government. Nationalists, anti-Semites, Church and Army, all who stood to lose by a shift to the left, must explain away every new fragment of truth as part of the conspiracy of their enemies; socialists, Jews, anti-clericals and anti-militarists saw their chance to ride to power on the Dreyfusist bandwagon. The cause was gradually contaminated by opportunists whom Proust, as a foundation-member, contemptuously called 'the Dreyfusards of the eleventh hour'. France was divided into two blocs, for whose enmity the guilt or martyrdom of the man on Devil's Island was a mere pretext. Injustice was now on both sides.

The split in society was also a split in high society. The Faubourg Saint-Germain, being royalist, nationalist and Catholic, was inevitably anti-Dreyfusist. Even the hostesses who remained neutral, whether from genuine doubt or from desire to keep their guests of both parties, were forced to choose one side or the other, for sooner or later their guests would quarrel about the Affair and refuse to meet one another again. A cartoon of Caran d'Ache represented a dining-room full of smashed crockery and diners sprawling in battle on the floor, with the caption: 'Somebody mentioned it.' There is no evidence that Proust's activities cost him a single invitation; but he deserves full credit for his courage, for he could not foresee that his Dreyfusism would not mean social death, any more than he could have foreseen he would come out of his duel with Jean Lorrain alive. In the event he was saved, socially, by the general liking he inspired in hostesses and guests, his ability to accept another person's point of view providing it was sincere, and the fact that, as Dr Proust's son, he was in theory a Catholic and, at most, only half-Jewish. But he made no secret of his convictions, and wrote a stern letter to the formidable Montesquiou warning him to refrain from anti-Semitic remarks in his presence.

The bourgeois salons, however, were either neutral or Dreyfusist. The Affair, it might be claimed, had almost begun at Mme Straus's. The rumour that she had worn black on the day after Dreyfus's condemnation was no doubt baseless; but her friend and former platonic lover, Joseph Reinach, was one of the chief agitators for revision. Reinach was an old boy of Condorcet, and had been one of the suspects in the Panama scandal through his relationship with his uncle, the crooked financier Baron Jacques de Reinach. He was a squat, bearded Jew of simian appearance; 'Reinach had a voice of wood and leather,' wrote his enemy Léon Daudet, 'and used to leap from chair to chair, in pursuit of bare-bosomed lady guests, with the gallantry of a self-satisfied gorilla.' "He was comic but nice," Proust told Jacques Émile Blanche, "although we did have to pretend he was a reincarnation of Cicero." Reinach revealed the truth about Dreyfus to the Straus's at their Trouville villa, the Clos des Mûriers, as early as August 1897. At one of her Saturday at-homes in October Mme Straus announced to her guests: "My friends, M. Reinach has an important announcement to make to you." Reinach then declared his certainty that the *bordereau* was written by Esterhazy, but spoiled his case by maintaining, sincerely but mistakenly, that the War Office had known all along that Dreyfus was innocent. The Byzantine scholar Gustave Schlumberger,[1] a bore with enormous feet, tried to defend the good faith of the Army, and was set upon by Hervieu, Porto-Riche and Émile Straus, who was apt to use unseemly language when crossed. Schlumberger left in a huff and broke with the Straus's, for which Proust never forgave him; and the same evening also cost them the friendship of Jules

[1] He is mentioned by M. d'Argencourt at Mme de Villeparisis's as one of the guests of the Duchesse de Guermantes (II, 213).

Lemaître, who henceforth confined himself to the nationalist salon of his mistress the Comtesse de Loynes, and of Forain, who soon afterwards started his anti-Semitic magazine *Psst*.

Mme Straus's salon, under Reinach's influence, became the G.H.Q. of Dreyfusism: it was here that her son Jacques Bizet, her nephews the Halévys and Proust had organised the first *Aurore* petition. Her noble guests, for the most part, remained loyal and continued to attend her Saturdays. But some awkwardness was inevitable, and the Affair marked the beginning of the decline of her salon; for like Zola, Picquart and Proust, Mme Straus was capable of sacrifice in the cause of truth. Princesse Mathilde, who was genuinely fond of the Straus's, made an attempt to convert them in December 1897. "General de Boisdeffre has assured me," she announced, "that the War Office has letters to Dreyfus in the Kaiser's own handwriting!" On 5 February 1898 at Mme Aubernon's—it was the very luncheon at which d'Annunzio exclaimed: "Read my books, madam, and let me get on with my food"—Mme Straus asked the diplomat Maurice Paléologue whether these dreadful letters existed. "If *one* exists, dear lady," he replied with irony, "I'm quite prepared to believe there are several"; and he went on to explain that emperors rarely or never wrote personally to spies.[1] The Haussonvilles, who despite their haughty bow were convinced of the importance of being fair-minded, were shaken by her arguments, and in April they too cross-examined Paléologue. He told them he had the gravest doubts about Dreyfus's guilt, and suspected the document quoted by Boisdeffre at the Zola trial (the *faux Henry*) of being a forgery. "Why, if you're right . . . ," they said, turning pale; but it was noticed that the perfidious M. d'Haussonville began thereafter to pronounce Mme Straus's name as 'Schtraus'.

For Mme Aubernon the Affair was merely an enthralling subject for discussion, like love or adultery, at her Wednesdays. She delighted to hear her pet Dreyfusists, Dr Pozzi, Brochard (the originals of Cottard and Brichot), Hervieu and Porto-Riche at grips with anti-Dreyfusist visitors such as René Bazin or Brunetière; and when asked, "What are you doing about your

---

[1] These letters were frequently appealed to as evidence by the anti-Dreyfusists, but never actually produced. In view of the activities of Major (by that time Colonel) Henry, and the undoubted good faith of Boisdeffre, they may well have existed as forgeries.

Jews?" by a hostess who was gradually eliminating hers, she grandly replied: "I'm keeping them on!" The Affair, however, was destined to be the poor, foolish lady's last pleasure in this world. Mme Aubernon was reduced to silence at last by a cancer of the tongue ("She's punished in the part that sinned," declared one of her enemies), and died on 2 September 1899, aged seventy-four. The faithful Dr Pozzi tended her to the last, and burst into tears as he closed her eyes. There were few people at her funeral, for at that time of year everyone was away on holiday; but when the 'faithful' returned to Paris they said to one another, scarcely knowing whether they spoke in relief or regret: "There'll never be another woman like her!"

For Mme Verdurin as a Dreyfusist, Proust had other hostesses in mind. Mme Ménard-Dorian in the Rue de la Faisanderie conducted a radical socialist salon which became known as the 'Fortress of Dreyfusism'. She had been a friend of Victor Hugo, whose grandson Georges married her daughter Pauline in 1895; and in her drawing-room no opinions were barred, so long as they were progressive and violent. Mme Claire de Saint-Victor, too, had known Hugo, for she was the daughter of his friend, the romantic critic Paul de Saint-Victor, for whose sake she had returned to her maiden name after the disappearance of her un-satisfactory husband. She was a tiny blonde, who made up for her short stature with a foaming, fantastically high coiffure. Mme Aubernon generously said of her salon: "It's just like mine!" Mme de Saint-Victor would burst into the drawing-rooms of her rivals like a lady missionary visiting cannibals, triumphantly brandish-ing an armful of Dreyfusist newspapers; and people called her 'Our Lady of the Revision'. But when Proust says of Mme Verdurin's salon, 'the Dreyfus Affair was over, but she still had Anatole France',[1] he is thinking of Mme Arman de Caillavet. The Affair cost Mme Arman the friendship of Jules Lemaître and Charles Maurras, but brought her the rising political stars of Clemenceau, Briand and Jaurès. Sometimes, indeed, she may have felt that M. France went too far. In July 1898, when Zola was struck off the rolls of the Légion d'Honneur, France quixotically handed in his own rosette; and all through the following winter, led on by Jaurès, he spoke at riotous public meetings of socialists and anarchists—"our voice will be the voice of justice and reason,

[1] III, 236

but it will sound like thunder!"—until hostile journalists began to call him not Monsieur France but Monsieur Prussia.

Mme Lemaire's salon remained neutral. At her reception on 25 May 1898 the long line of carriages waited once more outside 31 Rue de Monceau, while her flowering lilacs contemplated the tall trees of Prince Joachim Murat's garden over the way. Comtesse Aimery de la Rochefoucauld, Princesse Metternich and the Chevignés were there, only too happy to stand, in that amazing crush, with Dreyfusards such as Porto-Riche, Mme Straus, Reynaldo Hahn and Proust himself. Proust arrived, intentionally, after the music was over and Mme Réjane had recited, with his tailcoat several sizes too large, his eyes sparkling from lack of sleep and his voice choked with hay-fever. "What's happened so far?" he asked Albert Flament, and hurried off to Mme de Chevigné, who explained in her raucous voice that she had just dined with the Grand-Duchess Wladimir, "and she was *burning* to come on here with us!" They watched Mme de Chevigné talking with Mme Lemaire, the countess with her rows of pearls, ringletted forehead and bare nape, the hostess painted, wigged and untidy; yet each lady, confident of her supremacy in her own line, 'watched the other', as Flament wrote, 'with the amicable self-assurance which comes from a feeling of absolute equality'. "Mme Straus's Sunday lunches are so interesting," Proust told Flament: "I can't go to the actual lunch, because I'm never up in time, but I go round afterwards and talk about the Affair to Reinach and Dr Pozzi—their cigar-smoke is terribly bad for my asthma, but it's worth it."

At midsummer, as usual, Proust was ill. He had scarcely recovered when he was vouchsafed one of those dreadful warnings in which Providence is so generous, but which human nature, once they turn out to be merely warnings, prefers to forget. On a Wednesday in July Mme Proust was taken to a nursing-home and operated upon for cancer by Dr Proust's colleague Dr Louis Terrier. Only when the operation was under way did Dr Terrier realise the full gravity of her condition; he wrestled for nearly three hours with unpredictable complications, and declared afterwards that he would never have recommended surgical treatment if he had realised the danger it would involve. 'We can't think how poor Mama managed to carry that enormous weight about with her,' Proust wrote to Mme Catusse. For two days, to the distraction of Dr Proust, she lingered between life and death; and on the third day, when she was pronounced out of danger, her first words were a string of stammered witticisms to reassure the anxious Marcel. But the operation had been a success, and by the end of the year Mme Proust seemed completely recovered. She remained for two months in the nursing-home and in October went to Trouville with Dr Proust for convalescence.

Proust himself seems to have made, in the same month, a trip to Holland which is recalled in Jean Santeuil's visit to the seashore at Scheveningen, perhaps also in the mysterious and—so long as we do not know its key—absurd incident of the Dutch nun.[1] Meanwhile, on 21 August at St Petersburg, his childhood sweet-heart Marie de Benardaky had married Prince Michel Radziwill, a distant cousin of the Prince Léon Radziwill whom he was to know a few years later. It is probably that, just as Jean Santeuil meets Marie Kossichef in society ("I believe we used to play together in the Champs-Élysées," she says to the now indifferent Jean),[2] so Proust had seen Mlle de Benardaky after her 'coming-out'. The grown-up Marie, as her photograph shows, was dark and pretty; she had the rosy cheeks, and features at once frank and foxy, of Gilberte Swann. The new Princesse Radziwill was to have a daughter, Léontine, born in 1904; but her marriage was not happy, and was dissolved in 1915.

In August 1898 occurred the most astonishing event of the whole Dreyfus Affair. The Army had always assured the Government that it had the really crushing evidence against Dreyfus in reserve; and the new anti-revisionist war-minister, Cavaignac, decided to produce it. He was furnished with three documents, the 'canaille de D——' letter, which in fact did not refer to Dreyfus at all, a letter of 1896 which would have been completely irrelevant if the ingenious Colonel Henry had not altered the date to 1894 and the initial P—— to D——, and the *faux Henry* itself. He revealed these to the Chamber on 7 July. Picquart immediately denounced all three as forgeries and was duly rearrested on 12 July; the *faux Henry* was carefully inspected for the first time and found to be completely bogus; Henry was taken into custody on 30 August, and cut his throat from ear to ear in Mont-Valérien prison next day. Cavaignac and Boisdeffre, whose only fault had

[1] *Jean Santeuil*, Part VI, ch. VIII, and Part X, ch. IV
[2] *Jean Santeuil*, Part VIII, ch. I; cf. *A la Recherche*, III, 574, where the Narrator fails to recognise Gilberte at the Duchesse de Guermantes's.

been belief in what they wished to believe, furiously resigned on the spot. Esterhazy, seeing the game was up, fled the country.

At last the Government realised that revision was inevitable, and that the safest course would be, with the utmost possible delay, to permit it. The Dreyfus Case was put in the hands of the Court of Criminal Appeal, who sat from October to December 1898. When it became clear that the Court was coming to believe in Dreyfus's innocence, the proceedings were transferred, with the support of President Faure, to the United Appeal Courts. From March to May 1899 they re-examined the evidence with a meticulous patience which seemed misplaced only to those who remembered that the guiltless Dreyfus had now been on Devil's Island for over four years.

Meanwhile Picquart, too, was in grave danger. The Dreyfusards had been over-optimistic in assuming that, since he was now a civilian, he would be tried by a civil court. The Army was pressing for his case to be put before a court-martial, and it was only too likely, if they succeeded, that there would be two martyrs on Devil's Island. Picquart was denied access to his lawyer, Labori, who decided to try the effect of a new petition, which he organised with the help of the now militant Anatole France. This time it was France who called on Proust for help: he asked dear Marcel to secure from Mme Straus one or more of the biggest names from her salon, preferably that of Comte Othenin d'Haussonville himself. 'Perhaps he won't refuse, he has such a great heart, such an elevated mind,' Proust wrote to her hopefully, 'and yet, M. d'Haussonville would be too good to be true, so perhaps you could fall back on Ganderax or Dr Pozzi.' But poor Mme Straus, who had seen her salon suffer grievously for Dreyfus's sake, and was already approaching the intermittent nervous exhaustion by which she was to be tortured for the remaining twenty-eight years of her life,[1] could not even attempt so desperate an enterprise. Picquart's petition, however, was no less imposing than Dreyfus's at the time of *I Accuse*: among the signatures, amid a vast array of professors, artists, writers and even ambassadors, were those of France, Rostand, Porto-Riche, Brochard, Comte Mathieu de Noailles and the two originals of

[1] Mme Straus's facial tic had been particularly noticeable at Mme Lemaire's on 22 May. Her neurasthenia was hereditary, for her mother, sister and aunt had all died insane.

Berma, Réjane and Sarah Bernhardt. Every night from his cell in Cherche-Midi prison Picquart could hear bands of students from the Sorbonne shouting "*Vive* Picquart!" It was decided that his case should await the decision of the Appeal Court on Dreyfus; but the unfortunate consequence was that Picquart remained incarcerated for ten months. When Proust read the newspaper which contained the first list of signatures he found, to his extreme indignation, that his own name had been omitted. 'I know my name will add nothing to the list; but the fact of appearing in the list will add to my name,' he wrote to the editor; '... I believe that to honour Picquart is to honour the Army, since he incarnates its sublime spirit of sacrifice of the self to ends which surpass the individual.' However Proust might loathe the real Army of Henry and Boisdeffre, he never ceased to admire the ideal Army—to which he himself had belonged under Colonel Arvers and Captain Walewski at Orleans—of Picquart and Saint-Loup.

Even Henry's suicide ('the Affair, which used to be sheer Balzac, is now Shakespearean,' Proust had written to Mme Straus) could not convince the anti-revisionists. It was now the nationalist party-line to pretend that Henry's forgeries were a heroic act in defence of the State, and did not in the least affect the certainty of Dreyfus's guilt. Proust's acquaintance Charles Maurras became famous overnight for an article in the *Gazette de France* promising vengeance to the martyred Henry: 'Your ill-fated forgery will be acclaimed as one of your finest deeds of war!' This appeal to the doctrine that the end justifies the means began the resplendent career of propaganda—Catholic, royalist, anti-parliamentary and fascist—which ended, nearly fifty years later, in an extraordinary stroke of Nemesis: the aged Maurras found himself, like Dreyfus, imprisoned for life for betraying his country to the Germans. Now it was the turn of the anti-Dreyfusists to organise a list of names. The anti-Semitic *Libre Parole* opened a subscription, 'for Colonel Henry's widow against the Jew Reinach', which soon reached 130,000 francs. Contributions came not only from Barrès, the young Paul Valéry and Arthur Meyer, but from half the noble Faubourg, including the Ducs de Brissac, Luynes and La Rochefoucauld, the Duchesse d'Uzès, the Marquis's de Lubersac, Ludre and Luppé, and the Comtes de FitzJames, Ganay and Montesquiou (Robert's cousin Léon).

In opposition to the Dreyfusist Ligue des Droits de l'Homme, which was composed mainly of Sorbonne professors with a large proportion of Protestants, Maurras founded the Ligue de la Patrie Française,[1] which soon had fifteen thousand members, and survived long enough to become the foundation of fascism in France. Several of the most prominent, such as Jules Lemaître, the historian Vandal, Barrès, Forain, the poet Heredia and the Comtesse de Martel (the novelist Gyp) had been acquaintances of Proust in happier days. Their unofficial headquarters was the salon of the wealthy Comtesse de Loynes, on which the nationalist salon of Mme Swann at the time of the Affair is modelled. Mme de Loynes resembled Odette in that she had been a Second Empire cocotte, was at home (a most daring innovation) every day of the week at tea-time, and was given to benevolent but enigmatic silence while her guests talked. Jules Lemaître, her lover, was the Bergotte of her salon: "poor Lemaître, for him she'll never seem a day over fifty," someone said; and after her death in 1908 Adrien Hébrard, the editor of *Le Temps*, unfeelingly remarked: "Never mind, they'll meet again in a better *demi-monde*." But the salon of Mme de Loynes was political and literary, rather than aristocratic; and Proust is thinking of Mme Hayman's drawing-room six years before when he makes the Princesse d'Épinay, opening Odette's door in search of a sub-scription for the 'Patrie Française', find a fairy palace in which Louis de Turenne and the Marquis du Lau are cup-bearers serving orangeade and iced cakes.[2]

In December 1898 Proust was touched to receive a Christmas card from Marie Nordlinger, who had returned to England early in the summer before. He had ceased, like the Narrator, to believe in anniversaries; but now the memory of Christmasses past, 'of candle-light, of snowfalls, melancholy obstacles to some longed-for visitor, the scent of mandarin oranges absorbing the warmth of the room, the gaiety of frosts and fires, the perfumes of tea and mimosa', returned with a rush of emotion. 'All these things re-appear, coated with the delicious honey of our inner being, which we have unconsciously deposited on them during years in which we were under the spell of selfish ends; and now, suddenly, it makes our hearts beat.' And in gratitude he told Marie she was 'fresh and

---

[1] Brichot joined it, much to Mme Verdurin's annoyance, taking the opposite line from his original Brochard, who was a Dreyfusist (II, 583).
[2] II, 745

graceful as a branch of hawthorn'. The incident is one of several which show that Proust was now beginning, at last, to return to the secret springs of his early youth, the source of *A la Recherche*.

On the afternoon of 16 February 1899 the Angel of Death, this time in the guise of the lovely Mme Steinheil, called on yet another enemy of Dreyfus. She was admitted to President Faure's study in the Élysée Palace at 5.30. At 6.45 the President's secretary, hearing loud screams from the lady, broke the door in and found his master lying in a coma from a cerebral haemorrhage, still clutching the flowing hair of his stark-naked companion. Even Dr Potain could do nothing, and at 10 p.m. the father of Proust's playmates Antoinette and Lucie expired, without regaining consciousness. The nationalist newspapers decided it was, somehow, all a Jewish plot, and referred darkly to Judith and Delilah. The brutal Clemenceau wrote: 'Felix Faure is dead. There's still not a man the less in France, but there's a good situation vacant—I vote for Loubet.' Loubet, whom the anti-Dreyfusists hated because he had tried to hush up the Baron de Reinach scandal in the Panama crisis, and was known to be pro-English and a revisionist, was duly elected President of the Republic. For a few days the country was on the verge of revolution: on the 19th the new President was mobbed by Deroulède's nationalists and Guérin's anti-Semites, shouting their slogans of "Panama!" and "Aoh, yes!" (a favourite anti-English expression). On the 23rd, the day of Faure's funeral, the troops in the cortège were followed to their barracks by Déroulède, Guérin and Barrès, imploring them to march on the Élysée and impose a military dictatorship. Déroulède was arrested on a charge of high treason and subsequently acquitted; and this fiasco was the last serious threat to the cause of Dreyfusism.

On 25 February at the Vaudeville theatre Proust attended the first night of *Le Lys rouge*, an adaptation by Gaston de Caillavet of Anatole France's novel about love in high society. Both novel and adaptation had been written to Mme Arman's order, and the décor of the first act, as everyone noticed with satisfaction, was copied from her drawing-room. Proust arrived towards the end of the act and hurried to the dress-circle, where Mme Arman, her cheeks rouged carmine, her greying hair dyed copper-colour, and a toque trimmed with stuffed pink bull-finches perched on her vast forehead, took little trouble to conceal her ill-temper at the play's evident failure. "The actors don't seem real enough, don't you agree, Madame?" he murmured, and escaped to Mme Lemaire's box to bow to the rosy and golden Boni de Castellane, and kiss the diamonded hand of Boni's cross little wife. Gaston, who for the last ten years had found it difficult to be polite to Monsieur Trance, took offence at slighting references to his mother and his play in an article by the anti-Dreyfusard Pierre Véber. They fought with swords on 1 March at the Grande-Jatte, an island in the Seine beyond the Bois de Boulogne, and Gaston was slightly wounded in the arm. Proust passed on the congratulations of Dr and Mme Proust, who admired a good son even more than they deplored duelling, and took the opportunity to add: 'Please give your wife the respectful homage of her old admirer.'

He had already discovered a new social environment whose pleasures, a few years later, would come for him to surpass the splendours of the drawing-room. In a great restaurant he could observe, sit on plush in a corner free from draughts, be treated as a prince, be fantastically generous to young waiters, and talk endlessly in the small hours in a company almost exclusively male. On 4 March at Larue's in the Place de la Madeleine, while the gipsy orchestra played the waltz *Monte-Cristo* at 1 a.m. in a décor of blue, red and gold, he sat with Albert Flament and Robert de Flers in his favourite place at the far right corner, talking theatre: he had solved the problem of how, when an evening in society had ended and the guests departed, not to go straight home.

On 16 April Flament dined at one of Mme Arman's Sundays. When the inevitable discussion of the Affair became too heated—for M. Arman was 'Anti', and was apt to remark to Anatole France: "My dear anarchist, may I press you to a slice of this excellent ham?"—Mme Arman silenced the whole table with a formidable glare, while France changed the subject with a set-piece about Perugino and his pot of lapis-lazuli. At eleven o'clock, when the guests were beginning to leave, Proust arrived and fastened, with an air of affectionate absent-mindedness, on M. France. Mme Arman watched them. "What a pity Marcel won't work," she lamented to Flament, "he could write such a marvellous novel! But he fritters himself away. Don't you think he's a bit *too* fond of society?" And she added, in a tone at once vulgar and tyrannical, the very voice of Mme Verdurin, "but perhaps we could find a way of *making* him work?" Neither of the speakers was aware that Marcel had already written, by any standards but his own, a 'marvellous novel'. Flament objected that *Les Plaisirs et les Jours* was, all the same, a charming book. "It's charming, all right," she retorted, between her teeth; "but that's not enough. Baldassare Silvande, indeed!!"

Proust left with Flament. "I'll take you home," he promised, and chose, with mingled charity and procrastination, the most aged cabman and most decrepit horse in the Avenue Hoche; but instead of climbing in he said: "Follow us, please, while we walk on." The dark circles round his eyes grew larger; his white face wore an expression of appalling fatigue as he cross-examined Flament on the events of the evening and, by comparing his answers with those of M. France, constructed a stereoscopic picture of all that had happened before his arrival. The cabman fell asleep; he pressed a fistful of money into his hand ("don't you think the poor man looks just like that deaf M. de Saint-Hilaire, who always stands next to the door for fear anyone might speak to him?") and chose another. Flament rejected the offer of a drive through the Bois de Boulogne; they walked past the Parc Monceau, and Proust began to choke as the scent of leaves floated by: 'I don't want you to be tired out to-morrow—I know you get up in the morning *like other people*—" he remarked, "but I'm sure you must be hungry." After supping at Weber's in the Rue Royale they talked for an hour or two more at Flament's door, while the cabman snored on his high perch; and as Flament climbed the stairs, tottering with weariness, he saw Proust plunge at last into the darkness of the cab, as if to shelter from the dawn, while above the chimney-tops showed the accusing finger of a first pink cloud.

The next 'grand dinner at 9 Boulevard Malesherbes', as Proust and his mother were accustomed to call those harassing and expensive functions, was designed to give publicity to three poets, and incidentally to reflect notice upon Proust himself. The guests of honour on that 25 April were Montesquiou, Anatole France and Comtesse Anna de Noailles, who occupied the head of the table opposite Proust himself; and the others included Dr and Mme Proust, Mme Arman, Mme Lemaire, Comte Mathieu de Noailles and Léon Bailby, the editor of *La Presse*, in which a glowing account of the dinner was to appear on the 27th. Smaller fry, including Albert Flament, came after dinner to hear the young and lovely actress Cora Laparcerie reciting verses by M.

France, a selection from Montesquiou's *Les Perles Rouges* (a volume of sonnets on Versailles published on the following 6 June) and the first impassioned poems of Mme de Noailles. The poetess's husband Mathieu looked on, tall and thin with a narrow blond moustache, smiling politely but saying not a word. Flament was captivated by the new Muse: greatly daring, he spoke to her, and listened to a flood of enchanting images, like a river of diamonds. Her black hair hung to her eyebrows in a fringe which she alternately parted and smoothed down with a tiny hand decked with an enormous sapphire. Having said her piece, she enquired of each of the obscurer after-dinner guests: "Who's he? Does he write?"; and already she was calling Flament, as she called everybody, 'my dear'. M. France, he noticed, was beaming at the Comtesse, while Mme Arman pulled a grimace. Flament moved towards her to confide his emotions; but Mme Arman was not interested: "I've made M. France copy out the whole manuscript of *Le Lys Rouge*," she announced, "and we're going to give it to the Bibliothèque Nationale!"

Proust had met Anna de Noailles in Mme Arman's salon, where her success was dazzling but brief. "That little girl's a genius," declared Monsieur France; to which the jealous Mme Arman replied, for she felt that one genius was enough for any drawing-room: "When she's about, you don't exist!" She was the daughter of the Roumanian Princesse Rachel de Brancovan, the excitable Chopin-enthusiast, whom Proust had met at her Villa Bassaraba on Lake Geneva in August 1893, and who was the original of the elder Mme de Cambremer. Princesse Rachel, who lived in the Avenue Hoche near Mme Arman, was the widow of the Roumanian Prince Grégoire de Brancovan (1827-86) and daughter of Musurus Pacha, Turkish Ambassador in London in the 1850s and a descendant of a Greek family whose greatness dated from the mediaeval Byzantine Empire. Mme de Noailles had married Comte Mathieu in 1897 and was now twenty-three years old.[1] It was not till several years later, when his sudden

[1] She was a cousin-by-marriage of Montesquiou several times over, for his cousin Henri had married Mathieu de Noailles's sister Marie in 1889; his uncle Odon de Montesquiou was the husband of Princesse Rachel's cousin Princesse Marie Bibesco; and Anna de Noailles's sister Hélène had married in 1898 Prince Alexandre de Chimay, Mme Greffulhe's brother and the son of the late Prince Joseph de Chimay who had been the husband of Montesquiou's aunt Marie.

passion for her poetry played its part in the gradual liberation of his genius, that her friendship became important to Proust. For the time being he preferred her quiet, shy sister, Princesse Hélène de Chimay, with her gentle, short-sighted eyes and chestnut hair, and mistrusted, although she was an ardent Dreyfusard, the frighteningly brilliant Comtesse Anna. Meanwhile, as we have seen, he put her into *Jean Santeuil* as the Vicomtesse Gaspard de Réveillon.

The decision of the United Appeal Court on 3 June in favour of the re-trial of Dreyfus was followed by the release of Picquart (who had spent just under a year of the past seventeen months in gaol), the despatch of a cruiser to bring Dreyfus back from Devil's Island (he had been there for four years and four months), and the fall of the Government. The new Prime Minister was Waldeck-Rousseau, a revisionist and a moderate anti-clerical. He chose as War Minister General de Galliffet (Charles Haas's friend and the General de Froberville of *A la Recherche*), who was hated by the Right for his revisionism[1] and by the Left for his massacre of Communards in 1871. But the more decent elements in the Army respected him for his heroic cavalry charge at Sedan ("Why, sir, we'll charge as often as you like—so long as there's one of us left alive, that is") and his efficiency. During the wild disorder in the Chamber which greeted his first appearance he was observed to be taking names, and explained: "I thought I'd better invite these chaps to dinner." By a narrow majority, the revisionist ministry was allowed to survive, less for Dreyfus's sake than for fear of revolution and civil war; but in the event it lasted for three years, long enough not only for justice but, unfortunately, for revenge.

The new court-martial of Dreyfus began at Rennes in Brittany on 9 August. The wretched man's hair had turned white, and he was racked with malaria; solitary confinement had made it difficult for him to speak or understand the speech of others; and he had never even heard of Picquart or of the existence of Dreyfusism. Once more he created an unfortunate impression by his dejected manner, the toneless voice in which he exclaimed "I am innocent!" His case was mishandled tactically by Labori, and turned into an attack on the Army; and the judges, realising that

[1] He was not a Dreyfusist, and said: "I never liked the fellow, and I know damn all about his Case"; but for the sake of Army morale he was determined to put an end to the Affair, even at the price of seeing justice done.

to acquit Dreyfus would be to condemn their own superiors, were divided. On 9 September, by five votes to two, they pronounced the absurd and disgraceful verdict: "Guilty of high treason with extenuating circumstances." Dreyfus was sentenced to ten years' imprisonment and to the hideous ordeal of a second degradation. There was an outcry of savage delight from the nationalists, of grief and anger from the Dreyfusists. The Government were embarrassed: they had hoped for an end to the Affair, and now it could only go on for ever, in an interminable sequence of new appeals and new condemnations. They offered Dreyfus a free pardon, which he accepted under pressure from his brother Mathieu, who realised he would not survive another trial; but he made the proviso that he would not abandon the struggle to establish his innocence. The sensible Reinach concurred; Clemenceau, to whom Dreyfus was only a means to political ends, was furious; and the more idealistic of the young Dreyfusists, for whom Dreyfus was not so much a wronged and suffering human being as a symbol, felt themselves entitled to be bitterly disillusioned. 'We were ready to die for Dreyfus,' wrote Péguy, 'but Dreyfus isn't.'

Meanwhile Proust was at Évian on the Lake of Geneva with his father and mother, staying in the luxurious Splendide Hôtel. His passionate day-to-day interest in the Rennes trial, which was shared by Mme Proust but had to be tactfully kept from his anti-Dreyfusist father, did not prevent him from enjoying the social delights of the Lake. The Villa Bassaraba at Amphion was crammed with Brancovans, Noailles's, Chimays and Polignacs, all rabid Dreyfusards, except the poor Prince de Chimay, who did his best to keep out of the way. With them were the society novelist Abel Hermant, and, of all people, Léon Delafosse, now looking a somewhat ravaged angel. Princesse Rachel lived in the main villa, and the guests were scattered over the park in various annexes and châlets, so that on wet days a carriage was sent round to bring them to meals. After lunch the young people met in Mme de Noailles's room, where she usually received them reclining on a chaise-longue, or even in bed, with an extraordinary mingling of languor and effervescence—"I never knew a girl to toss about in bed so!" said Abel Hermant—and proceeded to read the poem she had invariably written the night before. Sometimes Proust would come to dine, and burn his anti-asthma powders beforehand in the châlet of her brother, Prince Constantin de Brancovan; but more often he would come much later. On fine evenings coffee was served on the terrace at the far end of the park, where the long road to Évian could be seen white in the moonlight. About midnight a carriage—Proust called it 'my Brancoach'—would be heard approaching; 'I'll bet anything that's Marcel Proust!" cried the Princesse; and on those evenings the session would be prolonged until three in the morning.

At Coudrée, with its giant plane-trees and box-alleys where Alfieri had wandered with the Countess of Albany a hundred years before, was Mme Bartholoni, a god-daughter of Chateaubriand. "I used to make him go down on all fours to play with me under the table, and I could hear his old knees cracking, but it never occurred to me to feel sorry." She had been a Second Empire beauty, and was still erect and majestic. In memory of her youth she dyed her hair bright red; when her daughters protested, she shouted: "not another word, or I'll dye it green!" Her youngest daughter, Kiki, was a tall, golden-haired, twenty-seven-year old Amazon—'like a heroine in a Scott novel', said the romantic young barrister Henry Bordeaux, who ten years earlier had been accustomed to rush to the schoolroom window with his comrades to see her pass when she rode into Thonon on horseback. All the young men on the lake were either in love with her or, like Proust, pretended to be. In return she took a sisterly interest in Proust's clothing: 'I can't think why you don't dress better, with a tailor like Eppler in the house," she declared.[1] Bordeaux, who was a member of the bar at Thonon and already a well-known novelist, met Proust one day at Coudrée and was delighted to find in him a fellow-enthusiast for Mlle Kiki, Dreyfus and the works of Chateaubriand. He lingered spellbound by Proust's carriage, missing boat after boat home, and remembered ever afterwards the hurt look in Proust's eyes when at last he broke away to catch the last steamer of the day.

Other social possibilities on the lake included the Adolphe de Rothschilds at Prégny near Geneva and the Haussonvilles at Coppet. But at Thonon there were two special friends of Proust, both Dreyfusards afflicted with anti-Dreyfusard fathers, Pierre

[1] The tailor Eppler had his shop on the ground floor of the Proust's home at 9 Boulevard Malesherbes, and in this, though perhaps in nothing else, helped to suggest Jupien.

de Chevilly and Vicomte Clément de Maugny. Maugny was
staying in his father's ancient and gloomy Château de Lausenette
—which reminded Proust of the ruinous castle in Gautier's *Le
Capitaine Fracasse*—high on the hills above Thonon. Evening
after evening they watched the summit of Mont Blanc turning
pink and crimson in the light of the vanished sun, and descended
to the lake to take the little train back into Thonon. A curious
letter of the previous 13 July, which Proust sent to Maugny with
a copy of *Les Plaisirs et les Jours*, shows that they had already
been friends and confidants for two years. Maugny has seen 'the
beginning and end of sorrows not so very different from those I
have tried to define in this book', has been 'intimately associated
with the very sources of my joys and griefs during these years',
and shows 'unfailing compassion for suffering he can scarcely
have understood'. There is an echo here of the emotions Proust
mentions in a letter to Reynaldo Hahn, apparently of this same
summer. 'I know all the more certainly that my affection for you
is a fixed star, when I see it shining still the same after so many
other fires have burned away.' Maugny, Chevilly and their friend
François d'Oncieu[1] are no doubt the young men whom Proust
remembered, in a letter twenty years later to Maugny's wife, as
'my three best friends, long before you knew Clément'.

The weeks at Évian made an important contribution to the
Narrator's two visits to Balbec. Mme de Cambremer's country-
house at Féterne is based on the Villa Bassaraba and is named
after the village of Féternes a few miles inland from Thonon; and
the name of Rivebelle, where the Narrator dines with Saint-Loup,
is a conflation of Riva-Bella, on the Normandy coast eight miles
west of Cabourg, and Belle-Rive, a group of villas on the lake
shore a mile east of Geneva. These borrowings are neither
accidental nor mechanical: the names are talismans to symbolise
the affinities Proust divined in sea-coast and lake-side. Mme
Proust and her son made the same mock-serious show as the
Narrator and his grandmother of shunning the dangers of unwanted society, whether noble (the Cambremers or Haussonvilles), bourgeois (there are unwelcome barristers at both Balbec
and Évian) or, one regrets to notice, Jewish. Mme Proust even
thought of leaving the district for Marcel's sake when they heard

[1] The original link between these three young men was, no doubt, that
each had a father who owned a château in Savoy.

that young Chefdebien was 'on the lake'; and after her departure Proust's letters to her are full of malicious allusions to those equivalents at Évian of the Blochs at Balbec, the Oulifs, Weisweillers and Biedermanns. He was all the more offended when he was himself confused with these, as when Chevilly's father remarked: "I suppose there are a lot of Jews at the Splendide? You really ought to stay at Thonon next year, the society's much less cosmopolitan there!" or M. Galard announced with an air of accusation: "I do believe you're Monsieur Weil's nephew!" There was a lift-boy, 'who did me a great many services'; and there was, above all, a little train.

We have seen little trains in Brittany, and on the way to Mme Aubernon's Cœur Volant near Paris, and shall find another at Cabourg. But the real 'little train' of his novel, as Proust explained long afterwards to Maugny's wife, was the one which crawled from Geneva to Thonon and Évian and back again, stopping at every village or group of villas, and even sometimes where, as at Amphion, there was nothing but a château. 'It was a nice, patient, good-tempered little train,' he wrote, 'which used to wait for late-comers as long as they liked, and even when it had already started didn't mind stopping again while, puffing as loudly as it did, they ran for it at full speed. Their full speed, however, was where the resemblance ceased; for the little train always moved with prudent deliberation. At Thonon there was a long wait, while the passengers shook hands with someone who was seeing his guests off, or another who'd come to buy newspapers, or a good many who, I always suspected, came only as an excuse to chat with their acquaintances. The stop at Thonon station was a form of social life like any other.'[1]

Dr and Mme Proust returned to Paris on 9 September, after a lingering embrace on the hotel terrace between Marcel and his mother, which was eyed with impatience by Dr Proust and with sentimental approval by M. Gougeon, first president of the court of appeal at Besançon. He is the original of M. Poncin at Balbec, who holds the same post at Caen (M. Gougeon himself had previously served at Rouen), and is addressed as 'Premier' by the barrister; he took a liking to Proust and on his departure a few days later gave him a pressing invitation to 'come and see my wife

---

[1] Proust used many of the actual words of this letter in his description of the little train at Balbec (II, 1110).

and me at Besançon'. The 9th was the day of the Rennes verdict
and at the Brancovans' that evening, as Proust inhaled his anti-
asthma powders in Constantin's room before dinner, he was
touched to hear Mme de Noailles weeping violently for Dreyfus
and crying "How could they do it? How could they bear to tell
him? What will the foreigners think of us now?" The harassed
Prince de Chimay had left, ostensibly for the opening of the
shooting season ("I don't think he'll find any game as worth
bagging as his wife," remarked Proust), but really to avoid
arguing about the Affair with his Dreyfusard in-laws. The Prince
de Polignac, however, Charles Haas's great friend, was most
affable, and enquired teasingly: "What's the good old syndicate
doing now, eh?"; for he pretended to believe Proust was in close
touch with the mythical secret society of Jews, free-masons and
atheists to which the anti-Dreyfusards were convinced their
opponents belonged. After dinner there were the usual paper-
games, but even here the Affair reared its head and Mme de
Noailles, asked to give circumstantial details about Bertillon (the
handwriting expert who gave preposterous evidence against
Dreyfus), shocked her young friend to the core by writing: 'I
don't know any, it isn't as if I'd ever been to bed with him.'

On the 19th Proust had an inflammation in his wrist, and was
given cold compresses by Dr Cottet, who resembled Dr Cottard
in name only, for he was charming and cultured, and impressed
his patient by showing that he knew Vigny's *La Maison du
Berger* by heart. Perhaps there is some mystery in this wrist.
When Charlotte Clissette is staying the night at Jean Santeuil's
home, he comes to her bedside at midnight and tells her: "My
wrist is hurting me." She takes his hand, saying "Let me massage
it for you"; 'the expression in her eyes gave him the idea that she
was aware of giving him pleasure, and that this was the reason
for her action'; but when he tries to kiss her she threatens to ring
the bell.[1] Clearly this is a prefiguration of the Narrator's attempt

[1] Part of the episode in *Jean Santeuil* is written on the back of an announcement for the wedding of Jeanne Bailby (sister of Léon Bailby, for whose
newspaper *La Presse* Proust was then writing an article) on 21 September
1899. Proust asked his mother about the date of the wedding on 12
September, complained next day of having no news, and thanked her on the
20th for her 'kind trouble'. He must have received the announcement, therefore, at some time after the 13th and before the 20th. See *Jean Santeuil*
vol. 3, 256-62

to kiss Albertine—who does indeed ring the bell—in her bed in the Grand Hôtel at Balbec. Perhaps the incident actually occurred with a guest, whether male or female, of Proust's at Évian; and possibly the guest was Maugny, who stayed the night at the Splendide Hôtel in Dr Proust's old room on 12 September. But probably the fact that Proust does not mention the pain in his wrist until the 19th rules out Maugny, unless he came a second time a week later. There can be no doubt, at least, that Proust's aching wrist is the same as Jean Santeuil's, and that the episode in *Jean Santeuil* was written at Évian.

One of the dilemmas of society on the lake was the necessity of seeing Coppet, with its relics of Mme de Staël, and the danger of meeting its châtelaine. Mme d'Haussonville ('Pauline', as Proust irreverently called her) was particularly formidable at this time of crisis in the Affair. When the Prince de Polignac's American wife (*née* Winnaretta Singer) saw her on the 9th she had, it is true, shown gracious pleasure on hearing Proust was at Évian: "Do tell me where he's staying, we're *such* good friends!"; but the next moment she remarked cuttingly to the Princesse: "I can *quite* understand you foreigners thinking as you do about the Affair!" The only solution was to go on a Thursday, when the house was thrown open to tourists, and Pauline would certainly be lunching out. On the 21st Constantin de Brancovan and Hermant set out from Amphion in one of the new motor-cars, and were joined by Proust, who preferred to travel by the little train for fear of draughts, at Geneva. Coppet was swarming with sightseers and Mme d'Haussonville, sure enough, was lunching in Geneva. They left a card on her, after seeing absolutely everything, and again on Mme de Rothschild at Prégny. When Proust once more insisted on taking the train at Geneva, Constantin was extremely wounding. "Draughts, indeed!" he exclaimed, "it's all your imagination! Why, your father always tells everybody there's nothing whatever the matter with you! He says your asthma's sheer hypochondria!" But Constantin, Proust later discovered, however insensitive he might be to the horrors of asthma, was right about motor-cars. When one felt only just well enough to get out of bed, he found, they would whisk one away to a longed-for place or person; if one felt too ill to get up at all, the friend would be brought to one's bedside; and they were driven by young and charming

chauffeurs. The motor-car, a few years later—such was the indirect consequence of the visit to Coppet—was to become an
indispensable factor in the liberation which enabled him to
conceive *A la Recherche*, and in the web of new habits which
enabled him to write it. Meanwhile Mme d'Haussonville sent a
most amiable letter of disappointment at missing her visitors, with
a whole page devoted to Proust himself and only a single line
for Abel Hermant, who was given to putting his aristocratic
acquaintances into his novels and making them commit the most
appalling crimes in the last chapter. Proust forwarded it to his
mother for safe keeping, remarking: 'Here is a letter from Pauline,
or How to show one's good-breeding gracefully.'

Autumn arrived at the end of September, rain swept the lake,
and the hotel was about to close. Just as at Rivebelle 'one could
be sure of two or three supplementary months of warmth after
the cold weather had reached Balbec',[1] so on the southward-
facing Swiss bank of the lake opposite Évian the sunlight was still
on the hillsides and the season just beginning; but Mme Proust
begged her son in vain to move there. The staff at the Splendide,
like their colleagues at Balbec, began to leave for Nice, headed
by the obliging lift-boy, who was unpopular with the rest, being
a Dreyfusard and a Jew. The omnibus-driver called on Proust to
shake hands and say, with a warmth that was all the more touching
since he had already received his tip: "Ever since I've worked in
hotels, I've never known anyone so kind to the 'employees'.[2]
We're all devoted to you, and I think it's a shame you're so ill,
because if anyone doesn't deserve to be, it's you!"

Proust had a momentary scare when he heard Anatole France
was thinking of him as a possible husband for his daughter
Suzanne. She was now a charming girl of eighteen, but permanently unsettled by the rift between her parents, who alternately
fought for her possession and neglected her.[3] 'I shall never do it,'

[1] I, 676

[2] "A charming euphemism," Proust observed to his mother, and used it
for the lift-boy at Balbec (I, 800).

[3] Suzanne ended by marrying Captain Henri Mollin, an assistant to the
Dreyfusist War Minister General André, on 10 December 1901: "the
young man speaks with due admiration of Picquart, and seems a decent
sort, so let us rejoice," said her prodigal father.

Proust wrote in alarm to his mother, adding 'Be very cautious if you talk about any matrimonial desires for me.' It may be inferred that Mme Proust had tried to find him a wife on previous occasions, and that he had made no objection in principle, whether from desire to please her, or to conceal his perversion, or from confidence that he could always refuse any actual candidate for his hand, or because he had not yet entirely renounced the possibility of marriage.

Early in October Maugny left for Paris, tiresomely announcing that he would tell Mme Proust her son would be perfectly well if he didn't take so much medicine. Proust saw more of Chevilly, and thought of moving on with him to Venice, where Coco de Madrazo (whose father Raymond de Madrazo had married Reynaldo's sister María in the previous June) had been staying with his aunt Mme Fortuny, the wife of the famous dress-designer. But he abandoned the idea when he heard that Coco had moved to Rome. One evening he drove with Chevilly's sister Marie on the way back from Mme Bartholoni's at Coudrée, and the movement of the carriage on the darkening road recalled Vigny's *Maison du Berger*, already recited by Dr Cottet, in which the poet rides in a shepherd's caravan with his beloved.

> *"Mais toi, ne veux-tu pas, voyageuse indolente,*
> *Rêver sur mon épaule, en y posant ton front?"*

he repeated daringly; for Marie was engaged to be married to the journalist Édouard Trogan, and he felt it safe to flirt with her. In *Sodome et Gomorrhe*[1] it is to Albertine that the Narrator addresses the same lines, as he tears open her raincoat in the little train after their meeting with Saint-Loup at Doncières. 'I don't know which of the two,' Proust wrote to Chevilly, 'those exquisite verses or your sister, seemed more poetic at that moment!' About 7 October he abandoned hope of Italy, broke a dinner-engagement with the Brancovans, and returned precipitately to Paris, where he fell ill and was visited every day by François d'Oncieu.

The Dreyfus Affair was over. On 19 September President Loubet had remitted the remainder of Dreyfus's sentence and

[1] II, 865

cancelled the order for his degradation[1]; on the 21st General de
Galliffet announced: 'The incident is closed'; and on 17 November
Waldeck-Rousseau tabled an amnesty bill covering all crimes or
misdemeanours committed in connection with the Affair.[2]
Dreyfus retired to his sister's house at Carpentras near Avignon
to recuperate. A year later, in November 1900, he appeared in
Paris and was mobbed by hostesses, much to their disappointment and his own disgust. "I hate all this moaning about my
sufferings," he remarked to Julien Benda. "I like to talk about my
Case *objectively*." When Mme Straus met him she could not resist
a malicious "How d'you do, Captain, I've been hearing such a lot
about you!"; and she was heard afterwards to utter the Duchesse
de Guermantes's epigram: "What a pity we can't choose someone
else for our innocent!"[3] Picquart's dislike of Jews mysteriously
returned; he refused to shake hands with Dreyfus, and took to
reading Drumont's *La Libre Parole*. The cynical Clemenceau
exclaimed: "If Drumont hadn't got in first, what a splendid anti-
Semitic newspaper Picquart and I could have run!" Léon Daudet
reported two remarks of Dreyfus which were none the less
apposite for being totally fictitious: "I've never had a moment's
peace since I left Devil's Island," and "Shut up, all of you, or I'll
confess."

The enchanting social scene on which Proust had moved for
six years was now riven asunder by complex antipathies; he
looked back on the Guermantes Way with disillusionment. Two
hostile groups confronted one another across a wide limbo of the
half-hearted and the indifferent. Not all were as violent as the
Marquis de Lubersac, a dreadful miser who thrashed his cabbies
and never paid Dr Proust's bills: such was his virulence, after he

[1] A new Dreyfusist petition was organised at this time by *L'Aurore*. A
list of signatures with the postmark 20 September 1899, shown at the Proust
Exhibition at the Wildenstein Gallery in October 1955 (*Catalogue*, No. 306),
has nothing to do with Proust, who was still at Évian, but includes the names
of several of his friends—Reynaldo Hahn, René Peter, Édouard Risler,
Méry Laurent and Anatole France. Possibly the canvasser was Robert
Proust, whose Dreyfusist activity at this time was causing Proust anxiety
('Please advise Robert to keep calm,' he wrote to Mme Proust on 10
September). Dr Robert Le Masle, who lent this list to the Proust exhibition,
was a personal friend of Robert Proust in later years.

[2] The bill was not finally carried until 24 December 1900; but in spite of
much skirmishing on either side no harm was done in the meantime.

[3] Cf. II, 239

became the lover of the royalist Mme Porgès (although she was born a Wodianer and came from Vienna) that he made each of his sons, one by one, fight duels with the young Rothschilds. Comtesse Potocka lectured Comte Étienne de Lorencez on patriotism, till he retorted: "Surely you, a Neapolitan Pole, aren't going to preach the love of France to the son of a French general?" The lovely Marie Finaly forgot her Jewish birth and adopted ("by way of keeping up with her in-laws," said Proust) the anti-Dreyfusist views of her husband's family, the Barbarins. An ambassador's son remarked to Proust's friend Louis de la Salle : 'Good Lord, are you a Dreyfusist? It won't do your career any good, you know!" Mme Greffulhe became secretly convinced of Dreyfus's innocence, and wrote to her friend the Kaiser begging him to grant her an audience in Berlin, and confide in her whether or not he had employed Dreyfus as a spy; but a large basket of orchids was the only answer Wilhelm II vouchsafed. It is very possible that the story told in *Sodome et Gomorrhe*[1] of the Prince and Princesse de Guermantes—how each unknown to the other asked Abbé Poiré to say a mass for Dreyfus—is true of Mme Greffulhe and her husband; and if so Abbé Poiré may be identified as their friend the Abbé Mugnier, a saintly and delightful high-society priest, whom we shall later find taking an interest in Proust's salvation. But Mme Greffulhe's motives were mixed, for she was becoming interested in politics, moving ever leftward, and had begun to invite those 'Dreyfusards of the eleventh hour', Barthou and Briand, to her dinners. Sometimes, however, as in the dying Charles Haas, Proust saw a genuine conscience in travail. It is probable that Haas, like Swann, risked his social position by proclaiming his belief in Dreyfus's innocence and his support for revision. But it is certain that he resembled Swann (who 'refused to sign, because his name sounded too Hebraic') in refraining from supporting the petition for Picquart. Swann, 'although he approved of revision, would have nothing to do with the campaign against the Army'[2]; and Haas, the veteran of 1870, as Jacques Émile Blanche records, joined the Marquis du Lau and other members of the Jockey Club in 'cutting' their fellow-clubman and former friend General de Galliffet, when he became the revisionist War Minister and undertook the reform of the Army.

The Dreyfus Case had broken the spell of the Guermantes

Way. Proust saw his hosts stripped of the poetry with which he himself had clothed them: a duchess was only an ordinary person wearing a tiara, a duke was only a bourgeois with an exaggerated hauteur or affability. He realised that in entering the heartless and empty world of the Guermantes, in searching there for something higher than himself, he had committed an absurdity and a sin. He punished himself. His asthma descended, like a gaoler or a guardian angel, never to leave him again. His face became haggard, anxious and bearded. Exiled in the desert island of his bedroom, a guiltless traitor to society, he must have felt very like Dreyfus. But 'going-out' ceased to be one of his chief preoccupations (though it always remained an occasional mixed pleasure), less because society had banished him, than because, like Coriolanus, he had banished *them*.

He had a further cause for despondency in the apparent failure of *Jean Santeuil*. He had written out his life, hoping that the answer to its mystery would somehow be revealed in the total, but the riddle remained unsolved. He had worked discontinuously, with innumerable fresh starts, as the fitful inspiration came; but the sterile, disjointed incidents did not add up to a novel. Each episode set out hopefully for the country of the imagination, which he knew ought to be always everywhere, and led him into a waste land. Four years of toil, as it seemed, nearly three hundred thousand words, were wasted.

Yet the imperfections of *Jean Santeuil* should not be exaggerated. It is a fragment made of fragments, a jigsaw puzzle with many of the pieces missing or refusing to fit; but another year's labour would have sufficed to join the episodes, to remove superfluous characters and incidents, and to produce a novel fit for publication. A revised *Jean Santeuil* would have been, in its theme and style and freshness, something new and surprising in French literature, yet not too new, not too far ahead of Anatole France and Barrès for the public to assimilate it: it might have made Proust's name, and rendered *A la Recherche* forever impossible. The best of *Jean Santeuil* is not noticeably immature, except to the modern reader, who is aware, with his knowledge of *A la Recherche*, that its maturity of talent is also the immaturity of genius. For such a reader there is in every page, besides the conscious brilliance, unconscious genius, the sense of a miracle about to happen: the overriding impression is of light and music, of endless discoveries always round the next corner, of sun, air and springtime. The bud contains the fruit, and Proust himself must have felt pride as well as disappointment in what he had achieved.

Perhaps he also realised, however, that *Jean Santeuil* is disfigured not only by technical lapses but by a moral fault which is inseparable from the main theme. It is a novel of revenges, of resentments felt and gratified, of self-adoration and self-pity. The hero is an ill-used young man, thwarted by unfeeling and philistine parents, insulted by wicked hostesses, self-satisfied snobs and pseudo-artists; a benevolent Providence ensures that he invariably scores off them all; and he is insufferably charming, handsome, intelligent and magnanimous. It is possible to commiserate with Proust's injured susceptibility, but not to admire its literary over-compensation in *Jean Santeuil*.

In no section of the novel is the flaw of hurt vanity so glaring as in the deplorable Part VIII, which consists of a series of incidents in which the hero is first socially outraged, and then has his revenge by being publicly patronised by the social superiors of his enemies. It is probable, however, that in their present form these are merely alternative sketches for what would have been, if Proust had revised his work, not more than two main episodes: a scene in which Jean is insulted by Mme Marmet and befriended by the Duchesse de Réveillon, and another in which he fights a duel and is championed by the Duc de Réveillon. Chapter V ('*Le Salon de Mme de Réveillon*') was written, as we have seen, at Kreuznach in August 1897, and internal evidence suggests that the remainder of Part VIII may have been written about the same time.[1] The whole section is particularly rich in material later used in *A la Recherche*. Mme Marmet is an early form of Mme Verdurin,[2]

[1] Datable allusions in Part VIII include the death of Verlaine (8 January 1896), vol. 3, p. 55; the death of Nathé Weil (30 June 1896), p. 125; Proust's duel with Lorrain (6 February 1897) suggests chapters X-XII; Nicolas II first uses the word 'alliance' (August 1897), p. 40.

[2] Mme Marmet has nothing in common with Proust's beloved, intelligent, warm-hearted, unsnobbish Mme Straus, with whom she has been identified merely because her son was Jean's schoolfellow, as Jacques Bizet was Proust's. But Jacques Baignères's mother Laure Baignères would fit equally well. In so far as she has a living original, Mme Marmet is probably Mme Hochon with a little of Mme Lemaire. But in the main Proust has merely borrowed her from the character of the same name in Anatole France's *Le Lys Rouge*.

M. Boissard of M. de Norpois, the Vicomte de Lomperolles of ̀
both Charlus (modelled solely on Baron Doasan without, as yet,
a trace of Montesquiou) and M. de Vaugoubert. An officer
returns Jean's salute in the street, like Saint-Loup, or Lieutenant
de Cholet at Orleans, with a hypocritical pretence of not recognising him. And the Duchesse de Réveillon, when Jean is
disgraced at Mme Marmet's, offers him her arm precisely as the
Queen of Naples was to give hers to the stricken Baron de
Charlus at Mme Verdurin's in *La Prisonnière*.[1] Bergotte in *Jean
Santeuil* is a painter who talks like Elstir; but a primitive form of
the novelist himself appears in Part X, chapter IX as Silvain
Bastelle. M. Bastelle is beset by the problem which obsesses the
dying Bergotte in *Le Temps Retrouvé*—the difficulty of redeem-
ing his moral evil by the creation of aesthetic good; but his vices
turn out, absurdly, to be nothing worse than drink and gluttony.

Jean's love for Mme Françoise S. in Part IX is based, as has
already been seen, on several different incidents in Proust's own
life: on Mme Hayman, Reynaldo Hahn, and the unidentifiable
love-affairs which produced, before he met Reynaldo, the scenes
of jealous cross-examination in the earlier stories of *Les Plaisirs
et les Jours*. The same material was used in *A la Recherche* for
both Odette and Albertine. Jean, like Swann, is tempted to open
his mistress's letter to an alleged uncle, knocks on the wrong
window and is confronted by two old gentlemen, associates his
love with the 'little phrase', and has a dream which marks the
end of his jealousy, and therefore of his love. Françoise, Odette
and Albertine alike are given to Lesbian love. But other incidents,
such as Jean's gift to Françoise of the agate marble, a present from
Marie Kossichef in the Champs-Élysées, belong in *A la Recherche*
not to Odette but to Albertine. It has been suggested that
Françoise, because her Christian name is the same with a feminine
ending, is intended for François d'Oncieu; but the identification
is quite impossible, for she is already called Françoise in *Les
Plaisirs et les Jours*, in stories written several years before Proust
met Oncieu.[2] In Part X Charlotte Clissette is another early
version of Albertine. Jean plays with her the game of ferret, not
at the seaside but in Paris (as he may have done with Marie

---

[1] *Jean Santeuil*, vol. 3, 93; *Pléiade*, III, 322.
[2] Cf. '*La Fin de la Jalousie*' and '*Mélancolique Villégiature de Mme de
Breyves*'.

Finaly), she is jealously guarded by an aunt, as was Albertine by Mme Bontemps, and she thwarts his attempt to kiss her in bed by threatening to ring the bell. Possibly the fact that Jean's love for Charlotte overlaps in time with the end of his love for Françoise is a further hint that the first Albertine was Marie Finaly; for Proust's brief passion for Marie Finaly closely followed his wooing of Mme Hayman.

Towards the end of *Jean Santeuil* appear signs that Proust had made, without realising their full meaning, the discoveries which were to lead to *A la Recherche*. In the last chapters of Part X, written not earlier than the autumn of 1898,[1] Jean shows a new compassion and understanding for his ageing father and mother. Proust had begun to forgive his parents, and the way was now open for the conception in *A la Recherche* of the Narrator's family as a symbol of absolute goodness, a counterbalance to the original sin which corrupts society and sexual love. Through this means the moral disequilibrium of *Jean Santeuil*, in which the unreal virtue of the hero is so unsatisfactory an atonement for the heartless aridity of the other characters, was to be resolved in his great novel.

A second discovery was still more far-reaching. In the Étreuilles section of *Jean Santeuil*, written in the summer of 1896, Jean experiences from time to time, in what is no doubt an un-altered reminiscence of Proust's own boyhood, a rudimentary form of unconscious memory. The apple-blossom at Étreuilles restores the precise sensation of seeing the blossom of the year before, buzzing flies or a noise of hammering heard in Paris bring back the very moment when he heard the same sounds at Étreuilles.[2] But his explanation of the experience ('the sensation of a past moment, in which we saw other such apple-trees, is concealed in it') is not adequate to the delight it causes ('Jean felt a happiness so intense, that he seemed on the point of fainting'). In the very latest parts of the novel, however, the true Proustian concept of unconscious memory is almost complete. Jean hears the little phrase once more, long after the end of his love for Françoise, and feels, even before he recognises it, 'a sensation of

[1] In chapter XI (vol. 3, 330) M. Santeuil remarks: "They say Colonel Picquart will get five years' imprisonment," an allusion to the expected court-martial of Picquart in October–November 1898.

[2] *Jean Santeuil*, vol. 1, 138, 149, 153, 164

vast freshness, as if he had become young again'.[1] The poems of
the Vicomtesse de Réveillon, which are those of Anna de Noailles
heard in the spring of 1899, show Jean that she, too, has known
'that profound essence of our being, which is restored instantaneously by a perfume, a ray of light falling into our room, and
so intoxicates us that we become indifferent to real life . . . and
are momentarily freed from the tyranny of the present'.[2] But the
mystery is studied most persistently in chapter IX of Part VI,
which describes an incident in Proust's stay at Évian in September
1899, and is therefore among the last passages Proust wrote
before he abandoned his abortive novel. While Jean is driving
back from Mme d'Alériouvres's villa on the Lake of Geneva—
evidently Princesse de Brancovan's Villa Bassaraba—and re-
proaching himself for his wasted life, the tracks of boats on the
lake recall those on the sea at Beg-Meil: 'his heart swelled, and the
life which he had thought so useless and unusable seemed enchanting and beautiful'. Once again he attempts to explain his
feeling, and this time, at least, makes a great advance: he sees that
he has experienced something more than a mere recrudescence of
the past, since his past pleasure at Beg-Meil was much smaller
than his present pleasure by the lake-shore. The meaning of his
experience lies in something incommensurable which has been
added to both past and present. But here Jean, and Proust with
him, lacks the essential clue, and can only enter upon a false path.
The unknown power, he decides, is poetic imagination, 'which
cannot work upon present reality, nor yet upon past reality as
restored to us by memory, but hovers only round the reality of
the past when it is entangled in the reality of the present'. Proust
(for in his excitement he has begun to use the word 'I') presses on,
and once or twice again touches upon the truth: 'what the poet
needs is memory, or not strictly speaking memory at all, but the
transmutation of memory into a reality directly felt'; 'from that
juxtaposition issues a sensation freed from the bonds of the
senses'; 'we are torn loose from the slavery of the present and
flooded with the intuition of an immortal life'. He even divines the
possibility of a work, the future *A la Recherche*, in which he would
write 'nothing of what I saw, or thought, or apprehended by
mere reasoning, or remembered by mere memory, but only of the
past brought to life in an odour or a sight which it causes to

[1] *Jean Santeuil*, vol. 3, 225   [2] *Ibid.*, vol. 2, 305-6

explode'. And the superiority of this pleasure to all other pleasures he has known 'is perhaps the token of the superiority of a state in which we have for our object an eternal essence'; 'our true nature is outside time, born to feed on the eternal'. 'We are justified in giving first place to the imagination, because we now realise that it is the organ that serves the eternal.'

Proust had now experienced, as a first reward for leaving the Guermantes Way, a complete form of 'unconscious memory'; but he was not yet equipped to understand its true nature. Time regained is surpassingly valuable not because it restores a fragment of past sensation—for this, since we were then as blinded by habit as we are now, is worth no more than the present—but because along with that fragment is released, from the unconscious mind in which it was buried and preserved, a vision of the absolute reality which only the unconscious mind can see. And further, in this momentary but endless admission to the world beyond time lies salvation, since there alone is the virtue we lose when we are born, and the joy which earthly love can only take away. Proust would not be granted the final revelation until Time, which so far he had only wasted, was, at last, Time Lost. He names 'le temps perdu' in the last section of his novel, but it still has only the meaning of time misspent: 'he thought unceasingly, with irritation and despair, of the time lost ('temps perdu') in the four years since he left school'.[1] The very last sentence of *Jean Santeuil*, like that of *A la Recherche*, contains the word 'time'—'the work of life and death, the work of time, continued unceasingly'—but here it is still only time the destroyer, sapping the life of the parents whom Jean, now that he is strong and they are weak, has at last forgiven. But even Proust's belief in the imagination was still misplaced; for in *A la Recherche* and perhaps in all great works of art, the true function of the imagination is, paradoxically, not to imagine—in the sense of inventing or transforming—but to see: to see the reality which is concealed by habit and the phenomenal world. He needed, and providentially found, a prophet who would tell him that 'the artist is only a scribe'.

[1] *Jean Santeuil*, vol. 3, 284

Chapter 14

SALVATION THROUGH RUSKIN

EXCEPT that it brought him joy unspoilt by suffering, Proust's passion for Ruskin took precisely the same course as his love-affairs or ardent friendships. There was a prelude of tepid acquaintance; a crystallisation and a taking fire; and a falling out of love, from which he emerged free, but changed and permanently enriched. The period of mere acquaintance was as protracted as the onset of devotion was sudden. He had learned of Ruskin at second-hand during his student-days at the École des Sciences Politiques from his master Paul Desjardins; and he read the brief translated extracts from Ruskin's works which appeared every year from 1893 to 1903 (with the exception of 1894 and 1901) in a periodical edited by Desjardins, the *Bulletin de l'Union pour l'Action Morale*, to which he was a regular subscriber. But he knew also from Montesquiou, who gave him a sumptuously bound copy of *The Gentle Art of Making Enemies* and was a friend of Whistler, of Ruskin's outrageous attack in 1877 on Whistler's *Nocturnes*; and this enemy of Elstir must have seemed less a prophet than a reactionary, a persecutor rather than an apostle of the religion of beauty. "I will walk with your Majesty," says the Duke of Brittany to the King of Portugal at the Opéra in *Jean Santeuil*; and "No, Brittany," replies the affable monarch, "I'd rather go with my young friend Jean; he can finish telling me about the libel-suit between Ruskin and Whistler, which fascinates me, and besides, it will be one in the eye for Mme Marmet."[1]

In 1897 appeared Robert de La Sizeranne's charmingly written and well-documented study, *Ruskin et la religion de la beauté*, which Proust seems to have read immediately[2]; for in that year[3]

---

[1] *Jean Santeuil*, vol. 3, 70

[2] He may have read La Sizeranne's book even before its publication in volume form, for it appeared serially in the *Revue des Deux Mondes* from December 1895 to April 1897.

[3] Ainslie's dating is confirmed by the existence of letters to him from Proust on the occasion of Alphonse Daudet's death in December 1897, after Ainslie's return to England.

Douglas Ainslie, an English friend of Robert de Billy, met Proust at the Daudets' in the Rue de Bellechasse, at 9 Boulevard Malesherbes, and in the Café Weber, where they argued about the relative merits of Ruskin and Pater. Proust arrived late at Weber's with the velvet collar of his greatcoat wrapped about his ears;"I can only stay a minute," he would announce, and then talk, as he did to Albert Flament, till dawn, growing ever more brilliant to stave off the moment of parting: 'to give of his best,' remarks Ainslie, 'he had to feel he was keeping an impatient cabman waiting'. Ainslie quoted a remark made to him by Pater in person: "I can't believe Ruskin could see more in St Mark's at Venice than I do!"; to which Proust retorted, with a despairing shrug of the shoulders: "What's the use! You and I will never see eye to eye about English literature!" Either at this time or a little later Proust read a less authoritative and much earlier study of Ruskin, J. A. Milsand's *L'Ésthétique anglaise*, which appeared in 1864, when only half of Ruskin's work had been written and before his philosophy reached its mature form.

In 1898 two other personal influences converged to join the undercurrent which, beneath the opposing stream of the Dreyfus Case, was directing Proust's thoughts towards Ruskin. In the autumn Robert de Billy visited Paris on leave from the French Embassy in London, where he served from 1896 to 1899. Billy described his recent visit to the romanesque churches of the Auvergne and Poitou, talked of Ruskin, and lent Proust his own copy of Émile Mâle's *L'Art religieux du XIIIe siècle en France*, which had just appeared. The book returned four years later, bereft of its cover and stained with patent medicines: Proust quoted it copiously in his Ruskin studies, and later used it for the iconography of Saint-André-des-Champs and Elstir's explanation of the sculptures in the 'Persian' church of Balbec.

Marie Nordlinger, too, during her stay in Paris from December 1896 to August 1898, was a valuable source of information about Ruskin. She found Proust had read 'everything by Ruskin that had been translated into French'—the extracts in the *Bulletin de l'Union pour l'Action Morale*, that is, and the extensive quotations in La Sizeranne's book. Proust, in turn, was delighted to discover that she came from Rusholme, the very suburb of Manchester in which Ruskin had delivered his lectures of *Sesame and Lilies*; so that henceforth the grey place-name of Manchester incongruously

took on a poetic aura hardly inferior to that of the golden Venice
or Vézelay. On her way home to England Mlle Nordlinger spent
two days at Rouen with Mme Hendlé, wife of the prefect of the
town and a relative of her father. She was met at the station by
the official landau with a cockaded footman, and drove straight
to the cathedral, where she talked to the stone-masons repairing
the porch, and to the near-by church of Saint-Ouen, where she met
the aged verger, Julien Édouard, who had guided Ruskin and his
friends in the autumn of 1880. A still more decisive example was
her visit, a little earlier, to Amiens: she had 'examined the
cathedral stone by stone, with Ruskin for my guide', and afterwards, in Paris, gave the eager Marcel an impromptu verbal
rendering of passages from the 'Separate Travellers' Edition'—
which constitutes a complete guide to the sculptures of the
cathedral—of Chapter Four of *The Bible of Amiens*.

In the summer of 1899 Proust discussed Ruskin with François
d'Oncieu, and lent him La Sizeranne's treatise before he went to
Évian. At first, in the lake-level society of the Brancovans and
Mlle Kiki, he felt no need of the book; but towards the end of
September, when with Clément de Maugny on the hills above
Thonon he faced the soaring Alps behind the lake, he was
conscious of the discrepancy between his own emotions and the
magnificent passage of *Praeterita*, quoted by La Sizeranne in his
first chapter, in which Ruskin describes his first sight of the Alps.[1]
He begged Mme Proust to rescue and send 'La Sizeranne's book
on Ruskin, so that I may see the mountains through the eyes of
that great man'. After a few days, before it came, he hurried back
to Paris: 'crystallisation' had occurred; his craving had turned
from the pinnacles of inaccessible ice to Ruskin himself. During
the illness which followed his return the faithful Oncieu called
every day to enquire after his health; and when he recovered they
went out together on expeditions in quest of Ruskin. 'Oncieu's
mind is free of prejudice and full of relish,' Proust wrote to
Chevilly, 'and he is so kind as to follow in my footsteps, which
lead him, however, only into perfectly respectable and high-

---

[1] 'There was no thought in any of us for a moment of their being clouds.
They were as clear as crystal, sharp on the pure horizon sky, and already
tinged with rose by the sinking sun. . . . I went down that evening from the
garden-terrace of Schaffhausen with my destiny fixed in all of it that was to
be sacred and useful.'

minded places such as the Louvre or the Bibliothèque Nationale.'
In that library he discovered a fragment of *The Seven Lamps of
Architecture* translated in the *Revue Générale* of October 1895,
nestling, as he noticed with amusement, between articles by two
of his summer acquaintances, Henry Bordeaux, and Chevilly's
sister's fiancé Édouard Trogan. Finding that no more translations from Ruskin existed, he began to read him, painfully but
successfully, in the original. A letter of 30 November asks Pierre
Lavallée, then a librarian at the École des Beaux-Arts, whether
his library possesses a copy of *The Queen of the Air* ('please leave
a note with the concierge—I never wake before two in the afternoon'); and whether or not Lavallée could supply the book,
Proust soon had a copy of his own.[1] *The Queen of the Air* was
chosen, no doubt, for the sake of the many superb and brilliantly
translated quotations from it in La Sizeranne: possibly for the
aphorism which fitted so aptly his new fervour and his abandonment of *Jean Santeuil*: 'A truly modest person admires the works
of others with eyes full of wonder, and with a joy that leaves him
no time to deplore his own.' Perhaps he was equally attracted by
the passages on the symbolism of flowers, including the lilies of
Florence, or on the limpid water of the Swiss lakes, which in
La Sizeranne's French astonishingly resemble, with their long
sentences winding in arabesque round the central column of their
meaning, his own prose in *Jean Santeuil*; for the influence of
Ruskin on Proust's later style came not so much from a desire
to write like Ruskin, as from a realisation that Ruskin already
wrote like himself.

On 5 December 1899, encouraged by unexpected praise of *Les
Plaisirs et les Jours* in a letter from Marie Nordlinger, he revealed
his momentous decision. Since they last met, a year and a half
before, he has been unhappy (he means, as always, unhappy in
love), and his creative powers have suffered from the deteriora-
tion in his health; his novel has failed ('*je travaille depuis très
longtemps à un ouvrage de très longue haleine, mais sans rien
achever*'), and he sometimes feels, he confesses, like Mr Casaubon
in *Middlemarch*, who wastes his life on a masterpiece he will never

---

[1] He appealed also to Marie Nordlinger, who sent him her copy of the
Queen of the Air with her own marginal annotations, early in January 1900;
but meanwhile he had acquired one by his own efforts, and gave her it in
exchange.

be able to finish. But for the past fortnight he has been busy 'on a little work, quite different from the sort of thing I usually write, on Ruskin and certain cathedrals.' Meanwhile, a few days before, Mlle Nordlinger's cousin Reynaldo Hahn had written to her what might seem a contradictory report, that Marcel was 'translating the fourth chapter of Ruskin's book on Amiens.' Ought we to deduce that he had already completed the first three chapters? Probably not, for this fourth chapter, to which the preceding three are merely introductory, gives a full guide to the cathedral and is complete in itself. As we have seen, Mlle Nordlinger, after her visit to Amiens eighteen months before, had made him an improvised translation from the 'Separate Travellers' Edition' of this very chapter; he had already begun, partly in emulation of La Sizeranne,[1] a series of pilgrimages to the cathedrals described by Ruskin, of which Amiens was the most accessible for a day-tripper from Paris; so on every account it was natural that he should turn first to this, of all sections of Ruskin's works. His first visit to Amiens had already taken place, in late October or early November, 'in the chill golden air of a French autumn morning',[2] with this same Chapter Four of *The Bible of Amiens* as guide.

Ruskin suggested two possible ways of approaching the cathedral: the first, 'if you are not afraid of an hour's walk', from the citadel on the chalk hill beyond the northernmost of the eleven streams into which the Somme here divides, causing Ruskin to call Amiens 'the Venice of France'; the second, 'if you cannot or will not walk, or if you really must go to Paris this afternoon, and supposing notwithstanding these weaknesses you are still a nice sort of person, for whom it is of some consequence which way you come at a pretty thing', from the Place Gambetta up the busiest street of the town, the Rue des Trois Cailloux. Proust, deciding that he belonged to this latter class, followed the pre-scribed way: past the *pâtisserie* on the left, where he followed Ruskin's advice to 'buy some bonbons or tarts, so as to get into a cheerful temper', and up the Rue Robert de Luzarches to the south façade of the cathedral. To the left of the porch he saw the beggars, and again obeyed Ruskin ('put a sou into every beggar's box who asks it there—it is none of your business whether they

[1] 'In Switzerland, Florence, Amiens, I have worked where Ruskin worked,' wrote La Sizeranne (*R.R.B.*, 9).
[2] *La Bible d'Amiens*, 246, footnote

should be there or not, nor whether they deserve the sou—be sure only whether you yourself deserve to have it to give; and give it prettily, and not as if it burnt your fingers'). The beggars were so ancient, he decided, that they might well be the same Ruskin saw nineteen years before. The master himself seemed to stand beside him and guide his hand; he remembered Frédéric Moreau, in *L'Éducation sentimentale*, tipping the harp-player on the Seine steamer after his first sight of Mme Arnoux, and Flaubert's words: 'it was no mere vanity that urged him to this act of charity, but a feeling of benediction, an almost religious impulse of the heart, in which he associated his companion'.

It was noon: 'the sun was paying his daily call on the Gilded Virgin, nowadays gilded by him alone; and it was to his passing caress that she seemed to address her age-old smile'. He stepped back; the sunshine on the rows of saints gave to one a halo round his forehead, to another a cloak of warm light about his shoulders. Over the transept the slender, immensely tall, slightly leaning spire seemed, as Ruskin suggested, to 'bend to the west wind'. The Virgin was surrounded by flowering sprays of stone hawthorn—like those in the *petit sentier* at Illiers in the Month of Mary—'from whose endless spring the wind of time seemed already to have blown a few petals'. She carried a live jackdaw in the crook of her hand; she smiled, he thought, remembering the ladies of the Faubourg Saint-Germain, like a celestial hostess in her doorway; and as he watched, a few boatmen, hurrying past to meet the high tide on the Somme, raised their eyes to her as the Star of the Sea. He entered the cathedral and wandered among the carved stalls of the choir—'there is nothing else so beautiful cut out of the goodly trees of the world,' wrote Ruskin. Proust had seen casts of them in Paris, which he was not allowed to touch, in the museum at the Trocadéro (where the Narrator saw replicas of the Virgin and Apostles of Balbec[1]); but now, by permission of the verger, he was allowed to tap the long harp-strings of the grain of the wood itself, which gave out 'a sound as of a musical instrument, that seemed to tell how tenuous they were and how indestructible'. He proceeded to the sculptures of the west front, which Ruskin called the Bible of Amiens. Of these he has little to say that is not in Ruskin; but he borrowed for the arms and motto of the Baron de Charlus[2] the figure of Christ trampling on

[1] I, 659   [2] III, 805

the lion and the dragon, and the verse of Psalm lviii, 4, to which Ruskin refers: '*Inculcabis super leonem et aspidem*.' He descended from the cathedral to the river, and looked back at the north front; the sun shone directly through the plain glass of the windows, and the cathedral, which till then had seemed an edifice of stone, seemed to become transparent, 'to hold between its pillars, erect and reaching to the sky, ghostly and immaterial giants of green gold and flame'. He hurried west along the river to the municipal slaughter-houses, to find the precise spot from which Ruskin had made his distant sketch of 'Amiens, All Souls' Day, 1880',[1] and back to catch his train for Paris. After his return he hung in his bedroom, next to the Mona Lisa, a photograph of the Gilded Virgin, whose smile was no less enigmatic than her companion's: 'the one has only the beauty of a masterpiece, but the Gilded Virgin has the melancholy of a memory'.

The visit to Amiens had been preceded by one to Bourges, where he saw the porch carved with hawthorn blossom even more profusely than the lintels round the Gilded Virgin. 'Bourges is the cathedral of hawthorn,' he wrote, and quoted Ruskin: 'never was such hawthorn; you would try to gather it forthwith, but for fear of being pricked.' But Ruskin told him no more about Bourges, or the still prouder cathedral near Illiers, which he also revisited at this time; 'the stones of Chartres and Bourges left unanswered a host of questions which I ponder unceasingly,' he lamented in his *Figaro* article of 13 February 1900.

On 20 January 1900 Ruskin died at Brantwood, his house on the shore of Lake Coniston. He had written his masterpiece *Praeterita* from 1885 to 1889, in the last level light of his declining genius, during the intervals between fits of violent mania; his last journey abroad was to France, Switzerland and Italy in 1888.[2] Thereafter he sank into lethargy and silence. His white prophetic beard grew ever longer, now he had ceased to prophesy; he neither

---

[1] He failed to find it, and no wonder; for there is no point on the banks of the Somme where the cathedral appears to the right of the river (and therefore east of the viewer) and Saint-Leu to the right of the cathedral, as shown in Ruskin's illustration, which in this respect is an imaginary view.

[2] Proust's vivid description in *Contre Sainte-Beuve*, 382-5, of seeing Ruskin at a Rembrandt exhibition at Amsterdam, presumably during his own trip to Holland in October 1898, is totally fictitious. Ruskin was entirely confined to Brantwood at this time; and Proust also seems to have forgotten the Master's lifelong dislike of all Dutch painting.

wrote nor spoke, and refused, like Aunt Léonie, to move, first from his house, at last even from his bedroom. But Proust's sorrow at the passing of his master was short-lived; 'my grief is healthy and full of consolations,' he told Marie Nordlinger, 'for I realise what a trivial thing death is, when I see how intensely this dead man lives, and how I admire and listen to his words, and seek to understand and obey him, more than I would for many who are living'.

He was consoled also by the knowledge that, during the brief wave of publicity that follows the death of a great author, his writings on Ruskin would have news-value; and he acted so promptly that his obituary—signed, however, only with his initials—appeared only a week later, on the 27th, in the *Chronique des arts et de la curiosité*. This periodical was a weekly supplement, containing current art news, to the *Gazette des Beaux-Arts*, edited by Charles Ephrussi, the lesser original of Swann. Ephrussi was eager for more, and Proust took the opportunity to announce in the obituary that 'the *Gazette des Beaux-Arts* will have the honour to give a just idea and impression of Ruskin's work in a forthcoming number'. He also contrived to be introduced, probably by Léon Daudet, to Gaston Calmette, the new editor of *Le Figaro*, in which Daudet was writing at this time. Calmette was exceptionally gifted with the charm and affability which are so unexpected yet so often to be found in editors. "But absolutely, my dear fellow—but certainly, but of course, I shall be only too delighted," he would repeat, in a deep, purring voice, darting a velvet glance under his pince-nez. During the next fourteen years he accepted numerous articles from Proust, who expressed his genuine liking, his overwhelming but uneasy gratitude, by invitations to dine with noble guests, expensive gifts, and finally by the dedication of *Du Côté de chez Swann*. Since *Le Figaro* was the favourite newspaper of the aristocracy, Proust's articles no doubt helped a little to make him known as a writer, but also, still more, to perpetuate his unfortunate reputation as a society amateur. Sometimes, with tongue in cheek, he would write under a pseudonym, and make his articles sly pastiches of the *Figaro* gossip-column clichés[1]; sometimes, as now, under his own name,

---

[1] Several such pastiches appear in *A la Recherche*, notably (though this is supposed to be published in *Le Gaulois*) the obituary on Swann, 'a Parisian whose wit was universally appreciated' (III, 199-200).

he made a successful compromise between the obligatory
'Parisian gaiety' and his own manner, and struck a note which can
often be heard in the full orchestra of *A la Recherche*.

He did not have so long to wait as the Narrator for the publication of his first article in *Le Figaro*—'that spiritual bread, still
warm and moist from the press and the mists of morning, which
we call a newspaper'.[1] *Pèlerinages Ruskiniens en France* appeared
on 13 February. He invited his fellow-countrymen to make
pilgrimages in honour of Ruskin, not to his grave at Coniston,
not even (Proust thinks, with a savour of sour grapes, of his
abortive plan to visit Venice from Évian the October before) to
Venice, but to Rouen and Amiens, where ('as in the tomb at
Rome which contains the heart of Shelley') they will find not his
lifeless body, but his soul. He drew attention once more to his
forthcoming articles in the *Gazette des Beaux-Arts*, appealed to
the friends with whom Ruskin had travelled to tell him what
would have been the contents of his unwritten books on Rouen
(*Domrémy*) and Chartres (*The Springs of Eure*), and alluded to
the Charity of Giotto at Padua, who reminds him at this moment,
'trampling on bags of gold and offering us wheat and flowers', not
of the kitchen-maid at Combray but of Ruskin himself.

Early in February, when he was writing his *Figaro* article, he
felt unsure of one of the facts he needed; and Léon Yeatman and
his wife Madeleine were roused from bed one night by Dr
Proust's man-servant with the extraordinary message: "Monsieur
Marcel has asked me to ask Monsieur: what became of Shelley's
heart?" One evening that spring the Yeatmans returned home and
found, to their astonishment, Proust sitting alone in the concierge's lodge: it was he who had pulled the cord to let them in.
"Your concierge is ill," he explained, "and her husband had to
go to the chemist's for medicine, so I offered to take his place.
Don't interrupt me now, I'm busy!" It was with the Yeatmans
that, at the same time, he visited Rouen. His purpose was not so
much to see the cathedral itself, of which Ruskin, in default of
the unwritten *Domrémy*, could tell him little, as to identify a
single small sculpture to which Ruskin had once referred in
passing. Nothing could show more clearly that at this stage his
interest in cathedrals was subsidiary to his passion for Ruskin:
if he searched Ruskin's work for all that Ruskin could tell him

[1] III, 568

about cathedrals, it was in order to visit the cathedrals for what they could tell him about Ruskin.

On the very day of Ruskin's death Proust happened to re-read in *The Seven Lamps of Architecture* the description of a little grotesque figure, 'vexed and puzzled in his malice; his hand is pressed hard against his cheek-bone, and the flesh of the cheek is *wrinkled* under the eye by the pressure'.[1] 'I was seized by the desire to see the little man of whom Ruskin speaks,' he wrote, 'and I went to Rouen as if in obedience to a testamentary request, as if he had bequeathed to the care of his readers the insignificant creature whom he had, by speaking of him, restored to life.'

Proust and his friends looked up at the west front. Row upon row of saints warmed themselves in the sunlight of the winter morning, soaring to seemingly uninhabited heights, where, nevertheless, a carved hermit lived in eternal isolation, or a St Christopher glanced back for ever, wry-necked, at the Christ-Child his burden. How, in this thronged city of stone, could they find one tiny mannikin? They walked, with little hope, to his abode in the north porch, the Portail des Libraires, where the mediaeval booksellers had once kept their stalls; and suddenly Yeatman's young wife—who luckily was a trained and talented sculptor—cried: "There's one that looks just like him!" It was the little stone man, not six inches in height, and crumbled by time, but keeping still his angry wrinkled cheek and the minute speck of malice in his eye. Like the surging naked souls in the Last Judgement above him, he seemed resurrected, and Ruskin with him. The party moved to Saint-Maclou near by, where there was another Last Judgement, with roaring flames pursuing souls whose anger and despair had reminded Ruskin of Orcagna and Hogarth; and to Saint-Ouen, where they talked to the verger Julien Édouard who had guided Ruskin in 1880 and Marie Nordlinger in 1898. "Monsieur Ruskin said our church was the finest gothic monument in the world," he told them, much to Proust's bewildered amusement. Armed as he was with *The Seven Lamps of Architecture*, he knew Ruskin had written peevishly of the lantern in the tower: 'it is one of the basest pieces of gothic in Europe . . . resembling, and deserving little more credit than, the burnt sugar ornaments of elaborate confectionery'; and he had called the shafts supporting the piers of the nave 'the

[1] Library Edition, vol. 8, 217

ugliest excrescence I ever saw on a gothic building!'[1] But the
success of the day was the stone man regained, a new emblem of
the indestructibility of unconscious memory, since the tiny
monster had reappeared not from the past of a living man, but
from the graves of two dead. 'I was moved to find him still
there,' wrote Proust, 'because I realised then that nothing dies that
once has lived, neither the sculptor's thought, nor Ruskin's.'

Thanks to his meeting with Ruskin, Proust was not unduly
grieved by his parting in March 1900 from the Mazarine Library.
It was now four and a half years since, in October 1895 at Beg-
Meil, he had requested and received leave till the end of the year
for his visit to Réveillon in the 'bad season'. Before 1895 was out
he had felt emboldened to ask for additional leave of a whole
year, which was granted, like a Christmas present, on 24
December. In 1896 his only visit to the Mazarine was to present
Les Plaisirs et les Jours to his colleagues. In December he
applied again, punctually and punctiliously, for a year's leave. It
was, he explained, through the Ministry's fault and from no
remissness of his own, that permission did not arrive until
January 1897; and he was wounded that M. Franklin, through
Paul Marais, had seen fit to send him a sharp letter of rebuke.
From a sense of delicacy he even abstained from using the
Mazarine for his own studies; and the only library in Paris which
he could never enter was the one to whose staff he belonged.
Every December he went through the same preposterous formal-
ity, the only purpose of which was to preserve in Dr Proust's
mind the conviction that his eldest son had, in a manner of speaking, a job. In 1899 a general inspection was held at the Mazarine:
it seemed odd that one of the three honorary unpaid attachés
should not have set foot in the library for so many years, and on
14 February 1900 Proust was peremptorily ordered to return to
work immediately. He refrained; on 1 March he was deemed to
have resigned; and so ended his imperceptible career as a librarian.

In *Du Côté de chez Swann* a journey to Venice is one of the
dreams of the Narrator's childhood. It is prevented by the sudden
illness which causes the family doctor to forbid not only Venice
but even a visit to the theatre to see Berma, and to prescribe
instead the daily outings in the Champs-Élysées, which alter the

---

[1] *The Seven Lamps* appeared in 1849. Julian Édouard's honour is saved
if we grant that Ruskin might have changed his mind by 1880.

Narrator's life by causing him to fall in love with Gilberte. A second obstacle, after many years during which he longs intermittently for Venice, is his life with Albertine, in spite of which he has decided at last to abandon her and go, only a moment before Françoise announces: "Mademoiselle Albertine has left." His desire is fulfilled only after Albertine is dead and forgotten. In Proust's own life, however, there is little trace of longing for Venice before the summer of 1899,[1] when he thought of going there from Évian, 'supposing I can find a companion', and was prevented partly because Coco de Madrazo happened to be in Rome and could not come, but mostly because of his sudden decision to return to Paris, read Ruskin in the original, and visit cathedrals. The Narrator's thoughts of Italy—of Venice, Florence and Padua—are splendid anachronisms, coloured solely by Proust's experience of Ruskin in the summer and autumn of 1899. The passages which the Narrator as a boy repeats to himself in his enthusiasm, without giving their source—'Venice is the school of Giorgione, the home of Titian', 'a city of marble and gold, embossed with jasper and paved with emerald', 'men majestic and terrible as the sea, wearing armour with glints of bronze beneath the folds of their bloodred mantles', 'rocks of amethyst like a coral reef in Indian seas'—are all quotations from Ruskin.[2] The Narrator's visions of Florence, which Proust was never to visit, were similarly derived from Ruskin, partly through La Sizeranne, partly from his own impressions of *Mornings in Florence* in the original. When he visited Venice it was in continuation of the same plan, less than a year old, which had dictated his winter pilgrimages to the cathedrals of France.

[1] There is only the view of inaccessible Italy from the Alp Grüm in 1893 (but Venice is not mentioned), and the conversation with Douglas Ainslie about Ruskin, Pater and Saint Mark's in 1897. Even at Évian his longing was divided between Venice for Ruskin's sake and the Italian lakes for Stendhal's—'I dream of the journeys I haven't made, which is one way of making them,' he wrote to Chevilly in October 1899 after his return to Paris, 'pending the accomplishment—by the law which always makes the vague hopes of our youth come true in later life, and which brought me to Thonon this summer—of our less unlikely pilgrimages to the shores where Fabrice del Dongo revelled.' He was never to see the Italian lakes.

[2] I, 391-3. The first three come from *Modern Painters*, vol. 5, pt. 9, ch. 9, perhaps borrowed from La Sizeranne, pp. 115-16. The last is from *The Stones of Venice*, vol. 2, ch. 1, §1, presumably read in the original, since La Sizeranne does not quote it.

He had probably intended to go on to Venice from Évian next October ('Constantin de Brancovan assures me it's the best possible time of year from the point of view of health,' he had told Mme Proust the year before). It was mere coincidence that a sudden opportunity allowed him to go in spring, only a little later than the season promised by the Narrator's father. In mid-April Reynaldo Hahn was in Rome with his mother and Coco: could he be persuaded to turn north to Venice? At first Proust hesitated: 'Marcel isn't quite sure whether he's going to Venice —look out, I think we're in for a shower of telegrams,' Reynaldo told his cousin Marie; but when he heard that Marie Nordlinger herself was in Florence (she had left Manchester on 20 April) and would be coming to Venice with Reynaldo, the scale was turned.

'It was on a radiant May morning,'[1] wrote Marie Nordlinger, 'that my aunt, Reynaldo and I saw Marcel and his mother arrive in Venice.' As the train crossed the plain of Lombardy Mme Proust had read aloud from *The Stones of Venice* the cherished passage about 'the coral reef in Indian seas'; and at first, 'because we cannot see things at once through the eyes of the body and the eyes of the mind', Proust was a little disappointed to find the façade of Saint Mark's less like pearls and rubies than Ruskin had given him to expect. But when, after an afternoon nap, he descended to the quays of Venice, imagination and reality had merged. That evening he sat with Mlle Nordlinger at Quadri's café in the square of Saint Mark's, correcting with her help the manuscript of his translation of *The Bible of Amiens*[2]; and next morning at ten o'clock, when his shutters were opened, his eyes were dazzled by the sunlight falling not, as usual, on the iron chimney-cowl of the next-door house in Paris, but on the golden angel over the campanile of Saint Mark's, 'who bore me on his flashing wings a promise of beauty and joy greater than he ever brought to Christian hearts, when he came to announce "glory to God in the highest, and peace on earth to men of good will".'

[1] Perhaps 'May morning' should not be taken literally. Proust sent Mlle Nordlinger a cutting, in which he acknowledged her help, from his article on Ruskin and Amiens in the *Mercure de France* for April. He would surely have sent it well before the end of the month; and as it reached her only the day before his arrival in Venice, this event should perhaps be dated to the last week in April. But she may have received the letter several days late, if it had to be forwarded from Florence.

[2] Chapter Four only, no doubt.

Their hotel was not two hundred yards from the Palace of the Doges, the Piazza, and the golden angel. For wherever Proust or his mother travelled, whether to Trouville, Cabourg, Versailles, Évian or Venice, they were invariably to be found in the very best hotel, the one at the head of Baedeker's list; and at Venice they stayed at the Hôtel Danieli, where Ruskin had been before them, and where Alfred de Musset, delirious with typhoid, had seen George Sand kissing his handsome physician. In front of the hotel was the Riva degli Schiavoni, paved with marble, leading in broad steps, the last of which the tide slowly climbed and descended, to the lagoon and the gondolas. Over the water was the Giudecca, and San Giorgio Maggiore, and on the near horizon the low dunes of the Lido. 'When I went to Venice I found,' Proust wrote some years later to Mme Straus, 'that my dream had become—incredibly but quite simply—my *address!*'

In the mornings, before the greatest heat of the day, he would set out with Reynaldo and Marie in a gondola along the Grand Canal, disembarking at each church or palace described by Ruskin. 'Blessed days,' he wrote in a footnote of *La Bible d'Amiens*, 'when with other disciples of the master I listened at the water's edge to his gospel, alighting at every one of the temples which seemed to rise from the sea expressly to offer us the object of his descriptions and the very image of his thoughts.' When they returned for lunch they could see, from as far off as the Dogana and Santa Maria della Salute, Mme Proust's shawl hung over the hotel balcony, weighed down by her book. For she preferred to stay behind and read, happy and astonished that her son was rising at ten in the morning to wander in the open air, happy too, perhaps, because he was spending the day not only with Reynaldo but with a beautiful girl. Since the deaths of Louis and Nathé Weil she had worn black; but now, when Marcel called up from the quay-side and she smiled back in welcome, she had a coquettish straw hat with a white tulle veil, as if to license his new-found joy in living.

In the afternoon the sun was already too hot for them to go further than the shady side of the Piazza, where they would sit with Mme Proust and Mlle Nordlinger's aunt at Florian's café eating the delicious honeycombed ice known as *granita*, and watching the pigeons with their iridescent breasts: "Pigeons are the lilacs of the animal kingdom,"[1] declared Marcel. Soon he would

[1] A remark reused for the pigeons in the Champs-Élysées (I, 408).

cross the square with Marie to work on Ruskin in the 'dazzling coolness' of Saint Mark's. Mlle Nordlinger remembered an afternoon when the sky darkened and a storm burst over Venice: she took shelter with Marcel in the great basilica, and translated for him the passage of *The Stones of Venice* in which Ruskin explains the decadence and fall of the Republic. In the mosaics of the domes of Saint Mark's are represented not only the prophets and the evangelists, but (for here the Bible of Venice differs from the Bible of Amiens) the very words of their texts. "The sins of Venice," repeated Marie, "were done with the Bible at her right hand. When in her last hours she threw off all shame and all restraint, be it remembered how much her sin was greater, because it was done in the face of the house of God, burning with the letters of His Law. Through century after century of gathering vanity and festering guilt, that white dome of Saint Mark's had uttered in the dead ear of Venice: 'Know thou, that for all these things God will bring thee into judgement.'" Proust took this tremendous warning, uttered in the oblivious voice of the young girl, to himself and defied it. When he came to write the last chapter of his introduction to *La Bible d'Amiens*, he had a logical answer ready. 'If Ruskin had been quite sincere with himself, he would not have thought the sins of the Venetians more inexcusable and more severely punished than those of other men, just because they had a church of many-coloured marble instead of a cathedral of limestone, or because the Palace of the Doges happened to be next-door to Saint Mark's instead of being at the other end of the town,' he ironically objected. But at the moment he was more serious. 'It was dark, and the mosaics shone only with their own material light, with an ancient, internal, terrestrial gold to which the Venetian sun had ceased to contribute. The emotion I felt on hearing these words, surrounded by all those angels illumined only by the environing darkness, was very strong.' And Marie Nordlinger noticed, as had Reynaldo on the day of the Bengal roses at Réveillon, that her companion was 'strangely moved, and exalted by a kind of ecstasy'.

In the evening it was more necessary than ever to evade the high moral standards of Mlle Nordlinger's aunt—'that charming Venetian aunt, fervent and meticulous, devoted to art, kindness and comfort, and so very full of goodwill towards the person who signs this letter,' he wrote to Marie Nordlinger some years later.

It was bad enough for a young man to get up so late in the morning ('She represented for me those *Mornings in Venice* which Ruskin never wrote and I never saw,' said Proust); but it was shocking for him to keep a young lady out so late at night. 'Nothing could soften her, nothing could budge the inflexibility of her principles,' and altogether, he irreverently decided, 'she was one of the most curious of all the *Stones of Venice*.' Nevertheless, the young people contrived to escape. The sun had set, even the north side of the Piazza was cool. They sat drinking coffee in the dusk outside Quadri's, and then took a gondola to the Lagoon. Reynaldo sang Venetian folk-songs, and Gounod's setting of Musset's

> *Dans Venise la rouge*
> *Pas un bateau qui bouge,*

while a yellow half-moon high over San Giorgio Maggiore sent a track of rippling light from the horizon to their trailing hands.

Influenced by a mistaken association of ideas between Florence, flowers and pollen, Proust had decided that Florence would be fatal for his hay fever, and the Ponte Vecchio, 'heaped with a profusion of hyacinths and anemones', remained forever only a vision of the Narrator. But Padua was only twenty-five miles by train from Venice, and contained treasures of painting praised by Ruskin even more highly than the Carpaccios which Proust had seen at the Accademia di Belle Arti, or, *Saint Mark's Rest* in hand, after a trip by gondola 'along a calm canal, a little before one reaches the tremulous infinity of the lagoon', at San Giorgio degli Schiavoni. Reynaldo was about to rejoin his mother and Coco in Rome, and consented to break his journey at Padua. So it was that Proust saw Giotto's frescoes, the Virtues and Vices of Padua, in the chapel of the Madonna dell'Arena. He knew them well already, not from childhood, like the Narrator to whom Swann gave the photographs of them which hung in the school-room at Combray, but only since the previous autumn, when he had found reproductions of Charity, Injustice, Infidelity and Envy in Ruskin's *Fors Clavigera*. These are the very figures which Proust introduced into *A la Recherche*: the sturdy, mannish Charity, with her gown billowing out at the waist, and carrying what might almost be asparagus in her basket, became an emblem of the pregnant kitchen-maid at Combray; Envy, with a serpent issuing from her distended mouth, reminded him of illustrations of cancer of the tongue in his father's medical books; M. de Palancy's monocle seemed to Swann at Mme de Saint-Euverte's a part intended to symbolise the whole, like the branch carried by Injustice to represent the forests in which he lurks; and Albertine playing diabolo on the promenade at Balbec resembled Infidelity, who carries, attached by a long cord, the idol or 'devil' which is the object of her guilty worship.[1] The Virtues and Vices of Padua, after which he once intended to call a whole section of his novel, were only the lowest rank of four frescoes; in the third row above was a Crucifixion, in which the suffering Christ was attended by diminutive weeping angels, who unlike most of their kind used their wings not as mere emblems, but for actual flying. When he wrote *Albertine Disparue*, late in the World War, and remembered Giotto's angels looping and nose-diving, he compared them to 'the young pupils of Garros'[2]—Roland Garros, the aviator killed in action in 1918, whose aerodrome he had visited with Agostinelli, who, he too, and four years sooner, was destined to die of flying.

Leaving the chapel, and crossing the Piazza dell'Arena under a sky which seemed scarcely brighter than the blue ceiling above the angels, they reached the Eremitani and saw Mantegna's fresco of the life of St James, 'one of the paintings I love best in the world,' Proust wrote to Montesquiou seven years later. One of the soldiers who stands aloof and brooding while St James is martyred is recalled by Swann at Mme de Saint-Euverte's, when he sees the gigantic footman who seemed 'as resolved to ignore the group of his comrades thronging about Swann, although he followed them vaguely with his cruel, grey-green eyes, as if the scene had been a Massacre of the Innocents or a Martyrdom of St James'.[3]

By the third week of May Reynaldo, Mlle Nordlinger and the high-principled aunt had left, and Proust's stay in Venice was nearly over. It is probable that a quarrel with his mother occurred at this time: not so much because it is described in *Albertine Disparue*,[4] for there the episode is aesthetically necessary, in order that the magic of Venice, like that of all other Names and Places, should fade at last; but because, like other incidents in Proust's life, it appears in *Contre Sainte-Beuve* briefly and without apparent purpose, and linked with another memory which is certainly real.[5]

---

[1] I, 80-2, 327, 886   [2] III, 648   [3] I, 324   [4] III, 651-5
[5] His remorse on his second visit to Venice, described below.

In *Albertine Disparue* the Narrator refuses to leave Venice with his mother, in *Contre Sainte-Beuve*[1] Proust threatens to leave without her: there is nothing to indicate which version is correct. 'I went downstairs;' he wrote in *Contre Sainte-Beuve*, 'I had given up the idea of going, but I wanted to prolong my mother's grief at thinking me gone. I stayed on the quay-side where she could not see me, while a boatman in a gondola sang a serenade to which the sun, about to disappear behind the Salute, had stopped to listen. I could feel the prolongation of my mother's anxiety, the suspense became unbearable, but I could not find the resolution to go and tell her: "I'm staying." It seemed the singer would never finish his song, nor the sun succeed in setting, as if my anguish, the dying light and the metal of the singer's voice had fused forever in a poignant, ambiguous and indissoluble alloy. The time would come when, if I tried to escape the memory of that bronze-like minute, I would not have, as then, my mother near me.' But the remorse in which Venice ended and receded left Proust determined to return, to enjoy pleasures of which the presence of his mother and friends had deprived him, and which were not mentioned anywhere in the works of Ruskin.

A few weeks before his arrival in Venice, on 1 April 1900, the *Gazette des Beaux-Arts* had published the first part of his long essay, *John Ruskin*, which was concluded in the issue of 1 August. This was the study already announced in the *Chronique des Arts et de la Curiosité* in January and in the *Figaro* article in February. Proust had finished it early in February, soon after the visit to Rouen with which it ends, and on the 8th he had written to Mlle Nordlinger: 'All my work on Ruskin is completed.' But it is possible that the first half was written as early as the summer of 1899, before he had begun to read Ruskin in the original. All the quotations from Ruskin in this section, with the exception of one from *The Bible of Amiens* and another from *The Seven Lamps*, which may have been added later, are borrowed with due acknowledgment from Milsand and La Sizeranne, and this suggests that he may have been writing at a time when he had no first-hand knowledge of Ruskin.[2] In the essay as a whole Proust expounds

[1] Pp. 123, 124

[2] Here, no doubt, is the article commissioned by Louis Ganderax for the *Revue de Paris*, to which Proust alludes in a letter to J. L. Vaudoyer in 1912. Ganderax, with his pathological inability to publish anything he could not

not only his opinion of the true nature of Ruskin's gospel but, what is still more important, describes the crucial effect of the revelation of Ruskin on his own view of art and human life.

The validity of Proust's opinion of Ruskin rests partly on the extent of his knowledge of English and of his acquaintance with Ruskin's works. His competence in both has been generally underestimated, not only by his critics but by his friends. "How on earth do you manage, Marcel," asked Constantin de Brancovan, "seeing that you don't know English?" 'He would have been hard put to it to order a cutlet in an English restaurant,' wrote Georges de Lauris, though he rightly added: 'he knew no English but Ruskin's, but he understood that in its most subtle shades of meaning.' Proust himself was under no illusions as to

have written himself, kept it, 'torn between the friendship he felt for me personally and the horror inspired in him by my writings', until 'the death of Ruskin made it no less admirable in news-value than it seemed detestable in prose-style'. Even so, Ganderax could not bring himself to use the article, and gave the same 'uniform, affectionate and regretful reason' as he had given for his rejection long ago of the group of sonnets and a short story later included in *Les Plaisirs et les Jours*: that he 'hadn't enough spare time to rewrite it'. In view of the improbability of Proust's having written a long study of Ruskin before the first onset of his enthusiasm in the summer of 1899, his words to Vaudoyer: 'the excellent Ganderax kept my verses, a short story and a study of Ruskin (commissioned!) waiting for years' need not all be taken literally. 'For years' no doubt refers to the sonnets and the story, but not to the Ruskin study, which Ganderax can hardly have kept for more than six months. Proust also expresses himself loosely when he tells Vaudoyer: 'this essay later became the preface to *La Bible d'Amiens*', since of the four sections of the preface the first is a foreword written last of all, the second is the *Mercure de France* article on Amiens written after his visit to the cathedral in October 1899, the latter half of the third describes his visit to Rouen in February 1900, and the fourth is based on his holiday in Venice in May 1900. The article written for Ganderax, therefore, can only be the first half of the third section, that is, the article in the *Gazette des Beaux-Arts* for 1 April 1900, reprinted in *Pastiches et Mélanges*, p. 149, line 17-p. 161, line 3. Even this, however, must have been considerably revised to make it topical, as it contains numerous allusions to the death of Ruskin on 20 January 1900. Perhaps Ganderax's procrastination suggested the Narrator's long wait for the appearance in *Le Figaro* of the article which he submitted soon after his first visit to Balbec, but which was not published until after the death of Albertine. No other article of Proust's was so long delayed; and both his first article in *Le Figaro* (*Pèlerinages Ruskiniens* of 13 February 1900) and the essay which corresponds to the Narrator's on the spires of Martinville (*Impressions de route en automobile* of 19 November 1907) appeared within a few weeks after they were written.

his competence in English: 'I'm so bad at languages,' he wrote to
Marie Nordlinger in August 1903; he bitterly lamented, in a letter
to Walter Berry in January 1918, his inability to talk English to
American soldiers met one night in Paris; 'I read English with
great difficulty,' he told Violet Schiff in 1919. He was always
prone to the typical mistakes of the beginner. In the *John Ruskin*
essay he translated Ruskin's '*a living soul*' by '*une âme aimante*',
because in English at least he was unaware of the difference
between living and loving; and twenty-two years later, only two
months before his death, he was horrified to learn that the title
chosen for the English translation of *Du Côté de chez Swann* was
Swann's Way: he thought the words could only mean 'in the
manner of Swann', and died in the pathetic belief that Scott-
Moncrieff's great work would be an ignorant travesty of *A la
Recherche*. He had no doubt begun English at the Lycée
Condorcet[1]; he continued while studying for his *licence ès lettres*,
in which he seems to have taken English as his first language[2];
and perhaps he learned a little from Edgar Aubert, and from
Willie Heath during their mornings in the Bois. But with the sole
exception of Ruskin he seems to have read all the English writers
he knew—Dickens, George Eliot, Shakespeare, Carlyle, Pater,
and later Stevenson, Kipling, Barrie, Wells and Hardy—in translation. He was exacting in his demands for help from his mother,
who knew English well, and from his English-speaking friends,
Mlle Nordlinger, Reynaldo Hahn, Robert de Billy, Robert
d'Humières (the translator of Kipling), and others. He corresponded with Ruskin's friends, Charles Newton Scott and
Alexander Wedderburn. In translating *The Bible of Amiens* he
was provided with a crib: according to Mlle Nordlinger, the
patient Mme Proust wrote for him a word-for-word translation
'in several red, green and yellow school exercise-books'.

Such are the ascertainable limitations of Proust's knowledge
of English: they may seem formidable, but they are, in fact,
irrelevant to his knowledge of Ruskin. Even if we assume that

[1] During Proust's first two years at Condorcet Mallarmé was English
master there. But Proust was only thirteen years old when Mallarmé left in
July 1884, and it is unlikely that he had begun English so early.

[2] It is known that he took German as his second language. He knew
enough of it to read and review two German books on Ruskin in 1903 and
1904. As he never shows any considerable knowledge of any others, it seems
likely that he took English as his first language.

in the general accuracy of his renderings he was largely indebted to Mme Proust, and that the occasional gross but trivial blunders are all his own, there can still be no doubt that for the elegance of his translation, the deep comprehension and sharing of Ruskin's inmost meaning and feeling, he owed nothing to his helpers. Proust's Ruskin may be compared to another great translation which, although not free from elementary but unimportant errors, is a masterly re-creation of its original: namely, Scott-Moncrieff's Proust. Until Proust's Ruskin manuscripts are published we can only guess at the respective parts played in *La Bible d'Amiens* and *Sésame et les Lys* by his own knowledge and intuition and by the conscripted assistance of his mother and friends. But concerning the extent of his knowledge of Ruskin's other works, as revealed by the hundreds of quotations in his essays and voluminous footnotes, certainty is possible. The quotations are mostly of his own choice; nearly all are taken from works which had not previously been translated into French; the few which had previously occurred in Milsand or La Sizeranne are mostly retranslated (except in the first section of *John Ruskin*) from the original; and they come from no fewer than twenty-six works, covering virtually the entire range of Ruskin's production. In the *Mercure de France* essay, *Ruskin à Notre-Dame d'Amiens*, he quotes *Praeterita*, *The Bible of Amiens*, *The Queen of the Air* and *Val d'Arno*; in the second section of *John Ruskin* he uses passages from *The Pleasures of England*, *The Seven Lamps of Architecture*, *Lectures on Architecture and Painting*, *The Stones of Venice* and *St Mark's Rest*.[1] In his notes to *La Bible d'Amiens* he draws from these and fourteen other works of Ruskin, including *The Two Paths*, *Unto this Last* and *Modern Painters*; and if only three more are added to the list in *Sésame et les Lys*, it is because the tale of Ruskin's works is by now, except for some half a dozen very minor pieces, complete. Mme Proust can hardly have supplied him with a home-made translation of all Ruskin; and his quotations are made with an ease and appositeness which imply a thorough knowledge of the books from which they are taken. The conclusion is inevitable, that Proust had read and digested

[1] This corroborates his claim in the letter to Marie Nordlinger of 8 February 1900, when he had recently finished these essays, to 'know by heart' *The Seven Lamps*, *The Bible of Amiens*, *Val d'Arno*, *Lectures on Architecture and Painting* and *Praeterita*.

in the original most of Ruskin's major works during his first
enthusiasm in 1899 and 1900, and the remainder by 1902, when
La Bible d'Amiens was completed.

The first section of *John Ruskin*, published in the *Gazette des
Beaux-Arts* of 1 April 1900 and probably written some eight
months before, is a discussion of the views of Milsand and La
Sizeranne. The quotations in it, as we have seen, are borrowed
with two exceptions from these authors, and it is only in the
second section of the essay that Proust shows an independent
knowledge of Ruskin's works. Nevertheless, the core of the whole
essay is the point at which, in this first section, he parts company
with La Sizeranne. He assents to La Sizeranne's concept of the
Religion of Beauty, but gives it a special meaning which, although
it is true of Ruskin, is henceforth Proust's own, and marks a
further advance towards the idea of Time Regained. The true
adorer of beauty, he writes, is not the man who 'spends his life
in the enjoyment which comes from the voluptuous contemplation of works of art'. 'Beauty cannot be loved fruitfully if it is
loved only for the pleasures it gives. Just as the search for
happiness for its own sake brings nothing but boredom, because
happiness can only be found by seeking something other than
happiness, so aesthetic pleasure is a mere by-product which comes
to us if we love beauty for itself, as something real which exists
outside ourselves and is infinitely more important than the joy
it gives us. Very far from being a dilettante or an aesthete, Ruskin
was one of those men of whom Carlyle speaks, whose genius
warns them of the vanity of all pleasure, and, at the same time,
of the presence near at hand of an eternal reality to be perceived
intuitively by their inspiration. . . . The Beauty to which he
consecrated his life was not conceived by him as an object of
enjoyment made for our delight, but as a reality infinitely more
important than life, for which he would have sacrificed his
own . . . The poet was, for Ruskin as for Carlyle, a kind of scribe
writing at the dictation of nature a more or less important part of
her secret; and the artist's primary duty is to add nothing of his
own to this divine message.' Here is the bridge between Jean
Santeuil's meditation by the Lake of Geneva and the final metaphysic of the Narrator. Only two elements are missing: unconscious memory, because Proust had still not solved its mystery,
and Time Lost, because he had as yet experienced only Time

Wasted. The meditation by the lake, which was a real event of September 1899, began, as has been seen, with a complete occurrence of unconscious memory; but this, since Proust proceeded to explain it mistakenly as an effect of poetic imagination, was a false start. In *John Ruskin*, however, although by temporarily abandoning the concept of unconscious memory he has retreated, he has also made a vital advance: the duty of the writer, he has decided, is not to imagine, but to perceive reality; the artist is a scribe; and since his task is 'infinitely more important than life', its fulfilment will bring salvation.

In defining the mission of Ruskin, Proust had discovered his own. Temporarily he put the knowledge away; for salvation, perhaps, is a state in which we cannot hope to live, but only, at best, to die. Nine years later he would begin to write the work that would kill and save him: meanwhile he had to live, if not in salvation, then touched, if possible, with grace. During his first worship of Ruskin it seemed sufficient to live as he supposed Ruskin had lived, in a perpetual adoration of gothic churches. This duty, in seeming anticlimax, is the subject of the second section of *John Ruskin*, which describes, as a pendant to the trip to Amiens in *Ruskin à Notre-Dame d'Amiens*, his visit to Rouen and the rediscovery of the stone mannikin. There was another aspect of Ruskin's way of life which attracted him: he learned from Collingwood's *Life and Works of John Ruskin*, published in 1893, of the master's habit of making his tours in the company of a chosen band of young friends; and in his *Figaro* article Proust appealed to these ('whom I have so often envied') for information on Ruskin's opinions of Chartres and Rouen. In the same way the Narrator envies Gilberte when Swann tells him that Bergotte 'is my daughter's great friend—they visit old towns and cathedrals and castles together'; and when he thinks of Gilberte he sees her 'in the porch of a cathedral, explaining to me the meaning of the statues, and introducing me as her friend to Bergotte'.[1] For the next three years Proust's answer to the question: 'What shall I do to be saved?' was: 'Visit cathedrals

---

[1] I, 99-100. Proust is thinking also of another Gilberte and Bergotte: of Jeanne Pouquet's journeys with Anatole France, who with Mme Arman and Gaston de Caillavet accompanied her on her honeymoon in Italy in the summer of 1893, and on other occasions. But the pagan and Grecian France cared little for the art of gothic churches.

with my friends.' Truth and happiness, he felt for a time, could be discovered by seeing the right places with the right persons. His illusion was less absurd and less unfruitful than it might seem: for although reality, in the metaphysic of *A la Recherche*, lies only in the utmost depths of our being which are in contact with eternity, images of reality are wherever we find them. Of the two false quests which for the Narrator were necessary stages in his recovery of Time Lost, and which he calls Names of People and Names of Places, Proust's pursuit of high society corresponded to the first, and his circular journey in the steps of Ruskin to the second.

Ruskin appears occasionally in *A la Recherche* under his own name. The Narrator's mother, seeing her son heartbroken by their parting as he sets out for Balbec with his grandmother, asks: "What would the church at Balbec say? Where's that enraptured tourist we read about in Ruskin?"[1] Bloch exhibits his vulgarity, when the Narrator reveals that the visit to Balbec 'fulfils one of my oldest desires, only less profound than that of going to Venice', by exclaiming: "Yes, you would! You'd like to drink sherbet with the pretty ladies"—as Proust had with Marie Nordlinger—"while you pretend to read *The Stones of Venighce* by Lord John Ruskin, that dreary old fossil, one of the most crashing bores who ever existed!"[2] At Venice the Narrator, like Proust himself, takes 'notes for some work I was doing on Ruskin'.[3] Jupien in his brothel jests upon 'a translation of Ruskin's *Sesame and Lilies* which I had sent to M. de Charlus': "if you see a light in my window you can come in, that's my Open Sesame," he says, "but if it's Lilies you're after, you'd better try elsewhere."[4] These words, as we shall see later, may actually have been spoken to Proust, some eighteen years afterwards, on a dark night in war-time Paris when the bombs were falling.

If Bergotte is in the habit of visiting gothic cathedrals, however, it is not because he has collected in passing—as he takes Renan's snail-shell nose, Bourget's words of advice, Bergson's name, and the magic of Barrès's prose—a trait from Ruskin. Just as much as in his social presence he is Anatole France, in the effect of his works on the Narrator Bergotte *is* Ruskin. 'One of the passages from Bergotte gave me a joy I was aware of feeling in a deeper region of myself,' the Narrator tells us, 'a region vaster

[1] I, 649   [2] I, 739   [3] III, 645   [4] III, 833

and simpler, from which all obstacles and separations seemed to have been removed.'[1] 'The universe suddenly regained an infinite value in my eyes,' wrote Proust in retrospect, at a time when his enthusiasm for Ruskin was cooling, 'and my admiration for Ruskin gave such importance to the things he had made me love that they seemed charged with something more precious than life itself.'[2] The quotations from Bergotte's works read at Combray: 'the inexhaustible torrent of beautiful appearances', 'the moving effigies which forever ennoble the venerable and delightful façades of cathedrals',[3] are like pastiches of Ruskin.

Ruskin also led Proust to one of the most striking aspects of Elstir. Elstir, no doubt, is a generalised Impressionist, just as Vinteuil and Bergotte are generalisations of the great composers and authors of Proust's youth; though each of the three is more supreme in his genius than any one actual artist of the time. In giving to Elstir powers which belonged to so many different painters—the cathedrals and Normandy cliffs of Monet, the race-course subjects of Degas, the gods and centaurs of Gustave Moreau, the firework nocturnes of Whistler, the bathing girls of Renoir—Proust suggested not only the contemporary reality of the imaginary painter, but also his superiority, since his greatness included theirs. But Elstir's salient quality is one in which he differs from the other impressionists. Both they and Elstir make it their task to reproduce the primal freshness of reality as seen in a first glance, before the viewer knows what it is he sees; but whereas Monet, for example, works by decomposing colours and their outlines, without wishing, however, to disguise the fact that it is a tree or a sail that he is showing us, Elstir's art lies in what the Narrator calls 'ambiguities' and 'metaphors': he reproduces the moment in which we are so far from knowing what it is we see, that we think it is something else. The charm of the pictures seen by the Narrator in Elstir's studio at Balbec lay 'in a kind of metamorphosis of the things they represented, analogous to what is called in poetry a metaphor; and if God the Father created

---

[1] I, 94   [2] Cf. *Pastiches et Mélanges*, 193
[3] I, 94. The phrase *'les belles apparences'*, however, was used more than once by Anatole France, and the whole comes from Leconte de Lisle's lines:

> *'La vie antique est faite inépuisablement*
> *Du tourbillon sans fin des apparences vaines.'*

Nevertheless, the Ruskinian flavour of Proust's adaptations is unmistakable.

things by naming them, it was by taking away their names, or giving them different ones, that Elstir created them anew'.[1] The most frequent metaphor in his seascapes was one which made sea seem land, and land seem sea. In these characteristics Elstir differs from any of the French impressionists, and resembles Turner, to whom Ruskin consecrated *Modern Painters*, the chief work of his youth. Proust knew, as early as 1900, Turner's album *The Rivers of France*, which he mentioned in *John Ruskin*. He borrowed from La Sizeranne in the same essay an anecdote of Turner in Ruskin's *The Eagle's Nest*: to a naval officer who complained that the ships in his view of Plymouth had no portholes, the painter retorted: "My business is to paint not what I know, but what I see."[2] 'My imagination,' says the Narrator, 'like Elstir reproducing some effect of perspective, painted for me not what I knew, but what I saw.'[3] 'Turner,' wrote Ruskin in *The Harbours of England*, 'was never able to recover the idea of positive distinction between sea and sky, or sea and land.' As Jean Autret has shown, Elstir's *Port of Carquethuit* is a combination of Turner's *Plymouth* and *Scarborough*, which Proust knew from the plates in *The Harbours of England* as published in 1904 in the Library Edition.[4] Turner's and Elstir's aesthetic of metaphor, the description of one thing in terms of another, is employed by Proust throughout *A la Recherche*. Elstir, indeed, is uniquely blessed, in that he has direct and immediate access to reality, without the intercession and long delay of unconscious memory; he alone can see reality in the present, when it is actually there. On the other hand, this very gift condemns him to perceive reality through one sense only, the vision of the eye; and moreover, he is cut off from the dimension of time, without which the metaphysical significance of reality remains invisible. Thus his art is still inferior to the full revelation of Time Regained: it cannot be more than a symbol of something greater which is out of its reach.

[1] I, 835   [2] *Pastiches et Mélanges*, 169   [3] II, 568
[4] J. Autret, *L'Influence de Ruskin sur Proust*, 130-6. M. Autret has also shown (*ibid.*, 119-24) that Proust was indebted for his knowledge of Botticelli's painting of Jethro's daughter Zipporah, of which Odette so obsessively reminds Swann, to the frontispiece of Ruskin's *Val d'Arno*. The figure reproduced by P. Abraham, *Proust*, pl. XVI, as Zipporah is in fact Moses' wife, whose features are nothing like Odette's. The real Zipporah is reproduced by Autret, *op. cit.*, 119.

At the end of *John Ruskin* Proust applied to Ruskin words which Ruskin had used of Turner: 'It is through those eyes, now closed for ever in the grave, that unborn generations will look upon nature.' Ruskin had given him new eyes, or, rather, restored the sight of his own, on which the years of Time Wasted, the vain pleasures of the Guermantes Way, the sterile sorrows of perverted love, the contamination of justice by politics in the Dreyfus Affair, had cast their temporary scales. But in one work, at least, Ruskin had shown himself aware of Time Regained: it was a book whose very title, *Praeterita*, might be literally translated as 'Things Past', or '*Temps Perdu*'. Ruskin had written the story of his childhood and youth, of the discovery of his vocation, at a time long afterwards when he had realised the meaning of his life; and his method was to re-create each moment, by a deliberate exercise of unconscious memory not unlike Proust's, so that the past should become eternally present. Proust knew *Praeterita* well: it was one of the works of Ruskin which in his letter to Mlle Nordlinger of 8 February 1900 he claimed to know by heart; and a few years later he began a translation of it which he soon abandoned. It is very likely that both the title and the theme of *A la Recherche* owed something to *Praeterita*. There is also at least one particular incident in *Praeterita* which Proust seems to have remembered. In the early summer of 1842 Ruskin set out for Switzerland by the devious way of Rouen, Chartres, Fontainebleau and Auxerre. On the day before he reached Fontainebleau he must have passed through, or very near to Illiers, where Adrien Proust was then a child of eight, and Louis Proust was still selling candles in the Place du Marché. 'The flat country between Chartres and Fontainebleau,' Ruskin recalled, 'with an oppressive sense of Paris to the north, fretted me wickedly.' That night he lay feverishly awake; at noon he 'tottered out, still in an extremely languid and woe-begone condition', into the forest, and lay in anguish on a sandy bank under a group of young trees. He tried in vain to sleep; until gradually 'the branches against the blue sky began to interest me, motionless as the branches of a tree of Jesse on a painted window. . . . Languidly, but not idly, I began to draw the tree; and as I drew the languor passed away: the beautiful lines insisted on being traced—without weariness. More and more beautiful they became, as each rose out of the rest, and took its place in the air.

With wonder increasing every moment, I saw that they "composed" themselves, by finer laws than any known of man. At last the tree was there, and everything that I had thought about trees, nowhere.'[1] This typically Proustian moment of truth surely played its part (though the incidents may none the less have actually occurred in Proust's own life) in the Narrator's questioning of the three trees near Balbec, and again in his sight from a railway-carriage of the trees striped with sunlight and shade, which seemed for ever to forbid, though in fact they preluded, his regaining of Time Lost.

Soon after the publication of the second half of *John Ruskin* on 1 August 1900 Dr and Mme Proust were once more at the Splendide Hôtel, Évian. Taking precautions to avoid what Mme Proust ingenuously called 'the Semitic element', they joined forces with the family of Dr Proust's colleague Dr Simon Duplay (whose son Maurice was to become Proust's friend a year or two later) to form, as Mme Proust put it, 'a miniature independent republican party of our own'. Each morning the now corpulent lady drank three glasses of medicinal water at the Spa; in the evening they attended the theatre at the casino, or played dominoes with the Duplays, to which pursuit Dr Proust brought such fiery energy, and such open joy when he won, as to recall Dr Cottard playing écarté at La Raspelière. He awaited Marcel's telegrams with ill-concealed anxiety, and when they arrived exclaimed: "There! Didn't I tell you everything would be all right!" From time to time distinguished acquaintances sought him out: the left-wing politician Jean Cruppi, a member of the Chamber of Deputies, a future Minister of Commerce, and husband of Mme Proust's cousin Louise Crémieux, was also 'on the lake'; and one Sunday a stout man with a red nose, Charles Dupuy, who had been prime minister in 1899 at the height of the Affair, popped up to slap Dr Proust jovially on the shoulder. Armand Nisard, Marie de Benardaky's uncle by marriage and an original of M. de Norpois, was at Évian on holiday from his post as ambassador at the Vatican. He was most affable, but since he was so deaf as to hear nothing that was said to him, and spoke

---

[1] *Praeterita*, vol. 2, ch. 4. Proust certainly knew this passage even before he read the original, for it is quoted by La Sizeranne, 28-9. Here again, Ruskin's prose in La Sizeranne's French is strikingly like the mature style of Proust.

so quietly as to be inaudible, conversation was difficult. The family thought he had shown far too little zeal a few years before, when Dr Proust had been an unsuccessful candidate for the Académie des Sciences Morales; and in this again he resembled M. de Norpois, who at Mme de Villeparisis's matinée sanctimoniously refuses to vote for the Narrator's father.[1] Marcel was to join them later: Mme Proust advised him to wait, because the hotel was brim-full and noisy; besides, as she would soon have to return to Paris on important business, they would risk crossing one another. Meanwhile he continued his Ruskin pilgrimages: 'when you don't write to me,' she remarked, 'I hope it's because you're off on some interesting, amusing or hygienic excursion'.

He arrived at Évian some time in September, while Dr Proust apparently moved on to Vichy; and in October, presumably about the 7th, when the Splendide Hôtel closed, he fulfilled his plan of the previous autumn and went to Venice from Évian, 'at the best possible time of year'. Of this mysterious second visit to Venice only a single fact is known: on 19 October 1900 Proust signed the visitors' register of the Armenian monastery on the Island of San Lazaro in the Lagoon.[2] But he mentioned it twice in *Contre Sainte-Beuve*[3]: 'the moment I saw Venice for the second time I remembered the evening when, after a quarrel with Mamma, I cruelly told her I was going away'; and: 'if I wept on the day when I again saw the window of her room, it was because it said to me "I remember your mother"'. Perhaps there was some other reason for his return to Venice and for his remorse when he arrived. The palaces, paintings and mosaics of Venice, the blazing sunlight reflected everywhere from cool green water, offered him novel aspects of art and nature which he may well have wished to experience again. But Venice also held less avowable though hardly less tempting charms, which the presence of his mother, Mlle Nordlinger, the strait-laced aunt and the quizzical Reynaldo had prevented him from exploring five months before. For the Narrator the very topography of Venice

[1] II, 225-6

[2] Except for a pleasant trip by *vaporetto* on the Lagoon, and a view of Venice from across the water, no particular motive can be guessed for his visit to San Lazaro. The Monastery was not one of the usual sights of Venice; Ruskin does not mention it; and although Byron spent some time with the Armenian monks there, Proust was not interested in Byron.

[3] p. 123

—the canal on whose yielding waters he seems 'to penetrate further and further into the depths of some secret thing', the moonlit *campo* which he discovers hidden in a labyrinth of narrow streets and can never find again—seems full of symbols of voluptuous desire and possession. He wanders alone, 'through humble *campi* and little abandoned *rii*', in search of the working-class girls whom Albertine might have loved when she was alive and in Venice.[1] Perhaps for Proust, too, Venice was linked with the Cities of the Plain; and perhaps he sought and found there on this second visit the sinister enchantments known to Byron and John Addington Symonds, Henry James, Housman and Baron Corvo, of which Ruskin had nothing to say.

The business on which Mme Proust was recalled to Paris in September was nothing less than the removal of the Proust family to a new home, into which they moved probably about 1 October, the beginning of the new quarter. They had been house-hunting all summer, and thought for a time of taking a second-floor apartment at 127 Boulevard Haussmann. The proprietor of the house, the Marquis des Réaulx, was understood to be unwilling to let to professional men; and Proust asked Pierre Lavallée, who was a friend of the marquis's grandson and tenant, Édouard de Monicault, to explain that Dr Proust had so nearly given up his practice that 'he now has fewer visitors than ordinary persons'. But in the end they decided upon 45 Rue de Courcelles, on the corner of the Rue Monceau, which satisfied their needs for more quiet, and living-space, and a more fashionable address to reflect the eminence Dr Proust had reached during the thirty years since his marriage.

At first sight there is little difference between the architecture of the Boulevard Malesherbes and that of the Rue de Courcelles. Both have the same unbroken line of dignified, seven-storey-high buildings, with iron balconies running along the upper floors. But the Boulevard Malesherbes was Second Empire, put up in the late 1860s and beginning to go down in the world; it was a little too showy, and already far too noisy. The Rue de Courcelles was Third Republic—the foundation-stone of No. 45 is dated 1881; it was solid, narrow, quiet, gloomy and treeless; and although less than half a mile from their old home, it ran, between the Boulevard Haussmann and the Avenue Hoche,

[1] III, 626-7, 650

through the outskirts of the aristocratic Quartier Monceau, a much more suitable district for a distinguished doctor.

This is the change of home which occurs at the beginning of *Le Côté de Guermantes*. Well might Françoise, who at this period of *A la Recherche* is based on the Proust's aged cook, Félicie Fitau, declare in the exile of this noiseless canyon that 'she found the twittering of the birds at daybreak insipid'.[1] But by a typical transposition Proust made the new house of the Narrator, in its most important features, more like his own old home than the new. The house of the Narrator's childhood, it is true, resembled 9 Boulevard Malesherbes in several ways: it was near the Champs-Élysées, had a Morriss column on the pavement opposite, and commanded a distant view of the Piranesi-like dome of Saint-Augustin. The Narrator's new home, like 45 Rue de Courcelles, is quiet, and situated on a steep hill (down which the Ladies with the Walking-Sticks clambered to tell the Duc de Guermantes that poor 'Mama' d'Osmond was dying). The height of the Rue de Courcelles, and its nearness to the Parc Monceau, gave it the better air which in the novel is needed for the Narrator's grandmother ('because, although we did not tell her the reason, she had not been at all well lately')[2] and in real life was desirable for Mme Proust. But it was 9 Boulevard Malesherbes which had a tailor's shop like Jupien's (M. Eppler's, of whom Kiki Bartholoni thought so highly) in the courtyard, and a ducal family as neighbours. At No. 3, only three doors away,[3] lived the Comte and Comtesse François de Maillé, nephew and niece-in-law of the octogenarian Dowager Duchesse de Maillé, whom Proust had so often seen, enthroned with other aged wallflowers, at the balls of his youth: her grey hair piled high over her forehead reminded him of the triple-tiered wig of judges under the *ancien régime*. Mme de Maillé was the niece of the Comtesse de Boigne, who had been dandled on the knees of Louis XVI and Marie Antoinette, and whose memoirs, first published in 1907, suggested those of Mme de Beausergent, the favourite reading of the Narrator's grandmother. The Comtesse de Boigne's nephew, M. d'Osmond,

[1] II, 9   [2] II, 10

[3] 'I was intimidated,' wrote Lucien Daudet of his first invitation to tea at 9 Boulevard Malesherbes, 'because I was under the impression that No. 9 formed part of the Hôtel Maillé, and therefore thought Marcel Proust lived in a house of vast size and extreme magnificence.'

for whose father in the 1850s she had written her memoirs (just
as Mme de Villeparisis's sister Mme de Beausergent had written
hers for the young Basin de Guermantes), was a frequent dinner-
host of Proust's parents; and when Proust went through the family
papers after their death he found M. d'Osmond's photograph and
a bundle of his letters. One of Montesquiou's innumerable
cousins, Madeleine de Montesquiou, had married Françoise de
Maillé in 1888. Here then, at 9 Boulevard Malesherbes—just as
the Guermantes's as châtelains of Combray were suggested by
the Goussencourts at Saint-Éman near Illiers—the Guermantes's
as neighbours of the Narrator in Paris were represented by the
Maillés. And according to his usual practice Proust left a clue
to the relationship, by giving the name Amanien ('Mama')
d'Osmond to the Guermantes cousin, whose death does not deter
the Duc de Guermantes from going to a fancy-dress ball,[1] and
who in earlier days had been one of Odette's lovers, and had
fought a duel with the jealous Swann.[2]

Proust returned from Venice towards the end of October 1900
to find the move already completed. His discomfort was none
the less extreme: as the Narrator remarks on the occasion, 'I
always found it as difficult to assimilate a new environment as I
found it easy to abandon an old.' But the next year is a barren
period in his biography, though not, it may be, in his life. Only
eight letters belonging to this time are available in print, and
there is a similar blank in the reminiscences of his friends. But
the lacuna may be to some extent real. He probably wrote fewer
letters because he was working on *La Bible d'Amiens*: the only
other comparable dearth of correspondence occurs in 1911, when
his concentration on the first version of *A la Recherche* was at its
height. Moreover, this year coincides with a break in his friendships: he had abandoned contact with many of his companions
of the 1890s, and had not yet found new. Perhaps he was too ill
to write: there is evidence of a serious illness in the autumn and
early winter of 1901. Whatever the reason, however, his life
vanishes into comparative obscurity during his first year in the
house where his parents were to die and Time was, at length, to
be lost.

[1] II, 575
[2] III, 300. "I had to act as Swann's second," says M. de Charlus, "and
Osmond never forgave me."

Chapter 15

SAINT-LOUP

AT 45 Rue de Courcelles Mme Proust continued to allow her son to give 'grand dinners'; and one of the grandest of all was that of 20 June 1901. The guests, among others, were Anatole France and his daughter Suzanne (now no longer dangerous, for she was about to become engaged to the Dreyfusard Captain Mollin); the Comte and Comtesse d'Eyragues (*née* Henriette de Montesquiou, Count Robert's cousin); Mme de Noailles with her husband Mathieu and her sister, Proust's favourite, Princesse Hélène de Caraman-Chimay; the old Comtesse de Brantes (the same whom Count Robert declared 'worth a whole Council of Trent'); Prince Constantin de Brancovan, Léon Daudet, Abel Hermant; and three young counts, Clément de Maugny, the Comte de Briey (whose mother laughed like Mme Verdurin), and Gabriel de La Rochefoucauld, of whom we shall hear more later. Mme de Noailles, whose first volume of poems, *Le Cœur Innombrable*, had appeared with sensational effect in May, was the guest of honour. Proust had already arranged through Reynaldo Hahn, who had just converted Sarah Bernhardt to these poems during a season of *Phèdre* at Brussels, for that great actress to give a reading from them on 30 May at Montesquiou's Pavillon des Muses; he had even persuaded Mme Proust, of all people, to attend, and the *Figaro* gossip-columnist to include her in 'among others recognised'. So the table decoration on 20 June consisted of nosegays culled from wild flowers mentioned in the poetess's verses, which Proust had ordered, at a price far steeper than that of orchids, from Lachaume and Vaillant-Rozier. Mme de Noailles was enraptured by the compliment: possibly, Gabriel de La Rochefoucauld maliciously surmised, she had hitherto known the flowers only by their pretty names; and as she poured out the jewelled river of her conversation, which left her no breath for eating, her eagle's head was turned continually towards 'dear Marcel'. He, too, ate little: it was his practice on these occasions, so that he might give undivided attention to his friends, to dine before their arrival; he sat with one guest during the soup-course, with another for the fish, and completed the round of the table during the nuts and fruit. Another guest was impressed by a still more remarkable feature of the dinner. Léon Daudet, now a violent nationalist and anti-Semite, realised with horror that Marcel had resolved to emulate Gégé Primoli by inviting the deadliest enemies to eat together. Most of his fellow-guests, except the Eyragues's and Mme de Brantes, were notorious Dreyfusards: 'I found myself sitting next to a ravishing young person whom I found on enquiry to be the daughter of a prominent Israelite banker; and I expected the crockery to begin flying at any moment. But rays of goodwill and sweet sympathy emanated from Marcel and darted in vertiginous spirals round the dining-room; and for two hours the utmost cordiality reigned over this banquet of the Atridae.' Daudet seized on his audacious friend in the drawing-room: "no one else in Paris could have performed such a miracle, Marcel," he cried. "Monsieur, the fact is, Monsieur," Proust modestly replied, "it all depends on the way in which, the moment they come into the room, people's characters interlock!"

Throughout this year Proust saw a good deal of Léon Daudet at the Café Weber, which (or Larue's) no doubt was the restaurant visited by the Narrator and Saint-Loup on a foggy night, where the Dreyfusards and nationalists sat at opposite sides of the room. At the Café Weber, however, the nationalists were not young noblemen, but Daudet himself, with the deadly Forain, laughing with a sound like broken glass, and his friend Caran d'Ache, the caricaturist, wearing one of his dazzling pink or buttercup-yellow suits, drawing faces on the tablecloth, and murmuring "That's vewwy dwoll, y'know." Louis de la Salle was there, now a convert to nationalism, obsessed with the idea, which he never carried out, of kicking Paul Hervieu's backside; and the critic Paul Souday, 'sullen as a neglected gumboil', sat alone and glowering. Proust entered, muffled summer and winter in an enormous greatcoat. He ordered two pears for himself, or half a dozen grapes, and whatever happened to be most expensive and out of season for his friends; he complained expiringly of insomnia and asthma; and he crossed to Daudet's table to begin a round of compliments: "Monsieur, oh, Monsieur, I did so enjoy your last book—have you finished that marvellous play yet, Monsieur?—excuse me, Madame, what is the exact colour of your charming wrap in daylight?" One evening at a nearby table the Marquis de Lagrenée, a retired diplomat and a renowned duellist, happened to call out to a friend: "Get along with you, you old Dreyfusard!" Proust took the remark to himself, and sent Daudet and Robert de Flers to demand either an apology or a duel: "he probably thinks I'm scared of him, just because he's good with a sword," he cried, white and trembling with rage, "but I'm not, I tell you, I'm not!" The aged Marquis was overcome with delight: "Oh, how splendid!" he cried, raising his nervous duellist's hands above his head, "what a simply delightful person your Monsieur Proust must be!" His joy was complete when it turned out that Daudet's grandmother had been his cousin Olga's very best friend; he came over to assure Proust that no offence had been intended—"It's such a pleasure to meet a young man who knows how to stand up for himself," he repeated. Among other habitués were the thin, bitter Paul Jean Toulet, author of the exquisite *Contrerimes*, and his inseparable friend the gourmet Curnonsky, who survived to commit suicide in the austere year of 1956. Proust and Toulet disliked one another: "I think, Monsieur, don't you agree, Monsieur, you'll ruin your stomach with all that whisky," insinuated Proust.

Sometimes on those June evenings they would emerge to find the Place de la Madeleine still glowing in the last mellow sunlight. "Look here, Daudet," Louis de la Salle would enquire, "what would Hermant say on the present occasion?"; and Daudet, who was almost as brilliant at imitations as Proust himself, would oblige in the tinny voice of Abel Hermant: "He would say, 'Hasn't annywan sin Constantan de Brencoven? I've been lookin' for him for *hours*! It's simply sickenin'!'" "Quite right. And what would Zola say?" "Zola would say: "Ve Madeleine dithappeared in a sheaf of golden light. Over vatht toiling Parith toppled thwatheth of thultry radianthe. Doctor Pathcal looked at Thuthanne. She looked at Jean. Vere wath a thilenthe."

Another member of Daudet's circle at the Cafe Wéber was the swarthy, black-bearded Debussy, whose music Proust had admired since the early 1890s, and was to venerate still more intensely, even at the expense of annoying the classicist Reynaldo, after the first performances of *Pelléas and Mélisande* in April 1902.

Unfortunately, less owing to any personal dislike than to their consciousness of the utter incompatibility of their musical aims, Hahn and Debussy were ineradicably convinced of one another's hatred and contempt; their salutations at the Café Weber became more and more distant, until they ceased altogether. Debussy was therefore inclined to distrust Proust and his group; and although Proust exerted all his charm in conversation ("He's longwinded and precious and a bit of an old woman," said Debussy), and once even saw Debussy home in his cab, their relations remained courteous but distant. Once Proust invited Debussy to dinner at 45 Rue de Courcelles, to meet a mixed company of writers and aristocrats; but Debussy, without ill-feeling, refused: "You see, I'm an absolute bear in company. I'd rather we just went on meeting at Weber's. Don't take it to heart, my dear sir, I was born like this!" So Proust was compelled to revere this Vinteuil from afar.

On 9 August 1901 Prince Edmond de Polignac died. Proust attended his funeral, and was moved by the tears of Princesse Hélène de Caraman-Chimay, and by the symbolism of the black pall with the scarlet princely crown, bearing only the letter 'P': the dead man had resigned all his individuality, and became a simple Polignac.[1] Prince Edmond would never talk again to Charles Haas (himself now near death) of their youth in the Second Empire, or walk across his studio with the splendid Comtesse Greffulhe to hear his own music played by a full orchestra. Proust remembered his kindness at Amphion, the recitals of Fauré's sonata, so like Vinteuil's, at the Rue Cortambert, his love of Venice—"the only city in the world where one can enjoy a conversation with the window open," the Prince would say—and he murmured, quoting *Hamlet*, "Good-night, sweet prince." On the 31st the bereaved Princesse Winnaretta asked Proust to call at tea-time to talk about her husband. One evening at Lady Brooke's he had met Swinburne, who shrilly declared: "I believe our families are related, and I'm flattered to

[1] Proust remembered this scene for the burial of Saint-Loup at Combray: 'the church of Saint-Hilaire was hung with black palls on which, below the princely crown, without any other initials to indicate Christian names or titles, stood out the "G" for the Guermantes he had in death once more become' (III, 851). Another image in the same paragraph—'the feudal turret, emptied of its books, had become warlike again'—derives from Proust's comparison of the Prince de Polignac to 'a castle keep converted into a library'.

meet you"; to which the astonished Prince, fully aware that genius takes precedence of noble birth, had gamely replied: "Believe me, I'm the more honoured of the two!"[1] During his last illness he had taken a dislike to his English night-nurse—"I don't want to talk to the Princess of Wales at three in the morning," he would complain; and when the Princesse described how she had sat up reading Mark Twain to her husband (she had retained her love for her native literature and was about to translate Thoreau's *Walden*) Proust thought with nostalgia of the nights of *François le Champi* with his mother at Auteuil.

By this time Mme and Dr Proust were at Zermatt. Proust had taken the opportunity, as he often did when his parents were away, to attempt to reform his lamentable hours: he went to bed at midnight and rose in time for an enormous lunch, 'every day a huge beef-steak without a morsel of waste, whole plates of fried potatoes, cream-cheese, gruyère, peaches and beer'. But as usual asthma intervened. 'I had to walk bent double, and light an anti-asthma cigarette at every tobacconist's I passed.' He consulted his father's colleague Dr Brissaud's *Hygiene for Asthmatics*: Dr Brissaud considered that asthma, in children at least, was often caused by worms; might he not have worms, like M. Homais in *Madame Bovary*? Ought he not to take enemas of mercury, as Dr Brissaud advised? or if that was too drastic, of something milder, such as calomel or glycerine? He had put on weight, but now, dreaming every night that he was holding his corpulence in, 'like a ball', to show his mother on her return, he lost it again. He was well enough, however, to resume his Ruskin pilgrimages. On 7 September he revisited Amiens, and went on to Abbeville to meet Léon Yeatman and see St Wulfram's Church, of which Ruskin had written: 'For cheerful, unalloyed, unwearying pleasure, the getting in sight of Abbeville on a fine summer afternoon, and rushing down the street to see St Wulfram again before the sun was off the towers, are things to cherish the past for—to the end.'[2] This was just such an afternoon: 'I was delighted to see the mines of summer's gold still virgin around me,'

[1] Swinburne had a fixed idea that his great-grandmother had been a Polignac, though this was contradicted by the poet's family. Cf. Gosse, *Life of Swinburne*, p. 3.

[2] *Praeterita*, vol. I, ch. 9, section 181, quoted by Proust in his introduction to *La Bible d'Amiens* (cf. *Pastiches et Mélanges*, p. 107).

Proust wrote to his mother. His excursions, however, had taken another trend; he was beginning to visit old churches that Ruskin never mentioned, for their own sake, not for Ruskin's. At this time he planned to go to Mantes and Caen with Robert de Billy, and to Illiers alone. Perhaps, he thought, his Ruskin studies were at last winning recognition: on 13 August an article by André Michel on Amiens Cathedral appeared in the *Journal des Débats*, though he looked in vain for any allusion to his own essay on the cathedral of the year before. Hopefully, he sent Michel a copy of the *Mercure de France* containing his essay; but his only reward was that Michel, in a second article on 10 September, referred sarcastically to 'people who visit Amiens not so much to admire or study the cathedral, as to make a devout Ruskinian pilgrimage', and to Ruskin himself as 'a well-meaning mystical Baedeker'.

During the years in which Proust had travelled the Guermantes Way, from 1892 to 1897, he had made no serious attempt—unless we except his pursuit in 1892 of Mme de Chevigné's nephews, Jacques and Gustave de Waru, because they had their aunt's hair, nose and eyes—to make friends among the young noblemen of the Faubourg Saint-Germain. As if to avert a blow to the heart more cruel than any he feared from titled hostesses, his affections had led him only to intelligent bourgeois youths, Willie Heath, Reynaldo Hahn and Lucien Daudet; and in *Jean Santeuil* he gave his hero, in Henri de Réveillon, a blue-blooded companion whose like he had never known. A new tendency is noticeable from 1898 to 1900, when he had already left the Guermantes Way, in his comradeship with Maugny, Chevilly and Oncieu; though these belonged only to the minor nobility, without any real footing in the Faubourg. But after a year's interval, in 1901, a new and momentous cycle of friendships began, coloured and partly instigated by his enthusiasm for Ruskin. Ruskin had brought him a new conception of art and nature; he now felt the possibility and the need of a corresponding new life of the heart, of companions whose physical and moral beauty would justify them as fit objects of aesthetic passion, and whose race made them living symbols of the cathedrals and castles of old France. By the autumn of 1901 he was already intimate with the first arrivals of the group of young noblemen who in *A la Recherche* merged into the gay, golden figure of Saint-Loup.

The first of these in order of time was Comte Aimery de La

Rochefoucauld's son Gabriel. Shortly before his attendance at
the Noailles dinner of 20 June Comte Gabriel had met Proust at
a society soirée; and his curiosity was sufficiently aroused to make
him ask the friend with whom he left: "What sort of a person is
this Proust?" "In my opinion his is the most remarkable literary
potentiality that has ever existed," declared the sententious
friend. 'I took the remark with friendly scepticism,' wrote Comte
Gabriel long afterwards; 'but I was reminded of it the next time
I met Proust, and in time I came to regard it as a prophecy.'
Proust, he found, seemed to have read everything; his conversation was full of the most piercing psychological observations,
and anecdotes of gentle but penetrating irony. Among those
treasured by Comte Gabriel was one of a society lady who, when
sitting next to Proust at dinner, had asked: "Have you ever heard
of a book called *Salammbo*?" Proust stared with childlike
astonishment in his eyes, but made no reply. "Come now, you're
interested in literature," she prodded, "so you must have heard
of it." "I believe it's by Flaubert," he murmured; but the lady,
mishearing, and feeling vaguely that she ought to be offended,
retorted: "It's beside the point whether it's by Paul Bert or anyone else, all that matters is that I quite liked it!"[1]

Gabriel de La Rochefoucauld was now twenty-six—a few
years too old, that is, for Proust to feel more than an ordinary
attraction towards him. As a boy he had played, a few years after
Proust and Marie de Benardaky, with Duc Agénor de Gramont's
daughter Élisabeth in the Tuileries gardens and the Champs-
Élysées. He and she had attended the same class for first communion, and exchanged sacred medallions; but when he wrote
love-letters to his little playmate she conscientiously showed
them to her mother. He resembled Saint-Loup in many ways: he
was a would-be intellectual, a Dreyfusard, and a scorner of the
aristocracy from which he sprang, particularly of his own father,
the overweening Comte Aimery; yet in speaking of persons of
birth below his own he was not entirely free from an instinctive
sense of his inalienable superiority, and the 'spirit of the Guermantes's seemed to pass over at a great height'.[2] He was tall, and
'bore in his forehead,' Proust wrote of him in 1904, 'like two

---

[1] Paul Bert (1833-86), a physiologist and Minister of Education in 1886,
was far from being a prominent literary figure. Proust used the anecdote for
Mme d'Arpajon at the Guermantes dinner (II, 489).   [2] II, 694

family jewels, his mother's bright eyes'. He was the only one of
Proust's aristocratic young friends whose blood had the supreme
nobility claimed by the Guermantes's; for the La Rochefoucaulds
were one of the first three ducal families of France, and he would
quote with a show of contempt his father's saying: "We're every
bit as good as the La Trémoïlles—they've been luckier, that's
all!" He was the son (instead of, like Saint-Loup, the nephew)
of the originals of the Prince and Princesse de Guermantes; and
he was a distant nephew of Comtesse Greffulhe, original of the
Duchesse, and of Montesquiou, original of Charlus. He was fond
of women and night-life, and was nicknamed, in contradistinction
from the *Maximes* of La Rochefoucauld, his ancestor, 'the La
Rochefoucauld of Maxim's'. Saint-Loup was banished to Tunisia
as a cure for his love of Rachel, and afterwards married Swann's
daughter Gilberte. Similarly, we shall find Comte Gabriel in 1904
travelling to Constantinople to recover from a tragic love-affair
and in 1905 marrying a girl of half-ducal, half-Jewish birth.

A few hundred yards further up the Rue de Courcelles, at
69, lived Princesse Rachel de Brancovan's cousin Princesse
Hélène Bibesco, widow of the Roumanian Prince Alexandre de
Bibesco. Like Princesse Rachel she was a virtuoso pianist, and
her salon was frequented by a galaxy of musicians, artists, writers
and aristocrats. In the past she had known Liszt, Wagner,
Gounod, Puvis de Chavannes, the royal Duc d'Aumale; her son
Antoine remembered Renan calling to autograph his books,
Saint-Saëns and Fauré playing piano duets with her, and the
polished cranium of Leconte de Lisle—'I wouldn't have thought
it possible for anyone to be so bald.' At the present time her guests
included Anatole France, Loti, Jules Lemaître, Maeterlinck,
Porto-Riche, Debussy and the painters Bonnard, Vuillard and
Odilon Redon. Proust was no doubt invited to her salon through
her niece, Mme de Noailles, or her nephew Constantin de
Brancovan, who was attending Bergson's lectures at the Sorbonne
with his cousins, her sons; and it was there that in 1900 he had
met the young Bibesco brothers. Prince Antoine Bibesco was not
altogether favourably impressed. He saw a very pale, slightly
stooping young man, with unkempt black hair and dark lacquer
eyes, who offered and quickly withdrew a drooping, childishly

flabby hand. A year later Antoine instructed him in the etiquette
of shaking hands: "You must grip powerfully, Marcel, like this,"
he explained; but "If I followed your example, people would take
me for an invert," Marcel objected.

In 1900 Antoine Bibesco was a virilely handsome young man
of twenty-three, with stern, chiselled features, implacable eyes,
and a slightly cruel twist in his thin lips. Perhaps his cruelty was
only apparent, or at worst, not merely gratuitous: he was a loyal
friend to the end of Proust's life; but he was inclined to be teasing
and revengeful, and when exasperated by Proust's excessive
demands or susceptibility he would wait his time and retaliate
without scruple. He was studying in Paris for the Roumanian
diplomatic service, but soon after their meeting he returned to
Roumania for his year's military service.

In the autumn of 1901 Antoine Bibesco returned to Paris, and
immediately introduced Proust to his friend Comte Bertrand de
Salignac-Fénelon—'the dearest of my friends,' says the Narrator,
calling him by name, 'the best, bravest and most intelligent of
men, Bertrand de Fénelon, whom no one who ever knew him
can forget'.[1] Fénelon, now aged twenty-three, was descended
from a brother of the famous bishop of Cambrai, the opponent of
Bossuet and author of *Télémaque* under Louis XIV. He shared
the blue eyes, the easy, aristocratic manner, the swift movements,
and, alas, thirteen years later, the death in battle of the Marquis
Robert de Saint-Loup. He was a Dreyfusard, an anti-clerical and
an intellectual. 'Bertrand de Fénelon left a glittering wake behind
him, and a great emptiness in the minds and hearts of his friends,'
wrote Georges de Lauris; 'we have not forgotten the amused and
affectionate irony of his gaze, the dauntless impetuosity which
we loved, and which he took with him into the battlefield. We
expected much of him, and were inclined to be afraid of his
verdicts, for he had no use for friendship without plain-speaking.
After long absences how enchanting were his returns, his lively
eyes, and open arms, and flying coat-tails, in the sunlight
before the war!'[2] Soon their group was joined by Comte

---

[1] II, 771
[2] It is possible (though neither source is quite reliable) that Proust met
Fénelon in 1899: Albert Flament mentions him among the habitués of the
Café Weber in that year, while Fernand Vandérem names him with Proust
as frequenting the salon of Mme Aubernon, who died in 1899. Similarly,

Georges de Lauris, who had met Fénelon in the Bibliothèque
Nationale, where Lauris was researching for a doctoral
thesis on Benjamin Constant, and Fénelon was studying political
history for the diplomatic service. Lauris had already met
Proust several times in society, notably amid the glass cup-
boards and gilded furniture of the salon of Mme Léon Fould,
the banker's wife. Proust also made friends this winter with
Antoine's brother Emmanuel, who was nicknamed, for his tall,
lissom shape and oriental eyes, *l'Almée*, that is, 'the dancing-girl'.
Emmanuel, he found, shared his passion for cathedrals, but loved
them directly, as did Robert de Billy, without the mediation of
Ruskin. Prince Emmanuel Bibesco and Billy, who in May 1899
had returned from the London embassy to work in the Ministry
of Foreign Affairs in Paris, helped Proust to win his independence
from Ruskin by encouraging a new series of visits to gothic
churches, to be enjoyed this time for their own sake. Proust liked
and admired Prince Emmanuel; but he did not pursue him, and
never reached the point of calling him '*tu*'.

Proust cannot be accused of introducing exalted ideas of
friendship into a circle innocent of such ways. The Bibesco
brothers and Fénelon already formed a secret society inaccessible
to the profane. They had a private language, and called one
another by anagrams and palindromes of their real names: the
Bibescos were the Ocsebibs, Fénelon was Nonelef, and Marcel,
when he arrived, could be none other than Lecram. Antoine,
from his addiction to the use of the telephone, was also known
as 'Telephas'; and he in turn, when he dared, would call Proust
'the Flatterer'. One of the chief duties of friendship, in their view,
lay in a constant exchange of deadly and inviolable confidences:
such a secret, therefore, was called a 'tomb'—*tombeau*—and
anyone who violated a *tombeau* was, obviously, a 'hyena'.
Friendship, however, was not a changeless phenomenon, but
subject to the mysterious vicissitudes of the stock-market: when
a friend was in a state of mounting prestige, he 'rose' like a share,
and when he seemed increasingly tiresome, he 'slumped'. One

Antoine Bibesco (whose memory, however, is often at fault) remembered
Proust as making friends with Emmanuel during his (Antoine's) absence on
military service in 1900-01. But it is quite clear from Proust's letters to
Antoine Bibesco between November 1901 and early March 1902 that at this
time Proust was as yet intimate with neither Emmanuel nor Fénelon.

of the most interesting pastimes of friendship was to introduce one friend to another, and see whether they took together, or disliked one another intensely: this was called 'operating a conjunction'. An indispensable element of conversation between friends was gossip, to which Proust was already no stranger: the code-word used as an assurance that one was correctly reporting the words of a third party was '*sic*'; and when a superlative was required one said: '*sicissime*'.

But the comradeship which for the others was a delightful secret game was for Proust a serious and heart-rending passion. Their playful group-friendship was uncongenial to him: he would have preferred an exclusive union with Antoine, or, failing him, with Nonelef. When the others went out together and he was confined to his bedroom, his despair was past bearing: 'I feel the jealousy of a masculine Andromeda chained to his rock,' he wrote to Antoine, 'tortured by the sight of Antoine Bibesco ever receding, ever disappearing and multiplying himself, ever past following.' Another complication, in December 1901, was that Antoine, having written a never-to-be-staged play, *La Lutte*, and made friends with the rising Jewish dramatist Henry Bernstein, was engrossed in an affair with an actress: 'supposing I felt particularly miserable about midnight,' wrote his rock-chained friend, 'I wish you'd tell me where you're likely to be, so long as it isn't in the arms of Salammbo'. Occasionally Antoine would try to console the sufferer with some material bribe; but 'Forgive me,' wrote the unappeasable Marcel, 'if, the day before yesterday, I was too preoccupied by the coil of mythological vipers in your mouth, and the dagger in your right hand, to notice that in your left you were handing me a box of chocolates!' Sometimes he tried to cow the fleeting Bibesco with severity: 'you were perfectly revolting yesterday evening, my dear Telephas, and your shares have slumped'. Soon for the first time Proust announces the paradoxical truth, which is one of the leit-motivs of *A la Recherche*, that friendship, like love, is an illusion: 'friendship is an unreal thing. Renan says we must avoid friendship with individuals, Emerson that we should progressively change every friendship for a better. It's true that equally great writers have said the opposite. But I am growing weary of insincerity and friendship, two things which are practically identical.'

For a time during that winter, perhaps only in the vain hope of provoking Antoine's jealousy, he thought of transferring his devotion to Fénelon. 'With Fénelon, I'm only at the hoping stage; but tell him I have a great deal of affection for him, and I should be delighted if in exchange he would give me a crumb of his own, which he scatters abroad over so many persons.' But the attempt was fruitless: 'soon Nonelef will be no more to me than twenty other people, and there will be no need to wrestle with that classic Siren with the seablue eyes, that direct descendant of Telemachus. . . . But the poor lad, of course, doesn't care a damn for me, and would be amazed if he knew he was the subject of all this heart-searching.' In fact, Proust was still too engrossed in Antoine to woo Nonelef. Nevertheless, it was in this winter of 1901-02 that Fénelon performed two memorable acts of friendship. The first was to take Proust, at his own request, to a brothel, where they arrived full of hope. But the girls, Proust complained, were less attractive than he expected, while the central heating left still more to be desired; and the whole establishment had to be turned upside down to provide hot-water bottles and extra bedclothes for this chilly client. Similarly, though the visit never actually occurs, Saint-Loup at the Princesse de Guermantes's soirée promises on his next leave to take the Narrator 'to a place where the women are quite amazing', and where he will meet the mysterious Mlle d'Orgeville.[1] One night at Larue's restaurant in the Place de la Madeleine Proust again complained of the cold; and it was Fénelon who executed Saint-Loup's famous run along the ledge behind the red-plush benches, carrying a greatcoat for his shivering friend. Proust was stirred to record the incident in a new chapter of *Jean Santeuil*, in which he called Fénelon 'Bertrand de Réveillon'.[2] It was the first addition to his novel for two years, and the last he was ever to make; but it was too soon to transfer the new power he had gained through Ruskin to an imaginative work, and the episode is one of the most ill-written (which is saying a great deal) in the whole novel.

[1] II, 694
[2] *Jean Santeuil*, vol. 1, pp. 289-98. Here Réveillon performs his feat only to reach his friend more quickly on entering. Perhaps this version is the truer to fact. As we shall see, Proust's overcoat was fetched in this athletic way by Jean Cocteau in or about 1911, and Proust may have combined the two incidents in *A la Recherche* (II, 411).

Early in 1902 Marie Nordlinger returned to Paris, after an absence of three and a half years, to work as a silversmith and enamellist at the Art Nouveau workshops for the jeweller Siegfried Bing. Once more she brought her gentle, unconscious guidance to influence Proust's life: on one of the first days of spring she visited the church of Saint-Loup-de-Naud near Provins, and borrowed from the Abbé Louis Nappe his treatise comparing the sculptures of its porch with those of Chartres. She passed the Abbé's book on to Marcel, and so touched off a new series of visits to gothic churches.

The first of these was to Chartres by rail, on a Sunday, probably 16 March 1902, with Fénelon and unnamed friends of Fénelon; though it was preceded by a still earlier trip by the Bibesco brothers in Emmanuel's motor-car, without Proust, to churches whose names are not revealed. 'I have, alas,' Proust remarked in a letter to Antoine on the Thursday before the journey to Chartres, 'no tempting automobile to offer you, but only a modest first-class railway ticket.' On Friday, to his great disappointment, Antoine declined the proposal; but he tried to make up for this unkindness by inviting Proust, for the first time, to call him '*tu*'. He also promised to see Proust that evening at Larue's, but spoilt even this by a further dig at his sensitive friend. So Proust's reply, the first letter in which he says *tu* to Antoine (thus providentially enabling the biographer to date the earlier letters in which he had written '*vous*') is one of bitter reproach. 'Let this be the last time you say "Don't be afraid, I shall only stay a minute", because my nerves are too much on edge to bear that particular irony again. I'm keeping your letter, and I shall compare it before your very eyes with one of Nonelef's, and I shall have something to say on the subject which you will think neither nice—though it is extremely so—nor just—though it is the truth itself!'

At Chartres that Sunday Proust studied the cathedral with the help of Mâle's book, and then went on alone to Illiers, arranging to rejoin his companions at Chartres the same evening. There may have been family reasons for the visit to Illiers; but there can be little doubt that Proust's own purpose was to see the church of Saint-Jacques with the new eyes given him by Ruskin. Previously he had always taken Saint-Jacques for granted. In the scene of Sunday mass at Étreuilles in *Jean Santeuil* there is no hint that the church might possess a beauty of its own, independent of the hot sunlight in the market-place, the townsfolk in their Sunday clothes, and the sound of the bells. But he now contributed something also of his own vision; for Ruskin would have remained indifferent to the humble merits of the eleventh-century romanesque door which matched that of the long-dead Louis Proust's house in the Rue du Cheval Blanc, or the massive roughstone walls, still encroached upon by the hatter's and other shops, of the market-place front; and the Master would have called down fire from heaven on the modern stained-glass and purple panelling of Abbé Carré, or the floor-tiles and altar 'in fifteenth-century style' of the good Canon Marquis, which seemed natural and kindly to Proust, because they had already been there in his childhood. The visit marks a further stage in Proust's recovery of his past, and his growing ability to perceive in it the truths of which his boyhood eyes had been only unconsciously aware.

On the way back from Chartres Proust had a violent attack of asthma, which prevented him from going to bed that night, but not from lunching, still sleepless, with Antoine at Weber's next morning: 'I've been longing for ages, I don't know why, to see you in that place at midday, when the sun is shining.'

It was after the Chartres visit that he began to take a moderate interest in Emmanuel Bibesco. At first he forbade Antoine to bring him to 45 Rue de Courcelles: 'I've nothing against him, of course, as he's charming, but I couldn't possibly see him, and Mama would never allow it, when I'm in bed undressed and wearing my untidy pullovers.' But soon he was writing: 'If your brother wants to see me we could all three meet in the evening, whenever he likes, or even in the daytime if he wants to visit country churches, but it will have to be before my hay-fever begins, that is, not later than 17 or 18 April.' This plan led to two other memorable journeys, the first of which was a direct consequence of Marie Nordlinger's example, and a logical sequel to the visit to Chartres.

On a Friday, probably 21 March, they set out in a cavalcade of two motor-cars: one of these, belonging to Emmanuel Bibesco, was enclosed, enabling Proust to travel without fear of draughts and asthma, while the other, Lucien Henraux's, was open and suitable for fresh-air fiends. They visited Provins and Saint-

Loup-de-Naud, a partly romanesque and partly gothic church, with the sculptured portal which showed, as Abbé Nappe had pointed out, such striking analogies with Chartres, and which Proust transferred to the imaginary church of Saint-André-des-Champs near Combray. The name of Saint-Loup was already familiar to him from the village near Illiers and the château on the Loire above Orleans; but this visit to the church of Saint-Loup-de-Naud, with the collective originals of the Marquis de Saint-Loup-en-Bray, was no doubt decisive for Proust's choice of his hero's name.

The other journey was the longest and best attended of all. On Good Friday, 28 March 1902, the automobiles set out to the north-east of Paris, bearing Proust, the two Bibescos, Fénelon, Lauris and Robert de Billy—perhaps, also, Lucien Henraux and Marquis François de Pâris. Proust solved the problem of getting up early enough by not going to bed at all; and at every stop on the way he fortified himself with a stiff *café-au-lait*, for which he insisted on giving an enormous tip. Their first call was at Saint-Leu-d'Esserent, a vast church on the Oise not far from Chantilly, mostly of twelfth-century and earlier date, with one romanesque and two gothic towers. Inside the church Antoine disgraced himself in Proust's eyes by singing the noisy Boulangist ditty, *En revenant de la revue*, with appropriate actions. They went on to the twelfth-century cathedral of Senlis, with its two belfries and exquisite spire. Lauris remembered Emmanuel here 'explaining to the attentive Marcel, but refraining from any appearance of giving a lecture, the features which characterise the church-towers of the Ile-de-France'. Proust already knew the spire from a water-colour painted by Marie Nordlinger in 1898, and was to see it two years later, far away over an endless forest, from the Duc de Gramont's château of Vallière: the town was to be sacked and the cathedral damaged, much to his grief, by the German invaders in September 1914. The friends reached their furthest point at Laon, eighty-seven miles from Paris. Laon, ostensibly, was the town at which Gilberte was staying, when the wind, 'the tutelary genius of Combray', seemed to waft her distant presence to the Narrator over the cornfields of the Méséglise Way; though in fact, as we have seen, Proust was thinking secretly of the village of Laons near Illiers, and perhaps of Mme Goupil's niece there. High in the belfries of the twin towers of the cathedral appear the sculptured heads of eight colossal oxen, carved in memory of the beasts who dragged the stones for the building— surely the strangest and most Proustian feature in all the cathedrals of France; and Emmanuel ingeniously arranged that his friends should have their first glimpse of the oxen when he led them suddenly round a street corner. The Narrator compares the proud race of the Guermantes's to 'a carved, mellow tower, rising over France before the cathedral nave had come to rest, like a Noah's Ark, on the hill of Laon, crammed with animals in the act of escaping through the towers, and with oxen grazing on the roof and looking down over the meadows of Champagne'.[1] Proust was delighted with the figures of the Liberal Arts in the porch, which he enumerated three years afterwards to Mme Catusse: 'Philosophy with the ladder of knowledge leaning against her bosom, Astronomy with eyes fixed on the heavens, Geometry with her compass and Arithmetic counting on her fingers, Logic with her wise serpent, but rather a banal Medicine, not as interesting as the one at Rheims who (if you will pardon my saying so) is examining a patient's urine in a vase.' In the same porch was a series of scenes from the life of the Virgin; and he borrowed these for the sculptures in the church at Balbec, which Elstir in his studio expounds to the Narrator.[2]

On the homeward journey that afternoon they stopped at Coucy, ten miles from Laon, to see the thirteenth-century castle, 'whose keep,' Proust had read in Viollet-le-Duc, 'is the finest specimen of mediaeval military architecture in France: beside this giant all others seem the merest spindles'. Here, too, Emmanuel contrived that they should first see the castle from a point at the foot of the hill, whence even its base showed high above the tree-tops. The friends climbed the spiral staircase of the great tower together. Marcel leaned on Fénelon's arm, while Fénelon, to encourage his asthmatic companion, and because the day was indeed Good Friday, sang the Good Friday-Spell motif from *Parsifal*. When they reached the platform at the top, one hundred and eighty feet from the ground, they gazed, in one of the eternal moments of which Time Lost is made, on the flowering apple- trees far below over the Ile-de-France, the last sunlight, the

[1] II, 13
[2] I, 840

endless green landscape of their youth.[1] Then night came, and cold; it was after midnight when they reached Paris, and Proust, utterly exhausted, took to his bed for several days.

By the middle of June his translation of *The Bible of Amiens* was nearly complete. On the 28th he asked Mme de Noailles to persuade her husband to lend him his Bible 'provided it isn't too enormous', for the quotations in the footnotes, at which he had been at work 'for the last few months'. 'At the moment of transcribing them I find they seem quite colourless, owing to the bad translation I've been using, and he told me he had an excellent Bible.' He adds that his 'documentation is now complete'. Perhaps it was at this time, when his erudition in Christian iconography was at its height, that Proust had the conversation recorded by Georges de Lauris with his former playmate of the Champs-Élysées, Lucie Faure, now Mme Goyau, an ardent Catholic and a scholarly student of Dante: 'he revealed a subtle and finely shaded mastery of the most difficult problems of religious philosophy and exegesis; could he have read the whole of the *Golden Legend*, and all the works of the learned Bollandists?'

He now sent his manuscript to the publisher Charles Ollendorff, who kept it for five months without deciding whether to accept or reject it, and then providentially went out of business to become editor of *Gil Blas*, leaving his successor to go bankrupt. 'If this hadn't happened,' Proust told Antoine Bibesco two years later, 'I doubt whether I'd ever have been able to recover my *Bible*, at once so cruelly scorned and so jealously detained.' But his memory was at fault when he told Antoine that Ollendorff 'had my Ruskin in his hands for a whole year before I could extract it from him'; for he had already recovered his manuscript and signed a contract with the *Mercure de France* for its publication as early as mid-December 1902.

On 29 June Proust wrote to Mme de Noailles: 'There's only one person who understands me, and that's Antoine Bibesco: I

[1] The tower of Coucy was blown up by the Germans in their retreat to the Hindenburg Line in March 1917. Perhaps it was the thought of this, among other such incidents, which made Proust allow the church of Saint-Hilaire to be destroyed in the Great War, when, as Gilberte wrote to the Narrator from Tansonville, 'for a year and a half the Germans held one half of Combray, the French the other' (III, 756), and according to the Baron de Charlus, 'the church was demolished by the French and English because the Germans were using it as an observation post' (III, 795).

hope he continues to do so! He is so intelligently kind to me, so
kind, and so intelligent.' But during July he transferred, or rather
extended, his pursuit from Antoine to Fénelon. It was one of the
stormiest and most disappointing of his friendships, the only one
on which he looked back with lasting bitterness, not because
he lost Fénelon, but because he never won him. The long-
accumulated strain on his nerves, added to the dual necessity of
lunching and dining with his friends without ceasing to stay up
all night, not infrequently prevented him from going to bed at
all; and when in total exhaustion at the beginning of August he
took to his bed in the evenings, it was not a return to the human
norm: on the contrary, he realised with horror, his life was a whole
twenty-four hours out of gear. Before leaving for Évian on 12
August Mme Proust took the extreme step of writing to Fénelon
to beg him to see her son regularly; but, Marcel grumbled,
'Fénelon has taken no notice of your requests—still, whatever
you do, don't begin again, because there's absolutely nothing
more to be said; and Bibesco is taken up every evening just now
by his double absorption in ham acting and making love.' 'I
never stop hearing new stories of women you've tried to assault,'
he rebuked Antoine, 'your violence is simply fantastic!' On the
14th, demoralised by lack of sleep, indigestion and a racing pulse,
he visited Dr Vaquez, who advised a régime of bed, trional and
cold tubs, and abstention from alcohol and morphine. "I never
could understand," said the wise doctor, "why invalids can't be
content with their own illnesses, instead of insisting on creating
new ones by making themselves unhappy over people who aren't
worth the trouble!" That night Proust dined at Larue's, alone
except for the waiters, under the glare of sixty electric lights:
Fénelon and Constantin de Brancovan had broken their promise
to join him, and he was again left in the lurch. But his woes were
alleviated by the kindness of old Félicie, of whom he wrote to
his mother in words which recall the Narrator's regard for
Françoise: 'Peace is restored, and a very affectionate one, between
Félicie and me. I'd far rather have her than Marie in a situation
like this. Marie is more educated, but less literary in her language,
and above all, Félicie's affection is so charming and simple.'

However, Proust and Fénelon had their times of laughter and
delight that summer. He recalled afterwards a day on which they
visited Mme Straus at her villa, Le Clos des Mûriers, at Trouville;

she took them over the clifftops in her motor-car to Honfleur, through the landscapes he had roamed with Marie Finaly ten years before. For once he enjoyed without asthma 'the mingled scent of leaves, milk and sea-salt'. And he remembered how every Sunday Bertrand would say: "Do find me the Stock Exchange column in *Le Figaro*, Marcel," and he would search in vain, because on Sundays there was no such column.

Early in September he thought of visiting his parents at Évian for the week-end—'I've been longing to see the beautiful lake again'—but he could not bring himself to leave the pleasures and miseries of Paris. The difficulty of persuading Marcel to take a holiday that year was only solved when Fénelon consented to go with him. After hastily reading up the Dutch and Flemish old masters in Antoine's copy of Fromentin's *Les Maîtres d'autrefois*, and buying another to take with him, he left with Bertrand on 2 October for Bruges. He heard the carillon, which reminded him of Mme Greffulhe's silvery laugh; and he met Harlette Comte, who was to marry his friend Fernand Gregh in March 1903. Soon he went on to Antwerp, where he was on the 9th, while Fénelon went on ahead to Amsterdam to book rooms on the Yeatmans' recommendation at the Hôtel de l'Europe. Even Proust found them fantastically expensive, though they had the advantage of being heated by hot-water pipes, to which he attributed his freedom from asthma during the whole visit; and Fénelon himself took to dining out, rather than pay ten francs for the *table d'hôte* dinner. Proust delighted once more in the seagulls of Amsterdam, of which Albertine says to Mme de Cambremer at Balbec: 'they smell the sea, they come to sniff the salt air even through the paving-stones';[1] and when he returned from the day's excursion he saw, like Albertine, 'the streets and towpaths brimming with a compact and joyful crowd'.[2] He visited Dordrecht on a showery day, and sent Reynaldo a sketch of the ivy-covered church, 'reflected in a network of sleeping canals, and in the tremulous, golden Meuse, in whose water the boats at evening disturb the images of red roofs and blue sky'. At Delft he saw 'an ingenuous little canal, bewildered by the din of seventeenth-century carillons and dazzled by the pale sunlight; it ran between a double row of trees stripped of their leaves by summer's end, and stroking with their branches

[1] II, 814   [2] III, 386

the mirroring windows of the gabled houses on either bank'. On 15 October he went to Vollendam by barge, 'through flatlands moaning in the wind, while on the banks the reedbeds bowed and raised their heads in endless undulation'. On the 17th, unlike the Narrator, who tells the Duchesse de Guermantes that on his visit to Holland, 'as I didn't want to confuse my impressions, and was short of time, I missed Haarlem', he visited Haarlem to see the paintings of Frans Hals[1]: 'why, even a person who saw them from the top of a tramcar would find them a real eye-opener,' the Duchesse shocks the Narrator by saying. Next day he rejoined Fénelon at The Hague, saw Vermeer's *View of Delft* at the Mauritshuis, and 'recognised it for the most beautiful painting in the world'. The Duc de Guermantes's impression of the picture was less vivid: when the Narrator enquires whether he knows the *View of Delft*, he replies with self-satisfaction: "If it's there to be seen, I certainly saw it!"[2] By now Proust was short of money; he explained to his parents, not for the first time in his life, that his pocket had been picked; and on 20 October he returned to Paris. His relations with Fénelon during these three weeks had been unwontedly serene. He would certainly have seized upon any new opportunity of complaining of him to Mme Proust, but instead he wrote: 'Fénelon was the *only person* with whom I could possibly have gone away ... he couldn't have been nicer.' His mother would have liked him to go on to Illiers; but in view of the season, for Illiers was at its most melancholy in autumn, and the critical situation of his private life, he refused: 'to stay at Illiers or anywhere else, especially just now, would be absolute madness'.

He returned to find Antoine Bibesco alarmed by the serious illness of his mother, who was in Roumania on the family estate of Corcova. At last, too late, a telegram arrived to call him to her side; she died on 31 October, and Antoine arrived too late to see her alive. Proust rose to the occasion with the peculiar intensity which he always showed when a friend was bereaved: he shared Antoine's grief to the point of making himself ill, he showed exquisite tact, utter unselfishness, an extraordinary insight into the mental processes of the mourner; yet it was as if the idea of a mother's death filled him with a strange, almost pleasurable

[1] At least, he told his mother he intended to do so; but he may have changed his mind.   [2] II, 523-4

excitement. When he saw Antoine's first letter, in which the very handwriting was shrunk by suffering, he was reminded of his own mother's voice on the telephone at Fontainebleau in 1896, after the deaths of Louis and Nathé Weil, 'broken and bruised, cracked and fissured, forever changed from the voice I had always known'. He offered to come to Corcova from February to June, if Antoine could assure him there were no flowers there to give him hay-fever; or to Munich for two days, if Antoine would meet him there half-way; but not till after 2 and 5 January, for the anniversaries of his grandmother's death and burial thirteen years before were still strictly kept in the family; or to Ragusa, Constantinople, or even Egypt. In the end, when all the inextricable web of planning and counter-planning could be spun no further, he stayed in Paris.

Antoine was not his only preoccupation during this November and December. Fénelon had been appointed attaché in the French embassy at Constantinople on 31 October, and was due to leave on 8 December: Proust, knowing his own inability to care long for the absent, did not disguise from himself that this meant the end of their friendship. Another cause for dejection was that his parents, exasperated by the ever-increasing expense of his social life, had insisted on putting him—at the age of thirty-one—on a fixed allowance. The Freudian equation of money and love was particularly strong in Proust: all his life he had expected and taken love and money from his parents, to spend on his friends and give to all who served him. It was as if his parents had decided to give him less love; and he was still more outraged by this betrayal than by what seemed to him the utter inadequacy of the allowance. Perhaps, however, their motive was not mere economy, but their knowledge that they had not long to live, and their desire to discipline the extravagant Marcel at the eleventh hour. His mother, too, who showed almost excessive indulgence when he was ill, was inclined to be jealous of his health, and of the social activities, friendships and freedom from home which it made possible. 'The truth is,' he told her with severity, 'that the moment I'm well, as the way of life which makes me well infuriates you, you demolish every-thing until I'm ill again. . . It's very sad not to be able to have affection and health both at once.' Her jealousy showed itself in all manner of petty restrictions and complaints, which, although

they were no doubt justifiable in themselves, would never have
occurred to her if he had been safely bedridden. He kept the
servants awake, and they in turn kept her awake; they were not
to wait on him at table, but must deposit a tray of food in his
bedroom and go away; they must not light a special fire in the
dining-room when his friends called; and worst of all, the bedside-
table on which he worked must be taken away ('I'd rather do
without chairs!'). Perhaps he was speaking the truth when he
told her that his despair at her unkindness was the sole cause of
his quarrel with Fénelon.

Fénelon and Lauris called one afternoon early in December,
and kept their overcoats on in the unheated dining-room: "I
daren't, Madame would have me dismissed," said Marie, when
asked to light a fire. In this gloomy situation Fénelon was moved
to say 'something extremely disagreeable'; whereupon Marcel
leaped upon him with clenched fists and, when restrained by
Lauris, seized Bertrand's beautiful new hat, stamped upon it, and
tore out the lining. With ludicrous pathos he kept the piece of
lining to show his mother, 'so that you can see I'm not exaggerating; but please don't throw it away, as I want to give it him
back in case it's still of any use to him'. Here is the original of
the incident in which the Narrator desecrates the new top-hat of
the Baron de Charlus.[1] The Baron has insulted him for not
consenting to his veiled overtures: it would be neat and logical
if the offence for which Proust punished Fénelon had been the
exact opposite, namely, an accusation of lack of virility. "Proust
was a Saturnian, and a very difficult friend," Fénelon told Paul
Morand twelve years later.

'Saturnian' was the euphemism in the slang of their group for
'homosexual'; we find Proust using the word on two other
occasions to the Bibesco brothers, but never to anyone else. 'I
have made some rather profound reflections on Saturnism,' he
airily informed Emmanuel Bibesco at about this time, 'which I
shall communicate to you at one of our next metaphysical
discussions. I need hardly add that they are of the utmost severity.
But one clings, all the same, to a philosophical curiosity about
people. Almost the only things worth knowing about a fool are
that he's an anti-Dreyfusard or a Saturnian.' Clearly, Emmanuel
was not supposed to be aware of Proust's own homosexuality;

[1] II, 559

nor was Antoine, when Proust objected to his recommendation of firmness in shaking hands: "but people would take me for an invert!" It is very likely that Proust's relations with all these noble young friends—not only those we have already met, but those, Albufera, Radziwill and Guiche, who are about to arrive—were entirely platonic. They may not have been willingly so; and his ill-success with Antoine and Fénelon may well have been due to his friends' realisation of the true nature of his frustrations. It is probable, too, with two possible exceptions, that all these young men were themselves normal. Marriage and the pursuit of women, it is true, are by no means incompatible with sexual inversion: Wilde and Gide were husbands and fathers, and Proust himself was to portray the woman-chasers and the married men of Sodom. But some weight must be given to the fact that a majority of Proust's friends—Gabriel de La Rochefoucauld, Antoine Bibesco, Lauris, Albufera, Radziwill and Guiche—were engaged in love-affairs with women during the first period of his friendship with them, and later married. Two, however, did not marry. It may or may not be significant that Emmanuel Bibesco was called the Dancing Girl, that there is no trace in the little we know of him of any affairs with women, and that he ultimately committed suicide: on the other hand, it is clear that Proust's feeling for him never went beyond liking. Fénelon, too, remained single: it seems not unlikely that it was to him that Paul Morand so scathingly referred when he alleged that 'the enchanting young man with fair hair and blue eyes, the darling of the ladies in 1900, who served as the model for Saint-Loup, was to end fairly and squarely in heterodoxy, or, as we called it in our jargon of those days, bi-metallism'. Fénelon perhaps suggested the descent into Sodom of Saint-Loup, as he suggested his redemption through death in battle. Did Proust, with his expert intuition in these matters, divine the truth even at this early period? Did their friendship end because Fénelon felt himself on the point of giving way, or because Proust himself made advances for which Fénelon was not yet prepared? However this may be, the swift Fénelon vanished into the East; his keen blue eyes and flying coat-tails were seen by his friends only in brief, yearly glimpses, on his summer leaves, and by Proust still more seldom. He half-forgot Bertrand instantly, and half-remembered him for ever.

Two other complications prevented him from visiting the bereaved Antoine in Roumania. Early in December he signed a contract with Alfred Vallette, editor of the *Mercure de France* and director of the publishing firm attached to that periodical, not only for *La Bible d'Amiens* but for a new translation of *Sesame and Lilies*. On the evening of his quarrel with his mother and Fénelon he had threatened, by way of revenge, to cancel the contract, but soon thought better of it. The manuscript of *La Bible d'Amiens*, which by now he had succeeded in extracting from Ollendorff, had to be revised and handed in on 1 February 1903. Also ('this marriage couldn't have come at a more inconvenient time') his brother Robert had become engaged to Mlle Marthe Dubois-Amiot, of 6 Rue de Messine and Aix-les-Bains; and Proust was faced with the dreadful duty of getting up in the daytime, first 'to make the acquaintance of the young lady, whom I haven't met yet', and then again in order to act as Robert's best man. He was also entrusted with the sending of invitations to the wedding, and was horrified to find, only a week before the great day, that no less than a hundred of these had failed to arrive. Perhaps his jealousy of his brother, repressed and replaced though it was by a genuine and lifelong affection, had risen at this crucial time nearer to the surface. Robert, for once, was the centre of attraction. He had taken his doctorate of medicine in February 1902, and was now in practice; he would soon be a husband and support a family of his own; he had proved his manhood and his normality as Marcel never would. A stay-at-home prodigal, a feeder among the swine of Sodom, Marcel saw with shame and indignation his allowance cut while the fatted calf was slain for his virtuous brother. Inevitably, he was ill for the wedding.

The ceremony took place on 2 February 1903 at noon, in the church of Saint-Augustin. In his capacity as best man Proust took the traditional collection for the poor after the service, assisted by his eighteen-year-old cousin Valentine Thomson. The girl's pleasure in her pretty dress and the bouquet of orchids Mme Proust had given her was spoiled by his distress and lamentable appearance. Marcel's white tie and tails were hidden beneath three overcoats and an indeterminate number of mufflers; his chest was wadded, his collar all too visibly caulked, with swathes of cotton-wool. Thus accoutred he was too bulky to pass along the pews; instead, he stood in the aisle looking like Tweedledum, 'his Lazarus-like face with its melancholy moustache rising like a surprise out of his woolly black cerements. He felt he had to explain himself, and to each row in turn he announced in a loud voice that he was not able to dress otherwise, that he had been ill for months, that he would be still more ill that evening, that it was not his fault.' After the midday reception at 6 Rue de Messine he took to his bed for a fortnight. 'Robert's wedding has been the death of me,' he wrote to Mme Catusse. But the ill wind of Saint-Augustin's brought him two fur coats, one from the good-hearted Robert as the obligatory present to his best man, and one from Antoine Bibesco, which he returned without opening the parcel: he did not wish to hurt Robert's feelings by accepting it, he explained, nor to let his parents think it a stratagem in his campaign against the meagreness of his allowance.

Since Antoine's absence and Fénelon's departure Proust had engaged in a new and even more than usually disappointing friendship with a certain 'M'. Antoine was thinking of a visit to Fénelon at Constantinople—'but if you won't come too, I shan't go'. In a letter of consent so provisional as to be almost a refusal Proust took the opportunity to tell Antoine and Bertrand some home-truths: 'it's curious that each of you has an opposite gift, yours being to dissipate mistrust, his to inspire it; so that you're both likely to make enemies, but yours will be people who don't know you and might well become your friends if you wished it, while Bertrand's enemies will always be his former friends. . . . This doesn't prevent me from being very fond of Bertrand. We're never more unjust than in those affections which we think must be prejudiced just because they're blind, and because for fear of liking him less we shut our eyes to the possible faults of the friend we cherish, and so prevent ourselves from seeing his virtues. I've had proof of this lately with M., whom I respected less the more I liked him, convinced as I was that because I was fond of him I was certain to be over-indulgent. Now I realise he was infinitely superior to the image of him constructed by my consciously indulgent, but therefore depreciatory affection. He would have had everything to gain from a severe, just and clearsighted friendship.' Proust's biting letter of dismissal to M. survives: 'I don't wish to see you any more, or to write to you, or to know you'; he keeps the inkstand M. has given him for

New Year's Day 1903, but intends to unscrew and return the
plaque so ironically engraved with 'Sweetest of blessings is a
genuine friend'; he is 'giving several little dinners soon, but if
anyone asks why you aren't there I'll explain that you're taken
up with your family, your mistress, your country-house and the
army' (for M., we are told, was at this time a sub-lieutenant in an
infantry regiment); and he signs the letter: 'I was, Your very
sincere friend, Marcel Proust.' In a letter to a common friend
about M. he quotes Barrès—'yet another lemon squeezed dry'.
'I hope you haven't passed on my kind regards to M., as they
would risk resembling those rays from a star which reach us only
after the star itself has ceased to shine.'

Spurred on by his mother ('You're quite impossible—instead
of admiring my positive resurrection and acquiescing in what
made it practicable, you have to insist on my setting to work
again'), he entered in December 1902 on a new cycle of literary
work. He added still further to his footnotes for *La Bible
d'Amiens*: one of his innumerable excuses for not going to
Roumania was the necessity of 'bringing thirty volumes of
Ruskin with me'. Constantin de Brancovan ('the latest person
to call me *tu*') had launched a new literary magazine, *La
Renaissance Latine*, and had accepted, as a substitute for the
articles he had originally requested, an abridgement of *La Bible
d'Amiens* which appeared in the issues for 15 February and 15
March 1903. But Proust had also been commissioned by Gaston
Calmette to write a series of articles on prominent hostesses and
their salons for *Le Figaro*. This was probably a delayed consequence of a curious incident in the previous August. He had
then tried in vain to arrange for Fénelon to write paragraphs for
the society gossip-columns of *Le Figaro*, and to persuade
Emmanuel Bibesco to supply information on his fellow-guests at
dinners and soirées ('of course, if you put in any made-up names
or other jokes it would make things so awkward for me that I
hope you'll refrain'); but Fénelon had been half-unwilling,
Emmanuel had refused outright, and the project fell through. The
first article in the series was on Princesse Mathilde (*Un Salon
historique: le salon de S.A.I. la Princesse Mathilde*), and appeared
on 25 February over the signature 'Dominique', a name Proust
had already given himself as the hero of the sketch '*L'Étranger*'
in *Les Plaisirs et les Jours*.

In March Proust felt obliged to give a series of dinners of gratitude at 45 Rue de Courcelles, the first for Calmette, another for Vallette, another for Cardane, secretary of *Le Figaro*, and yet others for Mme Lemaire, who was to be the subject of one of his forthcoming salon articles, and Hervieu, whom he had been meeting frequently with Lauris and the Bibescos at Mme de Pierrebourg's. These, no doubt, are the 'little dinners' to which he vengefully refrained from inviting 'M'. He had planned Calmette's dinner ('he would like to meet smart people') in January, but had been persuaded by his mother to postpone it till after Robert's wedding. When March came, however, Mme Proust was no better pleased with what she insultingly called 'this dinner of cocottes'; to Marcel's fury she used it as a menace to enforce a reform of his hours; 'if you don't change your hours, you shan't have your dinner!' He threatened to give it in a restaurant—'when I put myself in your place and imagine myself refusing you not one, but even a hundred dinners!'—but, although the sequel remains unknown, it is likely that he had his way. He did not know how little time the parents he exhausted with these exactions had still to live.

Chapter 16

TIME BEGINS TO BE LOST

BY the spring of 1903 three more young noblemen had joined the little band of Saint-Loups. Armand, Duc de Guiche, was the half-brother of Élisabeth de Gramont (since 1896 wife of Philibert, Marquis de Clermont-Tonnerre), and son of Duc Agénor by his second wife, Marguerite, daughter of Baron Charles de Rothschild: Guiche was therefore, despite his exalted birth on his father's side, half-Jewish. He was a tall, virile young man of twenty-three, with dark, curly hair, pale skin and violet eyes. He rode to hounds, played polo, painted, and already pursued the scientific studies which were to bring him international fame in the fields of optics and aerodynamics. Guiche met Proust early in March at Mme de Noailles's; he remembered how Reynaldo Hahn sang songs by Duparc and Fauré, chainsmoked, and broke into the Marseillaise when Mathieu de Noailles tiptoed in to say good-bye to his guests and leave for army manœuvres. Proust, however, was more interested in the antics of Lucien Daudet, who sat next to Guiche at dinner: demoralised by his noble company 'he chattered with unprecedented volubility and with all the joy of Mme Bovary crying "I've found a lover! I've found a lover!"' There was an awkward moment when Guiche asked, apparently in all innocence, "Have you a brother?" Lucien remained tongue-tied, for his brother, of course, was the now rabidly anti-Semitic Léon. He would have liked, Proust maliciously surmised, to reply: "No, certainly not, and if you should ever hear that someone named Daudet has been saying nasty things about Rothschilds and Jews, he's no relative of mine." But poor Lucien, transfixed by the implacable eyes of his hostess, could only burble a truthful but uninformative "Yes". Guiche had heard of Proust at Mme Straus's in his boyhood: "we invite him when we want someone witty to make up a fourteenth!" Struck by the brilliance of his conversation, he soon wrote to ask him to a party at his parent's house. 'My dear Proust', he began; but Proust answered: 'of course, I realise you can't call me "My dear Marcel", but you might at least put "My dear friend", which commits you to nothing, not even to friendship.' By April, however, their friendship had advanced far enough for Proust already to feel disappointed. He sent Guiche for an Easter present a copy of *Les Plaisirs et les Jours* with a melancholy inscription: 'To the Duc de Guiche, the true one rather than the real one, the one who might have been rather than the one who is. . . . I offer this portrait, now so poor a likeness, of a Marcel he has never known.'

Prince Léon Radziwill, nicknamed 'Loche', also aged twenty-three, was the son of Prince Constantin Radziwill,[1] whose remote cousin Prince Michel Radziwill had married Marie de Benardaky in 1897. The other branches of his large and wealthy family were scattered over Russia, Poland and Germany; and although the Constantin Radziwills were by now firmly rooted in France, Loche would complain: "It's very provoking, when I'm in Poland people talk about 'You Frenchmen', and when I'm in France they say 'You Poles'!" His aunt, Princesse Marie Radziwill, was one of the most prominent ladies in the court of the Kaiser, and devoted her life in vain to the promotion of friendship between France and Germany. She was also an aunt of Boni de Castellane, who once delighted and astonished her by taking her to the Ritz: "I'm particularly grateful to you for taking me to that inn, my dear," she said, "because I have never dined at an inn before." Loche was a young man of giant size, 'more like a block than a statue', with 'expressively inexpressive blue eyes', as Proust wrote one evening that autumn at Ermenonville, Prince Constantin Radziwill's château. The others had gone to bed, leaving Proust in the dining-room to write a character-sketch of Loche, and to freeze by the dying stove; he composed a wounded and wounding rigmarole of fifteen hundred words. Loche's voice, 'with its amusing slowness and false affability, seems clotted with foolishness and naïveté'; 'he would do anything for a friend except be his friend, in so far as that word

---

[1] Montesquiou, who might well have claimed to be the inventor of the clerihew, wrote:

'*It is most uncivil
To mention ladies to Constantin Radziwill.*'

Loche's father, as we shall see, was the original of the Prince de Guermantes in his later aspect as a homosexual.

implies preference, fidelity, security and perseverance'; most horrible of all, he once said of Ruskin that 'his greatest merit was his skill in making even the loftiest ideas agreeable and accessible to all!' 'Only an artist can see Loche's true merits, though women have an inkling of them, because they find him extremely attractive', and 'desire is a kind of sightless comprehension'. Clearly, Loche had sat for Proust's eternal friendship, but failed his examination.

At that time, however, the most important of all the new recruits of 1903 was Marquis (later Duc) Louis d'Albufera, known as 'Albu'. Albu was good-natured, loyal and simple, the only one of Proust's group of young noblemen who was a non-intellectual and an anti-Dreyfusard. He was aged twenty-six, an ardent motorist and traveller, and had made a journey to Tunisia at the time of Proust's winter friendship with M. Like Saint-Loup, he was in love with an actress; he had bought her a horse and buggy, and his delight in this spring was to sit on one of the iron chairs in the Avenue des Acacias and watch her drive up and down. Louisa de Mornand was a tall, willowy young person, with a long nose, arched eyebrows, and features of the most fascinating prettiness. She specialised in light comedy, first in soubrette parts, later in leads, and had a maid, Rachel, from whom Proust took the name of Saint-Loup's mistress. Proust himself immediately succumbed to Mlle de Mornand's charm partly because she was the beloved of a friend, but partly for her own sake; and their amical relationship survived through her subsequent love-affairs until the last years of his life. She made her début at the Théâtre des Mathurins in Tarride's *Coin du feu* on 17 April 1903 as the maid Victorine; and on 24 May at the same theatre she played a rather more important role in a curtain-raiser to the lyrical pantomime '*Rêve d'opium*' which featured the notorious Otéro, *la belle Otéro*, the rival in whoredom and diamonds of Liane de Pougy. On this prominent occasion Proust took it upon himself to organise her publicity: through Antoine Bibesco he asked the dramatist Edmond Sée and Abel Hermant, then dramatic critic of *Gil Blas*, to mention her appreciatively in their criticisms, if it was only to say: 'A friend of mine asks me to mention that Mlle de Mornant is a beauty and a charmer, and I don't mind if I do.' Since Proust here spelled her name wrongly, he can only have met her recently; but soon he was addressing her as *Chère amie*, which before long became *Ma petite Louisa*. Next month she was on holiday at Blois: 'how I should like to compare the charming embroidery of one of those blue or pink gowns that suit you so well with the stone lace-work of the castle!' She must not think he is making love to her; he knows that if he dared to try, she would only 'send me about my business'; and besides, he would 'rather die than raise my eyes to the adored beloved of a friend whose exquisite and noble heart makes him dearer to me every day'. Nevertheless, he signs his letter 'with something which would give me intoxicating pleasure if it were to happen otherwise than by letter, my dear Louisa—a tender kiss!' His wish was to come true a year later; meanwhile, 'if Albu is with you, you might ask him to stop calling me Proust!'

A few days before Antoine Bibesco's return to Paris in the second week of March Proust met the Princesse de Polignac, whom he had not seen since August 1901, at Princesse Hélène de Chimay's. He was pained to learn that she had just completed a French rendering of Thoreau's *Walden*,[1] which he and Antoine had planned to translate together in the early days of their friendship: 'it took me back to the delicious time of our meeting,' he told Antoine, 'and to hopes which since then have not entirely been realised'. The delivery of the manuscript of *La Bible d'Amiens* to the *Mercure de France*, which owing to Robert's wedding had already been postponed from 1 February to 1 March, probably took place about this time. To greet Antoine's return Proust had introduced him in an article on the salon of Mme Greffulhe intended for the Paris edition of the *New York Herald*, but transferred on Calmette's request to *Le Figaro*. In an interview at the *Figaro* offices on 15 April Calmette persuaded him, 'for reasons I cannot fathom', to postpone the article for a fortnight, and in the end never printed it—most deplorably, for all too little is known of Proust as Comtesse Greffulhe's guest. He asked instead for an essay, which Proust had already finished, on Mme Lemaire's salon; and Proust insisted on transferring to this the paragraph about Antoine, 'although Ettemlac and Enadrac [Calmette and Cardane] each separately begged me to do nothing of the kind, because the Mme Greffuhle article was

[1] Extracts from it appeared in the *Renaissance Latine* of 15 January 1904 over the Princesse's maiden name, W. Singer.

exquisite just as it was'. So on 11 May Antoine had the pleasure
of seeing himself in the morning's *Figaro* 'interrogated on the
Macedonian question', amid Mme Lemaire's lilacs, by the
eminent politician Paul Deschanel. 'Everyone who says "Prince"
to this young diplomat with a great future feels like a character
in Racine, so inevitably does his mythological appearance remind
them of Achilles or Theseus. M. Mézières, who is talking to him
now, looks like a high priest asking Apollo to deliver an oracle....
The prince's words, like the bees of Hymettus, are swift on the
wing and laden with delicious honey, but do not lack, for all
that, a certain sting!' At first, in the Mme Greffuhle article,
Proust had made Antoine talk not to Deschanel but to Paul
Hervieu, who could not be portrayed in Mme Lemaire's drawing-
room because he had quarrelled with the hostess. To make up
for this broken promise Proust took Hervieu to the second night
of the Caillavet and Flers comedy *Le Sire de Vergy* at the
Variétés on 16 April, where in his enthusiasm at his old friends'
success he 'narrowly missed blacking Hervieu's eye three times
over with my clapping hands'.

Since his outrush of sympathy in the previous autumn Proust's
ardour for Antoine had perceptibly cooled; he now pointedly
began his letters '*Mon cher Antoine*' instead of '*Mon petit
Antoine*'. Antoine was again, or still, in love with an actress;
Proust was making himself unhappy over Guiche and the
amiable but unforthcoming Albufera. Their friendship had gone
full circle and returned to its starting-point; yet, like two former
lovers tormenting one another with a meaningless renewal of
coquetry, they could not resist beginning again. This time
Antoine was the instigator; with his love of mystification and
playing with fire, he insisted on a pact that each should tell the
other his inmost secrets, and in particular should report any
scandal he might hear about his friend. It seemed to each,
naturally, that he gave away far too much in return for far too
little: 'I've made a thousand revelations to you, and you not the
least one to me,' complained Proust. Nevertheless, in his capacity
as the perfect friend, Antoine had betrayed at least two sufficiently
dangerous secrets. Porto-Riche, he confided, had said to him: "I
shouldn't see quite so much of Proust, if I were you, it will only
give you a bad reputation." And Léon Daudet had declared: "I
can tell you, as a doctor, that Marcel Proust's ill-health is due to

taking morphine.'[1] Soon Proust was racked with misgivings: 'I
see before me the dead, reproachful face of what might have been
but is not,' he wrote, remembering the words of Rossetti's sonnet
written ten years before by Edgar Aubert on the back of his
photograph, 'I mean, of the better person I might have been, if
to satisfy your curiosity at all costs I hadn't sold what no one
ought ever to have bought, and in fact the Devil alone can buy!'
The first move to break the bargain came from him: 'if you agree,
shall we renounce this cruel and impossible pact, which has
already made me so miserable?' But the habit had become too
strong—'the habit of not living for myself alone, of extending
the horizon of my life past the furthest frontiers of another
person, of allowing the stream of my existence to overflow into
this indiscernible prolongation of myself with all the gold and
mud it carried with it day by day, all the sights it had surprised
and reflected, the secrets that had been dropped in its waters'.
But now—he continued his river-metaphor—'just as a river cut
off by a high, impenetrable dike turns its course and fertilises
other lands, so I've been forced to pour into another confidant
what you refuse to accept from me, and to receive from him the
confidences which have become indispensable to me since you
gave me the habit of making them. Let's say no more—what I've
just written makes me blush for shame.' This letter, which marks
the end of the phase, can be dated to the first week in May 1903;
the new friend may be either Albufera or Guiche, or even,
already, 'Loche' Radziwill. But Proust's sufferings during these
two months need not be taken too tragically: in the whole series

[1] Léon Daudet had in fact taken his doctor's degree in the late 1880s, but
turned to writing without going into practice. His revelation was no doubt
made with the best intentions, from friendly concern, and without malice or
even untruth; for (a) the dangers of morphine were little understood at that
time. It was prescribed for asthma and other nervous ailments, and to take it
was thought at most an imprudence, certainly not a vice, unless it was taken
for mere pleasure; (b) Daudet of all people was particularly exercised about
the use of morphine, and had written a propaganda novel, La Lutte, against
the drug and doctors who prescribed it; (c) Proust undoubtedly took
morphine occasionally at this time, with his parents' knowledge, but disliked
it and never acquired the habit. (Cf. Mme Proust, 134 [20 Sept. 1899—but
this is only morphine ointment for his wrist at Évian]; ibid., 190 [15 Aug.
1902—'Dr Vaquez told me not to let myself be carried away by morphine
(he needn't worry!) or alcohol, which he considers equally detrimental in
all forms'].)

of eight letters of pain and alarm there is audible the note of sentimental enjoyment which the French call *marivaudage*, and Proust's friends called Proustification.

During this spring Proust seems to have resumed his trips by motor-car. He asked his mother to invite Robert Proust to lend his own car, promising to have it driven 'by a chauffeur from any firm he cares to name and feels he can trust', or by Albufera, 'who has driven all round France, Belgium, Germany and Switzerland'. It is not impossible that the visit to Saint-Leu-d'Esserent and Senlis took place at this time, rather than on the way to Laon and Coucy on 28 March 1902.[1]

On 9 June the ineffable Mme Lemaire gave a fancy-dress ball on the theme 'Athens in the time of Pericles'. 'Banquet, procession, dancing, *costume strictly Classical Greek*,' enjoined the invitation cards. Montesquiou, a little confused in his chronology, had arranged to come as the poet Anacreon in a purple robe, crowned with ivy, waving a golden lyre, and pelted with roses by a band of youthful disciples in very short white tunics. Could he have had a secret warning that his reception would be less serious than this almost sacred role demanded? He had shown less diffidence at her last ball, when as Haroun al Raschid, in a turban covered with turquoises borrowed from Sarah Bernhardt, he had gone the round of the rival salons before arriving, remarking to every hostess: "Your guests seem unusually ugly this evening!"; but now, purely and simply, he failed to show up. The agonised Empress of Roses sent Proust to telephone the aggrieved Count Robert, once, twice and thrice; but the line was dead. While he was behind the scenes Marie Nordlinger, Reynaldo Hahn and Coco de Madrazo had arrived, flinging themselves into the ball and calling "Have you seen Marcel yet?" every time their paths crossed. Suddenly, as Mlle Nordlinger danced past an alcove, a sepulchral voice exclaimed "Dieu, que vous êtes belle!"; and there, dressed not in 'strictly classical costume' but in white tie, tails and his new furlined overcoat, stood an embarrassed Marcel.

[1] Proust mentions Senlis in the letter to Antoine Bibesco quoted above (*Bibesco*, p. 129), and Saint-Leu in the quarrel with Antoine a month or two later (*Mme Proust*, 215), though in such a way as to leave it uncertain whether the visits were recent or a year old. The Laon and Coucy trip, at least, can only have been on Good Friday 1902, because in 1903 Fénelon was in Constantinople.

The Athenian maiden good-naturedly dismissed her partner to sit out with her utterly un-Greek friend; and as was his habit when overcome by the charm of a girl companion, he recited to her the whole of *La Maison du Berger*.

The return of Proust's hay-fever that summer brought a renewal of Mme Proust's indulgence and of the affection which, said her son, 'the contemptuous irony of your many harsh words in these last years had gone far to discourage me from cultivating'. 'It's a long time since I last thought of you with such a paroxysm of effusion,' he wrote one night, when he came home late and longed as of old, but forbore, to enter her room and kiss her in her sleep. One evening in late June, when he was already expecting the first proofs of *La Bible d'Amiens*, she magnanimously gave a little dinner for Antoine Bibesco. Proust primed his friend with a full list of the things he must not say: "No jokes about tipping, for one thing, and none of your stupid questions to Papa!" But the tact he demanded was too one-sided: in the middle of dinner he could not resist telling the dreadful story of Antoine singing '*En revenant de la revue*', with appropriate dance-steps, at Saint-Leu-d'Esserent; and Antoine, in return, began to say everything he had been begged not to say. "Don't you think, sir, that if Marcel wrapped up less? . . ." he began insinuatingly. Dr Proust was in full agreement, but it was not a subject he cared to discuss. Amid an electric silence the relentless Antoine proceeded with an anecdote of their latest night out: "and before I could stop him, Marcel tipped the waiter sixty francs!!" The storm broke; Dr Proust burst into rage, the dinner was spoiled, Marcel wept. Even Antoine was dismayed at the effect of his little revenge; but, as Proust truly told him, "my family affections are dearer to me than the affection of my friends, and I can't help mistrusting anyone who attacks me through them, just as I would someone who, in spite of a noble heart and other remarkable qualities, was liable at times under the influence of drink or for some similar reason to stick a knife into me". He swore never to forgive Antoine, and perhaps he never did. The factitious renewal of their secret game was ended; the bewitching phantom of the ideal friend had moved to other faces, and would never more wear Antoine Bibesco's.

Early in July Bertrand de Fénelon visited Paris for a month's leave. The nightly symposium of the friends at Weber's or

Larue's was now a broken habit, buried for ever in the past by the winter's absence of Antoine and Fénelon. Instead, with Lauris, Guiche, Albu, Gabriel de La Rochefoucauld and Loche Radziwill, they met every evening in Proust's bedroom for an agape of conversation, refreshed by iced cider or the famous beer from Pousset's tavern of which Proust was so fond. Élisabeth de Clermont-Tonnerre was amused and interested on hearing, no doubt from her half-brother Guiche, of these goings-on. She wrote inviting Proust to dinner. But he replied with more annoyance than gratification: 'I'm rather sad to find that someone has unveiled to you the absurd arrangements, the trivial mystery of my existence. I don't know whether it was done maliciously or not; in any case, whether intentionally or otherwise, this "someone" has succeeded in making me ridiculous in your eyes. Your documentation is admirable: everything, the words "nocturnal conversations", the very names of my principal visitors, even the vulgar but undeniable cider, proves the reliability of your information.' He accepted the young marquise's invitation so conditionally that nothing came of it, and their inevitable friendship was delayed for two years.

On 29 July the discussion in Proust's room was heated. For the first time since the Affair he found himself feeling passionately about politics. In June 1902 the Dreyfusist prime minister Waldeck-Rousseau had resigned, after being returned to office with a majority of violent anti-clericals who were too far to his left to accept his own more moderate policies. The new minister, Émile Combes, a militant atheist, who had studied for the priesthood in his youth and was nicknamed the 'Little Father', set himself to destroy the religious orders by a programme of forcible expulsion and confiscation. On that evening the diehard Albufera, devoted to the Church and still convinced of Dreyfus's guilt, was set upon by the progressive sceptics Fénelon and Lauris. "I can't bear the sight of priests reading the *Libre Parole*," declared Lauris; and Fénelon remarked with a snigger: "It's nice to see all these nuns obliged to take a trip for once in their lives!" Proust, when he tried to find common ground for both parties, was trampled in the struggle; and Lauris even accused him of insincerity for praising the conservative Denis Cochin's speeches against the Combes Laws in the Chamber. His friends went home still furious; but late that night Proust made his profession of

faith in a letter to Lauris. Over the ruins of the Church he saw
Saint-Jacques at Illiers; the exiled priests took on the face of the
good Canon Marquis; and the argument about politics led him
back to his childhood at Illiers, further than he had ever yet
penetrated into Time Lost.

Two days before, on 27 July, Dr Proust had visited Illiers, for
what was destined to be the last time, to preside over the prize-
giving at the boys' school. But Canon Marquis was absent: since
the anti-clerical laws of Jules Ferry in 1882 he had never been
invited, and Proust's uncle Jules Amiot, now deputy mayor and
a reader of both the priest-baiting *L'Intransigeant* and the anti-
Semitic *Libre Parole*, refused even to speak to the constant
visitor of his dead wife. Lauris and Fénelon supported the
expulsion of the religious orders in the name of French unity; but
would it forward unity if the Canon was exiled and Saint-Jacques
secularised? 'I remember that little town crouching to the earth,'
he wrote to Lauris, 'that avaricious earth, mother of avarice,
where the only impulse towards the sky—often dappled with
clouds, but often, too, of a heavenly blue, transfigured every
evening in the sunsets of the Beauce—is the exquisite spire of
the church; I remember the priest who taught me Latin and the
names of the flowers in his garden; and I think it unjust that he
should not be invited on prize-day as representing in the town
something harder to define than the social functions symbolised
by the chemist, the retired tax-collector, or the optician, yet none
the less worthy of respect—were it only for the intelligent, de-
materialised spire of his church, which points to the sunset, melts
so lovingly into the pink clouds, and strikes a stranger arriving
in the village as having a nobler air, more disinterestedness, more
intelligence and more love than other buildings,'—such as the
new, secular school—'however recent the laws that have erected
them . . . Supposing the religious orders were expelled, and the
fire of Catholicism quenched in France (if it could be quenched,
whereas in fact it is not by legislation that ideas and faiths perish,
but when the truth or social utility they possessed is corrupted
or diminished), then our clericalist unbelievers would only be
more violently anti-Semitic, anti-Dreyfusard, anti-liberal than
ever; they would be no fewer in number, but a hundred times
worse . . . You can't kill the Christian spirit by closing Christian
schools, and if it is destined to die, it will die even under a

theocracy.' He ended with a warning which history was to justify: 'at the present time the socialists commit the same error by being anti-clerical as the clericals in 1897 by being anti-Dreyfusard. They expiate their fault to-day; but we shall expiate ours to-morrow.' Lauris acknowledged long afterwards that Proust was right; and meanwhile Albufera, astonished that a Dreyfusard could be so fair-minded as to defend the Church in a time of persecution, asked him 'to explain the Affair to me so that I can share your conviction'. 'Only I haven't the heart to,' Proust told Lauris, 'and my one regret in being a Dreyfusard is that it saddens the loyal and noble Albufera.' But the chief consequence of that evening's argument was that Proust had been inspired, in his evocation of the church of Saint-Jacques, to see further into the meaning of Illiers than he could in *Jean Santeuil*. Illiers was now on the verge of becoming Combray, which, 'seen from the railway when we arrived there in the week before Easter, was nothing but a church epitomising the town'.

Early in August Dr and Mme Proust left for their last holiday together. After a few days at St Moritz, a week at Interlaken and a short stay at Ouchy, they arrived by the lake steamer on 18 August at Évian, where Dr Proust was to take a course of treatment. As in any other year the Hellbronners, Weisweillers and Duplays, the barrister Maître Ployel and the judge M. Gougeon were there. But the Splendide Hôtel was so appallingly noisy that Mme Proust recommended her son to go instead to Cabourg, 'because you used to find it suited your health so well'—advice which he only took, like a counsel from beyond the grave, four years later.

Meanwhile Proust was ill with asthma. In an interval between his attacks he dined with Antoine and his friends at Armenonville in the Bois de Boulogne, where Odette, to Swann's despair, listened with the little clan to the Vinteuil Sonata in the moonlight, and where Proust himself nine years before had invited Montesquiou and Delafosse in vain. The painter Vuillard was present and made a sketch of the gathering, 'a unique point of intersection between his admirable talent, which has so often kindled my memory, and one of the most delightful and perfect hours of my life,' as Proust wrote a year later when he asked to be allowed to buy the sketch—where is it now? Fénelon, too, fell ill in the last week of his leave, and was visited daily by Proust, himself choking with asthma and shivering with a high fever. He negotiated busily to prevent a duel between Jacques Bizet and a friend of Antoine and Bertrand, the playwright André Picard, but only at the expense of consenting to be Picard's second, which put him in the bad books of Bizet and the Straus's. Then, on 8 August, after a last supper with the departing and convalescent diplomat, he and Antoine put Bertrand into his train, 'looking as frisky as could be'. Antoine himself left a few days later for a post at the Roumanian Embassy in London, after a new quarrel which they had no time to make up. Proust had recently received his proofs from the *Mercure de France*, made a number of corrections suggested by Marie Nordlinger, and mislaid the whole batch: 'my publisher is annoyed,' he told her, 'and I am not sure whether he will want to publish the work of so un-business-like and boring a translator'. For a time he still hesitated where to go for his holiday. Should he join Lauris in Brittany, and see once more the Pointe du Raz?—'historically, geographically and literally, you know, it's Finisterre, the end of the world, a giant granite cliff round which the sea rages eternally, towering over the Bay of Ghosts, a place of funereal and illustrious malediction!' Or might he visit Mlle Nordlinger in the other half of Balbec, at Varange-ville near Dieppe, 'by the exquisite little graveyard, whose quiet-ness is a prelude to the unending silence enjoyed by its dead, which our living ears cannot detect, for they are distracted by this merely relative silence, deepened though it may be by the regular and repeated advance of the waves far below'? Suddenly, in the small hours of a morning in early September, after a fare-well dinner with Lauris, Albufera and Louisa de Mornand, he set out by a strangely devious route for Évian.

Feverish, asthmatic and exalted by his solitary journey, he was unable to sleep in the train as it ran in the moonlight past Melun, the Forest of Fontainebleau and Sens. Along the valley of the Yonne towards Auxerre the line threaded between steep, vine-clad hills and little towns, those to the east still silvery-black in the moonlight, those to the west already rose-pink in the rising sun. 'I was seized with a mad desire to ravish little sleeping towns—you notice I say *villes*, not *filles*, towns, not little sleeping girls,' he wrote to Lauris, using the sexual imagery which he so often associated with travel. He transferred this magical ride through hills lit simultaneously by moon and sun to the Narrator's night-journey with his grandmother to Balbec. At eleven in the morning he arrived at Avallon and took a carriage to Vézelay— 'a prodigious place in the middle of a kind of Switzerland, solitary on the top of a mountain which dominates the surrounding hills, visible for miles around in a landscape of the most extraordinary harmony; the church is enormous, more like a Turkish bath than Notre-Dame, built in alternating black and white stone, a delicious Christian mosque'. Here at Vézelay, with its union of Norman gothic and almost oriental romanesque, there is something of the 'Persian' church of Balbec. He returned to Avallon for the night, but could not sleep for fever. He walked the streets until it was time for the six a.m. train to Dijon, where he saw in the Hôtel de Ville, once the palace of the Dukes of Burgundy and now the Museum, the polychrome tombs of John the Fearless and Philip the Bold: he already knew the casts of these monuments at the Trocadéro, but 'you can't get any idea of them from the models, because the real thing is painted in so many colours'. Although he had now spent two days and nights without sleep, he continued 'my journey into death; at the stations people asked if they could get me anything, and when I saw my face in a mirror I didn't recognise it'. At dinner-time Maurice Duplay saw his spectral figure tottering from the hotel omnibus at Évian, amid the lightly-clad holiday makers, muffled in his fur-lined winter overcoat.

After a few days in bed Proust was so fully restored that, as he wrote with pride to Lauris and Robert de Billy, 'I'm up every day by two in the afternoon!' He was anxious for Lauris, who was in love with a married woman, and for Fénelon, now back in Constantinople, to whom the Bulgarian rebellion then raging in Macedonia was dangerously near. Mme de Noailles had already left Amphion; but he joined Albufera and Louisa de Mornand at Chamonix for a day's excursion on mule-back to Montanvert, where 'the agile Louisa displayed all her graces on the Mer de Glace'. He thought of the plan he had been discussing with his friends, to form a lay monastery for reading, writing and meditation: an echo of his dream ten years before, in the summer of Willie Heath, of 'living in a chosen circle of noble-minded men and women, far from the arrows of stupidity, vice and malice'. 'If only you could be the admirable abbess, habited all in white!' he wrote to Mme de Noailles; and to Lauris: 'don't tell a soul, because it wouldn't be a monastery if everybody came!' But Proust was destined, though not yet, for a different and even stranger form of solitude. At the end of September, however, on his way home, he visited a rather similar establishment, the fifteenth-century hospital at Beaune, with its nun nurses, all chosen from rich families, wearing their white summer habits and looking like his vision of Mme de Noailles as abbess. He thought of having himself admitted as an emergency case: had not Viollet le Duc said, 'the hospital at Beaune is so beautiful that it makes the tourist long to fall ill there'?; and yet, he wrote to Marie Nordlinger, 'if Viollet le Duc had been in my condition he wouldn't have spoken so lightly'. He dragged himself to Paris and was ill for a month, paying for each evening out with several evenings in bed.

The energetic and distinguished life of Dr Proust was now near its close. It was thirty-three years since the morning in August 1870, a few days before the Battle of Sedan and his marriage to Jeanne Weil, when he received from the Empress Eugénie the cross of chevalier of the Legion of Honour. He had risen through the rank of officer to that of commander; and many years later, when Proust himself received the cross, he remembered his awe as a boy when, on gala evenings, he watched his father putting on the red cravat of his decoration. In 1879 Dr Proust was elected to the seat in the Academy of Medicine left vacant by the death of his master Ambroise Tardieu; in 1884 he succeeded to the post of Fauvel, inventor of the *cordon sanitaire*, as Inspector-General of Sanitary Services; and in 1885 he became Professor of Hygiene in the Faculty of Medicine. Throughout his life he continued his intense activity as a teacher, a writer on medicine,[1] and a practising physician. Marcel was accustomed to invite his friends to consult his father on their ailments: 'would you like Papa to come and see you?' he asked Antoine Bibesco on the occasion of an indisposition in this same summer of 1903. Anatole France, however (perhaps when afflicted with the cyst

[1] His bibliography includes thirty-four items, covering a wide range of interests. Besides international hygiene he wrote on tuberculosis, rabies, deficiency diseases, paralysis, aphasia, various nervous and brain maladies, and occupational ailments, including (as his son must have noticed with a wry smile) 'saturnism', not in the sense familiar to Marcel and the Bibescos but meaning lead-poisoning.

for which he was operated on by Dr Pozzi in September 1899), was wary: "My dear young friend," he said, "I should never dare to consult your father; I'm not important enough for him; the only patients he takes on nowadays are *river-basins*!" But the sublime task to which Dr Proust had devoted his life was the exclusion of cholera from the frontiers of Europe. He was the leading spirit in a series of international conferences for the imposition, particularly at Suez, of the *cordon sanitaire*; and it must sadly be confessed that his chief opponent, partly for reasons of commercial convenience, partly from well-founded suspicion of French ambitions in Egypt, was the formidable power of England. At the Rome Sanitary Conference in 1885, thanks to England, little was accomplished; but at Venice in 1892 and Dresden in 1893 Dr Proust secured unanimous agreement of the powers, with the sole exception of England; and in this very year 1903 his life-work was crowned by the adhesion of that refractory nation and the formation of the International Office of Public Hygiene in Paris. "In those days," Casimir-Périer, then Minister of Foreign Affairs, had said in 1894, "the politicians had to practice a little medicine, and the doctors had to be politicians"; and everyone knew that he was alluding to Dr Proust and M. Barrère. Western civilisation owes a debt to Proust's father not only for producing one of its greatest novelists, but for the major part he played in the banishment of cholera from Europe.

His political colleague during those stirring years was Camille Barrère, afterwards ambassador at the Quirinal from 1897 to 1925, with his long face, aggressive oblong beard, and keen Norpois eyes. When *A l'Ombre des Jeunes Filles en Fleurs* was published in 1919 M. Barrère suspected, with extreme indignation, that M. de Norpois was meant for himself; 'simply because he used to dine with us every week when I was a child,' said Proust mendaciously, 'whereas M. de Norpois is a representative of a diplomatic type which is the exact opposite of M. Barrère, though no less utterly detestable!' But Proust also met other originals of M. de Norpois through his father. Gabriel Hanotaux, Foreign Minister from 1894 to 1898, had shown in Proust's student days M. de Norpois's infuriating confidence in the practicability of combining a diplomatic with a literary career. M. Hanotaux had every reason to think so; for he became a member of the Académie Française on 2 April 1897, wrote voluminously and boringly,

though not without talent, on historical subjects, and produced
newspaper articles on foreign affairs under the pseudonym
'Testis'.[1] Armand Nisard, ambassador at the Vatican from 1898
to 1904, had at least two features of M. de Norpois: he was Marie
de Benardaky's uncle by marriage, so that Proust might well
have been on the point of kissing his hand in gratitude for his
promise to put in a word for him with Marie's parents[2]; and he
was felt to have shown lack of zeal in supporting Dr Proust's
candidature for the Academy of Moral Sciences.[3]

Dr Proust's dining-room was also an ideally situated strategic
point for observing the natural history of doctors, and in particular the originals of Cottard, Du Boulbon, Dieulafoy and
Professor E. Dr Eugène-Louis Doyen (1859-1916), a surgeon of
sensationally original technique, with greying blond hair,
astonished blue eyes and an athletic figure, was a model for many
qualities of Cottard: his icy brutality, naïveté, inspired tactless-
ness, fury when contradicted by a patient, and total, incurable
ignorance in cultural and social matters. "With all her gifts," he
flabbergasted Proust by announcing, "Mme Greffulhe hasn't
managed to make her salon anything like as brilliant as Mme de
Caillavet's!" Dr Doyen regarded himself as Potain's superior—
"Potain's an old fool," he would say—an opinion shared by Mme
Verdurin.[4] The dates of his life fit those of Dr Cottard, who is
young in the 1880s and dies during the war. Professor Guyon,
the urologist and teacher of Robert Proust, was a tall, thin man
with white whiskers, from whose inexhaustible puns and clichés
Proust collected a store of hints for Cottard; and Auguste Broca
was another surgeon who, like Cottard, kept his students in fits
of laughter with puns, chestnuts and oaths. As we have seen,
Cottard, as a foundation-member of Mme Verdurin's 'little

---

[1] M. de Norpois at Venice, discussing with Prince Foggi the question of a
successor to the retiring Italian prime minister, remarks: "And has no one
pronounced the name of M. Giolitti?"—'words which supplied the chancel-
leries of Europe with food for conversation throughout the next twenty
years, and when at last forgotten were exhumed by persons signing themselves "One who Knows", "Testis", or "Machiavelli" ' (III, 635). Proust is
here at his usual trick of juxtaposing one of his characters with the name of
an original of the character; and the passage is immediately followed (III,
637) by a satirical account of the emotions on this occasion of yet another
model for M. de Norpois, M. Barrère himself.

[2] Cf. I, 477   [3] Cf. II, 225-6   [4] I, 188

nucleus' and an unfaithful husband, was Dr Pozzi at Mme Aubernon's; his pince-nez and involuntary wink were those of Proust's professor, Albert Vandal; but his name was taken from Dr Proust's fellow-student Cotard and Dr Cottet at Évian. The model for Dr du Boulbon was the favourite physician of the Faubourg Saint-Germain, Dr Le Reboulet; but a guest of Dr Proust, the warty-faced Dr Laboulbène, contributed to his name. Dr Dieulafoy, with his 'charmingly supple figure and face too handsome in itself', who is sent for simply to certify the grand-mother's last agony and, says the Narrator at the time of writing, 'is now no longer with us',[1] was a real person, Professor Georges Dieulafoy (1839-1911). He was Princesse Mathilde's doctor and guest, and Proust's friend Gabriel Astruc took him, no doubt with some good reason, for an original of Cottard. The wife of his brother Marcel, Mme Jane Dieulafoy, was a strange, mannish, emancipated little woman, who wore trousers and smoked cigars, but was much in demand by hostesses in her capacity as an eminent archaeologist and the excavator of Darius's palace at Susa.[2] Once, when she called at the *Revue de Paris* offices, the commissionaire announced her to Ganderax: "there's a gentleman downstairs who says he's a lady!"; and at a society dinner one evening, when she insisted on joining the men in the smoking-room, General de Galliffet took her by the arm and said: "Come along, my dear feller, let's go and have a p—s." Professor E., who automatically quotes poetry before examining the Narrator's grandmother, is Dr Édouard Brissaud, author of *Hygiene for Asthmatics*, 'our dear *médecin malgré lui*, on whom one almost has to use physical force to get him to talk medicine,' wrote Proust after consulting him in 1905.[3] Another friend of the Proust family and guest of Mme Aubernon was Dr Albert Robin, who told Proust: "I might be able to get rid of your asthma, but I wouldn't advise it; in your case it acts as an outlet, and saves you from having other

[1] II, 343

[2] 'M. Nissim Bernard's face,' remarks the Narrator on the occasion of his dinner with Bloch's family at Balbec, 'seemed to have been brought back from Darius's palace and restored by Mme Dieulafoy' (I, 774).

[3] Proust told Lucien Daudet in 1921 that there was 'something of Brissaud's type of doctor, more a sceptic and a clever talker than a clinician, in Du Boulbon'. But it was his habit not only to create a single character from several originals, but to distribute elements of a single real person over several characters.

diseases." He was renowned for the mysterious eccentricity of
his prescriptions: for example, to an old lady in whom he wished
to inculcate a certain complicated exercise of muscles and lungs,
he declared: "you must take off all your clothes, and then hop
round a table six feet in circumference, eating an artichoke one
leaf at a time"—'I've exaggerated this only very slightly,' remarks
Léon Daudet, who tells the story. Dr Robin was infatuated with
Liane de Pougy, who was jealous of his family and forbade him
to use the words 'my wife', 'my son'. "What must I say, then?"
"Say 'the monster', and 'the little monster'!" But the form in
which Proust knew this story was very different, whether because
it had been misreported to him, or because it had undergone a
significant transformation in his unconscious: he mistakenly
believed that Dr Robin called his child 'the little monster' not in
jest but in sadistic delight, 'because he couldn't obtain full sexual
pleasure in any other way'; and he told Louis de Robert that he
had used Dr Robin's example, among others, for the scene at
Montjouvain in which Mlle Vinteuil induces her friend to call her
dead father 'that old monkey'.[1] But the mingled admiration and
contempt with which Proust treats the medical profession in *A
la Recherche* is doubtless in part a reflection of his own feelings
towards his father.

Time had played its old, merciless trick on Dr Proust. He was
no longer the handsome, black-bearded man of forty, running in
the early mornings of the 1870s along the Rue La Fontaine to
catch the Auteuil-Madeleine omnibus, or meeting the young
Mme Proust with the infant Marcel and Robert in Louis Weil's
carriage outside the Hôtel-Dieu at the day's end; no longer even
the keen-eyed, pursed-lipped, Holbeinesque figure of Lecomte
du Nouy's portrait in 1885. A photograph of the Doctor outside
St Mark's at Venice, with the pigeons of the Piazza feeding at
his feet, perching in his hands, alighting on his shoulder, or
another in which he stands, morning-paper in hand, with the
fiercely-moustached Robert on the balcony of 45 Rue de
Courcelles, show a fading old gentleman with a short round
grey beard, looking rather like Edward the Seventh. He had
grown corpulent, like his wife; his voice was deep, but slightly
nasal; his habit of wearing his pince-nez far down his nose forced
him to tilt his head far back; his face wore a perspicacious,

[1] I, 162

indulgent smile, an expression of approaching repose. Contrary to usual report, Marcel had only the sharp-edged, delicately curved Jewish nose and swimming dark eyes of his mother: the mould of his face, especially the narrow, thick-lipped mouth, was startlingly like his father's.

Despite his occasional outbursts of rage, or sudden, arbitrary vetoes ('my father had a way of refusing to let me do things which were clearly allowed in the more liberal charters granted me by my mother and grandmother, because he was careless of "principles", and had no idea of "international law",' says the Narrator), Dr Proust had been a touchingly indulgent parent, more sensibly and equably so than Mme Proust. From sheer kindness and resignation he had allowed his bewildering son to lead the life he wished; he never withheld the money for his clothes, orchids, presents, 'little dinners' of fifteen persons, Ruskin pilgrimages, or twelve-hour cab-hires. Even the enormous bills of several hundred francs a month for cotton-wool, and medicaments for asthma, insomnia, rheumatisms and indigestions, although these hurt his professional conscience as well as his pocket, were paid with a sigh. He could understand neither Marcel's passion for society, nor society's passion for Marcel. "Is he really so charming? Why is he invited out so often?" he asked one of his son's noble hostesses; but there was no satisfactory answer. Yet he took pride in Marcel's literary career, such as it was, and consoled himself for his own failure to enter the Academy of Moral Sciences with the generous prophecy: "Marcel will belong to the Académie Française!"

On at least one occasion he made use of Marcel's talent. In his speech on 7 June 1903 at the unveiling of the monument to Pasteur at Chartres he compared the discoverer of the bacterial origin of disease to one of the sculptures in the cathedral. "In the porch of Chartres you will see a figure whose name is Magas, the magician of the Encyclopaedia of Chartres. Magas symbolises alchemy: he is the master of the science which summons from the domain of mystery so many extraordinary dreams, and transplants them into the real world we know." His audience must have been astonished by Dr Proust's knowledge of iconography; but we can hardly doubt that these Ruskinian words were written for him by his son. Dr Proust himself, however, may be given sole credit for the moving and eminently Proustian opening of his speech at the Illiers prize-giving on 27 July. "The emotion I feel on coming to your school sixty years after is something you will perhaps fail to understand," he said, "not because at fifteen one is less intelligent or comprehending than at my age; on the contrary I think one is able to understand a great deal more in boyhood. But there is one thing which is a closed book to the young, or which they can only guess at by a kind of presentiment, and that is the poetry and melancholy of memory." Perhaps father and son were not so different as they believed. Each disappointed his father, and achieved fame long after his father's death; each gave his life for a great aim, and died in the hour of its accomplishment.

On Sunday, 22 November, Dr Proust and Marcel had their last quarrel. 'We had an argument about politics,' Proust told Mme de Noailles a week later, 'and I said things I ought not to have said.[1] I feel as though I'd been hard on someone who could no longer defend himself. I don't know what I wouldn't give to have been more gentle and affectionate that evening. Papa's character was so much nobler than mine. I never stop complaining; but when Papa was ill his only thought was to keep us from knowing it.' And indeed, Dr Proust's last recorded words, probably spoken to Robert Proust a few weeks before, were these: "I've had a happy life. My only wish now is to leave it quietly and without pain."

On Monday, 23 November, Dr Proust took part, with his accustomed energy and lucidity, in a meeting of the Permanent Commission on Tuberculosis. In the afternoon he saw his patients and gave his usual consultations. Next day he called on Robert Proust at his new home, 136 Boulevard Saint-Germain, on his way to preside over an examination at the Faculty of Medicine; and Robert, alarmed at his father's look of harassed exhaustion, insisted on accompanying him to the nearby École de Médecine. Robert, who no doubt would have preferred to be with his pregnant wife, went to his laboratory; but a few minutes later he was summoned by an anxious attendant to the cloakroom, where his father was locked in a water-closet and could

[1] As father and son were in agreement on the injustice of the Combes Laws, and Marcel had moved well to the right of his position during the Affair, it is difficult to see what they can have found to argue about. Perhaps Dr Proust said something like: "Now you see what Dreyfusism leads to!"

not be made to reply. They broke the door in, and found the professor huddled on the floor, paralysed, unconscious and speechless. He was carried on a stretcher to 45 Rue de Courcelles. Marcel, of course, was still asleep; he remembered ever afterwards how his mother tapped on his bedroom door to say: "Forgive me for waking you, my dear, but your father has been taken rather ill at the École de Médecine."[1] Dr Proust died thirty-six hours later, early in the morning of Thursday, 26 November, without regaining consciousness. As she watched by his side, waiting for the end, Mme Proust wrote a journal, as she had done for her own father and mother, of her husband's illness. A few hours before, on the 25th, Robert's only child Suzy had been born.

Dr Proust's funeral procession to Saint-Philippe du Roule on the 28th was an imposing occasion. The mourners were led by Marcel and Robert, followed by the Council of the University and the entire Faculty and Academy of Medicine, the statesmen Méline, Fallières and Barthou, and other colleagues and friends of the doctor. Marcel's group was represented by Antoine Bibesco, Albufera, Baron Henri de Rothschild (who had helped to finance *Le Banquet* eleven years before) and Mathieu de Noailles. Marie Nordlinger was present, and remembered the frosty morning sunlight, and Marcel in full mourning at Robert's side, tottering with grief and fatigue. The farewell speech over Dr Proust's grave at Père La Chaise was delivered by Professor Debove, doyen of the Faculty of Medicine. "He was sceptic enough to be indulgent to people who left what we like to believe is the path of virtue, epicurean enough to enjoy life without taking the petty miseries of human existence too tragically, and stoic enough to face death without flinching," said Professor Debove rather finely.

Montesquiou, Mme de Noailles, her sister the Princesse de Chimay, Robert Dreyfus and many others wrote charming letters of sympathy. Proust noticed, without surprise, that his mother seemed her usual energetic self, apparently unchanged since the last day, only a week before, when her husband had still appeared strong and well. 'But I know the depth and violence and duration of the drama that is going on inside her,' he told

---

[1] Proust used the circumstances of his father's illness for the Narrator's grandmother's stroke in the public lavatory at the Champs-Élysées, and the words "Forgive me for waking you," for the Narrator's mother when she calls him (II, 335) to witness the grandmother's death-agony.

Mme de Noailles, 'and I can't help being afraid.' He had recently abandoned *La Bible d'Amiens*, perhaps from momentary bore- dom, or pique at Vallette's impatience, but more probably, as in the December before, to spite his parents. But his mother briskly intervened: "It was your father's one desire," she declared, "he waited from day to day to see it published"; and he wrote once more to Vallette, and resumed the endless task of imposing perfection on his proofs. For the last year or two Mme Proust had slept in a separate room; but she now moved to Dr Proust's bedroom, with its little cabinet from Indo-China and marquetry card-table and bureau, to spend every night with her dead husband for ever. Her time was short; she could not wait to keep, as she did for her parents according to Jewish custom, the 'year's end' of her loss. Every month, at first even every week, the three days of her husband's attack, death and burial were made sacred; and Marcel humoured her by observing them too, partly because it was a useful excuse when Montesquiou or others were pressing and he did not wish to go out.

'Life is beginning again,' he wrote to Mme de Noailles; but the life of every day had somehow become less real. The craving of his childhood, to enjoy his mother's love and be rid of his father, was ironically fulfilled when it was long outgrown. Her mourning presence was an embarrassment: she, not his father, was an un- wanted ghost in the house.

The old man was gone; the blowing of his nose, the rustle of his *Journal des Débats* would be heard no more; and it seemed that an indispensable condition of life in the present had been removed. Dr Proust returned, not as a benign, grey-bearded old man, but as a black, ascending shadow on the now demolished staircase at Auteuil. "You can see for yourself the child's un- happy," he declared; "after all, we're not gaolers! You'd better stay with him for the rest of the night." Proust realised with vertigo that only his stricken, weakening mother remained to keep him from falling into the past. He stood at last on the edge of the abyss of Time Lost.

VOLUME TWO

Et je compris que tous ces matériaux de l'œuvre littéraire, c'était ma vie passée.
PROUST, *Le Temps Retrouvé*

Chapter 1

VISITS FROM ALBERTINE
(*December 1903 – December 1904*)

'LIFE has begun again,' Proust had written to Mme de Noailles on 3 December 1903, a week after his father's death. Dr Proust was in his grave at Père Lachaise; but already the absence which at first had seemed calamitous was beginning to appear natural. Little outward change could be seen in Mme Proust: her manner that day was brisk and fortifying, and even the reappearance of her mourning-dress, so recently had she ceased to wear black for her father's and uncle's deaths seven years ago, was hardly noticeable. As before, or still more than before, she ran her son's errands while he slept, and ensured that the servants made no sound until, 'towards six o'clock in the afternoon, or as the common herd would put it, evening', he woke and rang his bell. In moments of leisure she sat in the drawing-room, reading Mme de Sévigné in her ebony Empire armchair, with Lecomte du Nouy's portrait of her husband propped on a black-draped easel beside her. The beautiful Jeanne Proust was now a plain, corpulent, middle-aged lady of fifty-five, with hair beginning at last to grey, and an expression of puzzled serenity which concealed undying grief for her dead and devouring anxiety for her son.

Not unreluctantly Proust imitated his mother: he ceased to weep, and put aside his pangs of genuine sorrow, his remorse for having been, as he confessed to Mme de Noailles, 'the dark side of Father's life'. It was unwise to remark upon the fact. "I don't think Marcel is unduly distressed at his father's death," observed the heartless Antoine Bibesco to a friend, who immediately sneaked; and Antoine, in a well-deserved letter of frantic anger, was told: 'you have committed an unforgivable crime, and I never want to see you again'. But Antoine was no stranger to these paroxysms of rage: he coolly called that very evening to discuss his new play, *Le Jaloux*, and was received as though nothing had happened by a gay and good-tempered Marcel. Even so, incidents of everyday life continued to recall the lost old man. Throughout that December and January letters of condolence from Anna de Noailles, with their sentiments and handwriting of 'disciplined tumult', arrived in succession; and Proust seemed to hear again outside his bedroom door his father's jovial shout: "Another letter from Mme de Noailles, my boy!", and his mother's scolding: "Really, my dear, must you spoil Marcel's pleasure by telling him in advance?"

With a comfortable feeling of obeying his father's last wish, pleasing his mother, and appeasing his impatient publisher, he fell again to correcting the proofs of *La Bible d'Amiens*, over which he had dawdled since July. He made a second resolution for his mother's sake: 'to enable myself soon to get up at the same time as you, drink my morning coffee with you, feel that our waking and sleeping hours are portioned out over one and the same expanse of time, would be, I mean *will* be, my delight'. Once in December he heroically went to bed at 1.30 a.m., some nine hours early by his time-scale; but he spent a sleepless night looking for a safety-pin to fasten the waist of his drawers, and devising a plan, never to be executed, for 'a new life in which we shall live to the same time-table, in the same rooms at the same temperature, in accordance with the same principles and—though contentment is now, alas, forbidden us—with mutual approbation'.

In some respects the new régime at 45 Rue de Courcelles was more liberal than the old. Never in his father's lifetime could Marcel have received, like the Narrator on the day of Albertine's first visit in Paris, a young girl in his bedroom; but in December, when the funeral bakemeats were hardly cold, Marie Nordlinger became a constant visitor. At first they worked on his Ruskin proofs at the huge oval dining-room table, the centre of so many 'grand dinner-parties' since the springtime of Willie Heath, with its red baize cloth and old-fashioned Carcel oil-lamp, for love of whose soft beams he extinguished the electric light. In January he was confined to bed with asthma and lumbago, 'and therefore prevented from having a young girl to visit me'; but soon he overcame his shyness of being seen by her in the sacred and chaotic bedroom from which he had excluded even Emmanuel Bibesco. His bed, when Mlle Nordlinger entered, was littered with dictionaries, Ruskins and exercise-books; cheap wooden pen-holders lay fallen on the floor; and Marcel reclined in a mare's nest of pillows, muffled in pullovers and cotton-wool, writing sometimes on the rickety bamboo bedside table ('my shallop'), sometimes, when that was piled too high with books, on paper held in mid-air. The room was suffocatingly hot; but soon old Félicie brought, with a plate of fancy cakes from Rebattet's, an ice or a glass of orangeade for Marie,[1] and a jug of boiling coffee for Master Marcel. Mlle Nordlinger poured out for him, taking care always to include the skin with the milk, for: "It's the cream, you see," he explained, "it's the best part of the milk!" They fell to work, discussing here a sentence, there a single word, whose possible synonyms Proust had prepared beforehand from his dictionaries. Orders were given that "no one is to be allowed in, except Monsieur Hahn"; and on the one occasion when the inquisitive Antoine Bibesco dared to gate-crash, he was made to rue it.

Towards midnight they began to talk; and Mlle Nordlinger remembered 'his strangely luminous, omnivorous eyes, alight with fun and mimicry, or suddenly suffused unaccountably, unashamedly with tears'. Starting from two Japanese *cloisonné* ear-rings hung on a chain from her neck—"May I touch them? Don't take them off! Where did Reynaldo get them?"—he cross-examined her on the mysteries of her craft. Later she found traces of their conversations in *A la Recherche*; and it is because Mlle Nordlinger worked as an enamellist for Siegfried Bing that the Narrator speaks of 'a crude blue, almost violet, suggesting the background of a Japanese *cloisonné*', or 'the polychrome enamel of pansies', or of the Prince de Borodino 'embedding glorious images beneath a royal blue enamel in the mysterious, illuminated and surviving reliquary of his eyes'.[2] They exchanged presents: Proust gave her Montesquiou's copy of Whistler's *The Gentle Art of Making Enemies*; and Marie brought her own water-colour of trees at Senlis, painted in 1898, which hung ever after by his bedside until, shortly before his death, Proust gave it to Reynaldo. In witty but sympathetic allusion to his love of the flowers he dared not smell, she gave him a twopenny packet of balsam seeds, a repoussé lily, a hawthorn flower in pink translucent enamel—'your grace is as fresh as a spray of hawthorn,' he had told her five years before. 'The seeds are flowers for the imagination, just as the Japanese dwarf trees at Bing's are trees for the imagination,' he wrote; and the dwarf trees reappeared in

---

[1] Similarly Albertine visualises the ice for which she longs on the morning of her visit to the Trocadéro as coming from Rebattet's (III, 128), and the Narrator offers her orangeade during her visit after the Princesse de Guermantes's soirée (II, 738).

[2] I, 169, 126; II, 132.

Albertine's lyrical monologue on ice-cream.[1] There can be no doubt, indeed, although his relationship with Mlle Nordlinger was one of comradely affection and nothing more, that her idyllic visits during this winter to his mother's home were remembered when, out of many girls and three young men, he created Albertine. But the impressions left by Marie Nordlinger were to be reinforced a few months later by the visits of a young woman with whom his relations were more physical.

Meanwhile, Proust conducted two hot but temporary quarrels. The first was with Antoine Bibesco, shortly before Antoine's departure with Emmanuel on 9 January for two months' leave in Egypt. Proust referred, in a letter to Mme de Noailles, the culprit's cousin, to his '*déboires sentimentaux*' with Antoine. Possibly he was jealous of his friend's prospective visit to Constantinople, where Bertrand de Fénelon still lingered after his transfer to the St Petersburg embassy on 23 November 1903. 'I wish you a very happy stay in Egypt, since I'm certain you'll never get there,' Proust wrote ironically on the eve of Antoine's departure. In fact Antoine went straight to Egypt, but from mid-February till his return to Paris at the end of March was at Constantinople.

The other victim was Constantin de Brancovan, who had rashly promised him the post of literary critic on the *Renaissance Latine*. On reflection Constantin realised that Marcel, being a genius, incessantly ill and now preoccupied with his Ruskin translations, would be totally unsuitable for a task which required a punctual hireling who would write in a manner to which the subscribers were accustomed. Late in December he appointed the versatile Gaston Rageot —'my Usurper,' as Proust called him—and informed Marcel only after the deed was done. Proust was wounded in his pride, his code of friendship, and in the vague longing which pursued him intermittently throughout his life to obtain a regular post as a journalist. He was particularly galled by Constantin's pretence to have acted for his own good ('you have doubted me, Marcel, but I forgive you'), to spare him 'the fatigue, toil and boredom of having to supply a monthly article'. He broke with Constantin in an interview at 45 Rue de Courcelles on 18 January, and on the 20th visited Mme de Noailles to receive her sympathy. But she seemed strangely reluctant to give it, and showed visible irritation when he asked permission to use her telephone, or when, as he left in the small hours, he explained

[1] III, 130.

from the bottom of her staircase that he could not find the switch to put out the electric light. Perhaps there was another reason for Constantin's decision. The *Renaissance Latine* was in some degree a family magazine—'the Brancovan chamber-pot, which the whole family fills so regularly,' said Montesquiou; and Rageot could be relied upon to praise Constantin's sister Anna's work less dithyrambically and more convincingly than Proust.[1]

It is time for a further glimpse of Montesquiou. A year ago, in January and February 1903, he had given a series of seven lectures in the United States, organised by Boni de Castellane's friend Miss Bessie Marbury. She was an intelligent American spinster who lived near Paris with her inseparable companion Miss Elsie de Wolfe (later the famous Lady Mendl of the 1920s); and because Miss de Wolfe was as thin as Miss Marbury was fat, Montesquiou nicknamed them Tanagra and Tonneau Gros. On the liner going over, the Count's tiffs with Yturri were overheard with smothered sniggers by unsympathetic bystanders. His lectures were given to diamonded and tiaraed audiences: "I understand you have a Steel King, an Oil King, a Railway King—but where is your Dream King, your Poetry King?" he began[2]; and he supplemented his earnings by selling *objets d'art* to his new converts. Proust assured him that his voyage was the most epoch-making feat of evangelisation since the Acts of the Apostles, and compared him and Yturri to Saint Paul and Timothy. In this January of 1904 the Count was summoned to Paris from his winter quarters at Nice to fight his second and last duel. Mme Ernesta Stern, an occasional hostess of Proust and Hahn, and a writer of mildly erotic novels, had become one of Montesquiou's *bêtes noires*. In a review of her latest volume he had ungallantly remarked of a chapter entitled 'How to choose a lover': 'this is absurd, because everyone knows she never bothers to choose.' He was challenged by her son Jean, a noted swordsman, and for once it seemed Count Robert had gone too far; but to his great pride he succeeded, by his previous stratagem of whirling his sword like the

---

[1] In July 1904 occurred a curious incident for which Fernand Gregh never forgave this obedient critic. Rageot had unwarily written a laudatory review of Gregh's new poems, *Les Clartés Humaines*, at a time when Mme de Noailles was consumed with baseless dread lest Gregh might be given the cross of the Legion of Honour before her; and at Constantin's orders he altered his article to a vigorous slating at the very moment of going to press.

[2] Charlus himself makes fun of the Steel King, saying the Iénas' title is no better than his (II, 564).

sail of a windmill, in baffling his opponent for nearly three-quarters
of an hour, and escaped with a mere scratch. The duel was fought on
18 January.

By sheer coincidence it was on that very day that Proust published
in *Le Figaro*, under the pseudonym Horatio,[1] an article entitled
'*Une Fête chez Montesquiou à Neuilly*'. In a brilliant parody of Saint-
Simon's *Mémoires* he evoked a typical fête at the Count's Pavillon
des Muses in the Boulevard Maillot; and the joke pleased him so well
that he included the same material fifteen years later in the much
longer Saint-Simon pastiche in *Pastiches et Mélanges*. Montesquiou
was uncertain whether to be gratified or annoyed. That he should be
treated as one of the great figures of the *grand siècle* was a just tribute
to his genius; but was not the satire a little more edged than could be
accounted for by the exigences of parody? Who on earth was
Horatio? He wrote a haughtily acrid letter to *Le Figaro*, addressed to
'Horatio', which Calmette showed to Proustbut did not print. Soon,
however, Count Robert changed his mind. In March, when Proust
and he were guests at the same dinner-party, he brought the conversation round to Mme de Noailles's short story '*L'Exhortation*',
published in the *Renaissance Latine* of 15 November 1903. "It's
not only sublime, marvellous and ravishing," he cried at the top
pitch of his eldritch voice, underlining his words with extraordinary
gestures, "it is the most beautiful thing I have ever read; indeed,
from all the height of my infallible taste, and all the breadth of my
infinite culture, I can say it is the most beautiful thing that has ever
been written!!" He proceeded to repeat the entire work from
memory, only interrupting himself to murmur aside: "What genius!
What *genius*!!" Outside in the street with Proust, who was acutely
embarrassed by the amazement of passers-by, he pointed to the
heavens and quoted: " 'The sky that evening was of a colour which
no words can describe,' " and stamped on the pavement with body
flung backwards until, as Proust told Mme de Noailles afterwards, 'I
was really afraid he'd sprain his ankles'. Then he changed the subject:
"Are you Horatio, Marcel?" he asked pointblank. Proust denied it.
"Because, as I couldn't discover who wrote the article, I've had a
small edition privately printed—with a few necessary corrections, of
course!" The agitated Marcel could only write to Mme de Noailles:
'What a blow! Not a word about Horatio, mind! *Tombeau, tombeau*,

[1] He had already used it in *Le Figaro* for his '*Salon de la Princesse de Polignac*'
(6 September 1903) and '*Salon de la Comtesse d'Haussonville*' (4 January 1904).

tombeau!' A little later, when Montesquiou found the identity of Horatio, disaster was averted: Proust whitened his lie by explaining that he had promised Calmette to keep the secret of his pseudonym; and Montesquiou, having once professed to take the article as a compliment, could only be doubly pleased to learn that he owed it to his 'dear Marcel'.

Although the *achevé d'imprimer* of *La Bible d'Amiens* was 15 February 1904, it was not too late for Proust to add last-minute corrections. In the small hours of that very day he sent two questionnaires to Mlle Nordlinger on passages which still perplexed him, ending with the ominous words: 'This old man'—meaning Ruskin—'is beginning to bore me.' The actual publication took place in the first week of March, and the book was first briefly mentioned, as 'the elegant and powerful translation which M. Marcel Proust has just given us', in an article on Alphonse Karr in *La Liberté* on 15 March by Robert de Flers. Reviews were for the most part as insensitive as for *Les Plaisirs et les Jours* eight years before. Few among the chorus of indolent reviewers realised that the meeting of Proust and Ruskin had produced a prose and a personality new in French literature, a work in which criticism had become a form of creative imagination, or that a great writer was here on the threshold of self-discovery. *La Bible d'Amiens*, in so far as it was noticed at all, only helped to confirm Proust's reputation as an amateur, a drawing-room dilettante.

Another disappointing feature of the reviews was that Proust's effort to organise them had brought its own punishment. With two unimportant exceptions[1] the book was not reviewed by anyone whom he had not persuaded to do so by entreaty or influence. Even the passing mention by his old friend Robert de Flers was made by request[2]; notices appeared in the *Chronique des Arts* (19 March) and *Le Figaro* (25 March) because Proust was a valued contributor to those papers. Another, in *Arts de la Vie* (March 1904) is to be explained by the fact that the editor Gabriel Mourey, himself a translator and critic of Ruskin, was a friend of Montesquiou, and was to publish the first section of *Sésame et les Lys* in his magazine a year later. Proust conveyed a hint to Léon Daudet that an article

---

[1] The only articles by persons not known to be friends or 'contacts' of Proust were those by Georges Richet in *Revue générale de la Bibliographie française*, 10 April 1904, and by Ernest Gaubert in *Revue universelle*, March 1905.

[2] 'It was nice of you to be so prompt,' Proust wrote in his glowing letter of thanks.

would be an acceptable return for the dedication of '*Ruskin à Notre-Dame d'Amiens*'. 'Never a word, and I still haven't swallowed it,' Proust wrote to Maurice Duplay a year later. He begged Mme de Noailles to ask Abel Hermant, the friend of Constantin de Brancovan, to 'insert ten words in one of his articles', and baited the hook with an invitation for Hermant to dine with his publisher Vallette ('a charming man who knows Henri de Regnier'). Perhaps owing to Proust's unwise quarrel with Constantin, Hermant's tardy compliance in *Gil Blas* on 4 September 1904 was worse than useless: without naming either Proust or his book he maliciously alluded to Mlle Nordlinger in a sentence about 'English gentlewomen who think it their duty to pore over the cornices of St Mark's because these happen to be mentioned by Ruskin.' Proust registered the insult and parodied it for Bloch's vulgar remark about 'drinking sherbet with lovely ladies while pretending to read *The Stones of Venighce* by Lord John Ruskin'.[1] The most satisfying notices, though even these were solicited, came from Proust's cousin-in-law Bergson and the historian Albert Sorel, who showed greater generosity than any of his friends in rallying to the aid of their former pupil. Bergson went so far as to read an official report on the book at the Académie des Sciences Morales on 28 May, remarking that the preface was 'an important contribution to the psychology of Ruskin', and that 'the style is so alive and so original that one would never suspect the work of being a translation'. Sorel gave Proust three whole columns in *Le Temps* on 11 July, including a sentence on his style which, for what it was worth, was perhaps the most penetrating thing said of him before the appearance of *Du Côté de chez Swann*: 'he writes, in moods of revery or meditation, a prose that is flexible, elusive and enveloping, opening on infinite vistas of colours and tones, yet always translucent, reminding one at times of the glass in which Gallé locks away the tendrils and arabesques of his engraving'.[2]

La *Bible d'Amiens* had originally been designed as a monument

[1] I, 739.

[2] The image drawn from Gallé may well have been suggested to Sorel by Proust himself. Proust shared Montesquiou's regard for Gallé's work and his son's, which he commissioned on several occasions for presents to friends, and twice mentioned with approval in *A la Recherche* (I, 803; II, 392). Proust's gratitude, by a characteristic transition, turned to admiration, and he referred in the preface to *Sésame et les Lys* to Sorel's article as 'perhaps the most powerful pages he has ever written'.

to Proust's voluntary and purposeful surrender to Ruskin, and dates from a period which had ended nearly two years before the publication of the volume. Most of the preface, as we have seen, was written between the summers of 1899 and 1900; the translation was finished in 1901, and the footnotes were added in the spring of 1902. But in the later Postscript to his preface Proust completed the drama by announcing his repudiation of Ruskin; and for the light it throws on the early stages of this liberation and the beginnings of *A la Recherche* his brief afterthought outweighs all the rest.[1]

In his meditation by the shore of Lake Geneva, a real incident of September 1899 which became one of the last-written episodes of *Jean Santeuil*, Proust had penetrated further than ever before into the nature of unconscious memory; but the revelation was premature and incomplete. Unable to advance further by his own power he abandoned his novel and entered, with relief and joy, the promised land of Ruskin, in which the real world is beautiful, and beauty is true and moral. For a time he surrendered completely to Ruskin, or rather to the undiscovered part of himself of which Ruskin first made him conscious. The dead Ruskin was a prophet, a guide, a father: Proust became his disciple, pilgrim and spiritual son. The first signs of a rift in this posthumous relationship came at Venice in May 1900, on the afternoon of thundercloud and storm when Marie Nordlinger read to him from *The Stones of Venice*, in the shelter of Saint Mark's, Ruskin's denunciation of the sins of the Venetians—doubly heinous, said Ruskin, because they were committed in sight of the word of God inscribed in the mosaics of their cathedral. Proust became aware that his union with Ruskin might be one-sided. Whether by a ludicrous coincidence or by a symbolic warning, he stood beneath those very mosaics, while the thunder of a vengeful deity or an angry Ruskin pealed above him; and the dead master denounced him through the young girl's voice for all his sins

---

[1] Possibly, since it continues a train of thought suggested in the last paragraph of the preceding section ('*John Ruskin*', written in the spring of 1900 and first published in the following August), and takes as its text an incident at Venice in May 1900, Proust may have had an inkling even at that early date of the future necessity of the Postscript. The conclusions which it states belong, however, to a period after the completion of the rest of the work; and its writing is firmly dated to May and June 1903 by the publication in the *Revue des Deux Mondes* on 15 June 1903 of Mme de Noailles's poem '*Déchirement*', which appeared, as Proust records, 'almost at the moment when I had finished writing these lines'. (*Pastiches et Mélanges*, p. 195, footnote.)

of sodomy, snobism and sacrilege. For a moment he was tempted to
plead guilty, and Marie Nordlinger saw him overcome by a trance
the opposite of that in which her cousin Reynaldo had found him on
the day of the Bengal roses at Réveillon. However, good sense
prevailed; for sin, in sinful man, is not a forfeiture but a condition of
salvation. He continued and completed his journey through Ruskin;
yet the accusation still rankled, and now in his Postscript he retaliated by accusing his master. He quoted Ruskin's charge against the
Venetians, and described the scene in Saint Mark's, the darkness, the
glowing mosaics and his own tell-tale emotion. But Ruskin, he said,
was mistaken in believing that the sins of Venice were more inexcusable because they were committed in the presence of her beautiful
cathedral. In this passage, Proust declared, indeed in the whole of
his life's work, Ruskin was himself guilty of the still more flagrant
sin of idolatry, of worshipping the graven image in preference to the
deity it represented, of pursuing the external beauty of symbols
rather than the truth they conceal. 'The doctrines Ruskin professed
were moral doctrines, not aesthetic, and yet he chose them for their
beauty. And as he wished to present them not as being beautiful, but
as being true, he was forced to lie to himself about the nature of the
reasons which made him adopt them.' Proust proceeded to make the
breach irreconcilable by comparing Ruskin in this respect to the
absurd Montesquiou. He did not venture to name Count Robert,
calling him merely 'one of the most justly celebrated of our contemporaries'; he alleged mendaciously that the sin of idolatry was
to be found 'only in his conversation, not in his books', whereas in
fact it is the fault which vitiates all Montesquiou's works in verse
and prose; and he wreathed the whole so successfully in compliments
that the Count did not take it amiss. 'This incomparable talker,'
Proust instanced, declared a house beautiful because Balzac once
lived in it, thought it a crime to give a passion-flower to a Jew
because its pistils and stamens mimicked the instruments of the
Crucifixion, and went into raptures over the dress of 'a society lady
his friend' (probably Mme Greffulhe) because 'it was in the very
style that the Princesse de Cadignan in Balzac wore when she saw
d'Arthez for the first time'.[1] Here is not only another declaration

---

[1] The same observation is made by M. de Charlus, who shares Montesquiou's
passion for Balzac, on Albertine's grey dress at La Raspelière; but the Narrator,
far from criticising the Baron's remark, silently rebukes Brichot for not appreci-
ating its interest (II, 1054-5).

of independence, another master left behind, but a first step, to be linked with the Saint-Simon parody of the following year, in the transformation of Montesquiou into the comic creation of Charlus.

Proust concludes by explaining that the revelation of Ruskin, through which 'the universe suddenly regained an infinite value in my eyes', is now a thing of the past; he can recall his passion for Ruskin only 'with the memory of facts which tells us "This is what you were," without allowing us to become it again, and assures us of the mere existence of a lost paradise instead of restoring it to us in recollection'. These words, and the whole marvellous passage in which they are embedded, mark a crucial step forward. Proust has now stated the difference between conscious and unconscious memory, and the supreme importance, though he still sees no way of attaining it, of the latter. By explaining the concept of 'idolatry' he has not only freed himself from Ruskin, and from a fault of which he was himself guilty throughout *Jean Santeuil*; he has discovered, though he is not yet aware of it, the theme of his future novel. 'Idolatry', and the casting aside of idolatry which is the only way to salvation, is the very subject of *A la Recherche du Temps Perdu*. The Narrator's vain pursuit of Names of Places and Names of People, of friendship, even of love, is idolatry, a worship of the ephemeral instead of the eternal. Idolatry is Time Lost; the truth behind the locked door of the image is Time Regained; and the key to the door is unconscious memory. *Jean Santeuil* and Ruskin were indispensable blind alleys, explored and left behind; and the way to *A la Recherche*, though long, was now becoming clear.

Copies of *La Bible d'Amiens* were sent to the whole circle of his friends and acquaintances, both sacred and profane, at one extremity to the Abbés Vignot and Hébert, at the other to Mlle de Mornand. Louisa's copy contained a startling inscription which shows, whatever may already have been the freedom of speech customary in their group, that her relations with Proust were taking a new turn. Mornand, he explains, is certainly *not* the present participle of *morner*, 'for this archaic verb had a meaning which I don't exactly remember, except that it was excessively improper.[1] And heaven knows how proper you are! Alas, for those who have had no success

---

[1] The meaning of *morner* (to blunt the point of a lance), if improper at all, is only Freudianly so.

with you—which includes everyone in the world—other women
cease to be attractive. Whence this couplet:

> *He who Louisa cannot win*
> *No refuge has but Onan's sin.'*

In April Mlle de Mornand took steps to save him from this sin.
She gave him two ravishingly pretty photographs of herself, one
signed 'your friend for always', and the other: 'the original, who is
very fond of her little Marcel', and invited him to collect them one
Sunday evening. Louisa was in bed, reading; her white arm, as she
turned the pages, rose like the stem of a lily from the sleeve of her
nightdress; and over her the blue and white canopy of her fourposter
spread like a summer sky striped with cirrus-clouds. As he lay beside
her Proust saw through the open door the crimson wallpaper of the
drawing-room, which seemed, when he looked up again, to turn the
azure bed-curtains green; and when he left, as he pointed out,
Sunday evening had already become Monday morning. Even without the lines which in the published text have been significantly
replaced by rows of dots, the final quatrains of the verses he sent her
in memory of the occasion leave little to the imagination:

> *'Her Sèvres Cupids nothing miss:*
> *Delicious and surprised they view*
> *Two mouths united in a kiss,*
> *Two hearts that are no longer two.*
>
> *The bed is blue, the salon red,*
> *But the azure jewel-case encloses,*
> *While nothing moves, and nought is said,*
> *A pearl whose hue is like a rose's.'*

The message on the photograph, he predicted, 'would have the
power to fix my wandering heart'. But it is unlikely that Mlle de
Mornand had ever heard from other friends in similar circumstances
the image with which he summed up his gratitude. 'I feel, meanwhile,' he said, 'happier than a child that has just been given its first
doll.'

For some time their relationship continued on its new footing.
'Ours was an *amitié amoureuse*,' Mlle de Mornand recalled more than
twenty years later, 'in which there was no element of a banal flirtation
nor of an exclusive liaison, but on Proust's side a strong passion

tinged with affection and desire, and on mine an attachment that was more than comradeship and really touched my heart.' For a year and a half Mlle Nordlinger was not the only girl visitor at 45 Rue de Courcelles. Usually in obedience to a letter or telephone-call, but sometimes inviting herself, Mlle de Mornand came 'so often and so charitably', as he reminded her that July, 'to roast in the suffocating heat of the dining-room, and to bring her ailing little Marcel the consolation of her affectionate smile'. Mme Proust was accustomed to retiring particularly early on the evenings of Louisa's visits, in order to leave the young couple undisturbed; and Marcel went into his mother's room to kiss her goodnight, or listened at her door ostensibly to find whether she was resting comfortably, but no doubt also to make sure that the coast was clear.

His carnal relationship with Louisa was unlikely to last for very long; and its close may be situated towards the July of 1904 when her more serious association with Albufera was in danger, and Proust out of disinterested friendship to them both was doing his best to preserve it. Later allusions in his letters, however, suggest that a limited dalliance continued: in September 1904, for example ('I'm dying to kiss you on both cheeks, and even on the nape of your lovely neck if you'll let me—I'll explain when I see you which part of you I wrote first and then crossed out') or in January 1905, when he makes a daring anatomical pun on the word 'button'. For the suspension of her regular visits which followed the death of his mother in September 1905 there are natural reasons, such as his need for solitude in his grief, his six weeks of confinement in a nursing-home, and Louisa's break with Albufera in the spring of 1906. It is significant, nevertheless, that this intimacy exactly covered the period of his life alone with his widowed mother, except for the first few months, when Mlle Nordlinger filled more platonically the same function. As in other actions of his life Proust was at once proving his mother's love by submitting it to a severe test, and punishing her, with more than a hint of sadism, for a feared or fancied refusal of love. He was arranging for other women, almost before her eyes, to bring him the goodnight kiss she had denied at Auteuil.

In her *amitié amoureuse* with Marcel Mlle de Mornand did not altogether depart from her position as the future original of Rachel-when-from-the-Lord. Proust thought of Louisa when he showed the Narrator astonished by not finding intense pleasure in dining and walking alone with Rachel, or by her seeming 'a mere dust-cloud of

flesh and dress-material', although she had driven Saint-Loup mad
with love.[1] But Mlle de Mornand also has a place among the originals
of Albertine, notably the Albertine who visited the Narrator and
surrendered to his embraces on the foggy evening when he was in
love with Mme de Stermaria; and this is only two pages after a
mention of Rachel's plot to rouse Saint-Loup's jealousy by accusing
the Narrator of 'making furtive attempts to have relations with her
during his absence'.[2] Albertine seems on this occasion to bring the
sea and sunlight of Balbec with her; and Mlle de Mornand was to be
associated a few years later with Trouville and Cabourg, the originals
of Balbec. Proust's silent, immobile love-making with Louisa recalls
the Narrator's with the sleeping Albertine in *La Prisonnière*. '*Louisa
reads herself to sleep*', he had written in his gallant verses on that
night in April,

> '*Lying on her side in bed,*
> *And eyes on book she cannot keep,*
> *But nods and droops her drowsy head*',

and it was in this apparently somnolent state that she had allowed
him to make love to her.

Meanwhile the visits of Mlle Nordlinger continued. Their work
on the proofs of *La Bible d'Amiens* was confined to December 1903
and the second week of February 1904. Early in January they had
already begun the translation of *Sesame and Lilies* for which Proust
signed a contract with the *Mercure de France* in December 1902.[3]
They worked as collaborators. Mlle Nordlinger was to have her
name with Proust's on the title-page and to share the proceeds,
not only from the *Mercure de France* but also from the prior publication of '*Trésors des Rois*' in *Arts de la Vie*, which was arranged with
Gabriel Mourey in May 1904. Proust had translated the beginning
and end of '*Trésors des Rois*' in six exercise-books, leaving blank
or underlining for her advice the phrases he was not sure of understanding. He completed the beginning in January, and had entirely

---

[1] III, 166, 175.

[2] II, 348.

[3] At first they intended to translate both the first two sections, '*Of Kings'
Treasuries*' and '*Of Queens' Gardens*'. By May 1904, however, they had decided
that the former would suffice, and it was not until February 1905 that Proust
again resolved to add the latter. There was never any question of adding the
third and last section, '*The Mystery of Life*'.

recast it by 7 February; while the end, although he immediately lost the three exercise-books containing it, was finished later in the same month. Mlle Nordlinger's share was the middle, finished late in April and 'turned upside-down', 'with affectionate respect', because he felt her French was too anglicised, by Proust in May. At the end of May he found his lost exercise-books and proceeded to a final revision of the whole, which was no doubt completed in June.

In April Mlle Nordlinger sent the most important of her symbolic gifts, a packet of the Japanese pellets of coloured pith which open, when dropped in a tumbler of water, into exquisite and jewel-like flowers. Proust was then suffering from asthma, and this 'fluviatile and inoffensive spring, these miraculous and hidden flowers' touched him profoundly, amid the desolation of the season he dared not see, with a memory of seasons buried in his childhood. 'Thanks to you,' he wrote, 'my dark electric room has had its Far-Eastern spring'; and he used the Japanese flowers, in the last paragraph of the opening chapter of *Swann*, as a simile for the revelation of unconscious memory, which draws 'all the flowers of Swann's garden, the water-lilies of the Vivonne, the good people of the village and their houses, the church and all Combray and the country round it from my cup of lime tea'.[1]

On 16 April, at the age of eighty, died Comte Thierry de Montes-quiou, Count Robert's father and vice-president of the Jockey Club, whom Proust had seen in the street, 'in the days when I was able to go out for walks', and regarded ever after with awe. Like Dr Proust, the fierce old gentleman had viewed a son's eccentricities with mingled contempt, bewilderment and pride: "I didn't do it on purpose," he had sardonically excused himself, when Count Robert reproached him with having 'made me what I am'. He had more than a vestige of his son's wit. "Thank God, they were very light ladies," he said, when run over by two cocottes in a pony-carriage. At the news of his father's operation for stone the year before Count Robert had very decently cancelled a fête in his garden at Neuilly and hurried to his bedside. "I'm sorry to have thrown this stone into your garden," said Count Thierry; whereas Uncle Wladimir de Montesquiou, apprehensively eyeing the very stone in question in its preserving-bottle, remarked simply: "I say, I shall have to be more careful about my health."

[1] I, 47-8.

Ever since her refusal to sympathise in his quarrel with her brother
Constantin, Proust had been 'exceedingly but very respectfully
annoyed' with Mme de Noailles. On 11 June, however, he received
her second novel, *Le Visage émerveillé*, and finished it at the moment
before dawn when, looking from his window, he saw a sky still so
dimly grey that he could not tell whether the growing light would
show it as blue or overcast. His anger vanished in a paroxysm of
flattery, which may be defended not so much by his knowledge that
for Mme de Noailles, as for Montesquiou, only the topmost pitch of
adulation would suffice, as by the fact that her novel had given him a
further insight into his own. Through the trellis of her metaphors he
glimpsed the landscape, vague and distant, but already bathed in a
radiance of joy and familiarity, of *A la Recherche*.

The theme of her novel—it was about a nun falling in love—was
no more likely to please him than it gratified her aunt Comtesse Odon
de Montesquiou, who exclaimed indignantly: "Why, it's a book
against convents!" From the beginning, indeed, her family had
shown themselves far from delighted at having a celebrated poetess
in their bosom. "So you've written some poetry, countess," the old
Marquis de Montsaulnin had remarked, "have you ever thought of
making a little volume, just to give to a few of your friends?" But
when *Le Cœur Innombrable* appeared her mother-in-law the Duchesse
de Noailles burst into tears and sobbed: "Now people will think *I*
wrote all that filth!" "She starts quoting Plutarch the moment she
comes into the room," complained another relative, "and I can't
allow that sort of thing in my house"—an accusation also made by
Mme de Gallardon against the Duchesse de Guermantes.[1] Proust
cannot have enjoyed the 'daring' theme of Mme de Noailles's novel:
he thoroughly approved of the nunneries he had visited at Beaune
and in the Netherlands, as manifestations of the aesthetic side of the
Church. The cause of 'the ecstasy with which,' he told her, 'every
step I have taken in this supernatural landscape has filled me' was her
unprecedented attempt to create a whole novel with the fervour and
imagery of poetry, to reveal a timeless beauty beneath the momentary surface of the phenomenal world. 'You remove from all things
the veil of grey mist which is nothing but the emanation of our own

---

[1] II, 447. Mme de Gallardon, an ignorant Courvoisier, says 'Aristotle', by
mistake for 'Aristophanes'. Mme de Noailles, a Roumanian princess, is 'the
young princess from the East' who marries a cousin of Saint-Loup and writes
poetry 'as beautiful as Victor Hugo's or Alfred de Vigny's' (II, 107).

mediocrity, and uncover an unknown universe, whose existence we had guessed in our hours of divination, where everything is truth and beauty,' he wrote in words which resemble the Narrator's after the final revelation in *Le Temps Retrouvé*. The phrases he quotes ('on the violet velvet petals [of pansies] is a yellow stain, sleek, alive and glossy, as if a wren's egg had fallen there and broken'—'the light, delicate, green spring-time' and so on) have little intrinsic merit; but he has picked out his own Proustian use of the 'three adjectives'. When he compared her organic unity of colour to a 'spring morning seen from a dining-room with tinted windows and a half-lowered blind, where the garden breezes enter the parlour whose walls are coated with whitewash and sunlight', the discovery of his own method in Mme de Noailles had penetrated to the depths where Aunt Amiot's house at Illiers survived in Time Lost.

The Paris season was over, but the weekly dinners in the country given by Guiche's father Duc Agénor de Gramont were just beginning. His first wife, Princesse Isabelle de Beauvau-Craon, had died bearing his daughter Élisabeth (now Marquise de Clermont-Tonnerre) in 1875; but three years later the impecunious Duc Agénor married Marguerite de Rothschild, the mother of Guiche, and with her untold wealth built the enormous château of Vallières at Mortefontaine. From the three-sided entrance hall the happy visitor could see, far over the trees of the forest of Ermenonville, the spire of Senlis, and to either side the islanded lakes on whose banks Rousseau had wandered. It was the polite thing to say: "You'd think we were in Scotland, yet it's only twenty miles from Paris!" Proust travelled by taxi; and alighting on the hot summer evening of 14 July, wearing top-hat, white tie and tails, he was horrified to find the other guests leaving in tweeds for a pike-fishing expedition on the lake. Guiche had neglected to warn him of the rural protocol of Vallière: diners were expected to arrive in country clothes, with a suitcase containing a mere dinner-jacket. Utterly downcast he advanced to enter his name in the visitors' book, and was encouraged to find that several old acquaintances had just signed in—Comtesse Rosa de FitzJames, the Aimery de La Rochefoucaulds, and the Comte de Cholet, his superior officer at Orleans fifteen years before, who had pretended like Saint-Loup to ignore his salute in the street, but had otherwise been a valued ally. As he hesitated Duc Agénor, recognising one of his son's intellectual friends, remarked with a grin in the words of the Duc de Guermantes on a similar occasion[1]: "Just your name will be sufficient, Monsieur Proust—no need to write a great thought." His evening was ruined, and the sight of thirty fellow-guests at dinner in 'smokings' could hardly add to his despair.

For a few weeks Proust and his friends had been united almost as in bygone years. The Bibesco brothers were still in London at the Roumanian Legation, but Fénelon was back on leave from St Petersburg, and Guiche or Albufera called every day. On the eve of Fénelon's departure Mme Proust allowed Marcel to entertain the group at home, not to dinner, for that would have been a breach of her mourning, but to supper; and soon after the disaster of Vallière there was a dinner with Guiche and the dramatist Tristan Bernard in the Bois de Boulogne. But Proust felt an atmosphere of eternal farewells, for Guiche and Albufera were engaged to be married in the autumn. Guiche's fiancée was none other than Mme Greffulhe's daughter Élaine, and Albufera's—for like Saint-Loup he was to marry a half-Jewish heiress—was Anna, daughter of Prince Victor d'Essling and his wife Paule, born a Furtado-Heine, at whose house in the Rue Jean-Goujon poor Charles Haas had been a constant visitor. "Nothing will be changed, Marcel," protested Albu; but Proust replied: "On the contrary, nothing will ever be the same again." The marriages of Gabriel de La Rochefoucauld and Loche Radziwill were to follow next year. It is a period in Proust's life which is represented in *A la Recherche* by the rumours of impending marriage, not only of Saint-Loup but of the Prince de Foix and his companions, in *Le Côté de Guermantes*.

Albufera might excusably have been on the watch for an opportunity to break with Louisa; but he was more in love than ever, and determined that with her, too, there should be 'nothing changed' by his marriage. Mlle de Mornand was now on holiday at Vichy, whence she allowed disquieting rumours to reach Albu. He called three times on Proust in the week of Vallières to ask his help and advice; and

---

[1] II, 549. The Duc de Gramont supplied one or two other hints for the Duc de Guermantes. Montesquiou remembered him as a fellow-schoolboy 'with blue eyes and golden, silky hair', in the 1860s at the Jesuit college at Vaugirard; and Basin de Guermantes was just such a boy when at school with his brother Charlus (II, 718; III, 716, 721). The Duc de Guermantes's icy reception of the Bavarian composer M. d'Herweck at the Princesse de Guermantes's soirée (II, 683) was no doubt suggested by Duc Agénor's greeting of the great d'Annunzio a few years later, when he extended two cold fingers of a limp hand and pronounced the words: "Good morning, Monsieur."

Proust duly sent three letters and a telegram to the recalcitrant Louisa. Before she left Paris, he reproached her, she had 'amused herself with anchoring Albu in his mistaken ideas'; and he reminded her how, even as early as the April of 1903, she and Albu had quarrelled in his presence at the Théâtre des Mathurins. Here is the original of the quarrels between Saint-Loup and Rachel in the restaurant and at the theatre (where, like Louisa at the Mathurins, she has only a 'walking-on' part), on the day of Mme de Villeparisis's matinée.

When on 17 July Proust dined with Mme de Noailles he thought again of *Le Visage émerveillé*, but this time with a different aspect in the foreground. In *La Nouvelle Espérance*, her last year's novel, the lover of the heroine Sabine had asked: "What do you need to be happy?"; and Sabine had replied: "Your love, and the possibility of being loved by everyone else." It is not a modest wish, and its granting was disastrous. Mme de Noailles was to pursue, like Proust himself, the changing star of love, ever burning her angelic wings; but unlike Proust, she could never learn wisdom from suffering, for she could never reach the hidden depths beneath her vanity. Except for the saving graces of her ardent love of life, her passionate spontaneity, though these only added to the tragedy of her destiny, she would never be much more, as a poet or person, than a female counterpart of Montesquiou. Her new novel, Proust knew, was a *roman à clef*: the nunnery was a convent school at Évian, its chapel was that of her mother-in-law's château at Champlâtreux ('you ought to have a special edition for railway bookstalls,' he told her, 'labelled Champlâtreux, five minutes' stop'); the enamoured Sister Catherine was Mme de Noailles herself, and the abbess who persuades her to give up her lover was the literary hostess, Mme de Noailles's great friend, Mme Bulteau. But Mme de Noailles did not give up her own lover, who was none other than Maurice Barrès.

Nothing could have been more unexpected than this illicit union between the Dreyfusard poetess and the greatest of Dreyfus's enemies. At the time of Rennes in 1899 Barrès had noted with amusement in his diary the rebuke of Comtesse Jean de Montebello to Mme de Noailles and her sister Hélène propagandising in her salon: "Call yourself French! Why, you're a couple of street-urchins from Byzantium!" Onlookers at their first meeting in the spring of 1903 noted that each of these brilliant people was dazzled by the other: 'they fell madly in friendship at first sight,' said Jacques Émile Blanche. Their marriage-partners acquiesced: Mme Barrès was deemed to have taken immensely to Mme de Noailles, and Comte Mathieu was supposed to delight in the company of Barrès. Only the Tharaud brothers, Barrès's secretaries, felt a jealous dislike for Mme de Noailles, which they prudently concealed until after the death of the parties concerned. 'Her body was too long for her legs,' they wrote, 'so that when she stood up she seemed much shorter than when she was sitting down; it was veiled in soft, bright fabrics, so that one was puzzled to know what happened between her tiny feet and her little white neck. . . . When she talked one felt battered by a hail of diamonds; she was an astonishing musical-box which was automatically set in motion the moment there were two or three people to listen.' But the time when Barrès would confess to them: "If only she'd keep quiet I might be able to listen to her!" had not yet come.

Proust had first met Barrès in the summer of 1892, when the tides of Boulangism and Panama were beginning to ebb. Barrès was then a thin, sallow-faced, still-young man of thirty, the nationalist member of the Chamber of Deputies for Nancy, and already a famous writer, commonly known as Prince of the Young. It was in this last capacity that he asked his electoral agent, Léon Yeatman's uncle, to arrange for him to meet some promising young writers; and the guests that evening were accordingly chosen from the group of *Le Banquet*, including Proust, Robert Dreyfus and Gregh. Their reactions to their prince were varied. Gregh, whom Barrès obligingly sent home in his own carriage, was amused and touched (for it was generally felt that Barrès had betrayed literature for politics) to find an open volume of Sainte-Beuve's poems in the side-pocket. Robert Dreyfus wrote for the July *Banquet* a laudatory article on Barrès as a sceptic, in which he attacked the mysticism of Proust's master Paul Desjardins. Proust rebuked him sharply: 'don't you see that Desjardins's faith is a shining light of reason compared with Barrès's scepticism?' As we have seen, the chapter of *Jean Santeuil* which described the first impact on his pupils of M. Beulier (modelled on Proust's revered Darlu) was intended as a counterblast to the opening scene of Barrès's *Les Déracinés*. Proust's uneasy dual attitude to Barrès corresponded to a fundamental division in Barrès himself, between the lyrical individualist and the power-seeking authoritarian. Proust admired the music of Barrès's prose and shared many of his beliefs—his love of France, his support of the persecuted Church as part of the greatness of France, his call to discipline and tradition. Yet by his determination, heroic as it was, to put his doctrines into practice by political action, Barrès was false to his own cause. His art became propaganda, his political faith—horrified as he would have been by the consequences he did not live to see— paved the way for fascism. His unshakeable belief in the guilt of Dreyfus was a symptom that he had come to prefer political expediency to truth and justice.

The rift between Barrès and Proust was not to be bridged by the dinner of 17 July. Proust took the opportunity to clear himself with regard to an anti-Semitic article in *La Libre Parole* during the Affair, in which his name was maliciously included in 'a list of young Jews who abominate Barrès'. "As I couldn't contradict it publicly without saying I wasn't a Jew, which although true would have upset my mother, I thought it useless to say anything," he explained; but it was clear from the expression on Barrès's face that he felt it would have been far from useless. The indomitable young man went on to rebuke the great novelist for a critical reference to Mme de Noailles's Dreyfusism in his glowing review of *Le Visage émerveillé* in *Le Figaro* for 9 July. "You wrote: 'her mistaken belief has been, to use La Fontaine's famous line on the condemnation of Fouquet, that *misfortune is a kind of innocence*'. But what she really meant was not that misfortune makes a man innocent, but that it's a double misfortune if he's found guilty when he's really innocent!" But Barrès merely gave his abrupt, sardonic laugh, and enquired: "What is the meaning of this sudden explosion of Dreyfusism?" Proust retired in disorder to the fireplace where, beneath a row of Mme de Noailles's favourite Tanagra figurines, he tried to retrieve the evening by a free consultation about his asthma with the young Roumanian doctor Nicolas Vaschide. Vaschide, he decided, was charming, although his medical theories were quite absurd (he took a lady clairvoyant round the hospitals with him to help in his diagnoses), and he was incapable of pronouncing his r's. Proust confided that he had recently visited Dr Merklen, who asserted that his asthma was only a nervous habit, and recommended a stay in Dr Dubois's sanatorium for nervous diseases at Berne: "he'll make you give up the asthma habit, just as they make people give up the morphine habit". Suddenly a crash was heard: Proust had inadvertently toppled over the very best of his hostess's Tanagras. "It's *nelvous*," observed the well-meaning but unhelpful Dr Vaschide. Overwhelmed by the disgrace of his accident Proust avoided Mme de Noailles for over a year; yet she came to treasure the broken figurine even more than its undamaged sisters, and in the exhibition of her relics at the Bibliothèque Nationale in 1953 it appeared as: 'No. 84. Tanagra broken by Marcel Proust.'

On Tuesday, 9 August, when Mme Proust was at Etretat with Robert Proust and her daughter-in-law Marthe, Proust took the train to Le Havre for a cruise on the steam-yacht *Hélène*, owned by Robert de Billy's wife's father, Paul Mirabaud. Proust made himself thoroughly but eccentrically at home in his solitary cabin: he asked for the porthole to be opened, ignited his anti-asthma powders, decided not to undress in the cold sea air, took an ineffective dose of trional, lay sleepless and fully clothed in his bunk till dawn, and finally emerged on the bridge to make the acquaintance of the crew and watch preparations for departure. They steamed along the Normandy coast over a calm, sunlit sea to Ouistreham, where Mme de Billy joined them, pink and charming, in a rowing-boat, and arrived that evening at Cherbourg, 'while a light breeze turned the sapphires of the sea to emeralds and set them in silver'. All day Proust had watched the moving panorama of the seaside resorts of his youth, the Trouville of Marie Finaly, the cliffs of Houlgate, the dunes and Grand Hôtel of Cabourg, from one of those butterfly-white yachts which he had seen and envied many years ago from the shore. The delightful voyage continued; he postponed again and again his secret intention of returning to Paris after the first two days. They lingered on Thursday at Cherbourg, and on Friday sailed by way of Guernsey to Saint-Malo. Three photographs show Proust sitting with Robert and the ladies, beneath a huge awning on the bridge, in the act of talking and gesticulating: he wears a black velvet jacket, a broadbrimmed felt hat, and a gloomy, drooping moustache. M. Mirabaud, 'an enormous Saxon god with blue eyes and flaxen hair', was a martyr to a weak heart, and a patient, like Proust, of Dr Merklen—"he's given me a new lease of life," the old man boasted. They compared notes on one another's ailments, and Proust impressed Billy by giving expert advice; but his keenest conversational pleasure was with the sailors, whom he cross-examined on their mysterious way of life and who, as Billy remembered, 'regretted his sudden departure as much as any of us'. For Proust decided on Saturday to leave next evening. He slept all day on Sunday, took the night train to Paris, and there slept again till Monday evening. The vicious circle of his upside-down life had begun again.

On 16 August, the day after his return, his article '*La Mort des*

Cathédrales' appeared in *Le Figaro*. The Combist movement for the separation of Church and State was now in full career, and the anticlerical Aristide Briand had proposed that, after the withdrawal of state subsidies from the Church, any cathedrals which proved uneconomic to maintain should be secularised and used as museums. Proust pointed out that the cathedrals, 'probably the noblest but indisputably the most original expression of the genius of France', owed their life to the continuance in them of divine worship. To withdraw this would be to kill them, to leave France 'a dry beach strewn with giant chiselled sea-shells, empty of the life which once inhabited them'. 'A performance of Wagner at Bayreuth,' he wrote, 'is a trivial thing compared with the celebration of high mass in Chartres Cathedral.' A Catholic admirer of Proust might regret that he supported the Church for its aesthetic and moral beauty, and wish him more than an *anima naturaliter Christiana*. On the other hand, if Proust had been a full believer he could never have written *A la Recherche*, which is an attempt to find salvation unaided, without the ready-made consolations of religion. But it would be erroneous to explain the limited nature of his Catholic sympathies by his half-Jewish birth: indeed, Proust was in the curious position of defending the Church against his anticlerical Aryan friends. '*La Mort des Cathédrales*' was a sequel to his heated discussion with Lauris and Fénelon in July 1903, and employed the same arguments, often the same words. As then, a memory of Illiers came to the surface: this time it was the way to Méréglise, 'between sainfoin fields and apple orchards, where at almost every step you see a spire soaring on the clear or stormy horizon, transfixing on days of rain and shine a rainbow which, like a mystic aureole reflected from the interior of the church, juxtaposes its rich, distinct, stained-glass colours on the neighbouring sky'.

Towards the middle of September it was agreed that Mme Proust should go on holiday to Trouville, Dieppe or Évian, and be joined later by Marcel. Rarely had his nervous inability to choose been so tormenting; each place had unique advantages—Dieppe would be convenient for Rouen Cathedral, Mme Straus and Charles Ephrussi would provide company at Trouville, at Évian he would feel most at home—and prohibitive disadvantages. He looked further, to Basle, Quimper, Caen, Chamonix (which Albu said was dry, while Billy maintained it was damp), even to Biskra in Algeria. On the 20th Mme Proust cut this Gordian knot by going alone to Dieppe, where

she battled for the last time with seaside wind and cold, still thinking
of her dead mother's delight in bad weather, and waited in vain for
Marcel. He had resolved to stay at home for a final effort to change
his hours by the only possible method: to stay awake for twenty-four
hours, and then go to bed half a day late. By a superhuman effort he
succeeded in rising at 9 a.m.; but the following night he could not
sleep for worrying about Dr Dubois and his sanatorium, the next
day he got up at 4 p.m., the next at 7 p.m. He had by now acquired a
dread, which would be lifelong, of seeing the light of day in times of
illness and unhappiness: 'If I'm to stay indoors and be ill, it's all one
to me at night, because I'm used to it, but in broad daylight, all alone,
and seeing the sunshine outside, it would be too nostalgic.' To avoid
the accusing eye of the sun he continued to rise at sunset. His letters
to his mother on his health had never been so anguished and interminable; but the good lady's replies were as sensible and reassuring
as ever. Her only note of alarm was when, at a moment of 'inexpres-
sible indisposition, despair, inability to move, incredible pulse', he
refused to see his barber, François Maigre (who, like Swann's,[1] was
accustomed to call at the house): 'no more of this looking like a
Frankish king,' she wrote almost sharply, "your hair gets in my eyes
when I think of you!'

Mlle Nordlinger had now almost completed a bronze portrait-
plaque of Dr Proust for his grave at Père Lachaise, which Proust
had persuaded his mother to commission in May, partly in the hope
of persuading his friend and helper to remain in Paris. She had called
with the first model on 8 August, when Proust had been confined to
bed by fever: 'I'll get up for five minutes to shake hands with you,'
he promised, 'and Mother will see you back to Auteuil.' On the
22nd, rather self-consciously, he had visited her for the second
view, without chaperone, in her summer home at Auteuil, 'where
the wasp wanders from rose to rose, drunk with its own mad flight,'
he wrote, confusing his hymenoptera. Then, soon after his mother's
departure for Dieppe, Proust invited Marie to call for a third discussion of the plaque. 'Your idea that your visit would be "improper"
in Mother's absence is perfectly enchanting, and made me laugh a
good deal,' he wrote on 24 September; 'if you were the young man
and I the girl there might be some sense in it—but even so, I managed
to see you alone at Auteuil!' In this situation is visible, as if at a
great distance, the absence of the Narrator's mother at Combray, and

[1] I, 380-1.

the arrival in his home of Albertine. But the year of 'visits from Albertine' was in its decline. On 24 October Mlle Nordlinger left for the United States to organise exhibitions of Japanese prints for her employer Siegfried Bing. Strangely enough, neither Mme Proust nor Marcel were satisfied with the portrait-plaque, though they duly installed it on 25 November, the day before the anniversary of Dr Proust's death, and even the artist herself shared their displeasure. In counterpoint to Lecomte du Nouy, who had painted the Doctor in 1882 as a keen-eyed, affable Holbein, she made him a Pisanello medallion in bronze. To the modern visitor on that utmost height of Père Lachaise, where the four Prousts, mother, father and sons, await the last regaining of Time, she seems to have caught, as successfully as her predecessor, the noble, energetic, Renaissance aspect of Adrien Proust; the handsome, unaged Doctor gazes for ever over the Biblical city of Paris, meditating simultaneously, as in life, on measures for halting a plague and on the portents of tomorrow's weather.

During that autumn Proust conducted a mild flirtation with *Le Figaro's* rival *Gil Blas*, the new daily newspaper owned by Paul Ollendorff, who two years before had failed to publish *La Bible d'Amiens*. On 9 September he tried to persuade Antoine Bibesco to write a publicity-notice in *Gil Blas* for Louisa de Mornand, who began a season at the Vaudeville on 16 September. 'What's needed is something utterly stupid, like "remember this name, it's ripe for stardom", or "the girl's mad about acting, she gives it all she's got" —I think you'd do it marvellously!' But Antoine failed to be moved by this testimonial, and Proust was forced to write the notice himself, and another early in December. He also contributed to the *Gil Blas* of 14 December a review of Fernand Gregh's *Études sur Victor Hugo* over the pseudonym 'Marc Antoine'. His most important contribution to *Gil Blas*, however, was rejected. This was a dialogue, entitled '*Vacances*' and dedicated to Robert de Flers, between a young man representing Proust himself and the ever-recurring Françoise—not the Narrator's servant, but the heroine who had already appeared in *Les Plaisirs et les Jours*, in *Jean Santeuil*, and in the imaginary letters which he had written with Flers for *La Presse* in the autumn of 1899,[1] and who was to become both Swann's Odette

---

[1] These letters, of which the first and third were written by Proust in the character of Bernard d'Algouvres, a society-man, and the second by Flers as his mistress Françoise de Breyves (already the heroine of '*Mélancolique villégiature*

and the Narrator's Albertine in *A la Recherche*. The young man is recovering from an unhappy love-affair, and debates with Françoise, on a September evening during a dinner on the island in the Bois de Boulogne, the possibility of consoling himself in her arms. '*Vacances*', in fact, is a primitive draft of the episode in which the Narrator, on a windy day in the same month of September, visits the island in the Bois, on which he hopes to dine to-morrow with Mme de Stermaria, with Albertine, then a poor second-best.[1]

The first night of Antoine Bibesco's *Le Jaloux* at the Théâtre Marigny[2] on 8 October clashed with the signing of Albufera's marriage-contract, which took place at the mansion of the bride's aunt's husband, Prince Joachim Murat, in the Rue de Monceau opposite Mme Lemaire's. This was the customary occasion for viewing the wedding-presents, prominent among which was Proust's own gift, a column discovered by Mme Proust at Bourcelet's antique-shop and converted into a lampstand. "Although the Murats' is the most magnificent private house in Paris, people will mistake our present for part of the furniture," declared her admiring son. The wedding was celebrated on the 11th; Albu and his bride left for the Bay of Naples; and poor Louisa, enjoying her first real success in Henri Bataille's *Maman Colibri* at the Vaudeville, wrote: 'my head is hard at work, but my heart is suffering.'

The noble fellowship of Proust's friends was dispersing. On 14

---

[1] II, 386-94.
[2] For two parodies of *Le Figaro's* dramatic criticism written by Proust on this occasion see *Lettres à Bibesco*, pp. 160-6.

---

de Madame de Breyves' in *Les Plaisirs et les Jours*), appeared on 19, 20 September and 12 October 1899 in the newspaper *La Presse*, of which their friend Léon Bailby was the editor. Proust introduced themes repeated from *Jean Santeuil* and reappearing in *A la Recherche*, such as the buzzing of flies suggesting a summer day, the colouring of cream cheese with strawberries, seagulls, jealousy, etc. The idea was a resurrection of a letter-novel planned in 1893 by Fernand Gregh, Daniel Halévy, Louis de La Salle and Proust, in which Gregh played the poet, Halévy the Abbé, La Salle the lover, and Proust himself the lady. No sinister interpretation need be given to any of these minor pieces, for the letter-novel written in collaboration is a recognised form in French literature, and someone, after all, has to write in the character of the heroine. If Flers had anything incriminating on his conscience, he would hardly have collaborated in the *La Presse* letters or accepted the dedication of '*Vacances*'. Nevertheless, in these two last pieces there may well be some connection with Proust's platonic friendship with Flers in 1893, however innocent.

November Guiche married Comtesse Greffulhe's twenty-two-year-old daughter Élaine at the Church of the Madeleine. Her mother was still in the full glory of her beauty; and as the bridal procession descended the steps Élisabeth de Clermont-Tonnerre heard a woman of the people say: "Lord strike me, you'd never believe she was the mother!" Guiche, wrote a reporter, was 'pale, with a gentle smile'—"it's the first time I've known you either pale or gentle," commented Proust, who made his way through the mob of guests to Mme Greffulhe and remarked: "it's my candid opinion that Guiche married your daughter (among other reasons, I quite admit) in the hope of getting your photograph!" The delighted comtesse gave her famous silvery laugh, 'so prettily that I felt tempted to say it ten times over,' and proudly repeated her daughter's latest verses in praise of her beauty. Élaine Greffulhe was a poet, and at the age of five and a half had published remarkable prose-lyrics for which her uncle Montesquiou had written a preface. When Proust asked Guiche what he would like for a wedding-present he jestingly replied: "I think I have everything, except a revolver." Proust took him at his word and gave him the grisly weapon, bought from the best gunsmith in Paris, Gastinne-Renette. It nestled, like a steel jewel, in a leather case painted in gouache by Coco de Madrazo with scenes and words from the bride's childhood poems, with seagulls (*'No more we'll drink the water of the sea, Because our tears have fallen in its waves'*), white ships and mountain-tops (*'The mountains seem like flowers to the ships, The peaks mistake the ships for fountains'*), and a flaming tiger (*' "Why don't people like you any more?" "Because I always eat them at the end of my stories." "Then don't tell me any stories." '*) Proust envied the happiness of the lovers, on honeymoon in the Forest of Fontainebleau at one of the bride's father's châteaux, all the more because the weather had turned bitterly cold. 'Cold weather is the most poignant of all backgrounds for happiness,' he wrote to Guiche, thinking perhaps of Marie de Benardaky and the snow in the Champs-Élysées; 'happiness that's numbed with cold, hunching its shoulders, shrinking back into its core, is for me the intensest of all.'

For Proust there was only the pilgrimage to Père Lachaise on the eve of the year's end of his father's death; and when, on the 28th, the anniversary of his funeral, he asked Mlle de Mornand to visit him 'at a quarter past midnight—I shan't tell Mother I've asked you, so that she'll think you've called on the spur of the moment', it was at her own urgent request, no doubt to talk about Albufera. He was tempted to spend Christmas Eve with the Greghs; but the fog was too thick, and he stayed at home imagining 'the lights of your house through the mist, like a crêche in the darkness'. He had the momentary presence of Fénelon, again on leave, to console him. Next Christmas Day, still more alone, he would be in a nursing-home weeping for his mother's death.

Chapter 2

DEATH OF A MOTHER
(*January – December 1905*)

IT was 1905, and Proust had entered unawares on the last year of
Time Lost. His friends were dispersed by marriage or the diplomatic service, and even Marie Nordlinger was three thousand miles
away in Detroit. He took refuge in work and illness. In principle
he had now accepted the unanimous advice of his doctors ('every
time I visit one the effort costs me several weeks in bed'), that only
a prolonged stay in a sanatorium would enable him to live a normal
life again; but he postponed the evil day, first until April, when his
hay fever would be due, then until autumn, when it would have
departed. All through January he kept to his bed, enjoying the first
fifteen volumes of the Library Edition of Ruskin, a New Year's gift
from Mme Proust; and early in February he began to translate '*Of
Queens' Gardens*', the second part of *Sesame and Lilies*, which a
year before he had decided to omit. Mlle Nordlinger was 'intensely
happy', he was wryly gratified to learn, and had made friends with
the railway-waggon millionaire Charles L. Freer, whose Whistler
collection was the finest in the world.[1] Proust had now banished
from his bedroom the aesthetic souvenirs of beauty of which Ruskin
would have approved, including even his photograph of the Gilded
Virgin of Amiens: 'tell your friend,' he wrote, 'that my room contains
in its intentional nudity only a single reproduction of a work of art—
Whistler's *Carlyle*, whose cloak is as serpentine in its folds as the
gown of Whistler's *Mother*.' He meditated on Ruskin's great
antagonist, of whom he had heard so much from Montesquiou and
Lucien Daudet, but whom he had met only once, on that evening at
Mme Laurent's 'when I made him say a few nice things about Ruskin, and appropriated his elegant grey gloves, which I've lost since'.
Was the opposition between Whistler and Ruskin, Elstir and Bergotte, quite irreconcilable? 'Whistler is right', he concluded, 'when

---

[1] Mlle Nordlinger had first met Freer in Paris a year before, when he visited
her employer Siegfried Bing.

he says in *Ten O'clock* that Art is distinct from morality; and yet
Ruskin, too, utters a truth, though on a different level, when he says
that all great art is a form of morality.'

On 9 February 1905 Gabriel de La Rochefoucauld married Odile
de Richelieu, an heiress of half-noble, half-Jewish birth.[1] Comte
Gabriel was no exception to the curious trick of destiny which made
so many of Proust's aristocratic friends foreshadow Saint-Loup's
unhappy love-affair, sojourn in the East, and semi-Jewish marriage.
During the year before Gabriel had been in love with a married
woman, and when in August to cure the pangs of jealousy he abandoned her for a trip to Constantinople with the novelist Loti, the
unfortunate lady committed suicide. 'Here is a secret that no one in
the world must know,' Proust wrote on 21 September 1904 to his
mother at Dieppe, 'it was for Gabriel de La Rochefoucauld that
Mme X killed herself.' Much to the indignation of both Proust and
Gabriel it was rumoured that Proust had helped him in his novel
about this tragic affair, *L'Amant et le Médecin*, which appeared in
1905 and scandalised the whole Faubourg Saint-Germain.[2]

In mid-February Proust refused an invitation from the Marquise
de Ludre, explaining that he was about to leave for Dr Dubois's
sanatorium at Berne. Instead, as a farewell to society, but also, he
confessed, by way of displaying his sanity to people who might
otherwise hint that he was being put away in a lunatic asylum, he
decided to give one last party. The 'grand dinners' of the past were
still forbidden in their house of mourning, but Mme Proust reluctantly consented to an afternoon-tea, which she did not honour with
her own presence, at 4 p.m. on 6 March. It was the last and not the
least brilliant of all such gatherings at 45 Rue de Courcelles. 'There
will be extremely few people,' he had reassured Mme Straus; but
these 'extremely few' included the Chevignés, the Ludres, Mme
Lemaire, Mme 'Cloton' Legrand (original of Mme de Villeparisis's

[1] Her mother was Alice Heine (1858-1925), who after the death of her husband Duc Armand de Richelieu (1847-80) married Prince Albert of Monaco in
1889, separated from him in 1902, and become one of the originals of the Princesse de Luxembourg in *A la Recherche*.

[2] There is no trace in this facile but workmanlike novel of Proust's influence
as a writer, still less of his actual hand. Proust himself, however, is introduced
rather unfavourably as one of the minor characters, the imaginary invalid Larti,
who has no use for women, quotes Schopenhauer, is about to visit Holland
with his great friend Hermois, and says: "It's no use hoping to get happiness
from love !"

enemy Mme Leroi), Guiche, Albufera and Gabriel de La Rochefoucauld with their mothers and young wives, Proust's adored
Princesse Hélène de Chimay, the Comtesses de Briey and d'Haussonville, and a dozen more. Reynaldo and the Comtesse de Guerne[1]
sang duets, and Proust took the opportunity to cross-examine Loche
Radziwill concerning a press-notice on Louisa de Mornand in the
Écho de Paris which Loche had promised to arrange. But when the
guests were gone and the candles out, while Proust wrote the report
of his party for next day's *Figaro*, choking in a fit of asthma, he
thought with remorse of the dreadful brawl among the servants
which the preparations for his party had caused the day before:
Lucien Henraux had intervened to save the life of Proust's 'faithful
Marie', their cook, who had left on the spot.[2] Worse followed, for
Montesquiou, like the wicked fairy Carabosse, unexpectedly had
wind of the party just in time to learn that he had not been invited.
Proust returned from the *Figaro* office after midnight to find a
scathing letter from Artagnan at his bedside. It was as if he welcomed
the campaign of nagging and reprisal which was to last all that
summer: Marcel mingled unpardonable impertinences with his
apologies, referring to 'that young and charming Clermont-
Tonnerre couple, who couldn't come', and to Montesquiou himself
as 'a fat, pink turbot, whom I might have served up to my guests,
but now can only watch receding behind the glass of the aquarium of
"Too Late"'. 'Your epithets are ill-chosen,' retorted the injured
Count, 'and serve only to dishonour those you purport to praise;
moreover, you seem unaware that the persons to whom you allude
as a "young couple" have children who will shortly be of an age to
partake of Holy Communion.'

Poor Mme Straus had been unable to come to the tea-party.
During the last year or two she had lapsed into a state of vague
neurasthenia from which she was never quite to emerge, and the once
beautiful lady who had so loved society, talk and bright lights was
now condemned intermittently to solitude, silence and darkened
rooms. In April she left for Territet, near Montreux, and was
attended by Dr Widmer, in whose nearby sanatorium called
Valmont Proust had now, for the moment, decided to take his rest-
cure in the autumn. Proust wrote frequently to cheer her with news

---

[1] Proust thanked her with an eulogistic article on her singing, '*La Comtesse
de Guerne*', signed 'Echo', in *Le Figaro* for 7 May 1905.

[2] For a similar catastrophe among the servants of Mme Cottard, cf. I, 597.

and mildly indelicate gossip ('it's not very proper, but then, we're both invalids'). As the guests streamed out from a concert on 27 April he had listened appreciatively to the loud voice of Mme de X (possibly Comtesse Diane de Saint-Paul?), 'who can't open her mouth without saying something unintentionally obscene'. "I don't think any of these pieces quite came off," she bellowed, "so I'm getting Plançon to do it for me—that'll be a real ecstasy! Next Thursday at ten, then—lovers of the noble art who may wish to be present, please note." An eddy of the crowd carried him out of earshot, and when he fought his way back he heard: "say what you like, my dear, Madeleine pays her cook two thousand, but I'd much rather spend it on my tenor. She likes it in her mouth, but I prefer it in my ear. Each to her taste, dear, this is a free country, ain't it?"

He made several half-hearted attempts to see Louisa de Mornand. On 9 March he had not dared, fearing she might be angry at the delay of her press-notice, to take her to a supper-party given by Reynaldo with the music-hall singer Fragson at the Café de l'Univers. Fragson, 'who is charming when you see him at close quarters', sang 'at the top of his voice till half-past three in the morning, when I left with a terrible attack of asthma, after swallowing all the dust and smoke in, so to speak, the Universe!'[1] If, as is possible, Proust and Louisa succeeded in meeting some time in May, this was the final occasion on which their tender relations can have been resumed; but Proust's last allusion to these as a pleasure of the recent past had been on New Year's Day, when Louisa sent him a gold bedside watch with a peacock-blue dial and the motto 'May I only number happy hours'. 'As I contemplated the case, never thinking that such a pretty thing could conceal something prettier still,' he wrote roguishly, 'a certain secret button (no improper suggestion intended!) seemed to invite a gentle pressure; and certainly there never was a button that kept more perfectly its promise of admission to paradise.'

Towards the end of April the second round in Montesquiou's campaign of nagging began. The Count commanded Proust's presence at his lecture 'On Fragments of Hugo's Fin de Satan' at the Théâtre Bour on 21 April, sent Yturri to wake him in the small hours of the afternoon, and wrote an angry letter when, in spite of all his

---

[1] Caricatures in comic papers of the period portray both Fragson and his rival Mayol, whose singing Proust was to admire a few years later, as homosexuals.

menaces, Proust failed to attend: 'your ill health doesn't prevent you from gracing the La Rochefoucauld orangeade,' he complained.[1] Count Robert made fun of Marcel's illegible handwriting, comparing it to the endless cavalcade of insects in the fable of Solomon's interview with Takia, Queen of the Ants, when she paraded her subjects before him. 'After seventy livelong days she announced: "that is all of this species, but there are sixty-nine others to come," whereupon Solomon declared the session closed.' Proust was not amused to find himself playing a mere ant to Montesquiou's Solomon. In return he compared the Count to Jupiter towering over a group of tiny mortals in Gustave Moreau's painting[2]; 'you always take the leading role for yourself,' he grumbled; to which Montesquiou airily riposted: 'I don't need to *take* the leading role, I already have it!' Early in May, with diabolical generosity, he intimated that since Proust was always too ill to come to his lectures, he would give one in Proust's own home, and allow him a month to round up the guests. After a week of insomnia and much wriggling Proust surrendered, and even showed some enthusiasm for the enormous labours of organising his punishment. The proposed lecture turned into a reading of '*The Handbell*', a savage essay on poor Mme Aubernon from Montesquiou's forthcoming *Professionelles Beautés*, and took place on 2 June in the presence of chosen friends and victims of the deceased lady, including Dr and Mme Pozzi, Mmes Lemaire and Laure Baignères, Albert Flament and Charles Ephrussi. After the function was over Proust stood with Yturri by the street-door bidding goodbye to his guests, while Montesquiou lingered above, still holding forth to those who had not succeeded in escaping. The ailing secretary went upstairs to beg his master to leave, in vain; and when he returned his face was so haggard that Proust could not resist tactlessly exclaiming: "How furious you look!" "No, I'm not furious," Yturri protested with a gentle smile, "I'm only tired." Proust was not to see him again in the land of the living. When even the Count had departed Proust hurried to the offices of *Le Gaulois* and the Paris edition of the *New York Herald* with his account of the evening for next morning's papers, which mendaciously began: 'A few select guests were given the surprise of hearing . . .', and the next two days were spent in a violent fit of asthma.

[1] Hence the ritual orangeade of the Guermantes (II, 31, 513; III, 868).

[2] The Narrator uses the same image of his own father as seen by Mme de Villeparisis (I, 701).

While the genuineness of Proust's ill-health in the first half of 1905 need not be doubted, it is certain that he used it, as so often before and after, for a pretext to ward off the visits of time-wasters like Montesquiou, to excuse his temporary neglect of others of whom he was fond, such as Mme Straus or Louisa, and to free himself for work and solitude. All through his life a period of protracted illness (though it might be as real as it was loudly proclaimed) was generally also a period of absorption in writing. Occasional allusions at this time in letters to less exacting correspondents give a very different picture from the incessant bouts of asthma which kept Count Robert from his door. 'I am leading a blissful life of rest, reading, and studious intimacy with mother,' he told Robert Dreyfus in May. In March, April and May the translation of '*Kings' Treasuries*', which he had written from January to June 1904 in collaboration with Marie Nordlinger, appeared in *Arts de la Vie*. 'I mean this translation to be as faithful as love and pity,' he told the editor Gabriel Mourey. During February and March he translated '*Of Queens' Gardens*', with help from Mme Proust, Robert d'Humières, and Ruskin's friend Charles Newton Scott—'the charming old English scholar whom I use as a Mary,' he wrote to the absent Marie Nordlinger. In April, with a renewed burst of energy, he wrote his most important work to date, the prefatory essay to *Sésame et les Lys* entitled '*Sur la Lecture*'.[1]

'My only purpose in this preface', Proust explains, 'is to meditate on the very subject discussed by Ruskin in '*Of Kings' Treasuries*', the utility of reading. Hence these pages in which Ruskin is scarcely mentioned constitute, nevertheless, a kind of indirect criticism of his doctrine.' The structure in space and time of the opening pages closely resembles the *Combray* chapter of *Swann*. He traverses long-lost Illiers, a boy of twelve again, in the places and hours of a single day's reading, from morning to bedtime, through all the rooms of Aunt Amiot's house to the pond-side and hornbeam spinney of the Pré Catelan. The value of reading in childhood, he suggests, lies not in the book itself (which was only Gautier's *Le Capitaine Fracasse*) but in the memories unconsciously preserved in it, which are 'so much more precious to our present judgment that, if we happen to turn the same pages today, it is only because they are the sole

---

[1] It was only in *Pastiches et Mélanges* (1919) that Proust decided, rather confusingly, to call this essay by the title of his later article in *Le Figaro* of 20 March 1907, '*Journées de Lecture*'.

surviving calendars of vanished days, and in the hope of seeing reflected in them the houses and pools that no longer exist.'[1] Ruskin's doctrine, that reading is valuable because it is 'a conversation with men far wiser and more interesting than those we have the opportunity to meet in everyday life', is in Proust's opinion unsatisfactory, because the difference between a book and a friend is not that the one is wiser than the other, but that in reading we retain the mental power which is peculiar to solitude and is dissipated by conversation. Even so, a book can never tell us what we wish to know, but only rouse in us the desire for knowledge; for 'we cannot receive truth from anyone, but must create it for ourselves', and 'reading is on the threshold of spiritual life: it can lead us in, but does not constitute that life in itself'. In special cases, Proust admits, reading still has its uses. It serves a mind paralysed by idleness or frivolous pleasures as a stimulus to enable it 'to descend spontaneously into its own depths, where the life of the spirit begins'. Another amenity of reading is that one may be encouraged, like Sainte-Beuve pursuing his researches on Port-Royal as far as Utrecht, to travel in quest of a rare book—and here Proust interpolates a magical impression of his own two visits to Holland; and finally, a book may be of value because, like the twin columns in the Piazzetta at Venice, it involuntarily preserves in the present a living fragment of a historic past.

Can this be all that Proust has to say in praise of reading? The beauty and brilliance of his essay have generally distracted attention from its curious bias. Ruskin had written *Sesame and Lilies* as an eulogy of reading: Proust's intention is to warn against its dangers, and '*Sur la Lecture*' is in fact an essay *against* reading. Supposing he had read at Illiers, instead of *Le Capitaine Fracasse*, a masterpiece of a great writer, would his response still have been adequate if he had valued the book only for its power to secrete an unconscious memory of the rooms and gardens in which he read it? A great book is an ocean, but Proust is determined to prove that it is only a diving-board. He does not hint at the true essence of reading, which is surely identical with the purpose of the writer: the communication of the state of vision in which the book was written, so that the writer's revelation becomes the reader's. Such was Proust's own aim in writing *A la Recherche*; and he did not intend his great novel merely to enable his readers to store up unconscious memories of the places

---

[1] The house is Louis Weil's at Auteuil, demolished in the late 1890s and the pool is that of the Pré Catelan at Illiers, already silted and dry.

in which they read it, nor even to goad idle minds into rejecting the book and thinking for themselves.

'*Sur la Lecture*' is far from representing Proust's normal opinion of the nature of reading: his earlier and later critical essays show that he was supremely able to hold his own vision of truth in abeyance in order to share a great writer's total experience. His preface offers, in fact, neither a general theory of reading nor the record of a permanent personal attitude. Instead, it marks a temporary but deeply motivated revulsion from the act of which it ironically pretends to be a panegyric; and its real meaning only emerges when it is seen as the private and cryptic expression of Proust's approach to literature at one particular period—the spring of 1905—and at no other.

For five and a half years, ever since he abandoned *Jean Santeuil* in the autumn of 1899, Proust had surrendered himself to the most arduous and self-abnegatory of all forms of reading: the translation and interpretation of an admired author. His faithful service to Ruskin was undertaken partly in order to enable him to write a better novel, partly as a punishment for having written a bad one; but now his penance was over, and it was time, he tried to believe, for his reward. Reading was no longer a moral duty, nor a spiritual pleasure, but a snare. 'It becomes dangerous', he warned, 'when we tend to make it a substitute for, rather than an incitement to the personal life of our mind, when truth no longer seems an ideal to be attained only by the inner progress of our thought and the effort of our heart, but a material object deposited between the leaves of books, like honey readymade by others.' The 'personal life of his mind', which he had relinquished but never forgotten during his years of bondage to Ruskin, lay in the writing of the ideal novel of which *Jean Santeuil* had been only the shadow on the walls of the Platonic cave. The secret meaning of '*Sur la Lecture*' is that Proust declares his emancipation not only from Ruskin but from all other authors, and resolves once more to write his novel.

'*Sur la Lecture*' is not only a record of the mental processes by which Proust liberated himself from Ruskin and prepared to resume his novel. It is also, in the narrative digression with which it opens, a preliminary trial for the subject, method and style of the novel itself. Proust had not yet formulated his theory of Time Regained in its mature and final form; yet, by a significant accident, he now found himself for the first time resurrecting Illiers, by means of the unconscious memories latent in *Le Capitaine Fracasse*, from the remote and buried past which he would afterwards call *le Temps Perdu*. Étreuilles in *Jean Santeuil* was Illiers seen directly, still clearly visible and available in the recent past; but in '*Sur la Lecture*' the village lost and found is already recognisable as Combray. Moreover, Proust's style has achieved a fundamental advance. The note of *A la Recherche* had already been audible in the Rheims, Amiens and Venice episodes of the *Bible d'Amiens* preface, or indeed, more distantly and by rare snatches, in almost everything he had ever written, from *Jean Santeuil* back to his seventeen-year-old essay in the *Revue Lilas* at Condorcet; but in '*Sur la Lecture*' the full orchestra of his mature prose is used and sustained. The authority and power of the final revelation were still to come; but there is a foretaste of these in his sense that he is at last saying something of supreme importance, that he is at last on the verge of his inheritance. His feeling of imminent victory was premature, but none the less prophetic.

'*Sur la Lecture*' appeared, as Proust had arranged with Constantin de Brancovan in mid-April, in the *Renaissance Latine* of 15 June. By a fortunate chance Mme de Noailles's third and last novel, *La Domination*, was published on the 9th; and Proust had time to send three letters of frenzied eulogy which on this occasion at least had an ulterior motive. Sure enough, the poetess returned the compliment with high praise of '*Sur la Lecture*'; and better still, on 19 June in *Le Figaro* came a favourable review by the influential critic André Beaunier, a friend of the Brancovan group, which, Proust told Mme de Noailles, 'I feel positive you must have dictated.' This indeed was almost the case, for Mme de Noailles had informed him: 'we read your essay with Beaunier yesterday evening', and he recognised in Beaunier's review the very phrases of his benefactress's letter. Proust himself wrote modestly to her of '*Sur la Lecture*': 'it's a kind of indigestible nougat, which has a bit of everything and sticks in your teeth'; and to Mme Straus, just back from Switzerland, 'don't read it, it has sentences a mile long which Dr Widmer would particularly forbid you'. But to trusted comrades he allowed something of his justified satisfaction to appear: 'if you didn't know I'd written it, I believe you'd think it quite original and well thought-out', he told Lauris, who had helped him with friendly advice during the process of composition.

Meanwhile, in the first week of June, Marie Nordlinger arrived from the United States on a flying visit to Paris. Her post at the Art

Nouveau workshops no longer existed: the establishment had closed during her absence, and her employer Siegfried Bing, once the friend of Goncourt and Whistler, was a dying man. When she called at 45 Rue de Courcelles for a last consultation on *Sésame et les Lys* she found Proust in bed, with his pallid face and burning eyes framed in a formidable black beard. 'His smile had gone, but I heard it still in his voice,' she recalled forty years after. "Give me a kiss, Marie," he murmured, "I've thought of you very often. Tell me all that's happened—did you see any beautiful things in America?" But there was time for nothing but Ruskin, and they worked on the manuscript until dawn. Marie Nordlinger was to see her friend only once more, in 1908, an occasion of which we have no record. 'You arrived in Paris like a Messiah, and left like a demon,' he wrote reproachfully.

On 15 June he visited the Whistler exhibition at the École des Beaux-Arts, and was impressed to find that so many of the finest paintings were the property of Mlle Nordlinger's millionaire friend Charles L. Freer. The experience had another personal aspect: there were landscapes of 'Venice in turquoise, Holland in topaz, Brittany in opal'[1]; and it was as if he saw paintings by Elstir of the places he would never see again. He packed his mother off to see the exhibition with a long list of everything she must not miss seeing, and subsided for three days into 'a terrible and indescribable state' of agitation and asthma. Another lost friend, whom Proust was only seldom to see again, was in Paris at the same time as Mlle Nordlinger; but to Bertrand de Fénelon Proust sent merely an icy 'kind regards' (*amitiés*) through Georges de Lauris.

Louisa de Mornand, still unhappy and ill from her year's parting with Albufera, had finished a season in Marcel Prévost's *Les Demi-Vierges* at the Vaudeville on 13 June. Her decision to spend the summer recess with her mother and sister at the Villa Saint-Jean near Trouville revived old memories in Proust. He wrote Louisa a series of letters recommending the places she must visit; and this evocation of the seacliffs of his youth and the summer of Marie Finaly encouraged the train of thought which led two years later to his decision to revisit Cabourg, and in this summer of 1905 to his first abortive work on a novel which introduced those same scenes. The places he described to Louisa were those of his wagonette-drives in 1892 with Mme Finaly and her family, from Les Frémonts over the high ground

[1] This last picture, Whistler's *La Plage d'Opale*, is recalled in *Du Côté de chez Swann* when Legrandin says that the Opal Bay is near Balbec (I, 138).

between Trouville and Honfleur, which became in *A l'Ombre* the Narrator's excursions in Mme de Villeparisis's carriage. 'If you visit the humble little church of Cricquebœuf, smothered in its ivy,' he told Louisa, 'give it an affectionate message from me; and say the same to a certain old peartree, broken-backed but untiring, like an aged servant, which holds up with all the strength of its gnarled but still green branches a tiny cottage, in whose only window smile the pretty faces of a group of girls; although,' he added ruefully, 'perhaps they are no longer pretty nor even girls, for all this was a long time ago.' Similarly, on the day of the trip to the ivy-covered church of Carqueville, just before the vision of the three trees near Hudimesnil, the Narrator is attracted by the village girls on the bridge.[1] The valley 'changed by moonlight into an opalescent lake', which he believes Louisa can see from her villa, is one of the 'three views' of Les Frémonts and of La Raspelière[2]; and Proust now recalled the night when he had walked back from Honfleur with Marie Finaly, with her arm round his neck to shield him with her cloak: 'at every step we stumbled into a pool of moonlight,' he told Louisa, without revealing that his companion had been a girl, 'and the valley seemed an endless lake'. Les Creuniers, where Louisa must not fail to walk, because 'all one's sorrows from there seem as small as the absurdly tiny people one sees far below on the sands', is the cliff of the same name near Balbec, which in Elstir's painting resembles a pink cathedral, and to which Andrée takes the Narrator on the day of the game of ferret.[3] As he wrote he saw Marie Finaly's green eyes again, and quoted to Louisa the poem of Baudelaire which he had sung that summer thirteen years ago: '*J'aime de vos longs yeux la lumière verdâtre*'.

On 24 June Proust entertained a party of friends in his bedroom, a rare event since his father's death and his long farewell to friendship. Albufera, Lauris and Robert de Billy were there, but Fénelon, though still on leave, was significantly absent, as was another member of their group. This was the day of Loche Radziwill's marriage-contract. Whatever his inward feelings, Proust had made a creditable display of goodwill in giving his blessing to the marriages of Albu-

[1] I, 715-17.
[2] The Narrator notices it during Cottard's game of écarté with Morel: 'it was almost too dark to see the sea through the windows on the right; but those to the left showed the valley, on which the moonlight had cast a fall of snow' (II, 974).
[3] I, 901, 921-5.

fera, Guiche and Gabriel de La Rochefoucauld; and when, a few weeks before, Loche Radziwill had announced his intention of marrying Guiche's nineteen-year-old cousin Claude de Gramont, he had shown no less altruism in his disapproval. Loche was not in love, and had no intention of giving up previous entanglements. "I'm doing it to please my mother," he explained. "You couldn't do anything more certain to hurt her, sooner or later," Proust retorted, "and I'm sure your mother is fond enough of you to put her pleasure in your happiness, and not in your leading a life of self-sacrifice." For a wedding present he gave Loche a twelfth-century alabaster figure of Christ, with an appropriate quotation from Ruskin engraved on the pedestal: 'You will be happy, but on one condition.' He sensed some irony in Loche's gift of a tie-pin in the shape of the Radziwill crest, a hunting-horn: Loche knew perfectly well that tie-pins were supposed to bring bad luck. "Vigny says that the sound of the horn is sad in the depths of the wood," Proust remarked, "but in the depths of my sickbed it sounds sadder still!" His premonition was soon fulfilled: only a week after his wedding on 27 June Loche left his wife, and their divorce, pronounced on 17 May 1906, was perhaps the speediest in the annals of the *Almanach de Gotha*.

The third round of Count Robert's punitive campaign was now being fought. Twice before, in 1893 and 1899, Proust had both promised and written an article on his exacting patron, but despite all his efforts had failed to find a willing editor.[1] On 4 June, as part of his thanks for the Count's reading from *Professionelles Beautés* on the 2nd, he had offered to write an essay on the book; and on the 25th he proposed 'for want of a more conspicuous theatre', to place it in *Arts de la Vie*. But the news which at any other time would have intensely gratified Count Robert came too late; for the first and last time in his life he was past caring for the strange discrepancy between his genius as a poet and its neglect by the critics.

It had generally been assumed that Gabriel d'Yturri, who had now been Montesquiou's secretary for twenty years, would live to serve his master for ever. For the past two years, however, his health had caused some disquiet. "Take care, Yturri," a doctor friend had warned him, "you have a dreadful smell of rotten apples." But the

---

[1] A short review of Montesquiou's *Le Pays des aromates* in the *Chronique des Arts* of 5 January 1901 did not count, as this minor piece (a preface to the catalogue of an exhibition of perfume-bottles) gave no opportunity for a general appraisal of Montesquiou's work.

doctor it was who died: "and now he's *feeding* apple-trees," the volatile Yturri would boast, "and I'm still here!"[1] Yturri's smell of apples, which was due to acetone in the breath, is one of the classic symptoms of diabetes, then an obscure and incurable disease; but at first no one was particularly alarmed.

> *'My Yturri, my Gabriel*
> *Often falls ill, always falls well'*,

wrote Montesquiou teasingly, and then (for meanness was not among his vices) sent him to spend the winter of 1904-5 in Algeria and Italy. In April Yturri was at Dr Noorden's sanatorium in Frankfort; but hearing of the Count's Good Friday lecture he insisted on returning—'Writing impossible, cured by enthusiasm', he tele-graphed—and begged his master not to meet him at the station because, he confessed pathetically, 'I'm ashamed of my ravaged face.' In mid-June, when the icy spring of 1905 changed to a heat-wave, poor Yturri began to stifle with the air-hunger which in diabetes marks the beginning of the end. Montesquiou surrendered to him the airiest room in the Pavillon des Muses; and here, on the big rotonda away from the Boulevard Maillot, Yturri received his last visitors, huddled in a silk dressing-gown, wafting the sultry air into his exhausted lungs with a fan, and complaining unjustly to all comers: "Mossou le Connte is leaving me to die like a dog!" Outside Montesquiou would explain to the departing enquirer: "I put my white tie and tails on, and pretend to go out, so that he won't think he's going to die; but he's annoyed if I go out, and still more annoyed if I stay in." On the afternoon of 5 July Yturri uttered his last words to his master. "Thank you for teaching me to understand all these beautiful things," he murmured, gazing at the bric-a-brac around him; then he sank into the final coma and died, watched over by the sleepless Count, at four in the following morning. It was a moment of truth for Montesquiou; for a while his vanity was pierced, and he felt real grief. Élisabeth de Clermont-Tonnerre found him in tears: "whenever I come home I see his little empty cycling-cap, his little empty cap," he sobbed, wringing his hands over his head.

---

[1] This doctor who died was perhaps Proust's own father. Paul Morand reports Proust as telling him in 1917 that Yturri had consulted Dr Proust, who informed Montesquiou: "He's a doomed man, but don't tell him so." "I shall have to tell him," replied the insolent Count, "because I have several messages for him to deliver in the next world."

He visited Yturri's crypt in the Cimetière des Gonards at Versailles daily, seeking comfort in the cool air and scented flowers of the tomb in which one day he would rejoin his friend; until about 10 August he accepted an invitation from the Duchesse de Rohan to recuperate among the pine-trees of her Domaine des Fées, near Bordeaux.

Proust followed the course of Yturri's illness with dismay, and twice sent his mother, willing but sorely distressed by the heat, to the Pavillon des Muses to enquire. He had always liked, as everyone did, the good-hearted, loyal and amusing Yturri; and now it seemed that something of his own life, as well as so much of the Count's, had vanished with him for ever. 'Those simple, every-day gestures of admiration on his part, of trust on yours,' he wrote to Montesquiou, 'are becoming for me, in the far-away, Giottoesque, golden glow in which they lie, almost sacred memories.' 'I know better than anyone else in the world what he means to you,' he wrote again, significantly. Nine years later Proust himself would be overwhelmed by a similar disaster. Meanwhile he rallied to the Count with letters of consolation, to which Montesquiou replied with poignant, unwonted simplicity; and he set to work in the second week of July on his essay for *Arts de la Vie*, which he called (in allusion to its subject, *Professionnelles Beautés*) '*A Professor of Beauty*'.

On 25 July came another death, that of the dear, kind Duchesse de Gramont, *née* Marguerite de Rothschild, Guiche's mother, who in 1893 with her sister Berthe, Princesse de Wagram, had been one of Proust's first hostesses in the Faubourg Saint-Germain.[1] He rose from his sickbed on the 28th to attend her funeral at Saint-Pierre-de-Chaillot, and there met Mme de Noailles, whom he had not seen since Guiche's wedding. She was present as a member of the family,[2] and with her was her mother, the excitable Princesse Rachel de Brancovan, who shocked him by beginning an acrimonious theological argument at the very foot of the altar. The Duchesse de Gramont was a converted Jewess and therefore, declared Princesse Rachel, was by no means certain of going to heaven. Proust went on to visit Dr Brissaud, 'our dear *Médecin malgré lui*', who insisted, like

---

[1] It was from one of her guests, Comte Léon de Tinseau, 'a sham literary man who was a perfect oaf,' that Proust borrowed the monocle of General de Froberville at Mme de Saint-Euverte's soirée.

[2] Her husband's brother Hélie de Noailles was married to the Duchesse's daughter Corisande.

Professor E, who was modelled on him, on talking literature, but at last deigned to recommend the sanatorium of Dr Sollier; and then he returned to bed with agonised thoughts of the poor Duchesse de Gramont. She shared the doubts of Princesse Rachel, and had died in the conviction that she would not be allowed to meet her beloved daughter Corisande in the next world. This was all too nearly the position between Proust himself, a baptised Catholic, and his mother, still Jewish; and it only made matters worse that neither he nor she believed in a life after death.

It was probably at this time that he held two conversations with Mme Proust which the Narrator has with his grandmother.[1] In the first she asked what he would do if she 'went away for a long time—perhaps for ever?', and he replied, hiding his emotion: "You know what a creature of habit I am. When I'm separated from people I love, I'm unhappy for the first few days—then I grow used to it, I organise my life differently, and I could bear it for months, years, for always." For they had no need, as he remarked in *Contre Sainte-Beuve*, to prove that each loved the other more than anything else in the world: on the contrary, they needed to pretend they were less fond of one another than appearances might suggest, and that whichever might survive the other would be able to go on living. A little later he remarked casually that the latest discoveries of science seemed to proclaim 'the bankruptcy of materialism', and to show that souls were immortal after all, and would be reunited after death. The fact remained, however, that she had asked his permission to die, and he, perforce, had given it.

In Proust's letters of late July and early August 1905 he mentions several times that he is 'working'; and then, for four weeks, there is one of the total gaps in his correspondence which tend to occur when he is absorbed in writing.[2] Veiled hints in his letters suggest that this mysterious new work was nothing less than a first version of the new novel, for which his six years of voluntary exile in the

---

[1] I, 727-8; in *Contre Sainte-Beuve*, 299-300, he has the same conversation with his mother.

[2] *Sésame et les Lys* was finished and delivered to the *Mercure de France* at the end of June; and when in July, after the arrival of the Library Edition of *Sésame* and of Marie Nordlinger's answers to his questions, he asked for the return of his manuscript, the insertion of a few corrections and additional footnotes can have taken little time. '*Un Professeur de Beauté*' was begun in mid-July, and must have been completed before the end of the month in time for its publication on 15 August.

world of Ruskin had been a preparation. In September 1904 he had informed Mlle Nordlinger of his refusal to translate Ruskin's *Saint Mark's Rest* for a Venetian publisher to whom Barrès had recommended him, 'because otherwise I shall die without ever having written anything by Myself'. In July 1905 he wrote to Antoine Bibesco: 'now that, for the first time after this long lethargy, I have turned my eyes inward towards my own thoughts, I feel how empty my life has been, and see hundreds of characters for a novel, a thousand ideas begging me to give them bodies, like the ghosts in the Odyssey that ask Ulysses for a drink of blood to bring them to life'.

Sufficient evidence exists for a conjectural reconstruction of at least some elements of this unknown novel. The essay '*Sur la Lecture*' may represent a draft for the opening scenes in the village of the Narrator's childhood, since it contains material which had already been used in *Jean Santeuil* and would reappear in *Du Côté de chez Swann*. Proust's letters to Louisa on the Trouville coast would serve as suggestions for episodes at the seaside, at some primitive form of Balbec; and the medical world, absent from *Jean Santeuil* but so prominent in *A la Recherche*, would make a substantial appearance, for he told Mme de Noailles after his visit to Dr Brissaud on 28 July: 'I'm going to write a book about doctors.' A fragment has been published in which the story of Jean and Françoise in *Jean Santeuil*, which became the love of Swann and Odette in *A la Recherche*, is already being told of a hero named Swann and a woman named Carmen. More surprisingly, another fragment shows Swann himself at 'Querqueville' on the seacoast of Normandy for two successive summers, in love like the Narrator with each member of a 'little band' in turn. Anna and Septimie, whom Swann jealously suspects of a Lesbian relationship, are equivalents of Albertine and Andrée, and the other girls, whose names are Maria, Célia and Arabelle, correspond to Gisèle and Rosemonde. Clearly Proust had transferred to Swann, who appears in the third person, a much larger proportion of the material of his own life later shared between Swann and the Narrator in *A la Recherche*; and the section on Swann and Odette in *Du Côté de chez Swann*, in which part of the same story is still told of Swann in the third person, is a surviving relic of the form taken by this intermediate version of his novel. The unexpectedly large part played by Swann suggests that the novel begun in 1905 looked not only forward to *A la Recherche* but backward to

Jean Santeuil. In *Jean Santeuil* the tale is told by and about the novelist C, and the narrator ostensibly closest to Proust himself is only the person who says 'I' in the introduction, who meets C in Brittany and is entrusted with the story of his life, but never appears again. In the 1905 novel Proust may have divided the material of his own life more equally between these two narrators: the novelist C became Swann, and his young friend was recognisable, for the first time, as the Narrator of *A la Recherche*. On this hypothesis the Narrator would begin with his village childhood and continue with his own love in the Champs-Élysées for Gilberte, who in this version may already have been Swann's daughter. He would hear from Swann and retell in the third person the story of Swann's loves not only for Carmen-Odette, but also for the little band; and this story within a story would have the function, as in *A la Recherche*, of foreshadowing the Narrator's own experience of the laws of love and jealousy. The novel would presumably have culminated in a final love-affair of the Narrator; though it is impossible to guess with whom, since the girl who was Charlotte in *Jean Santeuil* and became Albertine in *A la Recherche* was here loved by Swann.

Perhaps Proust himself regarded his 1905 novel only as an experiment, to be abandoned and rewritten as soon as he should find himself at last on the right track. He was writing with the old, ill-advised method of *Jean Santeuil*, in isolated fragments; and even the fragments read like mere notes, rather than considered workings-out of the episodes to which they relate. There is, surprisingly, no discernible advance in aesthetic merit upon *Jean Santeuil*. The Cities of the Plain are apparently still a subsidiary, not, as later, an essential theme. It is unlikely that the Two Ways, or Time Lost and Regained, or unconscious memory were, if they appeared at all, fundamental in the symbolism and structure of the novel; for when they appear three years later in *Contre Sainte-Beuve* it is still only in a tentative and rudimentary form. Indeed, a passage in one of his August letters to Louisa de Mornand at Trouville suggests that he was still using only voluntary and conscious memory as his technique for recovering lost time. Louisa, too, has been recalling the past, 'looking,' he writes, 'into the depths of your heart now calm and clear again, and there discerning ancient images'; and among these is Proust himself —'who means nothing to you, except as one involved in sweet and painful moments of your life . . . like the man who held the horse or stood by the carriage-door in some great historic event'. But, he adds, still apparently thinking only of conscious memory, 'our memory often presents us with "views" of the historic events of our own lives, which are not always easy to see clearly, like the views we strain our eyes to make out through the peep-hole in a pencase encrusted with shells, a souvenir of the seaside'.[1]

Early in September Proust's brief work on his novel was interrupted; it was time for the late summer holiday with his mother, which last year owing to his indecision had never taken place. During the year and nine months since his father's death their strange, half-loving, half-hostile relationship had become both closer and more equable. There is no sign of the serious quarrels of the past; Proust stayed more than ever before at home, and visits to friends, dinners at Larue's and evenings in high society were unprecedentedly rare. But his dream of union with his mother, now that his father was for ever out of the way, had failed to come true; it was as though neither of them quite wished it. Mme Proust transferred only a little of her wifely devotion to her son, but kept most of it for her cult of her dead husband. She never abandoned for Marcel's sake her weekly and monthly observance of the days of Dr Proust's stroke, death and funeral, or her insistence that there should be no more grand dinners, and little entertainment of guests, particularly on those fatal days. Marcel, on his side, did not succeed in his resolution to see more of his mother. On the contrary, he allowed his hours to become more unearthly than ever before, until in the spring and summer of 1905 he rose, if at all, at eight or nine in the evening, and Mme Proust was forced to dine at eleven p.m. if she wished to share his daily meal. She showed distress in the heatwave that killed poor Yturri; but otherwise her health had seemed good since a painful attack of nephritis in the winter of 1903-4, which she concealed from Marcel until it was over. When he had mentioned his anxiety to his brother Robert, Mme Proust was annoyed; henceforth he refrained from meddling, and left her health in Robert's hands. Proust has been accused of embittering his mother's life with his meticulous and harrowing letters about his health, and of shortening it by the daily errands which, especially in her last year, she ran for him all over Paris; but both charges are unjust. His complaining letters, whatever gloomy pleasure he may have taken in them, were written to her strict order, and if he neglected them he was sharply rebuked.

[1] Proust used this image of the view in the pencase for the Narrator's boyhood visions of Balbec (I, 389).

Similarly, when Mme Proust delivered a *Bible d'Amiens* in person to the astonished Léon Daudet, or saw Marie Nordlinger back to Auteuil, or journeyed twice in the heat-wave to Neuilly to enquire after Yturri, it was at her own request, not only to satisfy her need to serve, but as an excuse for exercise to reduce her corpulence, and an act of obedience to her dead mother's principles of hygiene. It was in the nature of this proud and formidable lady to rule by self-sacrifice; and when two human creatures live in so complete a state of symbiosis as Proust and his mother, neither can be held responsible, though each is partly the cause, for the actions of the other.

When, about 7 September, they left together for Évian, it was for Marcel's health rather than his mother's. It was agreed that at the end of their holiday she should see him safely installed for his rest-cure; for from Évian both Dr Widmer at Territet and Dr Dubois at Berne would be within easy reach. Only two hours after their arrival, when Proust was fully occupied in being ill himself, his mother had an attack of giddiness and vomiting: with his extensive knowledge of medicine he may have guessed the truth, that these were symptoms of a recurrence of her nephritis, brought on as is often the case by the jolting of a long train journey. Next morning, and every morning for the rest of those terrible few days, she tried to hide her partial paralysis and aphasia, which were two other recognised symptoms of her disease, and insisted on coming downstairs, helped by two servants of the hotel, to sit all day in the lounge. She refused food, and would not admit that she was ill, nor allow the analysis of her urine which would have revealed her condition. Proust telephoned for Mme Catusse, who was staying near by; but on her arrival, somewhat to his irritation, the sick lady only begged her old friend to take her photograph. It was not till later that he could interpret her strange mixture of eagerness, coquetry and reluctance: 'she was torn between the desire to leave me a last image of herself,' he explained to Mme Catusse five years afterwards, 'and the fear that it might be an unbearably sad one'. In his novel it is the grandmother at Balbec who, with the same purpose, persuades Saint-Loup to take her photograph, and is cruelly mocked by the Narrator.[1]

Proust sent for Robert, who decided to bring her back, while there was still time, to the medical facilities of Paris; and next morning, half carried, half dauntlessly walking, she was seen into the

[1] I, 786-7; II, 776-80.

railway-carriage by Mme Catusse. Moved by the wish to die at home
and to spare the distracted Marcel the sight of her agony, she forbade
him to come with her even to the station, and abdicated for ever her
care for her son. "I'm going back to Paris, because I'm useless and
can't help you when you're ill," she declared, almost sternly, as they
parted. For a few days he waited obediently, hoping, as he wrote to
Marie Nordlinger on the 13th, 'that all this will vanish like a bad
dream'; but soon a telegram from Robert summoned him to
Paris.

His mother, he found, showed signs of improvement: "if she gets
over this attack, she'll be as fit as ever," promised Dr Landowski.
Uraemia had been confirmed, but she still refused all food or medicine, and doggedly persisted in dressing and getting up every day.
She kept her lifelong air of absolute calm: 'none of us knows what
she is thinking or suffering,' Proust told Montesquiou, who, still
crushed by his own grief, was temporarily able to notice the sorrows
of other people. Mercifully her disease, instead of inflicting the usual
excruciating pain, took the alternative course of advancing paralysis
and coma. After a few days her apparent improvement ended, and she
began to die. When Dr Merklen called and announced: "Monsieur
Proust, I can recommend only one thing," Proust thought for one
wild moment that he was about to suggest a possible cure; but
Merklen, with a look of genuine sympathy which he always remembered with gratitude, concluded: "and that is, patience and resignation." When she was able to speak the poor lady would play, in a
voice distorted by aphasia, their old game of joking quotations from
the French classics. The nun who nursed her left them together for a
moment, and "*I never saw a better-timed departure*,"[1] she stammered.
"I couldn't bear to be without you," he cried, and "Don't be afraid,
my little boy," she replied, "your mother won't leave you; why, '*a
nice thing it would be, if I was at Étampes and my spelling went to
Arpajon*'."[2] Just before the end, as he fought to suppress his tears,
she frowned, pulled a smiling grimace, and whispered, so that he
guessed rather than heard the quotation from Corneille[3] with which
she had cheered their partings in his childhood: " '*if you're no
Roman, then deserve to be one!*' " In her final coma, as old Félicie told

[1] Molière, *Le Misanthrope*, act 3, scene 5.
[2] Labiche, *La Grammaire*, scene 15, spoken by a father who depends for his
spelling on a learned daughter.
[3] *Horace*, act 2, scene 3.

him afterwards, "Madame trembled like a leaf, although she was quite unconscious, whenever she heard your three rings on the bell, because however quietly you tried to ring that week you have a way which she couldn't mistake for anyone else's". And the nun-nurse remarked to him, with mingled admiration and disapproval, "for her you were still a child of four years old". On 26 September Mme Proust died, and suddenly Time was Lost.

For two days Marcel still had her to himself. She had taken no solid food since their arrival at Évian, and starvation had melted away the heaviness which of late years had made her face plain and middle-aged. The corpse by which he watched was that of a beautiful girl, the very image, he thought, of the portrait painted by Mme Beauvais in 1880. The young mother who had refused and granted his goodnight kiss at Auteuil was restored to him, risen from the abyss of Time. Now he gave her the same kiss again. 'Today I have her still, dead, but accepting my caresses—tomorrow I shall lose her for ever,' he told Mme de Noailles; and Reynaldo Hahn could never forget the horrifying sight of 'Marcel by Mme Proust's deathbed, weeping, and smiling through his tears at her body'.

Because Mme Proust had kept her Jewish religion out of respect for her parents, there was no church service, and the funeral procession, headed by Marcel, Robert, and her brother Georges Weil, left at noon on the 28th directly for Père Lachaise. The usual prohibition of flowers, however, was waived: 'the hearse could hardly be seen for wreaths,' observed the *Figaro* reporter, 'among the finest of which, we noticed, were those from the Marquis d'Albufera, Mme Félix Faure and Mme Gaston Thomson'. One of the most magnificent of all, which the reporter tactfully left unmentioned, came from Louisa de Mornand. Professors Berger, Brouardel, Dentu, Dieulafoy, Fournier, Hartmann and Pozzi attended in memory of her husband their colleague, and from the noble Faubourg the Noailles, Albufera, Chevigné and Grouchy couples came not only out of friendship for Marcel, but because they had been his parents' guests.

For a month Proust disappeared from the world of the living, almost as if he shared his mother's death. In this twilight half-life he lay in bed weeping incessantly and entirely deprived of sleep. The servants, from force of habit, tiptoed about the apartment as before; but he listened to the silence with horror, for it was a spectral relic of his mother, who had trained them not to disturb the sleep that was now forbidden him. Sometimes her bodiless voice murmured

unintelligibly in his ear, from beyond the grave: he had heard it
before, he realised, in the telephone at Fontainebleau nine years
since, when his mother spoke in a tone of mourning from an invisible
world, and he had felt a foreboding of her death. Although he now
thought of her unceasingly, he found to his despair that he could not
remember her face. He recalled that she, too, had known the same
torment, and confided that she could never call up the image of her
beloved mother, his grandmother, except by cruel flashes in sleep.
In his turn he twice suddenly saw her, in an instantaneous waking
vision, as a nightmare figure wrestling with her disease. Sometimes
he dozed; and his mind continued a hideous train of thought far more
terrible than the anguish of waking life, when he still had the protection of his reason. He remembered a moment in the last days before
her death, when she struggled in vain to speak: what had she tried to
say, what command had she left unuttered which might have saved
him?

Towards the end of October he began, by degrees, to sleep again,
at the cost of terrifying dreams. He left his bedroom for the first time
to revisit the empty rooms of their home; but in each one, as he
realised her absence anew, his mother seemed to die again; and he
explored, as he wrote to Mme de Noailles, 'unknown regions of grief,
which reach further and further into infinity with every step I take'.
Outside her bedroom he trod on a creaking board, which she would
hear in the small hours when he returned from an evening in society;
but he listened in vain for the kissing sound which she would then
make with her lips, meaning "Come and embrace me." For the last
time, in death, she had refused her goodnight kiss. At that moment
he decided to leave 'this house which is so sad because it used to be
so happy'; but he would have to wait nearly a year, for their annual
lease would not expire again until 30 September 1906.

Early in November, as if suddenly remembering an appointment,
Proust began to think again of his vow to enter a sanatorium. He had
succeeded, with unceasing feints and retreats, in procrastinating for
a year and a half, ever since Dr Merklen had ordered him to 'unlearn
your asthma'. At first he seemed only to renew his old tactics, plight-
ing his faith to half a dozen different doctors at a time. Dubois and
Sollier were close favourites, until a previous outsider, Dr Déjérine,
last heard of in December 1904, forged to the front. He promised to
cure Proust by three months of complete isolation; and as from
5 December 1905 Proust engaged a private room for three months

in the nursing-home of the Sisters of Sainte-Marie de la Famille in the Rue Blomet, of which Déjérine was the director.

Meanwhile his grief began to wane. He was taken unawares by feelings of possible happiness, followed by instant remorse. He resolved every day to go out for the first time tomorrow; but he was deterred by the memory of his mother meeting him at the door, before the servants could reply to his invariable question: "Is Madame still up?", and gazing anxiously to see whether he had returned in a fit of asthma. 'For grief isn't single,' he told Mme Straus on 9 November, 'because regret takes a different form every moment; suggested by the identity of a present impression with some moment of the past, a new disaster, an unknown sorrow strikes one down, as unbearable as the first onset of bereavement.' Proust's theories of grief and its intermittences, of unconscious memory as a source not only of joy but of anguish, were taught him by experience.

On 4 December, the very eve of his promised entry into the nursing-home in the Rue Blomet, Proust resolved to jilt Dr Déjérine. Sollier, he wildly surmised, might be persuaded to treat him at home, by the simple, well-tried, and totally ineffectual method of changing his hours of meals and sleep. Through Mme Straus he arranged for Sollier to call at 6.30 p.m. on 6 December. The young doctor was charming and optimistic: it was essential for Proust to enter his nursing-home, he explained, but in return he could effect a cure in only six weeks. Whether because he believed in this miracle, or because he felt there was not the least danger of its occurring, Proust allowed himself to be whisked off that very evening to Sollier's sanatorium at Boulogne-sur-Seine, otherwise Billancourt, a rural suburb between the western extremity of the Bois de Boulogne and the river.

Chapter 3

THE WATERSHED
(*December 1905 – January 1907*)

PSYCHIATRISTS are familiar with the patient who sets impossible conditions for his treatment, abandons it if he sees any risk of being cured, knows enough about the secret causes of his neurosis to be able to parry all attempts to detect them, and begins by establishing a feeling of intellectual superiority over his doctor. So it was to be with Sollier and Proust, who unconsciously preferred his asthma, and the way of life it necessitated, to the health of ordinary beings.

During the first half of 1905 he had conscientiously read up the works of French specialists in nervous ailments, and was interested to learn that the unconscious was responsible for all manner of diseases which hitherto had been supposed to be organic. One of these, according to Dr Brugelmann, was asthma; the very title of Dr Ribot's *Diseases of the Will* was a reproach which struck home; and Camus and Pagnier, in *The Isolation-Treatment in Psychotherapy*, with preface by Dr Déjérine himself, suggested what was in store for him at the Billancourt sanatorium. In a footnote to *Sésame et les Lys* he mentioned all these, and quoted from Dr Dubois's *The Psychoneuroses*, which he had borrowed from Fernand Gregh in 1903: 'Doctors used to say that a pessimist is a man with a bad stomach. Now Dr Dubois says outright that a man with a bad stomach is a pessimist. And it is no longer a question of curing his stomach to change his philosophy, but of changing his philosophy to cure his stomach.' The note of disrespectful irony is evident. It is as though Proust saw his physicians as substitutes for his dead father, saying in the very voice of Dr Proust: "there's nothing wrong with the boy, except lack of will-power"; and he behaved towards them, as to his father, with apparent submission but real evasion.

The charming Dr Sollier made an unfortunate start. In their first conversation after his arrival at Billancourt Proust asked whether he had read Bergson. "Yes, I felt I ought to, because we're both interes-

ted in the same field. But I found him terribly confused and narrow!"
'I felt a Da Vincian smile of intellectual pride passing over my face,'
Proust told Georges de Lauris afterwards, 'and this didn't contribute
to the success of my psychotherapeutic treatment.' Perhaps Proust
had more satisfying discussions with his doctor on a different subject.
He would have heard from Léon Daudet, who had been Sollier's
fellow-student, and like many ardent heterosexuals took a keen
interest in such matters, that Sollier was a specialist in the psycho-
pathology of women, and held advanced views on the statistics of
female homosexuality. "So-called frigidity in women," Sollier would
maintain, "is in three-quarters of all cases a symptom of Lesbianism." Isolation-treatment, indeed, as practised by Dr Sollier, was
delightfully devoid of rigour. Not only was Proust allowed to carry
on his enormous correspondence by dictation; in special cases, as to
Robert de Billy, or Louisa de Mornand, he could still write his own
letters. To Louisa he wrote to warn her against taking a new lover
until she was quite sure of herself—'Don't spoil one happiness until
you have another'—next to arrange a New Year's gift to Albu of a
travelling-watch for his automobile, and again to refuse a gift for
himself: 'unhappy friendships with people who gave me New Year
presents have made me almost superstitious, and in these sad days it
would seem like a bad omen'. The turn of the year, ever since his
love for Marie de Benardaky in the Champs-Élysées, had always
been a melancholy time, and now brought a recrudescence of his
grief for his mother. He remembered her question in his childhood:
"What would you like for a present on New Year's Day?" "I'd like
your love." "Why, you dear old ninny, that isn't a present—you have
that always." But now he had it no longer.

Early in January Dr Sollier became still more gracious. Proust
was now allowed to receive his friends on Tuesdays, Thursdays and
Saturdays from two to four in the afternoon. 'Insist when you arrive,
and if necessary ask to see Dr Sollier himself,' he told Robert de
Billy, who visited him before leaving, towards 9 January, to join the
French delegation at the Algeciras Conference. The isolation-
chamber at Billancourt had become a mere annexe to Proust's
bedroom at 45 Rue de Courcelles, and he was living precisely as
before, with asthma unabated, except that for the first time for five
years he was sleeping at night and breakfasting before noon. 'I'm
not climbing the hill, alas,' he complained to Billy, 'I'm going down it
at a gallop'; but soon the appointed six weeks were over, and about

20 January he returned home, 'fantastically ill'. The faithful Albufera
called every day to help with his correspondence; and in February
he was at home daily from five to ten to the few chosen friends whom
he allowed to know that he was fit to be seen: 'which constitutes a
great progress,' wrote Albu to Billy, 'and is an enormous pleasure
for us all'.

His sojourn at Billancourt had been not a cure, but a successful
and final escape from health. Nevertheless, although its effect on his
illness had been, as he unconsciously intended, almost negligible, its
symbolic importance was profound and manifold. He had fulfilled
his mother's last wish, and also defied her, since his obedience had
been useless. At the same time his continued ill health was an act of
piety: he would remain for ever in the state in which he had lived
with her, whereas if he had become a new man he would have been
parted from her eternally. Again, by retiring temporarily from the
world of the living he had shared in her death. But the Billancourt
cell had been a symbol not only of death but of approaching resurrection. In preparation for his new life of freedom he had retreated
into the life before birth, in a strange place where his mother was
invisible yet everywhere round him, and the father-figure of Dr
Sollier gently invited him to be made new and emerge. When he
came out, defenceless, bewildered and in pain, he was reborn, although more than a year would pass before he could gather his
strength and establish a new way of life. Already, however, he
thought less often of his mother, and only at sudden moments of
recollection with the old anguish. Dr Sollier had succeeded in curing
him of one thing: not his asthma, but his grief.

In *A la Recherche* his six weeks at Billancourt were magnified into
the Narrator's 'long years in a sanatorium, during which I had
completely renounced my idea of becoming a writer',[1] which lasted
from shortly after his visit to Gilberte de Saint-Loup at Tansonville
until the beginning of 1916, and again, 'in a new sanatorium which
was no more successful in curing me than the first', for a period of
'many years'.[2] This vast stretching of the thread of time was necessitated technically by Proust's wartime revision of his novel, in
which the insertion of the long chapter on the events of the World
War caused the revelation of Time Regained at the Princesse de
Guermantes's matinée to be transferred from the neighbourhood of
1912 to about the year 1922. Yet the significance of the brief real

[1] III, 723.   [2] III, 854.

and the long imaginary stay in a nursing-home was the same. The six weeks under Dr Sollier marked a fundamental division between the two eras of Proust's life, between the past thirty-four years with his mother and the coming seventeen years without her. Formerly he had lived, like the hero of *Jean Santeuil*, in a present which seemed destined, by the indefinite addition of day to day, to last for ever. When he returned from Billancourt to his empty home his whole previous life had become, by a total break of continuity, the past. On the far side of the barrier was the lost time in which his mother continued to give and withhold her infinite love; on the hither side he was alone in an unreal, ghostly and posthumous present which could be given meaning only by a recovery of the time he had squandered. The year of half-life that followed Billancourt formed a moorland plateau from which the rivers flowed on one side to his childhood, on the other to his death. He had reached the watershed between Time Lost and Time Regained.

For two months, between mid-February and mid-April 1906, Proust once again is lost to view, and the few surviving letters (one each to Mme de Noailles, Mme Catusse and Antoine Bibesco) are written to explain that he is too ill to write. He chose Dr Maurice Bize, who called every Friday, for his new physician. He corrected the proofs of *Sésame et les Lys*, the publication of which had been planned for October 1905, but delayed by his mother's death, and perhaps worked again on his novel.

On 5 May in the *Chronique des Arts* Proust reviewed a translation of Ruskin's *Stones of Venice* by his aunt Mathilde Peigné-Crémieux, Mme Proust's cousin and a sister of Mme Thomson. It was his only article during the prescribed year of his mourning, and no doubt he only allowed himself to write it in the knowledge that it would particularly have pleased his mother. He gave Aunt Mathilde a glowing review for 'this superb translation', but slyly pointed out how greatly her book would have been improved by the addition of footnotes. His passion for Ruskin momentarily revived, though the tables were turned: instead of admiring Venice for Ruskin's sake, he now praised Ruskin for his praise of Venice. 'The skies of Venice and the mosaics of St Mark's,' he wrote, 'take on colours still more miraculous than their own, since these are the hues of a marvellous imagination, carried across the world, as in an enchanted ship, by Ruskin's prose.' As he read the visionary city rose again from the sea of the past, and he thought, towards the end of May, of revisiting this Venice Preserved; 'but Venice is so much a graveyard of happiness for me,' he wrote ruefully to Mme Catusse, 'that I haven't the strength to go back'. For the rest of his life his nostalgia intermittently returned; and the Narrator's many years of longing for the Venice he had not yet seen were experienced by Proust after he had been there, and when he knew in his heart he would never return. Meanwhile, as he planned his imaginary journey, Aunt Mathilde played her part in the reawakening of his desire to live. 'Just recently,' he wrote to Léon Bélugou that summer, 'while reading one of Ruskin's travel books and feeling my heart beating with the desire to see the same places once more, I said to myself: "if I no longer cared for him, would he still be making the world beautiful for me, until I am consumed with longing and desolation whenever I look at a railway-timetable?" Yes, my affection for Ruskin has lasted. Only sometimes nothing chills it so much as reading him.' 'My original love,' he concluded, 'was more involuntary.'

Sésame et les Lys was published on 1 June. Marie Nordlinger had proved adamant in her self-effacing refusal to be treated as his collaborator, and her help, which had meant so much to him not only in itself but as a symbol of friendship and happier days, could be acknowledged only in a footnote. The preface was dedicated to his favourite Princesse Hélène de Chimay, '*Of Kings' Treasuries*' to Reynaldo Hahn, and '*Of Queens' Gardens*' to Suzette Lemaire. He sent a copy to Louisa de Mornand inscribed with Baudelaire's line '*O toi que j'eusse aimée, ô toi qui le savais*'—'*You whom I might have loved, as well you knew*'—and sat back with little hope to await reviews. He was still too downcast to organise, as he had for *La Bible d'Amiens*, the log-rolling publicity which he believed to be his only hope of fame in the world of letters. With an excess of modesty he even begged Calmette not to trouble Beaunier for a review, since that amiable critic had been only too generous the year before; but to his delighted embarrassment a brief notice by Beaunier appeared in *Le Figaro* on 5 June, followed by a front-page article on the 15th.

Since Beaunier's article was his one morsel of satisfaction, it was particularly maddening that Reynaldo, Lucien Daudet and Albufera all failed to notice it. The philistine Albu, who had not yet been persuaded to read even *La Bible d'Amiens*, went so far as to remark: "It's very odd, Marcel, considering Calmette is a friend of yours, that they haven't said a word about your book in *Le Figaro*!" "On the contrary, they've said all too much." "You must be mistaken, dear boy," replied Albu in the very words of the Duc de Guermantes denying the existence of the Narrator's article on the spires of Martinville,[1] "because my wife reads *Le Figaro* every morning from beginning to end, and there's been absolutely nothing about you!"

'The footnotes to *Sésame* are mere small-talk, and I'd rather do some really serious work,' Proust told Robert Dreyfus. In fact the footnotes, however slight their connection may sometimes be with Ruskin's text, contain some of Proust's most remarkable writing to date, and even when apparently trivial show his preoccupation with the 'really serious work' of his novel. His private life, which for him was so closely connected with his creative writing, persists in coming to the surface. Without naming the victim he quotes a Charlus-like remark of Montesquiou on the faithless Delafosse: "To think that I should be treated so by a person I trimmed into shape as a topiarist trims a yew-tree!"; and he recalls a saying of his mother, who continued to the end to discuss the possibility of his marriage: "I shouldn't mind if you chose someone who'd never heard of Ruskin, but I couldn't bear it if you married a woman who pronounced 'tramway' 'tramvay'!" The most significant note, however, is on the organic unity which underlies the apparent deviousness of Ruskin's construction. In the last paragraph of '*Kings' Treasuries*' Ruskin gathers together the diverse meanings latent in the Sesame of his title: it is a seed, a spiritual food, a magic word which opens a long-hidden, underground treasure-house, and so on. 'He passes from one idea to another,' comments Proust, 'without any apparent order. But in reality the fantasy which leads him follows its own profound affinities, which enforce upon him in spite of himself an overruling logic. Consequently we find in the end that he has obeyed a kind of secret plan, which when finally unveiled imposes its retrospective structure upon the work as a whole, so that we now see it splendidly towering to the final apotheosis.' When he wrote these words, probably in the spring of 1905, Proust may already have realised that his novel would demand, what *Jean Santeuil* had lacked, a majestic unity underlying its diversity, and a fugal or coda-like regathering of the themes at its conclusion. In his final paragraph, like Ruskin, he would repeat the keyword of his title, Time, and give it meanings not far distant from those of Sesame.

In the early summer Proust looked on with mixed feelings at the

[1] III, 583.

last act in the drama of the Dreyfus Affair. Officially Dreyfus was
still, in the words of the Rennes verdict in 1899, 'guilty with extenuating circumstances'; but the Appeal Court had been engaged ever
since 1903 in a leisurely new review of his case, and the triumph of
the Radical bloc in the May elections of 1906 made an early decision
so expedient as to be inevitable. The rehabilitation of Dreyfus,
however, was no longer an act of justice, but a political manœuvre
in the campaign of humiliation against the Church and Army which
Ruskin and Orleans had made dear to Proust. 'These elections have
been a sad blow to me,' he told Mme Catusse; and to the leftist
Reynaldo he grumbled: 'I see all your "unified socialist" friends are
in, and you must be as delighted as I'm furious—not that I wouldn't
gladly vote for you if you put up as a dear little hunnified socialist,
only I'd rather you didn't.' Suddenly, on 13 July, Dreyfus was
declared to have been innocent all along, and on the 20th, in a
grotesque reversal of his public degradation in the same place eleven
years before, he was invested with the cross of the Legion of Honour
before the assembled troops at the École Militaire. Proust's revulsion
from Dreyfus in the hour of victory is a measure of his former self-
identification with Dreyfus in the time of ostracism and martyrdom;
it also helps to explain the Narrator's almost neutral attitude to the
Affair in *A la Recherche*. 'In these ten years,' he wrote bitterly to
Mme Straus, 'we've all had many griefs, disappointments and agonies.
And for none of us will the hour ever strike when our griefs will be
changed to exultations, our disappointments to un-hoped-for
realisations, our agonies into delicious triumphs. I shall get iller and
iller, miss my lost ones more and more, and find all I ever dreamed
life might give me ever further out of reach. But for Dreyfus and
Picquart life has been as providential as a fairy-tale. The reason is
that *our* sorrows are based on truths, whether physiological, human
or emotional. But their misfortunes were the result of mere mistakes.
Blessed are the victims of mistakes, judicial or otherwise! For them
alone of mankind there is such a thing as restitution and reparation.'
Dreyfus was promoted to the rank of major, in which he served a
year for form's sake, and then resigned to live on his ample private
means. Picquart, who had been in compulsory retirement since 1898,
was more spectacularly made a general, and, on 26 October, War
Minister; but eight years of consciousness that in all the French
army he was the only man in step had turned his high-souled courage
in the heroic age of the Affair to priggish self-satisfaction, and as

minister he was neither competent nor popular. Proust wondered whether to favour him with a copy of *Sésame et les Lys*; but, he decided, 'when I think of the difficulty I had in smuggling *Les Plaisirs et les Jours* to him when he was in prison, it seems too easy now'.

As a further stage in his groping return to life he began to plan a summer holiday. At first, remembering his cruise on the *Hélène* two years before, he thought of 'hiring a little yacht', a project which in *A la Recherche* reappeared in the Narrator's intention of buying a yacht for Albertine. A host of bewildering and forbidding possibilities besieged him; and as in former years he would have unburdened his indecision upon his mother, so now he wrote repeatedly and interminably to Mme Straus. He was tempted to return to the Hôtel des Roches Noires at Trouville, but the thought of the mist in the valley, and the thinness of the partitions through which his mother had knocked good-morning in 1894, put him off. Where could he find absence of damp, dust, draughts and trees, abundance of lifts, bathrooms, fires and water-closets, and room for old Félicie whom, as the Narrator took Françoise to Balbec, he was determined to take with him? Knowing her friend as she did, Mme Straus cannot have been surprised to hear that he had resolved to stay at home, 'to rest from my journey, which was as exhausting to plan as it would have been to make', or, a few days later, that he had suddenly left alone for Versailles.

Probably at the suggestion of Reynaldo Hahn, who sometimes stayed there when in the throes of composition, he moved on 6 August into a suite at the Hôtel des Réservoirs. The hotel, an eighteenth-century mansion built for Mme de Pompadour, was separated from the northern wing of the Palace only by the reservoirs which still supplied the fountains and basins of the gardens. From its windows the guests surveyed the Bassin de Neptune and the beech-tree vistas beyond; and should they wish to walk in the park, two private exits led directly upon the gravel alleys and the lawns. Proust's apartment in the annexe was vast, sunless and extremely expensive, with lofty ceilings and innumerable tapestries, paintings and mirrors—'the sort of place where the guide tells you that Charles the Ninth died there, and you cast a furtive look around, longing to get out again into light and warmth and the comfortable present; but I not only can't get out, but even have to make the supreme surrender of sleeping there!' In these melancholy surroundings,

which habit soon changed into a familiar new home, he was to spend
nearly five months.

As a first step he surrounded himself with a band of zealous and
liberally-tipped servants: a hall-porter with powdered white hair,
his wife who made Proust's telephone-calls, a young favourite of
Reynaldo named Léon, another hall-porter whom Proust had
glimpsed previously as a footman of Montesquiou's distant uncle
the Duc de Fezensac, and the head-waiter, Hector, of whom there
may be something in Aimé, his counterpart at Balbec. With his
mind running on servants, Proust mistook a passer-by, who recognised him with frenzied gestures of delight as he drew his curtains
one evening, for his father's alcoholic ex-valet Eugène; but it was
another friend of Reynaldo, an eccentric Austrian painter named
Schlésinger. "Are you in Versailles for the day?" Proust enquired.
"No, I'm staying in the next room to yours," replied Herr Schlésinger, and proceeded to compliment Proust on his new beard: "it suits
you very well, in fact a beard always looks well when one's face is
beginning to show signs of age!" 'And the moral of that is,' Proust
wrote to Reynaldo quoting Pascal, 'that all the misfortunes of man
spring from his inability to live in a room alone!' But Proust himself,
preternaturally free from that inability, was beginning like his Aunt
Amiot at Illiers to create a life of constant drama simply by looking
out of his window.

His uncle Georges Weil was now dying, and one of Proust's
reasons for choosing Versailles was his wish to return the kindness
of this elder brother of his mother, who had called so often in the
evenings after Mme Proust's death to comfort his distracted nephew.
In flat disobedience to Dr Dubois, who had declared a few years
before that his illness was imaginary, Uncle Georges had taken to his
bed in June with uraemia; less fortunate than his sister, who had
died more gently of the same condition, he now experienced the
pain he had so often imagined, and lay in convulsions of ceaseless
agony. One day in mid-August Proust visited Paris to see him for
the last time, too late, for his uncle was already unable to recognise
him. On the way back he had a 'kind of accident' ('I don't like to
talk about it,' he told Mme Catusse) at the Gare Saint-Lazare, and
was rescued by a railway-employee whom he afterwards made vain
efforts to trace. Georges Weil died on the 23rd, and was buried in
the Jewish section of Père Lachaise on the 26th; but the fear of
repeating his unfortunate experience at the railway-station prevented

his nephew from returning to do his duty at the head of the funeral procession.

Another reason for his stay at Versailles was his impending move from 45 Rue de Courcelles, where his lease would expire on 30 September. He decided to leave arrangements for removal in his brother's hands, and to enlist his friends to find him a new home; and from this strategic retreat so near to Paris he would be able to carry on the necessary negotiations by post and telephone. All through September Georges de Lauris and other friends visited possible apartments and described them as vividly as possible by letter. Mme de Noailles was haled from dinner one evening by a telephone caller who introduced himself as the wine-waiter at the Hôtel des Réservoirs: "Monsieur Proust has asked me to ask Madame la Comtesse," he said, "whether she would advise him to take the apartment in the Boulevard Haussmann or the other one." 'My dialogue with this Invisible Man, and the weighty arguments of my well-pondered reply,' she wrote long afterwards, 'were perhaps among the factors which determined Marcel's final decision.' Towards 7 October he took a year's lease, destined to last for twelve and a half years, of the first-floor apartment at 102 Boulevard Haussmann. The house had belonged to his great-uncle Louis Weil; Proust had dined there often with his mother, and watched with her over the old man's death-bed ten years before; perhaps, for it is likely that the incident really occurred, he had also met the lady in pink there. He was even a part-proprietor of the house: Louis Weil had left the property to his nephew Georges and his niece Mme Proust; Georges Weil's share now belonged to his wife Émilie, while Mme Proust's had been divided between Marcel and Robert. Even so, he felt the apartment was beyond his means; but his mother had been there—'I couldn't steel myself to live in a house that mother had never known,' he explained—and it would be 'a transition between the Rue de Courcelles, which for me was the true and dear graveyard where she lay, and some place utterly strange and unknown.' Perhaps, too, he was attracted by its associations not only with Mme Proust, but with Louis Weil, the gay old man who had lived there in such scandalous freedom; and Proust may have foreseen that he would do the same, though mostly on the other side of the border between Paphos and Sodom.

Robert Proust had seen to the removal from 45 Rue de Courcelles, and the family furniture was now inconveniently dispersed between a carpet-store in the Place Clichy, a repository, and the empty ground-floor flat at 102 Boulevard Haussmann. It was time for the brothers to divide this part of their heritage; and for once Marcel's buried jealousy neared the surface, for it was as if he were now called upon to restore to Robert his fair share of their mother's love. His brother's utter unselfishness only thwarted his irresistible need to have a grievance. "Do whatever you please, Marcel," Robert repeated, "anything you decide will be quite perfect"; and when Marcel insisted on being advised he would say only: "Keep what you like, and sell or store the rest." Forgetting that he had taken 102 Boulevard Haussmann for the sake of old memories, he decided that only Robert's cruel refusal to accept his share of their unwieldy chattels had prevented him from economising in a smaller flat. He upbraided his brother: "you have forced me to alter my budget, my investments and my whole life," he said; but Robert's wife Marthe could be induced to covet only a few carpets and tapestries which Proust immediately decided he must keep. In November his little niece Suzy was ill with diphtheria. 'I like to think that perhaps a little of my mother and father survives in her', he declared, 'and it distresses me that she should begin her life so sadly.' But when the possibly plague-stricken Robert visited 102 Boulevard Haussmann, Marcel threatened to have the whole apartment fumigated; and when the hall-porter's wife reported, after telephoning his condolences to Marthe, that 'the lady seemed a bit short', he took severe umbrage. 'She's very nice, however, despite her uncertain temper,' he wrote magnanimously to Mme Catusse, 'and I must confess old Félicie assures me that, without being aware of it, I'm the last word in disagreeableness!'

During the three months from October to December Proust made his new apartment habitable by an infuriating but masterly exhibition of remote control. Becoming more than ever like his Aunt Amiot he succeeded, without leaving his bedroom, in badgering a host of people whom he never saw: Robert, Aunt Émilie, Mme Catusse, the architect, the manager, the concierge Antoine, the installers of electric light and wall-paper, the telephone-company, and the occupant of the flat above, who turned out to be an acquaintance named Arthur Pernolet. For a time he was determined to go to law, if only he could decide with whom: should it be with his aunt, who had improperly let the ground-floor flat to a professional man, Dr Gagey, or with Dr Gagey himself? Or could he persuade M.

Pernolet to be sufficiently aggrieved to do it for him? Early in December he began a lawsuit against the outgoing lady sub-lessor of his own flat, but on second thoughts withdrew it. The most delicious imbroglio of all was over the choice of furniture, in which he had the help of Mme Catusse, an expert on interior decoration. Every epic has its catalogue, the *Iliad* of ships, the *Pharsalia* of snakes; but Proust's catalogue of furniture, in which every single object from 45 Rue de Courcelles is in turn destined for every room in 102 Boulevard Haussmann, or given to servants, to Robert, to Dr Landowski, or sold, or popped into the basement, is an enormity which the biographer must spare the reader.

In the first few weeks of his stay he had risen when the sun was still setting over the green forests of Versailles; but soon it was dark when he awoke, it was therefore pointless to go outside the hotel, and for all those five months he never emerged. While he slept the majestic drama of the Versailles autumn was played unseen: the beech-avenues turned invisibly to gold, shed their leaves, and at last stood branch-deep in the mists of December. 'Am I really at Versailles?' he wrote to his old sweetheart Mme Gaston de Caillavet; 'I haven't left my bed, I haven't seen the palace, the Trianons, or anything; when I open my eyes it's already the dead of night, and I often wonder whether the room I lie in, lit by electricity and hermetically sealed, isn't anywhere in the world rather than at Versailles, where I haven't watched a single dead leaf whirling down over a single fountain!' One morning at sunrise, however, he must at least have looked from his window as he prepared for bed, and have seen the dying splendour of Versailles as an emblem of his own life; for he wrote to Mme Straus of 'these days when the great fall of the leaf outside matches so well all that is withered and dispersed in the heart'. He sent for Dr Bize: "you have a touch of anaemia because you won't open your windows," he was told, "and you're writing far too many letters!"

His isolation at Versailles, however, was neither complete nor uncheered. Something of these autumn months went into the Narrator's idyllic sojourn at Doncières: the season, the mist, the clangour of tramcars, the hotel which was, as Saint-Loup told the Narrator, 'an eighteenth-century palace with old tapestries, a real "historic dwelling" ',[1] the thin bugle-calls from the nearby barracks at dawn, the visits of friends; for Versailles too was a garrison-town and a

[1] II, 71.

peopled solitude. Lauris, Billy, Reynaldo and Mme Catusse came severally to dinner. "All this talk about meals brought to the annexe is a myth, they bring everything on the same tray, and it's all frozen when it arrives," Proust declared; so they dined without him in the high, white-panelled restaurant of the hotel, with the veined marble partition down the middle. The head-waiter was instructed to offer truffled partridges, quails *sur canapé*, the most expensive champagne; and Proust was furious if his guests ordered anything more modest. René Peter, a playwright friend of Reynaldo and Debussy and a native of Versailles, was a constant visitor. They collaborated in a fairy-tale pantomime, of which Proust supplied the idea and wrote two of the five acts: where is it now? He thought of writing another play with Peter, with a preposterous but significant plot, about a sadistic husband who, though in love with his wife, consorted with prostitutes, said infamous things about her to them, encouraged them to answer in kind, and was caught in the act by the injured lady, who left him, whereupon he committed suicide. As we have seen, this was an actual occurrence (except for the suicide) in the liaison of his father's colleague Dr Albert Robin with the courtesan Liane de Pougy. But the same form of cerebral sadism was a constant element in Proust's own ambivalent love-hatred for his mother, both in her lifetime and long after her death, and in the homosexual relationships with social inferiors with which, by a snobism in every sense inverted, he sought to profane her memory. He had used the theme, long before the misdemeanour of Dr Robin made it come true, in '*The Confession of a Young Girl*' in *Les Plaisirs et les Jours*, where the girl who is so evidently Proust himself kills her mother by allowing her vice to be detected, and then kills herself; and he was to use it again, reversing the sexes, in Mlle Vinteuil's desecration of her dead father at Montjouvain. But early in December, without letting her into the secret of its plot, he confessed to Jeanne de Caillavet: 'I haven't the courage to write my play.'

He had still further resources in the hotel itself, where other Parisians were enjoying the Versailles autumn. He visited the Comtesse d'Arnoux, whose nephew Henri Bardac was a friend of Reynaldo and had been studying for the diplomatic service at Oxford. With her he found a Norpois-like guest, the diplomat Jules Cambon, 'wrapped in a cloud of silence, old age and mystery, pierced only by the charm of his cunning eyes, like our Fénelon grown old, wrinkled and sly'. In the room above his own from August to

October a famous young beauty was staying, Miss Gladys Deacon, the original of the Miss Foster who is Number Three in the list of eligible heiresses discussed by the Prince de Foix and his group at the restaurant in the fog.[1] Her mother's lover, Émile Abeille, had been shot by her father in 1892 as he tried to leap from the window, and had left her 500,000 francs. Boni de Castellane, when he praised her beauty one evening at dinner, was told by the lady sitting next to him: "My dear Boni, I advise you to take jumping lessons." Mme de Clermont-Tonnerre, who was beginning to show signs of preferring intelligent girls to handsome men, thought her 'as beautiful as a Greek warrior, with eyes perhaps too large and blue', and was astonished when Miss Deacon began to talk brilliantly of *The Well-Beloved* and to explain the difference between Hardy and Meredith; while Montesquiou had pronounced her 'absolutely like an archangel!' Proust longed and feared to visit his dazzling neighbour, and was particularly galled when rumours reached him from all sides that he was seeing Miss Deacon every day. Late one evening he mustered all his daring and went up; but Miss Deacon had retired for the night, and he had to be content with a long conversation with her mother. One morning from his bed he glimpsed the lovely heiress in the courtyard, muffled in thick veils and climbing into an automobile. He was fascinated by her from afar for several years to come: 'I never saw a girl with such beauty, such magnificent intelligence, such goodness and charm,' he declared; and in 1910, at Mme de Clermont-Tonnerre's request, he tried half-heartedly and unsuccessfully to make a match between Miss Deacon and the divorced Loche Radziwill. Soon afterwards, however, she met the Ninth Duke of Marlborough, whom she married in 1921 after his long-delayed divorce from the former Consuelo Vanderbilt.

Despite its many logical motives and accidental consolations, however, Proust's incarceration at the Hôtel des Réservoirs remains one of the mysterious episodes of his life. It is not unlikely that he worked again on his novel; and perhaps his very denials at this time of his ability to write should be taken as confessions that he was doing so. 'A minimum of physical wellbeing is necessary not only for working,' he had written in June to Robert Dreyfus, 'but even for receiving poetic impressions from the outside world. And when one's illness ceases for a moment, and such impressions arise, then one enjoys them with the pleasure of a convalescent, without being

[1] II, 404.

able to divert the energy which is unceasingly occupied in repairing
the ravages of malady to make it available for incarnating what one
has felt.' To Marie Nordlinger he wrote from Versailles on 8 December: 'I have put an end to the era of translations, which was favoured
so by Mother; and as for translating myself, I no longer have the
courage.' But there are signs that he was also engaged in a more
sinister occupation.

During the following year it becomes clear that Proust's homosexuality had entered upon a further stage. He was now irrevocably
disillusioned with 'friendship', which for him meant an idealistic
search for happiness from a relationship, whether physical or platonic,
with his social equals—such as Robert de Flers, Reynaldo Hahn or
Lucien Daudet—or with social superiors, who had included the
whole group of young aristocrats whom he turned into Saint-Loup.
But the failure of friendship left his desires unabated; not only the
desire for carnal satisfaction, which he himself believed to be, in this
form, sinful although inescapable, but the nobler desire for reciprocal
kindness and devotion. Proust now proceeded to explore a further
and darker region of the Cities of the Plain, where lover and beloved
are master and servant, where guilt is justified by generosity, and
acceptance is guaranteed by gratitude. Even in the lifetime of his
parents there are traces of these protective and almost paternal
relationships: notably, in 1899, there was a certain 'young Poupetière' to whom, with Mme Proust's knowledge and approval, Proust
gave money and advice. There was now no need for concealment:
his mother's death had given him the freedom of Sodom; and from
1907 to the end of his life a succession of young men of the working-
classes, in the guise of man-servant, secretary or protégé, shared his
very home. The beginnings of this new freedom coincide with the
lifting of the anguish of his grief, and are visible at Versailles, where
it is evident from his letters to Reynaldo that Proust was seeing a
great deal of the young manservant Léon, and of a certain Robert
Ulrich, who intermittently during the next few years acted as his
secretary. For a nameless 'young man aged twenty-five, very
distinguished and pleasing in appearance, good handwriting, book-
keeping fair, charming manners, very serious-minded, but without
further education', he asked Robert de Billy to find a post in his
father-in-law's bank at the modest salary of '100 to 200 francs a
month'; and he continued his efforts to trace his good Samaritan of
the Gare Saint-Lazare.

On 27 December, when Proust had been announcing his imminent home-coming for the past six weeks and seemed likely to stay at Versailles for ever, he decided at an hour's notice to return to Paris. The concierge Antoine and Dr Proust's former manservant Jean Blanc could not conceal their consternation, for the apartment was far from ready, and the noisy alterations in Dr Gagey's flat below would take another month to complete. His new home, which he had not seen since Louis Weil's death ten years before, consisted, besides the 'usual offices', of a large bedroom and drawing-room facing the chestnut-trees of the boulevard, with a smaller bedroom, a dining-room and an ante-room upon the inner courtyard. Its appearance was both strange and familiar, for Mme Catusse had used all her ingenuity in—as Proust put it—her 'symphonic variations' on his parents' furniture. The floors were still bare, but he refused to allow the carpets to be laid until he recovered from the insomnia of arrival; he stopped the hapless Dr Gagey's renovations, and only consented on entreaty to allow their continuance in the late afternoon. But after a month of these petty obsessions with noise and the rights of property he was recalled to the real world of love and death, evil and atonement.

In the early summer of 1906 he had learned of the death of a certain Monsieur van Blarenberghe, whose wife had been an acquaintance of Mme Proust's. He remembered having dined in society with their son Henri, and could recall, if he tried, the young man's vaguely distinguished appearance, his smiling eyes and half-open mouth as he waited for applause after uttering a witticism. With an impulse of filial piety Proust wrote a letter of condolence on his dead mother's behalf, and in September at Versailles received a touching reply, four months delayed, for Henri van Blarenberghe had been travelling, under doctor's orders, to forget his grief. His father, he said, had been 'the centre of his life, the source of all his happiness'; he asked to be allowed to call on Proust, 'to shake your hand and talk about the past', and signed himself 'very affectionately yours'. It occurred to Proust that van Blarenberghe was not only an interesting fellow-mourner but also Chairman of the Chemins de Fer de l'Est, and rather self-seekingly he now wrote to him for help in tracing his saviour at the Gare Saint-Lazare, 'in whom a friend of mine is taking an interest', he mendaciously explained; but van Blarenberghe could tell him nothing, and suggested that he must have mistaken the name. 'What the year 1907 may have in store for me I do not know,' the young man added, 'but let us hope it may bring better things to us both, and that in a few months we may be able to meet.' This letter was written on 12 January, and Proust received it, forwarded from Versailles, on the 17th.

On the frosty afternoon of 25 January Proust settled down luxuriously in bed to enjoy his breakfast coffee and the day's *Figaro*. He skimmed the news of earthquakes and the latest government crisis, and was agreeably attracted by the leadline 'Murder by a Madman', when his pleasure turned to a sacred horror: the madman was none other than Henri van Blarenberghe, who had killed his mother the day before. The servants found Mme van Blarenberghe staggering downstairs, covered with blood: "Henri, what have you done? What have you done to me?" she cried, raising her arms in the air, and fell dead. The police broke through the locked door of her son's room, and found him still conscious on his bed. Henri van Blarenberghe had stabbed himself several times, and then shot himself inefficiently through the mouth: the left side of his face was blown away, his left eye hung on the pillow. The police-inspector shook him by the shoulder, shouting "Can you hear me? Answer, I say!"; but the murderer only opened his remaining eye, glared for a moment, and closed it for ever.

Five days later, on 30 January, Proust was asked by Calmette for a topical article on the crime[1]: he rested, without thinking of what he was about to write, until three in the morning, and then worked in a curious flow of inspiration until halted by writer's cramp and the din of Dr Gagey's workmen at eight, when he sent Ulrich with the article to the *Figaro* office. When the proofs arrived at eleven that evening he had no time to correct them, for he had just thought of 'an ending that was really rather good'. "Tell them they can cut whatever else they like, but they're not to alter a single word of the last paragraph," he instructed Ulrich; but when that young person returned to *Le Figaro* at midnight he found the sub-editor Cardane in an unaccommodating mood. "Does Monsieur Proust imagine that anyone will trouble to read his article besides himself, and the few people who happen to know him?" enquired Cardane, and complained that the new ending was "immoral, in fact it's a panegyric on

---

[1] Since Calmette could not have guessed unaided that Proust was personally acquainted with van Blarenberghe, or took a special interest in the theme of matricide, it may be inferred that his invitation had been prompted by Proust himself.

matricide!" Next morning, in exact contradiction to Proust's entreaty, '*The Filial Feelings of a Matricide*' appeared with the last paragraph omitted but the remainder intact.

Cardane was justified in prophesying the admiration of Proust's friends. Mme Straus's cousin, Ludovic Halévy, had the cuttings mounted and sumptuously bound: "your young friend Proust has written an astonishingly gifted article," he told Robert Dreyfus; and the dear Princesse de Chimay, when Proust told her over the telephone: "I'd rather have written that article of Antoine's than mine,"[1] retorted: "how can you be so *insincere*, Marcel!" and rang off in enthusiastic indignation. Van Blarenberghe's friends, on the other hand, were extremely annoyed. Cardane had been equally shrewd in his diagnosis of the final paragraph, though its omission scarcely affected the meaning of the essay as a whole.[2] Proust's purpose throughout was to show that the wretched van Blarenberghe had only done suddenly and directly what other men do indirectly and by degrees, and that we all kill our mothers. In defending van Blarenberghe he was defending himself; for the past year he had been accusing himself of van Blarenberghe's crime.

After his few months of wild grief in the autumn of 1905 the wound of his bereavement had seemed to heal; yet beneath it a deeper and more terrible wound, the hidden abscess of his guilt, remained. He had wept for his mother's death, but neglected to weep for her life. Their love, certainly, had been real: they were two noble creatures, united in a profound devotion; yet it was, equally, a mockery, for they had also been torn, each by the other, in an unending hostility. Every day for nearly thirty years, when he displayed his asthma, extorted her service, received her visits at his idle bedside, or left her to go with his friends, he had repeated the drama of the goodnight kiss at Auteuil. His mother in turn had been tainted for ever by that symbolic act of denial and surrender: always, whether she indulged his helplessness and soothed his hysteria, or whether she quarrelled with his extravagance, interfered with his

---

[1] An article by her cousin, Antoine Bibesco, on the Emir of Afghanistan, based on his automobile trip to Persia in the previous autumn, appeared in the *Figaro Literary Supplement* on 2 February.

[2] In the omitted ending Proust had written of the special veneration paid by the ancient Greeks to 'the tomb of Oedipus at Colonus and of Orestes at Sparta —that Orestes whom the Furies had pursued to the very feet of Apollo and Athene, crying: "We chase far from all altars sons who slew their mothers" '.

pleasures or showed jealousy of his moments of good health, she was prompted by anger as well as by love. He saw that, as surely as Henri van Blarenberghe had killed his mother, so too had he. His illness, his years on the Guermantes Way, even his homosexuality, had been not only substitutes for his mother's love but acts of revenge. He had taken her life, not with a dagger, but no less certainly; and as she swayed in the first onset of vertigo on the stairs at Évian she might have cried to her son like Mme van Blarenberghe: "What have you done to me?"

' "What have you done to me?" ' he wrote; 'if we allowed ourselves to think of it, there is perhaps no truly loving mother who could not, on the last day of her life, and often long before, address this reproach to her son. The fact is that we age and kill the heart that loves us by the anxiety we cause, by the uneasy tenderness we inspire and keep in a state of unceasing alarm. If we could see in a beloved body the slow work of destruction carried out by this anguished affection, the ravaged eyes, the hair which stayed indomitably black now defeated like the rest and turning white, the hardened arteries and obstructed kidneys, the courage vanquished by life, the slow, heavy step, the spirit that knows there is nothing left but despair, though once it rebounded tirelessly with unconquerable hopes, the inborn and seemingly immortal gaiety dried up for ever . . .': if, in a moment of lucid sanity like van Blarenberghe's when he saw his mother bleeding to death, we could see all these things, he concluded, then we too would shoot ourselves like him. 'In most men this agonising vision fades all too soon in the returning dawn of joy in life. But what joy, what reason for living, what life can bear to look it in the face? Which is true, it or joy? Which is the Truth?'

In a pretended generalisation he had described the exact symptoms of his own mother's slow torment and decline; and conversely he had condoned van Blarenberghe's matricide, which was also his own, by making it universal. Cardane was right indeed. In the preceding passage of his essay Proust compared van Blarenberghe to the tragic heroes of Sophocles, Shakespeare and Dostoevsky—to Ajax in his madness slaughtering the shepherds and their sheep, Oedipus tearing out his eyes at the sight of his mother-wife self-hanged for his sin, Lear bending over Cordelia dead, Dmitri Karamazov and the police-captain; and it was as if he saw van Blarenberghe's crime, and his own insight into its real nature, as an act of mythological, almost ritual dignity, as a moment of truth. The night on which he wrote '*Filial Feelings of a Matricide*' was a turning-point in Proust's life. For the first time he acknowledged his guilt, and was therefore able to forgive his mother; he had gone back beyond the evening at Auteuil when Time Lost began, into the world outside Time where his novel awaited him. He began to descend from the mountains of his mother's death, the watershed of his life, to make the long journey towards revelation and extinction. Which would come first? In the words of his question, which was the truth, it or joy?

Chapter 4

BALBEC REVISITED
(*February – December 1907*)

THE nervous tension caused by Proust's self-identification with a matricide was soon happily relieved by another, more natural death. Ever since the beginning of his stay at Versailles the mother of Georges de Lauris, whom he had never met, had been ill with a biliary calculus, and Proust had given not only condolence but, with visible pride, expert advice on the choice of a surgeon. On 15 February 1907 the afflicted lady died, and Proust took to himself the healing burden of Lauris's grief. 'When you have become accustomed to the dreadful truth,' he predicted, weeping as he wrote, 'that the time when you still had your mother is banished for ever into the past, you will feel her gently returning to life, coming back to take her place, her whole place, beside you.' 'The eyes of memory,' he wrote again, 'see nothing if we strain them too hard. Only try to live, to survive, leave the beloved images to grow in you without the help of your conscious will, and they will be reborn never to leave you again.' Such was his distress that his friends, Reynaldo, Albu, Maurice Duplay, wrote to console him as well as Lauris, and even the grim Marthe, his sister-in-law, telephoned her concern. Now he could identify himself with a son exempt from blame, and the martyred, accusing ghost of Mme Proust could become the 'beloved image' who was to inhabit *A la Recherche*. But he still continued to receive sympathetic letters from comparative strangers on his Van Blarenberghe article, including one from Mme Claire Dieulafoy ('not the man-woman, but her brother-in-law's wife,' he explained to Reynaldo), which was signed, instead of 'yours very sincerely', with a simple: 'May God have you in his keeping.'

All was now quiet in the flat below, where Dr Gagey had at last moved in; but the apartment adjoining Proust's in the house next door had been leased to a certain Madame Katz, whose new water-closets were being installed within a few inches of his pillow. The concierge Antoine took it upon himself to send the lady a letter pointing out that his sleepless lodger was 'the son of the famous Dr Proust', and to deliver it at one in the morning. Proust's entreaties and tips to the workmen were equally in vain; but providentially it turned out that Mme Katz's son, a judge, was a professional acquaintance of Émile Straus. 'If I were you, Marcel, I wouldn't let them raise a hammer till after midnight,' wrote Mme Straus with misplaced irony, for he was now rising a little after mid-day; and she invited M. Katz to lunch for negotiations. Even so the din continued throughout March: 'his cow of a mother is building God knows what,' Proust complained with unwonted discourtesy, 'something as majestic as the Great Pyramid, that I hear but can't see, and which must astound passers-by all the way from the Magasins du Printemps to Saint-Augustin!' Would the water-closets never be finished? 'She's changing the seats—I suppose she found they weren't wide enough.' Dr Bize ordered fresh air, for Proust had not been out of doors since the previous summer. In the earliest days of spring he took his first steps on his balcony, or up and down the pavement outside the house, and saw the sun: "I found it a very beautiful and very strange object," he said.

Meanwhile, in this pale sunlight of convalescence, he wrote a new article for Le Figaro, 'Journées de Lecture', which appeared on 20 March. His subject, once again, was the pleasures of reading; but he now took for his example, instead of Ruskin or the books of his childhood, the just-published memoirs of the Comtesse de Boigne. 'Journées de Lecture' is a practical demonstration of the paradox already announced in 'Sur la Lecture', that light reading is less harmful to the creative writer than the works of genius which may deceive him into believing that the truth he seeks has already been found; for most of its material, although the subscribers to Le Figaro could not have guessed it, would reappear in A la Recherche. In the long digression on the telephone-calls which interrupt his reading Proust thought of his conversation with his mother from Fontainebleau in October 1896, which he had already used in Jean Santeuil. The new treatment, however, retains hardly a vestige of the old; it is already in the mature style of his novel, complete with the superb invocation of 'the Ladies of the Telephone', 'the Danaids of the Invisible', 'the Daughters of Night', and 'the murmured words which I longed to kiss in their flight from lips forever turned to dust'. He was to use the whole passage, with only minor changes in wording, for the Narrator's interview from Doncières with his grandmother in Paris, with the

exception of a paragraph on 'the song of a passer-by, the horn of a
cyclist, a distant fanfare of trumpets', which he transferred to
Albertine's telephone-call on the night of the Princesse de Guermantes's soirée.[1] He recalls Bluebeard and Sister Anne on his magic-
lantern at Illiers[2]; and the Nereids who, 'though ravished from their
sea by an ancient sculptor, might think themselves sporting in it still
as they swim through the waves of their marble frieze', are already
the seanymph Glaukonome and her companions at Balbec.[3] A brief
remark on the magic of the names of places and people, which
mysteriously disperses when we experience the reality ('so that true
wisdom would consist in replacing all social relationships and nearly
all travel by study of the *Almanach de Gotha* and the railway
timetable'), contains for the first time the seeds of the same vast
theme in *A la Recherche*: for Proust's novel is the story of how the
enchantments of nature, society and love, symbolised in the names
of Balbec, Guermantes, Gilberte and Albertine, dissolve inevitably
into Time Lost. But the most extensive contributions to *A la Recherche* came from the book which formed the pretext for his
essay.

The five tall volumes of the Comtesse de Boigne's memoirs cover
the same immense period of time as the accompanying portraits,
which begin with a ringletted, pert-lipped, muslin-veiled beauty of
the First Empire, and end sixty years later with a hunched and sallow
octogenarian, like Mme de Villeparisis at Venice. Mme de Boigne
was born in 1781, and contrived, just in time, to be dandled on the
knees of Louis XVI and Marie Antoinette; she played an intimate
part in social and political life under Napoleon, Louis XVIII,
Charles X and Louis-Philippe, began to write her book in 1837, and
died in 1866, leaving her memoirs and all her wealth to her great-
nephew, the Marquis d'Osmond. Proust's interest in her work was
almost filial: the period of her story, the gentlewomanly, pleasantly
astringent prose-style, he felt, would have delighted his mother and
grandmother; and in his novel, as we have already seen, the memoirs
of the non-existent Mme de Beausergent, which next to Mme de
Sévigné's letters are the favourite literature of the Narrator's grandmother, are really those of the Comtesse de Boigne, which both
Mme Weil and Mme Proust had died too soon to read. But the

---

[1] *Jean Santeuil*, vol. 2, 178-81; *Chroniques*, 84-6; *Pléiade*, II, 133-6, 732.
[2] Cf. I, 10.
[3] Cf. I, 705.

fascination of Mme de Boigne was also unexpectedly personal. The Hôtel de Maillé, of which Proust's first home at 9 Boulevard Malesherbes had been an outlying wing, was inhabited by her great-great-nephew and his wife, the Comte and Comtesse François de Maillé; the dowager Duchesse de Maillé, whom he had seen as an aged wall-flower at her last society balls in the 1890s, was her niece; and her heir the Marquis d'Osmond, whose letters and photograph he had recently discovered in the papers of his dead parents, had frequently entertained Dr and Mme Proust as his dinner-guests. Proust introduced M. d'Osmond three times over into his novel; once in his own name as the friend of Charlus and Swann who dies so inconsiderately on the evening when the Duc and Duchesse are to attend a fancy-dress ball; again as the young Marquis de Beausergent in the Princesse de Guermantes's box at the Opera; and yet again as the Duc de Guermantes himself as a boy, for whom his aunt Mme de Beausergent, Mme de Villeparisis's sister, writes her memoirs.[1] Thanks to Mme de Boigne he thought again of the Maillés; and his future Duc and Duchesse de Guermantes could now develop a stage further from the Réveillons, their prototypes in *Jean Santeuil*, to become the nobles in whose house the Narrator lived, whose visitors he could watch from his window, and who were on nodding terms with his parents. The world of Mme de Boigne was familiar in other ways. Again and again in her pages he noticed the names of his friends and hostesses—Breteuil, FitzJames, Greffulhe, Guiche, La Rochefoucauld, Montesquiou, Noailles, Polignac, Potocka; but these were the great-grandparents of the people he knew, and in Mme de Boigne's memoirs the dimension of time seemed at once inexplicably lengthened and vertiginously foreshortened. Sometimes, too, he found a name long extinct and remembered it for his novel: he used Luxembourg for the raffish princess at Balbec, the Balzacian christian name Victurnien for the son of Mme de Surgis to whom M. de Charlus takes a fancy[2]; and he borrowed the title of Duchesse

---

[1] II, 575-89, III, 300; II, 55-6; III, 715. Proust makes a significant error when he states (*Chroniques*, 89) that his parents' friend, M. d'Osmond, whose portrait as a charming child with blond curls is among the illustrations to the memoirs, was the nephew for whom Mme de Boigne wrote her book. In fact M. d'Osmond was her great-nephew, and the memoirs were written for his father Comte Rainulphe d'Osmond, the Duchesse de Maillé's brother, who predeceased Mme de Boigne in 1862.

[2] II, 698-9. On this occasion M. de Charlus mentions Montesquiou, his own original, as one of the few people in the Faubourg who know their Balzac.

de Duras, borne by Mme Verdurin in her brief second marriage,[1] from the lady who had been in love ninety years before with the great Chateaubriand. His reading of Mme de Boigne, indeed, was perhaps an important factor in his decision to call his heroine Albertine. Albertine's name, like that of Saint-Loup, had many simultaneous sources: he knew it already from Marceline Desbordes-Valmore's poem, from his hostess Albertine de Montebello, from Clomesnil's rival Albertine Groscul, from Princesse Albertine de Broglie, who inherited it from Mme de Staël's daughter, her great-grandmother, and we shall find reason a little later to associate it with several young men. But in the memoirs of Mme de Boigne he found Mlle de Staël herself described at the age of eleven, a century ago, in terms which suggest the precocious Albertine of whom the Narrator hears her aunt Mme Bontemps speaking at Odette's at-home: ' "what's the matter, Albertine?" asked Mme de Boigne—"oh dear, everyone thinks I'm happy, and my heart is full of abysses!" ' And Mme de Boigne might have almost foreseen the enigmatic young girl on the front at Balbec when she wrote, a few years later: 'despite the somewhat daring colour of her hair, and a slight tendency towards freckles, Albertine de Staël was one of the most enchanting people I have ever met, and there was something angelic, pure and ideal in her face which I have never seen in any other'.[2]

Proust sent cuttings of 'Sentiments filiaux' and 'Journées de Lecture' to Marie Nordlinger, asking her to return them 'in case I ever decide to publish a volume of my articles'—a plan to which he was often to revert in the next few years, though it only reached fruition twelve years later, in Pastiches et Mélanges. Georges de Lauris delighted him by reading the latter article to his bereaved father, and by declaring it 'better than Francis Jammes'—an author whom Proust had first read in June 1906, and was to regard later as one of his own precursors. Even Montesquiou wrote to congratulate him, though only by way of a hint that he was still expecting a eulogy of Les Hortensias bleus, the first volume of the extremely expensive de luxe edition of his complete poetical works, for which he had insisted on Proust's taking out a subscription in the previous December. Count Robert called early in April to autograph his latest essays, Altesses sérénissimes, and held forth in a monologue as brilliant as ever. But the signs of approaching old age were visible

---

[1] III, 955.
[2] Boigne, Mémoires, vol. 1, 256, 413.

beneath the rouge and powder of his cheeks; and was there not a note of malice in Marcel's reassurance: 'it isn't age that gives you the pink, wrinkled face of a moss-rose, a flower which, as well you know, has a beauty of its own!'? The Count took umbrage, and Proust had to find excuses for his simile: 'in the now distant era when we used to meet at Mme Lemaire's on the first fine evenings of spring, and take off our overcoats under the lilacs, I saw you once with an exquisite flower in your button-hole, which you told me was a moss-rose,' he explained; and in the memory at least there was no prevarication, for he had used it long ago in *Jean Santeuil*, in a passage which mentioned Montesquiou by name.[1]

In the spring Proust performed a favour for Maurice Duplay, now director of the Théâtre de Cluny, by recommending a struggling actress, Mlle Macherez, to Louisa de Mornand. Louisa, who was now established in her new liaison with Robert Gangnat, the legal agent of the Société des Auteurs Dramatiques, was generous to 'this little Cinderella, who went home dazzled by your charm'. Perhaps it was at this time that Duplay took Proust to a favourite brothel. The manageress and her staff put on their politest manners, and Proust courteously co-operated, showing absolute belief that one young whore was indeed an actress 'resting', and another was 'a lady in society'. He even gave a family sideboard to 'Toinette', and found her a more respectable post as mannequin at Paquin's. Perhaps this pathetic but by no means ignoble habit of visiting brothels in quest of social relaxation, which belonged also to Swann and the Narrator,[2] was lifelong. As late as 1921 Paul Léautaud recorded Proust's way of driving with Odilon Albaret to one of these establishments, where he would ask two or three of the young ladies to step down, regale them with glasses of milk, and converse for hours in his darkling taxi on love, death and kindred subjects. Another of Duplay's revelations belongs apparently to the period before the death of Proust's parents: he felt 'a tender interest' in a young friend of Duplay's family, Mlle Hélène d'Ideville, 'whose mysterious beauty was like a painting by Leonardo', and who 'inspired in him ideas of marriage'. Here, perhaps, is a faint hint of Albertine in her socially presentable aspect, the niece of Mme Bontemps whom the Narrator's

[1] *Jean Santeuil*, vol. 1, 205. Similarly the Baron de Charlus, after eyeing the Narrator so strangely at Balbec, pretends to be busy arranging 'the moss-rose that hung in his button-hole' (I, 752).

[2] I, 373, 575-8.

mother is prepared to accept, however reluctantly, as her son's
fiancée.

On 11 April Proust made his first appearance in society for nearly
two years by attending the première of Reynaldo Hahn's orchestral
suite *Le Bal de Béatrice d'Este* at the Princesse de Polignac's.
Reynaldo conducted from his seat at the piano, and at his loudest
chords the tottering candlesticks seemed about to fall and set fire to
the paper roses on the dais[1]; but Proust forgot the danger of this
catastrophe when he noticed how Reynaldo's warning forefinger
a moment later 'became a magic baton which flew to the furthest
corner of the orchestra, just in time to wake a little sleeping triangle'.
Most of all, however, he was interested to see, after his long absence,
'how all the people I used to know have aged!' This musical At
Home supplied the first hint of another, at which the Narrator
realised, amid the wreckage of a world grown old around him, that
the recovery of Time Lost would be a race against death.

It was also in the spring of 1907 that Proust conducted his last
friendship with a beautiful young nobleman. The Marquis Illan de
Casa-Fuerte was the son of the Empress Eugénie's niece, the lovely
Flavie de Casa-Fuerte whom Montesquiou had adored nearly twenty
years before. His extraordinary good looks were of the kind which
seem (until, a whole generation late, they suddenly decompose into
old age) to last for ever: 'he was an incarnation of Dorian Gray',
wrote André Germain; and D'Annunzio, who knew him through
Montesquiou, used Illan as a model for Aldo, 'a young, fallen god', in
his novel *Forse chè si*. Proust and Illan had met when the young
marquis was still a schoolboy. Lucien Daudet had taken him one
evening to the Grand Guignol, saying mysteriously: "we shall be
meeting a friend of mine afterwards"; and there, on the pavement
outside the theatre, stood Proust in crumpled evening-clothes and
shaggy top-hat, with drooping moustache and enormous dark-
ringed eyes which seemed, said Illan, 'to eat up the rest of his face'.
They supped at Larue's, where Proust discussed his asthma and
insomnia: "I lie awake until morning, and it's only when I hear our
manservant saying to the cook: 'Hush, you'll wake Monsieur Marcel,'
that I fall into a deep sleep." When Illan began to visit 102 Boulevard

---

[1] Proust remembered this impression for the performance of the Vinteuil
Sonata at Mme de Saint-Euverte's soirée, when the forward young Mme de
Cambremer, much to Général de Froberville's admiration, dashes out to remove
the candlestick (I, 336).

Haussmann he shyly confessed that he, too, suffered from asthma, "particularly from the smell of horses, so I've had to give up riding!" Charmed by his host's lyrical description of the scents of flowers and leaves which caused *his* asthma, Illan declared: "I say, that's poetry!" to which Proust crossly replied: "You mean, it's torture." Next morning Illan received a long letter on 'the appalling attack caused by your perfume' which had followed his visit, together with a parcel containing so many packets of Legras anti-asthma powders that the Marquis, nearly thirty years later, remarked 'I still have several left'. In return Illan sent a pink coral box, in whose colour the coquettish Proust saw 'a delicate tinge of friendship': 'I have seen, desired, mourned it,' he wrote, 'deep in the gulfs of ocean, and high in the skies of summer, where seven o'clock in the evening stripped its last roses of their petals and left them strewn over the fields of the sea.'[1] Proust was equally delighted by his young friend's archaic Christian name. 'When the late Marquis de Casa-Fuerte wished to give his son a christening-gift', he wrote in an unpublished article,[2] 'he found no rarer or sweeter jewel in eleventh-century Spain—not even in the leather of Cordova, or Arab goblets with their pink and yellow-pink reflections—than the forename of Illan, which no one had borne since the capture of Toledo in 1085, and which seemed to have been preserved by a vein of marble lacework in some half-Moslem cathedral, lit by candles unextinguished for nearly a thousand years.' But their relationship was no more than a brief platonic flirtation between an older man and a youth accustomed to admiration from either sex; and if a parallel to Illan exists in *A la Recherche* it is the 'young Létourville' from whom the Narrator, after meeting him at the last matinée of the Princesse de Guermantes, is appalled to receive a letter signed 'your very respectful young friend'.[3]

Proust was fifteen years senior to the boyish marquis; he had abandoned all hope of satisfactory friendship within the aristocracy, and now sought, with the inverse snobism of the heart, only the

---

[1] An image used by Legrandin at Combray in his rhapsody on the sunsets of Balbec (I, 130).

[2] The passage probably belonged to the digression on Christian names in *'Journées de Lecture'* (an article which is known to have been severely cut), or to its promised sequel *'On Snobism and Posterity'* (cf. *Chroniques*, 87, 90) which was never published, although Proust actually sent it to *Le Figaro*.

[3] III, 927-8.

equally precarious devotion of the working-classes—for the time being, of his secretary Ulrich. Perhaps it was just as well that Ulrich was not particularly interested in men, and Proust was not displeased to discover that he had a mistress, who wrote to him: 'so just one more little peck, big fond lover, for this tiny morsel of a woman who isn't the usual sort, oh no, but's thine'. "As you see, she goes on to quote some poetry, beginning '*Love is such a peculiar feeling, It's all or it's nothing, is love*'", Ulrich pointed out: "now that, I'm quite certain, is by Victor Hugo"; and he added: "as a matter of fact, she isn't exactly pretty, but I go to bed with her because she's so extraordinarily intelligent, as you can tell from her letter."

The impact of Illan's beauty on Montesquiou was more serious. The Count felt, as he had with others of Marcel's friends, such as Delafosse, Reynaldo Hahn and Lucien Daudet, that here was his longed-for spiritual heir. André Germain was present at the reception on a radiant June afternoon, amid the roses of the Pavillon des Muses, of the Marquis and his young bride Béatrice, on whose forehead Count Robert imprinted a chaste kiss; and again at the dreadful scene which marked the inevitable end. A portrait of Illan in the Salon showed a great deal too much of his neck and shoulders and almost led, it was rumoured, to his expulsion from his club, the Cercle de l'Union. Montesquiou cursed painter, portrait and model in a paroxysm of fury which made the gallery and everyone in it tremble. Even the portrait had an unhappy ending: some years later Illan's second wife was urged by her maid on no account to enter the drawing-room where it was hung, "because a lady called this morning and cut Monsieur le Marquis's eyes out!"

The publication of Mme de Noailles's latest poems, *Les Éblouissements*, was now imminent. Already, in '*Journées de Lecture*', Proust had announced that the new volume would be equal to *Feuilles d'Automne* and *Les Fleurs du Mal* combined; and then, just as after giving a stupendous tip to a waiter he always had qualms lest it might not be quite enough, he telephoned the poetess to enquire whether there were other works of genius to which she would prefer hers to be compared. However, his admiration for her writing had never been more justified. *Les Éblouissements* was the product of her love for Barrès, a love now ending, for Barrès in a feeling that he could no longer cope with her interminable effervescence, for Mme de Noailles in a fury of injured vanity which ravaged the rest of her life; and these voluptuous, anguished and truly 'dazzling' poems, by their technical influence during the next few years upon Valéry and Cocteau, were to help to bridge the gap between symbolism and the twentieth century.[1]

Proust's review gave him more than usual trouble. His efforts to get it on the front page, to prevent drastic cutting, or banishment to the *Figaro Literary Supplement*, 'which is a foretaste of eternal oblivion', were in vain. One morning, while he was writing, the inside of his chimney collapsed; the concierge Antoine heroically performed first-aid repairs at the risk of asphyxiation; and then workmen mended the damage all day, in a cloud of plaster and brick-dust, while Proust lugubriously watched them from his bed. He wrote against the grain, for the still-subterranean rising of his own genius was now so far advanced that he would never again submit himself wholeheartedly to the literature of other writers, even of those greater than Mme de Noailles; and his mixed feelings are evident in the discords of irony and impatience which sound beneath the high pitch of his praise. But here and there a remark suggests that the revelation of *A la Recherche* is very near indeed. 'She knows,' he says, 'that a profound idea which has time and space enclosed within it is no longer subject to their tyranny, and becomes infinite in extent and duration'; and 'her metaphors substitute for a description of what exists a resurrection of what we have felt—which is the only reality of any interest'. Remembering the Japanese dwarf trees at Bing's, he sent Ulrich to buy three, which he contemplated at his bedside and used for his review, in words repeated by Albertine in her rhapsody on ice-cream, as a simile of the immensity which can be contained in a single line of poetry.[2] Not only his review, how-ever, but the very words of Mme de Noailles supplied hints for his novel. The poems on gardens, which formed one of the sincerest elements in her inspiration, since they reached back to her childhood

[1] To take Valéry only, and to quote only a few of many parallels, such lines as (p. 410):

> '*Tout l'azur chaque jour tombé dans ma poitrine*
> *S'élançait en gestes sans fin . . .*'

contain the essence of *La Jeune Parque*, while the seed of *Le Cimetière marin* is in (p. 5)

> '*Je crois voir, ses pieds nus appuyés sur les tombes,*
> *Un Éros souriant qui nourrit des colombes*'

or in (p. 386)

> '*Hélios . . . Tu me lances tes feux en t'écriant: Va vivre!*'

[2] III, 130; *Chroniques*, 187.

at Amphion and a lost time of innocence, were foreshadowings of
Combray; and he remembered three lines of a poem on Venice—

> 'La Dogana, le soir, montrant sa boule d'or
> Semble arrêter le temps et prolonger encor
> La forme du soleil qui descend dans l'abîme . . .

for the scene where the Narrator watches the sun frozen in the act of
setting over the dome of the Salute.[1]

His review appeared on 15 June in the outer darkness of the
Figaro Literary Supplement. He called on Calmette at midnight in the
Figaro offices (where midnight, as for himself, was the equivalent of
high noon elsewhere), and thanked him profusely for printing it at
all. "I should like to have you to dinner," he said unguardedly,
thinking, as he told Mme Straus, "that I might be well enough to
give a dinner in a few years, or before my death, which is perhaps
less distant"; but Calmette urbanely pulled out his notebook,
searched for a vacant date, and asked: "would July the first suit
you?"

The dinner of 1 July in a private room at the Ritz was Proust's
first and last 'grand dinner' for several years; it was also his first
recorded appearance at the hotel in the Place Vendôme from which he
was later to seem so inseparable that people would call him 'Proust
of the Ritz'. The guests, for whom Ulrich was deputed to telephone
all over Paris while his master slept, might well recall to an Anglo-
Saxon reader the words of Blake's *Island in the Moon*—'so all the
people in this book enter'd into the room'. The ladies included the
Comtesses de Brantes, Briey, Haussonville, Ludre and Noailles, and
Élisabeth de Clermont-Tonnerre, who brought her reactionary anti-
Dreyfusist husband Philibert; among the men, besides Calmette
himself, were Albu, Guiche, Jacques Émile Blanche, Proust's former
second Jean Béraud, Beaunier of *Le Figaro* and Emmanuel Bibesco.
The dinner, for which Guiche had chosen the food and wines, went
perfectly; the guests seemed delighted to see their resurrected host,
and old Mme de Brantes was true to form by being charming to
Proust and malicious to everyone else. After dinner came Illan de
Casa-Fuerte and Vicomte Robert d'Humières with their wives, Mme
de Chevigné, the Princesse de Polignac, Gabriel de La Rochefoucauld, Reginald Lister from the British Embassy, whom Proust
had known since the early '90s at Mme Straus's, and Ulrich himself;

[1] III, 1114; *Contre Sainte-Beuve*, 124.

and all adjourned to a gold and cherry-red drawing-room for music. Fauré had promised to play, but had been prevented only the day before by a sudden illness, the beginning of his subsequent deafness; and Proust had turned in desperation to his old friend Risler, who performed piano music by Beethoven, Chopin, Couperin and Fauré, and at Proust's special request the overture to the *Mastersingers* and the Liebestod from *Tristan*. Maurice Hayot, the professor of the violin at the Conservatoire, accompanied by Fauré's favourite pupil Mlle Hasselmans, played Fauré's Violin Sonata, one of the originals of Vinteuil's. Proust noted how Mme d'Haussonville swayed the long aigrette of her head-dress like a metronome, as much as to say "I know this piece backwards!"; and he used his observation for the dowager Marquise de Cambremer's rapture in the Vinteuil Sonata at Mme de Saint-Euverte's.[1] During the interval Élisabeth de Clermont-Tonnerre watched Proust and Mme de Noailles, two strange figures in furs, like a male and female Eskimo, circulating among the guests. "I gave Risler 1,000 francs," he whispered anxiously to the older ladies, "do you think it was enough?"; and "a great deal too much!" they replied in chorus, for he was spoiling their own market.

On 23 July in *Le Figaro* Proust published an obituary on Robert de Flers's grandmother, almost devoid of literary merit, but interesting because he is evidently mourning, in Mme de Rozière's name, for his own grandmother and mother. It is possible that this accidental equation of his beloved dead assisted in a fundamental feature of the structure of his novel—the taking-over by the Narrator's grandmother of many of the functions of Proust's own mother, above all of her death. Perhaps this article also revived his desire to revisit a place where he had grieved, sixteen years before, for his grandmother, and where he would now mourn again for his mother.

Dr Bize insisted that Proust should take a holiday immediately, for he had spent the past two years almost entirely in bed. On 1 August he was still hesitating, as he told Reynaldo, between 'Brittany, Cabourg, Touraine, Germany—and remaining in Paris'; but a few days later he made the choice which determined the future course of his novel and of his life. He had stayed at Cabourg as a child with his grandmother, and again with Mme Proust on his army leave in September 1890; when alone at Cabourg in September 1891 he had been overcome, like his Narrator, by a sudden renewal of

[1] I, 328.

grief for Mme Weil, who had died in January of the previous year;
a visit to Cabourg had been vaguely planned for August 1896; in
August 1903 his mother had unsuccessfully urged him to go there,
because 'you used to find it suited your health so well'; and only a
year ago Cabourg had been in his list of possibilities before he
finally decided on Versailles. When he left, about 7 August, for this
paradise of his past, it was in quest of the sunlit seas of Time Lost
and of the two dead women who would watch over him there: 'it
was the memory of Mother, who continues to guide me aright, that
led me to Cabourg,' he told Mme Catusse. But he also went to meet
a destiny which in years to come would complete and destroy the
circle of his being.

The visitor who beheld the stately hotels of the Cabourg seafront
would hardly guess that here was one of the ancient places of France.
The name, by a derivation which Brichot at La Raspelière would
certainly have explained if Mme Verdurin had not interrupted him
in time, came (like Caithness in Scotland) from the Norse root Cath,
a harbour-basin; it was here in 1058 that William of Normandy, the
future conqueror of England, hurled the troops of Henri I of France
into the sea, while the unhappy monarch, in the words of the minstrel
Wace,

> '*Mounting the hill of Bassebourg,*
> *Saw Varaville and saw Cabourg*'.[1]

But the modern Cabourg began in 1853 with the arrival of two
Paris financiers in search of a new site for a luxurious watering-place.
The railway age had made the Normandy coast accessible to holiday-
makers; Dieppe, Trouville and Deauville to the east had already
been discovered; but here the adventurers found a virgin expanse of
barren dunes and level sea-sands ripe for development. By the 1880s
an unreal city of villas and hotels had arisen, in a semicircle whose
diameter was the seafront, whose centre was the Grand Hôtel, and
whose radii were traced by a fan-work of avenues shaded with limes
and Normandy poplars. It was in this hinterland that the Narrator
visited Elstir's studio, 'on one of the newest avenues of Balbec, in
which his villa was perhaps the most sumptuously ugly of all'.[2] A
little past the frontier of the new town, nearly a mile inland from the

[1]   '*Monté fu de suz Basseborc,*
                          Vit Varaville e vit Caborc'.

[2] I, 833.

sea, was old Cabourg, a hamlet of thatched cottages and farmhouses, where ducks and hens ran among the fishnets hung to dry. Nevertheless, the equivalent near Cabourg of Balbec-le-Vieux or Balbec-en-Terre was not Cabourg-le-Vieux, but the mediaeval town of Dives, to which the road runs from Cabourg-le-Vieux eastward over the estuary of the little Dives river. Here, not as at Balbec 'more than five leagues away',[1] was the railway-station which served both Cabourg and Dives. The church of Dives was a huge, square-towered, fourteenth-century building which Proust as a boy with his grandmother must have visited, like the Narrator, on alighting from the train before going on to Cabourg or Trouville. The 'half-romanesque, almost Persian'[2] church of Balbec was transferred hither from Saint-Loup-de-Naud; but Dives, too, had its romanesque pillars and sculptured porch, and was famed, like the church of Balbec,[3] for its wooden figure of Christ miraculously cast ashore in A.D. 1001. This legend may have led the boy Proust to expect 'a church receiving at its base the last foam of angry waves'[4]; but the sea had receded long since, and Dives like Balbec-en-Terre was disappointingly far inland. To complete the Narrator's disillusionment Proust transferred to Balbec from his visit to Saint-Malo in the yacht *Hélène* the tramcars, the billiard-room and the statue of Admiral Duguay-Trouin.[5]

Cabourg is a little over 150 miles from Paris: the railway-journey from the Gare Saint-Lazare lasted only five and a half hours, and the 'beautiful, generous, one-twenty-two train' arrived in time for dinner the same evening. For the Narrator's long night-journey to the end of the world Proust thought of his own flight to Brittany with Reynaldo in 1895, and for the mountain valley lit simultaneously by sunrise and moon, of his sleepless train-ride through the gorges of the Yonne to Avallon in 1903. At Mézidon, eighteen miles before Cabourg, the traveller changed from the Paris-Cherbourg express to the local train which meandered, stopping at every village and small seaside-resort, past Cabourg-Dives to Trouville. Mézidon is Doncières in its aspect as junction-town for Balbec; and this 'Transatlantic' to Cabourg and Trouville was none other than the 'Little Train'. Just as the Narrator would set out with Albertine from Balbec, joined at every wayside station by members of 'the faithful', to Douville, the terminus for Mme Verdurin's La Raspelière,

[1] I, 658.   [2] I, 385.   [3] I, 658.
[4] I, 659.   [5] I, 659, 664; II, 772.

so Proust would journey past stations each with a name in '-ville', and symbolising a friend staying nearby, to Louisa de Mornand at Bénerville or Mme Straus's Clos des Mûriers at Trouville. Several of the names of places served by the Little Train at Balbec come from villages in the same district: Saint-Vaast, Douville, Angerville, Saint-Pierre-aux-Ifs are all here. Other names in the same exquisite litany—Hermonville, Saint-Mars-le-Vieux, Toutainville, Montmartin, Incarville, Infreville, Graincourt, Bricquebec, La Sogne, Fervaches—are taken with little or no change from parts of Normandy more or less distant from Cabourg: Proust had only to study his map and choose. A few, such as Hermenonville, Gourville, Marcouville and La Raspelière itself, come from near Illiers: 'these names seemed strange to me,' says the Narrator, 'although if I had read them in a book I should have seen that they had some connection with the names of places near Combray.'[1] We have already found two places in the country of Balbec, Féterne and Rivebelle, on the shores of Lake Geneva near Évian. There is, however, a Riva-Bella eight miles west of Cabourg, reached in Proust's time by a humbler relative of the Little Train known as a steam-tram, which plied through Le Homme-sur-Mer, Merville, Ouistreham, Riva-Bella and Lion-sur-Mer to Luc-sur-Mer. But Rivebelle as a beautiful apparition seen far across the bay from Balbec, enjoying a longer summer because it faces southward, is Le Havre on the opposite side of the Seine estuary, though this is not a holiday town but a busy port; and as a pleasure haunt with a superb restaurant Rivebelle is a synthesis of other resorts to the east of Cabourg, such as Houlgate, Villers-sur-Mer, Deauville or Trouville. The farm-restaurants of La Croix d'Heuland and Marie-Antoinette, with their cider and cherries, which the Narrator frequented with Albertine and the little band,[2] are both within a mile of Saint-Vaast on the Cabourg-Trouville railway. The Narrator praises by name another, more sumptuous farm-restaurant, that of Guillaume-le-Conquèrant at Dives,[3] which served, as Proust thought, the best cider of all.

In this very year Canon Joseph Marquis of Saint-Jacques at

---

[1] I, 661. Conversely the name Combray itself is that of a village fifteen miles south of Caen: we may be sure that when Proust saw it on his map it chimed with his knowledge of the town called Combres near Illiers, and so gave him the name for the village of the Narrator's childhood.

[2] I, 903-4; II, 837; III, 479.

[3] II, 35.

Illiers, who had taught the boy Marcel Latin and the names of the flowers in his presbytery garden, published his learned monograph *Illiers* in the series of *Archives historiques du diocèse de Chartres*. The good canon's interest in place-names is less exclusive than that of the curé of Combray; but he rather shakily discusses the derivations of Illiers (the Celtic Illia=*ville*), Montjouvin (rejecting a rival's *Mons Jovis*, but supplying no alternative), Tansonville (the *étançons* or props of the nearby bridge over the Thironne), La Rachepelière (from *arrache pieux*, alluding to the exploit of Eudes d'Arrachepel in removing stakes from a moat in a mediaeval siege),[1] and the like. Probably because Proust read this volume during or near the time of his visit to Cabourg, he made the curé of Combray, who is 'spending the last years of his life in writing a great work on Combray and its environs', publish 'a rather interesting little brochure', as the Dowager-Marquise de Cambremer tells the Narrator, on the place-names of Normandy.[2] It was not until twelve years later, however, in 1919, that Proust began his researches for Brichot's brilliant refutation of the poor curé's etymologies at La Raspelière,[3] and corresponded for this purpose with the great French authorities on place-names, Louis Dimier and Henri Longnon.

In the train from Paris that August Proust was joined by Dr Doyen, who remarked, exactly in the manner of Cottard, "Isn't it odd that Mme Greffulhe has never managed to round up such a brilliant salon as Mme Arman de Caillavet!" He stayed at the Grand Hôtel, which like its namesake at Balbec was an enormous edifice on the seafront, with 200 bedrooms, a lift, and a long dining-room from which a succession of plate-glass windows opened directly on the promenade, the sands, and the dazzling sea. Adjoining the hotel to the west was the casino, lined by a row of flagpoles and containing a theatre, a concert-hall, a ball-room and gambling tables. It was near this casino that Charlus eyed the Narrator so strangely, and within it that Bloch's cousin Esther Lévy behaved so scandalously with the actress Léa, the Narrator joined the little band in teasing the dancing-master, and Octave ('In the Soup') played baccarat.[4] To the east was the bathing-establishment of the hotel, where sea-water baths,

---

[1] Cf. II, 963, where M. de Cambremer gives a similar etymology for La Raspelière.

[2] I, 203; II, 809.

[3] II, 887-91, 913, 922.

[4] I, 751; I, 903; II, 902, 853; I, 893; I, 677.

cold showers and perhaps other pleasures were available, for it was here that the Narrator suspected Albertine of going for the same illicit purposes as Léa and her friends.[1] On the sands immediately below the hotel was the bandstand, where the Narrator hears a symphony concert on the morning of his introduction to the Princesse de Luxembourg.[2] At high tide the music mingled with the waves and seemed to come from under the sea; and the violins 'hummed like a swarm of bees that had strayed over the water'.[3]

For the first few days Proust was overcome by renewed grief for his mother. His 'intermittences of the heart' were more complex than those of the Narrator on his second arrival at Balbec: the Grand Hôtel was peopled with memories not only of his mother but of poor Mme Weil, now seventeen years in her grave, and his two bereavements joined here into one. It was symptomatic that his first excursion was to visit the motherless Georges de Lauris and his widower father at Houlgate, the next station past Dives-Cabourg of the little train. With unconscious cruelty he insisted on borrowing Georges's favourite photograph of his dead mother: "I want to look at it when I'm alone," he said; and he told Lauris that he had never been so unhappy: 'sorrow isn't meant to be stirred, one needs to keep still to give it time to settle and become serene and limpid again'.

The penance of grief, however, was not his primary object in returning to Cabourg. Mme Straus's son Jacques Bizet, his former schoolfellow, was now the director of a car-hire company, the Taximètres Unic de Monaco, with branches in Monaco, Paris and Cabourg. Proust saw the possibility of renewing in Normandy the visits by automobile to churches and cathedrals which he had enjoyed with the Bibesco brothers in the spring of 1902. He wrote before leaving to Emmanuel Bibesco for 'archeologico-spiritual advice', and again to Émile Mâle, after unsuccessfully sending Ulrich to beg him to call. At this time he intended to move on to Brittany, and this abortive plan may have helped in the fusion of Cabourg with Beg-Meil, and the situation of Balbec in a mysterious borderland between Normandy and the Atlantic promontories. Another request related still more directly to his novel, for he asked Mâle to recommend 'an old, untouched, Balzacian provincial town, which would be still more fruitful for my dreams than an ordinary cathedral, or even a sublime one'. Before the end of his first week at Cabourg he had

[1] III, 491.
[2] I, 698.   [3] I, 954; II, 780.

hired his taxi-cab and his three drivers, Jossien, Odilon Albaret, and Agostinelli.

Alfred Agostinelli was a native of Monaco, the son of Eugène Agostinelli, an Italian from Leghorn. His mother, *née* Marie Louise Bensa, of Provençal birth with, it is said, some Arab blood, had already borne ten children to a previous husband named Vittoré, before producing Alfred and his brother Émile. Alfred was a young man of eighteen,[1] whose round face, large, dark-ringed eyes and black moustache gave him a curious, fleeting resemblance to the master to whom he was later to cause such suffering. Agostinelli was photographed that summer, in his black rubber driving-cape and peaked cap, sitting with Albaret in one of the primeval Unic taxis by the public gardens behind the Grand Hôtel: his features show intelligence and ingratiating charm, with a perhaps deceptive hint of softness and indolence, but no sign of evil. It must be said at once that in all the evidence for Proust's relationship with Agostinelli during the next seven years there is nothing for which this honest and amiable young man can be blamed.

The next two months were among the strangest and perhaps the happiest—though he still repeated that he had never been 'so agitated, so sterile, so miserable'—in Proust's life. Every day he hurtled through the Normandy landscape, past frightened villages, immense panoramas of sea, green forests, fruiting hawthorns and apple-trees, beside this sleek and efficient young hireling. Poetic images arose in his mind, roused both by the beauty of Agostinelli's presence and by the mystery of his craft. 'His black rubber cape,' he wrote a few months later, 'and the hooded helmet which enclosed the fullness of his young, beardless face, made him resemble a pilgrim, or rather, a nun of speed.' As he deftly touched first one, then another secret lever, changing the tone and pitch of the engine's droning, he seemed like Saint Cecilia improvising some divine melody on her celestial organ; and the wheel over which he bowed so intently, a cross within a circle, seemed like an emblem carried by a stone saint in a cathedral to display the characteristic of his virtue on earth or the instrument of his death. 'May the steering-wheel of my young mechanic,' Proust prayed in vain, 'remain for ever the symbol of his talent, rather than the prefiguration of his martyrdom!' On they flared: Proust led, he told Lauris, 'the life of a cannon-ball in flight'; and when he alighted from the car, 'a kind of trembling like that of the motor continues to

[1] He was born on 11 October 1888.

hum and vibrate in me, and won't let my hand come to rest and obey me'. Asthma, despite the rush of wind and clouds of dust, had left him: at the cost of taking innumerable cups of coffee at wayside farmhouses, but little or no food, he was staying awake all day.

His first trip was to Caen, through the labyrinth of rivulets and marshlands west of the Dives, past Varavalle and Gonneville to the watershed above the Orne. The city was invisible in the vast blue plain below them: its position was marked by the spires of Saint-Étienne and Saint-Pierre, soon joined by that of Saint-Sauveur and the towers of La Trinité, which refused inexorably to draw nearer, yet as the road wound right and left seemed to change places in a ritual dance. An ancient memory returned to Proust: he saw again the movement of the village spires round the wide horizon of the Méréglise way, as they glided into ever-different angles of relationship with the steeple of Saint-Jacques at Illiers. Here at Caen the shifting spires were at the centre of a circle, at Illiers they had danced along its circumference; yet the two visions, united across a gulf of space and time, were miraculously the same. Suddenly he was driving through the city: the spires of Saint-Étienne, 'towering over us like giants with their full height, threw themselves so brutally in our way that we only just had time to avoid colliding with the porch'. A few days later he visited Bayeux Cathedral, which he preferred to the churches of Caen, although he complained to Émile Mâle that he had found the iconography of its sculptures bafflingly obscure. At Balleroy, ten miles south of Bayeux, he saw the château, built by Mansard, decorated by Mignard and famous for its tapestries by Boucher: it was one of the few châteaux of France still inhabited, like Guermantes by the Duc de Guermantes, by the family to whom the nearby village had long ago given its name. But Proust was ill-pleased with the late Comte de Balleroy, who had scattered among the Bouchers, which his son had framed in red damask, his own excruciating paintings of hunting-scenes.[1] He called on Marquis Charles d'Eyragues and his wife Henriette, Montesquiou's cousin,

[1] Proust used his memory of Balleroy for the Château de Guermantes. Saint-Loup informs the Narrator that its tapestries were not mediaeval as he supposed, but 'by Boucher, bought in the nineteenth century by an art-loving Guermantes, who had hung beside them the mediocre hunting-scenes which he had painted himself, in an ugly drawingroom draped with red plush' (II, 14, 15). Mme de Balleroy is the great-aunt of the Duchesse de Guermantes's niece, who sends the Narrator a declaration of love to which, crushed by the departure of Albertine, he can make no reply (III, 190, 449).

at their mansion in the market-place of Falaise, with its gardens descending to the rapid stream, and remembered the occasion next year in a charming paragraph of *Contre Sainte-Beuve*.[1] On another day they arrived late at Lisieux, twenty miles south-east of Cabourg and near the small town of Cambremer, which gave its name (pronounced 'Camembert' by the lift-boy) to the Cambremers in *A la Recherche*. When they reached the cathedral night had fallen, and Proust despaired of seeing the porch (through which Henry II of England had passed at his wedding to Eleanor of Guyenne in 1152), with its trees of stone mentioned by Ruskin; but the resourceful Agostinelli played his headlamps from leaf to leaf of the arboreal pillars, and night was turned to day.

Proust had visited Balleroy for the sake of its Bouchers with the artist Paul Helleu, who hoped to convert him to his theory that 'the primitives are worthless, my dear Marcel, because nobody knew how to paint before Rubens', and that painting reached its zenith in the eighteenth century. Helleu's own art was based on this belief, and Degas had called him 'a steam Watteau', a joke which the unfortunate Saniette at La Raspelière transfers to Elstir, saying that he prefers Helleu to Elstir as a moderniser of the eighteenth century.[2] Elstir, in fact, in one of his multitudinous aspects, is based on Helleu, from whose name (as well as Whistler's) his own is taken. The rather anomalous Elstirs which the Narrator sees on his first visit to the Hôtel de Guermantes—the 'man in evening-dress in his own drawing-room', and the same person 'in frock coat and top-hat at a regatta where he was obviously out of place'—were identified by Jacques Émile Blanche as paintings by Helleu.[3] Helleu was staying in Deauville at the time, perhaps in the very studio visited by the Narrator; and in this environment he must have seemed more than ever like his description by Léon Daudet's friend Paul Mariéton: 'he looks like an invitation to a funeral taking a holiday at the seaside'. He was a cadaverous, nervous, yellow-faced, black-bearded man, and always wore black; unlike Elstir, with his 'beautiful Gabrielle', whom Mme

---

[1] *Contre Sainte-Beuve*, 274-5.

[2] II, 938-9.

[3] II, 420-2. The mythological Elstirs which the Narrator sees on the same occasion, the poet walking with a Muse or riding on the back of a centaur, are pictures by Gustave Moreau, whom Proust had already discussed in similar words in an essay on Moreau written in 1898 (*Contre Sainte-Beuve*, 386-96) and again in his review of *Les Éblouissements* (cf. *Chroniques*, 178-9).

Verdurin called 'lower than the lowest street-woman',[1] he had
married a slim and charming lady who was perfectly presentable in
society and whom he loved devotedly. Proust had met him in the
1890s through Montesquiou, who had made Helleu's fortune in the
Faubourg Saint-Germain (perhaps to his detriment as an artist) by
persuading him to illustrate *Les Hortensias bleus*, and take a hundred
sketches of Comtesse Greffulhe in the intimacy of Bois-Boudran. In
La Bible d'Amiens, after praising Monet's studies of the façade of
Rouen Cathedral, Proust had remarked: 'but for interiors of cathedrals I know of none to equal in beauty those of the great painter
Helleu'. The Narrator's visit to Elstir's studio is based, then, on
Helleu at Cabourg, though the pictures he sees there were suggested
by those of Helleu's betters. Another painter staying at Cabourg,
however, posed during a moment for Elstir. Proust called on the
Bibescos' friend Vuillard in his studio, finding him at work in blue
overalls ('of a rather too pastel shade, I thought,' he wrote to
Reynaldo). Vuillard's opinions were the very opposite of Helleu's:
"a chap like Giotto, d'you see, or then again a chap like Titian, knew
every bit as much as Monet, or then again, a chap like Raphael, d'you
see ..." he repeated with intensity. 'He's no ordinary man, even if he
does say "chap" every twenty seconds,' was Proust's verdict, and he
made Elstir, discussing the sculptures of the church at Balbec,
deliver the same ideas in similar language: "the chap who carved that
façade of yours," Elstir tells the Narrator, "was every bit as fine a
fellow, you can take it from me, as the people you admire most
nowadays".[2] Another artist, the caricaturist Sem, was staying in the
district, and tried like Helleu to discourage Proust's love of the
Italian primitives. One night Proust brought him over the dark
Normandy roads in his taxi, all the way from Trouville to Cabourg.
At every turning they met a straying cow which threatened to charge
their car: "You invite me for a ride," grumbled Sem, "and then you
expect me to take part in a bull-fight in the heart of the pampas!"

   Proust complained bitterly of the noise and draught of the Grand
Hôtel—'I can't write you a proper letter amid the deafening and
melancholy tumult of this cruel and sumptuous hotel,' he told Émile
Mâle—and of his fellow-guests: 'unspeakable people', 'the common-
est set you could find anywhere', he wrote to Robert de Billy. But
throughout his life it was only in the theatrical but intensely real
environments of a luxury hotel, a society drawing-room or a great

restaurant, that he could feel at ease away from his own bedroom. 'This hotel is like a stage-setting for the third act of a farce,' he told Reynaldo; for around him was the delightful and appalling spectacle of Alfred Edwards, the gross, shady, Anglo-Levantine proprietor of *Le Matin*; his mistress, the Lesbian actress Lantelme (who may be compared to Léa at Balbec); his fifth, recently separated wife Misia Godebska; a previous wife, Mme Ralli; the Antarctic explorer Charcot, ex-husband of another ex-wife of Edwards; and Misia's first husband Thadée Natanson, one of Proust's editors on the now defunct *Revue Blanche*, all pretending not to notice one another's presence. One evening the heartening rumour circulated that Misia had shot Edwards stone-dead; but next morning, alas, he was seen to be in the best of health. Proust watched the menagerie around him with relish and entered into its curious pleasures: he attended polo matches, and every evening played baccarat, without success, in the casino.

His daily excursions were not all to gothic churches; along the stations of the little train stretched a garland of friends, the Guiches and Clermont-Tonnerres, Louisa with her new lover Robert Gangnat, and Mme Straus among the roses of her Clos des Mûriers at Trouville. Agostinelli, Albaret and Jossien were not his only male companions: he had dismissed old Félicie and Jean Blanc before leaving Paris, and hired as his manservant a portly young peasant, Nicolas Cottin, who with his wife Céline was to remain in Proust's service for seven years. Nicolas was already showing signs of his besetting fault: 'I have a horrifying suspicion that Nicolas drinks,' Proust wrote to Reynaldo. It may have been in this year that Proust visited the Château of Cantepie near Cambremer, the name of which he adapted for the Forest of Chantepie where M. de Cambremer 'went shooting every day for fifteen years and never wondered how it came by the name', and where the Narrator on his carriage-drives, first with Mme de Villeparisis and then several years later with Albertine, heard the singing birds on a hot day.[1] But from its owners, who were already acquaintances of his, he had borrowed the far more important name of Swann himself. The Swanns were an Anglo-French family whom Proust had met several years before; and they still remember his visit to Cantepie and his enquiring 'if Mr Swann

[1] II, 922. The forest is called Canteloup in *A l'Ombre* and Chantepie in *Sodome et Gomorrhe* (I, 720; II, 994-5), but the passage about the birds is identical.

would mind his using his name, which of course he did not mind in the least'.

Towards 20 September, when the Grand Hôtel was about to close for the winter, Proust set off late in a grey afternoon on his last and longest journey of the season with Agostinelli. The Clermont-Tonnerres had offered him a whole wing of their ancestral château at Glisolles near Évreux, promising with touching modesty: "you needn't even set eyes on us if you'd rather not!" Instead he decided to stay for a few days in Évreux itself and visit them from there. Near Évreux the car paused on the brink of a valley filled with white mist; and as they descended into the cold depths Proust felt his asthma, after six weeks' absence, suddenly returning. It was twilight when they reached Évreux, but he hurried to the cathedral, and found the stained-glass windows still lit from outside by the fading dusk: 'they contrived to steal from it jewels of light,' he wrote to Mme Straus, 'a purple that sparkled and sapphires made of fire'. As he told Jacques de Lacretelle many years later, he thought of the windows of Évreux for those of Saint-Hilaire at Combray, particularly for their quality of 'never shimmering more brightly than on days when the sun hardly showed itself, so that if it was dull outside you could be sure there would be fine weather inside'.[1] Then at the Hôtel Moderne he took not only an apartment for himself, but to ensure absolute quiet booked the empty one on the floor above. Here at last he was staying in an 'old Balzacian provincial town'; but Évreux was appallingly noisy, and his asthma grew worse. On the fourth day he set out for the Clermont-Tonnerres' château at Glisolles, an eighteenth-century building in pink sunburnt brick set in the woods and watermeadows of the little River Iton. The marquis and his wife had already given up hope when they heard from their drawing-room the wheels of a motor-car crunching on the gravel drive. "It looks like a taxi," declared Élisabeth. "Don't be absurd, m'dear." "Yes, it is, Philibert, a *red* taxi, and there's someone getting out"; and Proust alighted, panting and beaming, explaining that in order to calm his asthma he had been forced to drink seventeen cups of coffee on the way. He was introduced to their daughters Béatrix and Diane, two little girls with long curls, white frocks and bare arms, and talked about Turner's *Rivers of France*, which he promised to bring next day, and his intention to return to Paris by the valley of the Seine and to visit Monet's water-lily garden at Giverny. Occasionally he

[1] I, 59.

put in compliments on the beauty of their house, which they may have received like the Cambremers when the Narrator praises the draughts and broken windows of La Raspelière[1]: "It has the charm, at once primitive and refined, of a planter's or trout-fisherman's lodge which is also the studio of two artists," he declared. It was past midnight when Marquis Philibert guided his tottering steps down the stone staircase to the garden. "If you don't come again tomorrow you won't see our roses," complained the marquise; but Proust, delighted with his ingenuity, replied: "then I'll see them now," and Agostinelli directed his headlamps on the floodlit rose-beds of Glisolles. Next day *The Rivers of France* arrived in a parcel with several enormous Ruskins, but without Proust: distracted by the din of Évreux ('last night was like a witches' sabbath'), and abandoning the Seine estuary until next year, he had left suddenly in his taxi for Paris. There he endured three weeks of asthma and bed, deprived after a few days, during which he could hire him only twice, of his delightful companion; for Agostinelli, recalled by an illness of his brother Émile, had fled like a swallow to his sunny home in Monte Carlo, and would be seen no more till next summer. For the rest of the winter Proust was driven on his weekly nights out by Jossien, of whom he once asked, like the Narrator enquiring after the servant of Baroness Putbus: "do you think there would be any chance of one's going to bed with Monsieur Bizet's maid?" Jossien looked shocked: "you embarrass me, Monsieur," he replied, "because as a matter of fact she's my sister-in-law."

Towards the end of October Proust wrote the finest of his articles for *Le Figaro*, '*Impressions de route en automobile*', which appeared on 19 November. He combined into one five of his summer journeys with 'my chauffeur, the ingenious Agostinelli'—those to Caen, Bayeux, Lisieux, Évreux and Glisolles. The description of the moving steeples of Caen with which the article opens was adapted in *Du Côté de chez Swann* to become the Narrator's boyhood essay on the spires of Martinville seen from Dr Percepied's carriage.[2] This is

[1] II, 944.
[2] *Pastiches et Mélanges*, 92-4, corresponds to *Pléiade*, I, 181-2. The verbal changes are unimportant, consisting mainly in the omission of phrases which apply only to Caen and the motor-car, and the whole passage could not have been written at any earlier period, for it is in Proust's mature style. If there is any truth in the rumour that the Narrator's essay had already appeared twenty years earlier in the *Revue Lilas* at the Lycée Condorcet, it must have been in a very different form.

the article which the Narrator sends to *Le Figaro* a little before his dinner with Saint-Loup in the fog-bound restaurant in *Le Côté de Guermantes*, and which remains unpublished until several years later, after the death of Albertine.[1] Proust himself cannot have had to wait more than a week or two, if at all. Of all his letters of congratulation the prettiest, as he told Mme Straus, was from Agostinelli, to whom Nicolas had sent a copy of the article. The Narrator receives a similar letter, 'in a working-class hand and charming language', after the appearance of his essay on the spires of Martinville, and discovers later that it came from Théodore, the former choir-boy at Combray, who now lives (like Agostinelli) 'in the South'.[2]

Proust was not yet in love with Agostinelli, or he would not have acquiesced in their parting for a whole year. No doubt he had taken pleasure in his charming and youthful company, and perhaps a little of the Albertine with whom the Narrator drives through the country near Balbec may come from Agostinelli. But so much of this aspect of Albertine comes from Marie Finaly in 1892 and Marie de Chevilly in 1899, and so much more from the girl whom Proust was to meet at Cabourg in 1908, that little of her is left for Agostinelli. Albertine, as we shall find, can be identified with Agostinelli (and even then not entirely) only in 'the agony at sunrise' and in her life as a prisoner with the Narrator, which corresponds in Proust's life to events reaching from September 1913 to the spring of 1914. The character in *A la Recherche* who is based on the Agostinelli of 1907 is, after all, only the chauffeur whom the Narrator hires to drive himself and Albertine, and compares to 'a young Evangelist bowed over his wheel of consecration', in the very words Proust had used of 'the ingenious Agostinelli' in his *Figaro* article.[3]

At the end of September he had renewed his lease of 102 Boulevard Haussmann, still vowing that he would leave after another year. On 8 November he had an opportunity of acquiring the whole building, when his aunt's share, his own and Robert's were put up for auction. Instead he attended a soirée at Montesquiou's Pavillon

---

[1] II, 397; III, 567.

[2] III, 591, 701. Théodore in his capacity as a coachman who is a brother of Mme Putbus's maid (III, 307) resembles Jossien. But perhaps Proust may be thinking of himself and Agostinelli when he makes the Prince de Guermantes ask: "Why on earth doesn't X . . . go to bed with his coachman? Who knows, Théodore might be only too delighted to oblige, and perhaps he's extremely hurt that his master doesn't make any advances" (III, 306).

[3] II, 1028.

des Muses, where the creeping odour of dead leaves from the garden mingled with the scent of orange-blossom in the drawing-room, and the ghost of Yturri seemed to move among the guests. His aunt outbid her nephews: 'my income is halved,' he lamented to Montesquiou, and expressed doubts whether he ought not to have visited his lawyer that evening, rather than the Count—'The Cabinet of Ruses, instead of the Pavilion of Muses!' In fact, he was now rich, with an elder son's portion of the accumulated legacies of Louis and Nathé Weil, Dr and Mme Proust, and although he liked occasionally to complain that he was 'ruined', he would always remain wealthy. The fall in his income from the sale of his share in 102 Boulevard Haussmann was no doubt compensated by the rise in his capital.

On 26 December Proust published an anonymous article in *Le Figaro*, signed: D, on the recent death of his old ally, Gustave ('Sword-thrust') de Borda. By a regrettable lapse of taste his farewell to Borda was a parody of the banal society obituaries which Proust himself abominated, and later used for a last turn of the screw in the tragedy of the death of Swann.[1] As a crowning impertinence, when mentioning the ageing Borda's inability in his last years to grace the duelling-ground with his presence, he remarked: 'the last person, if our memory does not deceive us, whom he assisted in the quality of second, was our contributor M. Marcel Proust, who has always preserved a veritable cult for his memory'. A few weeks later Proust engaged in a sequence of very different parodies, which seemed to lead directly away from his novel, yet in fact formed the last turning but one in the circuitous way to *A la Recherche*.

[1] III, 199-200.

Chapter 5

PURIFICATION THROUGH PARODY
(January – October 1908)

IN January 1908 all Paris was delighted by one of those monumental frauds which, owing to the impudence of the swindler and the dignity of the victim, seem more farcical than deplorable. Sir Julius Wernher, a governor of the great diamond-mining company of De Beer's, had been approached in London three years before by a French electrical engineer named Lemoine with the shattering claim that he had invented a method of making diamonds. All that was needed was a furnace, a crucible, some common carbon, and a great deal of money; and after witnessing an experiment in which Lemoine seemed to produce a tiny but admittedly genuine diamond, Sir Julius parted by agonising degrees with a total of £64,000. From time to time Lemoine displayed still more diamonds, but could never be persuaded to reveal his formula. Sir Julius decided to prosecute. On 9 January 1908 Lemoine was interrogated in Paris by the magistrate Le Poittevin in the presence of his lawyer, who was none other than the great Labori, the champion of Dreyfus; and the Affair of the Diamonds immediately became world-famous. Lemoine had plotted to announce his discovery, to buy De Beer's shares during the consequent slump, and to make enormous profits when the market recovered. His diamonds were identified by the jewellers from whom they had been bought by his wife. The enquiry, and the daily fun, lasted till the end of March.

At first Proust felt some personal alarm. Ever since the summer after his mother's death he had been dabbling in the stock market, often with success, and part of his capital was invested with De Beer's. But soon the comedy of the situation seized his imagination. The Affair of the Diamonds was, as he had remarked to Mme Straus of the Dreyfus Affair, 'just like something in Balzac'; indeed, it was like something in Flaubert, Michelet, the Goncourt *Journal*, almost any writer one could imagine; and because it was quite unsuitable for serious treatment it would certainly have brought out the more vulnerable sides of them all. Proust had tried his hand at parody twice before, first in '*Mondanité et Mélomanie de Bouvard et Pécuchet*', written in 1895 and included in *Les Plaisirs et les Jours*, and again in his '*Fête chez Montesquiou à Neuilly*' of January 1904; and as it happened, parody was in the air this winter. *A la Manière de . . .*, an amusing but superficial volume of skits by Charles Müller and Paul Reboux (Fernand Gregh's friends and editors of *Les Lettres*), had been one of the successes of the season, and was familiar to readers of *Le Figaro* from a long extract in the issue for 26 January 1908. So it was not 'quite by accident', as Proust recalled long afterwards, that he 'chose this trivial law-suit one evening as the sole theme for a series of fragments in which I would try to imitate the manners of a number of authors'. The first group, consisting of Balzac, Émile Faguet, Michelet, and Edmond de Goncourt, appeared in the *Figaro* literary supplement on 22 February 1908; the second, Flaubert and Sainte-Beuve, on 14 March; and the last, Renan, on 28 March.

Proust's parodies are the funniest and most profound in the French language; they would also be the unkindest, were it not that he does full justice to the genius or talent of his victims, 'paying into other people's accounts,' as he claimed, 'ideas of which a more provident administrator of his own property would have preferred to keep the credit and the signature for himself'. Balzac's grandeur is suggested as unerringly as his ever-latent absurdity and moral vulgarity, and the Flaubert and Renan pastiches contain genuine beauty in a preposterous context. But hostility to his subjects, though all are writers whom he admired, is certainly present, and is keener and deeper than can be accounted for by the mere necessities of parody. 'I found it so amusing to perform literary criticism in action', Proust explained to Robert Dreyfus on 18 March 1908; but his idea of criticism was now, temporarily, very different from the definition he had put forward in *La Bible d'Amiens*. 'To help the reader to receive the full impact of the unique characteristics of a writer,' he had then declared, 'to set before his eyes a series of identical traits, which allow him to realise that these are the essential qualities of the author's genius, should be the first task of every critic.' Now, however, he had undertaken not only to detect those 'unique characteristics', but to make them appear ludicrous. Twelve years later, in his essay '*A propos du Style de Flaubert*' in the *Nouvelle Revue Française* of January 1920, he partly explained his motives. 'For writers intoxicated with Flaubert,' he remarked, 'I cannot recommend too highly the purgative, exorcising virtue of parody; we must make an intentional pastiche in order not to spend the rest of our lives in writing involuntary pastiche.' Perhaps he was serious in pleading his need for this homoeopathic remedy. Proust's Ruskin prefaces, and the *Figaro* articles of 1907, show that throughout the past eight years he had been intermittently in possession of the unique style of *A la Recherche*, not yet in its full power, but already showing little trace of influence from other writers. Nevertheless a curious regression to the derivative prose of *Jean Santeuil*, with its hints of Bourget, Anatole France, and ill-digested Balzac and Flaubert, is visible in the fragments of the lost novel of 1905-8, and is not quite outgrown, a year after the parodies, in the narrative portions of *Contre Sainte-Beuve*. It seems that the danger of imitation, which he had long overcome in other fields, was still formidable when he attempted narrative fiction. But a still deeper motive becomes visible when the parodies are considered in their historical place on Proust's way to *A la Recherche*. They clearly form part of the same series of advances towards free possession of his genius, which began in the summer of 1903 with his rejection of Ruskin, and continued in 1905 with his attack on the very act of reading in '*Sur la Lecture*'. There comes a time in the ascent of a great writer when, for the sake of his own future work, he must cease to admire even his greatest predecessors from a position of inferiority. Proust was now reaching the heights from which other summits appeared level with or lower than his own. His parodies were an antidote against the toxins of admiration.

He had risen from the weeping and anguish of the past two years, and now he laughed as if for the first time since the death of his mother. In the most hilarious moments of the Balzac pastiche—'Mme Firmiani sweated in her slippers, which were one of the masterpieces of Polish craftsmanship'—the sound of Proust's solitary glee in his midnight bedroom seems still audible. Not all his jokes were against his subjects. In the courtroom scene of the Flaubert parody, when Lemoine's lawyer Labori is speaking, Proust remembered the same Labori, passionate, noble and boring, at the Zola trial ten years before: 'he had a meridional accent,' he maliciously noted, 'appealed to the generous passions, and incessantly removed his pince-nez; and as she listened Nathalie felt the unrest which is caused by true eloquence; a delicious emotion assailed her, and the cambric on her bosom palpitated like a pigeon about to take flight'. Under the alias of Renan he took the opportunity to suggest his own concealed opinion of the contrast between Mme de Noailles's nostalgia for the innocence of Nature in her writing and her avid pursuit of the pleasures of society in her life—though this had been one of his own sins, the guilt of which he would acknowledge and atone in *A la Recherche*. 'What a false position her poetry must have given her in high society,' muses 'Renan'; 'but she appears to have realised this, and to have led, perhaps not without a certain degree of ennui, an utterly retired and simple life in the little orchard with which she so habitually holds conversations.' He also made fun of himself: 'Renan' quotes Ruskin, 'whom unfortunately we read only in the pitifully platitudinous translation which Marcel Proust has bequeathed to posterity'. The Goncourt pastiche turns on the diarist's gratification when informed by Lucien Daudet[1] that 'an eccentric friend of his named Marcel Proust', ruined by the slump in diamond shares, has committed suicide; Goncourt enjoys a brief vision of popular success from a tragedy on the subject, and is utterly crushed next morning by the news that Proust is still alive and kicking.

Proust's retreat to parody was a relaxation from the tensions of his novel, and a psychological preparation for his final attempt to write it. Nothing, at first sight, could seem more remote from the novel itself; yet in the Lemoine parodies he was in fact moving on several planes in the direction of *A la Recherche*. For the first time he had discovered himself as a comic writer. The Comic Spirit, which is almost entirely absent from *Les Plaisirs et les Jours* and *Jean Santeuil*, arrives in full force in the parodies, and is ever-present in *A la Recherche*, not only in the Narrator's view of the characters and the laws of human frailty which they reveal, but in his ironic attitude to himself, by which Proust redeemed the self-complacency and self-pity which had ruined *Jean Santeuil*. Parody itself, as a means of extracting the essence of other people and making it absurd, became one of the major ingredients of his novel. The Lemoine pastiches are a connecting link between Proust's early habit of performing 'imitations' (in which, as his friends have remarked, he would seem actually to *become* Montesquiou, Mme Lemaire, Mme Arman, or whoever was his victim of the moment), and the spoken words of the characters in *A la Recherche*. Charlus, Mme Verdurin, the Duchesse, Françoise and others do not merely speak as their models spoke:

---

[1] This is not only a compliment to Lucien Daudet, but a touch of verisimilitude, for the Goncourt *Journal* is full of meetings with Lucien and his family.

their conversation is a concentrated exaggeration, a pastiche in fact, of the words and manner of the real people on whom they are based. Charlus talks like Montesquiou, but more intensely so than Count Robert ever did, just as the Balzac parody is more Balzacian than Balzac himself. The parodies were a trial run for this use of pastiche in *A la Recherche*.

Other more direct parallels may be traced between the parodies and the novel. The Faguet is a sketch for certain aspects of Brichot, Mme de Villeparisis criticises the great writers she had known in her youth in the manner of Proust's Sainte-Beuve, Legrandin speaks like Proust's Renan. In the Balzac parody Proust's method of handling the symphonic complexities of a social occasion is a humorous imitation of Balzac's; yet he is now more successful than in similar episodes in *Jean Santeuil* (where he was imitating Balzac in all seriousness), and he was to use the same technique for the matinées and soirées, teas, concerts and dinners of *A la Recherche*. A single sentence of the imitation of Flaubert became one of the chief themes of the Narrator's youth at Combray. When the Narrator reads in an unnamed author, a little before his discovery of Bergotte, of 'a mountainous and fluviatile country, with many sawmills, and with clusters of violet and reddish flowers climbing over low walls'—a landscape in which a little later he imagines himself wandering hand in hand with the Duchesse de Guermantes, who, 'enamoured of me by a sudden caprice', shows him 'flowers leaning their violet and red spindles on low walls'[1]—Proust is thinking of a passage in his own Flaubert pastiche, about 'two clusters of violet flowers, descending to the swift water which they almost touched, along a reddish crumbling wall'. But the Lemoine pastiches actually appear in *A la Recherche* in a symbolic form, the clue to which is the appearance in each of a parody of the Goncourt *Journal*. During his visit to Gilberte at Tansonville the Narrator reads a passage (which is in fact another pastiche by Proust himself) from 'a volume of the unpublished *Journal* of the Goncourts', in which the diarist describes Cottard, Brichot and Swann at one of Mme Verdurin's Wednesdays long ago. The Narrator despairs of writing a great book, because 'Goncourt' has made these people appear more interesting than they ever seemed to himself; yet at the same time he rejects the Goncourt *Journal* and all literature of its kind, since he knows that his own rare glimpses of a reality behind the phenomenal world have been more valuable than

[1] I, 86, 172; II, 13.

anything visible to the 'naturalists' and their school, who can only copy the surface. Proust here called to mind his own situation in the spring of 1908. The Narrator's reading of a Goncourt parody, and Proust's writing of another, are symbolically the same; and both lay in a time of self-doubt and urgency which stood, unrealised, at the threshold of the revelation of Time Regained.

It was not Proust's fault that the Lemoine pastiches came to a temporary end. He had a further supply ready, including one of the dramatic critic Adrien Bernheim—'and even that isn't the lowest I've sunk,' he assured Robert Dreyfus. The Renan had given him particular pleasure: 'it came in such waves that I glued whole new pages on to the proofs,' he told Dreyfus; 'I'd adjusted my inner metronome to his rhythm, and I could have written ten volumes in the same style. You ought to thank me for my discretion in refraining.' He remembered the day nineteen years before when he had visited the serene old apostate and received his blessing. 'For Monsieur Marcel Proust,' Renan had written in the schoolboy's copy of his *Vie de Jésus*, 'whom I ask to keep an affectionate memory of me when I am no longer in this world'; and it is Renan—more even than France, Loti or Barrès, all three of whom were Renan's disciples—who is the chief original of Bergotte as 'the sweet singer with the snowy locks'. At midnight on 11 March Proust sent Ulrich to the *Figaro* offices with the manuscripts of Flaubert, Sainte-Beuve and Renan, and a letter begging Cardane to find room for all three on the following Saturday; but the implacable sub-editor postponed the Renan for a fortnight, till 28 March. A few days later Lemoine was released on bail, and in June the wretched man fled to Constantinople. The Affair of the Diamonds ceased to have news-value, and no more pastiches were required.

Perhaps Proust could publish his parodies as a book? In April he consulted Gaston de Caillavet and his wife in their home at 40 Boulevard de Courcelles, his first recorded visit to these old friends since their marriage in 1893. Remembering Marcel's insistence, in the far-off days when she was a girl and he was in love with her, on making friends with her father's servants, Jeanne teasingly asked his opinion of her present household. "I don't care for the concierge, though I didn't get to know him really well," he replied, "and I thought your page-boy, who's nothing like the one you had in the Rue de Miromesnil, rather mediocre." He was enraptured by this first sight of her pretty, thirteen-year-old daughter Simone, who when ordered to be nice replied: "I'm doing my best!" It was not, however, until Mlle de Caillavet was a few years older that he realised the deeper significance of this offspring of Gilberte and Saint-Loup. Gaston was thoroughly in favour of the plan to publish his parodies in volume form, and Jeanne offered to write on his behalf to Calmann-Lévy; but in the end Proust wrote his own letter, appealing to an entirely imaginary 'very high credit-balance' for *Les Plaisirs et les Jours*, offering to pay for the costs of printing, and adding with fatal modesty: 'I so hate to bother you that it would give me more pleasure if you did *not* publish these articles.' It was hardly surprising that Calmann-Lévy obligingly declined, as also did the *Mercure de France* and Fasquelle; and the premature appearance of *Pastiches et Mélanges* was once more averted.

The Lemoine Affair was only one of three scandals which fascinated Proust and all Paris that year. The last act in the decline and fall of the brilliant Boni de Castellane was now being played, and a whole epoch of Paris society seemed to end with the vanishing of his glory. For more than a decade he had received his multitudinous guests at the top of the red marble staircase in his Palais Rose; to each new arrival he directed a piercing ray from his lapis-lazuli eyes, and leaning slightly backwards in the manner of Saint-Loup[1] extended his gloved hand from a great distance, as if on the end of a barge-pole. "A nice place you've got here," remarked King Carlos of Portugal, and Boni replied, with equal truth and chivalry: "if it please your Majesty, it is the house of Mme de Castellane." To Boni it seemed unthinkable that the American millionairess to whom he had given his noble name, and whose wealth he was squandering with such exquisite taste, should not repay him with eternal gratitude and overlook his infidelities with prettier women. But his ugly little wife was about to put her foot down before the last of her fortune disappeared. "You can't divorce him," their friends exclaimed in horror; but "I don't see why not," she replied, adding in her still imperfect accent: "I 'ate 'im, I 'ate 'im!—*Je le hé, je le hé!!*" On 26 January 1906 she left Boni without warning, taking their two sons, and on 11 April she divorced him. Soon it was clear to everyone that the former Miss Anna Gould was determined not only to save her money but to gain a still better title by marrying Boni's cousin, Hélie de Talleyrand-Périgord, Prince de Sagan, who was nineteen years her senior. On 2 January 1908, at the funeral of their relative Charles

[1] I, 731.

de Talleyrand-Périgord, the furious Boni clubbed Cousin Hélie with his walking-stick as they emerged from the church. Proust's sympathies lay with Boni: 'Hélie ought to be spelled Élie,'[1] he observed maliciously to Reynaldo, 'like the Prophet, who in similar circumstances flew up into the heavens, a resource which unfortunately wasn't available to our Hélie. But in my opinion Gould for him spells principally Gold.' On 7 July Boni's ex-wife became Princesse Hélie de Sagan: and Boni, left destitute and besieged by creditors, found that by buying and selling antiques, and taking commissions from his fellow-aristocrats for interior decoration, he could still live in modest elegance. A little later Proust was introduced for the first time to Hélie de Talleyrand and the Duc de Brissac, but unluckily confused one with the other. Soon afterwards he happened to meet, as he thought, M. de Brissac, and took the opportunity to make a facetious remark on the new Mme de Talleyrand. "How exquisitely witty, I shall tell my wife," replied the supposed Duc, choking with rage. "But I don't think that could possibly interest Mme de Brissac," said Proust, making the gaffe worse; and it was only after long cogitation that he realised why the inexplicably angry gentleman had been holding a top-hat with the initials T. P. stamped in the lining. He used the incident in *A la Recherche* for the scene between the Narrator and Charlus after Mme de Villeparisis's matinée.[2]

The third scandal of that winter was the Eulenburg Affair in Germany, which combined the most deplorable features of both the Dreyfus Case and the persecution of Oscar Wilde: as in the former the course of justice was perverted by political intrigue, but as in the second the accused man was guilty, and his crime was homosexuality. Kaiser Wilhelm II had long been surrounded by a circle of intimate friends, known to their enemies as the Knights of the Round Table or the Camarilla,[3] who were hated by the Panger-

---

[1] i.e. Elijah.

[2] II, 277-8. The Narrator, seeing a G with ducal coronet in the Baron's top-hat, and forgetting that Charlus is a Guermantes, thinks he has inadvertently taken another guest's property. He then remarks that Saint-Loup is talking to 'that fool of a Duc de Guermantes'. "How very delightful, I shall tell my brother," exclaims the Baron, and the Narrator, supposing that his brother must surely have the same name, enquires: "Do you think that could interest M. de Charlus?"

[3] King Theodosius likewise, as M. de Norpois remarks when dining with the Narrator's parents, is 'surrounded by a camarilla' (I, 461).

manist war party not so much for their morals as for their pacifism and advocacy of friendship with France. Their leader, Prince Philip von Eulenburg, a married man in his sixties and the father of eight children, was attacked in October 1907 along with his dear friend General Cuno von Moltke (they called one another 'Phili' and 'Tutu') by the right-wing journalist Maximilian Harden. As in the Wilde Case the accuser was sued for libel, but produced evidence which resulted in the criminal prosecution of the plaintiff. The wretched Eulenburg was confronted with a boatman and a milkman, both now middle-aged, with whom he had had improper relations long ago in the 1880s. The milkman, as it turned out, was under the impression that the word Camarilla, which he heard used so often by Harden's lawyer but could not spell, was a technical term for a particular perversion. "If the Prince swears he never did Kramilla," he averred, "then he's a perjured liar." But although the poor Prince could never be convicted of Kramilla or anything else, since he always fainted at the critical moment, his political career was irretrievably ruined. The Kaiser abandoned his friends and was left with the militarists as his sole advisers; and the Eulenburg Affair was thus among the minor indirect causes of the First World War.

Proust took a keen interest in the Eulenburg Affair. Like many homosexuals, and like Charlus, he prided himself on his knowledge of all the prominent, undiscovered inverts of Europe: 'his documentation was remarkable,' says Robert de Billy, who assisted him in this hobby with inside information gained in his career as a diplomat. 'What do you think of that homosexuality trial?' Proust wrote to Billy about 10 November 1907; 'I think they've been hitting out rather at random, but it's absolutely true of several of the persons mentioned, notably the Prince, though some of the details are extremely comic.' The French people looked on with glee, forgetting that Eulenburg was their friend, and that the existence of homosexuality is far from impairing the fighting qualities of an enemy nation. The unhappy Prince was nicknamed 'Eulenbougre', Berlin became known as Sodom-on-Spree, and Billy told Proust that 'Do you speak German?' was now among the most familiar graffiti in the public conveniences of Paris. But Proust viewed the Affair with mingled feelings of grim amusement, scientific interest, and sympathy both human and personal; for the bell that tolled for Eulenburg tolled also for himself.

Since the beginning of 1908 Proust had been at work on yet

another version of his novel which, as we shall see, included when he abandoned it in the following November scenes at Combray, Balbec (then called Querqueville) and Venice.[1] On 3 February, just before he began the Lemoine pastiches, he wrote to Mme Straus of 'a rather long work to which I should like to devote myself'. On 14 May 1908, a week after Eulenburg's arrest, he spoke to Robert Dreyfus of a plan to write a topical article, in which he would use the Eulenburg Affair as the pretext for a general discussion of homosexuality. The apprehensive Dreyfus advised him to publish, if at all, only in the future collected volume of his essays; but on the 16th Proust suggested the *Mercure de France*, which had already printed in December 1907 and January 1908 two essays on the same theme by Remy de Gourmont, under the facetious title of '*L'Amour à l'envers*'. The article had by now turned into a short story, which must have nothing to do with the Affair, Proust explained, for 'art is too superior to life to be satisfied with copying it'; and his story, if allowed to 'participate in the contingency and unreality of an actual event', 'would seem banal and untrue, and deserve some blow in the face from outraged Existence, like Oscar Wilde saying that the greatest sorrow he had ever known was the death of Lucien de Rubempré in Balzac, and then learning soon afterwards, through his prosecution, that there are sorrows which are still more real'. Professor Vigneron has seen in this project for a short story the origin of *A la Recherche* itself. But the version of his novel on which Proust had now been engaged for several months was only the last in a series begun in the summer of 1905; and the essay discussed with Dreyfus can be identified not with the novel itself, but with the preliminary sketch for the first and second chapters of *Sodome et Gomorrhe* which forms Chapter Twelve, '*La Race Maudite*', of *Contre Sainte-Beuve*.[2]

[1] A letter (discussed by Professor Kolb in *Mercure de France*, 1 August 1956, 750-5) of January 1908 to Auguste Marguiller, sub-editor of the *Gazette des Beaux-Arts*, shows that Proust was then already writing or preparing the incident of his infant brother Robert and the pet goat at Combray, which he later embodied in the last published chapter of *Contre Sainte-Beuve*. Proust asked Marguiller to send on approval some English portrait-engravings including an animal, a genre to which he compares the scene of Robert and his pet. This incident is the first in the list of 'pages written' for the Combray episode in the novel-version of 1908 (*Contre Sainte-Beuve*, 14, 293).

[2] The reference to Wilde and Lucien de Rubempré is expanded in '*Sainte-Beuve et Balzac*' (*Contre Sainte-Beuve*, 217), but Wilde's fall is also mentioned in '*La Race Maudite*' and in *Sodome et Gomorrhe* (*ibid.*, p. 258 = II, 616). Wilde's remark occurs in his dialogue '*The Decay of Lying*', which Proust had read in

In May 1908, therefore, Proust had already begun his essay on the 'accursed race' of inverts, and had decided that elements of his novel should serve as its text in place of the Eulenburg Affair.

The other purpose of Dreyfus's visit had been to show Marcel his obituary on Ludovic Halévy—the son of Mme Straus's uncle Léon, and father of Proust's schoolfriends Élie and Daniel—who had died on 8 May. Proust thought with nostalgia of the summer Sundays early in the 1890s at the Halévys' long white country-house at Sucy, where with Gregh, Louis de La Salle, Jacques Bizet, Robert Dreyfus and Léon Brunschvicg he had flirted with the host's niece, Madeleine Breguet (who became Jacques Bizet's first wife and died under the surgeon's knife of Dr Pozzi) and her charming girl companions—another model for the 'little band'. "My father was a Jew, my mother was a Protestant, and they brought me up as a Catholic—I hope we all meet in the same heaven," M. Halévy used to say. Proust had intended, if Dreyfus and Beaunier had not forestalled him, to write an obituary of his own: 'it wouldn't have been as good as Beaunier's,' he told Mme Straus, 'but more precise, and corroborated by live memories'. Four days later, on 12 May, Robert de Billy's father-in-law, Paul Mirabaud, the 'blue-eyed Saxon god' of the yacht *Hélène*, succumbed to the heart-ailment which he had discussed with Proust during their cruise in 1904. The sea of Time Lost was rising, drawing so near that it threatened to drown even the present.

In June Proust meditated another never-to-be-published article, attacking the recent candidatures for the Académie Française[1] of the Byzantine historian Gustave Schlumberger, Mme Straus's old enemy, who had cut her in public ever since their quarrel over the Dreyfus Affair. Proust breathed horrible threats: 'I'll allude to his big feet, I'll drop all pretension to good taste, even to good faith.' But in the end he confined himself to the rather childish revenge of walking up and down in front of 'this prehistoric buffalo' at Princesse Marie Murat's soirée, announcing in a loud voice to all and sundry: "I'll say how d'you do to him when he says it to Mme Straus, not that she gives a damn about it, but *I do!!*" Mme de Chevigné assured him

[1] On 18 March and again on 1 May 1908.

_____

one of the two French translations of *Intentions* published in 1906. 'One of the greatest tragedies of my life,' says Vivian, 'is the death of Lucien de Rubempré. It is a grief from which I have never been able completely to rid myself.'

that she felt exactly the same, that she had told M. Schlumberger outright: "now you'll pay for all your mean tricks"; and to emphasise her good will she 'behaved exquisitely to a young girl of whom I'm fond'. Meanwhile 'the buffalo smiled like a ninny every time I walked past, thinking I was going to bow, and his enormous boots made fossil footprints on the carpet'.

The young girl was apparently Mlle Oriane de Goyon, whom Proust had long admired and now hoped to meet. He waited for a sponsor, acutely embarrassed by Mme Lemaire, who barked: "Suzette, show me this girl Marcel's talking about. H'm, she's extraordinarily ugly, and could do with a good wash!"; while Suzette Lemaire made matters worse by giggling loudly and crying: "Oh no, Mother, she's very pretty—come here, Marcel, look, she's just by the door!" André de Fouquières effected the introduction, but unfortunately was rather drunk, and teased Proust unmercifully: "What d'you say to those tiny cheeks, me lad? Like to pinch them, eh? Or how about a kiss—a really naughty one? Whassat? Want to bite those li'l' ribstone pippins? Qui' right, old man, besides, you're very smart today, got rid of your beard, I see." But Proust, although the young girl's fiancé was present, took his introduction seriously. He wrote pathetically to Lauris, the manuscript of whose novel *Ginette Chatenay* he was now reading, describing his joy at the meeting, and adding: 'you may guess how deep in me is the resonance of words in your novel like "what future does he see for our love?" ' This incident is the original of an episode in the version of Proust's novel then in progress, in which the Narrator attends a soirée given by the Duchesse de Marengo in the hope of meeting a girl whose beauty he admires.[1]

Nearly three years had passed since the death on 6 July 1905 of poor Yturri. Montesquiou had unveiled a statue over his grave, of an angel with finger on lips, trampling on the serpent of envy—'the

[1] *Figaro littéraire*, 16 November 1946. The Narrator listens with Swann to an orchestral suite in which the 'little phrase' is heard, reminding Swann not of the torments of his past love, but of the beauty of the moonlit Bois de Boulogne on the nights when he dined there with Odette and the Verdurins. Proust used elements of this scene four times in *A la Recherche*: the musical evening at Mme de Saint-Euverte's, Swann's remarks on the Vinteuil Sonata when his wife plays it to the Narrator, the soirée at the Princesse de Guermantes's when the Narrator converses with Swann, and the performance of the Vinteuil Septet at Mme Verdurin's in *La Prisonnière*, where he expects to meet Mlle Vinteuil and her friend.

Angel of Silence', he called it—in a tastefully spectacular ceremony on the following 20 November. For a time the Count was subjected to illnatured comment. The repulsive Ernest La Jeunesse wrote a cruel parody of his elegiac manner, with his foible for Latin tags and *rime riche*, beginning

> '*Ave, Caesar, morituri*
> *Te salutant!* Mort? Yturri?'

An idiotic rumour arose, because Montesquiou announced to everybody with noble melancholy: "I shan't be able to write any poetry for years now," that the dead secretary had written his master's verses for him; and indeed, the poet was to publish only prose until the First World War, when he burst into rhyme as prolifically as ever. In this third summer of their eternal parting it was time for a positively last farewell to Yturri, particularly as the Count had recently acquired a new secretary, Henri Pinard, to share his life and —as people noticed—his ever-thickening rouge and powder. On 27 June 1908 he gave a reading of *Le Chancelier des Fleurs*, a memorial volume in which he told the sad story of Yturri's last days, and quoted in full his letters of condolence from all the best people. The guests represented society, royalty, the arts and the Church, and included Comtesse Greffulhe, Judith Gautier, Mme Arman complete with Anatole France, Loti, Rodin, Dr Pozzi, the Abbé Mugnier and Barrès. The Grand Duke Wladimir, uncle of the Tsar and husband of Mme de Chevigné's inseparable friend the Grand Duchess Maria Pavlovna, arrived last but one, whereupon Montesquiou shouted: "Close all the doors!" "But Mme Greffulhe hasn't arrived," objected the new secretary, and "She'll be here at her usual time," replied her furious cousin. The Grand Duke was heard to enquire: "Why is she always an hour late? But then, perhaps she hasn't a clock!"; then he leaned his enormous frame against the wall next to Rodin ("no, I won't have a chair, I always feel safer in this house with my back against the wall!"), and the proceedings began. The air was heavy with the scent of huge lilies, and the drawn curtains shut out all but the single ray of sunlight in which Montesquiou nobly stood, reading, reading, reading, and reading, and dropping each leaf of manuscript into a bronze bowl when finished. "Uniquely beautiful," murmured Anatole France afterwards as, in the words of the reporter from *Le Figaro*, 'the motor-cars lined up outside the silent Pavilion dispersed noisily in the sunlight of a perfect day'.

Proust had not been invited, and rashly complained of it, with the inevitable result that Montesquiou called to give a private recital; and at two in the morning, without pity for the slumbers of Dr Gagey on the floor below, he stamped his heels on the floor and screamed: "and now, Scipio and Laelius, Orestes and Pylades, Cinq-Mars and De Thou, Edmond and Jules de Goncourt, Flaubert and Bouilhet, welcome me, for I am worthy, to your pre-eminent company!!" Proust read the volume, one of a hundred copies privately printed for distribution to the Count's particular friends, at his leisure. He noticed a letter on 'your cruel loss' from the German Ambassador, Prince von Radolin, and remarked bitterly to Reynaldo: 'he'd have done better to keep a little of his sympathy to give to Eulenburg'. But to Montesquiou he wrote, early in July, 'it's just like Bossuet', and added significantly: 'I am struggling, without making progress, on days when I'm not too ill, with a novel which will perhaps give you a little more esteem for me, if you have the patience to read it.' At the same time he also discussed his novel, and his intention of working on it at Cabourg, with his fellow-novelist Lauris.

He arrived at Cabourg on 20 July, but before starting work had two still more urgent matters to settle. First he must review Lucien Daudet's second novel,[1] *Le Chemin Mort*, the discreetly homosexual theme of which may have encouraged his own purpose; but on second thoughts he gave way to prudence, and his article remains unpublished and unknown. The annual problem of his fortnight of military training, which he seems to have succeeded in evading every year since his army service in 1889-90, would have caused him little concern, had it not been more serious this year, when his valet Nicolas Cottin was summoned for 1 August, the same day as himself. Poor Nicolas had a genuine weak chest, and his presence at Cabourg was indispensable to his invalid master. For himself Proust need only write to his father's friend Dr Duplay for a medical certificate[2]; but for Nicolas he asked his aunt Mme Thomson, whose husband was now Navy Minister, to approach General Dalstein, the military governor of Paris. He thought of going still higher, to Picquart himself, who had now been War Minister for nearly two years.

[1] The first was *La Fourmilière* (1907), which Proust had dutifully mentioned in his Goncourt pastiche (*Pastiches et Mélanges*, 38).

[2] Proust was transferred to the territorial army reserve on 11 November 1908.

'I'm afraid he's forgotten those who sent him presents and praise when he was in prison,' he wrote sadly to Mme Catusse; but he hinted to Reynaldo that any overtures he might feel able to make to Picquart, 'without turning your hair white about it', would be gratefully received. He sent Reynaldo 750 francs as alleged profits in a shares speculation; but Reynaldo, impervious to bribery, insisted on returning the money, just as he had refused 580 francs forwarded by Proust with the same excuse from Versailles two years before. To Nicolas such conduct seemed, on either side, hardly sane, and whenever his master spent too much money at Cabourg he remarked with heavy irony: "now we shall have to ask Monsieur Hahn to send us another lot". Soon Nicolas's ingratitude was punished; despite General Dalstein's promise a stern summons arrived, and he had to 'do his thirteen days'.

Once more Proust's friends were strung out, like beads on a rosary, along the line of the Little Train. Loche Radziwill was near by, with his new friend, the lovely actress Christiane Lorin; at Les Béquettes near Houlgate was Alexandre de Neufville, whom Proust had met at the Comte de Saussine's musical salon in 1893; Robert Gangnat had taken the Chalet Russe at Bénerville for Louisa de Mornand, her sister Suzanne and her mother; and the Guiches were in residence at their Villa Mon Rêve, also at Bénerville. One day Proust lunched there with the Clermont-Tonnerres, and quarrelled with a retired cavalry officer about literature. "I wouldn't dream of telling him he was an ass, if we were talking about military strategy," he complained in his most mournful tones, "so what right has he to turn up his nose at such a beautiful book?" But the sight of the little Clermont-Tonnerre girls soothed his ruffled feelings, as they demurely drank from their glasses of water, folded their table-napkins, kissed their Aunt Élaine, and said to him with wide eyes: "No, Monsieur, we don't remember seeing you at Glisolles." After lunch he strolled on the lawn, between the beds of sea-geraniums and the vast glittering of the sea, talking to their mother Élisabeth: 'he unlocked to me the treasures of his memory,' she recalled, 'and without realising it I was given a private view of his coming novel'. When he left the thin crescent-moon was shining in the west, and he quoted his favourite lines of Hugo's 'Booz endormi', which the Narrator recites to Albertine on their last drive together through moonlit Paris[1]:

<hr>

[1] III, 408.

'What god, what reaper of the eternal summer
Had left his task and carelessly discarded
This golden sickle in the field of stars?'

He passed by Louisa's Chalet Russe one evening without calling, on his way back from visiting Robert de Billy at the Finalys' villa, Les Frémonts, at Trouville. Billy hinted that he would like a room at the Grand Hôtel; but Proust had no intention of allowing his solitude to be disturbed, and explained, with the paradoxical and displeasing anti-Semitism which he shared with his mother, that the hotel was full, 'and with what people!—not a soul you could put a name to—and a few Israelite wholesale dealers are the haughty aristocracy of the place'. So Billy, as Proust urged, stayed at Les Frémonts; but Proust's visit to him helped to link the two Balbecs, the Trouville of Marie Finaly in 1892 and the Cabourg of sixteen years later.

Louisa had the four-years-married Albu still on her hook, just as Rachel continued to torment Saint-Loup after his marriage to Gilberte; and before making his promised visit Proust rebuked her sharply by post for her cruelty. He had received, he told her, heartbroken and furious letters from Albu, in the last of which the sufferer complained: 'I've sent her ten telegrams without getting any reply—I don't know even whether she's ill—all I want is to show my affection, but she doesn't answer, however I entreat her.' As a clinching argument Proust reminded Louisa that her birthday was approaching, and Albu might not dare to write, 'although he's gone to such trouble to find a present that would please you'. When Proust at last arrived at the Chalet Russe it was not entirely a courtesy visit. The young Gaston Gallimard, his future publisher, whose mother owned the nearby Manoir de Bénerville, happened to be calling on Gangnat and Louisa that afternoon. Gallimard saw a stranger approaching in a threadbare black suit and long velvet-lined cape, with a slightly soiled straw-hat tilted too far down over his forehead, and gathered from his dusty appearance and extreme exhaustion, and his story of the farmhouses at which he had been compelled to stop for coffee and recuperation, the absurd impression that he had walked the ten miles from Cabourg on foot.[1] Louisa joined them. The

---

[1] 'There was no other way of making the journey at the time,' Gallimard mistakenly explained in his account written fourteen years later; whereas in fact the Mézidon-Cabourg-Trouville railway of the Little Train had been running ever since 1883. Proust no doubt came by train and walked the distance of a little under a mile from Bénerville station.

astonished Gallimard saw the stranger stroking the nape of her
lovely neck, as if soothing a fractious colt, and heard him 'listing all
her faults, of which he seemed to have an expert knowledge, with a
teasing and benevolently interrogative manner, and scolding her in a
calm and controlled voice, but with an authority full of irony and a
patience which surprised me'. Gallimard knew, and saw Proust had
guessed, that Louisa had just been quarrelling with Gangnat: only
Proust and she can have been aware that he was admonishing
her for Albu's sake more than Gangnat's. It was not until the air
was thus cleared that he invited them all to dinner at the Grand
Hôtel.

Proust received his guests, who also included Louisa's sister,
Loche and Christiane, Alexandre de Neufville and others, in the
entrance hall, giving the Bénerville party fascinating word-portraits
and life-stories of the later arrivals. Young Gallimard felt a curious
excitement, as if he were about to witness some extraordinary event:
he was wrong, for nothing happened, yet he was right, for he was
dining at Balbec unawares, with the Narrator of *A la Recherche* and
several of his characters. A guest for whom Proust seemed to feel a
special kindness was an aged marquis, abandoned by his wife and
children, ruined by gambling and women, and crippled by locomotor
ataxia: he walked with sidelong lurches, and when sitting down
would aim elaborately for his chair, hurl himself towards it and miss,
except when Proust guided him. Proust led the conversation to
ground on which the unfortunate nobleman could feel at home, and
the guests, forgetting their embarrassment, found he was witty,
intelligent, and noble indeed. Proust put the marquis twice into *A la
Recherche*. In a curious rejected episode of *A l'Ombre* the Narrator
attends an organ recital in the casino at Balbec, and watches the
grotesque old man painfully climbing and descending, again and
again, 'like a clumsy, centenarian squirrel', to and from his seat on
the organ platform.[1] But in *Sodome et Gomorrhe* he is the impoverished Comte de Crécy, whom the Narrator invites to dinner and en-
courages to talk about wines and genealogy, because 'he considered
our Balbec agapes as an opportunity to converse on subjects which
were dear to him and of which he could not speak to anyone else',[2]

---

[1] I, 980-1. Proust wrote 'quinquagenarian', but it was one of his besetting
delusions (cf. III, 1143, note on 978) that this word meant a person in extreme
old age.
[2] II, 1085.

and who is later revealed by Charlus as the ex-husband of Odette.[1]
Meanwhile the guests devoured their roast chicken, watched
benignly by Proust, who having dined before their arrival sat with
legs crossed and chair turned sideways to the table. The conversation
veered towards travel, someone mentioned Constantinople, and
Proust quoted by heart a page of Loti on that city. "How magnificent," cried Gallimard, "and what an amazing memory you have!"
But Proust only smiled, and said later, as the guests departed: "you
should read the railway-timetable, it's finer still"; and he began to
recite a list of Names of Places.

It was during this visit that Proust met the mysterious young girl
whom he also saw from time to time in Paris, and a year later thought
of marrying. Not even her name is known, although she may be
alive to this day: 'I suppress her identity,' wrote Antoine Bibesco
forty years after, 'as she has begged me not to print her name.' The
evidence on Proust's relations with her is tantalisingly scanty, but
sufficient to show that she was, with Marie Finaly and Agostinelli,
one of the chief originals of Albertine. Her real presence is in Proust's
novel, in the Albertine of the 'little band'; but in his life the biographer can only draw attention, here and there, to her gracious
shadow. He also made the acquaintance of Camille Plantevignes,
a wealthy manufacturer of neck-ties who lived in Paris and was now
on holiday at Cabourg, of his son Marcel, Proust's namesake, who
was about to spend a year in Germany to learn the language, and of
two young men who were Marcel Plantevignes's friends. Meanwhile
he watched the passers-by, known or anonymous, on the promenade.
One evening he saw, silhouetted against the sunset in a pink gown,
the actress Lucy Gérard who had played with Louisa in Marcel
Prévost's Les Demi-vierges in 1905: 'I lingered to watch this exquisite
tinge of pink adding the complementary colour of the twilight to the
orange sky,' he told Louisa, 'and only returned to the hotel when I'd
caught cold and seen her fade into the horizon, to the utmost end of
which she glided like an enchanted sail.'

Perhaps it was in this summer that Paul Leclercq, one of Marcel's

---

[1] Odette, therefore, was perfectly entitled to call herself Odette de Crécy, and
Proust no doubt had in mind the dancer Cléo de Mérode to whom Reynaldo had
introduced him in 1895 and who, as she made a point of explaining, actually
belonged to a branch of the noble Austrian family whose name she bore—
whereas cocottes such as Liane de Pougy or Emilienne d'Alençon took names
which did not belong to them.

playfellows long ago in the Champs-Elysées, called at the Grand
Hôtel after a hot day's bicycling from Honfleur to Cabourg. A heap
of rugs and cushions on a sofa in the entrance-hall began as he
entered to stir, to protrude a hand, a foot, to stand up, and revealed
itself first as 'a sort of dishevelled crossing-sweeper in a huge black
greatcoat', and finally as Marcel. The restaurant was full of bare-
shouldered ladies and tail-coated gentlemen, and Leclercq wore
cycling-breeches and a Norfolk jacket. "Never mind, we'll dine in
my room, and I'll serve you myself so that the waiter shan't see
you," promised Proust; and sure enough he collected each course
from a tray in the lobby of his room, but only when the footsteps of
the waiter had died away in the soft-carpeted corridor. 'He thinks
being seen by a waiter in the wrong clothes would be as important
for me as it would be for him,' thought Leclercq with a pang of
amused affection, and decided that this was true courtesy.

Once more the season was ending. He negotiated unsuccessfully
to stay on in the Grand Hôtel after it closed for the winter, and
thought of revisiting Venice. Providentially the news arrived that
Georges de Lauris had broken a leg in a motor-car accident. Proust
saw the opportunity to combine a dramatic errand of mercy to his
friend with the secluded work and other pleasures which he had
enjoyed in the autumn of 1906, and left immediately for Versailles,
explaining, as he had during the illness of his uncle Georges Weil,
that his sole purpose was to be near the invalid. He travelled in one
of Jacques Bizet's taxis, driven by Agostinelli, and took the roundabout route by the Seine valley, via Pont-Audemer, Caudebec,
Saint-Wandrille and Jumièges, which he had planned the year
before. At Pont-Audemer in the church of Saint-Ouen he found hints
for the stained glass of Saint-Hilaire at Combray; and at the ruined
abbey of Jumièges he saw the Merovingian crypt and the paving of
abbots' tombs which he transferred likewise to Saint-Hilaire.[1]

At the Hôtel des Réservoirs he retired to his bed as before, ill both
with asthma and with the cafeine which he took as an antidote. He
visited Lauris once, in his third-floor bedroom in the Rue Washington, and found him looking the picture of health, but could never
again face the breathless ascent of his stairs; and twice more he came
to Paris to see his Cabourg friends, and enjoyed, as he confided in
Lauris, 'a few small pleasures with a girl who is new and dear to me
and with some young men friends who are new too'. Many as are

[1] I, 59-62, 103.

the possible meanings of '*de petits plaisirs*', Lauris can only have supposed Proust to imply that his 'small pleasures', with the girl at least, were those of love; and it is likely that Proust had in this October the same agreeable surprise as the Narrator, when Albertine in Paris granted him more than she had refused at Balbec. 'Young girls,' he wrote to Lauris early in the following January, 'are almost my only love, as if life weren't complicated enough anyway. You may say marriage was invented for this very purpose, but then the girl ceases to be a girl, one can only possess a girl once. I understand Bluebeard, he was a man who loved young girls.' But at Versailles he had still other enjoyments. Reynaldo stayed in the hotel for a few days and composed a new ballet for the Opéra, *La Fête chez Thérèse*, at his bedside, while Proust played dominoes with Agostinelli and Nicolas. At night, while his servants slept, he worked; and the revelation of Time Regained, gradual and imperfect but true, began to come to him at last.

Chapter 6

BY WAY OF SAINTE-BEUVE
(*November 1908 – August 1909*)

AFTER HIS three visits to Paris Proust was either too ill, as he alleged to the captive Lauris, or too engrossed in his writing, as may be suspected, to stir from his bed at Versailles. For a few days he lent Agostinelli and his taxi to friends, and then thriftily dismissed chauffeur and vehicle. He was still not sufficiently attached to the young man to invent excuses for keeping him near; and Agostinelli, returning as before like an autumn swallow to Monaco, vanished from his master's life for four years.

Early in November 1908 the re-paving of the Rue des Réservoirs below Proust's apartment drove him back to Paris, where he was afflicted by the noisy moving-in of Dr Williams, a dentist, on the floor above, and suffocated by a leak in his hot-water radiator, which compelled him to the unprecedented step of opening his windows to the winter night. Soon his asthma subsided, and he earnestly quoted to Lauris a maxim adapted by Ruskin from John ix, 4: 'work while you still have light, for soon the night cometh when no man can work'. 'I am already half-immersed in that night,' he added, 'and as I no longer have light I am setting to work.' Nevertheless, whether from dread of the long task ahead, from which only death would release him, or from an instinctive knowledge that the hour of beginning was still not arrived, he again avoided the direct way to his goal. Proust abandoned the 1905-8 novel, including even the promising new version on which he had worked since February in Paris, Cabourg and Versailles. He began to plan a book of very different intention; but in fact a deep intuition had now led him into the last turning of the way to *A la Recherche*.

As early as the previous spring, at the time of the first Lemoine pastiches, he had foreseen the necessity, though not the precise nature, of this new work. When he explained to Robert Dreyfus on 18 March 1908 that he wrote his parodies 'because I'm too lazy to write literary criticism, and because I found it so amusing to perform literary criticism in action', he added: 'but perhaps on the contrary my parodies will force me to write criticism, in order to explain them to people who don't understand them'. Now, towards the end of November 1908, he decided, as he informed Lauris and Mme de Noailles about a month later in almost identical words, to write a study of Sainte-Beuve: he had in mind two possible forms, either an essay in the classical manner like Taine's, or (a new idea which came when the first plan had already failed) an imaginary conversation with his mother, in which he would discuss his unwritten essay with her. But his ostensible subject was only a pretext for a wider theme. In exposing the philistinism of Sainte-Beuve, who was generally accepted as the most infallible of French critics, he would attack the false view of literature by which critics, the reading public, and all but the greatest writers had hitherto been blinded; and in showing the true nature of creative art he would simultaneously prepare the world for his own coming novel, and make the discoveries which would enable him to write it.

By way of preparation, as in 1905 before the composition of 'Sur la Lecture', he entered on a vast course of reading, which included not only the entire works of Sainte-Beuve, but the memoirs of Saint-Simon and of Chateaubriand, both of whom are among the great invisible presences in A la Recherche. Probably it was at this time that Proust wrote the brief fragment 'Chateaubriand', which contains ideas repeated by the Narrator in Le Temps Retrouvé: that Chateaubriand's moments of poetic vision, in which he seems to conquer death and time, are precursors of the theory of unconscious memory —'of the same species as the tasting of the madeleine', says the Narrator—and that such moments are in a sense more important than the great historical events which form the other subject of Mémoires d'Outre-Tombe, since the events are temporal, while the moments are eternal.[1]

In December he added a less avowable aspect of literature to his syllabus, by acquiring four obscene pamphlets at the sale of a respectable Protestant banker. The two 'secret, unclean and stupid Verlaines, of the kind of pornography that mortifies the senses', were Femmes and Hombres: the former a shameless lyric-cycle on the poet's heterosexual orgies, the latter a sodomitic counterpart which

---

[1] Contre Sainte-Beuve, 407-10; III, 728, 919-20.

reads like a versified prospectus for Jupien's brothel.[1] The others, a series of seven letters to Stendhal and a memoir on him entitled *H.B.*, were both by Mérimée. The notorious *H.B.* is a work of unexpected innocuousness, except for a gross frontispiece added by the wily publisher, showing Stendhal spying on the infidelity of his mistress; but its influence on Proust was none the less significant. He bought his four 'curious' books in quest of inspiration for the 'obscenity' which, as he announced to Lauris and others, he intended to introduce into both his Sainte-Beuve essay and his novel. The Narrator's three crucial revelations of sexual deviation are all associated with spying—not, like Stendhal in the scabrous engraving, through a keyhole, but by a characteristically Proustian symbol through a window. He becomes aware of Lesbianism by watching Mlle Vinteuil and her friend through the window at Montjouvain, of sodomy when he sees the meeting of Charlus and Jupien in the Duchesse's courtyard, and of solitary pleasure in the upstairs lavatory at Combray, where the Narrator himself is detected from outside by the flowering currant and the castle-keep of Roussainville. All these are probably based on real memories, and Proust had described, some fourteen years before, a similar scene to Stendhal's in *'Confession d'une Jeune Fille'*; but the earlier impressions were reinforced and crystallised for his novel by his reading at the crucial time of Mérimée's *H.B.* Moreover, although the Narrator's posthumous jealousy of Albertine was based on an experience in Proust's life which lay five years ahead, Proust doubtless did not forget Stendhal's confession to Mérimée that he 'felt a strange curiosity to know all my mistress's infidelities, insisted on being told every detail, and—in spite of the appalling suffering it caused me—took a certain pleasure in imagining her in all the situations which my informants described'.

Sainte-Beuve was less slow in coming than Proust pretended. Again and again he informed Lauris of his inability to set pen to paper: before the end of 1908 he had already started his essay three

[1]   '*Mes amants n'appartiennent pas aux classes riches,*
      Ce sont des ouvriers faubouriens ou ruraux.
      Leurs quinze et leurs vingt ans sans apprêts sont mal chiches
      De force assez brutale et de procédés gros. . . .'
wrote Verlaine in a catalogue of young men which included, by an odd coincidence, a namesake of Proust's chauffeur: '*Odilon, un gamin, mais monté comme un homme*'.

times 'in my head', but in January 1909 he alleged his increasing difficulty in remembering either his plan, or the works of Sainte-Beuve which he had read in his course of preparation. The truth was, as we shall see, that he wrote the first two-thirds of *Contre Sainte-Beuve* during this winter and spring, and when in June he at last admitted to Lauris that he had begun to work, his essay was not far from completion.

Meanwhile, recoiling in order to leap better, Proust put his clock a year back by writing yet more pastiches on the Lemoine Affair. The wretched maker of diamonds had fled to Constantinople in the previous June, and on his way was glimpsed incognito in the French embassy at Sofia by Robert de Billy—then *chargé d'affaires* in Bulgaria—as he waited despondently for a visa. In January 1909 Lemoine was tried in his absence. Calmette intimated that further pastiches would be welcome; but Proust had still another motive in his pique at an article in the *Journal des Débats* of 28 September 1908, in which Henri de Régnier had praised other parodists to the skies, but refrained from mentioning his former friend and fellow-member of the Cannibal Academy—'he quoted all our contemporary writers of parody, including several idiots,[1] but never a word about me'. Proust retaliated with a stinging pastiche of Régnier himself, doing full justice to the symbolist rococo of his prose-style, and insinuating that Régnier defrauded the public like Lemoine by manufacturing the false diamonds of literature. A Chateaubriand parody, a Maeterlinck, and a second Sainte-Beuve followed, but remain unpublished.[2] Soon Proust turned from Chateaubriand to an author who was to take an equal but opposite part in the literary sources of *A la Recherche*: 'I'm head over heels in Saint-Simon,' he told Lauris, 'though nothing could be more different from *Mémoires d'Outre-tombe*.' In February Proust wrote to Montesquiou asking to borrow

[1] This is hardly fair: Régnier in fact confined his examples to three verse parodists (Banville, Albert Sorel, and Tristan Bernard) who were by no means idiots; and prose parody was outside his subject.

[2] The Maeterlinck is included in the second of the exercise-books in which Proust wrote *Contre Sainte-Beuve*. The Chateaubriand and second Sainte-Beuve have not yet been reported. A Wellsian parody of Ruskin entitled '*La Bénédiction du Sanglier*', an 'introduction to Giotto's frescoes on the Lemoine Affair' in which the tourist-pilgrim to Paris is advised to travel by aeroplane ('Wilbur's bird'), probably belongs to this period. The brothers Wilbur and Orville Wright had given sensational exhibition flights in France in 1908. See *Nouvelle Nouvelle Revue Française*, 1 October 1953, 762-7.

the Saint-Simon pastiche, '*Fête chez Montesquiou à Neuilly*', which
he had written five years before. This he skilfully embedded, almost
without alteration, in the longer Saint-Simon parody in *Pastiches
et Mélanges*, together with material belonging to the year 1919; but it
was presumably in this February that he inserted the context relating
to the Lemoine Affair. In his Saint-Simon and Chateaubriand
parodies Proust was performing an act of homage as well as reducing
a literary influence to manageable proportions. The two writers had
travelled long before himself the Guermantes and the Méséglise
Ways, the former achieving a devastating vision of the vanity of
human relationships, the latter a recovery of the lost reality of his
own past. Both are invoked in the Narrator's meditations on his
coming novel in *Le Temps Retrouvé*, Chateaubriand, as we have
seen, for his anticipation of the discovery of unconscious memory,
and Saint-Simon when the Narrator resolves to write 'the Saint-
Simon's *Memoirs* of another epoch'.[1]

Early in March he promised, much to the Count's gratification,
a pastiche of Montesquiou himself. He met Jules Lemaître at Mme
Daudet's: "if an author's work can be taken apart and put together
again like that, one hardly dares go on writing—it's not only
extraordinary, it's terrifying!" said Lemaître, and affably urged him
to compose a Mérimée and a Voltaire. The Régnier pastiche appeared
in *Le Figaro* on 6 March; and Proust received a magnanimous note
from his victim, saying: 'I thought it a very good likeness!', and 'a
most intelligent and really pretty letter' from Barrès, remarking that
Proust had discovered 'a formula for criticism based on Buffon's
principle that form and content must not be separated'. Lemoine's
arrest in April happened to be witnessed by a Paris bookseller named
Puzin, whose assistant, however, was unable to give any further
information to reporters. "Lemoine?" the young man repeated,
"who's he?"; and he explained, pointing to a volume of Nietzsche
in his hand: "I never read newspapers, only books!" In a *Figaro*
article on 17 April Robert Dreyfus took the opportunity to mention
Proust's pastiches, 'in which he performs a marriage between the
solid substance of his fancy and the airy inspirations of topicality!',
and invited him to parody Nietzsche. In June Proust wrote for
Dreyfus's benefit an unpublished parody of the popular novelist
Paul Adam; but in July he exclaimed to his friend in unwontedly
strong language, '*Merde pour les pastiches!*'; and a brief '*Explanation*

[1] III, 919, 1044.

by H. Taine of the reasons why your talk of pastiches bores me to distraction' marked the end of the era of parodies. Nevertheless, during these eight months of apparent delay and evasion, he had never ceased to work on *Contre Sainte-Beuve*.

Early in March Proust had confided in Lauris that he hoped, 'if I am still alive', to publish his Sainte-Beuve essay in the autumn, 'because this full trunk in the middle of my brain is getting in my way, and I must decide either to make the journey or to unpack'. On 23 May he asked Lauris an epoch-making question: did the name Guermantes belong to the Pâris family, or was it 'extinct and available for a writer'? The châtelaine of Guermantes, François de Pâris's grandmother the Baronne de Lareinty, was an imposing, sharp-tongued old lady, whom Lauris forty years later remembered in her red armchair by the window, scanning the radiating avenues of the park for arriving guests, and exclaiming crossly when her son seemed indisposed, "He looks the image of a parsley omelette!" The château, a mellow edifice which exists to this day and is illustrated in standard works on French architecture, was built in the reign of Louis XIV for a wealthy financier named Paulin Prondre de Guermantes; for the majestic and poetic name which became a symbol of the last splendours of the French nobility was chosen by Proust, with deliberate irony, from a plebeian parvenu of the seventeenth century, who in turn had borrowed it from the nearby village.[1]

In June, having lamented for seven months his inability to begin, Proust at last declared to Lauris: 'I'm worn out from starting *Sainte-Beuve*—work is in full swing, though the results are deplorable.' This burst of creation was soon interrupted. 'My intention is to try to resume work on *Sainte-Beuve* from tomorrow onwards,' he told Lauris early in July; but in mid-August, when Lauris asked 'Is *Sainte-Beuve* finished?', Proust could still only reply: 'what a hurry you're in! I'll start again when I can.' Already, however, *Contre Sainte-Beuve* as we have it was probably completed, for a week or two later Proust considered his work far enough advanced to justify

---

[1] Proust alludes to this situation .wice in *A la Recherche*, once when the Narrator is disillusioned by learning from Saint-Loup that the Guermantes acquired their château only in the seventeenth century (II, 14), and again when Charlus informs him that Mme de Villeparisis's second husband was 'a certain little Monsieur Thirion', whose stolen name, once the property of a family extinct in 1702, belonged of right only to the small town of Villeparisis near Paris (II, 294). Villeparisis is, in fact, a little town near Meaux, not far from Guermantes itself.

seeking a publisher, and reported to Lauris: 'it's very long, between four and five hundred pages'. There is no record of further additions, and it was in this July, as we shall see, that he began *A la Recherche du Temps Perdu*.

Proust's work during the eighteen months from February 1908 to August 1909 may now be surveyed in chronological order. The new version of his novel, begun in February and abandoned in November 1908, survives in seventy-five unpublished loose leaves. These are said[1] to comprise the visit to Venice, a holiday at a seaside resort as yet unnamed, where the Narrator meets a much reduced little band of only two girls, and a long episode at Combray—a name which now appears for the first time—including the scene of the goodnight kiss and, again for the first time, the symbol of the Two Ways. Swann as the unwelcome visitor is called M. de Bretteville, and his other functions at Combray are filled by the Narrator's uncle; for although Proust had created and named Swann three years before, and had even at one time given to him episodes, such as the love-affair with the little band, which in *A la Recherche* belong to the story of the Narrator, he had not yet introduced him into the primal scenes of his novel. The first of the Ways was already called Méséglise, though the other was not yet Guermantes, but Villebon. Villebon is indeed a village with a fourteenth-century château, seven miles past Saint-Éman to the north of Illiers, and therefore in the same direction as the later Guermantes Way.

On a further twenty leaves of the same paper, and presumably written immediately after, are the three earliest sections of *Contre Sainte-Beuve*: the two prefaces (one to the 'classical essay', and the other to the imaginary conversation), and the essay '*Sur la méthode de Sainte-Beuve*'. This is none other than the 'classical essay in the manner of Taine' which Proust mentioned in December 1908 to Lauris and Mme de Noailles—indeed, he quotes Taine's essay on Sainte-Beuve in the first few paragraphs[2]—and its composition is further dated by the inclusion of the words from Saint John—'work while ye still have light'[3]—which Proust cited to Lauris early in November. The abandonment of his new work on his novel and the beginning of *Contre Sainte-Beuve* can be assigned, therefore,

[1] *Contre Sainte-Beuve*, 14. As at present reported, the order of the episodes in this manuscript is curiously reversed.
[2] *Contre-Sainte Beuve*, 133-4.
[3] *Ibid.*, 131.

to early November 1908, more than seven months before Proust's first admission to Lauris, in June 1909, that he had commenced his essay.

Proust's indictment of Sainte-Beuve is a development of his parody of the year before, in which the critic delivers on Proust's Flaubert pastiche the same perfidiously philistine judgements which Sainte-Beuve himself had uttered on Flaubert's *Salammbo*. Sainte-Beuve maintained that the supreme test of critical insight lay in ability to detect genius among one's contemporaries; yet he consistently underrated the truly original writers of his own time, such as Stendhal, Balzac, Baudelaire and Flaubert. Proust diagnoses the causes of this failure in Sainte-Beuve's false view of literature as a pleasant cultural recreation for a person of good breeding, in his journalist's habit of writing with his eye on the average intelligent reader—'he saw Mme de Boigne in her tall four poster, opening *Le Constitutionnel* in the wintry dawn'[1]—instead of looking in his own heart, but most of all in his famous method of using the external features of a writer's life and character to explain his work. 'An author's writing is inseparable from the rest of him,' declared Sainte-Beuve; and Stendhal, he pointed out, mediocre as his novels might be, was the soul of honour to his friends, while Baudelaire, however eccentric his poetry, was a perfect gentleman when one had the privilege of knowing him personally. Proust satirised Sainte-Beuve's method in Mme de Villeparisis's deflating anecdotes of Chateaubriand, Balzac, Vigny and Hugo. "I'm entitled to speak of them," she tells the Narrator at Balbec, "because they used to come to my father's house; and as Monsieur Sainte-Beuve, a man of great intelligence, used to say, one ought to take the word of people who've mixed with them and had the opportunity of forming a more exact opinion of their real worth."[2] And Proust condemns the method of Sainte-Beuve in a formula which applies equally to the understanding of another's work of art and to the now imminent creation of his own: 'a book is the product of a different self from the one we manifest in our habits, in society, in our vices. If we mean to try to understand this self it is only in our inmost depths, by endeavouring to reconstruct it there, that the quest can be achieved.' Sainte-Beuve, he concludes, 'found himself in the presence of reality and received from it a direct sensation' only in his early verses; and Proust ends with a metaphor which reappears in the dying Bergotte's vision of 'a

[1] *Ibid.*, 147, repeated III, 570.　　　　　　　　　　[2] I, 710-11, 721-3.

celestial balance, with his life in one scale and the little patch of yellow wall in the other'[1]: 'the poetry written by a critic outweighs, in the scales of eternity, all the rest of his work'.

Proust's verdict on Sainte-Beuve may well give pause to Proust's would-be biographer. Can it be that he has applied this shallow and falsifying 'method of Sainte-Beuve' to *A la Recherche* itself? Fortunately, however, the biographical approach to a work of art is the direct opposite of Sainte-Beuve's, in which a superficial impression of an author's outward behaviour is used as a corrective to an equally superficial impression of his work. The biographer's task, on the contrary, is to trace the formation and relationship of the very two selves which Proust distinguishes. He must discover, beneath the mask of the artist's every-day, objective life, the secret life from which he extracted his work; show how, in the apparently sterile persons and places of that external life, he found the hidden, universal meanings which are the themes of his book; and reveal the drama of the contrast and interaction between his daily existence and his incommensurably deeper life as a creator. *A la Recherche*, of all great works of art, cannot be fully understood until the life in time of which it is a symbolic reconstruction in eternity is known. So the biographer, if he fails, should blame his own faulty application of the biographical method, his deficiencies of talent and sensibility, but not the method itself. Proust himself was concerned at this time to vindicate his future novel as a work of creative imagination, and to forestall the philistine critics and readers who would mistake it for a *roman à clef*. But in different contexts, and particularly in *Le Temps Retrouvé* itself, he was ready to admit a much closer relation between the self that wrote his novel and 'the one we manifest in our habits, in society, in our vices', and so conceded some truth to Sainte-Beuve's belief that 'an author's work is inseparable from the rest of him'.

The section called '*Conclusion*' in the published *Contre Sainte-Beuve*, and placed at the end of the work, was not so called by Proust, and was neither last to be written nor intended as a conclusion. It alludes to the reading of Régnier and Maeterlinck which resulted, a few weeks later, in Proust's parodies of these authors, and must have been written, towards the end of December 1908, immediately after the essay on Sainte-Beuve's method to which it is a logical sequel. Proust now studies the nature of the true work of art

[1] III, 187.

in contemporary writers such as France, Régnier, Loti or Barrès (omitting to mention that he was now out of sympathy with all these), and the false in Romain Rolland's *Jean Christophe* and the neo-classicist poet Moréas. More important, he investigates artistic truth as it might be revealed in his own work 'if he were able to write', taking for the first time the position of his Narrator, who until the end of *A la Recherche* is a writer *manqué*; and although this is not literally true of Proust himself, who had written incessantly since his schooldays, it is true symbolically, because he had now worked for twenty years without being able to write *A la Recherche*. He claims, 'although, as I'd never been able to work, I could not be a writer', that he possesses two faculties necessary for creation. He can sense beneath the text of great literature the deeper undertone which is the creative self of the writer—'as soon as I began to read an author, I detected under the words the tune of the song, which in each author is different from that of every other'; and this, despite his inability to create, 'enabled me to produce parodies, because once a writer's tune is heard, the words soon follow'.[1] His other gift is the power to 'discover a profound affinity between two ideas or two sensations'; and for the separate being within him who only comes to life at such moments of revelation, 'existing and being happy are one and the same thing . . . it is he, and only he, who ought to write my books'. 'Why,' he asks, 'is reality restored to us by the coincidence of two identical sensations?'—but he can still give no satisfactory answer.

Once again, as in the vision by the Lake of Geneva in *Jean Santeuil* and in certain passages of his Ruskin prefaces, Proust was travelling in the right direction. But his objective 'essay in the manner of Taine' could take him no further. Soon his inspiration and his prose deteriorated, and he wrote in the margin of his manuscript: 'don't leave this horrible style unaltered!'[2] It was now, late in December 1908, when he realised that the problems of the creative imagination could not be satisfactorily handled in this abstract form, that he first thought of an alternative plan and asked the advice of

[1] The idea is an adaptation of Proust's remark to Robert Dreyfus in March 1908 on his Renan parody: 'I set my inner metronome to his rhythm, and the words came in floods.' But it is true of Proust's own work, which had failed because he had not yet fully discovered his own 'tune'. When he found it, in the summer of 1909, he immediately began *A la Recherche*.

[2] *Contre Sainte-Beuve*, 306.

Lauris and Mme de Noailles. His new idea was suggested by a digression in the essay on Sainte-Beuve's method, in which he contrasted the self-satisfaction of the great critic on seeing his weekly article in the Monday morning *Le Constitutionnel* with the more innocent joy of the beginner who—like Proust himself long ago—sees his own first article brought to his bedside by his mother.[1] He now decided to describe such a morning, and to bring the dead Mme Proust to life for a conversation in which, liberated from the rules of conventional criticism, he would unfold his essay to her in the mirror of his own past. For in order to show his view of art springing from its source in his own depths, he must first reconstruct his former and present self around it, complete with the environment of his lost family and the Faubourg Saint-Germain of his youth.

[1] *Contre Sainte-Beuve*, 146-7.

Chapter 7

THE TEA AND THE MADELEINE
(*January – December 1909*)

WITH the new year, after two months of unseasonable warmth and sunlight, came the first snow-fall of the winter. It was on or about 1 January 1909 that Proust returned, late at night, along the snow-covered Boulevard Haussmann, to experience one of the most momentous events of his life. As he sat reading by his lamp, still shivering with cold, Céline urged her master to take a cup of tea, an unfamiliar beverage for this addict of coffee; and when he idly dipped in it a finger of dry toast and raised the sodden mixture to his lips, he was overwhelmed once more by the mysterious joy which marked an onset of unconscious memory. He caught an elusive scent of geraniums and orange-blossom, mingled with a sensation of extraordinary light and happiness. Not daring to move, clinging to the taste on his palate, he pondered, until suddenly the doors of memory opened. The garden of his great-uncle Louis Weil at Auteuil had returned, miraculously preserved by the savour of the rusk soaked in tea which his grandfather Nathé Weil would give him when, a child in the summer mornings of the 1880s, he visited the old man in his bedroom. The experience, for Proust as for the Narrator, was of a familiar kind, which he had known at intervals all through his life. At that moment he saw it only as a symbol of his present theme, the nature of artistic creation; for the act of unconscious memory combined both the aspects of art of which he had written a few days before, the sensation in the depths of the self of a pure reality, and the discovery of an affinity between two feelings. He did not yet realise that this was the missing key, which he had sought ever since the beginning of *Jean Santeuil* in 1895, to the creation of his novel.

He now wrote the preface to the new version of *Contre Sainte-Beuve*. 'Every day,' he began, 'I attach less and less importance to the intellect. Every day I realise more that it is only by other means that a writer can regain something of our impressions, reach, that is, a particle of himself, the only material of art. What the intellect restores to us under the name of the past is not the past . . .' And by way of example he described four instances of involuntary memory, of which the first three, at least, were probably recent: the garden of Auteuil unfolding in his cup of tea, 'like the Japanese paper flowers which only come to life when we drop them in water'[1]; Venice preserved by his stumbling, 'last year, as I was crossing a courtyard', on an uneven paving-stone[2]; the trees near a railway-line, barred with sunlight and shadow, resurrected by the tinkling of a spoon on a saucer[3]; and the never-solved enigma of the group of trees, which would reappear to the Narrator during his drive in Mme de Ville-parisis's carriage near Balbec.[4] Now, at last, Proust interpreted the riddle of unconscious memory correctly: it was reality itself, freed from the mask of time and habit, 'a fragment of pure life preserved in its purity, which we can only know when it is so preserved, because, in the moment when we live it, it is not present to our memory, but surrounded by sensations which suppress it'. The whole vast structure of A la Recherche is enclosed in these seven pages of Proust's preface: within a few days he had experienced and sketched out the beginning of his novel in Time Lost and its end in Time Regained.

Such is the bewilderment produced by an unconscious memory before it is identified, Proust remarked in the new preface, that 'for a moment I was like a sleeper who wakes in the night and cannot tell where he is, or in what bed, in what house, what place, what year of his life he may be'. Once again a chance simile in one part of his

[1] A simile repeated in A la Recherche at the end of the madeleine incident (I, 47-8), and inspired by Marie Nordlinger's gift in April 1904.

[2] Cf. III, 867. There is no need to doubt that this, the first movement in the symphony of incidences of unconscious memory in Le Temps Retrouvé which cause the Narrator to begin his novel, actually occurred to Proust. Possibly 'last year' means the autumn of 1908, a time when he was thinking of Venice, and the courtyard may have been at Versailles in the Hôtel des Réservoirs. Neither Proust nor any other visitor could fail to stumble on the pavement of the basilica of Saint Mark, which undulates on the sea of time like the sea on which it is built; and the incident is as exquisitely appropriate to calling up the memory of Venice as it is likely to have occurred in real life.

[3] III, 855, 868. If this, too, is taken from real life, it may belong to one of Proust's two railway-journeys since the death of his mother, to Cabourg in 1907 and 1908. But in an early novel-fragment (1908?) the incident occurs in the Narrator's boyhood, on a train-journey to Combray (French Studies, vol. 3, no. 4 (Oct. 1949), 340).   [4] I, 717-19.

essay suggested the plan of the next, and was destined to expand still further in *A la Recherche*. As a prelude to his morning conversation with his mother he now decided to describe the mysteries of his sleep and awakening on that and other mornings: at the outset he would map the country of his unconscious mind, in the depths of which he would then situate the act of criticism and the act of creation.

Early in January 1909 Proust set aside the loose leaves on which he had so far worked, and proceeded to write the new version of his essay in seven school exercise books bound in black plush. The date is confirmed by the fact that the first two contain not only the account of his waking and the conversations with his mother, but the Maeterlinck and Régnier parodies written in the same month.

The first two chapters, '*Sommeils*' and '*Chambres*', contain the meditation on the various forms of sleep, the hallucinatory efforts to discover in which of the bedrooms of his past he has awoken, which later form the opening of *Du Côté de chez Swann*. Next, just as a seedling encloses in small compass the leaves, branches and flowers which will grow far apart in the mature plant, he produced material which would reappear in widely separate parts of *A la Recherche*. A long account of his solitary experiments in sex in the upstairs lavatory at Illiers, one of the passages of obscene beauty which formed part of his plan, is followed immediately by the lilacs of 'the park outside the town', which is not yet called Tansonville, and the tadpoles and mysterious fisherman of the river, which is not yet called the Vivonne.[1] One of the rooms in which he believes he has woken is at 'the château of Réveillon'; and the description of his life there was re-used, at opposite ends of *A la Recherche*, in the nocturnal walks of the Narrator with Gilberte de Saint-Loup at Tansonville.[2]

---

[1] The lavatory incident is given doubled force in *Swann* by being drastically abbreviated and split into two (I, 12, 158). The lilacs appear, much revised, at I, 135, the tadpoles and fisherman with little alteration at I, 168, 167. The mystery of the fisherman is solved in a rejected fragment: he is none other than the former lover of Mme Putbus's maid; but in *Swann* Proust wisely preferred to leave him as an enigma.

[2] *Contre Sainte-Beuve*, 71-2 = I, 6-7; III, 691-3. It is significant that even in *Jean Santeuil* Proust placed Réveillon (which in fact is a hundred miles, and on the other side of Paris, from Illiers) only a little way from the horizon of Étreuilles. 'I took them round by Montjouvain,' says the Duc de Réveillon (vol. 2, 244), and Henri one day 'has gone to Étreuilles with his father' (vol. 2, 23).

For the first time it is clear that these are the same walks which Jean Santeuil took at Réveillon with the Duchesse or Henri, and Proust himself at the real Réveillon of Madeleine Lemaire in the late summer of 1894; and Gilberte at this moment, alternately matronly and still young, is a fusion of Mme Lemaire herself fourteen years before (when Albert Flament had thought Proust 'infatuated' with her) and her charming daughter Suzette. At this stage in *Du Côté de chez Swann* the whole Combray episode intervenes, introduced by Swann's visit, the goodnight kiss, and the tasting of the madeleine. But Proust had already written a first version of this (though without the madeleine) in the novel-draft of the previous year; and in *Contre Sainte-Beuve* he leaps immediately to the moment when he sees, 'above the place I had assigned to my wardrobe, the streak of risen day',[1] and the kaleidoscope of Time Lost steadies into the grey daylight of the present.

In Chapter Three, '*Journées*', he is broad awake, yet the real world reaches his bedside only in the form of a natural metaphor, when the sound of passing tramcars, 'piercing with the auger of a fife the blue ice of a chill sunlit day', brings news of the unseen weather in the streets. The morning belongs to the very January in which Proust writes, but he has also unconsciously prophesied a future state. On winter mornings four years later he would listen as now before the sleep of the day, while in the next room Agostinelli rose for purposes of his own from the sleep of the night; and when Proust opened *La Prisonnière* with the beginning of a day with the captive Albertine, his material was ready to hand in *Contre Sainte-Beuve*. The description of Great-Uncle Louis's dining-room at Auteuil likewise reappears in *La Prisonnière*,[2] as does the evocation of the odour of motor-cars in the street, 'most intoxicating of country scents in summer', when the same smell of petrol makes the Narrator long to travel and leave Albertine, a moment before Françoise enters his bedroom with the news that Albertine, on the contrary, has left him; but in *Contre Sainte-Beuve* these country thoughts merge into the cornfields and poppies of the road to Méséglise, and the wind which seems to bring the Narrator a message from Gilberte. A little further on, now first used in a serious context, are the 'spindles of red flowers peering over a sunlit wall' from the Flaubert pastiche, which

---

[1] *Contre Sainte-Beuve*, 73 = I, 187.
[2] *Contre Sainte-Beuve*, 78-9 = *De David à Degas*, vii-viii. Cf. III, 168, 412.

the Narrator at Combray would associate with the Duchesse de Guermantes.[1]

Chapter Four, '*La Comtesse*', is a sketch for the Narrator's pursuit of the Duchesse de Guermantes, modelled on Proust's wooing of Mme de Chevigné in 1892; but in this primitive and inferior version she is only a countess, becomes his mistress, and visits friends with the mawkish names which Proust had favoured in *Les Plaisirs et les Jours* and *Jean Santeuil*: Princesse d'Alériouvres, Mme de Breyvres. Soon, however, he would find the names of his characters, and therefore be ready to create them. The unnamed concierge of his family works as a tailor in the shop in the countess's courtyard: here is a first faint appearance of Jupien. The family servant is called Françoise, a name which Proust had previously given only to women loved by his heroes.[2]

In Chapter Five, '*L'Article dans* Le Figaro', Proust has at last reached the central episode of the new essay, when his mother brings in the morning's *Figaro* with his article, tactfully leaves him to enjoy it alone, and re-enters for their morning conversation. The subject of the article is not revealed, and no single article of Proust's is intended: the scene represents countless similar occasions from the *Le Banquet* contributions of 1892 onwards. Nowhere else, whether in the surviving letters between mother and son, or in *Jean Santeuil*, or even in *A la Recherche* itself, is the intimacy and wit of their relationship so vividly preserved as in the protracted dialogue of *Contre Sainte-Beuve*. Proust had now brought his mother back to life, to collaborate in his new work as she had in his Ruskin translations, and in *A la Recherche* he would not let her die. The episode is a development of the fortuitous image of a conversation between mother and son in '*Sur la Méthode de Sainte-Beuve*'; and in *A la Recherche* it recurs when the Narrator's mother, some months after the death of Albertine, brings to his bedside his long-delayed article on the spires of Martinville in *Le Figaro*.[3] Soon the pink light of

---

[1] Material from this chapter (*Contre Sainte-Beuve*, 74-85) will be found in order of occurrence at III, 9, 82, 12, 27, 412; I, 145-6, 172.

[2] *Contre Sainte-Beuve*, 91. In the following chapters she is generally called Félicie, after her original in real life, Félicie Fitau; but on pp. 107, 113 she is again Françoise.

[3] *Contre Sainte-Beuve*, 146-7, 95-101 = III, 566-70. As we have seen, however, the Narrator's essay on the spires is an actual extract from Proust's *Figaro* article of 19 November 1907, which was written two years after his mother's death and published within a month or so of its composition.

dawn renews his longing to travel; and he recalls the vision seen by the Narrator on the night-train to Balbec, and by Proust himself on the way to Avallon in September 1903, of hills lit by moon and sun, and the rosy peasant-girl who brings coffee to the train.[1]

In Chapter Six, '*Le Rayon de Soleil sur le Balcon*', the conversation on the article continues, with a digression on the comedy of Saturday lunch (displaced in *A la Recherche* from Paris to Combray),[2] and another on the ray of sunlight on the balcony, and the boy Proust's first visit to Marie de Benardaky's home, which he used in the Narrator's love for Gilberte.[3] "Don't you agree that the piece about the telephone isn't too bad?" he asks his mother. Proust is thinking here both of the telephone-scene in '*Journées de Lecture*' (his *Figaro* article of 20 March 1907, which Mme Proust never saw), and of the episode in *Jean Santeuil* where Jean telephones his mother from Beg-Meil (written at Fontainebleau in October 1896), which Mme Proust had admired but thought 'terribly sad'. The 'piece about the telephone' would recur at Doncières.[4]

Chapter Seven, '*Conversation avec Maman*', the last in which the dialogue is fully sustained, includes four incidents from real life. The first, on his visits to Venice in May and October 1900, is a preliminary sketch for the Narrator's sojourn in Venice with his mother after the death of Albertine[5]; the second is the night at Auteuil when his mother read *François le Champi*, an episode afterwards transferred to Combray and joined to the story of the goodnight kiss. For two others, however, no place could be found in *A la Recherche*: one recalls Mme Proust quoting Molière and Labiche on her deathbed, to comfort her son; and in the other Reynaldo Hahn sings his setting of a chorus from Racine's *Esther* at the piano in Marcel's bedroom: 'my father did not dare to applaud; and my mother darted a furtive glance at him, to enjoy his happiness with a pang of emotion'.[6] Marcel now plans a new *Figaro* article to be called '*Contre Sainte-Beuve*,'[7] and summons his mother to hear it.

[1] I, 654-8.   [2] *Contre Sainte-Beuve*, 106-7 = I, 101-11.

[3] I, 396-9, 503-4; II, 637.   [4] II, 132-6.

[5] Cf. especially III, 623-5, 652-4. A later passage on Venice as imagined by his grandmother, *Contre Sainte-Beuve*, 290, corresponds to III, 628-9.

[6] A copy of Reynaldo's song from *Esther*, '*O douce paix*', dated 1896 and inscribed by him 'To Mme Adrien Proust, in memory of our friends in the *grand siècle*', was shown in the Proust exhibition at the Wildenstein Gallery (No. 332).

[7] This title, though it apparently occurs only here in Proust's manuscript, is therefore Proust's own.

In the ensuing studies of Gérard de Nerval, Baudelaire and Balzac, except that in the two latter he intermittently speaks to his mother, Proust reverts to his 'essay in classical form'. He shows that Sainte-Beuve's criticisms of these great writers are untrue not only of them, but of all great art; and conversely, when he refutes Sainte-Beuve by giving his own vision of their genius, his remarks are valid also for great literature in general, and for *A la Recherche* in particular. The writing of *Contre Sainte-Beuve* is symbolised in *A la Recherche* (just as the Lemoine pastiches are represented by the Narrator's disillusioned reading of the Goncourt *Journal* at Tansonville) by the Narrator's meditation on the nature of his coming novel at the Princesse de Guermantes's matinée. It is a consequence of Proust's train of thought at this time—about March and April 1909—that when the Narrator at last steps through the open door of Time Regained he meets Nerval and Baudelaire already there. Nerval's *Sylvie*, he reflects as he waits in the Prince de Guermantes's library,[1] 'contains a sensation analogous to the taste of the madeleine and the warbling of the thrush in Chateaubriand'; and he tries 'to remember the poems of Baudelaire which are based on a similar transposition of sensations, in order to establish my own place in that noble company, and to prove to myself that the work I no longer hesitated to undertake was worth the effort I was determined to consecrate to it'.

From Balzac, however, Proust gained mostly by reaction. 'He's an author you don't care for,' he observes to the dead Mme Proust, 'and you're not altogether mistaken. The vulgarity of his feelings is such that his life was inadequate to refine it.' Perhaps this assertion, which Proust elaborates with relentless documentation throughout the chapter,[2] is itself not quite exempt from the fault it condemns; but he has the grace to point out that Balzac's vulgarity is an indispen-

[1] III, 919-20. Proust quotes from Nerval's *Sylvie* a passage which is strikingly close to the theme of the early chapters of *Contre Sainte-Beuve*, and therefore to the opening of *Du Côté de chez Swann*: 'I went back to bed, but could find no rest there. As I lay half-sleeping, half-waking, all my youth returned in my memories. This state in which the mind still fights against the fantastic juxtapositions of dreams often allows one to see, crowded into a few minutes, the most striking pictures of a long period of one's life.' *Sylvie* must have formed part of Proust's reading in November 1908, and is therefore among the immediate sources not only of the second *Contre Sainte-Beuve*, but of *A la Recherche* itself.
[2] Proust himself is here guilty of adopting the 'method of Sainte-Beuve', since he uses Balzac's biography and letters not in order to throw light on the nature of his greatness, but to convict him of vulgarity.

sable condition of his power.[1] Partly, perhaps, because he had not discovered it himself, but had it thrust upon him in the mid-1890s by Reynaldo, Lucien Daudet and Montesquiou, Proust never admired Balzac's genius without reservations. But the vast plan of the *Comédie Humaine*, in which the ever-recurring characters are visible from all aspects at every stage of their lives, as they rise and sink in the infinite dimension of time, was not without influence on *A la Recherche*. The social episodes of Proust's novel in particular are profoundly Balzacian, though with an added angle of vision which is Proust's own. He already had an inkling of the way in which he would transcend his mighty model: he remarks—of an unnamed author, but in words which fit his own achievement in the soirées of *A la Recherche*—that 'his descriptions of evenings in high society are dominated by the mind of the writer, so that our own worldliness is purged, as Aristotle would say; whereas in Balzac's we feel an almost worldly satisfaction in being invited to be present'. A paragraph on Balzac's sudden realisation that all his previous novels had a mysterious interrelationship, and would form part of an enormous work to be called *La Comédie Humaine*, is repeated by the Narrator in his thoughts on Wagner's *Tristan* on the afternoon of Albertine's visit to the Trocadéro, and is not unrelated to Proust's own revelation of the unifying theme of his own novel.[2] At this moment Proust complains of Balzac's unduly materialistic use of two metaphysically significant titles, *Les Illusions Perdues* and *La Recherche de l'Absolu*. From this juxtaposition, and along the connecting link of the French proverb which mistakenly declares that Time Lost cannot be regained—'*Temps perdu ne se retrouve point*'—Proust must have found the title and theme of his novel. The Narrator's quest is for an absolute—Time Lost—which is indeed 'a matter of philosophy', and which both can and must be regained.[3]

Once more Proust's treatise was approaching a dead end. Revived

---

[1] Similarly the Narrator, in his meditation on the Goncourt *Journal* at Tansonville, reflects that Swann 'would rather have died a thousand deaths than use one of the vulgar expressions with which Balzac's letters are strewn'; and yet Swann, for all his refinement, 'would have been incapable of writing *La Cousine Bette* or *Le Curé de Tours*' (III, 720).

[2] *Contre Sainte-Beuve*, 206 = III, 160.

[3] *Contre Sainte-Beuve*, 207. Compare also Racine's lines in *Phèdre*, which Proust knew so well (act II, scene 5):

> '*Et Phèdre au labyrinthe avec vous descendue*
> *Se serait avec vous retrouvée ou perdue.*'

for a few chapters by the dramatic idyll of his waking and the resurrection of his mother, it had again relapsed into the sterile 'essay in the manner of Taine', with only, for form's sake, an occasional '*tu*' still addressed to the fading spectre of Mme Proust. For the second time Proust altered his plan: he would fashion living symbols of false art and true from the names and places of his recently discarded novel, and so contrast the lunar desert of his life in society with the lost sunlight of his childhood. Suddenly—the date is fixed to May 1909 by his letter to Lauris on François de Pâris—his critique of Sainte-Beuve was invaded by a legion of strangely rudimentary Guermantes, still hardly recognisable as their later selves, but clad at last in the feudal splendour of their names.

Yet again the new section was an unforeseen proliferation of a single branch of the old. Proust decided to study the various possible forms of a mis-directed passion for Balzac, as they might be displayed by the different members of the aristocratic family which had held his imagination ever since the Réveillons of *Jean Santeuil*. The Comte and Comtesse de Guermantes (for they are not yet Duc and Duchesse) live in the same mansion as the family of the Narrator (as he must at last be called, since he now begins to be distinguished by a larger element of fiction from the Proust of real life). The florist in the courtyard, like Jupien, has a republican sense of his own dignity, and addresses his landlord's visitor not as 'Monsieur le Vicomte' but as plain 'Monsieur Praus': "you may think yourself lucky it hasn't come to Citizen Praus," cries the furious nobleman to his guest, in the very words of the Duc de Guermantes.[1] The count has a brother, the Marquis de Quercy, who in the fullness of time will become the Baron de Charlus (himself, like Montesquiou, a fervent Balzac-lover), and an aunt, Mme de Villeparisis, who once met Balzac ('a very common person, who never had anything important to say'). Among their set is 'the young Marquise de Cardaillec, *née* Forcheville', who is a preliminary sketch for Gilberte as Mme de Saint-Loup: her reverence for the noble caste into which she has married has an aesthetic fervour which people attribute to her Forcheville blood, 'whereas I,' says the Narrator, 'knew it was the Swann in her'.[2] Each of these has an individual attitude towards

---

[1] *Contre Sainte-Beuve*, 231-2 = II, 32-3.

[2] For a similar misunderstanding by the uninitiate of Gilberte's background, see III, 960, 1010. Gilberte reads Balzac's *La Fille aux yeux d'or* at Tansonville, 'to keep up with my uncles' (III, 706).

Balzac, which already, however, concerns Proust less for the light
it throws on Balzac, than as a touchstone for the portrayal of his
characters. Sainte-Beuve and Balzac are receding into limbo: it is at
this point that Proust loses interest in the criticism of great art,
because he is so soon to create it. Yet it is strange that the noble
couple should have evolved so little in the fourteen years since *Jean
Santeuil*. The Comte has nothing of the Duc de Guermantes's
'Jupiterian' grandeur, the Comtesse has not acquired Oriane's
brilliance and glamour: they are still as homely, dowdy and stupid
as the Réveillons.[1] Proust even attributes to them the ceremony of
'showing the stereoscope', which in *A l'Ombre* he wisely transferred,
as a culminating bourgeois absurdity, to the Bloch family.[2] Here,
however, real life was odder, though less aesthetically appropriate,
than fiction; for this stereoscope was in fact the pride and joy of
Comte and Comtesse Greffulhe, when they regaled the guests at
Boisboudran with views of their travels in Egypt. "Is it *like*?" Mme
Greffulhe would breathlessly enquire. "But my dear, of course it is,"
cried Comtesse Jean de Montebello, "a photograph is always like!"
"Yes, I know, but is the local colour right?"; and yet another three-
dimensional picture of palms and camels would be popped into the
odious machine.

  At this point Proust used the substance of his past and future
novel for a theme which had nothing to do with Balzac, Sainte-
Beuve, or the principles of literary criticism. The Narrator sees M.
de Quercy crossing the courtyard: with his burly frame and dyed

  [1] Nevertheless, they have several minor characteristics of the Duc and
Duchesse. The Comte, besides his attitude towards the florist, and his patronis-
ing insistence on adjusting the Narrator's father's coat-collar (cf. II, 33),
habitually cries "But she's a cousin of mine!" (cf. II, 534), and has the Duc's
addiction to vulgar colloquialisms and bad French. His library, with its original
editions of writers of the 1840s, inspires the Narrator to the same conclusion as
that produced in *Le Temps Retrouvé* by the sight of *François le Champi* in the
library of the Prince de Guermantes: that if ever he became a collector of first
editions, these should be 'first' not in the bibliographical sense, but as being
those in which he had read the books for the first time in the garden at Combray,
in the days when his father used to cry: "Sit up straight!" (cf. III, 887). As for
the Comtesse, her first name is Floriane, at once like and infinitely unlike Oriane;
she has the Duchesse's intentionally provincial accent, saying: "*Elle est bête
comme* eun *oie*" (cf. II, 485; III, 43). But when asked if she has seen a certain
picture she is given the Duc's ineffable reply: "If it was there to be seen, I saw
it!" (cf. II, 524).
  [2] I, 748.

moustaches, like Charlus at the same moment, he resembles Baron
Doasan rather than Montesquiou.[1] Apprehensive, as in *A la Recherche*,
lest his invitation should be a mere practical joke, the Narrator
attends the Princesse de Guermantes's soirée,[2] and is amiably greeted
by his hostess, though strangely ignored by M. de Quercy, who
gives him only the little finger of his hand to shake.[3] Now M. de
Quercy, ceasing to resemble Doasan, has Montesquiou's pale
features and lofty oval forehead, his 'gaze glittering over the noble
line of his nose', his gesture of lifting his unruly hair with a delicate
hand; and the Narrator is overcome by the revelation that the unhappy nobleman not only looks like a woman but is one, since he
belongs to the race of men who love other men. 'A race accursed,'
Proust wrote; and the ensuing sentence of nearly fifteen hundred
words is the longest he, even he, ever wrote, as if he dared not pause,
lest he should come to a full stop indeed. In its anguished cruelty this
is Proust's indictment, in its angry sympathy his defence, in its tragic
beauty his confession of homosexuality. Here are many of the ideas
and even the very words of the more extended natural history of 'the
men-women, descendants of those inhabitants of Sodom who were
spared by the fire from heaven' in *Sodome et Gomorrhe*. He had
reached another of the major themes of his novel, though not for
the first time. The whole chapter is no doubt an adaptation of the
article in the form of a short story which Robert Dreyfus had
dissuaded him from publishing a year before, in May 1908; but the
character of M. de Quercy shows little advance beyond the ineffec-

---

[1] The encounter with the tailor-florist-concierge who will afterwards be
Jupien does not occur here; but one cannot be sure that it does not occur in
Proust's manuscript, concealed in the printed edition by the three dots with
which the paragraph (p. 247) ends, and perhaps revealed by the editorial statement that the tailor's name is Julliot (which is almost Jupien), though he is
unnamed in the published fragments.

[2] It is noticeable that the Princesse, not the Comtesse, is given the association with the Guermantes Way at Combray, the stained glass in the window
of Gilbert (here called Charles) the Bad, the magic lantern and Geneviève de
Brabant, which in *A la Recherche* belongs to the Duchesse; and the Narrator
even hopes that the glamour she thus retains will compensate for his disillusionment with the Comte and Comtesse her cousins (*Contre Sainte-Beuve*, 247-8,
252).

[3] In *A la Recherche* this incident of the grudging handshake is transferred to
the Narrator's glimpse of M. de Charlus in conversation with Odette at Mme de
Villeparisis's matinée (II, 270); though at the Princesse de Guermantes's soirée
the Baron's attitude is similarly distant (II, 639, 654).

tual Vicomte de Lomperolles in *Jean Santeuil*: the tremendous
Baron de Charlus still remains to be created. Proust already draws
the strange and moving parallel between the inverts and the Jews,
but does not yet compare them, as in *Sodome et Gomorrhe*, to a third
unjustly despised minority—the Dreyfusards.[1] Invert, Jew, Dreyfusard: was he not all three, triply rejected by his fellow-men? But
Proust's pleasure-pain in feeling solidarity with outcasts came
ultimately from the far-distant, ever-present moment when as a
child he thought himself rejected by his mother. In *Sodome et
Gomorrhe*, but not yet in *Contre Sainte-Beuve*, he dared to tell the last
secret of his guilt: the accursed people of Sodom, he wrote, 'are sons
without a mother, since they are obliged to lie to her all her life
long, and even in the hour when they close her eyes in death'.[2] Had
he lied to spare his mother, or rather to punish her by founding their
love upon a lie? Had he not chosen to lie, and chosen the sin that
compelled him to lie? At moments such as these he looked into the
pit of Sodom, and saw his own wraith imprisoned there.

Contre Sainte-Beuve was waning to its close. The penultimate
chapter, on the contrast between the poetry of the names of places
and people, and the emptiness of their reality, discusses one of the
chief themes of his novel, yet contains little material which he
thought worth including in *A la Recherche*.[3] But in the last chapter
of the published volume the Narrator and his mother converse once
more, and Proust ends his curious hybrid of critique and novel in a
magnificent dying fall. The Narrator visits Mme de Villeparisis at the
château of Guermantes, which is here modelled on Jumièges as seen
by Proust on his return from Cabourg in the previous autumn.
The pavement of abbots' tombstones will be found again in the
church of Saint-Hilaire at Combray[4]; the vision of the towers of
Guermantes rising over France before those of Chartres or Amiens
had been built would recur to the Narrator as a prelude to his
infatuation for the Duchesse.[5] On a walk with his hostess he sees,
beyond the furthest horizon of woods and fields, 'a tiny blue-grey

[1] *Contre Sainte-Beuve*, 265; II, 619.

[2] II, 615.

[3] However, the ancient lullaby, *Glory to the Lady of Guermantes*, which the
Narrator's nurse sings to him in his childhood, reappears in *Le Côté de Guermantes* (*Contre Sainte-Beuve*, 268 = II, 12), as does the meditation on Fantaisie,
the palace of Louis-Philippe's daughter (*Contre Sainte-Beuve*, 280-2 = II, 536).

[4] I, 103.

[5] *Contre Sainte-Beuve*, 287 = II, 13.

city dominated by twin spires': it is Chartres, 'that irregular, unforgettable, cherished and dreaded face'[1]; he is seized by a memory of partings there with his mother in childhood, and invents an excuse to return home to her. This incident, in which the Two Ways meet, and Time Lost is miraculously glimpsed across the dimension of space, is worthy of *A la Recherche*. No less mature, though in the field of pure comedy, is the episode (written, however, eighteen months before, in January 1908, as part of the novel-draft from which so much of *Contre Sainte-Beuve* is adapted) in which his infant brother Robert refuses to leave Combray without his pet goat, ruins the dress in which he is about to be photographed, and complains that "Marcel has had more chocolate blancmange than me!" But there was no room at Combray for such broad humour, nor in all his novel for Robert. Proust suppressed his brother: in *Du Côté de chez Swann* it is the Narrator who spoils his fine array, embracing the hawthorns of the *raidillon*[2]; and the mother's words of comfort in the scene of parting—"Regulus, on painful occasions, would show amazing fortitude"—were reserved for the Narrator's first departure to Balbec.[3] His mother, touched by this memory of his grief, asks what he would do if they were parted for ever—so had Mme Proust enquired, a few months before her death, and so would the Narrator's grandmother at Balbec[4]; and he tells her, in the last sentence of the published *Contre Sainte-Beuve*, that 'materialism is now discredited', and philosophers are beginning to teach 'that souls are immortal, and one day will meet again'. Within a few weeks he would begin the novel in which his mother would live again and never die, and would be absent on the afternoon of the Princesse de Guermantes's matinée only because 'she had to go to a little tea-party at Mme Sazerat's'.[5]

The origins and evolution of *Contre Sainte-Beuve* can now be seen more clearly. Proust's dissatisfaction with the accepted principles of literature had begun seven years before with his rejection of Ruskin for the sin of idolatry, and continued in 1905 with his attack on reading considered as an interference with individual vision in '*Sur la Lecture*'. The Lemoine pastiches of 1908-9 were

---

[1] Such a view of Chartres would be quite possible from the Villebon (i.e. Guermantes) country in the hills to the north of Illiers. Perhaps Proust also had in mind Jude's distant view of 'Christminster' in Hardy's *Jude the Obscure*.

[2] I, 145. [3] I, 650.
[4] I, 727-8. [5] III, 857.

similarly designed to free him from past admirations for writers who, although many of them would function as secondary influences in *A la Recherche*, could no longer be allowed to remain as primary influences. His parodies were also directed against the misuses of style as an artifice, an evasion of reality, an ornament for emptiness, an exploitation of the more easily accessible levels of a writer's individuality, a concession to the idle reader. But the main object of Proust's attacks had been himself: his complaints against the work of other authors were a projection of his disappointment with his own. A surrender to 'idolatry' (or worship of the graven image in place of the divinity it symbolises), an inability to penetrate beneath surface reality, an endeavour to compensate for lack of truth with beauty of style, had caused the failures of *Jean Santeuil* and the novel-drafts of 1905-8.[1] The solution was still to seek.

In *Contre Sainte-Beuve* Proust intended to demolish both the literature which was content with exterior reality, and the critical philosophy which hitherto had provided its justification. But his essay was also a quest for the secret key to his unwritten novel. The plot of the novel, indeed, was already fixed, since he had lived it once and written it twice without success: what he lacked was the hidden door to inner reality, which alone could give meaning to the narrative. In the four stages of *Contre Sainte-Beuve* Proust pursued his search ever deeper. He attempted to find his quarry first in a direct statement of doctrine; next in the freer region of his lost intimacy with his dead mother; then in a profounder understanding of the three great writers—Nerval, Baudelaire and Balzac—who had trodden the same path before him; and last in the whole world of his past, which was also the world of his novel. But the secret, however far he advanced, fled always beyond his grasp.

Like *Jean Santeuil*—though with ten years' store of riper maturity and keener insight—*Contre Sainte-Beuve* is a marvellous failure. Both are works of art at a stage only half-way advanced from chaos, since the finger of the creator has imposed only here and there the imperfect beginnings of order. The chapters tend to begin from nowhere and stop without having arrived, to form a series of separate dead ends rather than stages in a single road. Proust's Ruskin prefaces and the finest of his *Figaro* articles had shown a mastery of

---

[1] Proust himself wrote in his notes for *Contre Sainte-Beuve*: 'Idolatry in my preface to *La Bible d'Amiens*. The exact opposite now, and in '*Sur la Lecture*.'

construction and of his maturest style. *Contre Saint-Beuve*, despite many moments of still higher inspiration, marks a regression in both construction and style. Too often Proust abdicates, and allows the young man who wrote *Jean Santeuil*, or even the schoolboy who 'covered page after page with the speech of the Constable de Bourbon', to wander aimlessly.

Set in this disorderly substratum are many wonderful glimpses of the world of *A la Recherche*; and it was thought, when *Contre Sainte-Beuve* first appeared, that Proust's critique had somehow turned, half-unawares, into his novel; that the appearance of characters and events which are common to both could only be an invasion from the future work. The still fragmentary evidence suggests, however, that many, perhaps all or nearly all, of these are borrowings from the intermediate drafts of 1905-8, and not anticipations of the novel to come. Some episodes had already appeared in *Jean Santeuil*: Combray is the same as Étreuilles, the little girl in the Champs-Élysées belongs to both works, M. de Quercy is an expansion of the Vicomte de Lomperolles, the Comte and Comtesse de Guermantes are still close to the Duc and Duchesse de Réveillon. A list in one of Proust's note-books of 'pages written' for the novel-version of 1908[1] includes incidents which recur in the last two chapters of *Contre Sainte-Beuve*: the hortensias of the Normandy châteaux,[2] the palace of Fantaisie, Robert and the goat, the departure of the Narrator's mother. One of the few published passages from the intermediate novel shows the Narrator with M. de Quercy in a conversation which is a curious compound of interviews in *A la Recherche* with M. de Norpois and the Baron de Charlus, who at this early stage were one and the same character. M. de Quercy, like Norpois (and like Gabriel Hanotaux in 1895) recommends a diplomatic career and pours scorn upon the Narrator's ambition to write; but like Charlus (and like Montesquiou in 1893) he promises, at the price of an absolute but unexplained obedience, a life in common and the key to the secrets of society. Other passages, as has been seen, show Swann in love with Carmen (Odette), and with the little band at Querqueville (Balbec); but Swann, we are told, appears in the unpublished parts of *Contre Sainte-Beuve*, while Querqueville, still more significantly, though it is mentioned only once in passing,[3] is

---

[1] *Contre Sainte-Beuve*, 14.
[2] *Ibid.*, 274-6.
[3] *Ibid.*, 14, 269.

no doubt the same as the nameless seaside-resort in the draft of 1908.[1]
The Guermantes chapters of *Contre Sainte-Beuve* seem to postulate
a more detailed structure of characters and relationships as already
in existence elsewhere, that is, in Proust's abandoned novel. The
available evidence suggests that in characters, incidents and plot the
fictional part of *Contre Sainte-Beuve* is not so much a voyage of
exploration as a return to a country which Proust had already
discovered. In these respects, as in style and construction, Proust's
essay marks at the most a limited advance, certainly not a break-
through into the unknown. Yet—as will be seen shortly—in other
unobtrusive quarters, of whose full significance Proust was not
aware at the time of writing, *Contre Sainte-Beuve* held the true keys
to *A la Recherche*.

Meanwhile, throughout the stresses of *Contre Sainte-Beuve*,
Proust had kept in touch with his Cabourg friends. From May to
July he negotiated with Camille Plantevignes to obtain a job for a
rustic army-comrade of Georges de Lauris, Nogrette by name.
'Plantevignes of all ages' were so delighted with the young man
for his own sake that Proust felt half-disappointed, lest his own
merit in the case should seem impaired; for 'by pure chance I've been
able to be extremely nice to them, and I know they'd like to do a
great deal for me'. He maintained contact with the mysterious girl of
Cabourg. His remarks to Lauris early in 1909—when he expressed
his sympathy with Bluebeard, because 'he too loved girls', declared
'I love hardly any women but young girls, as if life weren't complicated enough without that', or confessed his sensual enjoyment on
reading how Chateaubriand 'was arrested when in bed with two
women'[2]—show that his thoughts still ran on the 'little pleasures'
he had experienced with her during his flying visits to Paris from
Versailles last October. In July, when he began to plan his annual
return to Cabourg, he confided in Lauris: 'Georges, if I leave Paris,
it will perhaps be with a woman.'[3]

---

[1] Querqueville, the first form of Balbec, was the seaside resort at which the
love-affair with the little band was experienced by Swann in the novel of 1905;
and it is mentioned also in a later but still primitive episode at Kreuznach, based
on Proust's stays there with his mother in July 1895 and August 1897 (BSAMP,
VIII, 447).

[2] Proust must have read this in the Goncourt *Journal*, 7 October 1866, which
seems to be the only printed source for the tradition.

[3] '... *avec une femme.*' The expression is ambiguous; it could mean, equally
well, 'with a wife.'

In the same July came a farcical yet touching encounter with a goddess of his past. Comtesse Greffulhe, in her capacity as president of the Société des Grandes Auditions Musicales de la France, requested 'a few lines, just as you feel, that is, exquisitely poetic!' for her annual concert-fête at Bagatelle in the Bois de Boulogne on 17 July. Proust declined, pleading illness and recent refusals of equally deserving cases (which included her own cousin Montesquiou). But instead of striking him off her list, the sympathetic noblewoman sent him a superb vine, cascading with grapes, in a pot: it was 'a speaking symbol', she declared, and if he would name his day and hour, she would visit his sickbed, 'hoping to find you restored to the very summit of your powers!' Proust, outreached for once, sent the unmanageable vegetable to Marie Nordlinger: 'I thought of throwing in some roses,' he maliciously told Reynaldo, 'so that I could quote Nerval's "*Trellis where vine is intertwined with rose*"; but it occurred to me that Mallarmé's "*When I have sucked the clarity of grapes*" would be more economical, because then there'd be no need for roses.' He swore Reynaldo to secrecy: 'otherwise the Élisabeth would hear in five minutes, because nowadays the moment anybody says anything unkind concerning anyone Montesquiou writes them a letter about it INSTANTANEOUSLY!'

Proust was now working with desperate energy on the last two of the seven black plush exercise-books of *Contre Sainte-Beuve*. His material was getting out of hand: still more characters, with ever less relevance to Sainte-Beuve, forced their way in from his old novel to wait on the brink of the new. In these last, unpublished fragments he wrote about Cottard, and Mme Verdurin's sacred monster Princesse Sherbatoff; he developed M. de Quercy, the future Charlus, and Montargis, the future Saint-Loup; Swann himself reappeared. On 29 June, when the living presence of the seven-years-dead Charles Haas was thus in his mind, he read in an article by Robert Dreyfus in *Le Figaro* of Haas as a brilliant young dandy in 1863, playing in amateur theatricals with the Pourtalès's, the Galliffets and Gaston de Saint-Maurice at the Château de Mouchy, and much to Dreyfus's bewilderment wept as he read. Would Mme Lemaire recognise herself in Mme Verdurin? and was his critique not becoming too much like a novel?

> '*I rather fear my novel on Sainte-Beuve*
> *May not entirely please our friend La Veuve*',

he told Reynaldo. On 6 July the electric light had glared for sixty
hours unextinguished in his bedroom, until even the scornful Nicolas
remarked with awe: "I think Monsieur must be an old Brahmin!"

It was during these first weeks of July 1909 that Proust began *A la
Recherche*: indeed, it is possible that his sixty sleepless hours from 4 to
6 July were caused not by the last throes of *Contre Sainte-Beuve*, but
by the first wave of inspiration on which his great novel was launched.
Just as in the autumn of 1899 he had renounced the barren *Jean
Santeuil* and turned joyfully to Ruskin, so he now abandoned the
waning *Contre Sainte-Beuve*; but this time the illumination came from
within. It was the most important single event of his life, both for
himself and for posterity.

All the material of his novel had long been available to him. He had
known its characters and experienced its plot—except for certain
episodes which were still in the unknown future—in a period of his
life which was now long past. He had even written it twice, in *Jean
Santeuil* and in the novel of 1905-7, and much of it (counting the new
draft of 1908 and *Contre Sainte-Beuve*) four times over. But the
identity of the last catalyst, which would fuse the whole and crystallise
its meaning, its metaphysic and its secret structure, remained an impenetrable mystery. The story he had told so often could only display
the vanity of human desire; it could only tell the terrible half-truth,
that desire is vain not because it is frustrated but because it is fulfilled,
and the people and places we love turn to ashes when we possess them.
Comparison between *A la Recherche* and the fruitless efforts of
Proust's past twenty years of ceaseless writing will show the nature of
the revelation which came to him in July 1909. In *A la Recherche*,
although he mapped the desert of experience more bitterly and
minutely than ever before, he showed that it leads, except for those
who stay in it, to the recovery of innocence, that the joy of our vision
is not cancelled by the disillusion of its attainment, that the truth of
salvation everywhere underlies the truth of sin and despair. Proust
had entered, at last and once for all, into Time Regained.

He had found it in real life, precisely as in *A la Recherche*, through
the incidents of unconscious memory which form the beginning and
end of his novel. He had eaten the madeleine and trodden on the
uneven paving-stone; he had forced them to release their messages
from Time Lost, of the scented garden at Auteuil and the sunlight of
Venice. At the time when they occurred, however, despite the
spiritual joy with which they were accompanied, these experiences

seemed mere opportune recurrences of similar events which had happened throughout his life, and had been recorded again and again in *Jean Santeuil*. He used them in January 1909, almost perfunctorily, for the second preface to *Contre Sainte-Beuve*, as useful parallels of his thesis in that work, the superiority of instinct over intellect. The profounder revelation came only in July, and was aesthetic rather than spiritual. The event in Proust's real life on which the eating of the madeleine in *A la Recherche* is based is not so much the actual occurrence of January 1909, as the moment of triumph in July when he realised that it was the key to his novel. *A la Recherche* would be a vast unconscious memory, embodying the whole of his past life, and extracting from it the truths which had been invisible in Time Lost.

In order to fit the incident for its new function as the gateway to his novel, he rearranged it. For the humble tea and rusk, which could only recall Auteuil and Nathé Weil, he substituted the lime-tea and madeleine which were associated with Illiers and would create Combray. Instead of Céline Cottin, as in real life, or Félicie Fitau, 'my old cook', as in *Contre Sainte-Beuve*,[1] his own mother brought him the enchanted potion, atoning for the kiss which had destroyed him by the clue to a work of art which would save him.

This new use of a minor incident—like the stone the builders rejected—for a greater purpose was a continuation of the curious instinctive process which we have seen at work in *Contre Sainte-Beuve*. A fortuitous and apparently unimportant image in one chapter would become, as Proust became conscious of its latent meaning, the inspiration for the next section of his essay: a brief digression in the 'classical' discussion of Sainte-Beuve's method suggested the conversation with his mother, the image in the second preface of the sleeper awakening provided his introductory chapters, the critique of Balzac introduced the Guermantes clan. The unconscious creative forces of *A la Recherche* were rising in *Contre Sainte-Beuve*, not in the incidents and characters, which were still unimproved repetitions of his earlier drafts, but in the structural devices which at the time seemed relevant only to his essay. The madeleine incident, which began his novel, was matched by the stumbling on the paving-stone, which ended it. The themes of waking in an unfamiliar room, lying in bed at early morning, longing for travel, the article in *Le Figaro* and the Narrator's conversation with his mother, became architectural motifs which recur throughout *A la Recherche*. During the seven months of

---

[1] *Contre Sainte-Beuve*, 53.

Contre Sainte-Beuve the hidden power of Time Regained had prepared, unknown to Proust, the symbolic patterns of *A la Recherche*.

The beginning of his novel delayed his departure for Cabourg several weeks past the usual time. His exhaustion was intensified by asthma, an abscess in a hollow tooth, and a mysterious fever, for which Dr Bize ordered fresh air. Suddenly, about 20 August, he left for Cabourg with Nicolas, and on the train had the unexpected pleasure of meeting 'Father Plantevignes', with whom he discussed the virtues of young Nogrette for two livelong hours.

For the sake of warmth and quiet he took a small, airless attic on the fourth floor of the Grand Hôtel, because it had a fireplace and no neighbours. Above was the roof, to one side an inner courtyard, and to the other only Nicolas, who had a palatial room with a private bathroom, 'for which', said Proust, 'I'm his sub-tenant'. Ulrich arrived to be his secretary; 'though so far,' he told Reynaldo, 'he's given me no cause to quote *'Ulrich, thine eyes have plumbed the ocean's depths'* '.[1] Last year he had risen early enough to visit the beach before dinner; but now he worked till far past dawn, rose at sunset, and first appeared at half-past nine in the vast restaurant whence other diners had long since fled. One evening he asked the gipsy orchestra 'whether they knew anything by Reynaldo Hahn?'; and when they obligingly struck up with Reynaldo's *Rêverie* he dissolved into tears, while twenty otherwise idle waiters put on expressions of deep concern, and the head-waiter hurried to fetch him a glass of water. Then he joined the young sons of his Cabourg friends in the casino next door, where one of his forms of innocent merriment was to make propaganda for the poetry of Mme de Noailles. 'The adolescents', as he called them, soon caught on. A student of mathematics quoted *'as sweet and savage as a Persian garden'* in the midst of a purely scientific discussion, and another enquired, in the name of optics, whether the sun could really *'insert his prism in a stained-glass window'*? The correct answer to "How was your golf today?" was " *'The course was full of maddened butterflies, Like jasmine blossoms poised on fluttering wings'*!" 'Great loves for you were born in those youthful hearts,' Proust assured the poetess.

A distressing letter, apparently of this year, from Proust to one of these 'adolescents' survives: it would be wrong to call it, as it has been called, a love-letter, still more to identify its insignificant recipient as 'one

---

[1] Adapted from Musset's sonnet to Ulrich Guttinguer.

who became in the end the very image of Albertine'. The temperature is low, the tone that of Montesquiou's melodious automatic nagging, or of Charlus's note to the headwaiter Aimé at Balbec[1]; this is merely a letter of aggrieved, unimportant, crestfallen platonic friendship, to a young man who has broken his promise to meet Proust on the sea-front from six to seven in the evening. Now Proust will refrain from inviting him to a party he is giving for 'the young people of Cabourg and others'; Alphonse Daudet and Anatole France never treated him like this; the young person has 'passed by and spoiled a famous oppor-tunity of friendship'; Proust will put him in his novel as an example of 'characters that will never know the elegance of missing a dance to give their company to a friend', and meanwhile 'bids him goodbye once and for all'. They probably made it up next morning. But this youth supplied, indeed, one small detail for Albertine at Balbec. 'I guessed your true nature,' says Proust, 'on the day when you told me with such energy: "I can't, because I've got to go to the Foucarts' party" '; and Albertine hurries off to tea at the golf club, crying to Andrée: "But you know Madame Durieux has invited you!"[2]

Another curious incident of the Narrator's first visit to Balbec, the appearance at the Grand Hôtel of the young man who has made him-self 'king of a tiny islet in Oceania' and his mistress the queen,[3] alludes to a person notorious in his time. Jacques Lebaudy, son of the sugar millionaire, acquired a plot of land in the Atlas Mountains, proclaimed himself Emperor of the Sahara, distributed titles of nobility, and made the singer Marguerite Dellier his Empress. In exile in the United States he proposed, like the Pharaohs his peers, to make their daughter his consort; whereupon the Empress shot him dead, and was acquitted by a sympathetic jury.

Proust's companions were not all male. He was now paying homage to Mlles Hélène and Colette, the young daughters of the Vicomte d'Alton, a nephew of the Aimée d'Alton who had been Musset's greatest love after George Sand, and had married the poet's brother after his death. 'Colette is ravishing,' Proust told Jean Louis Vaudoyer a year later, 'and resembles Aimée d'Alton in beauty, though in nothing else, for she is as virtuous as could be.' Proust gave Mlle Colette the gold handbag from Cartier's which the Narrator buys for Albertine, after 'finding out from M. de Charlus what the correct

<hr>

[1] II, 991-3.
[2] I, 894.
[3] I, 676-7; II, 113.

thing was at the moment', to use on the Little Train. [1] Another original
of Albertine, according to Mme de Clermont-Tonnerre, was Mlle
Bauche, the daughter of a manufacturer of safes and leader of a little
band of girls on the Cabourg promenade: 'she had a geranium-pink
complexion, and her sporting, unconventional behaviour was just like
Albertine's, although'—the Duchesse coyly adds—'the resemblance
went no further'. The same informant mentions Proust's visits to
Comtesse Berthier and her dazzling daughters Germaine and Yvonne
at their Villa Berthier in Cabourg, and how they asked, many years
later, whether the famous writer was any relative of their former
friend. "He's the very same person." "Impossible! Why, he never
even mentioned literature, and he used to make us die laughing with
his funny stories!" Perhaps the real Albertine was Colette d'Alton, or
another of these girls, or one whose name is still unknown in Proust's
story; but whoever she may have been, their relationship was now
reaching the extraordinary pitch of possible marriage.

Meanwhile Proust had written, just before leaving for Cabourg, to
offer *Contre Sainte-Beuve* to the *Mercure de France*; but Vallette, who
in April 1908 had rejected the Lemoine pastiches and a volume of
collected articles, declined the new work soon after Proust's arrival.
By a lucky chance Calmette happened to be staying near Cabourg,
and Proust decided to ask this most obliging of editors to find him a
publisher. When the interview took place, however, about 27 August,
he resolved to play for still higher stakes: without mentioning *Contre
Sainte-Beuve*, he confided that he was now writing a novel. The
amiable Calmette immediately offered to print it as a feuilleton serial
in *Le Figaro*. It now seemed prudent to keep the very existence of
Contre Sainte-Beuve a secret; and remembering with panic that he had
mentioned it to Beaunier, Proust begged Robert Dreyfus to explain
that the work accepted by Calmette was a novel and not the critical
essay; for if Beaunier thought it was the latter he might advise against
it, since only fiction could be considered suitable for a *Figaro* feuilleton. Dreyfus thought it pointless to warn Beaunier, and on 3 September Proust agreed. He reported to Mme Straus that he had 'just begun
—and just finished—a whole long book', and that he was about to set
to work again, after the interruption caused by his departure for
Cabourg. The book begun was *A la Recherche*, and the book finished
was *Contre Sainte-Beuve*. Already he was undecided about the *feuilleton*: he told Mme Straus that only part of his novel would appear in

[1] II, 1037.

Le Figaro, 'because it's too improper and too long', and Dreyfus that
he would probably wait until he could finish it in volume form.
Another remark at this time to Mme Straus explains Proust's curious
illusion, which he expressed to many friends during the coming
months, that the novel he had so recently begun would soon be completed. 'Although all of it's written,' he told her, 'a great many things
need recasting.' He still regarded *A la Recherche* as a mere revision,
under the new inspiration of Time Regained, of the work he had
drafted three times since 1905. In a sense he was right; but he did not
foresee that the task which now seemed to require only a few months
would in fact take thirteen years.

Mme Straus was staying again at her Trouville villa, the Clos des
Mûriers; but when she offered to visit her 'little Marcel', he put her off
with promises to visit her, and never came. Her afternoon call last
year, he explained, had been so spoiled by the draughts of the Grand
Hôtel, the din of the orchestra, and her husband's tactful disappearance to pay for their cups of chocolate, that it was only after she
departed in her motor-car that he had time to realise: 'I have been with
Mme Straus!' He envied her the company of Helleu, and quoted
Montesquiou's remark (for Helleu's great-grandfather had been a
member of the Council of Five Hundred), that 'few of the descendants
of his victims have as much breeding as this descendant of their
executioner!' He begged her to keep his presence at Cabourg secret
from Guiche and his wife, who were at Bénerville again.

When the season ended and his friends went away Proust hoped, as
he had planned the year before, to work on through October and
November in the solitude of the empty hotel. But the scheme fell
through (the manager desperately pleaded urgent repairs to cracks in
the walls), and towards the end of September he returned to Paris. He
arranged for a fair copy of the illegible beginning of *A la Recherche* to
be made, and invited Lauris to call and read it at his bedside; but as he
had not yet confided the secret of his novel to this friend, he pretended
that the manuscript would be 'the first paragraph, which is almost a
volume in itself, of the first chapter of *Contre Sainte-Beuve*'.

As it happened Proust first read his opening chapter in mid-
November to Reynaldo, who was enthusiastically encouraging. The
manuscript was now two hundred pages long; and he offered again to
read it to Lauris, announcing in the same letter (about 20 November
1909) that he would now return Lauris's set of Sainte-Beuve's *Port-
Royal*, 'because I shan't use it for several months'. This marked the

final postponement of *Contre Sainte-Beuve*, which he never mentioned
again. Instead he borrowed Mâle's *L'Art religieux de la fin du moyen-
âge en France*; and his sudden need for this volume suggests that he
was now describing Saint-Hilaire at Combray, or the sculptures of
Saint-André-des-Champs.[1] Early in December he received Lauris's
'divine letter' on the first manuscript-book of his novel, and sent him
the second and third. Lauris never forgot the 'enchanted amazement'
with which he had read the first few pages, in his little room opening
on the garden in the Rue de Berri, and how 'a whole new world
opened' before him.

The contents of the three manuscript-books may be deduced with
some certainty, for Lauris commented on Proust's apparent praise of
George Sand in the first. 'Don't infer that I like George Sand,' Proust
replied, 'it isn't intended as a piece of literary criticism, it's just like that
at that time, and the rest of the book will correct it.' The mother's
reading of George Sand to the Narrator as a child at Combray occurs
near the end of the opening chapter of *Swann*, and is in fact 'corrected'
by the meditation on *François le Champi* in the Prince de Guermantes's
library.[2] The first manuscript-volume contained therefore in all probability the whole chapter ('*Combray* I'); and the second and third
volumes must have comprised all or most of '*Combray* II', which is a
little more than twice as long again. This is confirmed by Proust's
enquiry, about mid-December, whether Lauris thinks the part he has
just read could be published separately, and whether, if he were to die
suddenly before finishing his work, Lauris would promise to arrange
this; for '*Combray*' in fact forms a separable unity.

Meanwhile, in November, he began to say goodbye to his friends
for the sake of his novel: to Louisa de Mornand ('I'm on the point of
cloistering myself for a long work'), to Montesquiou ('I have undertaken a kind of novel, the beginning of which will appear soon,
perhaps'), to Antoine Bibesco (saying that he hoped to finish by next
summer), and to Mme de Noailles ('desiring to put enough of myself
into it for you to know and esteem me a little'). On 27 November, by
way of a farewell appearance, he took three boxes at the Théâtre des
Variétés for Feydeau and Croisset's comedy *Le Circuit*. Marcel Plantevignes and the other two young men of Cabourg were his guests of
honour; and to these he added '(because these young people are a little
too young for me,' he told Louisa), all the unmarried survivors of his
closest friends: Lauris, Emmanuel Bibesco, Reynaldo, François de

[1] I, 59-67, 150-2.   [2] I, 39-43; III, 883-8.

Pâris, Fénelon,[1] Loche Radziwill with Christiane, and Louisa complete with Robert Gangnat.

In his letter of invitation to Lauris he revealed a stranger plan than this. 'A person who is dear to me is connected with them,' he wrote, mentioning the three young men of Cabourg, and added, in the formula with which a Frenchman would hint at a coming engagement: 'Georges, perhaps you will soon be hearing news of me—*vous apprendrez peut-être bientôt de moi du nouveau*'. 'Or rather,' he rectified, already retreating a little, 'I shall ask your advice. To make a very young and charming girl share my terrible life, even if she is not afraid of doing so—would it not be a crime?'

'I nearly married her, but in the end I didn't dare—I wouldn't have had the heart to make a young woman live with anyone so ill and so tiresome,' says the Narrator to Albertine of the imaginary woman for love of whom he is asking her to return with him to Paris.[2] 'No, I've too bad a character,' says the Narrator to Gilberte at Tansonville when she urges him to marry, 'and besides, I was engaged once, but couldn't go through with it.'[3] Proust was no doubt sincere in wishing, or half-wishing, or believing that he half-wished to marry the girl of Cabourg. His plan of marriage, however nebulous, came when the revelation of his novel had ended the sense of exile from humanity which, since the moonlight night at Auteuil in his childhood, he had tried in vain to heal. He saw for a moment a mirage of normal love, placation of his dead mother, liberation from pariah-hood, return to the sacraments of the human condition. Might he not possess all these, and still write his novel, which otherwise could bring salvation only at the price of solitude and death? But the vision of this last chance was illusory: not unheroically he turned his face, went his way, and spoke no more of marriage. What were the feelings of the young girl, who asked Antoine Bibesco 'not to print her name', whether she loved Proust and wished more seriously than he for this impossible union, will perhaps never be known.

[1] Fénelon was transferred from the French Embassy at Washington to the political and commercial section of the Foreign Ministry in Paris on 14 October 1909 until his posting to Rio de Janeiro on 21 May 1912.
[2] II, 1123.
[3] III, 707.

Chapter 8

MADEMOISELLE DE SAINT-LOUP

(*January 1910 – July 1912*)

EARLY in the new year of 1910 Proust read Thomas Hardy's *The Well-Beloved* in a recent French translation,[1] noticing with dismay, as he told Robert de Billy, that it resembled 'just the least little bit, though it's a thousand times better, what I'm writing now'. Proust had detected in Hardy's plot, in which the hero loves at different periods of his life a girl, her daughter, and her daughter's daughter, an affinity with his own; for *A la Recherche* was to be the story of three related loves in three separate epochs, Swann's for Odette and the Narrator's for Gilberte and Albertine, a structure of which a more primitive form had already appeared in *Jean Santeuil*. Hardy's view of love, according to which we pursue not a person, but a fleeting image of our own creation which is the same in all objects of our desire, was equally Proustian, as Hardy himself was to observe sixteen years later.[2] Proust asked Billy to approach his British colleague at Tangiers, Sir Reginald Lister, for information on the private lives of both Hardy and Barrie, apparently wondering whether they shared his own two principal vices: 'are they society men, and do they care for women?' he enquired.[3] *The Well-Beloved*, together with *Jude the Obscure* and *A Pair of Blue Eyes*, remained in Proust's mind throughout the writing of his novel. The Narrator in conversation with the captive Albertine illustrates his theory of the identical nature of all the works of a great artist, 'that unknown quality of a unique world which is perhaps the most authentic proof of genius', by the presence of the little phrase in every composition by Vinteuil, and again by the 'stonemason's geometry of Hardy's

[1] *La Bien-aimée*, tr. E. Paul-Margueritte, published in September 1909. *Jude l'Obscur* appeared in 1901, *Deux yeux bleus* in 1913.

[2] F. E. Hardy, *The Life of Thomas Hardy* (1962), p. 432.

[3] Proust had admired Barrie's *Margaret Ogilvie* in translation three years before. He may have been misled by the theme of mother-domination in Barrie's novel, and by the ironical glimpses of high society, or the intentionally platonic and formalistic representation of the hero's love for women, in Hardy's.

novels'; he invites her to consider the recurrence of the stonemason theme in *Jude*, *A Pair of Blue Eyes*, and *The Well-Beloved*, or 'the parallelism between *The Well-Beloved*, where the hero loves three women, and *A Pair of Blue Eyes*, where the heroine loves three men'.[1] The themes of *The Well-Beloved* are particularly present at the Princesse de Guermantes's matinée. The Narrator becomes suddenly aware of his age, like Jocelyn Pierston seeing his own timeworn face in the mirror[2]; like the Narrator before he stumbles on the paving-stone, Pierston, though for him there is to be no renovation, 'could no longer attach a definite sentiment to images of beauty revealed from the past'.[3] "You mistake me for my mother," says Gilberte,[4] a mistake which frequently occurs in *The Well-Beloved*; Odette's miraculous preservation of her youth is found to be due, like Marcia's, to 'beautifying artifices'[5]; "I wish you would speak to her—I'm sure you would like her," says the second Avice to Pierston of her daughter Avice the third, like Gilberte offering to introduce her daughter to the Narrator[6]; and at the same momentous party the Narrator sees gathered together the mother, daughter and granddaughter whom he has loved or may yet love, in the persons of Odette, Gilberte, and Mlle de Saint-Loup. Furthermore, at the very time when he read *The Well-Beloved*, Proust became aware of a similar situation in his own life.

For nearly ten years he had not seen Mme Arman de Caillavet. They had been estranged by what he referred to as a 'dissension', perhaps not unconnected with his habit of arriving so late at her Wednesdays that the guests, including Anatole France himself, would vanish with cries of "There's Marcel—that means we'll be here till two in the morning!" Mme Arman was sixty-three; she had ceased to dye her hair, which now rolled in noble white billows over her vast white forehead; but Monsieur France, rejuvenated by the self-satisfaction which she had toiled to give him, was only sixty-five and beginning to rove. On 30 April 1909 he sailed with Mme Arman's reluctant blessing for a lecture-tour in South America, guarded by two spies, his treacherous secretary Jean Jacques Brousson and her own manservant François. Perhaps his absence, 'in the antipodes,' she said, laughing wryly, 'surrounded by monkeys and parrots and

---

[1] III, 376-7.
[2] *The Well-Beloved*, 271.
[3] *Ibid.*, 324.
[4] III, 980.
[5] III, 948; *The Well-Beloved*, 328.
[6] III, 1028; *The Well-Beloved*, 237.

savages', would make him love her more; and besides, she was about to undergo an operation which would, she hoped, restore her lost youth and health. France sent many cablegrams but few letters. One evening, at last, Mme Arman assembled her guests to hear 'a letter from the Argentine'. " 'Yesterday we gave our first lecture . . .' " she began. "Charming! Who but M. France could have written that!" cried an unwary newcomer, only to be crushed by her indignant "Sir, this letter is not from M. France, but from my manservant François." But she also received anonymous letters, which spoke of an actress whom France had met on the boat and followed ever after, and a newspaper cutting, which mentioned the presence of 'M. and Mme France' at an official reception. The Abbé Mugnier began to call: perhaps God would give back her lover, or at least her peace? In July Brousson returned, unmasked, sacked and revengeful: the actress was Jeanne Brindeau, a lady of ample and well-preserved charms, and M. France had just sailed with her for Monte-Video, a city not hitherto included in his lecture itinerary.

On 28 August France returned crestfallen to captivity. He dismissed his concubine with all desirable brutality, and accompanied Mme Arman to the family estate at Capian for the vintage; but in October, still the eternal sightseer, he dragged her by motor-car to Toulouse, Montpellier, Carcassonne, and to Hendaye to call on Loti. Back at Capian she was cold and ill, so ill that France summoned Dr Widal (the same whose discovery of the dangers of salt in an invalid diet came too late to save the life of the Narrator's grandmother[1]) from Paris. Early in January, after nursing her devotedly, France brought her back to the Avenue Hoche. "Too old, too old," she lamented to her daughter-in-law Jeanne; "I'd better die, I haven't the courage to face what life has in store for me . . . but do stop crying, it upsets me!" France called, still unforgiven, and feeling that he too had a right to be ill: "Well, Madame, I'm off, my lumbago's hurting me," he grumbled, and stumped away. On the 12th, suddenly choking and speechless, Mme Arman scribbled on her bedside pad: 'Gaston quick, and M. Fr—', and died, regaining in death for a few ironic hours her promised youth, like Proust's mother five years before. "I could have stayed," wept France, "my lumbago wasn't as bad as all that . . . but when I saw her again she was dead. Her face was calm, her cheeks were soft, she looked as beautiful as she was at forty. It's I who am dead, not she— how could she desert me like this?" As he walked in her funeral

[1] II, 298.

cortège on the 14th he was heard to remark: "Pretty house, that, period 1830!"; but during the service at Saint-Philippe-du-Roule[1] he stood alone, avoiding the accusing glances of the others, and stifling his tears. Clemenceau, Gégé Primoli, the great Réjane, all the stars of her salon were present, including perhaps Proust himself, whose wreath of camelias, arum-lilies, lilac, roses and violets was on the hearse. He remembered how in life she would gaze at the flowers he brought her, bury her face in their fragrance, and ring imperiously for the servants to put them in water. 'Please try to put them near her,' he wrote to Gaston's wife, 'I'm drugging myself in the hope of being able to come to the funeral.'

Now he could ask again for the photograph of Jeanne which he had coveted nineteen years before, when he loved her. It came, and he saw a proud young woman, enthroned at the tennis-party in 1891 between the Dancognée and Daireaux girls, recognisable even now as the Jeanne he still knew. But the gawky, shyly grinning young man, who knelt at her feet and strummed on a tennis-racket for a guitar, was almost past recognition: it was himself, smiling from the depths of Time Lost, before he set foot in Sodom, surrendered to asthma, and wore his mother to her death. 'Was it taken *then*, or last summer? Nothing has changed but myself!' he told Jeanne. Emboldened, he wrote to her daughter Simone, now aged fifteen, who had so enchanted him two years before, and received a charming letter which seemed written in Chinese characters, he teasingly told her, 'as if water-coloured or landscape-gardened rather than written!' For a few weeks grandmother, daughter-in-law and granddaughter were in his thoughts together, just as in *The Well-Beloved*. He asked Mlle Simone, too, for a photograph, urged her to read *The Mill on the Floss*, and added in gloomy jest, alluding to the fate of Tom and Maggie Tulliver: 'no doubt I shall be drowned soon as well!'

The Seine was rising, swollen by the unprecedented rains which had fallen in central France since the day after Mme Arman's funeral. The angry brown river hurtled on, ever higher, carrying trees and dead cattle from the fields to the south, household furniture from the working-class suburbs, and barrels from the Quai de Bercy. By the 26th the metro was flooded, the electric trams had ceased to run, the

---

[1] Mme Arman received burial in the Catholic faith, but her grave was in the little Jewish section of the Montmartre cemetery, beside her parents the Lippmanns, where her husband and son, when their time came, did not choose to join her.

Zouave on the Pont de l'Alma stood breast-high in the roaring torrent, and half Paris was under water. Fifty thousand refugees sheltered in public buildings, while President Fallières tasted soup in improvised kitchens, congratulated the society ladies who cooked it, and talked sympathetically to cheering victims. The bears in the Jardin des Plantes were rescued in imminent danger of drowning; it was feared that the crocodiles might escape from their flooded pools; and the poor giraffe had to be left, knee-deep, to die of exposure. Sewers burst in the streets, or rose hideously in cellars, and rats fled through the boulevards. Plank bridges for pedestrians were built along the main thoroughfares, looters were ducked by infuriated crowds, and the police interrupted, in the nick of time, a lynching on the Pont d'Ivry. The carcase of a bullock was seen hurrying down-stream, with the corpse of its young herdsman still clutching its straw halter. Snow fell, and more rain. On the 28th, when the waters reached their highest point, a vast, malodorous lake stretched from the abandoned Gare Saint-Lazare far up the Boulevard Haussmann, rippling a little past Proust's apartment. The Parisians, except those who were homeless or ruined, grimly enjoyed a spectacle which had never been equalled since the great flood of 1746; and Proust himself, thrillingly marooned, took some pleasure in a drama which might have been entitled Proust on the Floss.

But when at last the river stayed away from his door, his troubles began—'though I daren't speak of myself when others have suffered so badly'. The cellars of 102 Boulevard Haussmann had to be pumped out; fumes from carbolic and stoves used for disinfection and drying gave him incessant fits of asthma; the wrecked lift must be repaired, and Dr Gagey's drains refitted; and because the workmen hammered all day in his sleep-time, he was compelled to take opium and veronal. He had albumen in his urine. It was 'only after the strangest prodigies, and looking like a mummy in a dress-suit', that he could attend the dress-rehearsal at the Opéra of *La Fète chez Thérèse*, the ballet on which Reynaldo had worked by his bedside at Versailles in October 1908, while he played dominoes with Agostinelli. Three times in February the river rose again above danger-level. "Even the Seine wants to see *Chantecler*," people said; for Rostand's brilliant comedy of the farmyard—in which Montesquiou was enraged to find himself satirised as the Peacock, *'prince of the unexpected adjective'*—was playing at the Porte Saint-Martin. For a time, as if he had not seen enough of streets turned into water-ways, Proust thought of leaving

for Venice; and then from March to June there is one of the characteristic gaps in his correspondence which mark a period of total absorption in his writing. In April he informed Mme Straus ('as if I hadn't
told you often enough!') that he was 'finishing a long work, which
may still take several months'. Proust was isolated by his novel still
more completely than by the great flood.

He was isolated, but not alone. At any moment of the day or night
two familiar demons could be brought to his bedside by the triple peal
of his bell. "There's your pal Valentin ringing," said Nicolas Cottin,
with heavy irony, calling his master by the baptismal first name which
Proust never used—"you won't let him put you in a state, will you,
dear?" "Céline, I can feel a gale blowing," Proust complained,
"you've left your larder door open again!" Nicolas was tall and
rotund, thicklipped and cleanshaven, with low forehead, narrow eyes,
and an expression of crafty stupidity; Céline was a jolly blonde; both
were still in their late twenties. The Cottins regarded their strange
employer with less respect than they displayed in his presence, but
perhaps with less contempt than they pretended when alone together.
Proust shed the loose leaves of his novel on the floor in the small
hours: it was one of Nicolas's duties to jab them in order with paper-
fasteners, and sometimes even to take down fresh passages from
dictation. "His rigmaroles are as big a bloody bore as he is," he told
Céline, "but mark my words, when he's dead he'll be a success all
right." The usual pay for a married couple was 150 francs monthly,
and Proust characteristically gave them double. But their service was
not without its rigours: Céline went to bed at 9.30 p.m., for she must
be up to give Monsieur his dawn coffee; while Nicolas, who was on
duty till 4 a.m., had become almost as nocturnal as his master, and
acquired a weak chest which Céline attributed to the suffocating heat
of Proust's bedroom. Proust dined at nine in the evening, on three
croissants from the Gare Saint-Lazare, boiling café au lait in a wadded
coffeepot, œufs Béchamel—"the sauce used to get in his beard!"—
fried potatoes in a little silver vegetable-dish, and stewed fruit according to season—"the same every day for weeks, and how we got tired
of stewed apples!" Often Monsieur Hahn would call, and play a few
dazzling notes on the grand-piano in the drawing-room before bursting in. "He's like the wind," Céline would say, and "He's like a
hurricane, Céline," Proust would reply. She remembered Albufera,
Antoine Bibesco and Loche Radziwill as the next most regular callers.
Monsieur never gave orders, except when he was angry, but always

said: "Would you be so obliging as to—"; and when he was too
asthmatic to speak he would write notes, which Nicolas kept:

> *'Since you preserve these missives for all time,*
> *Dear Nicolas, I'm forced to write in rhyme. . . .*
> *If not too weary is your wrist,*
> *Nicolas the nationalist,*
> *Bring me milk-coffee steaming hot. . . .'*

Proust called Céline 'the War-monger', because she once defiantly declared: "I'd love to see what war is like"—a wish destined to be granted.

In June Proust was lured from solitude by a new revelation of high
art. Diaghilev and the Russian Ballet had first exploded upon Paris for
an all-too-brief season in May 1909. In 1910 all Paris had awaited them
for a year, and their triumph was instant and tremendous. Proust went
with Reynaldo and the art-critic Jean Louis Vaudoyer to the opening
night at the Opéra on 4 June, when *Schéhérazade* was first performed.
The stage was a dazzling green tent with shadowy blue doors and a
vast orange carpet: 'I never saw anything so beautiful,' he told Reynaldo. Nijinsky, a boy of eighteen, entered with an eery, animal
crouch as the negro slave, and whirled away with Ida Rubinstein, the
Sultan's favourite wife; an orgy such as the Paris Opéra had never
before witnessed was interrupted by the Sultan's return, everyone was
hewn to pieces with scimitars, Nijinsky writhed in his unbelievable
horizontal death-leap, and the audience became raving mad. 'I don't
know how you could possibly see Nijinsky miming,' Proust objected
on reading Reynaldo's critique in *Le Journal*, 'because there were
always two hundred persons dancing in front of him.' *Schéhérazade*, it
is true, was a violent sensation rather than a masterpiece; but the
impact was made, and greater things followed in the succeeding years.

Meanwhile Proust and several of his friends discovered that among
the most intoxicating charms of the Russian Ballet was the personal
relationship which was permitted with the artists. Proust was not to
become a habitué until the following year; but he met Nijinsky, and
did not care for him, and Bakst, whom he 'admired prodigiously',
feeling that the great designer had made a point of being particularly
charming—'it's true he's charming to everybody, but I thought I
detected a *nuance*!' Montesquiou was seen at every performance with
his gold-headed cane, and worshipped the boyish Ida Rubinstein with
an adoration he had felt for no woman since the heyday of the Marquise de Casa-Fuerte seventeen years before. Reynaldo was com-

missioned to compose a ballet to a scenario by Cocteau, *Le Dieu Bleu*, for next season, and was invited to St Petersburg for the end of the winter. Cocteau, to whom Diaghilev one day would issue the momentous command: "Amaze me!", was first amazed by Diaghilev: the taxi which Diaghilev had so kindly lent him on the way home from Larue's seemed to take an extraordinarily long time over the journey, and at last deposited the bewildered stripling in the courtyard of the Hôtel des Réservoirs at Versailles. Vaudoyer, a romantically melancholy young man with pendulous moustaches, quoted Gautier's lines '*I am the spectre of the rose You wore last evening at the ball*' in his essay '*Variations on the Russian Ballet*' in the *Revue de Paris*, and wrote to Bakst suggesting that the poem might make a promising subject for a ballet. Already the camp-following of artists and intellectuals which formed an indispensable part of the Diaghilev circus was beginning to gather. Some, like Cocteau and Hahn, would bring their art, others, like Montesquiou and Vaudoyer, their publicity; some, like Proust himself, would give only their kindling admiration and conversation; but all would contribute to the incessant cross-fertilisation, devised by the strange and cunning genius of Diaghilev, by which the marvellous organism of the Ballets Russes grew and ripened, and for lack of which, many years after, it would wither away for ever.

In the next few years Proust frequented the Ballets Russes each summer. He was 'almost terrifying under the lights of the Opéra,' his future friend Edmond Jaloux remembered, 'with his fur coat, puffed face and black-rimmed eyes'; and to Jacques Porel he seemed 'like a yesterday's gardenia'. Above in the master's box sat the magician Diaghilev, scrutinising his dancers through a tiny mother-of-pearl lorgnette, and Misia Edwards beside him, with a tall white Persian aigrette in her head-dress. For a time Misia had struggled to regain the formidable Edwards from his mistress, the actress Lantelme; and we have seen Proust confronted by the grim farce of their triangular agonies at the Grand Hôtel of Cabourg in 1907. 'I had contrived to get a photograph of Lantelme,' she wrote in her memoirs; 'it adorned my dressing-table, and I made desperate efforts to look like her, dress my hair in the same way, wear the same clothes.' Proust used this situation for Gilberte's jealousy of Rachel and Saint-Loup at Tansonville: Gilberte has 'come across photographs of Rachel', and imitates her hair-style and dress 'in the hope of pleasing her husband'.[1] But Lantelme was drowned from Edwards' yacht in highly suspicious

[1] III, 682-3, 702.

circumstances in July 1911—"I hope she can swim," said Forain, on
first seeing his next mistress, the singer Lina Cavalieri—and Misia was
now the companion, later the wife, of the Spanish artist José Maria
Sert. "How very Spanish," remarked Degas on viewing one of his
huge and hideous frescoes in his Paris studio, "and in such a quiet
street, too!"; but Proust admired his costumes for *La Légende de
Joseph*, the Diaghilev ballet of 1914, and compared to them the
Fortuny and Carpaccio gowns which the Narrator buys for the captive Albertine.[1] Here at the Ballets Russes Misia became 'the ravishing
Princess Yourbeletieff' of Proust's novel, with her 'immense trembling aigrette, the like of which the Parisian ladies had never seen,
though they all tried to imitate it'.[2] "Are you a snob?" Misia asked
Proust; and he indignantly replied that, although he still saw an
occasional duke or prince, his favourite companions were a valet
(Nicolas) and a chauffeur (Odilon): "valets," he said, "are better
educated than dukes, and the chauffeur is more distinguished". Misia
asked him to share her box at the Opéra, and he wrote in accepting,
with thoughts of the final chapter of *Le Temps Retrouvé*: 'I find it
extremely interesting to see how people's faces grow older.'

After the ballet Proust and the dancers adjourned to supper at
Larue's, where Diaghilev devoured beefsteaks with Nijinsky, while
Proust wrote his letters sipping a humble whipped chocolate, and
Cocteau repeated the magnificent gesture of Saint-Loup, originated
in 1902 by the long-lost Fénelon. Proust recorded the occasion in
doggerel verses:

> '*To cover my shoulders with satin-lined mink,
> Without spilling one drop from his huge eyes' black ink,
> Like a sylph to the ceiling, or on snow a thin ski,
> Jean leaped on the table and dropped by Nijinsky.*'

Proust constructed Octave, the young dandy 'son of a rich manufacturer', whom the little band at Balbec nickname 'In the Soup', from
various youths in his Cabourg circle: from the artist Léonce de
Joncières, 'that amiable juvenile lead among the Tapirs, a belated
prolongation of Léandre or Octave'—those heroes of sentimental
comedy in the eighteenth century—'the most idiotic person I have
ever seen', as he wrote to Reynaldo, and from Marcel Plantevignes,
son of the manufacturer of neckties. But in his later aspect as the
genius whose 'little sketches, with his own costumes and décor, which

[1] III, 369, 647. In fact the costumes were by Bakst.   [2] II, 743; III, 236-7

have brought about in contemporary art a revolution at least equal to that achieved by the Ballets Russes' are 'perhaps the most extraordinary masterworks of our time', Octave is the Cocteau who created in 1917 and 1919 the revolutionary *Parade* and *Les Mariés de la Tour Eiffel*; while Andrée as Octave's fiancée is probably Jeanne, sister of Paul Iribe with whom Cocteau founded the avant-garde periodical *Le Mot* in 1916, Cocteau's temporary fiancée, and a heroine of *Le Grand Écart*.[1]

Still hoping for the indispensable publicity of serialisation, still believing that the end of his book was already in sight, Proust had recently sent his Combray chapter to *Le Figaro*. But the amiable editor, who a year before had positively begged for the new novel, was now disquietingly coy. 'Someone has managed to *alienate Calmette*, who used to like me so much,' he wrote to Antoine Bibesco about 20 May. In fact Calmette was genuinely impressed, but must have thought a fragment so dense in texture and so apparently destitute of action quite impossible as a feuilleton for his newspaper. Towards the end of June Proust called at one o'clock in the morning —'a most melancholy pilgrimage,' he told Lauris—to collect his rejected manuscript from the *Figaro* office.

As holiday-time approached he thought for a moment of persuading Lauris to accompany him to 'Paul Desjardins's lay abbey'. Desjardins, his revered philosophy teacher twenty years before, had recently founded the famous '*décades*', the discussion groups held for ten days each summer in the mediaeval abbey of Pontigny near Auxerre, which have been carried into our own time by Desjardins's daughter Anne Heurgon. Seventeen years ago with Willie Heath, and again in 1903 with Lauris himself, Proust had vaguely planned to found a secular monastery for writing and meditation. Might not Pontigny be the fulfilment of his dream?

Instead, on the afternoon of 17 July, assisted by the entire family of the concierge Antoine, Proust suddenly fled to Cabourg with Nicolas, reaching the Grand Hôtel on the stroke of midnight. His luggage had an unfamiliar air: it turned out to consist of the pretty hats of a lady who, at that very moment, would be gazing in horror at his cosy nightshirts somewhere in Brittany. The distracted Antoine had muddled the trunks at the Gare Saint-Lazare, and for twenty-four hours Proust was unable to go to bed, while poor Nicolas, very understandably, seized the occasion to go out and get drunk. After a

[1] I, 878; III, 604-7.

few days, however, Proust began to work. In the silence of the night his exultant cries to the absent Reynaldo of "O my Bunibuls, don't you agree that's rather nice!" disturbed his sleeping neighbours. He thought of summoning Ulrich to be his secretary, but discovered that the young man was in hiding after a thwarted attempt at abduction.

It is not unlikely that in the appropriate environment of Cabourg Proust now wrote of Balbec. During the eight months since the completion of the Combray chapter in November 1909 he would have had ample time to dispose of the Narrator's love for Gilberte in the Champs-Élysées and his visits to Odette's salon. Much of the material for the first visit to Balbec in *A l'Ombre* had already been worked over. At the time, perhaps as early as 1905, when Swann was to be the third-person hero of much of his novel, he had shown him in love with the little band at Querqueville; the night-journey, and the rosy peasant-girl selling coffee, had appeared in *Contre Sainte-Beuve*, as also had passing allusions which show that the Narrator's friendship with Montargis (Saint-Loup) at the same Querqueville (Balbec) had formed part of the earlier version of his novel. The little band known to Swann had borne mawkish names reminiscent of *Les Plaisirs et les Jours*, such as Arabelle, Célie, Solange; while Albertine and Andrée had appeared as Anna and Septimie, already suspect of a Lesbian intimacy which belongs to the second visit to Balbec in *Sodome et Gomorrhe*. Albertine and Andrée were not to be rechristened until some years later. But it is probable that the lovely name of Gisèle belongs to this summer, and that Proust took it from Diaghilev's revival that June of the old romantic ballet, which Proust reproached Reynaldo, in a letter from Cabourg, for calling 'the celebrated and insipid *Giselle*'.

Despite Calmette's refusal, which forced him to abandon hope of serial publication in a daily newspaper, Proust still thought of finding a welcome in a monthly magazine; but within a month of arrival at Cabourg he had advanced so far that too little time seemed left even for this. He asked Vaudoyer on 18 August 'whether a periodical like the *Grande Revue* would publish the greater part of my novel; but it will be finished so soon that I feel it's now too late to think of a magazine, which would necessarily involve a long delay'.

Meanwhile Proust was enacting some of the situations of his novel. Towards eleven in the evening he entered the casino and made for the baccarat table, where he was immediately surrounded by a band of pretty girls in holiday dresses. His cousin Valentine Thomson, who happened to be in Cabourg with her married sister Marguerite, watched with sympathetic concern as he shyly produced handfuls of twenty-franc gold pieces for the gay young creatures to gamble away. "They'd like anyone as sweet as you without all that money," she reproached him; but: "Poor young things," he explained, "it amuses them, and besides, they're so nice!" 'Marcel looked like an oriental sorcerer, with his black beard and black-rimmed eyes,' Mlle Thomson recalled long afterwards; and when *Al'Ombre* appeared she recognised the girls of Cabourg in the 'little band' of Balbec. One evening she walked arm in arm with Proust and Calmette, who was staying at the Villa des Tamaris at Houlgate. Suddenly Calmette pointed to her cousin and said: "Did you know that this chap's a genius? He's written a solid, magnificent thing." Valentine turned to Marcel, whose excessive humility was a family joke, expecting to see him protest and dissolve into confusion; but he was smiling remotely, with a look of assurance, although deeply moved, and the young woman realised that Calmette had not exaggerated.

In September, as the end of his holiday drew near, Proust gave the two d'Alton girls their annual present. This year it was a watch each, in periwinkle-blue enamel, on a neck-chain of gold, for which the Paris jeweller Cartier demanded the enormous sum of 4000 francs; so Proust arranged through Reynaldo's sister Maria, and with the expert advice of the elegantly impoverished Boni de Castellane, to buy the trinkets elsewhere at half the price. But the gifts to the two sisters were aimed only at one, apparently at Colette the elder. 'Perhaps you remember,' he wrote to Maria six years later, in the dark days of the war, when he consulted her on the Narrator's presents to Albertine, 'how once long ago you helped me to have fashionable trifles made for two girls, to one of whom I enjoyed giving them.'

Another gift had to be found at the same time, for Georges de Lauris had announced—'in a letter which might have been signed by Fromentin's Dominique or M. de Nemours in *La Princesse de Clèves*', as Proust remarked acidly to Reynaldo—his forthcoming marriage to Madeleine de Pierrebourg, the divorced wife of Proust's still earlier friend, Louis de La Salle. Lauris, after nine long years, was one of the last bachelor survivors of the group of noble young friends from whom Saint-Loup was created; his intimacy had been particularly precious of late, when Proust had made him, as a fellow-novelist, his chief confidant for the writing of *Contre Sainte-Beuve* and the beginning of *A la Recherche*: and Proust could not help feeling a secret bitterness at the coming end of an old comradeship. But he wrote a charming letter of congratulation: he had admired the bride for many years, and 'it would need a Mantegna to paint these nuptials of the Knight of the Ideal and the Rose Princess!' As a wedding-present Lauris suggested a clock for his study mantelpiece—'one whose chimes will tell me to write only books that will please you': 'and that,' Proust commented with the same note of acrimony to Reynaldo, 'rather complicates one's choice.'

At the beginning of October Proust returned from Cabourg, lamenting to Mme Catusse that he had only once been well enough to go on the beach. His mother's friend could not know that his incarceration was voluntary, and the sunlight on the sea had shone still more brilliantly in the pages he wrote than outside his shuttered windows and drawn blinds. He hoped to finish his novel soon, he told her, 'but the book lengthens ahead of me'; for the process of expansion and enrichment of his prearranged plan had now begun, and would continue until the day of his death. Now, while he worked through the hours before and after dawn, or slept from noon until late in the evening, he was no longer disturbed by the traffic of the Boulevard Haussmann, or the clatter of his servants and neighbours; for during his absence he had the famous cork walls installed in his bedroom, a device borrowed, according to Mme de Noailles, from Henry Bernstein. On his nights out, charioted by Odilon Albaret in his taxi, he visited Félix Mayol's concert-hall. Again, as on his return from Cabourg in 1907, he was fascinated by the shameless strutting and swaying of that effeminate singer, which reminded him of the dancing of the lovely Cléo de Mérode, by his facial likeness to the plump-cheeked Nicolas, and by the almost beautiful vulgarity of his song *Viens poupoule*, which the Narrator, when bringing the news of M. de Charlus's pretended duel, finds Morel singing at Doncières.[1] 'Mayol is *sublime*,' he told Reynaldo.

[1] II, 1065. The Narrator, when he brings Albertine captive to Paris, is likewise reminded of a former autumn when, after returning from a holiday, he went to hear Mayol, 'in order to regain contact with the forgotten pleasures of Paris', and finds himself humming Mayol's songs. Although tempted to go again he refrains, 'fearing the motley crowd at the café-concert might rouse Albertine's desires and regrets' (III, 1065-7). Charlus, however, was of a different mind: when the young bus-conductor, asked whether he is fond of concerts, confides that he 'goes to the Concert Mayol sometimes', the Baron exclaims: "I don't care for Mayol. I can't bear his effeminate manner, and I hate that sort on principle" (II, 1188).

Lauris's marriage on 27 October, at which Bertrand de Fénelon was best man, was followed by two deaths. Earlier in the year Proust had warned Louisa de Mornand that she was in danger of losing Robert Gangnat, who had discovered her affair with a well-known actor, and that the man's wife was having her followed in order to secure evidence for divorce. On 29 October this inextricable knot was cut by Gangnat's sudden death; his funeral was attended by his colleagues in the Society of Dramatic Authors, many of whom—Robert de Flers, Gaston de Caillavet, Francis de Croisset, Hervieu, Hermant—were friends of Proust; and Proust sent his condolences to Gangnat's mother: 'an absurd thing to do,' he told Flers, 'because I don't even know her, and no doubt she'll never see my letter, but I couldn't help myself.' To Louisa he wrote with sympathy barbed with bitter phrases: she had stirred in Albufera and Gangnat 'perhaps the two purest, most chivalrous, greatest devotions that any woman has yet inspired'; but 'I don't know how you will conduct your life henceforth, or whether your friends of tomorrow will be worthy of these two men'. He himself had felt for her—'you whom I loved so much, Louisa'—'that which cannot be forgotten, and nothing can efface'; but—'goodbye, dear favourite friend of long ago!' he concluded. On 7 November died Robert Dreyfus's elder brother Henri, who under the stage-name of Fursy had been a popular comedian, specialising in monologues. Proust remembered him in the Champs-Élysées nearly twenty-five years ago, benevolently watching their games. Thinking of his own bereavement and his own writing, he urged Robert to continue with his literary work; for 'in so doing you will live in a region of yourself where the barriers of Time and the body cease to exist, where there is no death because there is no Time and no body, and we live blissfully in the immortal company of those we love'.

In the summer of 1909 Montesquiou had fled from the Pavillon des Muses, with its mournful memories of the dead Yturri. His new secretary Henri Pinard took him to view a charming property at Le Vésinet, an outlying residential suburb ten miles north-west of Paris. "This is just what M. le Comte needs," said the painted secretary, and "If it isn't mine tomorrow, I shall die!!" declared the Count. His farewell fête at the Pavillon des Muses took place on 16 June 1909; of the nine celebrated actresses who were to represent the Nine Muses Ida Rubinstein (Terpsichore) and Segond-Weber (Thalia) failed to turn up; and although Montesquiou obligingly took the part of Thalia himself, the occasion was not altogether a success. So the Count

moved to the Palais Rose, as he called it after the former mansion of
the ruined Boni; though when people asked the reason for the name,
he would fix them in the eye and pronounce: "I call it the Palais Rose
because it is a palace, and because it is rose-pink."

At two o'clock in the morning of 12 December 1910 Proust rose
and dressed, and worked until dawn on his novel. The winter sun was
bright that day, although, as his shutters had been closed for months,
he would not have known it if Céline had not told him; and feeling a
sudden impulse to see the Palais Rose he ordered his taxi and emerged,
for the first time for several years, into the air of morning. On the way
he noticed a florist, and bought bouquets of out-of-season sweet-peas
for his host; but soon, overcome by their deadly perfume, he turned
back in a fit of asthma. He was to make further attempts to reach the
Palais Rose, but never succeeded; and many other persons likewise
found the pleasure of seeing the Count too dearly bought by the long
journey to Vésinet. Montesquiou's star was waning: at last, quite
literally, he had gone too far.

In February 1911, when Reynaldo was at St Petersburg with
Diaghilev and the dancers, Proust felt a sudden craving for music.
Subscribers to a curious invention known as the theatrophone could
ask the company's private exchange for any concert, opera or play on
the current list, and listen to the actual performance on their own
telephone. Lying in bed with the supernatural black trumpet pressed
to his ear, Proust heard *Pelléas et Mélisande* from the Opéra Comique
on the 21st. He repeated the experience on following evenings, and
when there was no performance sang the part of Pelléas to himself,
until he felt, as he told Reynaldo, the same bewitchment as when he
went every night to hear Mayol! He was haunted ever after by the
moment when Pelléas emerges from the subterranean cavern to the
air of the sea and the scent of roses. "It's just like *Pelléas*," says the
Narrator to Mme de Cambremer at Balbec, when she tells him of the
fragrance of roses borne on the sea-breeze at La Raspelière; "the scent
of roses is so strong in the score that I have asthma whenever I hear
it!" As a kind of penance Proust transferred to this pretentious lady
his own inadequate first-thoughts as expressed to Reynaldo, when he
was irrelevantly struck by the elements of Wagner, and even
Massenet, in the innovating genius of Debussy; and it is Mme de
Cambremer, not the Narrator, who 'began to hum something which
I suppose she mistook for Pelléas's farewell'.[1]

[1] II, 813-15. When the Narrator listens to the street-cries on the morning of

Reynaldo had arrived at a tragicomic crisis in the history of the Ballets Russes. At the end of January Nijinsky had danced in *Giselle* wearing an extraordinarily short tunic, designed by Benois and abbreviated by Bakst on the instructions of Diaghilev; and beneath this tunic he had been induced to discard an indispensable article of protective clothing. The Dowager-Empress could scarcely believe what she saw, or thought she saw; and although protocol demanded that she should pretend to have seen nothing, the revelation of Nijinski's protuberances was taken as a personal insult to the imperial family. He was dismissed immediately. On both sides the incident was a ludicrous but sinister pretext for a final rift. The court circles which controlled the Imperial Ballet were anxious to be rid of Diaghilev, feeling that he had turned the Maryinsky Theatre into a mere winter home for his private troupe; while Diaghilev, conversely, instead of being dependent on the services of dancers on summer leave from the Imperial Ballet, could now organise the Ballets Russes as an independent and permanent company. Proust sent his sympathy to Bakst and 'Vestris', as he insisted on nicknaming Nijinsky; but on hearing that the scandal had been a put-up job he withdrew his good wishes to the young dancer: 'he only interested me as a victim,' he told Reynaldo, 'and if he hasn't been victimised, then' (using his favourite rude word) '*merde* to him.'

In May 1911, a livid, bearded, fur-coated wallflower on a little gilt chair, Proust sat at the annual ball given by the newspaper *L'Intransigeant*, pursuing with his reproachful nocturnal eyes the fleeing Princesse Marthe Bibesco. Born a Lahovary, she had married her cousin Prince Georges Bibesco in 1902 at the age of sixteen; she was a cousin-german of Antoine and Emmanuel Bibesco and of Mme de Noailles, and was linked through her husband's family or her own with Mme Greffulhe, Montesquiou, Guiche, and half the noble Faubourg. In Paris this astonishingly young tree-nymph from Roumania, with her violet-green eyes and talent budding into power, was received as a reigning beauty and a genius; truly, for she was both, but to her own annoyance, for her wish was not to be discovered by others, but to find herself. Proust and Guiche saw her from afar at the Opéra in 1902, at a performance of *Tristan* sung by Litvinne and Van Dyck, and asked who she could be. "She's my cousin," said

Albertine's visit to the Trocadéro (III, 117), the monotonous song of the snail-seller reminds him of *Pelléas et Mélisande*.

Emmanuel to Marcel; and turning to Guiche he added: "She's your
cousin." "You mean yours?" "No, yours—mine too, of course!"
Emmanuel, that entwiner of destinies, sent Marcel her newly published first book, *Les Huit Paradis*, pretending it came from herself.
Proust wrote to Emmanuel in the Bibesco slang of his longing to:

> '*Tell to the Princess, be it said,*
> *Her beauty and her genius* (sic) . . .
> *She whom at* Tristan, *by Van Dyck*,
> *My eyes had much preferred unwed* . . .'

But the Princess, who had heard the words beauty and genius too
often, was not amused; and for opposite reasons she resented still
more the uncanny divination with which, in the letter he wrote her a
few days later, Proust praised her book, spoke of 'the childlike gaiety
which alone can aid you to bear the weight of your perpetual thought',
and warned her. So, at the ball three years later, his insistent and
uneasy presence reminded her (for she was perhaps the first person to
sense something supernatural in him), of a fantastic figure in a Hoffmann fairytale of her childhood, the night-owl Councillor Drossel-
mayer, whose apparition inside the grandfather-clock terrifies little
Clara:

> '*The clock is humming*
> *At midnight's tread,*
> *The Owl is coming,*
> *The King has fled!*'

She danced ever away from his melancholy eyes, till Fénelon,
suborned, danced her towards him. Was she writing another book,
Proust asked. She was writing, she replied, a book about happiness,
Alexandre Asiatique, the story of Alexander the Great considered as a
symbol of the greatest possible earthly bliss. Proust seemed appalled;
one should seek, he murmured, not for happiness, but for disaster! "I
have never made any money on the stock-exchange," he added, "but
the important thing in gambling is to lose." The Princess beckoned
to Fénelon and danced away. Proust had understood her already; but
the 'Labourer of the eleventh hour', as the Bibesco brothers and
Fénelon called this latecomer to their group, understood him afterwards with a poetic truth which no critic has equalled. 'He possessed
the keys of a world into which I refused to follow him that evening,'
she wrote after his death, 'but into which he has led me since.' Proust

and Princesse Marthe Bibesco were two natives of the same land; and their touching of finger-tips at the ball was more deeply significant than the embraces of those who danced together till dawn.

On 21 May 1911 Proust attended the dress-rehearsal of D'Annunzio's play *Le Martyre de Saint-Sébastien*, with décor by Bakst and music by Debussy, at the Théâtre du Châtelet. During the last act he sat next to Montesquiou: 'wired to the dynamos of your enthusiasm by the electrode of your wrist,' he told the Count later, 'I was convulsed in my seat, as if it had been an electric chair!'[1] Montesquiou regarded the whole occasion as a spectacular private party. He had known Gabriele d'Annunzio since the days of poor Yturri (whom D'Annunzio used to call 'the other Gabriel'), and had suggested the subject of his play. The saint, pierced by the arrows of the heathen— was he not the emblem of Count Robert, wounded by the incomprehension of critics and the treachery of friends? And the lovely boy of Perugino's *Saint Sebastian* in the Louvre, appealing in his distress to the protection of some higher being—was he not the disciple Count Robert had sought in vain, and the very image of Mme Rubinstein? Proust, too, was impressed by Ida Rubinstein: 'she's a cross between Clomesnil and Maurice de Rothschild,' he told Reynaldo, 'and her legs are sublime'. Various members of the noble audience offered their condolences for the ill-health which, they thought, prevented him from visiting them. Like the Narrator at the end of his novel, he found them changed for the worse: 'even the nicest ones,' he complained to Mme Straus, 'have taken to intelligence, which in society people is a mere co-efficient of stupidity, raising it to hitherto unknown powers. Only those who've had the sense to stay silly are still bearable!'

Proust left for his earliest and longest visit to Cabourg on 11 July. At first, unprecedentedly, the sea air failed to relieve his asthma, and in the darkling hour between sunset and electric light he listened from his bed to the fat members of a ladies' brass-band on the beach, playing waltzes on horns and cornets, 'till I'm ready to jump into the sea for melancholy!' He had toyed with the idea of bringing a young man whom he had met once at Constantin Ullmann's to act as his secretary. The young person's task, he explained, would be to take down the portion of his novel which was still in rough draft from dictation by

[1] 'At this moment,' says the Narrator, walking home from Mme de Villeparisis's matinée arm in arm with Charlus, 'I felt my arm jerked violently, as if by an electric shock' (II, 292).

shorthand, and to make a typewritten copy—or, if he happened to know neither shorthand nor typing, to copy it from dictation in long-hand. However, even the humble Nicolas was fit to do the latter, and when Proust found that a lady shorthand-typist was now attached to the Grand Hôtel, it seemed pointless to hire Constantin's friend at all. He sent an honorarium of 300 francs for his wasted hopes, but even so —'because I don't want to force you not to come, if you'd rather come'—half-invited him to Cabourg, with a salary of 400 francs a month, 250 more for meals, 'a nice room in my own apartment', and free mornings and afternoons. The unnamed youth was Albert Nah-mias, who became Proust's occasional secretary in the following winter. Proust turned to the hotel typist, an English lady named Miss Hayward, who gave every satisfaction except for her insular insistence on free week-ends. Soon he was able to write to Calmette: 'I have already dictated almost a quarter of "your" novel to a typist, and even this quarter, or rather fifth, is the length of a whole volume.'

The Plantevignes had deserted Cabourg for Chamonix, and are heard of no more; but the invariable d'Altons were present. Proust attended the Golf Club ball at the casino on 16 August, was received by the Vicomte d'Alton in his capacity as president of the club, and watched Mlle Colette lead off the first dance with Alexandre de Neuf-ville. He bowed to the Duc de Morny, whom he had met before through Reynaldo, 'but he stared at me with an air of such utter stupefaction that I refrained from insisting further'. The beautiful Maurice de Rothschild was there, 'but, nice as he's been to me, I must say he was absolutely impossible, and his wife was sheer torture'. One of Proust's favourite stories was of Montesquiou's request to Maurice de Rothschild for the loan of some diamonds to wear at a fancy-dress ball. Count Robert was outraged to receive only a very small brooch with the message: 'Please take great care of it, as it is a family jewel.' 'I was quite unaware that you had a family,' he replied haughtily, 'but I did think you had some jewels.'

Again Proust indulged in flutters at baccarat, and lost more heavily than ever, although this year he entrusted his bets to the banker. His only consolation was to quote to his friends (like the Narrator's mother in her letter from Combray during the captivity of Albertine,[1] and his own mother in the past) Mme de Sévigné's words on her erring son Charles: 'he has found a way of losing without gambling, and spending without having anything to show for it'. The young Jacques

[1] III, 141.

Porel, son of the great Réjane, was astounded to see him on the golf-course in his archiepiscopal violet velvet cloak, tottering and pale; but his interest was more in the players than in the game, the object of which he believed to be to get round in the greatest possible number of strokes. Andrée, in *A l'Ombre*, does a creditable round of seventy-seven: "That's a record," cries Albertine; but Octave 'In the Soup' remarks with negligent vainglory: "I scored eighty-two yesterday!"[1]

A few days after the Golf Club ball Calmette called to stand him a drink. "I'd rather have offered you one myself," Proust gently complained. "What does it matter, so long as we're together?" replied Calmette amiably. He had recently foiled another attempt of the army to call Proust up for a fortnight's training[2]; yet Proust sensed in him the wry embarrassment of a kindhearted editor towards a rejected contributor. 'I believe he can't bear the sight of me,' he told Reynaldo.

At the beginning of August Proust read excerpts from Maeterlinck's *On Death* in *Le Figaro*, and was shocked by what seemed to him a grossly material and negative conception of death and infinity. 'Death manifests itself in a way which is terribly positive,' he wrote to Lauris, and recalled how in conversation with Georges he had made fun of Maeterlinck's 'forty horsepower Infinite and motor-cars with the tradename Mystery'.[3] In this context he gave another glimpse of the progress of his novel: what he had written about death[4], he said, was finished long ago, and Lauris would be able to read it in the volume of 800 pages which he was now having transcribed for publication.

Proust returned to Paris towards the end of September, and immediately engaged in a grandiose speculation on the stock exchange, a continuation in a graver form, as he told Robert de Billy, of his gambling-fever in the baccarat-room at Cabourg: 'it may be that the stagnation of my solitary life is attracted by its opposite pole'.

[1] I, 878.

[2] At this setback the French army gave up the unequal struggle which had lasted for twenty years. Proust was informed on 6 September 1911 that his name was removed from the army reserve list, 'for reasons of health'.

[3] Similarly the Narrator, while playing *Tristan* on the piano on the afternoon when Albertine has gone to the Trocadéro, and wondering whether a great artist's originality may not be a mere illusion due to his technical skill, ironically longs for 'some downright material machine for exploring the infinite, some apparatus of 120 horsepower, registered trademark Mystery!' (III, 162). Maeterlinck's argument is that, since death consists in our removal from a finite world to an infinite one, we can look forward to an existence of infinite possibilities, far richer than our life on earth.

[4] Cf. I, 44, 82, 670-2.

Similarly Dostoevsky, laden with guilt and about to stake his salvation on the hope of becoming a great novelist, challenged destiny on the green-baize tables of Baden-Baden. Proust bought gold shares to the value of nearly 300,000 francs by the operation known as a time-bargain, in which the shares are to be paid for at a future date at a sum fixed beforehand. Gold had fallen, and Proust, in his capacity as a 'bull', hoped when the inevitable rise came to sell at a handsome profit. At each month's end the 'bull' may either 'liquidate', or 'carry over' until next month; but in the latter case, if his shares have continued to fall, he must pay a 'difference' to compensate their loss in value. Alas, gold continued inexplicably to slump; at the end of January 1912 Proust had to pay a large 'difference', and another on 29 February of this ill-omened leap-year. On 4 March he liquidated the whole transaction, with a loss of 40,000 francs, and next day, as if he alone had been holding it down, gold began to rise.

For these speculations Proust employed the young Albert Nahmias, whose father was the financial correspondent of *Le Gaulois*. Their relationship soon became affectionate: the letter in which he ordered 'liquidation' begins: '*Mon petit Albert*' and ends with '*tendresses*'. He also engaged Albert to supervise the typing of his novel, recommending him to use Miss Hayward of Cabourg, who was then wintering in Paris.[1] This new instalment of his typescript completed the first half of his novel, which he then hoped to publish in two large volumes. Meanwhile he began to revise this version for a second and final typescript to be submitted to a publisher in the autumn: 'I am finishing the last pages of my first chapter for the typist,' he told Robert de Billy in February 1912.

By way of atoning for his broken promise to publish Proust's novel as a serial, Calmette had offered to recommend it to the publisher Fasquelle, and to print suitable extracts in *Le Figaro* by way of advance publicity. The first of these appeared on 21 March, with the topical title (not of Proust's choosing, as he angrily explained to Lauris, Montesquiou and Vaudoyer), '*Au Seuil du Printemps*' (*On the Threshold of Spring*). This description of the hawthorns of Tansonville, round which he had ingeniously woven excerpts from the moon-

---

[1] He asked for the first page of the new instalment to be numbered 560: this section was presumably, therefore, the last in the volume which he had told Lauris would amount to 800 pages; and the two manuscript-books, one red and one blue, of which it consisted, probably contained the early version of the Narrator's first visit to Balbec, from what later became *A l'Ombre des Jeunes Filles en Fleurs*.

lit evenings of Swann's visit and the family walk, the hawthorns on the altar in the church, and the Narrator's farewell to his beloved flowers, was one of Proust's recent additions, although he had used the same memories sixteen years before in *Jean Santeuil*. 'It's an extract, re-arranged,' he told Lauris, who had read the original Combray chapter in November 1909, 'of a part of my book which you haven't yet seen, though it comes from the same chapter which you already know.'[1] He particularly hoped for the approval of Montesquiou. But the Count's praise was grudging and barbed: he referred to the mingling of sexual and religious imagery in the hawthorn episode as 'a hotchpotch of litanies and lechery', compared the whole article to Renan's *Souvenirs d'enfance et de jeunesse* (a great work, but one which Proust had no intention of emulating), and sent a picture-postcard of a gigantic haw-thorn at Artagnan. Proust replied ruefully but affably. For lechery and litanies, he said, he knew nothing to beat Fauré's *Romance sans Paroles*, 'which is the sort of music a pederast might hum when raping a choir-boy'; it was all too true that his articles would make people mistake his novel, 'which is so closely constructed and concentric', for mere *Memories of my Childhood*; and it was just like Montesquiou to have a hawthorn 'bigger than anyone else's and four times the size of mine'!

Reynaldo's mother, Mme Carlos Hahn, died on 25 March. She had written to Proust on New Year's Day, already ailing, during an absence of her son in Monte Carlo and Algeria, with news of 'Rey-naldo, our dear travelling pigeon'; and he had expressed in return his feelings of 'affectionate and filial respect'. It was about this time that he discovered the notebook in which his own mother had recorded the last illnesses of her parents and husband: 'narratives of such anguish,' he told Mme de Noailles, 'that one can hardly bear to go on living after reading them'. He quoted to Reynaldo, and perhaps now inserted in his novel, the words with which his mother had awakened him on the morning of his father's stroke.[2]

Proust's letters during these months in which he revised his novel for publication are full of hidden allusions to his work. He was fascinated by a satirical essay in Montesquiou's new volume, *Brelan de Dames*, on the blue-stocking Marquise de Blocqueville: 'I've often been puzzled,' he told the Count in March, 'to know why ladies like

---

[1] '*Au Seuil du Printemps*' is made up from *Pléiade*, I, 112, 114, 35, 114-15, 138-40, 144, in that order.

[2] II, 335. Cf. vol. I, *supra*, p. 335.

Mmes de Blocqueville, Beaulaincourt, Janzé, Chaponay, could never attract the same social élite (*gratin*) to which persons of less exalted origin find it so easy to treat themselves.' This was the situation of Mme de Villeparisis and her 'Three Fates', of whom these ladies were the originals.[1] He asked the Count to write poems on 'gowns, hats, wraps, apartments, shoes, jewellery', because 'I'd so enjoy comparing them with a chapter of my book on the same subject'—a reference, no doubt, to the Narrator's admiration for Odette and her clothing, when he watches her in the Bois or visits her salon. A few months before, in December 1911, he had visited the exhibition of Chinese painting at Durand-Ruel's with Lucien Henraux, and collected hints for his novel from Georges Rodier, a dilettante whom he had known long ago at Mme Lemaire's. 'He was aged, unrecognisable under his hat, eaten away, like unevenly melted honeycomb', he told Reynaldo. Proust described to him a black hat worn by Clomesnil when he saw her in the Bois twenty-three years before. "I know just what you mean," cried Rodier, "a hat *à la Rembrandt!*"; and in his novel Odette is seen 'walking up the rue d'Abbatucci' in a cape trimmed with skunk, a Rembrandt hat, and a bunch of violets in her corsage.[2] Indiscreetly he revealed that Clomesnil was not the only original of Odette ('I wish I hadn't mentioned the subject, for Laure Hayman's sake,' he told Reynaldo afterwards); but fortunately Rodier began to talk about Cocteau. "What I fear for him is society, he goes into society too much, if he goes into society he's lost!!", he repeated, like Legrandin meeting the Narrator on the way to Mme de Villeparisis's matinée[3]; 'but I saw he spoke,' Proust commented, 'not as a man about town deploring the cause of his weakness, but as a recluse giving the recipe for his virtue'.

One afternoon in April 1912 he rose from bed, wrapped his fur coat over his nightshirt, and drove by taxi to Rueil in search of apple-blossom. It was six o'clock when the car halted on a muddy road; the sky was grey after rain, and twilight was falling; gardeners were eyeing him and his chauffeur with astonished mistrust, mistaking them, he realised with horror, for the motor-bandits Bonnot and

---

[1] The Narrator asks the same question of M. de Charlus at the Verdurins' soirée, after the performance of the Vinteuil Septet; but 'he not only did not give me the solution of this little social problem, but seemed to be unaware of its very existence' (III, 293).

[2] I, 240.

[3] II, 153-4.

Garnier! But there, row after row, were the apple-trees which the Narrator sees on his second visit to Balbec, at the moment when his anguish for his dead grandmother is turning to a desire for renewed pleasures with Albertine: 'As far as the eye could reach they were in full bloom, scandalously luxurious, wearing ball-dresses with their feet in the mire, and taking no precautions against spoiling the most marvellous pink satin ever seen.'[1]

Comtesse Greffulhe had been sending Proust invitations, on and off, ever since her present of the potted vine two years before; and it is a measure of his revulsion from society that he had not seen her since Guiche's wedding in 1904. At last she succeeded, little knowing that he came for his novel's sake rather than hers, in attracting him to her box at the Opéra, on 9 May, the first night of the season of the Italian company from Monte Carlo. He met there for the first time the famous Mme Standish, the former friend of Edward VII: 'I thought her, making all necessary allowances for her age, amazing in her mummi-fied elegance, her artifical simplicity,' he told Robert de Billy, 'though the apple-trees in their flounces were even better dressed than Mme Standish.'[2] To the dazzling apparition of the Princesse and Duchesse de Guermantes at the Opéra in Le Côté de Guermantes he added the contrast between the flamboyant costume of Mme Greffulhe and the austere chicness of Mme Standish. The Duchesse at this moment, birdlike with her beaked nose, muslin plumage and swan's wing fan, is primarily Mme de Chevigné, as Proust had seen her at the theatre twenty years before, and described in the May 1892 number of Le Banquet[3]; but in the 'positively British precision' of her dress, which the Princesse considers 'too tailor-made',[4] she is also Mme Standish, who modelled her clothes on Queen Alexandra's and was nicknamed 'Missis' by the Faubourg. He sought instruction on the technical terms of their clothing from Jeanne de Caillavet, whom he had noticed in the audience, and from Mme Straus, not daring to ask Mme Greffulhe outright—'because if my characters turn out to poison people or commit incest later on, they'll think I mean them!' On second thoughts, however, he called several times on Mme Greffulhe, and on 27 June attended the last soirée of the season at her daughter the Duchesse de Guiche's, 'to refresh my memory of people's faces',

[1] II, 781.
[2] Mme Standish (1847-1933) was then sixty-four.
[3] Les Plaisirs et les Jours, 74-5.
[4] II, 54.

and saw both ladies again. He alludes to this occasion when, at the Princesse de Guermantes's soirée, the Narrator unexpectedly remarks that Mme Standish is 'a far greater lady than the Duchesse de Doudeauville',[1] or tells of the Duchesse and Princesse de Guermantes an anecdote which Proust repeated to Jeanne de Caillavet a few days later of Mme Greffulhe and Mme Standish.[2]

Proust's renewed interest in Gaston's wife, however, was motivated by deeper causes than her presence at the Opéra or her knowledge of fashions in ladies' dresses. A second extract from his novel, '*Un Rayon de Soleil sur le Balcon*', was to appear in *Le Figaro* on 4 June: it was the story of his love for Marie de Benardaky in the Champs-Élysées, much abridged and not yet wholly revised, but with the episode of the sunlight on the balcony already in its final form.[3] Gilberte was not only Marie, but also Jeanne: 'it's a memory of a childhood love-affair of mine,' he confided to her, 'not my love for you, it was before that—but still, you'll find amalgamated in it something of my feelings when I wasn't sure whether you'd be at the tennis-court'. It was twenty-two years since he had made friends with Gaston de Caillavet, the first original of Saint-Loup, and fallen in love with Jeanne, his fiancée. If he gazed into the well of Time Lost their young faces looked up at him, beside his own, although in this world he could only visit a middle-aged couple in the Avenue Hoche. But Time is not always a thief and destroyer, and now performed the miracle of the Two Ways, creating youth from age, one person from two loves, the last unifying theme of a great novel.

One evening towards the end of April, for the first time since Mme Arman's death and the great flood, Proust had called on the Caillavets. "Have Monsieur and Madame gone to bed?" he asked, for it was half-past eleven, "can they see me?" They had not the heart to refuse. "Madame," he began, "will you give me an enormous joy? I have not met your daughter for a very long time, perhaps I may never come here again, and when she is old enough to go to the ball I shall be too ill to go out. And so, Madame, I beg of you, let me see Mademoiselle Simone this evening." "But, Marcel, she went to bed hours ago." "Madame, I entreat you, go and see. If she's still awake, you can explain to her." Simone de Caillavet came down, a girl of sixteen, with

[1] II, 661.
[2] II, 1185; cf. *supra*, vol. 1, p. 152.
[3] *Chroniques*, 100-5. Cf. I, 395, 416-17, 413, 416, 398, 402, 411, 396, 404-5, 396-7.

her father's eyes, with cheeks, Proust told her mother, 'like petals of
an unknown flower', and a smile which he did not forget. 'I'm in love
with your daughter,' he wrote to Jeanne, with an exaggeration which
became truth in the world of his book; 'how cruel she is to be kind,
for it's her smile that made me fall in love, and has given its meaning to
all her person, and if she had been sulky I wouldn't have lost my
peace!' Was there any hope of her coming to Cabourg? He had met
her cousin there last year, 'little Prémonville, who promised to ask his
botany master for information'—about the flowers of Combray, no
doubt—'which turned out to be no use', and 'seemed to be in love
with her, as I am now'. Proust arranged to call again on his way to the
Duchesse de Guiche's soirée, and did not. But it is because Gaston's
wife and daughter were in his mind on that occasion that, in the last
scene of his novel, Gilberte says: "I'll bring my daughter to you, she's
over there talking to little Mortemart and other infants of no importance. I'm sure she'll make such a nice friend for you." And Mlle de
Saint-Loup, 'a young girl of about sixteen, whose tall figure measured
the lapse of time which I had refused to see', is none other than Simone
de Caillavet walking towards him across her parents' drawing-room.
'I thought her beautiful indeed,' says the Narrator, 'radiantly smiling,
still full of hopes, made out of the very years I had lost, she resembled
my youth.'[1]

[1] III, 1028, 1031-2.

Chapter 9

AGONY AT SUNRISE
(*August 1912 – August 1913*)

PROUST had almost convinced himself that his losses on the stock exchange would prevent him from visiting Cabourg. It was not until 7 August that he decided economy had gone far enough, ordered Nicolas to pack for the afternoon train, and released Céline to her native Burgundy. For the sake of quiet, perhaps also with a view to possible guests, he took five adjoining rooms on the top floor of the Grand Hôtel.

Once again he was surrounded by friends. The Strauses were at Trouville, the Guiches at Bénerville, Calmette, Mme Scheikévitch and Mme Gross (a friend of the Daudets) at Houlgate; and in Cabourg itself he had Reynaldo's friend Henri Bardac, Vaudoyer, the future surrealist poet Philippe Soupault, and young Albert Nahmias. His health and hours had improved, and he hoped once more, after four summers in which he had rarely left the hotel, to enjoy the pleasures of motoring in Normandy. But his ardour was chilled by a series of disasters: on the 11th Nahmias ran over a poor little girl, who died two days later, on the road to Caen; on the 25th Bardac killed another outright; and a few days later two local taxis were wrecked in a collision. In the end he prudently hired the hotel omnibus—'it's enormous and far from elegant,' he told Mme Straus, 'but it's safe, and the driver is very careful and clever'. Perhaps he made one of his mysterious flying visits to Brittany, for he wrote to Reynaldo in mid-August: 'I'm thinking of taking a house at dear little Beg-Meil in September, but it looks a very ugly one to me.'

This summer marked the zenith of his friendship with Albert Nahmias. He introduced Albert to Mme Gross, who declared: "Why, you're the image of Maurice Bernhardt!" "Ought I to regard that as an honour, Monsieur Proust," asked the disconcerted young man, "or as the contrary?"[1] Antoine Bibesco, in a conversation nearly forty

[1] On the whole it was probably meant as a compliment. Sarah Bernhardt's son was considered a little flighty, but charming and devoted to his mother.

years later, remembered Marcel's description of Albert on the front at Cabourg in the dusk, 'dressed all in fal-lals—*tout de fanfreluches habillé*', walking with his lovely sisters Anita and Estie, and declared that these formed the original 'little band', and that Albert was Albertine. No doubt there is some element of truth in this, although the little band and Albertine had many models, and there is no important aspect of either which cannot be traced to others. But it seems probable that the relationship between Proust and Albert Nahmias was neither profound nor painful, for Proust had been particularly cheerful since the spring, in the autumn he was engrossed in negotiations for his novel, and early in 1913 he became far more deeply interested in another young man. Perhaps Anita and Estie were among the girls with whom ('just to get the rust out of my joints,' he told Reynaldo apologetically) he danced every other evening in the casino.

Philippe Soupault, then a boy of fifteen, met Proust one evening on the terrace of the Grand Hôtel. A few minutes after the red sun disappeared into the western sea his strange host emerged, carrying a sunshade, and subsided into a wicker armchair past which the waiters walked on tiptoe. "Sunlight is bad for me," he explained; "once I came out when it was quite dark, and then the sun began to shine. It wasn't night at all, it was only a cloud! I suffered terribly." He had known the boy's mother in his schooldays. "I met her at a dancing class in the Rue de la Ville-l'Evêque, and your Aunt Louise, wasn't that her name? I can see her eyes now, the only eyes I've ever known that were *really* violet." Soupault disagreed. "You don't think so? Ah well, the sun must have been to blame, as always!" The boy had already begun his career as a writer, and said so, blissfully unaware that his host was another. Proust smiled gently.

Mme Scheikévitch, one of the most intelligent and influential of a new generation of hostesses, had seen Proust at Mme Lemaire's in 1905, and was sufficiently impressed to question Reynaldo, the Yeatmans and others who knew him; but their opinions tallied in only one point: "there's no one in the least like him!" More recently Reynaldo had announced that Proust was writing a great novel, and asked her to recommend it to her friend Adrien Hébrard, the editor of *Le Temps*, whom she addressed as 'Nounou'. She called at the Grand Hôtel one August evening with Calmette, and found Proust tottering under the chandeliers of the casino, battered straw hat in hand, wearing a winter overcoat, a voluminous dinner-jacket, several woollen waistcoats, and the grim black beard which he grew and shaved off so unpredictably—

'he seemed to put it on and take it off again like a comedian in a provincial music-hall,' said Cocteau. Calmette had a private word with his contributor: "Agreed, my dear fellow, I've spoken to Chevassu, you'll be in the Supplement," he cried, and vanished into the baccarat room.

That night, and on many others, Mme Scheikévitch and Proust talked long on the terrace under the stars. She mentioned his novel, too soon, for he interrupted with a deluge of compliments, and paid attention only when she changed the subject to Russian literature, which she had read in the original ever since her childhood in Moscow. "I worship Dostoevsky," said Proust. His face was emaciated, his eyes dark-ringed; he spoke of asthma, fumigations, the misery of never daring to smell a flower, the ignorance of people in high society, with examples. He gave astonishing imitations, and lapsed into harsh, helpless laughter. Pageboys arrived with news of engagements—with whom?—which he had sent them to arrange or cancel, or with letters which he stuffed unopened, after glancing at the handwriting on the envelopes, into his overcoat pockets crammed with unread newspapers and boxes of pills. At the moment of parting she ventured to say: "I've read everything you've published so far!"; and Proust, with a look of extreme disbelief, sat down again to put her through an examination which, she tells us, 'although it was full of catch-questions, I passed with honours'. She mentioned Hébrard, and this time Proust rose to the bait. "Reynaldo told me you'd recommended Suarès to him." "Yes, and Nounou thought Suarès would insist on doing something quite unheard of, but when he asked what he wanted to write, Suarès just said: 'I don't mind, what would you like?'!" On their next meeting they were already friends, and Proust tried to explain his novel; but she felt she was 'being shown the back of a tapestry, and would never understand the picture until I could see it from the front'. She spoke of her unhappy marriage with the son of the painter Carolus-Duran, which ended in attempted suicide and divorce, and wrung Proust's heart by telling how poor Mme Arman, in her grief for Monsieur France's infidelity, had called and said: "I want you to tell me just how you shot yourself."

Towards the end of the month, when Mme Scheikévitch left for Paris, rain fell every day, drumming on Proust's roof and pattering down his chimney; but the fine weather returned in September, together with a letter from his new friend on his latest article in *Le Figaro*—'it's organised and dense', she wrote. The article was

'*L'Église de Village*', a group of extracts from his Combray chapter on the church of Saint-Hilaire, and appeared on 3 September.[1] In his gratitude he paid her the supreme compliment of quoting the lines of Baudelaire which he associated with Marie Finaly, about the sunlight on the sea, and '*the greenish light of your long eyes*'. 'Fortunately I soon forget people I like,' he cautiously added; but Marie Scheikévitch was destined to be a lifelong friend to himself and his novel.

About 16 September Proust at last called on Mme Straus at Trouville. He asked her advice on his annual present to the d'Alton girls, to whom this year he had promised fur coats. Then she took him in her automobile to Honfleur, through the upland lanes which he had seen twenty years ago with Marie Finaly, ten years ago with herself and Fénelon. "It's my donkey-cart," she remarked, and "It's a magic coach for exploring the past," he replied. Two days later he returned to Paris, full of hope and energy, to face one of the great crises of his life. The new, corrected typescript of the first half of his novel was now ready for the press; he was determined to find a publisher in the autumn—preferably Fasquelle—and to see this first of two volumes (as he mistakenly believed) published early in the next spring.

The novel now consisted of two approximately equal halves, which together amounted to little more than a third of *A la Recherche* in its final form. The first half existed in three states: first, the original manuscript, secondly, the unrevised typescript begun by Miss Hayward at Cabourg in August 1911 and completed under the supervision of Albert Nahmias early in 1912; and thirdly the revised typescript made in the summer of 1912, which Proust now intended to submit to Fasquelle. The two typescripts each comprised about 700 pages, ending with the Narrator's return from his first visit to Balbec: they contained, that is, the equivalent of what afterwards became *Du Côté de chez Swann* and *A l'Ombre des Jeunes Filles en Fleurs*. *Swann* itself was to be enlarged in proof, notably in the episode of Swann's jealousy of Odette, but the additions were apparently of no great extent. *A l'Ombre*, however, amounted to less than half of its final length, the most surprising difference being the omission of all mentions of Albertine and the little band, who as yet did not appear until the

---

[1] *Chroniques*, 114-22. The passages which Proust interwove to form his article occur in their final revised and enriched form as follows: I, 63, 48, 62-3, 59-61, 63-4, 715 (here Proust quite unsuitably transfers to Saint-Hilaire his description of the ivy-covered church of Carqueville, which the Narrator sees near Balbec during a drive in Mme de Villeparisis's carriage), 64-7.

second half of the novel. This still existed only in the original rough manuscript, which Proust vaguely hoped to revise while the first volume was being printed, and to publish either simultaneously, or at latest in the next autumn. But this disaster, which would have left his novel immeasurably poorer in content, structure and texture, was to be averted by destiny, and by Proust's own steering of destiny.

At first he could only wait in growing distress. Calmette, who had promised to forward the typescript to his friend Fasquelle, and declared that Fasquelle would be only too glad to publish it intact as a personal favour to himself, —"absolutely, my dear fellow!"—had shown no sign of life since their meeting in August. Towards the middle of October Proust began to enlist the help of all possible friends. He asked Mme Straus to remind Calmette of his promise. The enigmatic editor told her he had spoken to Fasquelle, to whom Proust had only to deliver the typescript; but to Proust himself he remained strangely silent. Proust duly obeyed, and called at the *Figaro* office to thank Calmette. "Tell him I'm not in," said the editor, and left his grateful letters unanswered. Proust turned next to Lauris, Reynaldo, and Antoine Bibesco, who warned him that Fasquelle would refuse to publish the two separate volumes of the work simultaneously, that he would insist on omissions, that his favourite maxim was: "I can't have anything interfering with the *action*!" Could it be that Calmette was lying low out of embarrassment, because he had promised more than he could fulfil? Proust had set his heart upon Fasquelle, who was the publisher of Flaubert, Zola, and Rostand, and a specialist in the high-class bestsellers of whom Proust himself, for no ignoble motive, longed to be one. 'Wide publicity is a precious thing,' he had remarked pathetically to Vaudoyer last April, 'because it's only in the audience which it provides that chance can bring our words to the fraternal, forever unknown heart which will feel them as we have felt.' And to Mme Straus he confided his hope that Fasquelle would bring him 'a wider public, the sort of people who buy a badly printed volume before catching a train'. But now, as his hopes of Fasquelle waned, he decided to find a second string.

In February 1911 Antoine Bibesco had persuaded him to subscribe to the *Nouvelle Revue Française*, the brilliant literary magazine founded by Gide and Jacques Copeau in 1909, in which Gide's *Isabelle* was then appearing. 'Gide's story isn't bad,' he grumbled to Lauris, 'but it doesn't exactly bowl one over!' He was piously shocked to hear from Antoine in July 1912—a little late in the day—that Gide and his friend Henri Ghéon were practising homosexuals: 'which makes Ghéon's hypocrisy in his article on *Le Martyre de Saint-Sébastien* all the more revolting,' he told Reynaldo.[1] At Cabourg he complained to Vaudoyer of attacks in the NRF for September 1912 on Maeterlinck, and (again by Ghéon) on Cocteau as a mere 'boulevard' writer. Yet his failure to find a good word for the sour grapes of the NRF did not prevent him from deeply admiring other writers in that brilliant group, such as Jammes, Valéry Larbaud and Claudel. The NRF had recently launched their own publishing house, under the editorial direction of Gide, Copeau and Jean Schlumberger and the business management of Gaston Gallimard. Now, late in October, Antoine Bibesco offered to recommend his novel to Copeau, and Proust immediately felt that here, among the moderns of a new generation rather than with the best-selling Fasquelle, might be his spiritual home.

While still in doubt he wrote to Louis de Robert, his friend in the heroic days of the Dreyfus Affair. In the spring of 1911 Proust had renewed contact, feeling that they again had much in common; for Robert was now an invalid, and had written a talented novel about his own life, *Le Roman du Malade*, which had been successfully published by Fasquelle after its appearance as a *Figaro* serial. 'I've written a long book which I call a novel because it hasn't the casual element of memoirs,' he confided, pointing out that Robert, too, had produced 'a book that isn't a novel'. Did Robert think it might be wiser to renounce Fasquelle, and that 'a purely literary publisher such as the *Nouvelle Revue Française* might be more likely to persuade readers to accept a work which is completely different from the classical novel?' Robert thought the NRF's public would be too limited, but wrote a glowing letter of recommendation to Fasquelle.

Nevertheless, Proust allowed Antoine to make him an appointment with Copeau, to whom he explained his complex difficulties, and offered to submit the unrevised typescript (for the other was still with Fasquelle) to the NRF. Copeau advised him to apply direct to Gallimard, to whom Proust wrote accordingly on 2 November, recalling their friendship with the dead Robert Gangnat, and their meeting in Gangnat's villa at Bénerville in August 1908. He revealed frankly that his novel was already with Fasquelle, and offered, if the NRF would accept it, to pay the expenses of publication. Moreover,

[1] In his article on D'Annunzio's play (NRF for July 1911) Ghéon had perfidiously drawn attention to its epicene implications.

he confessed, his novel was 'extremely indecent'; indeed, part of the second volume would be a study of homosexuality. The old gentleman named M. de Fleurus or de Guray in the unrevised typescript—'I've changed the names several times'—who appeared at Combray as the supposed lover of Mme Swann, and was met by the hero at the seaside towards the end of the first volume, would turn out to be a pederast! 'I think the character is rather an original one,' Proust added consolingly, 'he's the virile pederast, in love with virility, loathing effeminate young men, in fact loathing all young men, just as a man who has suffered through women becomes a misogynist.' 'The metaphysical and moral viewpoint', it was true, 'is predominant all through the book'; but 'all the same, the old gentleman seduces a male concierge and keeps a pianist'.[1] Gallimard replied that if their opinion of the book was favourable, and Proust could obtain his release from Fasquelle, the NRF would be able to publish the first volume in two months' time, about 15 February. He offered to call for the typescript. 'You don't know how heavy it is,' replied Proust, and promised to send it; but Gallimard, on second thoughts, referred him back to Copeau.

Again Proust felt the need of the intervention of friends. He handed over his typescript to Antoine Bibesco, together with a manifesto in which he called his novel, apparently for the first time, *A la Recherche du Temps Perdu*.[2] He explained his work ('I hope you can make them understand my explanation,' he added) in terms paraphrased from *Le Temps Retrouvé*: it would employ not only plane psychology, but also psychology in space and time[3]; voluntary memory, being a function of the intellect and the sense of sight, can give us only the untruthful surface of the Past, whereas a scent or a taste involuntarily regained revive in us its extratemporal essence[4]; his book is a sequence of novels of the unconscious, and the artist should seek the primary material of his work in involuntary memories only; style is a question not of technique, but of vision.[5] Armed with all this Antoine and Emmanuel gave a dinner in mid-November to Copeau, Gide and Jean Schlumberger, the reading committee of the NRF, and left the type-

[1] In this unrevised version Proust had not given M. de Charlus his final name; Morel, who was then called Bobby Santois, was not yet a violinist but (like his chief original, Léon Delafosse) a pianist; and Jupien, called Julliot or Joliot, was still a concierge.

[2] However, it seems possible that Proust had already chosen his title in November 1909, when he asked Lauris 'not to reveal the subject or the title'.

[3] III, 1031.   [4] I, 44; III, 872.   [5] III, 895.

script with Gide. But by this second attempt to find a publisher Proust only doubled the anguish of waiting.

Du Côté de chez Swann ends with a passage, unique in Proust's novel, in which the Narrator emerges for a moment from the gulf of Time to observe the present in which he writes. 'On one of the first mornings of this November' he visits the Bois de Boulogne on his way to Trianon, hoping to see elegant ladies in their carriages, as in the year when he loved Gilberte and walked there with Mme Swann. To his horror, the carriages have turned to motor-cars 'driven by moustached mechanics'; the ladies are wearing—in the fashion of 1912— Greco-Saxon tunics and enormous hats 'covered with aviaries and vegetable-gardens'; and the gentlemen, worse still, instead of their former grey toppers wear no hats at all. It is twenty years too late. The sun goes in, he sees in the Avenue des Acacias the wandering spectres, grown old and terrible, of the ladies he had known, and the Bois has become a place of desolation and despair. Traces of Proust's intention to make this journey are visible in his letters of October 1912 to Mme Straus: he feels nostalgia for autumn, he says, and despite insomnia and fever would like to take her to tea at the Trianon Palace Hôtel at Versailles. But the motives of his expedition included not only his longing for autumn leaves and for tea with Mme Straus, but his decision to end the Gilberte episode in his novel with a comparison between the Bois of 1888, when he lay in wait there for Léonie Clomesnil, and the Bois of 1912. His journey may have taken place in Odilon Albaret's taxi a day or two after 10 November, when he told Mme Straus: 'the last dead leaves have fallen before I could see them ... if I'd been well I'd have gone to the Trianon Palace, where I sent Albaret to reconnoitre; for it's a good thing to publish one's impressions of the past, but to experience new ones is better still.'[1]

In these long weeks of waiting Proust called frequently on Mme Straus for tea and sympathy. More than once he had to complain of the unkindness of her husband. "There's one good thing about old So-and-So," remarked M. Straus pointedly, when he found 'dear Marcel'

---

[1] Similarly, the Narrator speaks (I, 422) of 'the spectacle of autumn, which ends so swiftly, before we can see it, and brings a nostalgia for dead leaves that turns to a fever and prevents us from sleeping'; and on his way back he is only prevented from calling on Odette by the realisation that she and the style of her drawing-room would have changed like everything else. As will be seen later, Proust intended this new episode as a finale to *'Chez Madame Swann'*, the first chapter of what is now *A l'Ombre*, and did not transfer it to its present position at the end of *Swann* until September 1913.

lolling exhausted in his drawing-room, "he always has the decency to stand up when I come in!" On 17 December she invited Proust with Calmette, Hervieu and her son Jacques Bizet to her box for the first night of *Kismet* (by Edward Knoblauch, translated by Jules Lemaître) at the Théâtre Sarah Bernhardt. Proust escorted her backstage to congratulate the star, Lucien Guitry, and while they talked hid modestly by an aged gentleman, 'trembling and sweetfaced', he thought, 'like an old man in the *Oresteia*'. He recognised Lemaître himself, transformed by old age and the illness of which he was to die twenty months later; but he was still more astonished when, behind the beard and invalid features superimposed upon the Marcel whom he had met as a schoolboy twenty-four years before, Lemaître recognised *him*. Meanwhile the irascible Jacques Bizet had smacked the face of Comte Hubert de Pierredon, with whom, despite the efforts of Calmette and Hervieu to smoothe things over, he fought a duel on the 20th. Proust felt he would have made a better peacemaker, and told Mme Straus how once, in the good old days, he had prevented a duel between Guiche and Albufera. When he returned home, as the final calamity of this imperfect evening, Nicolas pointed out that he was wearing a mere dinner-jacket over his white waistcoat.

At last, about 23 December, the NRF replied by rejecting both his novel and an extract which he had offered Copeau for their magazine. 'I read it with sustained interest,' wrote Copeau of the latter; but the novel, as Proust learned later, had scarcely been read at all. It was only to oblige the Bibesco brothers that the NRF had consented to the enormous breach of etiquette of considering a book which was already with another publisher. They knew Proust only as 'a snob, a literary amateur, the worst possible thing for our magazine', said Gide, who had met him in the alien world of the salons twenty years before. He wrote for *Le Figaro*, dedicated his book to Calmette, involved himself with the best-selling Fasquelle, and condemned his own work by offering to pay for its publication. Gide, idly opening the first volume of the typescript, found himself with extreme distaste among the pepsin and Vichy water bottles of Aunt Léonie's bedroom, was shocked by what he wrongly considered a solecism about 'the vertebrae in her forehead',[1] and read no further; while Schlumberger pointed out that this novel of 1400 pages would overstrain the

---

[1] I, 52. Proust, by a superb and entirely justified use of the trope known as metonymy, called the frontal bones in Aunt Léonie's forehead 'vertebrae' in order to suggest that they looked like vertebrae.

resources of their newly born publishing house. The book was clearly impossible. When the typescript was returned Proust convinced himself, quite mistakenly, that the parcel had never even been opened, and Albaret's fiancée Céleste Gineste, who had helped in its despatch, declared that the string was still tied with her own special knots.

While he still had hopes of the NRF, Proust had not dared to press Fasquelle too hard: 'I've tried to chloroform the situation,' he told Gallimard. But he was delighted to hear through Cocteau, early in November, that Edmond Rostand had only refrained from sending a telegram of congratulation on his *Figaro* article of 3 September because he assumed, knowing of Proust's friendship for his enemy Montesquiou,[1] that his compliments would be unwelcome. Rostand offered to write to Fasquelle, and his son Maurice actually did so. Calmette, overwhelmed to hear in Mme Straus's box at *Kismet* that Proust had tried to see Fasquelle in the daytime, and in vain, did his best to arrange an appointment in the evening; but the publisher did not reply. 'It was so easy to write my novel,' Proust told Louis de Robert with pathos, 'but how difficult it will be to publish it!'

Only a few days after his rejection by the NRF, about 28 December, Proust received his first direct communication from Fasquelle. The letter was courteous, sensible and firm: he 'could not undertake to publish a work of such length, and so different from what the public is accustomed to read'. Proust, with typical fairmindedness, was touched to see that Fasquelle had read his book with care and taken him seriously: 'I think he's wrong,' he told Louis de Robert magnanimously, 'but there's such a thing as being intelligently wrong.' However, three months of anxiety and intrigue had gone for nothing, and all was to begin again.[2]

Robert had already suggested his friend Humblot, the director of Ollendorff's and the publisher of Proust's friends Barrès, Régnier and Hermant, as a possible alternative to Fasquelle. Early in January he informed Humblot that Proust was a great writer, to publish whom would be one of the greatest honours of his career. A few days later Proust sent Humblot the typescript returned by Fasquelle, refraining,

---

[1] Montesquiou had revenged himself for the portrayal of his august person as the Peacock in *Chantecler* by writing an essay called '*Le Météore*'—'*The Shooting Star*'—on Rostand's rise to fame and the failure of this last play.

[2] On the other hand Fasquelle spoke so enthusiastically to Reynaldo of Proust's *Figaro* articles, which he had rejected in 1909, that Proust thought of offering them to him again, but did not do so.

on Robert's advice but against his own judgement, from mentioning its rejection by Fasquelle or his readiness to pay the costs of publication.

On the night of 14 January Proust called on Calmette at the *Figaro* office with a black moiré cigarette case from Tiffany's, with Calmette's monogram in brilliants, as a thank-offering for his incomplete and unsuccessful kindness. He dropped the dainty parcel in the editor's in-tray, shyly murmuring: "It's such a small thing, I hardly dare ..." Calmette gave an affectionate shrug of the shoulders; without mentioning gifts, novels, gratitude or Fasquelle, without seeming to notice the package, he spoke only of the imminent election for the Presidency of the Republic—"I hope Poincaré will get in," he remarked in his warm, modulated voice, "but then again, perhaps it will be Deschanel"—and ushered Proust to the door.

To another of his benefactors Proust was less forthcoming. Maurice Rostand, fired by Cocteau's enthusiasm, asked to be allowed to meet him, but was offered only a rendezvous in front of Notre-Dame at six o'clock in the morning, which he declined. This extraordinary proposal answered, however, to a real desire. On 17 January Proust had told Mme Straus of his longing to see the St Anne portal of Notre-Dame, 'where a human spectacle more charming than the one to which we are accustomed nowadays has been on view for the last eight centuries'. The St Anne portal, furthest to the right of the three which form the front entrance to the cathedral, contains scenes from the life of the Virgin which Proust no doubt needed for Elstir's explanation of the porch at Balbec in *A l'Ombre*. He made the excursion towards the 20th, wearing his fur coat over his night-shirt. The Last Judgement over the adjacent centre portal also caught his eye; and this lonely man, mistrustful of love, was deeply moved to see the carving of a married couple, in fear of being parted for all eternity, facing Christ the Judge with hand clasped in hand.[1]

Towards 10 February Louis de Robert received Humblot's answer. 'My dear fellow,' wrote this candid publisher, 'I may perhaps be dead from the neck up, but rack my brains as I may I can't see why a chap should need thirty pages to describe how he turns over in bed before going to sleep.' 'Fortune has knocked at your door and passed you by,' Robert grimly retorted, and insisted on Humblot's writing 'a more decent letter, fit for me to show my friend'. But Proust guessed the truth, and compelled Robert to show him the original which, much

[1] I, 840-1.

hurt, he rightly declared to be 'stupid and vulgar'. He now knew that he must give up all hope of finding a publisher who would take his novel for its own sake.

Proust indomitably began negotiations for the fourth time. His imprisonment in the ivory tower of his cork-lined bedroom prevented him from interviewing publishers; he felt, too, a sacred dread of even writing directly to beg these indifferent strangers to fulfil the deepest desire of his life. He looked for a new mediator, and found René Blum, whom he had known in the golden days of 1902 with Fénelon, Guiche, Lauris and the Bibesco brothers at the Café Weber. René, with his ironically affectionate smile, was known as 'the Blumet' in distinction from his more famous elder brother Léon, Proust's companion of *Le Banquet*. He was now the editorial secretary of the newspaper *Gil Blas*, for which he had just asked through Antoine Bibesco for an extract from Proust's novel, and was an intimate friend of the intelligent and energetic young publisher Bernard Grasset, who had produced Lauris's *Ginette Chatenay* in 1910. About 20 February Proust wrote to Blum asking him to propose to Grasset the publication of his novel at author's expense, the publisher to take a percentage of the published price, and the author to pay for publicity. A few days of gentlemanly bargaining followed: Grasset proposed to allow Proust half the published price, but Proust would take only three-sevenths; Grasset offered special royalties for de luxe copies, which Proust waived altogether; Grasset was willing to resign the translation rights of 500 francs for each translation, but Proust accepted only half. Finally it was agreed that the first edition should consist of 1200[1] copies at the published price of 3.50 francs, on which Proust was to receive a royalty of 1.50 francs per copy. On 11 March the contract was signed. The words 'author's expense', which had so deeply shocked the NRF, had acted on Grasset like a magic spell.[2] He

---

[1] This was later increased to 1750 copies.

[2] In justice to Grasset it must be recognised that Proust, although he thought he had been generous to his publisher and intended to be so, had in fact driven a hard bargain. Grasset at first proposed to sell this long volume of over 700 pages at 10 fr., allowing Proust 4 fr., and his profits were greatly curtailed by Proust's insistence (in the hope of wider circulation) on the low price of 3.50 fr. Again, Proust thought he was allowing Grasset 2 fr. per copy; but as the whole-sale price was only 2.10 fr. Grasset's real profit was a mere 60 centimes, and his gain on the whole edition would be the derisory sum of 720 fr. Grasset gained nothing from Proust's concession over the translation rights, as no translation was made until after the novel had passed to another publisher.

confessed later that he had published *Du Côté de chez Swann* without reading it.

Meanwhile Proust was treading a still more dolorous way than the road to publication, and carrying a heavier burden than his novel. During the eighteen months from January 1913 to June 1914 he suffered an agony at sunrise, and made captive in his apartment a male Albertine who fled from him and died.

For many years he had become immune to the exaltation and anguish of passionate love. The period when he was always in love had coincided with the years when he was always in society, and ended with the shock of the Dreyfus Case, the close of youth, the revelation of Ruskin, and the turn of the century. To Clément de Maugny in July 1899 he had written prophetically of 'storms that will never come again'; and he had last used such words as *chagrin, tristesse, peine*—which for him were synonyms of love—for his platonic relationships with Fénelon and Antoine Bibesco in 1902. Since then his needs for affection and physical pleasure had been satisfied—whether with women such as Louisa and the young girl of Cabourg, or with his young men of the working classes—without strong feeling or apparent suffering. During those years the deepest layers of his nature had been occupied first by grief for his mother, afterwards by the creation of his novel. But now the ghost of Mme Proust was temporarily laid, and his novel seemed complete. Without knowing it he was again, and for the last time, vulnerable to love.

One day in January 1913 Alfred Agostinelli, whom Proust had not seen since his return from Versailles in October 1908, called at 102 Boulevard Haussmann. "I've lost my job, Monsieur Proust," he announced, "and I've come to ask you to take me as your chauffeur." Proust objected that this would be unfair to Albaret, and then, struck by a fatal inspiration, suggested that the young man might care to become his secretary, and type the manuscript of the second half of his novel. Agostinelli mentioned that he now had a wife, the very Anna of whom Proust had heard five years before, as a mistress whom he hoped to marry; then, said Proust, she must come too. Anna turned out to be ugly and tiresome—"I can't think what he saw in her," Proust declared afterwards; but he was touched by her devotion to Alfred, and Alfred's to her. He allowed them a great deal of money, out of kindness, and then more still, in the hope of winning their affection, and because they spent it so fast. If he one day gave them fifty francs, he said, they would squander twenty on peaches, twenty on taxis, and next morning they would be penniless. Nor were their outlays always on this modest scale: "if I told you the way they lived, you *wouldn't believe me*," he lamented later to Émile Straus. Anna was madly jealous, and Agostinelli was assiduously unfaithful to her—"fortunately she never found out, or she'd have killed him," said Proust; and yet, "in all my life I've never seen a couple so tenderly united, so truly living each for the other". Anna did not conceal her dislike for Proust, who could not help returning it. Within a few weeks the situation had become impossible, unbearable and inescapable. About 12 February he wrote mysteriously to Mme de Noailles of 'sorrows (*chagrins*) which now discourage me'; and these cries of unexplained distress to his friends were to continue until the final tragedy.

Real life was less well constructed than his novel, and Proust began to experience *La Prisonnière* before he reached his agony at sunrise. The approach of spring, no less than the desire to escape from his captivity, made him long like the Narrator for Italy. He proposed to Mme de Noailles that they should go to Florence together, and suggested a meeting in Rome to Robert de Billy, who was now first secretary in the embassy there. When René Blum left on 25 February for a stay in Dr Widmer's sanatorium at Valmont, he thought of joining him, 'to change my hours', in order to go on and see Florence by daylight. Instead, with the inducement of keeping an eye on Agostinelli, he 'changed his hours' at home, and stayed awake during the day, but found this did not enable him to sleep at night. 'I think all the torments I suffer now might be a little less cruel,' he told Mme Straus early in March, 'if I told them to you. And they are of a kind which is sufficiently general and human to interest you, perhaps.'

The preoccupations of this spring were reflected in '*Vacances de Pâques*', the fourth and last extract from his novel in *Le Figaro*, which appeared on 25 March. He chose the passages from *Du Côté de chez Swann* and *Le Côté de Guermantes* in which the Narrator as a child longs for Florence, and remembers his longing several years later, when he is in love with the Duchesse de Guermantes. He introduced these with a prelude on the vernal sounds of tramcars and street-cries, which he now heard from his bed in the morning as he listened for the voice of Agostinelli; and he here used images first sketched in *Contre Sainte-Beuve* in the spring of 1909, and later splendidly elaborated in *La Prisonnière*.[1] He had not given up hope of publishing extracts in

[1] *Chroniques*, 106-13. Cf. I, 387-92; II, 143, 148; III, 9, 12, 116, 168, 409-10; *Contre Sainte-Beuve*, 74, 76, 79.

the *Nouvelle Revue Française,* although its editors had despised and rejected his novel; and it was to their address, although his admiration was sincere, that he inserted laudatory allusions to Claudel, Jammes, Ghéon and Larbaud in the same article.

Immediately after signing his contract with Grasset on 11 March Proust had paid a first instalment of 1750 francs for printing costs, promising another on receipt of the first complete author's copy. Once again the golden spell worked swiftly. The first galley-proofs arrived early in April, and by the 13th he was receiving daily batches, the margins of which he blackened with corrections and additions, glueing ever more insertions to top, bottom and sides. 'I've written a whole new book on the proofs,' he told Louis de Robert. His compunction lest he should ruin Grasset with this extra expense was relieved by the arrival early in May of the first forty-five revise galleys, together with a bill of 595 francs for excess corrections.

The last of the first galleys arrived at the same time, and necessitated a momentous decision. There were 95 in all, each of 8 pages, reaching to near the end of the first visit to Balbec and making a total, allowing for about five remaining galleys still to come, of approximately 800 pages instead of the 650 or 700 which he had estimated. Grasset objected, for technical and commercial reasons, since a volume of such inordinate size would be physically impossible and would reduce his profits on the whole work; and Louis de Robert thoroughly alarmed Proust by arguing that the public would refuse to read him unless he drastically shortened its length. He pleaded to be allowed to publish it unmutilated, in two parts cased in a cardboard box; but Grasset refused. He thought of omitting the Balbec chapter and stopping at the end of '*Chez Mme Swann*', making a total which he variously estimated as 660 or 680 pages, but which in fact would have been about 650. Even this sacrifice was not enough: a little over 500 pages was declared to be the maximum. This would comprise about a third of the novel, and he reverted accordingly to the alternative plan, which he had mentioned to Gallimard in the previous November, of dividing *A la Recherche* into three volumes. Page 500 fell towards the end of the first stage of the Narrator's love for Gilberte, when he plays with her in the Champs-Élysées in the snow, and the fateful 1st of January approaches, just before M. de Norpois 'came to dinner for the first time'. In search of an effective ending he transferred the magnificent episode of the sunlight on the balcony to this point; but when the proofs embodying this correction arrived, early in September, he found a still better plan. Reinstating 'the sunlight on the balcony' to its former position, just after the Narrator's first meeting with Gilberte in the Champs-Élysées, he ended the volume with the description of his visit to the Bois de Boulogne in November 1912, which had hitherto formed the end of '*Chez Mme Swann*'. *Du Côté de chez Swann* had thus reached its final form.

The publication of what afterwards became *A l'Ombre des Jeunes Filles en Fleurs* was thus delayed, not as it then seemed for twelve months, but in fact for nearly six years. But the disappointment which to Proust appeared at the time disastrous was to reveal itself as providential. The future *A l'Ombre*, like its successors, was as yet imperfect in content, style, structure and scale. It still lacked many of the finest and most indispensable episodes, such as the Narrator's 'irregular progress of oblivion' of Gilberte, or the appearance of Albertine and the little band, which was then intended for the summer after Mme de Villeparisis's matinée, during the second of three visits to Balbec. Its insufficient length, for it was afterwards more than doubled in size, would have left the remainder of *A la Recherche* top-heavy. The further experience of love and anguish, which would give Proust essential maturity and material, was still to come. The premature publication of *A l'Ombre* in 1913, still more that of *A l'Ombre* with the equally deficient *Le Côté de Guermantes* in 1914, which was to be averted by the outbreak of war, would have left the greatness of *A la Recherche du Temps Perdu* as we now know it irremediably compromised.

Meanwhile, amid the distractions of publication and unhappy love, Proust had forgotten last summer's promise of fur wraps to the d'Alton girls. During April and May he negotiated under Mme Straus's guidance with the furrier Corby, deciding at last, as one wanted a white fur and the other a dark, on white fox and grey: 'I don't like the sound of "mock ermine",' he told her, 'it savours of betrayal.' The first and second Balkan wars had been raging, with unprecedented and ill-omened slaughter, since the autumn of 1912. Once again he speculated on a falling market in the expectation of a rise which never came, paying his losses at the end of each month. He had staked several hundred thousand francs; and his 'liquidation' payment at the end of April was particularly heavy, since at that very moment the Austrian ultimatum to Montenegro for the evacuation of Scutari had roused fears of a European conflict. 'I'm a lovesick but ruined speculator,' he wrote to Mme Straus, in words which suggest that he had by

now carried out his hint, made early in March, of confiding in her the
reasons for his misery.

At this time he learned that Louis de Robert, like himself, was ill,
isolated and unhappily in love, though with a woman. Remembering
the great days when he had reconciled Louisa to Albufera, he offered
to help: 'I have made peace between friends, lovers, even married
couples,' he boasted, 'I have given prestige in the eyes of a coquette to
the wretched lover she disdained.' He volunteered to visit the lady, as
he had proposed to tackle Louisa at Vichy in 1904. 'When our squandered kindness fails, we must do the opposite, and cease to be kind,' he
recommended, and promised to make her 'long to love you, and fear
that it may be already too late.' But Robert declined this recipe of
doubtful efficacy.

Maurice Rostand had continued in vain to send enthusiastic letters.
At last, one evening in May, Proust invited the young man with Marie
Scheikévitch to midnight supper at Larue's after the Russian Ballet.
Mme Scheikévitch wore a bouquet of red roses on her bosom, as if
still stained with blood from her attempted suicide; and Proust, moved
by this tragic image, remembered the crimson-breasted doves seen
with Reynaldo and Pierre Lavallée in the Jardin des Plantes, eighteen
years before, and thought of calling his second volume 'Les Colombes
poignardées'. He ordered enormous strawberries, the most ruinously
expensive champagne, and borrowed from the head waiter, who
thanked him profusely, several hundred-franc notes of which he gave
one as a tip. They deposited Mme Scheikévitch half-asleep at her front
door, and went on to 102 Boulevard Haussmann where, in the antiquated lift, Proust suddenly became aware that his guest wore
perfume, and buried his face in a huge pocket handkerchief. Maurice
waited in the smaller of the two drawing-rooms, among the dust-
covers covered with dust, watched steadily by the portrait of a young
man in immaculate evening dress, faintly moustached and faintly
smiling, with luminous eyes. It was Blanche's painting of his host in
1892; and Maurice, trying to connect it with the spectral marionette in
the next room, whose dinner-clothes seemed, he thought, to have
been crumpled on purpose by a mad valet, noticed that the eyes were
the same. He entered the cork-lined bedroom, where he found his host
lying on the bed, amid drugs, invitations, prescriptions, neckties and
pyramids of books. Proust began to read aloud from sheets of proof:
"For a long time," he said, "I used to go to bed early . . ."

Proust's visit to Cabourg this year was late and brief. He lingered in Paris until August, immobilised by misery and illness. Partly because the subject was too painful, partly because his present life was bringing him new material for it, he felt unable to revise the proofs for the second half of his chapter about Swann in love with Odette, for which Grasset was beginning to press him. Poor Ulrich turned up one afternoon, out of work and starving. Proust telephoned Jacques Bizet's wife, asked her to find him a post as chauffeur, and declared: "I shan't be leaving Paris this year"; but an hour later he suddenly made his decision and fled to Cabourg with Agostinelli by motor-car, leaving Nicolas and Anna to follow next day. On the journey Agostinelli missed the way, and they arrived at the Grand Hôtel at five o'clock in the morning, in the first light of dawn.

For a few days Proust felt at home, and dutifully read his proofs. Then he spoke mysteriously of making a flying visit to Paris and returning; but he postponed this plan from day to day, and announced to Nicolas one Monday afternoon, as he set off with Agostinelli to Houlgate, that he had decided not to leave Cabourg before the end of the week. But when they reached Houlgate, according to Proust's account to Lauris a week later, Agostinelli said: "I can't bear to see you looking so sad. You'd better take the plunge, and catch the Paris train at Trouville without going back to the hotel!" Proust sent a message to Nicolas ordering him to pack and return immediately; Agostinelli added a note to Anna asking her to go with Nicolas: and the eloping couple fled to Paris.

The real situation behind this enigmatic crisis can only be guessed. Perhaps Proust's retreat to Paris with Agostinelli, like the Narrator's with Albertine, marks the point at which the lover first decided to make the beloved a prisoner in his home. It may also be that Proust's sufferings were hitherto caused only by his efforts to resist or conceal his own love, and to gain Agostinelli's; and the young man's behaviour at Cabourg, like Albertine's at Balbec, brought on the first pangs of jealousy and the need to remove him from temptation. But these possibilities do not explain why Proust should wish to visit Paris only for a few days, still less why he should arrange for Nicolas and Anna to follow only a few hours behind them. It is as though he were drawn to Paris by some anxiety unconnected with Agostinelli, which he hoped to allay, without relinquishing his watch upon the young man, and then return to the pleasures of Cabourg.

In the dawn which follows Albertine's terrible revelation on the little train of her intimacy with Mlle Vinteuil's friend, the Narrator

accounts for his unhappiness and his desire to take her with him to
Paris by a characteristic fiction. "When I came to Balbec," he tells her,
"I left behind a woman I was going to marry, who was ready to
sacrifice everything for me. For the last week I've been asking myself
day after day whether I'd have the courage not to send her a telegram
to say I was coming back. I've had that courage, but it made me so
unhappy I thought I would kill myself."[1] In his letter to Lauris
Proust gave exactly the same version of the reasons for his return:
'When I went to Cabourg,' he wrote, 'I left behind me a woman whom
I see rarely in Paris, but at least I know she's there, and at Cabourg I
felt far away and anxious. So I decided to put in a few days in Paris.'
Strange as it seems, it is probable that the story which the Narrator
told Albertine as a lie was at least partly true when Proust told it to
Lauris in real life; for this woman existed, and Lauris himself was one
of the few friends in whom Proust had confided about her. 'Would it
not be a crime,' he had asked Lauris four years before, when he was
thinking of marrying the mysterious girl of Cabourg, 'to make a
charming young girl share my dreadful life?'; and these are almost the
very words of the Narrator when he tells Albertine: "I nearly married
her, but I hadn't the heart to make a young woman live with someone
so ill and troublesome."[2] It is likely that the words Proust used to
Lauris and in his novel were also spoken to Agostinelli at Cabourg.
He may have fled to Paris in the desperate hope of curing his new love
for Agostinelli by reviving his old love for the young girl, or of using
her as a stratagem to compel Agostinelli to submission. However this
may be, the crisis at Cabourg was the equivalent in Proust's life of the
Agony at Sunrise. It marked the point of no return in his life as in his
novel; and it was the moment at which the girl of Cabourg united with
Agostinelli to form Albertine.

[1] II, 1118.   [2] II, 1123.

Chapter 10

AGOSTINELLI VANISHES
(*September 1913 – July 1914*)

PROUST reached Paris luggageless, without so much as a night-shirt in which to take to his bed, and instantly resumed work on his proofs. Ominously, he now inserted 'small details of the utmost importance which tighten the knots of jealousy round poor Swann'. He had lost weight alarmingly in the past months of distress, and Dr Bize ordered him to regain it by resting. Meanwhile he shaved his beard, revealing for the remainder of his life the moustached and age-less face of the lost young man of whom he wrote.

Early in September he sent a spare set of proofs to Lucien Daudet, who thus became the first person after Louis de Robert to read the whole volume. Robert, with the best of intentions, had plagued him with stupid objections: the book was too long-winded, the title too boring, the scene between Mlle Vinteuil and her friend too improper; why not just publish the *Combray* chapter separately? But Lucien read *Swann* with rapture far into the night, and his verdict, to Proust's great relief, was not only enthusiastic, but showed genuine under-standing. Proust gratefully accepted Lucien's offer to review him. A week or two later he sent proofs to Cocteau; Jean, too, was dazzled and dazzling, and promised a review.

The final instalment of the third and last complete set of proofs arrived towards the end of September, the whole volume went to press early in October,[1] and *Du Côté de chez Swann* was published on Friday, 14 November 1913.

[1] The last sheet of the second set, in which the volume ended with 'the sunlight on the balcony', was printed on 1 September; and it was therefore a little after this date that Proust inserted, from the end of '*Chez Mme Swann*', the episode in the Bois de Boulogne which formed the new ending. Meanwhile he had already received, corrected and returned most of the earlier sheets of the second set, from which the third set was printed from 31 July onwards. The last surviving portion of this third set, p. 432 (36 pages before the end of *Un Amour de Swann*), was printed on 28 August. Allowing time for Proust to correct and return the last of the second set and for the rest of the third set to be printed

Proust succeeded in arranging notices in nearly all the important Paris newspapers. Most were written by friends, or commissioned by editors who happened to be his friends. Mme Scheikévitch persuaded Hébrard to send Élie Joseph Bois to interview him for *Le Temps*; and Bois's description of 'the bedroom where the shutters are nearly always closed', and the 'two admirable eyes, alive and feverish, darting their rays beneath a forehead curtained with shaggy hair', gave the Paris public their first glimpse of Proust's environment and appearance. But the supposed 'interview', as published in *Le Temps* of 12 November, was not what it seemed, for in fact Proust handed to Bois a copy of the very manifesto which he had given Antoine Bibesco exactly a year ago to show to Gide and Copeau. This was reproduced almost word for word, with the addition of an occasional 'So you see', or 'How shall I put it?', and a tribute to Calmette of which Hébrard cut all but the opening words. 'I owe it to M. Calmette,' Proust wrote with bitter nostalgia and exaggeration, 'that I ever knew the joy of a young man who sees his first article in print. And then again, through enabling me by way of my articles to return the visits of people whom I then found it hard to do without, he helped me to make the transition from life in society to life in solitude.'

Swann was dedicated 'to M. Gaston Calmette, as a token of profound and affectionate gratitude'; yet Proust felt deeply hurt by Calmette's year-long silence, his ill-kept promise to win Fasquelle, his disregard of the cigarette-case from Tiffany's, his reluctance to print more than the four extracts from *Swann*. On 12 November he wrote Calmette an aggrieved letter: he was heartbroken that *Le Temps* had cut his eulogy, and sad ('but less so') that no advance notice had appeared in *Le Figaro*; would Calmette arrange for one, preferably without using the adjectives 'subtle' or 'delicate'? Calmette, with his characteristic gentle smile, handed the missive to Robert Dreyfus and said: "I'm sure you'll be very pleased to give Marcel Proust a specially kind notice!" Dreyfus did so, on 16 November. In Calmette's own copy Proust wrote: 'I have often felt that you care little for my writings. But should you ever have time to read a few pages of my

---

therefrom, it seems probable that he received the latter towards the end of September, and that the volume went to press about the beginning of October. A few leaves exist of a fourth and fifth set of proofs, printed 13-27 October, but there is no evidence that these sets were ever complete. Owing to the delay caused by these late alterations the *achevé d'imprimer* of the published volume is 8 November—less than a week before publication.

novel, especially in the second part,[1] I think you would at last make my acquaintance.' Calmette did not reply—'silence with him does duty equally well for gratitude and for many other feelings,' Proust told Dreyfus—but he did not neglect *Swann*. At Lucien's instigation the Empress Eugénie sent him a letter through her secretary: 'it would be *personally agreeable* to Her Imperial Majesty if M. Daudet's article could be published without omissions and in a prominent position.' Calmette obeyed, on 27 November, and on 8 December appeared yet another review by Francis Chevassu, the editor of the *Figaro* Literary Supplement. Meanwhile René Blum printed an advance notice in *Gil Blas* on 9 November, and a long extract from the soirée at Mme de Saint-Euverte's on the 18th.

Lucien Daudet's article was one of the most intelligent Proust ever received in his lifetime, and called attention to vital features of his work which are still not universally appreciated by Proustian critics. 'It evokes the author's presence for those who know him,' he wrote, 'and is capable of reconstituting it for those who do not . . . it attains an extraordinary moral grandeur . . . Monsieur Proust's analysis is so perfectly incorporated with a prodigious sensibility that the two qualities become indistinguishable . . . in the distant future it will seem one of the most astonishing manifestations of intelligence in the twentieth century.' *A la Recherche*, he concluded with an image worthy of Proust himself, would take its place with the great classics of the past, 'because every masterpiece is the cry of a precursor, and rallies beyond time, in the black frost of eternity, its companions yet to come'.

Cocteau's article appeared on 23 November in *Excelsior*, the editor of which, Pierre Lafitte, was a Cabourg acquaintance of Proust's, and had invited him to choose his own reviewer. Like Lucien, Cocteau saw *Swann* as a new classic; he spoke of the 'cousinship of master-pieces', and wrote: '*Swann* is a gigantic miniature, full of mirages, superimpositions of gardens, plays on space and time, broad cool touches in the style of Manet.' Maurice Rostand in *Comœdia* on 26 December told a charming anecdote of 'my partner in a tango the other evening, who talked about Odette de Crécy and quoted, almost accurately, more than thirty lines of *Swann*', but marred all, with an excess of zeal which infuriated Proust, by comparing him to Pascal, Shelley, Leonardo da Vinci, Goethe, Plato, Dostoevsky and Shake-speare. Jacques Emile Blanche in the *Echo de Paris* of 15 April 1914,

[1] '*Un Amour de Swann.*'

called *Swann* 'the book of insomnia, of a mind working in silence and darkness, but overflowing with life, diverse and one'. Each of the four made it clear that he was a personal friend of Proust: 'I think,' wrote Maurice Rostand, 'that if I had not the great pride and honour of being a friend of the author, I should be unable to rest till I had met him.' The public may have suspected, wrongly, that these reviewers admired this unknown novelist because they were his friends, whereas in fact they were his friends because they admired him.

The loyal Albufera, 'who never reads anything', made his inevitable *gaffe* in the manner of the Duc de Guermantes.[1] "My dear Louis, have you read my book?" enquired Marcel on the telephone. "Read your book? Have you written a *book*?" "Yes, of course, Louis, and I even sent you a copy." "Ah, my dear old Marcel, if you sent it me, I've certainly read it. I was just not quite sure whether it ever reached me!"

Paul Souday, whom Proust had seen in 1900 despised and glowering in the Café Weber, was now the official critic of *Le Temps*, and had been asked by Hébrard, again at Mme Scheikévitch's instigation, 'to give special attention to Marcel Proust's novel'. *Du Côté de chez Swann*, Souday declared on 10 December, was 'not positively boring, though a bit banal'; it 'swarmed with grammatical errors'; the chapter on Swann in love was nothing but 'an enormous digression', and Swann's passion for a cocotte showed 'a naïveté improbable in a Parisian of such extensive experience'. However, he admitted, 'Marcel Proust undoubtedly has a great deal of talent, though for that precise reason it will be deplored that he has spoiled such fine gifts by so many faults'; the novel contained 'precious elements with which he might have made an exquisite slim volume'; and Souday awaited the sequel 'with sympathy, and the hope that it will have a little more order, brevity, and a more chastened prose style'. Grasset telephoned Proust in such agitation that Nicolas exclaimed: "I thought war must have broken out!"; and Proust sent Souday a cutting letter in defence of his grammar. But by deigning to notice *Swann* at all this favourite critic of the philistine middle classes probably brought Proust more readers than any other reviewer; and Souday himself remained under the lifelong impression that he had 'discovered' Proust.

Swann was selling satisfactorily, and early in December Grasset decided to print a second edition, for which he offered to pay the expenses and give Proust a royalty of ten per cent. Grasset was alive to the publicity-value of literary prizes. 'I hear he fought a duel,' Proust

[1] II, 524; III, 583.

told Lucien, 'because the Academy gave a prize to Romain Rolland instead of to one of his authors'; and in his first negotiations with René Blum in February 1913 Proust had offered 'to put in for the Goncourt Prize or some other, if it would please Grasset', though not for the *Vie Heureuse* (which had an all-lady jury), 'because of the extreme licence and indecency of certain passages'. Grasset now asked him to apply for both. As it happened, Proust was too late for the *Vie Heureuse*, for the list was already closed, although he found he would have been ardently supported by Mme de Pierrebourg, Lauris's mother-in-law, who belonged to the committee. Louis de Robert recommended him to two members of the Goncourt Academy, Zola's disciple Paul Margueritte, and Rosny *aîné*, whom Proust had met at Cabourg in 1910, and suggested that he should send his book to Colette. But Proust, much as he admired her, had not seen Colette since Mme Arman's great quarrel with her in 1896 (which had led, because he tried to reconcile each party to the other, to his falling in disgrace with both), and felt it would be unethical to make up their difference with so ulterior a motive. Time was too short for further canvassing, and the Goncourt Prize was awarded on 3 December to a nonentity, as usual, although yet another novel of genius, Alain-Fournier's *Le Grand Meaulnes*, was among the official candidates. Rosny obligingly put in a minority vote of one for Proust, who was well pleased. 'Perhaps when they see my book was discussed by the jury,' he wrote hopefully to Robert, 'some people will think of reading it, and who knows whether among these there may not be some friend of my thoughts who otherwise would never have known them?'

Having longed for the NRF as for a promised land, and seen himself sternly barred at the threshold ('I felt I 'had come unto mine own, but mine own received me not',' he had told Copeau in the words of John i, 11), Proust was doubly hurt by Ghéon's review in the *Nouvelle Revue Française* of 1 January 1914. *Swann*, wrote Ghéon, contained 'poetry of the highest beauty, psychology of the newest, irony of the most original, a picture of "society" that no one had ever drawn before'; but it was 'a work of idle leisure, without organisation, form or selection, in short, the very opposite of a work of art'. He believed, or pretended to believe, that *Temps Perdu* meant only wasted time, not the Past. Proust angrily corrected him, and was dissatisfied with Ghéon's lame excuse, that he liked *Swann* so much that he had felt afraid to let himself go! But behind the scenes of the NRF the tide was turning. Reading between the lines of Ghéon's review, Gide began to mistrust his hasty judgement of twelve months before. Cocteau, too, told him that he had made a serious mistake, and must read *Swann* again, or rather, for the first time. During the first fortnight of January Gide and his colleagues did so, and the scales fell from their eyes.

'My dear Proust,' wrote Gide, with seductive but sincere repentance, about 13 January, 'for several days I have never left your book; I am supersaturating myself in it with rapture, revelling in it. The refusal of this book will always be the gravest mistake the NRF ever made—and (for I have the shame of being largely responsible for it) one of the most stinging regrets, nay, remorses, of my whole life.' Two months later[1] the editorial committee of the NRF sat in full sanhedrin and offered, 'with unanimity and enthusiasm', said Gide, to publish the remaining two volumes of *A la Recherche* and buy back the rights in the first volume from Grasset. The heartfelt apology, the entreaty for forgiveness, the full reparation which the injured dream of but rarely receive, had come beyond all hope to Proust.

He replied with dignified joy and gratitude, but asked for time to consider, and declared that he would not accept the offer if he found that it would hurt Grasset. He sent his contract to Émile Straus, who specialised in the legal problems of authors: could he break it without being liable to prosecution? Knowing that the Princesse de Polignac was a friend of Grasset, he asked Reynaldo, who was to see her on 3 April, to persuade her to sound the publisher informally on his behalf. On the same day, however, he received a letter from Grasset enquiring when he proposed to publish his second volume. He therefore countermanded his request to Reynaldo, and wrote to Grasset on the 4th, revealing his wish to transfer his novel to the NRF; 'I leave it to you to decide whether or not it suits you to grant it,' he said. In his alarm Grasset made the tactical error of trying to hold Proust to the terms of their contract, instead of appealing to his feelings. Proust showed that he was pained, and Grasset wrote again more wisely; Proust must do as he thought best, he released him from the contract, he wanted him to stay only of his own free will. Defeated in this contest of magnanimity, Proust told Gide ruefully that he would have to remain with Grasset.

This was not the first reversal of his defeats in December 1912. Fasquelle, seeing the unexpected success of *Swann*, had recently made overtures through Maurice Rostand for the publication of the remain-

[1] And not in January 1914, as has hitherto been thought, owing to Gide's faulty recollection.

ing volumes; but Proust had seen no reason to exchange one commercial publisher for another. The NRF's approach was far more tempting, for he regarded that brilliant and idealistic group as his spiritual home; but he refused for motives of honour, perhaps also of pride, in order to spurn them in turn and wait till they called him again. Yet his position with regard to Grasset was irremediably false. Grasset had consented to publish his novel for hire, unread, rather than for its own sake. He was a publisher of scrupulous honesty and high aims, but impelled, unlike the NRF, by ambition for the rise of his struggling firm more than by selfless love of literature or faith in the genius of his authors. Proust's fancied concessions in the matter of royalties had left him, as was no doubt his unconscious intention, with the impression that he owed nothing to Grasset. He seized every opportunity of believing that Grasset had the better of him: 'He's had me for a mug again—*j'ai été poire de nouveau*,' he told Vaudoyer inelegantly in December 1913.

Proust's campaign for his novel was now satisfactorily over: he had been reviewed widely and favourably, had made the Goncourt Academy aware of his existence, gained devoted readers known and unknown, and seen Fasquelle and the NRF repent their errors in vain. Even the sales were well above the average for a first novel by an unestablished author. Third and fourth editions were called for in January, and two more were to follow before the outbreak of war. Grasset himself showed his true opinion by his unwillingness to release Proust (for if he had not regarded him as a valuable asset, the NRF's offer would have seemed a heavensent opportunity to get rid of him), and by agreeing to print the remaining volumes at his own expense and with increased royalties. The mysterious chain-reaction which turns a *succès d'estime* into a bestseller had not taken place; but the common idea that the first publication of *Swann* was a failure, that it passed unnoticed or was a disappointment to Proust himself, is incorrect.

In February 1914, constrained by his political subsidisers to act out of character, Gaston Calmette had begun a ruthless campaign in *Le Figaro* against the progressive and Germanophile Minister of Finance, Joseph Caillaux, and his proposed income-tax. Calmette threatened to publish Caillaux's love-letters to the mistress he had later married; and on 16 March Mme Caillaux called at the *Figaro* office, produced a revolver and shot him. "Don't touch me, I'm a lady!" she cried, while Calmette's friends wept, and the gentle editor bled to death. The thugs of *L'Action Française*, led by the truculent Léon Daudet, raised street-riots with shouts of "Down with Caillaux!" and Barrès, meeting Daudet at Calmette's funeral, ironically enquired: "How the deuce did this happen to *him*, and not to *you*?" To Proust afterwards, as to many others, it seemed that the murder of Calmette, like a ritual sacrifice of a good man performed in vain, was the first warning of world war. The angel of death was abroad; but Proust, in this new era of violence, was to be revisited sooner than other men by that dark angel.

It is a measure of Proust's iron courage and inflexible ambition for his book that throughout these eight months of tireless manœuvre he was enduring the last agonies of his doomed love for Agostinelli. Thinking of his mother and his own coming into the world he compared his novel to a child, long borne in his own body, long protected in helpless infancy; yet he did his duty by *Swann* half mechanically, without joy, like a parent distracted by an adulterous passion. In letters about his book to Louis de Robert, Vaudoyer, Mme de Noailles, Montesquiou, Lucien Daudet, Mme Scheikévitch, Gabriel Astruc, René Blum and Mme Straus he could not resist alluding to the 'immense grief' which had deprived him, he said, of all the pleasure he hoped from its publication. He did not reveal the nature of his suffering; but Montesquiou guessed, and wrote one of the letters of genuine, winning sympathy with which this saturnine man revealed, sometimes, the goodness that still lingered in his corroded heart.

Proust's tortures, like the Narrator's with the captive Albertine, were twofold. The first was jealousy—but of whom and what? Was Agostinelli an invert, seeking relief from his employer's tyranny in less exacting encounters with younger men? It is possible, though there is no evidence to show it. But Proust's remark to Émile Straus, that Agostinelli loved his 'wife' Anna but was unfaithful to her—'which she didn't know, for she was madly jealous and would have killed him' —seems to suggest a more natural explanation: that Agostinelli's infidelities to wife and master were with women, and the pleasures which Proust dreaded because he could not give them were those of normal love. Perhaps Proust hurried Agostinelli to Paris in August 1913 because he had detected him in a seaside flirtation, and realised that not only the humble Anna but all women were his rivals. It was perhaps with the intention of having Agostinelli followed, as does Charlus with Morel,[1] and the Narrator (or so Albertine suspects)[2]

---

[1] III, 216-17.   [2] III, 334.

with Albertine, that Proust asked Albert Nahmias whether he had 'ever, for any reason, had anyone shadowed, and if so, have you kept the addresses of the detectives or maintained contact with them?' His second torment, like the Narrator's, was the knowledge that Agostinelli's captivity was nearing its end. Tried too far, despite his affection for this marvellous master, his gratitude for so much moral and financial kindness, the young man was planning to escape and live his own life in freedom.

There are happier incidents of Albertine's imprisonment which belong to Agostinelli's. The bathroom with frosted glass from which the Narrator listens to his beloved singing at her morning ablutions[1] was the one recorded by Cocteau at 102 Boulevard Haussmann, where Proust stood in his violet waistcoat, eating noodles, after a reading from *Swann*, and no doubt it was Agostinelli whom Proust heard there humming *'For melancholy is but folly'*. The pianola on which Albertine plays Rameau and Borodin was bought by Proust that autumn, not without difficulty in obtaining the 'rolls' he most desired: 'This is the first request we have had for this piece from any of our fifteen thousand subscribers during the past ten years,' replied the indignant makers, when he asked them for the piano transcription of Beethoven's Fourteenth Quartet.[2] Albertine, bending over the keys as formerly over the handlebars of her bicycle, is compared to Saint Cecilia at her organ; again Proust is thinking of Agostinelli whom he had likened in his motor-rides from Cabourg six years before, bowed upon his steering-wheel and touching the levers which changed the speed and tone of the engine, to 'Saint Cecilia improvising on a still more immaterial instrument'.[3] Albertine, says the Narrator, 'had become extremely intelligent. She used to say, though quite mistakenly: "I'm horrified to think that without you I should still be stupid. Don't deny it, you have opened a world of ideas to me that I never dreamed of, and whatever I've become I owe to you alone".'[4] The same apparent change had occurred in Agostinelli, and the same pathetic words were no doubt spoken by him. 'He was an extraordinary person,' Proust told Émile Straus, 'and possessed perhaps the

---

[1] III, 10-11.

[2] M. de Charlus shares their attitude when he rebukes Morel for playing the piano transcription of Beethoven's Fifteenth Quartet: "nothing is less suitable for the piano," he declares (II, 1009).

[3] III, 383; *Pastiches et Mélanges*, 96.

[4] III, 64.

greatest intellectual gifts I have ever known'; and to Gide he wrote of his 'delicious intelligence', 'this merit so marvellously incompatible with his station in life, which I discovered with amazement, though it added nothing to my affection for him, except that I enjoyed making him aware of it'.

We have seen, however, that the customary total identification of Albertine with Agostinelli goes beyond the facts. She already exists, long before Proust's first meeting with Agostinelli in 1907, in the heroine of '*Avant la Nuit*' in 1893, in the Françoise and Charlotte of *Jean Santeuil* in 1897, and in the 1905-6 version of his novel when the little band was wooed by Swann; and in all these the hero is tortured by jealousy of her Lesbianism. In *A la Recherche*, until the last episode of her story, she is based primarily upon female originals. In the first holiday at Balbec Albertine's chief model is Marie Finaly, in her visits to the Narrator's home she resembles Louisa de Mornand and Marie Nordlinger, and during the second visit to Balbec she is the young girl of Cabourg in 1908 and 1909. It is intrinsically probable, though factual evidence is lacking, that in all these episodes she is reinforced by Proust's memories of young men, particularly by the obscure incidents of 1892-3 and 1897-8, and by Albert Nahmias in 1911-12; but there is no aspect of her here—except perhaps the Narrator's jealousy—which cannot be explained by Proust's known relations with young women. Albertine becomes Agostinelli for the first time in the Agony at Sunrise and the captivity in Paris. Yet even here her origins remain complex and divided. By no possible process of 'transposition' can such themes as the project of marriage, the choice of Fortuny gowns, the Narrator's motionless lovemaking with the sleeping Albertine, be derived from Proust's relationship with a vigorous young chauffeur. All these come from his abortive engagement to the young girl of Cabourg. In his 'little pleasures' with her in Paris during the autumn of 1909 he no doubt displayed the passive and contemplative sexual behaviour which (as is shown also in his affair with Louisa de Mornand) he preferred with women, but not, it may be presumed, with young men; and the marine imagery with which the Narrator 'embarks on the sea of Albertine's sleep'[1] is a memory of their summers of 1908 and 1909 at Cabourg.

The main narrative of *La Prisonnière* and *Albertine Disparue*—the flight to Paris, the captivity, the escape, the death, the Narrator's posthumous jealousy and slow oblivion—indubitably retells the true

[1] III, 72.

story of Proust's love for Agostinelli. Yet it is as certain as it is strange that the earliest plot of *A la Recherche*, in the version finished six months before Agostinelli's unexpected reappearance in January 1913, followed a similar course. She was already intended at this same point of the novel, after the last return from Balbec, to become the Narrator's great love; the Narrator's jealous surveillance and cross-examinations were sketched out, twenty years before, in *'Avant la Nuit'* and in *Jean Santeuil*, parts IX and X; the scene in *Du Côté de chez Swann* between Mlle Vinteuil and her friend at Montjouvain was already designed to provoke, later in the novel, a revelation resembling the Agony at Sunrise; the process of oblivion was foretold in miniature by the Narrator's earlier love for Gilberte and Swann's for Odette; and Albertine's death, the only possible end to so desperate a love, was already adumbrated by the suicide of the Lesbian heroine of *'Avant la Nuit'*. It is as though Proust imposed upon his love for Agostinelli the pre-existing pattern not only of his total previous experience of love in his own life, but of the climax of his novel. Agostinelli was conducted along the road to his tragic end by the ineluctable mechanism of a work of art; he was killed by *A la Recherche*; and when he seemed to become a free agent, like Albertine in her flight to Touraine, he journeyed to his death. *A la Recherche* is a work consecrated by two human sacrifices, the deaths of Mme Proust and Agostinelli, for which Proust himself, in his own mind and in fact, was partly responsible.[1]

Soon after the return from Cabourg Agostinelli decided, and Anna agreed, that there was no future in his luxurious servitude to Proust. He had become a chauffeur when the motor-car still attracted the enterprise and mechanical ingenuity of the élite among the young of the working classes: he may be compared to the intelligent engineer Straker in *Man and Superman*. But the heroic age of the automobile was ending, and many of its protagonists were already numbered among the first pioneers—some among the first martyrs—of the air. In 1913, known to French aeronautical historians as *'l'Année glorieuse'*, the aviators of France flew by hops from Nancy to Cairo, crossed the Mediterranean to Algeria non-stop, made a speed record of 126 m.p.h., a height record of 20,000 feet, and looped the first loop. Aerodromes were opened near Paris, notably at Issy and Buc, and

---

[1] Cf. III, 496, 501. 'When I juxtaposed the deaths of my grandmother and Albertine I felt that my life was defiled by a double murder,' says the Narrator.

frequented by pupils, spectators, joy-riders, and the idle rich.[1] Agostinelli began to visit Buc and make friends with the airmen. A curious
incident in *Albertine Disparue*, so irrelevant that it seems to be an
undigested fragment from real life, no doubt belongs to this period.
Albertine declares that she has visited an airfield, where one of the
aviators is her friend; and Andrée (who here, and perhaps not infrequently elsewhere, seems to represent Anna) was so dazzled by the
compliments he paid Albertine, that she wanted to go up in his aeroplane.[2]

Before long, whether through his spies or because the young man
naïvely confided in him, Proust discovered Agostinelli's new interest,
and on several occasions accompanied him. 'Often,' says the Narrator,
'I liked to arrange that our outings should end—and it was also agreeable to Albertine, so devoted to every kind of sport—at one of these
aerodromes.' He was reminded by the aeroplanes—moored, departing, arriving, dragged to the starting-point by teams of mechanics—of
boats for hire on the beach at Cabourg; but here the element on which
the trippers sailed was the infinite sky. 'Soon the engine was started,
the machine began to move and gather impetus, and then abruptly to
rise, at a steep angle, in the tense and apparently immobilised ecstasy
of a horizontal speed suddenly transformed into a majestic and
vertical ascent'; while Albertine, like Agostinelli, 'beside herself with
joy, kept asking the mechanics to explain everything'.[3] Proust made
the acquaintance of two of Agostinelli's friends at Buc, Kasterine and
Sentmitchof, and wrote to Albert Nahmias to ask for a recommendation for 'a young man'—presumably Agostinelli himself—'who
believes he has made several inventions in the field of the aeroplane'.

It was probably in October 1913, when Proust's mysterious lamen-
tations to his friends recommenced, that Agostinelli announced his
intention to learn to fly. Possibly he would have been willing to train
at Buc, without entirely deserting his master; and it was perhaps only

---

[1] 'Although she is fifty-three,' wrote the diplomat Paléologue on 14 October
1913 of Cocteau's friend the Grand-Duchess Anastasia, 'she lives openly with
an Argentinian blackguard, dances at Magic City with all comers till two in the
morning and associates with the scum of the aerodromes.'

[2] III, 612. 'She no doubt hoped to turn my suspicions away from women,'
says the Narrator, 'because she thought I was less jealous of men.' Here is an
instance of 'transposition' which strongly suggests (because we can be quite
sure the aviator was a man) that Proust was chiefly jealous of Agostinelli's
relations with women.

[3] III, 105-6.

in the face of Proust's determined opposition that he realised that a complete break would be inevitable. This point may have been reached in mid-November, at the very time when *Du Côté de chez Swann* was published, when Proust told his friends that he was too unhappy to feel any pleasure at the appearance of his novel. The Narrator, weary of his sufferings, longs to see Venice and forget Albertine; and Proust asked Vaudoyer to recommend 'a quiet, isolated house in Italy', and confided to Mme Scheikévitch that she could wish him nothing but 'a kind of numbness which does not come'. In the first week of December Agostinelli fled. The date is fixed by a letter from Francis Jammes, comparing *Swann* to Shakespeare and Balzac, and speaking of its 'Tacitean phrases', which Proust received on 9 December: 'it would have given me such pleasure a month earlier,' he told Lucien Daudet, 'but as fate would have it, it arrived on a day when I was completely insane with misery'. Partly from a pathetic desire to find tranquillity and freedom in his old home, and in the bosom of his numerous family, partly because here was one of the chief aviation centres in France, Agostinelli sought refuge on his native Riviera. He took with him the money he had saved from Proust's gifts, which was amply sufficient for his plans.

In the first rage of betrayal, and with eery foresight, Proust cruelly wrote: 'you can tell your wife that if (which heaven forbid) you should have an aeroplane accident, she will find in me neither a protector nor a friend, and will never get a halfpenny from me'. In 1907, possibly divining in Agostinelli the passion for speed which is sometimes a disguised love of death, Proust had written with a similar presentiment: 'may the steering-wheel of my young mechanic remain for ever the symbol of his talent, rather than the prefiguration of his martyrdom!' Perhaps he now felt the base but irresistable wish, which many a desperate lover has known, to be freed from his torment by the death of the beloved. 'If Albertine could have been the victim of an accident and lived,' says the Narrator, 'I should have had an excuse for hurrying to her side; if she had died, I should have recovered my freedom to live.' And he remembers that Swann had felt the same desire to be freed from Odette by her death. 'If he had still been alive I could have informed him, a little later, that his wish was not only criminal, but absurd, that the death of the woman he loved would have freed him from nothing.'[1] Next, just as the Narrator dispatches Saint-Loup to Touraine to bribe Mme Bontemps and bring back Albertine, he sent

[1] III, 475-6; I, 355.

Albert Nahmias to persuade Agostinelli to return. The telegrams survive, dated from 3 December 1913 onwards and of extraordinary length, in which he advised Albert on the correct strategy for tackling the fugitive and his relatives, but forbade him, unlike the Narrator, to give money.

Agostinelli did not remain silent, and the tone of his letters is no doubt audible in the simple, dignified and affectionate letters of Albertine to the Narrator.[1] Proust had already been struck by his talent as a letter-writer in November 1907, when the young man's congratulations on '*Impressions de route en automobile*' had been 'the prettiest I received'. The words in which Albertine describes their last ride together, on the evening when they returned from Versailles— when they hear a sound like 'the droning of a wasp' in the sky, and Albertine says: "Look, there's an aeroplane, it's high up, very high," —may well be Agostinelli's: 'be sure that I for my part shall not forget our drive in that double twilight (since night was near, and we were about to part), and it will not fade from my memory until my night has fallen for ever.' 'I have letters from him,' Proust assured Gide afterwards, 'which are those of a great writer.' On 5 March, as Proust wrote a letter to Henry Bordeaux hinting of his anguish, he heard a lady neighbour 'indefatigably playing', instead of the airs from Massenet's *Manon* which torment the Narrator after Albertine's escape,[2] the *Appassionata* of Beethoven; 'but she does not render its sadness,' he added.

But the fugitive did not return. Proust suspected that Anna was mainly to blame: 'I did all I could to prevent him from flying,' he told Émile Straus, 'but his wife was convinced he was going to make a million.' However, it was not until nearly four months after his escape, when the flying season began again, that Agostinelli took the decisive step. Towards the end of March 1914 he enrolled at the flying school of the Garbero brothers at La Grimaudière near Antibes, under the absurd and pathetic pseudonym of Marcel Swann. Among his colleagues were Kasterine and Sentmitchof, his friends at Buc. During the next two months his progress was rapid, and on Saturday, 30 May 1914, at five o'clock in the afternoon, he made his second solo flight, carrying with him the 7000 francs which still remained from his master's gifts.

Joseph Garbero, the chief instructor, had warned the daring novice

[1] Albertine writes five letters, all quoted in full (III, 421, 452, 468, 477-8).
[2] III, 452.

to keep within the aerodrome; but Agostinelli, rashly exulting in the liberation of flight, ventured north-eastward over the sea.[1] He prepared to fly back, but forgot the necessity to gain height and speed for the turn; his monoplane stalled and crashed, along the dipping right wing, into the sea several hundred yards from land. The horrified watchers on the shore saw the young man standing on his seat in the sinking wreck, waving and shouting for help. Agostinelli had never learned to swim; and as a rowing-boat drew near, the plane and the tragic aviator sank.

Proust learned the disaster that evening in a despairing telegram from Anna, and read further details on page 7 of next morning's *Figaro*. A posthumous letter arrived from the dead Agostinelli, and Proust may well have felt, like the Narrator when Françoise brings him the letters posted by Albertine just before her riding accident, that he 'had in his eyes the look of a man whose mind is unbalanced'.[2] A day or two later Agostinelli's step-brother Jean Vittoré called at 102 Boulevard Haussmann, and Proust burst into tears in his arms.

Boats had searched till nightfall on Saturday, but the currents were strong and the body could not be found. On Sunday evening the wrecked aeroplane was hauled to the surface, empty. The Agostinellis issued a description of the drowned man, moved chiefly, as Proust darkly suspected, by desire of the money he had upon him: he was dressed in khaki overalls, a brown rubber helmet, a grey shirt, black trousers, and wore a gold signet-ring marked AA.[3] Anna repeatedly attempted suicide; and Proust, forgetting his threats, took her under his protection, and asked Émile Straus to put in a word for her with Prince Albert of Monaco. He was astonished to learn from the grasping family that she was not Agostinelli's legal wife, but only his mistress; however, in the same spirit of justice, he apologised to Émile Straus and through him to the Prince, but pointed out firmly that Anna was none the less deserving, since 'her love for the deceased and his relations with her were more affectionate than is the case in many lawful unions'.

On Sunday 7 June a fishing-boat found the corpse near Cagnes, six

---

[1] Proust alludes secretly to the death of Agostinelli, when he makes the Narrator at Balbec burst into tears on first seeing an aeroplane, 'which glided for a few moments over the sea' (II, 1029).

[2] III, 477.

[3] The mysterious rings which Albertine leaves behind her, each bearing a flying eagle, are likewise marked with her monogram (III, 63, 165, 463).

miles north-east from the scene of the crash, still in its khaki overalls, floating and decomposed. The funeral was at Nice next day; Anna, heavily veiled and supported by Émile and Agostinelli's father, was chief mourner; and the bearers were Hector and Joseph Garbero, Kasterine, and the dead man's other fellow-pupils. Proust sent a 400-franc wreath, 'as beautiful as could be, but they wished it had been of artificial flowers,' he complained afterwards. Such was the end of the brave, intelligent and well-meaning young man who was Proust's greatest love.

In his grief Proust descended into asthma and incessant fumigations, 'which help me to breathe, but would prevent anyone else,' he told Gide on 20 June, to ward off a proposed visit of condolence. Anna stayed at 102 Boulevard Haussmann at his invitation from about mid-June until early in July; they had both loved the same man, and were partners in suffering. 'As in the phenomenon of supersaturation,' he told Montesquiou, 'everything that hitherto was fluid and bearable grips me in an eternal vice. I only have the strength to restore to his poor widow the courage I lack for myself.' And to Lucien Daudet he wrote later: 'I knew what it was to hope, every time I took a taxi, that an oncoming motor-bus would run me over.' In this burning summer, while the doomed young men of Europe played their last games of tennis and love before nightfall, Proust watched with horror, like the Narrator, 'the declining sun coating the verticality of houses with a tawny distemper'. 'How slow the day is to die on these immeasurable evenings of summer!'[1]

Jealousy and separation had not impaired Proust's resolution in the publication and launching of *Swann*; no more could death and bereavement hinder the preparation of his next volume. On 4 April, when he made his unsuccessful proposal to Grasset to transfer his novel to the NRF, he answered Grasset's enquiry as to the date for the publication of his second volume. Before deciding in June 1913 to end the first volume with the episode of Gilberte in the Champs-Élysées he had already received galley-proofs equivalent to about 280 further pages, comprising the remainder of the Gilberte story ('*Chez Mme Swann*') and the whole of the first visit to Balbec. These, however, he must revise and enlarge, and at least two further sets of proofs would be required. The remainder of the volume, which at this time comprised the Narrator's love for the Duchesse de Guermantes, the visit to Doncières, and Mme de Villeparisis's matinée, was for the most part in

[1] III, 479, 481.

typescript[1]; the rest of the typing, the revision, printing and proof-correction of this section would take 'several months'. He therefore suggested October 1914 as a target-month for publication.

As before, he decided to publish extracts from his forthcoming volume; but now, after the success of *Swann*, there was no risk of refusal from unwilling editors, no need to disguise his fragments as topical articles for *Le Figaro*. In April Gide had invited him to contribute long excerpts to the *Nouvelle Revue Française*; and about 7 May Proust sent Rivière, as the first of two instalments, an abridged version of the first visit to Balbec, cut up and pasted together from last year's galleys. This comprised the night-journey, the arrival, the rides in Mme de Villeparisis's carriage, and the meetings with Saint-Loup and the Baron de Charlus, and was published in the NRF for 1 June 1914. Towards the end of May Proust asked Grasset to print second proofs from last year's corrected galleys of '*Chez Mme Swann*' and the first visit to Balbec, and sent the typescript for the remainder of his second volume (which he then intended to call *Le Côté de Guermantes*) for the printing of first proofs. As his second instalment for the NRF was now urgently required, he asked for the typescript to be printed first; and this was done, in 28 galleys numbered 1 to 28 and equivalent to about 224 pages, from 6 to 11 June. The preceding section ('*Chez Mme Swann*' and the first visit to Balbec) was then reprinted in 38 galleys numbered 29 to 66, equivalent to about 304 pages, from 12 to 22 June. From galleys 1 to 18 he made an abridged version of the first half of *Le Côté de Guermantes* as we now know it, comprising the move of the Narrator's family to the Hôtel de Guermantes, the gala at the Opéra Comique[2], the Narrator's love for the Duchesse, the autumn at Doncières,[3] and the visit with Saint-Loup to Rachel's villa, but omitting the matinée at Mme de Villeparisis's, which occupied galleys 19 to 28. He added the episode of the grandmother's stroke in the Champs-Élysées and her illness, which he had hitherto intended to place in his third volume between the Princesse de Guermantes's soirée and the last visit to Balbec. He had now decided that it should come immediately after Mme de Villeparisis's matinée and form the conclusion of his second volume, although he had not included it in

[1] It will be noticed that poor Agostinelli had in fact made some progress with the task of typing for which he was engaged in January 1913, since in the autumn of 1912 Proust's typescript had ended with the first visit to Balbec.

[2] Transferred in the final version of 1920 to the Opéra.

[3] Saint-Loup's garrison-town is nameless in this early version.

the material sent to Grasset. The new extracts were sent to Rivière about 13 June, and appeared in the NRF for 1 July.

Only '*Chez Mme Swann*' now remained unused. Proust's old friend Robert de Flers had replaced poor Calmette as editor of *Le Figaro*, and offered to publish it as a *feuilleton* serial in ten instalments. '*Odette mariée*: a long story by the author of that beautiful and great book, *Du Côté de chez Swann*' was announced as a coming attraction on the front page of *Le Figaro* on 15 July. But '*Odette mariée*' never appeared, *Le Côté de Guermantes* in this primitive and imperfect form was not published in October; and Proust was only one of many millions whose innocent hopes in that hot and ordinary July were not to be granted.

Chapter 11

THE DEATH OF SAINT-LOUP
(August 1914 – January 1916)

THE sky above Paris had never seemed so blue and crystalline—
for the factories were closed, and their chimneys had ceased to
smoke—as on the Sunday of Mobilisation Day, 3 August 1914, when
Proust saw his brother Robert off to Verdun at the Gare de l'Est.
Batteries of 75's had parked overnight in the Tuileries gardens, and
cavalry bivouacked on the boulevards, with their horses tethered to
the chestnut trees. The good Abbé Mugnier sat amid the tobacco-
smoke and clinking glasses of a café outside the Gare du Nord, hearing
confessions: "Quick, Monsieur l'Abbé, my train's nearly due out!"
Ferdinand Bac visited Colonel Walewski, once Proust's captain at
Orleans, now commander of the Versailles garrison, and offered his
services in vain. "To Berlin!" cried the marching soldiers; but Mme
Lemaire, grimly painting three white roses in a glass vase, remarked to
Henri Bardac: "I've heard all that before, in 1870."

Bac called on Comte Greffulhe at 8 rue d'Astorg, passing in the
courtyard a group of young men in caps and trilbies, sitting on suit-
cases, whom he seemed vaguely to know, and who seemed to know
him: they were the Count's footmen, about to leave for the war. He
entered the open door of the deserted mansion, climbed the state
staircase; and there, in his study at the end of the vast libary,[1] silhouetted black against the delicious sunlight of the summer garden, with its
flowers and birds and peace, was M. Greffulhe, ringing, ringing and
shouting: "Pierre — Jean — Jules! — Where's everybody? Why
doesn't anyone come?" The butler brought cold lunch from the
restaurant at the corner, and shook hands with his feudal master: "I
can't clear up, Monsieur le Comte," he explained, "I've got to go to
Belfort, you'll never see me again, we can't surrender a fortress, so
we'll have to blow ourselves up." "I shall be all alone," cried M.
Greffulhe, "but let Them come, They'll find me here, I'm not the sort

[1] The very library in which the Narrator sees *François le Champi* and meditates on Time Regained.

that runs away." Next day the streets were empty, and the Metro stopped; the young men, and the husbands, had gone to the Battle of the Frontiers.

The catastrophe of war was aggravated for Proust by upheavals in his household. He had quarrelled with Céline and dismissed her some months before,[1] but kept Nicolas; while Céline's place was filled by Odilon's wife Céleste, who came in from their home in the working-class suburb of Levallois, 'to run errands and do a little sewing'. Now Odilon was called up, and Proust arranged for Céleste to live in: "I've known you so long, Odilon," he said, "and your wife has only to take one of the servants' rooms." A few days later Nicolas had to go; Proust engaged a former valet, who likewise was summoned to the front; and a sickly youth recommended by Coco de Madrazo ('the door opened, and in walked Galloping Consumption in person,' he told Reynaldo) lasted no longer. Proust lingered in Paris, convinced that he must protect Robert's wife, and his ten-year-old niece Suzy; but late in August, liberated by their departure to Pau, he began to think of Cabourg.

During the first three weeks of war three German armies had poured across Belgium. On the 23rd they broke the French line at Charleroi, and next day forced the British retreat from Mons: the way to the capital was open, and 1870 seemed come again. On they flared, and in the next twelve days covered all but thirty of the hundred and eighty miles from the frontier to Paris.

The French public was kept unaware of disaster, although some noticed (like the Narrator)[2] that the sites of German defeats were drawing ever nearer; but on the 28th the famous communiqué, announcing that 'our line extends from the Somme to the Vosges', revealed that Paris was in danger. On the 29th distant guns were heard; on the 30th a solitary Taube dropped five bombs on the city; and on 2 September Von Kluck reached Senlis, only twenty-five miles away. Amiens, Laon, Coucy, Rheims, Saint-Leu-d'Esserent, Senlis! —the holy places of Proust's Ruskin pilgrimages twelve years before

[1] Perhaps the quarrel was connected with Agostinelli and Anna, and perhaps Françoise's hostility to Albertine was suggested by Céline's to Agostinelli. The break took place some time later than November 1913, when Céline was in hospital for an operation, and Proust sent her a copy of *Du Côté de chez Swann* inscribed: 'Greetings to the temporary invalid from the perpetual invalid.' Céleste helped at this time to send out the presentation copies of *Swann*.

[2] III, 750.

had all, within a few days, been desecrated by the enemy. On the night of the 2nd the government left for Bordeaux, and General Galliéni ominously promised he would defend Paris 'to the end'. A million people, women, children, the old, the infirm, the rich and the frightened, fled from the doomed city. Proust was both infirm and rich, though no coward; he stuck it out till the 4th, and then left for Cabourg.

Céleste not only agreed to come with him, but jestingly proposed to disguise herself as a man, an offer which he prudently rejected. The train took twenty-two hours instead of the peace-time five, and was crammed with fellow-fugitives. On the way he thought with anguish of Robert at Verdun, of his friends in danger, of poor Agostinelli. Agostinelli! Seven years ago at Cabourg, a young man of nineteen, a Saint Cecilia in his black cape, he had driven his sleepless master through the landscapes of peaceful Normandy; a year ago he had said: "I can't bear to see you looking so sad," and returned to captivity in Paris; and now he had ceased to exist, and his drowned body was corrupting far away into dust. Would not his ghost meet the master who had slain him, at Cabourg? Proust murmured to himself a favourite line of Verlaine: '*Ah! quand refleuriront les roses de septembre?* —When will September's roses flower again?'[1] At the Grand Hôtel he occupied room No. 147; and Céleste, revisiting the spot in 1953, recognised the little circular window at the end of the corridor, to which he would walk every evening in his dressing-gown, and watch the sun sinking below the sea-horizon.

He emerged at last from the Grand Hôtel to visit the hospital of Cabourg, now crowded with hundreds of wounded soldiers from the Marne. To his relief he found that most were only lightly injured: they ate, slept, walked and laughed. He went every day with gifts, fifty packs of playing-cards, sets of draughts, boxes of chocolates. Some of his new friends were coloured troops from Morocco and Senegal. One day he heard a tactless lady visitor greet her patient with: "Good morning, nigger!", to which the outraged black replied: "Me nigger, you old cow!!"; and he used the incident for Odette's anecdote of Mme Blatin viewing the Cinghalese in the Jardin d'Acclimatation.[2]

One day, when Proust was too ill to see them, Mme Greffulhe called with 'a gentleman', whom he learned later to have been Montesquiou. The Palais Rose had been commandeered by the Army, and the home-

---

[1] Verlaine, *Sagesse*, III, iii.
[2] I, 536.

less Count Robert had taken refuge in a hotel at Trouville. "We're all St Francises of Assisi now," he cried, as he trudged up the path of the Villa Mon Rêve at Bénerville to see Mme de Clermont-Tonnerre, carrying his own small suitcase and grey with dust; "I wanted to stay at home, and let the Germans shoot the author of twenty volumes on his own doorstep! Now, if I'm spared, perhaps I shall die the author of thirty volumes.[1] I couldn't bear to bury my pastels and hide my porcelain; so I offer my Palais Rose to Destiny." Isadora Duncan the dancer saw him pacing the seafront beneath her windows at the Hôtel de Normandie, and asked the Count to give her a baby, 'to soothe my nerves'; but he preferred to solace his own sorrows over bowl after bowl of humble mussels with Mme de Clermont-Tonnerre. Meanwhile Mme Straus, 'with the aid,' she said, 'of various duchesses who have strayed to this coast, and resident cocottes who are a great deal more efficient', was organising soup-kitchens for Belgian refugees. Montesquiou sighed for Artagnan: "I'd have peace and quiet there, I could eat my own eggs!" Soon, in the castle of his musketeer ancestor, he was hard at work producing war-elegies, with a fecundity he had never known since the death of Yturri. "If you hear me groaning," he told his servants, "it means I'm writing poetry and mustn't be disturbed."

Proust visited Mme Straus at the Clos des Mûriers, and for the last time saw M. Straus pruning his beloved roses, like M. Verdurin at La Raspelière. He engaged in a good-humoured disputation with a fellow-guest, the great Réjane (Berma herself), on the war-time banning of Wagner, which he deplored; "she called me a Boche, and nearly pushed me into a rosebush". About 12 October, all his money spent on gifts for the soldiers, he returned to Paris. On the train he was seized by an appalling attack of asthma, and Céleste, thinking him on the point of death, forced her way past the angry guard into the luggage-van to fetch his medicine. At Cabourg, where he had dreaded the revival of memories of Agostinelli, he had seemed, as he told Lucien Daudet, 'to feel a little less grief, and feared I was beginning to forget; but when I came home I was glad to find this was only a false alarm'. The 'intermittent progress of oblivion' had begun.

Meanwhile the vast events had occurred which made Germany's ultimate defeat inevitable, but also ensured that the war would last for

---

[1] As indeed he did.

several years. After sacking Senlis on 2 September, Von Kluck turned left to the Marne: in the next fortnight the remaining French armies must be surrounded, in a gigantic Sedan, and the six-weeks war of the Schlieffen Plan be punctually over. But a new French army, based on Paris, had been formed under General Maunoury (brother of the surgeon who operated on Proust's Aunt Amiot); and the British Expeditionary Force, which was thought broken and scattered far to the north, was south-east of Paris and ready to fight again. From the 6th to the 9th the German right flank was counter-attacked in the Battle of the Marne and driven back forty miles to the Aisne. A series of attempts by each side to outflank the other to the north developed into a race for the coast; by mid-November the line from Verdun to Flanders was stabilised, and four years of trench warfare began. Paris was never in danger again until the spring of 1918; but the French had lost five hundred thousand men.

Among those who fled to Bordeaux, not in fear but in tragic defiance, was Ferdinand Bac, who on alighting saw none other than Mme de Chevigné, exchanging embraces with the working-class family who had made room for her in their third-class carriage. There were no beds in the city; and as Bac and the countess settled in an empty train, they saw an endless line of cattle-trucks pass, loaded with haggard young men in clotted brown bandages, the wounded from the north. Weeping bitterly, Mme de Chevigné threw to them all she had: the remains of her modest dinner of rolls and gruyère, her silver cigarette-case, the contents of her handbag; and Bac saw in her face not only terror and despair, but an outburst of selfless love to which she had been many years a stranger. Bac went on to Bayonne, where he found Mme de Noailles at the hospital ("Here I am, it's all I'm good for, I recite poetry to them and write to their mothers"). At Pau he met Mme Straus; they walked past the cemetery, where a young woman knelt by a grave: "will scientists ever invent pills to cure a broken heart?" enquired Mme Straus.

Others, however, had left Paris in the opposite direction, to confront the enemy in their beloved, menaced châteaux. Mme Lemaire and Suzette waited dourly at Réveillon, which for a single day, on 5 September, the eve of the Marne, was within the fringe of the German advance. As they walked in the garden a German officer on horseback jumped the hedge, clapped his monocle to his eye, cried: "I wanted to see Madeleine Lemaire, and now I have!" and galloped away. That night a German detachment billeted in the château. Memories of

Réveillon and Suzette in 1895 had already served for the Narrator's last visit to Tansonville and walks with Gilberte; and the courage of mother and daughter at Réveillon in 1914 suggested Gilberte's heroic lingering at Tansonville in the war, which involved the transfer of Combray from the distant Beauce to the front line. Certain rivals, however, pretended that Mme Lemaire's behaviour in the war was, somehow, defeatist rather than brave; and Proust seems to reflect this calumny when the Narrator reports that Gilberte fled to Tansonville 'because the incessant Taube raids had terrified her so', and makes her praise 'the perfect breeding' of the German officers whom she is forced to billet.[1]

Proust was now harrowed by ceaseless anxiety for his relatives and friends. In October Robert Proust's field-hospital at Étain near Verdun was bombarded, and shell-fragments struck the table on which he operated; he was mentioned in despatches, promoted to captain, and continued to seek posts of utmost danger. Proust's youngest Mayer cousin was killed in the summer of 1915. The son of his former sweetheart Antoinette Faure died at Charleroi; Mme Scheikévitch lost her brother, whom Proust had glimpsed at Larue's; Charles Catusse was wounded in the Vosges, Henri Bardac on the Marne, Jacques Rivière was taken prisoner at Étain near Verdun on 24 August 1914, and Rivière's brother-in-law Alain-Fournier, the miraculous author of Le Grand Meaulnes, disappeared for ever on 22 September. Reynaldo was posted with Fernand Gregh and Robert Dreyfus to a regimental depot at Albi in Provence; but in spite of Proust's entreaties—'my little Albigensian, you must try to remain such'—he demanded to be sent to the front, and succeeded in November 1914. At Vauquois in the Meuse Reynaldo saw and risked death every day, intrepid for himself but anguished for others; he listened to the music of bombardment with the same invariable cigarette in his lips as when, at Mme Lemaire's twenty years before, he listened to his own; and he composed a gay regimental march which all the soldiers in the 31st used to whistle. Cocteau, wearing a beautiful uniform specially created by Poiret, joined a fantastic ambulance unit organised by Misia Edwards and her third husband-to-be, the Spanish

---

[1] III, 751. Proust adjusts the chronology and topography of the battle when he makes the Germans reach Tansonville 'after beating our troops at La Fère'— presumably La Fère-Champenoise, about thirty miles east of Réveillon, where the Germans won a temporary success in counter-attacking Foch on 8 September.

painter José Maria Sert. René Blum was an interpreter at Amiens, Lucien Daudet worked in a canteen at Tours, Jacques Bizet served at the Hôpital Saint-Martin, Lauris joined Gide at the Foyer Franco-Belge, a relief centre for Belgian refugees, and Albufera was Joffre's chauffeur. Loche Radziwill organised a Polish brigade, and finding that every volunteer wanted to be an officer, issued a standing order: 'There will also be privates in the Polish Army'.

At moments Proust imagined that he, too, would like to be pronounced fit for military service; but usually he felt it would be a disaster not only for himself but for his country: 'not to speak of the incapacity caused by my health, I ask myself what chaos I might not introduce into the services,' he told Mme Catusse. Three years before, on 6 September 1911, he had at last been struck off the territorial army lists in the rank of administrative officer in the Health Service; but the wartime regulations demanded that he should undergo a new medical examination. For a whole year he awaited the summons, sometimes pulling wires (Dr Pozzi had been most helpful in the very first month of war), sometimes with anxious resignation. He was, and always had been, fearless of danger; we shall find him later taking the same delight in air-raids as Cocteau or Apollinaire in shell-fire. But he was by now permanently unfit, both in body and in mind, for any way of life other than insomnia, asthma, fumigation, and confinement to bed for six and a half days in every week. Antoine Bibesco had expressed the fantastic unthinkability of Marcel's going to the wars, in an unfeeling telegram sent on Mobilisation Day: 'Hope they put you in the shock troops,' he wired.

Nevertheless, the war became part of his life. He deeply loved his country, its people, his friends and all who were dear to them, and suffered with their suffering. 'I have assimilated the war so completely, alas, that I can't isolate it,' he wrote to Princesse Soutzo later; 'it is not so much an object, for me, in the philosophical sense of the word, as a substance interposed between myself and all objects. As people used to love in God, I live in the war.' Then, no less profoundly, absorption in the war became a duty, a curiosity, an aspect of the search for truth; the war was a mysterious entity, sinister yet exhilarating, which it was imperative though impossible to fathom, like love or death. In his letters he explored and shared the longings, the anxiety, the grief of everyone he knew; he read seven newspapers every day, striving to pierce to the reality behind the communiqués, and followed the battles on a General Staff map. Proust particularly admired Henri

Bidou's daily articles, 'The Military Situation', in the Journal des Débats ('clear and remarkable, the only decent things I've read about the war')[1]; though when Bidou began to combine this sacred office with the secular post of dramatic critic on Le Journal, he remarked, a little shocked: "I wonder he doesn't get mixed up!" For Brichot's articles on the war, however, which Mme Verdurin ridicules ostensibly for their absurdity, but really because they have won him admittance to the salons of the noble Faubourg, Proust thought of Joseph Reinach's column in Le Figaro, under the pseudonym 'Polybe'.[2] 'The abuse of his ridiculous metaphors, his inability to forget anything he ever learned, his mock brevity, like a pinchbeck Michelet, prevent me from doing justice to his articles, though they are otherwise so serious and sound, so authoritative in their competence and inexhaustible knowledge,' Proust wrote to Mme Catusse in much the same language as the Narrator of poor Brichot, whose articles are 'decked with the paste jewels that we have seen him lavishing so often on the Faithful, yet rich in a very real erudition', and contain, exclaims the Narrator, 'such knowledge, such intelligence, such sound reasoning!' 'Polybe's friends laugh him to scorn,' reported Proust; and Mme Straus, for one, was not sorry to join in the fun against her former admirer, while M. Straus, all through the war, made a collection of 'Polybiana'.

Gaston de Caillavet was the first of Proust's friends to die during the war, though, as it happened, not in the war. Gaston had been painfully ill in Périgord since the summer, accepting his destiny with noble resignation; and Proust, to whose constant enquiries Jeanne had replied too reassuringly, was overwhelmed to read in Le Figaro on 14 January 1915 of his death. He wept, thinking of their friendship twenty-five years before, when Gaston's army year was nearly over and his own just beginning, of Gaston's first formal letters, which began 'Dear Sir', of their absurd rivalry for the love of Jeanne, and of Gaston's beautiful daughter Simone, whom he had not seen again,

---

[1] In conversation with the widowed Gilberte at the Princesse de Guermantes's matinée the Narrator regrets that Saint-Loup died too soon to read the article of Bidou ('for whom he had a profound admiration, and who visibly had a great influence on his military ideas') on the German offensive of March 1918 (III, 981).

[2] Characteristically Proust differentiates his character from the model by emphasising Brichot's anti-Dreyfusism, and mentioning that he never collected his articles into a volume; whereas Reinach, the arch-Dreyfusist, sedulously reprinted his in no fewer than nineteen volumes: La Guerre de 1914. Les commentaires de Polybe (1915-19). Cf. III, 789-93.

although whenever Gaston met him he would proudly say: "Come and see her, she's a marvel of intelligence!" He must talk to Jeanne; and soon after her return to Paris he arrived at 12 Avenue Hoche by taxi, after midnight, and was deeply hurt to find the house unlit, and deaf to his chauffeur's honking. Others, he darkly hinted, had a shorter memory than his for love and friendship, and there would be remarks on this subject in the next volume of his novel. Jeanne goodnaturedly arranged to visit 102 Boulevard Haussmann. As she entered in her widow's veils Marcel cried, bursting into tears: "My dear Gaston is dead!" and then, alternately sobbing and laughing at the images of Time Lost, took from a cardboard box laid ready on his bed the photographs of their past: Gaston as a soldier, himself as a soldier, himself at the tennis party in the Boulevard Bineau, Gaston again. "I must go, Marcel, I'm hurting you too much," said Jeanne as he wept still more bitterly at her account of Gaston's last days. Saint-Loup was dead, and Gilberte a widow. But Gaston was only the first in time of his Saint-Loups. Already Proust was alarmed for Fénelon, of whom no news had come since early in December.

After his return from Washington in October 1909 Bertrand de Fénelon had remained in Paris until May 1912, when he was transferred in succession to Rio de Janeiro, Havana and Christiania. He had served during 1908 at the French Legation in Peking, where he was photographed below a Chinese verandah, grave and bearded, with a Siamese cat on his shoulder. In April 1914, on his last leave in Paris, he asked to see the exquisite, seventeen-year-old Marguerite Lahovary, Princesse Marthe Bibesco's younger sister, whom he had met two years before and remembered; and all three visited the Musée Cernuschi, where he explained the beauty of Far-Eastern art to these Europeans of the Near East. 'A young girl passed by', wrote the princess later, 'on the bye-road which was leading Bertrand out of this life'. In August he was still in Christiania and could have stayed, for diplomats were exempt from mobilisation; but he demanded to be allowed to fight, and passed that autumn through England on his last journey. At the London embassy the young Paul Morand, who had recently read *Swann* with enthusiasm, questioned him about Proust, and was struck by the guarded manner in which Fénelon replied. 'He called up not so much Marcel's presence as his phantom,' said Morand, and he gave the impression that to know Proust was to belong to a particularly select secret society. But Fénelon was not entirely discreet; he remarked that Proust had "published two books at his own expense, and no doubt will remain unknown", and added: "he is a Saturnian, and a very difficult friend". 'Saturnian' had been the accepted slang for 'homosexual' in the Fénelon-Bibesco-Proust circle, but its meaning was perfectly understood elsewhere.

Fénelon's new comrades in the army noticed the same faint, ironic smile which his friends had known twelve years before. 'My constant aim, my only thought, is the liberation of our territory, the salvation of our nation and our country,' he wrote, 'and if I can make the least contribution to it, though unnoticed in the multitude, I shall feel I am happy and my task will be done.' Saint-Loup might have thought it more elegant to leave this resolve unexpressed; but perhaps it was still more elegant, when it came from the heart, to express it, and certainly no one had better right than Fénelon. 'He was always to the front, always in the post of most danger, always completely calm, even gay,' reported his superiors. His regiment was hurled into the useless First Battle of Artois in December 1914, and Fénelon was killed at Mametz on the 17th. For several months his fate remained obscure, and it was hoped he might have been taken prisoner. There was a mysterious rumour about a person in a motor-car, who claimed to have seen him alive, but could never be found again. At last, on 15 March 1915, Proust read in his morning *Figaro*: 'The sad news we have just received concerning Sub-Lieutenant de Salignac-Fénelon puts an end, alas, to the lingering hope that he might be found alive. After a desperate struggle, at the very moment when he was calling on the enemy to surrender, he received a mortal wound from a bullet in the head. The family photographs he carried on him seem to leave no doubt as to his identity.'

Proust had seen Fénelon rarely since 1902, and hardly at all since the party at *Le Circuit* on 27 November 1909. A last letter, in which Bertrand displayed his typical plain-speaking, had 'cooled my friendship for him still further,' he told Lauris. But for Fénelon, who died the death of Saint-Loup, he mourned as the Narrator for Saint-Loup: 'I am in tears, because they say now there is no hope of his being a prisoner,' he wrote to Lucien Daudet; 'I shall mourn him for ever,' he told Clément de Maugny. He had written his novel on the plan of his life, but now, with the vanishing of Agostinelli and Fénelon, life was beginning to write his novel.

Another heroic death that spring resembled the end of Saint-Loup. Vicomte Robert d'Humières, the proud and talented translator of Kipling and Conrad, who had helped Proust with Ruskin and reviewed *La Bible d'Amiens*,[1] was 'one of the Robert de Montesquious of this world, if I may use the expression,' wrote Ferdinand Bac. Bac had visited his lonely villa near Grasse in Provence; he noticed Henri Bataille's portrait of his host in youth as a cavalry-officer, with plumed helmet but bare, epicene chest, and the inscription: 'to my very dear friend Robert d'Humières'; in the garden stood an antique statue of Narcissus, 'pointing with an unequivocal gesture to the part of his body which he loved best'; and Humières's silent and self-effacing wife, with her infant daughter, seemed (like Gilberte at Tansonville) 'to carry in secret the burden of a vast, disappointed illusion'. Montesquiou wrote, in one of his venomous little couplets:

> *'With Humières you've left your son?*
> *Better make sure the light's still on.'*

Overwhelmed by an impending scandal Humières demanded to be posted to a Zouave regiment in the front line, and took the first opportunity of charging to his death. Proust read the news in the *Journal des Débats* on 13 May 1915, and linked his name with Fénelon's in letters to his friends: 'I weep day and night for Fénelon and Humières, as if I had left them only yesterday,' he told Mme Catusse. Perhaps, although there were many such, Humières was the invert to whom, as Proust remarked later to Paul Morand, 'love of men brought virility, and virility brought glory'. 'There are certain deaths I should like to discuss with you,' he told Robert de Billy, 'which I admire none the less, but which differ from the picture-postcard manner in which they are usually represented.'

Proust's life was more solitary in 1915 than ever before. His friends were far away, his hostesses had turned their mansions and châteaux into hospitals and their daughters into nurses, and all social life had ceased. He had increased his solitude by giving up his telephone in December 1914, ostensibly because of his 'ruin'; instead, Céleste used the telephone in a neighbouring café for her master's messages. Often during the spring he thought of retiring for a year, at the end of which the war would surely be over, to Nice or even to Venice, but waited in Paris for his ever-delayed medical board. In March he was distressed

---

[1] In *Chronique des arts et de la curiosité*, 12 March 1904. In return Proust reviewed Humières's *L'Ile et l'Empire de la Grande Bretagne* in the same periodical on 13 August 1904 (this article has not previously been noticed). The translation of Barrie's *Margaret Ogilvie*, which Proust mentioned admiringly in his *Figaro* article of 20 March 1907, '*Journées de Lecture*', was also by Humières.

by a malicious rumour that he had been heard to remark: "I haven't had time to think about the war yet, I'm still studying the Caillaux Affair." On 30 May, the first anniversary of Agostinelli's death, he asked Mme Catusse, then at her villa in Nice, to arrange for a wreath to be delivered to the dead man's sister and laid on his grave; but remembering the poor reception of the 400-franc wreath the year before, he pointedly ordered one to cost 40 francs only, 'as showy as possible'. Mlle Agostinelli, he explained apologetically, was living in sin, but her union was otherwise highly respectable, and had lasted for twenty years.[1] Ever since November 1914 Proust had been begging his friends on the Riviera—Gautier-Vignal, Mme Catusse, even Reynaldo's former secretary's cousin—to find a job for the destitute Émile Agostinelli.[2] In this May he at last succeeded in persuading Edmond Rostand to take him as chauffeur, but not for long; for Italy joined the war on 23 May, and Émile was killed a few months later at Gorizia on the Isonzo. He continued to keep benevolent ward over Anna, finding her excellent jobs in which she never stayed long. In October 1916 he refused her obstinate request to be recommended to Jacques Bizet for work in a munitions factory: it was too tiring for her, he explained to Mme Straus, and he would not be a party to it, 'any more than I consented to her poor husband's flying over the sea'. After this, in his published letters, the living Agostinellis are heard of no more; but no doubt his benevolence continued. Poor Nicolas Cottin caught pleurisy at the front in 1916 and died. Céline in her grief made no secret of her belief that the stifling air of 102 Boulevard Haussmann had given him his weak chest: 'You accuse me of Nicolas's death!' wrote Proust bitterly.

In June 1915 Proust visited Jacques Émile Blanche at Auteuil, where he complained of the cold; his host obligingly closed the window, lent him his cloak, and in delicate allusion to the opening chapter of *Swann* warmed him with an infusion of lime-tea. Since April Proust had been kindly but meddlesomely correcting the proofs of Blanche's

[1] Her lover was a certain Baron Duquesne, about whom Proust had heard from Agostinelli, and had recently asked for more from Gautier-Vignal, who knew the Baron as an old friend of his father. Proust seems to have used this relationship for the episode in which the squinting page-boy at Balbec tells of his sister's liaison with a wealthy man: "once she wanted to come home instead of staying respectable, but mother took the silly fool back to her friend, and quick too!" (II, 979-80).

[2] It is said that Émile Agostinelli took his brother's place as Proust's secretary for a time, presumably in July and August 1914.

Cahiers d'un Artiste, a talented and scandalous series of letters on the war, which introduced many of their society friends under disguised names, and ultimately reached six volumes. They worked on the proofs for a time; Proust recited the names of his friends dead at the war, lamented the ill-health 'which prevents me from doing my duty', and cried: "I ought to have fought like them!" Then, until dawn, he explained 'the architectural construction' of his novel; and as he revealed the significance in it of Sodom and Gomorrah, his voice grew louder, and Blanche, appalled, rose to shut the door that led to his sleeping household.

Montesquiou now arranged to read his first volume of war-poems, *Les Offrandes Blessées*, to a group of lucky friends at the Palais Rose. '188 elegies on the war,' Proust wrote in awe to Mme Catusse, 'he must have started on Mobilisation Day!' Proust evaded the reading, but not a punitive visit to his bedside in July, when the Count promised to go after five minutes and stayed for seven hours, chattering with the most astonishing and fatiguing brilliance. Montesquiou's own impressions were not altogether favourable: 'he's always ill, or rather, invariably in bed,' he wrote in his vengeful memoirs a few years later, recalling this visit, 'and one also notices jampots, not to mention chamber-pots'. Proust and Count Robert were destined never to meet again.

After being adopted as a mascot by a company of marines in Flanders, recommended for the *croix de guerre*, arrested as a spy, and rescued in the car of a general who happened to be a friend of his father (the Marines were wiped out next day), Cocteau had returned to Paris. Since the death of her husband in 1911 Mme de Chevigné had taken an apartment in Jean's family home at 10 rue d'Anjou, with its antiquated lift—"it dates from the period before lifts were invented," said Cocteau—and her star guest Joseph Reinach nicknamed her affectionately 'the Comtesse d'Anjou'. When Cocteau hugged her lapdog Kiss on the stairs, and the countess shouted: "Look out! I don't want him smothered in your facepowder!", they became great friends. In August Proust called on them both, and Jean found him sitting at midnight in the darkness on the top landing. "Why didn't you wait in my room, Marcel, you know I always leave the door ajar?" "Dear Jean," replied Marcel, "Napoleon had a man *shot* for waiting for him in his room."

At last, towards the same time, Proust was twice visited by medical majors, who to his horror were quite unaware, despite all his pulling of wires, that he was the invalid son of Dr Adrien Proust and the brother of Dr Robert Proust. "You're an architect, aren't you?" they said; but fortunately he was so obviously ill that they exempted him for six months. 'This is a recommendation which is certain to become more and more cogent until my death,' he commented grimly to Lucien.

Soon afterwards, at the urging of Coco de Madrazo and Lucien, he twice called on Comte Joachim Clary, a retired gentleman in waiting of the exiled Empress Eugénie, in his apartment in the Rue Galilée. Clary was half-blind, paralysed and slowly dying, and was tended by a faithful Japanese valet named Mineguishi, whom he had found on his travels working as a waiter in a hotel at Kyoto. No doubt Proust's memory of this situation reinforced his impression of the last days of the Prince de Sagan, when he wrote of Charlus stricken in sight and limbs under the care of Jupien. He rewarded Mineguishi with a signed copy of *Swann*, 'because I kept him up till the most unearthly hours'.

Two authors from whom Proust constructed a little of Bergotte died in the first period of the war: Jules Lemaître on 2 August 1914, and Paul Hervieu on 25 October 1915. With his red face and snow-white beard Lemaître had come to resemble 'a hot-house strawberry, nestling in January on a bed of cottonwool,' said Cocteau, whom Lemaître had met at Mme Scheikévitch's, and called, as the wise Prospero called his familiar spirit, 'my Ariel'. Lemaître's rôle as the sovereign guest and recognised lover of Mme de Loynes was curiously parallel to that of France in Mme Arman's salon, Hervieu's in Mme de Pierrebourg's, and Bergotte's in Mme Swann's. Proust had met Hervieu in the earliest days of his life in society, in the salons of Mmes Straus, Aubernon, Baignères and Arman, and had last seen him at Mme Straus's two months before. He remembered with remorse that he had never forgiven Hervieu's voting against his novel for the Académie Française prize in June 1914; and in one of his letters of condolence to the heartbroken Mme de Pierrebourg he told her, alluding to the death of Bergotte, that in his 'third volume' she would find a discussion of 'death, or rather this discord between the survival of the person we have lost and his apparent annihilation from the universe', which would bring her both pain and comfort.

On the outbreak of war Proust's publisher Grasset, together with most of his small staff and his printers, had been called to the army, and the appearance of Proust's second volume, originally planned for October 1914, was postponed for the duration of hostilities. Nevertheless, nearly the whole volume was already in print, in the proofs he had received in June, and the final pages were typed, perhaps by Émile Agostinelli, early in July. Proust had warned Grasset in April 1914 of 'the alterations which, knowing myself as I do, I am afraid I shall be forced to make', and this revision probably occupied his last visit to Cabourg and the autumn of 1914. The rewriting of the 'third' volume, which continued till the end of his life, was a natural continuation of the same process, and must have begun early in 1915. In April he confessed to Robert de Billy his hope that he would be rejected for military service, 'because I know how useless I should be, and because my last remains of health would be destroyed before I could finish my novel'; and in July he told Montesquiou: 'I am saving what little strength I have for the novel which, if God wills, I am in course of finishing.' By November 1915 he had completed a first version of *Albertine Disparue*, for he then covered the blank pages of Mme Scheikévitch's copy of *Swann* with a résumé of the whole Albertine episode, from the Narrator's first meeting with her at Balbec to his final oblivion after her death.[1] Proust's funeral march of separation and everlasting farewell has the note, more than any other section of his novel, of immediate experience rather than Time remembered; for he began *Albertine Disparue* when his grief for Agostinelli was still fresh, and wrote of oblivion as he attained it.

As the end of 1915 approached he felt his old melancholy for the dying year, but for a new reason. 'These sad days remind us,' he wrote to Antoine Bibesco, 'that the years return laden with the same natural beauty, but cannot bring back people. Alas, 1916 will have its violets and apple-blossom, but never again will there be a Bertrand de Fénelon.' Saint-Loup was dead, and youth and friendship lay with him in his unknown grave by the Somme.

---

[1] Embedded in this summary are two extracts from the quarrel and reconciliation scene after Mme de Cambremer's visit to Balbec (II, 833, 835), followed by seventeen passages on the Narrator's grief and jealousy after the death of Albertine, in the very order in which they occur in the novel (III, 419, 420, 430, 447, 475, 478, 483, 484, 490, 520 (cf. also 1104, note on 519), 529, 531 (note, p. 1104), 557, 558, 595-6, 601, 644).

Chapter 12

THE VINTEUIL SEPTET
(February 1916 – March 1917)

ON 21 February 1916 the atrocious agony of Verdun began, and persisted until 2 November. Of this, the longest and bloodiest battle of the war, Proust thought in the letter from Gilberte at Tansonville in 1916. The Battle of Méséglise has raged 'for more than eight months,' she remarks, 'the Germans have lost more than six hundred thousand men there', the obscure Roussainville has become a name as glorious as Austerlitz or Valmy, and the cornfield above the hawthorn path is now the famous Hill 307.[1] Perhaps Proust was unaware that nameless hills in the battle-zone were called after their height in metres; certainly, it was absurd to imply that the gentle eminence of the hawthorn path could be a thousand feet in height; but he knew that one of the focal points of the Verdun conflict, and the only significant objective of this altitude in all the Western Front north of the Vosges, was known as Hill 304.

On 25 February Gide called on Proust, whom he had not met since 1892. Among the subjects they discussed, besides homosexuality, were Proust's novel, the news that Rivière was rereading *Swann* with delight in his German prison-camp, and Grasset's inability to publish the second volume. Gide reopened the suggestion of migrating to the NRF, and Proust repeated that it was impossible, but with less conviction than two years before. A committee-meeting of the NRF on 14 April resulted in a new proposal to take over *A la Recherche*; and this unlooked-for second chance was another turning-point in Proust's long way to future fame.

Exactly two years had passed since the NRF's first repentant offer in the spring of 1914, and the situation was now fundamentally changed. It is likely that Proust had then refused not only out of loyalty to Grasset, but as a proud rebuke for their rejection of his novel in December 1912. By this second approach, however, the NRF had at last expiated their error. Moreover, since their printers

[1] III, 755-6.

were now at work again, they were able to propose immediate publication. Proust had resolved not to publish until the war was over; but even so, proofs could be printed and corrected meanwhile, and the volumes made ready for publication at the first suitable moment after the coming of peace. By deserting Grasset he might well gain as much as a year in his race against death. He resolved to accept, and to approach Grasset as before through the good offices of René Blum.

The negotiations with Grasset were difficult and painful. Moved by relentless determination in the higher cause of his novel, and suppressed guilt for abandoning the lesser duty towards his publisher, Proust for once displayed something less than his usual magnanimity. Remembering Grasset's almost excessive sympathy when told in July 1914 of his losses on the stock exchange, he decided to plead his imaginary ruin, and pretended that it was from need of money, and with the intention of publishing without delay, that he wished to accept the NRF's offer. He was convinced that he had behaved throughout with extraordinary generosity, that Grasset had failed him and was morally and financially in his debt. Owing to the moratorium imposed by the war Proust had received neither accounts nor royalties since April 1914. On the other hand, Grasset had already incurred considerable expense by printing nearly the whole of the second volume in proof, and making Proust's extensive corrections; he had given Proust an excellent contract, with 20 per cent royalties, for this and the rest of the work; and now he was expected to relinquish not only the future volumes but the already successful *Du Côté de chez Swann* without compensation, to sign away one of his most promising authors without protest, almost as an atonement for injury.

At first, however, Grasset was unfindable, for the two respectable ladies who now formed his only staff refused to give his address. As it happened, poor Grasset had fallen gravely ill with typhoid in the summer of 1915, and after six months in a military hospital had retired, semi-incognito, to a Swiss sanatorium at Neuchâtel. May and June were wasted in trying to trace him, with the aid of René Blum, Léon Bailby, Lauris, Albert Sorel's son, and a bribe to Grasset's concierge; and July and August passed in an exchange of letters through the slow posts to Switzerland. Grasset, though pained, was dignified and fair; he appealed to his illness, the war, the expenses he had already met for the second volume; he asked Proust to reconsider, but made no threat of standing on his legal rights. 'I have too much pride to retain an author who has lost confidence in me,' he told Blum, 'and I will facilitate the complete recovery of his freedom.' Even this was not enough. Sternly beginning 'Dear Sir' instead of his usual 'Dear Friend', Proust retorted with deep umbrage to fancied charges of egoism, shirking and lack of patriotism, resumed his strangely inaccurate wrangling over the proofs of vol. 2, and offered almost insultingly 'a small indemnity, though I don't see the reason for it'. Grasset saw that further argument would be useless, and made no effort to exculpate himself. 'The poor man makes me feel sorry for him, so I've been as conciliatory and cordial as I could,' he told Blum; and to Proust himself he wrote on 29 August; 'it was only natural that I should not renounce a valued author without showing my regret, and there was no reason here for your feelings to be hurt; but I do not wish to increase your troubles by any act of mine. Whatever the sacrifice, I forego publishing the second volume of *A la Recherche du Temps Perdu*.' Proust replied about 22 September, beginning once more 'Dear Friend'. Grasset had behaved admirably, Proust less so; but the transaction which was to enable him to perfect his novel and know the bliss of fame in his lifetime was accomplished.

A major reason for Proust's migration was the ever-increasing size of *A la Recherche*, which made the resumption of publication still more urgent. He had originally written two further volumes of the same length as *Du Côté de chez Swann*, but these, as he told Blum on 31 May 1916, had now become four. The evolution of his novel, from its premature completion in summer 1912 to its final published form, was already far advanced. The nature and significance of these changes must now be examined.

As to the extent of the alterations certainty is possible. *Du Côté de chez Swann* (525 pages in Grasset's edition) contains 170,000 words, and the remaining two volumes, each of approximately equal size and totalling about 340,000 words, would have brought the total of the 1912 version to 510,000 words. The second volume (originally called *Le Côté de Guermantes*) was intended to include what later became *A l'Ombre des Jeunes Filles en Fleurs* and *Le Côté de Guermantes*, comprising in the final version 445,000 words[1]: it was therefore considerably more than doubled. But the largest increase occurred in the last volume, containing the remainder of the novel, which ultimately reached 626,000 words, although as will be seen Proust transferred

[1] This and the following figures are reached by multiplying the number of pages in each section in the *Pléiade* edition by 400, the approximate number of words in each page.

two long episodes from it to positions earlier in the novel: it was therefore nearly quadrupled. The final version of *A la Recherche* contains
1,240,000 words; and the volumes after *Du Côté de chez Swann* were
enlarged from 340,000 words to 1,070,000.

The chapter-headings of the original second and third volumes
were printed opposite the title-page of *Du Côté de chez Swann* in 1913,
and give invaluable information on the contents and structure of the
1912 version. They read as follows: LE CÔTÉ DE GUERMANTES (Chez
Mme Swann.—Noms de pays: le pays.—Premiers crayons du baron
de Charlus et de Robert de Saint-Loup.—Noms de personnes: la
duchesse de Guermantes.—Le salon de Mme de Villeparisis.); LE
TEMPS RETROUVÉ (A l'ombre des jeunes filles en fleurs.—La princesse
de Guermantes.—M. de Charlus et les Verdurin.—Mort de ma
grand'mère.—Les intermittences du cœur.—Les "Vices et les
Vertus" de Padoue et de Combray.—Madame de Cambremer.—
Mariage de Robert de Saint-Loup.—L'Adoration perpétuelle).

The proofs of the second volume printed in June 1914 survive, and
although their present location remains unknown their contents have
been thoroughly studied by Professor Feuillerat, and can be compared in detail with the final version. They comprise 66 galleys,[1] each
containing the text of eight pages, a total of 528 pages.[2] The alterations
in the final version consist partly of retouching, in which Proust
clarifies, enriches and enhances his style and meaning, partly of
additions, which occur at almost every page and range from single
phrases to long new episodes. In *A l'Ombre des Jeunes Filles en Fleurs*,
which Proust enlarged from 98,000 to 210,000 words, the dinners with
Norpois and Bergotte, the Narrator's visits to Odette, Odette's tea-
party with Mme Cottard, the suppers at Rivebelle, the visits to Elstir's
studio at Balbec are greatly enlarged. New episodes include the meeting with Princesse Mathilde in the Bois,[3] the Narrator's glimpse of
Rachel in the brothel and his gift of Aunt Léonie's furniture to the
proprietress, his dinner with the Blochs at Balbec, and the superb
comparison of the glass-fronted restaurant at Rivebelle to an aqua-

[1] Galleys 15 and 16 are wanting, but once existed. Nos. 1-28 (224 pages)
comprise *Le Côté de Guermantes* (these, as already explained, were printed first
in order to supply the NRF extracts of July 1914); nos. 29-66 (304 pages)
comprise *A l'Ombre*.

[2] Proust's estimate that vol. 2 would be of approximately the same length as
Du Côté de chez Swann (525 pages) is thus confirmed.

[3] Proust was at work on this in April 1915, when he asked Lucien Daudet for
technical information on the Princesse's dress.

rium. None of these additions shows any intention to change the main narrative; still less, as some critics have maintained, do they inflate or disrupt it. Proust's revision, both here and throughout the remainder of his novel, springs from a new conception of the ideal scale of *A la Recherche*; his purpose, which he perfectly achieves, is not to expand it, but to bring it to its true magnitude.

Two further alterations in *A l'Ombre*, however, amount to major structural changes. The episode of the Narrator's quarrel with Gilberte, his sight of her at dusk in the Avenue des Champs-Élysées with a young man, (who long afterwards turns out to have been the actress Léa in disguise), and the 'irregular progress of oblivion', is absent from the 1912 version. By inserting it Proust not only deepens the significance of the Narrator's calf-love, but provides an indispensable link between Swann's love and oblivion of Odette at the beginning of *A la Recherche*, and the Narrator's of Albertine at the end. Most important and surprising of all is the omission from the 1912 version of all mention of Albertine and the little band; for the first visit to Balbec then included only the Narrator's relations with Mme de Villeparisis, Saint-Loup, Charlus and Elstir. The table of contents to Volume Three shows that originally there were three sojourns at Balbec, of which the meeting with Albertine and her friends was to form the second, situated in the summer after Mme de Villeparisis's matinée[1] and immediately before the Princesse de Guermantes's soirée. Proust now transferred most of this chapter[2] to the first visit to Balbec, into which he interwove it with consummate skill. The structural advantages of this change are manifest: the first visit to Balbec receives a new depth and beauty, it is fully counterpoised with what now becomes the second and last, and the great theme of the Narrator's love for Albertine ramifies throughout the novel instead of being confined to the last third.[3]

[1] This is why at Doncières (II, 124) and again at Mme de Villeparisis's matinée (II, 225, 276) the Narrator announces his next visit to Balbec for the following spring, whereas in the final version it takes place three years after the first.

[2] A meeting with Morel (then still called Santois) at a concert in the Casino was transferred to the later visit and situated at the railway-station at Doncières.

[3] With the same purpose in view Proust now inserted in *Chez Mme Swann* the first warning hints of the theme of Albertine. Gilberte remembers her at school: "she'll certainly turn out very 'fast' one day," adds Gilberte, "and meanwhile she has the most peculiar ways". Mme Bontemps at Odette's tea-party repeats her niece Albertine's insulting remark to the wife of the under-secretary of state for finance ("Your father was a dishwasher"—in the 1912 version the culprit is

Le Côté de Guermantes in the 1912 version totalled about 72,000 words, in the final version 235,000. Here, too, Proust added short or long passages to almost every page of the proof. These include the opening paragraph (beginning 'The twittering of the birds at dawn seemed insipid to Françoise'), the discussion of military strategy at Doncières with Saint-Loup and his friends, the marvellous rhapsodies on deafness, sleep and the Ladies of the Telephone, and the Narrator's first meeting with Morel. But the proofs end with Charlus escorting the Narrator home after Mme de Villeparisis's matinée, and the remainder of the volume, comprising the death of the grandmother, Albertine's visits, the Narrator's abortive longing for Mme de Stermaria, his dinner with Saint-Loup in the fog, the Duchesse de Guermantes's dinner, the quarrel with M. de Charlus, and the incident of the Duchesse's red shoes, constitutes an enormous addition of 120,000 words. The death of the grandmother was transferred, with a manifest gain in structural balance, from the third volume, where it occurred immediately before the third (afterwards the second) visit to Balbec; so, most probably, was the incident of Swann and the red shoes, since it forms a prelude to the story of the Princesse de Guermantes's soirée.

Grasset's proofs stopped short of the third volume, and the original manuscript, if it still survives, has not yet been revealed; but the 1912 version can still be reconstructed with a fair degree of probability by comparison of its chapter-headings (quoted above) with the final version, supplemented by inferences from *Jean Santeuil* and *Contre Sainte-Beuve*, where much of the same material had already been used.

The volume began, as we have seen, with the Narrator's early acquaintance with Albertine and the little band during a second visit to Balbec, which Proust afterwards incorporated, retaining its original title, in *A l'Ombre des Jeunes Filles en Fleurs*. Next came the Princesse

---

her unnamed daughter); and the Narrator, absorbed in his loss of Gilberte, refuses to accompany his father to an official dinner to which the Bontemps are bringing Albertine, 'a little girl still almost a child' (I, 512, 598, 626). A still more striking insertion links the yet-unknown Albertine with the last incident in her story: a description of Gilberte's handwriting (in which the letters Gi resemble an A, while the last syllable is 'indefinitely prolonged in a waving flourish') prepares for the telegram signed 'Albertine' and beginning 'My dear, you think I am dead, forgive me, I am very much alive . . .', which the Narrator receives at Venice after Albertine's death, and finds a few days later to have come from Gilberte (I, 502; III, 641, 656).

de Guermantes's soirée, which no doubt already included the discovery of the Baron de Charlus's homosexuality, the treatise on the
inhabitants of Sodom, and the Narrator's fear that he has not really
been invited, since these are already present in the corresponding
episode of *Contre Sainte-Beuve*. '*M. de Charlus et les Verdurin*' follows,
and evidently combined in a single episode the Baron's introduction
to the little clan, accompanied by Morel, and his final betrayal and
disgrace; and the whole must have taken place in Paris, since the chapter occurs in the interval between two visits to Balbec. If there was any
equivalent in this chapter of La Raspelière, it must have been in the
country near Paris, like Mme Aubernon's Cœur-Volant to which
Proust had travelled early in the 1890s on a little train, amid the
Charlus-like self-revelations of Baron Doasan. The scene in which the
Queen of Naples befriends the fallen Charlus had already appeared in
Jean Santeuil, though told of the hero Jean himself and the Duchesse
de Réveillon; but for reasons which will be seen shortly, the performance of the Vinteuil Septet did not originally form part of this chapter.
If we compare this primitive form of Charlus's tragedy with the final
version, it will be felt that here is one of the finest of Proust's structural
improvements. By interweaving the rise of the Baron's love for Morel
and his credit with the Verdurins into the second visit to Balbec, and
the decline and fall of both into *La Prisonnière*, Proust has transformed an isolated episode into one of the dominating themes of the
second half of *A la Recherche*, and has developed it in splendid and
terrible counterpoint to the parallel course of the Narrator's love for
Albertine.

The death of the Narrator's grandmother occurred next, im-
imediately preceding his grief for her in the following chapter. But in
this position her death was not only too far separated from the incidents which prepare it (the Narrator's cruelty when Saint-Loup
takes her photograph at Balbec, and the telephone-conversation at
Doncières), but too close to the episode of his grief, the significance of
which lies in its long delay. Proust saw the need for the transference of
this chapter to its final position immediately after Mme de Villeparisis's matinée as early as May 1914 (when he informed Rivière that
it would form the end of his second volume), and it duly appeared
there in the extracts in the NRF of July 1914.

The next chapter, '*Les Intermittences du cœur*', was enormously
lengthened: in the final version it covers nearly two thirds of *Sodome et
Gomorrhe*, the whole of *La Prisonnière*, and all but the last chapter of

Albertine Disparue, amounting in all to nearly 400,000 words, or much more than twice the whole of the original third volume of about 170,000 words. This enlargement was partly motivated, no doubt, by Proust's recent love, imprisonment, jealousy and loss of Agostinelli, to whose memory it is, in a sense, his monument. Yet the original version, as has been shown, must have taken much the same form—a summer at Balbec in which the Narrator falls in love with Albertine, and a winter in Paris in which he torments and loses her—and have had the same function, to prepare by a last and greatest disenchantment for the revelation of Time Regained. But the first size of this crucial episode was clearly far too meagre, and Proust's additions were justified not only because they included so many of the finest passages of *A la Recherche*, but because they were aesthetically and organically necessary for the scale of his novel. The first enlarged version was completed in 1915, in time for the excerpts dedicated to Mme Scheikévitch in November; but he continued his additions during the following years, and we shall find him still at work on the final text of *La Prisonnière* and *Albertine Disparue* at the time of his death.

'Les "Vices et les Vertus" de Padoue et de Combray' must have contained the Narrator's visit to Venice, which was already included in the 1908 version of his novel; moreover, the essential incidents of his arrival, sight of the Golden Angel, and quarrel at sunset with his mother, appear in *Contre Sainte-Beuve*; and in *Du Côté de chez Swann* the Narrator mentions Venice in the list of places where he has lived.[1] The chapter must at first have contained the Narrator's reflections on Giotto's Virtues and Vices in the Capella degli Scrovegni at Padua, and the new meanings they had acquired since Swann gave him photographs of these frescoes long ago at Combray. No doubt Proust decided that he had already exhausted the subject in *Du Côté de chez Swann*; and instead, he finally mentioned only the flying angels in the upper frescoes, which seemed to him in retrospect, as they looped the loop 'like the young pupils of Garros', to allude to Agostinelli's death and to the air-ace who in 1916 became Cocteau's great friend. But the long opening paragraph, in which the sunlight and shade of Venice seem to the Narrator a 'transposition in an entirely different and richer key' of Combray, is no doubt a relic of this earlier version.[2]

'*Madame de Cambremer*' described the unexpected marriage, soon after the Narrator's return from Venice, of Jupien's niece, now the

---

[1] I, 9.
[2] III, 648, 623-6.

adopted daughter of M. de Charlus who has given her the family title
of Mlle d'Oloron, to young Léonor de Cambremer, and her death a
few weeks later. In June 1915 Proust told Lucien Daudet that he
would find 'in the third volume of *Swann*' how 'a single unforeseen
alliance suffices to bring the whole *casus foederis* into play and start a
procession of great names', and would 'appreciate the official
announcement of the young Cambremer girl's death'.[1]

'*Mariage de Robert de Saint-Loup*' told the equally surprising union
of Saint-Loup to Gilberte, and the Narrator's visit to Tansonville. A
similar marriage had occurred in *Contre Sainte-Beuve*, that of 'the
young Marquise de Cardaillec, *née* Forcheville', whose passion for
Balzac comes, says the Narrator, 'from the Swann in her'; and both the
marriage and the sojourn at Tansonville were unobtrusively prepared
in the first pages of *Du Côté de chez Swann*, when the Narrator believes
he has awoken 'in my room at Mme de Saint-Loup's . . . at Tansonville'.[2] Gilberte, likewise, reads Balzac at Tansonville, 'to keep up
with my uncles'.[3]

The final episode, '*L'Adoration perpétuelle*', was an early version of
the Princesse de Guermantes's last matinée, and the title draws a
parallel between the Catholic rite of perpetual adoration of the Real
Presence in the Blessed Sacrament and the Narrator's discovery of the
undying truth of Time Regained, which he has been adoring unawares all through his life. Proust frequently maintained, by way of
illustrating the preordained architecture of his novel to foolish persons
(the tribe is not yet extinct) who thought he just put down anything
that came into his head, that he had written the last chapter immediately after the first. It is not quite certain whether this was literally
true, or whether he alluded only to the second preface to *Contre
Sainte-Beuve*, written in January 1909, in which the revelations of the
madeleine and the uneven paving-stone are told side by side, together
with the sight from a railway-carriage of trees striped with sunlight
and shade, and the tinkling teaspoon which restores the sound of a
hammer on the wagon-wheels. We have seen, however, that these and
other salient episodes of *Le Temps Retrouvé*—the paralysis of Char-

[1] Cf. III, 671, where the letter of intimation is summarised, with its procession
of great names, and the very phrase 'le *casus foederis* venant à jouer' is used.

[2] I, 6-7. Proust explained this passage to Lucien Daudet in August 1913, when
Lucien had just read it in the proofs of *Swann*: 'in the third volume Mlle Swann
marries Robert de Saint-Loup, whom you will meet in the second volume'.

[3] III, 706.

lus,[1] the Prince de Guermantes's library, the rediscovery of *François le Champi*, the Narrator's meditation on his future novel, the realisation that everyone he knew, including himself, has grown old, the apparition of Mlle de Saint-Loup—all date from the period 1909-12. In the first version, nevertheless, when the interval between the death of Albertine and the final matinée was at most ten years, his fellow-guests could only have aged a little, and Mlle de Saint-Loup could only have been a child. The intervention of war, and the consequent further ten years' delay which enabled Proust to revise his novel, aged his characters in the last chapter by two decades instead of one. Once again, just as he had used Agostinelli's death to reinforce the loss of Albertine, he took masterly advantage of a calamity unforeseeable when the first version was written. He inserted the magnificent chapter on 'M. de Charlus during the War', which contains the redemption of Saint-Loup, the ultimate degradation of Sodom, and the explanation of the long gap between the visit to Tansonville and the matinée of the Princesse de Guermantes. The Princesse's matinée became not only a revelation of eternal joy and salvation, but a danse macabre which warns of eternal damnation. The Narrator's elders totter along the precipice where Time falls into Death; by the narrowest margin the Narrator has time to write his work of art before he follows them; and the counterbalancing miracle of Time Regained is affirmed on the human plane by the sixteen-year-old Mlle de Saint-Loup, a personification of the continuity of youth and the spring of love.

In both quality and quantity Proust's additions to his novel were enormous and fundamental. The 1909-12 version stood only half-way in his progress to greatness, occupying a place as far above *Jean Santeuil* as below the final *A la Recherche du Temps Perdu*: it was no doubt a work of genius, but it was not yet a masterpiece. The alterations, however, were not directed primarily at the plot, plan or intention, which remained substantially the same; they were concerned mainly with textural enrichment, enlargement of scale, and structural unity. During the ten years of revision from 1913 to 1922 Proust achieved the ideal form towards which he had moved ever since *Les Plaisirs et les Jours*, and for which the 1909-12 version was only a preliminary study. He changed his novel into itself.

In the summer of 1916, however, this vast process of revision was still at an early stage—except, of course, for *Du Côté de chez Swann*, in

---

[1] Written before 1913, for the manuscript once gives his name in its early form as 'M. de Guercy' (III, 1132-860).

which it was perfectly and irrevocably completed in the seven months of proof-correction before publication, during April to October 1913. From May 1914, when the campaign in which he organised reviewing and publicity for *Swann* was closed, he worked on the revision and prepublication of the second volume planned for October, and no doubt continued despite the moratorium of the war. During the winter, however, he probably 'jumped' from some point in *Le Côté de Guermantes* to the middle of *Sodome et Gomorrhe*, preferring to write of Albertine while his grief for Agostinelli was still fresh. The extracts sent to Mme Scheikévitch in November 1915 show that a new version of the enormous expanse from the second (and now the last) visit to Balbec to the Narrator's oblivion of his dead mistress was by then already written. In the spring of 1916, when he asked Lucien Daudet in April for expert advice on the vanity-case which the Narrator gives Albertine for use on the Little Train,[1] he had evidently returned to *Sodome et Gomorrhe*. As yet he had only completed the first of many revisions, whether sustained or piecemeal.

One of the crucial metamorphoses of *A la Recherche* was inspired by experiences which began in 1907 and culminated in the spring of 1917. It is time to tell the strange story of the Vinteuil Septet.

The passion for music which had subsided during the years of the Dreyfus Affair and Ruskin had returned, momentarily with the violin and piano recital with which Proust regaled his guests at the Ritz on 1 July 1907, and in full force with the Russian Ballet in 1910 and the operas heard on the theatrophone in 1911. Next year, and until early in 1914, he became engrossed in the late quartets of Beethoven, which (although this was not Proust's reason) had suddenly become fashionable in Paris, and were one of the specialities of the newly reconstituted Quatuor Capet. Lauris accompanied him to the Salle Pleyel, where they sat in the private audition-room of the proprietress, screened from the public by a painted canvas partition; and after the concert Proust expressed his emotions with subtle simplicity to the astonished and delighted leader: never, Capet declared afterwards, had he heard

---

[1] Proust had already mentioned the subject to Mme Raymond de Madrazo (Reynaldo's sister Maria) in a letter of 18 February 1916. Later in the year (for the same letter mentions the recent death of Nicolas Cottin and Proust's efforts to aid the widowed and destitute Céline and her infant son), Proust told Albert Nahmias of his intention to consult him on 'the dresses girls wore when dining out at the seaside during our first years at Cabourg', and on the nicknames given to 'the little local train at Cabourg'.

so profound an appreciation both of Beethoven's genius and of the players' interpretation. One night, moved by an irresistible desire ('which perhaps concealed,' Lauris acutely remarked, 'some sign of a secret affinity between composer and hearer'), Proust summoned Capet and his colleagues to 102 Boulevard Haussmann, and listened in solitude to Debussy's quartet.

Among the most welcome features of the revival of the arts in the Paris of 1916, after two years of wartime austerity, was the foundation of the Quatuor Poulet, which specialised in the chamber music of César Franck, Fauré, Chausson, Ravel and Borodin. After a performance of the Franck quartet in November 1916 at the Concert Rouge in the Rue de Tournon, the viola player, Amable Massis, was approached by a pale, black-moustached stranger in a fur coat, who asked if the four musicians would be willing to play Franck's work privately in his apartment. Massis agreed; and a few days later, at the Mephistophelean hour of midnight, Proust arrived by taxi to rouse the young man from bed, despite the indignant resistance of his mother, and to claim his awful promise. Inside the taxi, while the chauffeur reassuringly winked and beamed, the alarmed Massis glimpsed a tureen of mashed potatoes, and a vast eiderdown beneath which Proust instantly crept. Off they drove to collect the leader and first violin, the twenty-year-old Gaston Poulet, the second violin Victor Gentil, and the 'cellist Louis Ruyssen, who made more fuss than anyone. Céleste, wearing formal black with white apron and starched cuffs, towering over her master, received them at 102 Boulevard Haussmann; "she wouldn't have much trouble in knocking *him* out," remarked Massis irreverently. Proust lay on his bed, with the manuscript of *A la Recherche* stacked and strewn on the floor beside him; the players propped their music on the furniture; and at one a.m., in the deep silence of the night and (as Poulet admitted) the superlative acoustics of the corklined bedroom, they performed the Franck quartet in D major. "Would you do me the immense kindness of playing the whole work again?" Proust entreated. The weary players, fortified with a supper of champagne and fried potatoes served by Céleste, did as he asked; and Proust, with cries of delight and congratulation, paid them on the spot from a Chinese casket stuffed with fifty-franc notes. Four taxis awaited them in the blacked-out street below; and next day, charmed with so courteous, appreciative and generous a listener, they sent him a round-robin of thanks. On other evenings they played Fauré's Piano Quartet in G minor, quartets by Mozart, Ravel and

Schumann, the late Beethoven quartets,[1] and the César Franck violin sonata, of which Proust insisted on hearing the third movement again and again. On 4 March 1917, at dinner with Morand and Princesse Soutzo at Larue's, he asked: "Would you like to hear some César Franck?" and, despite the head waiter's protests—"there's a war on, Monsieur Proust, they won't allow music in restaurants!"—he went off to round up the musicians. But at midnight he returned crestfallen and alone; he had woken Poulet ("it was just like Wells's *Food of the Gods*, I was nearly devoured by giant chickens (*poulets*)!" he cried); but Ruyssen was in hospital with appendicitis. Through Dr Pozzi's intervention he saved Massis, who was on convalescent leave after a serious wound, from returning to the front. He plotted to take the whole quartet to Venice, where he would live in a palace and listen to their music while dawn broke over the Grand Canal; but the disaster of Caporetto and the cooling of his enthusiasm put an end to this chimerical plan.

Proust constructed *A la Recherche* from his remembrance of the distant past, which he supplemented during the course of revision from analogous incidents in the present. Occasionally, however, like a scientist devising experiments to fill the gaps in his grand hypothesis, he deliberately sallied out to find the scenes and experiences he needed for his novel. We have seen him visiting Falaise in 1907 in search of 'an unspoiled Balzacian town', and in 1912 the countryside near Paris for the sight of Balbec apple blossom, and the autumnal Bois de Boulogne for a new conclusion to his first volume. But the most remarkable of all these quests was the obsessive listening to chamber-music which enabled him to create the Vinteuil Septet.

The Septet had long been present in *A la Recherche*, but in different places and primitive forms. It was played at first as a quartet at the Princesse de Guermantes's last matinée, where it is still faintly audible, even in the final version, as the music played in the drawing-room during the Narrator's meditation in the Prince's library: "the Princesse won't have the doors opened until it's finished," says the butler.[2] Wisely perceiving that its function was already taken in his concluding chapter by the revelations of the paving-stone and the tinkling saucer,

---

[1] In *A la Recherche* it is M. de Charlus who 'wanted to hear Beethoven's late quartets again, and had some musicians come to play them once a week' (I, 751).

[2] III, 859, 868, 869, 918.

and that it must come, as a miraculous harbinger, somewhere earlier in the novel, Proust then transferred it to the second of the visits to Balbec which, at this time, still numbered three in all. It was now a quintet, played incompetently at the Casino of Balbec by the very ladies whose concerts on the beach had been the torment of Proust's Cabourg evenings in 1911; and it was followed by an organ recital during which, by a hideous irony, a figure based on the paralytic old nobleman whom Proust had met there in 1908 (and who later became Odette's ex-husband, Pierre de Verjus, Comte de Crécy) clambered repeatedly up the steps to the organ, and turned out to be Vinteuil himself, decrepit and deranged, claiming his rightful place as composer beside the organist. Still later, when most of this second visit to Balbec was embodied in the first, the manuscript of this concert came to rest arbitrarily gummed to part of the Narrator's dinner with the Bloch family. Last of all, presumably in 1917, after his association with the Quatuor Poulet, Proust decided to place the episode in its final position, as the central feature of the soirée at which the Verdurins break with Charlus, and entirely rewrote it in its supremely beautiful last version.[1]

Like the Vinteuil Sonata, and like other fictional entities in Proust's novel, whether person, place or work of art, the Septet had many models. And yet, just as Swann borrowed lesser features from many people but was basically Charles Haas, and Balbec from many places but remained basically Cabourg, so the essential models of Vinteuil's music can be distinguished from the non-essential. Proust took a sly pleasure in multiplying the minor origins of the Sonata: he mentioned to Antoine Bibesco in 1913 the prelude to Act One of *Lohengrin*, and Fauré's *Ballade*, to Jacques de Lacretelle in 1918 both these and the Good Friday Spell from *Parsifal*, and 'something by Schubert'. But to each of these confidants he also revealed the profounder models, for the 'little phrase' in Saint-Saëns's Sonata in D Minor, and for the sonata as a whole in César Franck's Sonata in A Major.

The lesser originals of the Septet were not named by Proust, but the reader can still hear and identify them beneath his detailed description of the recital at the Verdurins'. The first movement evokes to the Narrator a seascape from dawn to midday. It begins 'on continuous plane surfaces like those of the sea, amid a harsh silence, an infinite void', and constructs before him, 'in the pink light of dawn, a new universe drawn from silence and night'; and it ends at noon, 'beneath a scorching and transitory sun', with 'a peal of clangorous and liberated bells'. Here, beyond doubt, is the first movement of Debussy's symphonic poem *La Mer*—'*De l'aube à midi sur la mer*'—from its mysterious opening chords in B minor to the last noonday carillon of trumpets and cymbals. Early in the Septet a tune on seven notes is heard, 'like a mystical cock-crow, an ineffable but over-shrill appeal to the eternal morning'; and Debussy's Quartet opens with just such a seven-noted cock-crow:

The same theme reappears, as 'a summons to a supraterrestrial joy', in the last movement of both the Vinteuil Septet and the Debussy Quartet.

But Proust himself revealed the deeper sources of the Septet. 'César Franck's quartet will appear in one of the later volumes,' he told Lacretelle. Franck's Quartet in D major, the very work for which Proust first brought the Quatuor Poulet to his lonely bedroom, was his last and greatest work, and its first performance, at the Salle Pleyel in February 1890, was the only public triumph the disappointed composer ever knew. But Franck's Piano Quintet in F minor was an equally important model. Unlike the Quartet it is haunted by exquisite, evanescent phrases which recall the Franck Sonata, or rather predict it, for the Sonata was written seven years after the Quintet. This is the work of which Proust thought when he imagined the Vinteuil Septet as pervaded by themes from the Vinteuil Sonata: 'in the midst of this music that was so new to me I found myself in the very heart of the Vinteuil Sonata,' says the Narrator; and in the last movement, 'again and again one phrase or another from the Sonata returned, but always changed, with different rhythm and harmony, the same and yet otherwise, as things return in one's own life'.[1] In the manuscript draft of the Vinteuil recital at the Balbec casino Proust had written, by way of a shorthand memorandum that this was indeed the work he had in mind: 'Franck's Quintet (call it something else)'.

[1] III, 249, 259.

PARALLEL PASSAGES IN THE
FRANCK QUINTET AND SONATA

The origins of Vinteuil as a native of Combray and an outraged father remain obscure.[1] But in his shy and noble character, with his displays of alternate humility and innocent vanity, and his situation as a composer, great, neglected, unique and unknown till after his death, he resembles César Franck and no other. Proust would have learned to revere Franck, as a recently dead and saintly master, in 1893 in the salon of Henri de Saussine, where Franck's disciple Vincent d'Indy reigned supreme.[2] He could have heard more from Gabriel Astruc, who tells the pathetic story of Franck bringing a manuscript to his music-publisher Enoch, and saying: "I know it won't sell, I'm forcing you to make sacrifices for me, don't give me too much money." And in a letter to Lucien Daudet of May 1916 Proust repeated the Vinteuil-like anecdote of the indignation of Franck's pupils when he was awarded the cross of the Légion d'Honneur not as a composer, but as teacher of the organ at the Conservatoire. "Not at all," expostulated Franck, "I'm very pleased"; and he added in a confidential whisper: "they told me I had very good chances for next year's list". To Reynaldo's sister Maria in February 1916 Proust explained: 'Vinteuil symbolises the great composer of César Franck's kind (*genre Franck*).'

The Queen of Naples, who champions the broken Charlus at the end of his disastrous soirée, was a historical character, the 'glorious sister of the Empress Élisabeth' of Austria and wife of Francis II, the last King of Naples. During the siege of Gaeta in 1861 the young queen manned the guns against the rebellious populace: "you know how this arm held the rabble at bay at Gaeta long ago," she says, as she

[1] Possibly he was the father of the unfortunate Mlle Joinville d'Artois, the original at Illiers of Mlle Vinteuil. The gentle and sad Ernest Guiraud, professor of advanced composition at the Conservatoire (in which post he was succeeded by Vincent d'Indy), wrote the recitatives for Bizet's *Carmen*, and frequented the salon of Bizet's widow, Mme Straus. Proust used the story of his naïve reply to Mme Straus, when asked if his natural daughter took after her mother ("I don't know, I never saw her dear mother without her hat on") in *A l'Ombre* (I, 859), and the first night of his posthumous opera *Frédégonde* on 18 December 1895 is one of the scenes of *Jean Santeuil* (vol. 3, pp. 66-73). Guiraud died in 1892. Possibly Guiraud and his daughter were among the models of Vinteuil and Mlle Vinteuil.

[2] Proust seems to have drawn many features which Franck and Vinteuil share from d'Indy's monograph *César Franck* (1906), e.g.: 'Franck's language is strictly individual, of an accent and quality hitherto unused, and recognisable among all other idioms. No musician would hesitate as to the authorship of one of his phrases, even if it were unknown to him.' D'Indy is here quoting an article by Paul Dukas in *Chronique des arts*, 1904, no. 33, p. 273.

offers it to the Baron. In the height of his insolent pride Charlus had jested cruelly at her fallen majesty: "she's come to your fête all the way from Neuilly," he boasts to Mme Verdurin, "which she finds a great deal less easy than leaving the Kingdom of the Two Sicilies"; and the exiled Queen in fact lived, during the early 1900s, in poverty-stricken retirement at Neuilly. During the war she joined the German Red Cross, and took cigarettes to French prisoners: "she's a frightful spy," cries Mme Verdurin in 1916, "if we had a more energetic government, that sort'd find itself in a concentration camp". After Proust's death, and a little before her own in 1925, the aged Queen listened with deep interest to a reading from La Prisonnière. "It's odd," she declared, "I never knew this Monsieur Proust, but he seems to know me very well, because he's made me act precisely as I think I would have done."[1]

The soirée at Mme Verdurin's has clear analogies with the Delafosse recital organised by Montesquiou at Baronne Adolphe de Roths-child's on 5 June 1897, when Count Robert was insulted by the Régniers, and quarrelled for ever with poor Delafosse. But that occasion, the insult, the consequent duel, and the vindictive break with the pianist, seemed to Montesquiou himself a personal triumph. The origins of this central event in A la Recherche must be sought deeper, in the otherwise unknown humiliation which Proust endeavoured unsuccessfully to exorcise in the most deplorable chapters of Jean Santeuil, where, in a series of equally preposterous alternative versions, Jean is outraged by Mme Marmet, a prototype of Mme Verdurin, and supported by the strong arm of the Duchesse de Réveillon.[2] A still crueller dishonour is remembered in the scene where Morel rejects the Baron to remain with the Verdurins. In 1896, during the series of quarrels which ended their passionate love and began their lifelong friendship, Reynaldo had angrily refused to leave a musical evening, and left Proust to go home alone and bitterly hurt. There is no more striking sign of Proust's moral maturity than the selfrighteous resentment with which he used the same episodes in Jean Santeuil, and the tragic grandeur to which he transformed them in La Prisonnière. Even so, these humiliations buried in the past of twenty years ago were still

---

[1] III, 322, 274, 765.
[2] Jean Santeuil, III, 66-102, 93. Mme Verdurin's double-edged exclamation concerning Charlus quoted in the same episode (III, 278)— 'Quelle tapette il a! Quelle tapette!"—was uttered in all innocence by Mme Alphonse Daudet, to the deep embarrassment of all present, to Montesquiou at a tea-party. Tapette means both 'chatter' and 'homosexual'.

too shameful to be laid to the account of the Narrator. Proust transferred them to the broad, bowed shoulders of the Baron de Charlus; and in the next chapter we shall find him casting upon the same mighty scapegoat the burden of still graver sins, committed in the very present, in the dark nights of war.

Chapter 23

THE PIT OF SODOM

(*March 1917 – November 1918*)

A NEW dynasty of friends was appearing, for whom Proust was inseparable from the novel for love of which they approached him; and he, in turn, cherished them partly for the sake of *A la Recherche du Temps Perdu*, which they would help to fame within his lifetime, and to immortality when he was dead. Proust had known Henri Bardac through Reynaldo for several years, but without realising, as he confessed to Lucien, that he was 'remarkably intelligent and excessively nice', until Bardac became an enthusiast for *Swann* and in September 1914 suffered a severe head-wound at the Battle of the Marne. In his hospital at Angers, where he was nursed by nuns of the Perpetual Adoration who also adored Proust's letters, Bardac received an enormous telegram beginning: 'Although the extent of my admiration for your heroism is equalled only by your antipathy towards myself', and continuing with a superb disquisition on the Perpetual Adoration, which at that time was the emblematic title of the last chapter of Proust's final volume. Bardac, an Oxford graduate, was soon posted to the French Embassy in London, where he spread the gospel of *Swann*. On leave in Paris in 1915 he became Proust's favourite visitor, though a little hard of hearing from his wound, and reduced him to helpless laughter with readings from Thackeray's *Yellowplush Papers*.[1] Bardac's was the wound-scar which the Narrator saw, 'more august and mysterious for me than a giant's footprint', on the forehead of Saint-Loup.[2]

London had received early news of *Swann* in an unsigned review by Mary Duclaux in the *Times Literary Supplement* for 4 December 1913. Mme Duclaux wrote with insight of Proust's 'images in which matter and memory are subtly combined in a sudden warm flood of life revived, without the intervention of the understanding'; she noticed the

---

[1] The burlesque letter of the Narrator's literary young footman, Joseph Périgot, owes much to these readings (II, 566-7).

[2] III, 757.

crucial significance of the Two Ways, and compared *Swann*, as a study
of a child's contact with a corrupt adult world, to Henry James's *A
Small Boy* and *What Maisie Knew*.[1] Perhaps the Master felt urged to
read *Swann* for himself after seeing this article. He obtained a copy
early in 1914 from his friend Edith Wharton, the distinguished American novelist in Paris, and was discovered immersed in it by Logan
Pearsall Smith. 'His letter to me showed how deeply it had impressed
him,' wrote Mrs Wharton, 'he seized upon *Swann* and devoured it in a
passion of curiosity and admiration ... he recognised a new mastery, a
new vision, and a structural design as yet unintelligible to him but as
surely there as hard bone under soft flesh in a living organism.' He
wrote Proust a magnificent letter, informing him that this was an
extraordinary book for so young an author (Proust was then forty-
two, and James seventy), and that it was a great pity he lived in
advance of his time. *Du Côté de chez Swann* was the greatest French
novel since *La Chartreuse de Parme*, he truly declared, but perhaps
(and here James was fortunately in error), Proust would suffer the
fate of Stendhal and not be recognised in his lifetime.[2]

Probably it was Mrs Wharton, for he was her lover (unless it was
Mme Scheikévitch, for she was his friend), who introduced Walter
Berry to *Swann*. Berry was a dignified, white-moustached, intelligent
and elderly American ('like an American in a Henry James novel,' said
Paul Morand), an expert in international law, an ardent propagandist
for the entry of the United States into the war, and president of the
American Chamber of Commerce in Paris. In May 1916 Berry was
delighted to find, at Belin's bookshop on the Left Bank, a volume
bound in 1709 with the arms of Paulin Prondre de Guermantes, and
sent it to the equally delighted Proust. Berry called and stayed till
dawn, learning the future history of the Guermantes family, and slyly
quoting Remy de Gourmont's saying: 'One only writes well about
things one hasn't experienced'—to which Proust, feeling that he must
stress the imaginative aspect of his work rather than its foundation in

[1] It would be arguable, however, that in *Du Côté de chez Swann* the child is
less innocent than the grown-ups.

[2] Proust proudly referred to this letter when he wrote to Lucien Daudet in
April 1918, of Léon Daudet's well meaning portrait of him in *Salons et Journaux*,
in which Proust is presented as a kind of eccentric, talented child: 'He doesn't
know what Henry James, whom he admires, said about me.' Lucien's comment,
that 'Henry James, despite his apparent benevolence, was in fact as I have been
told rather malicious, and what he had been reported to Proust as saying was
extremely unkind', is a sheer misapprehension.

reality, evasively replied: "That's my whole novel!" This prudent Franco-American, whose steadying influence on the passionate Mrs Wharton was mistakenly deplored by his rivals, became one of Proust's most useful and valued friends.

Among the proselytes converted by Bardac at the London embassy was the brilliant young Paul Morand, a friend of Cocteau, Giraudoux and the Bibescos. His verdict on *Swann* was reported to the author: "It beats Flaubert hollow!"; and in the spring of 1916, on leave in Bardac's Paris flat, Morand was woken by a night-visitor who proclaimed, 'in a ceremonious, bleating voice': "I am Marcel Proust." In August 1916 Morand was transferred to the Quai d'Orsay, and during the winter began a series of frequent visits to 102 Boulevard Haussmann. Many of the anecdotes then told to Morand by Proust reappear in *A la Recherche*. The bluff Grand Duke Paul, when taken to see the distinguished actress Mme Bartet, had applauded like thunder and roared: "Bravo, old girl!"—the very words with which, at the Princesse de Guermantes's soirée, the Grand Duke Wladimir his brother expresses his joy, 'clapping his hands as if he were at the theatre', when Mme d'Arpajon is drenched by the garden fountain.[1] The Marquise de Ganay owned a superb Cézanne, which her husband had never seen, because, he said: "It's in her bedroom, so I've never had occasion to!" So the Duc de Guermantes, when Oriane explains her plans for Swann's enormous photograph of the coinage of the Knights of Malta, declares: "If it's in your room, I may manage never to see it", 'without thinking of the revelation he so indiscreetly made of the negative character of his conjugal relations'.[2] The infatuation of Comte Greffulhe for the Comtesse de La Béraudière was now public property. Proust, wearing his wadded overcoat, had visited the couple on a hot evening in June 1913 in search of material for his novel. "He left as pleased as Punch," remarked the Count, "but he didn't fool me, I could see what he was after, I'm no child!" Proust returned in July 1915, to the fury of Montesquiou, whose pressing invitations to the Palais Rose he had eluded on the plea of ill-health: 'I had no idea my call on Mme de La Béraudière would cause me so much trouble,' he told Gautier-Vignal. In 1917 the aged Comte Greffulhe tried to keep his beloved a prisoner, with an unsuccess which reminded Proust of Agostinelli's captivity; but she evaded him, sending her concierge's wife to keep him company (Cocteau one day surprised the Count reading Hugo's *Légende des Siècles* to this amiable woman), or

[1] II, 658.   [2] II, 593.

ordering her chamber-maid to pace the bedroom-floor over the waiting nobleman, while she herself went out to call on friends, and the
unsuspecting M. Greffulhe wrote gallant verses to greet her reappearance:

> '*When I hear your tiny tootsies*
> *Pitter-patter, pitter-patter . . .*'[1]

It is said that he left her far too much money in his will, and his death in
1932 at the age of eighty-four was followed by family litigation.
Similarly there are rumours during the war, Saint-Loup reports, that
Oriane intends to divorce her husband[2]; and Odette in *Le Temps
Retrouvé* has become the Duc de Guermantes's mistress, is forced to
lunch, dine and spend every evening with him, eludes her sequestration
to mock him with her friends, and 'is certain to be his principal
legatee'.[3]

On 4 March 1917 Proust was introduced at Larue's to Morand's
friend and future wife, the Roumanian-Greek Princesse Hélène
Soutzo: 'he studied her black wrap and ermine muff,' wrote Morand,
'like an entomologist absorbed in the nervures of a firefly's wing,
while the waiters fluttered in circles around him'. It was on this evening that he went in search of the Quatuor Poulet, 'so that we can hear
some César Franck', and returned crestfallen. Rain lashed the windows of the Princesse's apartment at the Ritz while Proust, huddled in
his fur coat, his face 'the colour of endives blanched in a cellar', gave an
hour's monologue on Flaubert, 'which, as a concert of chamber-
music,' wrote Morand, 'was quite as good as the one we missed'. The
Princesse was as beautiful and witty as Morand had foretold; at Bucha-
rest, where she was rivalled and surpassed only by the incomparable
Princesse Marthe Bibesco, people had called her 'Minerva'; and
Proust, for almost the last time, was captivated by a fascinating young
woman who belonged to a friend.

He had not set foot in the Ritz since his grand dinner-party in July
1907, but now he began to dine there several times a week; and when
the lights in the vast restaurant were extinguished at 9.30, as wartime
regulations demanded, he vanished mysteriously aloft to Princesse
Soutzo's room. On 23 April he dined at the Ritz with Morand, Princesse Soutzo, Cocteau, and Mme de Chevigné, whom he had aban-

1   '*Quand j'entends vos petits petons*
             Trotte-menu, trotte-menu . . .'
2 III, 738.   3 III, 1015-20.

doned after his regular calls of last summer, alleging that he 'never went out in the evening'. In all innocence the Princesse mentioned his nightly visits: "the lift-boy brings him straight up, he doesn't have to be announced!" Mme de Chevigné was enraged, an 'appalling drama' ensued, and Proust, who had not forgotten her cruelty in the Avenue de Marigny twenty-five years before, wrote the poor lady a stern letter beginning: 'When a person you once loved turns out to be stupid . . .'

One of his last incarnations began; he was now famous as 'Proust of the Ritz'. The great hotel became his second home, a substitute for the palaces of Cabourg, Venice and Évian which he would never see again, and for the salons of the Faubourg, scattered by the war, whose surviving inmates now dined in strange company round him. At the Ritz he found again the movement and enigmas of a miniature world, the comfort and security of family life, the satisfaction of his lifelong craving for reciprocal service and gratitude. He wrote in his cork-lined bedroom, but went to the Ritz to live. "They don't hustle me, and I feel at home there", he said.

A group of very juvenile page-boys and very old waiters sur-rounded his table. "Who is the younger of the two ladies in the corner?" he asked, "I have to find out, because she's just like one of the characters in my book. I know the elder already—ah, if you could have seen her in my time!" The chamberlain of this court approached: "I haven't eaten anything for two days, Olivier," Proust declared, "I've been writing; but first I want very strong black coffee, double strength, so," he added earnestly, "you mustn't be afraid to charge me double for it on my bill." When he left his pockets were empty, and all but one of the staff had been fantastically tipped. "Would you be so kind as to lend me fifty francs?" he asked the door-man, who produced a wallet of banknotes with alacrity. "No, please keep it—it was for you"; and Proust repaid the debt with interest next evening.

The head-waiter at the Ritz, the celebrated Olivier Dabescat, was a Basque whom César Ritz had lured from Paillard's at the inauguration of his hotel in 1898. Olivier was tall, handsome, distinguished, and slightly sinister; in his devoted genius for his profession he displayed the sanctity of a high-priest, the tact of a diplomat, the strategy of a general, and the sagacity of a great detective. "I have given Monsieur the best table," he would whisper, a dozen times each evening, when-ever a favourite client entered; but of the Grand Duke Boris, im-poverished after the Revolution, he remarked with disdain: "that sort only drinks beer nowadays". 'For Proust Olivier was a kind of chief of secret police, and replaced Montesquiou as an informer,' thought the Duchesse de Clermont-Tonnerre, who saw them not only in private conference at the Ritz, but walking together in the Bois de Boulogne; 'I wonder what they found to talk about?' marvelled Mme Ritz in her memoirs. Proust gave him a set of *A la Recherche* inscribed 'To my friend Olivier, with my compliments'. "People say you help Monsieur Proust in his work, and that he owes a great deal of his novel to you," observed the social butterfly Gabriel Louis Pringué; and Olivier replied, proudly but discreetly: "So it is murmured." Aimé, the head-waiter of the Grand Hôtel at Balbec, although he owes a little also to Hector at the Hôtel des Réservoirs and to Charles at Larue's, is based chiefly on this equivocal and indispensable personage.

For five weeks in the spring of 1917 Proust was visited by Emmanuel Berl, a young writer-to-be, now invalided from the war, and tormented between a mistress, a fiancée, and the lifelong spell of the mysterious Sylvia. Berl was distantly related by marriage, as was Proust himself, to Bergson; he was a cousin of the poet Henri Franck who had loved Mme de Noailles and died in 1912; and he had read *Sésame et les Lys* in the trenches, and written an enthusiastic letter in which Proust, much moved, found grains of shrapnel embedded. As he entered Proust laid the manuscript-book on which he was working upon the tall bedside column of its companions, and taught, night after night, the black gospel of human solitude and the emptiness of human love. Berl, unconvinced, returned to Sylvia. He revisited Proust with the good news, that the true union of human hearts is possible; but Proust, towering like a thundercloud, turned upon the refractory disciple in one of his rare fits of monstrous rage. "You are stupid, stupider than Léon Blum!" he cried; and retiring to his frosted bathroom to dress for the Ritz he hurled abuse, cries of "Get out!" and at last even his slippers. The disciple left, for ever; but Berl was destined nevertheless, for he was more Proustian in practice than in theory, to work out for long years in his own person the ineluctable tragedy of the Narrator and Albertine.

At a tragic and embarrassing time for Roumanians, whose country declared war in August 1916 at the Allies' entreaty and was now defeated and occupied by Germany, Antoine Bibesco had arrived in Paris from London in January 1917. Antoine asked more questions than ever, and answered fewer, always under seal of secrecy. "I see my exports are getting bigger than my imports," Proust told him rue-fully, and complained: "Even when Antoine's only quoting Dostoevsky, he always says: 'but that's strictly between ourselves, isn't it?' And whenever I tip too heavily, he hurls himself on the waiters to find how much it was, and then tells them I've made a mistake, just to ruin my effect." "Do you find me altered in the last five years?" asked Antoine, as they supped on 17 March with Morand off Céleste's cider and chipped potatoes. "Yes, you're less." "Less what? Less intelligent? Less good-looking?" "Just less," replied the implacable Marcel. A few days later Antoine left for a fortnight in Spain; and every evening an enormous and inexplicable dish of ravioli arrived at 102 Boulevard Haussmann, followed at ten o'clock by a waiter who asked: "Was there enough ravioli, Monsieur?" "I haven't any enemies," lamented Proust at the Ritz on 30 March, "so I'm bound to suspect my friends"; and he darkly recalled telling Antoine how easy it was for him to dine at home, 'just by sending out for some ravioli'. The Roumanian General Iliesco was at their table: "Who's that chap in the white tie and dinner-jacket?" he asked, greatly intrigued, and declared his immediate intention of reading *Du Côté de chez Swann*. "What's it like?" he enquired, and Morand replied: "It isn't like anything, General."

In England, a little before the War, Prince Emmanuel Bibesco had taken greatly to Antoine's friend, the young Enid Bagnold. One day, as she sat with Antoine, a mysterious hand appeared round the edge of the door, offering a bouquet of withered flowers: it was Emmanuel who had seized this ambivalent posy, by way of introduction, from a vase in the hall. Emmanuel paid this brilliant girl the supreme compliment of admitting her to his passion for old churches; but she remembers a day when he hurried ahead to visit a village church in the home counties and returned saying: "We'll go back now, it's too beautiful for you to see." "The Bibesco brothers were my university," Miss Bagnold has said. Those who value her novels and plays for the unique originality of their fantastic yet classic vision, may nevertheless recognise in them a strand of lucid French imagination which appears also in the work of the Bibescos' friends, Giraudoux, Cocteau and Morand, even in Proust himself, and is connected in its origins with the unwritten art of that 'cruel and miraculous pair'.

In the spring of 1914 Emmanuel returned from a visit to Japan already touched by the cold finger of paralysis, and henceforth shunned the light of day and of life. The left side of his face was distorted; he announced day after day for his suicide, jesting at death as he had jested at life, guarded and frustrated by the distracted Antoine.

Now, in April 1917, he joined his brother in Paris, and visited for the last time the ancient mansions of the Marais, which spoke kindly to his own decay. On the 12th Antoine called on Proust with Morand: "I've left Emmanuel down in the cab," he said, "because he doesn't want people to see him." They descended, and Antoine with gentle authority prevented Emmanuel from giving up his place in the back seat: "The Bibesco brothers face the driver!" he declared. Proust and Morand took the two tip-up seats; but Emmanuel, with a laugh which made sobs rise in Marcel's throat, cried: "Cabman, drive backwards, so that Marcel Proust and Paul Morand may think they are facing forwards!" Proust, divining that Emmanuel was doomed, wept all that night, observed by Céleste: so Françoise watches the Narrator's tears for the death of Saint-Loup.[1]

Early in August Proust heard reassuring news: Morand had lunched with Emmanuel in London, Étienne de Beaumont had visited a church with him; but on the 22nd the death-devoted invalid evaded his friends and killed himself at Datchet. Miss Bagnold walked with Antoine all night on the Embankment, below the house in Grosvenor Road which the brothers had shared, to persuade him not to join Emmanuel. "Don't speak to me of this ever," said Antoine finally, "and don't speak of your silence." Proust's suffering, as he told Princesse Marthe Bibesco in April 1918, was 'double, uncured, I hope incurable; for I felt the sorrow of Antoine, and I had to accept the idea that I should never again see one of those who were among my dearest companions on this earth'. His grief for Emmanuel joined his loss of Fénelon. The sunlight of youth in which they had gazed, fifteen years before, from the tower of Coucy over the flowering apple-trees of the Ile de France, was extinguished for ever, and the darkness of war had reached its nadir.

On 13 October proofs of *A la Recherche* began to arrive from the NRF's printers, the firm of La Semeuse at Étampes. Imagining that all five volumes would now go to press, but even so exaggerating fantastically, Proust told his friends that he had 5000 pages to correct ('or rather 15,000, as there will be three sets of each'). The new edition of *Swann* was postponed to await simultaneous publication with *A l'Ombre* after the coming of peace[2]; but only two-thirds of *A l'Ombre* had been printed when, early in December 1917, the compositors of

---

[1] III, 849.

[2] The *achevé d'imprimer* is 14 June 1919. The process of enrichment and enlargement, which Proust had decided to apply successively to every volume

La Semeuse were conscripted. Gallimard and Copeau had just left on a propaganda mission to the United States; Rivière, after a gallant attempt to escape from his prison-camp at Hülseberg, was now ill and interned in Switzerland; Proust could only harass their deputy, the brave Mme Lemarié, and complain to Gide.

Meanwhile, not without pride, he pointed out to Lucien and to a new young friend, Jacques de Lacretelle, that it was 'futile to write novels, because life catches up with one!' Louis de Talleyrand-Périgord, aged fifty, married on 17 November 1917 the wealthy widow Cecilia Blumenthal, aged fifty-four, promising according to rumour to adopt the son of her first marriage and to surrender to the young man his own title of Duc de Montmorency. Purists in the Faubourg Saint-Germain felt this title was hardly his to give. It had been bestowed as recently as 1862 by the usurping Napoleon III upon the bridegroom's father, Adalbert de Talleyrand-Périgord, on the death of Adalbert's mother Anne, the last of the true Montmorencys. Proust felt obliged to delete from his novel an involuntarily prophetic remark of M. de Charlus, lest people should think he alluded to young M. Blumenthal. "They might just as well give it to M. Bloch!" the Baron was to have remarked, in denying Adalbert de Montmorency's right to the name. But he had his revenge in a far more important incident of A la Recherche, the amazing marriage of Mme Verdurin to the Prince de Guermantes,[1] which is founded on the strange rise of Mme Blumenthal. The Faubourg, however, could do nothing, except to nickname the bridegroom 'Momorenthal'.[2]

Proust had many other anxieties in the last months of 1917. His

[1] III, 955-6.
[2] In the event M. de Talleyrand-Périgord did not adopt his stepson, and kept the title of Duc de Montmorency for himself. His father Adalbert de Montmorency (1837-1915) is twice mentioned in A la Recherche (I, 640; III, 862) as a friend of Swann and Charlus; while both the Duc de Guermantes (II, 531, 592) and Charlus (III, 267) cast aspersions on his title.

of his novel, was already complete for Du Côté de chez Swann in November 1913. The text therefore remained unaltered, except for a few insignificant verbal corrections, and two equally small but more important amendments necessitated by later developments in A la Recherche. Saint-Loup's garrison-town was named for the first time Doncières (I, 9, 959); and in order to prepare for the war-chapter in his last volume, in which Combray would be in the front line, Proust altered the place-name Chartres (where Odette and Gilberte were supposed to be staying on the day of the family walk to Tansonville) to Rheims and Laon (I, 136, 145, 961).

brother Robert, always seeking the post of greatest danger, left for the
Italian front in mid-November soon after the disastrous defeat of
Caporetto.[1] Montesquiou had ominously begun to write his autobiography, spreading consternation in everyone who had ever known
him. Proust providently offered 'my own humble contribution of
observed absurdities', together with a list of persons to whom he had
recently spoken highly of Count Robert, and an invitation to dinner
with Princesse Soutzo; but the Count sent only a peal of magnificent,
enraged and incomprehensible thunders of rebuke from the Hôtel
Garnier, 'which he seems,' Proust told Lucien, 'to have chosen for his
Mount Sinai'. Princesse Soutzo was awaiting an operation for appendicitis, which she postponed month after month until Morand's
departure for the French Embassy in Rome on 10 December. Proust
gave her expert medical advice, visited her daily before and after her
operation, and made himself responsible for telegrams to the exiled
Morand. His relations with Mme Scheikévitch were permanently
strained by his resentment at a report of remarks she had made about
him to her friends after he dined with her at the Hôtel Crillon on 22
November, and by his concern, for which he thought her insuffi-
ciently grateful, at her financial losses from the October Revolution in
Russia. He mislaid his certificate of exemption from military service,
and feared arrest as a deserter during his midnight walks, or even at the
Ritz, where the police were showing an embarrassing interest in able-
bodied male diners. He was alarmed by new symptoms in his perpetual illness, on which Robert had warned him before departing: his
eyesight had been declining since early 1915, though he had never yet
risen early enough to see an oculist, and at times his heart seemed
about to burst from palpitations. Lastly, he must find ready money for
the interest-payments of 22,000 francs per annum on his 1911 shares-
loan of 275,000 francs,[2] for an old lady friend, 'whom it is my moral
obligation to assist in her great misfortune',[3] and perhaps for certain
obscurer purposes.

[1] Venice at this moment seemed in danger of capture, and Proust tried in vain
to induce one of the great daily newspapers to accept an article on Venice,
probably based on the Narrator's visit with his mother after Albertine's death.

[2] As he told Mme Catusse in 1916, this investment brought in about 32,780
francs, leaving the rather meagre net profit of 10,780 francs, or not quite 4 per cent.

[3] Not Mme Scheikévitch, to whom he mentioned this lady as an artist who
could no longer persuade the dealers to buy her work, but perhaps Mme
Lemaire, or Mme Hayman (now a talented sculptress), both of whom were in
reduced circumstances during the war.

Recently he had given away the less valuable portion of the family furniture, which had been stored for eleven years in a warehouse. 'I've made a crowd of unfortunates happy with it,' he told Mme Catusse. But the two best carpets of his parents' home were still at the Place Clichy store and the Bon Marché repository; and the dust-furred, disused dining-room of 102 Boulevard Haussmann contained a vast sideboard, crystal lustres, thirty leather chairs; he also had two tapestries, the family silver in unopened packing-cases, and a particularly precious suite of four Louis XVI armchairs and sofa. In November 1917 he enlisted the help of Walter Berry, Mme Catusse and Mme Straus, in one of those curious paroxysms of battening on his friends which intermittently formed part of the profound generosity of this most generous of men. Walter Berry ('he knows all the rich Americans') lost interest. Mme Catusse was indefatigable, but could only find a pair of antiquarian ladies, who opened the dining-room shutters at two in the afternoon ('such a thing has never happened since I came to live here,' he remarked with horror), and offered too little. The Strauses, however, sold the Louis XVI suite for the splendid sum of 10,000 francs, and the carpets, after storing them in their own home and displaying them to prospective purchasers, for 4000. Proust declared himself solvent again.

The last year of war began with a suave letter of New Year greetings from the grateful Olivier, and an exchange of wishes for victorious peace with Walter Berry: 'but meanwhile', Proust added, 'the universal anguish keeps us shut in the same Ark, and the Deluge is not yet over'. As on a New Year's Day nine years before, when he returned through white streets to eat the madeleine, snow had fallen on Paris; but now he emerged undaunted at midnight to walk alone, as was his strange new habit on evenings when he had dined at home. An oval moon, two days past the full, rode over the unlit city[1]; for this was the very night on which the Narrator walks through wartime Paris, when 'the rays of moonlight lay on the snow in the Boulevard Haussmann as if on a glacier in the Alps', and the boulevard seemed 'a field in Paradise, woven of petals from blossoming pear-trees'.[2] The first soldiers from the United States had arrived in Paris a week before; and as Proust trudged along this frozen meadow he was stopped by two American privates, who asked him the way to the Hôtel Bedford. In silence, for he could not speak English and they

[1] The moon was full on the night of 29/30 December 1917.
[2] III, 736.

spoke only broken French, and much moved at the thought of how far they had come to offer their lives, he led the young men (as he allusively told Berry) '*à la recherche de l'Hôtel Bedford*'. He pretended to them, and afterwards to Berry, that he was obliged to enquire the way, though he had good cause to know it well. The highly respectable Hôtel Bedford was, and is still, at No. 17 in the nearby Rue de l'Arcade, which runs from the Boulevard Haussmann opposite the Gare Saint-Lazare into the Boulevard Malesherbes by Proust's former home. At No. 11, only three doors further on, was Jupien's brothel, the Hôtel Marigny.

The proprietor was Albert Le Cuziat, a Breton born at Tréguier on 30 May 1881. As a boy of sixteen he had set out to seek his fortune, armed with a letter of recommendation from his parish priest to a brother-cleric in Paris, who found him a post as third footman with the Polish Prince D——. Albert was seen and appreciated by his master's friend and fellow-countryman Prince Constantin Radziwill, who begged him from Prince D—— and promoted him to first footman.

Prince Constantin, the father of Proust's friend Loche, was famous for the strength and beauty of his squad of twelve footmen, to each of whom he is said to have presented a pearl necklace. "Taking the good years with the bad," the Prince informed Montesquiou, "blackmail costs me 70,000 francs a year"; and Count Robert was fond of repeating the little epigram which has been quoted already:

> '*It is most uncivil*
> *To mention ladies to Constantin Radziwill*.'[1]

Prince Constantin was the evident original of the Prince de Guermantes, about whose activities Charlus is similarly indiscreet,[2] in his later aspect as an invert. He reappears in Jupien's brothel as the Prince de Foix, 'father of Saint-Loup's friend, and like his son a tall, handsome man, who gave his wife the impression that he passed a good deal of time at his club, but in fact spent hours at Jupien's gossiping to corner-boys about people in society'.[3]

While in his employment Albert spent a delightful evening with a young man who accosted him in the Rue Jouffroy, and behaved with the utmost kindness and generosity, but refrained from revealing his

---

[1]   '*Parler femmes est incivil*
                          Chez Constantin Radziwill.'

[2] III, 306-7.
[3] III, 827-8.

identity. A few days later the Prince gave a soirée, at which it was Albert's duty to announce the guests; and among these he recognised, at the moment of enquiring his name, which Albert then bawled out with astonished pride, the terrified features of his recent admirer, the Comte de S—. Proust used the story of Albert's adventure, after he heard it many years later from Albert himself, for the young Duc de Châtellerault at the Princesse de Guermantes's soirée, when the usher, 'who knew his heraldry well enough to complete for himself a title that seemed too modest, shouted with professional vehemence softened by intimate affection: "His Highness My Lord the Duke of Châtellerault!" '[1]

During a succession of posts as footman to the Prince d'Essling, Comtesse Greffulhe, Count Orloff and the Duc de Rohan, Albert acquired a profound devotion to the French nobility, particularly to the minority (neither larger nor smaller than in other layers of society) whose vice he shared and loved to assist. Proust met him towards 1911, when he served Count Orloff, and, attracted intellectually rather than physically by the personality of this still handsome but no longer young man, invited him to spend the evening at 102 Boulevard Haussmann. "How very witty!" he exclaimed at some remark of Albert's as they climbed the stairs, and Albert capped it with: "No, it was only staircase wit!"[2] He discovered that Albert possessed an extraordinary erudition on the etiquette and genealogy of the nobility, and tested him with imaginary situations from his novel. "The Duchesse de Guermantes is giving a dinner for a general and a bishop: to which should she give the place of honour?" "The bishop takes precedence," replied Albert immediately, "and must sit on the Duchesse's right." "And suppose she invited the Duchesse d'Uzès, who is the first Duchesse in France, and Princesse Murat, whose family although more recent was once royal?" "The Duchesse de Guermantes," Albert answered with equal decision, "would *never* ask the Duchesse d'Uzès and Princesse Murat on the same evening!" "You are as learned as Pico della Mirandola, and as witty as Mme du Deffand," cried Proust; and he called Albert 'my walking *Almanach de Gotha*'. He produced his cheque-book: "Please let me give you a modest indemnity for your trouble, say a hundred francs." Albert

[1] II, 634-7.
[2] Albert's little joke consisted of reversing the usual meaning of '*esprit d' escalier*', which signifies the brilliant retort that only occurs to one on the stairs after leaving, when it is too late to make it.

refused. "You are quite right, it isn't enough, I'll make it a hundred and fifty"; and Albert, who was not grasping, was obliged to accept before the figure mounted still higher. Proust sent Odilon and his taxi evening after evening to fetch Albert, paid by cheque for his valuable conversation on each occasion, and wrote letters for which the first footman was teased unmercifully by his colleagues.[1] After Proust's death Albert possessed several hundred of these, most of which were stolen and hawked to visiting inverts in the gay Paris of the 1920s, while the rest, he said, "I gave to my doctor, and other acquaintances."

It was towards the spring of 1917, after their relationship had presumably lapsed for several years during the reign of Agostinelli and the beginnings of war, that Albert discovered his true vocation. He was thirty-six, and could no longer serve his beloved superiors as in the days of youth; but he could be the cause of others' serving them, and his wide experience made him uniquely able to select both customers and staff. He decided to open a male brothel, gave notice to his last employer, the Duc de Rohan, and with the financial help of Proust took over the Hôtel Marigny, 11 Rue de l'Arcade, from its former proprietor M. Plaghki. The new establishment was partly furnished, especially in the entrance-hall and Albert's own bedroom, with the second-best chairs, sofas and carpets of Proust's dead parents. This was the furniture which he had stored in a warehouse ever since his removal from the family home in 1906, and now gave away, as he told Mme Catusse truly in October 1917, 'to make a crowd of unfortunates happy'. Similarly the Narrator presents 'some of the furniture inherited from Aunt Léonie, notably a huge sofa' to the proprietress of Bloch's heterosexual brothel, 'because she needed furniture, and I wanted to show my appreciation'. 'I never set eyes on it, because for want of space at home it was all piled in a warehouse,' he says.[2] For the financing of Jupien's brothel,[3] and for many of the incidents which the Narrator sees there, Proust preferred to transfer the responsibility from himself to the Baron de Charlus.

Here the tall Albert sat stiffly enthroned at the reception-desk, engrossed as the client entered in some textbook of genealogy, with bald head from which the golden hair had receded, pale forehead, thin lips, strangely sharp profile, and blue eyes still bright as the sky of his

[1] Charlus embarrasses Mme Verdurin's footman in the same way (III, 259).
[2] I, 578.
[3] III, 817.

native Brittany. Upstairs was his private room, which he called the Royal Chamber, because he was sovereign prince of this Sodom, or the Vatican Library, because it contained his little collection of books on history and heraldry. This is the room of which Jupien says, in words which must surely have been spoken by Albert to Proust (since in order to explain the allusion Proust is compelled to attribute his own translation of Ruskin's *Sesame and Lilies* to the Narrator): "I leave the light on in my little window to show that I'm at home, and you can come in: it's my Sesame. But if it's Lilies you're after, you'd better try elsewhere."[1] Partly because it amused him, partly out of professional secrecy, Albert never called his customers by their real names: one was Jean the Pole, another the Grand Duke,[2] and a particularly generous one was God's Gift on a Rainy Day (*'la Providence des Jours creux'*). Jupien has the same habit: his guests are nicknamed Monsieur Eugène, Monsieur Victor, Pamela the Enchantress, the Man in Chains (M. de Charlus himself), and he refers to his establishment, again probably in Albert's own words, as the Temple of Immodesty.[3] Perhaps not Verdun nor the Somme, but the nocturnal Hôtel Marigny in the Rue de l'Arcade, where zeppelins or gothas droned overhead in the starlight, and poor soldiers and lonely civilians entered to perform the ultimate act of hopeless men, was the true centre of the war.

Proust was virile himself, and had always preferred virility in young men; but in this terrible period of his descent into hell he was led, by certain long-quiescent and temporarily reviving impulses, to desire also violence and cruelty. By an irony as inevitable in vice as in love, these qualities were no less hard to find than the devotion and sympathy he had ceased to seek; and yet, on the other hand, it is clear that he himself desired only the mimic image of cruelty, not the reality.

Albert brought him, since a genuine butcher could not be found, a youth who was willing to pretend to be one. "Have you worked today?" asked Proust; "Did you kill an animal? An ox? Did it bleed much? Did you touch the blood?" So far the inarticulate young person had only mumbled, again and again, an unsatisfactory "Yes"; but now, gathering courage, he replied: "Of course I did, I put both hands right in it!" "Show me your hands," commanded Proust. Albert took him to a real butcher's shop, where Proust said to the apprentice: "Let

---

[1] III, 833. 'He alluded,' says the Narrator, 'to a translation of Ruskin's *Sesame and Lilies* which I had sent to M. de Charlus.'
[2] For a hidden allusion to this person, see III, 817.
[3] III, 815, 816, 821, 864.

me see how you kill a calf." These incidents reappear on the morning of Albertine's captivity in the butcher's boy, 'very tall and slim, fair-haired', who as he cuts up and weighs the superior and inferior portions of a side of beef seems 'a beautiful angel on Judgment Day, preparing the separation of the Good and Bad and the weighing of souls'[1]; again in Françoise's protégé, the 'timid and bloodstained' butcher's boy, who 'has just started work in the abattoirs', and whom she is anxious to save from going to the war[2]; and lastly in the 'ox-slaughterer, the man from the abattoirs', whom Jupien proposes to the Baron in place of the over-gentle Maurice, and who turns out to be only a hotel-employee.[3] Proust himself was not deceived. It is the lamentable paradox of Jupien's brothel, as of Albert's, that genuine evil is not to be had in it. Maurice, who flogs the Baron in chains, and is presented by Jupien as a murderer, is in fact only an irredeemably soft-hearted jeweller's apprentice; 'one of the most dangerous apaches in Belleville' is a dairy-boy; the rest of the inmates are working-class soldiers and airmen on leave from the front, patriotic, humanitarian, and ingenuously innocent, plying their hideous trade 'from mechanical habit, neglected education, need of money, and a preference for gaining it by a method which they supposed, perhaps wrongly, to be less laborious than working'.[4]

The conscious motives of this deplorable episode—perhaps the only truly deplorable episode—in Proust's life are not difficult to divine. In this pit of Sodom he was following his vice, which had begun with love for his equals (Reynaldo and Lucien), progressed through platonic affection for social superiors (Fénelon, Antoine Bibesco, and the rest) to physical affection for social inferiors (Ulrich and Agostinelli), and now ended, disillusioned with all, in a sterile intercourse with professional catamites. He was experimenting with evil—an evil which perhaps does not exist anywhere in the realm of natural or unnatural sex, except as a moral nullity, a mirage for the desperate—and testing his power to associate with it unscathed. He was buying cheaply, for money and without expense of time or emotion, not only pleasure but human society, albeit in its basest form; for Albert-Jupien's brothel, like the Little Train, was 'a form of society like any other'. Furthermore, like Toulouse-Lautrec sojourning for many months in a disorderly house, among the fallen women who would accept his deformed presence without contempt, he sought and found the last great paintings which would complete his art.

[1] III, 138.   [2] III, 750, 756-7.   [3] III, 817-18.   [4] III, 817-21.

Céleste reproached her master for associating with 'so disgusting a person' as Albert, but his excuse, however lame, was certainly part of the truth. "You are quite right, my dear Céleste," he said with a laugh, "but it can't be helped; he's indispensable for the information he brings me." Twice in the war years Proust had deliberately sought and found the experiences which would give him, at opposite poles of heaven and hell, the missing corner-stones in the edifice of his novel: the Vinteuil Septet, and Jupien's brothel.

But the worst remains. Proust's search for cruelty in these young men was only in part a conscious craving for the imaginary beauty of youthful strength and amorality. He was also performing symbolic acts of revenge for an injury inflicted in remote childhood, perhaps even further back than the kiss refused and extorted on the moonlight night at Auteuil. It was when he was only twenty-two months old, and his brother Robert was born, that it became for ever impossible for him to possess his mother's undivided love. Robert was not to blame, and Marcel had almost entirely forgiven his brother in very early years; but a diabolical part of him had never forgiven his mother. The deepest secret of Proust's life, the ultimate root of the very tensions which had produced his greatness of soul, his goodness and courage, his novel and his vice, now came to the surface. It revealed itself in acts which are at once abominable and absurd, but should be absolved with awe and sympathy by all his sinful fellow-humans. Perhaps these sins were even necessary for his salvation. The hitherto unresolved abscess of infantile aggression burst, by a fistula cut through forty-four years of time, leaving him free at last and ready to die. From the manner in which these terrible deeds appear in his novel it is clear, although their motives came from the lowest recesses of his unconscious, that this profound self-analyst was fully aware of their meaning.

The first was his gift to Albert's brothel of the furniture which had belonged to his dead parents. When the Narrator presents the proprietress of Bloch's brothel with Aunt Léonie's chairs and sofa, he is stricken with remorse on seeing them used by the inmates, 'tortured by the cruel contact to which I had delivered them without defence!' 'If I had caused the body of a dead woman to be violated,' he adds, 'I should not have suffered more.' The dead woman whose body Proust made and saw to be outraged was his own mother. 'I returned no more to visit the bawd,' says the Narrator, 'because they seemed to be alive and to beseech me, like the apparently inanimate objects in the Arabian

Nights, in which human souls are imprisoned who undergo martyrdom and beg for deliverance.'[1] But Proust returned again and again to visit Albert.

Throughout his life Proust was accustomed, as a not wholly innocent social game, to display to new friends his collection of photographs. He had done so to Lucien Daudet in 1895, when Lucien first came to tea in his bedroom and said, so disconcertingly: "I'd rather we talked!", and recently, on 16 December 1916, to Paul Morand on his first visit. But now this practice took a more sinister aspect. Proust arrived at the Hôtel Marigny with a packet of photographs, as Albert later told Maurice Sachs, 'of dear or illustrious lady-friends'. The butcher-boy or telegraph-messenger who was his companion for the evening would certainly have treated these with utter respect, since the sacred rite of viewing family photographs is nowhere regarded with deeper instinctive courtesy than among the proletariat. Instead, the young person had been sternly briefed by Albert, and when he saw the portrait of Proust's favourite Princesse Hélène de Chimay he dutifully cried: "And who the hell's this little tart?" Sometimes the image thus profaned was that of Mme Proust herself; and the primal scene at Montjouvain, where Mlle Vinteuil induces her friend to insult her father's portrait, was thus repeated in his own life by Proust.[2] It is true, however, of Proust as of Mlle Vinteuil (who dedicates her life equally to her vice and to the memory of her dead parent), that this atrocious deed was a symptom not only of hatred, but of wounded, lifelong love.

The story of Proust and the rats is circulated to this day, in preposterously elaborated forms, among the inverts of Paris and their foreign visitors. But of its basic truth there can unhappily be no doubt, since it is confirmed by independent witnesses, and still more conclusively by its unmistakable though disguised appearance in his novel. Maurice Sachs heard it from Albert Le Cuziat; Gide and Bernard Fay and Boni de Castellane from Proust himself; and between the wars it was possible and fashionable to meet the very chauffeur who declared, with a proud and beaming smile: "It was I who used to take the rats to Monsieur Marcel!" The wretched creatures were

---

[1] I, 578.

[2] It is therefore possible that Proust had already begun this sadistic ritual in 1912 or earlier, before the Montjouvain episode was written. But it is equally possible that the scene in his novel represents only a latent impulse, and that he did not put it into practice until his period of moral abasement in 1917-19.

pierced with hatpins or beaten with sticks, while Proust looked on.[1] The scene and its meaning appear in the Narrator's disquisition at Doncières on 'nightmares with their fantastic albums, in which our parents who are dead have met with a serious accident, that does not preclude a speedy recovery. Meanwhile we keep them in a little rat-cage, where they are smaller than white mice, covered with big red spots in each of which a feather is stuck, and address us with Ciceronian speeches.'[2] Here, alas, are the rats, their wounds and the hatpins, the wiremeshed rat-trap in which they were caught and brought to him,[3] and their very identity. No doubt his victims represented many things; for rats are among the most powerful, universal and complex symbols in the inferno of the unconscious, and are regarded with special libido and dread by homosexuals as emblems of anal aggression and anal birth.[4] But for Proust at this time they were chiefly his dead parents, who thus met through his revenge with a 'serious accident', and spoke to him, dwarfed by immeasurable time, of mysteries inaudible to his conscious memory.

He could not refrain from alluding further to the rats, once in a letter, and again in the episode of his novel to which they really

[1] According to Sachs, 'he had a live rat brought to him and stuck with hatpins while he watched'. According to Fay, as reported by André Germain, the rats had to be pursued and beaten by young men. Gide records: 'During a memorable night conversation (we had so few that I can remember each one) Proust explained to me his desire to conjoin the most disparate sensations and emotions for the purpose of orgasm. The pursuit of rats, among other devices, was to be justified in this intention; however that might be, Proust invited me to believe so.'

[2] II, 87.

[3] Perhaps this wire trap is the clue to the occasion of Proust's temptation and to the origin of the rats. Did they come from the rat-infested public abattoirs of La Villette, brought in a taxi by 'the man from the abattoirs' in the very cage in which they were caught? And had the man suggested, in the course of describing his work under Proust's cross-examination: "Would you like to see what we do with the rats?"

[4] In this infantile regression he also returned to the day when Ernestine had killed the chicken in the yard at Illiers, and thereby associated cruelty with the life of the family. He may have recreated this early memory still more closely, if there is any truth in a rumour recorded shortly after the war by Maurice Martin du Gard: that Proust, in a little hotel in the suburbs, took pleasure in having a chicken killed in the next room, with a young man dressed as a policeman beside him for protection. The detail of the suburban hotel is not necessarily false, for a tradition exists that Proust was interested in more brothels than one, like M. de Charlus (III, 832).

belonged. 'I am not afraid of the cannons and gothas,' he wrote to Princesse Soutzo in April 1918, 'but I *am* afraid of much less dangerous things, such as mice'; and the Narrator, leaving Jupien's brothel under bombardment in this same spring of 1918, meditates: 'one can be afraid of not sleeping, without being afraid of a serious duel; one can fear a rat, and not fear a lion'.[1]

It is probable that M. de Charlus's flagellation in chains remotely represents this most heinous of Proust's aberrations, and that here as elsewhere in the brothel scene the Baron is a mere scapegoat for Proust's own experiences. The masochistic form taken by Charlus's vice, though no more abject or absurd, is the most foreign to Proust's own sadistic desires, and was no doubt chosen for that reason; but it is by no means an uncommon one, and may have been adopted by some other customer of Albert's. Possibly, too, Proust may have thought here of Jean Lorrain, his opponent in his duel in 1897, and a minor original of Charlus[2]; for Lorrain's nocturnal excursions notoriously used to end, though not altogether in accordance with his wishes, in his being beaten up by his brutal companions. But Proust may well have selected it from one of the naïve natural histories of perversion then still current, such as Kraft-Ebbing's *Psychopathia sexualis*, one of which he read at this time, not without disapproval. "It seems that even vice has now become one of the exact sciences," he commented with rueful irony to Paul Morand.

Albert's brothel, then, was Jupien's, and Jupien in this episode of the novel is Albert. In his origins, however, Jupien has nothing to do with Le Cuziat. He already exists as tailor-concierge in passages of *Contre Sainte-Beuve* written in the spring of 1909, two years before Proust met Albert, and even then probably taken from an earlier version of the novel. In this aspect, as we have seen, Jupien is connected with the tailor Eppler in the courtyard of 9 Boulevard Malesherbes in Proust's boyhood; as Charlus's factotum he is suggested by Yturri, and as the paralysed Baron's male nurse he resembles Comte Clary's Japanese valet Mineguishi. During the process of revision, however, Proust seems to have retrospectively tinged Jupien's other

[1] III, 834. Similarly, defending himself without being accused, he then protested to Maugny that his nights out, 'though dangerous to my health' were 'absolutely innocent', and to Princesse Soutzo that he never went 'to any place unfit to be named'.

[2] Neither of the two chief originals of Charlus took a downward course. Montesquiou in his later years became ever more prim, while Doasan after his flighty youth seems to have been all talk and no sin.

appearances with something of Albert's wit and personality. The common idea that Albert was one of the chief originals of Albertine is evidently absurd: the two characters have nothing in common, and Albert himself, though he would have boasted if the contrary had been the case, always stated that he never had physical or emotional relations with Proust. However, it is not impossible that his name was a minor ingredient in the name of Albertine, along with those of Albert Nahmias, Alfred Agostinelli, and various women. Similarly, the character of Andrée already existed in the 1905-6 version of *A la Recherche*, where Swann himself meets the little band, and again in the 1907-8 version, where the Narrator meets only two girls at the seaside. In an early passage of *Albertine Disparue* she was called Germaine.[1] But Albert had a young soldier-friend named André, who visited 102 Boulevard Haussmann with him, and caused a jealous conflict between Proust and Albert which towards 1921, as Albert himself stated, brought the end of their long association. It is quite possible that this André is responsible not only for Andrée's name, but for some of the enigmatic by-play between the Narrator and Albertine's friend during and after Albertine's captivity; though here Anna Agostinelli is no doubt a more important original.

Without looking back, for fear of being turned into a pillar of salt, the reader may now at last be led away from the Hôtel Marigny. During the twelve months between the summers of 1917 and 1918, however, its environs were visited by the fire from heaven; and the Narrator himself, as he quits the scene of his appalling discovery during an air-raid, is reminded of the word '*Sodoma*' scrawled on a wall in the doomed city of Pompeii.[2]

On 27 July 1917, the night of the first great Gotha raid on Paris, Proust had dined at the Ritz with Morand, Princesses Soutzo and Violette Murat, Joseph Reinach ('he looks like Consul, the chimp that could smoke, dine and pay the bill, and at times a glimmer of almost human intelligence crosses his face,' remarked Proust), Réjane's son Jacques Porel, Étienne and Édith de Beaumont, and Cocteau. Beaumont telephoned for the latest hypnotist, a M. Delagarde: "the man's a complete ass," he assured the company, "but his fluid's absolutely terrific!" Sure enough M. Delagarde put Beaumont to sleep in a jiffy, and invited the guests to stick pins in his body, adding jovially but with gruesome ignorance of anatomy: "Only *do* try not to prick him in an artery!" Next came Princesse Murat: "could you cure me of

[1] III, 1106, notes on 546, 547.   [2] III, 806-7, 833.

grinding my teeth?" she asked ("a modest request," commented Proust); but she tactlessly began to come to of her own accord, while the hypnotist raced through the gestures of waking the subject in order to get there first. In the midst of their laughter and glee came the dreadful warning from the sirens on the Eiffel Tower. "Someone's trodden on the Eiffel Tower's toe, it's complaining," cried Cocteau. For a moment Proust ignored the interruption, still absorbed in the séance: "people in a trance always ask to be told their future," he observed, "for fear of being made to confess their past". Then he went out on the balcony. The sky was full of stars, a sheaf of search-lights at the peak of the great tower pointed into limitless space, and far away, in the direction of Le Bourget, tiny points of light soared into the air as the defending fighters took off to protect the city, and made new constellations. For more than an hour Proust stood there, entranced, for the first time since the final sunset of Cabourg and for the last time but one in all his life, by a scene of material beauty. When they descended, however, he was reminded of El Greco's *Burial of Count d'Orgaz*, in which the events of heaven and earth are presented on two separate planes; for while this apocalyptic vision was enacted in the sky, in the hall of the Ritz alarmed ladies in nightgowns were roaming, clutching their ropes of pearls to their bosoms, as in Feydeau's farce, *L'Hôtel du Libre Échange*." Among those recognised," remarks Saint-Loup in a conversation in which many of these images (constellations, apocalypse, El Greco, Feydeau) are repeated from a letter Proust wrote that night to Mme Straus, "the Duchesse de Guermantes superb in her nighty, the Duc de Guermantes indescribable in bath-robe and pink pyjamas".[1] Then came the merry cry of the bugles sounding the All Clear, the *berloque*:

'The *berloque*,' says the Narrator, 'like an invisible street-boy, discussed the good news at regular intervals, and threw its cry of joy high in the air.'[2]

The next great raid began a little before midnight on 30 January

[1] III, 758-9.   [2] III, 777.

1918, at the moment when Proust was leaving Gabriel de La Roche-foucauld's home in the Rue Murillo after a performance of Borodin's Second Quartet. Once again Proust had the opportunity of enjoying the same sublime spectacle, for his taxi broke down in the Avenue de Messine for half an hour, while he paced the pavement. When at last they reached 102 Boulevard Haussmann he kindly suggested to the aged driver: "I could put you up for the night in my drawing-room, if you're afraid to go home." But the old man was deaf, and oblivious of the raid raging about them. "Oh, no," he replied, "I'm off to Grenelle, it's only a false alarm, they haven't reached Paris at all." At that moment a bomb exploded near by, a little to the east, in a direction which might well have been the Rue de l'Arcade, though Proust learned afterwards that it was in the Rue d'Athènes, just behind the Gare Saint-Lazare. This was no doubt the very bomb which fell a few moments after the Narrator left Jupien's brothel, 'perhaps now already reduced to ashes'.[1]

On and after 23 March 1918 the Germans shelled Paris from positions seventy miles away, with the enormous naval guns which were collectively known as Big Bertha, after Krupp's wife. The Gothas stormed more violently than ever, and at each alert the lodgers at 102 Boulevard Haussmann trooped down to the cellar, headed by Céleste,[2] while Proust worked calmly upstairs, like the boy on the burning deck. "I don't know the way to the cellar," he said. Poor Céleste, distraught with fear and with the additional burden of nursing Odilon, who arrived in mid-April on sick-leave with quinsy, thought of leaving Proust's service. He threatened to replace her with the hated Céline, and annoyed her by refusing to take refuge in Mme Catusse's villa at Nice, or even at Cabourg. Céleste was ill all summer, but the bond between them was too strong to be broken by fear, or by anything except death.

The noble and intelligent Céleste had now served Proust for five and a half years, ever since the November of 1912 when she tied the parcel in which the typescript of Du Côté de chez Swann went to the NRF and returned rejected. She had married Odilon Albaret in March 1913, but during the reign of Céline had been summoned only for emergency tasks, such as the distribution of presentation copies of Swann in November 1913. When she first entered that dark bedroom,

<hr />

[1] III, 833.
[2] 'The All Clear sounded as I reached home, where I met Françoise coming up from the cellar,' says the Narrator on his return from Jupien's brothel (III, 840).

filled with the smoke of Legras powders, she had felt a twinge of eery dread, and thought of the gloomy metal-mines in her native Auxillac in Auvergne, where she lived with her brother François-Régis Gineste until 1904. Then Proust's profound goodness, reaching far deeper in him than anything that was imperfect, called to her generosity, his orphan need to her abnegation, and they were united in a strange and pure tie for ever. Céline, whose star was waning, called her 'the cajoler', '*l'enjôleuse*'. This is the word used by the jealous Françoise[1] of Marie Gineste and Céleste Albaret, the lady's maids at Balbec, to whom Proust by way of compliment gave the real names of Céleste and her unmarried sister, and the brilliant untutored conversation which is a pastiche of Céleste's, who accompanied him to Cabourg on his last visit in 1914.[2] From that time until his death she lived with him, fed, nursed and comforted him, taking the place of the young mother of his infancy. On the first Sunday of their life together she had dressed to go to mass. "Where are you going, how can you leave me all alone?" he had cried; "my dear Céleste, surely the good Lord is as likely to send you to heaven for nursing a sick man as for deserting him to go to mass!" And Céleste never went to mass again while Monsieur was alive.

Céleste, now aged twenty-seven, was tall, beautiful, and stately, 'like Lady de Grey forty years ago,' said Proust, having met that lofty English beauty, whom people called Ten Degrees below Freezing, at Mme Straus's in his youth. His friends called her 'the beautiful Céleste'; and hence, no doubt, the words "Look, there's the beautiful Françoise," with which Albertine warns the Narrator of her unexpected approach 'when my friend was lying naked by my side'[3]— words so inappropriate of the aged Françoise—were spoken in real life when Proust was disturbed with a companion by Céleste. Her voice was melodious, but in her not infrequent rages with husband or master 'it kept,' as the Narrator observes, 'the rhythm of her native torrents'.[4] 'Céleste sometimes reproached her husband with not understanding her,' says the Narrator of the lady's maid at Balbec, 'whereas I was amazed that he could endure her.'[5] "At that time,

[1] II, 848; III, 154.
[2] Many years after Proust's death Marie Scheikévitch repeated this episode of *Sodome et Gomorrhe* (II, 846-50) aloud to Céleste, who had never read her master's novel. "I said all these things to Monsieur not once but many times," commented the astonished Céleste.
[3] III, 822.   [4] II, 846, 850.   [5] II, 850.

Monsieur," the real Céleste told Proust of poor Odilon in the early days of their marriage, "he carried a bachelor-flat in his heart!" Proust was almost as proud as Céleste of the fact that her brother had married a niece of Monseigneur Nègre, Archbishop of Tours. He attributed the same archiepiscopal alliance to the lady's maid at Balbec in his novel,[1] and wrote in doggerel verses which he gave to Céleste:

> '*Tall, beautiful, refined and meagre,*
> *Now weary, now elate and eager,*
> *Charming prince alike and beggar,*
> *Scolding poor Marcel with rigour,*
> *Giving for honeyed words vinegar,*
> *Witty, brisk,* vitae integra,
> *She's the niece-in-law of Nègre!*'

Early in her service Céleste acquired, as had the unfortunate Agostinelli, a curious talent for poetic diction, and another peculiar to herself and her master for parody and impersonation, both of which she employed satirically against Monsieur and his friends.[2] "Monsieur Léger's verses are more like riddles than poems," she remarked of a volume by Morand's friend Saint-Léger Léger, the future Nobel Prize winner.[3] Of Morand himself she said: "You can see M. Morand's voice cutting out a silhouette of his face"; and of the hoarse-toned Mme de Chevigné: "That lady who has made Monsieur so unhappy has a voice like a railway-train when it goes into a tunnel." When Gide gave Proust a copy of his early work *Les Nourritures Terrestres*, in which all the sensual joys of the world are hymned in lyric prose to the imaginary friend Nathanaël, Céleste rose to the occasion. When Proust sent her to telephone Princesse Soutzo she returned saying: "Nathanaël, I will speak to thee of the lady-friends of Monsieur. First is she who has made him go out again after so many years, whence taxis to the Ritz, page-boys, tips, exhaustion...." 'I had to explain to her the other day that Napoleon and Bonaparte were one and the same person, I can't teach her to spell, she's never had the patience to read

---

[1] II, 850.

[2] 'She inserted in her little report of what purported to be a communication from the manager or one of my friends,' says the Narrator at Balbec, 'fictitious words which slyly depicted all the faults of Bloch, etc. In the form of a simple message which she had obligingly undertaken to deliver, she presented an inimitable portrait' (II, 849).

[3] Repeated by Céleste the lady's maid at Balbec (II, 849).

half a page of my book,' he told Gide, 'but she is full of extraordinary gifts.'

At the very time, in 1917-18, when Proust's association with Albert Le Cuziat was closest, he also saw a good deal of the Abbé Mugnier. No doubt he took a scientific, aesthetic and malicious pleasure in this strange counterpoint between a priest of evil and a priest of good; but he also felt a genuine need in his period of moral fall for a spiritual healer, even though, as in his relations with doctors who cared only for his body, he would always refuse to abdicate his own free will. The Abbé, with his selfless instinct for a soul in danger, came eagerly to meet him.

The Abbé Arthur Mugnier (1853-1944) was born at the Château of Lubersac, where his father was the architect in charge of the restoration of the Marquis's home. He was educated at the seminary of Nogent-le-Rotrou, twenty miles west of Illiers,[1] and ordained in Paris soon after the Siege. "My mother was overjoyed when I became a priest," he would say, "because she thought I would find peace—but I haven't! I've only had other people's troubles!" In 1896 he became vicar of the fashionable church of Sainte-Clothilde, in the heart of the Faubourg, and was seen at noble dinner-parties everywhere and always.

The Abbé was a witty, rosy-faced little man, with forget-me-not blue eyes behind pale pince-nez, a tuft of grey, smoke-coloured hair which he would twirl on his finger when puzzled, and an expression of harassed benignity. He lived in the utmost poverty, with humble food and threadbare soutane; he loved and cherished the poor, and heard confession, as he said, not only in his parish church but "in railway-stations, on benches, in streets and public gardens". Yet his true missions were elsewhere, instilled by his strange infancy in a great château, and by his passion for literature, which taught him that a great writer, as much as a priest, carries a vast burden of grace and sin along a dolorous path which leads out of this world. The souls of the French aristocracy were neither more nor less valuable to God, and perhaps in even greater peril, than those of the poor; and like Saint Paul to the pagan Greeks, or Father Damien to the lepers, the Abbé Mugnier became an Apostle to the Faubourg Saint-Germain. But he was no meddlesome or militant fisher for converts, for this wise and holy man, one of the rare saints of the twentieth century to be numbered with Gandhi or Albert Schweitzer, brought comfort and for-

[1] 'It ought to be renamed Nogent-l'Abbé!' Proust wrote to him in 1919.

giveness only to those who needed it. "She was far too pious to need converting," he said of a good Jewish lady; and when asked if he believed in hell he answered: "Yes, because it is a dogma of the Church —but I don't believe there is anyone in it." His other mission began when he sent Huysmans to the Trappists in 1892, and henceforth he specialised no less in sinful writers than in sinful nobles. Paul Bourget, who had begun to feel more Catholic than the Pope, complained: "he throws communion-bread to the sparrows!"; but the Abbé remarked: "I have two soutanes, Monsieur Bourget, would you like one?" After his death was found, tied in green cardboard folders, his correspondence from, among many others, Montesquiou, Cocteau, Bergson, Mme de Caillavet, Mauriac, Montherlant, Barrès, and Proust himself. In 1909, however, he had unwittingly offended the Church, when he endeavoured to reconvert the unfrocked and married priest, Hyacinthe Loyson, and was insulted by Loyson's son. "Now I know why priests must not marry," he cried, "it is because they have such unpleasant children!" As penance he was banished from Sainte-Clothilde and made a mere almoner to the Missionary Sisters of Saint Joseph of Cluny in the Rue Méchain, where he lived at No. 7 until his death. "In 1910 I had a nice neighbour on the floor above, very quiet, very polite," he would say, "his name was Lenin!" He deplored the war: "we ought to be fighting the Prussians inside us, our deadly sins," he said; but when asked if the Apocalypse had now come, he answered: "Not yet."

It is certain that two such indefatigable diners-out as Proust and the Abbé had met long before, though it is possible that each, for different reasons, may at first have misunderstood and avoided the other. Proust must have been aware of the Abbé's notorious devotion to the great Chateaubriand, whom none in our century have loved and known so passionately as the Abbé, his lifelong friend and spiritual ward Princesse Marthe Bibesco, and Proust himself. Early in the war, if not before, they had begun to make contact. 'I've just read Ruskin's *Sésame et les lys*, with an enchanting preface by Marcel Proust,' wrote the Princesse significantly to the Abbé on 11 June 1915, 'do you see him sometimes?' The Abbé was a friend of many of Proust's present friends, the Princesses Bibesco, Soutzo, and Marie Murat, Mme Scheikévitch, Morand, Blanche, the Beaumonts, Mme de Chevigné, Cocteau, Pierre de Polignac. On 5 June and 6 July 1917 Proust attended dinners at the Ritz, given by Princesse Soutzo, at which several of these and the Abbé were present. The Abbé, 'his quiff rising

like smoke from a censer,' said Morand, sportively produced an
edition of *Les Fleurs du Mal* to which Bourget had written a preface,
and remarked: "Now, with Bourget's preface, we shall have to call it
Les Fleurs du Bien!" In April 1918 Proust met the Abbé at Mme
Daudet's, saw him home, and a few evenings later met him again: 'I
like him very much,' he wrote to Lucien. The Abbé began to visit 102
Boulevard Haussmann, and Céleste always remembered two of his
typically profound sayings. When Proust asked his opinion of *Les
Fleurs du Mal* he replied, placing his hand on his heart: "They are
always with me, in here." And once when leaving for his convent, the
Abbé remarked with a similar double meaning: "I must hear the confessions of my mystic flappers—*mes poules mystiques.*" The Abbé
regarded indulgently Proust's love of high society, now almost
platonic: "He was a honey-bee of heraldic flowers," he told Lucien
Descaves. Proust pretended to be unaffected by the Abbé's interest in
his soul: "He talked to me about salvation," he told Blanche, "but I
said: 'I'd rather you talked about Comte Aimery de La Rochefoucauld'." In fact, like every great writer, Proust had undertaken to win
redemption through his work alone, to negotiate direct with God. But
we shall find him remembering the Abbé, and the Church whose
May-mass he had attended at Illiers, whose priests and cathedrals he
had defended in the dark hour of the Combes laws, at the moment of
death, in his own way.

All that spring and summer the Germans fought towards Paris and
died, reaching Château-Thierry on the Marne, only fifty miles away,
in June. As in 1914 many Parisians took refuge in the south. Princesse
Soutzo returned to Biarritz, where Proust thought vaguely of following her, but decided Céleste was too ill. He quoted Swann, who 'had
enough courage to stay, but not enough to go',[1] and longed regretfully 'to kiss your hand, and hear you assuring me that there isn't any
sugar on my moustache'. Her brother was in Paris, and he felt for a
moment his old curiosity to see 'this transposition into another sex of a
face one has loved'. So he had sought out the Waru brothers in 1892,
because they were Mme de Chevigné's nephews, and Jeanne
Pouquet's nephew 'little Prémonville' in 1911; and he had always
regretted never having met the brother of Marie de Benardaky ('she
was, perhaps without knowing it, the intoxication and despair of my
childhood,' he explained to the Princesse) before his death aged
eighteen early in the war, especially, perhaps, because the boy was of

extraordinary beauty and in the habit of dancing naked before his particular friends. Once again he was disquieted by new symptoms of ill-health, which seemed imaginary to his doctors, but were in fact premonitory visitations of death, now only four and a half years distant. He felt impediments in his speech, a hint of facial paralysis, and decided his brain was affected. In June he consulted Dr Babinski, the great neurologist, and asked him to perform a trepanotomy; but Babinski refused and succeeded in reassuring him.

On 13 June 1918 poor Dr Pozzi was murdered by a deranged patient. Proust thought with bewildered grief of the immense space of time during which he had known this gayer, more intelligent original of Dr Cottard, who had dined at 9 Boulevard Malesherbes when he was only fifteen, had invited him to the first precocious 'dinner in town' which his parents had been so reluctant for him to attend, had shone as the star of Mme Aubernon's soirées and tended her so devotedly in her last illness, and had rescued him in 1914 from military service. There was something portentous and supernatural in this abrupt calamity, and he wrote with magnificent imagery to Mme Straus: 'as at the death of Calmette, that innocent and mystic sacrificial victim, one felt the coming of war, so after the death of Pozzi one can't help wondering whether peace is near, whether these men were not the two bloodstained pillars which marked the beginning and end of the war'. And so it was to be.

After four months' interruption the flow of proofs of A l'Ombre from La Semeuse had begun again in mid-April. Even two years before, when Gallimard and Copeau had called to negotiate his migration to the NRF, and he showed them his corrections to the Grasset proofs of June 1914, Copeau had exclaimed: "Why, it's a new book!" But Proust persisted with his customary superb enlargement and enrichment of the text. This work continued until the autumn, and printing was finally completed on 30 November 1918.

On 10 April 1918 Jacques Émile Blanche offered to dedicate to Proust the first volume of his *Propos de Peintre*, a series of essays on the impressionist painters entitled *De David à Degas*, and asked him in return to introduce the book. Proust's preface, which he wrote in May, caused months of bickering between these two very susceptible friends. Proust, in a parable which was equally true of himself, represented Blanche as an artist who in his youth had preferred the pleasures of society, had been unwillingly forced to work by banishment from noble drawing-rooms, and had now reached fame through the law which grants recognition only after a generation of neglect. Blanche, on the contrary, felt that he had always consecrated himself to art alone, and was still by no means appreciated in accordance with his merits. This was the first of a series of critical writings in which Proust used material from the unpublished *Contre Sainte-Beuve*. He introduced the episode of great-uncle Louis Weil's cider-glasses and prismatic knife-rests,[1] and a concise version of his attack on Sainte-Beuve for contaminating his judgements on writers with considerations of their outward life, in which he accused Blanche of committing the same error in his essay on Manet. In the end Proust had his way, the proofs were passed by Blanche in January 1919, and the volume was published in the following March.

It was also in the first half of 1918, and probably during the gap in proof-reading from January to April, that Proust completed the war-chapter in *Le Temps Retrouvé*, his last major addition to his novel. The chapter is first mentioned in a letter to Grasset of 18 July, in which Proust demanded once more the long overdue royalties on *Du Côté de chez Swann* for the period since April 1914. Gallimard, during a flying visit to Paris from America in June, had arranged with Grasset to buy back *Swann* 'for a pretty high figure', and the remainder of Grasset's edition was now issued in new wrappers, with the NRF's own label affixed to the title-page; but Grasset naturally insisted on withholding the royalties until the further question of an indemnity for the remainder of the novel was settled. 'Two volumes called *Sodome et Gomorrhe*[2] have been written since the war began, and there is a section about the war,' Proust now told Grasset. Probably, however, the first half of this war-chapter, before the visit to Jupien's brothel, was written in the summer of the previous year, since nothing in it is based on events later than the first Gotha raid of 27 July 1917. At this time Proust expected to adhere to his original plan, in which the chapter was to describe the Narrator's visit to Paris in the summer of 1916, with a brief interpolation on his earlier visit in August 1914. The events of the war which he mentions here, such as the Battle of Tannenberg,[3] the sinking of the *Lusitania*,[4] French pressure on

---

[1] Proust scattered elements of this passage far and wide in *La Prisonnière* and *Albertine Disparue*. Cf. III, 168, 254, 411-12, 479.

[2] That is, *Sodome et Gomorrhe* as we now have it, and a further volume with the same title which was later divided into *La Prisonnière* and *Albertine Disparue*.

[3] 26-30 August 1914 (III, 760).

[4] 7 May 1915 (III, 772).

Roumania to join the war,[1] usually belong to the correct period; though allusions to King Constantine's withdrawal of troops to the Peloponnese[2] and the entry of the United States into the war[3] belong to the first half of 1917. However, since the only air attacks on Paris in 1916 had been by Zeppelin, Proust carefully turned the air-raid which the Narrator discusses with Saint-Loup, though modelled on the Gotha raid of July 1917, into a raid by Zeppelins.[4] It was not until the autumn of 1917 that Albert Le Cuziat opened his brothel at the Hôtel Marigny, and thus provided Proust with the material for the second half of his war-chapter. Accordingly he now introduced in the latter half of the Narrator's conversation with M. de Charlus and the visit to Jupien's brothel the environing events of that winter and the following spring, when he himself frequented the Hôtel Marigny: the bomb of 30 January 1918,[5] the incessant Gotha raids,[6] the bombardment by Big Bertha,[7] the German advance on Paris and the flight of refugees from the capital,[8] the crowds sheltering in the Metro and complaints of their scandalous behaviour,[9] and Françoise taking cover like Céleste in the cellar.[10] But these and many other anachronisms in *A la Recherche* are far from impairing the reality of Proust's novel; and the reader, assailed like the Narrator on waking by the malaise of wondering in what year he is, feels only the fluidity of time, and the possibility of eddies in its stream.

The same letter of 18 July to Grasset contains the first mention of *Pastiches et Mélanges*, the collection of Proust's Lemoine parodies, Ruskin prefaces and selected *Figaro* articles[11] which he had hoped to publish ever since 1908. He had arranged for its publication with Gallimard during his recent visit; and in order to ensure its simultaneous publication with *Swann* and *A l'Ombre* at the first suitable

[1] III, 785. Roumania declared war on 27 August 1916 (cf. III, 787).

[2] January 1917 (III, 729). King Constantine's abdication on 12 June 1917 is mentioned in the later section (III, 845).

[3] 6 April 1917 (III, 761, 794). The murder of Rasputin, however (29 December 1916), is mentioned as being still in the future (III, 777).

[4] III, 758-9.   [5] III, 833.   [6] III, 762, 777, 802, 809.
[7] III, 802.   [8] III, 806, 811.
[9] III, 834.   [10] III, 840.

[11] *'Sentiments filiaux d'un Parricide'* (1 February 1907) and *'Impressions de route en automobile'* (19 November 1907). Since it too was about churches, he added the latter, together with an abridged version of *'La Mort des Cathédrales'* (16 August 1904), to the preface to *La Bible d'Amiens*, and called the whole, in allusion to the cathedrals wrecked by the Germans, *'En mémoire des églises assassinées—In Memory of the Murdered Churches'*.

time after the end of the war, Proust asked the NRF to send it to a
different printer, since La Semeuse was still busy with *A l'Ombre*. He
had not kept copies of his articles, and was compelled to enquire their
dates from Robert Dreyfus, who was again on the staff of *Le Figaro*,
and to borrow cuttings (which arrived on an evening when he dined at
the next table at the Ritz to Mr Winston Churchill) from Lucien
Daudet. He took the occasion to ask Alfred Capus, the editor of *Le
Figaro* during Flers's absence on war-work, to renew the project of
printing extracts from *A l'Ombre* which had been thwarted by the
outbreak of war; but Capus was on holiday and did not reply, and in
the end, although the feuilleton was actually announced in *Le Figaro*,
the extracts were bespoken by the NRF.

The Germans retreated, fighting grimly to the end, preparing the
terrible legend which would bring the next war, that they were not
defeated but betrayed by their government. A million American
soldiers were in France, and Céleste no longer said, as she had the year
before: "I don't think much of America!" Proust did not go to
Cabourg, although Mme Straus was at Trouville: 'I thought I would
go,' he told her, 'and that we would talk together about everything
that one day, so suddenly, became the past.' He dined at the Ritz alone
with Mme de Chevigné: 'I don't regret having exasperated you twenty
years ago,' he wrote, politely forgetting that it was six years longer
still, 'and annoyed you sometimes since; you were as beautiful then as
today, not more, for you haven't changed.' He was introduced to
Mme Ritz, and met Princesse Soutzo's brother at last, 'a young prince
of the East surrounded by all the beauties of the Arabian Nights'.
Robert Proust returned from the quiescent Italian front, where his
wife Marthe had joined him as a nurse in the spring, to take part in the
last great battles of the war; and in October, during Robert's convalescence from a motor-accident on the Western Front, the brothers
met affectionately every day. Proust was persuaded by Henri Bardac
to call on the famous society clairvoyant and palmist Mme de Thèbes
for a character-reading; but the wise woman, after glancing at his face
and hands, observed only: "What do you expect from me, Monsieur?
It is for you to reveal my own character to me."[1] In November came,
as he wrote to Princesse Soutzo, 'the miraculous and vertiginous
Peace'.

[1] "It's instinct, divination in the style of Mme de Thèbes (you follow me?)
that is the decisive point in a great general, as in a great doctor," Saint-Loup
tells the Narrator at Doncières (II, 114).

Chapter 14

THE PRIZE
(*November 1918 – June 1920*)

THE men of Europe had struggled during four years towards a receding goal, with death everywhere on the way. Some, like Prince Paul Mourousy, a cousin of Princesse Soutzo, had fallen at the very end: 'The dead of the eleventh hour, who had only a day to wait not to be killed, are those who grieve us most of all,' Proust wrote to her. He was shocked by the wild rejoicing of the Paris mob on Armistice Day: 'we are weeping for so many dead,' he remarked to Mme Straus, 'that gaiety like this is not the form of celebration one would prefer'. Proust, as much as any civilian, had suffered for others' suffering and mourned for slaughtered friends; and yet for himself he had been curiously indifferent. He spent that long gulf of years, which now had vanished like a day, in an enclave outside the war, in the silent peace of his cork-lined bedroom, in the oblivious relaxation of Ritz or male brothel. But on that day of armistice he started again from where he had halted in August 1914. His novel was finished, his last duty was to see it published. Proust's own war now began, as he in turn struggled for four years towards a distant goal, with death everywhere on the way, and fell in the hour of victory.

First of all, however, pressed by the obscure necessity which drove him to make money each November and to strip himself of his worldly goods, he resumed the inextricable saga of his furniture-selling. He gave the inferior articles stored in the mews and spare bedrooms of 102 Boulevard Haussmann to a collection for refugees returning to the liberated areas of the north-east. The Strauses sold his remaining Smyrna carpet for 3000 francs in December, and he decided to part even with the historic carpet which the Shah of Persia had given Dr Proust in 1869. He persuaded Walter Berry to house tapestries and other furniture in the cellars of the American Chamber of Commerce, where prospective buyers could view them without disturbing his daytime sleep. He recommended his efforts to realise the uncashable

cheque of 30,000 francs on the banking firm of Warburg for the enemy
securities which he had surrendered on the outbreak of war, and
enlisted once more the help of his friends, Berry, Émile Straus,
Raphael Georges Lévy, even Princesse Marie Murat, whose Christmas
Eve dinner he attended at the Ritz. They went on to the flat of a
member of the Italian armistice delegation, where Cocteau sang
ditties of the 1900s to Coco de Madrazo's accompaniment, the enormous Hélène Vacaresco talked in verse to Jacques de Lacretelle,
Princesse Marie was effervescently witty; but in the end everyone
gathered round to listen to Marcel, while Jacques Émile Blanche egged
him on. He forgot his treasured walking-stick, sheathed in tattered
leather, a present from an old friend on the occasion of his wedding,
and returned home with laryngitis. A few weeks later, at a dinner in
honour of Lord Derby, he prudently kept his greatcoat on, but removed it when Lord Derby amiably teased him. Two years later he
was flattered to hear that Lord Derby had declared: "Of all the impressions my wife and I took home with us from Paris, Monsieur
Proust was the most indelible"; but he was chagrined to find that the
English statesman had added: "Yes, he was the first chap we'd ever
seen dining in a fur-coat."

La Semeuse, after completing A l'Ombre on 30 November 1918,
had already produced in vain the first six proof-sheets of Le Côté de
Guermantes before the final transfer of Proust's works to the press of
Louis Bellenand at Fontenay-aux-Roses early in December. Pastiches
et Mélanges went to press immediately, though he kept back the still
unfinished Saint-Simon pastiche, on which he had been working since
September. Except for the Balzac, which he nearly doubled in length,
the Figaro pastiches of 1908 and 1909 remained unaltered[1]; but the
Saint-Simon which he had written in 1904 as an ironical tribute to
Montesquiou, and adapted to the Lemoine Affair in February 1909,
was now transformed by further additions into a vast satire on Paris
society at the end of 1918. The new sub-plot is based on the preten-
tions of the Murats, who had never forgotten their brief season of

---

[1] The new passages in the Balzac are p. 12, l.32-p. 14, l.14; p. 14, l.30-33;
p. 15, l.11-21; p. 15, l.32-p.16, l.5; p. 16, l.32-p. 17, l.3; p. 17, l.27-p. 18, l.9,
and include a mention of Paul Morand as 'one of our most impertinent embassy
secretaries'. A reference in the Flaubert pastiche (p. 22) to 'cork padding in their
bedrooms to muffle the noise of neighbours' is prophetic, since it appeared in
Le Figaro on 14 March 1908, whereas Proust installed his cork walls only in
August 1910.

royalty in the First Empire, to the rank of sovereign princes,[1] and the counter-intrigues of 'Saint-Simon' to thwart them. Proust felt compunction at taking the family name of his good friend Princesse Marie Murat in vain, but decided not to ask her permission, since a refusal would have ruined his pastiche. He might have answered that the jest was really on Saint-Simon, and the titanic vanity which made all attempts to break the cobweb of social precedence seem, to that sombre genius, crimes against 'the most vital interests of the State, which is founded on the rights of the Dukes'. But the inmost, gleeful irony of the Saint-Simon pastiche is that Proust himself, the 'little Proust' who had travelled the Guermantes Way and emerged far beyond, is speaking of the Faubourg Saint-Germain from the stand-point of a social superior, with the bitter diction and violent syntax, and in the haughty person of the great memorialist. He took the opportunity, however, to add compliments to old and new friends: to Guiche, Albufera, Princesse Soutzo ('the only woman who, to my misfortune, has succeeded in making me leave my retirement'), Mme Straus, Olivier ('the King's head-butler, respectful and beloved by all'), José Maria Sert, Boni de Castellane and the Beaumonts. The last additions relate to incidents of January 1919, his meeting with Lord Derby ('whose affability is of a kind that the French do not possess and by which their hearts are won'), and Antoine Bibesco's engage-ment to Elizabeth Asquith. Antoine, to Marcel's enchanted embarrass-ment, brought Miss Asquith to his humble bedside, and 'Saint-Simon' remarks: 'she was probably the most intelligent woman in the world, and seemed like one of the beautiful portraits in fresco that one sees in Italy'. He promised, 'in another part of these Memoirs which will be chiefly consecrated to Mme de Chevigné', to speak further of Prin-cesse Soutzo and Mme Straus, and the pastiche ends with the words 'to be continued'. But this sequel, which he intended to publish at the same time as *Le Côté de Guermantes*, mentioned frequently and pro-bably began, remains still unknown.

In the middle of January 1919 arrived a calamity from which Proust never entirely recovered. No. 102 Boulevard Haussmann, with its memories of Great-Uncle Louis and Mme Proust, had seemed an inseparable annexe to his lost family home, a continuation of a way of life which reached back to his childhood. Now his aunt announced she had sold the building to a banker, M. Varin-Bernier, for conversion

[1] The same theme occurs several times in *A la Recherche* in passages which were presumably added about this time (I, 772; II, 518; III, 50, 275).

into a bank. To Marcel's protests she replied, with a deadly irony which shows that Mme Émilie Weil and her nephew-in-law had much in common, that she 'preferred the sweet name of aunt to that of landlady', and that should his health ever improve sufficiently for him to see her again, 'my decision will have the advantage of enabling us to discuss literature instead of the house!' He had never signed an extended lease; he owed her 20,000 francs for three years' rent, because in 1916 he had announced that he would be unable to pay her dues until the settlement of the famous Warburg cheque; and he feared that this debt would be claimed by the new proprietor. Encouraged by a newspaper-cutting sent by Albufera, which stated that civilian lodgers had a right to two years' notice, he thought of remaining; but preparations for the conversion began in February, the inner courtyard was to be covered over, the staircase reconstructed, he would be unable to sleep. He consulted Guiche, who not only interviewed the banker in his lair, but cancelled the debt and extracted a stiff indemnity: 'it was the greatest service a friend has ever rendered me,' he told Robert Dreyfus.

Early in March, at about the same season as the year before, the impediment in his speech returned, perhaps because it was connected with his springtime asthma, probably also, as his doctor assured him, because his state of anxiety had induced him to take too much veronal. 'It can't be general paralysis,' he told Berry, 'because all my reflexes are excellent, and I've never had venereal disease'; but he feared he might have the same malady as his mother, that he too might die speechless, and resolved if need be to shut himself away from all human contact, and die when his novel was finished. After three weeks, however, the mysterious symptoms vanished as before.

On 2 March Proust had been a fellow-guest of Princesse Soutzo at the Ritz with the young Harold Nicolson, a friend of Morand and Berry, who was now peace-making in Paris. He asked how the English delegation worked. "We generally meet at ten in the morning," began Nicolson; but Proust interrupted: "No, you're going too fast, begin again. You take the official motor-car, you get out at the Quai d'Orsay, you climb the stairs, you enter the committee-room. What happens then?" Nicolson told all to this 'white, unshaven, grubby' diner, who listened enthralled, exclaiming from time to time: "But be precise, *mon cher Monsieur*, don't be in such a hurry!" They met again on 30 April. "My dear friend, make an effort, try to be less incomprehensible!" Proust resumed, "you say an earl's daughter is called

Lady, and his brother Esquire?" "No, the Honourable." "So when you speak to him, you call him Honourable Sir?" persisted Proust, with a gaze of deep sadness and tortured perplexity. Nicolson suggested that this passion for detail was a sign of the literary temperament. "Certainly not!" exclaimed Proust crossly, and blew a kiss across the table to his favourite Gladys Deacon. Soon, however, they were discussing homosexuality, which Nicolson supposed must be 'a matter of glands or nerves'. "It is a matter of habit," replied Proust, and when Nicolson demurred he added, still more obscurely: "No, that was silly of me, what I meant was that it's a matter of delicacy." Nicolson decided that he was 'not very intelligent on the subject'.

Whether from habit or delicacy, Proust had been suffering for seven months from his first protracted love-affair since the passing of Agostinelli. 'I have embarked on a sentimental enterprise without possibility of joy or retreat, a perpetual source of fatigue, anguish and absurd expense,' he had told Mme Straus in November 1918. Writing to Walter Berry on the very night of the second dinner with Nicolson, he spoke of 'an unhappy love which is now finishing'. And on 7 May he invited Vaudoyer to dine at his bedside with Reynaldo and 'a youth I've been sheltering for several months, who won't be in our way because he never says anything'. This unloquacious young person was Henri Rochat, a Swiss employee of the Ritz, whom Proust had hired as secretary; and indeed he now occasionally dictated letters to Rochat, who wrote in a clear hand but with shaky spelling. Proust detected in his new captive 'an amazing gift for painting'. He took him to see the little still-life of two apples by Fantin Latour which hung in Jacques Émile Blanche's dining-room at Auteuil; but Blanche, although it was past eleven o'clock, was still out. One of the few traits of Rochat in Albertine as prisoner which can be differentiated from those of Agostinelli is her talent for painting, 'a touching recreation of the captive,' says the Narrator, 'which moved me so much that I complimented her'.[1] But Proust's belief that his 'unhappy love' was now ending was only a false alarm, for Rochat's captivity was to last for two years more.

Towards the middle of March Proust sent the final proofs of *Pastiches et Mélanges* to press, with a dedication to Walter Berry. "Why Berry?" asked Antoine Bibesco one evening at his bedside,

[1] III, 180, 68, 409. Morel, too, says the Narrator, had 'a magnificent handwriting, disfigured by the grossest spelling mistakes' (II, 1034).

and: "Because he won the war!" Proust replied. 'Antoine left full of sound doctrine, and I was delighted at this education of the masses through the spoken word,' Proust reported to Berry; for he liked to believe that his friend had been chiefly responsible for America's intervention, and therefore for victory.[1] Publication of his three books was promised for early May, and he therefore refused a gratifying request from Sydney Schiff for an extract to appear in the July number of his magazine *Art and Letters*. On 25 April, however, Proust unwillingly consented to postpone publication until early June, to allow Rivière to print the conclusion of the Narrator's love for Gilberte from *A l'Ombre* in the *Nouvelle Revue Française* for 1 June 1919. The NRF had ceased publication in August 1914, a month after the issue of 1 July 1914 containing extracts from *Le Côté de Guermantes*; and the gulf of nearly five years was thus appropriately bridged.

As the time for a decision on his new home approached, Proust flew agitatedly in decreasing circles from impossible dreams to possible realities. He thought of visiting Perugia, Siena and Pisa, of taking Mme Catusse's villa at Nice from May to November, of accepting Antoine and Elizabeth's invitation to stay with them in England (he had attended the dinner in honour of their engagement in March, and they were married on 30 April in London). He found a fifth-floor flat in the Rue de Rivoli, conveniently near the Ritz; the proprietor called on 10 May to ask his concierge: "Is M. Proust an honourable man and a quiet lodger?", and was told that he was both indeed. Proust asked the new manager of 102 Boulevard Haussmann to settle the lease, arranged thriftily for Guiche to sell his cork walls to a manufacturer of bottle-corks, and made Céleste burn 'precious autographs, manuscripts of which no other copy exists, photographs which have become rare'. But no one who really knew him can have been surprised when on 30 May, the day before his tenure of 102 Boulevard Haussmann expired, he suddenly resolved to move to 8 *bis* Rue Laurent-Pichat, the home of the great actress Réjane.

Her son Jacques Porel, who had glimpsed Proust in his violet cloak on the golf-course at Cabourg in 1911, and enthusiastically forced his mother to plough through *Du Côté de chez Swann* in 1914, was now an unemployed war-hero aged twenty-six. In May 1917, when Porel had been invalided from the army after being gassed at Ypres, Proust

---

[1] The dedication reads: 'To Monsieur Walter Berry, who from the first day of the war, before a still undecided America, pleaded the cause of France with incomparable energy and talent, and gained it.'

heard from Morand of his admiration for *Swann*, and sent Céleste ('a long fragile lady with a fixed smile, like an angel in a cathedral', Porel remembered) to summon the proselyte. "I like him, but he seems a bit flighty," Céleste reported, and ever afterwards Proust called his friend 'Porel the Flighty', and would say: "See that all the windows are shut, Céleste, or Monsieur Porel will fly away!" On this first visit Proust recalled the day in September 1914 at Trouville when Réjane, "that woman I madly admire, called me a Boche at Mme Straus's, and nearly pushed me into a rosebush"; and on the third, Porel says, 'he knew me better than my most intimate friends did'. He spoke so vividly of Balzac one evening when they dined together that Porel had the eery impression that Balzac himself would soon enter the restaurant and sit at their table. Dickens's *Bleak House*, Proust declared, was one of his favourite novels.[1] Porel noticed the pale Henri in the background, but felt that Proust had retired from life and love, that 'he enjoyed giving himself the sight of a young creature to whom he did service, and that was all'. He spoke often of homosexuality, but with remote objectivity, in the manner of Charlus to Brichot at Mme Verdurin's soirée in *La Prisonnière*: "*They* are so numerous nowadays that one might say it's *they* who are normal. For instance, So-and-so is normal, you can take my word for it, but X is abnormal, he likes women." Proust knew very well that Porel, in this sense, was 'abnormal', and it was to him that Porel first confided his love for the beautiful Anne-Marie, a war-nurse divorcée, whom he married on 11 March 1918. "I fear for you," Proust said, "when I see you preparing to advance into life, so young, with this marvellous burden on your arm." Now, in May 1919, on the second floor of 8 *bis* Rue Laurent-Pichat lived the great Réjane, aged sixty-two, still immensely celebrated and popular, but dying in harness; on the third floor were Porel and his wife with their seven-months old baby girl; and on the fourth floor was a vast furnished flat which Réjane kept for her estranged daughter, should she ever return, and which Porel providentially offered to Proust. He came, feeling that a fragment of his destiny was calling. Was he not entering the home of the dying Berma and her children?

It was a step towards his own death. By a strange coincidence the first new proofs of *Le Côté de Guermantes* came on the day of his departure, containing the description of the Narrator's despair when

[1] So was *Great Expectations*, and Proust was delighted when Lucien Daudet pointed out that the relationship between Magwitch and Pip resembled that between Charlus and Morel.

his family moved to a new apartment in the Guermantes mansion, where 'the twittering of the birds at daybreak seemed insipid to Françoise'. It was a memory of the Proust family's removal to 45 Rue de Courcelles in October 1900; but as he writhed in the asthma which always accompanied a change of residence Proust could savour the Narrator's remark, that he 'always found it as difficult to assimilate new things as he found it easy to abandon old'.[1] He did not regret 102 Boulevard Haussmann, but he was now homeless and uprooted for ever.

The house was made of paper, he declared, and noisier than the Gotha raids. At first the air seemed pure, but soon he decided that the trees of the Bois de Boulogne, only a quarter of a mile away, were giving him hay-fever; and the deluge of water when the actor Le Bargy performed his toilet in the house next door was muffled only by the sound of his own gasping for breath. Workmen arrived in Porel's apartment, and he shuddered at every hammer-blow. The lift was out of order, and on the stairs he would meet Réjane, panting also with her tired heart. The two invalids exchanged only a few words, but next day he talked endlessly of her with Porel, summoning his friend in this theatrical house by knocking thrice on the floor, in imitation of the three raps with which the curtain rises at the Comédie Française.

Thirty years had passed since Proust in his schooldays saw Réjane in the first night of *Germinie Lacerteux*. She was still as supreme in comedy as her friend Sarah Bernhardt in tragedy, and Proust created his Berma from both; but now she played only old women, sold the Théâtre Réjane which she had founded, and surrendered her great rôle in Sardou's *Madame Sans-Gêne* at the rueful request of Robert de Flers, who had married Sardou's daughter. During Proust's stay in her house she was resting, exhausted but bored, longing to live again and die on the stage. In the winter, with the reluctant consent of Dr Audistère and her son, she was to make a sensational return in Henri Bataille's *La Vierge Folle*, and in the spring of 1920 to play in a film which killed her.

It was on the tragedy of the Rue Laurent-Pichat that Proust based the terrible episode at the end of *Le Temps Retrouvé*, when the aged Berma sacrifices her life to the avarice of her daughter and son-in-law in a last revival of *Phèdre*, and the guests invited to her tea-party desert her for the Princesse de Guermantes's matinée.[2] As so often when he used a situation from real life, in his alteration of minor

[1] II, 9. [2] III, 856, 995-8, 1002-3, 1013-14.

details Proust meticulously alludes to the actual circumstances under
the pretext of disguising them. Instead of son and daughter-in-law
Berma's relatives are her daughter and son-in-law[1]; they live not in her
own house but next door; the hammer-blows of their house-
renovations, which 'interrupted the sleep of which the great tragic
actress had such need', are the same that disturbed the slumbers of a
great novelist; and for only the second time in the whole of *A la
Recherche* Proust here mentions Réjane herself by name.[2] In other
respects he reversed the real position, for Porel and his wife were
neither mercenary nor snobbish nor heartless; indeed, Porel's feckless
disregard for money, his intimacy on equal terms with such men as
Giraudoux, Morand, Cocteau, Fargue, his indifference to all but the
intellectual left wing of the nobility, his filial adoration of his mother,
were known to everyone. Proust can have had neither the fear nor the
intention of seeming to portray Porel and Anne-Marie, except by
contrast, and the appalling cruelty of the last days of Berma, the final
turn of the screw which completes the ruin of the Narrator's world,
was enforced by aesthetic necessity. And yet, just as the wounded
feelings which Proust cherished towards Montesquiou, Mme de
Chevigné and Fénelon form an essential part in the greatness of his
creation of Charlus, the Duchesse and Saint-Loup, so this incident is
bitterly leavened with his personal resentment for the annoyances of
his sojourn in the house of Réjane.[3]

Proust's discontent, however, was only intermittent. At the end of
the month for which he had agreed to come he decided to stay,
thought of taking a lease for three years, and in fact remained for four
months. 'He maintained that he was an unbearable lodger,' wrote
Porel, 'but in fact he was a charming neighbour.' He took a fancy to
Charmel, their eighty-year-old concierge, who dyed his hair yellow
and looked like an impoverished marquis, and delighted in Céleste's

---

[1] Even so, Proust forgets once and calls them 'her son and daughter-in-law'
(III, 995).

[2] III, 997. The other mention, a passing compliment, was no doubt added at
the same time (II, 495).

[3] It may be noted also that the description of Berma's son-in-law as 'ailing
and lazy' refers unkindly but not unfairly to Porel. Her doctor's excuse for
allowing Berma to return to the stage, that 'she enjoys it, so it will do her good'
(his real motive being that he is in love with the young wife), is founded on
Dr Audistère's reluctant decision, reported by Porel, that 'the worst danger of
all would be to impose upon this fearless and exacting woman a total cessation
of her activity' (III, 995).

reports of the old man's gallantry on the servants' staircase.[1] He received visits from Rivière, Morand, and Giraudoux, whose *La Nuit à Châteauroux* he greatly admired in the NRF for 1 June, but whose review of *A l'Ombre* he thought 'exquisite, crammed with wit, and utterly disappointing'. Soon he forgot his half-imaginary miseries in the proof-correction of *Le Côté de Guermantes* and the battle for his books.

Publication had been announced for 6 June, then for 15 June; and certain 'obstinate maniacs', as he severely informed Gallimard, had even called early in the month at the NRF offices in the Rue Madame hoping in vain to buy his new works. *A l'Ombre des Jeunes Filles en Fleurs*, *Pastiches et Mélanges* and the new edition of *Du Côté de chez Swann* appeared at last in the week beginning 23 June 1919.

The common belief that *A l'Ombre* was an instant success is almost as mistaken as the idea that the first publication of *Swann* was a failure. Whether on the NRF's advice, or from exhaustion, or because he had decided to leave his novel to find its destiny unaided, Proust had abandoned his practice of arranging to be reviewed by his friends. For old times' sake he made a single exception, and asked Robert de Flers for a front-page article in *Le Figaro*, suggesting the well-known names of Gide, Léon Blum, Louis de Robert, Edmond Jaloux and Francis de Miomandre as possible reviewers. But he unaccountably delayed even this proposal until the week before publication, and Flers could only offer a notice by Robert Dreyfus in the form of a front-page news-item, which appeared on Monday, 7 July. Proust gently complained that the print was too small, that Dreyfus had signed only with his pseudonym 'Bartholo', and had used the forbidden word 'meticulous'. He did not know until later that on the Sunday night Henri Vonoven, Cardane's successor as managing editor, had been horrified to find that the article had been printed by mistake on page 2, and stopped the presses and re-arranged the lay-out of the paper for Proust's and everyone's sake. During the first five months *A l'Ombre* was reviewed less promptly and little more extensively than *Swann* had been in the same period.[2] The NRF had issued six editions

---

[1] Proust gave Charmel's name to one of M. de Charlus's footmen (II, 559, 1062).

[2] Reviews appeared by Giraudoux in *Feuillets d'Art* for June, by Fernand Vandérem in *Revue de Paris* on 15 July, by Abel Hermant in *Le Figaro* on 3 and 23 August, by Francis de Miomandre in *Paris Magazine* and François Mauriac in *Revue des Jeunes* on 25 August, by André Billy in *L'Œuvre* on 26 August,

simultaneously, and these satisfied the brisk though not overwhelming demand until the beginning of December.

Nevertheless, Proust's situation had subtly but radically changed since 1913. With the end of the war, and the final signing of peace on 28 June 1919, came a universal feeling that France and the world were reborn, and the arts and intellectual life of mankind renewed. In fact the twentieth-century revolution in literature, as in music and painting, had taken place before and during the war, unnoticed except by the intelligentsia; but now at last it was possible for the new names to become famous and popular. The centre of gravity in French literature had shifted from Anatole France, Barrès, Bourget, Mme de Noailles, Rostand, to Gide, Claudel, Larbaud, Giraudoux, Valéry and Cocteau, all of whom were closely associated with and published by the NRF; and now Proust's name, thanks to his farseeing choice in 1916, was linked with theirs. *Swann* had won him passionate admirers, known and unknown, though few in number; and these, with his new comrades of the NRF, had enrolled an underground network of invisible converts. To all appearance *A l'Ombre* was a moderate success like *Swann*, the indolent reviewers blew hot and cold, and it seemed that the six editions would see the year out. In reality the air of Paris was saturated with his coming glory, as with an unnoticed inflammable vapour which awaited only the exploding spark; and Proust, with the uncanny insight into his destiny which he had shown throughout his life, but hitherto only in slow patience, divined what he must do. In September he informed Louis de Robert that he was applying for the Goncourt Prize.

Meanwhile he had passed the summer in lamenting that he had no first editions of *Al'Ombre* to send to Mme de Noailles, the Princesse de Chimay, Comtesse Greffulhe, Anatole France, Barrès, and many more. An undiscoverable bookseller had cornered them all, 'as if they were butter or coffee,' he complained. With strange procrastination he desultorily sent out third editions several months later. France, 'the first of my masters, the greatest and the best-loved', as Proust had inscribed in his copy of *Swann* six years before, was too old to appreciate his pupil: "Life is too short and Proust is too long," he sighed, and after Proust's death he declared not unkindly to a young

by Dominique Braga in *Crapouillot* on 1 September, by Jacques Émile Blanche in *Le Figaro* on 22 September, and by Gaston Rageot, Proust's former 'usurper', in *Le Gaulois* on 25 October.

friend: "I liked him, haven't seen him for twenty years, I don't understand his work, but that's my fault not his, I belong to the generation
before."

On 14 July, while Proust slept, the great victory procession of the
Allies marched down the nearby Avenue de la Grande Armée and
through the Arc de Triomphe, where Fernand Gregh watched with
Montesquiou. The Count had not relished his portrait in the Saint-
Simon pastiche, and later grumbled to Marcel about his third edition
of *A l'Ombre*: "But there's nothing rare about it!" Gregh introduced
his twelve-year-old son Didier; but Count Robert sharply announced:
"This boy reminds me of a person whom I loathed more than anyone
else in my life," and Gregh, looking in alarm at his child, recognised a
hint of the delicate features of Léon Delafosse.

On 24 July Proust asked Robert Dreyfus's advice on taking a
fourth-floor apartment in September at 156 Boulevard Malesherbes,
next door to Dreyfus himself, at the far northern end of the boulevard
and nearly a mile from the home of his youth; but on the 28th his
messenger found the 'To Let' notice gone. 'The foxes have holes, and
the birds of the air have nests, but the Son of Man has nowhere to lay
his head,' he quoted, and decided to apply to a house-agent. Jacques
Émile Blanche called on Réjane, unaware that Marcel lived in the same
house, and was astounded to hear old Charmel say: "Monsieur
Proust? Fourth floor!" "I've been at the point of death three times
today," Marcel began, but Blanche declared in a loud aside to Céleste:
"He looks the picture of health to me." "Oh, Monsieur," replied the
flustered Céleste, "we're too near the country!" It was true, however:
'I've put on weight,' Proust had told Princesse Soutzo last month,
'my eyes aren't so tired, I look a bit less old, now it's no use to me.'
And Blanche, as they talked gaily over wine and biscuits brought by
Céleste, decided that Marcel looked young indeed, about twenty-
nine, almost only twenty, like the innocent portrait by himself which
he had noticed on entering; 'but his cheeks were paler, bronzed by the
furnace in which he fused the metal of his book'. Prous t arranged to go
to Cabourg on 15 August in a friend's car; but he dined the night
before at the Ritz with Berry, the champagne was all too good, he
went to the Bois, 'sublime in silence, solitude and moonlight' to
recover from its effects; and deciding he was happiest in Paris, he let
the motor-car and Cabourg go for ever.

Réjane and the Porels left for Venice in September, enabling him to
stay a few weeks longer and find a new apartment. Boni de Castellane

called, and though Proust refused his invitation to dinner because Boni had been rude to his aunt Mme Thomson, he was amused to find himself treated for these last few days with paternal affection by the aged Charmel, who had been in service long ago with Boni's father, the late Marquis. On 1 October, after the carpet-layers and electricians had worked until one in the morning, he moved into his last home at 44 Rue Hamelin.

It was a quiet, narrow and gloomy street, running downhill from the Avenue Kléber halfway between the Arc de Triomphe and the Trocadéro, and dominated at its southern end by the incongruous skeleton of the Eiffel Tower beyond the Seine. The Rue Hamelin today seems shabby, even vaguely immoral; but in Proust's time it was still considered a moderately distinguished address, and contained one princess, five marquises, six countesses and a baron, not to mention Mme Standish in the Rue de Belloy just round the corner. Even Monsieur Virat, the baker on the ground floor and proprietor of No. 44, had his château in Seine-et-Marne and his name in *Bottin Mondain* with the nobs. Proust inhabited a small furnished apartment on the fifth floor, 'a vile hovel just large enough for my bedstead', he told Montesquiou, which cost 16,000 francs in rent. He made a present of felt slippers to the children who ran about on the floor above. But in the very discomfort of this bare, monastic dwelling there was something that comforted him, chimed with the sacrificial impulse which had made him sell his parents' furniture, and left him with no desire to change. He slept and worked in the brass bed of his childhood, with his manuscript piled on the mantelpiece and on the little bamboo bedside table, 'my shallop'; at last he was alone with his book.

In September Reynaldo Hahn had spent a few days at the Daudets' country house, La Roche, near Tours, with the mission of sounding Proust's prospects for the Goncourt Prize. He reported that 'they discussed the Prize a great deal, and Léon Daudet wouldn't even listen to what was said about the other candidates, but said he would vote for you whatever happened'. A few days later Rosny *aîné* wrote: 'Several of my fellow-members have asked me to find out whether, if the Prize was offered to you, you would accept it,' and when Proust politely demurred wrote again to insist. Proust sent *A l'Ombre* to each of the Ten, asked Louis de Robert and Robert de Flers to use their influence, and awaited developments. Léon Daudet undertook his crusade with truculent enthusiasm, not only from a genuine admiration for Proust's work, but also from emotions of family piety; for it was twenty-five years since 'little Marcel' had become the friend and protégé of himself, his mother, his brother Lucien, and his venerated father. Proust had maintained distant amicable relations with the Rosny brothers (though Rosny *jeune* did not always vote on the same side as Rosny *aîné*) since their meeting at Cabourg in 1910. "Proust is something new," Rosny *aîné* told his fellow-members. Of his two other wellwishers in 1913 only Céard remained, for Paul Margueritte had died in 1918. He had three certain votes, Daudet, Rosny *aîné* and Céard, and could only leave the rest to fortune.

The Goncourt Academy sat, or rather lunched, on 10 December, and on that afternoon Proust was wakened by a triumphant Léon Daudet bearing the following letter:

'*Monsieur et cher confrère,*
                                    We have the honour and pleasure to inform
you that you have been nominated today for the Goncourt Prize.

Elémir Bourges	Gustave Geffroy	J. H. Rosny, *aîné*
Léon Hennique	Léon Daudet	Paul Ajalbert
J. H. Rosny, *jeune*	Henry Céard.'	

Proust had received the narrow margin of six votes, while the remaining four had gone to *Les Croix de Bois*, a war novel by Roland Dorgelès.[1] Almost simultaneously up came Rivière, Gallimard, and the NRF's editorial manager Tronche, bursting with congratulations, and were introduced round Proust's bedside, on this historic but uneasy occasion, to Léon Daudet, their literary and political opposite. Next came hordes of journalists, eager one and all 'to offer you the front page of my paper', whom Proust imprudently dismissed unseen before subsiding into asthma.

The Prize brought the instantaneous explosion into fame towards which Proust had striven for thirty years. Next day there were twenty-seven articles in the newspapers, and the hundred-mark was passed before the end of January. He was well aware that his celebrity was due, at the moment, merely to the sensational award of the first post-war Goncourt Prize to an intellectual non-combatant of whom the

[1] Émile Bergerat and Lucien Descaves had voted by post. Bourges, Céard, Daudet and Rosny *aîné* voted for Proust. The names of his two other supporters have not been recorded, but (unless Rosny *jeune* was among them) they were probably Geffroy and Bergerat, with both of whom Proust is later found on good terms. Descaves and Hennique are known to have voted for Dorgelès, the latter protesting that Edmond de Goncourt's will had stipulated that preference should be given to younger writers.

general public had never heard: it was a tribute not to his genius but to his news-value. His name was familiar overnight to all the millions in France who read a daily newspaper. 'And I thought I was unknown,' he remarked ironically to Grasset. Many of the comments were preposterously irrelevant: the refusal of the prize to the ex-soldier Dorgelès was an insult to all patriotic Frenchmen, its award to Proust was a political recompense, engineered by the right-wing Daudet, for his services as an anti-Dreyfusard (!) and a supporter of the Church. He had been at school with Daudet at the Lycée Stanislas (of all places), he had bribed Bourges (whom he had never met) with sumptuous dinners; he was too rich to need the money; he was too old, for on the day of the Prize he was forty-eight, next day he was fifty-two, and by the end of the week he was fifty-eight—'I am resignedly awaiting the celebration of my hundredth birthday,' remarked Proust. Paul Morand arrived brandishing Dorgelès's novel with a paper band reading in large letters: 'Goncourt Prize', and in very tiny letters: 'Four votes out of ten'. "You must prosecute him for forgery, Marcel!" he cried; and Proust wrote in chagrin to Gallimard: 'I'm not sure whether this offence really comes under the law of forgery, but I do feel it's not playing the game.'

From the very beginning, however, there was no lack of more responsible comment. Rivière wrote in next day's *Excelsior*, Léon Daudet in his *L'Action Française* on the day after, Souday in *Le Temps* on 1 January 1920, that the Prize had never been given to a more distinguished novel.[1] The malice of the opposition journalists defeated its own ends by making him notorious. Even the voters for Dorgelès wrote apologetically: 'If you'd been a candidate for membership we'd have voted for you.' Several members of the Académie Française (though surely not as many as twenty, as Proust alleged) wrote: 'What a pity you have the Goncourt Prize, because we meant to award you our Grand Prix.' The NRF had been taken by surprise, and *A l'Ombre* instantly went out of print; but Gallimard made a rush order, and from 21 December onwards edition after edition was on sale, with the words 'Goncourt Prize', truthful this time, on the wrapper.

Henceforth Proust's fame was established, immense, and evergrowing. The immediate sensation, like the Prize itself, as he well

[1] In fact, with the sole exception of *Le Feu* (1917) by Henri Barbusse, Proust's former companion on *Le Banquet*, *A l'Ombre* was the only novel of lasting merit crowned by the Académie Goncourt from its foundation in 1903 until the award of the prize to Malraux's *La Condition Humaine* in 1933.

knew, was a vanity and a mockery, and unconnected with the reality of his novel; but its persistence was due to a widening and deepening conviction of his genius in the mind of the individual reader. In this aspect the Prize was an award of love, the closest possible earthly symbol of his dominion in eternity. 'I don't care if the Prize lowers me a little,' he defiantly told Souday, 'so long as it wins me readers.'

Proust spent the 5000 francs of the Prize within a few days on dinner-parties of gratitude. His financial position, however, had unexpectedly improved. In October he had mentioned to Robert de Billy, then on leave in Paris from his post as French plenipotentiary at Athens, his difficulty in realising the famous Warburg cheque. A pathetic misunderstanding ensued; for Billy, unaware that he was not the first but the last of Marcel's influential friends to be asked for help in the same affair, and believing Marcel was in real need of the money, promised to cash it through his own bank. Billy's bank, however, since the cheque was still under sequestration and not yet legal tender, would only accept it as security for an advance in which Billy must act as guarantor. In effect, Proust had unintentionally extorted a large and unwanted loan from Billy himself, and was as far as ever from cashing the Warburg cheque. In his embarrassment he further complicated their cross-purposes by writing: 'I have what I wanted, the proof that I was mistaken in you, and that you are the best and most generous of friends'; and Billy remained under the mistaken impression that Marcel had devised this request as a fantastic test of their friendship. Proust resumed his efforts in the New Year, but in vain; the law would not be hurried, and it was not until December 1920 that he received a first instalment, which he immediately turned over to Billy. A happier windfall was his discovery in December 1919 that he still possessed four Royal Dutch shares of the seventy he had sold in 1913, and that through subsequent bonus issues they had miraculously increased to twelve. Owing to the postwar rise in oil each was now worth 33,000 francs; and he bought Céleste a hat crowned with a stuffed bird of paradise on the strength of it.

In the *Nouvelle Revue Française* for 1 January 1920 appeared Proust's remarkable essay '*A propos du Style de Flaubert*', which he proposed to Rivière about 16 November 1919, delivered on 10 December, and intended for the never-published second volume of *Pastiches et Mélanges*. His appreciation of Flaubert, though severely limited ('he is a writer I do not greatly care for') is extraordinarily new and true, yet is directed to qualities (grammatical innovations, solidity of style, the substitution of impression for direct narrative, the sense of Time) which belong to his own work as much as to Flaubert's. His renewed attack on Sainte-Beuve for inability to detect genius in contemporary writers, his complaint that 'we have lost the ability to read', is secretly addressed to the readers and critics of *A la Recherche*; and he concludes by pointing out 'the rigorous though veiled construction' of his own novel, and quotes—as if knowing that otherwise he would never live to see their effect on his readers—the precedents for unconscious memory in Chateaubriand and Gérard de Nerval which were to appear in *Le Temps Retrouvé*. On 22 February Rivière suggested an article on Sainte-Beuve for the April NRF, and soon Proust received from the circulating library managed by Tronche a collection of Sainte-Beuve's works on loan; for his own books were now stored in a warehouse, and he had made the many quotations in '*A propos du Style de Flaubert*' from memory. But time was too short to fight again the long-won victory of *Contre Sainte-Beuve*, and after half-promising the article for July he abandoned the plan in May, though he was soon to return to the same subject elsewhere. He offered to lend money to Rivière, who was poor, anxious for his pregnant wife,[1] neurasthenic, exhausted by the toils of editing, and in need of a holiday; and he sent him to his cousin-in-law Dr Roussy, who gave excellent advice and refused a fee, saying: "I am only too happy to give Marcel this token of my friendship." Without informing Rivière Proust sent an honorarium of 100 francs, which Roussy gave to charity.

The proof-enrichment of *Le Côté de Guermantes* had been delayed by insomnia and fatigue, during which he could do nothing but play draughts with Henri Rochat, as does the Narrator with Albertine.[2] The mere correction of misprints, which for the ordinary writers of this world is the sole labour of seeing their books through the press, seemed more impossible than ever. In February he asked the NRF for help; and they appointed André Breton, then chieftain of the Dadaists and not yet king of the surrealists, who performed his task with the utmost negligence, but was so enraptured by the poetry of Proust's novel that he began to spread his fame among the Dadaist young. Late in March Gallimard asked Rivière to persuade Proust to publish the first volume of *Le Côté de Guermantes* separately, in order not to

[1] Alain Rivière, named after Rivière's dead brother-in-law Alain-Fournier, author of *Le Grand Meaulnes*, was born on 11 March 1920.
[2] III, 67, 71, 372.

keep the public waiting till past the end of the year. Proust consented and delivered the final proofs about 23 May. Meanwhile, early in April, appeared the *de luxe* edition of *A l'Ombre* which he had planned ever since February 1919. There were fifty copies at 300 francs apiece, each containing folding sheets of the manuscript or of the heavily revised Grasset proofs of 1914 from which the original edition had been printed, together with a reproduction of his portrait as a young man by Blanche. The Schiffs bought one, Princesse Soutzo another, Berry three, feeling that after he had pointedly asked their advice on its circulation they could do no less. All but twelve of the fifty copies, with their vital evidence on the evolution of Proust's text, remain still to be rediscovered.

On 4 May he attended the gala performance of the Russian Ballet at the Opéra. Bakst, his companions informed him, was now in hospital with general paralysis, Nijinski, whom he had seen dancing the negro slave at the first night ten years before, was insane; the glory seemed departed from *Schéhérazade*. Beside him sat a niece of Comte Othenin d'Haussonville; and there, in a nearby stall, was the old man himself, now seventy-seven, changed by the ocean of years from his slender, ironic affability into the virile figure of the hunting squire his father. 'I felt that the years had given his head, without modifying its curves, a majesty which it did not have to such a degree before,' he wrote to Mme Straus; and he used the model for the Duc de Guermantes at the end of his novel: 'lashed on all sides by the waves of suffering and anger at suffering,' says the Narrator, 'by the mounting tide of death that hemmed him in, his face, crumbling like a rock, kept the style and curves I had always admired'.[1]

He had kept in touch with Porel, and called at Rue Laurent-Pichat one evening, tottering and smiling in white tie and tails, when Ricardo Vinès was playing Debussy. Proust sat on the sofa with Léon Paul Fargue, while the pianist, his head buried in the keyboard, seemed to confide a secret to the composer; and glancing at the couple on the sofa Porel saw that Fargue, who became somnolent when supremely happy and was never happier than when Debussy was played, had fallen asleep on Proust's shoulder. When the news of the Goncourt Prize came Réjane had asked to be allowed to give him a present. "I'd like her photograph dressed as the Prince de Sagan in the Marquis de Massa's revue at the Épatant," declared Proust without hesitation, and Porel brought it next day. She wore full evening dress and top hat,

[1] III, 1017.

with the Prince's white hair, white gardenia, and monocle with the surprisingly broad black ribbon, but in her ears were pearl ear-rings. "Admire the intelligence of her interpretation," exclaimed Proust, "she is playing a male impersonation, but she has had the elegance to keep her ear-rings!"

On 14 June the dying Réjane had planned to see the first night of *Antony and Cleopatra* in Gide's translation at the Opéra. When the evening came she said only: "You ought to have taken Anne-Marie," and Porel, for in real life the great actress's children did not desert their mother, lamely replied: "Oh, you know, Shakespeare in summer, and in French!" A few moments later Réjane called his name, and died in his arms. Proust was at the Opéra in Princesse Soutzo's box with Henri Bardac, who reproached him a few days later for talking incessantly to his friends and paying no attention to the play; but Proust, raising his hands in protest, delivered so brilliant a lecture on Shakespeare, on the acting of Ida Rubinstein and Édouard de Max, the lighting in the banquet-scene, the conversation in the neighbouring boxes and incidents among the spectators below, that Bardac realised once more that Marcel always paid attention to everything. The news of Réjane's death arrived during the last interval, and Proust hurried to Rue Laurent-Pichat.

At this terrible moment, while Porel raved with grief, Proust stood pale and silent; as Porel was now, so had he been fifteen years before. At last he offered mechanically his customary words of consolation, which in the case of the guiltless and devoted Porel were true: that when at last the wound of separation was healed his mother would return, young and happy, and live for ever. Proust meditated all night in tense anguish, and at dawn found release in weeping. 'Keep what I said to you for the day when you will be able to use it,' he wrote to Porel, 'at present my words are meaningless for you, and may perhaps contradict bitter thoughts; but you will find them true, consoling and strengthening when you have made the journey from parting to memory, of which no one, alas, can spare you the cruel meanders.' At Porel's request he offered a tribute to Réjane for the NRF, which Rivière accepted with enthusiasm; but on reflection he found himself incapable of writing it. His words to Porel were not yet wholly true of himself. In his novel, just as he had projected his own homosexuality upon the other characters, and left the Narrator free of this gravest of sins, he had reconciled the mutual hatred between his mother and himself which persisted at the root of their love; he had cancelled her death, and made her young and happy for ever. But the redemption which was valid in the eternal world of art was still incomplete in the world of things, on this side of the grave. At Le Cuziat's brothel in the pit of Sodom he had hated and slain her again. In this world the Two Ways would meet only in the bed of death; he had killed his mother twice over, and it only remained to let her avenging spirit kill him.

Chapter 15

THE DARK WOMAN
(July 1920 – October 1921)

IN the summer of 1920, thinking no more of Cabourg, Proust half planned a holiday at Monte Carlo by royal invitation. Comte Pierre de Polignac, a new young friend from the last years of the war, had married Charlotte Grimaldi, Duchesse de Valentinois and adoptive crown princess of Monaco, on 19 March 1920. Her grandfather, the reigning Prince Albert (1848-1922) was a friend of the Strauses, through whom Proust had sought his protection for Agostinelli's widow in 1914; and Polignac, in allusion to an incident in the Saint-Simon parody in *Pastiches et Mélanges*, had gracefully remarked when announcing his engagement to Marcel: "Perhaps this will enable me to meet the lady who made that pretty retort to M. de Noyon!"[1] The match was made for dynastic reasons, for Prince Albert's second marriage to the gay Princesse Alice, born a Heine, widow of the Duc de Richelieu, and mother of Gabriel de La Rochefoucauld's wife Odile, had remained childless and ended in divorce; and the young Duchesse de Valentinois was the recently legitimised only child of his bachelor son Prince Louis from a morganatic liaison with an actress in 1898. In June the royal consort visited Proust, who found him 'still nicer than when he was only Polignac', and invited him to Monaco; but next month Proust took offence at his omission to order the *de luxe* edition of *A l'Ombre* and broke off their friendship.

Aided by the resemblance in the amiable levity of their lives between Princesse Alice and the Princesse de Sagan, his model for the Princesse de Luxembourg whom the Narrator meets at Balbec in *A*

---

[1] *Pastiches et Mélanges*, 79. Proust had quoted the anecdote of Mme Straus's reply to Gounod's remark that a passage in Massenet's *Hérodiade* was 'perfectly octagonal': "I was just about to say the same myself"; but for Gounod he substituted the Saint-Simonian name of M. de Noyon. François de Clermont-Tonnerre, Bishop of Noyon, was a frequent butt of Saint-Simon, who consistently alludes to him by his episcopal title.

l'Ombre,[1] Proust now added to the proofs of *Le Côté de Guermantes* a series of links between the fictitious Luxembourgs and the royal family of Monaco. Pierre de Polignac became the Comte de Nassau, who writes so sympathetically during the illness of the Narrator's grandmother, and whom the childless Grand Duke of Luxembourg adopts as his heir after his marriage to the 'enchanting and excessively rich' only daughter of another prince of the family.[2] The new heir is said by the young nobles dining in the restaurant in the fog to have announced to the Duchesse de Guermantes: "I make a point of everyone's getting up when my wife passes!" to which the Duchesse replies: "Well, that makes a change from her grandmother, because she expected the men to lie down"; and when staying at the Grand Hôtel at Balbec, it is rumoured, he insisted on having the Luxembourg flag flown on the seafront.[3] The conversation at the Guermantes dinner is equally malicious on the subject; and although the Narrator silently protests that 'all these stories were equally false', and that he 'never met a better, more intelligent, refined and in a word exquisite person than this Luxembourg-Nassau',[4] the new Duc de Valentinois must have cursed the day when he refused to subscribe to the *de luxe A l'Ombre.*

Le Côté de Guermantes, indeed, is particularly rich in the private allusions to the time of proofreading, more than twenty years later, with which Proust embellished his story of the late 1890s. The Narrator at Doncières meditates on the new world which is created, by the temporary loss of hearing, for 'the sick man whose ears have been hermetically stopped up'. In May 1919, foreseeing that he would be deprived for ever of his cork walls, Proust had decided, as he wrote to Mme de Noailles, 'to transport the means of defence into my ears'. Mme Simone the actress (whom he had met in 1903 when she was a friend of Antoine Bibesco and still married to Le Bargy) and Mme de Noailles herself recommended little balls of ivory, the Duchesse de Guiche advised cotton-wool soaked in vaseline; he tried both, but preferred the incomparable Boules Quies, those beneficent pellets of cotton-wool impregnated with pink medicated wax. In his delicious

[1] I, 698-703.
[2] II, 329-30.
[3] II, 410.
[4] II, 533-4, 537-9. 'Everything people say about him (that he thinks he's become a Little King, etc.) is stupid', Proust told Sydney Schiff, 'but unfortunately everyone says it and invents the most absurd tales'.

catalogue of sounds which are thus deadened the Narrator mentions
the bathwater of Le Bargy (whose wife, by a Proustian coincidence,
was thus responsible unawares for dulling the noise of her long-since-
divorced husband) and the hammering at Rue Laurent-Pichat; the
milk which he imagines 'a great writer' watching as it comes silently to
the boil stands on the same bedside electric hot-point on which Proust
made his coffee in the small hours; and it is in the voice of Céleste that
his servant tells him, when the saucepan boils over and 'his books and
watch are engulfed by the milky tidal-wave', that he 'has no more
sense than a child of five'.[1] 'I shall regret the black and white flowers on
a red background,' he had told Porel as he prepared to move to 44 Rue
Hamelin, 'but I have described them in my book.' And sure enough,
the Narrator's bathroom at Doncières is hung, like Proust's at Rue
Laurent-Pichat, with 'a violent red wallpaper sprinkled with black
and white flowers', whence he 'views the world as if from the heart of a
corn-poppy'.[2]

On 25 September 1920 Proust was awarded the cross of the Legion
of Honour. Various friends had asked if he would like it; he replied
that he would indeed; and his sponsors in approaching the Minister of
Public Education, André Honnorat, included Barrès, Regnier, Léon
Blum, Robert de Flers, Léon Daudet, Céard, Reynaldo Hahn, and
Paul Morand. Mme de Noailles and Colette received the same honour
on the same day. A wealthy art-dealer whom he had met before the
war at Cabourg sent him a superb cross set in brilliants, for dress-
wear: 'at most it will serve only to adorn my hearse, as I'm too ill to
attend royal dinners,' he told Mme Catusse. But now, in his glory, he
was not only a receiver but a giver of prizes. Mme Georges Blumenthal, a relative of the lady whose marriage had inspired the last avatar
of Mme Verdurin, invited him to join the committee for her newly
founded Blumenthal Prize, on which his eminent fellow-members
included Barrès, Bergson, the philosopher Émile Boutroux, Boylesve,
Gide, Robert de Flers, Edmond Jaloux, Mme de Noailles and Valéry.
Proust resolved to propose the noble-souled Rivière, who was in need
of money but still more of self-confidence, and to whom the 12,000
francs and prestige of the prize would give a little of both. On 30
September he arrived late at the Blumenthal committee, in pain from
otitis caused by his earplugs, swaying with the fatigue of his sleepless
day, nearly falling at one moment on Bergson, at another on Boylesve,

[1] II, 75-8.
[2] II, 89.

and afflicted once again by the mysterious impediment in his speech. 'In appearance and smile he looked like a lady palmist,' wrote Boylesve cruelly. Proust secured a unanimous vote for his friend: Rivière, less directly, had won a prize for him, and now he had won a prize for Rivière.

The next instalment of *A la Recherche* had been promised for 15 August,[1] postponed till 1 October because it seemed unwise to publish in the middle of the holiday season, reviewed from proofs by Léon Daudet in *L'Action Française* on 8 October, and delayed again for the printing of two pages of errata. *Le Côté de Guermantes I* at last appeared about 25 October, and was reviewed as the work of an unquestionably great writer, though with some foolish complaints about snobism. In the same way reviewers of *Sodome et Gomorrhe*, *La Prisonnière*, *Albertine Disparue* and *Le Temps Retrouvé* were to accuse Proust successively of obsession with homosexuality, inability to love, jealousy, and death; for it is the oldest trick in that parasitic trade to blame an author for writing about the subject of his book. Souday, however, deeply distressed Proust by calling him 'feminine' in *Le Temps* on 4 November. He retorted fiercely that if Souday wished to know whether or not he was effeminate he had only to ask the seconds who had attended him in his duel; and when Souday tried to bury the hatchet by sending a box of chocolates on New Year's Day, Proust cried: "Put these on the fire, Céleste, the man who sent them is capable of anything." But he magnanimously sent a grateful letter and a copy of the *de luxe A l'Ombre* in return.

Early in 1920 Paul Morand had published a volume of free verse, *Lampes à arc*, with a teasing and famous *Ode to Marcel Proust:*

> 'Shadow
> Born of the smoke of your fumigations
> Face and voice
> Eroded by the wear and tear of night
> Céleste
> With gentle rigour soaks me in the dark juice
> Of your room that smells of warm cork and dead hearth ...
> Proust, to what revels do you go by night'

—for Morand evidently had some inkling of his friend's visits to Albert's brothel—

[1] The date of the *achevé d'imprimer*, 17 August, is inconsistent with Proust's remark to Walter Berry on 7 August that the volume was then already stitched.

> *'That you return with eyes so tired and lucid?*
> *What terrors to us forbidden have you known*
> *That you return so kind and so indulgent*
> *Wise in the toil of souls and family secrets,*
> *Wise in the wound of love?'*

Not to be outdone, Proust contributed a preface to Morand's *Tendres stocks*, a volume of three short stories based on the love-affairs of the young diplomat in London during the early years of the war, which was to be published by the NRF in March 1921.[1] He wrote it in the first week of October 1920, after his alarming indisposition at the Blumenthal committee, and published it in the *Revue de Paris* on 15 November under the title '*Pour un ami. Remarques sur le style*'. Proust took as his text an article on Stendhal by Anatole France in the same magazine on 1 September, and respectfully but resolutely attacked the view of 'my dear master' that no good French had been written since the eighteenth century, and that style must be judged by a canon lost for ever in the French Revolution. For the third time he returned to the themes of *Contre Sainte-Beuve*, in particular to the arch-critic's misapprehension of Baudelaire. Style, Proust maintains, must be renewed in each new writer, since it consists not in adhesion to a classic model, but in the moment of identification between the author and his subject. He compared the writer, as does the Narrator in *Le Temps Retrouvé*,[2] to the optician who gives his patient a new vision of the world (for Proust had at last succeeded, after five years of failing sight, in consulting an optician), and pointed out, as does the Narrator to Albertine,[3] the unconscious symbolism with which Stendhal situated the prisons of Julien Sorel and Fabrice, where they attain spiritual freedom, in high places. He playfully represented Morand as a Minotaur devouring girls in the worldly labyrinth of luxury hotels, and offered to introduce him (it was a journey which Morand, with all his talent, was never quite to succeed in making) to the hotel of Balbec situated in the world of the imagination.

In the opening paragraph of his essay, however, Proust revealed the monster that lay in wait at the heart of his own labyrinth. 'A

---

[1] M. de Charlus refers during the war to 'the charming Morand, the delicious author of *Clarisse*' (III, 793)—*Clarisse*, which Proust had read in proof before appearance in the *Mercure de France* in May 1917, being the first story in *Tendres stocks*.

[2] III, 1033.

[3] III, 377.

strange woman,' he wrote, 'has chosen to make her home in my brain. She came and went; soon, from the commotion she caused, I began to know her habits; and besides, as is the way of a too forthcoming lodger, she insisted on striking up a personal acquaintance with me. I was surprised to find that she was not beautiful. I had always believed that Death was so, for otherwise, how could she get the better of us? However this may be, she seems to be out today—but not for long, to judge from all that she has left behind. And it would be wiser to profit from the respite she gives me otherwise than by writing a preface for a wellknown author who does not need one.'

For the last fifteen years Proust had been announcing his imminent death to his friends, who were duly amused. Mme de Chevigné teased him on his '*moribondage*', and Morand had written in his Ode:

'*I say: "You seem the picture of health," you reply:*
"*Dear friend, I have nearly died three times since morning.*" '

The death of his mother had shown that he too was mortal, his failure to regain health at Dr Sollier's sanatorium had destroyed his hope of recovery, the beginning of *A la Recherche* filled him with the apprehension natural to authors of being unable to see a long work through to the end; yet death had always seemed during these long years of reprieve to linger, receding rather than approaching, a little past the horizon of his novel. Now, however, recurrent warnings had convinced him that death was very near; and the preface for Morand marks Proust's irreversible realisation of his fate. His foreboding must be taken seriously, not only because it was sincere, but because it was true: he now had only two years to live. In his life as in his novel the white revelation of the madeleine was matched and concluded by the black revelation that salvation lies on the verge of the grave.

However, the deepest significance of the Morand preface lies not in the premonition of death, but in the form of Death's personification. That sombre noun, though masculine in Teutonic languages, is feminine in French, and it is natural that in France Death should seem a woman. But the hideous female lodging in Proust's brain took a strangely particular form, and may be recognised in other contexts in the final nightmares of his novel. The Narrator dreams during the captivity of Albertine that he is walking in a dark avenue; he hears a female cab-driver quarrelling with a policeman, 'reads in her voice the perfection of her features and the youth of her body', and hurries to take her cab: 'it was indeed a woman, but old, tall and stout, with white hair straying from under her cap, and a red leprosity on her face'.[1] Bergotte in his last illness has a hallucination of 'a hand with a wet towel, rubbed over his face by an evil woman'.[2] And the Narrator dreams he is talking to the dead Albertine, while 'at the far end of the room my grandmother moved to and fro, with part of her chin crumbled away like corroded marble'.[3] Nearly thirty years before, in his student days, Proust had written: 'Who knows whether, from our marriage with death, our conscious immortality may not be born?'[4] But now death, in a shape strangely but unmistakably like that of his own mother in her last years, had become a bride who did not accept the atonement of his novel, whose annihilating nuptials would be her final revenge for his crimes against her. 'This idea of death took up its abode in me as definitively as being in love. Not that I loved Death, I hated her,' says the Narrator at the end of *Le Temps Retrouvé*.[5] The real presence of death in Proust was now crystallised in the terrible figure known to psychoanalysts as the Dread Mother, whose monstrous image consummates and punishes the child's sin of love and hatred in the ultimate horror of the unconscious mind. It was with her that Proust would have to reckon in his last moments on earth, and we shall find the dark woman punctually reappearing at his bed of death.

During his October fever Proust composed another preface for a friend. In her leisure moments as a war-nurse Clément de Maugny's wife had prepared a volume of humorous drawings, *Au royaume du bistouri*, for which Proust had tried in vain to find a publisher in November 1917 and January 1919. He particularly appreciated the caption: "Wake up, there's a good boy, it's time for your sleeping-draught!"; and now, urged by the Maugnys who had secured a publisher in Geneva, he wrote a charming foreword, recalling his days by the lake with Clément in the distant summer of 1899, and describing the little train from Geneva to Évian in words he had used for the Little Train at Balbec. 'I have announced my death in a preface for Morand,' he told Mme de Maugny, coughing as he dictated to Rochat, and interrupted still further by poor Henri's question: "How do you spell cough?" Another old friend noted the significance of the Morand preface: 'The Strange Woman who took up her abode with you this winter is prowling around me,' wrote the ailing Mme Straus. How-

---

[1] III, 125.   [2] III, 184.   [3] III, 539.
[4] *Les Plaisirs et les Jours*, 187, first published in *Le Banquet*, July 1892.
[5] III, 1042.

ever, his otitis had been cured by the ear-specialist Dr Wicart; and he had at last acquired a pair of reading-spectacles, which he wore only in the privacy of his bedroom.

Early in January 1921 appeared the second volume of Jacques Émile Blanche's *Propos de peintre*, entitled *Dates*, with a long dedicatory foreword, woven from roses and thorns, in which this exceedingly touchy friend replied to Proust's amiable strictures in his preface to the first volume two years before. Blanche's eleven-page evocation of Montesquiou and his influence upon their youth was calculated to suggest to observant readers that the Baron de Charlus might be not unconnected with Count Robert. Worse still, and quite mistakenly in so far as concerned the volumes of *A la Recherche* then published, Blanche remarked: 'It seems to me that sometimes, and in your most beautiful pages, you borrow from one sex the features of the other; that in certain of your characters there is a partial substitution of gender, so that one might read "he" where you say "she".' But Blanche made a less unkind use of inside knowledge when he prophesied: 'You will sit beneath the dome of the Academy with Jacques Rivière, André Gide, Giraudoux and Morand when your fellow-academician Paul Claudel is President of the Republic.'

"Marcel will belong to the Académie Française," Dr Proust had declared long ago in moments of pride; and when his academician friends wrote in December 1919 to congratulate him on his Goncourt Prize, Proust began to cherish the vision of making his father's words come true. In May 1920 he asked Rivière whether the NRF would favour his candidature, 'supposing I had a good chance of success'; and Rivière, much taken aback, replied that they would be only too flattered, but that the time seemed premature: 'you are too vigorous, too positive, too truthful for these people, they are too fast asleep'. Proust sounded his chances. The Academy was then divided, as usual, into a hard core of retired politicians, generals, clerics, and fourth-rate belles-lettrists, and an outer fringe of writers and intellectuals with real merit; and several of the latter were his friends from early youth. Sure enough, Boylesve and Bordeaux gave their enthusiastic support; his cousin-in-law Bergson, Régnier and Barrès, whom he named to Jacques Boulanger in December 1920 as 'my promotors for the Academy', expressed encouragement. Half a dozen others, such as the newly elected Robert de Flers, his aged host Comte Othenin d'Haussonville, his boyhood masters Bourget and Anatole France, his father's colleague Gabriel Hanotaux, Darlu's friend the philosopher

Boutroux, Marcel Prévost, whom he had known ever since Louisa de Mornand acted in his *Les Demi-Vierges* fifteen years before, might well take a personal interest in him. Guiche, riding to hounds one day with Jacques Boulenger in the Forest of Ermenonville, was surprised to be informed (for though a duke, he was only a member of the Academy of Sciences, without influence on the Forty): "Marcel Proust says he'll have your help for the Academy!" Proust's willingness to sit on the Blumenthal committee, where Barrès, Bergson, Boutroux, Boylesve and Flers were his fellow-members, was doubtless part of his strategy; and in his Morand preface he meaningfully told the story of Baudelaire's abortive candidature and Sainte-Beuve's dissuasive perfidy; there was no need to point the moral.

Proust's dream was pathetic but not absurd: he would no doubt have obtained even in 1921 the preliminary token votes which are the time-honoured stepping-stone to eventual success, and if he had lived would have become an Academician not later than the 1930s. But death and his novel called more urgently; unless he could persuade the Academy to sit at midnight, how (as Barrès pointed out) could he attend its meetings?—and his project was last mentioned in a letter to Barrès in June 1921.

The publication of the second volume of *Le Côté de Guermantes* had been planned in July 1920 for December, and then, when the first volume was postponed till October, for February 1921. In January, however, Proust was still awaiting second proofs, *Sodome et Gomorrhe I* was still in manuscript, and he proposed 1 May as publication day. When the *Revue de Paris* had asked in August 1920 to print the volume as a serial, Proust refused, knowing the NRF's desire to keep their new great writer to themselves; but he was piqued by Rivière's apparent lack of zeal for extracts from the first volume,[1] and saw the opportunity to gain a wider public and extra money from occasional infidelities with other magazines. *'Une Agonie'*, the episode of the grandmother's death, appeared in the NRF for 1 January 1921, attracting many new subscribers, and was followed in February by *'Un Baiser'*, the story of Albertine's visit and her first kiss; but he reserved the dinner with Saint-Loup at the restaurant in the fog, which Rivière had also coveted, for the *Revue Hebdomadaire*, where it appeared on 21 January under the title *'Soirée de brouillard'*. He sent

[1] In fact Rivière had asked for extracts on 26 October 1919, Proust refused without giving reasons, and Rivière refrained from insisting, though he repeated the request, again without result, on 1 April 1920.

the manuscript of *Sodome et Gomorrhe I*, containing the meeting of
Charlus and Jupien and the treatise on male homosexuality, to Gallimard on 20 January, swearing him to secrecy; but to make it legible to
the printer Gallimard was compelled to have it typed, and it was on
this typescript that Proust made his final modifications, including the
deletion of a long, superb but superfluous introduction in an earlier
manner.[1] There was no time for him to see a final proof of *Le Côté de
Guermantes II*, or even a first proof of *Sodome et Gomorrhe I*. During
the third week of April all other work was abandoned in the NRF
offices, while Gallimard, Rivière and the deputy-editor Jean Paulhan,
a devoted working-party, corrected the proofs on his behalf; and the
volume was on sale, only one day late, on 2 May.[2]

The outcry that he had feared was not raised. The chapter on
Sodom was praised or justified as being 'moral' or 'scientific'. Rivière
himself, who first saw it only a fortnight before publication, declared
himself 'profoundly overwhelmed', and confessed to 'a vengeful
satisfaction in reading the terrible pages, made more terrible still by
their very equitability, in which you describe the men of Sodom'.
Rivière was still naïvely unaware that Proust was one of these, and
Rivière's loyal admiration for Gide's genius did not extend to Gide's
vice, still less to Gide's invert friends. 'I have listened too often to my
acquaintances falsifying the idea of love,' he wrote, 'not to feel a
delectable relief in hearing it discussed by someone as healthy and
balanced as you.' Rivière's words were echoed by Roger Allard, the
Gaston Rageot of the NRF, whose previous reviews had left Proust
far from satisfied: 'These pages of such burning eloquence, such harsh
and noble poetry,' wrote Allard in the NRF for September 1921,
'break the aesthetic spell of sexual inversion under which the arts and
literature have lain so long bewitched.' It is strange to reflect that if his
innocent friends had known the truth about Proust their opinion
might have changed, yet his burning pages would still have remained
the same, still have contained the moral fervour which they rightly
discerned in them, without seeing that it sprang from self-accusation.

Gide himself, however, whom Proust summoned in Odilon's taxi
on 13 and 17 May, was gravely displeased. To him this denunciation

[1] This passage, containing a vision of Balbec and Albertine called up by the
heat of the day, and a meditation on the mysteries of pollen suggested by the
Duchesse's rare shrub, was first published in BSAMP, tom. 6 (1956), 165-70.

[2] The *achevé d'imprimer* of 30 April is inconsistent with this fact, and must
have been post-dated by several days, like that to *Le Côté de Guermantes I*.

of sodomy by a native of Sodom could only seem an act of both treachery and hypocrisy. He found Proust much altered, grown so fat that he looked vaguely like the deceased Jean Lorrain, and shivering in a stifling room. 'I used to suspect him of trading on his ill-health to protect his work, which I thought perfectly legitimate,' he noted, 'but now I was able to convince myself that he was really very unwell.' Proust, who enjoyed letting his hair down with this great invert, and relished still more the irony of shocking him, led the conversation immediately to the subject of homosexuality. He had never loved women otherwise than spiritually, he declared, and had never experienced love except with men. Baudelaire, too, was a practising invert, he rashly maintained, for "the manner in which he speaks of Lesbianism, and even his need to speak of it, would alone suffice to convince me". In order to provide material for the heterosexual part of his novel, he confessed, he had transposed to the budding grove of girls 'all that was graceful, tender and charming' in his homosexual memories. Gide sorrowfully reproached him for 'seeming to have intended to stigmatise uranism'; "Will you never portray this form of Eros for us in the aspect of youth and beauty?" he asked. Proust lamely replied that he felt Charlus and Jupien 'were not so repulsive as all that', that for him beauty had little to do with desire, and that he must reserve youth for his transpositions, because young people were the easiest to transpose. These unfortunate evenings exposed and perpetuated the incompatibility between those two inverts of genius. 'I've annoyed many homosexuals with my last chapter,' Proust told Jacques Boulenger, 'and I'm sorry for it; but it isn't my fault that M. de Charlus is elderly, and I couldn't suddenly make him look like a Sicilian shepherd boy.' Gide wrote later in his *Journal* of Proust's 'camouflage', 'this offence against the truth', and called him 'the great master of dissimulation'. More seriously still, Proust's biased avowals, made partly to tease and partly to mollify his friend, have been conveniently accepted by his critics as his final and total diagnosis of his own abnormality and its relation to his novel. Seen in their context, and compared with the known facts of his life, they form only a fraction of a far more complicated truth. In his novel Proust rejected his own inversion, and created the Narrator from the lost but real heterosexual part of his own divided nature; he used homosexuality, like snobism and cruelty, as a symbol of universal original sin; if he had told the literal truth and made the Narrator love men, he would have destroyed the symbolic truth of his work. Proust was a remorseful, Gide a triumphant invert; and by Gide, whose art was based on confession, the great opposing sexual tensions of *A la Recherche* were mistaken for a figment of duplicity.

The publication of his latest two volumes had caused other and quite different imbroglios with Proust's friends. Albufera had recognised in the quarrel of Saint-Loup and Rachel the memory of his own brawls with Louisa at the Théâtre des Maturins in 1903, and severed relations with Marcel. Mme de Chevigné had been well pleased with her portrait in vol. 1 as the Duchesse de Guermantes with the cornflower hat and periwinkle eyes: 'all my next volume is about you,' Proust had told her last summer, and: 'if you like the Duchesse half as much as the Narrator does, who in the book is mad about her, I am recompensed'. But the second volume, the vast dinner-party in which the Duchesse displays her heartless vanity, the atrocious incident of Swann and the red shoes, and Proust's suspicious delay in sending her presentation copy, seemed a personal insult. Poor Mme de Chevigné did not realise that here the model had changed, and the Duchesse had temporarily become Mme Greffulhe, with a mixture, for her wit and the red shoes, of Mme Straus. Proust himself unkindly contributed to her misapprehension. At Mme Hennessy's dinner on 16 June, when his hostess and Guiche correctly suggested Mme Greffulhe, he 'protested with the utmost vivacity', declaring mendaciously that Mme Greffulhe was not the Duchesse, and truthfully that she was the Princesse de Guermantes. He spoke partly to avoid a dilemma, for Mme Greffulhe was Guiche's mother-in-law, he liked her and appreciated the obstinate goodwill with which during the last two decades she had persisted in inviting him to dinners which he never attended; and she could only be delighted to hear that she resembled the dazzling Princesse de Guermantes. But he was also determined that Mme de Chevigné should not escape. 'Except that the Duchesse de Guermantes is virtuous,' he cruelly wrote a few days later to Guiche, 'she resembles a little the tough hen whom I mistook long ago for a bird of paradise, and who could only repeat like a parrot: "FitzJames is expecting me!", when I tried to capture her under the trees of the Avenue Gabriel. By changing her into a mighty vulture, I at least prevent people from thinking her an old magpie.' Word reached Mme de Chevigné from malicious friends; in August she countered by accusing Proust of snobism, and demanded her copy, four months overdue, of this book about herself. 'Strange snobism,' he cried, 'which consists in never seeing anyone!' The book itself was his present to her; what did it matter which of them paid for her copy? Duchesses had protested to him: "She's no duchess, she's only a lady for little Jewish drawing-rooms!"; but: "She has more breeding than you," he had replied. It was not his fault if she disliked her portrait: 'I had to show that Places and People lose from contact, Balbec for Places, and Guermantes for People.'[1] Mme de Chevigné was goaded to make the only completely effective retort: she declined to read his book. 'When I was twenty she refused to love me,' he lamented to their mutual friend Cocteau, 'will she refuse to read me now I am forty' (in fact he was now just fifty) 'and have made from her all that is best in the Duchesse de Guermantes?' 'Fabre wrote a book about insects,' replied Jean, 'but he did not expect the insects to read his book.'

Proust remained unconsoled. Indeed, the French nobility, whom he had loved all his life, and whose great obituary he had written, were not insects. In the final glory of their sunset, which coincided with the fifty years of his own existence, they had fashioned in miniature the last social culture that our world has seen, a beautiful, fugitive and irreplaceable thing that history produced and history has destroyed. In their drawing-rooms flourished a gay elegance, a fantastic individuality, a chivalrous freedom, a living interplay of minds, morals and emotions. They gave their last young blood in the war, then perished because they had served art instead of power. It is our duty as twentieth-century barbarians to salute the nineteenth-century civilisation which we have overwhelmed. So did Proust; and in the retrospective light of Time Regained, where beauty is restored to the past and disillusion itself is shown to be an illusion, the poetry of the Faubourg Saint-Germain remains in Time Lost as dazzling as the sunlight of Combray, Balbec and Venice.

As for Mme de Chevigné, although the injustice of time had changed her outward form into that of an ogrish, pearl-bedizened old lady—the 'sacred fish' with 'cheeks composite like nougat' into which the Duchesse de Guermantes is transformed in *Le Temps Retrouvé*[2]—

[1] By an unfortunate accident the chapter-headings were omitted from *Le Côté de Guermantes I*, and have never been restored, although they were given in June 1919 as part of the list of forthcoming volumes in *Swann* and *A l'Ombre*. They were: *Noms de personnes: la duchesse de Guermantes; Saint-Loup à Doncières; Le salon de Mme de Villeparisis*. The first of these corresponds to the title of the Balbec chapter in *A l'Ombre*, *Noms de pays: le pays;* and by its omission one of the chief structural themes of *A la Recherche* was obscured.
[2] III, 927, 937.

for Proust she was still the swift young noblewoman he had pursued in the Avenue de Marigny, and his wounded feelings were unhealed. 'I remain as heartbroken as on the first day when she scorned me long ago,' he told Guiche, and to herself he wrote: 'to be misjudged at twenty years of distance'—again he minimised the date—'by the same person, in the same incomprehensible way, without possible excuse from the scandal-mongering of your too malevolent lady rivals, is one of the only great sorrows which can affect at the end of his life a man who has renounced everything'.

In his distress Proust felt resentment even against Mme de Chevigné's son-in-law, the amiable, talented and ambitious Francis de Croisset, who had married her daughter Marie in 1910. 'I'm not sending her my books,' he grumbled to Guiche, 'because as she met Croisset in my house[1] and chose him for her son-in-law, I feel that provides her with a sufficient fund of literature.' He had made a similar complaint against Croisset to Paul Morand in 1917, and it was no doubt at some time within this period that he used Croisset as his model for the final aspect of Bloch in A la Recherche. Croisset, whose real name was Franz Wiener, was a Belgian Jew born at Brussels in 1877 of a financier father and an English mother. Launched by Clemenceau and Octave Mirbeau, and assisted by his beautiful new name (borrowed from Flaubert's country home near Rouen), he had captured literary and social Paris by storm in the early years of the twentieth century, and had now taken the dead Gaston de Caillavet's place as Robert de Flers' partner in the writing of popular light comedies. 'Maeterlinck can't get into the Academy because he's a Belgian, Mme de Noailles because she's a woman, Porto-Riche because he's a Jew,' wrote Paul Léautaud in his journal, 'but Croisset's certain to be elected, although he's all three.'[2] In memory of his mother Croisset adopted an Anglophile attitude of distant, slightly sinister hauteur, and formal English dress. Similarly Bloch is received by Mme de Villeparisis as 'a young playwright, on whom she counted to procure, free of charge, actors and actresses who would perform at her next matinées'; and long afterwards, in Le Temps Retrouvé, he is

[1] This meeting was perhaps at Proust's tea-party on 6 March 1905, when Mme de Chevigné was present. Croisset is not mentioned in the lists of guests in the newspapers, but Proust was seeing him frequently at this time.

[2] On the other hand, Proust remarked to Lauris at Cabourg in August 1907: 'I see nothing at all of Croisset, entirely absorbed, I suppose, by his play, his mistress, and a thousand other complications.'

married, has taken the exquisitely absurd name of Jacques du Rozier, his face is 'totally transformed by English *chic*' and by the hauteur of his monocle, and he is known as 'the Guermantes Bloch, the crony of the Guermantes'.[1]

But the most perplexing problem of all was Montesquiou. How could Count Robert fail to recognise his august person in the Baron de Charlus, who spoke in his voice and with his superhuman insolence, who was the cousin of the Duchesse de Guermantes just as he was the cousin of Mme Greffulhe, who conducted in this volume the same monumental quarrel with the Narrator as his own with Marcel in 1893, and had displayed since the beginning of the novel increasing symptoms of the homosexuality which he now finally revealed in his encounter with Jupien? True, Proust had observed his usual precaution of mentioning character and model side by side, as if to prove that they could not possibly be the same. "We have an Empire card-room that came to us from Quiou-Quiou and is a sheer marvel," says the Duchesse at dinner. M. de Charlus himself knows and feels a proper respect for Count Robert; he quotes to the Narrator ("as the only eminent man in our world has said") his saying about 'the supreme test of excessive amiability'; and in the next volume (which Montesquiou was destined not to live to see), when the Baron compliments the lovely son of Mme de Surgis on his unique knowledge of Balzac, he corrects himself: "No, I'm wrong, there's a Polignac and a Montesquiou as well."[2] In vain! At the first apparition of the Baron on the seafront at Balbec in *A l'Ombre*, as Proust had learned a year before from Henri Bardac, Count Robert had smelled a rat.

Even before the war, when he knew Proust only distantly as a friend of Reynaldo, Bardac had discussed him with Montesquiou. "It is strange," said the Count, "that it should fall to me to enlighten you concerning a person whose bourgeois rank and racial descent are so closely analogous to your own. He was a product of Mme Lemaire's garden, to the weeding of which the Empress of Roses did not always give proper attention. I do not allude particularly to little Proust, who has an original turn of mind, and whose deference to my person is all that it should be. Beneath a timid exterior he is by no means destitute of enterprise. Indeed he would have done better to devote himself to the field of big business, in which his cheek would have been aided by his fractional atavism. You, who have never advanced far into the country of the mind, might well profit by his company. But if you

---

[1] II, 189-90; III, 350, 823, 944, 952-3, 959, 965.   [2] II, 521, 556, 699.

want information about society, you must go to others. He thinks
Mme X is a fashionable lady!"—here the ceiling reverberated shrilly
with the exploding rockets of Count Robert's laughter. "Still, to him
and his friend Daudet I have shown benevolence which Heaven has
spared me from extending to the third thief, a certain Hahn. You
would do well," he concluded, "to give Proust the address of your
tailor."

More recently, a few months after the publication of *A l'Ombre*,
Bardac had found Montesquiou filled with an enigmatic bitterness. He
spoke of 'shameless termites, burrowing their way through a world in
ruins', of 'barefaced opportunists, intriguing when everyone else is
weeping'. "And there's even talk of a Goncourt Prize!" he cried. Was
it not thanks only to his protection that certain distinguished persons
had taken an interest in a certain nobody? Had he ever grudged him
advice or instruction? And what did he get in return, but a note of
thanks for his congratulations, declining on grounds of alleged ill-
health the honour of his visit! "Who is that extraordinary fellow," he
hissed, "that incredible eccentric he meets on the promenade at Balbec?" Bardac tried to explain that each of the characters in Proust's
novel had several originals, which was true but uninformative. "I shall
leave you all my letters from Proust in my will!" screeched the Count
as he departed; but he forgot to do so. Bardac reported to Marcel, who
laughed, clasping his hands beneath his chin, and quoted grimly from
La Fontaine:

> " 'Romans, take heed, lest Heaven one day bestow
> On you our tears, on us your vengeful swords . . .' "

Proust decided that his best policy was to defend himself before he
was attacked. On 9 March 1921, nearly eight weeks before *Le Côté de
Guermantes II* was published, with the fatal quarrel scene and encounter of Charlus and Jupien, he promised Count Robert 'to
send the two *Guermantes*, and tell you the only two spurious keys
in the whole work, which unlock only two chapters'. The Count
replied by making his own intelligent guesses: Saint-Loup, he presumed, was Albufera plus Guiche, Swann was Charles Ephrussi, and
as for the Duc and Duchesse: 'are they really the two persons who leap
to the eye? They are, whether you meant it or not'—he alluded, of
course, to M. and Mme Greffulhe. Charlus, he cleverly surmised,
though it seemed too good to be true that he should think this model
sufficient, must be based on Vautrin, the sinister and vaguely homo-

sexual master-criminal in Balzac; and he duly and gratefully recognised himself as 'the only eminent person in our world', complaining
only that he would rather this eminent person had been named. In
return Proust revealed that Saint-Loup, in his walk along the benches
in the restaurant, was Fénelon, Swann was Haas, Mme de Villeparisis
was Mme de Beaulaincourt, and Charlus—ah, Charlus, at the moment
when he stared at the Narrator by the casino at Balbec, was Baron
Doasan, 'habitué of Mme Aubernon's salon, where I dined with him
twice or thrice, and rather of that kind'; but otherwise 'this character
was constructed in advance and entirely invented'. Montesquiou,
strangely pliant, acquiesced; he had 'never more than glimpsed the
Baron, with his waxed moustaches and waxed hair, who lacked all the
breeding you have bestowed on him'; how brave, and how rash, was
dear Marcel, 'to dare for the first time to choose as a direct subject the
vice of Tiberius or shepherd Corydon, the immense field of inversion,
hitherto banned, which is capable of enriching art with perilous and
beautiful works'. But Marcel was rich and famous, had a prize and a
cross, while he—: 'Dear Marcel, you know I never wrote but for
myself, and for those who understand me, as you always did so well.
Solitude widens round my work, and so does my pride. . . .'

Moved by compunction and dread—could not this unwonted
gentleness be a trap, devised to conceal who knows what horrible
vengeance that the Count might be preparing in his Memoirs?—
Proust planned a consolation and a bribe. He asked Jacques Boulenger
in April and again in July to invite Montesquiou to contribute to
L'Opinion or the *Revue de la Semaine*: 'he is a marvellous art critic,' he
wrote, 'and portrays as no one else can the work of a painter or sculptor he likes'. Illnatured persons, Proust explained, had spread the
rumour that Montesquiou was the model for Charlus, whereas,
'although I've known in high society an enormous number of inverts
whom no one suspected, in all the years I've known Montesquiou I've
never seen him show the least sign of it, whether alone or in company';
nevertheless, 'I believe he imagines, although he is too intelligent to
show it, that I intended to portray him, and the kindness of his letters
tortures me.' But Boulenger's invitation was too lukewarm, and Montesquiou, who could forgive an injury but not a benefaction, exploded
at last in a letter of insane fury, in which he continued to be perfectly
charming to Marcel, but said the most appalling things about Boulenger.

Meanwhile, all through May 1921, Paris had flocked to the loan exhibition of Dutch painting at the Jeu de Paume, which included two major works of Vermeer, the *Head of a Girl* and the *View of Delft*. Proust eagerly read the articles on Vermeer by Léon Daudet in the *Action Française* and by Vaudoyer in *L'Opinion*, probably also the essay on the exhibition by Clotilde Misme in the *Gazette des Beaux-Arts*. At last, about the 24th, he decided to go himself, and at 9.15 a.m., the hour when he usually retired to sleep, sent Odilon to fetch Vaudoyer as his escort. On the stairs of his home, seized by a terrifying giddiness, he swayed and paused, then pressed on. At the Jeu de Paume Vaudoyer had to take his arm and steer his tottering steps to the *View of Delft*. Proust had seen this painting, and 'knew I had seen the most beautiful picture in the world', at The Hague on 18 October 1902; he was perfectly capable of noticing the little patch of yellow on the wall unaided; but Vaudoyer's articles, in which he mentioned 'the gables like precious Chinese objects', and Mlle Misme's praise of 'the nuances of the bluish or red roofs, the pink walls, the sad green water and yellow river-bank', had no doubt served to guide his curiosity. In the lower right quarter of the painting, immediately to the left of the first turret on the shadowed water-gate, he saw a fragment of rooftop caught by the sunlight of that eternal summer evening, with the pent-roof of its distant attic window, and beneath it the 'little patch of yellow wall with a pent-roof', for which Bergotte dies and is redeemed.

Proust survived, and even found strength to proceed to the nearby exhibition of Ingres in the Rue de la Ville-l'Évêque—where he admired the view of Rome, long desired and never seen city, in the background of the portrait of François-Marius Granet—and to lunch at the Ritz. Then he returned home, still shaken and alarmed. "I don't know whether I shall ever be able to go out again," he said to Céleste, and then, seeing her distress and Odilon's, and remembering they were still hungry, he added: "Go and eat, you two. Take care of yourselves, I'm so fond of you. You are my children."

From the events of this day he added two incidents to *A la Recherche*, the warning of death that comes to the Narrator at the very end, when he 'narrowly escaped falling three times while going down-stairs',[1] and the death of Bergotte, which the Narrator learns on the day of Albertine's visit to the Trocadéro. In all the details of Bergotte's illness Proust is thinking of his own. Bergotte suffers from an artificial malady which has become real, consults several doctors and ironically compares their conflicting advices, rarely goes out, takes sleeping-

[1] III, 1039-42.

drugs in excess, and is attracted to the fatal exhibition, after 'a slight attack of uraemia', by reading the article of a critic who compares the 'little patch of yellow wall' to 'a precious Chinese work of art'.[1] Only the manner of Bergotte's death, however, dates from May 1921, for the great writer's imminent extinction was already prepared by the long account of his illness, which coincides with the death of the grandmother, in *Le Côté de Guermantes II*.[2] This, however, is itself a late insertion, and must have been added to the text in 1920,[3] for Bergotte's symptoms at this stage are drawn from the breakdown of Proust's own health in that year. Already, like Proust, Bergotte stumbles on the stairs; his sight is failing, he has an impediment in his speech; some say he has a cerebral tumour—the same imaginary tumour for which Babinski had refused to open Proust's brain; and his works, 'with an extraordinary power of expansion', have at last become known to the general public, like Proust's after the Goncourt Prize.[4]

From the bare room of 44 Rue Hamelin the family furniture, except for a few sacred or indispensable objects, had vanished for ever; it only remained for Proust to rid himself of his last worldly possession, poor Henri. Once already, in the summer of 1920, Henri had fled, though we have found him again writing his master's letters from dictation in the following October. Now, however, the young man was in serious trouble from a broken engagement to the daughter of a concierge, and it seemed best for everyone's sake that he should leave the country. Henri's last semi-public appearance was in March 1921, when Mauriac dined at Proust's bedside, and was uncomfortably aware of the sinister darkness of the room, the ambiguous young captive, the fur coat spread by way of a coverlet on the bed, and the waxen mask, 'in which only the hair seemed alive', through which his host watched them eating.

[1] III, 182-8.
[2] And again in *Sodome et Gomorrhe*, when Mme Verdurin announces mendaciously that she expects him at La Raspelière, on the very day when 'the morning papers revealed that his health was giving cause for serious alarm' (II, 970-1).
[3] Partly, at least, as late as October 1920. Proust here elaborates (II, 327) the comparison in the preface to *Tendres Stocks* (pp. 33-4) of Renoir with the oculist—whom Proust had then recently visited—who gives us a new vision and says: "Now look"—'and behold, the world (which was not created once and for all, but is re-created as often as a new artist appears) seems completely different from the one we knew already, but perfectly clear'. Cf. also III, 911.
[4] II, 325-9.

It was only necessary to find Henri a suitable place. Proust wrote to Robert de Rothschild, to Mme de Noailles's newest friend Henri Gans, who visited him often in this spring, and to Horace Finaly, the comrade of his student days, now director of the Banque de Paris et des Pays-Bas. 'I have to confess that this young man is rather idle,' he declared, 'and hasn't much of a head for figures, but . . .' Moved by this recommendation Finaly found him a post in a United States branch of the Banque de Paris et des Pays-Bas, and Henri sailed into exile on 4 June. His last plaintive remark was: "My only regret is that I've never seen Princesse Soutzo!" So Morel plans, if he should succeed in seducing the niece of Jupien (who in the earliest versions of *A la Recherche* was a concierge), and again, when he has decided to break their engagement, to 'b— off to an unknown destination'.[1] Jupien's niece had existed in Proust's novel at least as early as the completion of *Du Côté de chez Swann* in 1912-13, when the Narrator's grandmother sees her during a visit to Mme de Villeparisis, mistakes her for Jupien's daughter, and remarks: "The child is a pearl!"[2] Her sole function at that time was to perform, at the end of the novel, her surprising marriage with young Léonor de Cambremer. But now, aided by the strange coincidence that Henri's jilted fiancée was likewise the daughter of a concierge, Proust was able to insert into the future *La Prisonnière* the sad episode of Morel's betrayal of the tailor's niece. Perhaps other details, such as Morel's terrible cry of *"grand pied de grue"*, belong to Henri's love-affair. Thus in Henri Rochat there was not only a fragment of Albertine, but also another of Charlie Morel.

On 16 June Proust attended Mme Hennessy's dinner to celebrate the sensational engagement of the Duke of Marlborough, whose first duchess, the former Consuelo Vanderbilt, had consented after nearly ten years of obduracy to allow him to marry Miss Gladys Deacon. Proust was attracted by Mme Hennessy's plump arms, protested, as we have seen, when she suggested that the Duchesse de Guermantes was Mme Greffulhe, and was startled by the extravagant delight with which the elderly Princesse de Polignac greeted his remark: "Paul Morand likes you very much." 'I must ask you not to contradict me,' he wrote that very night to Morand, and added scrupulously: 'Of course, I didn't tell her you were in love with her!' Marlborough took a fancy to his fiancée's old admirer, and invited him to Blenheim. Proust objected that he was bedridden. "I'll put you in a sleeper at the

[1] III, 51, 195.   [2] I, 20.

Gare du Nord," replied the Duke, "I'll tuck you up in a cabin on the boat, and you can stay in bed at Blenheim." Meanwhile Proust ought to try the Coué system: "Just repeat to yourself: 'I feel marvellous', because if you believe you're well, you'll be well!" Proust tried, but felt worse than ever, and stayed in bed for four months.

In the NRF for June 1921 appeared the last of Proust's critical essays, 'A Propos de Baudelaire', written during the third week in April. A few ideas from the Baudelaire chapter of Contre Sainte-Beuve reappear, though without verbal reminiscences—a remark on the cruelty of Les Petites vieilles,[1] a comparison with Beethoven,[2] an unjustified complaint of the flatness of the last lines of Le Voyage and Le Cygne.[3] Once again, however, although no more profound and intuitively sympathetic study of Baudelaire has ever been written, Proust writes also of himself. He quotes Vigny's line 'La femme aura Gomorrhe et l'homme aura Sodome', explaining that it sprang 'from the poet's jealousy caused by the friendship of Mme Dorval for certain women'; and here is the epigraph and subject of the next part of Proust's novel. 'Perhaps, alas,' he remarks, again alluding to his own situation, 'one must carry imminent death in one's own body, be threatened with aphasia like Baudelaire, to achieve his lucidity in the midst of real suffering'. He recalls for the last time the line from Chant d'automne, 'J'aime de vos longs yeux la lumière verdâtre', and Fauré's melody, the leitmotivs of his love twenty-nine years before for Marie Finaly, who had died in the influenza epidemic of 1918. But he sensed a still more disturbing link between himself and Baudelaire in the poet's secret complicity with Lesbos, so unlike Vigny's angry horror, and in his enigmatic avowal:

> 'Car Lesbos entre tous m'a choisi sur la terre
> Pour chanter le secret de ses vierges en fleurs.'[4]

In the future volumes of his novel, Proust confided, this link between Sodom and Gomorrah would be 'entrusted to a brute, Charles Morel'; but 'what is comprehensible in Charles Morel remains profoundly mysterious in the author of Les Fleurs du Mal'. Proust

[1] Chroniques, 220, CSB, 179-80.
[2] Chroniques, 221, CSB, 186.
[3] Chroniques, 219, CSB, 190.
[4] It is probably owing to a reminiscence of this line (in which the plural is required by the rhyme) that Proust called his second volume A l'Ombre des Jeunes Filles en Fleurs, whereas ordinary French might prefer 'en fleur'.

refrained from announcing to the public the mistaken yet revealing explanation which he gave a few weeks later to Gide, that Baudelaire was himself a practising homosexual.[1] But the relations between male and female inverts, the affairs of Morel with Léa and Albertine,[2] which Proust perhaps inserted at this time and under the influence of these ideas, were to fulfil the circle of the mysterious round-dance of the sexes, and complete the unexpected but inevitable threads which join every character in *A la Recherche* to every other.

At the end of January 1921, when the printing of *Le Côté de Guermantes II* by Louis Bellenand at Fontenay-aux-Roses was still in progress, Proust proposed to Gallimard that *Sodome et Gomorrhe II* should be given to another press in order to save time, and printed not from the manuscript but from 'the detestable typescript', which had been made for him by a NRF typist. The first proofs, however, show considerable differences throughout from the surviving remains of this typescript. Proust must have devoted the intervals in the proof-revision of *Le Côté de Guermantes II* to these alterations, and the corrected typescript, now lost, cannot have gone to the new printer, F. Paillart of Abbeville, until March or April. Late in May Proust asked Gallimard to let him have the first proofs as soon as possible, 'because the volume will be the most difficult of all to recast', and on 5 June, the day after Henri's departure, he complained that he was still without proofs, 'although I sent you the text several months ago'. Proofs must have begun to arrive shortly afterwards, for at the end of August Rivière was able to read on holiday the first half of the volume in proof, up to the opening passages of the soirée at La Raspelière, and was aware that Proust was already well advanced with his corrections. This second stage of revision was even more important than the first, for the differences between the first proofs and the published volume, as we are told by the editor of the Pléiade text, 'extend not only to corrections of detail, but to the management of the narrative in general, and the order, length and form of its various elements'.

Among the additions, no doubt, was the appearance at La Raspelière of the Norwegian philosopher, who expounds Boutroux's and

[1] In fact few poets have been as exclusively heterosexual both in life and work as Baudelaire, whose obsession with Lesbianism was caused objectively by the homosexual infidelity of Jeanne Duval and other mistresses, and subjectively by its significance as one of the flowers of evil.

[2] III, 214-16, 598-600. These are certainly late additions, for Morel, who elsewhere appears in Proust's manuscript under his earlier name Santois, is here called Morel.

Bergson's views on soporifics, memory and immortality to the Narrator, and speaks French so haltingly but vanishes with such vertiginous rapidity.[1] This was the Swedish philosopher Algot Ruhe, a member of the Swedish Academy of Nine, the Swedish translator of Bergson, and the reviewer of *Du Côté de chez Swann* in the Stockholm *Var Tid* in 1917. Proust was introduced to him by Bergson, met him at Henri Bardac's, and tried in November 1921 to place a group of his prose-poems with Rivière, who found them 'not bad, but written in such uncertain French'. 'Let us hope,' wrote Proust to Rivière, 'that this eminent Swede will find no vestige of himself in the Norwegian philosopher, but I tremble for it.' The 'Norwegian' philosopher's reports on Bergson to the Narrator reflect a conversation between Proust and Bergson on insomnia and sleeping-drugs which was witnessed—probably during the Blumenthal Prize negotiations in September 1920 —by Edmond Jaloux. Jaloux listened with astonished admiration to these two supreme experts, Proust with his head thrown back and bulging chest, Bergson slender, bald and immaterial, 'like two black nightbirds', as they extracted from their malady such dazzling laws on the intellect and the unconscious, 'that insomnia seemed almost a blessing'.

In that autumn the seasonal relapse in Proust's health recurred. Towards 20 September he staggered and fell in his bedroom; soon afterwards he showed signs of uraemia, his mother's symptom and Bergotte's[2]; and early in October he poisoned himself accidentally by taking the enormous overdose of seven one-gramme cachets of veronal, dial and opium. He had thought each contained only a tenth of a gramme, he explained; but the ominous nature of such an error, in which a lapse of the conscious mind may well obey a destructive wish of the unconscious, is only too clear. This incident was not the first of its kind. A few years before, after Céleste had talked with her master until three in the morning, he had failed to ring at the usual time. All that day the bell remained silent; the chambermaid on the floor below urged her to go in, but Céleste did not dare to brave the wrath of her Ahasuerus and his cry from Racine's *Esther: "What reckless mortal comes to seek her death?"*[3] At two in the afternoon of the second day the summons sounded at last. "Ah, Monsieur, I was so worried about you!" she cried. "You had reason to be, Céleste." "I was afraid I'd never see you again." "You don't know how close you came to it." "I think he'd taken the largest possible dose of veronal he dared,"

[1] II, 930-1, 975-6, 984-5.   [2] III, 186.   [3] III, 120, 126.

Céleste told Miss Mina Curtiss many years later, "to be still sure of going on living while feeling and knowing what death was like." "We shall all meet again in the Valley of Jehoshaphat," Céleste would say, and: "Do you really believe people meet again when they're dead? If I thought I'd see Mother again I'd die this minute," her master replied. The heavenly scales, in which desire to complete *A la Recherche* was weighed against longing for the moment in which his sins would be instantaneously atoned and his mother's love eternally regained, trembled near the point of balance. So in these last years the visits of the Dark Woman punctually recurred in each spring and autumn, towards the times of his brother's birth and his mother's death; and Proust's life moved towards the brink in a slow and sinister rhythm, like the tolling of a great bell or the surging of an unknown sea.

Chapter 16

AN INDIAN SUMMER
(October 1921 – September 1922)

DURING the past fifteen years Proust must have been well aware of the existence in Paris of a coterie of charming and talented ladies who preferred their own society to that of men. The unjust stigma which condemned the natives of Sodom to a furtive or defiant criminality was spared them; they seemed to the world, as indeed they were, an innocent, proud, eccentric, indispensable leavening in a monotonous society. Their ranks were reconnoitred by the curious and benevolent, even temporarily joined by such eminent writers as Mme de Noailles and Colette. The great courtesans Liane de Pougy and Émilienne d'Alençon sought them for an idyllic holiday from professional duties. Certain repentant married ladies, including Proust's increasingly masculine friend Mme de Clermont-Tonnerre, the English feminist Anna Wickham, Yvonne Sabini, the drug-taking wife of the Italian commercial attaché in Paris, found them permanently preferable to their unsatisfactory husbands.

In the years before the war the nucleus of this little band was formed by Miss Natalie Clifford Barney, Lucie Delarue-Mardrus, Renée Vivien and her friend Evelina Palmer. Mme Delarue-Mardrus, a boyish brunette and a gifted poetess, was married to the fearsome, black-bearded Dr Mardrus, author of the magnificent translation of the *Arabian Nights* which the Narrator's mother, shocked by its impropriety and strange orthography, regrets having given to her son at Balbec.[1] Montesquiou, ravished by her poems and enraged by some lack of deference on the part of Mme de Noailles, invited both ladies to a grand fête. "A marvellous young Muse will now recite some of her verses!" he announced; but before Mme de Noailles could open her mouth she discovered she was not the Muse in question, for Mme Delarue-Mardrus had already begun to declaim. Count Robert henceforth took an avuncular interest in the whole group, and recorded in his secret diary a remark made to him by one of the sisterhood:"People

[1] II, 836-7.

call it unnatural—all I can say is, it's always come naturally to *me*!"
Renée Vivien, likewise ('a blonde young person with discouraged
shoulders', wrote Mme Delarue-Mardrus), was a talented Sapphic
poetess, and lived with her inseparable friend Miss Evelina Palmer, a
pre-Raphaelite American with auburn hair that reached to her ankles.
But the leader of them all was 'the wild girl from Cincinnati', as Joseph
Reinach's brother Salomon called her, the admirable Miss Barney.
Her father was an elegant clubman, descended from a Barney who
fought for France in the eighteenth century; she was educated at
the same odd boarding-school of Les Ruches in the Forest of
Fontainebleau (but several years later, when it was no longer under
the management of Mlles Souvestre and Dussaud) as her subsequent
friend, the wise and matchless authoress of *Olivia*; and she was and
remains celebrated as the Amazon, to whom the solitary and disfigured
Remy de Gourmont addressed his *Lettres à l'Amazone*. Mme Delarue-
Mardrus wrote of Miss Barney in her autobiography as 'the pure and
faithful companion whose pride, loyalty and greatness I esteem so
highly', and made her the heroine of her novel *L'Ange et les
Pervers*, 'where I have described and analysed at full length both
Natalie and the life into which she initiated me, in which it was not
until much later that I ceased to play more than the sexless rôle of the
angel'. Miss Barney had a feminine figure, golden hair, a pastel-
coloured skin, steely eyes, a biting smile, and a sudden blush.

The Amazon inhabited an ancient house at 20 Rue Jacob, once the
home of Racine's mistress the actress Champmeslé. Beneath the
garden trees stood an eighteenth-century pillared summerhouse,
called the Temple of Friendship and ambiguously barred, when it was
in need of repair, with a notice saying: 'DANGER'. Paul Morand visited
her in 1916, and commented: 'Very Fiesole 1895'. But after the
Armistice the headquarters of this little band became a brilliant salon,
and even Gide observed that "Miss Barney is one of the few people
one ought to see if one had time". Valéry, Rilke, Ezra Pound, T. S.
Eliot, Berenson, D'Annunzio and Pierre Louÿs were her friends.
She lived with the fearless purity of fire, devoted to the platonic
ideal of friendship which Proust had rejected, and wrote with an
intellectual passion and beauty of style for which posterity will
read and revere her. Her place among the great French women
writers of her time—Colette, Anna de Noailles, Princess Marthe
Bibesco—is assured, or at least deserved.

Proust and Miss Barney at last suspected they might have much in common, and at Morand's suggestion she sent him in September 1920 her *Pensées d'une Amazone* ('for Monsieur Marcel Proust, whose comprehension merits this unexpurgated copy'), and an invitation to the Temple of Friendship. Yet it seemed to him, rightly, that the realm over which Miss Barney was queen was a land of classic and literary idyll, Mitylene rather than Gomorrah. Nothing, he confessed, could be less like a response to her sweet singing than his coming *Sodome et Gomorrhe*: 'the divine peace of the *Eclogues* or *Symposium* does not reign there, but rather the dark despair of Vigny's line which I chose five years ago as an epigraph'[1]; and he prudently objected that the 'Temple of Love', as he called it by a natural confusion, would be too draughty in October. Nevertheless, he declared, he would like to discuss 'all that' with her. For a year these two exceptional people contemplated one another from a distance. 'I'm apprehensive of what you will say about Gomorrah,' she wrote after reading *Sodome et Gomorrhe I*, and: 'My Sodomites are all horrible,' he replied, 'but my Gomorrhans will all be charming.' In his letters to her Proust wrote with the particular tone which he reserved for persons of high and vigilant intelligence; he did not 'talk down' to Miss Barney. Their meeting, however, when at last towards November 1921 he visited the Rue Jacob, was not a success. It was very late at night, long past Miss Barney's bedtime; she sat draped in the white ermine chasuble which she used as a bedspread, while Proust, in his white shirtfront and black tail-suit, his dark eyes 'ringed with black by the vampires of solitude', looked 'like a corpse laid out in a coffin'; and she was uncomfortably conscious that he was watching her steadily without seeming to see her. He would speak of nothing but persons in high society, and the Belgian carillon of Mme Greffulhe's laugh, and neither of them was willing to be the first to mention 'all that'. When Miss Barney read his later volumes she thought Albertine and her friends 'not so much charming as improbable': 'not everyone,' she grimly declared, 'is able to infringe these Eleusinian mysteries'. In fact, she could tell Proust nothing that he wished to know and did not know already; for the impenetrable enigma which veils the relations of Albertine with the natives of Gomorrah is not a sign of ignorance on the part of the author, but an essential symbol of the mystery of love and jealousy.

In October 1921 Proust received a copy of Montesquiou's last

[1] *'La femme aura Gomorrhe et l'homme aura Sodome'*, from *'La Colère de Samson'*.

volume, *Élus et Appelés*, inscribed 'To Marcel Proust, author whom I
believe I judge rightly, friend whom I know I like truly'. This was
destined to be Count Robert's everlasting farewell to the 'dear
Marcel' whom, within his lights, he had respected and cherished for
nearly three decades. The Count's last years had been disenchanted
and sombre. 'I loved my fêtes better than my guests, who were perhaps
aware of the fact,' he confessed; and he never outlived the catastrophe
of his last grand pre-war party, a performance of Verlaine's *Les Uns et
les Autres* at the Palais Rose, when the few guests who turned up were
greatly outnumbered by the waiters. Alas, Mme Estradère, the gossip-
columnist of *Le Figaro*, who used the pen-name of Princesse de
Mésagne to which she was only vaguely entitled, had announced on
the authority of an anonymous letter that the fête was 'cancelled owing
to bad weather'.[1] "But here's the very letter!" cried the poor lady
when Montesquiou swooped for an explanation, "look, it begins
'Dear Princess'!" "Ah!—so you believed the rest!" exclaimed the
Count. He quarrelled with everyone, a process which he called
'widening, by cutting down the undergrowth of pointless friendships,
the avenues that lead to my solitude'. His despair of fame for his
writings was exacerbated by the incessant arrival of new names: 'no
sooner has one found leisure to enquire who André Gide is,' he complained, 'than one has to find out who André Suarès is!' He sold
Artagnan in 1919, after offering it in vain to all his rich, hated cousins.
In a last typically pure and remote love-affair he became enamoured of
the photograph of Prince Jean Sevastos, a clever, golden-haired boy
of seventeen, the stepson of his executor and physician Dr Paul-Louis
Couchoud, and courted him in a series of wary, melancholy and
moving letters, and with a box of crystallised violets. 'A photograph
is a mirror with a memory,' he wrote. Ought they to risk meeting? 'I
used to like being seen *very much*,' he admitted, 'but now I do not like
it *at all*. One only enjoys doing what one does well.' They met only
once, on 3 October 1920, when Montesquiou did the honours of the
Palais Rose for the young prince and his parents. But the boy was
bewilderingly reserved: was it shyness, or had he not understood
before that Count Robert was an elderly gentleman of sixty-six? 'You
will not know until later the meaning of that day,' wrote the Count, 'a
sad but human meaning, and not without beauty, if only the beauty
of sorrow.' "I'm looking for someone to close my eyes," he had

[1] M. de Charlus resolves to play this trick upon Mme de Mortemart (III,
271).

told Mme de Clermont-Tonnerre; but even that search had been in vain.

Montesquiou's final public appearance was in December 1920 at the baptism of his great-niece Corisande, the fifth and last offspring of Guiche and Élaine Greffulhe. "Are you the father of the child?" asked the verger, and "Certainly not!" cried the Count indignantly, muttering: "What a jazz-band baptism!" Then he approached Mme de Clermont-Tonnerre and spoke of their friend Marcel. "I, too, would like a little glory," he sighed, "I ought to start calling myself Montesproust." 'Guiche felt more exhausted after six hours of the Count's conversation,' she reported to Proust, 'than his wife after producing the baby.' Montesquiou retired to Dr Couchoud's clinic at Saint-Cloud with nephritis, emerged for his last amiable correspondence with Proust, and then, as summer ended, paced the Palais Rose taking his own blood-pressure and reading in it his death-warrant. "Shall I send for Dr Robin?" asked the faithful Henri Pinard. "What do you suppose Robin could do for me now?" replied Count Robert, "no, send for nobody, I'll die alone." He fled to the mimosas of Mentone—where Henri brought him *Élus et Appelés* fresh from the printer, saying: "Look, here is your newly-born!"—and died on 11 December 1921. A few loyal friends, Dr Couchoud who made a speech, Mme Delarue-Mardrus who recited a poem, Ida Rubinstein dissolved in tears, Mlle Breslau the painter, Mme de Clermont-Tonnerre, Coco de Madrazo, attended his funeral on the 21st. "We all owe him a great deal," said Mlle Breslau. He was buried in the Cimetière des Gonards at Versailles beside the waiting Yturri, beneath the statue of the Angel of Silence whose finger is ever on its lips.

The series of Proust's critical articles had been interrupted by a distressing contretemps. He had insisted, despite the author's justified forebodings, on arranging for the NRF to review Jacques Boulenger's *. . . Mais l'Art est difficile!*, a volume of collected criticism which contained three laudatory articles on Proust's own work. To the horror of them both, Louis Martin-Chauffier's review in the NRF for June 1921 was hostile, and contained a gratuitous insinuation that Boulanger had praised the work of René Boylesve in the hope of winning his vote for the Académie Française. Urged by Proust, Boulenger had expostulated forcibly in the July NRF; but Rivière, allowing for once his editorial duty to override his sense of justice, repeated the offence by supporting his contributor. On 19 and 26 August the ruffled Boulenger published articles on Flaubert in the *Revue de la Semaine*, in which he took Proust to task for a harmless criticism of himself in '*A propos de Baudelaire*',[1] and attacked his '*A propos du Style de Flaubert*'. Proust immediately wrote a new article on Flaubert, replying to Boulenger and apologising for the NRF's discourtesy, and offered it to Rivière, who accepted with evident reluctance and with requests for modifications. Proust withdrew the article, which still remains undiscovered, remarking regretfully: 'it would have enabled me to produce a volume of criticism by enabling me to continue my Flaubert'. In fact, although we shall find him making other abortive attempts to resume, this unhappy affair put an end to Proust's career as a critic.

Fortunately Rivière had asked before the storm for 'the finest fragment of your next volume'. '*Les Intermissions du cœur*', the story of the Narrator's second arrival at Balbec, his delayed grief for his grandmother, and his recovery when he sees the appleblossom on a showery day in spring, appeared in the NRF for October 1921, and was followed in December by '*En tram jusqu'à La Raspelière*', the episode of the journey in the little train to Mme Verdurin's soirée, into which Proust temporarily transferred a number of incidents, such as the Norwegian philosopher, which belong to the later part of that evening. Proust insisted on dedicating the latter extract to Jacques Boulenger, while Rivière in turn stipulated that only Boulenger's name should appear, without Proust's embarrassing reasons for the dedication. But he magnanimously arranged for a favourable review of the second volume of Boulenger's ... *Mais l'Art est difficile!* by Benjamin Crémieux in the January NRF. In December Proust gratefully lent Rivière money pending the payment of the last instalment of his Blumenthal prize. Meanwhile, however, others had profited from his irritation against the NRF. In July Boulenger had transmitted a request from Henri Duvernois, editor of the newly founded monthly *Les Œuvres Libres*, for a long extract from his novel. Proust accepted in September for the sake of independence, money, and the new readers who would be won by an occasional truancy from the closed shop of the NRF, and wrung Gallimard's reluctant consent. But Gallimard revealed immediately after that he was exceedingly distressed. 'Exclusivity is not laid down in the text of our agreement,' he admitted, 'but exists nonetheless in the mind of the contracting party!' 'I've never pronounced vows of obedience before Gallimard, nor even of

[1] 'And Jacques Boulanger, by far the best critic, and more than critic, of his generation, dares to tell us that Baudelaire's poetry is deficient in thought!' (*Chroniques*, 219).

chastity,' Proust grumbled to Boulenger, and called Gallimard and
Rivière 'my two dear torturers'; but he promised not to repeat his
dereliction, and privately resolved to do so never, or hardly ever. A
150-page extract from *Sodome et Gomorrhe II*, on the Narrator's love
for Albertine at Balbec and his growing suspicions of her Lesbianism,
appeared in the November *Œuvres Libres* under the disingenuous
title: '*Jalousie. A complete, unpublished novel by Marcel Proust*'.

In September and October Proust worked incessantly on the
second half of *Sodome et Gomorrhe II*, making his additions and corrections on the typescript already supplied by the NRF. At the end of
November he sent the completed text to Gallimard, declaring that he
passed it for publication without further proofs. He asked for larger
type to be used, and thwarted Gallimard's protests by pointing out the
economy gained by his abstention from proofs, and offering to allow
any excess costs to be subtracted from his credit balance. The work
was therefore printed, although this involved entirely resetting the
first half, with the attractive large type in which *A la Recherche* was
thereafter, until the Pléiade edition of 1954, most familiarly known to
Proust's readers. In this new form it became necessary to produce
Sodome et Gomorrhe II in three volumes instead of the usual two.
Publication was planned for 1 May 1922.

Proust immediately began work on *Sodome et Gomorrhe III*, as the
section afterwards called *La Prisonnière* was still entitled. At first he
believed it would be an exceptionally short volume, though in fact it
was to become one of the longest; in a moment of optimism he thought
he might publish it in October 1922, though in moods of pessimism at
the fancied slowness of the printers he feared that even *Sodome et
Gomorrhe II* might have to be postponed till May 1923. At the New
Year, after sending a present to the NRF lady typist, he decided to
engage one of his own. Since Henri Rochat's flight Céleste had written
many of Proust's letters from dictation, with spelling even more en-
dearingly weak than Henri's; but now her young niece Yvonne came
to live at 44 Rue Hamelin, where she typed his more formal correspondence and completed during the first half of 1922 a typescript of
La Prisonnière and *Albertine Disparue*. This youthful Parisian was the
very daughter of Françoise whose excruciating slang disconcerts the
Narrator and corrupts the pure and original diction of her mother.
She appears in her own typescript of *La Prisonnière*,[1] and is still with
the Narrator some fifteen years later, apparently unaged, in the war-

[1] III, 154-5.

chapter of *Le Temps Retrouvé*, when Françoise proudly adopts her abominable catch-phrase '*et patatipatali et patatapatala*'.[1] But Proust had met Céleste's niece several years before, perhaps as early as the summer of 1919, when, as he told Princesse Soutzo, 'the Albaret family multiplies around me'; for she already appears with her repertoire of slang in *Le Côté de Guermantes I*, in the spring after the Narrator's visit to Doncières, and again in the early part of *Sodome et Gomorrhe II*, on the evening of Albertine's visit after the Princesse de Guermantes's soirée.[2] During these years Céleste's sister Marie Gineste had also been intermittently with him to share Céleste's errands, and now entered his home for the rest of 1922. Another occasional inmate was the infant daughter of the baker-concierge below, who toddled up with his letters and once, he suspected, lost them, when her mother sprained her arm in February 1922. In April, when the little girl had measles and whooping-cough, he cautiously ordered all his correspondence to be fumigated in a formol-stove. The same child, in 1950 a still-young woman in charge of the pastry-shop on the ground-floor of 44 Rue Hamelin, well remembered her first visit to his room. "It was so dark, and he was so kind but strange, and I ran away! You see, Monsieur, I was so little." This charming and intelligent lady is no doubt the youngest person alive who has seen Proust plain, and when the twentieth century draws to a close will perhaps be the last.

The gaiety of the 1920s had begun, in time for Proust to glimpse a new age which he found too incongruous to insert in *A la Recherche*. At the Princesse de Guermantes's last matinée the music is still a dying echo of the Vinteuil Septet; but the evenings of 1922 were danced away to the unfamiliar syncopations of tango and ragtime, which to survivors of a past epoch seemed to symbolise a dislocation not only of rhythm but of morals. "And what do they do after they've finished dancing?" enquired a great lady, after watching with deep interest a couple interlocked in the first tango she had ever seen. Proust sat benign, holding court; and Fernand Gregh's daughter Geneviève, noticing the band of maidens and men round his throne, was reminded of the aged Voltaire revisiting Paris on the eve of death. He stayed all night at the Beaumonts' ball on New Year's Eve, though he missed their next on 27 February, when Mlle d'Hinnisdael, her sister and Princesse Marie Murat, dressed as picadors and matadors, slew a difficult bull who turned out to be Coco de Madrazo. He attended the Ritz

[1] III, 749.   [2] II, 147-8, 331, 341, 726-8.

ball on 15 January, and received a promised demonstration of the latest steps from Mlle d'Hinnisdael—'even when indulging in the most 1922 of dances, she still looks like a unicorn on a coat of arms!' He admired the chaste chivalry with which Morand, dancing with a lady in mauve, succeeded in disengaging his portliness from her person; he was introduced to the harpsichordist Wanda Landowska, 'just when she was in the act of biting Mlle Vacaresco in the buttock'; and then he fled to his private room upstairs and devoured a leg of lamb.

On 7 February he was observed by Maurice Martin du Gard at Princesse Soutzo's, tottering towards his dazzling hostess like a moth plunging into an electric light. Martin du Gard, the editor of *Les Écrits nouveaux*, had published last July a review of *Le Côté de Guermantes I* by André Germain, in which Proust was compared to 'an elderly governess who has become the mistress of the family footman'. Germain, a friend of Lucien Daudet, Montesquiou, Renée Vivien and Miss Barney, was a clever but hysterical young man who had never quite recovered from his brief mismarriage to Lucien's sister Edmée, and was tormented by the lifelong alternations of a fascinated liking and loathing for male and female inverts. In November Rivière had written a stern letter to Martin du Gard, announcing in the name of the NRF that 'we are all gravely displeased by M. André Germain's venomous article, and shall always regard any attack on Marcel Proust as an attack on ourselves'; but Proust himself, though determined to fight, had heard from Morand that the editor did not share his contributor's views, and specially asked the princess to invite him. "Proust wants a duel with sabres, but he doesn't want to take his overcoat off!" explained Morand, and disappeared. "It's true that this is hardly the weather for duelling," Proust agreed, "and supposing M. Germain goes to bed just when I get up? It's most awkward!" Reluctantly he allowed himself to be dissuaded from his homicidal intentions, but: "You and Morand are *most unkind*," he repeated. With a faint smile he cross-examined Martin du Gard on his most intimate beliefs—'a questioning that filled one with ecstasy, an absurd pride, and a tinge of terror'. He thanked Robert de Rothschild for a photograph of Fénelon—"the only one I have ever seen of that adorable person"—and tried to elucidate the mysteries of Fénelon's death to Martin du Gard; he declared that he himself was 'not just a novelist, but a moral poet', and insisted on sending his new acquaintance home in Odilon's taxi. "Number 8 *bis* Rue Laurent-Pichat," said Martin du Gard when asked for his address; for by a coincidence worthy of *A la*

Recherche itself he was a friend of Porel, and recently had taken Proust's place as lodger in the house of the dead Réjane.

The daily consequences of fame continued to amuse or exasperate Proust. He was annoyed when *Le Canard enchaîné* published an advertisement for 'the Swann pen, sole manufacturer Marcel Proust', but delighted when Mme Scheikévitch showed him a publicity item in *Le Figaro* which promised: 'You too can have the charming and supple figure of a young girl from "within a budding grove", if you buy our girdle!' When he noticed Morand's *Ouvert la Nuit* advertised in *Ève* as 'Not to be read by young girls' he commanded Gallimard to arrange the same publicity for himself; and on 28 May 1922 an announcement duly appeared in *Ève* of '*Sodome et Gomorrhe. Not to be read by young girls*'. Mme Bliss, he heard with mixed feelings, always kept the latest Marcel Proust on her drawing-room table, side by side with the latest Henry Bordeaux. An American girl wrote from the Villa Wolkonsky in Rome to inform him that she was extremely beautiful, and had read his works night and day for the past three years, but could not understand a word: 'Dear Marcel Proust,' she entreated, 'please tell me in two lines what you are trying to say.' An Italian journalist wrote: 'I enjoy everything in your books, but my wife has a marked preference for the meeting of M. de Charlus and Jupien, though she also likes the scene between Charlus and the cabman.' He was flattered by the comparison between himself and Einstein which Blanche had already suggested a year before in the preface to *Dates*, and on which the mathematician Camille Vettard had written an essay, '*Proust et Einstein*', published, after five months of effort on Proust's part, during which it was rejected by Rivière, accepted by Boulenger and withdrawn in a huff by the author, in the NRF for August 1922. Algot Ruhe, now an enthusiast for Einstein, as if egged on by his counterpart the 'Norwegian philosopher', wrote: 'You accelerate and decelerate the rotation of the earth, you are greater than God'. This, Proust himself felt, was going too far. 'Even if he'd merely said I was as great as God,' he objected to Guiche, 'it would still have been a bit much!' But the comparison with Einstein, if not with the Almighty, was attractive. *A la Recherche du Temps Perdu* was, indeed, the picture of a relativistic universe expanding and contracting in a curved space-time continuum; and when Benjamin Crémieux pointed out some apparent anachronisms in *Le Côté de Guermantes* Proust explained that these were due 'to the flattened form my characters take owing to their rotation in time'.

Proust continued his fruitless plans for articles. He had offered Rivière a 'burlesque obituary' on poor Joseph Reinach, who had died on 18 April 1921: 'what better service can one offer a dead man, than to make him live again?' When Léon Daudet dedicated his novel *L'Entremetteuse* to him in November 1921, Proust asked Boulenger to publish 'an extremely dithyrambic article' on his benefactor, which he wrote in the spring of 1922[1] but never submitted, for Daudet was political dynamite, and Boulanger could not be induced to accept with sufficient enthusiasm. He planned 'an anecdotic, high-society article' in memory of Montesquiou for an American magazine, but explained to Mme de Clermont-Tonnerre on 7 February 1922, with an unaccustomed lapse into callousness and bad taste, that he had abandoned it, fearing that Count Robert had only pretended to die, that his funeral was merely a last practical joke, and his coffin, like the Emperor Charles the Fifth's in the legend, was empty. The real reason for his abstention, no doubt, was the menace of the Count's posthumous memoirs, and the realisation that, if he should be compelled to ask for the suppression of any revelations concerning himself, it would be a tactical error to cast the first stone. If these memoirs were as many people, innocent and guilty, had reason to suspect, then indeed the terrible Count was not dead.

But the most important of these unprinted articles was an essay on Dostoevsky, which Proust proposed to Rivière in September 1921 and then abandoned, fearing it would interrupt his novel for too long. 'I am doing a great work,' he pleaded, quoting the prophet Nehemiah on the top of his ladder,[2] 'and I cannot come down.' Towards February 1922, however, when the centenary of the great Russian's birth was celebrated, he wrote a brief sketch,[3] which he developed into the superb monologue on Dostoevsky with which the Narrator interrupts Albertine at the pianola in *La Prisonnière*.[4] It was the last occasion but one on which he allowed an incident in the present to dictate an addition to his novel. The last of all, to anticipate a little, was in June 1922, when Paul Brach sent him a reproduction in *L'Illustration* of Tissot's painting of the Club in the Rue Royale in 1868, which was then being shown in an exhibition of Second Empire art at the

---

[1] *Contre Sainte-Beuve*, 438-41.
[2] *Nehemiah*, vi, 3.
[3] *Contre Sainte-Beuve*, 422-3, datable from the allusions to Gide's and Rivière's articles on Dostoevsky in the NRF for February 1922.
[4] III, 378-81.

Louvre.[1] 'Of the people in it I only knew Haas, Edmond de Polignac and Saint-Maurice,' he wrote, 'but what a pleasure to see them again!' And he added to *La Prisonnière* the apostrophe to 'dear Charles Swann' and the proud declaration; 'if everyone is talking of your presence in Tissot's painting of the balcony of the Club in the Rue Royale, along with Galliffet, Edmond de Polignac and Saint-Maurice, it is because people see there are several features which belong to you in the character of Swann.'[2]

His unavailing desire to write articles was to continue till the last months of his life. In June 1922 Robert de Flers asked him for a contribution on the centenary of Shelley's death, no doubt remembering the knowledge Marcel had shown of this subject long ago, in his Ruskin articles of 1900.[3] In July, realising that neither his Dostoevsky essay nor the Narrator's discourse to Albertine would be complete without mention of *The Possessed*, he arranged to borrow this novel from Morand, but without result. In the same month he offered Rivière an article in reply to remarks on his '*A propos du Style de Flaubert*' in Thibaudet's recently published biography, *Gustave Flaubert*, for which Rivière was still hoping as late as 20 September.

The publication of *Sodome et Gomorrhe II* on 2 May coincided with the Schiffs' long-awaited visit to Paris and the last but one of Proust's

---

[1] *L'Illustration*, 10 June 1922, p. 551.

[2] III, 200. Charles Haas himself had died just twenty years before, on 12 July 1902, a few months after his daughter's marriage. His funeral on the fifteenth at Saint-François-de-Sales (for he was a Catholic convert) was attended by the Ducs de Montmorency and de La Trémoille, the Marquis du Lau, Comte Othenin d'Haussonville, Baron Alphonse de Rothschild, Mme Meredith Howland, Comte Walewski (Proust's Prince de Borodino), and Comte Greffulhe. The obituary in *Le Gaulois*, in the style of Proust's parodied obituary of Swann (III, 199-200), called him 'one of the most sparkling conversationalists of his generation, and an art-connoisseur *di primo cartello*, whose place at the Jockey Club will be difficult to fill'. The aged Princesse de Polignac, during her exile in London in the Occupation, told the terrible and Proustian story of Haas sitting paralysed and speechless in his last illness, while his natural daughter Luisita scourged him with unnatural abuse. Proust himself intended to insert this incident, or something like it, in the visit to Gilberte at Tansonville in *Le Temps Retrouvé* (III, 697, 1118 *note*), where he wrote 'Cruelty on the death of her father (copy this from the manuscript-book in which it is written).'

[3] '*Pèlerinages ruskiniens en France*', in *Le Figaro*, 13 February 1900 (cf. *Chroniques*, 145) and '*Ruskin à Notre-Dame d'Amiens*', in *Mercure de France*, 1 April 1900 (cf. *Pastiches et Mélanges*, 102). In *Pastiches et Mélanges*, *loc. cit.*, Proust had shown his continued interest by adding a long footnote on Shelley's cremation.

spring and autumn accidents. He had begun to take adrenalin as a stronger substitute for cafeine when he wished to counteract the narcotic after-effects of veronal; and on the same day, to prepare himself for the Schiffs, he imprudently took an undiluted dose. His throat and stomach were burned as if with vitriol, he cried out with pain for three hours, and for a month lived on nothing but ice-cream and iced beer, which Odilon brought from the Ritz every morning and evening.

Violet and Sydney Schiff were a wealthy and highly intelligent English couple, patrons of art, literature and music, who had seen Proust briefly in the autumn of 1919. Sydney Schiff, a talented novelist who dedicated his *Richard Kurt* (1919) to Proust before their first meeting, and translated *Le Temps Retrouvé* after the death of Scott-Moncrieff, was bald, thin, alarmingly brisk and slightly deaf, with piercing spectacled eyes and a bristling moustache. He was now fifty-two, a year senior to Proust, while his wife was several years younger. Both had read *Du Côté de chez Swann* with enthusiasm in wartime London, and were passionate admirers of Proust's genius. Mrs Schiff was tall and softly graceful, with brown doe-like eyes and slender hands, an unfading Edwardian beauty: 'the angel Violet,' Proust called her, 'retiring, fragrant and miraculous flower'. Those who saw Violet Schiff before her tragic illness in the summer of 1961 will remember for ever the extraordinary youth in face and mind of this gentle and noble lady, the wisdom of her heart and voice, the love and bereavement with which she spoke of Proust, as if he had died yesterday or was still somehow present. "People don't understand that he was good," she repeated, "he was such a good man"; and for an uncanny moment an innocent, affectionate and living Marcel seemed to look from her eyes which saw him always.

On 28 April, fortified with injections of adrenalin, Proust had sallied to the Ritz, expecting to see the newly arrived Schiffs; but they were staying at Foyot's, near the Luxembourg Gardens, where he had eaten delicious lunches thirty years before, on the days of his law-examinations. On 2 May a new appointment was made, and it was for their sake that he took his overdose and, when the pain subsided, followed Mrs Schiff to the Ritz, where Olivier had been ordered 'to see that every window in the restaurant and gallery is shut tight'. He drank astonishing quantities of iced beer, and reproached Sydney Schiff for drinking so much champagne. On another evening he invited them to meet his sister-in-law Marthe and his niece Suzy at 44

Rue Hamelin, after delicately confessing his anxiety lest Suzy, now aged eighteen, should read *Sodome et Gomorrhe*—"and my next book will be even more terrible for an innocent young girl!" Proust deeply loved his brother's child, who for sixty years, it is often said, has devotedly returned his love. 'I like to think,' he had told Mme Catusse long before, 'that a little of my father and mother survives in her.' "What would you like me to give you?" he asked, when she was only six. "A pink flamingo," she replied; but to her lifelong regret, when Uncle Marcel was on the point of promising one, her mother interrupted with: "Don't listen to the child, she's out of her mind!" From her cot she heard, evening after evening, his spontaneous laughter, his voice vibrating with an unearthly intelligence and sensibility, as he talked to her parents. He had sent Robert a de luxe *A l'Ombre des Jeunes Filles en Fleurs* 'for the darling girl', feeling that this book, at least, was fit for the young, and to herself, '*Ma chère petite Suzy*', he wrote that she would receive a huge volume if he sent her all the letters he wrote to her every evening in his thoughts. "She takes after Robert, she already has his kindness of heart," he told Paul Morand. The Schiffs invited her to stay with them in England, and both she and they were amused by his shocked indignation at the idea of her travelling alone, so young, to so distant a country. A few years after his death she spoke of her unconsoled loss to the Abbé Mugnier. "Marcel Proust," mused that good man, "why, no one is less dead than he is"; and she realised henceforth that she was mistaken, that her uncle was alive for ever.

On 18 May, after the first night of Stravinsky's *Renard*, the Schiffs gave an enormous supper-party to Diaghilev and the dancers, and to the four men of genius whom they most admired, Picasso, Stravinsky, Proust and James Joyce. Proust had delighted in Picasso's décor for Cocteau's *Parade*, and in 1918 had watched with amused appreciation the unpacking of a crate of astounding white and blue cubist pictures, a present from Biarritz, in the flat of the painter's patron Mme Errasuriz. He remembered the incident for his novel: 'These ladies, touched by art as if by heavenly grace,' he wrote in *Le Temps Retrouvé*, 'lived in apartments filled with cubist paintings, while a cubist painter worked only for them and they lived only for him.'[1]

[1] III, 946. In a letter to Walter Berry in 1917 Proust pointed out the affinity between prehistoric cave-painting and the art of Picasso. 'Picasso is an artist whose work and person are by no means unknown to me,' he declared to Blanche in 1919 ;and in his preface to Blanche's *De David à Degas* he wrote of

Stravinsky he had known before the war, with the Russian dancers at Larue's; and now Proust approached him with the most unfortunate question that can possibly be put to a great composer after an anxious first night. "Do you like Beethoven?" "I detest him!" "But surely, the late quartets?" protested Proust. "Worst things he ever wrote!" snarled Stravinsky, who explained later; 'I should have shared his enthusiasm for Beethoven, were it not a commonplace among intellectuals of that time, and not a musical judgment but a literary pose.' Stravinsky could not know that Proust's comprehension of the late quartets was, for a layman, no less profound than his own, nor that the imprudent question was not mere small-talk, but a request for information on the Vinteuil Septet.

Joyce arrived at midnight, already the worse for wear, and improperly dressed because he did not possess a suit of tails. He settled morosely down, head buried in hands, to drink champagne. In October 1920, newly descended in Paris from Zurich, he had written to a friend: 'I observe a furtive attempt to run a certain M. Marcel Proust of here against the signatory of this letter. I have read some pages of his. I cannot see any special talent but I am a bad critic.' But now, perhaps glimpsing in this nocturnal stranger a faint but deified apparition of Leopold Bloom, or even a peer of his own,[1] he moved shyly to the door when Proust departed with the Schiffs. As they set off in Odilon's taxi Joyce obliviously opened a window and lit a cigarette, and Sydney Schiff hurriedly shut the one and asked Joyce to throw away the other. Joyce complained of his eyes, Proust of his stomach. Did M. Joyce like truffles? He did. Had he met the Duchesse de X? He had not. "I regret that I do not know M. Joyce's work," remarked Proust. "I have never read M. Proust," replied Joyce. When they reached 44 Rue Hamelin Proust said to Schiff, politely but firmly: "Please ask M. Joyce to let my taxi drive him home." Thus the two greatest novelists of the twentieth century met and parted. "If only we'd been allowed to meet and have a talk somewhere ...", remarked Joyce sadly afterwards. The failure of writers of genius to appreciate one another and one another's work is a common and unregrettable phenomenon of instinctive self-protection; for if one allowed himself

[1] In fact Joyce said later: "He looked like the hero of *The Sorrows of Satan*."

'the great and admirable Picasso, who has concentrated all Cocteau's features into a portrait of such noble rigidity that, when I contemplate it, even the most enchanting Carpaccios in Venice tend to take a second place in my memory'.

to be seized by the other's greatness he would risk contaminating his own. However, Joyce magnanimously embedded allusions to Proust's name and titles in *Finnegans Wake*,[1] a novel which like Proust's is circular or spiral in construction, and when it ends eternally begins again.

A new Blumenthal award was now imminent, and Proust again felt it his duty to secure at least one of the two prizes for a member of the NRF group. The first choice was Jean Paulhan, Rivière's assistant editor; but Proust begged Mme Blumenthal in vain to consider Paulhan's distinguished war-service, and to overlook his being two years beyond the age-limit of thirty-five. Proust next thought of the avant-garde poets André Salmon and André Breton, but finally fell back on Benjamin Crémieux and, for the second prize, the young, talented and impoverished Georges Gabory, who had corrected the proofs of *Sodome et Gomorrhe II* for a fee of 1000 francs, and was a protégé of Gide—'one of the most gifted of the young people I have had occasion to approach,' Gide assured Proust. At four in the afternoon of 13 June, when the jury met, the absent Proust was sleeping off the effects of a party at Mme Hennessy's the night before. Walter Berry had told him there would be no voting, but only a registration of candidates; yet voting took place after all, Crémieux and Maurice Genevoix were elected, and poor Gabory, to Gide's keen distress, was left in the cold. Gide suggested that Proust was duty-bound to help the young man financially, and Proust did so, 'to show that I know how to forgive an injury,' he told Rivière ruefully, 'for Gabory left all the misprints in my book that he pretended to correct!'[2]

As soon as he entered Mme Hennessy's apartment the evening before, Proust realised that he had been asked not to her 'chic' party

[1] 'Prost bitte!' (*FW* 424: 9); 'the prouts will invent a writing' (*FW* 482: 31); 'swansway' (*FW* 450: 5, 465: 35); 'two legglegels in blooms' (*FW* 587: 26); 'pities of the plain' (*FW* 564: 28).

[2] Gide suspected Proust of treachery, but Proust's correspondence shows that his conduct was entirely correct and open. He sincerely believed on Berry's authority that voting was postponed till a later meeting, but in any case had voted by post for both Crémieux and Gabory. Gide himself was a little to blame as his second vote went to Genevoix. It seems that the partisans of Crémieux and Genevoix had done a deal, and that each gave his second vote to the other's candidate, so that only Gide and Proust could spare a vote for Gabory. Moreover, Gabory had imprudently applied for the same prize as Crémieux, so that Proust's vote for Gabory was not even valid. However, Gabory in turn showed his lack of resentment by writing his *Essai sur Marcel Proust* (1926), one of the earliest and most sympathetic of French studies of Proust's work.

but to her 'mixed' one. A lady was singing '*I must depart forthwith*', which seemed scarcely polite; Gustave Schlumberger was snorting like a buffalo as he stumped relentlessly towards Thérèse d'Hinnisdael; the Princesse de Polignac, icy as a cold draught, was looking the image of Dante; and while Proust talked to Boni de Castellane he heard himself pointed out—"there, that dark man who looks ill and hasn't combed his hair, he's a genius!"—as "the famous Marcel Prévost, who wrote *Les Don Juanes*!" But Marcel Prévost himself, to whom letters intended for Proust had so often been misdirected, was there in person; and Proust half promised him *La Prisonnière* as a serial for his *Revue de France*, but withdrew the offer a few days later after an indignant outburst from Rivière.

A well-meaning friend, possibly Coco de Madrazo who adored her, had informed Laure Hayman, rather belatedly, that she was the original of Odette. While Proust was still suffering from his overdose of adrenalin she sent him a furious letter; he was a monster, she declared. He replied, without attempting to differentiate between their morals, that in her wealth of taste and intelligence she was the opposite of Odette, who was destitute of either; when he put Mme Straus's 'snowballs' in Odette's drawing-room, instead of accusing him of identifying her with Swann's wife, she had written to thank him; Odette in the Bois de Boulogne was Léonie Clomesnil; Mme Hayman was no more Odette than Baron Doasan was Charlus. Mme Hayman, after a mysterious sorrow towards 1900, had made a new career as a sculptress. She had lost her wealth and youth, but not her vitality and courage, and if she and Proust could have been reconciled these two old friends would have found much to say to one another. But Proust was deeply distressed by this pathetic incident, and complained to both Gabriel de La Rochefoucauld and Gallimard of the cruelty of 'a woman I loved thirty years ago'. 'Such letters, and having to reply to them, kill all work,' he wrote, 'not to mention pleasure, which I have long since renounced.'

The Schiffs had left a few days before Mme Hennessy's party. Proust posted to Sydney a sumptuous waistcoat he had admired, in grey velvet with a pattern of foliage, which Céleste insisted on sending first to the cleaner's ("it isn't good enough for Monsieur Schiff without!"). He recalled to them the two twin pageboys he had introduced to them at the Ritz, whose personality Sydney Schiff had thought so different ('but it's the same, and anyway perfectly null'), and revealed that one of them had gone off to Switzerland with Lord Northcliffe.

These brothers, alike in face but supposed unlike in nature, must surely be connected with the tomato-twins at Balbec, whose dissimilarity in character causes poor M. Nissim Bernard a black eye and a permanent dislike for the fruit they resemble.[1]

'Every day more rapidly,' Proust had written to Edmond Jaloux in the spring, when his real or fancied symptoms of uraemia had reappeared, 'I descend a rigid iron staircase that leads to the abyss.' But during this final summer all omens of doom ceased, as he halted unaware on the last step of the stairs. 'My giddiness, the weakness in my legs, my impediments of speech, have almost entirely vanished,' he told the departed Schiffs. Again, but as chimerically as Aunt Léonie when she thinks of visiting her beloved farmhouse at Mirougrain, he dreamed of a holiday away from Paris. At his bedside he gave lessons in French history to Céleste, Marie Gineste, Yvonne Albaret and Odilon, scolding them when he was displeased with the awful menace: "I'll drown you in an ocean of *merde*!" At the Ritz in his private room, where the manager M. Elles had now arranged for him to dine in the small hours, he held court for the last time with his retinue of pages. One evening, when he was explaining Molière's *Amphitryon* to a waiter who had studied the part of Sosie at the Conservatoire, the appropriate sound of a deluge was heard in the next room, as though an angry Jupiter had indeed arrived with his thunder; but no, Proust was informed, it was only Sir Philip Sassoon taking a bath.[2] The staff were proud of Proust's fame, and sometimes even gave him news of it. Vespis, the Italian head waiter in the grillroom, announced one evening in July: "The *Corriere della Sera*, it say Monsieur Proust's books are verra verra tiring, you must climb, climb always, but it's worth while, because you see so far from the top!" Vespis died a few weeks later: 'poor Vespis,' wrote Proust to Paul Brach, 'or happy Vespis, according to how you look at it—he's dead—is that a happy event? I don't know.'

On 15 July Proust allowed himself to be taken by Brach and Edmond Jaloux to the celebrated Bœuf sur le Toit, the night-resort of artists which Cocteau had discovered and consecrated. Jaloux called for him at the instant when Céleste was knotting her master's dress-tie

---

[1] II, 854-5.
[2] It was Sir Philip's mother, according to one of Montesquiou's favourite stories, who enquired of a lady in the Faubourg Saint-Germain—as does Mme Verdurin of M. de Charlus (II, 967): "Couldn't you recommend me some old nobleman, I've a vacancy for a hall-porter."

and bringing a hot drink. It was lukewarm, he complained; and then, seeing her feelings were hurt, Proust immediately assured her that she was right, that the tepid tisane was just what he needed in his state of health at the moment. The service at the Bœuf sur le Toit, Proust felt, was less perfect than at the Ritz. The roast chicken was excellent, but it was hurled at their heads by a hideous waiter whom he uncomfortably felt he had seen somewhere before. He talked of the future volumes of his novel, and revealed that Saint-Loup would become an invert like his uncle Charlus, "at the same age and for the same reasons". At the moment of tipping Proust summoned a distant waiter and rewarded him regally. "But he didn't do anything for us," protested Brach, and Proust replied: "Oh, but I saw such a sad look in his eyes, when he thought he wasn't going to get anything!" Jaloux left to go on to a soirée, and the evening began to take a sinister turn. Brach was joined by drunken friends, who engaged in hostile banter with a band of 'unbelievable pimps and queers' at the other end of the bar. The waiters, alas, and even the proprietor Moyse—"the tables this Moses keeps are apparently not those of the Law," commented Proust—seemed to favour the other side. Suddenly a completely canned young reveller lurched across to Proust, astonished by his fur coat and bowler, perhaps misunderstanding his conversation about Sodom, and picked a quarrel. Like an aged warrior, exulting in the vision of a final combat, Proust went through the motions of challenging to a duel, and exchanged names and addresses: the drunk was named Jacques Delgado, and lived in the Rue Greuze near the Trocadéro. But the etiquette of the 1890s would not do for the 1920s; his friends hurried to part the foes, explaining that it was all a joke, that he had nothing to do with their brawl, that Marcel could not possibly fight a person so far beneath him. Proust was led crestfallen away; but that night he indomitably wrote a challenge to swords, which Odilon carried at dawn to the Rue Greuze. M. Delgado was now cold sober, and sent so courteous an apology that Proust could only reply in kind. 'You owed me no excuses,' he wrote, 'and it is only the more delicate and elegant on your part to offer them. . . . The elevated sentiments of your letter give me precisely the pleasure I should have had after a duel; I mean, sir, that of shaking you very cordially by the hand.'

Among the subjects discussed at the Bœuf sur le Toit was the menace of Count Robert's posthumous memoirs. Proust had written in alarm to Henri Pinard and received a charming letter of vague reassurance. Would he be entitled, he asked Brach, if the memoirs contained an attack on himself, to prosecute Pinard? Edmond Jaloux was now literary editor to Grasset, who at this time was proposing to publish the memoirs; and on 21 October, when he was already dying, Proust wrote to Jaloux: 'it would be best to delete everything, even my name, if I do not survive the strange illness I have at this moment. Since in that case I should have good reason for being unable to reply, I prefer not to be mentioned.' His anxiety, however, and that of so many others, was needless. Montesquiou's *Les Pas effacés* might have been a masterpiece of brilliant venom, yet turned out, when published in 1923 not by Grasset but by Émile-Paul, to be only the lame apology of a disappointed man. In an interminable waste-land of verbiage and vanity, illuminated only rarely by a blazing image or thrust of a flashing swordblade that recalled his former power, Montesquiou's three volumes deplored the neglect of his greatness, praised the perspicacity of his admirers, extolled the beauty of his interior decoration, and quoted in full all the flattering things that had ever been said about him. His only damaging revelation about 'my dear Marcel' was that he had an untidy bedroom. He did not dispute Marcel's genius; he lamented only that it should have been recognised at the expense of his own, that persons other than himself should have the effrontery to claim they had been the first to discover it. 'They say this dear young man is very nice,' he wrote, 'but we were already aware of the fact!' The dreadful truth emerged at last: Count Robert's memoirs were not scandalous, but merely boring. The verdict of his beloved cousin Mme Greffulhe was generally felt to meet the case: 'it's not quite what one expects of a dead man,' she decided.

Proust's oldest friends were beginning, unawares, to see him for the last time. Lucien Daudet had called in June, to talk of distant times and express his profound dislike for one of Marcel's newest acquaintances. "Sympathies and antipathies aren't transmissible," said Marcel, "that is the saddest thing about friendships." Lucien spoke of the little ivory coffer, carved with a girl leaning on an urn and the words 'To Friendship', which Marcel had given him on New Year's Eve, 1896. "God!" cried Proust, "How could you keep it? How hideous it must be! Can you see anything prettier here that you'd like?" But Lucien wanted no rival to his ivory box. As he departed, with sobs rising in his throat, he tried to embrace his friend; but Proust recoiled in his bed, exclaiming: "No, don't, I haven't shaved." Then Lucien seized his left hand and kissed it, and bore away with him for ever the image of Marcel's black-rimmed eyes, fixed silently upon him through the open doorway.

In this June, when Antoine Bibesco briefly visited Paris from his post at the Roumanian Legation in Washington, occurred the last imperfect 'conjunction' between Proust and the Bibescos. Princesse Marthe Bibesco had dined with Proust and Walter Berry at the Ritz in 1920, unable at first to recognise, in this supernaturally young man with the small moustache and eyes extraordinarily animated with new life, whom she now heard for the first time laughing, the bearded and melancholy apparition of the ball nine years before. About the same time he had called on Antoine and his wife Elizabeth—'to ask her some questions about certain passages in Shakespeare'—at their apartment on the prow of the ship-like Ile Saint-Louis, where the gilded walls reminded him of the golden mosaics of Saint Mark's at Venice. Now Antoine brought the two princesses, without warning, to 44 Rue Hamelin after the theatre, and rang for the last time the unmistakable double peal of their youth at the doorbell. Céleste, when she opened the door, seemed inclined to close it again. "Monsieur has just had a terrible attack of asthma," she said, in the formal manner she had learned from her master, "he can hardly breathe. I'm afraid he may not be able to receive anyone, not even Prince Antoine, whose visits always give him such immense pleasure." Proust called from within; Céleste retired and returned; Antoine was to enter, but the ladies were asked to wait in the outer drawing-room. "Monsieur is very much afraid," she explained, "of the scent of princesses."

At the end of one of his last evenings in society Proust sat with Jeanne de Caillavet, his old love, now Jeanne Pouquet again, for she had married her cousin Maurice, whom Proust had glimpsed thirty years before in her mother's house. The guests were leaving, she was tired and began to go. His face took a haunting expression of gentleness, irony and pain as he said: "Very well, Madame, goodbye." "No, dear Marcel, au revoir, I'll come and visit you very soon." "No, Madame, goodbye. I shall never see you again. You think I look well? I'm dying. Look well! That's too funny!" and he burst into a forced, uncanny laugh. "Don't come, don't be offended, you're kind, but I don't want to see my friends any more," he said, as his eyes filled with tears, "I have very urgent work to do."

Jeanne's daughter Simone, now grown into a beautiful woman and a gifted writer, for whom Anatole France, in turn, had written a preface, had married Georges Stoïcesco, a Roumanian diplomat whom Proust had seen and disliked at Princesse Soutzo's; though M. Stoïcesco, we are assured, was in point of fact intelligent and charming.

With his feelings still wounded by her mother Proust was enraged to read in *Le Figaro* on 21 August that Mme Stoïcesco ('daughter of the second grand passion of my adolescence, the first being Mlle de Benardaky' and 'wife of the most detestable of Roumanians') had given 'a tea at Deauville in honour of the Shah of Persia and a *goûter* in honour of Prince and Princesse Christopher of Greece'. What, he asked, was the difference between a tea and a *goûter*? Why publish these delectable meals to the world, when the next page of *Le Figaro* revealed that millions were dying of famine in Russia after devouring the corpses of their children? He added to the manuscript of *Le Temps Retrouvé* the remark that Mlle de Saint-Loup 'later chose for husband an obscure man of letters'[1]; for he was not to know that Simone de Caillavet's second husband, at least, would be a most distinguished man of letters, his own biographer and the discoverer of the English to themselves, M. André Maurois.

Proust's urgent work was the preparation of *La Prisonnière* and *Albertine Disparue*. On 24 June he informed Gallimard that both were now typed in duplicate, though his revision, 'in which I am making changes and additions everywhere', was hardly begun. A fortnight later he agreed to Gallimard's request for both volumes to be announced for 1923, but still felt unable to fix a precise date. On 29 July he proposed to send in *La Prisonnière* for first proofs, with the double purpose of revising it on the galleys, and of seeing whether it would be short enough to publish simultaneously with *Albertine Disparue*. At the end of August he changed his plans, and re-engaged Yvonne Albaret, whom he had dismissed in June, to retype *La Prisonnière*. During the next ten weeks, which coincided with his last illness and death, Mlle Albaret copied three successive versions of the opening section of the volume, describing the morning of Albertine's visit to the Trocadéro and the street-cries of Paris, and also a long extract promised to *Les Œuvres Libres*, which gave an abridged version of the whole volume, omitting, with much else, the Verdurin soirée and the Vinteuil Septet, and was published posthumously in February 1923 under the title '*Précaution inutile*'.

Early in May Tronche had suggested that *Sodome et Gomorrhe III* and *Sodome et Gomorrhe IV* were inadequate titles for the coming volumes. "When people see a book with the same title as the one before," Tronche declared, "they'll say: 'Why, I've read that one already!' " It was thus not until just before the eleventh hour that

[1] III, 1028.

Proust chose new titles for the story of Albertine's captivity and death. Still in doubt, he forbore to spread the news. 'I'm thinking of calling my next volume *La Prisonnière*,' he told Jacques Boulenger in mid-May; but Gallimard was not informed until 25 June, while as late as 3 September the astonished Rivière could confess that he was 'terribly curious' to know what Proust meant by *La Prisonnière* and *La Fugitive*. Early in July, however, Proust learned that a volume of Rabindranath Tagore's poems was about to appear, in a translation by Mme de Brimont, under his own newborn title of *La Fugitive*. He knew the lady slightly, and thought of appealing to her better feelings; but no, 'it would be caddish, and too late anyway', he told Gallimard. He now resolved to abandon his title, and early in October reiterated his decision to Gallimard. The *Pléiade* editors have justifiably retained the title *La Fugitive*, since it is the only one for which documentary evidence from Proust's lifetime survives. On the other hand, of all titles it is the only one which, as equally certain documentary evidence shows, Proust would never have used. In the same October letter Proust revealed that he had made new plans for his title, and asked Gallimard to visit him to discuss the matter. Proust's published correspondence with Gallimard and Rivière during this month is incomplete, and does not indicate whether or not the visit took place; but we need have little doubt that when the NRF announced the volume as *Albertine Disparue* only a year later, they were following Proust's declared wishes.[1]

In August the famous '*décades*', the ten-day periods of literary and philosophical discussion organised by Paul Desjardins in the former monastery of Pontigny, were resumed for the first time since the war. Proust himself, as has been seen, had thought of attending in 1910, and earlier still his own half-serious, half-visionary plans for a lay monastery, with Willie Heath in 1893, with Lauris and Mme de Noailles as 'admirable abbess habited all in white' in 1903, had no doubt owed their inspiration to Desjardins. More recently, in the supposed extract from the Goncourt *Journal* which the Narrator reads at Tansonville in *Le Temps Retrouvé*, Proust had introduced a sympathetic allusion to Pontigny in the guise of a sojourn in Normandy of the Verdurins and their friends; and his satire here is directed at the absurdity of Gon-

---

[1] For these reasons the title *Albertine Disparue* has been used throughout the present biography. It may also be noticed that the typescript from which *Albertine Disparue* was printed has disappeared, and that Proust would surely have entered in it his final decision as to the title.

court and Mme Verdurin, not at Desjardins's noble dream come true,
for which he kept a nostalgic affection. 'They lodged a whole colony
of artists in an admirable mediaeval dwelling, a former monastery
rented by them for a mere nothing; and my mouth waters,' cries the
pretended diarist,[1] 'at the thought of the life Mme Verdurin confessed
to leading down there, each one working in his cell, and joining the
rest before lunch in the drawing-room, so enormous that it had two
fireplaces, for altogether superior conversation mingled with paper-
games.'

Among the thirty-five decadists of 1922 were Rivière, Gide, Marc
Allégret, Jean Schlumberger, Roger Martin du Gard, Charles du Bos,
the critic Ernst Robert Curtius who had already begun to make
Proust known in Germany, and the young André Maurois—'a
charming mind, alert, courteous and very prettily cultivated', noted
Gide with approval. 'Please give my homage to the Desjardins
family,' Proust asked Rivière, 'they are and will remain one of the
dearest and most respected parts of the years I have lived.' Proust's
spiritual presence was felt throughout Pontigny that year. His work
was frequently discussed in the formal conversations; Charles du Bos,
walking in the neighbouring forest and noticing the changing position
of the abbey church, was reminded of the Narrator's essay on the
moving spires of Martinville; and Rivière, whenever a foreign visitor
asked him to name the greatest living French writer, invariably
answered: "Proust!"

Among the foreign Proustians at Pontigny was Dorothy Bussy,
elder sister of Lytton Strachey and Gide's matchless translator and
friend. Proust's English admirers now included such elder men of
letters as Conrad, Arnold Bennett, Arthur Symons, Logan Pearsall
Smith, Edmund Gosse and George Saintsbury, young writers of the
new generation such as Aldous Huxley,[2] Middleton Murry, Compton
Mackenzie and J. C. Squire, and the entire Bloomsbury group: Virginia Woolf, Clive Bell, Desmond MacCarthy, Arthur Waley, Roger
Fry and Lytton Strachey. The sun of his glory in England had risen;
Proust himself felt its distant rays and began to respond, but with a shy
reluctance which would soon be cut short by death. Since April he had

[1] III, 713-14.
[2] Hearing of this Proust had slipped a characteristic 'visiting-card' into
Sodome et Gomorrhe: 'The illustrious Huxley, whose nephew'—he should
have said grandson—'now holds a preponderant place in the world of English
literature . . .' (II, 637).

intended to thank Murry for a new article[1] and 'an extremely nice letter', but he hesitated, unsure whether or not his benefactor should be addressed as Sir Middleton Murry. He felt too ill to accept an invitation from Jaloux early in June to dine with Murry and Katherine Mansfield, herself so soon to die.[2] T. S. Eliot, then the London correspondent of the NRF, had requested an extract from *A la Recherche* for *The Criterion*, but waited in vain for a reply: 'I am in deep despair at not yet having written to M. Eliot,' Proust told Sydney Schiff in August.

His last thoughts of England were unhappy. In December 1919 a nameless English lady had offered to translate *A la Recherche*, and Proust himself had then proposed Gilbert Cannan, translator of Romain Rolland's *Jean Christophe*, a gifted but ill-fated novelist who soon afterwards became insane. Providentially, however, and unknown to Proust, Charles Scott-Moncrieff had already resolved to devote his life to the translation of *A la Recherche du Temps Perdu*. After unavailingly offering *Swann's Way* in January 1920 to the short-lived magazine *Land and Water* as a serial, he persuaded Chatto and Windus to accept the whole of his magnificent *Remembrance of Things Past*. Early in September 1922 the Schiffs took alarm from an advance announcement, and convinced Proust that the titles, at least, were hopelessly inaccurate; for they incomprehensibly supposed the words *Swann's Way* to mean 'in the manner of Swann', and failed to recognise in *Remembrance of Things Past* the bold but exquisitely appropriate quotation from Shakespeare's Thirtieth Sonnet through which Scott-Moncrieff symbolised the transplanting of Proust's novel into English literature.[3] In his distress Proust thought of stopping the publication. 'I cherish my work,' he told Gallimard, 'and I won't have it ruined by Englishmen.'

Swann's Way was published in England in the third week of Sep-

---

[1] '*Marcel Proust. A new sensibility*', in the *Quarterly Review*, New York, July 1922, pp. 86-100, of which Murry sent Proust advance proofs.

[2] However, he sent Murry inscribed copies of *Le Côté de Guermantes II* and *Sodome et Gomorrhe II*, the latter 'with admiring and grateful homage from a writer whom you have always protected and supported, and who would like to have an hour's good health in order to thank you less briefly'.

[3] The Schiffs, who had erred only from loyalty to Proust, were quick to make amends. They became ardent admirers and personal friends of Scott-Moncrieff, and Sydney Schiff dedicated his translation of *Time Regained*: 'To the memory of my friend Charles Scott-Moncrieff, Marcel Proust's incomparable translator'.

tember.[1] Proust, despite his shaky acquaintance with the half-learned and half-forgotten English language, was relieved a little as he struggled through his own copy by the beauty he dimly perceived, still more, perhaps, by his press-cuttings from London reviews, which tended, though they praised both highly, to declare the translation superior to the original. Even so, when he thanked Scott-Moncrieff on 10 October for 'the trouble you have taken', and complimented him on his 'fine talent', his tone was still grudging and prickly. 'The verses you have inserted, and the dedication to your friends,' he remarked, 'are no substitute for the intentional ambiguity of my *Temps perdu*, which corresponds to the *Temps retrouvé* that appears at the end of my work.' As for *Swann's Way*, all would have been well, he suggested, if his translator had called it '*To Swann's Way*'! Scott-Moncrieff, equally ruffled, replied stiltedly in English—'because my knowledge of French, as you have shown me with regard to my titles, is too imperfect, too stunted a growth for me to weave from it the chaplet that I would fain offer you'—and stood by his guns.[2]

But Proust's strange visitor, who had come to warn every year in May, the month of his brother's birth, and September, the month of his mother's death, had now come to stay.

[1] The British Museum copyright copy was received on 19 September, and the first review appeared in the *Times Literary Supplement* on the 21st.

[2] The memory of his unlucky skirmish with Proust perhaps played some part in the sturdy independence which makes, quite as much as its fidelity, the greatness of his translation. Curtius, when he visited Scott-Moncrieff in Rome in 1928, was amused by the 'sarcastic want of respect' which seasoned his profound devotion to Proust's work, and remarked: 'He generally received me with some strong abuse of Albertine, whose moods and vices were at that time keeping him very busy.'

Chapter 17

THE TWO WAYS MEET
(*September – November 1922*)

NEW and unusually violent attacks of asthma on 2 and 3 September were followed on the 4th by repeated fits of vertigo, in which he fell again and again to the floor. Whenever he dared to step from his bed he swayed, turned and dropped, and soon his speech and memory were again affected. 'I have been deprived successively of speech, sight and movement,' he told Jaloux and Curtius, adding to the latter: 'We must never be afraid to go too far, for truth lies beyond.'

The causes of the symptoms which during the past five years had marked the approach of Proust's death are mysterious and were probably complex. He had ceased to believe that his brain was affected; no doubt his doctors were justified in blaming his alternate abuse of narcotic and stimulating drugs, and Proust himself may well have been right a year before in diagnosing chronic uraemia, a disturbance of metabolism arising not from kidney disease but from a malfunctioning of the central nervous system, which could have been caused by his drugs and would account medically for all his signs of uncoordination. But these symptoms, whatever their origin, combined to imitate, as he himself had noticed, those of his mother in her last illness. They included a psychosomatic factor which guided his physical ailments according to the self-destructive promptings of his inner guilt. The Dark Woman was punishing him with the sufferings he had caused; and conversely, by sharing his dead mother's torment he would be identified and united with her at last. For the present, however, Proust sought a more natural explanation. With some support from his doctors, he convinced himself truly or falsely that there were cracks in his chimney, and he was being poisoned by carbon monoxide fumes. Towards the middle of September he ventured several times to the Ritz for his four a.m. dinner, found his symptoms vanished when he left his unventilated bedroom, and felt his suspicions were confirmed. He gave orders that his fire must not be lit; and this most warmth-needing of men continued his journey to death in the still more dangerous environment of an unheated room. Henceforth all his actions combined to doom him. But the strange recurrent malady of his last years, though it had prepared for the end by undermining his powers of resistance, was not destined to be the cause of his death. He had sinned through his lungs when in childhood he used his asthma to compel his mother's love, and to punish her fancied refusal of love; and now he was to perish by his lungs, though not through asthma.

Never had he worked more obsessively at his novel. The opening section of *La Prisonnière* dissatisfied him, as has been seen, and from mid-August to late October he thrice rearranged the existing type-script, which Yvonne Albaret thrice typed again, until the themes of waking, the presence of Albertine, and the street-cries of Paris were interwoven and repeated in their final symphonic form.[1] The remain-der of the volume apparently contented him, as well it might, for only three minor additions were made to the typescript of the previous spring.[2] But the voice of duty to his editors sounded louder even than the knell of death. Early in August he had promised Rivière an extract on Albertine's sleep, '*Le Sommeil d'Albertine*', and another on the morning street-cries, '*Les Cris de Paris*', for the NRF. Towards the end of the month he wrung Gallimard's reluctant consent to the abridgement of *La Prisonnière*, '*Précaution Inutile*', in *Les Œuvres Libres*, for which the editor Henri Duvernois had offered the princely sum of 10,000 francs.[3] He began with the first NRF extract, adding, because it was too brief, another on the Narrator's waking entitled '*Mes Réveils*', and sent the contribution to Rivière on 24 September. "You're mad to work in a state like this," protested Dr Bize, and prescribed an injection of evatmine, for asthma, and cola as a heart stimulant. Readers of the November NRF must have been baffled to find that the naked girl slumbering at the Narrator's side was Gisèle;

[1] He was at work on the second of these revisions (which, counting the complete typescript as the first, he called the third) on 2 September, and on the third and last (which he called the fourth) on the 20th.

[2] Mme Verdurin's medicinal preparations for the torments of the Vinteuil Septet (III, 240-1), the quarrel with Albertine when she says, or nearly says, "*casser le pot*" (III, 338-40), and an enlargement of the final paragraph in which Françoise announces Albertine's departure (III, 415).

[3] Proust told Sydney Schiff in September that he had already lent 5000 francs in anticipation of this fee 'to help some infuriating unfortunates'. The last time he had lent money to 'unfortunates' was in November 1917, when he subsidised Albert Le Cuziat's brothel. Can Proust still have been assisting Albert, despite their break a year or two before? Or was he again helping Anna Agostinelli, or Céline Cottin?

for Proust had changed her name, and altered the title to '*La regarder dormir*', lest Duvernois should discover that his 'unpublished novel' had been shorn of one of its finest passages. The second extract, retitled '*Une Matinée au Trocadéro*', and enlarged by the death of Bergotte, appeared in January 1923 in the special number, *Hommage à Marcel Proust*, dedicated by the NRF to his memory. Next Proust began the still more formidable task of condensing his whole volume into 127 pages for *Les Œuvres Libres*, and of re-establishing the continuity he had broken by his NRF extracts. Even so, he found energy to negotiate from July to October with two collectors who competed to buy the manuscript and corrected proofs of *Sodome et Gomorrhe II*,[1] and to support Rivière's candidature for the Prix Balzac.[2]

Early in October, on a foggy evening, Proust attended a last soirée at the Beaumonts' and returned with a sore throat, which next day became a severe cold. The second stage of his last illness had begun. His fever rose, and bronchitis set in, with fits of incessant coughing. Towards the middle of the month, on Céleste's insistence, he sent for Dr Bize. "It's nothing serious yet," decided the good doctor, "I can

---

[1] Jacques Doucet offered 7000 francs in July. Proust hesitated, on learning that Doucet intended to bequeath his collection to the State. 'It isn't very agreeable,' Proust told the Schiffs, 'to think that when I am dead anyone who chooses will be able to study my manuscripts, compare them with the definitive text, and infer suppositions which will always be false on my method of work and the evolution of my thought . . . but I wonder whether I wouldn't do better to diminish my absurd and useless expenses by these 7000 francs, than to let myself be sensitive about this posthumous indiscretion.' Proust no doubt foresaw the prejudiced and destructive fallacies of Professors Feuillerat and Vigneron, which have done lasting harm to Proustian scholarship, rather than the devoted work of the *Pléiade* editors André Ferré and Pierre Clarac, which is the greatest of all monuments to his memory. In any case, Proust's misgivings related only to his textual critics, and those who quote them against his biographers are not entitled to do so. Towards the end of August Serge André, the owner of the periodicals edited by Jacques Boulenger, offered 10,000 francs; but Proust was too scrupulous to sell anything to a personal friend. The negotiations with Doucet were still in progress at the end of October, but were cut short by Proust's death, when the manuscript passed with the rest of his literary property to his brother Robert.

[2] Rivière submitted his novel *Aimée*, which he dedicated to Proust, but his honourable refusal to allow Proust to approach his political enemy Léon Daudet cost him the prize. The jury, presided by Paul Bourget, included Barrès, Boylesve, Bidou, Marcel Boulenger, Léon Daudet, Henri Duvernois, Georges Duhamel and Gaston Chérau, all of whom except the last two were personal friends of Proust.

cure you in a week or ten days, but you'll have to stop work, and above all take nourishment." Proust would do neither of these things. Take nourishment! So the family doctor had ordered, more than forty years ago, on the night of *François le Champi*; and his mother had said: "My child, that doctor may be cleverer than I am, but I know what is right." "Mother always nursed me better than any doctors," he told Céleste, "and she knew that fasting is the only thing for a fever."

So he fasted, taking only fruit and milk, but the fever still rose and the helpless coughing persisted. Céleste kept the pathetic, peremptory notes her master now wrote to her when he was too breathless to speak. 'I'm so heated with this coughing that I'll probably try to drink a hot tisane. Hot, not warmed up. But no over-ripe fruit (so I'd better have your grapes). . . .' 'I've just coughed more than three thousand times, my back and stomach are done for, everything. It's madness. I need very hot sheets and woollen pullovers. Remember, all your sheets have a smell that starts my useless coughing. I hope you'll take strict account of my order, otherwise I shall be more than angry.' 'Have we a drop of that port from Voisin's, that the Comte de Polignac said was just like milk?' 'Céleste, I want an empty teacup and some sugar.' 'Can someone run and get me a peach or an apricot from the Ritz?' The sleepless Céleste grew as thin as her master, and Dr Bize's seven days were nearly over.

Late on the afternoon of the 19th Proust disobeyed his doctor and his fever, dressed and went out for the last time. His strength failed, and he returned almost immediately, cold to the marrow, shuddering, racked with fits of sinister sneezing. He rested for a moment on his chaise-longue, and returned to bed, too harassed even to work that night. "Death pursues me, Céleste," he said, "I shan't have time to finish my corrections, and Gallimard is waiting." Next day Céleste telephoned for Dr Robert Proust, who was out, and Dr Bize, who came. Proust himself suspected, prematurely, that he had pneumonia.

He sent Odilon for Rivière that evening, but Rivière was busy and unaware of danger. 'My dear Jacques,' wrote Proust, 'you will never guess why I sent for you, and I'd rather no one else knew. It was to ask you to write to your brother for some medical information.' Rivière came next day, and his brother Dr Marc Rivière, a clinician in the Faculty of Medicine at Bordeaux, replied on 25 October. 'Cocci,' he explained, 'are punctiform, slightly ovoid microbes. When they are grouped in twos we have diplococci, when in chains streptococci, when in clusters staphylococci. Pneumococci belong to the class of diplococci, being usually found in pairs in sputum. Each species of coccus is always grouped in the same way, thus permitting its identification...' Proust had written in time past to Emile Mâle for iconography, to François de Pâris for the heraldry of the Guermantes, to Louis Dimier and Henri Longnon for Brichot's etymologies of Normandy place-names; now he had verified the sources of his death.

On the 25th he had received the advance proof of his NRF extract. Finding that the ending of '*Mes Réveils*' was not to his liking, and forgetting that he had given Rivière no instructions for altering it, he upbraided his friend with an uncharacteristic cruelty which showed only the extent of his exhaustion. 'You have deceived me,' he wrote, 'leave me alone, my suffering today has touched the brink of despair. I have lost faith in you.' The loyal Rivière, bearing no malice, stopped the presses at Abbeville and obeyed his orders. The day before, on 24 October, Proust had completed *La Prisonnière*, and from now until his death worked on the revision of *Albertine Disparue*. On the 28th he learned the news of Rivière's rejection at the Prix Balzac committee,[1] without understanding it—'I happened to be a little delirious'; and it was not until about 2 November that he sent his condolences, with ironical thanks to Dr Marc Rivière for 'his graceful Bordelaisian pastoral, which proves that every microbe is a sign of health'. A few minutes later he wrote to Gallimard: 'the kind of fury with which I have worked at *La Prisonnière* (ready, but needs to be reread—the best would be for you to have first proofs made for me to correct), especially in my terrible state of these days, has made the following volumes recede. But three days of rest may suffice. Goodbye, dear Gaston.' A little before he had sent '*Précaution Inutile*' to Duvernois: 'if I have another hour of strength I shall write to my dear Robert de Flers, and ask him to spare me "after a long and painful illness valiantly borne".... Anyway, I think I may still come through.... And now, expect no more of me but silence, and imitate mine.' These three letters, as far as is known, were the last Proust ever wrote. "November has come," he said to Céleste, "November, that took my father." Towards 8 November Proust contracted the pneumonia he had already suspected and foretold.

The baffled Dr Bize summoned Robert Proust. "Your brother is impossible to treat," he exclaimed, "I decline all responsibility if he goes on like this. What's the use of my coming to see him? He defies

[1] The prize was shared by Émile Baumann with *Job le Prédestiné* and Giraudoux with *Siegfried et le Limousin*, with a minority vote for Rivière.

all my orders!" "Then I shall have him forcibly treated," exploded Robert, "as a doctor I have the right. I'll have him taken to the Piccini clinic."[1] For the first time since 1906, when Robert had unselfishly refused to take his fair share of their mother's legacy, Proust quarrelled with his brother. Did Robert presume to save his life, which he must save unaided or not at all; did he dare to keep him from the rendezvous which lay at the end? "Let me alone," Marcel cried, blind with rage, "I won't leave my bedroom." Would he at least have a nurse, they pleaded. "I'll have no one but Céleste, she's the only one who understands me." Robert insisted, and Proust ordered his would-be saviours to leave. He rang for Céleste: "You are to promise not to let anyone in, neither doctor, nor nurse, nor my family. Everyone who might hinder my work must stay away. You are not to go out for a second, and if I get worse, you must stay by me. Do as I say, and don't torment me any more." In those days before the discovery of sulfa-drugs expert nursing was the only known treatment for pneumonia. Proust was now doomed.

Few persons were to see him again in this world. Tronche had called on 24 September to reveal that *Le Côté de Guermantes* and *Sodome et Gomorrhe II* were temporarily out of print—a form of news which seems gratifying to publishers but calamitous to authors. Rivière made a last visit to collect the typescript of *La Prisonnière* and, as Céleste believed, to receive instructions for *Albertine Disparue*, which may well have included the new title.[2] Reynaldo called every day to enquire, but left without being able to see his friend. The gay Morand came, and Proust was moved by his emotion. "I felt that Paul Morand has a heart of gold," he told Céleste, "though I didn't think so before. He must have found me much changed, he said such kind things, and I realised he was sad to see me like this. I didn't know he was fond of me; I am very fond of him too."

Proust began to prepare for the end. Remorseful for his unkindness to Dr Bize, and characteristically anxious to express repentance by a gift, he ordered Céleste to send the well-meaning doctor a basket of flowers. "That's one more thing put right, if I should die," he said.

[1] The Clinique Médicale de Paris, 6 Rue Piccini (only half a mile from 44 Rue Hamelin, on the far side of the Avenue du Bois de Boulogne), under the charge of Dr Louis Lamy.
[2] The title *Albertine Disparue* first appeared on the verso of the half-title of the first edition of *La Prisonnière*, which was printed and published in the autumn of the following year (*achevé d'imprimer* 14 November 1923).

Rather than explain why he had not asked his support for Rivière at the time of the Prix Balzac, he had not written to thank Léon Daudet for yet another article in his praise; so Daudet's wife, too, must have a present of flowers. In the summer of 1917 Marie Scheikévitch had given him a cigarette-lighter made from two English pennies, a present from her young brother at the front; "do you know," he remarked as he admired it, "you will find this in my novel."[1] Since the war his relations with Mme Scheikévitch had been strained; but now, as a gesture of reconciliation from beyond the grave, he told Céleste to return this sacred relic of their friendship after his death.

He thought of the saintly Abbé Mugnier's efforts to save his soul; he remembered, too, that he himself was a baptised and confirmed, though lapsed Catholic. Had he not fought against injustice to the Church in the dark days of the Combes laws, and expressed in his novel a profound love for the humble gothic churches which, perhaps, are a truer symbol of faith than the corrupt souls of men? Yet he could not show a conformity which he did not feel. "Send for the good Abbé Mugnier," he said with mingled irony and reverence, "half an hour after I die. You will see how he'll pray for me. And find the rosary that Lucie Faure brought me from Jerusalem, and put it between my fingers when I'm dead." He looked at Céleste's hands. "To think that those little hands will close my eyes," he said, "Céleste, you have nursed me as though you were my own mother."

Sleep had left him, and in his long hours of waking he imagined the sudden arrival in his bedroom of staff from the Piccini clinic, sent by Robert to take him away by force. He wrote to Reynaldo and Morand asking them to prevent this fell arrest; and poor Robert consented, on condition that he should be allowed to call every day. From the 15th Robert Proust was almost constantly near Marcel, sharing devotedly in Céleste's nursing. Another anxiety seized Proust: "Céleste, it is horrible to think that doctors insist on torturing a dying man. They will want to give me injections when I'm too weak to resist, just to prolong my sufferings for a few hours. You must swear to prevent them." Céleste hesitated, and he gave her a terrible look. "If you don't," he hissed, "I'll come back to haunt you."

Pneumonia, when uninterrupted by modern remedies, lasts for up

---

[1] In his list of wartime jewellery carried by fashionable ladies on the home front the Narrator mentions 'cigarette-lighters made of two English pennies, to which a soldier in his dugout had contrived to give so beautiful a patina that Queen Victoria's profile seemed traced by Pisanello' (III, 724).

to ten days, ending in a crisis followed by the death or rapid recovery of the sufferer; but the crisis is often preceded a day or two before by a 'false crisis', after which the patient's condition temporarily and illusorily improves. Proust's 'false crisis' came on 16 November, and on the 17th, declaring himself much better, he sent for Robert. "Tomorrow will be the ninth day," he said, "and if I get past it I'll show my doctors what sort of a man I am. Five days more, and we shall see whether they were right in trying to prevent me from working. But it remains to be seen whether I can survive these five days." Robert asked him to take nourishment. Proust smiled. "If, like my doctors, you want me to eat," he told Céleste, "you can cook me a fried sole. I'm sure it won't do me any good, but I want to please you." But this ritual sole, which Mme Proust had prescribed for his convalescence at the time of *François le Champi*, was prudently forbidden by Robert, and Marcel gracefully acquiesced. "I'm going to do a good night's work," he said, as Robert departed, "and I'll keep Céleste by me to help."

At least two of the products of this last night have survived. One is written on the back of an envelope stained by a spilt tisane, in a tragically changed and quavering hand; only a few phrases are legible or intelligible, but enough to show that this was an expanded version of a few sentences in the Narrator's mother's conversation with her Combray friends on the marriage of Saint-Loup and Gilberte, near the end of *Albertine Disparue*.[1] Towards three in the morning, exhausted and suffocating, he called Céleste, in whose hand many of the November additions to the manuscript of *Albertine Disparue* are written, to take dictation. "Now I'm in the same condition myself, I want to add some notes to the death of Bergotte," he said. The only relic of these, written in the clear, unhurried, misspelt autograph of Céleste, is a satirical observation on the imbecility of doctors, drawn perhaps by Proust from the remarks of the previous day. 'And then one day everything changes. We are now allowed everything that was declared unsuitable, all that was forbidden us. "But I couldn't have champagne, for instance?" "Why, certainly, if you feel like it." Unable to believe our ears, we send for the very brands we had most strictly denied ourselves; and it is such things as this that impart a certain slight vulgarity to the unbelievable frivolousness of the dying.'

[1] '*Le vieux qui entretenait la mère . . . d'avoir épousé Mlle de Forcheville . . . cependant que la personne qui avait l'air de vouloir . . . trouva qu'elle était elle et était une autre (G. de Forcheville).*' Cf. III, 676.

His other insertions may have been less insignificant, for as he finished his face lit up with joy. "Céleste, I think what I've made you write was very good. Above all, don't forget to add it in the proper place." But Céleste forgot, or could not find the place, and the insertions were never made.[1] His strength suddenly failed, and the doctors told her next day that the abscess in his lungs must have burst at that moment. "I must stop, I can't do any more," he said. Céleste noticed that he was clutching at the bedclothes, drawing the scattered leaves of his manuscript towards him, and recognised, wise in peasant lore, the uncanny reflex action known as 'plucking', an infallible sign of the close and inevitable end.

When the dawn of Saturday, 18 November 1922, came he was still conscious. At six he asked for milk, adding with a smile: "Always just to please you." At ten he sent Odilon to the Ritz for iced beer: "Like everything else, it will come too late," he said. He drew breath with appalling difficulty; his face was white and emaciated, his black beard had grown again; and his eyes, with an extraordinary intensity, seemed to gaze on things invisible. "Leave me, I want to be alone," he murmured. Céleste stood by the inner door, concealed by the blue satin bedscreen, but he sensed her presence. "Why are you waiting, Céleste?" "I'm afraid to leave Monsieur." "Don't lie, Céleste, you know she's come." Proust was staring at the other door, the one through which visitors came, through which, indeed, a last visitor had just entered. "She's big, very big," he cried, "she's very big, very dark! She's all in black, she's ugly, she frightens me." "You needn't be afraid, I'm here, I'll make her go away." "No, don't touch her, Céleste! No one must touch her! She's merciless, she's getting more horrible every moment." It was more than time to send for the doctors.

Robert Proust hurried from his hospital, followed by Dr Bize, the long cortège of orderlies with cupping-glasses, bladders of oxygen, hypodermic syringes, and Odilon with the beer. With angry eyes Proust ignored the invaders, and murmured: "Thank you, my dear Odilon, for getting the beer." He submitted in silence to an injection from Dr Bize, while Robert clasped his hand; but as Céleste raised the bedclothes she felt his fingers, pinching her wrist till the blood came,

[1] In the *Pléiade* text of *La Prisonnière* (III, 182-8) the death of Bergotte is printed unchanged from the typescript made by Yvonne Albaret in the previous spring, while the passage on Gilberte is in the original version, without indication of any alternative.

and heard his voice whispering: "Ah, Céleste, why did you let them?" The doctors performed their useless ritual in vain. The cupping-glasses, intended to draw the broken abscess and stimulate his failing heart, would not hold on his dying skin. At three in the afternoon Robert raised his brother gently on the pillows: "I'm disturbing you, my dear boy," he said, "I'm afraid I'm hurting you." "Oh, yes, my dear Robert," replied Marcel, in his last conscious words; but a little later he was heard to say: "Mother". The Dark Woman, raised five years before by the unaccepted offering of his novel and his descent into the final pit of Sodom, had come and gone. He had forgiven Robert, who by his birth had hurt him indeed; and now only the young mother, restored from before the beginning of Time Lost, before she had ever seemed to withhold her love, remained. At half-past five, calm and motionless, his eyes still wide open, Proust died.

Soon Reynaldo would come, to write hurried *pneus* to Marcel's friends, and telephone; "Is that you, Lucien? Marcel has just died." For two days more the endless, bewildered procession of mourners would enter to see Proust for the last time and bid him farewell. Morand and Gabriel Astruc, indeed, came the same evening, followed a little before midnight by Fernand Gregh, who stayed to watch over the dead man while Reynaldo rested, and the noises of the great city gradually died away. Marcel, he reflected, was the first of the *Banquet* group to die—the first, except for Jacques Bizet, who, fallen into alco-holism and morphinomania and tortured by a cruel mistress, had shot himself a fortnight before. But Gregh remembered most clearly the young Marcel of thirty years ago, ringing from house to house in the Boulevard Haussmann to find him in the first fervour of their friend-ship; in love with the enchanting Marie Finaly; and once at Trouville, in the dark-room at the Manoir de la Cour Brûlée, inexplicably faint-ing while Gregh and Jacques Bizet developed their negatives.

Marthe and Suzy Proust, Robert Dreyfus, Mme de Noailles, Lucien Daudet, Lauris, Robert de Billy, Proust's cousins Valentine Thomson and her sister Marguerite, Jaloux, Porel and Cocteau came next day. When the weeping Céleste offered to lead him in, Dreyfus had not the heart to see the body, and left with the kinder memory of the boy Marcel in the Champs-Élysées, darting to meet Marie de Benardaky. Mme de Noailles came with Henri Gans; Marcel's face was proud and indolent, she thought, as though death had not succeeded in attracting his attention. Lucien saw a smile of victory, Lauris Marcel's look of infinite goodness—'never was so much goodness accompanied by so much intelligence,' he wrote—while Billy noticed how each of the friends, stricken at heart, kept to himself rather than intrude on the suffering of the others. Porel slipped a cameo ring, given by Anatole France to Réjane after the first night of *Le Lys Rouge*, on Marcel's finger. Cocteau observed the twenty manuscript volumes of *A la Recherche du Temps Perdu*, piled neatly on the mantelpiece by Céleste, 'continuing to live, like the ticking watch on the wrist of a dead soldier'. But Jaloux, perhaps rightly, was struck by the impression that Proust 'was more dead than other dead men—he was totally absent'. Céline Cottin turned up and thought, with her streak of malice: "Thin and pale as ever, legs still like matchsticks." Helleu, Dunoyer de Segonzac, the sculptor Wlérick, the surrealist photographer Man Ray came at Robert's invitation to make portraits of the majestic head and folded hands. Helleu, who had been the Count's friend as well as Proust's, remarked to Céleste: "Why did he write like that about Montesquiou? Montesquiou died of it", and was horror-struck by the look of vengeful delight in Céleste's face.

Proust's funeral-service would be at noon on Tuesday, 21 November, at the nearby church of Saint-Pierre-de-Chaillot, with the military honours due to a chevalier of the Légion d'Honneur. In that enormous concourse, where Antoinette Faure-Berge stood with Comte Greffulhe, Pierre Lavallée with Princesse Marie Murat, Reynaldo's sister Maria with Diaghilev, he was surrounded by all the friends of all his life, as though a throng of ghosts had risen to do honour to a living man. Ravel's *Pavane for a Dead Infanta* was played, the Abbé Delepouve pronounced absolution, the bells tolled, and the mourners waited for their carriages. Barrès, bowler-hatted, his umbrella dangling from his elbow, said to Mauriac: "Ah, well, he was our young man." Reynaldo recognised a familiar face in the crowd: "Good Lord, there's Céline," he thought. Astruc and Léon Daudet, sworn enemies for thirty-five years since Astruc had written disrespectfully of Alphonse Daudet in *L'Événement*, hailed the same taxi and pardoned one another. Fernand Gregh's little dog Flipot had escaped and taken refuge, amid the vulgar laughter of sightseers, under Proust's hearse; and suddenly the desperate animal darted away through the torrent of motor-cars, never to be seen again. They buried Proust with his father and mother, beneath Marie Nordlinger's plaque of the bearded Doctor Proust, at the summit of Père Lachaise. For a few years, until no one came, the Abbé Mugnier held an anniversary mass in his memory at Saint-Pierre-de-Chaillot.

Meanwhile, however, the dead writer lay on his white bed, with a bunch of violets in his clasped hands, holy water and a sprig of box at his side. Daylight and fresh air flooded his bedroom for the first time, and funereal flowers which did not rouse his asthma surrounded him. The look of peace and returned youth, the faint smile left his face, replaced by the hollow cheeks and stark grin of dissolution. But the great circle commenced by his birth, which the spiritual triumph of *A la Recherche du Temps Perdu* had left still imperfect, was now at last entire. His novel, by leaving his deepest guilt unatoned, had led to his most terrible sin; but salvation is completed only in the material world, at the moment of forgiveness and being forgiven, which for Proust was the moment of death. Now not only his work but his life was eternally alive. As he predicted, the Two Ways had met. The Méséglise and Guermantes Ways, the self we are born with and the self which we acquire, always join at last, for the rarest and greatest in a work of art, in death for everyone; but to find their point of unity we must first travel them, in the world of people, places and things, in Time.

THE END

BIBLIOGRAPHY

MARCEL PROUST. VOLUMES ONE AND TWO

This bibliography is limited to books and articles containing the primary sources on which the present biography is based. Each entry is preceded by the abbreviated form used for the source-references given in the Notes.

MAJOR WORKS BY PROUST

BA   *La Bible d'Amiens* (Mercure de France, Paris, 1904).

C   *Chroniques* (Gallimard, Paris, 1927).

CG   *Correspondance générale*. 6 vols. (Plon, Paris, 1930-36).

CSB   *Contre Sainte-Beuve* (Gallimard, Paris, 1954).

I., II, III *A la Recherche du Temps Perdu*. Ed. Pierre Clarac and André Ferré. 3 vols. (*Bibliothèque de la Pléiade*, Gallimard, Paris, 1954.)

JS   *Jean Santeuil*. 3 vols. (Gallimard, Paris, 1952).

PJ   *Les Plaisirs et les Jours* (Gallimard, Paris, 1924).

PM   *Pastiches et Mélanges* (Gallimard, Paris, 1919).

SL   *Sésame et les Lys* (Mercure de France, Paris, 1906).

LETTERS AND MINOR WORKS OF PROUST, MEMOIRS, MISCELLANEOUS WORKS, ARTICLES

Abraham   Abraham, Pierre. *Proust* (Rieder, Paris, 1930).

Adam   *Adam International Review*, no. 260 (1957). *Marcel Proust. A world symposium*. ed. Miron Grindea.

Adam (Barney)   *Adam International Review*, no. 269 (1963). *The Amazon of Letters. A world tribute to Natalie Clifford Barney*. ed. Miron Grindea.

Adam, A.   Adam, Antoine. 'Le Roman de Proust et le problème des clefs', *Revue des sciences humaines*, jan. mars 1952, 49-90.

Adam, H. P.   Adam, H. P. *Paris sees it through* (Hodder & Stoughton, London, 1919).

Adelson   Adelson, Dorothy. 'The Vinteuil Sonata', *Music and Letters*, vol. 23 (July 1942), 228-33.

Albalat   Albalat, Antoine. *Trente ans de Quartier Latin* (Malfère, Paris, 1930).

Alden   Alden, Douglas W. *Marcel Proust and his French Critics* (Lymanhouse, Los Angeles, 1940).

Ambrière   Ambrière, F. 'Gaston Calmette et les écrivains du Figaro', *Nouvelles littéraires*, 17 Sept. 1932.

Amiel   Amiel, Denys. 'Une Lettre inédite de Proust (à Denys Amiel)', *Nouvelles littéraires*, 31 Dec. 1927.

Amphitrion   Amphitrion. 'Marcel Proust à la recherche d'un bastone perduto', *Nuova antologia*, 16 March 1935, 319-20.

Astruc   Astruc, Gabriel. *Le Pavillon des fantômes* (Grasset, Paris, 1929).

Augustin-Thierry   Augustin-Thierry, A. *La Princesse Mathilde* (Albin Michel, Paris, 1950).

Autret   Autret, Jean. *L'Influence de Ruskin sur la vie, les idées et l'oeuvre de Marcel Proust* (Droz, Genève, 1955).

Bac (A) Bac, Ferdinand. *Intimités de la Troisième République*, 2 vols. (Hachette, Paris, 1935).

Bac (B) ——, ——. *La Princesse Mathilde* (Hachette, Paris, 1928).

Baedeker Baedeker, Karl. *Le Nord-Ouest de la France*. 8me éd. (Baedeker, Leipzig, 1908).

Balsan Balsan, Consuelo Vanderbilt. *The Glitter and the Gold* (Heinemann, London, 1953).

Bardac (A) Bardac, Henri. 'Madeleine Lemaire et Marcel Proust', *Revue de Paris*, août 1949, 137-42.

Bardac (B) ——, ——. 'Proust et Montesquiou,' *Revue de Paris*, sept. 1948, 142-6.

Barney (A) Barney, Natalie Clifford. *Aventures de l'esprit* (Émile Paul, Paris, 1929).

Barney (B) ——, ——. *Souvenirs indiscrets* (Flammarion, Paris, 1960).

Barrès Barrès, Maurice. *Mes cahiers*. 14 vols. (Plon, Paris, 1929-57).

Baumont Baumont, Maurice. *L'Affaire Eulenbourg et les origines de la guerre mondiale* (Payot, Paris, 1933).

Bell Bell, Clive. *Old Friends* (Chatto & Windus, London, 1956).

Benda Benda, Julien. *La Jeunesse d'un clerc* (Gallimard, Paris, 1937).

Benoist-Méchin Benoist-Méchin, Jacques. *Retour à Marcel Proust* (Amiot, Paris, 1957).

Bérence Bérence, Fred. 'Une Héroïne de Proust. Souvenirs inédits sur la reine Marie de Naples', *Nouvelles littéraires*, 26 sept. 1946.

Bergson Bergson, Henri. 'Rapport sur un ouvrage de M. Marcel Proust: *La Bible d'Amiens* de Ruskin', *Académie des Sciences morales et politiques, Séances et travaux*, vol. 162, juillet 1904, 491-2.

Berl (A) Berl, Emmanuel. *Sylvia* (Gallimard, Paris, 1952).

Berl (B) ——, ——. 'Une Lettre de Marcel Proust à Emmanuel Berl', *Table ronde*, sept. 1953, 9-11.

Berl (C) ——, ——. *Présence des morts* (Gallimard, Paris, 1956).

Bertaut Bertaut, Jules. *L'Opinion et les mœurs* (Éditions de France, Paris, 1931).

Bibesco, A (A) Bibesco, Prince Antoine. 'The Heartlessness of Marcel Proust', *Cornhill Magazine*, no. 983 (summer 1950), 421-8.

Bibesco, A (B) ——, ——. *Lettres de Marcel Proust à Bibesco* (Éditions de Clairefontaine, Lausanne, 1949).

Bibesco, M (A) Bibesco, Princesse Marthe. *Au Bal avec Marcel Proust* (Gallimard, Paris, 1928).

Bibesco, M (B) ——, ——. *La Duchesse de Guermantes. Laure de Sade, comtesse de Chevigné* (Plon, Paris, 1951).

Bibesco, M (C) ——, ——. *Le Voyageur voilé* (La Palatine, Genève, 1947).

Bibesco, M (D) ——, ——. 'Marcel Proust et la mémoire', *Hommes et mondes*, jan. 1956, 183-93.

Bibesco, M (E) ——, ——. *La vie d'une amitié*. 3 vols. (Plon, Paris, 1951-7).

Billy Billy, Robert de. *Marcel Proust. Lettres et conversations* (Éditions des Portiques, Paris, 1930).

Bisson Bisson, L. A. 'Deux inédits de Proust', *French Studies*, vol. 2, no. 4 (Oct. 1948), 341-7.

Blanche (A) Blanche, Jacques Émile. *Mes modèles* (Stock, Paris, 1928).

Blanche (B) ——, ——. *La Pêche aux souvenirs* (Flammarion, Paris, 1949).

Blanche (C) ——, ——. *Propos de peintre*. 3 vols. (Émile Paul, Paris, 1919-28).

Blanche (D) ——, ——. 'Souvenirs sur Marcel Proust', *Revue hebdomadaire*, 21 juillet 1928, 259-70.

Blanche (E) ——, ——. *Portraits of a Lifetime* (Dent, London, 1937).

Blum Blum, René. *Comment parut Du Côté de chez Swann. Lettres de Marcel Proust à René Blum, Bernard Grasset et Louis Brun* (Kra, Paris, 1930).

Boigne Boigne, Comtesse C. de. *Récits d'une tante*. 5 vols. (Plon, Paris, 1907-8).
Bonnefont Bonnefont. *Les Parisiennes chez elles* (Flammarion, Paris, 1895).
Bonnet Bonnet, Henri. *Marcel Proust de 1907 à 1914* (Nizet, Paris, 1959).
Bordeaux (A) Bordeaux, Henry. *Histoire d'une vie* (Plon, Paris, 1951-00).
Bordeaux (B) ——, ——. 'Souvenirs sur Proust et Boylesve', *Œuvres libres*, no. 288 (juillet, 1951), 98-146.
Bourcet Bourcet, M. *Un Couple de tragédie. Le duc et la duchesse d'Alençon* (Perrin, Paris, 1939).
Bourdet (A) Bourdet, D. *Pris sur le vif* (Plon, Paris, 1957).
Bourdet (B) ——, ——. 'Images de Paris (César Ritz)', *Revue de Paris*, sept. 1948, 152-3.
Boylesve Boylesve, René. *Feuilles tombées* (Dumas, St. Étienne, 1947).
Brach Brach, Paul. *Quelques lettres de Marcel Proust* (Flammarion, Paris, 1928).
Briand (A) Briand, Charles. *Le Secret de Marcel Proust* (Lefèbvre, Paris, 1950).
Briand (B) ——, ——. 'Lettres inédites à Marcel Proust', *Combat*, 17 nov., 1 déc. 1949.
Brousson Brousson, J. J. *Les Vêpres de l'avenue Hoche* (Cadran, Paris, 1932).
BSAMP *Bulletin de la Société des amis de Marcel Proust.*
Buffenoir Buffenoir, H. *Grandes dames contemporaines* (Librairie du Mirabeau, Paris, 1893).
Bugnet Bugnet, Charles. 'Lettres de Proust au capitaine Charles Bugnet', BSAMP, III, (1953), 5-22.

Casa-Fuerte Casa-Fuerte, Marquis Illan de. 'Marcel Proust et les parfums', *Revue hebdomadaire*, août 1935, 355-62.
Castellane (A) Castellane, Marquis Boniface de. *L'Art d'être pauvre* (Crès, Paris 1926).
Castellane (B) ——, ——. *Comment j'ai découvert l'Amérique* (Crès, Paris, 1925).
Castillon Castillon du Perron, M. *La Princesse Mathilde* (Amiot-Dumont, Paris, 1953).
Cattaui (A) Cattaui, Georges. *Marcel Proust. Documents iconographiques* (Cailler, Genève, 1956).
Cattaui (B) ——, ——. *L'Amitié de Proust* (Gallimard, Paris, 1935).
Cattaui (C) ——, ——. *Marcel Proust* (Julliard, Paris, 1952).
Catusse Catusse, Mme A. *Marcel Proust. Lettres à Mme C.* (Janin, Paris, 1946).
Chalupt Chalupt, René. 'Petite musique de nuit à la façon de Marcel Proust', *Revue internationale de musique*, no. 11 (aut. 1951), 497-500.
Chapman Chapman, Guy. *The Dreyfus Case* (Hart-Davis, London, 1955).
Charavay Librairie Charavay, Paris. *Lettres de Marcel Proust à Reynaldo Hahn. Vente 16, 17 déc. 1958.*
Charensol Charensol, G. 'À Combray à la recherche de Marcel Proust', *Nouvelles littéraires*, 29 août 1946.
Clermont-Tonnerre (A) Clermont-Tonnerre, Duchesse Élisabeth de. *Marcel Proust* (Flammarion, Paris, 1948).
Clermont-Tonnerre (B) ——, ——. *Mémoires*. 4 vols. (Grasset, Paris, 1928-35).
Clermont-Tonnerre (C) ——, ——. *Robert de Montesquiou et Marcel Proust* (Flammarion, Paris, 1925).
Cocteau (A) Cocteau, Jean. *La Difficulté d'être* (Morihien, Paris, 1947).
Cocteau (B) ——, ——. *Journal d'un inconnu* (Grasset, Paris, 1953).
Cocteau (C) ——, ——. *Opium* (Stock, Paris, 1930).
Cocteau (D) ——, ——. *Poésie critique*, vol. 1 (Gallimard, Paris, 1959).
Corpechot Corpechot, Lucien. *Souvenirs d'un journaliste.* vol. 3 (Plon, Paris, 1937).
Couvreur Couvreur, J. 'Avec Céleste Albaret', *Le Monde*, 9 juillet 1953.

Craft Craft, R. *Conversations with Stravinsky* (Faber & Faber, London, 1959).

Crémieux Crémieux, Benjamin. *Du Côté de chez Marcel Proust* (Lemarget, Paris, 1929).

Crosland Crosland, Margaret. *Jean Cocteau* (Nevill, London, 1955).

Curtiss (A) Curtiss, Mina. *Letters of Marcel Proust* (Chatto & Windus, London, 1950).

Curtiss (B) ——, ——. 'Céleste', *Cornhill Magazine*, vol. 164 (spring, 1950), 306-17.

Daudet, Mme A. Daudet, Mme Alphonse. *Souvenirs de famille et de guerre* (Charpentier, Paris, 1920).

Daudet, Léon (A) Daudet, Léon. *Au temps de Judas* (Nouvelle Librairie Nationale, Paris, 1920).

Daudet, Léon (B) ——, ——. *Devant la douleur* (Nouvelle Librairie Nationale, Paris, 1915).

Daudet, Léon (C) ——, ——. *Écrivains et artistes*, vol. 3 (Capitole, Paris, 1928).

Daudet, Léon (D) ——, ——. *L'Entre-deux-guerres* (Nouvelle Librairie Nationale, Paris, 1915).

Daudet, Léon (E) ——, ——. *Fantômes et vivants* (Nouvelle Librairie Nationale, Paris, 1914).

Daudet, Léon (F) ——, ——. *Paris vécu.* 2 vols. (Gallimard, Paris, 1929, 30).

Daudet, Léon (G) ——, ——. *Salons et journaux* (Nouvelle Librairie Nationale, Paris, 1917).

Daudet, Léon (H) ——, ——. *Vers le roi* (Nouvelle Librairie Nationale, Paris, 1921).

Daudet, Léon (I) ——, ——. *Quand vivait mon père* (Grasset, Paris, 1940).

Daudet, Lucien (A) Daudet, Lucien. *Autour de soixante lettres de Marcel Proust* (Gallimard, Paris, 1929).

Daudet, Lucien (B) ——, ——. *Dans l'ombre de l'Impératrice Eugénie* (Gallimard, Paris, 1935).

Davray Davray, Jean. *Collection J. D. . . . Vente à Paris 6, 7 déc. 1961.*

DBF *Dictionaire de biographie française* (Letouzey & Ané, Paris, 1933-00).

Défense *Défense de Marcel Proust* (Rouge et le Noir, Paris, 1930).

Deffoux Deffoux, Léon. *Chronique de l'Académie Goncourt* (Firmin-Didot, Paris, 1929).

Delarue-Mardrus Delarue-Mardrus, Lucie. *Mes mémoires* (Gallimard, Paris, 1938).

Delattre Delattre, Floris. 'Bergson et Proust', *Études bergsoniennes*, vol. 1 (1948), 7-127.

Delay Delay, Jean. *La Jeunesse d'André Gide*, vol. 2 (Gallimard, Paris, 1957).

Descaves Descaves, Lucien. *Deux amis. Huysmans et l'abbé Mugnier* (Plon, Paris, 1946).

Dreyfus (A) Dreyfus, Robert. *De Monsieur Thiers à Marcel Proust* (Plon, Paris, 1939).

Dreyfus (B) ——, ——. *Souvenirs sur Marcel Proust* (Grasset, Paris, 1926).

Drumont Drumont, Édouard. *La France juive.* 2 vols. (Flammarion, Paris, 1886).

Du Bled Du Bled, Victor. *La Société française depuis cent ans.* vol. 2. *Mme Aubernon et ses amis* (Bloud & Gay, Paris, 1924).

Du Bos Du Bos, Charles. *Journal, 1921-1923* (Corréa, Paris, 1946).

Dujardin Dujardin, Marie. 'Proust à Venise', *Le Figaro*, 10 oct. 1931.

Dumesnil Dumesnil, René. 'L'Abbé Mugnier', *Mercure de France*, mars 1949, 398-409.

Duplay (A) Duplay, Maurice. 'Proust avant Proust', *Nouvelles littéraires*, 3 oct. 1957.

Duplay (B) ——, ——. 'Marcel Proust tel que je l'ai connu', *Figaro littéraire*, 19 nov. 1960.

Duplay (C) ——, ——. 'Marcel Proust. Lettres à M. Duplay', *Revue nouvelle*, juin 1929, 1-13.
Dupont Dupont, Alfred. *Précieux autographes composant la collection de M. Alfred Dupont. Vente 22 nov. 1962. Paris.*

East East, C. J. *The Armed Strength of France* (War Office, London, 1877).
Elkin Mathews Elkin Mathews Ltd. *Catalogue* no. 117 (July-August 1950).
Ellmann Ellmann, Richard. *James Joyce* (Oxford University Press, London, 1959).

Fauchier-Magnan Fauchier-Magnan, A. *C'était hier* (Scorpion, Paris, 1960).
Fernandez Fernandez, Ramon. *A la gloire de Proust* (Nouvelle Revue Critique Paris, 1944).
Ferré (A) Ferré, André, *Les Années de collège de Marcel Proust* (Gallimard, Paris, 1959)..
Ferré (B) ——, ——. *La Géographie de Marcel Proust* (Sagittaire, Paris, 1939).
Feuillerat Feuillerat, Albert. *Comment Marcel Proust a composé son roman* (Yale University Press, New Haven, 1934).
Flament Flament, Albert. *Le Bal du Pré Catelan* (Fayard, Paris, 1946).
Flament (B) ——, ——. 'Souvenir de l'abbé Mugnier', *Revue des deux mondes*, mars 1950, 144-51.
Fleury Fleury, Maurice de. 'Deux lettres inédites de Marcel Proust à Maurice de Fleury', BSAMP, V(1955), 6-8.
Fouquier Fouquier, Baron Marcel. *Jours heureux d'autrefois* (Albin Michel, Paris, 1941).
Fouquières (A) Fouquières, Comte André de. *Cinquante ans de panache* (Horay, Paris, 1951).
Fouquières (B) ——, ——. *Mon Paris et ses parisiens* (Horay, Paris, 1953-00).
Fouquières (C) ——, ——. 'Fantômes du Faubourg Saint-Honoré', *Œuvres libres*, no. 353 (déc. 1956), 75-112.

Gabory Gabory, Georges. *Essai sur Marcel Proust* (Le Livre, Paris, 1926).
Gaillard Gaillard, Roger. *Vie d'un joueur* (Calmann-Lévy, Paris, 1953).
Garver Garver, Milton. 'An Unpublished Letter of Proust', *Modern Language Notes*, vol. 47 (1932), 519-21.
Germain (A) Germain, André. *La Bourgeoisie qui brûle* (Sun, Paris, 1951).
Germain (B) ——, ——. *Les Clés de Proust* (Sun, Paris, 1953).
Germain (C) ——, ——. *Les Fous de 1900* (Plon, Paris, 1954).
Germain (D) ——, ——. *De Proust à Dada* (Sagittaire, Paris, 1924).
Germain (E) ——, ——. *La Vie amoureuse de D'Annunzio* (Fayard, Paris, 1954).
Ghika Ghika, Prince Matila. *Couleur du monde.* 2 vols. (Éditions du Vieux-Colombier, Paris, 1956).
Gibbs-Smith Gibbs-Smith, Charles H. *The Aeroplane* (H.M. Stationery Office, London, 1960).
Gide (A) Gide, André. *Journal, 1889-39. Bibliothèque de la Pléiade* (Gallimard, Paris, 1941).
Gide (B) ——, ——. *Marcel Proust. Lettres à André Gide* (Ides et Calendes, Neuchâtel, 1949).
Goncourt Goncourt, Edmond and Jules de. *Journal.* 4 vols. (Imprimerie Nationale, Monaco, 1956).
Goron Goron, Lucien. 'L'Horizon de Combray', BSAMP, I(1950), 19-33.
Gramont Gramont, Armand, duc de. 'Souvenirs sur Marcel Proust,' BSAMP, VI (1956), 171-80.
Grandjean Grandjean, Charles. 'Lettres de Marcel Proust à Charles Grandjean', BSAMP, VI (1956), 137-57.

Grasset (A) Grasset, Bernard. 'Souvenirs sur Émile Clermont', *Revue hebdomadaire*, 9 avr. 1938, 129-51.

Grasset (B) ——, ——. *Textes choisis* (Table Ronde, Paris, 1953).

Gregh (A) Gregh, Fernand. *L'Age d'or* (Grasset, Paris, 1947).

Gregh (B) ——, ——. *L'Age d'airain* (Grasset, Paris, 1951).

Gregh (C) ——, ——. *L'Age de fer* (Grasset, Paris, 1956).

Gregh (D) ——, ——. *Mon amitié avec Marcel Proust* (Grasset, Paris, 1958).

Grigoriev Grigoriev, S. L. *The Diaghilev Ballet* (Constable, London, 1953).

Guichard (A) Guichard, Léon. *Introduction à la lecture de Proust* (Nizet, Paris, 1956).

Guichard (B) ——, ——. 'Un Article inconnu de Marcel Proust', RHLF, vol. 39 (1949), 161-75.

Guillot de Saix Guillot de Saix. 'Trente ans après. Céleste servante au grand cœur nous raconte les derniers jours de Proust', *Nouvelles littéraires*, 20 nov. 1952.

Guth Guth, Paul. 'A l'ombre de Marcel Proust. Comment Céline . . . et Nicolas Cottin voyaient leur maître', *Figaro littéraire*, 25 sept. 1954.

Gyp (A) Gyp (pseud. of Comtesse M. A. de Martel). *Du temps des cheveux et des chevaux* (Calmann-Lévy, Paris, 1929).

Gyp (B) ——. *La Joyeuse enfance de la Troisième Republique* (Calmann-Lévy, Paris, 1931).

Hahn (A) Hahn, Reynaldo. *La Grande Sarah* (Hachette, Paris, 1930).

Hahn (B) ——, ——. *Marcel Proust. Lettres à Reynaldo Hahn.* ed. Philip Kolb. (Gallimard, Paris, 1956).

Hahn (C) ——, ——. *Notes. Journal d'un musicien* (Plon, Paris, 1933).

Hahn (D) ——, ——. 'Proust et Ruskin', *Le Figaro*, 21 avril 1945.

Hahn, M. Hahn, Maria. 'Huit lettres inédites de Marcel Proust à Maria Hahn', BSAMP, III (1953), 23-8.

Halévy Halévy, Daniel. *Pays parisiens* (Grasset, Paris, 1932).

Halicka Halicka, Alice. *Hier. Souvenirs* (Pavois, Paris, 1946).

Hayman Hayman, Laure. *Lettres et vers de Marcel Proust à Mesdames Laure Hayman et Louisa de Mornand* (Andrieux, Paris, 1928).

Hermant (A) Hermant, Abel. *Souvenirs de la vie frivole* (Hachette, Paris, 1933).

Hermant (B) ——, ——. *Souvenirs de la vie mondaine* (Hachette, Paris, 1935).

HLB *Harvard Library Bulletin.*

Hommage *Hommage à Marcel Proust* (NRF) (Gallimard, Paris, 1927).

Hommage (DV) *Hommage à Marcel Proust* (Disque Vert, Bruxelles, 1952).

Hommage (RN) *Hommage à Marcel Proust* (Rouge et le Noir, Paris, 1928).

Humières Humières, Comte Robert d'. *Le Livre de la beauté* (Mercure de France, Paris, 1921).

Indy Indy, Vincent d'. *César Franck* (Alcan, Paris, 1930).

Jaloux Jaloux, Edmond. *Avec Marcel Proust* (Palatine, Genève, 1953).

Jammes Francis Jammes & Arthur Fontaine. *Correspondance* (Gallimard, Paris, 1959).

Jones Jones, Stanley. 'Two Unknown Articles by Marcel Proust', *French Studies*, vol. 4, no. 3 (July 1950), 239-51.

Joyce Joyce, James. *Letters of James Joyce.* ed. Stuart Gilbert (Faber & Faber, London, 1957).

Keim Keim, Albert. *Le Demi-siècle* (Albin Michel, Paris, 1950).

Kolb (A) Kolb, Philip. *La Correspondance de Marcel Proust* (University of Illinois Press, Urbana, 1949).

Kolb (B) ——, ——. 'The Genesis of Jean Santeuil', *Adam*, 112-9.

Kolb (C) ——, ——. 'An Enigmatic Proustian Metaphor', *Romanic Review*, vol. 54, no. 3 (Oct. 1963) 187-97.

Kolb (D) —— ——. 'Le "Mystère" des gravures anglaises recherchées par Proust', *Mercure de France* (1 août 1956), 750-5.

Kolb (E) —— ——. 'Proust et Ruskin: nouvelles perspectives', *Cahiers de l'Association Internationale des Études Françaises* XII (1961), 259-73.

Labori Labori, Marguerite. *Labori* (Attinger, Paris, 1947).

Lacretelle Lacretelle, Jacques de. *Les Maîtres et les amis* (Wesmael-Charlier, Paris, 1959).

La Faye La Faye, J. de. *La Princesse Mathilde* (Émile Paul, Paris, 1928).

Landau Landau, Baron Horace de. *Sale Catalogue, Sotheby's, 12-13 July 1948.*

Lannes Lannes, Roger. *Jean Cocteau* (Seghers, Paris, 1945).

Larcher Larcher, P. L. *Le Parfum de Combray* (Mercure de France, Paris, 1945).

Larnac Larnac, Jean. *La Comtesse de Noailles* (Sagittaire, Paris, 1931).

La Rochefoucauld La Rochefoucauld, Comte Gabriel de. *Constantinople avec Loti* (Éditions de France, Paris, 1928).

La Sizeranne La Sizeranne, Comte Robert de. *Ruskin et la religion de la beauté* (Hachette, Paris, 1897).

Lauris (A) Lauris, Marquis Georges de. *A un ami* (Amiot-Dumont, Paris, 1948).

Lauris (B) ——, ——. *Souvenirs d'une belle époque* (Amiot-Dumont, Paris, 1948).

Léautaud Léautaud, Paul. *Journal littéraire* (Mercure de France, Paris, 1954-00).

Leclercq Leclercq, Paul. 'Marcel Proust au temps de la bicyclette', *Figaro littéraire*, 7 fév. 1931.

Le Goff Le Goff. M. *Anatole France à la Béchellerie* (Albin Michel, Paris, 1947).

Le Masle Le Masle, Robert. *Le Professeur Adrien Proust* (Lipschutz, Paris, 1935).

Le Masle (B) ——, ——. 'Un Familier de Proust (Odilon Albaret)', *Nouvelles littéraires*, 17 nov. 1960.

Levaillant Levaillant, J. 'Note sur le personnage de Bergotte', *Revue des sciences humaines*, jan.-mars 1952, 33-48.

Lieven Lieven, Prince P. *The Birth of the Ballets Russes* (Allen & Unwin, London, 1936).

Lifar Lifar, Serge. *A History of Russian Ballet* (Hutchinson, London, 1954).

Lister Lister, Barbara. *The House of Memories* (Heinemann, London, 1929).

Louÿs Louÿs, Pierre. *Poésie*. 2 vols. (Albin Michel, Paris, 1945).

Lowery Lowery, Bruce. *Marcel Proust et Henry James* (Plon, Paris, 1964).

Lubbock Lubbock, Percy. *Portrait of Edith Wharton* (Cape, London, 1947).

Marquis Marquis, Chanoine Joseph. *Illiers* (Archives Historiques du Diocèse de Chartres, Chartres, 1907).

Martin du Gard Martin du Gard, Maurice. *Les Mémorables.* vol. 1 (Flammarion, Paris, 1957).

Massis Massis, Henri. *Le Drame de Marcel Proust* (Grasset, Paris, 1937).

Maupassant Maupassant, Guy de. *Correspondance inédite* (Wepler, Paris, 1951).

Mauriac, C. Mauriac, Claude. *Marcel Proust par lui-même* (Éditions du Seuil, Paris, 1954).

Mauriac, F. Mauriac, François. *Du côté de chez Proust* (Table Ronde, Paris, 1947).

Maurois Maurois, André. *A la recherche de Marcel Proust* (Hachette, Paris, 1949).

Maurois (B) ——, ——. *Mémoires.* vol. 1 (Flammarion, Paris, 1948).

Mérimée Mérimée, Prosper. *Lettres à Mme de Beaulaincourt* (Calmann-Lévy, Paris, 1936).

Mérode Mérode, Cléo de. *Le Ballet de ma vie* (Horay, Paris, 1955).

Mille   Mille, Pierre. *Mes trônes et mes dominations* (Éditions des Portiques, Paris, 1930).

Missoffe   Missoffe, Michel. *Gyp et ses amis* (Flammarion, Paris, 1932).

Mondor   Mondor, Henri. *Vie de Mallarmé* (Gallimard, Paris, 1941).

Monnin-Hornung   Monnin-Hornung, J. *Proust et la peinture* (Droz, Genève, 1951).

Montesquiou (A)   Montesquiou, Comte Robert de. 'Cahiers secrets', *Mercure de France*, vol. 211 (15 avr. 1929), 296-322.

Montesquiou (B)   ——, ——. 'Netzkés', *Mercure de France*, vol. 221 (juillet 1930), 48-64.

Montesquiou (C)   ——, ——. 'Papillotes mondaines', *Mercure de France*, vol. 212 (juin 1929), 557-9.

Montesquiou (D)   ——, ——. *Les Pas effacés.* 3 vols. (Émile Paul, Paris, 1923).

Montesquiou (E)   ——, ——. *Les Quarante bergères* (Librairie de France, Paris, 1925).

Montesquiou (F)   ——, ——. 'Lettres inédites au prince Sevastos', *Revue de Paris*, juillet 1947, 128-42.

Montesquiou (G)   ——, ——. *Le Chancelier des fleurs* (Privately printed, Paris, 1908).

Montfort   Montfort, Eugène. *Vingt-cinq ans de littérature française.* 2 vols. (Librairie de France, Paris, 1922-5).

Morand (A)   Morand, Paul. *Journal d'un attaché d'ambassade* (Table Ronde, Paris, 1949).

Morand (B)   ——, ——. *Le Visiteur du soir* (Palatine, Genève, 1949).

Morand (C)   ——, ——. *L'Eau sous les ponts* (Grasset, Paris, 1954).

Morand (D)   ——, ——. *Mes débuts* (Cahiers libres, Paris, 1933).

Morand (E)   ——, ——. *Tendres stocks* (Gallimard, Paris, 1921).

Morand (F)   ——, ——. 'Une Agonie', *Nouvelles littéraires*, 25 nov. 1922.

Mornand   Mornand, Louisa de. 'Mon amitié avec Marcel Proust', *Candide*, 1 nov. 1928.

Mourey   Mourey, Gabriel. 'Proust, Ruskin et Walter Pater' *Monde Nouveau*, août-sept. 1926, 702-14, Oct. 1926, 896-909.

Nichols   Nichols, Beverley. *The Sweet and Twenties* (Weidenfeld & Nicolson, London, 1958).

Nicolson (A)   Nicolson, Sir Harold. *Peacemaking* (Constable, London, 1933).

Nicolson (B)   ——, ——. 'Proust et l'Angleterre', *Figaro littéraire*, 15 oct. 1955.

Nicolson (C)   ——, ——. 'Marcel Proust et l'Angleterre', *Revue hebdomadaire*, juin 1936, 7-21.

NNRF   *Nouvelle nouvelle revue française.*

Nordlinger (A)   Riefstahl-Nordlinger, Marie. *Marcel Proust. Lettres à une amie* (Éditions du Calame, Manchester, 1942).

Nordlinger (B)   ——, ——. 'Proust as I knew him', *London Magazine*, Aug. 1954, 51-61.

Nordlinger (C)   ——, ——. 'Et voici les clefs du Jean Santeuil de Marcel Proust' *Figaro littéraire*, 14 juin 1952.

Nordlinger (D)   ——, ——. 'Proust and Ruskin', *Wildenstein*, 57-63.

Nordlinger (E)   ——, ——. 'Memories of Marcel Proust', *The Listener*, 28 April 1960, 749-51.

Nordlinger (F)   ——, ——. 'Fragments de journal', BSAMP, VIII (1958), 521-7.

Nordlinger (G)   ——, ——. 'Chez Céleste', *Studies in French Literature presented to P. Mansell Jones* (Manchester University Press, Manchester, 1961), 263-5.

NRF   *Lettres à la NRF* (*Cahiers Marcel Proust*, VI), (Gallimard, Paris, 1932).

Oberlé   Oberlé, Jean. *La Vie d'artiste* (Denoel, Paris, 1956).

Paléologue   Paléologue, Maurice. *Journal de l'Affaire Dreyfus* (Plon, Paris, 1955).

Paléologue (B)   ——, ——. *Journal, 1913-1914* (Plon, Paris, 1947).

Patin   Patin, J. 'Mme Madeleine Lemaire', *Figaro littéraire*, 10 avril 1928.

Péguy   Péguy, Charles. *Notre jeunesse* (Ollendorff, Paris, 1910).

Penrose   Penrose, Roland. *Picasso: his life and work* (Gollancz, London, 1958).

Peter (A)   Peter, René. *Claude Debussy* (Gallimard, Paris, 1931).

Peter (B)   ——, ——. *L'Académie Française et le xxe siècle* (Librairie des Champs-Élysées, Paris, 1949).

Peter (C)   ——, ——. *La Vie secrète de l'Académie Française.* 5 vols. (Librairie des Champs-Élysées, Paris, 1934-40).

Pierre-Quint   Pierre-Quint, Léon. *Marcel Proust. Sa vie, son œuvre* (Kra, Paris, 1925).

Pierre-Quint (B)   ——, ——. 'Deux lettres de Marcel Proust', *Europe*, nov. 1947, 67-9.

Poniatowski   Poniatowski, Prince Stanislaus. *D'un siècle à l'autre* (Presses de la Cité, Paris, 1948).

Porel (A)   Porel, Jacques. *Fils de Réjane.* 2 vols. (Plon, Paris, 1951-2).

Porel (B)   ——, ——. 'Proust locataire de Réjane', *Figaro littéraire*, 22 juin 1957.

Porto-Riche   Porto-Riche, Georges de. 'Lettres de Marcel Proust à Porto-Riche', *Table ronde*, juin 1954, 93-101.

Pouquet (A)   Pouquet, Jeanne Maurice. *Quelques lettres de Marcel Proust* (Hachette, Paris, 1928).

Pouquet (B)   ——, ——. *Le Salon de Madame Arman de Caillavet* (Hachette, Paris, 1926).

Pringué   Pringué, Gabriel Louis. *Trente ans de dîners en ville* (Édition Revue Adam, Paris, 1948).

Proust, Mme   Proust, Mme Adrien. *Marcel Proust. Correspondance avec sa Mère.* ed. Philip Kolb. (Plon, Paris, 1953).

Rachilde   Rachilde (Mme Alfred Vallette). *Portraits d'hommes* (Mercure de France, Paris, 1930).

Radziwill   Radziwill, Princesse Marie. *Lettres au général de Robilant.* 4 vols. (Plon, Paris, 1933-4).

Regnier (A)   Regnier, Henri de. *De mon temps* (Mercure de France, Paris, 1933).

Regnier (B)   ——, ——. *Nos rencontres* (Mercure de France, Paris, 1931).

Reinach   Reinach, Joseph. *Histoire de l'Affaire Dreyfus.* 7 vols. (Fasquelle, Paris, 1901-11).

Renard   Renard, Jules. *Journal* (Gallimard, Paris, 1948).

RHLF   *Revue d'histoire littéraire de la France.*

Ritz   Ritz, Marie L. *César Ritz* (Tallandier, Paris, 1948).

Rivière   Rivière, Jacques. *Marcel Proust et Jacques Rivière. Correspondance, 1914-1922.* ed. Philip Kolb. (Plon, Paris, 1955).

RL   *Renaissance Latine.*

Robert (A)   Robert, Louis de. *Comment débuta Marcel Proust* (Gallimard, Paris, 1925).

Robert (B)   ——, ——. *De Loti à Proust* (Flammarion, Paris, 1928).

Robert (C)   ——, ——. *Lettres à Paul Faure* (Denoël, Paris, 1943).

Rose   Rose, Sir Francis. *Saying Life* (Cassell, London, 1961).

Rosny   Rosny, J. H., aîné. *Portraits et souvenirs* (Compagnie Française des Arts Graphiques, Paris, 1945).

Rostand (A)   Rostand, Maurice. *Confessions d'un demi-siècle* (Jeune Parque, Paris, 1948).

Rostand (B)   ——, ——. 'Rencontre avec Marcel Proust', *Revue de Paris*, fév. 1948, 95-8.

Sachs (A) Sachs, Maurice. *Le Sabbat* (Corréa, Paris, 1946).
Sachs (B) ——, ——. 'L'Air du mois', *NRF*, 1 juillet 1938, 863-4.
Salmon Salmon, André. *Souvenirs sans fin* (Gallimard, Paris, 1955-00).
Scheikévitch (A) Scheikévitch, Marie. *Souvenirs d'un temps disparu* (Plon, Paris, 1935).
Scheikévitch (B) ——, ——. 'Marcel Proust and his Céleste', *London Mercury*, vol. 37 (April 1938), 601-10.
Scheikévitch (C) ——, ——. 'Marcel Proust et Céleste', *Œuvres libres*, no. 168 (1960), 37-52.
Schiff Schiff, Violet. 'A Night with Proust', *London Magazine*, Sept. 1956.
Schiff, S. Schiff, Sydney. *Céleste* (Blackamore Press, London, 1930).
Schlumberger Schlumberger, Gustave. *Mes souvenirs.* 2 vols. (Plon, Paris, 1934).
Scott-Moncrieff Scott-Moncrieff, C. K. *Memories and Letters* (Chapman & Hall, London, 1931).
Seillière Seillière, Baron Ernest. *Marcel Proust* (Nouvelle Revue Critique, Paris, 1931).
Sert Sert, Misia. *Misia* (Gallimard, Paris, 1952).
Sévrette Sévrette, J. *Cabourg et ses environs* (Hachette, Paris, 1882).
Sorel Sorel, Cécile. *La Confession de Célimène* (Presses de la Cité, Paris, 1949).
Souday Souday, Paul. *Marcel Proust* (Kra, Paris, 1927).
Souza Souza, Sybil de. 'Un des premiers états de *Swann*', *French Studies*, vol. 3, no. 4 (Oct. 1949), 335-44.
Suffel Suffel, Jacques. *Anatole France* (Éditions du Myrte, Paris, 1946).

Tharaud (A) Tharaud, Jérôme, and Jean. *Mes années chez Barrès* (Plon, Paris, 1928).
Tharaud (B) ——, ——. *Le Roman d'Aïssé* (Self, Paris, 1946).
Thomas Thomas, Louis. *Le Général de Galliffet* (Dorbon, Paris, 1910).
Thomson Thomson, Valentine. 'My Cousin Marcel Proust', *Harpers Magazine*, vol. 164 (May 1932), 710-20.

Univers L'Univers de Proust. (Le Point, no. 55/56.) (Le Point, Mulhouse, 1959).
Uzès Uzès, Anne, Duchesse d'. *Souvenirs* (Plon, Paris, 1939).

Vandérem Vandérem, Fernand, *Gens de qualité* (Plon, Paris, 1938).
Védrines Védrines, Louis. 'Séjours vénitiens', BSAMP, IV (1954), 57-60.
Vigneron Vigneron, Robert. 'Genèse de Swann', *Revue d'histoire de la philosophie et d'histoire générale de la civilisation*, 15 jan. 1937, 67-115.
Viollet-le-Duc Viollet-le-Duc, Eugène E. *Dictionnaire raisonné d' architecture française* (Paris, 1863).

Wharton Wharton, Edith. *A Backward Glance* (Appleton-Century, New York, 1934).
Wildenstein Wildenstein Gallery, London. *Marcel Proust and His Time* (1955).
Wisely Wisely, G. A. K. *Handbook of the French Army* (War Office, London, 1891).

Yeatman Yeatman, Léon. 'Lettre de Marcel Proust à Léon Yeatman', *Nouvelles littéraires*, 25 juillet 1936.

Zillhardt Zillhardt, M. *L.-C. Breslau et ses amis* (Éditions des Portiques, Paris, 1932).
Zola Zola, Émile. *Livre d'hommage des lettres françaises à Émile Zola* (Société Libre d'Éditions des Gens de Lettres, Paris, 1898).

REFERENCES TO SOURCES

The sources used in each paragraph are grouped separately, preceded by the page number and first words of the paragraph. For the full titles of the works cited, see Bibliography. Volume numbers of these are given in roman numerals, page numbers in arabic.

VOLUME ONE

CHAPTER 1 THE GARDEN OF AUTEUIL

Page and Paragraph

1 *The doorway* . . . Larcher, 41; *Le Masle*, 9, 32-3.
1 *The heroic* . . . *Le Masle*, 33-5.
2 *Adrien Proust* . . . *Le Masle*, 34-6, 38, 40, 43; CG, VI, 218.
3 *Mlle Weil* . . . *Proust, Mme*, 5; Cattaui (B), 188.
3 *Within* . . . JS, I, 172, 174; *Briand* (A), 19.
4 *After* . . . *Le Masle*, 36-7.
4 *At first* . . . Curtiss (A), 3; Lauris (A), 24; *Daudet, Lucien* (A), 180.
4 *Their Paris* . . . *Proust, Mme*, 86, 123.
5 *The first* . . . *Le Masle*, 37; *Hommage*, 17; Cattaui (A), 5; *Daudet, Lucien* (A), 21 *Proust, Mme*, 6, 49.
6 *The other* . . . Curtiss (B), 164; I, 52, 77; *Proust, Mme*, 75.
7 *Auteuil* . . . Goncourt, 24 May 1871.
8 *It was* . . . Blanche (C), I, vi; *Proust, Mme*, 36, 221; Thomson, 713-4.
8 *During* . . . Blanche (C), I, vii-viii, xii; *Le Masle*, 37; III, 411-12.
10 *He wrote* . . . I, 27-43; CSB, 125-6; *Proust, Mme*, 176; JS, III, 306-11; *Le Masle*, 37.
12 *During* . . . *Hommage*, 18.

CHAPTER 2 THE GARDEN OF ILLIERS

13 *Marcel's* . . . *Le Masle*, 11-12, 32; Mauriac, C, 147.
13 *Her daughter* . . . *Le Masle*, 21, 40; Larcher, 43.
13 *They took* . . . JS, I, 135-6, 140; C, 114; I, 63.
14 *His bed* . . . PM, 230-6.
15 *Marcel* . . . PM, 226-30; JS, I, 140, 160, 176; I, 122.
16 *It was* . . . *Le Masle*, 22, 24; Goron, 32.
16 *Gradually* . . . I, 69, 105-7; Lauris (A), 63; *Le Masle*, 13, 16; Goron, 21; Marquis, 210.
17 *Ernestine* . . . *Le Masle*, 23; Goron, 20; JS, I, 139-41; I, 54.
18 *The door* . . . I, 12, 72; *Le Masle*, 19-20; PM, 227; JS, I, 161-2.
19 *The garden* . . . I, 14; Larcher, 51.
19 *Past* . . . I, 43, 45, 49, 56, 83, 135; *Le Masle*, 16; Larcher, 43, 46; PM, 230.
20 *In the* . . . Larcher 42; I, 58.
21 *The church* . . . I, 63-6; PM, 229; CSB, 289.

21 *The church* . . . I, 61-2, 105; *Le Masle*, 12-13, 16-18; *Larcher*, 17, 18, 32, 34;
    Goron, 29; *Marquis*, 200; JS, I, 230.
23 *As they* . . . JS, I, 144, 155, 174, 217; *Larcher*, 58, 109; CSB, 64-6; I, 12, 58; *Le
    Masle*, 16; *Goron*, 20.
24 *After* . . . *Larcher*, 55; II, 154.
25 *Up the* . . . *Goron*, 47-8; I, 139, 922; JS, I, 204; *Larcher*, 86-7.
25 *Uncle* . . . PM, 236; JS, I, 144-5, 168, 174, 189, 201; *Larcher*, 87; *Le Masle*, 27.
26 *Above* . . . *Larcher*, 87; *Le Masle*, 27-8; I, 135; *Goron*, 48, 53; JS, I, 183-4, 189,
    193, 202, 211.
27 *There is* . . . *Goron*, 32.
27 *Sometimes* . . . I, 133-5, 147; III, 691; *Larcher*, 48; *Le Masle*, 53; JS, III, 310.

                    CHAPTER 3 THE TWO WAYS

29 *A few* . . . *Larcher*, 91.
30 *Méréglise* . . . II, 473-4.
30 *The church* . . . *Larcher*, 87, 90.
31 *The Méréglise* . . . I, 134; *Goron*, 23, 30; JS, I, 206-7
32 *At Combray* . . . *Larcher*, 102-3; *Charensol*.
32 *Her name* . . . *Larcher*, 99-100; *Charensol*.
33 *In his* . . . *Goron*, 30; *Larcher*, 100-1; I, 147-8.
33 *Saint-Éman* . . . *Larcher*, 104.
34 *At* . . . *Goron*, 29; *Larcher*, 106-7.
35 *It was* . . . I, 48, 58, 109, 146, 904; II, 531; *Ferré* (B), 88; *Larcher*, 41; *Hommage*,
    190.
36 *The most* . . . *Blanche* (C), I, xi; *Proust, Mme*, 125; PM, 226, 228-30.
37 *It was* . . . *Le Masle*, 26.
37 *Sometimes* . . . *Curtiss* (A), 336; *Daudet, Léon* (E), 114-15; *Nordlinger* (B), 54;
    Schlumberger, II, 171; *Peter* (B), 22; *Mondor*, 814.
38 *Illiers* . . . JS, I, 86, 137-8, 149, 163-4.
38 *But Illiers* . . . *Proust, Mme*, 5; JS, I, 201, 221; PM, 236-7; *Lauris* (A), 63; III,
    692.

          CHAPTER 4 THE GARDEN OF THE CHAMPS-ÉLYSÉES

40 *Marcel's* . . . *Cattaui* (A), 16, 12, 19, 14, 15.
41 *For the* . . . *Dreyfus* (B), 340.
41 *His parents* . . . *Dreyfus* (B), 19-22.
41 *There is* . . . *Briand* (A), 167-8; *Dreyfus* (B), 23; JS, I, 117-21; *Cattaui* (A), 37.
43 *Perhaps* . . . *Hommage*, 191; *Bibesco, M* (C), 102; *Morand* (B), 81; I, 405; *Dreyfus*
    (B), 16-17; *Maurois*, 20.
43 *Lucie* . . . *Gyp* (B), 204-7; BSAMP, VII (1957), 272.
44 *Marie* . . . CG, V, 190-1; *Clermont-Tonnerre* (A), 92; *Flament*, 230; *Fouquières*
    (B), I, 113; *Germain* (A), 186.
45 *Except* . . . *Dreyfus* (B), 11; *Dreyfus* (A), 42-4; *Hommage*, 191; *Abraham*, pl. VI;
    I, 492-4; II, 310.
46 *In the* . . . *Dreyfus* (B), 14, 16; JS, I, 90; *Gyp* (B), 206-7.
46 *Soon* . . . *Dreyfus* (B), 12; C, 101; JS, I, 89-90, 97-8; I, 396-9.
47 *In December* . . . JS, I, 94-6; *Hommage*, 191; I, 398-9.
47 *Every* . . . JS, I, 93; I, 400-1.
48 *In February* . . . JS, I, 98-9, 104; CSB, 111-12, 115; *Germain* (B), 139-40.
49 *In the* . . . JS, I, 101-9; CG, V, 190-1; PJ, 185.

CHAPTER 5 BALBEC AND CONDORCET

51 *An inventory* ... *Cattaui* (A), 20.
51 *His* ... *Cattaui* (A), 20.
52 *Illiers* ... *Hommage*, 7; *Proust, Mme*, 5; *Maurois*, 21; *Cattaui* (A), 34; C, 135; *Gide* (A), 694.
53 *In 1887* ... *Catusse*, 13-15.
54 *In the* ... JS, I, 118-19; *Dreyfus* (B), 24; *Clermont-Tonnerre* (A), 16; *Proust, Mme*, 1-3; *Catusse*, 132.
55 *In October* ... CG, IV, 169, 171.
55 *Maxime* ... CG, IV, 3, 171-2; *Maurois*, 33-5; *Astruc*, 25-6; *Dreyfus* (B), 30; *Daudet, Léon* (A), 115.
56 *In the* ... *Dreyfus* (B), 25; CG, IV, 169, 171; *Gregh* (A), 136.
56 *There is* ... *Cattaui* (A), 25; *Dreyfus* (B), 24; *Wildenstein*, no. 231.
57 *Early* ... *Proust, Mme*, 4-7.
57 *The servants* ... *Proust, Mme*, 5; CG, IV, 178-80; CG, V, 222; *Hommage*, 191; *Astruc*, 132.
58 *He was* ... *Proust, Mme*, 6, 8; *Dreyfus* (B), 48.
59 *In October* ... PJ, 16; *Gregh* (A), 141-3; JS, I, 241-5; CG, IV, 252; *Hommage*, 18.
60 *Meanwhile* ... *Gregh* (A), 142; *Dreyfus* (B), 68-72.
61 *The most* ... *Dreyfus* (B), 56-9; *Pierre-Quint*, 30.
62 *His school* ... *Halévy*, 122-3; *Curtiss* (A), 3-4; *Blanche* (D); CG, IV, 173-4.
63 *He might* ... *Briand* (A), 161; CG, VI, 202; CG, III, 101-2; CG, I, 108.
63 *The key* ... *Gregh* (A), 169, 185-7; *Germain* (B), 50; *Dreyfus* (A), 20; CG, VI, 3.
64 *When the* ... *Dreyfus* (B), 23, 46, 55.

CHAPTER 6 BERGOTTE AND DONCIÈRES

65 *Proust* ... CG, IV, 137; *Pouquet* (A), 5, 6; *Gregh* (A), 175-6; I, 547.
65 *His hostess* ... *Pouquet* (B), 4, 9-10.
65 *In 1889* ... *Gregh* (A), 175; *Germain* (B), 54.
66 *Like* ... *Pouquet* (B), 8, 228-31.
66 *Her husband* ... *Gregh* (A), 179; *Morand* (A), 224; *Scheikévitch* (A), 55-7; *Mille*, 95.
67 *Mme* ... *Pouquet* (B), 49-53; *Du Bled*, 233.
67 *For a* ... *Pouquet* (B), 55, 57, 121, 123; *Suffel*, 190-1; *Morand* (A), 223-4; *Clermont-Tonnerre* (A), 140.
68 *Anatole* ... *Pouquet* (B), 58; *Billy*, 90-1; *Wildenstein*, no. 360; *Clermont-Tonnerre* (A), 100; *Levaillant*, 38, 43, 45; I, 474.
69 *To the* ... *Cattaui* (A), 37.
70 *On* ... *Clermont-Tonnerre* (B), I, 4; *Regnier* (A), 42; *Gregh* (A), 173, 182.
71 *Perhaps* ... *Pouquet* (B), 15, 66, 84-105; *Pouquet* (A), 24; CG, IV, 137
71 *The period* ... *Wisely*, 5; *East*, 16-18; *Cattaui* (A), 28-9; *Wildenstein*, no. 230.
72 *His way* ... *Hommage*, 18; *Proust, Mme*, 28, 36; *Clermont-Tonnerre* (A), 27; *Lauris* (B), 83; *Guichard*, 175; JS, III, 59-62; *Wildenstein*, no. 27.
73 *In theory* ... *Proust, Mme*, 89; JS, II, 287-91, 316.
73 *In February* ... *Billy*, 21-3.
74 *Incredible* ... *Proust, Mme*, 21, 44, 64; *Curtiss* (A), 101; JS, II, 316; *Dreyfus* (B), 150; *Gregh* (A), 218-19.
75 *Meanwhile* ... *Proust, Mme*, 10-14, 16-19, 26, 29, 31, 36, 43-4.
75 *His* ... *Proust, Mme*, 9, 17, 20, 27.
76 *Almost* ... CG, IV, 137-8; *Pouquet* (A), 9-10.
77 *One* ... *Pouquet* (A), 11, 16.

77 *Soon* . . . *Pouquet* (A), 12-16; CG, IV, 141-2.
78 *In the* . . . *Proust, Mme,* 36; *Daudet, Lucien* (A), 152; *Cattaui* (A), 30-33.
78 *That* . . . *Proust, Mme,* 31-2, 36-7, 45; *Blanche* (B), 173; *Goncourt,* 28 Jan. 1895;
    Maupassant, 243-67.
79 *For the* . . . *Proust, Mme,* 45, 49; *Bugnet,* 12; *Maurois,* 49; *Hahn* (B), 225.

CHAPTER 7 THE STUDENT IN SOCIETY

On 20 . . . *Proust, Mme,* 51; *Billy,* 23-6, 89; *Delattre,* 39; *Le Masle,* 36; *Daudet,
    Léon* (E), 297; *Hommage,* 25.
81 *Meanwhile* . . . *Pouquet* (A), 18-21.
81 *That winter* . . . *Pouquet* (A), 16, 20-1; *Maurois,* 53-4.
82 *In the* . . . *Pouquet* (A), 17; *Cattaui* (A), 38, 39; CG, IV, 119.
82 *After* . . . *Pouquet* (A), 22; *Suffel,* 216-17; *Clermont-Tonnerre* (B), I, 12.
83 *In September* . . . *Maurois,* 21; *Blanche* (C), I, v-vi; *Seillière,* 9, 189; *Clermont-
    Tonnerre* (A), 105.
84 *Another* . . . *Blanche* (C), I, iv-vi; *Morand* (A), 239; *Cattaui* (A), 49; *Wildenstein,*
    no. 170; *Hommage,* 61.
85 *Towards* . . . *Hommage,* 29; *Pouquet* (A), 17.
85 *Laure* . . . *Fouquières* (B), I, 139-41; *Poniatowski,* 257; *Flament,* 213; *Dreyfus* (B),
    249.
86 *When* . . . CG, V, 222; *Poniatowski,* 257-9; *Dreyfus* (B), 44-6; *Maurois,* 42;
    Flament, 213; *Wildenstein,* no. 97, 343; CG, V, 210; I, 616; *Pouquet* (A), 17.
87 *Unlike* . . . CG, V, 209, 211, 215, 219; CG, VI, 15; *Blanche* (A), 119; NRF, 213.
88 *Jeanne* . . . CG, VI, 4-6, 11, 14.
89 *The social* . . . *Clermont-Tonnerre* (B), I, 200, II, 112, 198, 200, 203; *Blanche* (A),
    103; *Dreyfus* (A), 20; CG, VI, 126; *Hahn* (B), 220.
89 *Émile* . . . *Gregh* (A), 168-9; *Dreyfus* (A), 18-20; *Clermont-Tonnerre* (A), 99;
    Lauris (B), 156; *Schlumberger,* I, 303-4.
90 *Mme* . . . *Gregh* (A), 168-9; *Hermant* (B), 236; *Clermont-Tonnerre* (B), II, 200;
    Dreyfus (A), 21, 27, 30; CG, VI, 84, 263; CG, I, 237.
91 *Mme* . . . *Hermant* (B), 233; *Gregh* (A), 168; *Flament,* 156.
91 *In the* . . . *Blanche* (A), 109; *Lauris* (B), 153-5; *Hommage,* 49; *Dreyfus* (A), 22-3;
    Clermont-Tonnerre (B), II, 198-9; *Gregh* (A), 195; *Goncourt,* 25 March 1894;
    Schlumberger, I, 305; *Schlumberger,* II, 163-4; CG, VI, 250.
92 *Among* . . . *Clermont-Tonnerre* (A), 99; *Clermont-Tonnerre* (B), II, 198, 201
    Schlumberger, I, 305.
92 *Charles* . . . *Seillière,* 128; *Clermont-Tonnerre* (A), 59; *Gregh* (A), 160; *Gyp* (B),
    42, 90-100, 116-19; *Halévy,* 80-2; *Dreyfus* (B), 249-50; *Cattaui* (A), 104-9, 113-4,
    117, 120; *Wildenstein,* no. 78; *Brach,* 9; *Schlumberger,* I, 322, 379; *Astruc,* 155,
    307; *Clermont-Tonnerre* (C), 237; *Gregh* (A), 160; *Le Gaulois,* 16, 17 July 1902.
93 *Haas* . . . *Clermont-Tonnerre* (C), 236; *Fouquières* (A), 75; *Montesquiou* (D), II,
    87; *Clermont-Tonnerre* (A), 60; *Gregh* (D), 45; *Astruc,* 90; *Seillière,* 128; *Hahn*
    (C), 189.
94 *In some* . . . *Germain* (B), 79; *Blanche* (A), 116.
94 *In his* . . . CG, VI, 167; *Astruc,* 310; *Clermont-Tonnerre* (A), 61; C, 19.
95 *Another* . . . *Augustin-Thierry,* 232; *Billy,* 42; *Hahn* (C), 11, *Hermant* (B),
    169-70; *Regnier* (A), 23; *Scheikévitch* (A), 47; C, 14-18; I, 338.
96 *The Princess* . . . *Hermant* (B), 175-7; *Augustin-Thierry,* 302; *Schlumberger,* II,
    159; *Blanche* (A), 53; *La Faye,* 267.
97 *In* . . . C, 14-27; *Goncourt,* 18 Sept. 1890; *Augustin-Thierry,* 307-9; *Bac* (B),
    207-10; *Hermant* (B), 180.
98 *Mme Lydie* . . . DBF, vol. 4, col. 1, 2; *Vandérem,* 15, 25; *Du Bled,* 159, 162-3,

243; *Pouquet* (B) 51; *Goncourt*, 22 May 1895; *Gregh* (A), 243, 266; *Hermant* (B), 97.

99 *Mme Aubernon* ... *Gregh* (A), 266, 268; *Lauris* (B), 150; *Montesquiou* (D), II, 301; *Du Bled*, 159, 188-92; *Vandérem*, 15; *Billy*, 44.

100 *Mme* ... *Lauris* (B), 150; *Du Bled*, 160, 163, 171, 173, 208, 234, 264; *Fouquier* 117; *Gregh* (A), 268; *Vandérem*, 20-23; *Blanche* (A), 109.

100 *In some* ... *Montesquiou* (D), II, 301.

101 *The doctor* ... *Daudet, Léon* (G), 220; *Du Bled*, 231, 236, 248; *Clermont-Tonnerre* (A), 147.

101 *The pedant* ... *Blanche* (A), 101; *Vandérem*, 37; *Du Bled*, 233, 238; *Gregh* (A), 145; *Daudet, Léon* (B), 251-5.

102 *Brochard* ... *Du Bled*, 181-2, 251; *Blanche* (B), 169-71; *Blanche* (A),102-3; *Gregh* (A), 266; *Vandérem*, 20-23; CG, I, 282, 284; CG, V, 221-2.

103 *The train* ... *Vandérem*, 49-51; *Du Bled*, 162-3.

104 *Mme* ... CG, VI, 205, 261.

104 *To complete* ... *Gregh* (A), 263; *Du Bled*, 230; *Lauris* (B) 258; *Clermont-Tonnerre* (B), I, 207.

105 *The last* ... C, 29-32; *Wildenstein*, no. 203-12.

106 *She was* ... *Flament*, 55, 104; *Bardac* (A), 140; *Gregh* (A), 271; *Cattaui* (A), 99; *Fouquières* (A), 69; PJ, 11; *Curtiss* (A), 337.

106 *As a* ... *Bardac* (A), 139; C, 37; *Scheikévitch* (A), 45; *Clermont-Tonnerre* (A), 208; *Clermont-Tonnerre* (C), 136.

107 *If a* ... *Fouquières* (A), 198-9; PM, 78; *Hahn* (B), 48; C, 37.

CHAPTER 8 THE DUCHESSE AND ALBERTINE

109 *Either* ... *Dreyfus* (A), 17; *Lauris* (B), 157; *Flament*, 156-7; C, 31.

109 *He had* ... *Hahn* (B), 47; *Bibesco, M* (B), 153; I, 178; II, 12; *Billy*, 45, 78-9, 106; *Pierre-Quint*, 46; *Bibesco, M* (C), 111; *Blanche* (A), 108; *Bibesco, M* (A), 46.

111 *Mme de* ... *Lister*, 76-7; *Bibesco, M* (B), 20, 32, 38, 73, 79-80, 99, 101; *Hahn* (C), 87; *Schlumberger*, II, 198-9.

112 *Comtesse* ... *Flament*, 156; *Sert*, 118; PJ, 74-5; *Bibesco, M* (B), 12, 13, 49-50, 67 *Bibesco, M* (C), 111; *Montesquiou* (E), 88-9.

113 *In May* ... PJ, 74-5.

113 *Le Banquet* ... *Hommage*, 36; *Gregh* (A), 148-9; *Dreyfus* (A), 16.

114 *Le Banquet* ... *Dreyfus* (B), 73, 82-3; NRF, 7-8.

115 *And yet* ... PJ, 68, 75, 185-6, 216, 236; C, 135.

115 *She was* ... *Proust, Mme*, 10-14; 17; *Gregh* (A), 164; *Billy*, 65; *Clermont-Tonnerre* (A), 33; *Poniatowski*, 523.

116 *Mme Hugo* ... *Landau*, 1; *Gregh* (A), 163-5; CG, V, 156; *Astruc*, 5-6.

117 *Early* ... *Billy*, 40-1; CG, IV, 184; *Gregh* (A), 165-6; *Cattaui* (A), 44, 56; CG V, 158, 160, 167.

117 *Horace* ... *Gregh* (A), 164-7; *Gregh* (B), 256; *Billy*, 46; *Proust, Mme*, 143.

118 *A curious* ... CG, V, 158; *Billy*, 44-5, 105.

CHAPTER 9
FIRST GLIMPSES OF THE CITIES OF THE PLAIN

120 *In the* ... *Bibesco, A* (B), 81

121 *His new* ... *Billy*, 37-9, 43, 48, 51, 101; *Bibesco, A* (B), 123.

122 *The three* ... *Billy*, 43, 48

122 *In August* ... *Billy*, 39, 43, 48, 53.

122 *Instead* ... *Billy*, 40, 43, 102-3, 106; CG, IV, 29.

123 *It was* ... *Billy*, 53; PJ, 12, 15.

123 *They* ... PJ, 11-13; CG, IV, 4; *Billy*, 29, 52; BSAMP, VII (1957), 276.
124 *Meanwhile* ... CG, I, 3, 97.
124 *Montesquiou* ... *Montesquiou* (D), I, 17-88; *Gregh* (A), 205; *Daudet, Lucien* (A), 200.
125 *Montesquiou* ... *Clermont-Tonnerre* (C), 25-6, 59; *Montesquiou* (D), II, 15-78, 87-95, 107-27, 185-91; *Mondor*, 434-5.
127 *Montesquiou was* ... *Clermont-Tonnerre* (C), 22-4, 34, 68; CG, I, 200, 225; *Regnier* (B), 180.
127 *Montesquiou had* ... *Morand* (A), 312; *Castellane* (B), 334; *Zillhardt*, 134, 136; *Clermont-Tonnerre* (C), 57-8, 154-5; *Corpechot*, 39; *Montesquiou* (G), 119-34.
128 *The conversation* ... *Clermont-Tonnerre* (C), 23, 48, 82, 85, 213; *Corpechot*, 36; *Gregh* (A), 204; *Daudet, Léon* (E), 282; *Blanche* (A), 121; *Blanche* (B), 195; *Montesquiou* (D), I, 80; *Schlumberger*, II, 172; *Morand* (A), 312.
129 *Montesquiou* ... *Clermont-Tonnerre* (C), 39, 59-60, 74, 167; *Montesquiou* (D), II, 105-6; *Germain* (B), 10; *Clermont-Tonnerre* (A), 167; III, 214, 818.
129 *The first* ... *Clermont-Tonnerre* (C), 54-5; *Blanche* (A), 102; *Montesquiou* (D), I, 279, II, 168; *Montesquiou* (G), 13, 16, 34; *Gregh* (A), 203; *Germain* (B), 8; *Clermont-Tonnerre* (A), 167.
130 *In one* ... *Zillhardt*, 140-2; *Blanche* (B), 195; *Blanche* (A), 7; *Montesquiou* (D), II, 229-31; *Goncourt*, 7 July 1891; *Cattaui* (A), 142.
131 *Montesquiou* ... *Montesquiou* (D), II, 296-300, III, 66-8; *Blanche* (B), 199.
132 *For a* ... *Clermont-Tonnerre* (B), II, 137-8; *Blanche* (B), 196-9.
133 *Early in* ... CG, I, 3-4; *Blanche* (B), 195; *Montesquiou* (D), II, 183, 198, 210-11; CSB, 434.
134 *It was* ... CG, I, 5-6; *Goncourt*, 7 July 1891, 15 Aug. 1896; *Montesquiou* (D), II, 209.
134 *The reasons* ... CG, I, 20, 23, 26, 35-7, 97, 250, 286-7; *Goncourt*, 21 March 1895; *Blanche* (B), 198; *Corpechot*, 235; *Montesquiou* (D), III, 287; *Daudet, Lucien* (A), 185.
135 *The quarrel* ... *Billy*, 49-51, 106, 145; PJ, 223-5; *Gregh* (A), 278, 297.
136 *In September* ... CG, VI, 51, 56; *Proust, Mme*, 53-4.
137 *With an* ... *Proust, Mme*, 52-3; BSAMP, VI, 141-53; *Billy*, 51; CG, VI, 195-6; *Pierre-Quint*, 33; *Fouquier*, 17.
138 *His progress* ... *Gregh* (A), 187-8; *Billy*, 52-4.
138 *Any attempt* ... PJ, 113-34, 211-15, 222-7.
139 *Another* ... *Revue Blanche*, Dec. 1893; PJ, 49-55; *Proust, Mme*, 142.
140 *It was* ... *Billy*, 76-7; *Gregh* (A), 226-7, 231; *Peter* (B), 25-8; *Delay*, II, 130.
141 *In November* ... CG, I, 43-6, 49, 51; *Renard*, 141.
141 *With all* ... CG, I, 8-9, 47, 111-12.
142 *Meanwhile* .. *Montesquiou* (D), III, 25; *Goncourt*, 10, 17 Jan. 1894; CG, I, 85, 132; CG, IV, 212.
143 *In February* ... CG, I, 14, 50; *Rachilde*, 214; *Montesquiou* (D), II, 286-91; *Wildenstein*, no. 287; *Le Ménestrel*, 29 April 1894.
144 *Léon* ... *Rachilde*, 215-16; CG, I, 52-3; *Montesquiou* (D), II, 288, 294-5; *Gregh* (D), 35-6.
145 *Meanwhile* ... *Montesquiou* (D), II, 294-5; CG, I, 52-3, 67, 89-90, 96-8.
145 *He was* ... *Montesquiou* (D), II, 283, 292-4; *Regnier* (B), 161-3; *Bisson*, 342-4; *Goncourt*, 31 May, 17 June 1894; CG, I, 69, 98.

CHAPTER 10 THE GUERMANTES WAY

147 *The agate* ... *Blanche* (B), 201-2; *Fouquier*, 50; *Fouquières* (A), 35; *Flament*, 105-6; *Montesquiou* (D), I, 238; *Mondor*, 767; *Seillière*, 172.

148 *Her . . .* Blanche (B), 203.

148 *He was . . .* Blanche (B), 202-5; Clermont-Tonnerre (B), II, 25-7; Morand (A), 300; Flament, 259.

149 *Comtesse . . .* Blanche (B), 202; Clermont-Tonnerre (B), II, 24-5, 131; Morand (A), 289; Montesquiou (C), 558; Clermont-Tonnerre (A), 47; Goncourt, 5 Feb. 1894; Flament, 182; Wildenstein, no. 122, 123 bis; Montesquiou (D), II, 145-9.

149 *The Countess . . .* Germain (B), 129; Montesquiou (D), II, 147, 154; Goncourt, 25 April 1891, 20 June, 6 July, 8 August 1894; Clermont-Tonnerre (B), II, 22-3; Fouquières (A), 283.

150 *As we . . .* Clermont-Tonnerre (C), 136; Clermont-Tonnerre (B), II, 18-21, 24. 27; Clermont-Tonnerre (A), 87; Hommage, 191; Schlumberger, II, 218; Castellane (B), 97; Fouquières (B), I, 243; Seillière, 193; Morand (A), 59.

151 *Another . . .* Thomas, 65-6, 84-101, 119-37, 226-30; Schlumberger, II, 184; Blanche (B), 54; Fouquières (A), 49-50; CG, VI, 47; Castellane (B), 152.

152 *In several . . .* CG, IV, 124-7; Wildenstein, no. 122.

152 *A later . . .* Clermont-Tonnerre (B), II, 68; Germain (B), 129-30.

153 *For the . . .* Fouquières (A), 79-80; Montesquiou (D), I, 275-9; Gramont, 175; Montesquiou (A), 305; Morand (A), 112.

154 *The Prince . . .* Fouquières (A), 48-9; Castellane (A), 25, 59-60, 75-6; Fouquier, 53, 58; Castellane (B), 92-7; Astruc, 82.

155 *The Princesse . . .* Fouquières (A), 48-9; Seillière, 9, 189; Drumont, II, 178.

156 *The Prince . . .* Clermont-Tonnerre (A), 109; Seillière, 149; Fouquières (A), 50; Castellane (B), 110.

156 *In 1895 . . .* Castellane (B), 1-37, 198; Clermont-Tonnerre (B), I, 151, II, 65-6.

156 *Boni . . .* Clermont-Tonnerre (A), 92, 165-6; Clermont-Tonnerre (B), II, 64; Bibesco, M (B), 150; Schlumberger, II, 197; Seillière, 133; Castellane (B), 100, 185; Goncourt, 21 Sept. 1887; CG, I, 282, 284; Hommage, 30; Mérimée, xxxi; Blanche (A), 121.

158 *Mme de . . .* Seillière, 132-3; CG, I, 212, 282, 284; Clermont-Tonnerre (C), 220.

159 *In real . . .* Clermont-Tonnerre (A), 166; Blanche (B), 165; Clermont-Tonnerre (C), 60-1; Hahn (B), 38.

159 *The gratin . . .* Schlumberger, II, 179-80; CG, I, 47; Seillière, 191; Fouquières (B), I, 104-5; Germain (B), 31-2.

160 *Another . . .* Fouquier, 120-4; Schlumberger, II, 81; Lister, 83.

160 *When . . .* Castellane (B), 110; Clermont-Tonnerre (B), II, 62, 72-3; Montesquiou (D), II, 230; Schlumberger, II, 196.

161 *Another . . .* Fouquières (A), 75, Schlumberger, II, 177; Clermont-Tonnerre (B), II, 48; Hahn (B), 164; Fouquières (B), I, 47-8; Germain (B), 138; Germain (A), 185-6; Fouquier, 125.

161 *Comtesse . . .* Fouquières (A), 59-60; Poniatowski, 26; Hahn (C), 100; Catusse, 47; Castellane (B), 98-9; Germain (B), 138.

162 *One of . . .* Fouquières (A), 97-8; Fouquières (B), I, 169; PM, 80, 83; Clermont-Tonnerre (B), I, 90; Morand (A), 312, 315.

163 *Next . . .* Uzès, vii, ix, xiv, xvii, xix, xxv, xxvii, xxxiii-iv, 7, 88; Fouquier, 29, 47; Castellane (B), 112; Clermont-Tonnerre (B), I, 149.

164 *One of . . .* Clermont-Tonnerre (C), 236; C, 40-5; Blanche (B), 249; Goncourt, 18 April 1894.

164 *Another . . .* Clermont-Tonnerre (B), I, 109; Fouquières (A), 73; Fouquier, 113-16; Bibesco, M (B), 104; C, 52-3, Proust, Mme, 120; CG, III, 86.

166 *One of . . .* Blanche (B), 145, 158-65, 171-3; Flament, 280-1; Du Beed, 198; Fouquier, 123; C, 56-9; Hahn (C), 267.

CHAPTER 11 DESCENT INTO THE CITIES OF THE PLAIN

169 *During* ... CG, I, 28, 62, 72, 77; Hahn (B), 23.

169 *Before* ... Schlumberger, II, 226; Gregh (A), 191-2; Drumont, II, 213; Daudet, Léon (E), 237; Astruc, 81, 177; Billy, 89.

170 *In August* ... Clermont-Tonnerre (C), 24-5; CG, I, 28.

170 *Hahn* ... Hahn (B), 13-14; Goncourt, 18 Dec. 1893; C, 36-7; Flament, 51, 159.

171 *Réveillon* ... Baraac (A), 139-40; Hommage, 33-4.

172 *Proust's stay* ... Hahn (B), 24-9; CG, I, 9-10; CG, IV, 11-12; PJ, 48; Proust, Mme, 56-7; Catusse, 136.

172 *Proust's mention* ... Nordlinger (A), vi; CG, IV, 10; Wildenstein, no. 142, 293 bis; Flament, 206-8; CG, I, 48.

173 *Hahn's* ... CSB, 328-31; NRF, 66-8.

173 *It was* ... Hahn (C), 141; Hommage, 190; Bibesco, A (B), 153; Hahn, M, 28; Adelson, 232; JS, III, 146-151, 212-27; Louys, II, 541; Germain (B), 105.

175 *Meanwhile* ... PJ, 11, 16; BSAMP, VI, 151, 155; CG, I, 24-5, 99-100.

176 *La Confession* ... PJ, 141-159; JS, I, 189, 198, 211.

177 *By the* ... CG, I, 18-20, 27, 32-3; Hahn (B), 45; Clermont-Tonnerre (B), II, 56; Kolb (A), 13; Le Gaulois, 29 May 1895; CG, IV, 16; PJ, 135-40.

178 *Proust* ... CG, IV, 4, 12, 13; Hahn (C), 139; Blum, 60; PJ, 177-9; CG, I, 14.

179 *In June* ... Hahn (B), 15, 35, 37; NRF, 278-80; Suffel, 158, 160; CG, IV, 15; CG, I, 107; Daudet, Lucien (A), 18; Porto-Riche, 95-6.

180 *Early* ... Billy, 95-7, 194; Kolb (A), 244.

180 *After* ... Hahn (B), 24, 48, 51; CG, I, 16; CG, IV, 13; PJ, 17-48.

181 *Soon* ... Hahn (B), 48-50; Hahn, M, 24; Le Gaulois, 24 Aug. 1895; PJ, 232-4; Proust, Mme, 64.

182 *No doubt* ... CG, IV, 54; CG, I, 58; Hahn (A), 135; Yeatman; III, 173; Kolb (B), 113; JS, II, 171-3.

183 *Their* ... Nordlinger (B), 52-3; Nordlinger (C); Billy, 96-7; CG, I, 58-9; JS, II, 182, 186-7, 189, 193, 210.

183 *Among* ... Nordlinger (B), 53; Nordlinger (C); JS, I, 34-6, II, 194-207; Lauris (A), 83; Flament, 70

184 *His return* ... Hahn (A), 135; CG, IV, 25; NRF, 278-9.

185 *Whether* ... JS. II, 241, 243, 245-6, 298, 302, 332-7; Hahn, M., 24; NRF, 280.

185 *Another* ... Flament, 39-42; Goncourt, 12 Dec. 1895.

186 *After* ... Daudet, Lucien (A), 10-12; Renard, 181; Germain (B), 17-18, 165-8.

187 *In the* ... Daudet, Lucien (A), 14, 18-19, 27.

187 *Lucien* ... Daudet, Lucien (A), 26-7, 30-32, 41; CG, I, 51-2; Hahn (B), 29; Germain (B) 13, 19, 26; Bardae (B), 144.

189 *Meanwhile* ... Hahn (B), 54-6.

189 *Only* ... CG, I, 90-1; CG, VI, 15; PJ, 8, 9.

190 *Les Plaisirs* ... Revue Blanche, 1 July 1896, 46-8; Revue de Paris, 15 July 1896; Revue encyclopédique. 22 Aug. 1896, 582-4; Suffel, 194-6; Kolb (A), 300.

CHAPTER 12 THE EARLY YEARS OF *JEAN SANTEUIL*

192 *The appearance* ... Kolb (A), 169; CG, V, 212; Catusse, 36; CG, VI, 62.

192 *In* ... CG, V, 212-14; Wildenstein, no. 82, 85.

193 *Next* ... Le Figaro, 2 July 1896; Cattaui (A), 5; I, 12; Crémieux, 99; Blanche (C), I., xi; Proust. Mme, 67-9, 243; JS, I, 107-8, III, 125, 245; CG, I, 55, 124; Hahn (B), 60.

216 *Although* ... Castellane (B), 163-6, 178; Hahn (B), 59.

216 *M. Groult* ... Flament, 138, 159-63; Clermont-Tonnerre (C), 79-80; Hahn (C), 15; Zillhardt, 162-6; Fouquier, 122-3.

194 *In August* . . . Hahn (B), 61-2, 66, 68; JS, II, 214-221.
194 *On the* . . . Proust, Mme, 63, 95; Hahn (B), 57, 60, 62, 65-6, 68.
194 *In September* . . . Proust, Mme. 71-5, 78, 80-2.
195 *Early* . . . Proust, Mme, 76; Flament, 85-6; Times, 7 Oct. 1896, 3; Clermont-Tonnerre (B), II, 13; I, 431, 458, 460.
196 *Another* . . . Clermont-Tonnerre (A), 220.
196 *On 19* . . . Daudet, Lucien (A), 32; Daudet, Léon (F), I, 135; Daudet, Léon (G), 301; Daudet, Léon (C), 20-2; Proust, Mme, 84-101; JS, II, 177.
197 *On 20* . . . Proust, Mme, 84-5, 88, 91; Bibesco, A (B), 65; JS, II, 178-81; II, 132-6.
198 *Proust* . . . Kolb (B), 114-15; Hahn (B), 53, 66; Proust, Mme, 75, 77, 95; Dreyfus (B), 150.
200 *The narrative* . . . JS, I, 78, 125-31.
201 *The Easter* . . . JS, I, 136, 140, 146, 163-4, 167, 174, 176, 181, 184, 188-9, 203-10, 219-22.
202 *Part IV* . . . JS, II, 11-15, 31.
204 *Most* . . . JS, II, 263, 276; Proust, Mme, 95.
205 *I mean* . . . Hahn (B), 53.
206 *Henri's* . . . JS, II, 242.
206 *And so* . . . Proust, Mme, 75.
206 *In December* . . . Nordlinger (A), v-vi; Wildenstein, no. 58, 60, 280; Cattaui (A), 130; Nordlinger (B), 51, 54; Hahn (B), 66; Hahn (C), 19, 31.
208 *Lorrain* . . . Astruc, 81; Renard, 241; Gregh (A), 213; Germain (C), 58; Hahn (C), 43.
208 *It was* . . . Montesquiou (D), III, 79-80; Flament, 228.
209 *It was* . . . Wildenstein, no. 238; Dreyfus (B), 152; Pouquet (A), 28; C, 73-4; CG, III, 133; Hahn (C), 154; Robert (A), 79.
210 *After* . . . Montesquiou (A), 316; Kolb (A), 17; Bourcet, 297; Uzès, 69-72; Fouquières (B), I, 72-4; Montesquiou (D), III, 9-16, 81-2, 294-6; Clermont-Tonnerre (C), 85-6; Regnier (B), 163-5.
212 *The recital* . . . Montesquiou (D), II, 292, 295; Gregh (D), 36; Germain (B), 17; Pierre-Quint, 64; CG, I, 113-14; Rachilde, 214-15; Blanche (E), 157; Chapman, 52-3.
213 *Meanwhile* . . . Dreyfus (B), 116, 119-29; Gregh (A), 250, 272; Daudet, Léon (F), I, 117; Daudet, Léon (A), 116-20; Keim, 87; Pouquet (A), 24.
214 *A few* . . . Flament, 109-113.
214 *On 24* . . . Le Figaro, 26 May 1897; Le Gaulois, 25 May 1897; CG, I, 129-30; CG, VI, 15.
215 *It was* . . . Proust, Mme, 103; Guillot de Saix.
216 *Proust* . . . See after 193 above, 216 *Although*.
216 *M. Groult* . . . Ibid.
217 *Later (In July)* . . . Nordlinger (B), 60; CG, I, 108, 128.
217 *During* . . . Mondor, 416-17; Montesquiou (D), III, 174-5.
218 *It was* . . . Regnier (A), 76; Nordlinger (B), 54.
218 *Mme* . . . Regnier (A), 74; Mondor, 485-6, 780-1, 802; Hahn (C), 66; Nordlinger (A), 34, 85.
219 *In August* . . . Proust, Mme, 109, 121; Kolb (B), 117.
219 *On 16* . . . Daudet, Lucien (A), 13, 129, 179; CSB, 339-42; Lauris (A), 34.
220 *For three* . . . Daudet, Lucien (A), 34; NRF, 69-70; Daudet, Léon (F), I, 42.

CHAPTER 13 THE DREYFUS CASE

221 *On 26* . . . Paléologue, 1-52, 65, 186; Chapman, 45-111.
221 *The case* . . . Chapman, 53-7, 65, 97, 117, 152, 367.

222 *In July* . . . *Chapman*, 117-142.
223 *Suddenly* . . . *Chapman*, 155-79; *Reinach*, II, 36, 373; *Paléologue*, 79-81.
223 *I was* . . . CG, III, 71; *Gregh* (A), 290-1; *Nordlinger* (B), 52; II, 152; *Chapman*, 181; *Reinach*, III, 244-5; *Zola*, II, 34-7, 43, 52, 54; *Mondor*, 760; *Regnier* (B), 107.
224 *From 7* . . . *Chapman*, 190, 194-5; *Reinach*, II, 413.
224 *A few* . . . *Maurois*, 95; JS, II, 117, 134; *Robert* (B); CG, VI, 49; *Catusse*, 114; *Billy*, 126.
225 *Zola* . . . *Chapman*, 187, 189, 195; *Paléologue*, 109; JS, II, 123, 134, 142-8; *Hahn* (B), 69.
226 *The intervention* . . . *Chapman*, 197, 203.
226 *Already* . . . *Billy*, 150.
226 *The split* . . . *Gregh* (A), 288; CG, I, 100-1.
227 *The bourgeois* . . . *Clermont-Tonnerre* (B), I, 202; *Chapman*, 30, 91-2; *Daudet, Léon* (C), 23; *Daudet, Léon* (A), 13-16; *Blanche* (A), 115; *Gregh* (A), 286, 293; *Schlumberger*, I, 306-8.
228 *Mme* . . . *Paléologue*, 102-5, 120-4, 134, 146; *Gregh* (A), 169.
228 *For Mme* . . . *Paléologue*, 60-1, 89-91; *Vandérem*, 27-8, 53-4; *Du Bled*, 241, 266; DBF, vol. 4, col. 2; CG, VI, 205.
229 *For Mme* . . . *Clermont-Tonnerre* (A), 76; *Hermant* (B), 146-7; *Daudet, Léon* (A), 132-5; *Schlumberger*, II, 148-9; *Vandérem*, 41; *Du Bled*, 175-6; *Lauris* (B), 169; *Suffel*, 257, 263
230 *Mme* . . . *Flament*, 155-9.
230 *At* . . . *Nordlinger* (A), 3; CG, I, 59-60; *Lauris* (A), 108; *Catusse*, 22-4; CG, IV, 186; *Proust, Mme*, 104.
231 *Proust* . . . *Proust, Mme*, 104; *Jones*, 243; CSB, 382-5.
231 *In August* . . . *Paléologue*, 126-7; *Chapman*, 212-13, 221-8.
232 *At last* . . . *Chapman*, 233, 236, 238, 258-65.
232 *Meanwhile* . . . *Chapman*, 240-2; CG, VI, 16-17; *Schlumberger*, I, 301; *Wildenstein*, no. 250.
233 *Even* . . . CG, VI, 17; *Chapman*, 228, 247; *Reinach*, IV, 439-42.
233 *In* . . . *Chapman*, 250; *Gregh* (A), 259-62; *Hermant* (B), 163; *Castellane* (B), 221.
234 *In* . . . *Nordlinger* (A), 1-3.
235 *On the* . . . *Paléologue*, 174-6; *Chapman*, 253-7.
235 *On 25* . . . *Flament*, 198-9; CG, IV, 107-8; *Pouquet* (B), 193; *Pouquet* (A), 29; *Kolb* (A), 128.
236 *He had* . . . *Flament*, 202.
236 *On 16* . . . *Flament*, 217-19; *Suffel*, 273.
237 *Proust* . . . *Flament*, 219, 22.
237 *The next* . . . *Flament*, 261-2; *Kolb* (A), 20; CG, I, 104-5.
238 *Proust* . . . *Pouquet* (B), 196.
239 *The decision* . . . *Chapman*, 264, 269, 272, 275, 375; *Thomas*, 99, 247; *Radziwill*, II, 340.
239 *The new* . . . *Chapman*, 277, 285-305; *Paléologue*, 194-5; *Péguy*, 63-4.
240 *Meanwhile* . . . *Curtiss* (A), 92; *Hermant* (B), 220-6; *Labori*, 121.
241 *At* . . . *Bordeaux* (A), II, 47-8; *Bordeaux* (B), 100-2; *Hermant* (B), 202; CG, V, 131; *Proust, Mme*, 123.
241 *Other* . . . *Hermant* (B) 226; *Proust, Mme*, 119-23; CG, V, 89-90, 121-2, 131; *Hahn* (B), 69.
242 *The weeks* . . . *Proust, Mme*, 119, 121-3, 126, 129-30, 140-1, 150.
243 *We have* . . . *Proust, Mme*, 158, 161; CG, V, 122-3.
243 *Dr and* . . . *Proust, Mme*, 105, 110, 112, 115, 146, 153.
244 *On the* . . . *Proust, Mme*, 113, 116, 118, 128, 133-4, 136; *Kolb* (B), 118.

245 *One of* ... Proust, Mme, 106, 128, 138-9, 143; Hermant (B), 227; C, 51; Daudet, Léon (G), 221-3; II, 1005-6; Bibesco, M (B), 125.
246 *Autumn* ... Proust, Mme, 153, 157-8, 160.
246 *Proust* ... Proust, Mme, 156-7; Pouquet (B), 125.
247 *Early* ... Proust, Mme, 150, 158, 160-1; CG, V, 129-31.
247 *The Dreyfus* ... Chapman, 303, 312, 320, 343, 375; Benda, 202; Clermont-Tonnerre (B), I, 202; CG, VI, 84; Barrès, II, 209; Proust, Mme, 106.
248 *The enchanting* ... Morand (A), 299; Schlumberger, I, 326; Hahn (C), 268; Proust, Mme, 143; CG, IV 243; Germain (B), 43; Blanche (B), 257; Blanche (A), 116.

CHAPTER 14 SALVATION THROUGH RUSKIN

256 *Except* ... Autret, 15, 170; Proust, Mme, 111; Nordlinger (A), 32, 83, 85, 117.
256 *In 1897* ... Hommage, 279-80; Billy, 128; PM, 150.
257 *In 1898* ... Billy, 111.
257 *Marie* ... Nordlinger (D), 58-9; Nordlinger (A), 93.
258 *In the* ... Proust, Mme, 148-9, 156; CG, V, 121-2, 130-1; La Sizeranne, 23, 71, 106, 130, 135-7; CG, IV, 21; Nordlinger (A), 8, 10, 20, 114.
259 *On 5* ... Nordlinger (A), 5, 6; Nordlinger (D), 59.
260 *Ruskin* ... PM, 110-12, 116-17.
261 *It was* ... PM, 68-70, 111-12, 117, 120-4; CSB, 76; BA, 286-8.
262 *The visit* ... PM, 115; C, 147.
262 *On 20* ... Nordlinger (A), 9.
263 *He was* ... Daudet, Léon (G), 42; Daudet, Léon (D), 162.
264 *He did* ... C, 145-9.
264 *Early* ... Scheikévitch (A), 127.
265 *On the* ... PM, 173-4.
265 *Proust* ... Scheikévitch (A), 127-8; PM, 162, 174-6; Nordlinger (A), 19; Kolb (A), 303-4.
266 *Thanks* ... NRF, 280-3; CG, I, 57-8; III, 419; Proust, Mme, 150; CG, V, 130.
268 *He had* ... Proust, Mme, 161; Nordlinger (B), 56; Kolb (A), 305.
268 *It was* ... Nordlinger (A), ix, 20-1; Nordlinger (D), 61; CSB, 119-20, 122, 270; Dujardin; Gide (B), 56; Kolb (A), 305; PM, 109; CG, VI, 123.
269 *In the mornings* ... BA, 245; CSB, 122-3; III, 625.
269 *In the afternoon* ... Nordlinger (B), 56; BA, 306-7; Nordlinger (A), ix; PM, 184-5; Ruskin, Stones of Venice, II, iv, 71.
270 *In the* ... Nordlinger (A), 91-2, 106; Nordlinger (B), 56; Nordlinger (E), 751.
271 *Influenced* ... Nordlinger (A), 21; I, 388, 390; BA, 219; Kolb (A), 305; Lauris (A), 131.
272 *Leaving* ... III, 648; CG, I, 12.
272 *By the* ... Kolb (A), 305.
273 *A few* ... Nordlinger (A), 15; Autret, 23, 26; CG, IV, 44-5.
274 *The validity* ... Lauris (A), 22; Nordlinger (A), viii, 23; CG, V, 35; CG, III, 13, 56; Autret, 38; NRF, 248-9; Adam, 48; Wildenstein, no. 259, 260, 301; Lauris (A), 21-2; Bibesco, A (B), 124; Nordlinger (D), 59; Billy, 129-30; Proust, Mme, 278-9; Hahn (B), 37; Hahn (D); SL, 7.
275 *Such are* ... Autret, 32, 39, 58, 76; Nordlinger (A), 14.
277 *The first* ... PM, 153-6; III, 890.
278 *In* ... C, 147; Wildenstein, no. 303.
279 *If Bergotte* ... Levaillant, 44-5, 51; JS, I, 125; PM, 193.
282 *At the* ... PM, 180; Nordlinger (A), 14; Billy, 137.

283 *Soon . . .* Proust, Mme, 163-70; Fouquières (B), I, 59-60; Germain (B), 140; Maurois, 156.
284 *He . . .* Proust, Mme, 155-6, 161, 169-70; Dujardin; Védrines, 59-60.
285 *The business . . .* Proust, Mme, 170; CG, IV, 22.
286 *This is . . .* Castellane (B), 137-8; C, 89; Daudet, Lucien (A), 14.
287 *Proust . . .* II, 19; Proust, Mme, 204.

CHAPTER 15 SAINT-LOUP

288 *At 45 . . .* Le Figaro, 21 June 1901; Duplay (C), 4; Lauris (A), 27; Hommage, 64, 191; Proust, Mme, 156, 173; Kolb (A), 22, 69; Hahn (A), 170-3; CG, II, 32-3; Le Gaulois, 12 May, 1901; Daudet, Léon (G), 302-3; Daudet, Léon (A), 66.
289 *Throughout . . .* Daudet, Léon (F), I, 182-4; Daudet, Léon (A), 51; Daudet, Léon (G), 298, 300-1, 304.
290 *Sometimes . . .* Daudet, Léon (G), 312-13.
290 *Another . . .* Peter (A), 98-9; Daudet, Léon (G), 308-9; Hahn (B), 227.
291 *On 9 . . .* Bibesco, A (B), 35; C, 39-44; Morand (A), 112; Proust, Mme, 176.
292 *By this . . .* Proust, Mme, 172-5, 177, 179, 181; C, 146.
293 *The first . . .* Hommage, 63-4; Clermont-Tonnerre (C), 207.
294 *Gabriel . . .* Clermont-Tonnerre (B), I, 105; C, 59; La Rochefoucauld, 25; Montesquiou (A), 313.
295 *A few . . .* Bibesco, A (B), 29-30, 160; Bibesco, M (A), 63; Hermant (B), 212.
296 *In 1900 . . .* Bibesco, A (B), 31-2; Cattaui (A), 157; Billy, 172-3.
296 *In the . . .* Bibesco, M (A), 31; Flament, 221; Vandérem, 42; Lauris (A), 9, 10; Lauris (B), 105; Clermont-Tonnerre (A), 35; Billy, 121; Kolb (A), 295.
297 *Proust . . .* Bibesco, M (A), 11, 12, 18, 25-7, 54.
298 *But the . . .* Bibesco, M (A), 15, 18; Bibesco, A (B), 78, 80-2.
298 *For a . . .* Bibesco, M (A), 20, 169; Bibesco, A (A), 424; CG, I, 281.
300 *Early . . .* Nordlinger (D), 59, 61; Nordlinger (F), 521.
300 *The first . . .* Bibesco, M (A), 31, 128-9; Bibesco, A (B), 97.
300 *At . . .* Bibesco, A (B), 97.
301 *On the . . .* Bibesco, A (B), 86-7.
301 *It was . . .* Bibesco, M (A), 38, 196-7.
301 *On a . . .* Bibesco, M (A), 39.
302 *The other . . .* Billy, 122; Lauris (A), 18-20; Bibesco, M (A), 37, 47, 49; Hommage, 41; Proust, Mme, 215; Nordlinger (D), 59; Adam, 18; BA, 296, 326; Catusse, 27-8.
303 *On the . . .* Billy, 122; Hommage, 41; Lauris (A), 19-20; Viollet-le-Duc, VI, 114.
304 *By the . . .* CG, II, 39-40; Lauris (A), 11.
304 *He now . . .* Lauris (A), 21; Bibesco, A (B), 71, 144-5.
304 *On 29 . . .* CG, II, 43-4; CG, IV, 189; Proust, Mme, 186-91; Bibesco, A (B), 122.
305 *However . . .* CG, VI, 261; CG, V, 158; CG, IV, 148-9; PJ, 238.
306 *Early . . .* Proust, Mme, 197-202; Bibesco, A (B), 88; Wildenstein, no. 182; Jones, 245; PM, 254-6; Hahn (B), 70; CG, IV, 86.
307 *He returned . . .* Bibesco, A (B), 59-60; 64-5, 70-2, 94-6, 99-100; Bibesco, M (A), 85-6.
308 *Antoine . . .* Kolb (A), 272; Proust, Mme, 202-4; Bibesco, A (B), 84-5.
309 *Fénelon . . .* Proust, Mme, 203-4; Hommage, 80.
309 *Saturnian . . .* Bibesco, A (B), 30, 47, 119; Clermont-Tonnerre (A), 36; Morand (A), 227; Morand (B), 26.
311 *Two . . .* Bibesco, A (B), 66, 68, 71; Proust, Mme, 200, 204-5; CG, IV, 189.
311 *The ceremony . . .* Thomson, 717; Catusse, 19-20; Bibesco, A (B), 83-5.
312 *Since . . .* Bibesco, M (A), 23, 126-7; Bibesco, A (B), 100; Briand (A), 351-3, 372.

313 *Spurred* . . . Proust, Mme, 194, 208; Bibesco, *A* (B), 39-40, 71, 102, 104; C, 14-27; PJ, 207-10.
314 *In March* . . . Proust, Mme, 206-10.

CHAPTER 16 TIME BEGINS TO BE LOST

315 *By the* . . . Bibesco, M (C), 10, 13, 15, 21; Clermont-Tonnerre (A), 36, 38; C, 58; Gramont, 171; Bibesco, *A* (B), 98-9.
316 *Prince* . . . Poniatowski, 610; Castellane (A), 41; Hommage, 309-13; Montesquiou (C), 558; Montesquiou (B), 60; Halicka, 66.
317 *At that* . . . CG, I, 202; Proust, Mme, 213; C, 45; Briand (A), 372-3; Clermont-Tonnerre (A), 35; CG, V, 149-51, 181; Bibesco, *A.* (B), 135-6.
318 *A few* . . . Bibesco, *A* (B), 100, 104, 107-8; C, 34; CG, IV, 115.
319 *Since* . . . Bibesco, *A* (B), 120, 123, 126, 128-9; Gregh (A), 161; Hommage, 36; CG, V, 176.
321 *During* . . . Proust, Mme, 213.
321 *On 9* . . . Nordlinger (B), 57-8; Clermont-Tonnerre (C), 71-2, 94.
322 *The return* . . . Proust, Mme, 212, 214-16.
322 *Early* . . . Clermont-Tonnerre (C), 11-14.
323 *On 29* . . . Lauris (A), 23, 62, 66, 70.
324 *Two* . . . Le Masle, 31-2, 62-4; Lauris (A), 23, 65, 69, 71, 84.
325 *Early* . . . Proust, Mme, 218, 220-1, 224, 226-8.
325 *Meanwhile* . . . Bibesco, *A* (B), 123, 127-8, 137; Nordlinger (A), 22-3; Proust, Mme, 225; Lauris (A), 45, 82-3.
326 *Feverish* . . . Lauris (A), 46-7; CSB, 102; I, 655-8; Proust, Mme, 229; Duplay (A).
327 *After* . . . Lauris (A), 48-9; Billy, 121, 145; CG, II, 53-4; PM, 256, 268; Nordlinger (A), 24; Catusse, 121; CG, V, 202.
328 *The energetic* . . . CG, V, 72; Le Masle, 39-44, 57-9; Bibesco, *A* (B), 143; Proust, Mme, 136, 149.
329 *His* . . . Crémieux, 166; Morand (A), 56; Thomas, 168; Maurois, 156.
330 *Dr Proust's* . . . Daudet, Léon (G), 40-1; Hahn (B), 142; Daudet, Léon (B), 81-4; Le Masle, 51; Montesquiou (D), II, 193-5; Schlumberger, II, 149, 152; Clermont-Tonnerre (A), 147; Bac (B), 205; Astruc, 307; Gregh (A), 202; Morand (A), 122; Keim, 84; CG, II, 140; Daudet, Lucien (A), 36; Guichard, 176; Clermont-Tonnerre (C), 146; Goncourt, 7 June 1896; Robert (A), 74-5.
332 *Time* . . . Le Masle, 48-50; Cattaui (A), 55; Mauriac, C, 9; Thomson, 712; Fleury, 6-7.
333 *Despite* . . . I, 36; Le Masle, 50-2; Pierre-Quint, 60; Clermont-Tonnerre (A), 29.
333 *On at* . . . Le Masle, 31, 55.
334 *On Sunday* . . . CG, II, 49-50; Le Masle, 49.
334 *On Monday* . . . Le Masle, 44; CG, V, 215; Hahn (B), 223; CG, II, 190.
335 *Dr Proust's* . . . Le Masle, 45, 49; Nordlinger (F), 527; Nordlinger (B), 58.
335 *Montesquiou* . . . CG, I, 121; CG, II, 48-9, 51-2; CG, IV, 190; Catusse, 40, 4-34, 56.
336 *Life* . . . CG, II, 51.
336 *The old* . . . I, 36.

REFERENCES TO SOURCES

VOLUME TWO

CHAPTER 1 VISITS FROM ALBERTINE

Page and Paragraph

1 *Life has* . . . CG, II, 48-50; *Proust, Mme*, 145, 235.

1 *Not unreluctantly* . . . CG, II, 49, 56-7; *Bibesco, A* (A), 425; RL, 15/11/1904.

2 *With a* . . . CG, II, 51; *Proust, Mme*, 231-2.

2 *In some* . . . *Proust, Mme*, 196; *Nordlinger* (A), 26-40; *Nordlinger* (B), 57-9;
    Nordlinger (D), 59, 62; *Hommage*, 39; CG, II, 57; *Daudet, Lucien* (A), 48,
    51, 239; *Maurois*, 128.

3 *Towards* . . . *Nordlinger* (A), ix-x, 3, 28-30, 32, 35, 116-18; *Nordlinger* (B), 57-9;
    Nordlinger (D), 62; *Adam*, 18; *Montesquiou* (D), II, 209.

4 *Meanwhile* . . . CG, II, 59; *Bibesco, A* (B), 105; *Kolb* (A), 73; *Annuaire diplo-
    matique*, 1914, 291.

4 *The other* . . . CG, II, 58-64, 70-2; *Clermont-Tonnerre* (A), 34; *Gregh* (B), 55-9;
    Gregh (D), 96-100; *Montesquiou* (A), 314.

5 *It is* . . . CG, I, 84-5, 106, 148-9; *Castellane* (A), 77-88; *Nichols*, 215-16; *Hahn* (B),
    39, 40; *Montesquiou* (A), 314; *Montesquiou* (D), II, 86, III, 116-19; *Montesquiou*
    (G) 80; *Kolb* (A), 23; *Bac* (A, II, 89, III, 119-32; *Fouquières* (C), 107-9;
    Zillhardt, 147-8; *Clermont-Tonnerre* (C), 90-2.

6 *By sheer* . . . CG, I, 157, 172, 216-17; CG, II, 72, 100-5; NRF, 49; PM, 73-8;
    C, 39-54; *Montesquiou* (G), 82.

7 *Although* . . . *Nordlinger* (A), 55-8; *Kolb* (A), 126.

7 *Another* . . . CG, II, 103-5; CG, IV, 96-7, 185; *Billy*, 32-3; *Curtiss* (A), 101;
    Duplay (C), 1-3; *Alden*, 6, 160; *Nordlinger* (A), 79; *Bergson*; PM, 241; CG, II,
    185; *Gregh* (D), 89-91.

8 *La Bible* . . . PM, 195.

9 *In his* . . . PM, 182-92.

11 *Proust* . . . PM, 193, 195.

11 *Copies* . . . CG, IV, 29. *Maurois*, 116.

12 *In April* . . . CG, V, 152-4; *Wildenstein*, no. 81, pl. 8; *Mauriac*, C, 59.

12 *For some* . . . CG, V, 172-4, 176-7, 181, 188, 198, 203; *Curtiss* (A), 87; *Mornand*.

13 *His* . . . CG, V, 174.

13 *In her* . . . CG, V, 152.

14 *Meanwhile* . . . *Nordlinger* (A), 26-7, 31, 37-9, 41-8, 55-8, 62-7.

15 *In April* . . . *Nordlinger* (A), x, 45, 118-19; *Nordlinger* (B), 58.

15 *On 16* . . . CG, I, 78-9; *Montesquiou* (D), I, 204, 206, 208; *Clermont-Tonnerre*
    (C), 119; *Zillhardt*, 139-40.

16 *Ever since* . . . CG, II, 73.

16 *The theme* . . . CG, II, 73-92; CG, VI, 187; *Clermont-Tonnerre* (B), II, 217;
    Bibesco, M (E), I, 77; *Morand* (A), 200; *Lauris* (B), 173.

17 *The Paris* . . . CG, II, 93; CG, V, 197, 202; *Clermont-Tonnerre* (B), I, 134, 165;
    Clermont-Tonnerre (C), 14-15; *Bibesco, A* (B), 89; *Hahn* (B), 140; *Morand* (A),
    188-9; *Montesquiou* (D), II, 46-7; BSAMP, VI, 175-7.

18 *For a* . . . *Bibesco, A* (B), 89.

18 *Albufera* . . . CG, V, 196-203.
19 *When on* . . . CG, II, 83, 89; Noailles, *Nouvelle espérance*, 266.
19 *Nothing* . . . Barrès, II, 108; *Blanche* (A), 53; *Tharaud* (B), 12-14, 58.
20 *Proust* . . . *Dreyfus* (B), 108-11; *Gregh* (B), 259.
21 *The rift* . . . CG, II, 93-4, 109-10, 134; CG, IV, 199-200; *Bibesco, A* (B), 89-91;
     Kolb (A), 76.
22 *On Tuesday* . . . *Proust, Mme,* 237-45; *Billy,* 72, 136, 143-4, 147, 181; CG, VI,
     22; *Nordlinger* (A), 70-2.
23 *On 16* . . . C, 150-69.
23 *Towards* . . . *Proust, Mme,* 247-75.
24 *Mlle Nordlinger* . . . *Nordlinger* (A), 61-2, 68-78, 120-1; *Proust, Mme,* 246, 294;
     Kolb (A), 312; CG, V, 167, 216-7.
25 *During* . . . CG, I, 125, 131-2; CG, V, 174-5, 184; *Bibesco, A* (B), 144-5; C, 170-1;
     Gregh (D), 107-9; *Cattaui* (C), 40; HLB, II (1949), 257-67; *Jones; Proust,
     Mme,* 143-4.
26 *The first* . . . CG, V, 168, 172-3; *Bibesco, A* (B), 160-70; *Bibesco, M* (C), 27;
     Proust, Mme, 251, 273, 276-7.
26 *The noble* . . . *Bibesco, M* (C), 25-46; BSAMP, VI, 177; *Montesquiou* (D), II, 155;
     Proust, Mme, 247; *Wildenstein,* no. 240.
27 *For Proust* . . . CG, V, 167, 171-3; *Gregh* (D), 109-13.

CHAPTER 2 DEATH OF A MOTHER

29 *It was* . . . CG, VI, 20, 25; *Montesquiou* (D), II, 243-62; *Nordlinger* (A), 82-5;
     Nordlinger (F), 525-6; *Proust, Mme,* 279.
30 *On 9* . . . *Proust, Mme,* 257-8; *Clermont-Tonnerre* (B), I, 105; BSAMP, VI, 175;
     La Rochefoucauld, 1, 6.
30 *In mid-February* . . . CG, I, 221-4; CG, V, 181-4; CG, VI, 17-18; *Kolb* (A), 300-1;
     Clermont-Tonnerre (C), 89, 107-9.
31 *Poor* . . . CG, I, 215; CG, VI, 18-28.
32 *He made* . . . CG, V, 162-3, 165-6, 168-9, 182-4, 188-9, 198.
32 *Towards* . . . CG, I, 74-6, 125-9, 133-46, 156-8, 215-7; CG, VI, 29, 33; *Kolb* (A),
     27; *Montesquiou* (D), II, 284-5, 301.
34 *While* . . . CG, I, 216; CG, IV, 193, 196-8; CG, VI, 27, 35; *Bibesco, A* (B), 124;
     Billy, 130; *Autret,* 62; *Mourey; Nordlinger* (A), 84; SL, 7.
34 *My only* . . . PM, 226, 244, 250, 252; SL, 7.
36 *For five* . . . PM, 254.
37 *Sur la* . . . CG, II, 111-33, 147-9; CG, IV, 208; CG, VI, 27, 36; *Lauris* (A), 59,
     77.
37 *Meanwhile* . . . *Nordlinger* (A), x, 86; *Nordlinger* (B), 61; *Proust, Mme,* 293.
38 *On 15* . . . CG, I, 245-7; CG, II, 124; *Lauris* (A), 60, 77; *Nordlinger* (A), 86-91,
     94; BSAMP, VIII, 455; *Proust, Mme,* 293-6.
38 *Louisa* . . . CG, V, 155-65.
39 *On 24* . . . CG, V, 42; *Clermont-Tonnerre* (A), 40-1; *Proust, Mme,* 298.
40 *The third* . . . CG, I, 42, 152, 157, 216, 246; *Hommage* (RN), 11-12; *Garver,*
     519-20.
40 *It had* . . . CG, I, 149-52; *Clermont-Tonnerre* (C), 110-12; *Germain* (B), 10;
     Montesquiou (G), 185-219; *Morand* (A), 199; *Zillhardt,* 136-7.
42 *Proust* . . . CG, I, 152-6, 159.
42 *On 25* . . . CG, II, 138-42; CG, V, 161; *Hommage,* 191.
43 *In Proust's* . . . CG, V, 161; *Bibesco, A* (B), 131-2; SL, 7-8; *Nordlinger* (A), 79-80,
     89-91, 93, 96-7; *Proust, Mme,* 262.
44 *Sufficient* . . . CG, II, 140; *Maurois,* 153-4.

45 *Perhaps* ... CG, V, 164.
46 *Early in* ... CG, I, 134; CG, V, 161; *Daudet, Lucien* (A), 153-4, 168; *Lauris* (A), 54, 59; *Proust, Mme*, 241, 264, 298, 300.
47 *When* ... CG, I, 160; CG, VI, 38; *Billy*, 153-4; *Catusse*, 32-4; *Hahn* (B), 232; *Nordlinger* (A), 101-2.
47 *Proust* ... *Catusse*, 151; *Lauris* (A), 150; *Nordlinger* (A), 101-2.
48 *His mother* ... CG, I, 120, 161, 163; CG, VI, 38-9; *Catusse*, 33-4, 111; CSB, 302; *Hahn* (B), 232; III, 404; *Porto-Riche*, 94; *Thomson*, 714.
49 *For two* ... CG, II, 106-7; CG, V, 177-8; *Catusse*, 51; *Hahn* (C), 99.
49 *Because* ... *Figaro*, 29/9/1905.
49 *For* ... CG, I, 162-3; CG, VI, 40-2; *Lauris* (A), 124; II, 134, III, 466.
50 *Towards* ... CG, II, 108; CG, VI, 40-1.
50 *Early* ... CG, II, 109, 140; CG, VI, 19, 41-4.
51 *Meanwhile* ... CG, VI, 40-1.
51 *On 4* ... CG, V, 196; CG, VI, 42-4; *Nordlinger* (A), 123.

CHAPTER 3 THE WATERSHED

52 *During* ... *Gregh* (A), 304-6; *Gregh* (D), 88-92; SL, 106.
52 *The charming* ... CG, II, 150; CG, V, 151-2, 154-5, 195-6; CG, VI, 45; *Billy*, 164; *Daudet, Léon* (I), 137; *Daudet, Lucien* (A), 97; *Lauris* (A), 205-6.
53 *Early* ... *Billy*, 159-62; *Bonnet*, 21; *Catusse*, 98.
55 *For two* ... CG, II, 157-9; CG, IV, 193, 202; *Bibesco, A* (B), 166-7; *Catusse*, 98; *Hahn* (B), 78-9; *Nordlinger* (A), 90.
55 *On 5* ... *Catusse*, 30; *Clermont-Tonnerre* (C), 148-9; *Proust, Mme*, 278-84.
56 *Sésame* ... CG, IV, 204, 206; *Maurois*, 116; *Nordlinger* (A), 79, 91; SL, 7.
56 *Since* ... CG, I, 202; CG, IV, 267.
57 *The footnotes* ... CG, IV, 202; SL, 68, 89, 201.
57 *In the* ... CG, II, 152-3; CG, VI, 47-50; *Catusse*, 31; *Hahn* (B), 80.
59 *As a* ... CG, VI, 50-9; *Billy*, 145.
59 *Probably* ... CG, VI, 60-1; *Hahn* (B), 122; *Lauris* (A), 38-9.
60 *As a* ... *Hahn*, (B), 94-9; *Proust, Mme*, 262.
60 *His uncle* ... CG, V, 217; CG, VI, 52, 60; *Billy*, 144-5, 210; *Catusse*, 32-6, 59; *Gregh* (D), 88-9, 91-2; *Hahn* (B), 98; PM, 215.
61 *Another* ... CG, II, 188; CG, IV, 114; CG, VI, 62-3, 65-6; *Catusse*, 36, 55; *Lauris* (A), 101, 103, 106-7; *Nordlinger* (A), 105; *Porto-Riche*, 94.
61 *Robert* ... *Catusse*, 39-40, 42, 49-51, 74-80.
62 *During* ... CG, IV, 146; CG, VI, 65-6; *Catusse*, 38-85; *Lauris* (A), 105; *Nordlinger* (A), 105.
63 *In the* ... CG, IV, 112; CG, VI, 65; *Catusse*, 55; *Lauris* (A), 111.
63 *His isolation* ... *Billy*, 210; *Catusse*, 36-7; *Hahn* (B), 97, 99-100, 102, 108-9; *Lauris* (A), 39, 91-6.
64 *He had* ... CG, VI, 67; *Castellane* (B), 104; *Clermont-Tonnerre* (A), 38-42; *Clermont-Tonnerre* (B), II, 54-5; *Clermont-Tonnerre* (C), 64; *Bibesco, M* (E), 8-9; *Fouquières* (B), I, 251; *Fouquières* (C), 86; *Schlumberger*, II, 183.
65 *Despite* ... CG, IV, 202-3; *Nordlinger* (A), 105.
66 *During* ... *Billy*, 150, 152; *Hahn* (B), 99, 101, 111, 119-21; *Proust, Mme*, 113, 125, 128, 132-3, 136, 141; PM, 215.
67 *On 27* ... CG, VI, 71; *Catusse*, 82, 87-90.
67 *In the* ... *Catusse*, 91; PM, 211-16.
68 *On the* ... PM, 217-21.
68 *Five* ... CG, IV, 213-16; *Dreyfus* (B), 202; *Hahn* (B), 124-5.

69 *Cardane* ... CG, IV, 273; *Ambrière; Dreyfus* (B), 202; *Bibesco, A* (B), 179; *Hahn* (B), 127-30.
69 *After* ... PM, 223-4.

CHAPTER 4 BALBEC REVISITED

72 *The nervous* ... *Lauris* (A), 87-125.
72 *All was* ... CG, I, 192; CG, VI, 68-75; *Catusse*, 87, 89-93; *Maurois*, 129.
73 *Meanwhile* ... C, 83-91.
74 *The five* ... *Boigne*, I, 256, 413; C, 89-90.
76 *Proust* ... CG, I, 159, 199-201, 225-6; CG, IV, 164; *Briand* (B); *Hahn* (B), 123; *Nordlinger* (A), 109; *Lauris* (A), 143-5; *Robert* (A), 39-41, 45-6.
77 *In the* ... CG, V, 186-7; *Duplay* (B); *Hahn* (B), 125-6, 128; *Léautaud*, III, 379.
78 *On 11* ... *Hahn* (B), 132-4.
78 *It was* ... CG, I, 184; *Billy*, 31; *Casa-Fuerte; Elkin Mathews; Germain* (E), 200 HLB, VII (1953), 152.
79 *Proust* ... *Hahn* (B), 131-2.
80 *The impact* ... CG, I, 198-9, 226; *Germain* (B), 20-1.
80 *The publication* ... CG, II, 170-3; C, 86-7.
81 *Proust's* ... CG, I, 202; CG, II, 164-9; CG, VI, 78; C, 177-92; *Lauris* (A), 126.
82 *His review* ... CG, II, 174-6; CG, VI, 75-85.
82 *The dinner* ... CG, IV, 111-12, 216-17; CG, VI, 75-85; *Billy*, 171-2; *Brach*, 9; *Clermont-Tonnerre* (C), 137, 139; *Hahn* (B), 136-8, 237; *Morand* (B), 40.
83 *On 23* ... C, 67-72.
83 *Dr Bize* ... CG, VI, 50, 56, 58; *Catusse*, 99; *Hahn* (B), 57; *Proust, Mme*, 224; *Sévrette*, 87, 157.
84 *The visitor* ... *Sévrette*, 43-4, 48-69, 120-131.
85 *Cabourg* ... CG, VI, 250; *Baedeker*, 221-2; *Clermont-Tonnerre* (C), 234; I, 385.
86 *In this* ... CG, III, 298; *Lauris* (A), 63; *Marquis*.
87 *In* ... *Hahn* (B), 142; *Sévrette*, 224.
88 *For the* ... *Lauris* (A), 122-3, 130-5.
88 *The penance* ... CG, VI, 86-7; *Bibesco, A* (B), 42-3; *Billy*, 112-17; *Hahn* (B), 139-40; *Lauris* (A), 131; *Le Masle* (B).
89 *Alfred* ... *Adam*, 81; *Cattaui* (A), 63; *Curtiss* (A), 220; *Vigneron*, 102.
89 *The next* ... CG, I, 220; *Bibesco, A* (B), 43; *Lauris* (A), 130-1; PM, 96-7.
90 *His first* ... *Bibesco, A* (B), 42; *Billy*, 115-17, 153; *Catusse*, 17; *Daudet, Lucien* (A), 229; *Lauris* (A), 131-3; *Le Masle* (B); II, 825.
91 *Proust* ... *Astruc*, 308; *Brach*, 37; *Corpechot*, 63-73; *Curtiss* (A), 353; *Daudet, Léon* (I), 248; *Flament*, 178-82; *Fouquières* (B), I, 225; *Goncourt*, 4/6/1890, 5/2/1894; *Hahn* (B), 145-6; BA, 32; *Lauris* (A), 131-2; I, 850; *Clermont-Tonnerre* (B), II, 114.
92 *Proust* ... *Billy*, 117, 153, 212; *Hahn* (B), 144-6.
93 *His daily* ... CG, VI, 85, 88; *Annuaire des châteaux*, 1906-7, II, 175; *Billy*, 153; *Hahn* (B), 113, 138, 146; *Lauris* (A), 133.
94 *Towards* ... CG, III, 5-6; CG, IV, 219-20; CG, VI, 85-90; *Billy*, 153, 212-3; *Catusse*, 99; *Clermont-Tonnerre* (C), 101-5, 139; *Clermont-Tonnerre* (B), IV, 9; *Hahn* (B), 135, 143-4, 148, 150; *Hommage*, 190; PM, 91; *Zillhardt*, 147-50.
95 *Towards* ... PM, 91-9.
96 *At the* ... CG, VI, 171; *Billy*, 175; *Catusse*, 102, 104.
97 *On 26* ... C, 73-4.

CHAPTER 5 PURIFICATION THROUGH PARODY

98 *In January* ... *Times, Figaro*, Jan.-March, 1908.
98 *At first* ... *Billy*, 138; *Hahn* (B), 86-7, 98, 100, 112-13, 115; PM, 11, 37.

99 *Proust's* . . . Lauris (A), 243-4; C, 204; PM, 108.
100 *He had* . . . PM, 15, 20-1, 49, 57.
102 *Other* . . . III, 708; PM, 22.
103 *It was* . . . CG, IV, 228-30; BSAMP, VIII, 457-9; *Wildenstein*, no. 360.
103 *Perhaps*... CG, IV, 115-19; *Dreyfus* (B), 234; *Gregh* (D), 140; *Lauris* (A), 181, 206.
104 *The Lemoine* . . . CG, VI, 96; *Clermont-Tonnerre* (B), II, 62-8; *Fouquier*, 164; *Hahn* (B), 151-2; *Morand* (A), 162; *Morand* (B), 105; *Porel* (A), II, 29.
105 *The third* . . . Baumont, 240, et passim.
106 *Proust* . . . Billy, 175-6.
106 *Since* . . . CG, IV, 234-5; CG, VI, 97; *Dreyfus* (B), 239; *Vigneron*, 73-9.
108 *The other* . . . CG, IV, 230-4; CG, VI, 103-5; *Billy*, 72, 143, 168, 174, 208, 219; *Dreyfus* (B), 239; *Gregh* (A), 273; *Gregh* (B), 13; *Kolb* (A), 251; *Sachs* (A), 64; *Uzès*, 163.
108 *In June* . . . CG, VI, 198-202; *Porto-Riche*, 96; *Schlumberger*, II, 113-16, 190.
109 *The young* . . . Hahn (B), 171-2; Lauris (A), 195.
109 *Nearly* . . . Bac (A), II, 190-8; *Bertaut*, 388; *Clermont-Tonnerre* (C), 112; *Figaro*, 28, 29/6/1908; *Germain* (B), 11; *Montesquiou* (D), III, 45, 75; *Montesquiou* (G).
111 *Proust* . . . CG, I, 171-5, 226-7; Hahn (B), 153; Lauris (A), 128-9.
111 *He arrived* . . . Catusse, 113-14; *Daudet, Lucien* (A), 202; *Hahn* (B), 98-100 112-13, 154-6, 185; *Kolb* (A), 44; *Kolb* (F).
112 *Once more* . . . Clermont-Tonnerre (C), 133-5, 139; Hahn (B), 156.
113 *He passed* . . . CG, V, 194; Billy, 209.
113 *Louisa* . . . CG, V, 179-80, 193-5; *Bottin mondain*, 1910, 805; *Hommage*, 56-9; NRF, 90; *Sévrette*, 57, 220.
114 *Proust* . . . CG, V, 195; Hahn (B), 156-7; *Hommage*, 58-9; *Mérode*, 66-9.
115 *It was* . . . CG, IV, 98; CG, V, 180; *Bibesco, A* (A), 164; *Bottin, Paris*, 1907, 647; *Fouquières* (B), I, 259; *Lauris* (A), 151, 176.
115 *Perhaps* . . . Leclercq: Dreyfus (B), 17.
116 *Once more* . . . CG, VI, 105-9; *Billy*, 114, 116, 160-1; CSB, 284-8; *Clermont-Tonnerre* (C), 105; *Hommage*, 190; *Kolb* (A), 272; *Lauris* (A), 147, 150-2.
116 *At the* . . . CG, VI, 105-9; Billy, 160-1; Hahn (B), 162; Lauris (A), 147, 150-2.

CHAPTER 6 BY WAY OF SAINTE-BEUVE

118 *After* . . . CG, VI, 108; Lauris (A), 150-2.
118 *Early* . . . Lauris (A), 146-9, 155-7.
118 *As early* . . . CG, II, 45-6; CG, IV, 227; Lauris (A), 158.
119 *By way* . . . Lauris (A), 15-16, 154, 160
119 *In December* . . . Lauris (A), 138, 154, 161; C, 226.
120 *Sainte-Beuve* . . . Lauris (A), 153-4, 160.
121 *Meanwhile* . . CG, I, 204-5; CG, IV, 244; *Billy*, 169-70; *Lauris* (A), 154, 163, 170-1; CSB, 15; PM, 32-5.
122 *Early in March he* . . . CG, I, 210, 217-8; CG, IV, 237-8; *Briand* (B); *Dreyfus* (B), 244-5; *Daudet, Lucien* (A), 58; PM, 32-5.
123 *Early in March Proust* . . . Clermont-Tonnerre (A), 163; *Lauris* (A), 170; *Lauris* (B), 63-6; *Schlumberger*, II, 370, 393.
123 *In June* . . . Lauris (A), 166, 176, 181, 199.
124 *Proust's* . . . CSB, 14-15.
124 *On a* . . . CSB, 14-15.
125 *Proust's* . . . CSB, 136-9, 172-4.
126 *The section* . . . CG, IV, 229-30; CSB, 301-13.
127 *Once again* . . . CG, II, 45-6; Lauris (A), 158.

CHAPTER 7 THE TEA AND THE MADELEINE

129 *With the* . . . CSB, 53-4; *Figaro*, 30/12/1908—3/1/1909.
129 *He now* . . . CSB, 53-9.
130 *Such is* . . . CSB, 56-7.
131 *Early in* . . . CSB, 15.
131 *The first* . . . *Flament*, 41; NNRF, 1/2/1953, 377-84.
134 *In Chapter* . . . *Proust, Mme*, 91.
135 *From Balzac* . . . *Billy*, 97; *Daudet, Lucien* (A), 37-8.
137 *Yet again* . . . *Schlumberger*, II, 200.
138 *At this* . . . CSB, 15.
141 *The origins* . . . CSB, 29.
142 *Like* . . . JS, I, 114-15.
143 *Set* . . . *Maurois*, 153-9.
144 *Meanwhile* . . . *Lauris* (A), 139, 164-7, 173, 176, 180-1, 208.
145 *In the* . . . CG, VI, 118; *Hahn* (B), 173-5; *Nordlinger* (B), 60-1.
145 *Proust* . . . CG, IV, 238, 241; *Dreyfus* (B), 248-50; CSB, 15; *Hahn* (B), 174.
148 *The beginning* . . . CG, IV, 239, 244-5; *Lauris* (A), 180-1, 196-7.
148 *For the* . . . CG, II, 68; CG, VI, 115; *Duplay* (C), 9-10; *Kolb* (A), 265; *Hahn* (B), 175-6; *Lauris* (A), 182-3; I, 878.
148 *A distressing* . . . *Hommage* (DV), 11-20.
149 *Another* . . . *Fouquier*, 288-9; *Fouquiéres* (C), 82-4.
149 *Proust's* . . . CG, IV, 37; *Clermont-Tonnerre* (A), 123-4.
150 *Meanwhile* . . . CG, IV, 246-9; CG, VI, 116-17; *Lauris* (A), 181.
151 *Mme Straus* . . . CG, IV, 248; CG, VI, 115-18.
151 *When the* . . . *Lauris* (A), 32, 169, 177-8, 217.
151 *As it* . . . *Lauris* (A), 32, 169, 177-8.
152 *The contents* . . . *Lauris* (A), 177-8, 186.
152 *Meanwhile* . . . CG, I, 224; CG, II, 67; CG, IV, 203-4; CG, VI, 162; *Annuaire diplomatique*, 1914, 291; *Bibesco, A* (B), 139-40; *Lauris* (A), 168-9.
153 *In his* . . . *Lauris* (A), 168.
153 *I nearly* . . . *Bibesco, A* (A), 424.

CHAPTER 8 MADEMOISELLE DE SAINT-LOUP

154 *Early in* . . . *Billy*, 180-1; *Kolb* (E).
155 *For nearly* . . . CG, IV, 123; *Maurois*, 135; *Pouquet* (B), 249-53; *Scheikévitch* (A), 64, 67-73; *Suffel*, 297-305.
156 *On 28* . . . CG, IV, 108, 121; *Bac* (A), III, 82; *Pouquet* (B), 253-68; *Scheikévitch* (A), 73-4.
157 *Now he* . . . CG, IV, 120, 141-4.
157 *The Seine* . . . *Times*, Jan. 1910; *Schlumberger*, II, 124-6.
158 *But when* . . . CG, I, 168-9; CG, VI, 123-5; *Gregh* (A), 204; *Gregh* (B), 242; *Hahn* (B), 176-7; *Lauris* (A), 202-3.
159 *He was* . . . *Guth*.
160 *In June* . . . CG, IV, 35-7; *Hahn* (B), 188; *Lauris* (A), 209.
160 *Meanwhile* . . . *Cocteau* (A), 50; *Corpechot*, 247-56; *Hahn* (B), 203; *Lieven*, 121; *Montesquiou* (D), III, 122-4.
161 *In the* . . . CG, V, 70, 133; *Cocteau* (A), 47; *Bibesco, M.* (A), 181-2; *Fouquier*, 240, 296; *Hahn* (B), 144-5; *Jaloux*, 16-17; *Morand* (A), 38; *Morand* (B), 110; *Porel* (A), II, 113; RHLF, avril-juin 1930, 305-6; *Sert*, 131-40.
162 *After* . . . *Astruc*, 133, 308; *Bibesco, M* (A), 181-2; *Cocteau* (C), 64; *Hahn* (B), 142, 146; *Morand* (B), 110; *Sert*, 131-40.

163 *Still* ... *Bibesco, A* (B), 159; *Lauris* (A), 179.
163 *As holiday* ... *Lauris* (A), 209.
163 *Instead* ... *Catusse*, 150; *Duplay* (C), 9–10; *Kolb* (A), 265; *Hahn* (B), 183–8.
164 *It is* ... CSB, 102–3, 269; *Hahn* (B), 184–5; *Maurois*, 153.
164 *Despite* ... CG, IV, 39.
164 *Meanwhile* ... *Hahn* (B), 187; *Thomson*, 719.
165 *In September* ... *Daudet, Lucien* (A), 165–7; *Hahn* (B), 189; *Hahn, M*, 33;
    Kolb (A), 206.
165 *Another* ... *Cattaui* (A), 139; *Hahn* (B), 191–2; *Lauris* (A), 211–13.
166 *At the* ... CG, II, 213; CG, IV, 250; *Catusse*, 149–51; *Hahn* (B), 147–8, 189,
    192–3.
167 *Lauris's* ... CG, IV, 236, 245, 253–5, 257; CG, V, 204–7; *Bibesco, A* (B), 87;
    Figaro, 28 Oct., 31 Oct., 3 Nov. 1910; *Kolb* (A), 275; *Pouquet* (A), 34–5.
167 *In the* ... CG, I, 224; *Clermont-Tonnerre* (C), 118, 155; *Montesquiou* (D), III,
    120–7, 133–40.
168 *At two* ... CG, I, 195–6.
168 *In February* ... *Annuaire de la Presse*, 1908, 41; *Bibesco, A* (B), 92; *Cocteau* (A),
    102; *Billy*, 72; *Hahn* (B), 196, 199–205; *Lauris* (A), 234–5.
169 *Reynaldo* ... *Hahn* (B), 196, 200, 203; *Lieven*, 126–9.
169 *In May* ... *Bibesco, M* (A), 1–11, 52–62, 111–15; *Bibesco, M* (C), 63–6; *Ghika*,
    I, 193–4.
171 *On 21* ... CG, I, 230–1; CG, VI, 128; *Clermont-Tonnerre* (B), II, 257; *Clermont-
    Tonnerre* (C), 150–2; *Corpechot*, 48–55; *Montesquiou* (D), III, 155–61, 167;
    Montesquiou, Têtes couronnées (1916), 49–94; *Hahn* (B), 206.
171 *Proust* ... BSAMP, IV, 9–11, VII, 281, IX, 7–10; *Ambrière; Hahn* (B), 207;
    Kolb (C), 192; *Pierre-Quint* (B), 68–9.
172 *The Plantevignes* ... CG, IV, 127; *Hahn* (B), 211–13.
172 *Again* ... CG, I, 243; *Billy*, 214, 218; *Guth; Hommage*, 88; *Lauris* (A), 29;
    Porel (A), I, 317.
173 *A jew* ... CG, VI, 127; *Ambrière; Hahn* (B), 186, 212–13.
173 *At the* ... *Blum*, 37; *Gregh* (D), 104–5; *Kolb* (A), 276; *Lauris* (A), 220–2.
173 *Proust* ... CG, I, 238, 243; *Billy*, 188, 213–18; *Hahn* (B), 219; *Lauris* (A), 230–1;
    Maurois, 139–40.
174 *For these* ... *Astruc*, ix, 164, 182; *Billy*, 218; BSAMP, VII, 280–1; *Maurois*,
    139–40.
174 *By way* ... CG, I, 167, 212, 228–9, 236–7, 243; CG, IV, 43; *Lauris* (A), 226–31.
175 *Reynaldo's* ... *Hahn* (B), 220–3.
175 *Proust's* ... CG, I, 168, 212; *Hahn* (B), 217–18; II, 195–8.
176 *One afternoon* ... CG, I, 237; CG, IV, 124–7; *Billy*, 186.
177 *Comtesse* ... CG, IV, 124–7; CG, VI, 129–30; *Billy*, 186; *Catusse*, 113.
178 *Proust's* ... CG, IV, 119–20, 126–8.
178 *One evening* ... *Pouquet* (A), 45–6; CG, IV, 119–20, 126–8; *Cattaui* (A), 161;
    Maurois, 133.

CHAPTER 9 AGONY AT SUNRISE

180 *Proust* ... CG, IV, 50–1, 126, 148; *Billy*, 185; *Hahn* (B), 229; *Hommage*, 61.
180 *Once again* ... CG, IV, 51–2; CG, VI, 111–13, 119–20; *Hahn* (B), 226, 228, 230.
180 *This summer* ... *Adam*, 24; *Hahn* (B), 231–2, 228.
181 *Philippe* ... *Hommage*, 60–2.
181 *Mme Scheikévitch* ... *Bac* (A), III, 84; *Cocteau* (A), 103; *Scheikévitch* (A), 44,
    129–36.
182 *That night* ... *Hahn* (B), 226, 231–2; *Scheikévitch* (A), 90, 129–36.

182 *Towards* ... CG, V, 225-6; CG, VI, 112-13.
183 *About* 16 ... CG, VI, 131-2.
183 *The novel* ... NRF, 96, 99-100, 107; *Robert* (A), 26.
184 *At first* ... CG, IV, 45; CG, VI, 133-44; *Robert* (A), 23-6.
184 *In February* ... CG, IV, 53; *Hahn* (B), 227; *Lauris* (A), 235.
185 *While* ... *Robert* (A), 23-8; *Robert* (B), 161-3.
185 *Nevertheless* ... CSB, 15; *Lauris* (A), 177; NRF, 89-106; III, 1116, 1242.
186 *Again Proust* ... *Bibesco, A* (B), 174-7, 181.
187 *Du Côté* ... CG, VI, 132-3, 137-8, 140-1.
187 *In these* ... CG, VI, 144-53; *Robert* (A), 37-9; *Figaro*, 21/12/1912.
188 *At last* ... *Bibesco, A* (B), 178-80; *Bonnet*, 127; BSAMP, VII, 307-9, VIII, 517-20; *Gide* (B), 9-11; *Kolb* (C); NRF, 98; *Robert* (A), 52.
189 *While he* ... CG, VI, 134, 142, 154-6; NRF, 106-7; *Robert* (A), 29-33, 37.
189 *Only a* ... CG, VI, 154-5; CG, II, 192-3; *Bibesco, A* (B), 179; *Blum*, 38; *Robert* (A), 34-5, 37, 51.
189 *Robert* ... *Robert* (A), 12-13, 35-6, 44.
190 *On the* ... CG, VI, 155, 157, 159-60, 162-3; *Hahn* (B), 239.
190 *To another* ... CG, VI, 157-8; *Daudet, Lucien* (A), 89-90; *Hahn* (B), 237; *Rostand* (B), 55.
190 *Towards* 10 ... *Robert* (A), 13-15, 50-1, 55-9.
191 *Proust* ... CG, IV, 57-8, 62-3; *Bibesco, M* (A), 29; *Blum*, 28-55, 228-9; *Grasset* (A), 9; *Grasset* (B), 194; *Massis*, 7-8; *Robert* (A), 15, 52-3, 59.
192 *For many* ... CG, V, 90.
192 *One day* ... CG, VI, 242, 244-5; CG, II, 193; *Robert* (A), 63-4.
193 *Real* ... CG, II, 198; CG, VI, 122, 145; *Billy*, 191; *Blum*, 47, 51.
194 *Immediately* ... CG, IV, 56, 58; *Blum*, 51; *Robert* (A), 62-3; *Duplay* (C), 10.
194 *The last* ... CG, IV, 56; *Blum*, 49; *Daudet, Lucien* (A), 69, 79-80; *Lauris* (A), 184-5; *Robert* (A), 16-17, 63, 65-7, 75; *Robert* (C), 79; NRF, 95, 100-1, 105; *Vigneron*, 107.
195 *Meanwhile* ... CG, VI, 132, 145-6, 164; *Robert* (A), 84; *Robert* (B), 175.
196 *At this* ... *Robert* (A), 64, 83-6; *Robert* (C), 65-78.
196 *Maurice* ... CG, IV, 4; CG, V, 226-7; *Blum*, 60; *Hahn* (B), 237; *Robert* (A), 46, 53, 59-60; *Rostand* (B), 55-7; *Scheikévitch* (A), 136-7.
196 *Proust's* ... *Hahn* (B), 240-1.
197 *For a* ... *Daudet, Lucien* (A), 68-9, 74; *Kolb* (A), 51; *Lauris* (A), 223-4.
197 *In the* ... *Lauris* (A), 168, 223.

CHAPTER 10 AGOSTINELLI VANISHES

199 *Proust* ... *Cocteau* (A), 103; *Daudet, Lucien* (A), 65-6, 74, 76, 78; *Duplay* (C), 10-11; *Lauris* (A), 224.
199 *Early in* ... *Blum*, 59; *Cocteau* (A), 105-6; *Daudet, Lucien* (A), 65-6, 68-80; *Robert* (A), 62-77; *Robert* (B), 166-8.
199 *The final* ... CG, IV, 99; *Dreyfus* (B), 294-7; I, xxxix, 959.
200 *Proust* ... *Blum*, 75-7; *Dreyfus* (B), 285-94; *Scheikévitch* (A), 139-41.
200 *Swann* ... CG, IV, 98-9, 260-1; *Ambrière*; *Dreyfus* (B), 294-9; *Daudet, Lucien* (A), 81.
201 *Lucien* ... *Daudet, Lucien* (A), 80-6; *Robert* (A), 80.
201 *Cocteau's* ... *Alden*, 10; *Daudet, Lucien* (A), 73; *Hahn* (B), 188; *Rivière*, 19; *Robert* (A), 80.
202 *The loyal* ... CG, I, 188-9, 201-2; *Blum*, 129-30.
202 *Paul* ... CG, I, 265; CG, III, 62-3; CG, IV, 64-5; CG, V, 229-30; *Scheikévitch* (A), 141; *Souday*, 7-16.

202 *Swann* . . . CG, IV, 62-4; *Blum*, 44; *Daudet, Lucien* (A), 73; *Billy*, 72; *Robert* (A), 78-82; *Robert* (B), 170-1.
203 *Having* . . . *Briand* (A), 523; *Cocteau* (B), 112; *Gide* (B), 14-15, 21, 41.
204 *My dear* . . . *Gide* (A), I, 398; *Gide* (B), 9-12; *Kolb* (C), 187-97.
204 *He replied* . . . CG, VI, 251-2; *Blum*, 150-9, 169; *Gide* (B), 13-17, 19-23, 30, 36.
204 *This was* . . . CG, IV, 62-4; *Blum*, 151, 171; *Gide* (B), 20.
205 *Proust's* . . . *Astruc*, 309; *Blum*, 178, 209; *Gide* (B), 30.
205 *In February* . . . CG, VI, 165-6, 203; *Bordeaux* (A), III, 353; *Daudet, Léon* (F), I, 109; *Gregh* (B), 159-61; *Lauris* (B), 222-3; *Morand* (A), 153; *Schlumberger*, II, 239.
206 *It is* . . . CG, I, 248; CG, II, 204; CG, IV, 60-2, 65; CG, V, 228; III, 1032; *Robert* (A), 77; *Figaro Littéraire*, 25/11/1939; CG, VI, 189; *Astruc*, 310; *Blum*, 123; *Daudet, Lucien* (A), 95.
206 *Proust's* . . . CG, VI, 244; *Maurois*, 140-1.
207 *There are* . . . CG, VI, 189, 242; *Cocteau* (A), 105-6; *Gide* (B), 39; III, 372-3, 382-3.
208 *The main* . . . III, 501, 902; *Jammes*, 286-7; *Rivière*, 3.
209 *Soon after* . . . CG, III, 321; *Gibbs-Smith*, 84-7; *Paléologue* (B), 208; *Schlumberger*, II, 242.
210 *Before long* . . . CG, III, 321; RHLF, Jan.-March, 1933, 159.
210 *It was* . . . CG, IV, 61, 64-5; CG, V, 228; CG, VI, 242, 245; *Daudet, Lucien* (A), 95; *Jammes*, 286-7.
211 *In the* . . . CG, VI, 242; *Bonnet*, 165; *Dupont*, no. 137; PM, 97.
212 *Agostinelli* . . . CG, VI, 247; *Bordeaux* (A), III, 186; *Gide* (B), 38; III, 406-7.
212 *But the* . . . CG, VI, 242-245; III, 321; PM, 95-6; *Vigneron*, 100-1.
212 *Joseph* . . . *Vigneron*, 100-1.
213 *Proust* . . . CG, VI, 241-2; *Adam*, 81, 83; *Figaro*, 31/5/1914.
213 *Boats* . . . CG, VI, 241-7; *Bordeaux* (A), III, 87; *Vigneron*, 107-8.
213 *On Sunday* . . . *Catusse*, 133-5; *Vigneron*, 107-8.
214 *In his* . . . CG, I, 270-1; *Astruc*, 310-11; *Bordeaux* (A), III, 87; *Daudet, Lucien* (A), 109; *Gide* (B), 43.
214 *Jealousy* . . . CG, V, 41; *Blum*, 155-7, 207; *Gide* (B), 34; NRF, 103.
215 *As before* . . . CG, VI, 166-7; *Gide* (B), 36-7, 45; *Feuillerat*, 5, 23-107; I, xxiii; *Rivière*, 3-18.
216 *Only* . . . CG, IV, 263; CG, V, 95-6.

CHAPTER 11 THE DEATH OF SAINT-LOUP

217 *The sky* . . . *Bac* (A), III, 177-87; *Bardac* (A), 141; *Daudet, Lucien* (A), 135
217 *Bac called* . . . *Bac* (A), III, 197-211.
218 *The catastrophe* . . . CG, VI, 171; *Guth; Hahn* (B), 249-50; *Nordlinger* (G), 265; *Scheikévitch* (C), 41.
218 *The French* . . . *Hahn* (B), 250.
219 *Céleste* . . . *Bordeaux* (A), III, 87; *Catusse*, 115, 118; *Hahn* (B), 250; *Kolb* (A), 290; *Figaro*, 5/9/1914; *Scheikévitch* (C), 43.
219 *He emerged* . . . BSAMP, III, 28; BSAMP, V, 15; *Catusse*, 117.
219 *One day* . . . CG, VI, 172-3; *Clermont-Tonnerre* (C), 178-81; *Bac* (A), III, 298; *Dreyfus* (A), 33.
220 *Proust* . . . *Catusse*, 119; *Gregh* (A), 168; *Daudet, Lucien* (A), 109-10; *Hermant* (B), 243; *Kolb* (A), 290; *Morand* (A), 175; *Porel* (A), I, 270, 317, 320; *Porel* (B); I, 431.
220 *Meanwhile* . . . *Le Masle*, 24.
221 *Among* . . . *Bac* (A), III, 229-286, 313-14.

221 *Others* . . . *Bardac* (A), 141-2; *Gregh* (A), 271; *Patin; Schlumberger*, II, 157.
222 *Proust* . . . CG, III, 318, 320; CG, V, 230-1; CG, VI, 171-2; *Astruc*, 313; *Bardac* (B), 143; *Billy*, 195; *Blum*, 165; *Crosland*, 40-1; BSAMP, III, 29; *Daudet, Lucien* (A), 100, 107, 113, 133; *Gregh* (B), 165-8, 173-81; *Catusse*, 115-27, 140; *Gide* (A), 514, 527, 534, 537; *Lannes*, 27-8; *Lauris* (A), 240, 242, 248; *Lauris* (B), 187-90; *Halicka*, 66; *Guth; Poniatowski*, 610; *Sert*, 199.
223 *At moments* . . . CG, III, 317; CG, VI, 171-2; *Billy*; 197; *Catusse*, 116, 120, 124; *Daudet, Lucien* (A), 104; *Morand* (A), 200; *Morand* (B), 15.
223 *Nevertheless* . . . CG, VI, 175-7, 189, 193-5, 206; *Daudet, Lucien* (A), 106, 135, 141; *Catusse*, 137; *Hahn* (B), 255; *Hommage*, 82; *Lauris* (A), 240; *Morand* (A), 39, 173, 314; *Morand* (B), 81-2.
224 *Gaston* . . . *Pouquet* (A), 75-82; CG, IV, 109, 129-36.
225 *After his* . . . CG, IV, 131, 134; *Annuaire diplomatique*, 1914, 291; *Bibesco, A* (B), 47, 119; *Bibesco, M* (A), 136-8; *Billy*, 137; *Hommage*, 80; *Morand* (B), 13.
226 *Fénelon's* . . . *Bibesco, M* (A), 137; *Pouquet* (A), 64, 77-8.
226 *Proust* . . . CG, V, 92; *Billy*, 195; *Daudet, Lucien* (A), 140; *Lauris* (A), 241-7.
226 *Another* . . . CG, V, 92, 159; *Bac* (A), III, 91-7; *Billy*, 194; BSAMP, III, 29-30; C, 87; *Catusse*, 135; *Figaro*, 4/8/1915; *Montesquiou* (C), 558; *Morand* (A), 301; *Proust, Mme*, 211; *Humières*, 15-19; *Wharton*, 288-9; *Porel* (A), I, 283-4.
227 *Proust's* . . . CG, III, 317, 322; CG, VI, 168-9, 248; *Adam*, 82; *Billy*, 198; *Blum*, 199, 206; *Catusse*, 124-7, 133-6; *Daudet, Lucien* (A), 111, 135-6, 139-45; *Guth; Hahn* (B), 255; *Lauris* (A), 244.
228 *In June* . . . CG, III, 112-15; *Hommage*, 52.
229 *Montesquiou* . . . CG, I, 252; CG, III, 255-6; *Catusse*, 137; *Montesquiou* (D), II, 286.
229 *After being* . . . CG, III, 320; *Bibesco, M* (B), 15; *Crosland*, 41; *Cocteau* (C), 163; *Porel* (A), I, 349.
229 *At last* . . . CG, III, 112, 116, 126, 317-18, CG, IV, 67, 135; CG, V, 231-2; BSAMP, III, 27; *Daudet, Lucien* (A), 123-4, 137; *Catusse*, 116, 120, 124-5.
230 *Soon* . . . *Adam*, 51; BSAMP, IV, 86-7; *Daudet, Lucien* (A), 96, 115, 137, 148.
230 *Two authors* . . . CG, VI, 248-9; *Astruc*, 314; *Bac* (A), III, 79-90; *Gide* (A), I, 514; *Lauris* (A), 236-7, 249-51, 259-69; *Lauris* (B), 243-79; *Scheikévitch* (A), 89-90.
230 *On the* . . . CG, I, 257; CG, V, 233-41; *Billy*, 197; *Blum*, 156, 163; *Lauris* (A), 236-7.
231 *As the* . . . *Bibesco, A* (B), 149-50.

CHAPTER 12 THE VINTEUIL SEPTET

232 *On 25* . . . *Blum*, 166-71, 205; *Gide* (A), 543, 553; *Gide* (B), 52-3.
232 *Exactly* . . . *Blum*, 169-70.
233 *The negotiations* . . . *Blum*, 166-70, 178-9, 224.
233 *At first* . . . *Blum*, 174-219.
234 *A major* . . . *Blum*, 169.
235 *The chapter-headings* . . . I, xxiii.
235 *The proofs* . . . *Daudet, Lucien* (A), 143, 145; *Feuillerat*, 2-5, 23-68, 275-92; *Lauris* (A), 184; *Robert* (A), 67.
236 *Two further* . . . *Feuillerat*, 36-42, 68, 140-50, 282-4, 290-2; I, 981-2, II, 861-3.
237 *Le Côté* . . . *Feuillerat*, 69-70, 77-80, 107, 292, 294-6, 302.
237 *The volume* . . . CSB, 247-66; JS, III, 93.
238 *The death* . . . *Rivière*, 7.
238 *The next* . . . CG, V, 233-41.

239 *Les Vices* . . . CSB, 14-15, 120-4; III, 648.
239 *Madame de* . . . *Daudet, Lucien* (A). 118-19.
240 *Mariage de* . . . CSB, 244-6; *Daudet, Lucien* (A), 71-2.
240 *The final* . . . CG, III, 72, 202; *Amiel; Crémieux*, 159; CSB, 53-9.
241 *In the* . . . CG, I, 270; CG, V, 233-41; BSAMP, III, 33; *Gide* (B), 45; *Lauris* (A), 236-7; *Dupont*, no. 137.
242 *The passion* . . . CG, IV, 73; CG, VI, 189-90; *Bibesco, A* (B), 147; BSAMP, III, 31; *Hahn* (B), 235; *Lauris* (A), 36-7; *Maurois*, 314; *Robert* (A), 48.
243 *Among* . . . CG, III, 119-20, 323; *Catusse*, 131; *Daudet, Lucien* (A), 153; *Chalupt*; BSAMP, XI, 424-9, 432-4; *Morand* (A), 121, 185; *Morand* (B), 29; *Morand* (D), 62-4.
244 *The Septet* . . . *Maurois*, 172; I, 978-82, III, 1083 (252).
245 *Like the* . . . *Bibesco, A* (B), 153-4; *Hommage*, 190.
245 *The lesser* . . . III, 250, 261.
246 *But Proust* . . . *Hommage*, 190; I, 979, III, 249, 259.
248 *The origins* . . . *Adam*, 99; *Astruc*, 225; BSAMP, III, 33; *Daudet, Lucien* (A), 171; *Indy*, 65; *Schlumberger*, I, 305.
248 *The Queen* . . . *Bérence; Castellane* (B), 215; *Cattaui* (A), 101; III, 322, 765; *Sachs* (B).
249 *The soirée* . . . *Germain* (B), 163; *Hahn* (B), 55.

CHAPTER 13 THE PIT OF SODOM

251 *A new* . . . *Bardac* (B), 143; *Cattaui* (A), 166; *Daudet, Lucien* (A), 115, 174; *Morand* (B), 12-14, 20; *Nordlinger* (D), 60.
251 *London* . . . CG, III, 54; *Adam*, 47; *Cattaui* (B), 69; *Curtiss* (B), 311-12; *Daudet, Lucien* (A), 231; *Hommage*, 73; *Wharton*, 323-4.
252 *Probably* . . . CG, V, ii-iii, 241-2; *Cattaui* (A), 174; *Clermont-Tonnerre* (A), 273-4; *Daudet, Lucien* (A), 170; *Hommage*, 71-2; *Lauris* (B), 214; *Lubbock*, 47-50, 205-9; *Morand* (A), 172; *Scheikévitch* (A), 152; BSAMP, VI, 178-9.
253 *Among* . . . CG, I, 256; CG, III, 319; *Adam, A*, 90; *Cattaui* (A), 68, 167; *Clermont-Tonnerre* (B), II, 26, 187-8; *Bac* (A), II, 292-9; *Fouquières* (A), 193, 227; *Hahn* (B), 244; *Morand* (A), 111-13, 161, 203, 300; *Morand* (B), 9-30, 36; *Pouquet* (A), 66; *Schlumberger*, II, 265.
254 *On 4* . . . *Ghika*, I, 165; *Morand* (A), 185-6; *Morand* (B), 37, 48-9, 53; PM, 69.
254 *He had* . . . CG, V, 36; *Bibesco, M* (C), 76, 100; *Morand* (A), 239, 243.
255 *One of* . . . BSAMP, VI, 173; *Bibesco, M* (C), 78.
255 *A group* . . . *Cocteau* (C), 166; *Hommage*, 78; *Pierre-Quint*, 76-7.
255 *The head-waiter* . . . *Benoist-Méchin*, 189-90; *Bourdet* (B), 152-3; *Castellane* (A), 144-7; *Clermont-Tonnerre* (A), 209; *Clermont-Tonnerre* (B), I, 167, II, 245, IV, 17; *Clermont-Tonnerre* (C), 142; *Fouquier*, 162; *Pringué*, 75; PM, 82; *Ritz*, 224-5.
256 *For five* . . . *Berl* (A), 32, 59-60, 106-7, 130-7, 153-8; *Berl* (B); *Larnac*, 113-16.
256 *At a* . . . *Bibesco, A* (B), 152-3; *Morand (A)*, 149, 161, 164-5, 199-203, 218-19, 223.
257 *In England* . . . *Times*, 11/9/51.
257 *In the* . . . *Bibesco, A* (B), 35-7; *Bibesco, M* (A), 137-8; *Morand* (A), 227, 230.
258 *Early in* . . . CG, V, 143-7, 248; CG, VI, 193; *Bibesco, A* (B), 37; *Daudet, Lucien* (A), 139-41; *Morand* (B), 60; *Times*, 11/9/1951.
258 *On 13* . . . CG, I, 261, 270; CG, IV, 151; CG, V, 256; CG, VI, 186; *Catusse*, 147, 152; *Daudet, Lucien* (A), 202-3, 208, 213; *Duplay* (C), 12-13; *Gide* (B), 47-9, 66-73; *Kolb* (A), 60; *Morand* (B), 68, 71; *Lacretelle*, 114; *Rivière*, 23; NRF, 37.

259 *Meanwhile . . .*   Daudet, Lucien (A), 203; *Germain* (B), 55-6; *Lacretelle*, 116; III, 1141; PM, 59.

259 *Proust . . .*   CG, I, 234-5, 254, 257, 267, 269-70; CG, IV, 151; CG, V, 6, 20-1, 33, 36-7, 97, 105, 249-50, 253-7, 261; CG, VI, 184, 187; *Blum*, 187, 217; *Catusse*, 129, 132, 145, 152, 173, 200; *Daudet, Lucien* (A), 153-4, 209; *Lacretelle*, 115; *Morand* (B), 66-79.

261 *Recently . . .*   CG, V, 21-2, 250-1; CG, VI, 180-8, 196, 198, 201; *Catusse*, 152-74; *Morand* (B), 66-8.

261 *The last . . .*   CG, V, 33-8; *Adam*, 68; *Bottin, Paris*, 1916-7, II, 1129; *Daudet, Lucien* (A), 233; *Morand* (B), 66, 76-7.

262 *The proprietor . . .*   Bottin, Paris, 1919, II, 756, 1129; *Guichard* (A), 168; *Sachs* (A), 280.

262 *Prince . . .*   Barney (B), 123-4; *Clermont-Tonnerre* (A), 209-10; *Clermont-Tonnerre* (C), 142-3; *Fouquier*, 272-3; *Halicka*, 66; *Montesquiou* (B), 60; *Montesquiou* (C), 558.

262 *While . . .*   Sachs (A), 281-2.

263 *During . . .*   Guichard (A), 168-9; *Sachs* (A), 280-1; *Sachs* (B).

264 *It was . . .*   Bottin, Paris, 1916-7, II, 1129; *Guichard* (A), 169-70; *Sachs* (A), 280-3.

264 *Here the . . .*   Sachs (A), 279-80; *Sachs* (B).

265 *Albert . . .*   Guichard (A), 169-70; *Sachs* (A), 285; *Sachs* (B), 864.

266 *The conscious . . .*   Adam, 80-1; II, 1110.

268 *Throughout . . .*   Daudet, Lucien (A), 15; *Germain* (B), 71, 149; *Hommage*, 188-9; *Morand* (A), 112; *Sachs* (A), 285; *Sachs* (B), 864.

268 *The story . . .*   Germain (B), 71-2; *Germain* (C), 248; *Gide* (A), II, 1223; *Martin du Gard*, 244; *Rose*, 118; *Sachs* (A), 285.

269 *He could . . .*   CG, V, 105; *Morand* (B), 76, 82.

270 *It is . . .*   Goncourt, 3 June 1891; *Morand* (C), 54; *Rachilde*, 79-92.

270 *Albert's . . .*   CSB, 14, 15, 86, 232; *Guichard* (A), 170-1; *Maurois*, 153; *Sachs* (A), 282-3.

271 *On 27 . . .*   CG, VI, 176-9; *Adam, H. P.*, 316; *Curtiss* (A), 249; *Morand* (A), 324-5.

272 *The next . . .*   CG, VI, 197-8.

273 *On and . . .*   CG, V, 98; *Blum*, 224-5; *Catusse*, 175-6; *Daudet, Lucien* (A), 98; *Morand* (B), 80, 82, 87-8.

273 *The noble . . .*   Couvreur; *Curtiss* (B), 313; *Morand* (A), 111; *Scheikévitch* (B), 607-8; *Scheikévitch* (C), 40.

274 *Céleste . . .*   CG, VI, 278, 280; *Castellane* (B), 6; *Clermont-Tonnerre* (C), 207; *Daudet, Lucien* (A), 138, 187; *Fouquier*, 161-2; *Fouquières* (A), 96; *Gregh* (D), 43; *Guillot de Saix*; *Hahn* (B), 83, 145; *Montesquiou* (A), 300, 311; *Morand* (A), 306; *Morand* (B), 54.

275 *Early in . . .*   Gide (B), 61-2; *Morand* (A), 243, 277, 299.

276 *The Abbé . . .*   Bibesco, M (E), I, 2, 4.

276 *The Abbé was . . .*   Bibesco, M (E), I, 1, 6, 28, 174, 181, II, 7; *Clermont-Tonnerre* (B), II, 52-3, 202; *Descaves*, 41, 131, 139-40; *Dumesnil*; *Flament* (B); *Fouquières* (A), 127-9; *Germain* (B), 217, 219; *Lauris* (B), 197-201; *Morand* (A), 299.

277 *It is . . .*   Bibesco, M (E), I, 6, 12-17, 326; *Bibesco, M* (D), 192-3; *Blanche* (A), 137-8; *Curtiss* (B), 313-14; *Descaves*, 152; *Daudet, Lucien* (A), 214; *Fouquières* (A), 72; *Morand* (A), 283, 306.

278 *All that . . .*   CG, III, 147; CG, IV, 126, 143; CG, V, 102, 190-1, 256-8; CG, VI, 193; *Bibesco, M* (A), 46; *Clermont-Tonnerre* (A), 91-2; *Daudet, Lucien* (A), 224; *Fouquières* (B), I, 114; *Morand* (B), 80-91; *Nouvelle Revue Française*, 1/1/1928, 87-8; *Pouquet* (B), 246.

279 *On 13* ... CG, III, 102; CG, VI, 202-7.
279 *After* ... Daudet, Lucien (A), 224, 227; Lacretelle, 110-1; NRF, 115.
279 *On 10* ... CG, III, 121-5, 127-58; Blanche (C), I, vii-viii; CSB, 78-9; Daudet,
     Lucien (A), 231.
280 *It was* ... Blum, 179, 220-31; NRF, 37.
281 *The same* ... CG, IV, 263; CG, V, 44; CG, VI, 206, 224; Blum, 228; Daudet,
     Lucien (A), 211, 220-1; Lacretelle, 112.
282 *The Germans* ... CG, III, 150; CG, V, 97; CG, VI, 206, 224; Bibesco, M (B),
     162-4; Daudet, Léon (G), 271; Daudet, Lucien (A), 229; Catusse, 143-4, 176;
     Fernandez, 205; Hommage, 91; Morand (A), 305; Morand (B), 91-3.

CHAPTER 14 THE PRIZE

283 *The men* ... CG, VI, 214; Morand (B), 93.
283 *First* ... CG, III, 213-14; CG, V, 6-20, 45-9, 136; CG, VI, 212-27; Billy, 202;
     Blum, 204; Clermont-Tonnerre (C), 204-5; Guth.
284 *La Semeuse* ... CG, V, 13; CG, VI, 207, 210-11, 215, 218, 224, 233, 257, 263;
     Bibesco, A (B), 52; Bibesco, M (A), 157; Morand (B), 105-6; NRF, 114; PM,
     15, 22, 69-72, 79-80, 82-6; Rivière, 27-8.
285 *In the* ... CG, IV, 77, 270; CG, V, 6-10, 16, 51, 54, 102-3; CG, VI, 226-8,
     256-7, Billy, 119; Catusse, 177.
286 *Early in* ... CG, IV, 74, 77, 264; CG, V, 29-31; Catusse, 177; Morand (B),
     100-3.
286 *On 2* ... Bibesco, M (A), 197; Nicolson (A), 275-6, 318-9; Nicolson (B);
     Nicolson (C).
287 *Whether* ... CG, III, 205; CG, IV, 75; CG, V, 55-7; CG, VI, 220; Blanche
     (A), 136-7; Blanche (B), 127; Pierre-Quint, 113-14; Rivière, xvii, 48, 70, 103,
     105.
287 *Towards* ... CG, III, 3-5; CG, V, 52-4; Rivière, 21-2, 26-33.
288 *As the* ... CG, II, 213, CG, III, 6-8; CG, IV, 76-8; CG, V, 29, 32, 56; Cattaui
     (B), 184; Catusse, 178-80, 183-4, 186, 188-92; Scheikévitch (B), 604; Scheiké-
     vitch (C), 44.
288 *Her son* ... CG, V, 60; Catusse, 186; Hommage, 88-9; Morand (A), 175, 278;
     Morand (B), 18, 41; Porel (A), I, 317-31, 334; Porel (B).
289 *It was* ... NRF, 121.
290 *The house* ... CG, III, 7-8; CG, IV, 268, 273; CG, V, 60-1; Catusse, 193;
     Martin du Gard, 201-2; Porel (A), I, 330-1, 364, II, 77; Porel (B).
290 *Thirty* ... CG, VI, 3; Porel (A), I, 364, 370-3.
290 *It was* ... Porel (A), I, 372.
291 *Proust's* ... CG, III, 193, 221; CG, V, 61; Catusse, 186; HLB, VII (1953),
     157-60; NRF, 121; Porel (A), I, 330-1, II, 77.
292 *Publication* ... CG, V, 56; Kolb (A), 217; NRF, 122-3; Rivière, 32.
292 *The common* ... CG, IV, 266-78; Dreyfus (B), 210-36; NRF, 111-12.
293 *Nevertheless* ... Robert (B), 169-72.
293 *Meanwhile* ... CG, I, 276-8; CG, III, 11; CG, IV, 79; Astrue, 314; Blum, 244;
     Bibesco, A (B), 156; Catusse, 194, 196; Le Goff, 243, 332; Lacretelle, 102;
     Suffel, 381.
294 *On 14* ... CG, I, 276-9; Gregh (A), 205; Gregh (B), 249; Gregh (D), 37.
294 *On 24* ... CG, I, 275; CG, IV, 273-7; CG, V, 66; Blanche (C), II, xxxvii-xl;
     Billy, 202; Morand (B), 109, 112.
294 *Réjane* ... Charavay, no. 102; HLB, VII (1953), 157-60; Porel (A), I, 365-7.

295 *It was* . . . CG, I, 287-8, 290; *Abraham*, pl. XXXVI; *Bottin, Paris,* 1919, II, 1370; *Bottin-Mondain,* 1919, 1125, 1608, 1653; *Catusse,* 197; *Daudet, Lucien* (A), 48, 239; *Maurois,* 128, 320; *Pierre-Quint,* 112-13.

295 *In September* . . . CG, III, 71, 214, 216, 218; *Billy,* 72; *Daudet, Lucien* (A), 161; *Deffoux,* 121-3; *Maurois,* 292; *Robert* (B), 169-72; RHLF, jan.-mars, 1932, 160.

296 *The Goncourt* . . . CG, III, 71, 200, 216, 230; CG, IV, 159; *Alden,* 32, 162; *Deffoux,* 121-3, 136; *Lacretelle,* 123, 125; *Montfort,* II, 25; NRF, 217; *Rivière,* 73; *Wildenstein,* no. 257.

296 *The Prize* . . . CG, III, 71, 166-7, 200-1, 216-17; *Alden,* 29-36, 176-8; *Blum,* 237; NRF, 127.

297 *From the* . . . CG, III, 70, 201; NRF, 129, 229; *Rivière,* 76-7.

297 *Henceforth* . . . CG, III, 71.

298 *Proust* . . . CG, V, 7-9, 14-15, 23, 28, 31-2, 56-7; CG, VI, 195-6, 198-9; *Billy,* 233-43; *Catusse,* 201-2; *Pierre-Quint,* 109.

298 *In the* . . . CG, III, 208, 298; C, 193-211; *Rivière,* 60-77, 80, 86-7, 89, 91-4, 99, 101-3, 106, 142.

299 *The proof-enrichment* . . . CG, III, 8-11, 15-16, 18-20, 209; CG, V, 59-60, 68; *Bibesco, M* (B), 154; BSAMP II, 36; *Gide* (B), 78; *Lacretelle,* 112-13; *Morand* (B), 132-3; NRF, 124, 130; I, xxiv; *Rivière,* 85, 103, 108.

300 *On 4* . . . CG, VI, 234-5.

300 *He had* . . . BSAMP, VII, 278-9; *Castellane* (B), 197; *Porel* (A), I, 331-2, 342-3.

301 *On 14* . . . *Hommage,* 92-3; *Porel* (A), I, 332, 374.

301 *At this* . . . CG, V, 105; *Lacretelle,* 121; *Porel* (A), I, 332; *Rivière,* 109-10, 116, 118, 120, 127.

CHAPTER 15 THE DARK WOMAN

303 *In the* . . . CG, III, 17, 20, 24-5; CG, VI, 232; *Fouquières* (C), 84-5; *Germain* (B), 101; *Morand* (A), 306; *Morand* (B), 117; *Rivière,* 91, 137; *Schlumberger,* II, 55-8; *Wildenstein,* no. 124.

303 *Aided* . . . *Clermont-Tonnerre* (A), 105.

304 *Le Côté* . . . CG, II, 214-5; CG, III, 21-2, 219; CG, V, 87; CG, VI, 137; *Billy,* 119; III, 137; RHLF, avril-juin, 1930, 306; *Rivière,* 108.

305 *On 25* . . . CG, III, 21-2, 81-3, 217; CG, IV, 100, 280; CG, V, 72, 82, 106; *Bibesco, A* (B), 54; *Boylesve,* 266-7; *Catusse,* 201; *Jaloux,* 134-6; *Journal officiel,* 1920, 14250; *Daudet, Lucien* (A), 238; NRF, 133-4; *Rivière,* 136-7; *Porto-Riche,* 100.

306 *The next* . . . CG, III, 86-91; CG, V, 69; *Alden,* 54-6; NRF, 39, 119; *Rivière,* 147-8; *Scheikévitch* (B), 604.

306 *Early in* . . . CG, III, 77; CG, V, 71, 120-1; *Morand* (A), 222-3; *Morand* (B), 41, 58, 115; *Morand* (C), 46; *Morand* (D), 56-7.

307 *In the* . . . *Morand* (E), 9-11.

308 *For the* . . . CG. I, 198; CG, IV, 38, 203; CG, VI, 81, 106; *Bibesco, M* (B), 119, 123; *Billy,* 160; *Hahn* (B), 196; *Lauris* (A), 186.

309 *During* . . . CG, III, 21-2, 256; CG, IV, 105, 263; CG, V, 95-7, 102-6, 117-24; CG, VI, 272; *Blum,* 217; *Catusse,* 200; *Curtiss* (A), 281; BSAMP, XII, 530; *Mauriac, F,* 24; NRF, 132; *Morand* (B), 79.

310 *Early in* . . . CG, III, 159-62, 170-3; *Blanche* (C), II, xv, xli; *Rivière,* 167.

310 *Marcel* . . . CG, III, 228; CG, V, 159, 169; *Bordeaux* (A), III, 88; BSAMP, VI, 178; *Écrits de Paris,* jan. 1951, 108; *Le Masle,* 50; *Morand* (E), 16-22; *Rivière,* 105-7, 167; *Tharaud* (A), 180-3.

311 *Proust's* . . . *Écrits de Paris,* jan. 1951, 108.

311 *The publication* . . . Mauriac, F, 26; NRF, 119, 137; *Rivière*, 55, 61, 63, 67, 92, 129, 133, 149, 154-74, 188, 190, 192.

312 *The outcry* . . . *Rivière*, 83, 95-6, 98, 111-12, 121, 188, 193, 197.

312 *Gide* . . . CG, III, 244-6; *Gide* (A), I, 691-4, 705, 848.

314 *The publication* . . . CG, I, 282; CG, VI, 232; *Bibesco, M* (B), 119-21, 138-41, 149-50, 153-4; *Bibesco, M* (C), 110-11; *Bibesco, M* (D), 189-90; BSAMP, XIII, 5; *Clermont-Tonnerre* (C), 228; *Cocteau* (C), 163; *Cocteau* (D), I, 125, 130.

315 *As for* . . . Bibesco, M (C), 110.

316 *In his* . . . CG, I, 142, 144; CG, II, 136; CG, III, 255; *Bibesco, M* (B), 158; *Bibesco, M* (C), 111; *Fouquières* (C), 102-5; *Gregh* (B), 195; *Germain* (B), 32; *Kolb* (A), 300-1; *Lauris* (A), 133; *Léautaud*, 11/5/1923; *Morand* (A), 206, 225; *Proust, Mme*, 267, 284.

317 *Even before* . . . Bardac (B), 143-4.

318 *More recently* . . . Bardac (B), 143-4; *Montesquiou* (D), III, 285, 288-93.

318 *Proust* . . . CG, I, 280-7; *Clermont-Tonnerre* (C), 218-27

319 *Moved* . . . CG, I, 282, 287-90; CG, III, 240, 253-7, 259-61; *Bibesco, M* (C), 111-12; *Clermont-Tonnerre* (C), 244-5.

319 *Meanwhile* . . . CG, IV, ii-iii, 86-91; *Gazette des Beaux-Arts*, mai, 1921, 271-2; *Gide* (B), 58.

320 *Proust* . . . CG, IV, 69; *Bibesco, M* (C), 99; *Guillot de Saix*.

321 *From the* . . . CG, III, 18, 27; *Mauriac, F*, 30, 34, 36, 41, 43.

322 *It was* . . . CG, II, 210; CG, III, 27, 202, 205; CG, V, 121; *Morand* (B), 124-5; NRF, 144; *Pierre-Quint*, 113-14.

322 *On 16* . . . CG, III, 28; CG, V, 74; *Adam*, 34; *Balsan*, 98, 186, 189; *Morand* (B), 123-4.

323 *In the* . . . C, 214-16, 220, 229-30; II, 1032; *Rivière*, 185-92.

324 *At the* . . . NRF, 144-8, 196-7; II, 1173-6; *Rivière*, 201-18.

324 *Among* . . . Bardac (B), 144; *Hommage*, 307; *Jaloux*, 18-19; *Rivière*, 239-42.

325 *In that* . . . CG, I, 253; CG, III, 28; *Barney* (A), 65; *Curtiss* (B), 314; *Guillot de Saix*; NRF, 149-50, 156-7; *Rivière*, 216; *Scheikévitch* (B), 604.

CHAPTER 16 AN INDIAN SUMMER

327 *During* . . . Cattaui (A), 153; *Fouquières* (A), 94; *Fouquières* (B), I, 18; *Germain* (A), 95-111; *Morand* (A), 51, 76, 107, 215-16; *Paléologue* (B), 309.

327 *In the* . . . Barney (B), 31; *Clermont-Tonnerre* (B), II, 213-6, 236-7; *Clermont-Tonnerre* (C), 69-70; *Delarue-Mardrus*, 143-4; *Germain* (A), 95-111, 292; *Germain* (C), 154-66; *Montesquiou* (A), 311; *Morand* (A), 215-16; *Schlumberger* I, 63-4.

328 *The Amazon* . . . Barney (A), 60; *Bourdet* (A), 239-45; *Gide* (A), I, 196-7; *Morand* (A), 107, 124, 167, 309-10; *Pringué*, 55, 81.

329 *Proust* . . . Barney (A), 59-74; *Wildenstein*, no. 346.

330 *In October* . . . Clermont-Tonnerre (C), 156-7, 191; *Fauchier-Madran*, 116-17; *Gaillard*, 135, 196-205; *Germain* (B), 22-3; *Gregh* (B), 196; *Montesquiou* (D), I, 62, III, 63, 190-3, 230; *Montesquiou* (F).

331 *Montesquiou's* . . . CG, I, 281, 283, 290; *Barney* (B), 123; *Clermont-Tonnerre* (C), 212-16, 240-3.

331 *The series* . . . CG, III, 199, 202, 226, 233-7, 250-1, 256-8, 263-5, 267, 302-3; *Rivière*, 198-200, 205-7, 209.

332 *Fortunately* . . . CG, III, 259, 265, 267, 275, 286; *Blum*, 240-1; NRF, 157-60, 165-6; *Rivière*, 198, 209, 231-6, 243-4.

333 *In September* . . . NRF, 163-4, 171-2, 175-8, 184-5, 192.

333 *Proust* . . . CG, III, 33-5, 174, 181, 184, 283; CG, IV, 136-7; CG, V, 25, 267; *Billy*, 203; *Maurois*, 309; *Morand* (B), 109, 130-1; NRF, 178, 185-6, 199, 203, 224; *Rivière*, 251.

334 *The gaiety* . . . CG, V, 25; *Bibesco, M* (C), 104; *Gregh* (B), 257; *Morand* (B), 125-6, 130; NRF, 193; *Schlumberger*, II, 342.

335 *On 7* . . . CG, III, 273; *Germain* (A), 59-72, 95-111; *Germain* (B), 207-10, 234-5, 247; *Germain* (D), 13-14; *Martin du Gard*, I, 195-202; *Morand* (B), 126-7; NRF, 218-9; *Rivière*, 229-30.

336 *The daily* . . . CG, III, 182-94, 284-6, 289-92; CG, V, 25, 77; *Bibesco, M* (C), 105; *Blanche* (C), II, xliii; *Crémieux*, 167-8; *Kolb* (A), 227; *Morand* (B), 129; NRF, 181, 210, 215, 232, 237, 244; *Riviere*, 242, 244-9, 256-9; *Scheikévitch* (A), 161.

337 *Proust* . . . CG, III, 274-8, 281-5, 287, 289, 292; CG, V, 80; *Clermont-Tonnerre* (C), 244-5; *Rivière*, 189.

337 *But the* . . . *Brach*, 27-8; *Cattaui* (A), 106-7; *Gaulois*, 16/7/1902; NRF, 173-4; *Proust, Mme*, 71; *Rivière*, 218.

338 *His unavailing* . . . CG, IV, 103; NRF, 225, 236, 242, 246; *Rivière*, 263, 266 268, 277, 284.

338 *The publication* . . . CG, III, 38; CG, IV, 90; CG, V, 23-4, 84, 113-15; NRF, 214, 224; *Rivière*, 251.

339 *Violet* . . . CG, III, 20, 51. 57; *Adam*, 6-12; *Hommage*, 274; *Schiff*.

339 *On 28* . . . CG, III, 31-3, 36-8, 51; *Adam*, 11-12; BSAMP, IX, 18-24; *Catusse*, 42; *Morand* (B), 33; *Schiff*; *Wildenstein*, no. 258, 316.

340 *On 18* . . . CG, III, 158; CG, V, 40; *Bell*, 179-80; *Blanche* (C), I, xxii; *Cocteau* (C), 165-6; *Craft*, 89; *Monnin-Hornung*, 14-16; *Penrose*, 208; *Porel* (A), II, 321; *Schiff*.

341 *Joyce* . . . *Adam*, 64-5; *Bell*, 179-80; *Ellman*, 523-4; *Joyce*, 148.

342 *A new* . . . CG, V, 81-5; *Crémieux*, 161-3; *Gabory*, 36; *Gide* (B), 86-96; *Jaloux*, 132-3; NRF, 203, 206, 209, 221; *Rivière*, 252, 254-7; *Salmon*, III, 73-5.

342 *As soon* . . . CG, III, 42, 221-2, 293; CG, V, 84-6, 134; *Bibesco, M* (C), 100, 115-17; NRF, 221, 253; *Rivière*, 257, 259-60; *Robert* (A). 26.

343 *A well-meaning* . . . CG, V, 221-3; *Hayman; Hommage*, 70; NRF, 213-14; I, 634.

343 *The Schiffs* . . . CG, III, 42; *Adam*, 11; *Wildenstein*, no. 239.

344 *Every day* . . . CG, III, 45, 301; CG, V, 82, 134; *Brach*, 27-8, 32-3; *Crémieux*, 165; *Jaloux*, 138, 140, 143-4; *Montesquiou* (A), 313; *Pierre-Quint*, 114-15.

344 *On 15* . . . *Brach*, 33-8; *Briand* (A), 515-16; BSAMP, VI, 135; *Hommage*, 150; *Jaloux*, 11, 13, 86, 149-51; *Kolb* (A), 230; NRF, 231, 243; *Oberlé*, 108-10.

345 *Among* . . . *Brach*, 38; *Clermont-Tonnerre* (C), 192; *Jaloux*, 152; *Mauriac, F*, 49-56; *Montesquiou* (D), III, 285-94; *Pierre-Quint*, 211.

346 *Proust's* . . . *Daudet, Lucien* (A), 27, 241.

347 *In this* . . . CG, III, 45; *Bibesco, A* (B), 52-5; *Bibesco, M* (A), 153-60, 195-200; NRF, 220.

347 *At the* . . . *Pouquet* (A), 94-5.

347 *Jeanne's* . . . CG, III, 55; *Adam*, 12; *Bibesco, M* (C), 101-2; *Bibesco, M* (E), II, 62; *Kolb* (A), 97; *Maurois* (B), I, 210-19, 230-7; *Morand* (B), 111.

348 *Proust's* . . . CG, IV, 161; *Abraham*, LII-LVI; BSAMP, III, 17-18; *Crémieux*, 169; NRF, 224-5, 234-5, 246, 256, 265; *Œuvres Libres*, février 1923, 235-6; III, 1057-8; *Rivière*, 284.

348 *Early in* . . . CG, III, 290-1; I, xxxii-iii, III, 1094; NRF, 225, 235, 271; *Rivière*, 272, 275, 277, 278.

349 *In August* . . . CG, II, 54; *Lauris* (A), 49, 209; PJ, 12-13.

350 *Among the thirty-five* . . . *Du Bos*, 164; *Gide* (A), I, 741; *Maurois* (B), I, 185-91; *Rivière*, 271, 274.

350 *Among the foreign* ... CG, III, 34, 48, 54, 58; *Adam*, 12, 43; *Hommage*, 243-78;
   Jaloux, 147; NRF, 195, 261; *Sotheby*, 26/11/1957, no. 261.
351 *His last* ... CG, III, 56; *Adam*, 48; *Hommage*, 277; NRF, 113, 125, 248-9;
   Scott-Moncrieff, 149-56; *Schiff*, S, 39.
351 *Swann's* ... *Adam*, 48; *Scott-Moncrieff*, 152-4, 179.

CHAPTER 17 THE TWO WAYS MEET

353 *New* ... CG, III, 312-3; NRF, 247, 249, 255, 262, 265; *Rivière*, 281-2.
353 *The causes* ... CG, III, 56; *Bibesco*, M (C), 101; *Jaloux*, 149; *Kolb* (A), 98, 270;
   NRF, 265; *Pierre-Quint*, 121; *Scheikévitch* (A), 164-5.
354 *Never* ... CG. III, 49-51, 56-7; NRF, 250-6, 261-3, 265-7; I, xxvii; *Rivière*,
   270-87, 302.
355 *Early in* ... *Couvreur*; CSB, 125-6; *Daudet, Lucien* (A), 57; *Maurois*, 325;
   Pierre-Quint, 121; *Rivière*, 291-2, 297; *Scheikévitch* (A), 163-4.
356 *So he* ... *Davray*, no. 31; *Guillot de Saix*; *Scheikévitch* (A), 161-2.
356 *Late on* ... *Guillot de Saix*; *Scheikévitch* (A), 164.
356 *He sent* ... CG, III, 298, 304; *Clermont-Tonnerre* (C), 234; III, 224; *Rivière*,
   292-4, 300-2.
357 *On the* ... CG, IV, 161-2; *Guillot de Saix*; NRF, 272-3; *Rivière*, 295-303.
357 *The baffled* ... *Gregh* (A), 162; *Gregh* (D), 48; *Maurois*, 325; *Scheikévitch* (A),
   165-6.
358 *Few* ... *Cattaui* (C), 138; *Guillot de Saix*; NRF, 228-9, 269-70, 273; *Rivière*,
   288, 293; *Scheikévitch* (A), 165-6.
358 *Proust* ... *Guillot de Saix*; NRF, 271-2; *Rivière*, 269, 272-3, 275-7, 279, 287-8,
   290, 298-9; *Scheikévitch* (A), 145, 154-5, 166.
359 *He thought* ... *Bibesco*, M (D), 192-3; *Bibesco*, M (E), I, 85-6; *Cattaui* (A), 135;
   Cattaui (C), 138; *Curtiss* (B), 314, 316-17; *Fouquières* (A), 72; *Guillot de Saix*;
   Maurois, 294.
359 *Sleep* ... *Guillot de Saix*; *Maurois*, 325-7; *Scheikévitch* (A), 165-6.
359 *Pneumonia* ... CSB, 125; *Guillot de Saix*; *Scheikévitch* (A), 167.
360 *At least* ... *Daudet, Léon* (C), III, 37; *Guillot de Saix*; *Hommage*, 66; *Mauriac,
   F*, 60; *Pierre-Quint*, 122; *Scheikévitch* (A), 167-8; *Thomson*, 720; *Wildenstein*,
   no. 319.
361 *When the* ... *Guillot de Saix*; *Scheikévitch* (A), 168.
361 *Robert* ... *Guillot de Saix*; *Rivière*, 305; *Scheikévitch* (A), 168-9.
362 *Soon* ... *Astruc*, 317; *Daudet, Lucien* (A), 242; *Dreyfus* (B), 340; *Gregh* (B),
   253-8; *Guillot de Saix*; *Morand* (B), 30; *Rivière*, 305; *Sachs* (A), 61-8.
362 *Marthe* ... CG, II, 11-14, 210; *Abraham*, XXXVI; *Astruc*, 317; *Barrès*, XIV,
   215-6; *Billy*, 251-2; *Cattaui* (A), 74-80; *Cocteau* (A), 105; *Cocteau* (D), I,
   129-32; *Daudet, Lucien* (A), 242; *Dreyfus* (B), 340-1; *Gregh* (B), 258; *Gregh*
   (D), 34-5; *Guth*; *Hommage*, 41; *Jaloux*, 27-8; *Porel* (A), I, 333; *Thomson*,
   720.
363 *Proust's* ... *Astruc*, 80-1, 322-3; *Bibesco*, M (E), I, 86; *Clermont-Tonnerre* (C),
   174; *Duplay* (B); *Figaro*, 22/11/1922; *Gregh* (B), 258; *Guth*; *Mauriac, F*, 9;
   Montesquiou (D), II, 284.
364 *Meanwhile* ... *Cattaui* (A), 74; *Jaloux*, 28; *Morand* (F).

SUPPLEMENTARY SELECT ANNOTATED BIBLIOGRAPHY

Source references to works here listed are given by the name of the author or, where appropriate, by a prefixed abbreviation. References to the present biography are made in the form MP followed by the volume and page number.

PROUST'S WORKS AND CORRESPONDENCE

Pléiade I, II, III   *A la Recherche du Temps Perdu.* Ed. Pierre Clarac and André Ferré. 3 vols. (*Bibliothèque de la Pléiade*, Gallimard, Paris, 1954.)

A la Recherche du Temps Perdu. Ed. J. Y. Tadié. (Gallimard, Paris, 1987- .) (With introductions, annotations, variants and unpublished drafts, for which exclusive copyright is retained, this is henceforth the authoritative edition *par excellence.* To be completed in 4 vols.)

A la Recherche du Temps Perdu. Ed. J. Milly and B. Brun. 10 vols. (Garnier-Flammarion, Paris, 1987.) (Of textual and editorial importance next only to the Tadié-Gallimard edition.)

A la Recherche du Temps Perdu. Ed. B. Raffalli. 3 vols. (Laffont, Paris, 1987.) (With the celebrated 'Quid de Proust', a Proustological compendium, and translated as *The Book of Proust* by J. Dalley, Chatto and Windus, London, 1989.)

Remembrance of Things Past. Trans. C. K. Scott Moncrieff and T. Kilmartin. 3 vols. (Chatto and Windus, London, and Random House, New York, 1981; also Penguin Books, Harmondsworth, 1983.) (The authoritative English translation, correcting Scott Moncrieff's errors and replacing his unreliable original by the scholarly and enlarged *Pléiade* 1954 text.)

Alla ricerca del tempo perduto. (Mondadori, Milan, 1983- .) (The first fully annotated edition of Proust's novel in any language, and a translation second only to Scott Moncrieff's in beauty of style.)

Albertine disparue. Ed. Nathalie Mauriac. (Grasset, Paris, 1987; English translation by T. Kilmartin, *Albertine Gone*, Chatto and Windus, 1989.) (Text from Proust's hitherto lost typescript of June 1922, rediscovered in 1986, with his last corrections, including, as I predicted, the change of title from *La Fugitive.*)

Pléiade IV   *Jean Santeuil; Les Plaisirs et les jours.* Ed. P. Clarac & Y. Sandre. (*Bibliothèque de la Pléiade*, Gallimard, Paris, 1971).

Pléiade V   *Contre Sainte-Beuve, Pastiches et mélanges, essais et articles.* Ed. P. Clarac & Y. Sandre. (*Bibliothèque de la Pléiade*, Gallimard, Paris, 1971.) (Unfortunately includes only one of the three alternative forms of *Contre Sainte-Beuve*, the critical essay, omitting the Narrator's conversation with his mother, and the novel which became a primitive version of *A la Recherche.* A new maximised edition of *CSB* is now much needed. The English version by Sylvia Townsend Warner, *By Way of Sainte-Beuve*, based on the original text published by Gallimard in 1954, is a translation of genius (Chatto and

Windus, London, 1958; reprinted as a Hogarth Press paperback, 1984, with a helpful introduction by T. Kilmartin.)

Cahier de 1908   *Le Cahier de 1908*. Ed. P. Kolb. (*Cahiers Marcel Proust*, n.s. no. 8, Gallimard, Paris, 1976.) (A notebook containing memoranda for the future *A la Recherche* and for *Contre Sainte-Beuve*, including evidence (pp. 49, 50, 135) that the character already in 1908 analogous to Albertine was to be kept by the Narrator as a captive, and the first mention of Le Cuziat, added towards 1911 to a list of manservants in noble families (pp. 116, 198).)

TR   *Textes retrouvés*. Ed. P. Kolb. (*Cahiers Marcel Proust*, n.s. no. 3, Gallimard, Paris, 1971.) (Includes texts lacking in *Pléiade* V, and vice-versa, so that both works are indispensable, and a bibliography of publications of Proust texts and letters 1892-1971 comprising 381 items.)

CK   *Correspondance*. Ed. P. Kolb. (Plon, Paris, 1970-   .) (In progress; vol. 16, comprising year 1917, published 1988.)

LR   *Lettres retrouvées*. Ed. P. Kolb. (Plon, Paris, 1966.) (A collection of 67 unsent letters, apparently stolen by a secretary and later acquired and misused by Charles Briand. Most important is the letter to Agostinelli, written unawares on the very day and hour of his death, 5 p.m. 30 May 1914.)

BIBLIOGRAPHIES

(See also bibliographies by P. Kolb in Proust, *Textes retrouvés*, above, and by H. Bonnet, *Marcel Proust de 1907 à 1904*, below, and current annual lists in RHLF.)

Chantal, René de. *Marcel Proust. Critique littéraire*, vol. 2, pp. 645-736. (Presses de l'Université de Montréal, Montreal, 1967.)

Gibson, R. 'Proust et la critique anglo-saxonne', in *Cahiers Marcel Proust*, n.s. no. 11, Gallimard, Paris, 1982. (Comprising 359 items from 1913 to 1979, including the correct attribution to Mary Duclaux, *née* Robinson, of the anonymous review of *Du côté de chez Swann* in *Times Literary Supplement* 4 December 1914, later included in her *Twentieth Century French Writers*, 1919, pp. 253-6, but hitherto wrongly assigned to A. B. Walkley.)

Graham, Victor E. *Bibliographie des études sur Marcel Proust et son œuvre*. (Droz, Geneva, 1976.) (2274 items.)

Russell Taylor, Elisabeth. *Marcel Proust and his Contexts. A critical bibliography of English-language scholarship*. (Garland Publishing, New York & London, 1981.) (1393 items.)

BIOGRAPHICAL MATERIAL

(Memoirs by Proust's friends, associates or contemporaries, modern biographies of these, and other source-works relevant to Proust's life and world.)

Adam   *Adam International Review*. Ed. Miron Grindea. Special Proust numbers I-VIII: no. 260 (1957); nos. 297-8 (1961); nos. 310-12 (1966); nos. 349-51 (1971); nos. 364-6 (1972); nos. 394-6 (1976); nos. 449-55 (1984); nos. 452-4 (1984), so numbered and dated. (These special Proust issues, containing unique primary and critical material and *inédits*, ought to be in every academic or Proustian library, but are not. Complete sets are said to be still available from 28 Emperor's Gate, London, sw7.)

Albaret   Albaret, Céleste. *Monsieur Proust*. (Laffont, Paris, 1973.) (Céleste is an incomparable witness to all she herself saw of Proust or heard him say, but apt to deny all else as mere invention. Much of her memories had been disclosed in published interviews and used in this biography. Much is new, notably her revelations on Proust's association with Le Cuziat and his brothel, including even his spying on the Man in Chains. My name appears in the index as 'Harold D. Painter'.)

Bareau, Juliet Wilson. 'Édouard Vuillard at les princes Bibesco', in *Revue de l'art*, no. 74 (1986) 37-46. (With full discussion of Vuillard's contacts with Proust, including Proust's visit towards 31 August 1907 to his studio—not at Cabourg but at Amfreville seven miles west—which provided hints for Elstir.)

Bibesco, Princesse Marthe. *Le Confesseur et les poètes*. (Grasset, Paris, 1970.) (Letters to the Abbé Mugnier from Proust, Cocteau, Montesquiou.)

Bibliothèque Nationale. *Marcel Proust. Catalogue de l'exposition*, juin 1965. (Paris, 1965.) (Still a valuable primary source, citing many unpublished documents.)

Curtiss, Mina. *Other People's Letters*. (Macmillan, London, 1978.) (An audacious, wittily endearing foray into post-Occupation Paris in quest of Proust letters and memories. Mina Curtiss met Daniel Halévy, Céleste, Suzy Mante-Proust, Dr Lemasle (an associate, as Mme Scheikévitch told her, of "Albert, the Jupien of the novel", and a collector of Proust's letters "to various low-life types"—perhaps the very letters which Le Cuziat said: "I gave to my doctor"?)—and Antoine Bibesco, aged 69, for whom she underwent what lesser women might have thought a fate worse than death: "Enfin to talk about Proust in a horizontal position was as relaxing, as useful, as the thought of his ghost in the room was amusing.")

De Cossart, Michael. *The Food of Love. Princesse Edmond de Polignac and her salon*. (Hamish Hamilton, London, 1978.) (The social, musical and lesbian worlds of Princesse Winnaretta often and illuminatingly intermingle with Proust's.)

Diesbach, Ghislain de. *La Princesse Bibesco*. (Perrin, Paris, 1986.) (A large-scale, documented, sensitive biography of Marthe Bibesco, though underrating her works on Proust and her unfinished masterpiece *La Nymphe Europe*.)

Duplay, Maurice. *Mon ami Marcel Proust. Souvenirs intimes.* (*Cahiers Marcel Proust*, n.s. no. 5, Gallimard, Paris, 1972.)

Forssgren, Ernest. 'Les mémoires d'un valet de chambre', in *Cahiers Marcel Proust*, n.s. no. 7, pp. 119-42 (Gallimard, Paris, 1975.) (Written in old age by a Swedish manservant who attended Proust at Cabourg in September 1914 and reappeared in Paris in September 1922. Céleste summed him up as "so infatuated with himself that he must have thought he was the King of Sweden at least, if not God", and reports Proust as saying: "You know, Céleste, he annoys me and bores me, this Ernest." See *Albaret* 45, 50. Forssgren himself says Proust told him: "Ernest, in all my life I have never known a person I liked as much as I like you.")

Gautier-Vignal, Louis. *Proust connu et inconnu*. (Laffont, Paris, 1976.) (Memoirs of one of the last survivors who saw Marcel plain. Reviewed by me in *Adam*, 1976.)

Gimpel, René. *Journal d'un collectionneur-marchand de tableaux*. (Calmann-Lévy, Paris, 1973.) (Gimpel was the art-dealer, met at Cabourg in 1908, who gave Proust a jewelled cross for his Légion d'Honneur in September 1920. See *Gimpel* 296-7, *MP* II 305.)

Gold, Arthur and Fizdale, Robert. *Misia*. (Macmillan, London, 1980.) (The biography of Misia Godebska, later Natanson, later Edwards, later Sert, friend of Proust and Diaghilev, original of Princesse Yourbeletieff in *A la Recherche*.)

Harding, James. *Agate*. (Methuen, London, 1986.) (For James Agate as a frequenter of Le Cuziat's brothel see pp. 49-54, also further references by Agate himself in *Ego* I, IV 187, V 57-8. Harding mentions 'my old friend Marcel Jouhandeau' as 'another satisfied customer', with reference to Jouhandeau's *La Vie comme une fête*, 1977, pp. 139-40 for 'further details of Proust's *ébats charnels*'.)

Jullian, Philippe. 'Charles Haas', in *Gazette des beaux-arts* (1971), 239-56. (A documented biography of the original of Proust's Swann, revealing that his great love and mother of his daughter Luisita (1881-1956) was marquise Adélaïde d'Audiffret, *née* Arellano.)

——, ——. *Robert de Montesquiou. Un prince 1900.* (Perrin, Paris, 1965.) (With rich source material from Montesquiou archives, by a delightful writer who calls his subject 'Saint-Charlus'.)

Plantevignes, Marcel. *Avec Marcel Proust.* (Nizet, Paris, 1966.) (An old man's sunlit though repetitious memories of Proust at Cabourg. It was this 'other Marcel', as Proust called him, who was startled like the Narrator by the sudden apparition of an aeroplane when riding on the seashore, and supplied the title of *A l'ombre des jeunes filles en fleurs* and the bluetits in the blossoming appletrees. See pp. 304, 351-2, 544, 669; *Pléiade* II 781, 1028. The language and rhythm of Proust's talk have never been more convincingly transcribed. Reviewed by me in *Adam*, 1966.)

Samuels, Ernest. *Bernard Berenson. The making of a legend.* (Harvard University Press, Cambridge Mass., London, 1987.) (Berenson met Proust only once, at Walter Berry's on 30 April 1918, describing him as 'a dark rather long-haired man ... In voice and diction singularly like Montesquiou.' See pp. 233-4, 629. But this fine biography includes much on common friends including Montesquiou, Gladys Deacon, Lucien Henraux.)

Sebba, Anne. *Enid Bagnold.* (Weidenfeld and Nicolson, London, 1986.) (A writer, character and hostess with a touch of greatness, much involved with Antoine and all the Bibescos.)

Vickers, Hugo. *Gladys, Duchess of Marlborough.* (Weidenfeld and Nicolson, London, 1979.) (A brilliant life of Proust's longlived pin-up Gladys Deacon, 1881-1977.)

CRITICISM, PASTICHE, TEXTUAL STUDIES

Assouline, Pierre & Taillandier, François. 'Le 5 octobre Proust vous appartient!', in *Lire*, no. 145 (oct. 1987), 43-61. (A survey of new editions and unpublished manuscripts of *A la Recherche* in the month of its entry into 'public domain'.)

Bardèche, Maurice. *Marcel Proust romancier.* 2 vols. (Les Sept Couleurs, Paris, 1971.) (An important pioneer study in use and citation of Proust's unpublished manuscript drafts as evidence for the evolution of *A la Recherche*.)

Bonnet, Henri. *Marcel Proust de 1907 à 1914.* 2 vols. (Nizet, Paris, 1971, 1976.) (With extensive bibliographies, including an updated summary of Proust manuscripts in the Bibliothèque Nationale, in vol. 2, pp. 105-16.)

Johnson, Pamela Hansford. *Six Proust Reconstructions.* (Macmillan, London, 1958.) (Radio plays dramatising in sympathetic pastiche episodes which Proust did not include in *A la Recherche* but almost might have; a work, as Proust said of his own pastiches, 'of criticism in action'.)

Moss, Howard. *The Magic Lantern of Marcel Proust.* (Macmillan, New York, 1962; Faber and Faber, London, 1963.)

Mouton, Jean. *Proust.* (*Les écrivains devant Dieu.*) (Desclée de Brouwer, Paris, 1968.) (A rehabilitation of Proust, writer and man, as an *anima naturaliter christiana*.)

Pinter, Harold. *The Proust Screenplay.* (Eyre Methuen, London, 1978.) (The totality of

Proust's novel condensed, without apparent distortion, into an as yet unperformed filmscript by a master of words.)

Shattuck, Roger. *Proust's Binoculars*. (Random House, New York, 1963; Chatto and Windus, London, 1964.) (Having read and recommended this and Howard Moss's book—see above—for their English publishers 25 years ago, I recommend them still to all readers.)

Stern, Frances. *A Concordance to Proust*. (Adam Books, 28 Emperor's Gate, London, 1987.) (A bold essay in intertextuality, proposing consecutive verbal parallels between *Du côté de chez Swann* and Dante's *Inferno*, Racine's *Phèdre*, Goethe's *Faust*, and Wagner's *Parsifal*. Although I feel regretfully unable to concede the objective reality of these parallels as presented, or Proust's actual use of them whether consciously or unconsciously, the juxtaposition of texts makes magnificent reading. As to the general presence of all four works in Proust's mind and novel, Stern "is surely right"—see my article in *Adam* 1984.)

Winton, later Finch, Alison. *Proust's Additions. The making of A la Recherche du Temps Perdu*. 2 vols. (Cambridge University Press, Cambridge, 1977.) (A study of Proust's post-1914 manuscript drafts and their evolution through his vast additions to the final version.)

BY GEORGE D. PAINTER

(I have ventured to include here, for completeness and for relevance to this biography, the following list of my own articles, reviews and other fugitive publications on Proust during the past forty years.)

Review (unsigned) of H. March, *The Two Worlds of Marcel Proust*, in *The Listener*, 19 May 1949.

Review of F. C. Green, *The Mind of Proust*, in *The Listener*, 8 December 1949.

Review (unsigned) of Proust, *Letters to a Friend* (*G. de Lauris*), in *The Listener*, 16 February 1950.

Review (unsigned) of Proust, *Letters*, trans. Mina Curtiss, in *The Listener*, 21 December 1950. ("In her translation Proust's real voice, as in Scott Moncrieff his ideal voice, speaks again".)

Reviews (unsigned) of P. A. Spalding, *A Reader's Handbook to Proust*, in *New Statesman*, 26 January 1952, and *The Listener*, 22 May 1952.

Review (unsigned) of Proust, *Letters to Antoine Bibesco*, in *The Listener*, 10 December 1953.

'Time Retained' (review of *Jean Santeuil*, trans. G. Hopkins), in *The Listener*, 6 October 1955.

'Proust's Way', in *Marcel Proust. Letters to his Mother*. Trans. and ed. George D. Painter (Rider, London, 1956.) (A brief preliminary sketch for the present biography.)

'Plays on Proust' (review of Pamela Hansford Johnson, *Six Proust Reconstructions*, in *New Statesman*, 5 April 1958.

Review of *Adam* no. 260, in *The Listener*, 21 January 1960.

Maurois, André, *The Chelsea Way, or Marcel in England. A Proustian Parody*. Trans. (from *Le Côté de Chelsea*) with introduction and notes by George D. Painter (Weidenfeld and Nicolson, London, 1966).

'Proust, Paul Desjardins et Pontigny', in *Entretiens sur Marcel Proust. Centre culturel international de Cerisy-la-Salle*, pp. 279-83 (Éditions Mouton, Paris, 1966).

'The Sunlight of Balbec' (review of M. Plantevignes, *Avec Marcel Proust*, in *Adam*, nos. 310-12 (1966), 127-8.

'Proust's Letters to Sydney and Violet Schiff', in *British Museum Quarterly*, vol. 32, nos. 3-4 (1968), 65-74.

Review of Proust, *Time Regained*, trans. Andreas Mayor, in *The Listener*, 26 February 1970.

'Centenary of Proust', in *Journal of the Franco-British Society*, vol. 27, no. 100 (summer 1971), 10-11.

'Proust and Virginia Woolf', in *Adam*, nos. 364-6 (1972), 17-23.

'Proust Known and Unknown' (review of L. Gautier-Vignal, *Proust connu et inconnu*), in *Adam*, nos. 394-6 (1976), 12-14.

'Proust and Chateaubriand', in Royal Society of Literature, *Essays by Divers Hands*, n.s. vol. 41 (1980), 68-82.

'Remembrance of Pamela and Proust', in *Adam*, nos. 440-2 (1982), 21-3. (On my meetings with Pamela Hansford Johnson, later Lady Snow, and her writings on Proust. The same issue includes her Proust pastiche 'Albertine at the Royal Court'.)

Grosskurth, Phyllis. An Interview with George Painter, in *Salmagundi*, no. 61 (fall 1983), 22-41 (Skidmore College, Saratoga Springs, N.Y.).

'Threads through Proust's Labyrinth' (advance notice of Frances Stern, *Concordance to Proust*), in *Adam*, nos. 449-55 (1984), 4-5.

INDEXES

VOLUME I
VOLUME II

(VOLUME I)

Two separate indexes are provided, the first of real persons and places, the second of fictitious characters and places in Proust's novel, A la Recherche du Temps Perdu. In order to facilitate the tracing of discussions in the text of Proust's models in real life, cross-references from each index to the other have been given, where applicable, in capitals and parentheses; but the reader should remember that these discussions are sometimes necessarily incomplete, and are subject to supplementation in the second and final volume.

I. PERSONS AND PLACES

Abbeville, 292-3
Adam, Antoine, xv
——, Paul, 209
Agostinelli, Alfred, 31, 220, 272
Aigle, Marquise d', 150
Ainslie, Douglas, 256-7, 267
Aix-les-Bains, 79, 311
Albaret, Céleste, 6, 41, 215
Albufera, Marquis Louis d' (SAINT-LOUP), 310, 317-27, 335
Alençon, Émilienne d' (RACHEL), 163
Alexandra, Queen, 151, 162-3
——, Tzarina (EUDOXIE, Queen), 196
Allard, Adeline, 186
——, Marthe, 186
Amiens, 258, 260-4, 278, 292-3
Amiot, André, 19
——, Jules (ADOLPHE, Uncle), 12-19, 25-7, 36, 201, 324
——, Mme ——, *née* Élisabeth Proust (LÉONIE, Aunt), 12-19, 21, 36
Amsterdam, 262, 306
Anaxagoras, 164
Angelico, Fra, 187
Angélique, servant, 57, 75
Annunzio, Gabriele d', 99, 131, 228
Antwerp, 306
Arenberg, Prince Auguste d' (AGRIGENTE, Prince d'), 92, 150
——, Princesse ——, 150
Arman de Caillavet, Albert (VERDURIN, M.), 65-7, 236
——, Mme ——, *née* Léontine Lippmann (VERDURIN, Mme), 65-71, 76-7, 101, 106, 125, 169, 190-1, 194, 210, 214, 223, 235-8, 278, 330

——, Gaston (SAINT-LOUP), 71, 76-7, 81-3, 85, 114, 210, 214, 235-6, 278, 319
——, Mme ——, *née* Jeanne Pouquet (GILBERTE), 77-9, 81-3, 85, 87, 109, 137, 278
——, Simone (SAINT-LOUP, Mlle de), 83
Artagnan, Château d', 125
——, d', musketeer, *see* Batz
Astruc, Gabriel, 94
Aubernon, Georges, 98
——, Mme ——, *née* Lydie de Nerville (VERDURIN, Mme), 67, 85, 98-104, 106, 117, 151, 155, 177, 208, 228-9, 296, 331
——, Raoul, 98
Aubert, Edgar, 121-4, 135-8, 275, 319
Aurore, L', 228, 248
Autret, Jean, xv, 281
Avallon, 327

Baignères, Arthur, 116
——, Mme ——, *née* Charlotte de Formeville, 121
——, Henri, 64
——, Mme ——, *née* Laure Boillay (LEROI, Mme), 64, 83-5, 99, 121, 136, 186, 251
——, Jacques, 64, 71, 138, 251
Bailby, Jeanne, 244
——, Léon, 237, 244
Bailleau-le-Pin (ROUSSAINVILLE), 24
Balzac, Honoré de, 23, 70, 167, 183, 196, 233
Banquet, Le, 113-15, 138 ;0, 190, 335

Barbarin, Thomas de, 118, 243
Barbey d'Aurevilly, Jules, 131
Barbusse, Henri, 114
Barrère, Camille (NORPOIS), 63, 329-30
Barrès, Maurice (BERGOTTE), 70, 97, 131, 138, 148, 202-3, 209, 211, 220, 224, 233-5, 249, 279, 313
Barrie, James, 275
Bartet, Mlle, 124, 145
Bartholoni, Mme, 241, 247
——, Kiki, 241, 286
Barthou, Louis, 249, 335
Bassaraba, Villa (FÉTERNE), 240-5, 254
Bastian, Mme, 221
Batz, Charles de, d'Artagnan, 125, 127, 210
Baudelaire, Charles, 46, 118, 136, 141
Bauer, Henri, 213
——, Mgr, 152
Bauffremont, family, 125
Bazin, René, 228
Beaulaincourt, Comte de, 157
——, Comtesse Sophie de (VILLE-PARISIS, Mme de), 155-9
Beaune, 328
Becque, Henri, 102
Beg-Meil (BALBEC), 79, 182-4, 198-200, 204, 207, 254, 266
Belle-Isle, 182
Belle-Rive (RIVEBELLE), 242
Bénac, André, 182, 198
Benardaky, Marie de (GILBERTE), 43-50, 175, 193, 231, 283, 316, 330
——, Nelly de, 44-6, 157
——, Nicolas de (SWANN), 44, 48
——, Mme — de, (ODETTE), 44, 48
Benda, Julien, 248
Benedetti, Comte (NORPOIS), 96
Béraud, Jean (ELSTIR), 105, 166, 209, 211, 214
Bergson, Henri (BERGOTTE), 68, 80, 279, 295
Bernhardt, Sarah (BERMA), 46, 69, 129, 145, 182, 232, 288, 321
Bernstein, Henry, 298
Berry, Walter, 275
Bert, Paul, 294
Berthelot, Daniel, 140
——, Philippe, 140
Bertillon, Alphonse, 244
Bibesco, Prince Antoine, 197, 295-314, 317-23, 328, 335
——, Prince Emmanuel, 295-314

——, Princesse Hélène, 295, 306-7
Bible d'Amiens, 258, 260, 268-77, 287, 292, 304, 311, 313, 318, 322, 336
Biedermann, family, 243
Billy, Comte Robert de, 73-4, 80-1, 94, 109, 117-18, 121-3, 135-8, 141, 170, 180, 198, 225, 257, 275, 293, 297, 302, 327
——, Comtesse ——, *née* Jeanne Mirabaud, 180
Bing, Siegfried, 300
Bischoffsheim, Raphael, 86
Bizet, Georges, 41, 89
——, Jacques, 41, 56, 60-1, 64, 71, 89, 114, 117, 213, 223, 251, 326
Bjoernson, Mlle, 65
Blanc, Jean, 215
Blanche, Dr Antoine, 84-5
——, Mme —, 84, 164
——, Jacques Émile (ELSTIR), 62, 84-85, 88, 94, 101, 132, 135, 148, 164, 166, 170, 175, 213, 227, 249
Bloch, Albert, 224
Blocqueville, Marquise Adélaïde de, 158
Blum, Léon, 114, 138, 140, 190
Boegner, M., 73
Boigne, Comtesse de (BEAUSERGENT), 158, 286
Boileau, 7
Boisboudran, Château de, 148-9
Boisdeffre, General de, 225-8, 231
Boissonnas, Jean, 80, 122
Boldini, Jean, 129, 210-11
Bonaparte, Princesse Mathilde, *see* Mathilde
Bonnard, Pierre, 295
Borda, Gustave de, 210, 214
Bordeaux, Henry, 241, 259
Botticelli, 15, 58, 86, 281
Boulanger, General Georges, 43, 163, 204, 302
Bourges, 262
Bourget, Paul (BERGOTTE), 68, 87, 91, 96, 115, 161, 166, 279
Brancovan, Anna de, *see* Noailles
——, Prince Constantin de, 241, 244-245, 268, 274, 288, 290, 295, 305, 313
——, Prince Grégoire de, 238
——, Hélène de, *see* Chimay
——, Princesse Rachilde de (CAMBREMER), 136, 212, 238, 240-1, 295
Brantes, Marquise de, 161, 177, 288-9

Breteuil, Comte Henri de (BRÉAUTÉ), 111-12, 150-1, 160, 216
——, Comtesse —, née Garner, 112, 151
Briand, Aristide, 229, 249
Briey, Comte de, 288
——, Mme de (VERDURIN), 288
Brissac, Duc de, 233
Brissaud, Dr Édouard (E., Professor), 292, 331
Broca, Auguste (COTTARD), 330
Brochard, Victor (BRICHOT), 67, 84, 101-4, 228, 232, 234
Broglie, Princesse Albertine de, 165
Brooks, Mme Romaine, 159
Bruges, 150, 306
Brunet, Maitre, 137
Brunetière, Ferdinand, 228
Brunschwicg, Léon (BLOCH), 43, 71
Bulletin de l'Union pour l'Action Morale, 256-7
Byron, Lord, 284-5

Cabourg (BALBEC), 52-3, 75, 79, 83, 117, 325
Caen, 31, 202, 293
Caillavet, see Arman de Caillavet
Calmann Lévy, 175, 194, 199
Calmette, Gaston, 220, 263, 313-14, 318
Cambronne, 90
Camondo, Abraham, 117
——, Nissim (BERNARD), 117
Camus (CAMUS), 20, 30
Caraman-Chimay, see Chimay
Caran d'Ache, 89, 289
Cardane, 314, 318
Carlyle, Thomas, 183, 275, 277
Caro, Elme, 166
Carpaccio, 271
Carré, Abbé Louis, 22, 301
Casa-Fuerte, Marquise Flavie de, 129, 132, 188
——, Illan de, 129
Casimir-Périer, Pierre, 329
Castellane, Marquis Antoine de, 215
——, Comte Boni de (SAINT-LOUP), 154-7, 160, 214-16, 236, 316
——, Comtesse —, née Anna Gould, 153, 216, 236
——, Maréchal Boniface de, 148, 156
——, Comtesse Jean de, née Dorothée de Talleyrand-Périgord (GUER-MANTES, Princesse de), 153

Castiglione, Comtesse de, 129
Catusse, Mme Anatole, 53-5, 172, 231, 303, 312
Cavaignac, Godefroi de, 231
Cazalis, Henri (LEGRANDIN), 37, 79, 103, 194
Céleste, see Albaret
Cerisier, baker, 197
Chabrillan, Comtesse de, 153
Chambord, Comte de, 111, 165
Chaponay, Mme de (ALIX), 158
Charcot, Jean Martin, 2
Chardin, Jean, 207
Charpentier, Gustave, 224
Chartres, 1, 3, 13-14, 18, 75, 178, 262, 264, 278, 282, 300-1, 333
Chateaubriand, Francois René de, 36, 148, 156, 241
Châteaudun, 3, 20, 36
Chauffard, Dr, 2
Chefdebien, M., 243
Chénier, André, 55
Chevigné, Comte Adhéaume de, 111, 155, 163, 230
——, Comtesse —, née Laure de Sade (GUERMANTES, Duchesse de), 92, 109-15, 119, 150, 155, 159-61, 166, 230
Chevilly, Marie de (ALBERTINE), 247, 259
——, Pierre de, 242-3, 247, 258, 267, 293
Chimay, family, 125
——, Prince Alexandre de, 238, 240, 244
——, Princess —, née Hélène de Brancovan, 238-9, 244, 288, 291, 318, 335
——, Ghislaine de, 149
——, Prince Joseph de, father, 147, 163
——, —, son, 147
——, Princesse —, née Clara Ward, 147
——, Princesse Marie de, 147
Cholet, Lieutenant Comte de (SAINT-LOUP), 73, 252
Chronique des Arts et de la Curiosité, 263, 273
Clairin, Georges (BRICHOT), 105-6, 223
Clemenceau, Georges, 203, 221, 223, 229, 235, 240, 248

Clermont-Tonnerre, Marquis Philibert de, 315
——, Marquise ——, *née* Élisabeth de Gramont, 170, 294, 315, 323
Clomesnil, Léonie (ODETTE), 57-8
Cochin, Denis, 323
Cocteau, Jean, 299
Cœur-Volant, (RASPELIÈRE, La), 102-4
Coislin, Comte de, 157
Colette, Mme, 210
Collingwood, W. G., 278
Combes, Émile, 323, 334
Comte, Harlette, *see* Gregh
Contades, Marquis de, 157
——, Antoine de, 157
Contre Sainte-Beuve, 6, 141, 262, 272-3, 284
Coppée, François, 131, 218
Coppet, Château de, 92, 245
Corneille, Pierre, 55, 141
Corvo, Baron, 285
Costa de Beauregard, Comte, 111, 150
Cotard, Dr (COTTARD), 2, 331
Cottet, Dr (COTTARD), 244, 331
Coucy, 303-4
Coudrée, 241, 247
Cour Brûlée, Manoir de la (RASPELIÉRE, La), 104, 117
Crémieux, Louise, *see* Cruppi
Criqueboeuf (CARQUEVILLE), 117
Cruppi, Jean, 283
——, Mme ——, *née* Louise Crémieux, 283
Cucheval, Victor, 55-7, 164
Curnonsky, 290
Cuyp, Albert, 178

Daireaux, Mlles, 82
Damoiseau (BORANGE), 20-1, 25
Dancogné, Mlles, 82
Dante Alighieri, 187, 304
Darblay, Louis, 77
Darlu, Alphonse (BERGOTTE), 59, 60, 74, 81, 113, 120, 179, 202, 223-6
Daudet, Alphonse (BERGOTTE), 53, 185-7, 209, 219-20, 256-7
——, Mme ——, 186
——, Edmée, 187
——, Léon, 101, 186, 196, 209, 227, 248, 263, 288-90, 315, 319-20, 332
——, Lucien, 6, 180, 186-9, 196, 220, 293, 315, 331
Dauphiné, François, 55-6

Debove, Dr., 335
Debussy, Claude (VINTEUIL), 172-3, 208, 290-1, 295
Decaze, Duc, 164
Degas, Edgar (ELSTIR), 89, 91, 131, 280
Delafosse, Léon (MOREL), 143-6, 169, 176, 188, 210-13, 240, 325
Delaunay, Élie, 89, 91
Delft, 307-8
Delion, hatter, 94
Denis, Maurice, 140
Déroulède, Paul, 235
Desbordes-Valmore, Marceline, 142-5, 193
Deschanel, Paul, 319
Desjardins, Paul, 80, 223, 256
Desvaux, gunsmith, 20
Detaille, Édouard, 105, 151
Dickens, Charles, 39, 121, 275
Dieppe, 52, 84, 181, 194, 201, 326
Dieulafoy, Dr Georges (COTTARD; DIEULAFOY), 331
——, Jane, 331
——, Marcel, 331
Dijon, 327
Doasan, Baron Jacques (CHARLUS), 102-4, 129, 130, 148, 151, 155, 176, 208, 252
Dordrecht, 306
Dostoevsky, 12, 70
Douglas, Lord Alfred (MOREL), 170, 176
Doyen, Dr Eugène Louis (COTTARD), 330
Dreyfus, Captain Alfred, 221-2, 239-240, 247-8
——, Mathieu, 223, 240
——, Robert, 41-3, 46, 55, 57, 75, 114-15, 210, 213, 335
—— Affair, 85, 94, 118, 147, 200, 203-4, 212, 218, 220-50, 282, 324-5
Drumont, Édouard, 170, 220, 248
Dubois-Amiot, Marthe, *see* Proust
Dumas, Alexandre, the Elder, 125, 194
——, ——, the Younger, 66, 95, 106
Duncan, Isadora, 129
Duplay, Maurice, 283, 312-14, 327
——, Simon, 283, 312, 317, 325
Dupré, M., 56
Dupuy, Charles, 283
Dürer, Albrecht, 95
Duse, Eleanora, 129

Edmond, Charles, 179
Édouard, Julien, 258, 265-6
Edward VII, 93, 113, 151, 162, 216
Eiffel, M., 58
Eliot, George, 39, 70, 121, 196, 259, 275
Emerson, Ralph Waldo, 298
Enesco, Georges, 136
Épeautrolles, 201
Ephrussi, Charles (SWANN), 95-6, 263
Eppler (JUPIEN), 5, 241, 286
Ermenonville, Château d', 316
Esnault, draper, 3
Esterhazy, Major, 222-4, 227, 231
Eugénie, Empress, 3, 152, 157, 162, 188, 328
Evans, Dr Thomas, 217
Évian (BALBEC). 240-7, 254, 283-4, 305-6, 325-8
Évreux, 36
Eyragues, Comtesse Charles d', née Henriette de Montesquiou, 288-9

Falguière, Joseph, 149
Fallières, Armand, 335
Faudoas, Mme de, 128
Faure, Antoinette (GILBERTE), 43, 50-1, 172
——, Félix, 43, 195, 223, 232, 235
——, Mme Félix, 44
——, Lucie, 43-4, 75, 304
Fauré, Gustave (VINTEUIL), 118, 132, 136, 164, 172-3, 291, 295, 315
Fauvel, Dr, 2, 328
Fénelon, Comte Bertrand de (SAINT-LOUP), 202, 296-313, 321-7
Fermont, M., 183
Féternes (FÉTERNE), 242
Fifine, servant, 81
Figaro, Le, 66, 170, 190, 210. 223, 262-4, 273-4, 278, 288, 306, 313-14, 318-19
Finaly, family (BLOCHS), 121-2, 140
——, Horace (BLOCH), 75, 115-19
——, Hugo (BLOCH, Senior), 116
——, Mme — (BLOCH, Mme), 116
——, Marie (ALBERTINE; BLOCH, Mlle), 115-19, 136, 140, 243, 253, 306
Fitau, Félicie (FRANÇOISE), 187, 195, 286, 305
FitzJames, Comte Robert de, 110, 155, 160-1, 233
——, Comtesse —, née Rosa de Gutmann, 93, 113, 146, 161

Flament, Albert, 86, 113, 185-6, 214, 230, 236-8, 296
Flaubert, Gustave, 12, 70, 74, 95, 97 208, 261, 292, 294, 315
Flers, Comte Robert de, 114, 122-3, 210, 223, 236, 290, 319
Fleury, Comte de (NORPOIS), 157
Florence, 258, 260, 267, 271
Fogazzaro, Antonio, 99
Fontainebleau (DONCIÈRES), 74-5, 196-9, 205, 282, 308
Forain, Jean Louis, 91, 131, 209, 213-214, 226, 228, 234, 288
Fortuny, Mme, 247
Fould, Mme Léon, 297
Fragonard, Jean Honoré, 216
France, Anatole (BERGOTTE), 44, 59, 65-70, 75, 92, 101, 115, 128, 175, 177, 179, 190, 203, 209, 213-14, 220, 223, 229-30, 232, 235-8, 246, 248-9, 251, 278-80, 288, 295, 328-9
——, Mme —, 67
——, Suzanne, 246-7, 288
Franck, César (VINTEUIL), 173
Franklin, Alfred, 180, 184, 198, 266
Frémonts, Les (RASPELIÈRE, La), 83-5, 104, 116-18, 122
Freud, Sigmund, 2
Frohsdorf, 111
Fromentin, Eugène, 306
Fürstenberg, Prince Karl Egon von, 86, 153

Galbois, Baronne de (MONTERIENDER; VARAMBON), 97-8
Gallé, Émile, 131, 223
Galliffet, General Marquis Gaston de (FROBERVILLE), 93-4, 151-2, 155, 239, 248-9, 331
——, Marquise —, 84
Gallou, Ernestine (FRANÇOISE), 14-20, 201
Galopin, Dr (GALOPIN; PERCEPIED), 20
——, Mlle, see Goupil
Ganay, Marquis de, 93
——, Comte de, 233
Ganderax, Louis, 90-2, 96, 141, 232, 273-4, 331
Garner, Miss, see Breteuil
Garros, Roland, 272
Gaucher, Maxime, 55-6, 59
Gaulois, Le, 146, 173, 181, 190, 215, 263

Gautier, Théophile, 26, 39, 219, 242
Gazette de France, 233
— des Beaux-Arts, 95, 263-4, 273-4, 277
Geneviève de Brabant, 23, 112, 202
Germain, André, 129, 153, 187
——, Mme, 208
Gervex, Henri (ELSTIR), 166, 218
Ghirlandaio, 187
Gide, André, 53, 120, 138, 140, 170, 224
Gil Blas, 304, 317
Gillou, Mme Albert, 91
Giotto, 264, 271-2
Giraud, Julien, 41
Goethe, 78, 196
Golo, 23, 202
Goncourt, Edmond de, 7-8, 64, 95, 98, 126, 131, 149-50, 157-8, 185
Gontaut-Biron, Comte Joseph de, 111
Gougeon, M. (PONCIN), 243-4, 325
Gould, Anna, see Castellane
Gounod, Charles, 52, 54, 172, 271, 295
Goupil, Mme, née Galopin (GOUPIL, Mme), 20, 29
——, Mlle, 29, 302
Goussencourt, family (GUERMANTES), 22, 34
Grainger, Percy, 212
Gramont, Duc Agénor de (GUER-MANTES, Duc de), 125, 142, 150, 302, 315
——, Duchesse —, née Marguerite de Rothschild, 142, 315
——, Élisabeth de, see Clermont-Tonnerre
Grancey, Comte Charles de, 123
Greco, El, 207
Greffulhe, Charles, 148
——, Cordélia, 148, 156
——, Comte Henri (GUERMANTES, Duc de), 147-50, 206
——, Comtesse —, née Élisabeth de Chimay (GUERMANTES, Duchesse de), 66, 93, 98, 129, 142-54, 164, 216, 243, 291, 295, 306, 318, 330
Gregh, Fernand, 59, 66, 70, 75, 101, 104, 114-18, 138, 140, 169, 190, 213, 223
——, Mme —, née Harlette Comte, 306
Grey, Lady de, Marchioness of Ripon, 92

Groult, Camille, 216
Guérin, Jules, 235
Guerne, Comtesse Marie de, 166
Guiche, Duc Armand de (SAINT-LOUP), 310, 315-16, 319-20, 323
Guiraud, Ernest, 92
Guyon, Dr (COTTARD), 330
Gyp, see Martel, Comtesse de

Haarlem, 307
Haas, Charles (SWANN), 39, 44, 90-6, 104, 111, 126, 128, 138, 150-1, 155, 160-2, 164, 174, 249, 291
——, Luisita, 94-5
Hague, The, 307
Hahn, Carlos, 217
——, Mme —, 268, 271
——, Clarita, see Seminario
——, Maria, 180-5, 219, 247
——, Reynaldo, 111, 162, 166, 170-89, 194, 198, 203-7, 210, 213-14, 217-20, 230, 242, 248, 252, 260, 268-72, 275, 284, 288, 290-1, 293, 306, 315, 321
Halévy, Daniel, 56, 60-3, 75, 114, 176, 199, 223
——, Élie, 81, 223
——, Léon, 89
——, Ludovic, 91
Hals, Frans, 306
Hanotaux, Gabriel (NORPOIS), 63, 179, 185, 195, 329-30
Hardy, Thomas, 70, 275
Harrison, Alexander (ELSTIR), 183-4, 207
Hata, gardener, 134
Haussonville, Comte Othenin de (GUERMANTES, Duc de), 92, 165-6, 228, 232
——, Comtesse —, née Pauline d'Har-court (CAMBREMER), 164-6, 245-6
Hayman, Laure (ODETTE), 49, 85-8, 94, 153, 174, 187, 192, 252-3
Heath, Willie, 123-4, 137-8, 175-6, 178, 275, 293, 327
Hébert, Ernest (ELSTIR), 149, 152
Hébrard, Adrien, 234
Hellbronner, family, 325
Helleu, Paul (ELSTIR), 131, 149
Hendlé, Mme, 258
Hennequeville, 117
Henraux, Lucien, 301-2
Henry, Major Joseph, 221-5, 228, 231-3
Herbert, Michael, 86

Heredia, José Maria de, 97, 131, 133, 138, 140, 175, 208, 234
——, Hélène de, 140
——, Louise de, 140
——, Marie de, *see* Regnier
Hermant, Abel, 91, 101, 240, 244-5, 288, 290, 317
Hérold, Ferdinand, 140
Hervey de Saint-Denis, Marquis d', 159
——, Marquise d' (ORVILLERS, Princesse d'), 146, 159-60
Hervieu, Paul (SWANN), 75, 91, 104, 125, 220, 227-8, 289, 314, 319
Hesiod, 191
Hochon, Mme (VERDURIN), 195, 251
Holland, 204, 231, 306-7
Homer, 54-5
Honfleur, 117-18, 306
Housman, A. E., 285
Howland, Mme Meredith, 135, 139, 146, 212
Hugo, Georges, 133, 229
——, Victor, 133, 229
Humières, Vicomte Robert d', 275
Huysmans, Joris Karl, 102, 126, 131

Ibsen, Henrik, 81, 100
Illiers (COMBRAY), 1, 3, 7, 10, 13-39, 52, 191, 197, 282, 293, 300-1, 307, 324-5, 334
——, Basin d', 23, 155
——, Florent d', 21-3
——, Geoffroy d' (GILBERT THE BAD), 23-4
——, Miles d', 23
Indy, Vincent d' (VINTEUIL), 173
Intransigeant, L', 324
Isabella, Queen of Spain, 113
Izoulet-Loubatière, Jean, 183

James, Henry, 285
Jammes, Francis, 38
Janzé, Vicomtesse Alix de (ALIX), 158
Jaucourt, Marquise de, 216
Jaurès, Jean, 221, 229
Jean Santeuil, 3, 6, 7, 10-11, 38, 42, 45, 47, 49, 59, 62, 69, 73, 75, 79, 85, 88, 115, 118, 139, 165, 174-8, 181-5, 189, 193, 197-207, 215, 219-20, 225, 231, 239, 244-5, 250-6, 259, 277-8, 293, 299-301, 325
Joan, of Arc, 23, 42

Joinville d'Artois, Juliette (VINTEUIL, Mlle), 32-3
Journal, Le, 207, 209
—— *des Débats*, 197, 293, 336
Journées de Lecture, 36
Jouvenel, Baronne de, 104
Juigné, Marquis de, 156

Karageorgevitch, 86
Keyserling, Count Hermann, 161
Kipling, Rudyard, 275
Kolb, Philip, xv, 191
Krauss, Gabrielle, 108
Kreuznach, 180, 219, 251

Labiche, Eugène, 99
Labori, Fernand, 225, 232, 239
Laboulbène, Dr (DU BOULBON), 331
Laffitte, Charles, 148
La Fontaine, Jean de, 216
La Gandara, Antoine, 85, 129, 131, 220
Lagrenée, Marquis de, 290
La Jeunesse, Ernest, 213-14
Lamartine, Alphonse de, 44, 46, 158
Landau, Baron Horace de (BERNARD, Nissim), 116-17
Laon, 29, 302-3
Laons, 29, 302
Laparcerie, Cora, 237
Larcher, Mme, 19
——, P. L., xv
Larochefoucauld, acrobat, 127, 134
La Rochefoucauld, family, 125
——, Comte Aimery de (GUERMANTES, Prince de), 130, 153-4, 161, 294-5
——, Comtesse ——, 146, 154, 295
——, Vicomte Charles de, 86
——, Comte Gabriel de (SAINT-LOUP) 154, 166, 288, 294-5, 310, 323
——, Duc Sosthène de, 233
La Salle, Comte Louis de, 43, 75, 114, 117, 123, 135-6, 139, 199, 223, 243, 289-90
La Sizeranne, Robert de, 256-60, 267, 273, 276-7, 281, 283
La Tour, Quentin de, 91
La Trémoïlle, Duc Charles de, 160, 163
——, Duchesse ——, 160, 166
Lau, Marquis du, 93, 111, 150, 161, 187, 234, 249

Laurent, Méry (ODETTE), 217-19, 248
Lauris, Comte Georges de (SAINT-
    LOUP), 105, 274, 296-7, 302-4, 309-
    10, 314, 323-7
——, Comtesse ——, née Madeleine de
    Pierrebourg (GILBERTE), 105
Lavallée, Pierre, 75, 122-3, 172, 178-91,
    203, 259, 285
Lecomte du Nouy, Jules, 332
Leconte de Lisle, Charles, 46, 54, 56,
    131, 133, 280, 295
Legrand, Gaston, 159
——, Mme — (LEROI), 159
——, Georges, 135
Legué, M. (CAMUS), 19
Leibnitz, 59
Lemaire,   Madeleine   (VERDURIN;
    VILLEPARISIS), 88, 105-9, 124, 138,
    145, 157, 170-5, 177, 181-2, 185-6,
    190, 194-5, 203-6, 209, 213, 219, 230,
    232, 236-7, 251, 314, 318-19, 321
——, Suzette, 106, 185, 203, 219
Le Masle, Dr Robert, 248
Léon, Princesse de, see Rohan
Le Reboulet, Dr (DU BOULBON), 101,
    331
Leroy-Beaulieu, Anatole, 80
Lévy, Raphaël Georges, 140
Libre Parole, La, 233, 248, 324
Lillebonne, Béatrix de 165
Lintilhac, Eugène, 61
Lisieux (DONCIÈRES), 36, 74
Lister, Barbara, 112
——, Sir Reginald, 92
Lobre, Maurice, 131
Loir, River (VIVONNE), 15, 24-8, 31-4,
    39, 202
Lorencez, Comte Étienne de, 249
Lorrain, Jean, 138, 207-12, 251
Loti, Pierre, 54, 57, 70, 295
Loubet, Émile, 235, 247
Louÿs, Pierre, 138, 140, 209, 224
Loynes, Comtesse de (ODETTE), 228,
    234
Lubersac, Marquis de, 233, 248
Ludre, Marquis de, 233
Lundi, 60
Luppé, Marquis de, 233
Luynes, family, 153
——, Duc Honoré de, 195, 233
Lytton, Lord, 92

M., see Duplay, Maurice

Madrazo, Frédéric (Coco) de (SKI),
    107, 207 247, 267-8 271, 321
——, Raymond de, 247
Maeterlinck, Maurice, 295
Maillé, Duchesse de, 158, 286-7
——, Comte François de, 158, 286-7
Malakoff, Mlle de, 48
Mâle, Émile, 257, 300
Mallarmé, Étienne, 38, 126, 131, 133,
    138, 178, 217-19, 276
Manet, Édouard, 217-18
Mantegna, Andrea, 272
Manuel, Eugène, 55
Marais, Paul, 180, 266
Marchéville (MARTINVILLE), 30
Marie, servant, 305, 309
Marquis, Canon Joseph (CURÉ), 17, 22,
    301, 324
Marsy, Mlle, 148, 155, 160
Martel, Comtesse de, alias Gyp, 44,
    46, 234
Martin, M., 56
Mathilde, Princesse (PARME, Princesse
    de), 84, 92-8, 157, 160, 228, 313
Maugny, Comte Clément de, 242, 245
    247, 258, 288, 293
——, Comtesse ——, 242-3
Maunoury, General Joseph, 161
Maupassant, Guy de, 79, 84, 166
Maurras, Charles, 190-2, 229, 233-4
Mayrargues, M., 73
Meilhac, Henri, 91
Meissonier, Ernest, 52
Méline, Jules, 335
Ménard, gardener, 24-5
——, Victor (THÉODORE), 24
Ménard-Dorian, Mme (VERDURIN),
    229
——, Pauline, 229
Ménestrel, Le, 144
Mercure de France, 268, 276, 293, 304,
    311, 318, 326
Méréglise (MÉSÉGLISE), 15, 27, 29-31
Mérimée, Prosper, 95, 157
Merle, M., 77
Metternich, Princesse, 162, 212, 230
Meyer, Arthur, 233
Mézidon (DONCIÈRES), 75
Mézières, Alfred, 319
Michel, Henri, 293
Milsand, J. A., 257, 273, 276-7
Mirabaud, Paul, 180
Molé, Comte Mathieu, 156

Molière, 7, 18, 44, 98, 101
Mollin, Captain Henri, 246, 288
Monaco, Princesse Alice de (LUXEM-BOURG, Princesse de), 84
Monet, Claude (ELSTIR), 91, 207, 223, 280
Monicault, Édouard de, 285
Monnier, Henri, 89
Mont Dore, 194, 204
Montebello, Comtesse Albertine de, 165
——, Marquis Gustave de (VAU-GOUBERT), 195-6
——, Marquise ——, (VAUGOUBERT, Mme de), 196
Montesquiou, Comte Bertrand de, 162
——, Comte Gontran de, 128, 142, 154
——, Comtesse ——, née Pauline de Sinéty, 142
——, Henriette de, see Eyragues
——, Comte Léon de, 233
——, Madeleine de, 287
——, Marie de, see Chimay
——, Raimond-Aimeri de, 125
——, Comte Robert de (CHARLUS), 66, 85, 93-4, 99, 101-3, 106, 108, 124-36, 141-54, 159, 161-2, 164, 167-70, 175-9, 185-8, 193-4, 208-17, 227, 237-8, 252, 256, 272, 288, 295, 316, 321, 325, 335-6
——, Comte Thierry de, 125, 128
Montjouvin (MONTJOUVAIN), 31-3
Montluc, Blaise de, 125
Moore, George, 218
Morand, Paul, 310
Moreau, Gustave (ELSTIR), 131, 280
Mornand, Louisa de (RACHEL), 317-18, 326-7
Morris, William, 15
Mortemart, family, 125, 163
Mozart, 52, 172
Mugnier, Abbé Arthur (POIRÉ), 161, 249
Mun, Comte Albert de, 150
Murat, Prince Joachim, 96, 106
——, Princesse Lucien, née Marie de Rohan, 160
Musset, Alfred de, 46, 52, 54, 97, 158, 269, 271
Musurus Pacha, 238

Napoleon I, 72, 95-7
Nappe, Abbé Louis, 300, 302

Natanson, Alexandre, 138
——, Thadée, 138, 140
Nattier, Jean Marc, 91, 216
Nerville, Mme de, 98
Neuberger, Mlle, 80
New York Herald, Paris edition, 318
Nibor, Yann, 145, 182
Nicolas II, Tzar (THEODOSIUS), 73, 97, 195-6, 251
Nisard, Armand (NORPOIS), 195, 283-284, 330
Noailles, Comte Mathieu de, 232, 237-8, 304, 315, 335
——, Comtesse ——, née Anna de Brancovan, 136, 205, 237-41, 244, 254, 288, 295, 304, 315, 327-8, 334-6
Nordlinger, Marie, 206-7, 217-18, 234-5, 257-60, 263, 265, 268-76, 279, 282, 284, 300-2, 321-2, 326, 328, 335

Offenbach, Jacques, 78, 91
Ollendorff, Charles, 304, 311
Oncieu, François d', 242, 247, 252, 258-9, 293
Orleans (DONCIÈRES), 72-9, 115, 191, 205
Osmond, Marquis Osmond d' (BEAU-SERGENT; OSMOND), 158, 286-7
Ostend, 75, 115
Otéro, Mlle, 317
Oulif, family, 243

Paderewski, Ignace, 136
Padua, 264, 271-2
Pailleron, Édouard, 67, 90
Paléologue, Maurice, 228
Panizzardi, 212, 224
Paris, Comte de, 93
Pâris, Marquis François de, 302
Parrot, Dr, 2
Pasteur, Louis, 333
Pater, Walter, 257, 267, 275
Péguy, Charles, 240
Percepied, postman (PERCEPIED), 20
Perdreau, Abbé (PERDREAU), 17
Perroneau, J. B., 216
Peter, René, 248
Petit-Abbeville, 181
Petronius, 55, 190
Picard, André, 326
Picquart, Georges, 222-6, 231-3, 239, 248, 253
Pierrebourg, Baron Aimery de, 104

Pierrebourg, Baronne Aimery de, *née* Marguerite Thomas-Galline (ODETTE), 104, 314
——, Madeleine de, *see* Lauris
Pierson, Mme, 195
Pipereau (PIPERAUD, Dr), 19
Piranesi, 4
Plaisirs et les Jours, Les, 59, 69, 74, 113-15, 138-40, 143, 172, 174-82, 185, 189-94, 207-9, 213-14, 225, 237, 242, 252, 259, 266, 274, 314, 316
Ployel, Maître (BARRISTER), 325
Poilly, Mme de, 208
Polignac, Prince Edmond de (BERGOTTE), 93, 164, 181, 240, 244, 291-2
——, Princesse ——, *née* Winaretta Singer, 93, 164, 245, 291-2, 318
Pomaré, Queen of Tahiti, 99
Poniatowski, Prince André, 116
Popelin, Claudius, 97
Porgès, Mme Jules, 153, 249
Porto-Riche, Georges de, 91, 96, 214, 227-8, 230, 232, 295, 319
Portraits de Peintres, 177-8
Potain, Dr, 2, 235, 330
Potocka, Comtesse Emmanuela, 135, 146, 166, 249
Potter, Paul, 178
Pougy, Liane de, 317, 332
Pouquet, Eugène, 81
——, Mme ——, 77-8, 81
——, Jeanne, *see* Arman de Caillavet, Mme Gaston.
Pourtalès, Comtesse Mélanie de, 93, 146, 161-2
Pozzi, Dr Samuel (COTTARD), 63, 96, 101, 166, 211, 228-30, 232, 329, 331
——, Mme —— (COTTARD, Mme), 101
Pré Catelan (TANSONVILLE), 23, 25-7, 39, 171, 176, 201, 219
Presse, La, 237, 244
Primoli, Comte Joseph, 96, 289
Proust, Dr Adrien, 1-5, 14-15, 47, 50, 72-5, 78-9, 86, 136-8, 197, 215, 223, 230-1, 236-7, 243, 245, 248, 253, 266, 283-7, 322-5, 328-36
——, Mme ——, 3-12, 14, 28, 47, 54, 57-8, 73-9, 116, 136, 172, 177, 180, 192-9, 215, 230-1, 236-7, 243-4, 247, 253, 258, 268-9, 272-3, 275-6, 283-8, 301, 305-9, 314, 322, 325, 332-6
——, Élisabeth, *see* Amiot

——, Louis, 1, 13, 282, 301
——, Mme ——, *née* Virginie Torcheux, 1, 3, 13, 17, 75
——, Robert, 5-6, 26, 40-1, 54, 57-8, 75, 172, 223, 248, 311-12, 320, 332-5
——, Mme ——, *née* Marthe Dubois-Amiot, 311-12, 334
——, Suzy, 335
Provins (DONCIÈRES), 199, 205, 301
Puvis de Chavannes, Pierre, 105, 295

Quillard, Pierre (BLOCH), 224

Rabaud, Henri, 114
Rachel, servant, 317
Rachepelière, La (RASPELIÈRE, La), 104
Racine, Jean, 55, 69, 141, 319
Radziwill, Prince Constantin (GUERMANTES, Prince de), 316
——, Prince Léon (SAINT-LOUP), 231, 310, 316-17, 320, 323
——, Princesse Marie, 316
——, Prince Michel, 231, 316
Réaulx, Marquis des, 285
Redon, Odilon, 295
Regnier, Henri de, 70, 130, 135, 140, 211
——, Mme ——, *née* Marie de Heredia, 140-1, 211
Reichenberg, Mlle, 145, 155
Reinach, Baron Jacques de, 227, 235
——, Joseph, 89, 225-8, 230, 233, 240
Reiter, Eugène, 114
Réjane, Mme (BERMA), 230, 232
Rembrandt, 262
Remiremont, convent of, 165
Rémusat, M. de, 64
Renaissance Latine, 313, 318
Renan, Ernest (BERGOTTE), 68-9, 95-96, 182, 295, 298
Renard, Jules, 92, 186, 208, 224
Renoir, Auguste (ELSTIR), 280
Renvoyzé, Mme, 73, 205
Réveillon (RASPELIÈRE, La), 106, 170-172, 179, 185, 202-5, 219, 266
Revue Blanche, 138, 141-2, 170, 190
—— *Bleue,* 55
—— *de Paris,* 91, 141, 190, 205, 273-4
—— *de Seconde,* 60-1
—— *des Deux Mondes,* 90, 141, 205, 256
—— *Encyclopédique,* 190
—— *Générale,* 259

Revue Hebdomadaire, 181
—— *Lilas*, 61, 64, 113
—— *Verte*, 61, 113
Rheims, 9, 75, 303
Rigo, Jancsi, 147
Rimbaud, Arthur, 40, 91
Risler, Édouard (DECHAMBRE), 75, 177-8, 248
Riva-Bella (RIVEBELLE), 242
Robert, Hubert, 28
——, Louis de, 225, 332
Robin, Dr Albert, 218, 331-2
Rochefort, Henri 185
Rohan, Duc Alain de (GUERMANTES, Duc de), 161
——, Duchesse ——, *née* Herminie de Verteillac, 12, 160-1
Ronsard, Pierre de, 23
Rossetti, Dante Gabriel, 119, 121, 319
Rostand, Edmond, 232
Rothschild, family, 89, 92, 116
——, Baronne Adolphe de, 211, 241, 245
——, Baron Alphonse de, 89, 156
——, Baron Charles de, 315
——, Baron Edmond de, 89
——, Baron Gustave de, 89
——, Henri de, 114, 335
Rouen, 258, 264-6, 278
Roussainville (ROUSSAINVILLE-LE-PIN), 24
Rouvier, Maurice, 203
Rubinstein, Ida, 129
Ruskin, John (BERGOTTE), 69, 219, 256-87, 292-3, 300-1, 317, 333. See also *Bible d'Amiens*; *Sésame et les Lys*.

Sade, Laura de, 112
——, Marquis de, 112
Sagan, Prince Boson de, 132, 148, 154-156, 215-16
——, Princesse ——, *née* Jeanne Seillière (LUXEMBOURG, Princesse de), 84, 151, 155-6
Saint-Augustin, church, 4, 286, 311-312
Saint-Éman (GUERMANTES), 22, 30-4
Saint-Hilaire, Illiers, 27
——, M. de, 237
Saint-Jacques, Illiers, 14, 17, 20-6, 300-1, 324
Saint-Leu-d'Esserent, 302, 321-2

Saint-Louis d'Antin, church, 4
Saint-Loup, near Illiers, 37, 302
——, Château de, 73, 302
——, Claire de, 37
Saint-Loup-de-Naud, 37, 300-2
Saint-Maurice, Gaston de, 93-4
Saint-Moritz, 122, 135, 139, 169-70, 325
Saint-Paul, Marquise de (SAINT-EUVERTE), 107-8
Saint-Saëns, Camille (VINTEUIL), 170-174, 295
Saint-Simon, Duc Louis de, 18, 125, 167
Sainte-Beuve, Charles, 95, 179
Saivrin, Captain, 73
Salies-de-Béarn, 52-4, 57
Sand, George, 10-11, 51, 219, 269, 292
Sandt and Laborde, tailors, 5
Sargent, John, 132, 212
Saussine, Comte Henri de, 143, 172
Schiff, Violet, 275
Schlumberger, Gustave, 162, 227
Schwartz, Gabrielle, 43, 82
Schwartzkoppen, Colonel, 212, 221-2, 224
Schwob, Marcel, 209
Scott, Charles Newton, 275
——, Sir Walter, 241
Scott-Moncrieff, C. K., 275-6
Sée, Edmond, 317
Seminario, Clarita, *née* Hahn, 181
Senlis, 302, 320
Sésame et les Lys, 279, 313
Sévigné, Mme de, 3, 76, 167
Shakespeare, William, 99, 116-19, 196, 233, 275, 291
Shelley, Percy Bysshe, 264
Sorel, Albert, 80
Souday, Paul, 289
Staël, Mme de, 92, 165, 245
——, Albertine de, 165
Standish, Mme, 152, 162-3
Steinheil, Mme, 235
Stendhal, 70, 267
Stevenson, Robert Louis, 275
Straus, Émile, 64, 89-91, 96, 227-8
——, Mme ——, *née* Geneviève Halévy (GUERMANTES, Duchesse de; ODETTE), 41, 49, 64, 79, 84, 88-94, 96, 99, 104, 114-15, 117, 121, 169, 172, 177, 210, 215, 227-30, 232, 248, 251, 269, 305, 315, 326

Surtees, R. S., 219
Swinburne, A. C., 291-2
Symonds, John Addington, 285

Taine, Hippolyte, 95-7
Tansonville (TANSONVILLE), 22
Tardieu, Dr, 2, 328
Temps, Le, 70, 114, 190, 274
Terrier, Dr Louis, 231
Thierry, Augustin, 39, 51
Thironne, River (VIVONNE), 31
Thomson, Gaston, 8
——, Mme —, née Henriette Peigné-
  Crémieux, 8
——, Valentine, 8, 311-12
Thonon, 241-3
Thoreau, Henry David, 292, 318
Tinan, Jean de, 43, 246
Tinayre, Marcelle, 90
Tissot, James, 93-4, 151
Tolstoy, Leo, 70, 194
Toulet, Paul Jean, 290
Trarieux, Gabriel, 82, 114, 117, 137
Trogan, Édouard, 247, 259
Trouville (BALBEC), 52, 83-4, 104,
  116-18, 136, 139, 151, 172, 191, 305
Turenne, Comte Louis de (BRÉAUTÉ),
  92, 96, 150-1, 155, 160-1, 215, 234
Turner, J. M. W. (ELSTIR), 281-2
Twain, Mark, 292

Universel, L', 67, 190
Uzanne, Octave, 209
Uzès, Duchesse Anne d', 163-4, 233
——, Jacques d' (SAINT-LOUP), 163-4

Valéry, Paul, 140-1, 233
Vallette, Alfred, 311, 314, 336
Vallière, Château de, 302
Vandal, Comte Albert (COTTARD), 80,
  234, 331
Vandérem, Fernand, 296
Van Dyck, 123, 178
Vaquez, Dr Henri, 305, 320
Vaudoyer, Jean Louis, 273-4
Vaufreland, M., 166
Véber, Pierre, 236
Venice, 247, 258, 260, 266-73, 279,
  284-5, 291, 329, 332
Verlaine, Paul, 46, 60, 131, 138, 160,
  171, 207, 251
Vermeer, Jan, 95, 203, 306
Versailles (DONCIÈRES), 7, 74, 197

Vézelay, 258, 327
Victoire, servant, 57-8
Vignot, Abbé Pierre, 122
Vigny, Alfred de, 64, 244, 247, 322
Villiers de l'Isle Adam, Comte Auguste,
  131, 190
Vinci, Leonardo da, 124
Viollet-le-Duc, Eugène, 303, 328
Vollendam, 307
Vuillard, Jean Édouard, 295, 325
Vulpian, Dr, 2

Wagner, Richard, 172-3, 295, 303
Wagram, Princesse Alexandre de, née
  Berthe de Rothschild, 96, 142, 145
Waldeck-Rousseau, René, 239, 248,
  323
Wales, Prince of, see Edward VII
Walewska, Maria, 72
Walewski, Captain (BORODINO, Prince
  de), 72, 205
Waru, Comte Gustave de (SAINT-
  LOUP), 110, 113, 123, 293
——, Comte Jacques de, 110, 159, 293
——, Comte Pierre de, 110
Watteau, Antoine, 178, 216
Wedderburn, Alexander, 275
Weede, Mme de, 221
Weil, Georges, 192
——, Jeanne, see Proust, Mme Adrien
——, Louis (ADOLPHE, Uncle), 4, 11,
  18, 36, 54, 57, 85-7, 94, 172, 181,
  192-3, 243, 332
——, Nathé, 3, 36, 57, 193, 200-1,
  251
——, Mme —, née Adèle Berncastel
  (GRANDMOTHER), 3 ,18, 36, 52, 54,
  57, 75-6, 83
Weisweiler, family, 243, 325
Wells, Herbert George, 275
Whistler, James McNeill (ELSTIR), 84,
  131, 207, 219, 256, 280
Wilde, Oscar, 84, 169-70, 176
Wilhelm II, Kaiser, 228, 249
Willy (pseud. of Henri Gauthier-
  Villars), 210
Winterhalter, Franz, 161
Wladimir, Grand Duchess, 113, 152,
  160, 230
Wolff, Albert, 169-70

Yeatman, Léon, 199, 213, 219, 223,
  264-5, 292, 306

Yeatman, Mme —, 264-5
Ysaye, Eugène, 173
Yturri, Gabriel d' (JUPIEN), 103, 126-130, 144, 182, 212

Zandt, Amélie van, 193
——, Marie van, 193
Zola, Émile, 220, 223-6, 229, 290

II. CHARACTERS AND PLACES

Adolphe, Uncle, (AMIOT, Jules; WEIL, Louis), 86-7, 94, 191-3
Albaret, Céleste (ALBARET), 41
Albertine (AGOSTINELLI, Alfred; CHEVILLY, Marie de; FINALY, Marie) 5, 117, 139-40, 143, 165, 172, 174, 177, 189, 210, 245, 247, 252-3, 267, 272, 285, 306
Alix (CHAPONAY; JANZÉ), 158
Argencourt, M. de, 227
Arpajon, Mme d', 294

Balbec (CABOURG; ÉVIAN; TROUVILLE), 31, 52, 75, 82, 104, 117-19, 136, 172, 184, 191, 242-6, 257, 261, 279, 283, 303, 326-7
Barrister (PLOYEL, Maître), 325
Beausergent, Mme de (BOIGNE), 158, 286-7
——, Marquis de (OSMOND), 158
Bergotte (BARRÈS; BERGSON; BOURGET; DARLU; DAUDET, Alphonse; FRANCE; LEMAÎTRE; RENAN; RUSKIN), 67-70, 87, 95, 164, 190, 203, 220, 234, 252, 278-80
Berma (BERNHARDT; RÉJANE), 69
Bernard, Nissim (CAMONDO, Nissim; LANDAU), 116, 331
Bloch (BRUNSCHWICG; FINALY, Horace; QUILLARD), 46, 54, 58, 64, 156, 165, 176, 201, 203, 224-5, 243, 279
——, Mlles, 140
——, senior (FINALY, Hugo), 93
Bontemps, Mme, 63, 253
Borange (DAMOISEAU), 21
Borodino, Prince de (WALEWSKI), 72, 162, 205
Bréauté, Hannibal de (BRETEUIL; TURENNE), 150-1
Brichot (BROCHARD; CLAIRIN), 101, 106, 234

Cambremer, Dowager Marquise de (BRANCOVAN), 238

——, Marquise de, née Legrandin (HAUSSONVILLE), 90, 158, 163
Camus (CAMUS; LEGUÉ), 20
Carquethuit, 183
Carqueville (CRIQUEBOEUF), 117
Céline, Aunt, 36
Champieu, 35
Charlus, Baron Palamède de (DOASAN; LA ROCHEFOUCAULD, Aimery de; MONTESQUIOU, Robert de; SAGAN), 66, 80, 93, 101-3, 107-8, 116, 120, 124-36, 144, 147, 152-5, 159, 168, 178, 212, 252, 261, 287, 304, 309
Combray (ILLIERS), 7, 10, 35-7, 61, 83, 191, 271
Cottard, Dr (BROCA; COTARD; COTTET; DIEULAFOY; DOYEN; GUYON; POZZI; VANDAL), 2, 63, 80, 101, 107, 188, 283, 330-1
——, Mme (POZZI, Mme), 101, 188
Courvoisier, family, 165
Crécy, Pierre de Verjus, comte de, 104
Curé, of Combray (MARQUIS), 17

Dechambre (RISLER), 178
Dieulafoy, Dr (DIEULAFOY), 330-1
Doncières (FONTAINEBLEAU; LISIEUX; MÉZIDON; ORLEANS; PROVINS; VERSAILLES), 74-5, 178, 191, 196-9, 204-5
Du Boulbon, Dr (LA BOULBÈNE; LE REBOULET), 101, 330-1

E., Professor (BRISSAUD), 330-1
Elstir (BÉRAUD; BLANCHE; GERVEX; HARRISON; HÉBERT; HELLEU; MAUPASSANT; MONET; MOREAU; TURNER; WHISTLER), 79, 85, 152, 166, 183, 193, 207, 252, 280-1, 303
Épinay, Princesse d', 234
Eudoxie, Queen (ALEXANDRA, Tzarina), 196
Eulalie, 17

Faffenheim, Prince von (EPHRUSSI), 95
Fates, Three, 158
Féterne (FÉTERNES; BASSARABA), 242
Flora, Aunt, 36
Forcheville, 107
Françoise (FITAU; GALLOU), 10, 17-19, 35, 156, 286
Froberville, General de (GALLIFFET), 151

Galopin, pastrycook (GALOPIN), 20
Gilbert, the Bad (ILLIERS, Geoffroy d'), 22-3
Gilberte (ARMAN DE CAILLAVET, Mme Gaston; BENARDAKY, Marie de; FAURE, Antoinette; GOUPIL, Mlle; HAAS, Luisita; LAURIS, Madeleine de), 25-6, 29, 34, 37, 39, 69, 77-8, 82-3, 95, 105, 137, 231, 278, 295, 302, 304
Gisèle, 55
Goupil, Mme (GOUPIL), 20
Grandmother (WEIL, Mme Nathé), 18, 76, 83, 92, 101, 193, 198, 286, 335
Great-aunt, 36, 193
Guermantes, Château de (SAINT-ÉMAN), 22
——, family, 18, 23, 154, 287, 295
——, village and Way (SAINT-ÉMAN), 22, 33-4
——, Basin, Duc de (GREFFUHLE; HAUSSONVILLE; ILLIERS, Basin d'; SAGAN; STRAUS), 23, 30, 90, 94, 148, 155, 158, 166, 306
——, Oriane, Duchesse de (CHEVIGNÉ; GOUSSENCOURT; GREFFUHLE; ROHAN; STRAUS), 20, 22-3, 90-1, 93, 109-13, 116, 135, 142, 146-52, 161, 166, 191, 248, 306
——, Prince de (La ROCHEFOUCAULD, Aimery de; RADZIWILL, Constantin de), 153-4, 249, 316
——, Princesse de (CASTELLANE, Comtesse Jean de; GREFFUHLE), 66, 152-3, 249

Hunolstein, Mme (Tiny) d', 154

Iéna, family, 96

Jupien (EPPLER; YTURRI), 5, 155, 279

Legrandin (CAZALIS), 25, 37-8, 134, 184

Léonie, Aunt (AMIOT), 17-18, 20-2, 32, 37, 176, 202, 263
Leroi, Mme (BAIGNÈRES, Laure; LEGRAND), 99, 159
Luxembourg, Prince de, 216
——, Princesse de (MONACO; SAGAN), 84, 155

Marquise, lavatory-attendant, 45
Marsantes, Mme de, 116
Martinville-le-Sec (CAEN; MARCHÉVILLE), 20, 30-1, 60-1, 202, 274
Méséglise, village and Way (MÉRÉGLISE), 29-34, 148
Mirougrain (MIROUGRAIN), 31-3
Monteriender, Comtesse de (GALBOIS), 98
Montjouvain (MONTJOUVIN), 31-3, 202, 332
Morel, Charles (DELAFOSSE), 102, 129, 143-6, 173, 193, 212

Naples, Queen of, 252
Nassau, Princesse de, see Orvillers
Norpois, M. de (BARRÈRE; BENEDETTI; FLEURY; HANOTAUX; NISARD), 2, 63, 68, 78, 96, 105, 134, 157, 188, 195, 252, 283-4, 329-30

Octave, Uncle (AMIOT, Jules), 37
Odette (ARMAN DE CAILLAVET, Léontine; CLOMESNIL; HAYMAN; LAURENT; LOYNES; PIERREBOURG; STRAUS), 49, 58, 68, 86-8, 94, 104, 139, 146, 169, 174, 190, 192-3, 200, 217-8, 234, 252, 281, 287
Orgeville, Mlle d', 299
Orvillers, Princesse d' (HERVEY DE SAINT-DENIS), 159
Osmond, Amanien d' (OSMOND), 154, 158, 286-7

Palancy, M. de, 187, 272
Parme, Princesse de (MATHILDE), 97
Percepied, Dr. (GALOPIN; PERCEPIED), 20, 27, 30
——, Mlle (GOUPIL), 20, 22
Perdreau, Abbé (PERDREAU), 17
Poiré, Abbé (MUGNIER), 249
Poncin, M. (GOUGEON), 243-4
Rachel (ALENÇON, E. de; MARSY; MORNAND), 156, 164, 295, 317

Raspelière, La (CŒUR VOLANT; COUR BRULÉE; FRÉMONTS; RACHEPELIÈRE; RÉVEILLON), 83, 103-4, 106, 117, 171

Rivebelle (BELLE-RIVE; RIVA BELLA), 183, 242, 246

Roussainville-le-Pin (BAILLEAU-LE-PIN; ROUSSAINVILLE), 24

Saint-André-des-Champs, 18, 35-6, 257, 302

Saint-Euverte, Marquise Diane de (SAINT-PAUL), 73, 107, 272

Saint-Hilaire (SAINT-JACQUES; SAINT-HILAIRE), 21, 304

Saint-Loup, Robert de (ARMAN DE CAILLAVET, Gaston; CASTELLANE, Boni de; CHOLET; FÉNELON, Bertrand de; LA ROCHEFOUCAULD, Gabriel de; LAURIS, Georges de; SAINT-LOUP; UZÉS, Jacques d'), 37, 64, 71, 73, 83, 105, 113, 154, 164, 202, 205, 225, 252, 289, 291, 293-6, 299, 302, 310, 317

——, Mlle de (ARMAN DE CAILLAVET, Simone), 83

Sazerat, Mme, 157

Sherbatoff, Princesse, 99

Ski (MADRAZO, Frédéric de), 107

Swann, Charles (BENARDAKY, Nicolas de; EPHRUSSI, Charles; HAAS, Charles; HERVIEU, Paul; STRAUS, Émile), 10, 37, 39, 58, 80, 89-95, 104, 126, 139, 148, 160, 169, 174, 181, 187, 200, 249, 252, 263, 271-2, 278, 281, 287

——, Mme Charles, see Odette

——, the elder, 98

——, Gilberte, see Gilberte

Tansonville (PRÉ CATALAN; TANSONVILLE), 25-7, 176, 201

Théodore (MÉNARD, Victor), 24

Theodosius II, King (NICOLAS II), 195-6

Thiberzy, 35

Varambon, Mme de (GALBOIS), 97-8

Vaugoubert, M. de (MONTEBELLO), 195-6, 252

——, Mme de (MONTEBELLO), 196

Verdurin, M. (ARMAN DE CAILLAVET, Albert), 67

——, Mme (ARMAN DE CAILLAVET, Mme Albert; AUBERNON, Mme; LEMAIRE, Madeleine; MÉNARD-DORIAN; SAINT-VICTOR), 65-6, 99-104, 106-8, 136, 191, 229, 236, 251-2, 288, 330

Verjus, see Crecy

Vieuvicq (VIEUVICQ), 30

Villeparisis, Mme de (BEAULAINCOURT, LEMAIRE), 68, 95, 105, 154-9, 165

Vinteuil (DEBUSSY; FAURÉ; FRANCK; D'INDY; SAINT-SAËNS), 27, 33, 37, 173, 280, 291

——, Mlle (JOINVILLE D'ARTOIS), 31-33, 177, 332

——, Sonata, 38, 98, 164, 169, 173-4, 325

Vivonne (LOIR; THIRONNE), 31

(VOLUME II)

Two separate indexes are provided, the first of real persons and places, the second of fictitious characters and places in Proust's novel, A la Recherche du Temps Perdu. In order to facilitate the tracing of discussions in the text of Proust's models in real life, cross-references from each index to the other have been given, where applicable, in capitals and parentheses. For this special purpose the two indexes should be used in conjunction with one another, and with the corresponding indexes in Volume One.

I. PERSONS AND PLACES

Abeille, Émile, 65
Action Française, 206, 297, 306, 320
Adam, Paul, 122
Agostinelli, Alfred (ALBERTINE), 89-96, 115-18, 132, 158, 192-3, 197-8, 206-15, 218-20, 226, 228, 231, 239, 241-2, 253, 264, 266, 271, 275, 287, 303
——, Anna (ANDRÉE), 192-3, 197, 206, 210, 212-14, 218, 228, 271, 303
——, Émile, 89, 95, 214, 228, 231
——, Eugène, 89, 214
——, Mme —, 89, 228
——, Mlle, 228
Ajalbert, Paul, 296
Albaret, Céleste (ALBARET, Céleste; FRANÇOISE), 189, 218-20, 227, 243, 257-8, 267, 273-6, 278, 281-2, 288-9, 291-2, 294, 298, 305-6, 320, 325-6, 333-4, 343-5, 347, 356-63
——, Odilon, 77, 88, 93, 120, 162, 166, 187, 189, 193, 218, 264, 273-5, 312, 320, 335, 339, 341, 344-5, 356, 361
——, Yvonne (FRANÇOISE'S DAUGHTER, 333-4, 344, 348, 354, 361
Albufera, Marquis Louis d' (SAINT-LOUP), 13, 18-19, 23, 26, 28, 31, 38-40, 49, 53-4, 56-7, 72, 82, 113-14, 159, 167, 188, 196, 202, 223, 285-6, 314, 318
——, Marquise —, *née* Anna d'Essling, 18, 26, 31, 49, 57
Alençon, Émilienne d' (RACHEL), 115, 327
Alexandra, Queen, 177
Allard, Roger, 312
Allégret, Marc, 350
Alton, Aimée, d', 149

——, Colette d' (ALBERTINE), 149-50, 165, 172, 183, 195
——, Hélène d', 149, 165, 172, 183, 195
——, Vicomte d', 149, 172
Amiens, 29, 140, 218
Amiot, Mme Jules, *née* Élisabeth Proust (LÉONIE, Aunt), 17, 60, 62, 221
Anastasia, Grand Duchess, 210
André, Serge, 355
——, soldier (ANDRÉE), 271
Annunzio, Gabriele d', 18, 78, 171, 185, 328
Antoine, concierge, 62, 67, 72-3, 81, 163
Apollinaire, Guillaume, 223
Aristotle, 16, 136
Arman de Caillavet, Albert (VERDURIN, M.), 157
——, Mme —, *née* Léontine Lippmann (VERDURIN, Mme), 87, 101, 110, 155-7, 178, 182, 203, 230, 277
——, Gaston (SAINT-LOUP), 103-4, 156-7, 167, 178-9, 224-5, 316
——, Mme —, *née* Jeanne Pouquet (GILBERTE), 63-4, 103-4, 156-7, 177-9, 224-5, 316
——, Simone (SAINT-LOUP, Mlle de), 103-4, 157, 178-9, 224-5, 347-8
Arnoux, Comtesse d', 64
Arrachepel, Eudes d', 87
Artagnan, Château d', 31, 175, 220, 330
Art and Letters, 288
Arts de la Vie, 7, 14, 34, 40, 42
Asquith, Elizabeth, *see* Bibesco
Astruc, Gabriel, 206, 248, 362-3
Aubernon, Mme Lydie (VERDURIN, Mme), 33, 230, 238, 279, 319

Audistère, Dr, 290-1
Auteuil (COMBRAY), 24, 35, 47, 49, 69, 71, 129-30, 132, 134, 146-7, 153, 228, 267, 287
Avallon, 85, 134

Babinski, Dr Joseph, 279, 321
Bac, Ferdinand, 217, 221, 227
Bagnold, Enid, 257-8
Baignères, Mme Laure, 33, 230
Bailby, Léon, 26, 233
Bakst, Léon, 160-2, 169, 171, 300
Balleroy, Château de (GUERMANTES), 90
——, Comte de, 90
Balzac, Honoré de, 10, 75, 88, 94, 98-100, 102, 107, 125, 135-8, 142, 211, 240, 244, 284, 289, 317-19
Banquet, Le, 20, 177, 191, 297, 309, 362
Banville, Théodore de, 121
Barbusse, Henri, 297
Bardac, Henri (SAINT-LOUP), 64, 180, 217, 222, 251, 253, 282, 301, 317-18, 325
Barney, Natalie Clifford, 327-9, 335
Barrès, Maurice (BERGOTTE), 19-21, 44, 80, 103, 110, 122, 127, 189, 206, 277, 293, 305, 310-1, 355, 363
——, Mme —, 19
Barrie, James, 154, 227
Bartet, Julia, 253
Bataille, Henri, 26, 227
Bauche, Mlle (ALBERTINE), 150
Baudelaire, Charles, 39, 56, 80, 125, 135, 142, 183, 278, 307, 311, 313, 323-4, 332
Baumann, Émile, 357
Bayeux, 90, 95
Beaulaincourt, Comtesse Sophie de (VILLEPARISIS, Mme de), 176, 379
Beaumont, Comte Étienne de, 258, 271, 277, 285, 334, 355
——, Comtesse —, née Edith de Taisne, 271, 277, 285, 334, 355
Beaune, 16
Beaunier, André, 37, 56, 82, 108, 150
Beauvais, Mme, 49
Beauvau-Craon, Isabelle de, see Gramont
Beethoven, Ludwig van, 83, 207, 212, 242-4, 323, 341
Beg-Meil (BALBEC), 88, 134, 180
Bell, Clive, 350
Bellenand, Louis, printer, 284, 324

Bélugou, Léon, 56
Benardaky, Marie de (GILBERTE), 27, 53, 134, 178, 278, 348, 362
Bénerville, 86, 112-14, 151, 180, 185, 220
Bennett, Arnold, 350
Benois, Alexandre, 169
Béraud, Jean, 82
Berenson, Bernard, 328
Berger, Dr, 49
Bergerat, Émile, 296
Bergson, Henri, 8, 52-3, 256, 277, 305, 310-1, 325
Berl, Emmanuel, 256
Berne, 21, 30, 47
Bernard, Tristan, 18, 121
Bernhardt, Maurice, 180
——, Sarah (BERMA), 180, 290
Bernheim, Adrien, 103
Bernstein, Henry, 166
Berry, Walter, 252-3, 261-2, 283-4, 286-8, 294, 300, 306, 340, 342, 347
Berthier, Comtesse, 150
——, Germaine, 150
——, Yvonne, 150
Bibesco, Prince Antoine, 1, 3, 4, 18, 25, 26, 44, 55, 69, 88, 92, 115, 152-3, 159, 163, 169-70, 180-1, 184-6, 188, 191-2, 200, 223, 225, 231, 245, 253, 256-8, 266, 285, 287-8, 304, 347
——, Princesse —, née Elizabeth Asquith, 285, 288, 347
——, Prince Emmanuel, 2, 4, 18, 82, 88, 92, 152, 169-70, 186, 188, 191, 253, 257-8
——, Prince Georges, 169
——, Princesse —, née Marthe Lahovary, 169-71, 225, 254, 258, 277, 329, 347
Bible d'Amiens, La, 2-3, 7-11, 14-15, 25, 37, 47, 56, 92, 99, 142, 227, 281
Bidou, Henri, 223-4, 355
Billy, André, 292
——, Robert de, 22, 23, 39, 53-4, 64, 66, 92, 106, 108, 113, 121, 154, 173-174, 177, 193, 227, 231, 298, 362-3
——, Mme —, née Jeanne Mirabaud, 22
Bing, Siegfried, 3, 25, 29, 38, 81
Biskra, 23
Bize, Dr Maurice, 55, 63, 73, 83, 148, 199, 354-8, 361
Bizet, Georges, 248
——, Jacques, 88, 95, 108, 116, 188, 197, 223, 228, 362

——, Mme ——, *née* Madeleine Breguet, 108

——, Mme ——, *née* Frankel, 197

Blake, William, 82

Blanc, Jean, 67, 93

Blanche, Jacques Émile, 19-20, 82, 91, 196, 201-2, 228-9, 277-80, 284, 287, 293-4, 300, 310, 336, 340

Blarenberghe, M. van, 67

——, Mme ——, 67-70

——, Henri van, 67-70

Bliss, Mme, 336

Blocqueville, Marquise Adelaide de (FATES), 175-6

Blum, Léon, 191, 256, 292, 305

——, René, 191, 193, 201, 203, 206, 223, 233-4

Blumenthal, Mme Ferdinand, *née* Cecilia Ullmann (VERDURIN, Mme), 259

——, Mme Georges, 305, 342

Boigne, Comtesse de (BEAUSERGENT, Mme de), 73-6, 125

Bois, Élie Joseph, 200

Bonnot, bandit, 176

Borda, Gustave de, 97

Bordeaux, Henry, 212, 310-11, 336

Boris, Grand Duke, 255

Borodin, Alexander, 207, 243, 273

Bossuet, 111

Boucher, François, 90-1

Boulenger, Jacques, 310-12, 319, 331-3, 336-7, 349

——, Marcel, 355

Bourcelet, antique-dealer, 26

Bourges, Élémir, 295-6

Bourget, Paul, 100, 277-8, 293, 310, 355

Boutroux, Émile, 305, 311, 324

Boylesve, René, 305-6, 310-11, 331, 355

Brabant, Geneviève de, 139

Brach, Paul, 337-8, 344-5

Braga, Dominique, 293

Brancovan, Prince Constantin de, 4-5, 8, 16, 37

——, Princesse Rachel de, 42-3

Brantes, Mme de, 82

Breguet, Madeleine, *see* Bizet

Breslau, L. C., 331

Breton, André, 299, 342

Briand, Aristide, 23

Briey, Comtesse de, 31, 82

Brimont, Mme de, 349

Brindeau, Jeanne, 156

Brissac, Duc de, 105

——, Duchesse de, 105

Brissaud, Dr Édouard (E., Professor), 42-4

Brittany, 38, 45, 83, 88, 180

Broglie, Princesse Albertine de, 76

Brouardel, Dr, 49

Brousson, Jean Jacques, 155-6

Brugelmann, Dr, 52

Brunschvicg, Léon (BLOCH), 108

Buc, 209-10, 212

Buffon, 122

Bulteau, Mme, 19

Bussy, Dorothy, *née* Strachey, 328, 350

Cabourg (BALBEC), 14, 22, 38, 83-94, 111-18, 130, 140, 148-53, 161, 163-6, 171-4, 179-83, 192, 196-8, 201, 203, 207-10, 218-20, 231, 242, 245, 255, 272-4, 282, 294, 303, 305, 316

Caen, 23, 90, 95, 180

Caillaux, Joseph, 205-6, 228

——, Mme ——, 205, 228

Caillavet, *see* Arman de Caillavet

Calmann-Lévy, 104

Calmette, Gaston, 6-7, 56, 68, 82, 121, 150, 163-5, 172-4, 180-2, 188-90, 204-5, 216, 279

Cambon, Jules (NORPOIS), 64

Cambremer (CAMBREMER), 91, 93

Camus, Dr, 52

Canard Enchaîné, Le, 338

Cannan, Gilbert, 351

Cantepie, Château de (CHANTEPIE), 93

Capet, Quartet, 242-3

Capus, Alfred, 282

Cardane, 68-70, 103, 292

Carlos, King of Portugal, 104

Carlyle, Thomas, 29

Carolus-Duran, 182

Carpaccio, Vittore, 162, 341

Cartier, jeweller, 149, 165

Casa-Fuerte, Marquise Flavie de, 78, 160

——, Marquis Illan de, 78-80, 82

——, Marquise ——, 80, 82

Castellane, Marquis Boni de (SAINT-LOUP), 5, 65, 104-5, 165, 168, 268, 285, 294-5, 343

——, Marquise ——, *née* Anna Gould, 104-5

Catusse, Mme Anatole, 47-8, 55-6, 58, 60, 62-4, 67, 84, 166, 223-4, 227-9, 260-1, 264, 274, 288, 305, 340

——, Charles, 222

Cavalieri, Lína, 162
Céard, Henry, 296, 305
Céleste, see Albaret
Céline, see Cottin
Cézanne, Paul, 253
Chamonix, 23, 172
Champmeslé, Mlle, 328
Chaponay, Mme de (ALIX), 176
Charcot, Jean, 93
Charles, headwaiter (AIMÉ), 244, 256
Charmel, concierge (CHARMEL), 291-2, 294-5
Chartres, 23, 140-1, 259
Chateaubriand, François René de, 76, 119, 121-2, 125, 135, 144, 277, 299
Chatto and Windus, publishers, 351
Chausson, Ernest, 243
Chérau, Gaston, 355
Chevassu, Francis, 182, 201
Chevigné, Comte Adhéaume de, 30, 49
——, Comtesse —, née Laure de Sade (GUERMANTES, Duchesse de), 30, 49, 82, 108-10, 133, 177, 221, 229, 254-5, 275, 277-8, 282, 285, 291, 308, 314-16
——, Marie de, 316
Chevilly, Marie de (ALBERTINE), 96
Chimay, Princesse Alexandre de, née Hélène de Brancovan, 19, 31, 56, 69, 268, 293
Cholet, Comte de (SAINT-LOUP), 17
Chopin, Frédéric, 83
Chronique des Arts et de la Curiosité, 7, 40, 55, 227
Churchill, Winston, 282
Clarac, Pierre, 355
Clary, Comte Joachim, 230, 270
Claudel, Paul 185, 194, 293, 310
Clemenceau, Georges, 157, 316
Clermont-Tonnerre, Marquis Philibert de, 31, 82, 93-5, 112
——, Marquise —, née Élisabeth de Gramont, 17, 27, 31, 41, 65, 82-3, 93-5 112, 150, 220, 256, 327, 331, 337
——, Béatrix de, 94, 112
——, Diane de, 94, 112
——, François de, Bishop of Noyon, 303
Clomesnil, Léonie (ODETTE), 171, 176, 187, 343
Clos des Mûriers (RASPELIÈRE), 86, 93, 151, 220
Cocteau, Jean (OCTAVE), 81, 161-3, 176, 182, 185, 189-90, 199, 201, 207,

210, 222-3, 229-30, 239, 253-4, 257, 271-2, 277, 284, 291, 293, 315, 340-1, 344, 362-3
Colette, Mme, 203, 305, 327-8
Combes, Émile, 23, 278, 359
Combres (COMBRAY), 86
Combray (COMBRAY), 86
Comœdia, 201
Conrad, Joseph, 226, 350
Constantine, King of Greece, 281
Consul, chimpanzee, 271
Contre Sainte-Beuve, 43, 45, 91, 100, 107, 118-52, 163, 165, 193, 237-40, 270, 280, 299, 307, 323
Copeau, Jacques, 184-6, 188, 200, 203, 259, 279
Corby, furrier, 195
Corelli, Marie, 341
Corriere della Sera, 344
Cottin, Nicolas, 93, 96, 111-12, 117, 146, 148, 159-60, 162-3, 166, 172, 180, 188, 197, 202, 218, 228, 242
——, Mme Céline (FRANÇOISE), 93, 129, 147, 159-60, 168, 180, 218, 228, 242, 260, 273-4, 363
Couchoud, Dr Paul Louis, 330-1
Coucy, 218, 258
Couperin, François, 83
Crapouillot, Le, 293
Crémieux, Benjamin, 332, 336, 342
Creuniers, Les (CREUNIERS), 39
Cricquebœuf (CARQUEVILLE), 39
Criterion, The, 351
Croisset, Francis de (BLOCH), 152, 167, 316-17
Curtiss, Mina, 326
Curtius, Ernst Robert, 350, 352-3

Dabescat, Olivier (AIMÉ), 255-6, 261, 285, 339
Daireaux, Mlles, 157
Dalstein, General, 111-12
Dancognée, Mlles, 157
Darlu, Alphonse, 20, 310
Daudet, Alphonse, 149, 296, 363
——, Mme —, 122, 249, 278, 296
——, Edmée, 335
——, Léon, 7-8, 47, 53, 91, 206, 252, 295-7, 305-6, 337, 355, 359, 363
——, Mme—, née Marthe Allard, 359
——, Lucien, 29, 56, 66, 78, 80, 101, 111, 136, 199, 201, 203, 206, 211, 214, 220, 223, 226, 230, 235, 240, 242, 248,

251-2, 259-60, 266, 268, 278, 282, 289, 296, 318, 335, 346, 362

Deacon, Gladys (FOSTER, Miss), 65, 287, 322

——, Mme, 65

Deauville, 84, 86

Debussy, Claude (VINTEUIL), 64, 168, 171, 243, 246, 300

Degas, Edgar, 91, 162

Déjérine, Dr Jules, 50-2

Delafosse, Léon (MOREL), 57, 80, 186, 249, 294

Delagarde, hypnotist, 271-2

Delarue-Mardrus, Lucie, 327-8, 331

Delepouve, Abbé, 363

Delgado, Jacques, 345

Dellier, Marguerite, 149

Dentu, Dr, 49

Derby, Edward Stanley, Lord, 284-5

Desbordes-Valmore, Marceline, 76

Descaves, Lucien, 278, 296

Deschanel, Paul, 190

Desjardins, Paul, 20, 163, 349-50

Diaghilev, Serge, 160-2, 164, 168-9, 340, 363

Dickens, Charles, 289

Dieppe (BALBEC), 23-4, 30, 84

Dieulafoy, Mme Claire, 72

——, Dr Georges (DIEULAFOY), 49

——, Mme Jane, 72

Dimier, Louis, 87

Dives, 85-6

Doasan, Baron Jacques (CHARLUS), 139, 238, 270, 319, 343

Dorgelès, Roland, 296-7

Dostoevsky, Feodor, 70, 174, 182, 201, 256-7, 337-8

Doucet, Jacques, 355

Doudeauville, Duchesse de, 178

Douville, 86

Doyen, Dr Eugène Louis (COTTARD), 87

Dreyfus, Alfred; Dreyfus Affair, 19-20, 58, 82, 98, 105, 185, 192, 242, 297

——, Henri, 167

——, Robert, 20, 34, 57, 65, 69, 99, 103, 107-8, 118-19, 122-3, 127, 139, 145, 150-1, 167, 222, 282, 286, 292, 294, 362

Dubois, Dr Paul, 21, 23, 30, 47, 50, 52

Du Bos, Charles, 350

Duchesne, Monsignor, 328

Duguay-Trouin, Admiral, 85

Duhamel, Georges, 355

Dukas, Paul, 249

Duncan, Isadora, 220

Dunoyer de Segonzac, 363

Duplay, Dr Simon, 111

——, Maurice, 8, 72, 77

Duquesne, Baron, 228

Durand-Ruel, 176

Duras, Duchesse de, 75-6

Dussaud, Mlle, 328

Duval, Jeanne, 324

Duvernois, Henri, 332, 354-5

Écho de Paris, 31, 201

Écrits Nouveaux, Les, 335

Edward VII, King, 177

Edwards, Alfred, 93, 161-2

——, Mme —, *née* Misia Godebska (YOURBELETIEFF, Princesse), 93, 161-162, 222

Einstein, Albert, 336

Eliot, George, 157

——, Thomas Stearns, 328, 351

Elles, M., manager of Ritz Hotel, 344

Émile-Paul, publisher, 346

Enoch, music-publisher, 248

Ephrussi, Charles (SWANN), 23, 33, 318

Eppler, tailor (JUPIEN), 270

Ermenonville, 17

Ernestine, *see* Gallou

Errasuriz, Mme, 340

Essling, Prince Victor d', 18, 262

——, Princesse —, *née* Paule Furtado-Heine, 18

——, Anna d', *see* Albufera

Estradère, Mme, called Princesse de Mésagnes, 330

Etretat, 22

Eugène, valet, 60

Eugénie, Empress, 201, 230

Eulenburg, Prince Philip von, 105-7, 111

Ève, 336

Évian, 19, 23, 47-9, 70, 86, 255, 309

Évreux, 94-5

Excelsior, 201, 297

Eyragues, Marquis Charles d', 90-1

——, Marquise —, *née* Henriette de Montesquiou, 90-1

Fabre, Jean Henri, 315

Faguet, Émile, 102

Falaise, 91, 244

Fallières, Armand, 157

Fantin-Latour, 287
Fargue, Léon Paul, 291, 300
Fasquelle, Eugène, 104, 183-6, 189-90, 200, 204-5
Faure, Mme Félix, 49
——, Antoinette, 222, 363
——, Lucie, 359
Fauré, Gabriel (VINTEUIL), 83, 175, 243, 245, 323
Fay, Bernard, 268-9
Félicie, see Fitau
Fénelon, Comte Bertrand de (SAINT-LOUP), 4, 18, 23, 28, 39, 64, 153, 162, 167, 170, 183, 191-2, 225-7, 231, 258, 266, 291, 319, 335
Ferré, André, 355
Feuillerat, Albert, 235, 355
Feuillets d'Art, 292
Feydeau, Georges, 152, 272
Fezensac, Duc de, 60
Figaro, Le, 6-7, 23, 25, 31, 34, 37, 49, 56-7, 68-9, 73, 79, 81-3, 95-7, 99, 100, 103, 110, 122, 133-4, 142, 145, 147, 150-1, 163, 173-4, 178, 182, 185, 188-190, 193, 200-1, 205, 213, 215-16, 224, 226, 281-2, 284, 292-3, 330, 336, 347
Finaly, Horace (BLOCH), 322
——, Mme Hugo (VILLEPARISIS, Mme de), 38, 113
——, Marie (ALBERTINE), 38-9, 96, 113, 115, 183, 208, 323, 362
Fitau, Félicie (FRANÇOISE), 3, 48-9, 59, 93, 133, 147
FitzJames, Comte Robert de, 314
——, Comtesse ——, née Rosa Gutmann, 17
Flament, Albert, 33, 132
Flaubert, Gustave, 98-100, 102-3, 125, 132, 184, 253-4, 284, 298-9, 316, 331-2, 338
Flers, Marquis Robert de, 7, 25-6, 66, 83, 167, 216, 282, 290, 292, 295, 305, 310-11, 316, 338
Florence, 193
Fontainebleau, 27, 50, 73, 134
Forain, Jean Louis, 162
Fortuny, 208
Fouquet, Nicolas, 21
Fouquières, André de, 109
Fournier, Alain, 203, 222, 299
——, Dr, 49
Fragson, singer, 32
France, Anatole (BERGOTTE), 100, 103,

110, 127, 149, 155-7, 182, 230, 293-4, 307, 311, 347, 363
Franck, César (VINTEUIL), 243-7, 254
——, Henri, 256
Freer, Charles L., 29, 38
Frémonts, Les (RASPELIÈRE), 38-9, 113
Fromentin, Eugène, 165
Fry, Roger, 350

Gabory, Georges, 342
Gagey, Dr Émile, 62, 67, 72, 111, 158
Gallé, Émile, 8
Galliéni, General, 219
Galliffet, General Marquis Gaston de, 145, 338
Gallimard, Gaston, 113-15, 185-6, 194, 259, 279-81, 292, 296-7, 299, 324, 332-3, 336, 344, 348-9, 351, 354, 356-7
Gallou, Ernestine (FRANÇOISE), 269, 312
Ganay, Marquis de, 253
——, Marquise de, 253
Gangnat, Robert, 77, 93, 112-14, 153, 167, 185
Gans, Henri, 322, 362
Garbero, Hector, 212, 214
——, Joseph, 212, 214
Garnier, bandit, 177
Garros, Roland, 239
Gastine-Rennette, gunsmith, 27
Gaubert, Ernest, 7
Gaulois, Le, 33, 174, 293, 338
Gautier, Juliette, 110
——, Théophile, 34-6, 161
Gautier-Vignal, Comte Louis, 228, 253
Gazette des Beaux-Arts, 107, 320
Geffroy, Gustave, 296
Genevoix, Maurice, 342
Gentil, Victor, 243-4
Gérard, Lucy, 115
Germain, André, 78, 80, 269, 335
Ghéon, Henri, 185, 194, 203
Gide, André, 184-8, 200, 203-4, 207, 212, 214-15, 223, 232, 259, 268-9, 275-6, 292-3, 301, 305, 310, 312-14, 324, 328, 337, 342, 350
Gil Blas, 8, 25, 181, 201
Gineste, Céleste, see Albaret
——, François-Régis, 274
——, Marie (GINESTE, Marie), 274, 334, 344
Giotto, 42, 92, 121, 239
Giraudoux, Jean, 253, 257, 291-3, 210, 357

Giverny, 94
Glisolles, 94-5, 112
Godebska, Misia, see Edwards
Goethe, 201
Goncourt, Edmond de, 38, 98, 101-3, 111, 135-6, 144, 290, 296, 349-50
Gontaut-Biron, Mlle de, 109
Gosse, Edmund, 350
Gounod, Charles, 303
Gourmont, Remy de, 107, 252, 328
Gramont, Duc Agénor de (GUERMANTES, Duc de), 17-18
——, Duchesse ——, née Marguerite de Rothschild, 17, 42-3
——, Claude de, 40
——, Corisande de, see Noailles
Grande Revue, 164
Granet, François Marius, 320
Grasset, Bernard, 191-2, 194, 197, 202-5, 215-16, 230-4, 237, 279-82, 297, 300, 346
Greco, El, 272
Greffulhe, Comte Henri (GUERMANTES, Duc de), 138, 217-18, 253-4, 318, 338, 363
——, Comtesse ——, née Élisabeth de Chimay (GUERMANTES, Duchesse de; GUERMANTES, Princesse de), 10, 18, 27, 31, 87, 92, 110, 138, 145, 169, 177-8, 219, 254, 262, 293, 314, 317-18, 329, 330, 346
—— Elaine, see Guiche
Gregh, Fernand, 5, 20, 25-6, 28, 52, 99, 108, 222, 294, 362-3
——, Didier, 293
——, Geneviève, 334
Grey, Lady de, Marchioness of Ripon, 274
Groscul, Albertine, 76
Gross, Mme, 180
Grouchy, Vicomte de, 49
Guermantes, Château de, and village (GUERMANTES), 123
Guerne, Comtesse Marie de, 31
Guernsey, 22
Guiche, Duc Armand de (SAINT-LOUP), 17-18, 27, 31, 40, 42, 82, 93, 112, 151, 169-70, 177, 180, 188, 191, 285-6, 288, 311, 314, 316, 318, 331, 336
——, Duchesse ——, née Elaine Greffulhe, 18, 27, 31, 93, 112, 151, 177, 179, 180, 304, 331
——, Corisande de, 331

Guiraud, Ernest (VINTEUIL), 248
——, Mlle (VINTEUIL, Mlle), 248
Guitry, Lucien, 188

Haas, Charles (SWANN), 18, 145, 319, 338
——, Luisita (GILBERTE), 338
Hahn, Mme Carlos, 175
——, Maria, see Madrazo
——, Reynaldo, 3, 10, 31-2, 49, 56, 58-60, 64, 66, 72, 78, 80, 83, 85, 92, 93, 105, 111-12, 115, 117, 134, 136, 145-6, 148, 151-2, 158-66, 168-9, 171-3, 175-6, 180-2, 184, 189, 196, 204, 218, 222, 228, 249, 251, 266, 287, 295, 305, 317-18, 358-9, 362-3
Halévy, Daniel, 26, 108
——, Élie, 108
——, Léon, 108
——, Ludovic, 69, 108
Hanotaux, Gabriel (NORPOIS), 143, 210
Harden, Maximilian, 106
Hardy, Thomas, 65, 141, 154-5, 157
Hartmann, Dr, 49
Hasselmans, Mlle, 83
Haussonville, Comte Othenin d' (GUERMANTES, Duc de), 300, 310, 338
——, Comtesse ——, née Pauline d'Harcourt (CAMBREMER), 6, 31, 82-3
Havre, Le (RIVEBELLE), 22, 86
Hayman, Laure (ODETTE), 176, 260, 343
Hayot, Maurice, 83
Hayward, Miss, 172, 174, 183
Heath, Willie, 2, 163, 349
Hébert, Abbé, 11
Hébrard, Adrien, 181-2, 200, 202
Hector, headwaiter (AIMÉ), 60, 256
Hélène, yacht, 22, 59, 108
Helleu, Paul (ELSTIR), 91-2, 151, 363
——, Mme (ELSTIR, Mme), 91-2
Hennessy, Mme Jean, née Marguerite de Mun, 322, 342-3
Hennique, Léon, 296
Henraux, Lucien, 31, 176
Hermant, Abel (BLOCH), 8, 167, 189, 292
Hervieu, Paul (BERGOTTE), 167, 188, 230
Heurgon, Anne, 163
Hinnisdäel, Thérèse d', 334-5, 343
Hoffmann, E. T. A., 170
Holbein, 25
Holland, 35, 38
Homer, 44
Honfleur, 39, 116, 183

Honnorat, André, 305
Houlgate, 86, 88, 112, 165, 197
Howland, Mme Meredith, 338
Hugo, Victor, 16, 25, 32, 80, 112-13, 125, 253
Humblot, M., 189-90
Humières, Vicomte Robert d' (SAINT-LOUP), 34, 82, 226-7
——, Vicomtesse —, 82, 227
Huxley, Aldous, 350
——, Thomas H., 350
Huysmans, Joris Karl, 277

Ideville, Hélène d'(ALBERTINE), 77
Iliesco, General, 257
Illiers (COMBRAY), 17, 23, 34, 35-7, 60, 74, 86-7, 89, 124, 131, 141, 147, 248, 269, 276, 278
Illustration, L', 337
Impressions de route en automobile, 89, 95-6, 212, 281
Indy, Vincent d' (VINTEUIL), 248
Ingres, 320
Intransigeant, L', 169
Iribe, Jeanne (ANDRÉE), 163
——, Paul, 163

Jaloux, Edmond, 161, 292, 305, 325, 344-6, 351, 353, 362-3
James, Henry, 252
Jammes, Francis, 76, 185, 194, 211
Janzé, Vicomtesse Alix de (ALIX), 176
Jean Santeuil, 9, 11, 20, 25-6, 36-7, 44-5, 55, 57, 75, 77, 100-21, 127, 129, 131-4, 137-43, 146-7, 154, 175, 208-9, 237-8, 241, 248-9
Joffre, Marshal, 223
Joinville d'Artois, Juliette (VINTEUIL, Mlle), 248
Joncières, Léonce de (OCTAVE), 162
Jossien, chauffeur, 88, 93, 95, 96
Journal, Le, 160
Journal des Débats, 121
Journées de Lecture, 34, 73-6, 79-80, 134, 227. See also Sur la Lecture
Joyce, James, 340-2
Jumièges, 116, 140

Karr, Alphonse, 7
Kasterine, aviator, 210, 212, 214
Katz, Mme, 72-3
——, M., 73
Kipling, Rudyard, 226

Kluck, Marshal von, 218, 221
Knoblauch, Édouard, 188
Kolb, Philip, 107
Kraft-Ebbing, 270
Kreuznach, 144
Krupp, Bertha, 273

La Béraudière, Comtesse de (ODETTE), 253-4
Labiche, Eugène, 48, 134
Labori, Fernand, 98, 100
Lacretelle, Jacques de, 94, 245-6, 259, 284
Lafitte, Pierre, 201
La Fontaine, Jean de, 21, 318
Lahovary, Marguerite, 225
La Jeunesse, Ernest, 110
Lamy, Louis, 358
Land and Water, 351
Landowska, Wanda, 335
Landowski, Dr Ladislas, 48, 63
Lantelme, Ginette (LÉA; RACHEL), 93, 161
Laon, 218, 259
Larbaud, Valéry, 185, 194, 293
Lareinty, Baronne de, 123
La Rochefoucauld, Comte Aimery de (GUERMANTES, Prince de), 17, 278
——, Comtesse —, 17, 31, 33
——, Comte Gabriel de (SAINT-LOUP), 18, 30-1, 40, 82, 273, 303, 344
——, Comtesse —, née Odile de Richelieu, 30-1, 303
La Salle, Louis de, 26, 108, 165
La Trémoille, Duc Charles de, 338
Lau, Marquis du, 338
Lauris, Comte Georges de (SAINT-LOUP), 23, 37, 39, 53, 61, 64, 72, 76, 88-9, 109, 111, 116-25, 128, 137, 144, 151-3, 163, 165-7, 173-5, 184, 186, 191, 197-8, 203, 223, 226, 233, 242-3, 316, 349, 362-3
——, Comtesse —, née Madeleine de Pierrebourg, 165-6
——, Marquis de, senior, 76, 88
——, Marquise de, 72, 88
Lavallée, Pierre, 196, 363
Léautaud, Paul, 77, 316
Le Bargy, actor, 290, 304-5
——, Mme Simone, 304-5
Lebaudy, Jacques (OCEANIA), 149
Leclercq, Paul, 115-16
Lecomte du Nouy, Jules, 1, 25

Le Cuziat, Albert (JUPIEN), 262-71, 276, 282, 302, 306, 354

Legrand, Mme Gaston, *née* Clothilde de Fournes (LEROI, Mme), 30

Lemaire, Madeleine (VERDURIN, Mme), 29, 30, 32-3, 77, 101, 109, 132, 145, 176, 181, 217, 221-2, 260, 317

——, Suzette (GILBERTE), 56, 109, 132, 221-2

Lemaître, Jules (BERGOTTE), 122, 188, 230

Lemarié, Mme, 259

Lemoine, swindler, 98-104, 121-3, 135, 141, 150, 281, 284

Lenin, 277

Léon, 60, 66

Leonardo da Vinci, *see* Vinci

Le Poittevin, magistrate, 98

Lettres, Les, 99

Lévy, Raphael Georges, 284

Liberté, La, 7

Libre Parole, La, 21

Lisieux, 95

Lister, Sir Reginald, 82, 154

Litvinne, Mme, 169

Longnon, Henri, 87, 357

Lorin, Christiane, 112, 114, 153

Lorrain, Jean (CHARLUS), 270, 312

Loti, Pierre, 30, 103, 110, 115, 127, 156

Louÿs, Pierre, 328

Loynes, Comtesse de (ODETTE), 230

Loyson, Hyacinthe, 277

Lubersac, Marquis, de, 276

Ludre, Marquise de, 30, 82

MacCarthy, Desmond, 350

Macherez, Mlle, 77

Mackenzie, Compton, 350

Madrazo, Frédéric (Coco) de, 27, 218, 230, 331, 343

——, Mme Raymond de, *née* Maria Hahn, 165, 242, 248, 363

Maeterlinck, Maurice, 121, 126, 131, 173, 185, 316

Maigre, François, 23

Maillé, Duchesse de, 75

——, Comte François de, 75

——, Comtesse —, 75

Mâle, Émile, 88, 90, 92, 152, 357

Mallarmé, Stéphane, 145

Malraux, André, 297

Manet, Édouard, 201

Mansfield, Katherine, 351

Mantegna, Andrea, 166

Marbury, Bessie, 5

Mardrus, Dr Joseph, 327

Margueritte, Paul, 203

Marguiller, Auguste, 107

Maria Pavlovna, Grand Duchess, 110

Marie, cook, 31

Mariéton, Paul, 91

Marlborough, Charles Spencer-Churchill, Duke of, 65, 322-3

——, Duchess of, *née* Consuelo Vanderbilt, 65, 322

Marquis, Canon Joseph (CURÉ), 86-7

Martin-Chauffier, Louis 331

Martin du Gard, Maurice, 269, 335-6

——, Roger, 350

Massa, Marquis de, 300

Massenet, Jules, 168, 212, 303

Massis, Amable, 243-4

Mathilde, Princesse, 235

Matin, Le, 93

Maugny, Comte Clément de, 192, 226, 270, 309

——, Comtesse —, 309

Maunoury, General, 221

Mauriac, François, 277, 292, 321, 363

Maurois, André, 348, 350

——, Mme —, *see* Arman de Caillavet, Simone

Max, Édouard de, 301

Mayer, cousin of Proust, 222

Mayol, Félix, 32, 166, 168

Mercure de France, publishing firm and magazine, 14, 43, 104, 107, 150

Meredith, George, 65

Méréglise (MÉSÉGLISE), 23, 90

Mérimée, Prosper, 120, 122

Merklen, Dr Pierre, 21-2, 48, 50

Mérode, Cléo de, 115, 166

Mézidon (DONCIÈRES), 85, 113

Michelet, Jules, 98, 224

Mineguishi, valet (JUPIEN), 230, 270

Miomandre, Francis de, 292

Mirabaud, Paul, 22, 66, 108

Mirbeau, Octave, 316

Misme, Clotilde, 320

Molière, 48, 134, 344

Moltke, General Cuno von, 106

Monaco, 88-9, 118, 303

——, Prince Albert of (LUXEMBOURG), 30, 213, 303

——, Princess Alice of, formerly

Duchesse Armand de Richelieu, *née* Heine (LUXEMBOURG, Princesse de), 30, 303

Monaco, Princesse Charlotte of, 303

——, Prince Louis of, 303

Monet, Claude, 92, 94

Montebello, Comtesse Jean de, *née* Albertine de Briey, 19, 76, 138

Montesquiou, Comtesse Odon de, *née* Princesse Marie Bibesco, 16

——, Comte Robert de (CHARLUS), 3, 5-8, 10-11, 15-16, 18-19, 27, 29, 31-4, 40-2, 48, 57, 60, 65, 75-8, 80, 90, 92, 96-7, 101-2, 109-11, 122, 136, 137, 139, 143, 145, 149, 152, 158, 160-1, 167-9, 171-2, 174-6, 189, 206, 214, 219-20, 227, 229, 231, 249, 253, 256, 260, 262, 270, 277, 284, 291, 294-5, 310, 317-9, 327-8, 329-31, 335, 337, 344-6, 363

——, Comte Thierry de, 15

——, Comte Wladimir de, 15

Montherlant, Henri de, 277

Montjouvin (MONTJOUVAIN), 87

Montmorency, Duc de, *see* Talleyrand-Périgord

Montsaulnin, Marquis de, 16

Morand, Paul, 41, 225-7, 244, 252-4, 260, 268, 270-1, 275, 277-8, 284, 286, 289, 291-2, 297, 305-11, 316, 321-2, 328-9, 335-6, 338, 340, 358-9

Moréas, Jean, 127

Moreau, Gustave (ELSTIR), 33, 91

Mornand, Louisa de (RACHEL), 11-14, 18-19, 25-8, 31-2, 34, 38-9, 44-6, 49, 53, 56, 77, 86, 93, 112-15, 152-3, 167, 192, 196, 208, 311, 314

——, Mme de, 38, 112

——, Suzanne de, 38, 112, 114

Morny, Duc de, 172

Mort des Cathédrales, La, 23, 281

Mot, Le, 163

Mourey, Gabriel, 7, 14, 34

Mourousy, Prince Paul, 283

Moyse, 345

Mozart, 243

Mugnier, Abbé Arthur, 110, 156, 217, 276-8, 340, 359, 363

Muller, Charles, 99

Murat, Prince Joachim, 26

——, Princesse —, *née* Cécile d'Elchingen, 26

——, Princesse Lucien, *née* Marie d'Elchingen, 108, 263, 277, 284-5, 335, 363

——, Princesse Violette, 271-2

Murry, John Middleton, 350-1

Musset, Alfred de, 149

——, Paul de, 149

Nahmias, Albert (ALBERTINE), 171-2, 174, 180-1, 183, 207-8, 210, 212, 242, 271

——, Anita, 181

——, Estie, 181

Naples, Marie, Queen of (NAPLES, Queen of), 248-9

Napoléon I, 229, 275

—— III, 259

Natanson, Thadée, 93

Nègre, Monseigneur, 275

Nerval, Gérard de, 135, 142, 145, 299

Neufville, Alexandre de, 112, 114, 172

New York Herald, Paris edition, 33

Nicolas, *see* Cottin

Nicolas II, Tsar, 110

Nicolson, Harold, 286-7

Nietzsche, Friedrich, 122

Nijinsky, Vaslav, 160, 162, 169, 300

Noailles, Marquis Hélie de, 42

——, Marquise —, *née* Corisande de Gramont, 42-3

——, Duchesse de, 16

——, Comte Mathieu de, 20, 49

——, Comtesse —, *née* Anna de Brancovan, 1-2, 4-9, 16-17, 19-22, 37, 42, 44, 49, 50, 55, 61, 80-3, 91, 101, 119, 124, 128, 148, 152, 166, 169, 175, 193, 206, 221, 293, 304-5, 322, 327-9, 349, 362

Nogrette, young, 144, 148

Noorden, Dr, 41

Nordlinger, Marie (ALBERTINE), 2-4, 7-10, 13-15, 23-4, 29, 34, 37-8, 43-4, 47-8, 56, 66, 76, 130, 145, 208, 363

Northcliffe, Alfred Harmsworth, Lord, 343

Nouvelle Revue Française, publishing firm and magazine, 99, 184-9, 194, 203-5, 215-16, 232-4, 238, 258, 273, 279-82, 287, 292-3, 296-9, 301, 310-12, 323, 331-2, 336, 349, 351, 354-5, 357

NRF, *see Nouvelle Revue Française*

Odilon, *see* Albaret

Œuvre, L', 292

Œuvres Libres, Les, 332-3, 348, 354-5
Olivier, *see* Dabescat
Ollendorff, Paul, 25, 190
Opinion, L', 319-20
Orleans (DONCIÈRES), 58, 217
Orloff, Comte, 262
Osmond, Marquis Osmond d' (OS-MOND), 74-5
——, Comte Rainulphe d', 75
Ouistreham, 22, 86

Padua, 239
Pagnier, Dr, 52
Paillart, F., printer, 324
Paléologue, Maurice, 210, 327
Palmer, Evelina, 327-8
Paquin, modist, 77
Pâris, Marquis François de, 123, 137, 152-3, 357
Paris Magazine, 292
Pascal, Blaise, 60, 201
Pastiches et Mélanges, 6, 9, 34, 76, 104, 122, 281, 287, 292, 298, 303, 338
Paul, Grand Duke, 253
Paulhan, Jean, 312, 342
Peigné-Crémieux, Mathilde, 53-6
Pernolet, Arthur, 62-3
Perugino, 171
Peter, René, 64
Picasso, Pablo, 340-1
Picquart, Georges, 58-9, 111-2
Pierrebourg, Baronne Aimery de (ODETTE), 203, 230
——, Madeleine de, *see* Lauris
Pierredon, Comte Hubert de, 188
Pinard, Henri, 110, 167, 331, 345-6
Pisanello, 25, 359
Plaghki, M., 264
Plaisirs et les Jours, Les, 7, 25-6, 59, 64, 99, 101, 104, 133, 164, 241, 309
Plançon, Pol, 32
Plantevignes, Camille, 115, 144, 148, 172
——, Marcel (OCTAVE), 115, 152, 162, 172
Plato, 201
Pleyel, Mme, 242
Poincaré, Raymond, 190
Polignac, Prince Edmond de, 317, 338
——, Princesse ——, *née* Winnaretta Singer, 6, 78, 82, 204, 322, 338, 343
——, Comte Pierre de (NASSAU), 277, 303-4, 356
Pompadour, Mme de, 59

Pont-Audemer, 116
Pontigny, 163, 349-50
Porel, Jacques, 161, 172-3, 271, 288-91, 300-1, 305, 336, 363
——, Mme ——, 289-91, 301
Porto-Riche, Georges de, 316
Pougy, Liane de, 64, 115, 327
Poulet, Gaston, 243-6, 254
Pound, Ezra, 328
Poupetière, young, 66
Pouquet, Jeanne, *see* Arman de Caillavet, Mme Gaston
——, Maurice, 347
Pozzi, Dr Samuel (COTTARD), 33, 49, 108, 110, 223, 244, 279
——, Mme ——, 33
Pré Catelan (TANSONVILLE), 34-5
Prémonville, little, 179, 278
Presse, La, 25-6
Prévost, Marcel, 38, 115, 311, 343
Primoli, Comte Joseph, 157
Pringué, Gabriel Louis, 256
Professeur de Beauté, Un, 40, 42-3
Prondre de Guermantes, Paulin (GUER-MANTES), 123, 252
Proust, Dr Adrien, 1-2, 24-5, 27, 41, 46, 52, 60, 62, 64, 67, 73, 75, 97, 134, 175, 230, 264, 283, 310, 340, 357, 363
——, Mme ——, 1-2, 13, 18, 21-30, 34, 42-3, 46-55, 57, 60-2, 64, 66, 69, 70, 73-5, 83-4, 88, 97, 113, 119, 128, 130, 133-7, 140-1, 144, 147, 172, 175, 192, 209, 256, 264, 267-9, 301-2, 308-9, 316, 325-6, 340, 352-4, 356, 358, 360-3
——, Robert, 22, 25, 46-9, 61-3, 107, 141, 143, 217-19, 222, 230, 260, 267, 282, 340, 352, 355-63
——, Mme ——, *née* Marthe Dubois-Amiot, 22, 62, 72, 218, 282, 339-40, 363
——, Suzy, 62, 218, 339-40, 363
Puzin, bookseller, 122

Rachepelière, La (RASPELIÈRE), 87
Racine, Jean, 134, 136, 325, 328
Radolin, Prince Hugo von, 111
Radziwill, Prince Constantin (FOIX, Prince de, father; GUERMANTES, Prince de), 262-3
——, Princesse ——, 40
——, Prince Léon (Loche) (FOIX, Prince de, son), 18, 31, 39-40, 65, 112, 114, 153, 159, 223, 262

Rageot, Gaston, 4-5, 293, 312
Ralli, Mme, 93
Rameau, 207
Raphael, 92
Rasputin, Grigor, 281
Ravel, Maurice, 243, 363
Ray, Man, 363
Rebattet, confectioner, 3
Reboux, Paul, 99
Régnier, Henri de, 8, 121-2, 126-7, 131, 189, 249, 310
——, Mme —, *née* Marie de Heredia, 249
Reinach, Joseph (BRICHOT), 224, 229, 271, 337
——, Salomon, 328
Réjane, Mme (BERMA), 157, 172, 220, 271, 288-91, 294, 300-1, 336, 363
Renaissance Latine, 4-6, 37
Renan, Ernest (BERGOTTE), 99, 101-3, 127, 175
Renoir, Auguste, 321
Réveillon, Château de (TANSONVILLE), 10, 131-2, 221-2
Revue Blanche, 93
—— *de France*, 343
—— *de la Semaine*, 319, 331
—— *de Paris*, 292, 307, 311
—— *des Deux Mondes*, 9
—— *des Jeunes*, 292
—— *générale de la Bibliographie Fran-çaise*, 7
—— *Hebdomadaire*, 311
—— *Lilas*, 37, 95
—— *Universelle*, 7
Rheims, 37, 218, 259
Ribot, Dr, 52
Richelieu, Duc Armand de, 30
——, Duchesse —, *see* Monaco
——, Odile de, *see* La Rochefoucauld
Richet, Georges, 7
Rilke, Rainer Maria, 328
Risler, Edouard, 83
Ritz, Hôtel, 82, 242, 254-6, 260, 271-2, 277, 282-4, 286-8, 320, 334, 339, 343-5, 347, 356, 361
——, César, 255
——, Mme —, 256, 282
Riva-Bella (RIVEBELLE), 86
Rivière, Jacques, 215-16, 222, 232, 238, 259, 288, 292, 296-9, 301, 305-6, 310-12, 325-6, 331-3, 335-8, 342, 349-50, 354-9

——, Mme —, 299
——, Alain, 299
——, Dr Marc, 356-7
Robert, Louis de, 185, 189-90, 194, 196, 199, 203, 206, 292-3, 295
Robin, Dr Albert, 64, 331
Rochat, Henri (ALBERTINE; MOREL), 287, 289, 299, 309, 321-2, 324, 333
Rodier, Georges (LEGRANDIN), 176
Rodin, Auguste, 110
Rohan, Duc Alain de, 263-4
——, Duchesse Herminie de, 42
Rolland, Romain, 203, 351
Rosny *aîné*, 203, 295-6
Rosny *jeune*, 296
Rostand, Edmond, 158, 184, 189, 228, 293
——, Maurice, 189-90, 196, 201-2, 204
Rothschild, Baronne Adolphe de, 249
——, Baron Alphonse de, 338
——, Maurice de, 171-2
——, Robert de, 332, 335
Rouen, 23, 37, 92
Rousseau, Jean-Jacques, 17
Roussy, Dr Gustave, 299
——, Mme —, *née* Marguerite Thom-son, 165, 362
Rozière, Mme de, 83
Rubens, 91
Rubinstein, Ida, 160, 167, 171, 301, 331
Ruhe, Algot (NORWEGIAN PHILOSO-PHER), 325, 336
Ruskin, John, 2, 7-11, 29-30, 34-8, 40, 44, 55-8, 73, 91, 95, 100, 101, 118, 121, 127, 133, 141-2, 146, 192, 226, 242, 265, 277, 281, 338; *see also* *Bible d'Amiens; Sésame et les Lys*
Ruyssen, André, 243-4

Sabini, Yvonne, 327
Sachs, Maurice, 268-9
Sagan, Prince Boson de (CHARLUS), 230, 300-1
——, Princesse —, *née* Jeanne Seillière (LUXEMBOURG, Princesse de), 303
——, Prince Hélie de, 104-5
Saint-Éman (GUERMANTES), 124
Saint-Jacques, church of (SAINT-HILAIRE), 86, 90
Saint-Léger Léger, Alexis, 275
Saint-Leu-d'Esserent, 218
Saint-Loup-de-Naud, 85

Saint-Malo, 22, 85
Saint-Maurice, Gaston de, 145, 338
Saint-Paul, Marquise Diane de, 32
Saint-Saëns, Camille, 245
Saint-Simon, Duc Louis de, 6, 119, 121-2, 284-5, 294, 303
Sainte-Beuve, Charles, 20, 35, 102-3, 118-52, 280, 299, 307, 311
Saintsbury, George, 350
Salmon, André, 342
Sand, George, 134, 138, 149, 152, 217, 241, 356, 360
Sardou, Victorien, 290
Sassoon, Sir Philip, 344
Saussine, Comte Henri de, 112, 248
Scheikévitch, Marie, 180-3, 196, 200, 202, 206, 211, 222, 230-1, 239, 242, 252, 260, 274, 277, 336, 359,
Schiff, Sydney, 288, 300, 304, 338-41, 343-4, 351, 354-5
——, Mrs ——, née Violet Beddington, 300, 338-41, 343-4, 351, 355
Schlésinger, M., 60
Schlumberger, Gustave, 108-9, 343
——, Jean, 185-6, 188, 350
Schubert, Franz, 245
Schumann, Robert, 244
Scott, Charles Newton, 34
Scott-Moncrieff, Charles K., 339, 351-2
Segond-Weber, Mme, 167
Sem, caricaturist, 92
Semeuse, La, printers, 258-9, 279, 282, 284
Senlis, 3, 17, 218, 220
Sentiments Filiaux d'un Parricide, 68-72, 76, 281
Sentmitchoff, aviator, 210, 212
Sert, José Maria, 162, 222-3, 285
Sésame et les Lys, 7-8, 14, 29, 34-8, 43, 55-7, 59, 256, 265, 277
Sevastos, Prince Jean, 330
Sévigné, Mme de, 1, 74, 172
Shakespeare, William, 70, 201, 211, 301, 351
Shelley, Percy Bysshe, 201, 338
Smith, Logan Pearsall, 252, 350
Sollier, Dr Paul, 43, 50-5, 308
Sophocles, 70
Sorel, Albert, 8, 121, 233
——, Albert Émile, 233
Souday, Paul, 202, 297-8, 306
Soupault, Philippe, 180-1
Soutzo, Princesse Hélène, 223, 244, 254-5, 260, 270-1, 275, 277-8, 282-3, 285-6, 294, 301, 322, 334-5, 347
Souvestre, Mlle, 328
Squire, John C., 350
Stael, Mme de, 76
——, Albertine de, 76
Standish, Mme, 177-8, 295
Stendhal, 120, 125, 252, 307
Stern, Jean, 5-6
——, Mme Louis, née Ernesta de Hirschel, 5
Stoïcesco, Georges, 347-8
——, Mme ——, see Arman de Caillavet, Simone
Strachey, Lytton, 350
Straus, Émile, 73, 151, 180, 187-8, 193, 204, 206-8, 212-13, 220, 224, 261, 283-4, 303
——, Mme ——, née Geneviève Halévy, 23, 30-2, 34, 37, 51, 59, 60, 63, 69, 73, 82, 86, 88, 93-4, 96, 98, 107-8, 150-1, 159, 171, 177, 180, 183-4, 187-90, 193, 195-6, 206, 220-1, 224, 228, 230, 248, 261, 272, 274, 279, 282-3, 285, 287, 289, 300, 303, 309, 314, 343
Stravinsky, Igor, 340-1
Suarès, André, 181, 330
Sur la Lecture, 34-7, 44, 73, 100, 119, 141-2
Swann, family (SWANN), 93-4
Symons, Arthur, 350

Tacitus, 211
Tagore, Rabindranath, 349
Taine, Hippolyte, 119, 122, 124, 127, 137
Talleyrand-Périgord, Adalbert de, 279
——, Charles de, 104-5
——, Hélie de, see Sagan
——, Louis de, 259, 338
Tansonville (TANSONVILLE), 87
Temps, Le, 8, 181, 200, 297, 306
Thackeray, William Makepeace, 251
Tharaud, Jean, 20
——, Jérôme, 20
Thèbes, Mme de, 282
Thibaudet, Albert, 338
Thomson, Gaston, 111
——, Mme ——, née Henriette Peigné-Crémieux, 49, 55, 111, 295
——, Marguerite, see Roussy
——, Valentine, 164-5, 362
Tiffany, jeweller, 190, 200
Times Literary Supplement, 251-2, 352

Tinseau, Comte Léon de (FROBERVILLE) 42
Tissot, James, 337-8
Titian, 92
Toulouse-Lautrec, Henri de, 266
Tronche, M., 296, 299, 348, 358
Trouville (BALBEC), 14, 22, 23, 38-9, 44-5, 59, 84-6, 92-3, 113, 151, 180, 183, 197, 220, 282, 289, 362
Turner, Joseph M. W., 94-5

Ullmann, Constantin, 171-2
Ulrich, Robert, 66, 68, 80-2, 88, 103, 148, 164, 197, 266
Uzès, Duchesse Anne d', 263

Vacances, 25-6
Vacaresco, Hélène, 284, 335
Valéry, Paul, 81, 293, 305, 328
Vallette, Alfred, 2, 8, 150
Vallière, Château de, 17
Valmont, sanatorium, 31, 193
Vandérem, Fernand, 292
Van Dyck, tenor, 169-70
Var Tid, 325
Varin-Bernier, banker, 285-6
Vaschide, Nicolas, 21
Vaudoyer, Jean Louis, 149, 160-1, 164, 174, 180, 184-5, 205-6, 211, 287, 320
Venice, 9-10, 35, 37-8, 55-6, 74, 82, 107, 116, 124, 130, 134, 146, 211, 227, 237, 239, 244, 255, 260, 315, 341
Verdun, 217, 219, 221-2, 232, 265
Verlaine, Paul, 119-20, 219, 330
Vermeer, 320-1
Versailles (DONCIÈRES), 42, 59-68, 84, 111, 116-18, 130, 144, 161, 187, 193, 212, 217, 331
Vespis, headwaiter, 344
Vettard, Camille, 336
Vigneron, Robert, 107, 355
Vignot, Abbé Pierre, 11
Vigny, Alfred de, 16, 40, 125, 323, 329
Villebon (GUERMANTES), 124, 141
Villeparisis (VILLEPARISIS), 123
Villers-sur-mer, 86
Vinci, Leonardo da, 53, 77, 201
Vinès, Ricardo, 300
Virat, M., 295
Vittoré, Jean, 213

Vivien, Renée, 327-8, 335
Voltaire, 122, 334
Vonoven, Henri, 292
Vuillard, Édouard (ELSTIR), 92

Wagner, Richard, 23, 83, 136, 168-70, 173, 220, 245
Wagram, Princesse Alexandre de, née Berthe de Rothschild, 42
Walewski, Colonel (BORODINO, Prince de), 217, 338
Waley, Arthur, 350
Warburg, bankers, 284, 286, 298
Waru, Comte Gustave de, 278
——, Comte Jacques de, 278
Watteau, Antoine, 91
Weil, Georges, 49, 60-1, 116
——, Mme ——, née Émilie Oulmann, 61-2, 96-7, 285-6
——, Louis, 35, 61, 67, 97, 129, 132, 280, 285
——, Nathé, 97, 129, 147
——, Mme —— (GRANDMOTHER), 50, 74, 83-4, 88
Wells, Herbert George, 61, 121, 244
Wernher, Sir Julius, 98
Wharton, Edith, 252-3
Whistler, James McNeill (ELSTIR), 3, 29-30, 38
Wicart, Dr, 310
Wickham, Anna, 327
Widal, Dr Fernand, 156
Widmer, Dr, 31, 37, 47, 193
Wilde, Oscar, 78, 105-8
Wilhelm II, Kaiser, 105-6
Williams, Dr, 118
Wladimir, Grand Duke, 110, 253
Wlérick, 363
Wolfe, Elsie de, 5
Woolf, Virginia, 350
Wright, Orville, 121
——, Wilbur, 121

Yeatman, Léon, 21, 181
Yturri, Gabriel d' (JUPIEN), 5, 32-3, 40-2, 46-7, 97, 109-11, 167, 171, 220, 270, 331

Zola, Émile, 100, 184, 203

II. CHARACTERS AND PLACES

Aimé (CHARLES; DABESCAT; HECTOR), 60, 149, 256

Albaret, Céleste (ALBARET, Céleste), 274-5

Albertine (AGOSTINELLI, Alfred; ALTON, Colette d'; BAUCHE, Mlle; CHEVILLY, Marie de; FINALY, Marie; IDEVILLE, Hélène d'; MORNAND, Louisa de; NAHMIAS, Albert; NORDLINGER, Marie; ROCHAT, Henri), 2-4, 10, 14, 25-6, 44-5, 59, 74, 76-7, 81, 85-8, 90, 93, 96, 112, 115, 117, 120, 132-4, 136, 149-50, 153-4, 162, 164-6, 169, 172-3, 177, 181, 183, 192, 195, 197-8, 206-14, 218, 231, 236-9, 241-2, 256, 260, 266, 271, 274, 287, 299, 307-9, 311-12, 317, 320, 322, 324, 333-4, 337-8, 348-9, 352, 354-5

Alix (CHAPONAY, JANZÉ), 176

Andrée (AGOSTINELLI, Anna; ANDRÉ; IRIBE, Jeanne), 39, 44, 149, 163-4, 173, 210, 271, 329

Arpajon, Mme d', 253

Balbec (CABOURG; DIEPPE; ÉVIAN; TROUVILLE), 14, 39, 44-6, 59, 60, 74-7, 79, 83-94, 107, 113, 117, 130, 134, 141, 143-4, 149, 162, 164-5, 168, 177, 190, 194-5, 197-8, 208, 213-15, 228, 231, 235-9, 242, 245-6, 256, 274-5, 303, 307, 309, 312, 315-16, 318-19, 332-3, 344

Balleroy, Mme de, 90

Beausergent, Mme de (BOIGNE), 74-5

——, Marquis de (OSMOND), 75

Bergotte (BARRÈS; BERGSON; BOURGET; DARLU; DAUDET, Alphonse; FRANCE; LEMAÎTRE; RENAN; RUSKIN), 29, 102, 103, 125-6, 230, 235, 309, 320-1, 325, 355, 360-1

Berma (BERNHARDT; RÉJANE), 220, 289-91

——'s daughter (POREL, Mme Jacques), 289-91

——'s son-in-law (POREL, Jacques), 289-91

Bernard, Nissim (CAMONDO; LANDAU), 344

Blatin, Mme, 219

Bloch (BLOCH; BRUNSCHVICG, Léon; CROISSET, Francis de; FINALY, Horace; HERMANT, Abel; QUILLARD, Pierre), 8, 138, 235, 245, 259, 264, 267, 275, 316-17

Bontemps, Mme, 76-7, 211, 236-7

Borodino, Prince de (WALEWSKI), 3, 338

Brichot (BROCHARD; CLAIRIN; REINACH, Joseph), 10, 84, 87, 102, 224, 289, 357

Butcher's boy, 265-6

Cambremer, Dowager Marquise de (BRANCOVAN, Princesse Rachel de), 87, 231

——, Marquis de (CAMBREMER), 7, 95

——, Marquise de, née Legrandin (HAUSSONVILLE), 78, 83, 95, 168

——, family, 91

——, Léonor de, 239, 322

Canteloup, Forest of, see Chantepie

Carqueville (CRICQUEBOEUF), 39, 183

Chantepie, Forest of (CANTEPIE), 93

Charlus, Baron Palamède de (DOASAN; LA ROCHEFOUCAULD, Comte Aimery de; LORRAIN, Jean; MONTESQUIOU, Robert de; SAGAN, Prince Boson de; WILDE), 5, 10-11, 57, 75, 77, 101-2, 105-6, 115, 120, 123, 137, 139-40, 143, 145, 149, 166, 171, 186, 206-7, 215, 230, 236-41, 244-5, 249-50, 259, 262, 264-6, 269-70, 281, 289, 291-2, 307, 310, 312-13, 317-19, 330, 336, 343-345

Charmel (CHARMEL), 292

Châtellerault, Duc de, 263

Chauffeur, Narrator's (AGOSTINELLI, Alfred; ALBARET, Odilon), 96

Combray (AUTEUIL; COMBRAY; COMBRES; ILLIERS), 15, 24, 34, 37, 44, 79, 82, 86, 94, 96, 102, 107, 116, 120, 124, 130, 132-4, 138-41, 143, 147, 152, 172, 179, 183, 186, 221, 239, 315, 360

Cottard, Dr (BROCA; COTARD; COTTET; DIEULAFOY; DOYEN; GUYON; POZZI; VANDAL), 87, 102, 145, 279

——, Mme, 31, 235

Courvoisier, family, 16

Crécy, Pierre de Verjus, Comte de, 114-15, 245

Creuniers, Les (CREUNIERS), 39
Curé, of Combray (MARQUIS), 87

Doncières (FONTAINEBLEAU; LISIEUX; MÉZIDON; ORLEANS; PROVINS; VERSAILLES), 63-4, 73, 85, 134, 166, 214-215, 236-8, 259, 269, 282, 304-5, 334
Douville (DOUVILLE), 85-6
Durieux, Mme, 149

E., Professor (BRISSAUD), 43
Elstir (BÉRAUD; BLANCHE; GERVEX; HARRISON; HÉBERT; HELLEU; MAUPASSANT; MONET; MOREAU; TURNER; VUILLARD; WHISTLER), 29, 38-9, 84, 91-2, 190, 235-6
——, Mme (HELLEU, Mme), 91-2

Fates, Three (BLOCQUEVILLE; CHAPONAY; JANZÉ), 176-7
Féterne (BASSARABA; FÉTERNES), 86
Foix, Prince de, father (RADZIWILL, Prince Constantin), 262
——, ——, son (RADZIWILL, Prince Léon), 18, 65, 262
Forcheville, Comte de, 137
Foster, Miss (DEACON, Gladys), 65
Françoise (ALBARET, Céleste; COTTIN, Céline; FITAU; GALLOU), 25, 59, 101, 132-3, 213, 218, 237, 258, 265, 281, 290, 333-4, 354
——'s daughter (ALBARET, Yvonne), 333-4
Froberville, General de (GALLIFFET; TINSEAU), 42, 78

Gallardon, Mme de, 16
Gilbert, the Bad (ILLIERS, Geoffroy d'), 139
Gilberte (ARMAN DE CAILLAVET, Mme Gaston; BENARDAKY, Marie de; EDWARDS, Misia; FAURE, Antoinette; GOUPIL, Mlle; HAAS, Luisita; LAURIS, Madeleine de; LEMAIRE, Suzette), 18, 30, 45, 54, 74, 102, 104, 113, 131, 132, 134, 137, 153-5, 161, 164, 178, 187, 194-5, 209, 214, 221, 224-5, 227, 232, 236-7, 240, 259, 288, 338, 360-1
Gineste, Marie (GINESTE), 274
Gisèle, 44, 164
Grandmother (PROUST, Mme Adrien; WEIL, Mme Nathé), 43, 47, 73, 83-4, 134, 141, 156, 177, 209, 215, 237-8, 309-11, 322, 332

Guermantes, Château, village, Way, (BALLEROY; GUERMANTES; JUMIÈGES; SAINT-ÉMAN; VILLEBON), 90, 122-4, 139-41, 364
——, family, 33, 74, 137, 144, 147, 252, 315, 317, 357
——, Basin, Duc de (GRAMONT, Agénor de; GREFFULHE, Comte; HAUSSONVILLE, Othenin de; ILLIERS, Basin d'), 18, 57, 75, 105, 137-8, 202, 253-4, 300, 318
——, Oriane, Duchesse de (CHEVIGNÉ; GOUSSENCOURT; GREFFULHE; ROHAN, Duchesse de; STRAUS, Mme), 16, 75, 101, 102, 133, 137-8, 177-8, 193, 214-15, 237, 253-4, 263, 272, 291, 304, 312, 314-15, 317-18
——, Prince de (LA ROCHEFOUCAULD, Aimery de; RADZIWILL, Prince Constantin; TALLEYRAND-PÉRIGORD, Louis de), 96, 135, 138, 152, 241, 244, 259, 262
——, Princesse de (CASTELLANE, Comtesse Jean de; GREFFULHE, Mme), 3, 54, 74-5, 109, 135, 139, 141, 154, 177-8, 215, 224, 236-8, 240-1, 244, 253, 263, 290, 314, 334

Herweck, M. d', 18
Hudimesnil, 39

Iéna, family, 5

Jupien (EPPLER; LE CUZIAT; MINEGUISHI; YTURRI), 120, 133, 137, 139, 186, 230, 239, 262-72, 280-1, 312-13, 317-8, 322, 336
——'s niece, 239-40, 322

Léa (LANTELME), 87-8, 93, 236, 324
Legrandin (CAZALIS; RODIER), 79, 102, 176
Léonie, Aunt (AMIOT, Mme Jules), 60, 188, 235, 264, 267, 344
Leroi, Mme (BAIGNÈRES; LEGRAND), 31
Létourville, little, 79
Lévy, Esther, 87
Lift-boy, 91
Little Band, 44, 86, 87, 108, 115, 124, 144, 162, 165, 181, 183, 195, 236-7, 271
Little Train, 85-6, 150, 242, 266
Luxembourg, Grand Duke of (MONACO, Prince Albert of), 304

——, Princesse de (MONACO, Princess Alice of; SAGAN, Princesse de), 30, 75, 83, 303-4, 309, 332

Martinville-le-Sec (CAEN; MARCHÉVILLE), 57, 90, 95-6, 133, 350
Maurice, inmate of Jupien's brothel, 266
Méséglise, village and Way (MÉRÉGLISE), 122, 124, 132, 232, 364
Mirougrain (MIROUGRAIN), 344
Montjouvain (MIROUGRAIN; MONTJOUVIN); 87, 120, 131, 209, 268
Morel, Charles (DELAFOSSE; Léon; ROCHAT, Henri), 166, 186, 206-7, 236-8, 249, 287, 289, 322-4
Mortemart, Mme de, 330

Naples, Queen of (NAPLES, Marie, Queen of), 238, 248-9
Nassau, Comte de (POLIGNAC, Pierre de), 304
Norpois, M. de (BARRÈRE; BENEDETTI; CAMBON; FLEURY; HANOTAUX; NISARD), 105, 143, 194, 235
Norwegian philosopher (RUHE, Algot), 324-5, 332

Oceania, king of an islet in (LEBAUDY, Jacques,) 149
Octave, 'In the Soup' (COCTEAU; JONCIÈRES; PLANTEVIGNES, Marcel), 87, 162-3, 173
Odette (ARMAN DE CAILLAVET, Léontine; CLOMESNIL; HAYMAN; LA BÉRAUDIÈRE; LAURENT, Méry; LOYNES; PIERREBOURG; STRAUS, Mme), 25, 44-5, 61, 76, 109, 115, 139, 143, 154-5, 164, 176, 183, 186-7, 197, 201, 209, 211, 219, 230, 235-6, 245, 254, 259, 343
Osmond, Amanien d' (OSMOND), 75

Page-boy, squinting, 228
Percepied, Dr, 95
Putbus, maid of Baroness, 95-6, 131

Rachel (ALENÇON, Émilienne d'; LANTELME; MARSY; MORNAND, Louisa de), 13-4, 19, 113, 161, 215, 235, 314
Raspelière, La (CLOS DES MÛRIERS; CŒUR VOLANT; COUR BRULÉE; FRÉMONTS; RACHEPELIÈRE; RÉVEILLON), 10, 39, 84, 85-7, 91, 95, 168, 220, 238, 321, 324, 332

Rivebelle (BELLE-RIVE; HAVRE; RIVABELLA), 86, 235
Rosemonde, 44
Roussainville, 120, 232

Saint-André-des-Champs, 152
Sainte-Euverte, Marquise Diane de (SAINT-PAUL), 78, 83, 109, 201
Saint-Hilaire (ÉVREUX; SAINT-JACQUES; SAINT-HILAIRE), 94, 116, 152, 183
Saint-Loup, Marquis Robert de (ARMAN DE CAILLAVET, Gaston; CASTELLANE, Boni de; CHOLET; FÉNELON, Bertrand de; LA ROCHEFOUCAULD, Gabriel de; LAURIS, Georges de; SAINT-LOUP; UZÈS, Jacques d'; WARU), 14, 16-19, 30, 63, 66, 76, 90, 96, 104-5, 113, 123, 145, 161-2, 164-5, 178, 211, 215-16, 224-6, 231, 236-8, 240-1, 251, 254, 258-9, 262, 272, 281-2, 291, 311, 314, 318-19, 345, 360
——, Mlle de (ARMAN DE CAILLAVET, Simone), 104, 155, 178, 240, 348
——, Mme de, see Gilberte
Saniette, 91
Sazerat, Mme, 141
Sherbatoff, Princesse, 145
Stermaria, Mme de, 14, 26, 237
Surgis, Marquise de, 75, 317
——, Victurnien de, 75, 317
Swann, Charles (BENARDAKY, Nicolas de; EPHRUSSI, Charles; HAAS, Charles; HERVIEU, Paul, STRAUS, Émile), 23, 44-5, 75, 77, 93-4, 97, 109, 124, 132, 136-7, 143-5, 154, 164, 183, 197, 199, 202, 209, 211, 236, 239, 245, 253, 259, 278, 314, 318-19, 338
——, Mme ——, see Odette
——, Gilberte, see Gilberte

Tansonville (PRÉ CATELAN; RÉVEILLON; TANSONVILLE), 54, 102, 131, 135-7, 153, 161, 174, 221, 227, 232, 240-1, 259, 338
Théodore (AGOSTINELLI, Alfred; MÉNARD, Victor), 96
Theodosius, King, 105
Thirion, M. de, see Villeparisis, M. de
Twins, Tomato, 343-4

Verdurin, M. (ARMAN DE CAILLAVET, Albert; STRAUS, Émile), 220, 238, 245-9

——, Mme (ARMAN DE CAILLAVET, Mme Albert; AUBERNON, Mme; BLUMENTHAL, Cecilia; LEMAIRE, Madeleine; MÉNARD-DORIAN; SAINT-VICTOR), 76, 84, 92, 101, 102, 109, 145, 176, 224, 238, 245-9, 259, 264, 289, 305, 321, 332, 344, 349-50, 354

Verjus, *see* Crécy

Villeparisis, Mme de (BEAULAINCOURT; FINALY, Mme Hugo; LEMAIRE, Madeleine; VILLEPARISIS), 19, 30, 33, 38-9, 74-5, 93, 102, 105, 123, 125, 130, 137, 139-40, 171, 176, 183, 195, 214-15, 236-8, 316, 319, 322

——, M. de, 123

Vinteuil (BEETHOVEN; DEBUSSY; FAURÉ; FRANCK; GUIRAUD; INDY; SAINT-SAËNS), 64, 154, 245, 248

——, Mlle (GUIRAUD, Mlle; JOINVILLE D'ARTOIS), 64, 109, 120, 197, 199, 209, 248, 268

——, Septet, 109, 176, 238, 242-9, 267, 334, 341, 348, 354

——, Sonata, 78, 83, 109, 245-7

Vivonne (LOIR; THIRONNE), 15, 131

Yourbeletief, Princesse (EDWARDS, Mme), 162

FOR THE BEST IN PAPERBACKS, LOOK FOR THE 🐧

In every corner of the world, on every subject under the sun, Penguin represents quality and variety – the very best in publishing today.

For complete information about books available from Penguin – including Puffins, Penguin Classics and Arkana – and how to order them, write to us at the appropriate address below. Please note that for copyright reasons the selection of books varies from country to country.

In the United Kingdom: Please write to *Dept E.P., Penguin Books Ltd, Harmondsworth, Middlesex, UB7 0DA.*

If you have any difficulty in obtaining a title, please send your order with the correct money, plus ten per cent for postage and packaging, to *PO Box No 11, West Drayton, Middlesex*

In the United States: Please write to *Dept BA, Penguin, 299 Murray Hill Parkway, East Rutherford, New Jersey 07073*

In Canada: Please write to *Penguin Books Canada Ltd, 2801 John Street, Markham, Ontario L3R 1B4*

In Australia: Please write to the *Marketing Department, Penguin Books Australia Ltd, P.O. Box 257, Ringwood, Victoria 3134*

In New Zealand: Please write to the *Marketing Department, Penguin Books (NZ) Ltd, Private Bag, Takapuna, Auckland 9*

In India: Please write to *Penguin Overseas Ltd, 706 Eros Apartments, 56 Nehru Place, New Delhi, 110019*

In the Netherlands: Please write to *Penguin Books Netherlands B.V., Postbus 195, NL–1380AD Weesp*

In West Germany: Please write to *Penguin Books Ltd, Friedrichstrasse 10–12, D–6000 Frankfurt/Main 1*

In Spain: Please write to *Longman Penguin España, Calle San Nicolas 15, E–28013 Madrid*

In Italy: Please write to *Penguin Italia s.r.l., Via Como 4, I-20096 Pioltello (Milano)*

In France: Please write to *Penguin Books Ltd, 39 Rue de Montmorency, F-75003 Paris*

In Japan: Please write to *Longman Penguin Japan Co Ltd, Yamaguchi Building, 2–12–9 Kanda Jimbocho, Chiyoda-Ku, Tokyo 101*

A CHOICE OF PENGUINS

The Secret Lives of Trebitsch Lincoln Bernard Wasserstein

Trebitsch Lincoln was Member of Parliament, international spy, right-wing revolutionary, Buddhist monk – and this century's most extraordinary conman. 'Surely the final work on a truly extraordinary career' – Hugh Trevor-Roper. 'An utterly improbable story ... a biographical coup' – *Guardian*

Out of Africa Karen Blixen (Isak Dinesen)

After the failure of her coffee-farm in Kenya, where she lived from 1913 to 1931, Karen Blixen went home to Denmark and wrote this unforgettable account of her experiences. 'No reader can put the book down without some share in the author's poignant farewell to her farm' – *Observer*

In My Wildest Dreams Leslie Thomas

The autobiography of Leslie Thomas, author of *The Magic Army* and *The Dearest and the Best*. From Barnardo boy to original virgin soldier, from apprentice journalist to famous novelist, it is an amazing story. 'Hugely enjoyable' – *Daily Express*

The Winning Streak Walter Goldsmith and David Clutterbuck

Marks and Spencer, Saatchi and Saatchi, United Biscuits, GEC ... The UK's top companies reveal their formulas for success, in an important and stimulating book that no British manager can afford to ignore.

Bird of Life, Bird of Death Jonathan Evan Maslow

In the summer of 1983 Jonathan Maslow set out to find the quetzal. In doing so, he placed himself between the natural and unnatural histories of Central America, between the vulnerable magnificence of nature and the terrible destructiveness of man. 'A wonderful book' – *The New York Times Book Review*

Mob Star Gene Mustain and Jerry Capeci

Handsome, charming, deadly, John Gotti is the real-life Mafia boss at the head of New York's most feared criminal family. *Mob Star* tells the chilling and compelling story of the rise to power of the most powerful criminal in America.

A CHOICE OF PENGUINS

The Assassination of Federico García Lorca   Ian Gibson

Lorca's 'crime' was his antipathy to pomposity, conformity and intolerance. His punishment was murder. Ian Gibson – author of the acclaimed new biography of Lorca – reveals the truth about his death and the atmosphere in Spain that allowed it to happen.

Between the Woods and the Water   Patrick Leigh Fermor

Patrick Leigh Fermor continues his celebrated account – begun in *A Time of Gifts* – of his journey on foot from the Hook of Holland to Constantinople. 'Even better than everyone says it is' – Peter Levi. 'Indescribably rich and beautiful' – *Guardian*

The Hunting of the Whale   Jeremy Cherfas

'*The Hunting of the Whale* is a story of declining profits and mounting pigheadedness … it involves a catalogue of crass carelessness … Jeremy Cherfas brings a fresh eye to [his] material … for anyone wanting a whale in a nutshell this must be the book to choose' – *The Times Literary Supplement*

Metamagical Themas   Douglas R. Hofstadter

This astonishing sequel to the bestselling, Pulitzer Prize-winning *Gödel, Escher, Bach* swarms with 'extraordinary ideas, brilliant fables, deep philosophical questions and Carrollian word play' – Martin Gardner

Into the Heart of Borneo   Redmond O'Hanlon

'Perceptive, hilarious and at the same time a serious natural-history journey into one of the last remaining unspoilt paradises' – *New Statesman*. 'Consistently exciting, often funny and erudite without ever being overwhelming' – *Punch*

When the Wind Blows   Raymond Briggs

'A visual parable against nuclear war: all the more chilling for being in the form of a strip cartoon' – *Sunday Times*. 'The most eloquent anti-Bomb statement you are likely to read' – *Daily Mail*

FOR THE BEST IN PAPERBACKS, LOOK FOR THE 🐧

BIOGRAPHY AND AUTOBIOGRAPHY IN PENGUIN

Just for William Nicholas Woolley and Sue Clayton

Originating as a film for the award-winning BBC2 documentary series *Forty Minutes*, *Just for William* is the story of William Clayton, diagnosed with leukaemia at the age of nine – and the story of a family who refused to give up hope in the battle against one of the deadliest diseases of all.

The Secret Lives of Trebitsch Lincoln Bernard Wasserstein

Trebitsch Lincoln was Member of Parliament, international spy, right-wing revolutionary, Buddhist monk – and this century's most extra-ordinary conman. 'An utterly improbable story ... a biographical scoop' – *Guardian*

Tolstoy A. N. Wilson

'One of the best biographies of our century' – Leon Edel. 'All his skills as a writer, his fire as a critic, his insight as a novelist and his experience of life have come together in this subject' – Peter Levi in the *Independent*

Fox on the Run Graeme Fowler

The intimate diary of a dramatic eighteen months, in which Fowler became the first Englishman to score a double century in India – before being cast down by injury and forced to come to terms with loss of form. 'One of the finest cricket books this year' – *Yorkshire Post*. Winner of the first Observer/Running Late Sports Book Award.

Backcloth Dirk Bogarde

The final volume of Dirk Bogarde's autobiography is not about his acting years but about Dirk Bogarde the man and the people and events that have shaped his life and character. All are remembered with affection, nostalgia and characteristic perception and eloquence.

Jackdaw Cake Norman Lewis

From Carmarthen to Cuba, from Enfield to Algeria, Norman Lewis brilliantly recounts his transformation from stammering schoolboy to the man Auberon Waugh called 'the greatest travel writer alive, if not the greatest since Marco Polo'.